T0305518

INTERNATIONAL
FINANCIAL
STATEMENT
ANALYSIS

CFA Institute is the premier association for investment professionals around the world, with more than 150,000 CFA charterholders worldwide in 165+ countries and regions. Since 1963 the organization has developed and administered the renowned Chartered Financial Analyst® Program. With a rich history of leading the investment profession, CFA Institute has set the highest standards in ethics, education, and professional excellence within the global investment community and is the foremost authority on investment profession conduct and practice. Each book in the CFA Institute Investment Series is geared toward industry practitioners along with graduate-level finance students and covers the most important topics in the industry. The authors of these cutting-edge books are themselves industry professionals and academics and bring their wealth of knowledge and expertise to this series.

INTERNATIONAL FINANCIAL STATEMENT ANALYSIS

Fourth Edition

Thomas R. Robinson, CFA

Elaine Henry, CFA

Michael A. Broihahn, CFA

WILEY

CONTENTS

CHAPTER 5
Understanding Cash Flow Statements 163

CHAPTER 8
Long-Lived Assets

PREFACE

International Financial Statement Analysis is a practically oriented introduction to financial statement analysis. Each chapter covers one major area of financial statement analysis and is written by highly credentialed experts. By taking a global perspective on accounting standards, with a focus on international financial reporting standards (IFRS), and by selecting a broad range of companies for illustration, the book well equips the reader for practice in today's global marketplace.

The content was developed in partnership by a team of distinguished academics and practitioners, chosen for their acknowledged expertise in the field, and guided by CFA Institute. It is written specifically with the investment practitioner in mind and is replete with examples and practice problems that reinforce the learning outcomes and demonstrate real-world applicability.

The CFA Program Curriculum, from which the content of this book was drawn, is subjected to a rigorous review process to assure that it is:

- Faithful to the findings of our ongoing industry practice analysis
- Valuable to members, employers, and investors
- Globally relevant
- Generalist (as opposed to specialist) in nature
- Replete with sufficient examples and practice opportunities
- Pedagogically sound

The accompanying workbook is a useful reference that provides Learning Outcome Statements, which describe exactly what readers will learn and be able to demonstrate after mastering the accompanying material. Additionally, the workbook has summary overviews and practice problems for each chapter.

We hope you will find this and other books in the CFA Institute Investment Series helpful in your efforts to grow your investment knowledge, whether you are a relatively new entrant or an experienced veteran striving to keep up to date in the ever-changing market environment. CFA Institute, as a long-term committed participant in the investment profession and a not-for-profit global membership association, is pleased to provide you with this opportunity.

THE CFA PROGRAM

If the subject matter of this book interests you, and you are not already a CFA charterholder, we hope you will consider registering for the CFA Program and starting progress toward earning the Chartered Financial Analyst designation. The CFA designation is a globally recognized standard of excellence for measuring the competence and integrity of investment professionals.

To earn the CFA charter, candidates must successfully complete the CFA Program, a global graduate-level self-study program that combines a broad curriculum with professional conduct requirements as preparation for a career as an investment professional.

Anchored by a practice-based curriculum, the CFA Program Body of Knowledge reflects the knowledge, skills, and abilities identified by professionals as essential to the investment decision-making process. This body of knowledge maintains its relevance through a regular, extensive survey of practicing CFA charterholders across the globe. The curriculum covers 10 general topic areas, ranging from equity and fixed-income analysis to portfolio management— all with a heavy emphasis on the application of ethics in professional practice. Known for its rigor and breadth, the CFA Program curriculum highlights principles common to every market so that professionals who earn the CFA designation have a thoroughly global investment perspective and a profound understanding of the global marketplace.

ACKNOWLEDGMENTS

Authors
We would like to thank the many distinguished authors who contributed outstanding chapters in their respective areas of expertise:

Michael A. Broihahn, CFA

Jack T. Ciesielski, CFA, CPA

Timothy S. Doupnik, PhD

Elizabeth A. Gordon

Elaine Henry, PhD, CFA

Elbie Louw, CFA

Thomas R. Robinson, PhD, CFA

Karen O'Connor Rubsam, CPA, CFA

Thomas I. Selling, PhD, CPA

Hennie van Greuning, CFA

Susan Perry Williams, PhD

Reviewers
Special thanks to all the reviewers, curriculum advisors, and question writers who helped to ensure high practical relevance, technical correctness, and understandability of the material presented here.

Production
We would like to thank the many others who played a role in the conception and production of this book: the Curriculum and Learning Experience team at CFA Institute, with special thanks to the Curriculum Directors, past and present, who worked with the authors and reviewers to produce the chapters in this book; the Practice Analysis team at CFA Institute; and the Credentialing Product Marketing team at CFA Institute.

ABOUT THE CFA INSTITUTE INVESTMENT SERIES

CFA Institute is pleased to provide you with the CFA Institute Investment Series, which covers major areas in the field of investments. We provide this best-in-class series for the same reason we have been chartering investment professionals for more than 50 years: to lead the investment profession globally by promoting the highest standards of ethics, education, and professional excellence for the ultimate benefit of society.

The books in the CFA Institute Investment Series contain practical, globally relevant material. They are intended both for those contemplating entry into the extremely competitive field of investment management as well as for those seeking a means of keeping their knowledge fresh and up to date. This series was designed to be user friendly and highly relevant.

We hope you find this series helpful in your efforts to grow your investment knowledge, whether you are a relatively new entrant or an experienced veteran ethically bound to keep up to date in the ever-changing market environment. As a long-term, committed participant in the investment profession and a not-for-profit global membership association, CFA Institute is pleased to provide you with this opportunity.

THE TEXTS

Corporate Finance: A Practical Approach is a solid foundation for those looking to achieve lasting business growth. In today's competitive business environment, companies must find innovative ways to enable rapid and sustainable growth. This text equips readers with the foundational knowledge and tools for making smart business decisions and formulating strategies to maximize company value. It covers everything from managing relationships between stakeholders to evaluating merger and acquisition bids, as well as the companies behind them. Through extensive use of real-world examples, readers will gain critical perspective into interpreting corporate financial data, evaluating projects, and allocating funds in ways that increase corporate value. Readers will gain insights into the tools and strategies used in modern corporate financial management.

Equity Asset Valuation is a particularly cogent and important resource for anyone involved in estimating the value of securities and understanding security pricing. A well-informed professional knows that the common forms of equity valuation—dividend discount modeling, free cash flow modeling, price/earnings modeling, and residual income modeling—can all be reconciled with one another under certain assumptions. With a deep understanding of the underlying assumptions, the professional investor can better understand what other investors assume when calculating their valuation estimates. This text has a global orientation, including emerging markets.

International Financial Statement Analysis is designed to address the ever-increasing need for investment professionals and students to think about financial statement analysis from a global perspective. The text is a practically oriented introduction to financial statement analysis that is distinguished by its combination of a true international orientation, a structured presentation style, and abundant illustrations and tools covering concepts as they are introduced in the text. The authors cover this discipline comprehensively and with an eye to ensuring the reader's success at all levels in the complex world of financial statement analysis.

Investments: Principles of Portfolio and Equity Analysis provides an accessible yet rigorous introduction to portfolio and equity analysis. Portfolio planning and portfolio management are presented within a context of up-to-date global coverage of security markets, trading, and market-related concepts and products. The essentials of equity analysis and valuation are explained in detail and profusely illustrated. The book includes coverage of practitioner-important but often neglected topics, such as industry analysis. Throughout, the focus is on the practical application of key concepts with examples drawn from both emerging and developed markets. Each chapter affords the reader many opportunities to self-check his or her understanding of topics.

One of the most prominent texts over the years in the investment management industry has been Maginn and Tuttle's *Managing Investment Portfolios: A Dynamic Process*. The third edition updates key concepts from the 1990 second edition. Some of the more experienced members of our community own the prior two editions and will add the third edition to their libraries. Not only does this seminal work take the concepts from the other readings and put them in a portfolio context, but it also updates the concepts of alternative investments, performance presentation standards, portfolio execution, and, very importantly, individual investor portfolio management. Focusing attention away from institutional portfolios and toward the individual investor makes this edition an important and timely work.

The New Wealth Management: The Financial Advisor's Guide to Managing and Investing Client Assets is an updated version of Harold Evensky's mainstay reference guide for wealth managers. Harold Evensky, Stephen Horan, and Thomas Robinson have updated the core text of the 1997 first edition and added an abundance of new material to fully reflect today's investment challenges. The text provides authoritative coverage across the full spectrum of wealth management and serves as a comprehensive guide for financial advisers. The book expertly blends investment theory and real-world applications and is written in the same thorough but highly accessible style as the first edition.

Quantitative Investment Analysis focuses on some key tools that are needed by today's professional investor. In addition to classic time value of money, discounted cash flow applications, and probability material, there are two aspects that can be of value over traditional thinking. The first involves the chapters dealing with correlation and regression that ultimately figure into the formation of hypotheses for purposes of testing. This gets to a critical skill that challenges many professionals: the ability to distinguish useful information from the overwhelming quantity of available data. Second, the final chapter of *Quantitative Investment Analysis* covers portfolio concepts and takes the reader beyond the traditional capital asset pricing model (CAPM) type of tools and into the more practical world of multifactor models and arbitrage pricing theory.

All books in the CFA Institute Investment Series are available through all major booksellers. All titles also are available on the Wiley Custom Select platform at http://customselect.wiley.com, where individual chapters for all the books may be mixed and matched to create custom textbooks for the classroom.

INTERNATIONAL FINANCIAL STATEMENT ANALYSIS

CHAPTER 1

INTRODUCTION TO FINANCIAL STATEMENT ANALYSIS

Elaine Henry, PhD, CFA
Thomas R. Robinson, PhD, CFA

LEARNING OUTCOMES

After completing this chapter, you will be able to do the following:

- describe the roles of financial reporting and financial statement analysis;
- describe the roles of the statement of financial position, statement of comprehensive income, statement of changes in equity, and statement of cash flows in evaluating a company's performance and financial position;
- describe the importance of financial statement notes and supplementary information—including disclosures of accounting policies, methods, and estimates—and management's commentary;
- describe the objective of audits of financial statements, the types of audit reports, and the importance of effective internal controls;
- identify and describe information sources that analysts use in financial statement analysis besides annual financial statements and supplementary information;
- describe the steps in the financial statement analysis framework.

1. INTRODUCTION

Financial analysis is the process of examining a company's performance in the context of its industry and economic environment in order to arrive at a decision or recommendation. Often, the decisions and recommendations addressed by financial analysts pertain to providing capital to companies—specifically, whether to invest in the company's debt or equity securities and at what price. An investor in debt securities is concerned about the company's ability to pay interest and to repay the principal lent. An investor in equity securities is an owner with a residual interest in the company and is concerned about the company's ability to pay dividends and the likelihood that its share price will increase.

Overall, a central focus of financial analysis is evaluating the company's ability to earn a return on its capital that is at least equal to the cost of that capital, to profitably grow its operations, and to generate enough cash to meet obligations and pursue opportunities.

Fundamental financial analysis starts with the information found in a company's financial reports. These financial reports include audited financial statements, additional disclosures required by regulatory authorities, and any accompanying (unaudited) commentary by management. Basic financial statement analysis—as presented in this chapter—provides a foundation that enables the analyst to better understand other information gathered from research beyond the financial reports.

This chapter is organized as follows: Section 2 discusses the scope of financial statement analysis. Section 3 describes the sources of information used in financial statement analysis, including the primary financial statements (statement of financial position or balance sheet, statement of comprehensive income, statement of changes in equity, and cash flow statement). Section 4 provides a framework for guiding the financial statement analysis process. A summary of the key points concludes the chapter.

2. ROLES OF FINANCIAL REPORTING AND FINANCIAL STATEMENT ANALYSIS

The role of financial statements issued by companies is to provide information about a company's performance, financial position, and changes in financial position that is useful to a wide range of users in making economic decisions. The role of financial statement analysis is to use financial reports prepared by companies, combined with other information, to evaluate the past, current, and potential performance and financial position of a company for the purpose of making investment, credit, and other economic decisions. Managers within a company perform financial analysis to make operating, investing, and financing decisions but do not necessarily rely on analysis of related financial statements. They have access to additional financial information that can be reported in whatever format is most useful to their decision.

In evaluating financial reports, analysts typically have a specific economic decision in mind. Examples of these decisions include the following:

- Evaluating an equity investment for inclusion in a portfolio.
- Evaluating a merger or acquisition candidate.
- Evaluating a subsidiary or operating division of a parent company.
- Deciding whether to make a venture capital or other private equity investment.
- Determining the creditworthiness of a company in order to decide whether to extend a loan to the company and if so, what terms to offer.
- Extending credit to a customer.
- Examining compliance with debt covenants or other contractual arrangements.
- Assigning a debt rating to a company or bond issue.
- Valuing a security for making an investment recommendation to others.
- Forecasting future net income and cash flow.

These decisions demonstrate certain themes in financial analysis. In general, analysts seek to examine the past and current performance and financial position of a company in order to form expectations about its future performance and financial position. Analysts are also concerned about factors that affect risks to a company's future performance and financial position. An examination of performance can include an assessment of a company's profitability (the ability to earn a profit from delivering goods and services) and its ability to generate positive cash flows (cash receipts in excess of cash disbursements). Profit and cash flow are not equivalent. Profit (or loss) represents the difference between the prices at which goods or services are provided to customers and the expenses incurred to provide those goods and services.

In addition, profit (or loss) includes other income (such as investing income or income from the sale of items other than goods and services) minus the expenses incurred to earn that income. Overall, profit (or loss) equals income minus expenses, and its recognition is mostly independent from when cash is received or paid. Example 1 illustrates the distinction between profit and cash flow.

EXAMPLE 1   Profit versus Cash Flow

Sennett Designs (SD) sells furniture on a retail basis. SD began operations during December 2017 and sold furniture for €250,000 in cash. The furniture sold by SD was purchased on credit for €150,000 and delivered by the supplier during December. The credit terms granted by the supplier required SD to pay the €150,000 in January for the furniture it received during December. In addition to the purchase and sale of furniture, in December, SD paid €20,000 in cash for rent and salaries.

1. How much is SD's profit for December 2017 if no other transactions occurred?
2. How much is SD's cash flow for December 2017?
3. If SD purchases and sells exactly the same amount in January 2018 as it did in December and under the same terms (receiving cash for the sales and making purchases on credit that will be due in February), how much will the company's profit and cash flow be for the month of January?

Solution to 1: SD's profit for December 2017 is the excess of the sales price (€250,000) over the cost of the goods that were sold (€150,000) and rent and salaries (€20,000), or €80,000.

Solution to 2: The December 2017 cash flow is €230,000, the amount of cash received from the customer (€250,000) less the cash paid for rent and salaries (€20,000).

Solution to 3: SD's profit for January 2018 will be identical to its profit in December: €80,000, calculated as the sales price (€250,000) minus the cost of the goods that were sold (€150,000) and minus rent and salaries (€20,000). SD's cash flow in January 2018 will also equal €80,000, calculated as the amount of cash received from the customer (€250,000) minus the cash paid for rent and salaries (€20,000) *and* minus the €150,000 that SD owes for the goods it had purchased on credit in the prior month.

Although profitability is important, so is a company's ability to generate positive cash flow. Cash flow is important because, ultimately, the company needs cash to pay employees, suppliers, and others in order to continue as a going concern. A company that generates positive cash flow from operations has more flexibility in funding needed for investments and taking advantage of attractive business opportunities than an otherwise comparable company without positive operating cash flow. Additionally, a company needs cash to pay returns (interest and dividends) to providers of debt and equity capital.

The expected magnitude of future cash flows is important in valuing corporate securities and in determining the company's ability to meet its obligations. The ability to meet short-term obligations is generally referred to as **liquidity**, and the ability to meet long-term obligations is generally referred to as **solvency**. Cash flow in any given period is not, however, a complete measure of performance for that period because, as shown in Example 1, a company may be obligated to make future cash payments as a result of a transaction that generates positive cash flow in the current period.

Profits may provide useful information about cash flows, past and future. If the transaction of Example 1 were repeated month after month, the long-term average monthly cash flow of SD would equal €80,000, its monthly profit. Analysts typically not only evaluate past profitability but also forecast future profitability.

Exhibit 1 shows how news coverage of corporate earnings announcements places corporate results in the context of analysts' expectations. Panel A shows the earnings announcement, and Panel B shows a sample of the news coverage of the announcement. Earnings are also frequently used by analysts in valuation. For example, an analyst may value shares of a company by comparing its price-to-earnings ratio (P/E) to the P/Es of peer companies and/or may use forecasted future earnings as direct or indirect inputs into discounted cash flow models of valuation.

EXHIBIT 1   An Earnings Release and News Media Comparison with Analysts' Expectations

Panel A: Excerpt from Apple Earnings Release

Apple Reports Second Quarter Results
Revenue Grows 16 Percent and EPS Grows 30 Percent to New March Quarter Records
New $100 Billion Share Repurchase Authorization Announced, Dividend Raised by 16 Percent

Cupertino, California—May 1, 2018—Apple today announced financial results for its fiscal 2018 second quarter ended March 31, 2018. The Company posted quarterly revenue of $61.1 billion, an increase of 16 percent from the year-ago quarter, and quarterly earnings per diluted share of $2.73, up 30 percent. International sales accounted for 65 percent of the quarter's revenue.

"We're thrilled to report our best March quarter ever, with strong revenue growth in iPhone, Services and Wearables," said Tim Cook, Apple's CEO. "Customers chose iPhone X more than any other iPhone each week in the March quarter, just as they did following its launch in the December quarter. We also grew revenue in all of our geographic segments, with over 20 percent growth in Greater China and Japan."

"Our business performed extremely well during the March quarter, as we grew earnings per share by 30 percent and generated over $15 billion in operating cash flow," said Luca Maestri, Apple's CFO. "With the greater flexibility we now have from access to our global cash, we can more efficiently invest in our US operations and work toward a more optimal capital structure. Given our confidence in Apple's future, we are very happy to announce that our Board has approved a new $100 billion share repurchase authorization and a 16 percent increase in our quarterly dividend."

EXHIBIT 1   (Continued)

The Company will complete the execution of the previous $210 billion share repurchase authorization during the third fiscal quarter.

Reflecting the approved increase, the Board has declared a cash dividend of $0.73 per share of Apple's common stock payable on May 17, 2018 to shareholders of record as of the close of business on May 14, 2018.

The Company also expects to continue to net-share-settle vesting restricted stock units.

From the inception of its capital return program in August 2012 through March 2018, Apple has returned $275 billion to shareholders, including $200 billion in share repurchases. The management team and the Board will continue to review each element of the capital return program regularly and plan to provide an update on the program on an annual basis.

Apple is providing the following guidance for its fiscal 2018 third quarter:

- revenue between $51.5 billion and $53.5 billion
- gross margin between 38 percent and 38.5 percent
- operating expenses between $7.7 billion and $7.8 billion
- other income/(expense) of $400 million
- tax rate of approximately 14.5 percent

Apple will provide live streaming of its Q2 2018 financial results conference call beginning at 2:00 p.m. PDT on May 1, 2018 at www.apple.com/investor/earnings-call/. This webcast will also be available for replay for approximately two weeks thereafter.

Source: https://www.apple.com/newsroom/2018/05/apple-reports-second-quarter-results/ (retrieved 3 November 2018).

Panel B: Excerpt from News Article: Apple Second Quarter 2018 Earnings Release

Apple reported quarterly earnings and revenue on Tuesday that beat expectations, but sold fewer iPhones than expected.

Shares rose as much 5 percent after hours, as investors digested the company's better-than-expected outlook for the current quarter, and a hefty capital return program.

The soft iPhone sales were still up from a year ago, and Apple CEO Tim Cook said in a statement that customers "chose iPhone X more than any other iPhone each week in the March quarter."

- Earnings per share: $2.73 vs. $2.67, adjusted, expected by a Thomson Reuters consensus estimate
- Revenue: $61.1 billion vs. $60.82 billion expected by Thomson Reuters consensus
- iPhone unit sales: 52.2 million vs. 52.54 million expected by a StreetAccount estimate
- Fiscal Q3 revenue guidance: $51.5 billion to $53.5 billion vs. $51.61 billion expected by Thomson Reuters consensus

Net income was $13.82 billion, up from $11.03 billion a year ago. A year ago, Apple earned $2.10 a share on revenue of $52.9 billion.

Source: https://cnbc.com/2018/05/01/apple-earnings-q2-2018.html (retrieved November 3, 2018).

Analysts are also interested in the financial position of a company. The financial position can be measured by comparing the resources controlled by the company (**assets**) in relation to the claims against those resources (**liabilities** and **equity**). The combination of liabilities and equity used to finance its assets represents the capital structure of the company. An example of a resource is cash. In Example 1, if no other transactions occur, the company should have €230,000 more in cash at December 31, 2017 than at the start of the period. The cash can be used by the company to pay its obligation to the supplier (a claim against the company) and may also be used to make distributions to the owner (who has a residual claim against the company's assets, net of liabilities).

Financial position and capital structure are particularly important in credit analysis, as depicted in Exhibit 2. Panel A of the exhibit is an excerpt from the company's annual earnings release highlighting the cumulative profitability, strong cash flow, strong balance sheet, and strong return on invested capital. Panel B of the exhibit is an excerpt from an August 2017 news article about an increase in the credit rating of Southwest Airlines due to a long history of profitability and a conservative capital structure.

EXHIBIT 2

Panel A: Excerpt from Earnings Announcement by Southwest Airlines

Southwest Airlines Reports Fourth Quarter and Record Annual Profit; 44th Consecutive Year of Profitability

> DALLAS, Jan. 26, 2017 /PRNewswire/ -- Southwest Airlines Co. (NYSE:LUV) (the "Company") today reported its fourth quarter and annual 2016 results:
>
> Fourth quarter net income of $522 million, or $.84 per diluted share, compared with fourth quarter 2015 net income of $536 million, or $.82 per diluted share.
>
> Excluding special items, fourth quarter net income of $463 million, or $.75 per diluted share, compared with fourth quarter 2015 net income of $591 million, or $.90 per diluted share. This exceeded the First Call fourth quarter 2016 consensus estimate of $.70 per diluted share.
>
> Record annual net income of $2.24 billion, or $3.55 per diluted share, compared with 2015 net income of $2.18 billion, or $3.27 per diluted share.
>
> Excluding special items, record annual net income of $2.37 billion, or $3.75 per diluted share, compared with 2015 net income of $2.36 billion, or $3.52 per diluted share.
>
> Annual operating income of $3.76 billion, resulting in an operating margin of 18.4 percent.
>
> Excluding special items, annual operating income of $3.96 billion, resulting in an operating margin of 19.4 percent.
>
> Record annual operating cash flow of $4.29 billion, and record annual free cash flow of $2.25 billion.
>
> Returned $1.97 billion to Shareholders in 2016, through a combination of $222 million in dividends and $1.75 billion in share repurchases.
>
> Annual return on invested capital (ROIC) of 30.0 percent.
>
> Gary C. Kelly, Chairman of the Board and Chief Executive Officer, stated, "We are delighted to report record annual profits for 2016, our 44th consecutive year of profitability. Our total operating revenues reached a record $20.4 billion, with sustained demand for our legendary low fares and superior Customer Service. Our profit

EXHIBIT 2   (Continued)

margins were very strong, and our ROIC was a near-record 30.0 percent. Our record profits and balance sheet discipline generated record free cash flow, allowing us to return significant value to our Shareholders. Operationally, our performance was also very solid. We carried a record number of Customers while improving our ontime performance, baggage delivery rate, and net promoter score. My thanks and congratulations to the superb People of Southwest for these outstanding results, which earned them $586 million in profit sharing during 2016.

"We ended the year with a solid fourth quarter 2016 performance. Total operating revenues grew 2.0 percent, year-over-year, to a fourth quarter record $5.1 billion, exceeding our expectations as of the beginning of the fourth quarter. Travel demand and close-in yields improved post-election. In addition, December business travel was stronger than anticipated leading up to the holiday period. Based on current bookings and revenue trends, we estimate first quarter 2017 operating unit revenues will be flat to down one percent, year-over-year. This represents a continued and sequential improvement from the 2.9 percent operating unit revenue year-over-year decline in fourth quarter 2016, which is an encouraging start to the year.

"As expected, our fourth quarter unit costs increased, year-over-year, due to higher fuel costs, pay increases from amended union contracts, and additional depreciation expense associated with the accelerated retirement of our Boeing 737-300 aircraft. While inflationary cost pressures are expected in 2017 due to the union contract pay increases, we are continuing our efforts to drive offsetting cost efficiencies through fleet modernization and ongoing technology investments in our operations.

…"As we close out a year of record results, we begin 2017 with momentum and enthusiasm. We are on track to open a new international terminal in Fort Lauderdale, along with the launch of new service, this June. We are on track to launch the new Boeing 737-8 in the fall. And, we are encouraged by recent revenue trends, as well as the prospects for continued economic growth and moderate fuel prices. We are excited about our current outlook for another strong year with opportunities to win more Customers and reward our People and our Shareholders."

Source: http://www.southwestairlinesinvestorrelations.com/news-and-events/news-releases/ 2017/01-26-2017-111504198 (retrieved November 3, 2018)

Panel B: Excerpt from News Article About Southwest Airlines

Southwest Wins Another Credit Rating Upgrade

Citing its "consistent record of profitability," S&P Global Ratings upgraded Southwest Airlines (LUV) on Monday to a triple-B-plus rating from triple-B.

This line from the report sums up the rationale for the upgrade nicely:

Southwest is the only U.S. airline that has recorded 44 consecutive years of profitability and remains the largest low-cost airline in the world.

The credit rating agency commends the airline for its record despite headwinds including, "multiple industry cycles, the evolution of the large U.S. hub-and-spoke airlines into more efficient and financially secure competitors, the emergence of

(continued)

EXHIBIT 2   (Continued)

ultra-low-cost airlines, the acquisition and integration of AirTran Holdings Inc. in 2011, and the company's entry into more congested but lucrative metropolitan airports such as New York's LaGuardia Airport."

In June, Moody's upgraded Southwest to A3, one notch higher than S&P's new rating on its credit scale. Moody's Senior Credit Officer Jonathan Root wrote then, "the upgrade to A3 reflects Moody's expectation that Southwest will continue to conservatively manage its capital structure, allowing it to sustain credit metrics supportive of the A3 rating category."

Source: https://www.barrons.com/articles/southwest-wins-another-credit-rating-upgrade-1502747699 (retrieved November 3, 2018).

In conducting financial analysis of a company, the analyst will regularly refer to the company's financial statements, financial notes, and supplementary schedules and a variety of other information sources. The next section introduces the primary financial statements and some commonly used information sources.

3.   PRIMARY FINANCIAL STATEMENTS AND OTHER INFORMATION SOURCES

In order to perform an equity or credit analysis of a company, an analyst collects a great deal of information. The nature of the information collected will vary on the basis of the individual decision to be made (or the specific purpose of the analysis) but will typically include information about the economy, industry, and company, as well as information about comparable peer companies. Information from outside the company will likely include economic statistics, industry reports, trade publications, and databases containing information on competitors. The company itself provides core information for analysis in its financial reports, press releases, investor conference calls, and webcasts.

Companies prepare financial reports at regular intervals (annually, semiannually, and/or quarterly depending on the applicable regulatory requirements). Financial reports include financial statements along with supplemental disclosures necessary to assess the company's financial position and periodic performance.

Financial statements are the result of an accounting process that records a company's economic activities, following the applicable accounting standards and principles. These statements summarize the accounting information, mainly for users outside the company (such as investors, creditors, analysts, and others) because insiders have direct access to the underlying financial data summarized in the financial statements and to other information that is not included in the financial reporting process.

Financial statements are almost always audited by independent accountants, who provide an opinion on whether the financial statements present fairly the company's performance and financial position, in accordance with a specified, applicable set of accounting standards and principles.

3.1. Financial Statements and Supplementary Information

A complete set of financial statements includes a statement of financial position (i.e., a balance sheet), a statement of comprehensive income (i.e., a single statement of comprehensive income or an income statement and a statement of comprehensive income), a statement of changes in equity, and a statement of cash flows.[1] The balance sheet portrays the company's financial position at a given point in time. The statement of comprehensive income and statement of cash flows present different aspects of a company's performance over a period of time. The statement of changes in equity provides additional information regarding the changes in a company's financial position. In addition, the accompanying required notes, or footnotes, are considered an integral part of a complete set of financial statements.

Along with the required financial statements, a company typically provides additional information in its financial reports. In many jurisdictions, some or all of this additional information is mandated by regulators or accounting standards boards. The additional information provided may include a letter from the chairman of the company, a report from management discussing the results (typically called management discussion and analysis [MD&A] or management commentary), an external auditor's report providing assurances, a governance report describing the structure of the company's board of directors, and a corporate responsibility report. As part of his or her analysis, the financial analyst should read and assess this additional information along with the financial statements. The following sections describe and illustrate each financial statement and some of the additional information.

3.1.1. Balance Sheet (Statement of Financial Position)

The **balance sheet** (also called the **statement of financial position** or **statement of financial condition**) presents a company's financial position by disclosing the resources the company controls (assets) and its obligations to lenders and other creditors (liabilities) at a specific point in time. **Owners' equity** (sometimes called "net assets") represents the excess of assets over liabilities. This amount is attributable to the company's owners or shareholders. Owners' equity is the owners' residual interest in (i.e., residual claim on) the company's assets after deducting its liabilities.

The relationship among the three parts of the balance sheet (assets, liabilities, and owners' equity) can be expressed in the following equation form: Assets = Liabilities + Owners' equity. This equation (sometimes called the accounting equation or the balance sheet equation) shows that the total amount of assets must equal or *balance* with the combined total amounts of liabilities and owners' equity. Alternatively, the equation may be rearranged as follows: Assets − Liabilities = Owners' equity. This formulation emphasizes the residual claim aspect of owners' equity. Depending on the form of the organization, owners' equity may be referred to as "partners' capital" or "shareholders' equity" or "shareholders' funds."

Exhibit 3 presents the balance sheet of the Volkswagen Group from its Annual Report 2017.

---

[1] The names of the financial statements are those in IAS 1. Commonly used terms for these financial statements are indicated in parentheses. Later chapters will elaborate on each of these financial statements.

EXHIBIT 3   Balance Sheet of the Volkswagen Group (Excerpt)

€ million	Dec. 31, 2017	Dec. 31, 2016
Assets		
Noncurrent assets		
Intangible assets	63,419	62,599
Property, plant, and equipment	55,243	54,033
Lease assets	39,254	38,439
Investment property	468	512
Equity-accounted investments	8,205	8,616
Other equity investments	1,318	996
Financial services receivables	73,249	68,402
Other financial assets	8,455	8,256
Other receivables	2,252	2,009
Tax receivables	407	392
Deferred tax assets	9,810	9,756
	262,081	**254,010**
Current assets		
Inventories	40,415	38,978
Trade receivables	13,357	12,187
Financial services receivables	53,145	49,673
Other financial assets	11,998	11,844
Other receivables	5,346	5,130
Tax receivables	1,339	1,126
Marketable securities	15,939	17,520
Cash, cash equivalents, and time deposits	18,457	19,265
Assets held for sale	115	–
	160,112	**155,722**
Total assets	**422,193**	**409,732**
Equity and Liabilities		
Equity		
Subscribed capital	1,283	1,283
Capital reserves	14,551	14,551
Retained earnings	81,367	70,446
Other reserves	560	(1,158)
Equity attributable to Volkswagen AG hybrid capital investors	11,088	7,567
Equity attributable to Volkswagen AG shareholders and hybrid capital investors	108,849	92,689
Noncontrolling interests	229	221
	109,077	**92,910**
Noncurrent liabilities		
Financial liabilities	81,628	66,358
Other financial liabilities	2,665	4,488
Other liabilities	6,199	5,664
Deferred tax liabilities	5,636	4,745

EXHIBIT 3   (Continued)

€ million	Dec. 31, 2017	Dec. 31, 2016
Provisions for pensions	32,730	33,012
Provisions for taxes	3,030	3,556
Other provisions	20,839	21,482
	152,726	**139,306**
Current liabilities		
Put options and compensation rights granted to noncontrolling interest shareholders	3,795	3,849
Financial liabilities	81,844	88,461
Trade payables	23,046	22,794
Tax payables	430	500
Other financial liabilities	8,570	9,438
Other liabilities	15,961	15,461
Provisions for taxes	1,397	1,301
Other provisions	25,347	35,711
	160,389	**177,515**
Total equity and liabilities	**422,193**	**409,732**

Note: Numbers are as shown in the annual report and may not precisely add because of rounding.

Source: Volkswagen 2017 annual report.

In Exhibit 3, the balance sheet is presented with the most recent year in the left column and the earlier year in the right column. Although this is a common presentation, analysts should be careful when reading financial statements. In some cases, the ordering may be reversed, with the earlier year(s) on the left and the most recent year on the far right.

At 31 December 2017, Volkswagen's total resources or assets were €422 billion. This number is the sum of non-current assets of €262 billion and current assets of €160 billion.[2] Total equity was €109 billion. Although Volkswagen does not give a total amount for all the balance sheet liabilities, it can be determined by adding the non-current and current liabilities, €153 billion + €160 billion = €313 billion.[3]

Referring back to the basic accounting equation, Assets = Liabilities + Equity, we have €422billion = €313 billion + €109 billion. In other words, Volkswagen has assets of €422 billion, owes €313 billion, and thus has equity of €109 billion. Using the balance sheet and applying financial statement analysis, the analyst can answer such questions as

- Has the company's liquidity (ability to meet short-term obligations) improved?
- Is the company solvent (does it have sufficient resources to cover its obligations)?
- What is the company's financial position relative to the industry?

---

[2] Current assets are defined, in general, as those assets that are cash or cash equivalents; are held for trading; or are expected to be converted to cash (realized), sold, or consumed within 12 months or the company's normal operating cycle. All other assets are classified as non-current.

[3] Current liabilities are defined, in general, as those that are expected to be settled within 12 months or the company's normal operating cycle. All other liabilities are classified as non-current.

Volkswagen, a German-based automobile manufacturer, prepares its financial statements in accordance with International Financial Reporting Standards (IFRS). IFRS require companies to present balance sheets that show current and non-current assets and current and non-current liabilities as separate classifications. However, IFRS do not prescribe a particular ordering or format, and the order in which companies present their balance sheet items is largely a function of tradition.

As shown, Volkswagen presents non-current assets before current assets, owners' equity before liabilities, and non-current liabilities before current liabilities. This method generally reflects a presentation from least liquid to most liquid. In other countries, the typical order of presentation may differ. For example, in the United States, Australia, and Canada, companies usually present their assets and liabilities from most liquid to least liquid. Cash is typically the first asset shown, and equity is presented after liabilities.

As a basis for comparison, Exhibit 4 presents the balance sheet of Walmart, Inc. (Walmart) from its 2018 annual report, with a fiscal year end of January 31.

EXHIBIT 4   Walmart Consolidated Balance Sheet

	As of January 31	
(Amounts in $ millions)	2018	2017
ASSETS		
Current assets:		
Cash and cash equivalents	6,756	6,867
Receivables, net	5,614	5,835
Inventories	43,783	43,046
Prepaid expenses and other	3,511	1,941
Total current assets	59,664	57,689
Property and equipment:		
Property and equipment	185,154	179,492
Less accumulated depreciation	(77,479)	(71,782)
Property and equipment, net	107,675	107,710
Property under capital lease and financing obligations:		
Property under capital lease and financing obligations	12,703	11,637
Less accumulated amortization	(5,560)	(5,169)
Property under capital lease and financing obligations, net	7,143	6,468
Goodwill	18,242	17,037
Other assets and deferred charges	11,798	9,921
Total assets	204,522	198,825
LIABILITIES AND EQUITY		
Current liabilities:		
Short-term borrowings	5,257	1,099
Accounts payable	46,092	41,433
Accrued liabilities	22,122	20,654
Accrued income taxes	645	921
Long-term debt due within one year	3,738	2,256
Capital lease and financing obligations due within one year	667	565

EXHIBIT 4   (Continued)

(Amounts in $ millions)	As of January 31	
	2018	2017
Total current liabilities	78,521	66,928
Long-term debt	30,045	36,015
Long-term capital lease and financing obligations	6,780	6,003
Deferred income taxes and other	8,354	9,344
Commitments and contingencies		
Equity:		
Common stock	295	305
Capital in excess of par value	2,648	2,371
Retained earnings	85,107	89,354
Accumulated other comprehensive loss	(10,181)	(14,232)
Total Walmart shareholders' equity	77,869	77,798
Noncontrolling interest	2,953	2,737
Total equity	80,822	80,535
Total liabilities and equity	204,522	198,825

Source: Walmart 2018 annual report.

As of January 31, 2018, Walmart has total assets of $205 billion. Liabilities and other non-equity claims total $124 billion, and equity is $81 billion.

3.1.2. Statement of Comprehensive Income

The statement of comprehensive income can be presented as a single statement of comprehensive income or as two statements, an income statement and a statement of comprehensive income that begins with profit or loss from the income statement. The Volkswagen Group chose the latter form of presentation.

3.1.2.1. Income Statement   The income statement presents information on the financial performance of a company's business activities over a period of time. It communicates how much **revenue** and other income the company generated during a period and the expenses it incurred to generate that revenue and other income. Revenue typically refers to amounts charged for the delivery of goods or services in the ordinary activities of a business. Other income may include gains that may or may not arise in the ordinary activities of the business, such as profit on a business disposal. **Expenses** reflect outflows, depletions of assets, and incurrences of liabilities that decrease equity. Expenses typically include such items as cost of sales (cost of goods sold), administrative expenses, and income tax expenses and may be defined to include losses. Net income (revenue plus other income minus expenses) on the income statement is often referred to as the "bottom line" because of its proximity to the bottom of the income statement. Net income may also be referred to as "net earnings," "net profit," and "profit or loss." In the event that expenses exceed revenues and other income, the result is referred to as "net loss."

Income statements are reported on a consolidated basis, meaning that they include the income and expenses of subsidiary companies under the control of the parent (reporting) company. The income statement is sometimes referred to as a **statement of operations** or **profit and loss (P&L) statement**. The basic equation underlying the income statement is Revenue + Other income − Expenses = Income − Expenses = Net income.

In general terms, when one company (the parent) controls another company (the subsidiary), the parent presents its own financial statement information consolidated with that of the subsidiary. (When a parent company owns more than 50 percent of the voting shares of a subsidiary company, it is presumed to control the subsidiary and thus presents consolidated financial statements.) Each line item of the consolidated income statement includes the entire amount from the relevant line item on the subsidiary's income statement (after removing any intercompany transactions). However, if the parent does not own 100 percent of the subsidiary, it is necessary for the parent to present an allocation of net income to the minority interests. Minority interests, also called non-controlling interests, refer to owners of the remaining shares of the subsidiary that are not owned by the parent. The share of consolidated net income attributable to minority interests is shown at the bottom of the income statement along with the net income attributable to shareholders of the parent company. Exhibit 5 presents the income statements of the Volkswagen Group from its 2017 annual report.

EXHIBIT 5   Income Statement of the Volkswagen Group (Excerpt)

€ million	2017	2016
Sales revenue	**230,682**	**217,267**
Cost of sales	(188,140)	(176,270)
Gross result	**42,542**	**40,997**
Distribution expenses	(22,710)	(22,700)
Administrative expenses	(8,254)	(7,336)
Other operating income	14,500	13,049
Other operating expenses	(12,259)	(16,907)
Operating result	**13,818**	**7,103**
Share of the result of equity-accounted investments	3,482	3,497
Interest income	951	1,285
Interest expenses	(2,317)	(2,955)
Other financial result	(2,022)	(1,638)
Financial result	**94**	**189**
Earnings before tax	**13,913**	**7,292**
Income tax income/expense	(2,275)	(1,912)
Current	(3,205)	(3,273)
Deferred	930	1,361
Earnings after tax	11,638	5,379
of which attributable to		
Noncontrolling interests	10	10
Volkswagen AG hybrid capital investors	274	225
Volkswagen AG shareholders	11,354	5,144
Basic earnings per ordinary share in €	**22.63**	**10.24**

EXHIBIT 5   (Continued)

€ million	2017	2016
Diluted earnings per ordinary share in €	**22.63**	**10.24**
Basic earnings per preferred share in €	**22.69**	**10.30**
Diluted earnings per preferred share in €	**22.69**	**10.30**

Note: The numbers are as shown in the annual report and may not add because of rounding.

Source: 2017 Volkswagen annual report.

Exhibit 5 shows that Volkswagen's sales revenue for the year ended December 31, 2017 was €231 billion. Subtracting cost of sales from revenue gives gross profit (called "gross results" by Volkswagen) of €43 billion. After subtracting operating costs and expenses, and adding other operating income, the company's operating profit (called "operating result" by Volkswaen) totals €14 billion. Operating profit represents the results of the company's usual business activities before deducting interest expense or taxes. Operating profit (also called operating income in addition to operating result) is thus often referred to as earnings before interest and taxes (EBIT).

Next, operating profit is increased by Volkswagen's share of the profits generated by certain of its investments (€3.5 billion) plus interest income of €1.0 billion, and decreased by losses from its other financial activities (€2.0 billion) and by interest expense of €2.3 million, resulting in profit (earnings) before tax of €13.9 billion. Total income tax expense for 2017 was €2.3 billion, resulting in profit after tax (net income) of €11.6 billion. After allocating the profits attributable to minority interest ownership in Volkswagen subsidiary companies, the profit attributable to shareholders of Volkswagen for 2017 was €11.4 billion.

Companies present both basic and diluted earnings per share on the face of the income statement. Earnings per share numbers represent net income attributable to the class of shareholders divided by the relevant number of shares outstanding during the period. Basic earnings per share is calculated using the weighted-average number of common (ordinary) shares that were actually outstanding during the period and the profit or loss attributable to the common shareowners. Diluted earnings per share uses **diluted shares**—the number of shares that would hypothetically be outstanding if potentially dilutive claims on common shares (e.g., stock options or convertible bonds) were exercised or converted by their holders—and an appropriately adjusted profit or loss attributable to the common shareowners.

Volkswagen has two types of shareholders, ordinary and preferred, and presents earnings per share information for both, although there is no requirement to present earnings per share information for preferred shareowners. Volkswagen's basic earnings per ordinary share was €22.63. A note to the company's financial statements explains that this number was calculated as follows: €11.4 billion profit attributable to shareholders of Volkswagen, of which €6.8 billion is attributable to ordinary shareholders and the balance is attributable to preferred shareholders. The €6.8 billion attributable to ordinary shareholders divided by the weighted-average number of ordinary shares of 0.295 billion shares equals basic earnings per share of €22.63. Similar detail is provided in the notes for each of the earnings per share numbers.

An analyst examining the income statement might note that Volkswagen was profitable in both years. The company's profits increased substantially in 2017, primarily because of higher sales and lower other operating expenses (footnotes reveal this was largely due to $4 billion less in litigation expenses in 2017). The analyst might formulate questions related to profitability, such as the following:

- Is the change in revenue related to an increase in units sold, an increase in prices, or some combination?
- If the company has multiple business segments (for example, Volkswagen's segments include passenger cars, light commercial vehicles, and financial services, among others), how are the segments' revenue and profits changing?
- How does the company compare with other companies in the industry?

Answering such questions requires the analyst to gather, analyze, and interpret information from a number of sources, including, but not limited to, the income statement.

3.1.2.2. Other Comprehensive Income   Comprehensive income includes all items that impact owners' equity but are not the result of transactions with shareowners. Some of these items are included in the calculation of net income, and some are included in other comprehensive income (OCI). When comprehensive income is presented in two statements, the statement of comprehensive income begins with the profit or loss from the income statement and then presents the components of OCI.

Exhibit 6 presents an excerpt from the statement of comprehensive income of the Volkswagen Group from its 2017 annual report.

EXHIBIT 6   Statement of Comprehensive Income of the Volkswagen Group (Excerpt)

€ million	Fiscal Year Ended December 31, 2017
Earnings after tax	**11,638**
Pension plan remeasurements recognized in other comprehensive income	
Pension plan remeasurements recognized in other comprehensive income, before tax	785
Deferred taxes relating to pension plan remeasurements recognized in other comprehensive income	(198)
Pension plan remeasurements recognized in other comprehensive income, net of tax	588
Share of other comprehensive income of equity-accounted investments that will not be reclassified to profit or loss, net of tax	96
Items that will not be reclassified to profit or loss	**683**
Exchange differences on translating foreign operations	
Unrealized currency translation gains/losses	(2,095)
Transferred to profit or loss	(4)
Exchange differences on translating foreign operations, before tax	(2,099)
Deferred taxes relating to exchange differences on translating foreign operations	(8)
Exchange differences on translating foreign operations, net of tax	(2,107)
Cash flow hedges	
Fair value changes recognized in other comprehensive income	6,137
Transferred to profit or loss	(558)

EXHIBIT 6   (Continued)

€ million	Fiscal Year Ended December 31, 2017
Cash flow hedges, before tax	5,579
Deferred taxes relating to cash flow hedges	(1,597)
Cash flow hedges, net of tax	3,982
Available-for-sale financial assets	
Fair value changes recognized in other comprehensive income	56
Transferred to profit or loss	62
Available-for-sale financial assets, before tax	118
Deferred taxes relating to available-for-sale financial assets	(25)
Available-for-sale financial assets, net of tax	93
Share of other comprehensive income of equity-accounted investments that may be reclassified subsequently to profit or loss, net of tax	(346)
Items that may be reclassified subsequently to profit or loss	**1,622**
Other comprehensive income, before tax	4,133
Deferred taxes relating to other comprehensive income	(1,828)
Other comprehensive income, net of tax	**2,305**
Total comprehensive income	**13,943**

Source: Volkswagen 2017 annual report.

Exhibit 6 shows total comprehensive income for 2017 was €13.9 billion, which is the sum of earnings after tax of €11.6 billion, reported on the income statement, and other comprehensive income of €2.3 billion. The items in OCI reflect changes in the company's equity that are not considered to be profit or loss, some of which may be reclassified as such in the future such as unrealized currency translation gains and losses. The statement of comprehensive income will be discussed in greater detail in a later chapter.

3.1.3. Statement of Changes in Equity

The statement of changes in equity, sometimes called the "statement of changes in owners' equity" or "statement of changes in shareholders' equity," primarily serves to report changes in the owners' investment in the business over time. The basic components of owners' equity are paid-in capital and retained earnings. Retained earnings include the cumulative amount of the company's profits that have been retained in the company. In addition, non-controlling or minority interests and reserves that represent accumulated OCI items are included in equity. The latter items may be shown separately or included in retained earnings. Volkswagen includes reserves as components of retained earnings.

The statement of changes in equity is organized to present, for each component of equity, the beginning balance, any increases during the period, any decreases during the period, and the ending balance. For paid-in capital, an example of an increase is a new issuance of equity, and an example of a decrease is a repurchase of previously issued stock. For retained earnings, income (both net income as reported on the income statement and OCI) is the most common increase, and a dividend payment is the most common decrease.

Volkswagen's balance sheet in Exhibit 3 shows that equity at the end of 2017 totaled €109 billion, compared with €93 billion at the end of 2016. The company's statement of changes in equity presents additional detail on the change in each line item. Exhibit 7 presents an excerpt of the statement of changes in equity of the Volkswagen Group from its 2017 annual report. For purposes of brevity, several interim columns were excluded from the presentation.

EXHIBIT 7   Statement of Changes in Equity of the Volkswagen Group (Excerpt)

€ million	Subscribed capital	Capital reserves	Retained earnings	Total equity
Balance at 1 January 2017	1,283	14,551	70,446	92,910
Earnings after tax	–	–	11,354	11,638
Other comprehensive income, net of tax	–	–	586	2,305
Total comprehensive income	–	–	11,940	13,943
Capital increases	–	–	–	3,481
Dividends payment	–	–	–1,015	–1,332
Capital transactions involving a change in ownership interest	–	–	–	–
Other changes	–	–	–4	75
Balance at December 31, 2017	1,283	14,551	81,367	109,077

Note: Numbers are as shown in the annual report and may not add and cross-add because of the exclusion of columns and due to rounding.

In Exhibit 7, as shown in the far right column, total equity is increased during the year by total comprehensive income of €13.9 billion and by capital infusions of €3.5 billion; it is decreased by dividends of €1.3 billion; and, finally, slightly increased by €75 million of other changes. Explanatory notes on equity are included in the notes to the consolidated financial statements.

3.1.4. Cash Flow Statement

Although the income statement and balance sheet provide measures of a company's success in terms of performance and financial position, cash flow is also vital to a company's long-term success. Disclosing the sources and uses of cash helps creditors, investors, and other statement users evaluate the company's liquidity, solvency, and financial flexibility. **Financial flexibility** is the ability of the company to react and adapt to financial adversity and opportunities.

The cash flow statement classifies all cash flows of the company into three categories: operating, investing, and financing. Cash flows from **operating activities** generally involve the cash effects of transactions involved in the determination of net income and, hence, comprise the day-to-day operations of the company. Cash flows from **investing activities** are associated with the acquisition and disposal of long-term assets, such as property and equipment. Cash flows from **financing activities** relate to obtaining or repaying capital to be used in the business. IFRS permit more flexibility than US GAAP in classifying dividend and interest receipts and payments within these categories.

Exhibit 8 presents Volkswagen's statement of cash flows for the fiscal years ended December 31, 2017 and 2016.

EXHIBIT 8   Cash Flow Statement of the Volkswagen Group: 1 January to 31 December

€ million	2017	2016
Cash and cash equivalents at beginning of period	**18,833**	**20,462**
Earnings before tax	13,913	7,292
Income taxes paid	(3,664)	(3,315)
Depreciation and amortization of, and impairment losses on, intangible assets, property, plant and equipment, and investment property	10,562	10,100
Amortization of and impairment losses on capitalized development costs	3,734	3,586
Impairment losses on equity investments	136	130
Depreciation of and impairment losses on lease assets	7,734	7,107
Gain/loss on disposal of noncurrent assets and equity investments	(25)	(222)
Share of the result of equity-accounted investments	274	377
Other noncash expense/income	(480)	716
Change in inventories	(4,198)	(3,637)
Change in receivables (excluding financial services)	(1,660)	(2,155)
Change in liabilities (excluding financial liabilities)	5,302	5,048
Change in provisions	(9,443)	5,966
Change in lease assets	(11,478)	(12,074)
Change in financial services receivables	(11,891)	(9,490)
Cash flows from operating activities	**(1,185)**	**9,430**
Investments in intangible assets (excluding development costs), property, plant and equipment, and investment property	(13,052)	(13,152)
Additions to capitalized development costs	(5,260)	(5,750)
Acquisition of subsidiaries	(277)	(119)
Acquisition of other equity investments	(561)	(309)
Disposal of subsidiaries	496	(7)
Disposal of other equity investments	24	2,190
Proceeds from disposal of intangible assets, property, plant and equipment, and investment property	411	351
Change in investments in securities	1,376	(1,245)
Change in loans and time deposits	335	(2,638)
Cash flows from investing activities	**(16,508)**	**(20,679)**
Capital contributions	3,473	–
Dividends paid	(1,332)	(364)
Capital transactions with noncontrolling interest shareholders	–	(3)
Proceeds from issuance of bonds	30,279	14,262
Repayments of bonds	(17,877)	(23,601)
Changes in other financial liabilities	3,109	19,455
Lease payments	(28)	(36)
Cash flows from financing activities	**17,625**	**9,712**
Effect of exchange rate changes on cash and cash equivalents	(727)	(91)
Net change in cash and cash equivalents	**(796)**	**(1,628)**
Cash and cash equivalents at end of period	**18,038**	**18,833**

After showing the beginning cash balance, the operating activities section starts with profit before tax,[4] €13.9 billion for 2017, subtracts actual income tax payments, and then adjusts for the effects of non-cash transactions, accruals and deferrals, and transactions of an investing and financing nature to arrive at the amount of cash generated from operating activities: a negative €1.2 billion (a net use of cash). This approach to reporting cash flow from operating activities is termed the indirect method. The direct method of reporting cash flows from operating activities discloses major classes of gross cash receipts and gross cash payments. Examples are cash received from customers and cash paid to suppliers and employees.

The indirect method emphasizes the different perspectives of the income statement and cash flow statement. On the income statement, income is reported when earned, not necessarily when cash is received, and expenses are reported when incurred, not necessarily when paid. The cash flow statement presents another aspect of performance: the ability of a company to generate cash flow from running its business. Ideally, for an established company, the analyst would like to see that the primary source of cash flow is from operating activities as opposed to investing or financing activities.

The sum of the net cash flows from operating, investing, and financing activities and the effect of exchange rates on cash equals the net change in cash during the fiscal year. For Volkswagen, the sum of these four items was a negative €796 million in 2017, decreasing the company's cash and cash equivalents from €18.8 billion at the beginning of the period to €18.0 billion at the end of the period.

3.1.5. Financial Notes and Supplementary Schedules

The notes (also sometimes referred to as footnotes) that accompany the four financial statements are required and are an integral part of the complete set of financial statements. The notes provide information that is essential to understanding the information provided in the primary statements. Volkswagen's 2017 financial statements, for example, include more than 100 pages of notes.

The notes disclose the basis of preparation for the financial statements. For example, Volkswagen discloses that its fiscal year corresponds to the calendar year; its financial statements are prepared in accordance with IFRS as adopted by the European Union; the statements are prepared in compliance with German law; the statements are denominated in millions of euros unless otherwise specified; and the figures have been rounded, which might give rise to minor discrepancies when they are added. Volkswagen also states that its financial statements are on a consolidated basis—that is, including Volkswagen AG and all of the subsidiary companies it controls.

The notes also disclose information about the accounting policies, methods, and estimates used to prepare the financial statements. As will be discussed in later chapters, both IFRS and US GAAP allow some flexibility in choosing among alternative policies and methods when accounting for certain items. This flexibility aims to meet the divergent needs of many businesses for reporting a variety of economic transactions. In addition to differences in accounting policies and methods, differences arise as a result of estimates needed to record and measure transactions, events, and financial statement line items.

---

[4]Other companies may choose to begin with net income.

Overall, flexibility in accounting choices is necessary because, ideally, a company will select those policies, methods, and estimates that are allowable and most relevant and that fairly reflect the unique economic environment of the company's business and industry. Flexibility can, however, create challenges for the analyst because the use of different policies, methods, and estimates reduces comparability across different companies' financial statements. Comparability occurs when different companies' information is measured and reported in a similar manner over time. Comparability helps the analyst identify and analyze the real economic differences across companies, rather than differences that arise solely from different accounting choices. Because comparability of financial statements is a critical requirement for objective financial analysis, an analyst should be aware of the potential for differences in accounting choices even when comparing two companies that use the same set of accounting standards.

For example, if a company acquires a piece of equipment to use in its operations, accounting standards require that the cost of the equipment be reported as an expense by allocating its cost, less any residual value, in a systematic manner over the equipment's useful life. This allocation of the cost is known as **depreciation**. Accounting standards permit flexibility, however, in determining the manner in which each year's expense is determined. Two companies may acquire similar equipment but use different methods and assumptions to record the expense over time. An analyst's ability to compare the companies' performance is hindered by the difference. Analysts must understand reporting choices in order to make appropriate adjustments when comparing companies' financial positions and performance.

A company's significant accounting choices (policies, methods, and estimates) must be discussed in the notes to the financial statements. For example, a note containing a summary of significant accounting policies includes how the company recognizes its revenues and depreciates its non-current tangible assets. Analysts must understand the accounting choices a company makes and determine whether they are similar to those of other companies identified and used as benchmarks or comparables. If the policies of the companies being compared are different, the analyst who understands accounting and financial reporting can often make necessary adjustments so that the financial statement data used are more comparable.

For many companies, the financial notes and supplemental schedules provide explanatory information about every line item (or almost every line item) on the balance sheet and income statement, as illustrated by the note references in Volkswagen's balance sheet and income statement in Exhibits 3 and 5. In addition, note disclosures include information about the following (this is not an exhaustive list):

- financial instruments and risks arising from financial instruments,
- commitments and contingencies,
- legal proceedings,
- related-party transactions,
- subsequent events (i.e., events that occur after the balance sheet date),
- business acquisitions and disposals, and
- operating segments' performance.

EXHIBIT 9   Notes to the Consolidated Financial Statements of the Volkswagen Group: Selected Data on Operating Segments (Excerpt)

€ million	Passenger cars	Commercial vehicles	Power engineering	Financial services	Total segments	Reconciliation	Volkswagen Group
Sales revenue from external customers	169,513	27,632	3,280	30,191	230,618	64	230,682
Intersegment sales revenue	18,892	7,568	3	3,541	30,004	–30,004	–
Total sales revenue	188,405	35,200	3,283	33,733	260,621	–29,939	230,682
Depreciation and amortization	11,363	2,557	371	6,797	21,089	-147	20,941
Impairment losses	704	2	0	574	1,280	0	1,280
Reversal of impairment losses	14	1	–	41	56	–	56
Segment result (operating result)	12,644	1,892	-55	2,673	17,153	–3,335	13,818
Share of the result of equity-accounted investments	3,390	83	1	9	3,482	–	3,482
Net interest result and other financial result	–1,920	–220	-2	–180	–2,321	–1,067	–3,388
Equity-accounted investments	6,724	753	18	710	8,205	–	8,205
Investments in intangible assets, property, plant and equipment, and investment property	15,713	1,915	159	421	18,208	104	18,313

22

An analyst uses a significant amount of judgment in deciding how to incorporate information from note disclosures into the analysis. For example, such information as financial instrument risk, contingencies, and legal proceedings can alert an analyst to risks that can affect a company's financial position and performance in the future and that require monitoring over time. As another example, information about a company's operating segments can be useful as a means of quickly understanding what a company does and how and where it earns money. The operating segment data shown in Exhibit 9 appear in the notes to the financial statements for Volkswagen. (The totals of the segment data do not equal the amounts reported in the company's financial statements because the financial statement data are adjusted for intersegment activities and unallocated items. The notes provide a complete reconciliation of the segment data to the reported data.) From the data in Exhibit 9, an analyst can quickly see that most of the company's revenues and operating profits come from the sale of passenger cars. Over 80 percent of the company's revenues was generated by this segment This segment accounted for over 90 percent of the company's total segment operating profits.

Experience using the disclosures made by a company and its competitors typically enhances an analyst's judgment about the relative importance of different disclosures and the ways in which they can be helpful.

3.1.6. Management Commentary or Management's Discussion and Analysis

Publicly held companies typically include a section in their annual reports where management discusses a variety of issues, including the nature of the business, past results, and future outlook. This section is referred to by a variety of names, including management report(ing), management commentary, operating and financial review, and management's discussion and analysis. Inclusion of a management report is recommended by the International Organization of Securities Commissions and frequently required by regulatory authorities, such as the US Securities and Exchange Commission (SEC) or the UK Financial Reporting Council (FRC). In Germany, management reporting has been required since 1931 and is audited.

The discussion by management is arguably one of the most useful parts of a company's annual report besides the financial statements themselves; however, other than excerpts from the financial statements, information included in the management commentary is typically unaudited. When using information from the management report, an analyst should be aware of whether the information is audited or unaudited.

To help improve the quality of the discussion by management, the International Accounting Standards Board (IASB) issued an IFRS Practice Statement "Management Commentary" that includes a framework for the preparation and presentation of management commentary. The framework provides guidance rather than sets forth requirements in a standard. The framework identifies five content elements of a "decision-useful management commentary": 1) the nature of the business; 2) management's objectives and strategies; 3) the company's significant resources, risks, and relationships; 4) results of operations; and 5) critical performance measures.

In the United States, the SEC requires listed companies to provide an MD&A and specifies the content.[5] Management must highlight any favorable or unfavorable trends and identify

---

[5] Relevant sections of SEC requirements are included for reference in the FASB ASC. The FASB ASC does not include sections of SEC requirements that deal with matters outside the basic financial statements, such as the MD&A.

significant events and uncertainties that affect the company's liquidity, capital resources, and results of operations. The MD&A must also provide information about the effects of inflation, changing prices, or other material events and uncertainties that may cause the future operating results and financial condition to materially depart from the current reported financial information. In addition, the MD&A must provide information about off-balance-sheet obligations and about contractual commitments such as purchase obligations. Management should also discuss the critical accounting policies that require them to make subjective judgments and that have a significant impact on reported financial results.

The management commentary, or MD&A, is a good starting place for understanding information in the financial statements. In particular, the forward-looking disclosures, such as those about planned capital expenditures, new store openings, or divestitures, can be useful in projecting a company's future performance. However, the commentary is only one input for the analyst seeking an objective and independent perspective on a company's performance and prospects.

The management report in Volkswagen's 2017 annual report includes much information of potential interest to an analyst. The lengthy report contains sections such as Goals and Strategies, Internal Management and Key Performance Indicators, Structure and Business Activities, Corporate Governance, Remuneration, Executive Bodies, Disclosures Required under Takeover Law, Diesel Issue, Business Development, Shares and Bonds, Results of Operations, and Report on Risks and Opportunities.

3.1.7. Auditor's Reports

Financial statements presented in companies' annual reports are generally required to be audited (examined) by an independent accounting firm in accordance with specified auditing standards. The independent auditor then provides a written opinion on the financial statements. This opinion is referred to as the audit report. Audit reports may vary in different jurisdictions, but the minimum components, including a specific statement of the auditor's opinion, are similar. Audits of financial statements may be required by contractual arrangement, law, or regulation.

International standards on auditing (ISAs) have been developed by the International Auditing and Assurance Standards Board (IAASB). This body has emerged from the International Federation of Accountants. ISAs have been adopted by many countries and are referenced in audit reports issued in those countries. Other countries, such as the United States, specify their own auditing standards. With the enactment of the Sarbanes–Oxley Act of 2002 in the United States, auditing standards for public companies are promulgated by the Public Company Accounting Oversight Board.

Under international standards for auditing (ISAs), the overall objectives of an auditor in conducting an audit of financial statements are

A. To obtain reasonable assurance about whether the financial statements as a whole are free from material misstatement, whether due to fraud or error, thereby enabling the auditor to express an opinion on whether the financial statements are prepared, in all material respects, in accordance with an applicable financial reporting framework; and

B. To report on the financial statements, and communicate as required by the ISAs, in accordance with the auditor's findings.[6]

---

[6]See the International Auditing and Assurance Standards Board (IAASB) *Handbook of International Quality Control, Auditing, Review, Other Assurance, and Related Services Pronouncements.*

Publicly traded companies may also have requirements set by regulators or stock exchanges, such as appointing an independent audit committee within its board of directors to oversee the audit process. The audit process provides a basis for the independent auditor to express an opinion on whether the information in the audited financial statements presents fairly the financial position, performance, and cash flows of the company in accordance with a specified set of accounting standards.

Audits are designed and conducted using sampling techniques, and financial statement line items may be based on estimates and assumptions. This means that the auditors cannot express an opinion that provides absolute assurance about the accuracy or precision of the financial statements. Instead, the independent audit report provides *reasonable assurance* that the financial statements are *fairly presented*, meaning that there is a high probability that the audited financial statements are free from *material* error, fraud, or illegal acts that have a direct effect on the financial statements.

The independent audit report expresses the auditor's opinion on the fairness of the audited financial statements, and specifies which financial statements were audited, the reporting entity, and the date. An *unqualified* audit opinion states that the financial statements give a "true and fair view" (international) or are "fairly presented" (international and US) in accordance with applicable accounting standards. This is also referred to as an "unmodified" or a "clean" opinion and is the one that analysts would like to see in a financial report. There are several other types of modified opinions. A *qualified* audit opinion is one in which there is some scope limitation or exception to accounting standards. Exceptions are described in the audit report with additional explanatory paragraphs so that the analyst can determine the importance of the exception. An *adverse* audit opinion is issued when an auditor determines that the financial statements materially depart from accounting standards and are not fairly presented. Finally, a *disclaimer of opinion* occurs when, for some reason, such as a scope limitation, the auditors are unable to issue an opinion.

The audit report also describes the basis for the auditor's opinion and, for listed companies, includes a discussion of Key Audit Matters (international) and Critical Audit Matters (US).[7] Key Audit Matters are defined as issues that the auditor considers to be most important, such as those that have a higher risk of misstatement, involve significant management judgment, or report the effects of significant transactions during the period. Critical Audit Matters are defined as issues that involve "especially challenging, subjective, or complex auditor judgment" and similarly include areas with higher risk of misstatement or involving significant management judgement and estimates.

Exhibit 10 presents the independent auditor's report for Volkswagen. Note that Volkswagen received an unqualified audit opinion (i.e., clean or unmodified opinion) from PricewaterhouseCoopers for the company's fiscal year ended December 31, 2017.

---

[7] Discussion of Key Audit Matters in the auditor's report is required by the International Standard on Auditing (ISA) ISA 701, effective in 2017, issued by the International Audit and Assurance Standards Board. Discussion of Critical Audit Matters in the auditor's report is required by the Auditor Reporting Standard AS 3101, effective for large filers' fiscal years ending on or after June 30, 2019, issued by the Public Company Accounting Oversight Board.

EXHIBIT 10   Volkswagen's Independent Audit Report
_____

On completion of our audit, we issued the following unqualified auditor's report dated February 23, 2018. This report was originally prepared in German. In case of ambiguities the German version takes precedence:

    To VOLKSWAGEN AKTIENGESELLSCHAFT, Wolfsburg
    REPORT ON THE AUDIT OF THE CONSOLIDATED FINANCIAL STATEMENTS AND OF THE GROUP MANAGEMENT REPORT

Audit Opinions

We have audited the consolidated financial statements of VOLKSWAGEN AKTIENGESELLSCHAFT, Wolfsburg, and its subsidiaries (the Group), which comprise the income statement and the statement of comprehensive income, the balance sheet, the statement of changes in equity and the cash flow statement for the financial year from January 1 to December 31, 2017, and notes to the consolidated financial statements, including a summary of significant accounting policies. In addition, we have audited the group management report of VOLKSWAGEN AKTIENGESELLSCHAFT, which is combined with the Company's management report, for the financial year from January 1 to December 31, 2017. We have not audited the content of those parts of the group management report listed in the "Other Information" section of our auditor's report in accordance with the German legal requirements.

In our opinion, on the basis of the knowledge obtained in the audit,

- the accompanying consolidated financial statements comply, in all material respects, with the IFRSs as adopted by the EU, and the additional requirements of German commercial law pursuant to § [Article] 315e Abs. [paragraph] 1 HGB [Handelsgesetzbuch: German Commercial Code] and, in compliance with these requirements, give a true and fair view of the assets, liabilities, and financial position of the Group as at December 31, 2017, and of its financial performance for the financial year from January 1 to December 31, 2017, and
- the accompanying group management report as a whole provides an appropriate view of the Group's position. In all material respects, this group management report is consistent with the consolidated financial statements, complies with German legal requirements and appropriately presents the opportunities and risks of future development. Our audit opinion on the group management report does not cover the content of those parts of the group management report listed in the "Other Information" section of our auditor's report.

    Pursuant to § 322 Abs. 3 Satz [sentence] 1 HGB, we declare that our audit has not led to any reservations relating to the legal compliance of the consolidated financial statements and of the group management report.

Basis for the Audit Opinions

We conducted our audit of the consolidated financial statements and of the group management report in accordance with § 317 HGB and the EU Audit Regulation (No. 537/2014, referred to subsequently as "EU Audit Regulation") and in compliance with German Generally Accepted Standards for Financial Statement Audits promulgated by the Institut der Wirtschaftsprüfer [Institute of Public Auditors in Germany] (IDW). Our responsibilities under those requirements and principles are further described in the "Auditor's Responsibilities for the Audit of the Consolidated

EXHIBIT 10   (Continued)

Financial Statements and of the Group Management Report" section of our auditor's report. We are independent of the group entities in accordance with the requirements of European law and German commercial and professional law, and we have fulfilled our other German professional responsibilities in accordance with these requirements. In addition, in accordance with Article 10 (2) point (f) of the EU Audit Regulation, we declare that we have not provided non-audit services prohibited under Article 5 (1) of the EU Audit Regulation. We believe that the audit evidence we have obtained is sufficient and appropriate to provide a basis for our audit opinions on the consolidated financial statements and on the group management report.

Emphasis of Matter – Diesel Issue

We draw attention to the information provided and statements made in section "Key Events" of the notes to the consolidated financial statements and in section "Diesel Issue" of the group management report with regard to the diesel issue including information about the underlying causes, the noninvolvement of members of the board of management as well as the impact on these financial statements.

Based on the results of the various measures taken to investigate the issue presented so far, which underlie the consolidated financial statements and the group management report, there is still no evidence that members of the Company's board of management were aware of the deliberate manipulation of engine management software before summer 2015. Nevertheless, should as a result of the ongoing investigation new solid knowledge be obtained showing that members of the board of management were informed earlier about the diesel issue, this could eventually have an impact on the consolidated financial statements and on the group management report for financial year 2017 and prior years.

The provisions for warranties and legal risks recorded so far are based on the presented state of knowledge. Due to the inevitable uncertainties associated with the current and expected litigation it cannot be excluded that a future assessment of the risks may be different.

Our opinions on the consolidated financial statements and on the group management report are not modified in respect of this matter.

Source: Volkswagen 2017 annual report

In the United States, under the Sarbanes–Oxley Act, the auditors must also express an opinion on the company's internal control systems. This information may be provided in a separate opinion or incorporated as a paragraph in the opinion related to the financial statements. The internal control system is the company's internal system that is designed, among other things, to ensure that the company's process for generating financial reports is sound. Although management has always been responsible for maintaining effective internal control, the Sarbanes–Oxley Act greatly increases management's responsibility for demonstrating that the company's internal controls are effective. Management of publicly traded companies in the United States are now required by securities regulators to explicitly accept responsibility for the effectiveness of internal control, evaluate the effectiveness of internal control using suitable control criteria, support the evaluation with sufficient competent evidence, and provide a report on internal control.

Although these reports and attestations provide some assurances to analysts, they are not infallible. The analyst must always use a degree of healthy skepticism when analyzing financial statements.

3.2. Other Sources of Information

The information described in Section 3.1 is generally provided to shareholders at least annually. In addition, companies also provide information on management and director compensation, company stock performance, and any potential conflicts of interest that may exist between management, the board, and shareholders. This information may appear in the company's annual report or other publicly available documents. Public companies often provide this information in proxy statements, which are distributed to shareholders about matters that are to be put to a vote at the annual (or special) meeting of shareholders.

Interim reports are also provided by the company either semiannually or quarterly, depending on the applicable regulatory requirements. Interim reports generally present the four primary financial statements and condensed notes but are not audited. These interim reports provide updated information on a company's performance and financial position since the last annual period.

Companies also provide relevant current information on their websites, in press releases, and in conference calls with analysts and investors. One type of press release, which analysts often consider to be particularly important, is the periodic earnings announcement. The earnings announcement often happens well before the company files its formal financial statements. Such earnings announcements are often followed by a conference call in which the company's senior executives describe the company's performance and answer questions posed by conference call participants. Following the earnings conference call, the investor relations portion of the company's website may post a recording of the call accompanied by slides and supplemental information that was discussed.

When performing financial statement analysis, analysts should review all these company sources of information as well as information from external sources regarding the economy, the industry, the company, and peer (comparable) companies. Information on the economy, industry, and peer companies is useful in putting the company's financial performance and position in perspective and in assessing the company's future. In most cases, information from sources apart from the company is crucial to an analyst's effectiveness. For example, an analyst studying a consumer-oriented company will typically seek direct experience with the products (taste the food or drink, use the shampoo or soap, visit the stores or hotels). An analyst following a highly regulated industry will study the existing and expected relevant regulations. An analyst following a highly technical industry will gain relevant expertise personally or seek input from a technical specialist. In sum, thorough research goes beyond financial reports.

The next section presents a framework for using all this information in financial statement analysis.

4. FINANCIAL STATEMENT ANALYSIS FRAMEWORK

Analysts work in a variety of positions within the investment management industry. Some are equity analysts whose main objective is to evaluate potential investments in a company's equity securities (i.e., the shares or stock it issues) as a basis for deciding whether a prospective investment is attractive and what an appropriate purchase price might be. Others are credit analysts who evaluate the credit-worthiness of a company to decide whether (and on what terms) a loan should be made or what credit rating should be assigned. Analysts may also be involved in a variety of other tasks, such as evaluating the performance of a subsidiary company, evaluating a private equity investment, or finding stocks that are overvalued for purposes of taking a short position.

This section presents a generic framework for financial statement analysis that can be used in these various tasks. The framework is summarized in Exhibit 11.[8]

EXHIBIT 11   Financial Statement Analysis Framework

Phase	Sources of Information	Output
1. Articulate the purpose and context of the analysis.	• The nature of the analyst's function, such as evaluating an equity or debt investment or issuing a credit rating. • Communication with client or supervisor on needs and concerns. • Institutional guidelines related to developing specific work product.	• Statement of the purpose or objective of analysis. • A list (written or unwritten) of specific questions to be answered by the analysis. • Nature and content of report to be provided. • Timetable and budgeted resources for completion.
2. Collect input data.	• Financial statements, other financial data, questionnaires, and industry/economic data. • Discussions with management, suppliers, customers, and competitors. • Company site visits (e.g., to production facilities or retail stores).	• Organized financial statements. • Financial data tables. • Completed questionnaires, if applicable.
3. Process data.	• Data from the previous phase.	• Adjusted financial statements. • Common-size statements. • Ratios and graphs. • Forecasts.
4. Analyze/interpret the processed data.	• Input data as well as processed data.	• Analytical results.
5. Develop and communicate conclusions and recommendations (e.g., with an analysis report).	• Analytical results and previous reports. • Institutional guidelines for published reports.	• Analytical report answering questions posed in Phase 1. • Recommendation regarding the purpose of the analysis, such as whether to make an investment or grant credit.
6. Follow-up.	• Information gathered by periodically repeating above steps as necessary to determine whether changes to holdings or recommendations are necessary.	• Updated reports and recommendations.

---

[8] Components of this framework have been adapted from van Greuning and Bratanovic (2003, p. 300) and from Benninga and Sarig (1997, pp. 134–156).

The following sections discuss the individual phases of financial statement analysis.

4.1. Articulate the Purpose and Context of Analysis

Prior to undertaking any analysis, it is essential to understand the purpose of the analysis. An understanding of the purpose is particularly important in financial statement analysis because of the numerous available techniques and the substantial amount of data.

Some analytical tasks are well defined, in which case articulating the purpose of the analysis requires little decision making by the analyst. For example, a periodic credit review of an investment-grade debt portfolio or an equity analyst's report on a particular company may be guided by institutional norms such that the purpose of the analysis is given. Furthermore, the format, procedures, and/or sources of information may also be given.

For other analytical tasks, articulating the purpose of the analysis requires the analyst to make decisions. The purpose of an analysis guides further decisions about the approach, the tools, the data sources, the format in which to report the results of the analysis, and the relative importance of different aspects of the analysis.

When facing a substantial amount of data, a less experienced analyst may be tempted to just start making calculations and generating financial ratios without considering what is relevant for the decision at hand. It is generally advisable to resist this temptation and thus avoid unnecessary or pointless efforts. Consider these questions: If you could have all the calculations and ratios completed instantly, what conclusion would you be able to draw? What question would you be able to answer? What decision would your answer support?

The analyst should also define the context at this stage. Who is the intended audience? What is the end product—for example, a final report explaining conclusions and recommendations? What is the time frame (i.e., when is the report due)? What resources and resource constraints are relevant to completion of the analysis? Again, the context may be predefined (i.e., standard and guided by institutional norms).

Having clarified the purpose and context of the financial statement analysis, the analyst should next compile the specific questions to be answered by the analysis. For example, if the purpose of the financial statement analysis (or, more likely, the particular stage of a larger analysis) is to compare the historical performance of three companies operating in a particular industry, specific questions would include the following: What has been the relative growth rate of the companies, and what has been their relative profitability?

4.2. Collect Data

Next, the analyst obtains the data required to answer the specific questions. A key part of this step is obtaining an understanding of the company's business, financial performance, and financial position (including trends over time and in comparison with peer companies). For historical analyses, financial statement data alone are adequate in some cases. For example, to screen a large number of companies to find those with a minimum level of profitability, financial statement data alone would be adequate. But to address more in-depth questions, such as why and how one company performed better or worse than its competitors, additional information would be required. As another example, to compare the historical performance of two companies in a particular industry, the historical financial statements would be sufficient to determine which had faster-growing sales or earnings and which was more profitable. However, a broader comparison with overall industry growth and profitability would obviously require industry data.

Furthermore, information on the economy and industry is necessary to understand the environment in which the company operates. Analysts often take a top-down approach whereby they 1) gain an understanding of the macroeconomic environment, such as prospects for growth in the economy and inflation, 2) analyze the prospects of the industry in which the company operates, based on the expected macroeconomic environment, and 3) determine the prospects for the company given the expected industry and macroeconomic environments. For example, an analyst may need to forecast future growth in earnings for a company. Past company data provide the platform for statistical forecasting; however, an understanding of economic and industry conditions can improve the analyst's ability to forecast earnings.

4.3. Process Data

After obtaining the requisite financial statement and other information, the analyst processes these data using appropriate analytical tools. For example, processing the data may involve computing ratios or growth rates; preparing common-size financial statements; creating charts; performing statistical analyses, such as regressions or Monte Carlo simulations; performing equity valuation; performing sensitivity analyses; or using any other analytical tools or combination of tools that are available and appropriate for the task. A comprehensive financial analysis at this stage would include the following:

- Reading and evaluating financial statements for each company being analyzed. This includes reading the notes and understanding what accounting standards have been used (for example, IFRS or US GAAP), what accounting choices have been made (for example, when to report revenue on the income statement), and what operating decisions have been made that affect reported financial statements (for example, leasing versus purchasing equipment).
- Making any needed adjustments to the financial statements to facilitate comparison when the unadjusted statements of the subject companies reflect differences in accounting standards, accounting choices, or operating decisions. Note that commonly used databases do not always make such analyst adjustments.
- Preparing or collecting common-size financial statement data (which scale data to directly reflect percentages [e.g., of sales] or changes [e.g., from the prior year]) and financial ratios (which are measures of various aspects of corporate performance based on financial statement elements). On the basis of common-size financial statements and financial ratios, analysts can evaluate a company's relative profitability, liquidity, leverage, efficiency, and valuation in relation to past results and/or peers' results.

4.4. Analyze/Interpret the Processed Data

Once the data have been processed, the next step—critical to any analysis—is to interpret the output. The answer to a specific question is seldom the numerical answer alone. Rather, the answer relies on the analyst's interpretation of the output, and the use of this interpreted output to support a conclusion or recommendation. The answers to the specific analytical questions may themselves achieve the underlying purpose of the analysis, but usually a conclusion or recommendation is required. For example, an equity analysis may require a buy, hold, or sell recommendation or a conclusion about the value of a share of stock. In support of the decision, the analysis would cite such information as target value, relative performance, expected future performance given a company's strategic position, quality of management, and whatever other information influenced the decision.

4.5. Develop and Communicate Conclusions/Recommendations

Communicating the conclusion or recommendation in an appropriate format is the next step. The appropriate format will vary by analytical task, by institution, and/or by audience. For example, an equity analyst's report would typically include the following components:

- summary and investment conclusion;
- earnings projections;
- valuation;
- business summary;
- risk, industry, and competitive analysis;
- historical performance; and
- forecasts.

The contents of reports may also be specified by regulatory agencies or professional standards. For example, the CFA Institute *Standards of Practice Handbook* (*Handbook*) dictates standards that must be followed in communicating recommendations. According to the *Handbook*:

> Standard V(B) states that members and candidates should communicate in a recommendation the factors that were instrumental in making the investment recommendation. A critical part of this requirement is to distinguish clearly between opinions and facts. In preparing a research report, the member or candidate must present the basic characteristics of the security(ies) being analyzed, which will allow the reader to evaluate the report and incorporate information the reader deems relevant to his or her investment decision making process.[9]

The *Handbook* requires that limitations to the analysis and any risks inherent to the investment be disclosed. Furthermore, it requires that any report include elements important to the analysis and conclusions so that readers can evaluate the conclusions themselves.

4.6. Follow-Up

The process does not end with the report. If an equity investment is made or a credit rating is assigned, periodic review is required to determine if the original conclusions and recommendations are still valid. In the case of a rejected investment, follow-up may not be necessary but may be useful in determining whether the analytical process is adequate or should be refined (for example, if a rejected investment turns out to be successful in the market, perhaps the rejection was due to inadequate analysis). Follow-up may involve repeating all the previous steps in the process on a periodic basis.

5. SUMMARY

The information presented in financial and other reports, including the financial statements, notes, and management's commentary, helps the financial analyst to assess a company's performance and financial position. An analyst may be called on to perform a financial analysis

---

[9] *Standards of Practice Handbook* (2014, p. 169).

for a variety of reasons, including the valuation of equity securities, the assessment of credit risk, the performance of due diligence on an acquisition, and the evaluation of a subsidiary's performance relative to other business units. Major considerations in both equity analysis and credit analysis are evaluating a company's financial position, its ability to generate profits and cash flow, and its potential to generate future growth in profits and cash flow.

This chapter has presented an overview of financial statement analysis. Among the major points covered are the following:

- The primary purpose of financial reports is to provide information and data about a company's financial position and performance, including profitability and cash flows. The information presented in the reports —including the financial statements and notes and management's commentary or management's discussion and analysis—allows the financial analyst to assess a company's financial position and performance and trends in that performance.
- The primary financial statements are the statement of financial position (i.e., the balance sheet), the statement of comprehensive income (or two statements consisting of an income statement and a statement of comprehensive income), the statement of changes in equity, and the statement of cash flows.
- The balance sheet discloses what resources a company controls (assets) and what it owes (liabilities) at a specific point in time. Owners' equity represents the net assets of the company; it is the owners' residual interest in, or residual claim on, the company's assets after deducting its liabilities. The relationship among the three parts of the balance sheet (assets, liabilities, and owners' equity) may be shown in equation form as follows: Assets = Liabilities + Owners' equity.
- The income statement presents information on the financial results of a company's business activities over a period of time. The income statement communicates how much revenue and other income the company generated during a period and what expenses, including losses, it incurred in connection with generating that revenue and other income. The basic equation underlying the income statement is Revenue + Other income – Expenses = Net income.
- The statement of comprehensive income includes all items that change owners' equity except transactions with owners. Some of these items are included as part of net income, and some are reported as other comprehensive income (OCI).
- The statement of changes in equity provides information about increases or decreases in the various components of owners' equity.
- Although the income statement and balance sheet provide measures of a company's success, cash and cash flow are also vital to a company's long-term success. Disclosing the sources and uses of cash helps creditors, investors, and other statement users evaluate the company's liquidity, solvency, and financial flexibility.
- The notes (also referred to as footnotes) that accompany the financial statements are an integral part of those statements and provide information that is essential to understanding the statements. Analysts should evaluate note disclosures regarding the use of alternative accounting methods, estimates, and assumptions.
- In addition to the financial statements, a company provides other sources of information that are useful to the financial analyst. As part of his or her analysis, the financial analyst should read and assess this additional information, particularly that presented in the management commentary (also called management report[ing], operating and financial review, and management's discussion and analysis [MD&A]).

- A publicly traded company must have an independent audit performed on its annual financial statements. The auditor's report expresses an opinion on the financial statements and provides some assurance about whether the financial statements fairly present a company's financial position, performance, and cash flows. In addition, for US publicly traded companies, auditors must also express an opinion on the company's internal control systems.
- Information on the economy, industry, and peer companies is useful in putting the company's financial performance and position in perspective and in assessing the company's future. In most cases, information from sources apart from the company are crucial to an analyst's effectiveness.
- The financial statement analysis framework provides steps that can be followed in any financial statement analysis project. These steps are:
  - articulate the purpose and context of the analysis;
  - collect input data;
  - process data;
  - analyze/interpret the processed data;
  - develop and communicate conclusions and recommendations; and
  - follow up.

REFERENCES

Benninga, Simon Z., and Oded H. Sarig. 1997. *Corporate Finance: A Valuation Approach*. New York: McGraw-Hill Publishing.

International Auditing and Assurance Standards Board (IAASB). *Handbook of International Quality Control, Auditing, Review, Other Assurance, and Related Services Pronouncements*, Standard 200, available at www.ifac.org/IAASB.

van Greuning, Hennie, and Sonja Brajovic Bratanovic. 2003. *Analyzing and Managing Banking Risk: A Framework for Assessing Corporate Governance and Financial Risk*. Washington, DC: World Bank.

PRACTICE PROBLEMS

1. Providing information about the performance and financial position of companies so that users can make economic decisions *best* describes the role of:
   A. auditing.
   B. financial reporting.
   C. financial statement analysis.

2. Which of the following *best* describes the role of financial statement analysis?
   A. To provide information about a company's performance.
   B. To provide information about a company's changes in financial position.
   C. To form expectations about a company's future performance and financial position.

3. The role of financial statement analysis is *best* described as:
   A. providing information useful for making investment decisions.
   B. evaluating a company for the purpose of making economic decisions.
   C. using financial reports prepared by analysts to make economic decisions.

4. A company's financial position would *best* be evaluated using the:
   A. balance sheet.
   B. income statement.
   C. statement of cash flows.

5. A company's profitability for a period would *best* be evaluated using the:
   A. balance sheet.
   B. income statement.
   C. statement of cash flows.

6. The financial statement that presents a shareholder's residual claim on assets is the:
   A. balance sheet.
   B. income statement.
   C. cash flow statement.

7. A company's profitability over a period of time is *best* evaluated using the:
   A. balance sheet.
   B. income statement.
   C. cash flow statement.

8. The income statement is *best* used to evaluate a company's:
   A. financial position.
   B. sources of cash flow.
   C. financial results from business activities.

9. Accounting policies, methods, and estimates used in preparing financial statements are *most likely* to be found in the:
   A. auditor's report.
   B. management commentary.
   C. notes to the financial statements.

10. Information about management and director compensation are *least likely* to be found in the:
    A. auditor's report.
    B. proxy statement.
    C. notes to the financial statements.

11. Information about a company's objectives, strategies, and significant risks are *most likely* to be found in the:
    A. auditor's report.
    B. management commentary.
    C. notes to the financial statements.

12. Which of the following *best* describes why the notes that accompany the financial statements are required? The notes:
    A. permit flexibility in statement preparation.
    B. standardize financial reporting across companies.
    C. provide information necessary to understand the financial statements.

13. What type of audit opinion is preferred when analyzing financial statements?
    A. Qualified.
    B. Adverse.
    C. Unqualified.

14. An auditor determines that a company's financial statements are prepared in accordance with applicable accounting standards except with respect to inventory reporting. This exception is *most likely* to result in an audit opinion that is:
    A. adverse.
    B. qualified.
    C. unqualified.

15. An independent audit report is *most likely* to provide:
    A. absolute assurance about the accuracy of the financial statements.
    B. reasonable assurance that the financial statements are fairly presented.
    C. a qualified opinion with respect to the transparency of the financial statements.

16. Interim financial reports released by a company are *most likely* to be:
    A. monthly.
    B. unaudited.
    C. unqualified.

17. Which of the following sources of information used by analysts is found outside a company's annual report?
    A. Auditor's report.
    B. Peer company analysis.
    C. Management's discussion and analysis.

18. Ratios are an input into which step in the financial statement analysis framework?
    A. Process data.
    B. Collect input data.
    C. Analyze/interpret the processed data.

19. Which phase in the financial statement analysis framework is *most likely* to involve producing updated reports and recommendations?
    A. Follow-up.
    B. Analyze/interpret the processed data.
    C. Develop and communicate conclusions and recommendations.

CHAPTER 2

FINANCIAL REPORTING STANDARDS

Elaine Henry, PhD, CFA
Jan Hendrik van Greuning, DCom, CFA
Thomas R. Robinson, PhD, CFA

LEARNING OUTCOMES

After completing this chapter, you will be able to do the following:

- describe the objective of financial reporting and the importance of financial reporting standards in security analysis and valuation;
- describe the roles of financial reporting standard-setting bodies and regulatory authorities in establishing and enforcing reporting standards;
- describe the International Accounting Standards Board's conceptual framework, including qualitative characteristics of financial reports, constraints on financial reports, and required reporting elements;
- describe general requirements for financial statements under International Financial Reporting Standards (IFRS);
- describe implications for financial analysis of alternative financial reporting systems and the importance of monitoring developments in financial reporting standards.

1. INTRODUCTION

Financial reporting standards provide principles for preparing financial reports and determine the types and amounts of information that must be provided to users of financial statements, including investors and creditors, so that they may make informed decisions. This chapter focuses on the context within which these standards are created. An understanding of the underlying framework of financial reporting standards, which is broader than knowledge of specific accounting rules, will allow an analyst to assess the valuation implications of financial statement elements and transactions—including transactions, such as those that represent new developments, which are not specifically addressed by the standards.

Section 2 of this chapter discusses the objective of financial reporting and the importance of financial reporting standards in security analysis and valuation. Section 3 describes the roles of financial reporting standard-setting bodies and regulatory authorities and several of the financial reporting standard-setting bodies and regulatory authorities. Section 4 describes the International Financial Reporting Standards (IFRS) framework[1] and general requirements for financial statements. Section 5 compares IFRS and alternative reporting systems, and Section 6 discusses the importance of monitoring developments in financial reporting standards. A summary of the key points concludes the chapter.

2. THE OBJECTIVE OF FINANCIAL REPORTING

The financial reports of a company include financial statements and other supplemental disclosures necessary to assess a company's financial position and periodic financial performance. Financial reporting is based on a simple premise. The International Accounting Standards Board (IASB), which sets financial reporting standards that have been adopted in many countries, said in its *Conceptual Framework for Financial Reporting* (*Conceptual Framework*) that the objective of financial reporting is to provide financial information that is useful to users in making decisions about providing resources to the reporting entity, where those decisions relate to equity and debt instruments, or loans or other forms of credit, and in influencing management's actions that affect the use of the entity's economic resources.[2]

A fully articulated framework is an essential first step to guide the development of a set of standards. Previously, financial reporting standards were primarily developed independently by each country's standard-setting body. This independent standard-setting process created a wide range of standards, some of which were quite comprehensive and complex (rules-based standards) and others that were more general (principles-based standards). The globalization of capital flows and various accounting scandals increased awareness of the need for more uniform, high-quality global financial reporting standards and provided the impetus for stronger coordination among the major standard-setting bodies. Such coordination is also a natural outgrowth of the increased globalization of capital markets.

Developing financial reporting standards is complicated because the underlying economic reality is complicated. The financial transactions and financial position that companies aim to present in their financial reports are also complex. Furthermore, uncertainty about various aspects of transactions often results in the need for accruals and estimates, both of which necessitate judgment. Judgment varies from one preparer to the next. Accordingly, standards are needed to achieve some amount of consistency in these judgments. Even with such standards, there usually will be no single correct answer to the question of how to reflect economic reality in financial reports. Nevertheless, financial reporting standards try to limit the range of acceptable answers to increase consistency in financial reports.

---

[1] The body of standards issued by the International Accounting Standards Board (IASB) is referred to as International Financial Reporting Standards.
[2] In March 2018, the IASB updated the *Conceptual Framework for Financial Reporting* originally adopted in 2010.

The IASB and the US-based Financial Accounting Standards Board (FASB) have developed similar financial reporting frameworks, which specify the overall objectives and qualities of information to be provided. Financial reports are intended to provide information to many users, including investors, creditors, employees, customers, and others. As a result, financial reports are *not* designed solely with asset valuation in mind. However, financial reports provide important inputs into the process of valuing a company or the securities a company issues. Understanding the financial reporting framework—including how and when judgments and estimates can affect the numbers reported—enables an analyst to evaluate the information reported and to use the information appropriately when assessing a company's financial performance. Clearly, such an understanding is also important in assessing the financial impact of business decisions by, and in making comparisons across, entities.

3. STANDARD-SETTING BODIES AND REGULATORY AUTHORITIES

A distinction must be made between standard-setting bodies and regulatory authorities. Standard-setting bodies, such as the IASB and FASB, are typically private sector, self-regulated organizations with board members who are experienced accountants, auditors, users of financial statements, and academics. The requirement to prepare financial reports in accordance with specified accounting standards is the responsibility of regulatory authorities. Regulatory authorities, such as the Accounting and Corporate Regulatory Authority in Singapore, the Securities and Exchange Commission (SEC) in the United States, and the Securities and Exchange Commission of Brazil have the legal authority to enforce financial reporting requirements and exert other controls over entities that participate in the capital markets within their jurisdiction.

In other words, *generally*, standard-setting bodies set the standards, and regulatory authorities recognize and enforce the standards. Without the recognition of the standards by the regulatory authorities, the private-sector standard-setting bodies would have no authority. Note, however, that regulators often retain the legal authority to establish financial reporting standards in their jurisdiction and can overrule the private-sector standard-setting bodies.

This section provides a brief overview of the IASB and the FASB. The overview is followed by descriptions of the International Organization of Securities Commissions, the US Securities and Exchange Commission, and capital markets regulation in the European Union. The topics covered in these overviews were chosen to serve as examples of standard-setting boards, securities commissions, and capital market regulation. After reading these descriptions, the reader should be able to describe the functioning and roles of standard-setting bodies and regulatory authorities in more detail than is given in the introduction to this section.

3.1. Accounting Standards Boards

Accounting standards boards exist in virtually every national market. These boards are typically independent, private, not-for-profit organizations. There are certain attributes that are typically common to these standard setters—the IASB and the FASB are discussed in this section as primary examples.

3.1.1. International Accounting Standards Board

The IASB is the independent standard-setting body of the IFRS Foundation, an independent, not-for-profit private sector organization. The Trustees of the IFRS Foundation reflect a diversity of geographical and professional backgrounds. The Trustees appoint the members of the IASB and are accountable to a monitoring board composed of public authorities that include representatives from the European Commission, IOSCO, the Japan Financial Services Agency, and the US SEC, with the chairman of the Basel Committee on Banking Supervision as an observer.

The Trustees of the IFRS Foundation make a commitment to act in the public interest. The principal objectives of the IFRS Foundation are to develop and promote the use and adoption of a single set of high quality financial standards; to ensure the standards result in transparent, comparable, and decision-useful information while taking into account the needs of a range of sizes and types of entities in diverse economic settings; and to promote the convergence of national accounting standards and IFRS. The Trustees are responsible for ensuring that the IASB is and is perceived as independent.

The members of the IASB are appointed by the Trustees on the basis of professional competence and practical experience and reflect a diversity of geographical and professional backgrounds. The members deliberate, develop, and issue international financial reporting standards,[3] assisted by advice on the standards, and their application, from advisory bodies whose members represent a wide range of organizations and individuals that are affected by and interested in international financial reporting.

The IASB has a basic process that it goes through when deliberating, developing, and issuing international financial reporting standards. A simplified version of the typical process is as follows. An issue is identified as a priority for consideration and placed on the IASB's agenda. After considering an issue, which may include soliciting advice from others including national standard-setters, the IASB may publish an exposure draft for public comment. After reviewing the input of others, the IASB may issue a new or revised financial reporting standard. These standards are authoritative to the extent that they are recognised and adopted by regulatory authorities.

3.1.2. Financial Accounting Standards Board

The FASB and its predecessor organizations have been issuing financial reporting standards in the United States since the 1930s. The FASB operates within a structure similar to that of the IASB. The Financial Accounting Foundation oversees, administers, and finances the organization. The Foundation ensures the independence of the standard-setting process and appoints members to the FASB and related advisory entities.

The FASB issues new and revised standards to improve standards of financial reporting so that decision-useful information is provided to users of financial reports. This is done through a thorough and independent process that seeks input from stakeholders and is overseen by the Financial Accounting Foundation. The steps in the process are similar to those described for the IASB. The outputs of the standard-setting process are contained in the FASB Accounting Standards Codification™ (Codification).[4] The Codification, organized by topic, is the source of

---

[3] Although the name of the IASB incorporates "Accounting Standards" and early standards were titled International Accounting Standards (IAS), the term "International Financial Reporting Standards" (IFRS) is being used for new standards. The use of the words "financial reporting" recognizes the importance of disclosures outside of the core financial statements, such as management discussion of the business, risks, and future plans.

[4] The Codification combines literature issued by various standard setters, including the FASB, the Emerging Issues Task Force (EITF), the Derivative Implementation Group (DIG), and the American Institute of Certified Public Accountants (AICPA).

authoritative US generally accepted accounting principles to be applied to non-governmental entities.

US GAAP, as established by the FASB, is officially recognized as authoritative by the SEC; however the SEC retains the authority to establish standards. Although it has rarely overruled the FASB, the SEC does issue authoritative financial reporting guidance including Staff Accounting Bulletins. These bulletins reflect the SEC's views regarding accounting-related disclosure practices and can be found on the SEC website. Certain portions—but not all portions—of the SEC regulations, releases, interpretations, and guidance are included for reference in the FASB Codification.

3.2. Regulatory Authorities

The requirement to prepare financial reports in accordance with specified accounting standards is the responsibility of regulatory authorities. Regulatory authorities are governmental entities that have the legal authority to enforce financial reporting requirements and exert other controls over entities that participate in the capital markets within their jurisdiction. Regulatory authorities may require that financial reports be prepared in accordance with one specific set of accounting standards or may specify acceptable accounting standards. For example in Switzerland, Swiss-based companies listed on the main board of the Swiss Exchange have to prepare their financial statements in accordance with either IFRS or US GAAP if they are multinational.[5] Other registrants in Switzerland could use IFRS, US GAAP, or Swiss GAAP.

3.2.1. International Organization of Securities Commissions

While technically not a regulatory authority, the International Organization of Securities Commissions (IOSCO) regulates a significant portion of the world's financial capital markets. This organization has established objectives and principles to guide securities and capital market regulation.

IOSCO was formed in 1983 and consists of ordinary members, associate members, and affiliate members. Ordinary members are the securities commission or similar governmental regulatory authority with primary responsibility for securities regulation in the member country.[6] The members regulate more than 95 percent of the world's financial capital markets in more than 115 jurisdictions, and securities regulators in emerging markets account for 75 percent of its ordinary membership.

IOSCO's comprehensive set of *Objectives and Principles of Securities Regulation* is updated as required and is recognized as an international benchmark for all markets. The principles of securities regulation are based upon three core objectives:[7]

---

[5] https://www.iasplus.com/en/jurisdictions/europe/switzerland.
[6] The names of the primary securities regulator vary from country to country. For example: China Securities Regulatory Commission, Egyptian Financial Supervisory Authority, Securities and Exchange Board of India, Kingdom of Saudi Arabia Capital Market Authority, and Banco Central del Uruguay.
[7] *Objectives and Principles of Securities Regulation*, IOSCO, May 2017.

- protecting investors;
- ensuring that markets are fair, efficient, and transparent; and
- reducing systemic risk.

IOSCO's principles are grouped into ten categories, including principles for regulators, for enforcement, for auditing, and for issuers, among others. Within the category "Principles for Issuers," two principles relate directly to financial reporting:

1. There should be full, accurate, and timely disclosure of financial results, risk, and other information that is material to investors' decisions.
2. Accounting standards used by issuers to prepare financial statements should be of a high and internationally acceptable quality.

Historically, regulation and related financial reporting standards were developed within individual countries and were often based on the cultural, economic, and political norms of each country. As financial markets have become more global, it has become desirable to establish comparable financial reporting standards internationally. Ultimately, laws and regulations are established by individual jurisdictions, so this also requires cooperation among regulators. Another IOSCO principle deals with the use of self-regulatory organizations (SROs), which exercise some direct oversight for their areas of competence and should be subject to the oversight of the relevant regulator and observe fairness and confidentiality.[8]

To ensure consistent application of international financial standards (such as the Basel Committee on Banking Supervision's standards and IFRS), it is important to have uniform regulation and enforcement across national boundaries. IOSCO assists in attaining this goal of uniform regulation as well as cross-border co-operation in combating violations of securities and derivatives laws.

3.2.2. The Securities and Exchange Commission (US)

The US SEC has primary responsibility for securities and capital markets regulation in the United States and is an ordinary member of IOSCO. Any company issuing securities within the United States, or otherwise involved in US capital markets, is subject to the rules and regulations of the SEC. The SEC, one of the oldest and most developed regulatory authorities, originated as a result of reform efforts made after the stock market crash of 1929, sometimes referred to as simply the "Great Crash."

A number of laws affect reporting companies, broker/dealers, and other market participants. From a financial reporting and analysis perspective, the most significant pieces of legislation are the Securities Acts of 1933 and 1934 and the Sarbanes–Oxley Act of 2002.

- **Securities Act of 1933** (The 1933 Act): This act specifies the financial and other significant information that investors must receive when securities are sold, prohibits misrepresentations, and requires initial registration of all public issuances of securities.
- **Securities Exchange Act of 1934** (The 1934 Act): This act created the SEC, gave the SEC authority over all aspects of the securities industry, and empowered the SEC to require periodic reporting by companies with publicly traded securities.

---

[8] *Objectives and Principles of Securities Regulation*, IOSCO, May 2017.

- **Sarbanes–Oxley Act of 2002**: This act created the Public Company Accounting Oversight Board (PCAOB) to oversee auditors. The SEC is responsible for carrying out the requirements of the act and overseeing the PCAOB. The act addresses auditor independence (it prohibits auditors from providing certain non-audit services to the companies they audit); strengthens corporate responsibility for financial reports (it requires executive management to certify that the company's financial reports fairly present the company's condition); and requires management to report on the effectiveness of the company's internal control over financial reporting (including obtaining external auditor confirmation of the effectiveness of internal control).

Companies comply with these acts principally through the completion and submission (i.e., filing) of standardized forms issued by the SEC. There are more than 50 different types of SEC forms that are used to satisfy reporting requirements; the discussion herein will be limited to those forms most relevant for financial analysts.

Most of the SEC filings are required to be made electronically, so filings that an analyst would be interested in can be retrieved online from one of many websites, including the SEC's own website. Some filings are required on the initial offering of securities, whereas others are required on a periodic basis thereafter. The following are some of the more common information sources used by analysts.

- **Securities Offerings Registration Statement**: The 1933 Act requires companies offering securities to file a registration statement. New issuers as well as previously registered companies that are issuing new securities are required to file these statements. Required information and the precise form vary depending upon the size and nature of the offering. Typically, required information includes: 1) disclosures about the securities being offered for sale, 2) the relationship of these new securities to the issuer's other capital securities, 3) the information typically provided in the annual filings, 4) recent audited financial statements, and 5) risk factors involved in the business.
- **Forms 10-K, 20-F, and 40-F**: These are forms that companies are required to file *annually*. Form 10-K is for US registrants, Form 40-F is for certain Canadian registrants, and Form 20-F is for all other non-US registrants. These forms require a comprehensive overview, including information concerning a company's business, financial disclosures, legal proceedings, and information related to management. The financial disclosures include a historical summary of financial data (usually 10 years), management's discussion and analysis (MD&A) of the company's financial condition and results of operations, and audited financial statements.
- **Annual Report**: In addition to the SEC's annual filings (e.g., Form 10-K), most companies prepare an annual report to shareholders. This is not a requirement of the SEC. The annual report is usually viewed as one of the most significant opportunities for a company to present itself to shareholders and other external parties; accordingly, it is often a highly polished marketing document with photographs, an opening letter from the chief executive officer, financial data, market segment information, research and development activities, and future corporate goals. In contrast, the Form 10-K is a more legal type of document with minimal marketing emphasis. Although the perspectives vary, there is considerable overlap between a company's annual report and its Form 10-K. Some companies elect to prepare just the Form 10-K or a document that integrates both the 10-K and annual report.
- **Proxy Statement/Form DEF-14A**: The SEC requires that shareholders of a company receive a proxy statement prior to a shareholder meeting. A proxy is an authorization from

the shareholder giving another party the right to cast its vote. Shareholder meetings are held at least once a year, but any special meetings also require a proxy statement. Proxies, especially annual meeting proxies, contain information that is often useful to financial analysts. Such information typically includes proposals that require a shareholder vote, details of security ownership by management and principal owners, biographical information on directors, and disclosure of executive compensation. Proxy statement information is filed with the SEC as Form DEF-14A.

- **Forms 10-Q and 6-K**: These are forms that companies are required to submit for interim periods (quarterly for US companies on Form 10-Q, semiannually for many non-US companies on Form 6-K). The filing requires certain financial information, including unaudited financial statements and a MD&A for the interim period covered by the report. Additionally, if certain types of non-recurring events—such as the adoption of a significant accounting policy, commencement of significant litigation, or a material limitation on the rights of any holders of any class of registered securities—take place during the period covered by the report, these events must be included in the Form 10-Q report. Companies may provide the 10-Q report to shareholders or may prepare a separate, abbreviated, quarterly report to shareholders.

EXAMPLE 1   Initial Registration Statement

In 2004, Google filed a registration statement with the US SEC to register its initial public offering of securities (Class A Common Stock). In addition to a large amount of financial and business information, the registration statement provided a 20-page discussion Google's business and industry.

Which of the following is *most likely* to have been included in Google's registration statement?

A. Interim unaudited financial statements
B. Assessment of risk factors involved in the business
C. Projected cash flows and earnings for the business

Solution: B is correct. Information provided by companies in registration statements typically includes disclosures about the securities being offered for sale; the relationship of these new securities to the issuer's other capital securities; the information typically provided in the annual filings; recent audited financial statements; and risk factors involved in the business. Companies provide information useful in developing projected cash flows and earnings but do not typically include these in the registration statement, nor do they provide unaudited interim statements in the initial registration statement.

A company or its officers make other SEC filings—either periodically, or, if significant events or transactions have occurred, in between the periodic reports noted above. By their nature, these forms sometimes contain the most interesting and timely information and may have significant valuation implications.

- **Form 8-K:** In addition to filing annual and interim reports, SEC registrants must report material corporate events on a more current basis. Form 8-K (6-K for non-US registrants) is the "current report" companies must file with the SEC to announce such major events as acquisitions or disposals of corporate assets, changes in securities and trading markets, matters related to accountants and financial statements, corporate governance and management changes, and Regulation FD disclosures.[9]
- **Forms 3, 4, 5, and 144**: Forms 3, 4, and 5 are required to report beneficial ownership of securities. These filings are required for any director or officer of a registered company as well as beneficial owners of greater than 10 percent of a class of registered equity securities. Form 3 is the initial statement, Form 4 reports changes, and Form 5 is the annual report. Form 144 is notice of the proposed sale of restricted securities or securities held by an affiliate of the issuer. These forms can be used to examine purchases and sales of securities by officers, directors, and other affiliates of the company, who collectively are regarded as corporate insiders.
- **Form 11-K**: This is the annual report of employee stock purchase, savings, and similar plans. It might be of interest to analysts for companies with significant employee benefit plans because it contains more information than that disclosed in the company's financial statements.

In jurisdictions other than the United States, similar legislation exists for the purpose of regulating securities and capital markets. Regulatory authorities are responsible for enforcing regulation, and securities regulation is intended to be consistent with the IOSCO objectives described in the previous section. Within each jurisdiction, regulators will either establish or, more typically, recognize and adopt a specified set or sets of accounting standards. The regulators will also establish reporting and filing requirements. IOSCO members have agreed to cooperate in the development, implementation, and enforcement of internationally recognised and consistent standards of regulation.

3.2.3. Capital Markets Regulation in Europe

Each individual member state of the European Union (EU) regulates capital markets in its jurisdiction. There are, however, certain regulations that have been adopted at the EU level. Importantly the EU agreed that from 2005 consolidated accounts of EU listed companies would use International Financial Reporting Standards. The endorsement process by which newly issued IFRS are adopted by the EU reflects the balance between the individual member state's autonomy and the need for cooperation and convergence. When the IASB issues a new standard, the European Financial Reporting Advisory Group advises the European Commission on the standard, and the Standards Advice Review Group provides the Commission with an opinion about that advice. Based on the input from these two entities, the Commission prepares a draft endorsement regulation. The Accounting Regulatory Committee votes on the proposal; and if the vote is favorable, the proposal proceeds to the European Parliament and the Council of the European Union for approval.[10]

---

[9] Regulation Fair Disclosure (FD) provides that when an issuer discloses material non-public information to certain individuals or entities—generally, securities market professionals such as stock analysts or holders of the issuer's securities who may trade on the basis of the information—the issuer must make public disclosure of that information. In this way, the rule aims to promote full and fair disclosure.

[10] *Source:* European Commission. http://ec.europa.eu/internal_market/accounting/legal_framework/ias_regulation_en.htm.

Two bodies related to securities regulation established by the European Commission are the European Securities Committee (ESC) and the European Securities and Market Authority (ESMA). The ESC consists of high-level representatives of member states and advises the European Commission on securities policy issues. ESMA is an EU cross-border supervisor established to co-ordinate supervision of the EU market. As noted earlier, regulation still rests with the individual member states, and, therefore, requirements for registering shares and filing periodic financial reports vary from country to country. ESMA is one of three European supervisory authorities; the two others supervise the banking and insurance industries.

4. THE INTERNATIONAL FINANCIAL REPORTING STANDARDS FRAMEWORK

As previously discussed, the IASB *Conceptual Framework for Financial Reporting* sets forth the concepts that underlie the preparation and presentation of financial statements for external users. The framework is designed to: assist standard setters in developing and reviewing standards; assist preparers of financial statements in applying standards and in dealing with issues not specifically covered by a standard; assist auditors in forming an opinion on financial statements; and assist users in interpreting financial statement information. The objective of financial reporting is the provision of financial information that is useful to current and potential providers of resources in making decisions and all other aspects of the framework flow from that central objective.

The providers of resources are considered to be the primary users of financial reports and include investors, lenders, and other creditors. The purpose of providing the financial information is to be useful in making decisions about providing resources. Other users may find the financial information useful for making economic decisions. The types of economic decisions differ by users, so the specific information needed differs as well. However, although these users may have unique information needs, some information needs are common across all users. Information is needed about the company's financial position: its resources and its financial obligations. Information is needed about a company's financial performance; this information explains how and why the company's financial position changed in the past and can be useful in evaluating potential changes in the future. The third common information need is the need for information about a company's cash. How did the company obtain cash (by selling its products and services, borrowing, other)? How did the company use cash (by paying expenses, investing in new equipment, paying dividends, other)?

Information that is helpful to users in assessing future net cash inflows to the entity includes information about the economic resources of (assets) and claims against (liabilities and equity) the entity, and about how well the management and governing board have utilized the resources of the entity. Users need to consider information from other sources as well in making their decisions. Although financial reports do not show the value of an entity, they are useful in estimating the value of an entity.

4.1. Qualitative Characteristics of Financial Reports

Flowing from the central objective of providing information that is *useful* to providers of resources, the *Conceptual Framework* identifies two fundamental qualitative characteristics that make financial information useful: relevance and faithful representation.[11] The concept of materiality is discussed within the context of relevance.

1. *Relevance*: Information is relevant if it would potentially affect or make a difference in users' decisions. The information can have predictive value (useful in making forecasts), confirmatory value (useful to evaluate past decisions or forecasts), or both. In other words, relevant information helps users of financial information to evaluate past, present, and future events, or to confirm or correct their past evaluations in a decision-making context. *Materiality:* Information is considered to be material if omission or misstatement of the information could influence users' decisions. Materiality is a function of the nature and/ or magnitude of the information.

2. *Faithful representation*: Information that faithfully represents an economic phenomenon that it purports to represent is ideally complete, neutral, and free from error. Complete means that all information necessary to understand the phenomenon is depicted. Neutral means that information is selected and presented without bias. In other words, the information is not presented in such a manner as to bias the users' decisions. Free from error means that there are no errors of commission or omission in the description of the economic phenomenon, and that an appropriate process to arrive at the reported information was selected and was adhered to without error. Faithful representation maximizes the qualities of complete, neutral, and free from error to the extent possible.

Relevance and faithful representation are the fundamental, most critical characteristics of useful financial information. In addition the *Conceptual Framework* identifies four enhancing qualitative characteristics: comparability, verifiability, timeliness, and understandability.

1. *Comparability*: Comparability allows users "to identify and understand similarities and differences of items." Information presented in a consistent manner over time and across entities enables users to make comparisons more easily than information with variations in how similar economic phenomena are represented.

2. *Verifiability*: Verifiability means that different knowledgeable and independent observers would agree that the information presented faithfully represents the economic phenomena it purports to represent.

3. *Timeliness*: Timely information is available to decision makers prior to their making a decision.

4. *Understandability*: Clear and concise presentation of information enhances understandability. Information should be prepared for, and be understandable by, users who have a reasonable knowledge of business and economic activities, and who are willing to study the information with diligence. Information that is useful should not be excluded simply because it is difficult to understand, and it may be necessary for users to seek assistance to understand information about complex economic phenomena.

---

[11] *Conceptual Framework for Financial Reporting.*

Financial information exhibiting these qualitative characteristics—fundamental and enhancing—should be useful for making economic decisions.

4.2. Constraints on Financial Reports

Although it would be ideal for financial statements to exhibit all of these qualitative characteristics and thus achieve maximum usefulness, it may be necessary to make tradeoffs across the enhancing characteristics. The application of the enhancing characteristics follows no set order of priority, and each enhancing characteristic may take priority over the others. The aim is an appropriate balance among the enhancing characteristics.

A pervasive constraint on useful financial reporting is the cost of providing and using this information. Optimally, benefits derived from information should exceed the costs of providing and using it. Again, the aim is a balance between costs and benefits.

A limitation of financial reporting involves information that is not included. Financial statements, by necessity, omit information that is non-quantifiable. For example, the creativity, innovation, and competence of a company's work force are not directly captured in the financial statements. Similarly, customer loyalty, a positive corporate culture, environmental responsibility, and many other aspects about a company may not be directly reflected in the financial statements. Of course, to the extent that these items result in superior financial performance, a company's financial reports will reflect the results.

EXAMPLE 2   Balancing Qualitative Characteristics of Useful Information

A tradeoff between enhancing qualitative characteristics often occurs. For example, when a company records sales revenue, it is required to simultaneously estimate and record an expense for potential bad debts (uncollectible accounts). Including this estimated expense is considered to represent the economic event faithfully and to provide relevant information about the net profits for the accounting period. The information is timely and understandable; but because bad debts may not be known with certainty until a later period, inclusion of this estimated expense involves a sacrifice of verifiability. The bad debt expense is simply an estimate. It is apparent that it is not always possible to simultaneously fulfill all qualitative characteristics.

Companies are *most likely* to make tradeoffs between which of the following when preparing financial reports?

A. Relevance and materiality
B. Timeliness and verifiability
C. Relevance and faithful representation

Solution: B is correct. Providing timely information implies a shorter time frame between the economic event and the information preparation; however, fully verifying information may require a longer time frame. Relevance and faithful representation are fundamental qualitative characteristics that make financial information useful. Both characteristics are required; there is no tradeoff between these. Materiality is an aspect of relevance.

4.3. The Elements of Financial Statements

Financial statements portray the financial effects of transactions and other events by grouping them into broad classes (elements) according to their economic characteristics. Three elements of financial statements are directly related to the measurement of financial position: assets, liabilities, and equity.

1. **Assets**: A present economic resource controlled by the entity as a result of past events. An economic resource is a right that has the potential to produce economic benefits. Assets are what a company owns (e.g., inventory and equipment).
2. **Liabilities**: A present obligation of the entity to transfer an economic resource as a result of past events. An obligation is a duty or responsibility that the entity has no practical ability to avoid. Liabilities are what a company owes (e.g., bank borrowings).
3. **Equity** (for public companies, also known as "shareholders' equity" or "stockholders' equity"): Assets less liabilities. Equity is the residual interest in the assets after subtracting the liabilities.

The elements of financial statements directly related to the measurement of performance (profit and related measures) are income and expenses.

- **Income**: Increases in assets, or decreases in liabilities, that result in increases in equity, other than those relating to contributions from holders of equity claims. Income includes both revenues and gains. Revenues represent income from the ordinary activities of the enterprise (e.g., the sale of products or provision of services). Gains may result from ordinary activities or other activities (the sale of surplus equipment).
- **Expenses**: Decreases in assets, or increases in liabilities, that result in decreases in equity, other than those relating to distributions to holders of equity claims. Expenses include those related to operating activities such as cost of goods sold and operating expenses including wages, rents, and other items. Losses are also considered expenses and can result from the sale of assets at less than their carrying values, impairments of asset values and, a variety of other items.

4.3.1. Underlying Assumptions in Financial Statements

Two important assumptions underlie financial statements: accrual accounting and going concern. These assumptions determine how financial statement elements are recognized and measured.

The use of "accrual accounting" assumes that financial statements should reflect transactions in the period when they actually occur, not necessarily when cash movements occur. For example, a company reports revenues *when they are earned (when the performance obligations have been satisfied)*, regardless of whether the company received cash before or after delivering the product, at the time of delivery.

"Going concern" refers to the assumption that the company will continue in business for the foreseeable future. To illustrate, consider the value of a company's inventory if it is assumed that the inventory can be sold over a normal period of time versus the value of that same inventory if it is assumed that the inventory must all be sold in a day (or a week). Companies with the intent to liquidate or materially curtail operations would require different information for a fair presentation.

4.3.2. Recognition of Financial Statement Elements

Recognition means that an item is included in the balance sheet or income statement. Recognition occurs if the item meets the definition of an element and satisfies the criteria for recognition. Recognition is appropriate if it results in both relevant information about assets, liabilities, equity, income, and expenses, and a faithful representation of those items, because the aim is to provide information that is useful to investors, lenders, and other creditors.

4.3.3. Measurement of Financial Statement Elements

Measurement is the process of determining the monetary amounts at which the elements of the financial statements are to be recognized and carried in the balance sheet and income statement. The following alternative bases of measurement are used to different degrees and in varying combinations to measure assets and liabilities:

- **Historical cost**: Historical cost is simply the amount of cash or cash equivalents paid to purchase an asset, including any costs of acquisition and/or preparation. If the asset was not bought for cash, historical cost is the fair value of whatever was given in order to buy the asset. When referring to liabilities, the historical cost basis of measurement means the amount of proceeds received in exchange for the obligation.
- **Amortised cost**: Historical cost adjusted for amortisation, depreciation, or depletion and/ or impairment.
- **Current cost**: In reference to assets, current cost is the amount of cash or cash equivalents that would have to be paid to buy the same or an equivalent asset today. In reference to liabilities, the current cost basis of measurement means the undiscounted amount of cash or cash equivalents that would be required to settle the obligation today.
- **Realizable (settlement) value**: In reference to assets, realizable value is the amount of cash or cash equivalents that could currently be obtained by selling the asset in an orderly disposal. For liabilities, the equivalent to realizable value is called "settlement value"—that is, settlement value is the undiscounted amount of cash or cash equivalents expected to be paid to satisfy the liabilities in the normal course of business.
- **Present value (PV)**: For assets, present value is the present discounted value of the future net cash inflows that the asset is expected to generate in the normal course of business. For liabilities, present value is the present discounted value of the future net cash outflows that are expected to be required to settle the liabilities in the normal course of business.
- **Fair value**: This is defined as an exit price, the price that would be received to sell an asset or paid to transfer a liability in an orderly transaction between market participants at the measurement date. This may involve either market measures or present value measures depending on the availability of information.

4.4. General Requirements for Financial Statements

The *Conceptual Framework* provides a basis for establishing standards and the elements of financial statements. However, the framework does not address the general contents of the financial statements, which are addressed in International Accounting Standard (IAS) No. 1, *Presentation of Financial Statements*. IAS No. 1 specifies the required financial statements, general features of financial statements, and structure and content of financial statements.[12] These general requirements are illustrated in Exhibit 1 and described in the subsections below.

---

[12] For US GAAP, financial statement presentation is covered in Sections 205 through 280 of the Accounting Standards Codification.

EXHIBIT 1   IASB General Requirements for Financial Statements

Required Financial Statements
- Statement of financial position (Balance sheet)
- Statement of comprehensive income (Single statement or Income statement + Statement of comprehensive income)
- Statement of changes in equity
- Statement of cash flows
- Notes, summarizing accounting policies and disclosing other items
- In certain cases, Statement of financial position from earliest comparative period

General Features
- Fair presentation
- Going concern
- Accrual basis
- Materiality and aggregation
- No offsetting
- Frequency of reporting
- Comparative information
- Consistency of presentation

Structure and Content
- Classified balance sheet
- Minimum specified information on face
- Minimum specified note disclosures
- Comparative information

In the following sections, we discuss the required financial statements, the general features underlying the preparation of financial statements, and the specified structure and content in greater detail.

4.4.1. Required Financial Statements

Under IAS No. 1, a complete set of financial statements includes:[13]

- a statement of financial position (balance sheet);
- a statement of comprehensive income (a single statement of comprehensive income or two statements, an income statement and a statement of comprehensive income that begins with profit or loss from the income statement);
- a statement of changes in equity, separately showing changes in equity resulting from profit or loss, each item of other comprehensive income, and transactions with owners in their capacity as owners;[14]
- a statement of cash flows; and
- notes comprising a summary of significant accounting policies and other explanatory notes that disclose information required by IFRS and not presented elsewhere and that provide information relevant to an understanding of the financial statements.

---

[13] IAS No. 1, *Presentation of Financial Statements*, paragraph 10.
[14] Examples of transactions with owners acting in their capacity as owners include sale of equity securities to investors, distributions of earnings to investors, and repurchases of equity securities from investors.

Entities are encouraged to furnish other related financial and non-financial information in addition to that required. Financial statements need to present fairly the financial position, financial performance, and cash flows of an entity.

4.4.2. General Features of Financial Statements

A company that applies IFRS is required to state explicitly in the notes to its financial statements that it is in compliance with the standards. Such a statement is only made when a company is in compliance with *all* requirements of IFRS. In extremely rare circumstances, a company may deviate from a requirement of IFRS if management concludes that complying with IFRS would result in misleading financial statements. In this case, management must disclose details of the departure from IFRS.

IAS No. 1 specifies a number of general features underlying the preparation of financial statements. These features clearly reflect the *Conceptual Framework*.

- *Fair Presentation*: The application of IFRS is presumed to result in financial statements that achieve a fair presentation. The IAS describes fair presentation as follows:

  Fair presentation requires the faithful representation of the effects of transactions, other events, and conditions in accordance with the definitions and recognition criteria for assets, liabilities, income, and expenses set out in the *Framework*.[15]

- *Going Concern*: Financial statements are prepared on a going concern basis unless management either intends to liquidate the entity or to cease trading, or has no realistic alternative but to do so. If not presented on a going concern basis, the fact and rationale should be disclosed.
- *Accrual Basis*: Financial statements (except for cash flow information) are to be prepared using the accrual basis of accounting.
- *Materiality and Aggregation*: Omissions or misstatements of items are material if they could, individually or collectively, influence the economic decisions that users make on the basis of the financial statements. Each material class of similar items is presented separately. Dissimilar items are presented separately unless they are immaterial.
- *No Offsetting*: Assets and liabilities, and income and expenses, are not offset unless required or permitted by an IFRS.
- *Frequency of Reporting*: Financial statements must be prepared at least annually.
- *Comparative Information*: Financial statements must include comparative information from the previous period. The comparative information of prior periods is disclosed for all amounts reported in the financial statements, unless an IFRS requires or permits otherwise.
- *Consistency*: The presentation and classification of items in the financial statements are usually retained from one period to the next.

4.4.3. Structure and Content Requirements

IAS No. 1 also specifies structure and content of financial statements. These requirements include the following:

---

[15] IAS No. 1, *Presentation of Financial Statements*, paragraph 15.

- *Classified Statement of Financial Position (Balance Sheet)*: requires the balance sheet to distinguish between current and non-current assets, and between current and non-current liabilities unless a presentation based on liquidity provides more relevant and reliable information (e.g., in the case of a bank or similar financial institution).
- *Minimum Information on the Face of the Financial Statements*: specifies the minimum line item disclosures on the face of, or in the notes to, the financial statements. For example, companies are specifically required to disclose the amount of their plant, property, and equipment as a line item on the face of the balance sheet. The major line items included in financial statements are covered in other chapters.
- *Minimum Information in the Notes* (or on the face of financial statements): specifies disclosures about information to be presented in the financial statements. This information must be provided in a systematic manner and cross-referenced from the face of the financial statements to the notes. The required information is summarized in Exhibit 2.
- *Comparative Information*: For all amounts reported in a financial statement, comparative information should be provided for the previous period unless another standard requires or permits otherwise. Such comparative information allows users to better understand reported amounts.

EXHIBIT 2   Summary of IFRS Required Disclosures in the Notes to the Financial Statements

Disclosure of Accounting Policies	• Measurement bases used in preparing financial statements • Significant accounting policies used • Judgments made in applying accounting policies that have the most significant effect on the amounts recognized in the financial statements
Sources of Estimation Uncertainty	• Key assumptions about the future and other key sources of estimation uncertainty that have a significant risk of causing material adjustment to the carrying amount of assets and liabilities within the next year
Other Disclosures	• Information about capital and about certain financial instruments classified as equity • Dividends not recognized as a distribution during the period, including dividends declared before the financial statements were issued and any cumulative preference dividends • Description of the entity, including its domicile, legal form, country of incorporation, and registered office or business address • Nature of operations and principal activities • Name of parent and ultimate parent

5. COMPARISON OF IFRS WITH ALTERNATIVE REPORTING SYSTEMS

The adoption of IFRS as the required financial reporting standard by the EU and other countries has advanced the goal of global convergence. Nevertheless, there are still significant differences in financial reporting in the global capital markets. Arguably, the most critical are the differences that exist between IFRS and US GAAP. Following the EU adoption of IFRS (in 2005), a significant number of the world's listed companies use one of these two reporting standards.

In general, the IASB and FASB work together to coordinate changes to accounting standards and reduce differences between the standards. A joint IASB/FASB project initiated in 2004 aimed to develop an improved, common conceptual framework. In late 2010, convergence of the conceptual frameworks was put on hold. In December 2012, the IASB reactivated the conceptual framework as an IASB project. As of year-end 2018, there are no new projects on the convergence agenda.

As more countries adopt IFRS, the need for analysts to consider other financial reporting systems will be reduced. Analysts are likely to encounter financial statements that are prepared on a basis other than IFRS. Differences between IFRS and US GAAP remain and affect the framework as well as numerous financial reporting standards (see Exhibit 3). Curriculum readings on individual financial statements and specific topics provide a more detailed review of related differences in IFRS and US GAAP.

EXHIBIT 3   Differences between IFRS and US GAAP

Basis for Comparison	US GAAP	IFRS
Developed by	Financial Accounting Standard Board (FASB)	International Accounting Standard Board (IASB)
Based on	Rules	Principles
Inventory valuation	FIFO, LIFO, and Weighted Average Method	FIFO and Weighted Average Method
Extraordinary items	Shown below (at the bottom of the income statement)	Not segregated in the income statement
Development cost	Treated as an expense	Capitalized, only if certain conditions are satisfied
Reversal of Inventory	Prohibited	Permissible, if specified conditions are met

Source: https://keydifferences.com/difference-between-gaap-and-ifrs.html.

For analyzing financial statements created under different standards, reconciliation schedules and disclosures regarding the significant differences between the reporting bases—historically available in some jurisdictions—were particularly helpful. For example, the SEC historically required reconciliation for foreign private issuers that did not prepare financial statements in accordance with US GAAP. In 2007, however, the SEC eliminated the reconciliation requirement for companies that prepared their financial statements according to IFRS. Although the disclosures related to any such differences were sometimes dauntingly long, the numerical reconciliations of net income and shareholders' equity appeared in charts that were relatively easy to use. Because reconciliation disclosures are no longer generally available, an analyst comparing two companies that use different reporting standards must be aware of areas where accounting standards have not converged. In many cases, a user of financial statements prepared under different accounting standards does not have enough information to make specific adjustments required to achieve comparability. Instead, an analyst must maintain caution in interpreting comparative financial measures produced under different accounting standards and monitor significant developments in financial reporting standards, as these can have important implications for comparing the performance of companies and security valuation.

6. MONITORING DEVELOPMENTS IN FINANCIAL REPORTING STANDARDS

In studying financial reporting and financial statement analysis in general, the analyst must be aware that reporting standards are evolving. Analysts need to monitor ongoing developments in financial reporting and assess their implications for security analysis and valuation. The need to monitor developments in financial reporting standards does not mean that analysts should be accountants. An accountant monitors these developments from a preparer's perspective; an analyst needs to monitor from a user's perspective. More specifically, analysts need to know how these developments will affect financial reports.

Analysts can remain aware of developments in financial reporting standards by monitoring new products or transactions, actions of standard setters and other groups representing users of financial statements (such as CFA Institute), and company disclosures regarding critical accounting policies and estimates.

6.1. New Products or Types of Transactions

New products and new types of transactions can have unusual or unique elements to them such that no explicit guidance in the financial reporting standards exists. New products or transactions typically arise from economic events, such as new businesses (e.g., fintech), or from a newly developed financial instrument or financial structure. Financial instruments, whether exchange traded or not, are typically designed to enhance a company's business or to mitigate inherent risks. However, at times, financial instruments or structured transactions have been developed primarily for purposes of financial report "window dressing."

Although companies might discuss new products and transactions in their financial reports, the analyst can also monitor business journals and the capital markets to identify such items. Additionally, when one company in an industry develops a new product or transaction, other companies in the industry often do the same. Once new products, financial instruments, or structured transactions are identified, it is helpful to gain an understanding of the business purpose. If necessary, an analyst can obtain further information from a company's management, which should be able to describe the economic purpose, the financial statement reporting, significant estimates, judgments applied in determining the reporting, and future cash flow implications for these items.

6.2. Evolving Standards and the Role of CFA Institute

The actions of standard setters and regulators are unlikely to be helpful in identifying new products and transactions, given the lag between new product development and regulatory action. Monitoring the actions of these authorities is nonetheless important for another reason: Changes in regulations can affect companies' financial reports and, thus, valuations. This is particularly true if the financial reporting standards change to require more explicit identification of matters affecting asset/liability valuation or financial performance. For example, one regulatory change required companies to include a provision for expenses associated with the grant and vesting of employee stock option grants as an expense in the income statement. Prior to the required expensing, an analyst could only assess the dilutive effect to shareholders associated with stock option grants by reviewing information disclosed in the notes to the financial statements.

To the extent that some market participants do not examine financial statement details and thus ignore some items when valuing a company's securities, more explicit identification could affect the value of the company's securities. Additionally, it is plausible to believe that management is more attentive to and rigorous in any calculations/estimates of items that appear in the financial statements, compared to items that are only disclosed in the notes.

The IASB (www.iasb.org) and FASB (www.fasb.org) provide a great deal of information on their websites regarding new standards and proposals for future changes in standards. In addition, the IASB and FASB seek input from the financial analyst community—those who regularly use financial statements in making investment and credit decisions. When a new standard is proposed, an exposure draft is made available, and users of financial statements can draft comment letters and position papers for submission to the IASB and FASB in order to evaluate the proposal.

CFA Institute is active in supporting improvements to financial reporting. Volunteer members of CFA Institute serve on several liaison committees that meet regularly to make recommendations to the IASB and FASB on proposed standards and to draft comment letters and position papers. The comment letters and position papers of these groups on financial reporting issues are available at www.cfainstitute.org/advocacy.

In 2007, CFA Institute issued a position paper titled *A Comprehensive Business Reporting Model: Financial Reporting for Investors*, which provides a suggested model for significantly improving financial reporting. The position paper remains relevant in stating:

> Corporate financial statements and their related disclosures are fundamental to sound investment decision making. The well-being of the world's financial markets, and of the millions of investors who entrust their financial present and future to those markets, depends directly on the information financial statements and disclosures provide. Consequently, the quality of the information drives global financial markets. The quality, in turn, depends directly on the principles and standards managers apply when recognizing and measuring the economic activities and events affecting their companies' operations....
>
> Investors require timeliness, transparency, comparability, and consistency in financial reporting. Investors have a preference for decision relevance over reliability..."analysts need to know economic reality—what is really going on—to the greatest extent it can be depicted by accounting numbers." Corporate financial statements that fail to reflect this economic reality undermine the investment decision-making process.[16]

Among other principles, the proposed model stresses the importance of information regarding the current fair value of assets and liabilities, of neutrality in financial reporting, and of providing detailed information on cash flows to investors through the choice of the so-called direct format for the cash flow statement.

In summary, analysts can improve their investment decision making by keeping current on financial reporting standards. In addition, analysts can contribute to improving financial reporting by sharing their perspective as users with standard-setting bodies, which typically invite comments concerning proposed changes.

---

[16] *A Comprehensive Business Reporting Model: Financial Reporting for Investors*, CFA Institute Centre for Financial Market Integrity, July 2007, p. 1, 2.

7. SUMMARY

An awareness of financial reporting and underlying financial reporting standards can assist in security valuation and other financial analysis. This chapter describes the conceptual objectives of financial reporting standards, the parties involved in standard-setting processes, and the implication for analysts in monitoring developments in reporting standards.

Some key points of the chapter are summarized below:

- The objective of financial reporting is to provide financial information about the reporting entity that is useful to existing and potential investors, lenders, and other creditors in making decisions about providing resources to the entity.
- Financial reporting requires policy choices and estimates. These choices and estimates require judgment, which can vary from one preparer to the next. Accordingly, standards are needed to ensure increased consistency in these judgments.
- Private-sector standard-setting bodies and regulatory authorities play significant but different roles in the standard-setting process. In general, standard-setting bodies make the rules, and regulatory authorities enforce the rules. However, regulators typically retain legal authority to establish financial reporting standards in their jurisdiction.
- The IFRS framework sets forth the concepts that underlie the preparation and presentation of financial statements for external users.
- The objective of fair presentation of useful information is the center of the IASB's *Conceptual Framework*. The qualitative characteristics of useful information include fundamental and enhancing characteristics. Information must exhibit the fundamental characteristics of relevance and faithful representation to be useful. The enhancing characteristics identified are comparability, verifiability, timeliness, and understandability.
- *IFRS Financial Statements*: IAS No. 1 prescribes that a complete set of financial statements includes a statement of financial position (balance sheet), a statement of comprehensive income (either two statements—one for net income and one for comprehensive income—or a single statement combining both net income and comprehensive income), a statement of changes in equity, a cash flow statement, and notes. The notes include a summary of significant accounting policies and other explanatory information.
- Financial statements need to reflect certain basic features: fair presentation, going concern, accrual basis, materiality and aggregation, and no offsetting.
- Financial statements must be prepared at least annually, must include comparative information from the previous period, and must be consistent.
- Financial statements must follow certain presentation requirements including a classified statement of financial position (balance sheet) and minimum information on both the face of the financial statements and in the notes.
- A significant number of the world's listed companies report under either IFRS or US GAAP.
- In many cases, a user of financial statements will lack the information necessary to make specific adjustments required to achieve comparability between companies that use IFRS and companies that use US GAAP. Instead, an analyst must maintain general caution in interpreting comparative financial measures produced under different accounting standards and monitor significant developments in financial reporting standards.
- Analysts can remain aware of ongoing developments in financial reporting by monitoring new products or types of transactions; actions of standard setters, regulators, and other groups; and company disclosures regarding critical accounting policies and estimates.

PRACTICE PROBLEMS

1. Which of the following is *most likely* not an objective of financial statements?
   A. To provide information about the performance of an entity.
   B. To provide information about the financial position of an entity.
   C. To provide information about the users of an entity's financial statements.

2. International financial reporting standards are currently developed by which entity?
   A. The IFRS Foundation.
   B. The International Accounting Standards Board.
   C. The International Organization of Securities Commissions.

3. US generally accepted accounting principles are currently developed by which entity?
   A. The Securities and Exchange Commission.
   B. The Financial Accounting Standards Board.
   C. The Public Company Accounting Oversight Board.

4. A core objective of the International Organization of Securities Commissions is to:
   A. eliminate systemic risk.
   B. protect users of financial statements.
   C. ensure that markets are fair, efficient, and transparent.

5. According to the *Conceptual Framework for Financial Reporting*, which of the following is *not* an enhancing qualitative characteristic of information in financial statements?
   A. Accuracy.
   B. Timeliness.
   C. Comparability.

6. Which of the following is *not* a constraint on the financial statements according to the *Conceptual Framework*?
   A. Understandability.
   B. Benefit versus cost.
   C. Balancing of qualitative characteristics.

7. The assumption that an entity will continue to operate for the foreseeable future is called:
   A. accrual basis.
   B. comparability.
   C. going concern.

8. The assumption that the effects of transactions and other events are recognized when they occur, not when the cash flows occur, is called:
   A. relevance.
   B. accrual basis.
   C. going concern.

9. Neutrality of information in the financial statements most closely contributes to which qualitative characteristic?
   A. Relevance.
   B. Understandability.
   C. Faithful representation.

10. Valuing assets at the amount of cash or equivalents paid or the fair value of the consideration given to acquire them at the time of acquisition most closely describes which measurement of financial statement elements?
    A. Current cost.
    B. Historical cost.
    C. Realizable value.

11. The valuation technique under which assets are recorded at the amount that would be received in an orderly disposal is:
    A. current cost.
    B. present value.
    C. realizable value.

12. Which of the following is *not* a required financial statement according to IAS No. 1?
    A. Statement of financial position.
    B. Statement of changes in income.
    C. Statement of comprehensive income.

13. Which of the following elements of financial statements is *most* closely related to measurement of performance?
    A. Assets.
    B. Expenses.
    C. Liabilities.

14. Which of the following elements of financial statements is *most* closely related to measurement of financial position?
    A. Equity.
    B. Income.
    C. Expenses.

15. Which of the following disclosures regarding new accounting standards provides the *most* meaningful information to an analyst?
    A. The impact of adoption is discussed.
    B. The standard will have no material impact.
    C. Management is still evaluating the impact.

CHAPTER **3**

UNDERSTANDING INCOME STATEMENTS

Elaine Henry, PhD, CFA
Thomas R. Robinson, PhD, CFA

LEARNING OUTCOMES

After completing this chapter, you will be able to do the following:

- describe the components of the income statement and alternative presentation formats of that statement;
- Describe general principles of revenue recognition and accounting standards for revenue recognition;
- calculate revenue given information that might influence the choice of revenue recognition method;
- describe general principles of expense recognition, specific expense recognition applications, and implications of expense recognition choices for financial analysis;
- describe the financial reporting treatment and analysis of non-recurring items (including discontinued operations, unusual or infrequent items) and changes in accounting policies;
- distinguish between the operating and non-operating components of the income statement;
- describe how earnings per share is calculated and calculate and interpret a company's earnings per share (both basic and diluted earnings per share) for both simple and complex capital structures;
- distinguish between dilutive and antidilutive securities and describe the implications of each for the earnings per share calculation;
- convert income statements to common-size income statements;
- evaluate a company's financial performance using common-size income statements and financial ratios based on the income statement;
- describe, calculate, and interpret comprehensive income;
- describe other comprehensive income and identify major types of items included in it.

1. INTRODUCTION

The income statement presents information on the financial results of a company's business activities over a period of time. The income statement communicates how much revenue the company generated during a period and what costs it incurred in connection with generating that revenue. The basic equation underlying the income statement, ignoring gains and losses, is Revenue minus Expenses equals Net income. The income statement is also sometimes referred to as the "statement of operations," "statement of earnings," or "profit and loss (P&L) statement." Under both International Financial Reporting Standards (IFRS) and US generally accepted accounting principles (US GAAP), the income statement may be presented as a separate statement followed by a statement of comprehensive income that begins with the profit or loss from the income statement or as a section of a single statement of comprehensive income.[1] This chapter focuses on the income statement, and the term *income statement* will be used to describe either the separate statement that reports profit or loss used for earnings per share calculations or that section of a statement of comprehensive income that reports the same profit or loss. The chapter also includes a discussion of comprehensive income (profit or loss from the income statement plus other comprehensive income).

Investment analysts intensely scrutinize companies' income statements. Equity analysts are interested in them because equity markets often reward relatively high- or low-earnings growth companies with above-average or below-average valuations, respectively, and because inputs into valuation models often include estimates of earnings. Fixed-income analysts examine the components of income statements, past and projected, for information on companies' abilities to make promised payments on their debt over the course of the business cycle. Corporate financial announcements frequently emphasize information reported in income statements, particularly earnings, more than information reported in the other financial statements.

This chapter is organized as follows: Section 2 describes the components of the income statement and its format. Section 3 describes basic principles and selected applications related to the recognition of revenue, and Section 4 describes basic principles and selected applications related to the recognition of expenses. Section 5 covers non-recurring items and non-operating items. Section 6 explains the calculation of earnings per share. Section 7 introduces income statement analysis, and Section 8 explains comprehensive income and its reporting. A summary of the key points and practice problems in the CFA Institute multiple choice format complete the chapter.

2. COMPONENTS AND FORMAT OF THE INCOME STATEMENT

Exhibits 1, 2, and 3 show the income statements for Anheuser-Busch InBev SA/NV (AB InBev), a multinational beverage company based in Belgium, Molson Coors Brewing Company (Molson Coors), a US-based multinational brewing company, and Groupe Danone (Danone), a French food manufacturer.[2] AB InBev and Danone report under IFRS, and

---

[1] International Accounting Standard (IAS) 1, *Presentation of Financial Statements*, establishes the presentation and minimum content requirements of financial statements and guidelines for the structure of financial statements under IFRS. Under US GAAP, the Financial Accounting Standards Board Accounting Standards Codification ASC Section 220-10-45 [Comprehensive Income–Overall–Other Presentation Matters] discusses acceptable formats in which to present income, other comprehensive income, and comprehensive income.
[2] Following net income, the income statement also presents **earnings per share**, the amount of earnings per common share of the company. Earnings per share will be discussed in detail later in this chapter, and the per-share display has been omitted from these exhibits to focus on the core income statement.

Molson Coors reports under US GAAP. Note that both AB InBev and Molson Coors show three years' income statements and list the years in chronological order with the most recent year listed in the left-most column. In contrast, Danone shows two years of income statements and lists the years in chronological order from left to right with the most recent year in the right-most column. Different orderings of chronological information are common.

On the top line of the income statement, companies typically report revenue. **Revenue** generally refers to the amount charged for the delivery of goods or services in the *ordinary activities* of a business. Revenue may also be called sales or turnover.[3] For the year ended 31 December 2017, AB InBev reports $56.44 billion of revenue, Molson Coors reports $13.47 billion of revenue (labeled "sales"), and Danone reports €24.68 billion of revenue (labeled "sales").

Revenue is reported after adjustments (e.g., for cash or volume discounts, or for other reductions), and the term **net revenue** is sometimes used to specifically indicate that the revenue has been adjusted (e.g., for estimated returns). For all three companies in Exhibits 1 through 3, footnotes to their financial statements (not shown here) state that revenues are stated net of such items as returns, customer rebates, trade discounts, or volume-based incentive programs for customers.

In a comparative analysis, an analyst may need to reference information disclosed elsewhere in companies' annual reports—typically the notes to the financial statements and the Management Discussion and Analysis (MD&A)—to identify the appropriately comparable revenue amounts. For example, excise taxes represent a significant expenditure for brewing companies. On its income statement, Molson Coors reports $13.47 billion of revenue (labeled "sales") and $11.00 billion of net revenue (labeled "net sales"), which equals sales minus $2.47 billion of excise taxes. Unlike Molson Coors, AB InBev does not show the amount of excise taxes on its income statement. However, in its disclosures, AB InBev notes that excise taxes (amounting to $15.4 billion in 2017) have been deducted from the revenue amount shown on its income statement. Thus, the amount on AB InBev's income statement labeled "revenue" is more comparable to the amount on Molson Coors' income statement labeled "net sales."

EXHIBIT 1   Anheuser-Busch InBev SA/NV Consolidated Income Statement (in Millions of US Dollars) [Excerpt]

	12 Months Ended December 31		
	2017	2016	2015
Revenue	$56,444	$45,517	$43,604
Cost of sales	(21,386)	(17,803)	(17,137)
Gross profit	35,058	27,715	26,467
Distribution expenses	(5,876)	(4,543)	(4,259)
Sales and marketing expenses	(8,382)	(7,745)	(6,913)
Administrative expenses	(3,841)	(2,883)	(2,560)
Other operating income/(expenses)	854	732	1,032
Restructuring	(468)	(323)	(171)
Business and asset disposal	(39)	377	524
Acquisition costs business combinations	(155)	(448)	(55)

(continued)

---

[3] **Sales** is sometimes understood to refer to the sale of goods, whereas *revenue* can include the sale of goods or services; however, the terms are often used interchangeably. In some countries, the term "turnover" may be used in place of revenue.

EXHIBIT 1   (Continued)

	12 Months Ended December 31		
	2017	2016	2015
Impairment of assets	—	—	(82)
Judicial settlement	—	—	(80)
Profit from operations	17,152	12,882	13,904
Finance cost	(6,885)	(9,216)	(3,142)
Finance income	378	652	1,689
Net finance income/(cost)	(6,507)	(8,564)	(1,453)
Share of result of associates and joint ventures	430	16	10
Profit before tax	11,076	4,334	12,461
Income tax expense	(1,920)	(1,613)	(2,594)
Profit from continuing operations	9,155	2,721	9,867
Profit from discontinued operations	28	48	
Profit of the year	9,183	2,769	9,867
Profit from continuing operations attributable to:			
Equity holders of AB InBev	7,968	1,193	8,273
Non-controlling interest	1,187	1,528	1,594
Profit of the year attributable to:			
Equity holders of AB InBev	7,996	1,241	8,273
Non-controlling interest	$1,187	$1,528	$1,594

Note: reported total amounts may have slight discrepancies due to rounding

EXHIBIT 2   Molson Coors Brewing Company Consolidated Statement of Operations (in Millions of US Dollars) [Excerpt]

	12 Months Ended		
	Dec. 31, 2017	Dec. 31, 2016	Dec. 31, 2015
Sales	$13,471.5	$6,597.4	$5,127.4
Excise taxes	(2,468.7)	(1,712.4)	(1,559.9)
Net sales	11,002.8	4,885.0	3,567.5
Cost of goods sold	(6,217.2)	(2,987.5)	(2,131.6)
Gross profit	4,785.6	1,897.5	1,435.9
Marketing, general and administrative expenses	(3,032.4)	(1,589.8)	(1,038.3)
Special items, net	(28.1)	2,522.4	(346.7)
Equity Income in MillerCoors	0	500.9	516.3
Operating income (loss)	1,725.1	3,331.0	567.2
Other income (expense), net			
Interest expense	(349.3)	(271.6)	(120.3)
Interest income	6.0	27.2	8.3
Other income (expense), net	(0.1)	(29.7)	0.9
Total other income (expense), net	(343.4)	(274.1)	(111.1)
Income (loss) from continuing operations before income taxes	1,381.7	3,056.9	456.1
Income tax benefit (expense)	53.2	(1,055.2)	(61.5)

EXHIBIT 2   (Continued)

	12 Months Ended		
	Dec. 31, 2017	Dec. 31, 2016	Dec. 31, 2015
Net income (loss) from continuing operations	1,434.9	2,001.7	394.6
Income (loss) from discontinued operations, net of tax	1.5	(2.8)	3.9
Net income (loss) including noncontrolling interests	1,436.4	1,998.9	398.5
Net (income) loss attributable to noncontrolling interests	(22.2)	(5.9)	(3.3)
Net income (loss) attributable to Molson Coors Brewing Company	$1,414.2	$1,993.0	$395.2

EXHIBIT 3   Groupe Danone Consolidated Income Statement (in Millions of Euros) [Excerpt]

	Year Ended December 31	
	2016	2017
Sales	21,944	24,677
Cost of goods sold	(10,744)	(12,459)
Selling expense	(5,562)	(5,890)
General and administrative expense	(2,004)	(2,225)
Research and development expense	(333)	(342)
Other income (expense)	(278)	(219)
Recurring operating income	3,022	3,543
Other operating income (expense)	(99)	192
Operating income	2,923	3,734
Interest income on cash equivalents and short-term investments	130	151
Interest expense	(276)	(414)
Cost of net debt	(146)	(263)
Other financial income	67	137
Other financial expense	(214)	(312)
Income before tax	2,630	3,296
Income tax expense	(804)	(842)
Net income from fully consolidated companies	1,826	2,454
Share of profit of associates	1	109
Net income	1,827	2,563
Net income – Group share	1,720	2,453
Net income – Non-controlling interests	107	110

Differences in presentations of items, such as expenses, are also common. **Expenses** reflect outflows, depletions of assets, and incurrences of liabilities in the course of the activities of a business. Expenses may be grouped and reported in different formats, subject to some specific requirements.

At the bottom of the income statement, companies report net income (companies may use other terms such as "net earnings" or "profit or loss"). For 2017, AB InBev reports $9,183 million "Profit of the year", Molson Coors reports $1,436.4 million of net income including noncontrolling interests, and Danone reports €2,563 million of net income. Net income is often referred to as the "bottom line." The basis for this expression is that net income is the final—or bottom—line item in an income statement. Because net income is often viewed as the single most relevant number to describe a company's performance over a period of time, the term "bottom line" sometimes is used in business to refer to any final or most relevant result.

Despite this customary terminology, note that each company presents additional items below net income: information about how much of that net income is attributable to the company itself and how much of that income is attributable to noncontrolling interests, also known as minority interests. The companies consolidate subsidiaries over which they have control. Consolidation means that they include all of the revenues and expenses of the subsidiaries even if they own less than 100 percent. Noncontrolling interest represents the portion of income that "belongs" to the minority shareholders of the consolidated subsidiaries, as opposed to the parent company itself. For AB InBev, $7,996 million of the total profit is attributable to the shareholders of AB InBev, and $1,187 million is attributable to noncontrolling interests. For Molson Coors, $1,414.2 million is attributable to the shareholders of Molson Coors, and $22.2 million is attributable to noncontrolling interests. For Danone, €2,453 million of the net income amount is attributable to shareholders of Groupe Danone and €110 million is attributable to noncontrolling interests.

Net income also includes **gains** and **losses,** which are increases and decreases in economic benefits, respectively, which may or may not arise in the ordinary activities of the business. For example, when a manufacturing company sells its products, these transactions are reported as revenue, and the costs incurred to generate these revenues are expenses and are presented separately. However, if a manufacturing company sells surplus land that is not needed, the transaction is reported as a gain or a loss. The amount of the gain or loss is the difference between the carrying value of the land and the price at which the land is sold. For example, in Exhibit 1, AB InBev reports a loss (proceeds, net of carrying value) of $39 million on disposals of businesses and assets in fiscal 2017, and gains of $377 million and $524 million in 2016 and 2015, respectively. Details on these gains and losses can typically be found in the companies' disclosures. For example, AB InBev discloses that the $377 million gain in 2016 was mainly from selling one of its breweries in Mexico.

The definition of income encompasses both revenue and gains and the definition of expenses encompasses both expenses that arise in the ordinary activities of the business and losses.[4] Thus, **net income** (profit or loss) can be defined as: a) income minus expenses, or equivalently b) revenue plus other income plus gains minus expenses, or equivalently c) revenue plus other income plus gains minus expenses in the ordinary activities of the business minus other expenses, and minus losses. The last definition can be rearranged as follows: net income equals (i) revenue minus expenses in the ordinary activities of the business, plus (ii) other income minus other expenses, plus (iii) gains minus losses.

In addition to presenting the net income, income statements also present items, including subtotals, which are significant to users of financial statements. Some of the items are specified by IFRS but other items are not specified.[5] Certain items, such as revenue, finance costs,

---

[4] IASB *Conceptual Framework for Financial Reporting (2010)*, paragraphs 4.29 to 4.32.
[5] Requirements are presented in IAS 1, *Presentation of Financial Statements.*

and tax expense, are required to be presented separately on the face of the income statement. IFRS additionally require that line items, headings, and subtotals relevant to understanding the entity's financial performance should be presented even if not specified. Expenses may be grouped together either by their nature or function. Grouping together expenses such as depreciation on manufacturing equipment and depreciation on administrative facilities into a single line item called "depreciation" is an example of a **grouping by nature** of the expense. An example of **grouping by function** would be grouping together expenses into a category such as cost of goods sold, which may include labour and material costs, depreciation, some salaries (e.g., salespeople's), and other direct sales related expenses.[6] All three companies in Exhibits 1 through 3 present their expenses by function, which is sometimes referred to "cost of sales" method.

One subtotal often shown in an income statement is **gross profit** or **gross margin** (that is revenue less cost of sales). When an income statement shows a gross profit subtotal, it is said to use a **multi-step format** rather than a **single-step format**. The AB InBev and Molson Coors income statements are examples of the multi-step format, whereas the Groupe Danone income statement is in a single-step format. For manufacturing and merchandising companies, gross profit is a relevant item and is calculated as revenue minus the cost of the goods that were sold. For service companies, gross profit is calculated as revenue minus the cost of services that were provided. In summary, gross profit is the amount of revenue available after subtracting the costs of delivering goods or services. Other expenses related to running the business are subtracted after gross profit.

Another important subtotal which may be shown on the income statement is **operating profit** (or, synonymously, operating income). Operating profit results from deducting operating expenses such as selling, general, administrative, and research and development expenses from gross profit. Operating profit reflects a company's profits on its business activities before deducting taxes, and for non-financial companies, before deducting interest expense. For financial companies, interest expense would be included in operating expenses and subtracted in arriving at operating profit because it relates to the operating activities for such companies. For some companies composed of a number of separate business segments, operating profit can be useful in evaluating the performance of the individual business segments, because interest and tax expenses may be more relevant at the level of the overall company rather than an individual segment level. The specific calculations of gross profit and operating profit may vary by company, and a reader of financial statements can consult the notes to the statements to identify significant variations across companies.

Operating profit is sometimes referred to as EBIT (earnings before interest and taxes). However, operating profit and EBIT are not necessarily the same. Note that in each of the Exhibits 1 through 3, interest and taxes do not represent the only differences between earnings (net income, net earnings) and operating income. For example, AB InBev separately reports its share of associates' and joint ventures' income and Molson Coors separately reports some income from discontinued operations.

Exhibit 4 shows an excerpt from the income statement of CRA International, a company providing management consulting services. Accordingly, CRA deducts cost of services (rather than cost of goods) from revenues to derive gross profit. CRA's fiscal year ends on the Saturday nearest December 31st. Because of this fiscal year timeframe, CRA's fiscal year occasionally

---

[6]Later chapters will provide additional information about alternative methods to calculate cost of goods sold.

comprises 53 weeks rather than 52 weeks. Although the extra week is likely immaterial in computing year-to-year growth rates, it may have a material impact on a quarter containing the extra week. In general, an analyst should be alert to the effect of an extra week when making historical comparisons and forecasting future performance.

EXHIBIT 4   CRA International Inc. Consolidated Statements of Operations (Excerpt)
(in Thousands of Dollars)

	Fiscal Year Ended		
	Dec. 30, 2017	Dec. 31, 2016	Jan. 2, 2016
Revenues	$370,075	$324,779	$303,559
Costs of services (exclusive of depreciation and amortization)	258,829	227,380	207,650
Selling, general and administrative expenses	86,537	70,584	72,439
Depreciation and amortization	8,945	7,896	6,552
GNU goodwill impairment	—	—	4,524
Income from operations	15,764	18,919	12,394

Note: Remaining items omitted

Exhibits 1 through 4 illustrate basic points about the income statement, including variations across the statements—some of which depend on the industry and/or country, and some of which reflect differences in accounting policies and practices of a particular company. In addition, some differences within an industry are primarily differences in terminology, whereas others are more fundamental accounting differences. Notes to the financial statements are helpful in identifying such differences.

Having introduced the components and format of an income statement, the next objective is to understand the actual reported numbers in it. To accurately interpret reported numbers, the analyst needs to be familiar with the principles of revenue and expense recognition—that is, how revenue and expenses are measured and attributed to a given accounting reporting period.

3. REVENUE RECOGNITION

Revenue is the top line in an income statement, so we begin the discussion of line items in the income statement with revenue recognition. Accounting standards for revenue recognition (which we discuss later in this section) became effective at the beginning of 2018 and are nearly identical under IFRS and US GAAP. The revenue recognition standards for IFRS and US GAAP (IFRS 15 and ASC Topic 606, respectively) were issued in 2014 and resulted from an effort to achieve convergence, consistency, and transparency in revenue recognition globally.

A first task is to explain some relevant accounting terminology. The terms revenue, sales, gains, losses, and net income (profit, net earnings) have been briefly defined. The IASB *Conceptual Framework for Financial Reporting* (2010),[7] referred to hereafter as the *Conceptual*

---

[7] The IASB is currently in the process of updating its *Conceptual Framework for Financial Reporting*.

Framework, further defines and discusses these income statement items. The *Conceptual Framework* explains that profit is a frequently used measure of performance and is composed of income and expenses.[8] It defines **income** as follows:

> Income is increases in economic benefits during the accounting period in the form of inflows or enhancements of assets or decreases of liabilities that result in increases in equity, other than those relating to contributions from equity participants.[9]

In IFRS, the term "income" includes revenue and gains. Gains are similar to revenue, but they typically arise from secondary or peripheral activities rather than from a company's primary business activities. For example, for a restaurant, the sale of surplus restaurant equipment for more than its carrying value is referred to as a gain rather than as revenue. Similarly, a loss typically arises from secondary activities. Gains and losses may be considered part of operating activities (e.g., a loss due to a decline in the value of inventory) or may be considered part of non-operating activities (e.g., the sale of non-trading investments).

In the following simple hypothetical scenario, revenue recognition is straightforward: a company sells goods to a buyer for cash and does not allow returns, so the company recognizes revenue when the exchange of goods for cash takes place and measures revenue at the amount of cash received. In practice, however, determining when revenue should be recognized and at what amount is considerably more complex for reasons discussed in the following sections.

3.1. General Principles

An important aspect concerning revenue recognition is that it can occur independently of cash movements. For example, assume a company sells goods to a buyer on credit, so does not actually receive cash until some later time. A fundamental principle of accrual accounting is that revenue is recognized (reported on the income statement) when it is earned, so the company's financial records reflect revenue from the sale when the risk and reward of ownership is transferred; this is often when the company delivers the goods or services. If the delivery was on credit, a related asset, such as trade or accounts receivable, is created. Later, when cash changes hands, the company's financial records simply reflect that cash has been received to settle an account receivable. Similarly, there are situations when a company receives cash in advance and actually delivers the product or service later, perhaps over a period of time. In this case, the company would record a liability for **unearned revenue** when the cash is initially received, and revenue would be recognized as being earned over time as products and services are delivered. An example would be a subscription payment received for a publication that is to be delivered periodically over time.

---

[8] *Conceptual Framework*, paragraph 4.24. The text on the elements of financial statements and their recognition and measurement is the same in the IASB *Conceptual Framework for Financial Reporting* (2010) and the IASB *Framework for the Preparation and Presentation of Financial Statements* (1989).

[9] Ibid., paragraph 4.25(a).

3.2. Accounting Standards for Revenue Recognition

The converged accounting standards issued by the IASB and FASB in May 2014 introduced some changes to the basic principles of revenue recognition and should enhance comparability.[10] The content of the two standards is nearly identical, and this discussion pertains to both, unless specified otherwise. Issuance of this converged standard is significant because of the differences between IFRS and US GAAP on revenue recognition prior to the converged standard. The converged standard aims to provide a principles-based approach to revenue recognition that can be applied to many types of revenue-generating activities.

The core principle of the converged standard is that revenue should be recognized to "depict the transfer of promised goods or services to customers in an amount that reflects the consideration to which the entity expects to be entitled in an exchange for those goods or services." To achieve the core principle, the standard describes the application of five steps in recognizing revenue:

1. Identify the contract(s) with a customer
2. Identify the separate or distinct performance obligations in the contract
3. Determine the transaction price
4. Allocate the transaction price to the performance obligations in the contract
5. Recognize revenue when (or as) the entity satisfies a performance obligation

According to the standard, a contract is an agreement and commitment, with commercial substance, between the contacting parties. It establishes each party's *obligations* and *rights,* including payment terms. In addition, a contract exists only if collectability is probable. Each standard uses the same wording, but the threshold for probable collectability differs. Under IFRS, probable means more likely than not, and under US GAAP it means likely to occur. As a result, economically similar contracts may be treated differently under IFRS and US GAAP.

The performance obligations within a contract represent promises to transfer distinct good(s) or service(s). A good or service is distinct if the customer can benefit from it on its own or in combination with readily available resources and if the promise to transfer it can be separated from other promises in the contract. Each identified performance obligation is accounted for separately.

The transaction price is what the seller estimates will be received in exchange for transferring the good(s) or service(s) identified in the contract. The transaction price is then allocated to each identified performance obligation. Revenue is recognized when a performance obligation is fulfilled. Steps three and four address amount, and step five addresses timing of recognition. The amount recognized reflects expectations about collectability and (if applicable) an allocation to multiple obligations within the same contract. Revenue is recognized when the obligation-satisfying transfer is made.

Revenue should only be recognized when it is highly probable that it will not be subsequently reversed. This may result in the recording of a minimal amount of revenue upon sale when an estimate of total revenue is not reliable. The balance sheet will be required to reflect the entire refund obligation as a liability and will include an asset for the "right to returned goods" based on the carrying amount of inventory less costs of recovery.

---

[10] *IFRS 15 Revenue from Contracts with Customers* and FASB ASC Topic 606 (Revenue from Contracts with Customers).

When revenue is recognized, a contract asset is presented on the balance sheet. It is only at the point when all performance obligations have been met except for payment that a receivable appears on the seller's balance sheet. If consideration is received in advance of transferring good(s) or service(s), the seller presents a contract liability.

The entity will recognize revenue when it is able to satisfy the performance obligation by transferring control to the customer. Factors to consider when assessing whether the customer has obtained control of an asset at a point in time:

- Entity has a present right to payment,
- Customer has legal title,
- Customer has physical possession,
- Customer has the significant risks and rewards of ownership, and
- Customer has accepted the asset.

For a simple contract with only one deliverable at a single point in time, completing the five steps is straight-forward. For more complex contracts—such as when the performance obligations are satisfied over time, when the terms of the multi-period contracts change, when the performance obligation includes various components of goods and services, or when the compensation is "variable"—accounting choices can be less obvious. The steps in the standards are intended to provide guidance that can be generalized to most situations.

In addition, the standard provides many specific examples. These examples are intended to provide guidance as to how to approach more complex contracts. Some of these examples are summarized in Exhibit 5. Note that the end result for many examples may not differ substantially from that under revenue recognition standards that were in effect prior to the adoption of the converged standard; instead it is the conceptual approach and, in some cases, the terminology that will differ.

EXHIBIT 5   Applying the Converged Revenue Recognition Standard

The references in this exhibit are to Examples in IFRS 15 *Revenue from Contracts with Customers* (and ASU 2014-09 (FASB ASC Topic 606)), on which these summaries are based.

Part 1 *(ref. Example 10)*.

Builder Co. enters into a contract with Customer Co. to construct a commercial building. Builder Co. identifies various goods and services to be provided, such as pre-construction engineering, construction of the building's individual components, plumbing, electrical wiring, and interior finishes. With respect to "Identifying the Performance Obligation," should Builder Co. treat each specific item as a separate performance obligation to which revenue should be allocated?

The standard provides two criteria, which must be met, to determine if a good or service is distinct for purposes of identifying performance obligations. First, the customer can benefit from the good or service either on its own or together with other readily available resources. Second, the seller's "promise to transfer the good or service to the customer is separately identifiable from other promises in the contract." In this example, the second criterion is not met because it is the building for which the customer has contracted, not the separate goods and services. The seller will integrate all the goods and services into a combined output and each specific item should not be treated as a distinct good or service but accounted for together as a single performance obligation.

(continued)

EXHIBIT 5   (Continued)

Part 2 *(ref. Example 8)*.

Builder Co.'s contract with Customer Co. to construct the commercial building specifies consideration of $1 million. Builder Co.'s expected total costs are $700,000. The Builder incurs $420,000 in costs in the first year. Assuming that costs incurred provide an appropriate measure of progress toward completing the contract, how much revenue should Builder Co. recognize for the first year?

The standard states that for performance obligations satisfied over time (e.g., where there is a long-term contract), revenue is recognized over time by measuring progress toward satisfying the obligation. In this case, the Builder has incurred 60% of the total expected costs ($420,000/$700,000) and will thus recognize $600,000 (60% × $1 million) in revenue for the first year.

This is the same amount of revenue that would be recognized using the "percentage-of-completion" method under previous accounting standards, but that term is not used in the converged standard. Instead, the standard refers to performance obligations satisfied over time and requires that progress toward complete satisfaction of the performance obligation be measured based on input method such as the one illustrated here (recognizing revenue based on the proportion of total costs that have been incurred in the period) or an output method (recognizing revenue based on units produced or milestones achieved).

Part 3 *(ref. Example 8)*.

Assume that Builder Co.'s contract with Customer Co. to construct the commercial building specifies consideration of $1 million *plus* a bonus of $200,000 if the building is completed within 2 years. Builder Co. has only limited experience with similar types of contracts and knows that many factors outside its control (e.g., weather, regulatory requirements) could cause delay. Builder Co.'s expected total costs are $700,000. The Builder incurs $420,000 in costs in the first year. Assuming that costs incurred provide an appropriate measure of progress toward completing the contract, how much revenue should Builder Co. recognize for the first year?

The standard addresses so-called "variable consideration" as part of determining the transaction price. A company is only allowed to recognize variable consideration if it can conclude that it will not have to reverse the cumulative revenue in the future. In this case, Builder Co. does not recognize any of the bonus in year one because it cannot reach the non-reversible conclusion given its limited experience with similar contracts and potential delays from factors outside its control.

Part 4 *(ref. Example 8)*.

Assume all facts from Part 3. In the beginning of year two, Builder Co. and Customer Co. agree to change the building floor plan and modify the contract. As a result the consideration will increase by $150,000, and the allowable time for achieving the bonus is extended by 6 months. Builder expects its costs will increase by $120,000. Also, given the additional 6 months to earn the completion bonus, Builder concludes that it now meets the criteria for including the $200,000 bonus in revenue. How should Builder account for this change in the contract?

Note that previous standards did not provide a general framework for contract modifications. The converged standard provides guidance on whether a change in a contract is a new contract or a modification of an existing contract. To be considered a new contract, the change would need to involve goods and services that are distinct from the goods and services already transferred.

In this case, the change does not meet the criteria of a new contract and is therefore considered a modification of the existing contract, which requires the company to reflect the impact on a cumulative catch-up basis. Therefore, the company must update its transaction price

EXHIBIT 5   (Continued)

and measure of progress. Builder's total revenue on the transaction (transaction price) is now $1.35 million ($1 million original plus the $150,000 new consideration plus $200,000 for the completion bonus). Builder Co.'s progress toward completion is now 51.2% ($420,000 costs incurred divided by total expected costs of $820,000). Based on the changes in the contract, the amount of additional revenue to be recognized is $91,200, calculated as (51.2% × $1.35 million) minus the $600,000 already recognized. The additional $91,200 of revenue would be recognized as a "cumulative catch-up adjustment" on the date of the contract modification.

Part 5 *(ref. Example 45).*

Assume a Company operates a website that enables customers to purchase goods from various suppliers. The customers pay the Company in advance, and orders are nonrefundable. The *suppliers* deliver the goods directly to the customer, and the Company receives a 10% commission. Should the Company report Total Revenues equal to 100% of the sales amount (gross) or Total Revenues equal to 10% of the sales amount (net)? Revenues are reported gross if the Company is acting as a Principal and net if the Company is acting as an Agent.

In this example, the Company is an Agent because it isn't primarily responsible for fulfilling the contract, doesn't take any inventory risk or credit risk, doesn't have discretion in setting the price, and receives compensation in the form of a commission. Because the Company is acting as an Agent, it should report only the amount of commission as its revenue.

Some related costs require specific accounting treatment under the new standards. In particular, incremental costs of obtaining a contract and certain costs incurred to fulfill a contract must be capitalized under the new standards (i.e., reported as an asset on the balance sheet rather than as an expense on the income statement). If a company had previously expensed these incremental costs in the years prior to adopting the converged standard, all else equal, its profitability will initially appear higher under the converged standards.

The disclosure requirements are quite extensive. Companies are required at year end[11] to disclose information about contracts with customers disaggregated into different categories of contracts. The categories might be based on the type of product, the geographic region, the type of customer or sales channel, the type of contract pricing terms, the contract duration, or the timing of transfers. Companies are also required to disclose balances of any contract-related assets and liabilities and significant changes in those balances, remaining performance obligations and transaction price allocated to those obligations, and any significant judgments and changes in judgments related to revenue recognition. Significant judgments are those used in determining timing and amounts of revenue to be recognized.

The converged standard is expected to affect some industries more than others. For example, industries where bundled sales are common, such as the telecommunications and software industries, are expected to be significantly affected by the converged standard.

4. EXPENSE RECOGNITION

Expenses are deducted against revenue to arrive at a company's net profit or loss. Under the IASB *Conceptual Framework*, **expenses** are "decreases in economic benefits during the

---

[11] Interim period disclosures are required under IFRS and US GAAP but differ between them.

accounting period in the form of outflows or depletions of assets or incurrences of liabilities that result in decreases in equity, other than those relating to distributions to equity participants."[12]

The IASB *Conceptual Framework* also states:

> The definition of expenses encompasses losses as well as those expenses that arise in the course of the ordinary activities of the enterprise. Expenses that arise in the course of the ordinary activities of the enterprise include, for example, cost of sales, wages and depreciation. They usually take the form of an outflow or depletion of assets such as cash and cash equivalents, inventory, property, plant and equipment.
>
> Losses represent other items that meet the definition of expenses and may, or may not, arise in the course of the ordinary activities of the enterprise. Losses represent decreases in economic benefits and as such they are no different in nature from other expenses. Hence, they are not regarded as a separate element in this *Conceptual Framework*.
>
> Losses include, for example, those resulting from disasters such as fire and flood, as well as those arising on the disposal of non-current assets.[13]

Similar to the issues with revenue recognition, in a simple hypothetical scenario, expense recognition would not be an issue. For instance, assume a company purchased inventory for cash and sold the entire inventory in the same period. When the company paid for the inventory, absent indications to the contrary, it is clear that the inventory cost has been incurred and when that inventory is sold, it should be recognized as an expense (cost of goods sold) in the financial records. Assume also that the company paid all operating and administrative expenses in cash within each accounting period. In such a simple hypothetical scenario, no issues of expense recognition would arise. In practice, however, as with revenue recognition, determining when expenses should be recognized can be somewhat more complex.

4.1. General Principles

In general, a company recognizes expenses in the period that it consumes (i.e., uses up) the economic benefits associated with the expenditure, or loses some previously recognized economic benefit.[14]

A general principle of expense recognition is the **matching principle.** Strictly speaking, IFRS do not refer to a "matching principle" but rather to a "matching concept" or to a process resulting in "matching of costs with revenues."[15] The distinction is relevant in certain standard setting deliberations. Under matching, a company recognizes some expenses (e.g., cost of goods sold) when associated revenues are recognized and thus, expenses and revenues are matched. Associated revenues and expenses are those that result directly and jointly from the same transactions or events. Unlike the simple scenario in which a company purchases inventory and sells all of the inventory within the same accounting period, in practice, it is more

---

[12] IASB *Conceptual Framework*, paragraph 4.25(b).
[13] Ibid., paragraphs 4.33–4.35.
[14] Ibid., paragraph 4.49.
[15] Ibid., paragraph 4.50.

likely that some of the current period's sales are made from inventory purchased in a previous period or previous periods. It is also likely that some of the inventory purchased in the current period will remain unsold at the end of the current period and so will be sold in a following period. Matching requires that a company recognizes cost of goods sold in the same period as revenues from the sale of the goods.

Period costs, expenditures that less directly match revenues, are reflected in the period when a company makes the expenditure or incurs the liability to pay. Administrative expenses are an example of period costs. Other expenditures that also less directly match revenues relate more directly to future expected benefits; in this case, the expenditures are allocated systematically with the passage of time. An example is depreciation expense.

Examples 1 and 2 demonstrate matching applied to inventory and cost of goods sold.

EXAMPLE 1   The Matching of Inventory Costs with Revenues

Kahn Distribution Limited (KDL), a hypothetical company, purchases inventory items for resale. At the beginning of 2018, Kahn had no inventory on hand. During 2018, KDL had the following transactions:

Inventory Purchases		
First quarter	2,000	units at $40 per unit
Second quarter	1,500	units at $41 per unit
Third quarter	2,200	units at $43 per unit
Fourth quarter	1,900	units at $45 per unit
Total	7,600	units at a total cost of $321,600

KDL sold 5,600 units of inventory during the year at $50 per unit, and received cash. KDL determines that there were 2,000 remaining units of inventory and specifically identifies that 1,900 were those purchased in the fourth quarter and 100 were purchased in the third quarter. What are the revenue and expense associated with these transactions during 2018 based on specific identification of inventory items as sold or remaining in inventory? (Assume that the company does not expect any products to be returned.)

Solution: The revenue for 2018 would be $280,000 (5,600 units × $50 per unit). Initially, the total cost of the goods purchased would be recorded as inventory (an asset) in the amount of $321,600. During 2018, the cost of the 5,600 units sold would be expensed (matched against the revenue) while the cost of the 2,000 remaining unsold units would remain in inventory as follows:

Cost of Goods Sold		
From the first quarter	2,000 units at $40 per unit =	$80,000
From the second quarter	1,500 units at $41 per unit =	$61,500
From the third quarter	2,100 units at $43 per unit =	$90,300
Total cost of goods sold		$231,800

Cost of Goods Remaining in Inventory

From the third quarter	100 units at $43 per unit =	$4,300
From the fourth quarter	1,900 units at $45 per unit =	$85,500
Total remaining (or ending) inventory cost		$89,800

To confirm that total costs are accounted for: $231,800 + $89,800 = $321,600. The cost of the goods sold would be expensed against the revenue of $280,000 as follows:

Revenue	$280,000
Cost of goods sold	231,800
Gross profit	$48,200

An alternative way to think about this is that the company created an asset (inventory) of $321,600 as it made its purchases. At the end of the period, the value of the company's inventory on hand is $89,800. Therefore, the amount of the Cost of goods sold expense recognized for the period should be the difference: $231,800.

The remaining inventory amount of $89,800 will be matched against revenue in a future year when the inventory items are sold.

EXAMPLE 2   Alternative Inventory Costing Methods

In Example 1, KDL was able to specifically identify which inventory items were sold and which remained in inventory to be carried over to later periods. This is called the **specific identification method** and inventory and cost of goods sold are based on their physical flow. It is generally not feasible to specifically identify which items were sold and which remain on hand, so accounting standards permit the assignment of inventory costs to costs of goods sold and to ending inventory using cost formulas (IFRS terminology) or cost flow assumptions (US GAAP). The cost formula or cost flow assumption determines which goods are assumed to be sold and which goods are assumed to remain in inventory. Both IFRS and US GAAP permit the use of the first in, first out (FIFO) method, and the weighted average cost method to assign costs.

Under the **FIFO method**, the oldest goods purchased (or manufactured) are assumed to be sold first and the newest goods purchased (or manufactured) are assumed to remain in inventory. Cost of goods in beginning inventory and costs of the first items purchased (or manufactured) flow into cost of goods sold first, as if the earliest items purchased sold first. Ending inventory would, therefore, include the most recent purchases. It turns out that those items specifically identified as sold in Example 1 were also the first items purchased, so in this example, under FIFO, the cost of goods sold would also be $231,800, calculated as above.

The **weighted average cost method** assigns the average cost of goods available for sale to the units sold and remaining in inventory. The assignment is based on the average cost per unit (total cost of goods available for sale/total units available for sale) and the number of units sold and the number remaining in inventory.

For KDL, the weighted average cost per unit would be

$321,600/7,600 units = $42.3158 per unit

Cost of goods sold using the weighted average cost method would be

5,600 units at $42.3158 = $236,968

Ending inventory using the weighted average cost method would be

2,000 units at $42.3158 = $84,632

Another method is permitted under US GAAP but is not permitted under IFRS. This is the last in, first out (LIFO) method. Under the **LIFO method**, the newest goods purchased (or manufactured) are assumed to be sold first and the oldest goods purchased (or manufactured) are assumed to remain in inventory. Costs of the latest items purchased flow into cost of goods sold first, as if the most recent items purchased were sold first. Although this may seem contrary to common sense, it is logical in certain circumstances. For example, lumber in a lumberyard may be stacked up with the oldest lumber on the bottom. As lumber is sold, it is sold from the top of the stack, so the last lumber purchased and put in inventory is the first lumber out. Theoretically, a company should choose a method linked to the physical inventory flows.[16] Under the LIFO method, in the KDL example, it would be assumed that the 2,000 units remaining in ending inventory would have come from the first quarter's purchases:[17]

Ending inventory 2,000 units at $40 per unit = $80,000

The remaining costs would be allocated to cost of goods sold under LIFO:

Total costs of $321,600 less $80,000 remaining in ending inventory = $241,600

Alternatively, the cost of the last 5,600 units purchased is allocated to cost of goods sold under LIFO:

1,900 units at $45 per unit + 2,200 units at $43 per unit + 1,500 units at $41 per unit = $241,600

An alternative way to think about expense recognition is that the company created an asset (inventory) of $321,600 as it made its purchases. At the end of the period, the value of the company's inventory is $80,000. Therefore, the amount of the Cost of goods sold expense recognized for the period should be the difference: $241,600.

---

[16] Practically, the reason some companies choose to use LIFO in the United States is to reduce taxes. When prices and inventory quantities are rising, LIFO will normally result in higher cost of goods sold and lower income and hence lower taxes. US tax regulations require that if LIFO is used on a company's tax return, it must also be used on the company's GAAP financial statements.

[17] If data on the precise timing of quarterly sales were available, the answer would differ because the cost of goods sold would be determined during the quarter rather than at the end of the quarter.

Exhibit 6 summarizes and compares inventory costing methods.

EXHIBIT 6   Summary Table on Inventory Costing Methods

Method	Description	Cost of Goods Sold When Prices Are Rising, Relative to Other Two Methods	Ending Inventory When Prices Are Rising, Relative to Other Two Methods
FIFO (first in, first out)	Costs of the earliest items purchased flow to cost of goods sold first	Lowest	Highest
LIFO (last in, first out)	Costs of the most recent items purchased flow to cost of goods sold first	Highest*	Lowest*
Weighted average cost	Averages total costs over total units available	Middle	Middle

*Assumes no LIFO layer liquidation. **LIFO layer liquidation** occurs when the volume of sales exceeds the volume of purchases in the period so that some sales are assumed to be made from existing, relatively low-priced inventory rather than from more recent purchases.

4.2. Issues in Expense Recognition

The following sections cover applications of the principles of expense recognition to certain common situations.

4.2.1. Doubtful Accounts

When a company sells its products or services on credit, it is likely that some customers will ultimately default on their obligations (i.e., fail to pay). At the time of the sale, it is not known which customer will default. (If it were known that a particular customer would ultimately default, presumably a company would not sell on credit to that customer.) One possible approach to recognizing credit losses on customer receivables would be for the company to wait until such time as a customer defaulted and only then recognize the loss (**direct write-off method**). Such an approach would usually not be consistent with generally accepted accounting principles.

Under the matching principle, at the time revenue is recognized on a sale, a company is required to record an estimate of how much of the revenue will ultimately be uncollectible. Companies make such estimates based on previous experience with uncollectible accounts. Such estimates may be expressed as a proportion of the overall amount of sales, the overall amount of receivables, or the amount of receivables overdue by a specific amount of time. The company records its estimate of uncollectible amounts as an expense on the income statement, not as a direct reduction of revenues.

4.2.2. Warranties

At times, companies offer warranties on the products they sell. If the product proves deficient in some respect that is covered under the terms of the warranty, the company will incur an expense to repair or replace the product. At the time of sale, the company does not know the amount of future expenses it will incur in connection with its warranties. One possible approach would be for a company to wait until actual expenses are incurred under the warranty and to reflect the expense at that time. However, this would not result in a matching of the expense with the associated revenue.

Under the matching principle, a company is required to estimate the amount of future expenses resulting from its warranties, to recognize an estimated warranty expense in the period of the sale, and to update the expense as indicated by experience over the life of the warranty.

4.2.3. Depreciation and Amortisation

Companies commonly incur costs to obtain long-lived assets. **Long-lived assets** are assets expected to provide economic benefits over a future period of time greater than one year. Examples are land (property), plant, equipment, and **intangible assets** (assets lacking physical substance) such as trademarks. The costs of most long-lived assets are allocated over the period of time during which they provide economic benefits. The two main types of long-lived assets whose costs are *not* allocated over time are land and those intangible assets with indefinite useful lives.

Depreciation is the process of systematically allocating costs of long-lived assets over the period during which the assets are expected to provide economic benefits. "Depreciation" is the term commonly applied to this process for physical long-lived assets such as plant and equipment (land is not depreciated), and **amortisation** is the term commonly applied to this process for intangible long-lived assets with a finite useful life.[18] Examples of intangible long-lived assets with a finite useful life include an acquired mailing list, an acquired patent with a set expiration date, and an acquired copyright with a set legal life. The term "amortisation" is also commonly applied to the systematic allocation of a premium or discount relative to the face value of a fixed-income security over the life of the security.

IFRS allow two alternative models for valuing property, plant, and equipment: the cost model and the revaluation model.[19] Under the cost model, the depreciable amount of that asset (cost less residual value) is allocated on a systematic basis over the remaining useful life of the asset. Under the cost model, the asset is reported at its cost less any accumulated depreciation. Under the revaluation model, the asset is reported at its fair value. The revaluation model is not permitted under US GAAP. Although the revaluation model is permitted under IFRS, as noted earlier, it is not as widely used and thus we focus on the cost model here. There are two other differences between IFRS and US GAAP to note: IFRS require each component of an asset to be depreciated separately and US GAAP do not require component depreciation; and IFRS require an annual review of residual value and useful life, and US GAAP do not explicitly require such a review.

The method used to compute depreciation should reflect the pattern over which the economic benefits of the asset are expected to be consumed. IFRS do not prescribe a particular method for computing depreciation but note that several methods are commonly used, such as the straight-line method, diminishing balance method (accelerated depreciation), and the units of production method (depreciation varies depending upon production or usage).

---

[18] Intangible assets with indefinite life are not amortised. Instead, they are reviewed each period as to the reasonableness of continuing to assume an indefinite useful life and are tested at least annually for impairment (i.e., if the recoverable or fair value of an intangible asset is materially lower than its value in the company's books, the value of the asset is considered to be impaired and its value must be decreased). IAS 38, *Intangible Assets* and FASB ASC Topic 350 [Intangibles–Goodwill and Other].

[19] IAS No. 16, *Property, Plant, and Equipment.*

The **straight-line method** allocates evenly the cost of long-lived assets less estimated residual value over the estimated useful life of an asset. (The term "straight line" derives from the fact that the annual depreciation expense, if represented as a line graph over time, would be a straight line. In addition, a plot of the cost of the asset minus the cumulative amount of annual depreciation expense, if represented as a line graph over time, would be a straight line with a negative downward slope.) Calculating depreciation and amortisation requires two significant estimates: the estimated useful life of an asset and the estimated residual value (also known as "salvage value") of an asset. Under IFRS, the residual value is the amount that the company expects to receive upon sale of the asset at the end of its useful life. Example 3 assumes that an item of equipment is depreciated using the straight-line method and illustrates how the annual depreciation expense varies under different estimates of the useful life and estimated residual value of an asset. As shown, annual depreciation expense is sensitive to both the estimated useful life and to the estimated residual value.

EXAMPLE 3   Sensitivity of Annual Depreciation Expense to Varying Estimates of Useful Life and Residual Value

Using the straight-line method of depreciation, annual depreciation expense is calculated as:

$$\frac{\text{Cost} - \text{Residual value}}{\text{Estimated useful life}}$$

Assume the cost of an asset is $10,000. If, for example, the residual value of the asset is estimated to be $0 and its useful life is estimated to be 5 years, the annual depreciation expense under the straight-line method would be ($10,000 − $0)/5 years = $2,000. In contrast, holding the estimated useful life of the asset constant at 5 years but increasing the estimated residual value of the asset to $4,000 would result in annual depreciation expense of only $1,200 [calculated as ($10,000 − $4,000)/5 years]. Alternatively, holding the estimated residual value at $0 but increasing the estimated useful life of the asset to 10 years would result in annual depreciation expense of only $1,000 [calculated as ($10,000 − $0)/10 years]. Exhibit 7 shows annual depreciation expense for various combinations of estimated useful life and residual value.

EXHIBIT 7   Annual Depreciation Expense (in Dollars)

Estimated Useful Life (Years)	Estimated Residual Value					
	0	1,000	2,000	3,000	4,000	5,000
2	5,000	4,500	4,000	3,500	3,000	2,500
4	2,500	2,250	2,000	1,750	1,500	1,250
5	2,000	1,800	1,600	1,400	1,200	1,000
8	1,250	1,125	1,000	875	750	625
10	1,000	900	800	700	600	500

Generally, alternatives to the straight-line method of depreciation are called **accelerated methods** of depreciation because they accelerate (i.e., speed up) the timing of depreciation. Accelerated depreciation methods allocate a greater proportion of the cost to the early years of an asset's useful life. These methods are appropriate if the plant or equipment is expected to be used up faster in the early years (e.g., an automobile). A commonly used accelerated method is the **diminishing balance method**, (also known as the declining balance method). The diminishing balance method is demonstrated in Example 4.

EXAMPLE 4   An Illustration of Diminishing Balance Depreciation

Assume the cost of computer equipment was $11,000, the estimated residual value is $1,000, and the estimated useful life is five years. Under the diminishing or declining balance method, the first step is to determine the straight-line rate, the rate at which the asset would be depreciated under the straight-line method. This rate is measured as 100 percent divided by the useful life or 20 percent for a five-year useful life. Under the straight-line method, 1/5 or 20 percent of the depreciable cost of the asset (here, $11,000 − $1,000 = $10,000) would be expensed each year for five years: The depreciation expense would be $2,000 per year.

The next step is to determine an acceleration factor that approximates the pattern of the asset's wear. Common acceleration factors are 150 percent and 200 percent. The latter is known as **double declining balance depreciation** because it depreciates the asset at double the straight-line rate. Using the 200 percent acceleration factor, the diminishing balance rate would be 40 percent (20 percent × 2.0). This rate is then applied to the remaining undepreciated balance of the asset each period (known as the **net book value**).

At the beginning of the first year, the net book value is $11,000. Depreciation expense for the first full year of use of the asset would be 40 percent of $11,000, or $4,400. Under this method, the residual value, if any, is generally not used in the computation of the depreciation each period (the 40 percent is applied to $11,000 rather than to $11,000 minus residual value). However, the company will stop taking depreciation when the salvage value is reached.

At the beginning of Year 2, the net book value is measured as

Asset cost	$11,000
Less: Accumulated depreciation	(4,400)
Net book value	$6,600

For the second full year, depreciation expense would be $6,600 × 40 percent, or $2,640. At the end of the second year (i.e., beginning of the third year), a total of $7,040 ($4,400 + $2,640) of depreciation would have been recorded. So, the remaining net book value at the beginning of the third year would be

Asset cost	$11,000
Less: Accumulated depreciation	(7,040)
Net book value	$3,960

For the third full year, depreciation would be $3,960 × 40 percent, or $1,584. At the end of the third year, a total of $8,624 ($4,400 + $2,640 + $1,584) of depreciation would have been recorded. So, the remaining net book value at the beginning of the fourth year would be

Asset cost	$11,000
Less: Accumulated depreciation	(8,624)
Net book value	$2,376

For the fourth full year, depreciation would be $2,376 × 40 percent, or $950. At the end of the fourth year, a total of $9,574 ($4,400 + $2,640 + $1,584 + $950) of depreciation would have been recorded. So, the remaining net book value at the beginning of the fifth year would be

Asset cost	$11,000
Less: Accumulated depreciation	(9,574)
Net book value	$1,426

For the fifth year, if deprecation were determined as in previous years, it would amount to $570 ($1,426 × 40 percent). However, this would result in a remaining net book value of the asset below its estimated residual value of $1,000. So, instead, only $426 would be depreciated, leaving a $1,000 net book value at the end of the fifth year.

Asset cost	$11,000
Less: Accumulated depreciation	(10,000)
Net book value	$1,000

Companies often use a zero or small residual value, which creates problems for diminishing balance depreciation because the asset never fully depreciates. In order to fully depreciate the asset over the initially estimated useful life when a zero or small residual value is assumed, companies often adopt a depreciation policy that combines the diminishing balance and straight-line methods. An example would be a deprecation policy of using double-declining balance depreciation and switching to the straight-line method halfway through the useful life.

Under accelerated depreciation methods, there is a higher depreciation expense in early years relative to the straight-line method. This results in higher expenses and lower net income in the early depreciation years. In later years, there is a reversal with accelerated depreciation expense lower than straight-line depreciation. Accelerated depreciation is sometimes referred to as a conservative accounting choice because it results in lower net income in the early years of asset use.

For those intangible assets that must be amortised (those with an identifiable useful life), the process is the same as for depreciation; only the name of the expense is different. IFRS state that if a pattern cannot be determined over the useful life, then the straight-line method should be used.[20] In most cases under IFRS and US GAAP, amortisable intangible assets are amortized

---

[20] IAS 38, *Intangible Assets.*

using the straight-line method with no residual value. **Goodwill**[21] and intangible assets with indefinite life are not amortised. Instead, they are tested at least annually for impairment (i.e., if the current value of an intangible asset or goodwill is materially lower than its value in the company's books, the value of the asset is considered to be impaired, and its value in the company's books must be decreased).

In summary, to calculate depreciation and amortization, a company must choose a method, estimate the asset's useful life, and estimate residual value. Clearly, different choices have a differing effect on depreciation or amortization expense and, therefore, on reported net income.

4.3. Implications for Financial Analysis

A company's estimates for doubtful accounts and/or for warranty expenses can affect its reported net income. Similarly, a company's choice of depreciation or amortization method, estimates of assets' useful lives, and estimates of assets' residual values can affect reported net income. These are only a few of the choices and estimates that affect a company's reported net income.

As with revenue recognition policies, a company's choice of expense recognition can be characterized by its relative conservatism. A policy that results in recognition of expenses later rather than sooner is considered less conservative. In addition, many items of expense require the company to make estimates that can significantly affect net income. Analysis of a company's financial statements, and particularly comparison of one company's financial statements with those of another, requires an understanding of differences in these estimates and their potential impact.

If, for example, a company shows a significant year-to-year change in its estimates of uncollectible accounts as a percentage of sales, warranty expenses as a percentage of sales, or estimated useful lives of assets, the analyst should seek to understand the underlying reasons. Do the changes reflect a change in business operations (e.g., lower estimated warranty expenses reflecting recent experience of fewer warranty claims because of improved product quality)? Or are the changes seemingly unrelated to changes in business operations and thus possibly a signal that a company is manipulating estimates in order to achieve a particular effect on its reported net income?

As another example, if two companies in the same industry have dramatically different estimates for uncollectible accounts as a percentage of their sales, warranty expenses as a percentage of sales, or estimated useful lives as a percentage of assets, it is important to understand the underlying reasons. Are the differences consistent with differences in the two companies' business operations (e.g., lower uncollectible accounts for one company reflecting a different, more creditworthy customer base or possibly stricter credit policies)? Another difference consistent with differences in business operations would be a difference in estimated useful lives of assets if one of the companies employs newer equipment. Or, alternatively, are the differences seemingly inconsistent with differences in the two companies' business operations, possibly signaling that a company is manipulating estimates?

Information about a company's accounting policies and significant estimates are described in the notes to the financial statements and in the management discussion and analysis section of a company's annual report.

---

[21]Goodwill is recorded in acquisitions and is the amount by which the price to purchase an entity exceeds the amount of net identifiable assets acquired (the total amount of identifiable assets acquired less liabilities assumed).

When possible, the monetary effect of differences in expense recognition policies and estimates can facilitate more meaningful comparisons with a single company's historical performance or across a number of companies. An analyst can use the monetary effect to adjust the reported expenses so that they are on a comparable basis.

Even when the monetary effects of differences in policies and estimates cannot be calculated, it is generally possible to characterize the relative conservatism of the policies and estimates and, therefore, to qualitatively assess how such differences might affect reported expenses and thus financial ratios.

5. NON-RECURRING ITEMS AND NON-OPERATING ITEMS

From a company's income statements, we can see its earnings from last year and in the previous year. Looking forward, the question is: What will the company earn next year and in the years after?

To assess a company's future earnings, it is helpful to separate those prior years' items of income and expense that are likely to continue in the future from those items that are less likely to continue.[22] Some items from prior years are clearly not expected to continue in the future periods and are separately disclosed on a company's income statement. This is consistent with "An entity shall present additional line items, headings, and subtotals . . . when such presentation is relevant to an understanding of the entity's financial performance."[23] IFRS describe considerations that enter into the decision to present information other than that explicitly specified by a standard. Both IFRS and US GAAP specify that the results of discontinued operations should be reported separately from continuing operations. Other items that may be reported separately on a company's income statement, such as unusual items, items that occur infrequently, effects due to accounting changes, and non-operating income, require the analyst to make some judgments.

5.1. Discontinued Operations

When a company disposes of, or establishes a plan to dispose of, one of its component operations and will have no further involvement in the operation, the income statement reports separately the effect of this disposal as a "discontinued" operation under both IFRS and US GAAP. Financial standards provide various criteria for reporting the effect separately, which are generally that the discontinued component must be separable both physically and operationally.[24]

In Exhibit 1, AB InBev reported profit from discontinued operations of $28 million in 2017 and $48 million in 2016. In Exhibit 2, Molson Coors reported income from discontinued operations of $1.5 million and $3.9 million in 2017 and 2015, respectively, and a loss from discontinued operations of $2.8 million in 2016.

---

[22] In business writing, items expected to continue in the future are often described as "persistent" or "permanent," whereas those not expected to continue are described as "transitory."

[23] IAS No. 1, *Presentation of Financial Statements*, paragraph 85.

[24] IFRS No. 5, *Non-Current Assets Held for Sale and Discontinued Operations*, paragraphs 31–33.

Because the discontinued operation will no longer provide earnings (or cash flow) to the company, an analyst may eliminate discontinued operations in formulating expectations about a company's future financial performance.

5.2. Unusual or Infrequent Items

IFRS require that items of income or expense that are material and/or relevant to the understanding of the entity's financial performance should be disclosed separately. Unusual or infrequent items are likely to meet these criteria. Under US GAAP, material items that are unusual or infrequent, and that are both as of reporting periods beginning after December 15, 2015, are shown as part of a company's continuing operations but are presented separately. For example, restructuring charges, such as costs to close plants and employee termination costs, are considered part of a company's ordinary activities. As another example, gains and losses arising when a company sells an asset or part of a business, for more or less than its carrying value, are also disclosed separately on the income statement. These sales are considered ordinary business activities.

Highlighting the unusual or infrequent nature of these items assists an analyst in judging the likelihood that such items will reoccur. This meets the IFRS criteria of disclosing items that are relevant to the understanding of an entity's financial performance. In Exhibit 2, Molson Coors' income statement showed a separate line item for "Special Items, net." The company's footnotes provide details on the amount and explain that this line includes revenues or expenses that either they "do not believe to be indicative of [their] core operations, or they believe are significant to [their] current operating results warranting separate classification." In Exhibit 3, the income statement of Danone shows an amount for "Recurring operating income" followed by a separate line item for "other operating income (expense)," which is not included as a component of recurring income. Exhibit 8 presents an excerpt from Danone's additional disclosure about this non-recurring amount.

EXHIBIT 8   Highlighting Infrequent Nature of Items—Excerpt from Groupe Danone footnotes to its 2017 financial statements

---

NOTE 6. Events and Transactions Outside the Group's Ordinary Activities [Excerpt]

"Other operating income (expense) is defined under Recommendation 2013-03 of the French CNC relating to the format of consolidated financial statements prepared under international accounting standards, and comprises significant items that, because of their exceptional nature, cannot be viewed as inherent to Danone's current activities. These mainly include capital gains and losses on disposals of fully consolidated companies, impairment charges on goodwill, significant costs related to strategic restructuring and major external growth transactions, and incurred or estimated costs related to major crises and major litigation. Furthermore, in connection with Revised IFRS 3 and Revised IAS 27, Danone also classifies in Other operating income (expense) (i) acquisition costs related to business combinations, (ii) revaluation profit or loss accounted for following a loss of control, and (iii) changes in earn-outs related to business combinations and subsequent to the acquisition date.

"In 2017, the net Other operating income of €192 million consisted mainly of the following items:

(continued)

EXHIBIT 8   (Continued)

(in € millions)	Related income (expense)
Capital gain on disposal of Stonyfield	628
Compensation received following the decision of the Singapore arbitration court in the Fonterra case	105
Territorial risks, mainly in certain countries in the ALMA region	(148)
Costs associated with the integration of WhiteWave	(118)
Impairment of several intangible assets in Waters and Specialized Nutrition Reporting entities	(115)
Remainder of table omitted	

In Exhibit 8, Danone provides details on items considered to be "exceptional" items and not "inherent" to the company's current activities. The exceptional items include gains on asset disposals, receipts from a legal case, costs of integrating an acquisition, and impairment of intangible assets, among others. Generally, in forecasting future operations, an analyst would assess whether the items reported are likely to reoccur and also possible implications for future earnings. It is generally not advisable simply to ignore all unusual items.

5.3. Changes in Accounting Policies

At times, standard setters issue new standards that require companies to change accounting policies. Depending on the standard, companies may be permitted to adopt the standards prospectively (in the future) or retrospectively (restate financial statements as though the standard existed in the past). In other cases, changes in accounting policies (e.g., from one acceptable inventory costing method to another) are made for other reasons, such as providing a better reflection of the company's performance. Changes in accounting policies are reported through retrospective application[25] unless it is impractical to do so.

Retrospective application means that the financial statements for all fiscal years shown in a company's financial report are presented as if the newly adopted accounting principle had been used throughout the entire period. Notes to the financial statements describe the change and explain the justification for the change. Because changes in accounting principles are retrospectively applied, the financial statements that appear within a financial report are comparable.

Example 5 presents an excerpt from Microsoft Corporation's Form 10-K for the fiscal year ended 30 June 2018 describing a change in accounting principle resulting from the new revenue recognition standard. Microsoft elected to adopt the new standard 1 July 2017, earlier than the required adoption date. Microsoft also elected to use the "full retrospective method," which requires companies to restate prior periods' results. On its income statement, both 2016 and 2017 are presented as if the new standard had been used throughout both years. In the footnotes to its financial statements, Microsoft discloses the impact of the new standard.

---

[25] IAS No. 8, *Accounting Policies, Changes in Accounting Estimates and Errors,* and FASB ASC Topic 250 [Accounting Changes and Error Corrections].

EXAMPLE 5   Microsoft Corporation Excerpt from Footnotes to the Financial Statements

The most significant impact of the [new revenue recognition] standard relates to our accounting for software license revenue. Specifically, for Windows 10, we recognize revenue predominantly at the time of billing and delivery rather than ratably over the life of the related device. For certain multi-year commercial software subscriptions that include both distinct software licenses and SA, we recognize license revenue at the time of contract execution rather than over the subscription period. Due to the complexity of certain of our commercial license subscription contracts, the actual revenue recognition treatment required under the standard depends on contract-specific terms and in some instances may vary from recognition at the time of billing. Revenue recognition related to our hardware, cloud offerings (such as Office 365), LinkedIn, and professional services remains substantially unchanged. Refer to Impacts to Previously Reported Results below for the impact of adoption of the standard in our consolidated financial statements.

(In $ millions, except per share amounts)	As Previously Reported	New Revenue Standard Adjustment	As Restated
Income Statements			
Year Ended June 30, 2017			
Revenue	89,950	6,621	96,571
Provision for income taxes	1,945	2,467	4,412
Net income	21,204	4,285	25,489
Diluted earnings per share	2.71	0.54	3.25
Year Ended June 30, 2016			
Revenue	85,320	5,834	91,154
Provision for income taxes	2,953	2,147	5,100
Net income	16,798	3,741	20,539
Diluted earnings per share	2.1	0.46	2.56

Question: Based on the above information, describe whether Microsoft's results appear better or worse under the new revenue recognition standard.

Solution: Microsoft's results appear better under the new revenue recognition standard. Revenues and income are higher under the new standard. The net profit margin is higher under the new standard. For 2017, the net profit margin is 26.4% (= 25,489/96,571) under the new standard versus 23.6% (= 21,204/89,950) under the old standard. Reported revenue grew faster under the new standard. Revenue growth under the new standard was 5.9% [= (96,571/91,154) − 1] compared to 5.4% [= (89,950/85,320) − 1)] under the old standard.

Microsoft's presentation of the effects of the new revenue recognition enables an analyst to identify the impact of the change in accounting standards.

Note that the new revenue recognition standard also offered companies the option of using a "modified retrospective" method of adoption. Under the modified retrospective approach, companies were not required to revise previously reported financial statements. Instead, they adjusted opening balances of retained earnings (and other applicable accounts) for the cumulative impact of the new standard.

In contrast to changes in accounting policies (such as whether to expense the cost of employee stock options), companies sometimes make *changes in accounting estimates* (such as the useful life of a depreciable asset). Changes in accounting estimates are handled prospectively, with the change affecting the financial statements for the period of change and future periods. No adjustments are made to prior statements, and the adjustment is not shown on the face of the income statement. Significant changes should be disclosed in the notes. Exhibit 9 provides an excerpt from the annual Form 10-K of Catalent Inc., a US-based biotechnology company, that illustrates a change in accounting estimate.

EXHIBIT 9   Change in Accounting Estimate

Catalent Inc. discloses a change in the method it uses to calculate both annual expenses related to its defined benefit pension plans. Rather than use a single, weighted-average discount rate in its calculations, the company will use the spot rates applicable to each projected cash flow.

Post-Retirement and Pension Plans

...The measurement of the related benefit obligations and the net periodic benefit costs recorded each year are based upon actuarial computations, which require management's judgment as to certain assumptions. These assumptions include the discount rates used in computing the present value of the benefit obligations and the net periodic benefit costs. . . .

Effective June 30, 2016, the approach used to estimate the service and interest components of net periodic benefit cost for benefit plans was changed to provide a more precise measurement of service and interest costs. Historically, the Company estimated these service and interest components utilizing a single weighted-average discount rate derived from the yield curve used to measure the benefit obligation at the beginning of the period. Going forward, the Company has elected to utilize an approach that discounts the individual expected cash flows using the applicable spot rates derived from the yield curve over the projected cash flow period. The Company has accounted for this change as a change in accounting estimate that is inseparable from a change in accounting principle and accordingly has accounted for it prospectively.

Another possible adjustment is a *correction of an error for a prior period* (e.g., in financial statements issued for an earlier year). This cannot be handled by simply adjusting the current period income statement. Correction of an error for a prior period is handled by restating the financial statements (including the balance sheet, statement of owners' equity, and cash flow statement) for the prior periods presented in the current financial statements.[26] Note disclosures are required regarding the error. These disclosures should be examined carefully because they may reveal weaknesses in the company's accounting systems and financial controls.

[26] Ibid.

5.4. Non-Operating Items

Non-operating items are typically reported separately from operating income because they are material and/or relevant to the understanding of the entity's financial performance. Under IFRS, there is no definition of operating activities, and companies that choose to report operating income or the results of operating activities should ensure that these represent activities that are normally regarded as operating. Under US GAAP, operating activities generally involve producing and delivering goods, and providing services, and include all transactions and other events that are not defined as investing or financing activities.[27] For example, if a non-financial service company invests in equity or debt securities issued by another company, any interest, dividends, or profits from sales of these securities will be shown as non-operating income. In general, for non-financial services companies,[28] non-operating income that is disclosed separately on the income statement (or in the notes) includes amounts earned through investing activities.

Among non-operating items on the income statement (or accompanying notes), non-financial service companies also disclose the interest expense on their debt securities, including amortization of any discount or premium. The amount of interest expense is related to the amount of a company's borrowings and is generally described in the notes to the financial statements. For financial service companies, interest income and expense are likely components of operating activities. (Note that the characterization of interest and dividends as non-operating items on the income statement is not necessarily consistent with the classification on the statement of cash flows. Specifically, under IFRS, interest and dividends received can be shown either as operating or as investing on the statement of cash flows, while under US GAAP interest and dividends received are shown as operating cash flows. Under IFRS, interest and dividends paid can be shown either as operating or as financing on the statement of cash flows, while under US GAAP, interest paid is shown as operating and dividends paid are shown as financing.)

In practice, companies often disclose the interest expense and income separately, along with a net amount. For example, in Exhibit 1, ABN InBev's 2017 income statement shows finance cost of $6,885 million, finance income of $378 million, and net finance cost of $6,507 million. Similarly, in Exhibit 3, Danone's 2017 income statement shows interest income of €130, interest expense of €276, and cost of net debt of €146.

For purposes of assessing a company's future performance, the amount of financing expense will depend on the company's financing policy (target capital structure) and borrowing costs. The amount of investing income will depend on the purpose and success of investing activities. For a non-financial company, a significant amount of financial income would typically warrant further exploration. What are the reasons underlying the company's investments in the securities of other companies? Is the company simply investing excess cash in short-term securities to generate income higher than cash deposits, or is the company purchasing securities issued by other companies for strategic reasons, such as access to raw material supply or research?

---

[27] FASB ASC *Master Glossary.*

[28] Examples of financial services companies are insurance companies, banks, brokers, dealers, and investment companies.

6. EARNINGS PER SHARE

One metric of particular importance to an equity investor is earnings per share (EPS). EPS is an input into ratios such as the price/earnings ratio. Additionally, each shareholder in a company owns a different number of shares. IFRS require the presentation of EPS on the face of the income statement for net profit or loss (net income) and profit or loss (income) from continuing operations.[29] Similar presentation is required under US GAAP.[30] This section outlines the calculations for EPS and explains how the calculation differs for a simple versus complex capital structure.

6.1. Simple versus Complex Capital Structure

A company's capital is composed of its equity and debt. Some types of equity have preference over others, and some debt (and other instruments) may be converted into equity. Under IFRS, the type of equity for which EPS is presented is referred to as ordinary. **Ordinary shares** are those equity shares that are subordinate to all other types of equity. The ordinary shareholders are basically the owners of the company—the equity holders who are paid last in a liquidation of the company and who benefit the most when the company does well. Under US GAAP, this ordinary equity is referred to as **common stock** or **common shares**, reflecting US language usage. The terms "ordinary shares," "common stock," and "common shares" are used interchangeably in the following discussion.

When a company has issued any financial instruments that are potentially convertible into common stock, it is said to have a complex capital structure. Examples of financial instruments that are potentially convertible into common stock include convertible bonds, convertible preferred stock, employee stock options, and warrants.[31] If a company's capital structure does not include such potentially convertible financial instruments, it is said to have a simple capital structure.

The distinction between simple versus complex capital structure is relevant to the calculation of EPS because financial instruments that are potentially convertible into common stock could, as a result of conversion or exercise, potentially dilute (i.e., decrease) EPS. Information about such a potential dilution is valuable to a company's current and potential shareholders; therefore, accounting standards require companies to disclose what their EPS would be if all dilutive financial instruments were converted into common stock. The EPS that would result if all dilutive financial instruments were converted is called **diluted EPS**. In contrast, **basic EPS** is calculated using the reported earnings available to common shareholders of the parent company and the weighted average number of shares outstanding.

Companies are required to report both basic and diluted EPS as well as amounts for continuing operations. Exhibit 10 shows the per share amounts reported by AB InBev at the bottom of its income statement that was presented in Exhibit 1. The company's basic EPS ("before dilution") was $4.06, and diluted EPS ("after dilution") was $3.98 for 2017. In addition, in the

---

[29] IAS No. 33, *Earnings Per Share*.
[30] FASB ASC Topic 260 [Earnings Per Share].
[31] A warrant is a call option typically attached to securities issued by a company, such as bonds. A warrant gives the holder the right to acquire the company's stock from the company at a specified price within a specified time period. IFRS and US GAAP standards regarding earnings per share apply equally to call options, warrants, and equivalent instruments.

same way that AB InBev's income statement shows income from continuing operations separately from total income, EPS from continuing operations is also shown separately from total EPS. For 2017, the basic and diluted EPS from continuing operations were $4.04 and $3.96, respectively. Across all measures, AB InBev's EPS was much higher in 2017 than in 2016. An analyst would seek to understand the causes underlying the changes in EPS, a topic we will address following an explanation of the calculations of both basic and diluted EPS.

EXHIBIT 10   AB InBev's Earnings Per Share

	12 Months Ended December 31		
	2017	2016	2015
Basic earnings per share	$4.06	$0.72	$5.05
Diluted earnings per share	3.98	0.71	4.96
Basic earnings per share from continuing operations	4.04	0.69	5.05
Diluted earnings per share from continuing operations	$3.96	$0.68	$4.96

6.2. Basic EPS

Basic EPS is the amount of income available to common shareholders divided by the weighted average number of common shares outstanding over a period. The amount of income available to common shareholders is the amount of net income remaining after preferred dividends (if any) have been paid. Thus, the formula to calculate basic EPS is:

$$\text{Basic EPS} = \frac{\text{Net income} - \text{Preferred dividends}}{\text{Weighted average number of shares outstanding}} \qquad (1)$$

The weighted average number of shares outstanding is a time weighting of common shares outstanding. For example, assume a company began the year with 2,000,000 common shares outstanding and repurchased 100,000 common shares on 1 July. The weighted average number of common shares outstanding would be the sum of 2,000,000 shares × 1/2 year + 1,900,000 shares × 1/2 year, or 1,950,000 shares. So the company would use 1,950,000 shares as the weighted average number of shares in calculating its basic EPS.

If the number of shares of common stock increases as a result of a stock dividend or a stock split, the EPS calculation reflects the change retroactively to the beginning of the period.

Examples 6, 7, and 8 illustrate the computation of basic EPS.

EXAMPLE 6   A Basic EPS Calculation (1)

For the year ended 31 December 2018, Shopalot Company had net income of $1,950,000. The company had 1,500,000 shares of common stock outstanding, no preferred stock, and no convertible financial instruments. What is Shopalot's basic EPS?

Solution: Shopalot's basic EPS is $1.30 ($1,950,000 divided by 1,500,000 shares).

EXAMPLE 7   A Basic EPS Calculation (2)

For the year ended December 31, 2018, Angler Products had net income of $2,500,000. The company declared and paid $200,000 of dividends on preferred stock. The company also had the following common stock share information:

Shares outstanding on January 1, 2018	1,000,000
Shares issued on April 1, 2018	200,000
Shares repurchased (treasury shares) on October 1, 2018	(100,000)
Shares outstanding on December 31, 2018	1,100,000

1. What is the company's weighted average number of shares outstanding?
2. What is the company's basic EPS?

Solution to 1: The weighted average number of shares outstanding is determined by the length of time each quantity of shares was outstanding:

$1,000,000 \times$ (3 months/12 months) =	250,000
$1,200,000 \times$ (6 months/12 months) =	600,000
$1,100,000 \times$ (3 months/12 months) =	275,000
Weighted average number of shares outstanding	1,125,000

Solution to 2: Basic EPS = (Net income − Preferred dividends)/Weighted average number of shares = ($2,500,000 − $200,000)/1,125,000 = $2.04

EXAMPLE 8   A Basic EPS Calculation (3)

Assume the same facts as Example 7 except that on December 1, 2018, a previously declared 2-for-1 stock split took effect. Each shareholder of record receives two shares in exchange for each current share that he or she owns. What is the company's basic EPS?

Solution: For EPS calculation purposes, a stock split is treated as if it occurred at the beginning of the period. The weighted average number of shares would, therefore, be 2,250,000, and the basic EPS would be $1.02 [= ($2,500,000 − $200,000)/2,250,000].

6.3. Diluted EPS

If a company has a simple capital structure (in other words, one that includes no potentially dilutive financial instruments), then its basic EPS is equal to its diluted EPS. However, if a company has potentially dilutive financial instruments, its diluted EPS may differ from its basic EPS. Diluted EPS, by definition, is always equal to or less than basic EPS. The sections below describe the effects of three types of potentially dilutive financial instruments on diluted EPS: convertible preferred, convertible debt, and employee stock options. The final section explains why not all potentially dilutive financial instruments actually result in a difference between basic and diluted EPS.

6.3.1. Diluted EPS When a Company Has Convertible Preferred Stock Outstanding

When a company has convertible preferred stock outstanding, diluted EPS is calculated using the **if-converted method**. The if-converted method is based on what EPS would have been if the convertible preferred securities had been converted at the beginning of the period. In other words, the method calculates what the effect would have been if the convertible preferred shares converted at the beginning of the period. If the convertible shares had been converted, there would be two effects. First, the convertible preferred securities would no longer be outstanding; instead, additional common stock would be outstanding. Thus, under the if-converted method, the weighted average number of shares outstanding would be higher than in the basic EPS calculation. Second, if such a conversion had taken place, the company would not have paid preferred dividends. Thus, under the if-converted method, the net income available to common shareholders would be higher than in the basic EPS calculation.

Diluted EPS using the if-converted method for convertible preferred stock is equal to net income divided by the weighted average number of shares outstanding from the basic EPS calculation plus the additional shares of common stock that would be issued upon conversion of the preferred. Thus, the formula to calculate diluted EPS using the if-converted method for preferred stock is:

$$\text{Diluted EPS} = \frac{(\text{Net income})}{\left(\begin{array}{c}\text{Weighted average number of shares} \\ \text{outstanding} + \text{New common shares that} \\ \text{would have been issued at conversion}\end{array}\right)} \quad (2)$$

A diluted EPS calculation using the if-converted method for preferred stock is provided in Example 9.

EXAMPLE 9   A Diluted EPS Calculation Using the If-Converted Method for Preferred Stock

For the year ended December 31, 2018, Bright-Warm Utility Company (fictitious) had net income of $1,750,000. The company had an average of 500,000 shares of common stock outstanding, 20,000 shares of convertible preferred, and no other potentially dilutive securities. Each share of preferred pays a dividend of $10 per share, and each is convertible into 5 shares of the company's common stock. Calculate the company's basic and diluted EPS.

Solution: If the 20,000 shares of convertible preferred had each converted into 5 shares of the company's common stock, the company would have had an additional 100,000 shares of common stock (5 shares of common for each of the 20,000 shares of preferred). If the conversion had taken place, the company would not have paid preferred dividends of $200,000 ($10 per share for each of the 20,000 shares of preferred). As shown in Exhibit 11, the company's basic EPS was $3.10, and its diluted EPS was $2.92.

EXHIBIT 11   Calculation of Diluted EPS for Bright-Warm Utility Company Using the If-Converted Method: Case of Preferred Stock

	Basic EPS	Diluted EPS Using If-Converted Method
Net income	$1,750,000	$1,750,000
Preferred dividend	−200,000	0
Numerator	$1,550,000	$1,750,000
Weighted average number of shares outstanding	500,000	500,000
Additional shares issued if preferred converted	0	100,000
Denominator	500,000	600,000
EPS	**$3.10**	**$2.92**

6.3.2. Diluted EPS When a Company Has Convertible Debt Outstanding

When a company has convertible debt outstanding, the diluted EPS calculation also uses the if-converted method. Diluted EPS is calculated as if the convertible debt had been converted at the beginning of the period. If the convertible debt had been converted, the debt securities would no longer be outstanding; instead, additional shares of common stock would be outstanding. Also, if such a conversion had taken place, the company would not have paid interest on the convertible debt, so the net income available to common shareholders would increase by the after-tax amount of interest expense on the debt converted.

Thus, the formula to calculate diluted EPS using the if-converted method for convertible debt is:

$$\text{Diluted EPS} = \frac{\begin{array}{c}(\text{Net income} + \text{After-tax interest on} \\ \text{Convertible debt} - \text{Preferred dividends})\end{array}}{\begin{array}{c}(\text{Weighted average number of shares} \\ \text{outstanding} + \text{Additional common} \\ \text{shares that would have been} \\ \text{issued at conversion})\end{array}} \tag{3}$$

A diluted EPS calculation using the if-converted method for convertible debt is provided in Example 10.

EXAMPLE 10   A Diluted EPS Calculation Using the If-Converted Method for Convertible Debt

Oppnox Company (fictitious) reported net income of $750,000 for the year ended December 31, 2018. The company had a weighted average of 690,000 shares of common stock outstanding. In addition, the company has only one potentially dilutive security:

$50,000 of 6 percent convertible bonds, convertible into a total of 10,000 shares. Assuming a tax rate of 30 percent, calculate Oppnox's basic and diluted EPS.

Solution: If the debt securities had been converted, the debt securities would no longer be outstanding, and instead an additional 10,000 shares of common stock would be outstanding. Also, if the debt securities had been converted, the company would not have paid interest of $3,000 on the convertible debt, so net income available to common shareholders would have increased by $2,100 [= $3,000(1 − 0.30)] on an after-tax basis. Exhibit 12 illustrates the calculation of diluted EPS using the if-converted method for convertible debt.

EXHIBIT 12   Calculation of Diluted EPS for Oppnox Company Using the If-Converted Method: Case of a Convertible Bond

	Basic EPS	Diluted EPS Using If-Converted Method
Net income	$750,000	$750,000
After-tax cost of interest		2,100
Numerator	$750,000	$752,100
Weighted average number of shares outstanding	690,000	690,000
If converted	0	10,000
Denominator	690,000	700,000
EPS	**$1.09**	**$1.07**

6.3.3. Diluted EPS When a Company Has Stock Options, Warrants, or Their Equivalents Outstanding

When a company has stock options, warrants, or their equivalents[32] outstanding, diluted EPS is calculated as if the financial instruments had been exercised and the company had used the proceeds from exercise to repurchase as many shares of common stock as possible at the average market price of common stock during the period. The weighted average number of shares outstanding for diluted EPS is thus increased by the number of shares that would be issued upon exercise minus the number of shares that would have been purchased with the proceeds. This method is called the **treasury stock method** under US GAAP because companies typically hold repurchased shares as treasury stock. The same method is used under IFRS but is not named.

For the calculation of diluted EPS using this method, the assumed exercise of these financial instruments would have the following effects:

• The company is assumed to receive cash upon exercise and, in exchange, to issue shares.
• The company is assumed to use the cash proceeds to repurchase shares at the weighted average market price during the period.

---

[32]Hereafter, options, warrants, and their equivalents will be referred to simply as "options" because the accounting treatment for EPS calculations is interchangeable for these instruments under IFRS and US GAAP.

As a result of these two effects, the number of shares outstanding would increase by the incremental number of shares issued (the difference between the number of shares issued to the holders and the number of shares assumed to be repurchased by the company). For calculating diluted EPS, the incremental number of shares is weighted based upon the length of time the financial instrument was outstanding in the year. If the financial instrument was issued prior to the beginning of the year, the weighted average number of shares outstanding increases by the incremental number of shares. If the financial instruments were issued during the year, then the incremental shares are weighted by the amount of time the financial instruments were outstanding during the year.

The assumed exercise of these financial instruments would not affect net income. For calculating EPS, therefore, no change is made to the numerator. The formula to calculate diluted EPS using the treasury stock method (same method as used under IFRS but not named) for options is:

$$
\text{Diluted EPS} = \frac{(\text{Net income} - \text{Preferred dividends})}{\begin{bmatrix} \text{Weighted average number of shares} \\ \text{outstanding} + (\text{New shares that would} \\ \text{have been issued at option exercise} - \\ \text{Shares that could have been purchased} \\ \text{with cash received upon exercise}) \times \\ (\text{Proportion of year during which the} \\ \text{financial instruments were outstanding}) \end{bmatrix}} \tag{4}
$$

A diluted EPS calculation using the treasury stock method for options is provided in Example 11.

EXAMPLE 11   A Diluted EPS Calculation Using the Treasury Stock Method for Options

Hihotech Company (fictitious) reported net income of $2.3 million for the year ended June 30, 2018 and had a weighted average of 800,000 common shares outstanding. At the beginning of the fiscal year, the company has outstanding 30,000 options with an exercise price of $35. No other potentially dilutive financial instruments are outstanding. Over the fiscal year, the company's market price has averaged $55 per share. Calculate the company's basic and diluted EPS.

Solution: Using the treasury stock method, we first calculate that the company would have received $1,050,000 ($35 for each of the 30,000 options exercised) if all the options had been exercised. The options would no longer be outstanding; instead, 30,000 shares of common stock would be outstanding. Under the treasury stock method, we assume that shares would be repurchased with the cash received upon exercise of the options. At an average market price of $55 per share, the $1,050,000 proceeds from option exercise, the company could have repurchased 19,091 shares. Therefore, the incremental number of shares issued is 10,909 (calculated as 30,000 minus 19,091). For the diluted EPS calculation, no change is made to the numerator. As shown in Exhibit 13, the company's basic EPS was $2.88, and the diluted EPS was $2.84.

EXHIBIT 13   Calculation of Diluted EPS for Hihotech Company Using the Treasury Stock Method: Case of Stock Options

	Basic EPS	Diluted EPS Using Treasury Stock Method
Net income	$2,300,000	$2,300,000
Numerator	$2,300,000	$2,300,000
Weighted average number of shares outstanding	800,000	800,000
If converted	0	10,909
Denominator	800,000	810,909
EPS	**$2.88**	**$2.84**

As noted, IFRS require a similar computation but do not refer to it as the "treasury stock method." The company is required to consider that any assumed proceeds are received from the issuance of new shares at the average market price for the period. These new "inferred" shares would be disregarded in the computation of diluted EPS, but the excess of the new shares that would be issued under options contracts minus the new inferred shares would be added to the weighted average number of shares outstanding. The results are the same as the treasury stock method, as shown in Example 12.

EXAMPLE 12   Diluted EPS for Options under IFRS

Assuming the same facts as in Example 11, calculate the weighted average number of shares outstanding for diluted EPS under IFRS.

Solution: If the options had been exercised, the company would have received $1,050,000. If this amount had been received from the issuance of new shares at the average market price of $55 per share, the company would have issued 19,091 shares. IFRS refer to the 19,091 shares the company would have issued at market prices as the inferred shares. The number of shares issued under options (30,000) minus the number of inferred shares (19,091) equals 10,909. This amount is added to the weighted average number of shares outstanding of 800,000 to get diluted shares of 810,909. Note that this is the same result as that obtained under US GAAP; it is just derived in a different manner.

6.3.4. Other Issues with Diluted EPS

It is possible that some potentially convertible securities could be **antidilutive** (i.e., their inclusion in the computation would result in an EPS higher than the company's basic EPS). Under IFRS and US GAAP, antidilutive securities are not included in the calculation of diluted EPS. Diluted EPS should reflect the maximum potential dilution from conversion or exercise of potentially dilutive financial instruments. Diluted EPS will always be less than or equal to basic EPS. Example 13 provides an illustration of an antidilutive security.

EXAMPLE 13   An Antidilutive Security

For the year ended 31 December 2018, Dim-Cool Utility Company (fictitious) had net income of $1,750,000. The company had an average of 500,000 shares of common stock outstanding, 20,000 shares of convertible preferred, and no other potentially dilutive securities. Each share of preferred pays a dividend of $10 per share, and each is convertible into three shares of the company's common stock. What was the company's basic and diluted EPS?

Solution: If the 20,000 shares of convertible preferred had each converted into 3 shares of the company's common stock, the company would have had an additional 60,000 shares of common stock (3 shares of common for each of the 20,000 shares of preferred). If the conversion had taken place, the company would not have paid preferred dividends of $200,000 ($10 per share for each of the 20,000 shares of preferred). The effect of using the if-converted method would be EPS of $3.13, as shown in Exhibit 14. Because this is greater than the company's basic EPS of $3.10, the securities are said to be antidilutive, and the effect of their conversion would not be included in diluted EPS. Diluted EPS would be the same as basic EPS (i.e., $3.10).

EXHIBIT 14   Calculation for an Antidilutive Security

	Basic EPS	Diluted EPS Using If-Converted Method	
Net income	$1,750,000	$1,750,000	
Preferred dividend	−200,000	0	
Numerator	$1,550,000	$1,750,000	
Weighted average number of shares outstanding	500,000	500,000	
If converted	0	60,000	
Denominator	500,000	560,000	
EPS	**$3.10**	$3.13	←Exceeds basic EPS; security is antidilutive and, therefore, **not** included. **Reported diluted EPS = $3.10**.

6.4. Changes in EPS

Having explained the calculations of both basic and diluted EPS, we return to an examination of changes in EPS. As noted above, AB InBev's fully diluted EPS from continuing operations increased from $0.68 in 2016 to $3.96 in 2017. In general, an increase in EPS results from an increase in net income, a decrease in the number of shares outstanding, or a combination of both. In the notes to its financial statements (not shown), AB InBev discloses that the weighted average number of shares for both the basic and fully-diluted calculations was greater in 2017 than in 2016. Thus, for AB InBev, the improvement in EPS from 2016 to 2017 was driven by an increase in net income. Changes in the numerator and denominator explain the changes in EPS arithmetically. To understand the business drivers of those changes requires further research. The next section presents analytical tools that an analyst can use to highlight areas for further examination.

7. ANALYSIS OF THE INCOME STATEMENT

In this section, we apply two analytical tools to analyze the income statement: common-size analysis and income statement ratios. The objective of this analysis is to assess a company's performance over a period of time—compared with its own past performance or the performance of another company.

7.1. Common-Size Analysis of the Income Statement

Common-size analysis of the income statement can be performed by stating each line item on the income statement as a percentage of revenue.[33] Common-size statements facilitate comparison across time periods (time series analysis) and across companies (cross-sectional analysis) because the standardization of each line item removes the effect of size.

To illustrate, Panel A of Exhibit 15 presents an income statement for three hypothetical companies in the same industry. Company A and Company B, each with $10 million in sales, are larger (as measured by sales) than Company C, which has only $2 million in sales. In addition, Companies A and B both have higher operating profit: $2 million and $1.5 million, respectively, compared with Company C's operating profit of only $400,000.

How can an analyst meaningfully compare the performance of these companies? By preparing a common-size income statement, as illustrated in Panel B, an analyst can readily see that the percentages of Company C's expenses and profit relative to its sales are exactly the same as for Company A. Furthermore, although Company C's operating profit is lower than Company B's in absolute dollars, it is higher in percentage terms (20 percent for Company C compared with only 15 percent for Company B). For each $100 of sales, Company C generates $5 more operating profit than Company B. In other words, Company C is relatively more profitable than Company B based on this measure.

The common-size income statement also highlights differences in companies' strategies. Comparing the two larger companies, Company A reports significantly higher gross profit as a percentage of sales than does Company B (70 percent compared with 25 percent). Given that both companies operate in the same industry, why can Company A generate so much higher gross profit? One possible explanation is found by comparing the operating expenses of the two companies. Company A spends significantly more on research and development and on advertising than Company B. Expenditures on research and development likely result in

---

[33]This format can be distinguished as "vertical common-size analysis." As the chapter on financial statement analysis discusses, there is another type of common-size analysis, known as "horizontal common-size analysis," that states items in relation to a selected base year value. Unless otherwise indicated, text references to "common-size analysis" refer to vertical analysis.

products with superior technology. Expenditures on advertising likely result in greater brand awareness. So, based on these differences, it is likely that Company A is selling technologically superior products with a better brand image. Company B may be selling its products more cheaply (with a lower gross profit as a percentage of sales) but saving money by not investing in research and development or advertising. In practice, differences across companies are more subtle, but the concept is similar. An analyst, noting significant differences, would do more research and seek to understand the underlying reasons for the differences and their implications for the future performance of the companies.

EXHIBIT 15

Panel A: Income Statements for Companies A, B, and C ($)

	A	B	C
Sales	$10,000,000	$10,000,000	$2,000,000
Cost of sales	3,000,000	7,500,000	600,000
Gross profit	7,000,000	2,500,000	1,400,000
Selling, general, and administrative expenses	1,000,000	1,000,000	200,000
Research and development	2,000,000	—	400,000
Advertising	2,000,000	—	400,000
Operating profit	2,000,000	1,500,000	400,000

Panel B: Common-Size Income Statements for Companies A, B, and C (%)

	A	B	C
Sales	100%	100%	100%
Cost of sales	30	75	30
Gross profit	70	25	70
Selling, general, and administrative expenses	10	10	10
Research and development	20	0	20
Advertising	20	0	20
Operating profit	20	15	20

Note: Each line item is expressed as a percentage of the company's sales.

For most expenses, comparison to the amount of sales is appropriate. However, in the case of taxes, it is more meaningful to compare the amount of taxes with the amount of pretax income. Using note disclosure, an analyst can then examine the causes for differences in effective tax rates. To project the companies' future net income, an analyst would project the companies' pretax income and apply an estimated effective tax rate determined in part by the historical tax rates.

Vertical common-size analysis of the income statement is particularly useful in cross-sectional analysis—comparing companies with each other for a particular time period or comparing a company with industry or sector data. The analyst could select individual peer companies for comparison, use industry data from published sources, or compile data from databases based on a selection of peer companies or broader industry data. For example, Exhibit 16 presents median common-size income statement data compiled for the components of the S&P 500 classified into the 10 S&P/MSCI Global Industrial Classification System (GICS) sectors using 2017 data. Note that when compiling aggregate data such as this, some level of aggregation is necessary and less detail may be available than from peer company financial statements. The performance of an individual company can be compared with industry or peer company data to evaluate its relative performance.

EXHIBIT 16   Median Common-Size Income Statement Statistics for the S&P 500 Classified by S&P/MSCI GICS Sector Data for 2017

	Energy	Materials	Industrials	Consumer Discretionary	Consumer Staples	Health Care
Number of observations	34	27	69	81	34	59
Gross Margin	37.7%	33.0%	36.8%	37.6%	43.4%	59.0%
Operating Margin	6.4%	14.9%	13.5%	11.0%	17.2%	17.4%
Net Profit Margin	4.9%	9.9%	8.8%	6.0%	10.9%	7.2%

	Financials	Information Technology	Telecommunication Services	Utilities	Real Estate
Number of observations	63	64	4	29	29
Gross Margin	40.5%	62.4%	56.4%	34.3%	39.8%
Operating Margin	36.5%	21.1%	15.4%	21.7%	30.1%
Net Profit Margin	18.5%	11.3%	13.1%	10.1%	21.3%

Source: Based on data from Compustat. Operating margin based on EBIT (earnings before interest and taxes.)

7.2. Income Statement Ratios

One aspect of financial performance is profitability. One indicator of profitability is **net profit margin**, also known as **profit margin** and **return on sales**, which is calculated as net income divided by revenue (or sales).[34]

$$\text{Net profit margin} = \frac{\text{Net income}}{\text{Revenue}}$$

Net profit margin measures the amount of income that a company was able to generate for each dollar of revenue. A higher level of net profit margin indicates higher profitability and is thus more desirable. Net profit margin can also be found directly on the common-size income statements.

For AB InBev, net profit margin based on continuing operations for 2017 was 16.2 percent (calculated as profit from continuing operations of $9,155 million, divided by revenue of $56,444 million). To judge this ratio, some comparison is needed. AB InBev's profitability can be compared with that of another company or with its own previous performance. Compared with previous years, AB InBev's profitability is higher than in 2016 but lower than 2015. In 2016, net profit margin based on continuing operations was 6.0 percent, and in 2015, it was 22.9 percent.

---

[34] In the definition of margin ratios of this type, "sales" is often used interchangeably with "revenue." "Return on sales" has also been used to refer to a class of profitability ratios having revenue in the denominator.

Another measure of profitability is the gross profit margin. Gross profit (gross margin) is calculated as revenue minus cost of goods sold, and the **gross profit margin** is calculated as the gross profit divided by revenue.

$$\text{Gross profit margin} = \frac{\text{Gross profit}}{\text{Revenue}}$$

The gross profit margin measures the amount of gross profit that a company generated for each dollar of revenue. A higher level of gross profit margin indicates higher profitability and thus is generally more desirable, although differences in gross profit margins across companies reflect differences in companies' strategies. For example, consider a company pursuing a strategy of selling a differentiated product (e.g., a product differentiated based on brand name, quality, superior technology, or patent protection). The company would likely be able to sell the differentiated product at a higher price than a similar, but undifferentiated, product and, therefore, would likely show a higher gross profit margin than a company selling an undifferentiated product. Although a company selling a differentiated product would likely show a higher gross profit margin, this may take time. In the initial stage of the strategy, the company would likely incur costs to create a differentiated product, such as advertising or research and development, which would not be reflected in the gross margin calculation.

AB InBev's gross profit (shown in Exhibit 1) was $35,058 million in 2017, $27,715 million in 2016, and $26,467 million in 2015. Expressing gross profit as a percentage of revenues, we see that the gross profit margin was 62.1 percent in 2017, 60.9 percent in 2016, and 60.7 percent in 2015. In absolute terms, AB InBev's gross profit was higher in 2016 than in 2015. However, AB InBev's gross profit *margin* was lower in 2016 than in 2015.

Exhibit 17 presents a common-size income statement for AB InBev, and highlights certain profitability ratios. The net profit margin and gross profit margin described above are just two of the many subtotals that can be generated from common-size income statements. Other "margins" used by analysts include the **operating profit margin** (profit from operations divided by revenue) and the **pretax margin** (profit before tax divided by revenue).

EXHIBIT 17   AB InBev's Margins: Abbreviated Common-Size Income Statement

| | 12 Months Ended December 31 | | | | | |
| | 2017 | | 2016 | | 2015 | |
	$	%	$	%	$	%
Revenue	56,444	100.0	45,517	100.0	43,604	100.0
Cost of sales	(21,386)	(37.9)	(17,803)	(39.1)	(17,137)	(39.3)
Gross profit	**35,058**	**62.1**	**27,715**	**60.9**	**26,467**	**60.7**
Distribution expenses	(5,876)	(10.4)	(4,543)	(10.0)	(4,259)	(9.8)
Sales and marketing expenses	(8,382)	(14.9)	(7,745)	(17.0)	(6,913)	(15.9)
Administrative expenses	(3,841)	(6.8)	(2,883)	(6.3)	(2,560)	(5.9)
Portions omitted						
Profit from operations	**17,152**	**30.4**	**12,882**	**28.3**	**13,904**	**31.9**
Finance cost	(6,885)	(12.2)	(9,382)	(20.6)	(3,142)	(7.2)
Finance income	378	0.7	818	1.8	1,689	3.9
Net finance income/(cost)	(6,507)	(11.5)	(8,564)	(18.8)	(1,453)	(3.3)
Share of result of associates and joint ventures	430	0.8	16	0.0	10	0.0

EXHIBIT 17   (Continued)

| | 12 Months Ended December 31 | | | | | |
| | 2017 | | 2016 | | 2015 | |
	$	%	$	%	$	%
Profit before tax	**11,076**	**19.6**	**4,334**	**9.5**	**12,461**	**28.6**
Income tax expense	(1,920)	(3.4)	(1,613)	(3.5)	(2,594)	(5.9)
Profit from continuing operations	**9,155**	**16.2**	**2,721**	**6.0**	**9,867**	**22.6**
Profit from discontinued operations	28	0.0	48	0.1		—
Profit of the year	**9,183**	**16.3**	**2,769**	**6.1**	**9,867**	**22.6**

The profitability ratios and the common-size income statement yield quick insights about changes in a company's performance. For example, AB InBev's decrease in profitability in 2016 was not driven by a decrease in gross profit margin. Gross profit margin in 2016 was actually slightly higher than in 2015. The company's decrease in profitability in 2016 was driven in part by higher operating expenses and, in particular, by a significant increase in finance costs. The increased finance costs resulted from the 2016 merger with SABMiller. Valued at more than $100 billion, the acquisition was one of the largest in history. The combination of AB InBev and SABMiller also explains the increase in revenue from around $45 billion to over $56 billion. The profitability ratios and the common-size income statement thus serve to highlight areas about which an analyst might wish to gain further understanding.

8. COMPREHENSIVE INCOME

The general expression for net income is revenue minus expenses. There are, however, certain items of revenue and expense that, by accounting convention, are excluded from the net income calculation. To understand how reported shareholders' equity of one period links with reported shareholders' equity of the next period, we must understand these excluded items, known as **other comprehensive income**. Under IFRS, other comprehensive income includes items of income and expense that are "not recognized in profit or loss as required or permitted by other IFRS." **Total comprehensive income** is "the change in equity during a period resulting from transaction and other events, other than those changes resulting from transactions with owners in their capacity as owners."[35]

Under US GAAP, **comprehensive income** is defined as "the change in equity [net assets] of a business enterprise during a period from transactions and other events and circumstances from non-owner sources. It includes all changes in equity during a period except those resulting from investments by owners and distributions to owners."[36] While the wording differs, comprehensive income is conceptually the same under IFRS and US GAAP.

Comprehensive income includes *both* net income and other revenue and expense items that are excluded from the net income calculation (collectively referred to as Other Comprehensive Income). Assume, for example, a company's beginning shareholders' equity is €110 million, its net income for the year is €10 million, its cash dividends for the year are €2 million,

---

[35] IAS 1, *Presentation of Financial Statements.*
[36] FASB ASC Section 220-10-05 [Comprehensive Income–Overall–Overview and Background].

and there was no issuance or repurchase of common stock. If the company's actual ending shareholders' equity is €123 million, then €5 million [€123 − (€110 + €10 − €2)] has bypassed the net income calculation by being classified as other comprehensive income. If the company had no other comprehensive income, its ending shareholders' equity would have been €118 million [€110 + €10 − €2].

Four types of items are treated as other comprehensive income under both IFRS and US GAAP. (The specific treatment of some of these items differs between the two sets of standards, but these types of items are common to both.)

1. Foreign currency translation adjustments. In consolidating the financial statements of foreign subsidiaries, the effects of translating the subsidiaries' balance sheet assets and liabilities at current exchange rates are included as other comprehensive income.
2. Unrealized gains or losses on derivatives contracts accounted for as hedges. Changes in the fair value of derivatives are recorded each period, but certain changes in value are treated as other comprehensive income and thus bypass the income statement.
3. Unrealized holding gains and losses on a certain category of investment securities, namely, available-for-sale debt securities under US GAAP and securities designated as "fair value through other comprehensive income" under IFRS. (Note: IFRS, but not US GAAP, also includes a category of equity investments designated at fair value through other comprehensive income.)
4. Certain costs of a company's defined benefit post-retirement plans that are not recognized in the current period.

In addition, under IFRS, other comprehensive income includes certain changes in the value of long-lived assets that are measured using the revaluation model rather than the cost model. Also, under IFRS, companies are not permitted to reclassify certain items of other comprehensive income to profit or loss, and companies must present separately the items of other comprehensive income that will and will not be reclassified subsequently to profit or loss.

The third type of item listed above is perhaps the simplest to illustrate. Holding gains on securities arise when a company owns securities over an accounting period, during which time the securities' value increases. Similarly, holding losses on securities arise when a company owns securities over a period during which time the securities' value decreases. If the company has not sold the securities (i.e., has not realized the gain or loss), its holding gain or loss is said to be unrealized. The question is: Should the company exclude unrealized gains and losses from income; reflect these unrealized holding gains and losses in its income statement (i.e., statement of profit and loss); or reflect these unrealized holding gains as other comprehensive income?

According to accounting standards, the answer depends on how the company has categorized the securities. Categorization depends on what the company intends to do with the securities (i.e., the business model for managing the asset) and on the cash flows of the security. Unrealized gains and losses are excluded from income for debt securities that the company intends to hold to maturity. These held-to-maturity debt securities are reported at their amortized cost, so no unrealized gains or losses are reported. For other securities reported at fair value, the unrealized gains or losses are reflected either in the income statement or as other comprehensive income.

Under US GAAP, unrealized gains and losses are reflected in the income statement for: (a) debt securities designated as **trading securities**; and (b) all investments in equity securities (other than investments giving rise to ownership positions that confer significant influence over the investee). The trading securities category pertains to a debt security that is acquired with the intent of selling it rather than holding it to collect the interest and principal payments.

Also, under US GAAP, unrealized gains and losses are reflected as other comprehensive income for debt securities designated as **available-for-sale** securities. Available-for-sale debt securities are those not designated as either held-to-maturity or trading.

Under IFRS, unrealized gains and losses are reflected in the income statement for: (a) investments in equity investments, unless the company makes an irrevocable election otherwise; and (b) debt securities, if the securities do not fall into the other measurement categories or if the company makes an irrevocable election to show gains and losses on the income statement. These debt and equity investments are referred to as being measured at *fair value through profit or loss*. Also under IFRS, unrealized gains and losses are reflected as other comprehensive income for: (a) "debt securities held within a business model whose objective is achieved both by collecting contractual cash flows and selling financial assets"; and (b) equity investments for which the company makes an irrevocable election at initial recognition to show gains and losses as part of other comprehensive income. These debt and equity investments are referred to as being measured at *fair value through other comprehensive income*. Accounting for these securities is similar to accounting for US GAAP's available-for-sale debt securities.

Even where unrealized holding gains and losses are excluded from a company's net income (profit and loss), they are *included* in other comprehensive income and thus form a part of a company's comprehensive income.

EXAMPLE 14   Other Comprehensive Income

Assume a company's beginning shareholders' equity is €200 million, its net income for the year is €20 million, its cash dividends for the year are €3 million, and there was no issuance or repurchase of common stock. The company's actual ending shareholders' equity is €227 million.

1. What amount has bypassed the net income calculation by being classified as other comprehensive income?
   A. €0.
   B. €7 million.
   C. €10 million.

2. Which of the following statements *best* describes other comprehensive income?
   A. Income earned from diverse geographic and segment activities.
   B. Income that increases stockholders' equity but is not reflected as part of net income.
   C. Income earned from activities that are not part of the company's ordinary business activities.

Solution to 1: C is correct. If the company's actual ending shareholders' equity is €227 million, then €10 million [€227− (€200 + €20 − €3)] has bypassed the net income calculation by being classified as other comprehensive income.

Solution to 2: B is correct. Answers A and C are not correct because they do not specify whether such income is reported as part of net income and shown in the income statement.

EXAMPLE 15   Other Comprehensive Income in Analysis

An analyst is looking at two comparable companies. Company A has a lower price/earnings (P/E) ratio than Company B, and the conclusion that has been suggested is that Company A is undervalued. As part of examining this conclusion, the analyst decides to explore the question: What would the company's P/E look like if total comprehensive income per share—rather than net income per share—were used as the relevant metric?

	Company A	Company B
Price	$35	$30
EPS	$1.60	$0.90
P/E ratio	21.9×	33.3×
Other comprehensive income (loss) $ million	($16.272)	$(1.757)
Shares (millions)	22.6	25.1

Solution: As shown in the following table, part of the explanation for Company A's lower P/E ratio may be that its significant losses—accounted for as other comprehensive income (OCI)—are not included in the P/E ratio.

	Company A	Company B
Price	$35	$30
EPS	$1.60	$0.90
OCI (loss) $ million	($16.272)	$(1.757)
Shares (millions)	22.6	25.1
OCI (loss) per share	$(0.72)	$(0.07)
Comprehensive EPS = EPS + OCI per share	$ 0.88	$0.83
Price/Comprehensive EPS ratio	39.8×	36.1×

Both IFRS and US GAAP allow companies two alternative presentations. One alternative is to present two statements—a separate income statement and a second statement additionally including other comprehensive income. The other alternative is to present a single statement of other comprehensive income. Particularly in comparing financial statements of two companies, it is relevant to examine significant differences in comprehensive income.

9. SUMMARY

This chapter has presented the elements of income statement analysis. The income statement presents information on the financial results of a company's business activities over a period of time; it communicates how much revenue the company generated during a period and what costs it incurred in connection with generating that revenue. A company's net income and its components (e.g., gross margin, operating earnings, and pretax earnings) are critical inputs into both the equity and credit analysis processes. Equity analysts are interested in earnings because equity markets often reward relatively high- or low-earnings growth companies with above-average or below-average valuations, respectively. Fixed-income analysts examine the components of income statements, past and projected, for information on companies' abilities to make promised payments on their debt over the course of the business cycle. Corporate financial announcements frequently emphasize income statements more than the other financial statements.

Key points to this chapter include the following:

- The income statement presents revenue, expenses, and net income.
- The components of the income statement include: revenue; cost of sales; sales, general, and administrative expenses; other operating expenses; non-operating income and expenses; gains and losses; non-recurring items; net income; and EPS.
- An income statement that presents a subtotal for gross profit (revenue minus cost of goods sold) is said to be presented in a multi-step format. One that does not present this subtotal is said to be presented in a single-step format.
- Revenue is recognized in the period it is earned, which may or may not be in the same period as the related cash collection. Recognition of revenue when earned is a fundamental principal of accrual accounting.
- An analyst should identify differences in companies' revenue recognition methods and adjust reported revenue where possible to facilitate comparability. Where the available information does not permit adjustment, an analyst can characterize the revenue recognition as more or less conservative and thus qualitatively assess how differences in policies might affect financial ratios and judgments about profitability.
- As of the beginning of 2018, revenue recognition standards have converged. The core principle of the converged standards is that revenue should be recognized to "depict the transfer of promised goods or services to customers in an amount that reflects the consideration to which the entity expects to be entitled in an exchange for those goods or services."
- To achieve the core principle, the standard describes the application of five steps in recognizing revenue. The standard also specifies the treatment of some related contract costs and disclosure requirements.
- The general principles of expense recognition include a process to match expenses either to revenue (such as, cost of goods sold) or to the time period in which the expenditure occurs (period costs such as administrative salaries) or to the time period of expected benefits of the expenditures (such as depreciation).
- In expense recognition, choice of method (i.e., depreciation method and inventory cost method), as well as estimates (i.e., uncollectible accounts, warranty expenses, assets' useful life, and salvage value) affect a company's reported income. An analyst should identify differences in companies' expense recognition methods and adjust reported financial statements where possible to facilitate comparability. Where the available information does not permit adjustment, an analyst can characterize the policies and estimates as more or less conservative and thus qualitatively assess how differences in policies might affect financial ratios and judgments about companies' performance.
- To assess a company's future earnings, it is helpful to separate those prior years' items of income and expense that are likely to continue in the future from those items that are less likely to continue.
- Under IFRS, a company should present additional line items, headings, and subtotals beyond those specified when such presentation is relevant to an understanding of the entity's

financial performance. Some items from prior years clearly are not expected to continue in future periods and are separately disclosed on a company's income statement. Under US GAAP, unusual and/or infrequently occurring items, which are material, are presented separately within income from continuing operations.
- Non-operating items are reported separately from operating items on the income statement. Under both IFRS and US GAAP, the income statement reports separately the effect of the disposal of a component operation as a "discontinued" operation.
- Basic EPS is the amount of income available to common shareholders divided by the weighted average number of common shares outstanding over a period. The amount of income available to common shareholders is the amount of net income remaining after preferred dividends (if any) have been paid.
- If a company has a simple capital structure (i.e., one with no potentially dilutive securities), then its basic EPS is equal to its diluted EPS. If, however, a company has dilutive securities, its diluted EPS is lower than its basic EPS.
- Diluted EPS is calculated using the if-converted method for convertible securities and the treasury stock method for options.
- Common-size analysis of the income statement involves stating each line item on the income statement as a percentage of sales. Common-size statements facilitate comparison across time periods and across companies of different sizes.
- Two income-statement-based indicators of profitability are net profit margin and gross profit margin.
- Comprehensive income includes *both* net income and other revenue and expense items that are excluded from the net income calculation.

PRACTICE PROBLEMS

1. Expenses on the income statement may be grouped by:
   A. nature, but not by function.
   B. function, but not by nature.
   C. either function or nature.

2. An example of an expense classification by function is:
   A. tax expense.
   B. interest expense.
   C. cost of goods sold.

3. Denali Limited, a manufacturing company, had the following income statement information:

Revenue	$4,000,000
Cost of goods sold	$3,000,000
Other operating expenses	$500,000
Interest expense	$100,000
Tax expense	$120,000

Denali's gross profit is equal to:
   A. $280,000.
   B. $500,000.
   C. $1,000,000.

4. Under IFRS, income includes increases in economic benefits from:
   A. increases in liabilities not related to owners' contributions.
   B. enhancements of assets not related to owners' contributions.
   C. increases in owners' equity related to owners' contributions.

5. Fairplay had the following information related to the sale of its products during 2009, which was its first year of business:

Revenue	$1,000,000
Returns of goods sold	$100,000
Cash collected	$800,000
Cost of goods sold	$700,000

   Under the accrual basis of accounting, how much net revenue would be reported on Fairplay's 2009 income statement?
   A. $200,000.
   B. $900,000.
   C. $1,000,000.

6. Apex Consignment sells items over the internet for individuals on a consignment basis. Apex receives the items from the owner, lists them for sale on the internet, and receives a 25 percent commission for any items sold. Apex collects the full amount from the buyer and pays the net amount after commission to the owner. Unsold items are returned to the owner after 90 days. During 2009, Apex had the following information:
   • Total sales price of items sold during 2009 on consignment was €2,000,000.
   • Total commissions retained by Apex during 2009 for these items was €500,000.
   How much revenue should Apex report on its 2009 income statement?
   A. €500,000.
   B. €2,000,000.
   C. €1,500,000.

7. A company previously expensed the incremental costs of obtaining a contract. All else being equal, adopting the May 2014 IASB and FASB converged accounting standards on revenue recognition makes the company's profitability initially appear:
   A. lower.
   B. unchanged.
   C. higher.

8. During 2009, Accent Toys Plc., which began business in October of that year, purchased 10,000 units of a toy at a cost of £10 per unit in October. The toy sold well in October. In anticipation of heavy December sales, Accent purchased 5,000 additional units in November at a cost of £11 per unit. During 2009, Accent sold 12,000 units at a price of £15 per unit. Under the first in, first out (FIFO) method, what is Accent's cost of goods sold for 2009?
   A. £120,000.
   B. £122,000.
   C. £124,000.

9. Using the same information as in Question 8, what would Accent's cost of goods sold be under the weighted average cost method?
   A. £120,000.
   B. £122,000.
   C. £124,000.

10. Which inventory method is least likely to be used under IFRS?
    A. First in, first out (FIFO).
    B. Last in, first out (LIFO).
    C. Weighted average.

11. At the beginning of 2009, Glass Manufacturing purchased a new machine for its assembly line at a cost of $600,000. The machine has an estimated useful life of 10 years and estimated residual value of $50,000. Under the straight-line method, how much depreciation would Glass take in 2010 for financial reporting purposes?
    A. $55,000.
    B. $60,000.
    C. $65,000.

12. Using the same information as in Question 16, how much depreciation would Glass take in 2009 for financial reporting purposes under the double-declining balance method?
    A. $60,000.
    B. $110,000.
    C. $120,000.

13. Which combination of depreciation methods and useful lives is most conservative in the year a depreciable asset is acquired?
    A. Straight-line depreciation with a short useful life.
    B. Declining balance depreciation with a long useful life.
    C. Declining balance depreciation with a short useful life.

14. Under IFRS, a loss from the destruction of property in a fire would most likely be classified as:
    A. continuing operations.
    B. discontinued operations.
    C. other comprehensive income.

15. A company chooses to change an accounting policy. This change requires that, if practical, the company restate its financial statements for:
    A. all prior periods.
    B. current and future periods.
    C. prior periods shown in a report.

16. For 2009, Flamingo Products had net income of $1,000,000. At 1 January 2009, there were 1,000,000 shares outstanding. On 1 July 2009, the company issued 100,000 new shares for $20 per share. The company paid $200,000 in dividends to common shareholders. What is Flamingo's basic earnings per share for 2009?
    A. $0.80.
    B. $0.91.
    C. $0.95.

17. For its fiscal year-end, Calvan Water Corporation (CWC) reported net income of $12 million and a weighted average of 2,000,000 common shares outstanding. The company paid $800,000 in preferred dividends and had 100,000 options outstanding with an average exercise price of $20. CWC's market price over the year averaged $25 per share. CWC's diluted EPS is *closest* to:
    A. $5.33.
    B. $5.54.
    C. $5.94.

18. A company with no debt or convertible securities issued publicly traded common stock three times during the current fiscal year. Under both IFRS and US GAAP, the company's:
    A. basic EPS equals its diluted EPS.
    B. capital structure is considered complex at year-end.
    C. basic EPS is calculated by using a simple average number of shares outstanding.

19. Laurelli Builders (LB) reported the following financial data for year-end December 31:

Common shares outstanding, January 1	2,020,000
Common shares issued as stock dividend, June 1	380,000
Warrants outstanding, January 1	500,000
Net income	$3,350,000
Preferred stock dividends paid	$430,000
Common stock dividends paid	$240,000

Which statement about the calculation of LB's EPS is *most* accurate?
    A. LB's basic EPS is $1.12.
    B. LB's diluted EPS is equal to or less than its basic EPS.
    C. The weighted average number of shares outstanding is 2,210,000.

20. Cell Services Inc. (CSI) had 1,000,000 average shares outstanding during all of 2009. During 2009, CSI also had 10,000 options outstanding with exercise prices of $10 each. The average stock price of CSI during 2009 was $15. For purposes of computing diluted earnings per share, how many shares would be used in the denominator?
    A. 1,003,333.
    B. 1,006,667.
    C. 1,010,000.

21. For its fiscal year-end, Sublyme Corporation reported net income of $200 million and a weighted average of 50,000,000 common shares outstanding. There are 2,000,000 convertible preferred shares outstanding that paid an annual dividend of $5. Each preferred share is convertible into two shares of the common stock. The diluted EPS is *closest to*:
    A. $3.52.
    B. $3.65.
    C. $3.70.

22. When calculating diluted EPS, which of the following securities in the capital structure increases the weighted average number of common shares outstanding without affecting net income available to common shareholders?
    A. Stock options.
    B. Convertible debt that is dilutive.
    C. Convertible preferred stock that is dilutive.

23. Which statement is *most* accurate? A common-size income statement:
    A. restates each line item of the income statement as a percentage of net income.
    B. allows an analyst to conduct cross-sectional analysis by removing the effect of company size.
    C. standardizes each line item of the income statement but fails to help an analyst identify differences in companies' strategies.

24. Selected year-end financial statement data for Workhard are shown below.

	$ millions
Beginning shareholders' equity	475
Ending shareholders' equity	493
Unrealized gain on available-for-sale securities	5
Unrealized loss on derivatives accounted for as hedges	−3
Foreign currency translation gain on consolidation	2
Dividends paid	1
Net income	15

Workhard's comprehensive income for the year:
A. is $18 million.
B. is increased by the derivatives accounted for as hedges.
C. includes $4 million in other comprehensive income.

25. When preparing an income statement, which of the following items would *most likely* be classified as other comprehensive income?
A. A foreign currency translation adjustment.
B. An unrealized gain on a security held for trading purposes.
C. A realized gain on a derivative contract not accounted for as a hedge.

CHAPTER 4

UNDERSTANDING BALANCE SHEETS

Elaine Henry, PhD, CFA
Thomas R. Robinson, PhD, CFA

LEARNING OUTCOMES

After completing this chapter, you will be able to do the following:

- describe the elements of the balance sheet: assets, liabilities, and equity;
- describe uses and limitations of the balance sheet in financial analysis;
- describe alternative formats of balance sheet presentation;
- distinguish between current and non-current assets and current and non-current liabilities;
- describe different types of assets and liabilities and the measurement bases of each;
- describe the components of shareholders' equity;
- convert balance sheets to common-size balance sheets and interpret common-size balance sheets;
- calculate and interpret liquidity and solvency ratios.

1. INTRODUCTION

The balance sheet provides information on a company's resources (assets) and its sources of capital (equity and liabilities/debt). This information helps an analyst assess a company's ability to pay for its near-term operating needs, meet future debt obligations, and make distributions to owners. The basic equation underlying the balance sheet is Assets = Liabilities + Equity.

Analysts should be aware that different types of assets and liabilities may be measured differently. For example, some items are measured at historical cost or a variation thereof and others at fair value.[1] An understanding of the measurement issues will facilitate analysis. The balance sheet measurement issues are, of course, closely linked to the revenue and expense

---

[1] IFRS and US GAAP define "fair value" as an exit price, i.e., the price that would be received to sell an asset or paid to transfer a liability in an orderly transaction between market participants at the measurement date (IFRS 13, FASB ASC Topic 820).

recognition issues affecting the income statement. Throughout this chapter, we describe and illustrate some of the linkages between the measurement issues affecting the balance sheet and the revenue and expense recognition issues affecting the income statement.

This chapter is organized as follows: In Section 2, we describe and give examples of the elements and formats of balance sheets. Section 3 discusses current assets and current liabilities. Section 4 focuses on assets, and Section 5 focuses on liabilities. Section 6 describes the components of equity and illustrates the statement of changes in shareholders' equity. Section 7 introduces balance sheet analysis. A summary of the key points and practice problems in the CFA Institute multiple-choice format conclude the chapter.

2. COMPONENTS AND FORMAT OF THE BALANCE SHEET

The **balance sheet** (also called the **statement of financial position** or **statement of financial condition**) discloses what an entity owns (or controls), what it owes, and what the owners' claims are at a specific point in time.[2]

The financial position of a company is described in terms of its basic elements (assets, liabilities, and equity):

- **Assets** (A) are what the company owns (or controls). More formally, assets are resources controlled by the company as a result of past events and from which future economic benefits are expected to flow *to* the entity.
- **Liabilities** (L) are what the company owes. More formally, liabilities represent obligations of a company arising from past events, the settlement of which is expected to result in a future outflow of economic benefits *from* the entity.
- **Equity** (E) represents the owners' residual interest in the company's assets after deducting its liabilities. Commonly known as **shareholders' equity** or **owners' equity**, equity is determined by subtracting the liabilities from the assets of a company, giving rise to the accounting equation: $A - L = E$ or $A = L + E$.

The equation $A = L + E$ is sometimes summarized as follows: The left side of the equation reflects the resources controlled by the company, and the right side reflects how those resources were financed. For all financial statement items, an item should only be recognized in the financial statements if it is probable that any future economic benefit associated with the item will flow to or from the entity and if the item has a cost or value that can be measured with reliability.[3]

The balance sheet provides important information about a company's financial condition, but the balance sheet amounts of equity (assets, net of liabilities) should not be viewed as a measure of either the market or intrinsic value of a company's equity for several reasons. First, the balance sheet under current accounting standards is a mixed model with respect to measurement. Some assets and liabilities are measured based on historical cost, sometimes with adjustments, whereas other assets and liabilities are measured based on a fair value, which represents its current value as of the balance sheet date. The measurement bases may have a significant effect on the amount reported. Second, even the items measured at current value reflect the value that was current at the end of the reporting period. The values of those items obviously can change after the balance sheet is prepared. Third, the value of a company is a function of

---

[2]IFRS uses the term "statement of financial position" (IAS 1 *Presentation of Financial Statements*), and US GAAP uses the terms "balance sheet" and "statement of financial position" interchangeably (ASC 210-10-05 [Balance Sheet–Overall–Overview and Background]).

[3] *Conceptual Framework for Financial Reporting (2018).*

many factors, including future cash flows expected to be generated by the company and current market conditions. Important aspects of a company's ability to generate future cash flows—for example, its reputation and management skills—are not included in its balance sheet.

2.1. Balance Sheet Components

To illustrate the components and formats of balance sheets, we show the major subtotals from two companies' balance sheets. Exhibit 1 and Exhibit 2 are based on the balance sheets of SAP Group and Apple Inc. SAP Group is a leading business software company based in Germany and prepares its financial statements in accordance with IFRS. Apple is a technology manufacturer based in the United States and prepares its financial statements in accordance with US GAAP. For purposes of discussion, Exhibits 1 and 2 show only the main subtotals and totals of these companies' balance sheets. Additional exhibits throughout this chapter will expand on these subtotals.

EXHIBIT 1   SAP Group Consolidated Statements of Financial Position (Excerpt) (in millions of €)

	December 31	
Assets	2017	2016*
Total current assets	11,930	11,564
Total non-current assets	30,567	32,713
Total assets	42,497	44,277
Equity and liabilities		
Total current liabilities	10,210	9,675
Total non-current liabilities	6,747	8,205
Total liabilities	16,957	17,880
Total equity	25,540	26,397
Equity and liabilities	42,497	44,277

Note: Numbers exactly from the annual report as prepared by the company, which reflects some rounding.

* Numbers are the reclassified numbers from the SAP Group 2017 annual report.

Source: SAP Group 2017 annual report.

EXHIBIT 2   Apple Inc. Consolidated Balance Sheets (Excerpt)* (in millions of $)

Assets	September 30, 2017	September 24, 2016
Total current assets	128,645	106,869
[All other assets]	*246,674*	*214,817*
Total assets	375,319	321,686
Liabilities and shareholders' equity		
Total current liabilities	100,814	79,006
[Total non-current liabilities]	*140,458*	*114,431*
Total liabilities	241,272	193,437
Total shareholders' equity	134,047	128,249
Total liabilities and shareholders' equity	375,319	321,686

**Note*: The italicized subtotals presented in this excerpt are not explicitly shown on the face of the financial statement as prepared by the company.

Source: Apple Inc. 2017 annual report (Form 10K).

SAP Group uses the title Statement of Financial Position and Apple uses the title Balance Sheet. Despite their different titles, both statements report the three basic elements: assets, liabilities, and equity. Both companies are reporting on a consolidated basis, i.e., including all their controlled subsidiaries. The numbers in SAP Group's balance sheet are in millions of euros, and the numbers in Apple's balance sheet are in millions of dollars.

Balance sheet information is as of a specific point in time. These exhibits are from the companies' annual financial statements, so the balance sheet information is as of the last day of their respective fiscal years. SAP Group's fiscal year is the same as the calendar year, and the balance sheet information is as of December 31. Apple's fiscal year ends on the last Saturday of September, so the actual date changes from year to year. About every six years, Apple's fiscal year will include 53 weeks rather than 52 weeks. This feature of Apple's fiscal year should be noted, but in general, the extra week is more relevant to evaluating statements spanning a period of time (the income and cash flow statements) rather than the balance sheet, which captures information as of a specific point in time.

A company's ability to pay for its short-term operating needs relates to the concept of **liquidity**. With respect to a company overall, liquidity refers to the availability of cash to meet those short-term needs. With respect to a particular asset or liability, liquidity refers to its "nearness to cash." A liquid asset is one that can be easily converted into cash in a short period of time at a price close to fair market value. For example, a small holding of an actively traded stock is much more liquid than an investment in an asset such as a commercial real estate property, particularly in a weak property market.

The separate presentation of current and non-current assets and liabilities facilitates analysis of a company's liquidity position (at least as of the end of the fiscal period). Both IFRS and US GAAP require that the balance sheet distinguish between current and non-current assets and between current and non-current liabilities, and present these as separate classifications. An exception to this requirement, under IFRS, is that the current and non-current classifications are not required if a liquidity-based presentation provides reliable and more relevant information. Presentations distinguishing between current and non-current elements are shown in Exhibits 1 and 2. Exhibit 3 in Section 2.3 shows a liquidity-based presentation.

2.2. Current and Non-Current Classification

Assets that are held primarily for the purpose of trading or that are expected to be sold, used up, or otherwise realized in cash within one year or one operating cycle of the business, whichever is greater, after the reporting period are classified as **current assets**. A company's operating cycle is the average amount of time that elapses between acquiring inventory and collecting the cash from sales to customers. (When the entity's normal operating cycle is not clearly identifiable, its duration is assumed to be one year.) For a manufacturer, the operating cycle is the average amount of time between acquiring raw materials and converting these into cash from a sale. Examples of companies that might be expected to have operating cycles longer than one year include those operating in the tobacco, distillery, and lumber industries. Even though these types of companies often hold inventories longer than one year, the inventory is classified as a current asset because it is expected to be sold within an operating cycle. Assets not expected to be sold or used up within one year or one operating cycle of the business, whichever is greater, are classified as **non-current assets** (long-term, long-lived assets).

Current assets are generally maintained for operating purposes, and these assets include— in addition to cash—items expected to be converted into cash (e.g., trade receivables), used up (e.g., office supplies, prepaid expenses), or sold (e.g., inventories) in the current operating cycle. Current assets provide information about the operating activities and the operating capability of the entity. For example, the item "trade receivables" or "accounts receivable" would indicate that a company provides credit to its customers. Non-current assets represent the infrastructure from which the entity operates and are not consumed or sold in the current period. Investments in such assets are made from a strategic and longer-term perspective.

Similarly, liabilities expected to be settled within one year or within one operating cycle of the business, whichever is greater, after the reporting period are classified as **current liabilities**. The specific criteria for classification of a liability as current include the following:

- It is expected to be settled in the entity's normal operating cycle;
- It is held primarily for the purpose of being traded;[4]
- It is due to be settled within one year after the balance sheet date; or
- The entity does not have an unconditional right to defer settlement of the liability for at least one year after the balance sheet date.[5]

IFRS specify that some current liabilities, such as trade payables and some accruals for employee and other operating costs, are part of the working capital used in the entity's normal operating cycle. Such operating items are classified as current liabilities even if they will be settled more than one year after the balance sheet date. All other liabilities are classified as **non-current liabilities**. Non-current liabilities include financial liabilities that provide financing on a long-term basis.

The excess of current assets over current liabilities is called **working capital**. The level of working capital provides analysts with information about the ability of an entity to meet liabilities as they fall due. Although adequate working capital is essential, excessive working capital should be invested so that funds that could be used more productively elsewhere are not inappropriately tied up.

A balance sheet with separately classified current and non-current assets and liabilities is referred to as a **classified balance sheet**. Classification also refers generally to the grouping of accounts into subcategories. Both companies' balance sheets that are summarized in Exhibits 1 and 2 are classified balance sheets. Although both companies' balance sheets present current assets before non-current assets and current liabilities before non-current liabilities, this is not required. IFRS does not specify the order or format in which a company presents items on a current/non-current classified balance sheet.

2.3. Liquidity-Based Presentation

A liquidity-based presentation, rather than a current/non-current presentation, is used when such a presentation provides information that is reliable and more relevant. With a liquidity-based presentation, all assets and liabilities are presented broadly in order of liquidity.

Entities such as banks are candidates to use a liquidity-based presentation. Exhibit 3 presents the assets portion of the balance sheet of HSBC Holdings plc (HSBC), a global financial services company that reports using IFRS. HSBC's balance sheet is ordered using a liquidity-based presentation. As shown, the asset section begins with cash and balances at central banks. Less liquid items such as "Interest in associates and joint ventures" appear near the bottom of the asset listing.

---

[4] Examples of these are financial liabilities classified as held for trading in accordance with IAS 39, which is replaced by IFRS 9 effective for periods beginning on or after January 1, 2018.
[5] IAS 1, *Presentation of Financial Statements*, paragraph 69.

EXHIBIT 3   HSBC Holdings plc Consolidated Statement of Financial Position (Excerpt: Assets Only) as of December 31 (in millions of US $)

Consolidated balance sheet—USD ($) $ in Millions	Dec. 31, 2017	Dec. 31, 2016
Assets		
Cash and balances at central banks	$180,624	$128,009
Items in the course of collection from other banks	6,628	5,003
Hong Kong Government certificates of indebtedness	34,186	31,228
Trading assets	287,995	235,125
Financial assets designated at fair value	29,464	24,756
Derivatives	219,818	290,872
Loans and advances to banks	90,393	88,126
Loans and advances to customers	962,964	861,504
Reverse repurchase agreements – non-trading	201,553	160,974
Financial investments	389,076	436,797
Prepayments, accrued income, and other assets	67,191	63,909
Current tax assets	1,006	1,145
Interests in associates and joint ventures	22,744	20,029
Goodwill and intangible assets	23,453	21,346
Deferred tax assets	4,676	6,163
Total assets	2,521,771	2,374,986

Source: HSBC Holdings plc 2017 Annual Report and Accounts.

3. CURRENT ASSETS AND CURRENT LIABILITIES

This section examines current assets and current liabilities in greater detail.

3.1. Current Assets

Accounting standards require that certain specific line items, if they are material, must be shown on a balance sheet. Among the current assets' required line items are cash and cash equivalents, trade and other receivables, inventories, and financial assets (with short maturities). Companies present other line items as needed, consistent with the requirements to separately present each material class of similar items. As examples, Exhibit 4 and Exhibit 5 present balance sheet excerpts for SAP Group and Apple Inc. showing the line items for the companies' current assets.

EXHIBIT 4   SAP Group Consolidated Statements of Financial Position (Excerpt: Current Assets Detail) (in millions of €)

Assets	As of December 31 2017	2016
Cash and cash equivalents	€4,011	€3,702
Other financial assets	990	1,124
Trade and other receivables	5,899	5,924
Other non-financial assets	725	581

EXHIBIT 4   (Continued)

	As of December 31	
Assets	2017	2016
Tax assets	306	233
Total current assets	11,930	11,564
Total non-current assets	30,567	32,713
Total assets	**42,497**	**44,277**
Total current liabilities	10,210	9,674
Total non-current liabilities	6,747	8,205
Total liabilities	16,958	17,880
Total equity	25,540	26,397
Total equity and liabilities	**€42,497**	**€44,277**

Source: SAP Group 2017 annual report.

EXHIBIT 5   Apple Inc. Consolidated Balance Sheet (Excerpt: Current Assets Detail) *
(in millions of $)

Assets	September 30, 2017	September 24, 2016
Cash and cash equivalents	$20,289	$20,484
Short-term marketable securities	53,892	46,671
Accounts receivable, less allowances of $58 and $53, respectively	17,874	15,754
Inventories	4,855	2,132
Vendor non-trade receivables	17,799	13,545
Other current assets	13,936	8,283
Total current assets	128,645	106,869
[All other assets]	*246,674*	*214,817*
Total assets	**375,319**	**321,686**
Total current liabilities	100,814	79,006
[Total non-current liabilities]	*140,458*	*114,431*
Total liabilities	241,272	193,437
Total shareholders' equity	134,047	128,249
Total liabilities and shareholders' equity	**$375,319**	**$321,686**

*Note: The italicized subtotals presented in this excerpt are not explicitly shown on the face of the financial statement as prepared by the company.

Source: Apple Inc. 2017 annual report (Form 10K).

3.1.1. Cash and Cash Equivalents

Cash equivalents are highly liquid, short-term investments that are so close to maturity,[6] the risk is minimal that their value will change significantly with changes in interest rates. Cash and cash equivalents are financial assets. Financial assets, in general, are measured and reported at either **amortized cost** or **fair value**. Amortized cost is the historical cost (initially recognised

---

[6] Generally, three months or less.

cost) of the asset adjusted for amortization and impairment. Under IFRS and US GAAP, fair value is based on an exit price, the price received to sell an asset or paid to transfer a liability in an orderly transaction between two market participants at the measurement date.

For cash and cash equivalents, amortized cost and fair value are likely to be immaterially different. Examples of cash equivalents are demand deposits with banks and highly liquid investments (such as US Treasury bills, commercial paper, and money market funds) with original maturities of three months or less. Cash and cash equivalents excludes amounts that are restricted in use for at least 12 months. For all companies, the Statement of Cash Flows presents information about the changes in cash over a period. For the fiscal year 2017, SAP Group's cash and cash equivalents increased from €3,702 million to €4,011 million, and Apple's cash and cash equivalents decreased from $20,484 million to $20,289 million.

3.1.2. Marketable Securities

Marketable securities are also financial assets and include investments in debt or equity securities that are traded in a public market, and whose value can be determined from price information in a public market. Examples of marketable securities include treasury bills, notes, bonds, and equity securities, such as common stocks and mutual fund shares. Companies disclose further detail in the notes to their financial statements about their holdings. For example, SAP Group discloses that its other financial assets consist of items such as time deposits, other receivables, and loans to employees and third parties. Apple's short-term marketable securities, totaling $53.9 billion and $46.7 billion at the end of fiscal 2017 and 2016, respectively, include holdings of US treasuries, corporate securities, commercial paper, and time deposits. Financial assets such as investments in debt and equity securities involve a variety of measurement issues and will be addressed in Section 4.5.

3.1.3. Trade Receivables

Trade receivables, also referred to as accounts receivable, are another type of financial asset. These are amounts owed to a company by its customers for products and services already delivered. They are typically reported at net realizable value, an approximation of fair value, based on estimates of collectability. Several aspects of accounts receivable are usually relevant to an analyst. First, the overall level of accounts receivable relative to sales (a topic to be addressed further in ratio analysis) is important because a significant increase in accounts receivable relative to sales could signal that the company is having problems collecting cash from its customers.

A second relevant aspect of accounts receivable is the allowance for doubtful accounts. The allowance for doubtful accounts reflects the company's estimate of the amount of receivables that will ultimately be uncollectible. Additions to the allowance in a particular period are reflected as bad debt expenses, and the balance of the allowance for doubtful accounts reduces the gross receivables amount to a net amount that is an estimate of net realizable value. When specific receivables are deemed to be uncollectible, they are written off by reducing accounts receivable and the allowance for doubtful accounts. The allowance for doubtful accounts is called a **contra account** because it is netted against (i.e., reduces) the balance of accounts receivable, which is an asset account. SAP Group's balance sheet, for example, reports current net trade and other receivables of €5,899 million as of December 31, 2017. The amount of the allowance for doubtful accounts (€74 million) is disclosed in the notes[7] to

---

[7] Note 13 SAP Group 2017 Annual report.

the financial statements. Apple discloses the allowance for doubtful accounts on the face of the balance sheet; as of September 30, 2017, the allowance was $58 million. The $17,874 million of accounts receivable on that date is net of the allowance. Apple's disclosures state that the allowance is based on "historical experience, the age of the accounts receivable balances, credit quality of the Company's customers, current economic conditions, and other factors that may affect customers' abilities to pay." The age of an accounts receivable balance refers to the length of time the receivable has been outstanding, including how many days past the due date.

Another relevant aspect of accounts receivable is the concentration of credit risk. For example, SAP Group's annual report discloses that concentration of credit risk is limited because they have a large customer base diversified across various industries, company sizes, and countries. Similarly, Apple's annual report notes that no single customer accounted for 10 percent or more of its revenues. However, Apple's disclosures for 2017 indicate that two customers individually represented 10% or more of its total trade receivables, and its cellular network carriers accounted for 59% of trade receivables. Of its vendor non-trade receivables, three vendors represent 42%, 19%, and 10% of the total.[8]

EXAMPLE 1   Analysis of Accounts Receivable

1. Based on the balance sheet excerpt for Apple Inc. in Exhibit 5, what percentage of its total accounts receivable in 2017 and 2016 does Apple estimate will be uncollectible?
2. In general, how does the amount of allowance for doubtful accounts relate to bad debt expense?
3. In general, what are some factors that could cause a company's allowance for doubtful accounts to decrease?

Solution to 1: ($ millions) The percentage of 2017 accounts receivable estimated to be uncollectible is 0.32 percent, calculated as $58/($17,874 + $58). Note that the $17,874 is net of the $58 allowance, so the gross amount of accounts receivable is determined by adding the allowance to the net amount. The percentage of 2016 accounts receivable estimated to be uncollectible is 0.34 percent [$53/($15,754 + $53)].

Solution to 2: Bad debt expense is an expense of the period, based on a company's estimate of the percentage of credit sales in the period, for which cash will ultimately not be collected. The allowance for bad debts is a contra asset account, which is netted against the asset accounts receivable.

To record the estimated bad debts, a company recognizes a bad debt expense (which affects net income) and increases the balance in the allowance for doubtful accounts by the same amount. To record the write off of a particular account receivable, a company reduces the balance in the allowance for doubtful accounts and reduces the balance in accounts receivable by the same amount.

---

[8] Page 53, Apple Inc 2017 10-K.

Solution to 3: In general, a decrease in a company's allowance for doubtful accounts in absolute terms could be caused by a decrease in the amount of credit sales.

Some factors that could cause a company's allowance for doubtful accounts to decrease as a percentage of accounts receivable include the following:

- Improvements in the credit quality of the company's existing customers (whether driven by a customer-specific improvement or by an improvement in the overall economy);
- Stricter credit policies (for example, refusing to allow less creditworthy customers to make credit purchases and instead requiring them to pay cash, to provide collateral, or to provide some additional form of financial backing); and/or
- Stricter risk management policies (for example, buying more insurance against potential defaults).

In addition to the business factors noted above, because the allowance is based on management's estimates of collectability, management can potentially bias these estimates to manipulate reported earnings. For example, a management team aiming to increase reported income could intentionally over-estimate collectability and under-estimate the bad debt expense for a period. Conversely, in a period of good earnings, management could under-estimate collectability and over-estimate the bad debt expense with the intent of reversing the bias in a period of poorer earnings.

3.1.4. Inventories

Inventories are physical products that will eventually be sold to the company's customers, either in their current form (finished goods) or as inputs into a process to manufacture a final product (raw materials and work-in-process). Like any manufacturer, Apple holds inventories. The 2017 balance sheet of Apple Inc. shows $4,855 million of inventories. SAP Group's balance sheet does not include a line item for inventory, consistent with the fact that SAP Group is primarily a software and services provider.

Inventories are measured at the lower of cost and net realizable value (NRV) under IFRS. The cost of inventories comprises all costs of purchase, costs of conversion, and other costs incurred in bringing the inventories to their present location and condition. NRV is the estimated selling price less the estimated costs of completion and costs necessary to complete the sale. NRV is applicable for all inventories under IFRS. Under US GAAP, inventories are also measured at the lower of cost and NRV unless they are measured using the last-in, first-out (LIFO) or retail inventory methods. When using LIFO or the retail inventory methods, inventories are measured at the lower of cost or market value. US GAAP defines market value as current replacement cost but with upper and lower limits; the recorded value cannot exceed NRV and cannot be lower than NRV less a normal profit margin.

If the net realizable value or market value (under US GAAP, in certain cases) of a company's inventory falls below its carrying amount, the company must write down the value of the inventory. The loss in value is reflected in the income statement. For example, within its

Management's Discussion and Analysis and notes, Apple indicates that the company reviews its inventory each quarter and records write-downs of inventory that has become obsolete, exceeds anticipated demand, or is carried at a value higher than its market value. Under IFRS, if inventory that was written down in a previous period subsequently increases in value, the amount of the original write-down is reversed. Subsequent reversal of an inventory write-down is not permitted under US GAAP.

When inventory is sold, the cost of that inventory is reported as an expense, "cost of goods sold." Accounting standards allow different valuation methods for determining the amounts that are included in cost of goods sold on the income statement and thus the amounts that are reported in inventory on the balance sheet. (Inventory valuation methods are referred to as cost formulas and cost flow assumptions under IFRS and US GAAP, respectively.) IFRS allows only the first-in, first-out (FIFO), weighted average cost, and specific identification methods. Some accounting standards (such as US GAAP) also allow last-in, first-out (LIFO) as an additional inventory valuation method. The LIFO method is not allowed under IFRS.

3.1.5. Other Current Assets

The amounts shown in "other current assets" reflect items that are individually not material enough to require a separate line item on the balance sheet and so are aggregated into a single amount. Companies usually disclose the components of other assets in a note to the financial statements. A typical item included in other current assets is prepaid expenses. **Prepaid expenses** are normal operating expenses that have been paid in advance. Because expenses are recognized in the period in which they are incurred—and not necessarily the period in which the payment is made—the advance payment of a future expense creates an asset. The asset (prepaid expenses) will be recognized as an expense in future periods as it is used up. For example, consider prepaid insurance. Assume a company pays its insurance premium for coverage over the next calendar year on December 31 of the current year. At the time of the payment, the company recognizes an asset (prepaid insurance expense). The expense is not incurred at that date; the expense is incurred as time passes (in this example, one-twelfth, 1/12, in each following month). Therefore, the expense is recognized, and the value of the asset is reduced in the financial statements over the course of the year.

SAP's notes to the financial statements disclose components of the amount shown as other non-financial assets on the balance sheet. The largest portion pertains to prepaid expenses, primarily prepayments for operating leases, support services, and software royalties. Apple's notes do not disclose components of other current assets.

3.2. Current Liabilities

Current liabilities are those liabilities that are expected to be settled in the entity's normal operating cycle, held primarily for trading, or due to be settled within 12 months after the balance sheet date. Exhibit 6 and Exhibit 7 present balance sheet excerpts for SAP Group and Apple Inc. showing the line items for the companies' current liabilities. Some of the common types of current liabilities, including trade payables, financial liabilities, accrued expenses, and deferred income, are discussed below.

EXHIBIT 6   SAP Group Consolidated Statements of Financial Position
(Excerpt: Current Liabilities Detail) (in millions of €)

	As of December 31	
	2017	2016
Assets		
Total current assets	11,930	11,564
Total non-current assets	30,567	32,713
Total assets	42,497	44,277
Equity and liabilities		
Trade and other payables	1,151	1,281
Tax liabilities	597	316
Financial liabilities	1,561	1,813
Other non-financial liabilities	3,946	3,699
Provisions	184	183
Deferred income	2,771	2,383
Total current liabilities	10,210	9,674
Total non-current liabilities	6,747	8,205
Total liabilities	16,958	17,880
Total equity	25,540	26,397
Total equity and liabilities	€42,497	€44,277

Source: SAP Group 2017 annual report.

EXHIBIT 7   Apple Inc. Consolidated Balance Sheet (Excerpt: Current Liabilities Detail)*
(in millions of $)

Assets	September 30, 2017	September 24, 2016
Total current assets	128,645	106,869
[All other assets]	*246,674*	*214,817*
Total assets	375,319	321,686
Liabilities and shareholders' equity		
Accounts payable	49,049	37,294
Accrued expenses	25,744	22,027
Deferred revenue	7,548	8,080
Commercial paper	11,977	8,105
Current portion of long-term debt	6,496	3,500
Total current liabilities	100,814	79,006
[Total non-current liabilities]	*140,458*	*114,431*
Total liabilities	241,272	193,437
Total shareholders' equity	134,047	128,249
Total liabilities and shareholders' equity	375,319	321,686

Note: The italicized subtotals presented in this excerpt are not explicitly shown on the face
of the financial statement as prepared by the company.

Source: Apple Inc. 2017 annual report (Form 10K).

Trade payables, also called **accounts payable**, are amounts that a company owes its vendors for purchases of goods and services. In other words, these represent the unpaid amount as of the balance sheet date of the company's purchases on credit. An issue relevant to analysts is the trend in overall levels of trade payables relative to purchases (a topic to be addressed further in ratio analysis). Significant changes in accounts payable relative to purchases could signal potential changes in the company's credit relationships with its suppliers. The general term "trade credit" refers to credit provided to a company by its vendors. Trade credit is a source of financing that allows the company to make purchases and then pay for those purchases at a later date.

Financial liabilities that are due within one year or the operating cycle, whichever is longer, appear in the current liability section of the balance sheet. Financial liabilities include borrowings such as bank loans, notes payable (which refers to financial liabilities owed by a company to creditors, including trade creditors and banks, through a formal loan agreement), and commercial paper. In addition, any portions of long-term liabilities that are due within one year (i.e., the current portion of long-term liabilities) are also shown in the current liability section of the balance sheet. According to its footnote disclosures, most of SAP's €1,561 million of current financial liabilities is for bonds payable due in the next year. Apple shows $11,977 million of commercial paper borrowing (short-term promissory notes issued by companies) and $6,496 million of long-term debt due within the next year.

Accrued expenses (also called accrued expenses payable, accrued liabilities, and other non-financial liabilities) are expenses that have been recognized on a company's income statement but not yet been paid as of the balance sheet date. For example, SAP's 2017 balance sheet shows €597 million of tax liabilities. In addition to income taxes payable, other common examples of accrued expenses are accrued interest payable, accrued warranty costs, and accrued employee compensation (i.e., wages payable). SAP's notes disclose that the €3,946 million line item of other non-financial liabilities in 2017, for example, includes €2,565 million of employee-related liabilities.

Deferred income (also called **deferred revenue** or **unearned revenue**) arises when a company receives payment in advance of delivery of the goods and services associated with the payment. The company has an obligation either to provide the goods or services or to return the cash received. Examples include lease payments received at the beginning of a lease, fees for servicing office equipment received at the beginning of the service period, and payments for magazine subscriptions received at the beginning of the subscription period. SAP's balance sheet shows deferred income of €2,771 million at the end of 2017, up slightly from €2,383 million at the end of 2016. Apple's balance sheet shows deferred revenue of $7,548 million at the end of fiscal 2017, down slightly from $8,080 million at the end of fiscal 2016. Example 2 presents each company's disclosures about deferred revenue and discusses some of the implications.

EXAMPLE 2   Analysis of Deferred Revenue

In the notes to its 2017 financial statements, SAP describes its deferred income as follows:

> Deferred income consists mainly of prepayments made by our customers for cloud subscriptions and support; software support and services; fees from multiple-element arrangements allocated to undelivered elements; and amounts ... for obligations to perform under acquired customer contracts in connection with acquisitions.

Apple's deferred revenue also arises from sales involving multiple elements, some delivered at the time of sale and others to be delivered in the future. In addition, Apple recognizes deferred revenue in connection with sales of gift cards as well as service contracts. In the notes to its 2017 financial statements, Apple describes its deferred revenue as follows:

> The Company records deferred revenue when it receives payments in advance of the delivery of products or the performance of services. This includes amounts that have been deferred for unspecified and specified software upgrade rights and non-software services that are attached to hardware and software products. The Company sells gift cards redeemable at its retail and online stores. . . . The Company records deferred revenue upon the sale of the card, which is relieved upon redemption of the card by the customer. Revenue from AppleCare service and support contracts is deferred and recognized over the service coverage periods. AppleCare service and support contracts typically include extended phone support, repair services, web-based support resources and diagnostic tools offered under the Company's standard limited warranty.

1. In general, in the period a transaction occurs, how would a company's balance sheet reflect $100 of deferred revenue resulting from a sale? (Assume, for simplicity, that the company receives cash for all sales, the company's income tax payable is 30 percent based on cash receipts, and the company pays cash for all relevant income tax obligations as they arise. Ignore any associated deferred costs.)
2. In general, how does deferred revenue impact a company's financial statements in the periods following its initial recognition?
3. Interpret the amounts shown by SAP as deferred income and by Apple as deferred revenue.
4. Both accounts payable and deferred revenue are classified as current liabilities. Discuss the following statements:
   A. When assessing a company's liquidity, the implication of amounts in accounts payable differs from the implication of amounts in deferred revenue.
   B. Some investors monitor amounts in deferred revenue as an indicator of future revenue growth.

Solution to 1: In the period that deferred revenue arises, the company would record a $100 increase in the asset Cash and a $100 increase in the liability Deferred Revenues. In addition, because the company's income tax payable is based on cash receipts and is paid in the current period, the company would record a $30 decrease in the asset Cash and a $30 increase in the asset Deferred Tax Assets. Deferred tax assets increase because the company has paid taxes on revenue it has not yet recognized for accounting purposes. In effect, the company has prepaid taxes from an accounting perspective.

Solution to 2: In subsequent periods, the company will recognize the deferred revenue as it is earned. When the revenue is recognized, the liability Deferred Revenue will decrease. In addition, the tax expense is recognized on the income statement as the revenue is recognized, and thus the associated amounts of Deferred Tax Assets will decrease.

Solution to 3: The deferred income on SAP's balance sheet and deferred revenue on Apple's balance sheet at the end of their respective 2017 fiscal years will be recognized as revenue, sales, or a similar item in income statements subsequent to the 2017 fiscal year, as the goods or services are provided or the obligation is reduced. The costs of delivering the goods or services will also be recognised.

Solution to 4A: The amount of accounts payable represents a future obligation to pay cash to suppliers. In contrast, the amount of deferred revenue represents payments that the company has already received from its customers, and the future obligation is to deliver the related services. With respect to liquidity, settling accounts payable will require cash outflows whereas settling deferred revenue obligations will not.

Solution to 4B: Some investors monitor amounts in deferred revenue as an indicator of future growth because the amounts in deferred revenue will be recognized as revenue in the future. Thus, growth in the amount of deferred revenue implies future growth of that component of a company's revenue.

4. NON-CURRENT ASSETS

This section provides an overview of assets other than current assets, sometimes collectively referred to as non-current, long-term, or long-lived assets. The categories discussed are property, plant, and equipment; investment property; intangible assets; goodwill; financial assets; and deferred tax assets. Exhibit 8 and Exhibit 9 present balance sheet excerpts for SAP Group and Apple Inc. showing the line items for the companies' non-current assets.

EXHIBIT 8   SAP Group Consolidated Statements of Financial Position (Excerpt: Non-Current Assets Detail) (in millions of €)

	As of December 31	
Assets	2017	2016
Total current assets	11,930	11,564
Goodwill	21,274	23,311
Intangible assets	2,967	3,786
Property, plant and equipment	2,967	2,580
Other financial assets	1,155	1,358
Trade and other receivables	118	126
Other non-financial assets	621	532
Tax assets	443	450
Deferred tax assets	1,022	571
Total non-current assets	30,567	32,713
Total assets	**42,497**	**44,277**
Total current liabilities	10,210	9,674
Total non-current liabilities	6,747	8,205
Total liabilities	**16,958**	**17,880**
Total equity	**25,540**	**26,397**
Total equity and liabilities	**€42,497**	**€44,277**

Source: SAP Group 2017 annual report.

EXHIBIT 9   Apple Inc. Consolidated Balance Sheet (Excerpt: Non-Current Assets Detail)*
(in millions of $)

Assets	September 30, 2017	September 24, 2016
Total current assets	128,645	106,869
Long-term marketable securities	194,714	170,430
Property, plant and equipment, net	33,783	27,010
Goodwill	5,717	5,414
Acquired intangible assets, net	2,298	3,206
Other non-current assets	10,162	8,757
[All other assets]	*246,674*	*214,817*
Total assets	375,319	321,686
Liabilities and shareholders' equity		
Total current liabilities	100,814	79,006
[Total non-current liabilities]	*140,458*	*114,431*
Total liabilities	241,272	193,437
Total shareholders' equity	134,047	128,249
Total liabilities and shareholders' equity	375,319	321,686

*Note: The italicized subtotals presented in this excerpt are not explicitly shown on the face of
the financial statement as prepared by the company.
Source: Apple Inc. 2017 annual report (Form 10K).

4.1. Property, Plant, and Equipment

Property, plant, and equipment (PPE) are tangible assets that are used in company operations and expected to be used (provide economic benefits) over more than one fiscal period.
Examples of tangible assets treated as property, plant, and equipment include land, buildings, equipment, machinery, furniture, and natural resources such as mineral and petroleum
resources. IFRS permits companies to report PPE using either a cost model or a revaluation
model.[9] While IFRS permits companies to use the cost model for some classes of assets and the
revaluation model for others, the company must apply the same model to all assets within a
particular class of assets. US GAAP permits only the cost model for reporting PPE.

Under the cost model, PPE is carried at amortized cost (historical cost less any accumulated depreciation or accumulated depletion, and less any impairment losses). Historical cost
generally consists of an asset's purchase price, plus its delivery cost, and any other additional
costs incurred to make the asset operable (such as costs to install a machine). Depreciation and
depletion refer to the process of allocating (recognizing as an expense) the cost of a long-lived
asset over its useful life. Land is not depreciated. Because PPE is presented on the balance sheet
net of depreciation and depreciation expense is recognised in the income statement, the choice
of depreciation method and the related estimates of useful life and salvage value impact both a
company's balance sheet and income statement.

Whereas depreciation is the systematic allocation of cost over an asset's useful life,
impairment losses reflect an unanticipated decline in value. Impairment occurs when the

---

[9] IAS 16, *Property, Plant and Equipment*, paragraphs 29-31.

asset's recoverable amount is less than its carrying amount, with terms defined as follows under IFRS:[10]

- Recoverable amount: The higher of an asset's fair value less cost to sell, and its value in use.
- Fair value less cost to sell: The amount obtainable in a sale of the asset in an arms-length transaction between knowledgeable willing parties, less the costs of the sale.
- Value in use: The present value of the future cash flows expected to be derived from the asset.

When an asset is considered impaired, the company recognizes the impairment loss in the income statement in the period the impairment is identified. Reversals of impairment losses are permitted under IFRS but not under US GAAP.

Under the revaluation model, the reported and carrying value for PPE is the fair value at the date of revaluation less any subsequent accumulated depreciation. Changes in the value of PPE under the revaluation model affect equity directly or profit and loss depending upon the circumstances.

In Exhibits 8 and 9, SAP reports €2,967 million of PPE, and Apple reports $33,783 million of PPE at the end of fiscal year 2017. For SAP, PPE represents approximately 7 percent of total assets, and for Apple PPE represents approximately 9 percent of total assets. Both companies disclose in the notes that PPE are generally depreciated over their expected useful lives using the straight-line method.

4.2. Investment Property

Some property is not used in the production of goods or services or for administrative purposes. Instead, it is used to earn rental income or capital appreciation (or both). Under IFRS, such property is considered to be **investment property**.[11] US GAAP does not include a specific definition for investment property. IFRS provides companies with the choice to report investment property using either a cost model or a fair value model. In general, a company must apply its chosen model (cost or fair value) to all of its investment property. The cost model for investment property is identical to the cost model for PPE: In other words, investment property is carried at cost less any accumulated depreciation and any accumulated impairment losses. Under the fair value model, investment property is carried at its fair value. When a company uses the fair value model to measure the value of its investment property, any gain or loss arising from a change in the fair value of the investment property is recognized in profit and loss, i.e., on the income statement, in the period in which it arises.[12]

Neither SAP Group nor Apple discloses ownership of investment property. The types of companies that typically hold investment property are real estate investment companies or property management companies. Entities such as life insurance companies and endowment funds may also hold investment properties as part of their investment portfolio.

4.3. Intangible Assets

Intangible assets are identifiable non-monetary assets without physical substance.[13] An identifiable asset can be acquired singly (can be separated from the entity) or is the result of specific

---

[10] IAS 36, *Impairment of Assets*, paragraph 6. US GAAP uses a different approach to impairment.

[11] IAS 40, *Investment Property*.

[12] IAS 40, *Investment Property*, paragraph 35.

[13] IAS 38, *Intangible Assets*, paragraph 8.

contractual or legal rights or privileges. Examples include patents, licenses, and trademarks. The most common asset that is not a separately identifiable asset is accounting goodwill, which arises in business combinations and is discussed further in Section 4.4.

IFRS allows companies to report intangible assets using either a cost model or a revaluation model. The revaluation model can only be selected when there is an active market for an intangible asset. These measurement models are essentially the same as described for PPE. US GAAP permits only the cost model.

For each intangible asset, a company assesses whether the useful life of the asset is finite or indefinite. Amortization and impairment principles apply as follows:

- An intangible asset with a finite useful life is amortized on a systematic basis over the best estimate of its useful life, with the amortization method and useful life estimate reviewed at least annually.
- Impairment principles for an intangible asset with a finite useful life are the same as for PPE.
- An intangible asset with an indefinite useful life is not amortized. Instead, at least annually, the reasonableness of assuming an indefinite useful life for the asset is reviewed, and the asset is tested for impairment.

Financial analysts have traditionally viewed the values assigned to intangible assets, particularly goodwill, with caution. Consequently, in assessing financial statements, analysts often exclude the book value assigned to intangibles, reducing net equity by an equal amount and increasing pretax income by any amortization expense or impairment associated with the intangibles. An arbitrary assignment of zero value to intangibles is not advisable; instead, an analyst should examine each listed intangible and assess whether an adjustment should be made. Note disclosures about intangible assets may provide useful information to the analyst. These disclosures include information about useful lives, amortization rates and methods, and impairment losses recognised or reversed.

Further, a company may have developed intangible assets internally that can only be recognized in certain circumstances. Companies may also have assets that are never recorded on a balance sheet because they have no physical substance and are non-identifiable. These assets might include management skill, name recognition, a good reputation, and so forth. Such assets are valuable and are, in theory, reflected in the price at which the company's equity securities trade in the market (and the price at which the entirety of the company's equity would be sold in an acquisition transaction). Such assets may be recognised as goodwill if a company is acquired, but are not recognised until an acquisition occurs.

4.3.1. Identifiable Intangibles

Under IFRS, identifiable intangible assets are recognised on the balance sheet if it is probable that future economic benefits will flow to the company and the cost of the asset can be measured reliably. Examples of identifiable intangible assets include patents, trademarks, copyrights, franchises, licenses, and other rights. Identifiable intangible assets may have been created internally or purchased by a company. Determining the cost of internally created intangible assets can be difficult and subjective. For these reasons, under IFRS and US GAAP, the general requirement is that internally created identifiable intangibles are expensed rather than reported on the balance sheet.

IFRS provides that for internally created intangible assets, the company must separately identify the research phase and the development phase.[14] The research phase includes activities

---

[14] IAS 38, *Intangible Assets*, paragraphs 51–67.

that seek new knowledge or products. The development phase occurs after the research phase and includes design or testing of prototypes and models. IFRS require that costs to internally generate intangible assets during the research phase must be expensed on the income statement. Costs incurred in the development stage can be capitalized as intangible assets if certain criteria are met, including technological feasibility, the ability to use or sell the resulting asset, and the ability to complete the project.

US GAAP prohibits the capitalization as an asset of most costs of internally developed intangibles and research and development. All such costs usually must be expensed. Costs related to the following categories are typically expensed under IFRS and US GAAP. They include:

- internally generated brands, mastheads, publishing titles, customer lists, etc.;
- start-up costs;
- training costs;
- administrative and other general overhead costs;
- advertising and promotion;
- relocation and reorganization expenses; and
- redundancy and other termination costs.

Generally, acquired intangible assets are reported as separately identifiable intangibles (as opposed to goodwill) if they arise from contractual rights (such as a licensing agreement), other legal rights (such as patents), or have the ability to be separated and sold (such as a customer list).

EXAMPLE 3   Measuring Intangible Assets

Alpha Inc., a motor vehicle manufacturer, has a research division that worked on the following projects during the year:

Project 1:   Research aimed at finding a steering mechanism that does not operate like a conventional steering wheel but reacts to the impulses from a driver's fingers.

Project 2:   The design of a prototype welding apparatus that is controlled electronically rather than mechanically. The apparatus has been determined to be technologically feasible, salable, and feasible to produce.

The following is a summary of the expenses of the research division (in thousands of €):

	General	Project 1	Project 2
Material and services	128	935	620
Labor			
• Direct labor	—	630	320
• Administrative personnel	720	—	—
Design, construction, and testing	270	450	470

Five percent of administrative personnel costs can be attributed to each of Projects 1 and 2. Explain the accounting treatment of Alpha's costs for Projects 1 and 2 under IFRS and US GAAP.

Solution: Under IFRS, the capitalization of development costs for Projects 1 and 2 would be as follows:

		Amount Capitalized as an Asset (€'000)
Project 1:	Classified as in the research stage, so all costs are recognized as expenses.	NIL
Project 2:	Classified as in the development stage, so costs may be capitalized. Note that administrative costs are not capitalized.	(620 + 320 + 410 + 60) = 1,410

Under US GAAP, the costs of Projects 1 and 2 are expensed.

As presented in Exhibits 8 and 9, SAP's 2017 balance sheet shows €2,967 million of intangible assets, and Apple's 2017 balance sheet shows acquired intangible assets, net of $2,298 million. SAP's notes disclose the types of intangible assets (software and database licenses, purchased software to be incorporated into its products, customer contracts, and acquired trademark licenses) and notes that all of its purchased intangible assets other than goodwill have finite useful lives and are amortized either based on expected consumption of economic benefits or on a straight-line basis over their estimated useful lives which range from 2 to 20 years. Apple's notes disclose that its acquired intangible assets consist primarily of patents and licenses, and almost the entire amount represents definite-lived and amortizable assets for which the remaining weighted-average amortization period is 3.4 years as of 2017.

4.4. Goodwill

When one company acquires another, the purchase price is allocated to all the identifiable assets (tangible and intangible) and liabilities acquired, based on fair value. If the purchase price is greater than the acquirer's interest in the fair value of the identifiable assets and liabilities acquired, the excess amount is recognized as an asset, described as **goodwill**. To understand why an acquirer would pay more to purchase a company than the fair value of the target company's identifiable assets net of liabilities, consider the following three observations. First, as noted, certain items not recognized in a company's own financial statements (e.g., its reputation, established distribution system, trained employees) have value. Second, a target company's expenditures in research and development may not have resulted in a separately identifiable asset that meets the criteria for recognition but nonetheless may have created some value. Third, part of the value of an acquisition may arise from strategic positioning versus a competitor or from perceived synergies. The purchase price might not pertain solely to the separately identifiable assets and liabilities acquired and thus may exceed the value of those net assets due to the acquisition's role in protecting the value of all of the acquirer's existing assets or to cost savings and benefits from combining the companies.

The subject of recognizing goodwill in financial statements has found both proponents and opponents among professionals. The proponents of goodwill recognition assert that goodwill is the present value of excess returns that a company is expected to earn. This group claims that determining the present value of these excess returns is analogous to determining the present value of future cash flows associated with other assets and projects. Opponents of goodwill recognition claim that the prices paid for acquisitions often turn out to be based on unrealistic expectations, thereby leading to future write-offs of goodwill.

Analysts should distinguish between accounting goodwill and economic goodwill. Economic goodwill is based on the economic performance of the entity, whereas accounting goodwill is based on accounting standards and is reported only in the case of acquisitions. Economic goodwill is important to analysts and investors, and it is not necessarily reflected on the balance sheet. Instead, economic goodwill is reflected in the stock price (at least in theory). Some financial statement users believe that goodwill should not be listed on the balance sheet, because it cannot be sold separately from the entity. These financial statement users believe that only assets that can be separately identified and sold should be reflected on the balance sheet. Other financial statement users analyze goodwill and any subsequent impairment charges to assess management's performance on prior acquisitions.

Under both IFRS and US GAAP, accounting goodwill arising from acquisitions is capitalized. Goodwill is not amortized but is tested for impairment annually. If goodwill is deemed to be impaired, an impairment loss is charged against income in the current period. An impairment loss reduces current earnings. An impairment loss also reduces total assets, so some performance measures, such as return on assets (net income divided by average total assets), may actually increase in future periods. An impairment loss is a non-cash item.

Accounting standards' requirements for recognizing goodwill can be summarized by the following steps:

A. The total cost to purchase the target company (the acquiree) is determined.
B. The acquiree's identifiable assets are measured at fair value. The acquiree's liabilities and contingent liabilities are measured at fair value. The difference between the fair value of identifiable assets and the fair value of the liabilities and contingent liabilities equals the net identifiable assets acquired.
C. Goodwill arising from the purchase is the excess of a) the cost to purchase the target company over b) the net identifiable assets acquired. Occasionally, a transaction will involve the purchase of net identifiable assets with a value greater than the cost to purchase. Such a transaction is called a "bargain purchase." Any gain from a bargain purchase is recognized in profit and loss in the period in which it arises.[15]

Companies are also required to disclose information that enables users to evaluate the nature and financial effect of business combinations. The required disclosures include, for example, the acquisition date fair value of the total cost to purchase the target company, the acquisition date amount recognized for each major class of assets and liabilities, and a qualitative description of the factors that make up the goodwill recognized.

Despite the guidance incorporated in accounting standards, analysts should be aware that the estimations of fair value involve considerable management judgment. Values for intangible assets, such as computer software, might not be easily validated when analyzing acquisitions.

---

[15] IFRS 3 *Business Combinations* and FASB ASC 805 [Business Combinations].

Management judgment about valuation in turn impacts current and future financial statements because identifiable intangible assets with definite lives are amortized over time. In contrast, neither goodwill nor identifiable intangible assets with indefinite lives are amortized; instead, as noted, both are tested annually for impairment.

The recognition and impairment of goodwill can significantly affect the comparability of financial statements between companies. Therefore, analysts often adjust the companies' financial statements by removing the impact of goodwill. Such adjustments include:

- excluding goodwill from balance sheet data used to compute financial ratios, and
- excluding goodwill impairment losses from income data used to examine operating trends.

In addition, analysts can develop expectations about a company's performance following an acquisition by taking into account the purchase price paid relative to the net assets and earnings prospects of the acquired company. Example 4 provides an historical example of goodwill impairment.

EXAMPLE 4   Goodwill Impairment

Safeway, Inc., is a North American food and drug retailer. On February 25, 2010, Safeway issued a press release that included the following information:

> Safeway Inc. today reported a net loss of $1,609.1 million ($4.06 per diluted share) for the 16-week fourth quarter of 2009. Excluding a non-cash goodwill impairment charge of $1,818.2 million, net of tax ($4.59 per diluted share), net income would have been $209.1 million ($0.53 per diluted share). Net income was $338.0 million ($0.79 per diluted share) for the 17-week fourth quarter of 2008.
>
> In the fourth quarter of 2009, Safeway recorded a non-cash goodwill impairment charge of $1,974.2 million ($1,818.2 million, net of tax). The impairment was due primarily to Safeway's reduced market capitalization and a weak economy....The goodwill originated from previous acquisitions.
>
> Safeway's balance sheet as of 2 January 2010 showed goodwill of $426.6 million and total assets of $14,963.6 million. The company's balance sheet as of January 3, 2009 showed goodwill of $2,390.2 million and total assets of $17,484.7 million.

1. How significant is this goodwill impairment charge?
2. With reference to acquisition prices, what might this goodwill impairment indicate?

Solution to 1: The goodwill impairment was more than 80 percent of the total value of goodwill and 11 percent of total assets, so it was clearly significant. (The charge of $1,974.2 million equals 82.6 percent of the $2,390.2 million of goodwill at the beginning of the year and 11.3 percent of the $17,484.7 million total assets at the beginning of the year.)

> *Solution to 2:* The goodwill had originated from previous acquisitions. The impairment charge implies that the acquired operations are now worth less than the price that was paid for their acquisition.

As presented in Exhibits 8 and 9, SAP's 2017 balance sheet shows €21,274 million of goodwill, and Apple's 2017 balance sheet shows goodwill of $5,717 million. Goodwill represents 50.1 percent of SAP's total assets and only 1.5 percent of Apple's total assets. An analyst may be concerned that goodwill represents such a high proportion of SAP's total assets.

4.5. Financial Assets

IFRS define a financial instrument as a contract that gives rise to a financial asset of one entity, and a financial liability or equity instrument of another entity.[16] This section will focus on financial assets such as a company's investments in stocks issued by another company or its investments in the notes, bonds, or other fixed-income instruments issued by another company (or issued by a governmental entity). Financial liabilities such as notes payable and bonds payable issued by the company itself will be discussed in the liability portion of this chapter. Some financial instruments may be classified as either an asset or a liability depending on the contractual terms and current market conditions. One example of such a financial instrument is a derivative. **Derivatives** are financial instruments for which the value is derived based on some underlying factor (interest rate, exchange rate, commodity price, security price, or credit rating) and for which little or no initial investment is required.

Financial instruments are generally recognized when the entity becomes a party to the contractual provisions of the instrument. In general, there are two basic alternative ways that financial instruments are measured subsequent to initial acquisition: fair value or amortized cost. Recall that fair value is the price that would be received to sell an asset or paid to transfer a liability in an orderly market transaction.[17] The **amortized cost** of a financial asset (or liability) is the amount at which it was initially recognized, minus any principal repayments, plus or minus any amortization of discount or premium, and minus any reduction for impairment.

Under IFRS, financial assets are subsequently measured at amortized cost if the asset's cash flows occur on specified dates and consist solely of principal and interest, and if the business model is to hold the asset to maturity. The concept is similar in US GAAP, where this category of asset is referred to as **held-to-maturity**. An example is an investment in a long-term bond issued by another company or by a government; the value of the bond will fluctuate, for example with interest rate movements, but if the bond is classified as a held-to-maturity investment, it will be measured at amortized cost on the balance sheet of the investing company. Other types of financial assets measured at historical cost are loans to other companies.

Financial assets not measured at amortized cost subsequent to acquisition are measured at fair value as of the reporting date. For financial instruments measured at fair value, there are two basic alternatives in how net changes in fair value are recognized: as profit or loss on the income statement, or as other comprehensive income (loss) which bypasses the income statement. Note that these alternatives refer to *un*realized changes in fair value, i.e., changes in the value of a financial asset that has not been sold and is still owned at the end of the period. Unrealized gains and losses are also referred to as holding period gains and losses. If a financial

---

[16] IAS 32, *Financial Instruments: Presentation*, paragraph 11.
[17] IFRS 13 *Fair Value Measurement* and US GAAP ASC 820 *Fair Value Measurement*.

asset is sold within the period, a gain is realized if the selling price is greater than the carrying value, and a loss is realized if the selling price is less than the carrying value. When a financial asset is sold, any realized gain or loss is reported on the income statement.

Under IFRS, financial assets are subsequently measured at fair value through other comprehensive income (i.e., any unrealized holding gains or losses are recognized in other comprehensive income) if the business model's objective involves both collecting contractual cash flows and selling the financial assets. This IFRS category applies specifically to debt investments, namely assets with cash flows occurring on specified dates and consisting solely of principal and interest. However, IFRS also permits equity investments to be measured at fair value through other comprehensive income if, at the time a company buys an equity investment, the company decides to make an irrevocable election to measure the asset in this manner.[18] The concept is similar to the US GAAP investment category **available-for-sale** in which assets are measured at fair value, with any unrealized holding gains or losses recognized in other comprehensive income. However, unlike IFRS, the US GAAP category available-for-sale applies only to debt securities and is not permitted for investments in equity securities.[19]

Under IFRS, financial assets are subsequently measured at fair value through profit or loss (i.e., any unrealized holding gains or losses are recognized in the income statement) if they are not assigned to either of the other two measurement categories described above. In addition, IFRS allows a company to make an irrevocable election at acquisition to measure a financial asset in this category. Under US GAAP, all investments in equity securities (other than investments giving rise to ownership positions that confer significant influence over the investee) are measured at fair value with unrealized holding gains or losses recognized in the income statement. Under US GAAP, debt securities designated as trading securities are also measured at fair value with unrealized holding gains or losses recognized in the income statement. The trading securities category pertains to a debt security that is acquired with the intent of selling it rather than holding it to collect the interest and principal payments.

Exhibit 10 summarizes how various financial assets are classified and measured subsequent to acquisition.

EXHIBIT 10   Measurement of Financial Assets

Measured at Cost or Amortized Cost	Measured at Fair Value through Other Comprehensive Income	Measured at Fair Value through Profit and Loss
• Debt securities that are to be held to maturity. • Loans and notes receivable • Unquoted equity instruments (in limited circumstances where the fair value is not reliably measurable, cost may serve as a proxy (estimate) for fair value)	• "Available-for-sale" debt securities (US GAAP); Debt securities where the business model involves both collecting interest and principal and selling the security (IFRS) • Equity investments for which the company irrevocably elects this measurement at acquisition (IFRS only)	• All equity securities unless the investment gives the investor significant influence (US GAAP only) • "Trading" debt securities (US GAAP) • Securities not assigned to either of the other two categories, or investments for which the company irrevocably elects this measurement at acquisition (IFRS only)

---

[18] IFRS 7 *Financial Instruments: Disclosures*, paragraph 8(h) and IFRS 9 *Financial Instruments*, paragraph 5.7.5.

[19] US GAAP ASU 2016-01 and ASC 32X *Investments*.

To illustrate the different accounting treatments of the gains and losses on financial assets, consider an entity that invests €100,000,000 on January 1, 200X in a fixed-income security investment, with a 5 percent coupon paid semi-annually. After six months, the company receives the first coupon payment of €2,500,000. Additionally, market interest rates have declined such that the value of the fixed-income investment has increased by €2,000,000 as of 30 June 200X. Exhibit 11 illustrates how this situation will be portrayed in the balance sheet and income statement (ignoring taxes) of the entity concerned, under each of the following three measurement categories of financial assets: assets held for trading purposes, assets available for sale, and held-to-maturity assets.

EXHIBIT 11   Accounting for Gains and Losses on Marketable Securities

IFRS Categories	Measured at Cost or Amortized Cost	Measured at Fair Value through Other Comprehensive Income	Measured at Fair Value through Profit and Loss
US GAAP Comparable Categories	*Held to Maturity*	*Available-for-Sale Debt Securities*	*Trading Debt Securities*
Income Statement for Period January 1–June 30, 200X			
Interest income	2,500,000	2,500,000	2,500,000
Unrealized gains	—	—	2,000,000
Impact on profit and loss	2,500,000	2,500,000	4,500,000
Balance Sheet as of June 30, 200X			
Assets			
Cash and cash equivalents	2,500,000	2,500,000	2,500,000
Cost of securities	100,000,000	100,000,000	100,000,000
Unrealized gains on securities	—	2,000,000	2,000,000
	102,500,000	104,500,000	104,500,000
Liabilities			
Equity			
Paid-in capital	100,000,000	100,000,000	100,000,000
Retained earnings	2,500,000	2,500,000	4,500,000
Accumulated other comprehensive income	—	2,000,000	—
	102,500,000	104,500,000	104,500,000

In the case of held-to-maturity securities, the income statement shows only the interest income (which is then reflected in retained earnings of the ending balance sheet). Because the securities are measured at cost rather than fair value, no unrealized gain is recognized. On the balance sheet, the investment asset is shown at its amortized cost of €100,000,000. In the case of securities classified as Measured at Fair Value through Other Comprehensive

Income (IFRS) or equivalently as Available-for-sale debt securities (US GAAP), the income statement shows only the interest income (which is then reflected in retained earnings of the balance sheet). The unrealized gain does not appear on the income statement; instead, it would appear on a Statement of Comprehensive Income as Other Comprehensive Income. On the balance sheet, the investment asset is shown at its fair value of €102,000,000. (Exhibit 11 shows the unrealized gain on a separate line solely to highlight the impact of the change in value. In practice, the investments would be shown at their fair value on a single line.) In the case of securities classified as Measured at Fair Value through Profit and Loss (IFRS) or equivalently as trading debt securities (US GAAP), both the interest income and the unrealized gain are included on the income statement and thus reflected in retained earnings on the balance sheet.

In Exhibits 4 and 8, SAP's 2017 balance sheet shows other financial assets of €990 million (current) and €1,155 million (non-current). The company's notes disclose that the largest component of the current financial assets are loans and other financial receivables (€793 million), and the largest component of the non-current financial assets is €827 million of available-for-sale equity investments.

In Exhibits 5 and 9, Apple's 2017 balance sheet shows $53,892 million of short-term marketable securities and $194,714 million of long-term marketable securities. In total, marketable securities represent more than 66 percent of Apple's $375.3 billion in total assets. Marketable securities plus cash and cash equivalents represent around 72 percent of the company's total assets. Apple's notes disclose that most of the company's marketable securities are fixed-income securities issued by the US government or its agencies ($60,237 million) and by other companies including commercial paper ($153,451 million). In accordance with its investment policy, Apple invests in highly rated securities (which the company defines as investment grade) and limits its credit exposure to any one issuer. The company classifies its marketable securities as available for sale and reports them on the balance sheet at fair value. Unrealized gains and losses are reported in other comprehensive income.

4.6. Deferred Tax Assets

Portions of the amounts shown as **deferred tax assets** on SAP's balance sheet represent income taxes incurred prior to the time that the income tax expense will be recognized on the income statement. Deferred tax assets may result when the actual **income tax payable** based on income for tax purposes in a period exceeds the amount of income tax expense based on the reported financial statement income due to temporary timing differences. For example, a company may be required to report certain income for tax purposes in the current period but to defer recognition of that income for financial statement purposes to subsequent periods. In this case, the company will pay income tax as required by tax laws, and the difference between the taxes payable and the tax expense related to the income for which recognition was deferred on the financial statements will be reported as a deferred tax asset. When the income is subsequently recognized on the income statement, the related tax expense is also recognized, which will reduce the deferred tax asset.

Also, a company may claim certain expenses for financial statement purposes that it is only allowed to claim in subsequent periods for tax purposes. In this case, as in the previous example, the financial statement income before taxes is less than taxable income. Thus, income taxes payable based on taxable income exceeds income tax expense based on accounting net income before taxes. The difference is expected to reverse in the future when the income reported on the financial statements exceeds the taxable income as a deduction for the expense becomes allowed for tax purposes. Deferred tax assets may also result from carrying forward unused tax losses and credits (these are not temporary timing differences). Deferred tax assets are only to be recognized if there is an expectation that there will be taxable income in the future, against which the temporary difference or carried forward tax losses or credits can be applied to reduce taxes payable.

5. NON-CURRENT LIABILITIES

All liabilities that are not classified as current are considered to be non-current or long-term. Exhibits 12 and 13 present balance sheet excerpts for SAP Group and Apple Inc. showing the line items for the companies' non-current liabilities.

Both companies' balance sheets show non-current unearned revenue (deferred income for SAP Group and deferred revenue for Apple). These amounts represent the amounts of unearned revenue relating to goods and services expected to be delivered in periods beyond 12 months following the reporting period. The sections that follow focus on two common types of non-current (long-term) liabilities: long-term financial liabilities and deferred tax liabilities.

EXHIBIT 12   SAP Group Consolidated Statements of Financial Position (Excerpt: Non-Current Liabilities Detail) (in millions of €)

	as of December 31	
	2017	2016
Assets		
Total current assets	11,930	11,564
Total non-current assets	30,567	32,713
Total assets	42,497	44,277
Total current liabilities	10,210	9,674
Trade and other payables	119	127
Tax liabilities	470	365
Financial liabilities	5,034	6,481
Other non-financial liabilities	503	461
Provisions	303	217
Deferred tax liabilities	240	411
Deferred income	79	143
Total non-current liabilities	6,747	8,205
Total liabilities	16,958	17,880
Total equity	25,540	26,397
Total equity and liabilities	€42,497	€44,277

Source: SAP Group 2017 annual report.

EXHIBIT 13   Apple Inc. Consolidated Balance Sheet (Excerpt: Non-Current Liabilities Detail)*
(in millions of $)

Assets	September 30, 2017	September 24, 2016
Total current assets	128,645	106,869
[All other assets]	*246,674*	*214,817*
Total assets	375,319	321,686
Liabilities and shareholders' equity		
Total current liabilities	100,814	79,006
Deferred revenue, non-current	2,836	2,930
Long-term debt	97,207	75,427
Other non-current liabilities	40,415	36,074
[Total non-current liabilities]	*140,458*	*114,431*
Total liabilities	241,272	193,437
Total shareholders' equity	134,047	128,249
Total liabilities and shareholders' equity	375,319	321,686

Note: The italicized subtotals presented in this excerpt are not explicitly shown on the face of the
financial statement as prepared by the company.
Source: Apple Inc. 2017 annual report (Form 10K).

5.1. Long-term Financial Liabilities

Typical long-term financial liabilities include loans (i.e., borrowings from banks) and notes
or bonds payable (i.e., fixed-income securities issued to investors). Liabilities such as loans
payable and bonds payable are usually reported at amortized cost on the balance sheet. At
maturity, the amortized cost of the bond (carrying amount) will be equal to the face value
of the bond. For example, if a company issues $10,000,000 of bonds at par, the bonds are
reported as a long-term liability of $10 million. The carrying amount (amortized cost) from
the date of issue to the date of maturity remains at $10 million. As another example, if a
company issues $10,000,000 of bonds at a price of 97.50 (a discount to par), the bonds
are reported as a liability of $9,750,000 at issue date. Over the bond's life, the discount of
$250,000 is amortized so that the bond will be reported as a liability of $10,000,000 at
maturity. Similarly, any bond premium would be amortized for bonds issued at a price in
excess of face or par value.

In certain cases, liabilities such as bonds issued by a company are reported at fair value.
Those cases include financial liabilities held for trading, derivatives that are a liability to the
company, and some non-derivative instruments such as those that are hedged by derivatives.

SAP's balance sheet in Exhibit 12 shows €5,034 million of financial liabilities, and the
notes disclose that these liabilities are mostly for bonds payable. Apple's balance sheet shows
$97,207 million of long-term debt, and the notes disclose that this debt includes floating- and
fixed-rate notes with varying maturities.

5.2. Deferred Tax Liabilities

Deferred tax liabilities result from temporary timing differences between a company's income
as reported for tax purposes (taxable income) and income as reported for financial statement

purposes (reported income). Deferred tax liabilities result when taxable income and the actual income tax payable in a period based on it is less than the reported financial statement income before taxes and the income tax expense based on it. Deferred tax liabilities are defined as the amounts of income taxes payable in future periods in respect of taxable temporary differences.[20] In contrast, in the previous discussion of unearned revenue, inclusion of revenue in taxable income in an earlier period created a deferred tax asset (essentially prepaid tax).

Deferred tax liabilities typically arise when items of expense are included in taxable income in earlier periods than for financial statement net income. This results in taxable income being less than income before taxes in the earlier periods. As a result, taxes payable based on taxable income are less than income tax expense based on accounting income before taxes. The difference between taxes payable and income tax expense results in a deferred tax liability—for example, when companies use accelerated depreciation methods for tax purposes and straight-line depreciation methods for financial statement purposes. Deferred tax liabilities also arise when items of income are included in taxable income in later periods—for example, when a company's subsidiary has profits that have not yet been distributed and thus have not yet been taxed.

SAP's balance sheet in Exhibit 12 shows €240 million of deferred tax liabilities. Apple's balance sheet in Exhibit 13 does not show a separate line item for deferred tax liabilities; however, note disclosures indicate that most of the $40,415 million of other non-current liabilities reported on Apple's balance sheet represents deferred tax liabilities, which totaled $31,504 million.

6. EQUITY

Equity is the owners' residual claim on a company's assets after subtracting its liabilities.[21] It represents the claim of the owner against the company. Equity includes funds directly invested in the company by the owners, as well as earnings that have been reinvested over time. Equity can also include items of gain or loss that are not recognized on the company's income statement.

6.1. Components of Equity

Six main components typically comprise total owners' equity. The first five components listed below comprise equity attributable to owners of the parent company. The sixth component is the equity attributable to non-controlling interests.

1. *Capital contributed by owners* (or common stock, or issued capital). The amount contributed to the company by owners. Ownership of a corporation is evidenced through the issuance of common shares. Common shares may have a par value (or stated value) or may be issued as no par shares (depending on regulations governing the incorporation). Where par or stated value requirements exist, it must be disclosed in the equity section

---

[20] IAS 12, *Income Taxes*, paragraph 5.
[21] IASB *Conceptual Framework (2018)*, paragraph 4.4 (c) and FASB ASC 505-10-05-3 [Equity–Overview and Background].

of the balance sheet. In addition, the number of shares authorized, issued, and outstanding must be disclosed for each class of share issued by the company. The number of authorized shares is the number of shares that may be sold by the company under its articles of incorporation. The number of issued shares refers to those shares that have been sold to investors. The number of outstanding shares consists of the issued shares less treasury shares.

2. *Preferred shares.* Classified as equity or financial liabilities based upon their characteristics rather than legal form. For example, perpetual, non-redeemable preferred shares are classified as equity. In contrast, preferred shares with mandatory redemption at a fixed amount at a future date are classified as financial liabilities. Preferred shares have rights that take precedence over the rights of common shareholders—rights that generally pertain to receipt of dividends and receipt of assets if the company is liquidated.

3. *Treasury shares* (or treasury stock or own shares repurchased). Shares in the company that have been repurchased by the company and are held as treasury shares, rather than being cancelled. The company is able to sell (reissue) these shares. A company may repurchase its shares when management considers the shares undervalued, needs shares to fulfill employees' stock options, or wants to limit the effects of dilution from various employee stock compensation plans. A repurchase of previously issued shares reduces shareholders' equity by the amount of the cost of repurchasing the shares and reduces the number of total shares outstanding. If treasury shares are subsequently reissued, a company does not recognize any gain or loss from the reissuance on the income statement. Treasury shares are non-voting and do not receive any dividends declared by the company.

4. *Retained earnings.* The cumulative amount of earnings recognized in the company's income statements that have not been paid to the owners of the company as dividends.

5. *Accumulated other comprehensive income* (or other reserves). The cumulative amount of *other* comprehensive income or loss. The term comprehensive income includes both a) net income, which is recognized on the income statement and is reflected in retained earnings, and b) other comprehensive income which is not recognized as part of net income and is reflected in accumulated other comprehensive income.[22]

6. *Noncontrolling interest* (or minority interest). The equity interests of minority shareholders in the subsidiary companies that have been consolidated by the parent (controlling) company but that are not wholly owned by the parent company.

Exhibits 14 and 15 present excerpts of the balance sheets of SAP Group and Apple Inc., respectively, with detailed line items for each company's equity section. SAP's balance sheet indicates that the company has €1,229 million issued capital, and the notes to the financial statements disclose that the company has issued 1,229 million no-par common stock with

---

[22] IFRS defines Total comprehensive income as "the change in equity during a period resulting from transactions and other events, other than those changes resulting from transactions with owners in their capacity as owners. (IAS 1, Presentation of Financial Statements, paragraph 7. Similarly, US GAAP defines comprehensive income as "the change in equity [net assets] of a business entity during a period from transactions and other events and circumstances from nonowner sources. It includes all changes in equity during a period except those resulting from investments by owners and distributions to owners." (FASB ASC *Master Glossary*.)

a nominal value of €1 per share. SAP's balance sheet also indicates that the company has €1,591 of treasury shares, and the notes to the financial statements disclose that the company holds 35 million of its shares as treasury shares. The line item share premium of €570 million includes amounts from treasury share transactions (and certain other transactions). The amount of retained earnings, €24,794 million, represents the cumulative amount of earnings that the company has recognized in its income statements, net of dividends. SAP's €508 million of "Other components of equity" includes the company's accumulated other comprehensive income. The notes disclose that this is composed of €330 million gains on exchange differences in translation, €157 million gains on remeasuring available-for-sale financial assets, and €21 million gains on cash flow hedges. The balance sheet next presents a subtotal for the amount of equity attributable to the parent company €25,509 million followed by the amount of equity attributable to non-controlling interests €31 million. Total equity includes both equity attributable to the parent company and equity attributable to non-controlling interests.

The equity section of Apple's balance sheet consists of only three line items: common stock, retained earnings, and accumulated other comprehensive income/(loss). Although Apple's balance sheet shows no treasury stock, the company does repurchase its own shares but cancels the repurchased shares rather than holding the shares in treasury. Apple's balance sheet shows that 5,126,201 thousand shares were issued and outstanding at the end of fiscal 2017 and 5,336,166 thousand shares were issued and outstanding at the end of fiscal 2016. Details on the change in shares outstanding is presented on the Statement of Shareholders' Equity in Exhibit 16, which shows that in 2017 Apple repurchased 246,496 thousand shares of its previously issued common stock and issued 36,531 thousand shares to employees.

EXHIBIT 14   SAP Group Consolidated Statements of Financial Position (Excerpt: Equity Detail) (in millions of €)

Assets	as of December 31	
	2017	2016
Total current assets	11,930	11,564
Total non-current assets	30,567	32,713
Total assets	42,497	44,277
Total current liabilities	10,210	9,674
Total non-current liabilities	6,747	8,205
Total liabilities	16,958	17,880
Issued capital	1,229	1,229
Share premium	570	599
Retained earnings	24,794	22,302
Other components of equity	508	3,346
Treasury shares	(1,591)	(1,099)
Equity attributable to owners of parent	25,509	26,376
Non-controlling interests	31	21
Total equity	25,540	26,397
Total equity and liabilities	€42,497	€44,277

Source: SAP Group 2017 annual report.

EXHIBIT 15   Apple Inc. Consolidated Balance Sheet (Excerpt: Equity Detail) (in millions of $)
(Number of shares are reflected in thousands)

Assets	September 30, 2017	September 24, 2016
Total current assets	128,645	106,869
[All other assets]	*246,674*	*214,817*
Total assets	375,319	321,686
Liabilities and shareholders' equity		
Total current liabilities	100,814	79,006
[Total non-current liabilities]	*140,458*	*114,431*
Total liabilities	241,272	193,437
Common stock and additional paid-in capital, $0.00001 par value: 12,600,000 shares authorized; 5,126,201 and 5,336,166 shares issued and outstanding, respectively	35,867	31,251
Retained earnings	98,330	96,364
Accumulated other comprehensive income/(loss)	(150)	634
Total shareholders' equity	134,047	128,249
Total liabilities and shareholders' equity	375,319	321,686

Source: Apple Inc. 2017 annual report (10K).

6.2. Statement of Changes in Equity

The **statement of changes in equity** (or statement of shareholders' equity) presents information about the increases or decreases in a company's equity over a period. IFRS requires the following information in the statement of changes in equity:

- total comprehensive income for the period;
- the effects of any accounting changes that have been retrospectively applied to previous periods;
- capital transactions with owners and distributions to owners; and
- reconciliation of the carrying amounts of each component of equity at the beginning and end of the year.[23]

Under US GAAP, the requirement as specified by the SEC is for companies to provide an analysis of changes in each component of stockholders' equity that is shown in the balance sheet.[24]

Exhibit 16 presents an excerpt from Apple's Consolidated Statements of Changes in Shareholders' Equity. The excerpt shows only one of the years presented on the actual statement. It begins with the balance as of September 24, 2016 (i.e., the beginning of fiscal 2017) and presents the analysis of changes to September 30, 2017 in each component of equity

---

[23] IAS 1, *Presentation of Financial Statements*, paragraph 106.
[24] FASB ASC 505-10-S99 [Equity–Overall–SEC materials] indicates that a company can present the analysis of changes in stockholders' equity either in the notes or in a separate statement.

that is shown on Apple's balance sheet. As noted above, the number of shares outstanding decreased from 5,336,166 thousand to 5,126,201 thousand as the company repurchased 246,496 thousand shares of its common stock and issued 36,531 thousand new shares which reduced the dollar balance of Paid-in Capital and Retained earnings by $913 million and $581 million, respectively. The dollar balance in common stock also increased by $ 4,909 million in connection with share-based compensation. Retained earnings increased by $48,351 million net income, minus $12,803 million dividends, $33,001 million for the share repurchase and $581 million adjustment in connection with the stock issuance. For companies that pay dividends, the amount of dividends are shown separately as a deduction from retained earnings. The statement also provides details on the $784 million change in Apple's Accumulated other comprehensive income. Note that the statement provides a subtotal for total comprehensive income that includes net income and each of the components of other comprehensive income.

EXHIBIT 16   Excerpt from Apple Inc.'s Consolidated Statements of Changes in Shareholders' Equity (in millions, except share amounts which are reflected in thousands)

	Common Stock and Additional Paid-In Capital		Retained Earnings	Accumulated Other Comprehensive Income/(Loss)	Total Shareholders' Equity
	Shares	Amount			
Balances as of September 24, 2016	5,336,166	31,251	96,364	634	128,249
Net income	—	—	48,351	—	48,351
Other comprehensive income/(loss)	—	—	—	(784)	(784)
Dividends and dividend equivalents declared	—	—	(12,803)	—	(12,803)
Repurchase of common stock	(246,496)	—	(33,001)	—	(33,001)
Share-based compensation	—	4,909	—	—	4,909
Common stock issued, net of shares withheld for employee taxes	36,531	(913)	(581)	—	(1,494)
Tax benefit from equity awards, including transfer pricing adjustments		620	—	—	620
Balances as of September 30, 2017	5,126,201	35,867	98,330	(150)	134,047

7. ANALYSIS OF THE BALANCE SHEET

This section describes two tools for analyzing the balance sheet: common-size analysis and balance sheet ratios. Analysis of a company's balance sheet can provide insight into the company's liquidity and solvency—as of the balance sheet date—as well as the economic resources the company controls. **Liquidity** refers to a company's ability to meet its short-term financial commitments. Assessments of liquidity focus on a company's ability to convert assets to cash and to pay for operating needs. **Solvency** refers to a company's ability to meet its financial obligations over the longer term. Assessments of solvency focus on the company's financial structure and its ability to pay long-term financing obligations.

7.1. Common-Size Analysis of the Balance Sheet

The first technique, vertical common-size analysis, involves stating each balance sheet item as a percentage of total assets.[25] Common-size statements are useful in comparing a company's balance sheet composition over time (time-series analysis) and across companies in the same industry. To illustrate, Panel A of Exhibit 17 presents a balance sheet for three hypothetical companies. Company C, with assets of $9.75 million is much larger than Company A and Company B, each with only $3.25 million in assets. The common-size balance sheet presented in Panel B facilitates a comparison of these different sized companies.

EXHIBIT 17

Panel A: Balance Sheets for Companies A, B, and C

($ Thousands)	A	B	C
ASSETS			
Current assets			
Cash and cash equivalents	1,000	200	3,000
Short-term marketable securities	900	—	300
Accounts receivable	500	1,050	1,500
Inventory	100	950	300
Total current assets	2,500	2,200	5,100
Property, plant, and equipment, net	750	750	4,650
Intangible assets	—	200	—
Goodwill	—	100	—
Total assets	3,250	3,250	9,750
LIABILITIES AND SHAREHOLDERS' EQUITY			
Current liabilities			
Accounts payable	—	2,500	600
Total current liabilities	—	2,500	600
Long-term bonds payable	10	10	9,000
Total liabilities	10	2,510	9,600
Total shareholders' equity	3,240	740	150
Total liabilities and shareholders' equity	3,250	3,250	9,750

---

[25] As discussed in the curriculum reading on financial statement analysis, another type of common-size analysis, known as "horizontal common-size analysis," states quantities in terms of a selected base-year value. Unless otherwise indicated, text references to "common-size analysis" refer to vertical analysis.

EXHIBIT 17   (Continued)

Panel B: Common-Size Balance Sheets for Companies A, B, and C

(Percent)	A	B	C
ASSETS			
Current assets			
Cash and cash equivalents	30.8	6.2	30.8
Short-term marketable securities	27.7	0.0	3.1
Accounts receivable	15.4	32.3	15.4
Inventory	3.1	29.2	3.1
Total current assets	76.9	67.7	52.3
Property, plant, and equipment, net	23.1	23.1	47.7
Intangible assets	0.0	6.2	0.0
Goodwill	0.0	3.1	0.0
Total assets	100.0	100.0	100.0
LIABILITIES AND SHAREHOLDERS' EQUITY			
Current liabilities			
Accounts payable	0.0	76.9	6.2
Total current liabilities	0.0	76.9	6.2
Long-term bonds payable	0.3	0.3	92.3
Total liabilities	0.3	77.2	98.5
Total shareholders' equity	99.7	22.8	1.5
Total liabilities and shareholders' equity	100.0	100.0	100.0

Most of the assets of Company A and Company B are current assets; however, Company A has nearly 60 percent of its total assets in cash and short-term marketable securities while Company B has only 6 percent of its assets in cash. Company A is more liquid than Company B. Company A shows no current liabilities (its current liabilities round to less than $10 thousand), and it has cash on hand of $1.0 million to meet any near-term financial obligations it might have. In contrast, Company B has $2.5 million of current liabilities, which exceed its available cash of only $200 thousand. To pay those near-term obligations, Company B will need to collect some of its accounts receivables, sell more inventory, borrow from a bank, and/or raise more long-term capital (e.g., by issuing more bonds or more equity). Company C also appears more liquid than Company B. It holds over 30 percent of its total assets in cash and short-term marketable securities, and its current liabilities are only 6.2 percent of the amount of total assets.

Company C's $3.3 million in cash and short-term marketable securities is substantially more than its current liabilities of $600 thousand. Turning to the question of solvency, however, note that 98.5 percent of Company C's assets are financed with liabilities. If Company C experiences significant fluctuations in cash flows, it may be unable to pay the interest and principal on its long-term bonds. Company A is far more solvent than Company C, with less than 1 percent of its assets financed with liabilities.

Note that these examples are hypothetical only. Other than general comparisons, little more can be said without further detail. In practice, a wide range of factors affect a company's liquidity management and capital structure. The study of optimal **capital structure** is a fundamental issue addressed in corporate finance. Capital refers to a company's long-term debt and equity financing; capital structure refers to the proportion of debt versus equity financing.

Common-size balance sheets can also highlight differences in companies' strategies. Comparing the asset composition of the companies, Company C has made a greater proportional investment in property, plant, and equipment—possibly because it manufactures more of its products in-house. The presence of goodwill on Company B's balance sheet signifies that it has made one or more acquisitions in the past. In contrast, the lack of goodwill on the balance sheets of Company A and Company C suggests that these two companies may have pursued a strategy of internal growth rather than growth by acquisition. Company A may be in either a start-up or liquidation stage of operations as evidenced by the composition of its balance sheet. It has relatively little inventory and no accounts payable. It either has not yet established trade credit, or it is in the process of paying off its obligations in the process of liquidating.

EXAMPLE 5   Common-Size Analysis

Applying common-size analysis to the excerpts of SAP Group's balance sheets presented in Exhibits 4, 6, 8, and 12, answer the following: In 2017 relative to 2016, which of the following line items increased as a percentage of assets?

A. Cash and cash equivalents.
B. Total current assets.
C. Total financial liabilities
D. Total deferred income.

Solution: A, B, and D are correct. The following items increased as a percentage of total assets:

- Cash and cash equivalents increased from 8.4 percent of total assets in 2016 (€3,702 ÷ €44,277) to 9.4 percent in 2017 (€4,011 ÷ €42,497).
- Total current assets increased from 26.1 percent of total assets in 2016 (€11,564 ÷ €44,277) to 28.1 percent in 2017 (€11,930 ÷ €42,497).
- Total deferred income increased from 5.7 percent of total assets in 2016 ((€ 2,383 + €143) ÷ €44,277) to 6.7 percent in 2017 ((€ 2,771 +€79) ÷ €42,497).

Total financial liabilities decreased both in absolute euro amounts and as a percentage of total assets when compared with the previous year.

Note that some amounts of the company's deferred income and financial liabilities are classified as current liabilities (shown in Exhibit 6), and some amounts are classified as non-current liabilities (shown in Exhibit 12). The total amounts—current and non-current—of deferred income and financial liabilities, therefore, are obtained by summing the amounts in Exhibits 6 and 12.

Overall, aspects of the company's liquidity position are somewhat stronger in 2017 compared to 2016. The company's cash balances as a percentage of total assets increased. While current liabilities increased as a percentage of total assets and total liabilities remained approximately the same percentage, the mix of liabilities shifted. Financial liabilities, which represent future cash outlays, decreased as a percentage of total assets, while deferred revenues, which represent cash received in advance of revenue recognition, increased.

Common-size analysis of the balance sheet is particularly useful in cross-sectional analysis—comparing companies to each other for a particular time period or comparing a company with industry or sector data. The analyst could select individual peer companies for comparison, use industry data from published sources, or compile data from databases. When analyzing a company, many analysts prefer to select the peer companies for comparison or to compile their own industry statistics.

Exhibit 18 presents common-size balance sheet data compiled for the 10 sectors of the S&P 500 using 2017 data. The sector classification follows the S&P/MSCI Global Industrial Classification System (GICS). The exhibit presents mean and median common-size balance sheet data for those companies in the S&P 500 for which 2017 data were available in the Compustat database.[26]

Some interesting general observations can be made from these data:

- Energy and utility companies have the largest amounts of property, plant, and equipment (PPE). Telecommunication services, followed by utilities, have the highest level of long-term debt. Utilities also use some preferred stock.
- Financial companies have the greatest percentage of total liabilities. Financial companies typically have relatively high financial leverage.
- Telecommunications services and utility companies have the lowest level of receivables.
- Inventory levels are highest for consumer discretionary. Materials and consumer staples have the next highest inventories.
- Information technology companies use the least amount of leverage as evidenced by the lowest percentages for long-term debt and total liabilities, and highest percentages for common and total equity.

Example 6 discusses an analyst using cross-sectional common-size balance sheet data.

---

[26] An entry of zero for an item (e.g., current assets) was excluded from the data, except in the case of preferred stock. Note that most financial institutions did not provide current asset or current liability data, so these are reported as not available in the database.

EXHIBIT 18   Common-Size Balance Sheet Statistics for the S&P 500 Grouped by S&P/MSCI GICS Sector (in percent except No. of Observations; data for 2017)

Panel A. Median Data

	10 Energy	15 Materials	20 Industrials	25 Consumer Discretionary	30 Consumer Staples	35 Health Care	40 Financials	45 Information Technology	50 Telecommunication Services	55 Utilities	60 Real Estate
Number of observations	34	27	68	81	33	59	64	64	4	29	30
Cash and short-term investments	6.8%	6.3%	8.1%	8.3%	4.1%	11.2%	6.2%	22.7%	1.2%	0.7%	1.4%
Receivables	5.8%	8.8%	12.9%	6.8%	6.5%	9.7%	20.4%	9.6%	3.7%	3.6%	2.0%
Inventories	1.6%	8.9%	6.9%	14.9%	9.6%	4.3%	0.0%	1.3%	0.3%	1.7%	0.0%
Total current assets	16.1%	26.0%	30.5%	41.5%	29.1%	31.4%	N.A.	48.7%	8.6%	7.3%	10.8%
PPE	73.3%	36.3%	12.5%	19.8%	17.2%	8.1%	0.9%	6.2%	35.0%	72.0%	33.4%
Intangibles	1.6%	27.9%	33.3%	16.8%	41.9%	37.6%	2.8%	26.4%	49.6%	6.2%	1.0%
Goodwill	0.7%	20.0%	28.3%	11.3%	26.2%	22.8%	2.2%	22.3%	26.0%	4.8%	0.0%
Accounts payable	5.7%	7.3%	6.2%	8.0%	8.0%	3.1%	27.0%	2.7%	2.5%	3.0%	1.3%
Current liabilities	10.9%	16.5%	22.5%	25.8%	25.0%	16.5%	N.A.	21.2%	11.5%	11.5%	7.1%
LT debt	27.3%	31.4%	28.0%	28.7%	32.3%	24.3%	6.4%	22.9%	46.8%	32.5%	43.4%
Total liabilities	49.3%	64.2%	65.5%	64.9%	63.8%	59.2%	86.7%	59.9%	75.8%	71.8%	53.3%
Common equity	47.3%	33.8%	34.5%	34.7%	36.2%	39.4%	12.6%	39.3%	23.9%	27.7%	40.4%
Preferred stock	0.0%	0.0%	0.0%	0.0%	0.0%	0.0%	0.0%	0.0%	0.0%	0.0%	0.0%
Total equity	47.3%	33.8%	34.5%	34.7%	36.2%	39.4%	13.2%	39.3%	23.9%	28.0%	41.8%

EXHIBIT 18 (Continued)

Panel B. Mean Data

	10	15	20	25	30	35	40	45	50	55	60
	Energy	Materials	Industrials	Consumer Discretionary	Consumer Staples	Health Care	Financials	Information Technology	Telecommunication Services	Utilities	Real Estate
Number of observations	34	27	68	81	33	59	64	64	4	29	30
Cash and short-term investments	6.9%	7.4%	9.2%	12.9%	7.3%	15.4%	11.2%	28.3%	3.6%	1.3%	2.9%
Receivables	6.6%	10.5%	15.2%	9.0%	7.7%	11.2%	31.5%	11.8%	5.0%	3.8%	3.8%
Inventories	3.4%	9.3%	7.8%	18.3%	10.6%	6.3%	3.8%	4.1%	0.3%	1.6%	0.1%
Total current assets	17.7%	28.8%	32.9%	40.6%	27.8%	36.4%	N.A.	49.4%	10.1%	8.6%	16.1%
PPE	68.0%	36.9%	24.5%	25.1%	21.6%	11.2%	2.1%	10.3%	39.0%	69.9%	34.9%
Intangibles	7.8%	26.6%	35.6%	23.0%	43.6%	43.9%	11.4%	31.1%	48.2%	6.8%	10.3%
Goodwill	5.4%	18.4%	26.8%	14.6%	24.6%	27.3%	7.7%	24.5%	25.9%	5.7%	5.7%
Accounts payable	5.9%	8.1%	7.1%	11.8%	9.8%	8.1%	35.9%	5.1%	3.1%	2.9%	2.0%
Current liabilities	11.8%	17.0%	23.0%	26.8%	24.6%	21.2%	N.A.	26.1%	11.9%	11.8%	12.8%
LT debt	28.3%	31.2%	29.4%	31.3%	32.4%	28.5%	10.3%	24.8%	47.5%	35.0%	44.8%
Total liabilities	50.3%	63.4%	67.1%	67.5%	68.3%	60.1%	80.1%	61.8%	77.6%	73.9%	54.5%
Common equity	46.4%	34.2%	32.3%	32.3%	30.9%	38.9%	18.2%	37.5%	22.2%	24.7%	40.2%
Preferred stock	0.0%	0.0%	0.1%	0.0%	0.0%	0.1%	0.4%	0.3%	0.0%	0.3%	2.2%
Total equity	46.4%	34.2%	32.4%	32.3%	30.9%	39.0%	18.5%	37.8%	22.2%	25.0%	42.3%

PPE = Property, plant, and equipment, LT = Long term.
Source: Based on data from Compustat.

EXAMPLE 6   Cross-Sectional Common-Size Analysis

Jason Lu is comparing two companies in the computer industry to evaluate their relative financial position as reflected on their balance sheets. He has compiled the following vertical common-size data for Apple and Microsoft.

Cross-Sectional Analysis: Consolidated Balance Sheets (as Percent of Total Assets)

	Apple	Microsoft
	September 30, 2017	June 30, 2017
ASSETS:		
Current assets:		
Cash and cash equivalents	5.4	3.2
Short-term marketable securities	14.4	52.0
Accounts receivable	4.8	8.2
Inventories	1.3	0.9
Vendor non-trade receivables	4.7	0.0
Other current assets	3.7	2.0
Total current assets	34.3	66.3
Long-term marketable securities	51.9	2.5
Property, plant, and equipment, net	9.0	9.8
Goodwill	1.5	14.6
Acquired intangible assets, net	0.6	4.2
Other assets	2.7	2.6
Total assets	100.0	100.0
LIABILITIES AND SHAREHOLDERS' EQUITY:		
Current liabilities:		
Accounts payable	13.1	3.1
Short-term debt	3.2	3.8
Current portion of long-term debt	1.7	0.4
Accrued expenses	6.9	2.7
Deferred revenue	2.0	14.1
Other current liabilities	0.0	2.6
Total current liabilities	26.9	26.8
Long-term debt	25.9	31.6
Deferred revenue non-current	0.8	4.3
Other non-current liabilities	10.8	7.3
Total liabilities	64.3	70.0
Commitments and contingencies		
Total shareholders' equity	35.7	30.0
Total liabilities and shareholders' equity	100.0	100.0

Source: Based on data from companies' annual reports.

From this data, Lu learns the following:

- Apple and Microsoft have high levels of cash and short-term marketable securities, consistent with the information technology sector as reported in Exhibit 18. Apple also has a high balance in long-term marketable securities. This may reflect the success of the company's business model, which has generated large operating cash flows in recent years.
- Apple's level of accounts receivable is lower than Microsoft's and lower than the industry average. Further research is necessary to learn the extent to which this is related to Apple's cash sales through its own retail stores. An alternative explanation would be that the company has been selling/factoring receivables to a greater degree than the other companies; however, that explanation is unlikely given Apple's cash position. Additionally, Apple shows vendor non-trade receivables, reflecting arrangements with its contract manufacturers.
- Apple and Microsoft both have low levels of inventory, similar to industry medians as reported in Exhibit 18. Apple uses contract manufacturers and can rely on suppliers to hold inventory until needed. Additionally, in the Management Discussion and Analysis section of their annual report, Apple discloses $38 billion of noncancelable manufacturing purchase obligations, $33 billion of which is due within 12 months. These amounts are not currently recorded as inventory and reflect the use of contract manufacturers to assemble and test some finished products. The use of purchase commitments and contract manufacturers implies that inventory may be "understated." Microsoft's low level of inventory is consistent with its business mix, which is more heavily weighted to software than to hardware.
- Apple and Microsoft have a level of property, plant, and equipment that is relatively close to the sector median as reported in Exhibit 18.
- Apple has a very low amount of goodwill, reflecting its strategy to grow organically rather than through acquisitions. Microsoft's level of goodwill, while higher than Apple's, is lower than the industry median and mean. Microsoft made a number of major acquisitions (for example, Nokia in 2014) but subsequently (in 2015) wrote off significant amounts of goodwill as an impairment charge.
- Apple's level of accounts payable is higher than the industry, but given the company's high level of cash and investments, it is unlikely that this is a problem.
- Apple's and Microsoft's levels of long-term debt are slightly higher than industry averages. Again, given the companies' high level of cash and investments, it is unlikely that this is a problem.

7.2. Balance Sheet Ratios

Ratios facilitate time-series and cross-sectional analysis of a company's financial position. **Balance sheet ratios** are those involving balance sheet items only. Each of the line items on a vertical common-size balance sheet is a ratio in that it expresses a balance sheet amount in relation to total assets. Other balance sheet ratios compare one balance sheet item to another. For example, the current ratio expresses current assets in relation to current liabilities as an indicator of a company's liquidity. Balance sheet ratios include **liquidity ratios** (measuring the company's ability to meet its short-term obligations) and **solvency ratios** (measuring the company's ability to meet long-term and other obligations). These ratios and others are discussed in a later chapter. Exhibit 19 summarizes the calculation and interpretation of selected balance sheet ratios.

EXHIBIT 19   Balance Sheet Ratios

Liquidity Ratios	Calculation	Indicates
Current	Current assets ÷ Current liabilities	Ability to meet current liabilities
Quick (acid test)	(Cash + Marketable securities + Receivables) ÷ Current liabilities	Ability to meet current liabilities
Cash	(Cash + Marketable securities) ÷ Current liabilities	Ability to meet current liabilities
Solvency Ratios		
Long-term debt-to-equity	Total long-term debt ÷ Total equity	Financial risk and financial leverage
Debt-to-equity	Total debt ÷ Total equity	Financial risk and financial leverage
Total debt	Total debt ÷ Total assets	Financial risk and financial leverage
Financial leverage	Total assets ÷ Total equity	Financial risk and financial leverage

---

EXAMPLE 7   Ratio Analysis

For the following ratio questions, refer to the balance sheet information for the SAP Group presented in Exhibits 1, 4, 6, 8, and 12.

1. The current ratio for SAP Group at December 31, 2017 is *closest* to:
   A. 1.17.
   B. 1.20.
   C. 2.00.
2. Which of the following liquidity ratios decreased in 2017 relative to 2016?
   A. Cash.
   B. Quick.
   C. Current.
3. Which of the following leverage ratios decreased in 2017 relative to 2016?
   A. Debt-to-equity.
   B. Financial leverage.
   C. Long-term debt-to-equity.

Solution to 1: A is correct. SAP Group's current ratio (Current assets ÷ Current liabilities) at December 31, 2017 is 1.17 (€11,930 million ÷ €10,210 million).

Solution to 2: B and C are correct. The ratios are shown in the table below. The quick ratio and current ratio are lower in 2017 than in 2016. The cash ratio is slightly higher.

Liquidity Ratios	Calculation	2017 € in Millions	2016 € in Millions
Current	Current assets ÷ Current liabilities	€11,930 ÷ €10,210 = **1.17**	€11,564 ÷ €9,674 = **1.20**
Quick (acid test)	(Cash + Marketable securities + Receivables) ÷ Current liabilities	(€4,011 + €990 + €5,899) ÷ €10,210 = **1.07**	(€3,702 + €1,124 + €5,924) ÷ €9,674 = **1.11**
Cash	(Cash + Marketable securities) ÷ Current liabilities	€4,011 ÷ €10,210 = **0.39**	€3,702 ÷ €9,674 = **0.38**

Solution to 3: A, B, and C are correct. The ratios are shown in the table below. All three leverage ratios decreased in 2017 relative to 2016.

Solvency Ratios			
Long-term debt-to-equity	Total long-term debt ÷ Total equity	€5,034 ÷ €25,540 =**19.7%**	€6,481 ÷ €26,397 = **24.6%**
Debt-to-equity	Total debt ÷ Total equity	(€1,561 + €5,034) ÷ €25,540 = **25.8%**	(€ 1,813 + €6,481) ÷ €26,397 = **31.4%**
Financial Leverage	Total assets ÷ Total equity	€42,497 ÷ €25,540 = **1.66**	€44,277 ÷ €26,397 = **1.68**

Cross-sectional financial ratio analysis can be limited by differences in accounting methods. In addition, lack of homogeneity of a company's operating activities can limit comparability. For diversified companies operating in different industries, using industry-specific ratios for different lines of business can provide better comparisons. Companies disclose information on operating segments. The financial position and performance of the operating segments can be compared to the relevant industry.

Ratio analysis requires a significant amount of judgment. One key area requiring judgment is understanding the limitations of any ratio. The current ratio, for example, is only a rough measure of liquidity at a specific point in time. The ratio captures only the amount of current assets, but the components of current assets differ significantly in their nearness to cash (e.g., marketable securities versus inventory). Another limitation of the current ratio is its sensitivity to end-of-period financing and operating decisions that can potentially impact current asset and current liability amounts. Another overall area requiring judgment is determining whether a ratio for a company is within a reasonable range for an industry. Yet another area requiring judgment is evaluating whether a ratio signifies a persistent condition or reflects only a temporary condition. Overall, evaluating specific ratios requires an examination of the entire operations of a company, its competitors, and the external economic and industry setting in which it is operating.

8. SUMMARY

The balance sheet (also referred to as the statement of financial position) discloses what an entity owns (assets) and what it owes (liabilities) at a specific point in time. Equity is the owners' residual interest in the assets of a company, net of its liabilities. The amount of equity is increased by income earned during the year, or by the issuance of new equity. The amount of equity is decreased by losses, by dividend payments, or by share repurchases.

An understanding of the balance sheet enables an analyst to evaluate the liquidity, solvency, and overall financial position of a company.

- The balance sheet distinguishes between current and non-current assets, and between current and non-current liabilities unless a presentation based on liquidity provides more relevant and reliable information.
- The concept of liquidity relates to a company's ability to pay for its near-term operating needs. With respect to a company overall, liquidity refers to the availability of cash to pay those near-term needs. With respect to a particular asset or liability, liquidity refers to its "nearness to cash."
- Some assets and liabilities are measured on the basis of fair value, and some are measured at historical cost. Notes to financial statements provide information that is helpful in assessing the comparability of measurement bases across companies.
- Assets expected to be liquidated or used up within one year or one operating cycle of the business, whichever is greater, are classified as current assets. Assets not expected to be liquidated or used up within one year or one operating cycle of the business, whichever is greater, are classified as non-current assets.
- Liabilities expected to be settled or paid within one year or one operating cycle of the business, whichever is greater, are classified as current liabilities. Liabilities not expected to be settled or paid within one year or one operating cycle of the business, whichever is greater, are classified as non-current liabilities.
- Trade receivables, also referred to as accounts receivable, are amounts owed to a company by its customers for products and services already delivered. Receivables are reported net of the allowance for doubtful accounts.
- Inventories are physical products that will eventually be sold to the company's customers, either in their current form (finished goods) or as inputs into a process to manufacture a final product (raw materials and work-in-process). Inventories are reported at the lower of cost or net realizable value. If the net realizable value of a company's inventory falls below its carrying amount, the company must write down the value of the inventory and record an expense.
- Inventory cost is based on specific identification or estimated using the first-in, first-out or weighted average cost methods. Some accounting standards (including US GAAP but not IFRS) also allow last-in, first-out as an additional inventory valuation method.
- Accounts payable, also called trade payables, are amounts that a business owes its vendors for purchases of goods and services.
- Deferred revenue (also known as unearned revenue) arises when a company receives payment in advance of delivery of the goods and services associated with the payment received.
- Property, plant, and equipment (PPE) are tangible assets that are used in company operations and expected to be used over more than one fiscal period. Examples of tangible assets

include land, buildings, equipment, machinery, furniture, and natural resources such as mineral and petroleum resources.

- IFRS provide companies with the choice to report PPE using either a historical cost model or a revaluation model. US GAAP permit only the historical cost model for reporting PPE.
- Depreciation is the process of recognizing the cost of a long-lived asset over its useful life. (Land is not depreciated.)
- Under IFRS, property used to earn rental income or capital appreciation is considered to be an investment property. IFRS provide companies with the choice to report an investment property using either a historical cost model or a fair value model.
- Intangible assets refer to identifiable non-monetary assets without physical substance. Examples include patents, licenses, and trademarks. For each intangible asset, a company assesses whether the useful life is finite or indefinite.
- An intangible asset with a finite useful life is amortized on a systematic basis over the best estimate of its useful life, with the amortization method and useful-life estimate reviewed at least annually. Impairment principles for an intangible asset with a finite useful life are the same as for PPE.
- An intangible asset with an indefinite useful life is not amortized. Instead, it is tested for impairment at least annually.
- For internally generated intangible assets, IFRS require that costs incurred during the research phase must be expensed. Costs incurred in the development stage can be capitalized as intangible assets if certain criteria are met, including technological feasibility, the ability to use or sell the resulting asset, and the ability to complete the project.
- The most common intangible asset that is not a separately identifiable asset is goodwill, which arises in business combinations. Goodwill is not amortized; instead it is tested for impairment at least annually.
- Financial instruments are contracts that give rise to both a financial asset of one entity and a financial liability or equity instrument of another entity. In general, there are two basic alternative ways that financial instruments are measured: fair value or amortized cost. For financial instruments measured at fair value, there are two basic alternatives in how net changes in fair value are recognized: as profit or loss on the income statement, or as other comprehensive income (loss), which bypasses the income statement.
- Typical long-term financial liabilities include loans (i.e., borrowings from banks) and notes or bonds payable (i.e., fixed-income securities issued to investors). Liabilities such as bonds issued by a company are usually reported at amortized cost on the balance sheet.
- Deferred tax liabilities arise from temporary timing differences between a company's income as reported for tax purposes and income as reported for financial statement purposes.
- Six potential components that comprise the owners' equity section of the balance sheet include: contributed capital, preferred shares, treasury shares, retained earnings, accumulated other comprehensive income, and non-controlling interest.
- The statement of changes in equity reflects information about the increases or decreases in each component of a company's equity over a period.
- Vertical common-size analysis of the balance sheet involves stating each balance sheet item as a percentage of total assets.
- Balance sheet ratios include liquidity ratios (measuring the company's ability to meet its short-term obligations) and solvency ratios (measuring the company's ability to meet long-term and other obligations).

PRACTICE PROBLEMS

1. Resources controlled by a company as a result of past events are:
   A. equity.
   B. assets.
   C. liabilities.

2. Equity equals:
   A. Assets − Liabilities.
   B. Liabilities − Assets.
   C. Assets + Liabilities.

3. Distinguishing between current and non-current items on the balance sheet and present-ing a subtotal for current assets and liabilities is referred to as:
   A. a classified balance sheet.
   B. an unclassified balance sheet.
   C. a liquidity-based balance sheet.

4. Shareholders' equity reported on the balance sheet is *most likely* to differ from the market value of shareholders' equity because:
   A. historical cost basis is used for all assets and liabilities.
   B. some factors that affect the generation of future cash flows are excluded.
   C. shareholders' equity reported on the balance sheet is updated continuously.

5. The information provided by a balance sheet item is limited because of uncertainty regarding:
   A. measurement of its cost or value with reliability.
   B. the change in current value following the end of the reporting period.
   C. the probability that any future economic benefit will flow to or from the entity.

6. Which of the following is *most likely* classified as a current liability?
   A. Payment received for a product due to be delivered at least one year after the balance sheet date.
   B. Payments for merchandise due at least one year after the balance sheet date but still within a normal operating cycle.
   C. Payment on debt due in six months for which the company has the unconditional right to defer settlement for at least one year after the balance sheet date.

7. The *most likely* company to use a liquidity-based balance sheet presentation is a:
   A. bank.
   B. computer manufacturer holding inventories.
   C. software company with trade receivables and payables.

8. All of the following are current assets *except*:
   A. cash.
   B. goodwill.
   C. inventories.

9. The *most* likely costs included in both the cost of inventory and property, plant, and equipment are:
    A. selling costs.
    B. storage costs.
    C. delivery costs.

10. Debt due within one year is considered:
    A. current.
    B. preferred.
    C. convertible.

11. Money received from customers for products to be delivered in the future is recorded as:
    A. revenue and an asset.
    B. an asset and a liability.
    C. revenue and a liability.

12. An example of a contra asset account is:
    A. depreciation expense.
    B. sales returns and allowances.
    C. allowance for doubtful accounts.

13. The carrying value of inventories reflects:
    A. their historical cost.
    B. their current value.
    C. the lower of historical cost or net realizable value.

14. When a company pays its rent in advance, its balance sheet will reflect a reduction in:
    A. assets and liabilities.
    B. assets and shareholders' equity.
    C. one category of assets and an increase in another.

15. Accrued expenses (accrued liabilities) are:
    A. expenses that have been paid.
    B. created when another liability is reduced.
    C. expenses that have been reported on the income statement but not yet paid.

16. The initial measurement of goodwill is *most likely* affected by:
    A. an acquisition's purchase price.
    B. the acquired company's book value.
    C. the fair value of the acquirer's assets and liabilities.

17. Defining total asset turnover as revenue divided by average total assets, all else equal, impairment write-downs of long-lived assets owned by a company will *most likely* result in an increase for that company in:
    A. the debt-to-equity ratio but not the total asset turnover.
    B. the total asset turnover but not the debt-to-equity ratio.
    C. both the debt-to-equity ratio and the total asset turnover.

18. A company has total liabilities of £35 million and total stockholders' equity of £55 million. Total liabilities are represented on a vertical common-size balance sheet by a percentage *closest* to:
    A. 35%.
    B. 39%.
    C. 64%.

19. For financial assets classified as trading securities, how are unrealized gains and losses reflected in shareholders' equity?
   A. They are not recognized.
   B. They flow through income into retained earnings.
   C. They are a component of accumulated other comprehensive income.

20. For financial assets classified as available for sale, how are unrealized gains and losses reflected in shareholders' equity?
   A. They are not recognized.
   B. They flow through retained earnings.
   C. They are a component of accumulated other comprehensive income.

21. For financial assets classified as held to maturity, how are unrealized gains and losses reflected in shareholders' equity?
   A. They are not recognized.
   B. They flow through retained earnings.
   C. They are a component of accumulated other comprehensive income.

22. The non-controlling (minority) interest in consolidated subsidiaries is presented on the balance sheet:
   A. as a long-term liability.
   B. separately, but as a part of shareholders' equity.
   C. as a mezzanine item between liabilities and shareholders' equity.

23. The item "retained earnings" is a component of:
   A. assets.
   B. liabilities.
   C. shareholders' equity.

24. When a company buys shares of its own stock to be held in treasury, it records a reduction in:
   A. both assets and liabilities.
   B. both assets and shareholders' equity.
   C. assets and an increase in shareholders' equity.

25. Which of the following would an analyst *most likely* be able to determine from a common-size analysis of a company's balance sheet over several periods?
   A. An increase or decrease in sales.
   B. An increase or decrease in financial leverage.
   C. A more efficient or less efficient use of assets.

26. An investor concerned whether a company can meet its near-term obligations is *most likely* to calculate the:
   A. current ratio.
   B. return on total capital.
   C. financial leverage ratio.

27. The most stringent test of a company's liquidity is its:
   A. cash ratio.
   B. quick ratio.
   C. current ratio.

28. An investor worried about a company's long-term solvency would *most likely* examine its:
   A. current ratio.
   B. return on equity.
   C. debt-to-equity ratio.

29. Using the information presented in Exhibit 4, the quick ratio for SAP Group at 31 December 2017 is *closest* to:
    A. 1.00.
    B. 1.07.
    C. 1.17.

30. Using the information presented in Exhibit 14, the financial leverage ratio for SAP Group at December 31, 2017 is *closest* to:
    A. 1.50.
    B. 1.66.
    C. 2.00.

Questions 31 through 34 refer to Exhibit 1.

EXHIBIT 1   Common-Size Balance Sheets for Company A, Company B, and Sector Average

	Company A	Company B	Sector Average
ASSETS			
Current assets			
Cash and cash equivalents	5	5	7
Marketable securities	5	0	2
Accounts receivable, net	5	15	12
Inventories	15	20	16
Prepaid expenses	5	15	11
Total current assets	35	55	48
Property, plant, and equipment, net	40	35	37
Goodwill	25	0	8
Other assets	0	10	7
Total assets	100	100	100
LIABILITIES AND SHAREHOLDERS' EQUITY			
Current liabilities			
Accounts payable	10	10	10
Short-term debt	25	10	15
Accrued expenses	0	5	3
Total current liabilities	35	25	28
Long-term debt	45	20	28
Other non-current liabilities	0	10	7
Total liabilities	80	55	63
Total shareholders' equity	20	45	37
Total liabilities and shareholders' equity	100	100	100

31. Based on Exhibit 1, which statement is *most likely* correct?
    A. Company A has below-average liquidity risk.
    B. Company B has above-average solvency risk.
    C. Company A has made one or more acquisitions.

32. The quick ratio for Company A is *closest* to:
    A. 0.43.
    B. 0.57.
    C. 1.00.

33. Based on Exhibit 1, the financial leverage ratio for Company B is *closest* to:
    A. 0.55.
    B. 1.22.
    C. 2.22.

34. Based on Exhibit 1, which ratio indicates lower liquidity risk for Company A compared with Company B?
    A. Cash ratio.
    B. Quick ratio.
    C. Current ratio.

CHAPTER 5

UNDERSTANDING CASH FLOW STATEMENTS

Elaine Henry, PhD, CFA
Thomas R. Robinson, PhD, CFA
J Hennie van Greuning, DCom, CFA
Michael A. Broihahn, CPA, CIA, CFA

LEARNING OUTCOMES

After completing this chapter, you will be able to do the following:

- compare cash flows from operating, investing, and financing activities and classify cash flow items as relating to one of those three categories given a description of the items;
- describe how non-cash investing and financing activities are reported;
- contrast cash flow statements prepared under International Financial Reporting Standards (IFRS) and US generally accepted accounting principles (US GAAP);
- distinguish between the direct and indirect methods of presenting cash from operating activities and describe arguments in favor of each method;
- describe how the cash flow statement is linked to the income statement and the balance sheet;
- describe the steps in the preparation of direct and indirect cash flow statements, including how cash flows can be computed using income statement and balance sheet data;
- convert cash flows from the indirect to the direct method;
- analyze and interpret both reported and common-size cash flow statements;
- calculate and interpret free cash flow to the firm, free cash flow to equity, and performance and coverage cash flow ratios.

1. INTRODUCTION

The cash flow statement provides information about a company's *cash receipts* and *cash payments* during an accounting period. The cash-based information provided by the cash flow statement contrasts with the accrual-based information from the income statement. For example, the income statement reflects revenues when earned rather than when cash is collected; in contrast, the cash flow statement reflects cash receipts when collected as opposed to when the revenue was earned. A reconciliation between reported income and cash flows from operating activities provides useful information about when, whether, and how a company is able to generate cash from its operating activities. Although income is an important measure of the results of a company's activities, cash flow is also essential. As an extreme illustration, a hypothetical company that makes all sales on account, without regard to whether it will ever collect its accounts receivable, would report healthy sales on its income statement and might well report significant income; however, with zero cash inflow, the company would not survive. The cash flow statement also provides a reconciliation of the beginning and ending cash on the balance sheet.

In addition to information about cash generated (or, alternatively, cash used) in operating activities, the cash flow statement provides information about cash provided (or used) in a company's investing and financing activities. This information allows the analyst to answer such questions as:

- Does the company generate enough cash from its operations to pay for its new investments, or is the company relying on new debt issuance to finance them?
- Does the company pay its dividends to common stockholders using cash generated from operations, from selling assets, or from issuing debt?

Answers to these questions are important because, in theory, generating cash from operations can continue indefinitely, but generating cash from selling assets, for example, is possible only as long as there are assets to sell. Similarly, generating cash from debt financing is possible only as long as lenders are willing to lend, and the lending decision depends on expectations that the company will ultimately have adequate cash to repay its obligations. In summary, information about the sources and uses of cash helps creditors, investors, and other statement users evaluate the company's liquidity, solvency, and financial flexibility.

This chapter explains how cash flow activities are reflected in a company's cash flow statement. The chapter is organized as follows. Section 2 describes the components and format of the cash flow statement, including the classification of cash flows under International Financial Reporting Standards (IFRS) and US generally accepted accounting principles (GAAP) and the direct and indirect formats for presenting the cash flow statement. Section 3 discusses the linkages of the cash flow statement with the income statement and balance sheet, and the steps in the preparation of the cash flow statement. Section 4 demonstrates the analysis of cash flow statements, including the conversion of an indirect cash flow statement to the direct method and how to use common-size cash flow analysis, free cash flow measures, and cash flow ratios used in security analysis. A summary of the key points and practice problems in the CFA Institute multiple-choice format conclude the chapter.

2. COMPONENTS AND FORMAT OF THE CASH FLOW STATEMENT

The analyst needs to be able to extract and interpret information on cash flows from financial statements. The basic components and allowable formats of the cash flow statement are well established.

- The cash flow statement has subsections relating specific items to the operating, investing, and financing activities of the company.
- Two presentation formats for the operating section are allowable: direct and indirect.

The following discussion presents these topics in greater detail.

2.1. Classification of Cash Flows and Non-Cash Activities

All companies engage in operating, investing, and financing activities. These activities are the classifications used in the cash flow statement under both IFRS and US GAAP and are described as follows:[1]

- **Operating activities** include the company's day-to-day activities that create revenues, such as selling inventory and providing services, and other activities not classified as investing or financing. Cash inflows result from cash sales and from collection of accounts receivable. Examples include cash receipts from the provision of services and royalties, commissions, and other revenue. To generate revenue, companies undertake such activities as manufacturing inventory, purchasing inventory from suppliers, and paying employees. Cash outflows result from cash payments for inventory, salaries, taxes, and other operating-related expenses and from paying accounts payable. Additionally, operating activities include cash receipts and payments related to **dealing securities** or **trading securities** (as opposed to buying or selling securities as investments, as discussed below).
- **Investing activities** include purchasing and selling long-term assets and other investments. These long-term assets and other investments include property, plant, and equipment; intangible assets; other long-term assets; and both long-term and short-term investments in the equity and debt (bonds and loans) issued by other companies. For this purpose, investments in equity and debt securities exclude a) any securities considered cash equivalents (very short-term, highly liquid securities) and b) securities held for dealing or trading purposes, the purchase and sale of which are considered operating activities even for companies where this is not a primary business activity. Cash inflows in the investing category include cash receipts from the sale of non-trading securities; property, plant, and equipment; intangibles; and other long-term assets. Cash outflows include cash payments for the purchase of these assets.
- **Financing activities** include obtaining or repaying capital, such as equity and long-term debt. The two primary sources of capital are shareholders and creditors. Cash inflows in this category include cash receipts from issuing stock (common or preferred) or bonds and cash receipts from borrowing. Cash outflows include cash payments to repurchase stock (e.g., treasury stock) and to repay bonds and other borrowings. Note that indirect borrowing using accounts payable is not considered a financing activity—such borrowing is classified as an operating activity. The new IFRS standard relating to lease accounting (IFRS 16) affects how operating leases are represented in the cash flow statement.[2] Under IFRS 16, operating leases are treated similarly to finance leases—that is, the interest component of lease payments will be reflected in either the operating or financing section, and the principal component of lease payments is included in the financing section.

---

[1] IAS 7 *Statement of Cash Flows*.

[2] IFRS 16 is effective for fiscal years beginning January 1, 2019, with earlier voluntary adoption allowed.

EXAMPLE 1   Net Cash Flow from Investing Activities

A company recorded the following in Year 1:

Proceeds from issuance of long-term debt	€300,000
Purchase of equipment	€200,000
Loss on sale of equipment	€70,000
Proceeds from sale of equipment	€120,000
Equity in earnings of affiliate	€10,000

On the Year 1 statement of cash flows, the company would report net cash flow from investing activities *closest* to:

A. (€150,000).
B. (€80,000).
C. €200,000.

Solution: B is correct. The only two items that would affect the investing section are the purchase of equipment and the proceeds from sale of equipment: (€200,000) + €120,000 = (€80,000). The loss on sale of equipment and the equity in earnings of affiliate affect net income but are not cash flows. The issuance of debt is a financing cash flow.

IFRS provide companies with choices in reporting some items of cash flow, particularly interest and dividends. IFRS explain that although for a financial institution interest paid and received would normally be classified as operating activities, for other entities, alternative classifications may be appropriate. For this reason, under IFRS, interest received may be classified either as an operating activity or as an investing activity. Under IFRS, interest paid may be classified as either an operating activity or a financing activity. Furthermore, under IFRS, dividends received may be classified as either an operating activity or an investing activity, and dividends paid may be classified as either an operating activity or a financing activity. Companies must use a consistent classification from year to year and disclose separately the amounts of interest and dividends received and paid, and where the amounts are reported.

Under US GAAP, discretion is not permitted in classifying interest and dividends. Interest received and interest paid are reported as operating activities for all companies.[3] Under US GAAP, dividends received are always reported as operating activities, and dividends paid are always reported as financing activities.

EXAMPLE 2   Operating versus Financing Cash Flows

On December 31, 2018, a company issued a £30,000 180-day note at 8 percent and used the cash received to pay for inventory and issued £110,000 long-term debt at 11

---

[3] FASB ASC Topic 230 [Statement of Cash Flows].

percent annually and used the cash received to pay for new equipment. Which of the following *most* accurately reflects the combined effect of both transactions on the company's cash flows for the year ended December 31, 2018 under IFRS? Cash flows from:

A. operations are unchanged.
B. financing increase £110,000.
C. operations decrease £30,000.

Solution: C is correct. The payment for inventory would decrease cash flows from operations. The issuance of debt (both short-term and long-term debt) is part of financing activities and would increase cash flows from financing activities by £140,000. The purchase of equipment is an investing activity. Note that the treatment under US GAAP would be the same for these transactions.

Companies may also engage in non-cash investing and financing transactions. A non-cash transaction is any transaction that does not involve an inflow or outflow of cash. For example, if a company exchanges one non-monetary asset for another non-monetary asset, no cash is involved. Similarly, no cash is involved when a company issues common stock either for dividends or in connection with conversion of a convertible bond or convertible preferred stock. Because no cash is involved in non-cash transactions (by definition), these transactions are not incorporated in the cash flow statement. However, because such transactions may affect a company's capital or asset structures, any significant non-cash transaction is required to be disclosed, either in a separate note or a supplementary schedule to the cash flow statement.

2.2. A Summary of Differences between IFRS and US GAAP

As highlighted in the previous section, there are some differences in cash flow statements prepared under IFRS and US GAAP that the analyst should be aware of when comparing the cash flow statements of companies prepared in accordance with different sets of standards. The key differences are summarized in Exhibit 1. Most significantly, IFRS allow more flexibility in the reporting of such items as interest paid or received and dividends paid or received and in how income tax expense is classified.

US GAAP classify interest and dividends received from investments as operating activities, whereas IFRS allow companies to classify those items as either operating or investing cash flows. Likewise, US GAAP classify interest expense as an operating activity, even though the principal amount of the debt issued is classified as a financing activity. IFRS allow companies to classify interest expense as either an operating activity or a financing activity. US GAAP classify dividends paid to stockholders as a financing activity, whereas IFRS allow companies to classify dividends paid as either an operating activity or a financing activity.

US GAAP classify all income tax expenses as an operating activity. IFRS also classify income tax expense as an operating activity, unless the tax expense can be specifically identified with an investing or financing activity (e.g., the tax effect of the sale of a discontinued operation could be classified under investing activities).

EXHIBIT 1   Cash Flow Statements: Differences between IFRS and US GAAP

Topic	IFRS	US GAAP
Classification of cash flows:		
• Interest received	Operating or investing	Operating
• Interest paid	Operating or financing	Operating
• Dividends received	Operating or investing	Operating
• Dividends paid	Operating or financing	Financing
• Bank overdrafts	Considered part of cash equivalents	Not considered part of cash and cash equivalents, and classified as financing
• Taxes paid	Generally operating, but a portion can be allocated to investing or financing if it can be specifically identified with these categories	Operating
Format of statement	Direct or indirect; direct is encouraged	Direct or indirect; direct is encouraged. A reconciliation of net income to cash flow from operating activities must be provided regardless of method used

Sources: IAS 7; FASB ASC Topic 230; and "IFRS and US GAAP: Similarities and Differences," PricewaterhouseCoopers (November 2017), available at www.pwc.com.

Under either set of standards, companies currently have a choice of formats for presenting cash flow statements, as discussed in the next section.

2.3. Direct and Indirect Methods for Reporting Cash Flow from Operating Activities

There are two acceptable formats for reporting **cash flow from operating activities** (also known as **cash flow from operations** or **operating cash flow**), defined as the net amount of cash provided from operating activities: the direct and the indirect methods. The *amount* of operating cash flow is identical under both methods; only the *presentation format* of the operating cash flow section differs. The presentation format of the cash flows from investing and financing is exactly the same, regardless of which method is used to present operating cash flows.

The **direct method** shows the specific cash inflows and outflows that result in reported cash flow from operating activities. It shows each cash inflow and outflow related to a company's cash receipts and disbursements. In other words, the direct method eliminates any impact of accruals and shows only cash receipts and cash payments. The primary argument in favor of the direct method is that it provides information on the specific sources of operating cash receipts and payments. This is in contrast to the indirect method, which shows only the net result of these receipts and payments. Just as information on the specific sources of revenues and expenses is more useful than knowing only the net result—net income—the analyst gets additional information from a direct-format cash flow statement. The additional information is useful in understanding historical performance and in predicting future operating cash flows.

The **indirect method** shows how cash flow from operations can be obtained from reported net income as the result of a series of adjustments. The **indirect format** begins with net income. To reconcile net income with operating cash flow, adjustments are made for non-cash items, for non-operating items, and for the net changes in operating accruals. The main argument for the indirect approach is that it shows the reasons for differences between net income and operating cash flows. (However, the differences between net income and operating cash flows are equally visible on an indirect-format cash flow statement and in the supplementary reconciliation required under US GAAP if the company uses the direct method.) Another argument for the indirect method is that it mirrors a forecasting approach that begins by forecasting future income and then derives cash flows by adjusting for changes in balance sheet accounts that occur because of the timing differences between accrual and cash accounting.

IFRS and US GAAP both encourage the use of the direct method but permit either method. US GAAP encourage the use of the direct method but also require companies to present a reconciliation between net income and cash flow (which is equivalent to the indirect method).[4] If the indirect method is chosen, no direct-format disclosures are required. The majority of companies, reporting under IFRS or US GAAP, present using the indirect method for operating cash flows.

Many users of financial statements prefer the **direct format**, particularly analysts and commercial lenders, because of the importance of information about operating receipts and payments in assessing a company's financing needs and capacity to repay existing obligations. Preparers argue that adjusting net income to operating cash flow, as in the indirect format, is easier and less costly than reporting gross operating cash receipts and payments, as in the direct format. With advances in accounting systems and technology, it is not clear that gathering the information required to use the direct method is difficult or costly. CFA Institute has advocated that standard setters require the use of the direct format for the main presentation of the cash flow statement, with indirect cash flows as supplementary disclosure.[5]

2.3.1. An Indirect-Format Cash Flow Statement Prepared under IFRS

Exhibit 2 presents the consolidated cash flow statement prepared under IFRS from Unilever Group's 2017 annual report. The statement, covering the fiscal years ended December 31, 2017, 2016, and 2015, shows the use of the indirect method. Unilever is an Anglo-Dutch consumer products company with headquarters in the United Kingdom and the Netherlands.[6]

EXHIBIT 2   Unilever Group Consolidated Cash Flow Statement (€ millions)

	For the year ended December 31		
	2017	2016	2015
Cash flow from operating activities			
Net profit	6,486	5,547	5,259
Taxation	1,667	1,922	1,961
Share of net profit of joint ventures/associates and other income (loss) from non-current investments and associates	(173)	(231)	(198)
Net finance costs:	877	563	493

(continued)

---

[4] FASB ASC Section 230-10-45 [Statement of Cash Flows–Overall–Other Presentation Matters].

[5] *A Comprehensive Business Reporting Model: Financial Reporting for Investors*, CFA Institute Centre for Financial Market Integrity (July 2007), p. 13.

[6] Unilever NV and Unilever PLC have independent legal structures, but a series of agreements enable the companies to operate as a single economic entity.

EXHIBIT 2   (Continued)

	For the year ended December 31		
	2017	2016	2015
Operating profit	8,857	7,801	7,515
Depreciation, amortization and impairment	1,538	1,464	1,370
Changes in working capital:	(68)	51	720
Inventories	(104)	190	(129)
Trade and other current receivables	(506)	142	2
Trade payables and other liabilities	542	(281)	847
Pensions and similar obligations less payments	(904)	(327)	(385)
Provisions less payments	200	65	(94)
Elimination of (profits)/losses on disposals	(298)	127	26
Non-cash charge for share-based compensation	284	198	150
Other adjustments	(153)	(81)	49
Cash flow from operating activities	**9,456**	**9,298**	**9,351**
Income tax paid	(2,164)	(2,251)	(2,021)
Net cash flow from operating activities	**7,292**	**7,047**	**7,330**
Interest received	154	105	119
Purchase of intangible assets	(158)	(232)	(334)
Purchase of property, plant, and equipment	(1,509)	(1,804)	(1,867)
Disposal of property, plant, and equipment	46	158	127
Acquisition of group companies, joint ventures, and associates	(4,896)	(1,731)	(1,897)
Disposal of group companies, joint ventures, and associates	561	30	199
Acquisition of other non-current investments	(317)	(208)	(78)
Disposal of other non-current investments	251	173	127
Dividends from joint ventures, associates, and other non-current investments	138	186	176
(Purchase)/sale of financial assets	(149)	135	(111)
Net cash flow (used in)/from investing activities	**(5,879)**	**(3,188)**	**(3,539)**
Dividends paid on ordinary share capital	(3,916)	(3,609)	(3,331)
Interest and preference dividends paid	(470)	(472)	(579)
Net change in short-term borrowings	2,695	258	245
Additional financial liabilities	8,851	6,761	7,566
Repayment of financial liabilities	(2,604)	(5,213)	(6,270)
Capital element of finance lease rental payments	(14)	(35)	(14)
Buy back of preference shares	(448)	—	—
Repurchase of shares	(5,014)	—	—
Other movements on treasury stock	(204)	(257)	(276)
Other financing activities	(309)	(506)	(373)
Net cash flow (used in)/from financing activities	**(1,433)**	**(3,073)**	**(3,032)**
Net increase/(decrease) in cash and cash equivalents	**(20)**	**786**	**759**
Cash and cash equivalents at the beginning of the year	**3,198**	**2,128**	**1,910**
Effect of foreign exchange rate changes	(9)	284	(541)
Cash and cash equivalents at the end of the year	**3,169**	**3,198**	**2,128**

Beginning first at the bottom of the statement, we note that cash increased from €1,910 million at the beginning of 2015 to €3,169 million at the end of 2017, with the largest increase occurring in 2016. To understand the changes, we next examine the sections of the statement. In each year, the primary cash inflow derived from operating activities, as would be expected for a mature company in a relatively stable industry. In each year, the operating cash flow was more than the reported net profit, again, as would be expected from a mature company, with the largest differences primarily arising from the add-back of depreciation. Also, in each year, the operating cash flow was more than enough to cover the company's capital expenditures. For example, in 2017, the company generated €7,292 million in net cash from operating activities and—as shown in the investing section—spent €1,509 million on property, plant, and equipment. The operating cash flow was also sufficient to cover acquisitions of other companies.

The financing section of the statement shows that each year the company returned more than €3.3 billion to its common shareholders through dividends and around €500 million to its debt holders and preferred shareholders via interest and dividends. In 2017, the company used cash to repurchase about €5 billion in common stock in and generated cash from increased borrowing. The increase in short-term borrowings (€2,695 million) and additional financial liabilities (€8,851 million) exceeded the cash repayment of liabilities (€2,604 million).

Having examined each section of the statement, we return to the operating activities section of Unilever's cash flow statement, which presents a reconciliation of net profit to net cash flow from operating activities (i.e., uses the indirect method). The following discussion of certain adjustments to reconcile net profit to operating cash flows explains some of the main reconciliation adjustments and refers to the amounts in 2017. The first adjustment adds back the €1,667 million income tax expense (labeled "Taxation") that had been recognized as an expense in the computation of net profit. A €2,164 million deduction for the (cash) income taxes paid is then shown separately, as the last item in the operating activities section, consistent with the IFRS requirement that cash flows arising from income taxes be separately disclosed. The classification of taxes on income paid should be indicated. The classification is in operating activities unless the taxes can be specifically identified with financing or investing activities.

The next adjustment "removes" from the operating cash flow section the €173 million representing Unilever's share of joint ventures' income that had been included in the computation of net profit. A €138 million inflow of (cash) dividends received from those joint ventures is then shown in the investing activities section. Similarly, a €877 million adjustment removes the net finance costs from the operating activities section. Unilever then reports its €154 million (cash) interest received in the investing activities section and its €470 million (cash) interest paid (and preference dividends paid) in the financing activities section. The next adjustment in the operating section of this indirect-method statement adds back €1,538 million depreciation, amortization, and impairment, all of which are expenses that had been deducted in the computation of net income but which did not involve any outflow of cash in the period. The €68 million adjustment for changes in working capital is necessary because these changes result from applying accrual accounting and thus do not necessarily correspond to the actual cash movement. These adjustments are described in greater detail in a later section.

In summary, some observations from an analysis of Unilever's cash flow statement include:

- Total cash increased from €1,910 million at the beginning of 2015 to €3,169 million at the end of 2017, with the largest increase occurring in 2016.
- In each year, the operating cash flow was more than the reported net profit, as would generally be expected from a mature company.

- In each year, the operating cash flow was more than enough to cover the company's capital expenditures.
- The company returned cash to its equity investors through dividends in each year and through share buybacks in 2017.

2.3.2. A Direct-Format Cash Flow Statement Prepared under IFRS

In the direct format of the cash flow statement, the cash received from customers, as well as other operating items, is clearly shown.

Exhibit 3 presents a direct-method format cash flow statement prepared under IFRS for Telefónica Group, a diversified telecommunications company based in Madrid.[7]

EXHIBIT 3 Telefónica Group Consolidated Statement of Cash Flows (€ millions)

For the years ended December 31	2017	2016	2015
Cash flows from operating activities			
Cash received from operations	63,456	63,514	67,582
Cash paid from operations	(46,929)	(47,384)	(50,833)
Net interest and other financial expenses net of dividends received	(1,726)	(2,143)	(2,445)
Taxes paid	(1,005)	(649)	(689)
Net cash flow provided by operating activities	**13,796**	**13,338**	**13,615**
Cash flows from investing activities			
(Payments on investments)/proceeds from the sale in property, plant, and equipment and intangible assets, net	(8,992)	(9,187)	(10,256)
Proceeds on disposals of companies, net of cash and cash equivalents disposed	40	767	354
Payments on investments in companies, net of cash and cash equivalents acquired	(128)	(54)	(3,181)
Proceeds on financial investments not included under cash equivalents	296	489	1,142
Payments made on financial investments not included under cash equivalents	(1,106)	(265)	(426)
(Payments)/proceeds on placements of cash surpluses not included under cash equivalents	(357)	42	(557)
Government grants received	2	—	7
Net cash used in investing activities	**(10,245)**	**(8,208)**	**(12,917)**
Cash flows from financing activities			
Dividends paid	(2,459)	(2,906)	(2,775)
Proceeds from share capital increase	2	—	4,255
Proceeds/(payments) of treasury shares and other operations with shareholders and with minority interests	1,269	(660)	(1,772)
Operations with other equity holders	646	656	83

---

[7] This statement excludes the supplemental cash flow reconciliation provided at the bottom of the original cash flow statement by the company.

EXHIBIT 3   (Continued)

For the years ended December 31	2017	2016	2015
Proceeds on issue of debentures and bonds, and other debts	8,390	5,693	1,602
Proceeds on loans, borrowings, and promissory notes	4,844	10,332	8,784
Repayments of debentures and bonds and other debts	(6,687)	(6,873)	(3,805)
Repayments of loans, borrowings, and promissory notes	(6,711)	(8,506)	(9,858)
Financed operating payments and investments in property, plant, and equipment and intangible assets payments	(1,046)	(1,956)	(126)
Net cash flow used in financing activities	**(1,752)**	**(4,220)**	**(3,612)**
Effect of changes in exchange rates	(341)	185	(1,000)
Effect of changes in consolidation methods and others	(2)	26	—
Net increase (decrease) in cash and cash equivalents during the period	**1,456**	**1,121**	**(3,914)**
Cash and cash equivalents at January 1	3,736	2,615	6,529
Cash and cash equivalents at December 31	5,192	3,736	2,615

As shown at the bottom of the statement, cash and cash equivalents decreased from €6,529 million at the beginning of 2015 to €5,192 million at the end of 2017. The largest decrease in cash occurred in 2015. Cash from operations was the primary source of cash, consistent with the profile of a mature company in a relatively stable industry. Each year, the company generated significantly more cash from operations than it required for its capital expenditures. For example, in 2017, the company generated €13.8 billion cash from operations and spent—as shown in the investing section—only €9 billion on property, plant, and equipment, net of proceeds from sales. Another notable item from the investing section is the company's limited acquisition activity in 2017 and 2016 compared with 2015. In 2015, the company made over €3 billion of acquisitions. As shown in the financing section, cash flows from financing were negative in all three years, although the components of the negative cash flows differed. In 2015, for example, the company generated cash with an equity issuance of €4.2 billion but made significant net repayments of debts resulting in negative cash from financing activities.

In summary, some observations from an analysis of Telefónica's cash flow statement include:

- Total cash and cash equivalents decreased over the three-year period, with 2015 showing the biggest decrease.
- Cash from operating activities was large enough in each year to cover the company's capital expenditures.
- The amount paid for property, plant, and equipment and intangible assets was the largest investing expenditure each year.
- The company had a significant amount of acquisition activity in 2015.
- The company paid dividends each year although the amount in 2017 is somewhat lower than in prior years.

2.3.3. Illustrations of Cash Flow Statements Prepared under US GAAP

Previously, we presented cash flow statements prepared under IFRS. In this section, we illustrate cash flow statements prepared under US GAAP. This section presents the cash flow statements of two companies, Tech Data Corporation and Walmart. Tech Data reports its operating activities using the direct method, whereas Walmart reports its operating activities using the more common indirect method.

Tech Data Corporation is a leading distributor of information technology products. Exhibit 4 presents comparative cash flow statements from the company's annual report for the fiscal years ended January 31, 2016 through 2018.

EXHIBIT 4   Tech Data Corporation and Subsidiaries Consolidated Cash Flow Statements (in Thousands)

Years Ended January 31	2018	2017	2016
Cash flows from operating activities:			
Cash received from customers	$42,981,601	$29,427,357	$28,119,687
Cash paid to vendors and employees	(41,666,356)	(28,664,222)	(27,819,886)
Interest paid, net	(86,544)	(22,020)	(20,264)
Income taxes paid	(131,632)	(84,272)	(85,645)
Net cash provided by operating activities	**1,097,069**	**656,843**	**193,892**
Cash flows from investing activities:			
Acquisition of business, net of cash acquired	(2,249,849)	(2,916)	(27,848)
Expenditures for property and equipment	(192,235)	(24,971)	(20,917)
Software and software development costs	(39,702)	(14,364)	(13,055)
Proceeds from sale of subsidiaries	0	0	20,020
Net cash used in investing activities	**(2,481,786)**	**(42,251)**	**(41,800)**
Cash flows from financing activities:			
Borrowings on long-term debt	1,008,148	998,405	—
Principal payments on long-term debt	(861,394)	—	(319)
Cash paid for debt issuance costs	(6,348)	(21,581)	—
Net borrowings on revolving credit loans	(16,028)	3,417	5,912
Cash paid for purchase of treasury stock	—	—	(147,003)
Payments for employee withholdings on equity awards	(6,027)	(4,479)	(4,662)
Proceeds from the reissuance of treasury stock	1,543	733	561
Acquisition of earn-out payments	—	—	(2,736)
Net cash provided by (used in) financing activities	**119,894**	**976,495**	**(148,247)**
Effect of exchange rate changes on cash and cash equivalents	94,860	3,335	(15,671)
Net (decrease) increase in cash and cash equivalents	(1,169,963)	1,594,422	(11,826)
Cash and cash equivalents at beginning of year	2,125,591	531,169	542,995
Cash and cash equivalents at end of year	**$955,628**	**$2,125,591**	**$531,169**
Reconciliation of net income to net cash provided by operating activities:			
Net income	$116,641	$195,095	$265,736
Adjustments to reconcile net income to net cash provided by operating activities:			
Depreciation and amortization	150,046	54,437	57,253
Provision for losses on accounts receivable	21,022	5,026	6,061

EXHIBIT 4   (Continued)

Years Ended January 31	2018	2017	2016
Stock-based compensation expense	29,381	13,947	14,890
Loss on disposal of subsidiaries	—	—	699
Accretion of debt discount and debt issuance costs	3,326	835	839
Deferred income taxes	(4,261)	(11,002)	2,387
Changes in operating assets and liabilities:			
Accounts receivable	(554,627)	(91,961)	(297,637)
Inventories	(502,352)	(20,838)	(219,482)
Prepaid expenses and other assets	32,963	66,027	(44,384)
Accounts payable	1,704,307	459,146	426,412
Accrued expenses and other liabilities	100,623	(13,869)	(18,882)
Total adjustments	980,428	461,748	(71,844)
Net cash provided by operating activities	$1,097,069	$656,843	$193,892

Tech Data Corporation prepares its cash flow statements under the direct method. The company's cash increased from $543 million at the beginning of 2016 to $956 million at the end of January 2018, with the biggest increase occurring in 2017. The 2017 increase was driven by changes in both operating cash flow and financing cash flow. In the cash flows from operating activities section of Tech Data's cash flow statements, the company identifies the amount of cash it received from customers, $43 billion for 2018, and the amount of cash that it paid to suppliers and employees, $41.7 billion for 2018. Cash receipts increased from $29.4 billion in the prior year, and cash paid also increased substantially. Net cash provided by operating activities was adequate to cover the company's investing activities in 2016 and 2017 but not in 2018, primarily because of increased amounts of cash used for acquisition of business. Related to this investing cash outflow for an acquisition, footnotes disclose that the major acquisition in 2018 accounted for the large increase in cash receipts and cash payments in the operating section. Also related to the 2018 acquisition, the financing section shows that the company borrowed more debt than it repaid in both 2017 and 2018. In 2017, borrowings on long-term debt were $998.4 million, and net borrowings on revolving credit loans were $3.4 million. In 2018, the company generated cash by borrowing more long-term debt than it repaid but used cash to pay down its revolving credit loans. There are no dividend payments, although in 2016, the company paid $147 million to repurchase its common stock.

Whenever the direct method is used, US GAAP require a disclosure note and a schedule that reconciles net income with the net cash flow from operating activities. Tech Data shows this reconciliation at the bottom of its consolidated statements of cash flows. The disclosure note and reconciliation schedule are exactly the information that would have been presented in the body of the cash flow statement if the company had elected to use the indirect method rather than the direct method. For 2018, the reconciliation highlights an increase in the company's accounts receivable, inventory, and payables.

In summary, some observations from an analysis of Tech Data's cash flow statement include:

• The company's cash increased by over $412 million over the three years ending in January 2018, with the biggest increase occurring in 2017.

- The company's operating cash was adequate to cover the company's investments in 2016 and 2017, but not in 2018 primarily because of a major acquisition.
- Related to the 2018 acquisition, the financing section shows an increase in long-term borrowings in 2017 and 2018, including a $998 million increase in 2017.
- The company has not paid dividends in the past three years, but the financing section shows that in 2016 the company repurchased stock.

Walmart is a global retailer that conducts business under the names of Walmart and Sam's Club. Exhibit 5 presents the comparative cash flow statements from the company's annual report for the fiscal years ended January 31, 2018, 2017, and 2016.

EXHIBIT 5   Walmart Cash Flow Statements Fiscal Years Ended January 31 ($ millions)

Fiscal Year Ended January 31	2018	2017	2016
Cash flows from operating activities:			
Consolidated net income	10,523	14,293	15,080
Adjustments to reconcile income from continuing operations to net cash provided by operating activities:			
Depreciation and amortization	10,529	10,080	9,454
Deferred income taxes	(304)	761	(672)
Loss on extinguishment of debt	3,136	—	—
Other operating activities	1,210	206	1,410
Changes in certain assets and liabilities, net of effects of acquisitions:			
Receivables, net	(1.074)	(402)	(19)
Inventories	(140)	1,021	(703)
Accounts payable	4,086	3,942	2,008
Accrued liabilities	928	1,280	1,466
Accrued income taxes	(557)	492	(472)
Net cash provided by operating activities	28,337	31,673	27,552
Cash flows from investing activities:			
Payments for property and equipment	(10,051)	(10,619)	(11,477)
Proceeds from disposal of property and equipment	378	456	635
Proceeds from the disposal of certain operations	1,046	662	246
Purchase of available for sale securities	—	(1,901)	—
Investment and business acquisitions, net of cash acquired	(375)	(2,463)	—
Other investing activities	(58)	(122)	(79)
Net cash used in investing activities	(9,060)	(13,987)	(10,675)
Cash flows from financing activities:			
Net change in short-term borrowings	4,148	(1,673)	1,235
Proceeds from issuance of long-term debt	7,476	137	39
Payments of long-term debt	(13,061)	(2,055)	(4,432)
Payment for debt extinguishment or debt prepayment cost	(3,059)	—	—
Dividends paid	(6,124)	(6,216)	(6,294)

EXHIBIT 5   (Continued)

Fiscal Year Ended January 31	2018	2017	2016
Purchase of Company stock	(8,296)	(8,298)	(4,112)
Dividends paid to noncontrolling interest	(690)	(479)	(719)
Purchase of noncontrolling interest	(8)	(90)	(1,326)
Other financing activities	(261)	(398)	(676)
Net cash used in financing activities	(19,875)	(19,072)	(16,285)
Effect of exchange rates on cash and cash equivalents	487	(452)	(1,022)
Net increase (decrease) in cash and cash equivalents	(111)	(1,838)	(430)
Cash and cash equivalents at beginning of year	6,867	8,705	9,135
Cash and cash equivalents at end of year	**6,756**	**6,867**	**8,705**
Supplemental disclosure of cash flow information			
Income taxes paid	6,179	4,507	8,111
Interest paid	2,450	2,351	2,540

Walmart's cash flow statement indicates the following:

- Cash and cash equivalents declined over the three years, from $9.1 billion at the beginning of fiscal 2016 to $6.8 billion at the end of fiscal 2018.
- Operating cash flow was relatively steady at $27.6 billion, $31.7 billion, and $28.3 billion in fiscal 2016, 2017, and 2018, respectively. Further, operating cash flow was significantly greater than the company's expenditures on property and equipment in every year.
- Over the three years, the company used significant amounts of cash to pay dividends and to repurchase its common stock. The company also repaid borrowing, particularly in fiscal 2018.

Walmart prepares its cash flow statements under the indirect method. In the cash flows from operating activities section of Walmart's cash flow statement, the company reconciles its net income for 2018 of $10.5 billion to net cash provided by operating activities of $28.3 billion. The largest adjustment is for depreciation and amortization of $10.5 billion. Depreciation and amortization expense requires an adjustment because it was a non-cash expense on the income statement. As illustrated in previous examples, depreciation is the largest, or one of the largest, adjustments made by many companies in the reconciliation of net income to operating cash flow.

Whenever the indirect method is used, US GAAP mandate disclosure of how much cash was paid for interest and income taxes. Note that these are line items in cash flow statements using the direct method, so disclosure does not have to be mandated. Walmart discloses the amount of cash paid for income tax ($6.2 billion) and interest ($2.5 billion) at the bottom of its cash flow statements.

3. THE CASH FLOW STATEMENT: LINKAGES AND PREPARATION

The indirect format of the cash flow statement demonstrates that changes in balance sheet accounts are an important factor in determining cash flows. The next section addresses the linkages between the cash flow statement and other financial statements.

3.1. Linkages of the Cash Flow Statement with the Income Statement and Balance Sheet

Recall the accounting equation that summarizes the balance sheet:

$$\text{Assets} = \text{Liabilities} + \text{Equity}$$

Cash is an asset. The statement of cash flows ultimately shows the change in cash during an accounting period. The beginning and ending balances of cash are shown on the company's balance sheets for the previous and current years, and the bottom of the cash flow statement reconciles beginning cash with ending cash. The relationship, stated in general terms, is as shown below.

Beginning Balance Sheet at December 31, 20X8	Statement of Cash Flows for Year Ended December 31, 20X9		Ending Balance Sheet at December 31, 20X9
Beginning cash	Plus: Cash receipts (from operating, investing, and financing activities)	Less: Cash payments (for operating, investing, and financing activities)	Ending cash

In the case of cash held in foreign currencies, there would also be an impact from changes in exchange rates. For example, Walmart's cash flow statement for 2018, presented in Exhibit 5, shows overall cash flows from operating, investing, and financing activities that total $(111) million during the year, including $487 million net effect of exchange rates on cash and cash equivalents.

The body of Walmart's cash flow statement shows why the change in cash occurred; in other words, it shows the company's operating, investing, and financing activities (as well as the impact of foreign currency translation). The beginning and ending balance sheet values of cash and cash equivalents are linked through the cash flow statement.

The current assets and current liabilities sections of the balance sheet typically reflect a company's operating decisions and activities. Because a company's operating activities are reported on an accrual basis in the income statement, any differences between the accrual basis and the cash basis of accounting for an operating transaction result in an increase or decrease in some (usually) short-term asset or liability on the balance sheet. For example, if revenue reported using accrual accounting is higher than the cash actually collected, the result will typically be an increase in accounts receivable. If expenses reported using accrual accounting are lower than cash actually paid, the result will typically be a decrease in accounts payable or another accrued liability account.[8] As an example of how items on the balance sheet are related to the income statement and/or cash flow statement through the change in the beginning and ending balances, consider accounts receivable:

Beginning Balance Sheet at December 31, 20X8	Income Statement for Year Ended December 31, 20X9	Statement of Cash Flows for Year Ended December 31, 20X9	Ending Balance Sheet at December 31, 20X9
Beginning accounts receivable	Plus: Revenues	Minus: Cash collected from customers	Equals: Ending accounts receivable

[8]There are other less typical explanations of the differences. For example, if revenue reported using accrual accounting is higher than the cash actually collected, it is possible that it is the result of a decrease in an unearned revenue liability account. If expenses reported using accrual accounting are lower than cash actually paid, it is possible that it is the result of an increase in prepaid expenses, inventory, or another asset account.

Knowing any three of these four items makes it easy to compute the fourth. For example, if you know beginning accounts receivable, revenues, and cash collected from customers, you can compute ending accounts receivable. Understanding the interrelationships among the balance sheet, income statement, and cash flow statement is useful not only in evaluating the company's financial health but also in detecting accounting irregularities. Recall the extreme illustration of a hypothetical company that makes sales on account without regard to future collections and thus reports healthy sales and significant income on its income statement yet lacks cash inflow. Such a pattern would occur if a company improperly recognized revenue.

A company's investing activities typically relate to the long-term asset section of the balance sheet, and its financing activities typically relate to the equity and long-term debt sections of the balance sheet. The next section demonstrates the preparation of cash flow information based on income statement and balance sheet information.

3.2. Steps in Preparing the Cash Flow Statement

The preparation of the cash flow statement uses data from both the income statement and the comparative balance sheets.

As noted earlier, companies often only disclose indirect operating cash flow information, whereas analysts prefer direct-format information. Understanding how cash flow information is put together will enable you to take an indirect statement apart and reconfigure it in a more useful manner. The result is an approximation of a direct cash flow statement, which—while not perfectly accurate—can be helpful to an analyst. The following demonstration of how an approximation of a direct cash flow statement is prepared uses the income statement and the comparative balance sheets for Acme Corporation (a fictitious retail company) shown in Exhibits 6 and 7.

EXHIBIT 6 Acme Corporation Income Statement Year Ended December 31, 2018

Revenue (net)		$23,598
Cost of goods sold		11,456
Gross profit		12,142
Salary and wage expense	$4,123	
Depreciation expenses	1,052	
Other operating expenses	3,577	
Total operating expenses		8,752
Operating profit		3,390
Other revenues (expenses):		
Gain on sale of equipment	205	
Interest expense	(246)	(41)
Income before tax		3,349
Income tax expense		1,139
Net income		$2,210

EXHIBIT 7   Acme Corporation Comparative Balance Sheets December 31, 2018 and 2017

	2018	2017	Net Change
Cash	$1,011	$1,163	$(152)
Accounts receivable	1,012	957	55
Inventory	3,984	3,277	707
Prepaid expenses	155	178	(23)
Total current assets	6,162	5,575	587
Land	510	510	—
Buildings	3,680	3,680	—
Equipment*	8,798	8,555	243
Less: accumulated depreciation	(3,443)	(2,891)	(552)
Total long-term assets	9,545	9,854	(309)
Total assets	$15,707	$15,429	$278
Accounts payable	$3,588	$3,325	$263
Salary and wage payable	85	75	10
Interest payable	62	74	(12)
Income tax payable	55	50	5
Other accrued liabilities	1,126	1,104	22
Total current liabilities	4,916	4,628	288
Long-term debt	3,075	3,575	(500)
Common stock	3,750	4,350	(600)
Retained earnings	3,966	2,876	1,090
Total liabilities and equity	$15,707	$15,429	$278

*During 2018, Acme purchased new equipment for a total cost of $1,300. No items impacted retained earnings other than net income and dividends.

The first step in preparing the cash flow statement is to determine the total cash flows from operating activities. The direct method of presenting cash from operating activities is illustrated in sections 3.2.1 through 3.2.4. Section 3.2.5 illustrates the indirect method of presenting cash flows from operating activities. Cash flows from investing activities and from financing activities are identical regardless of whether the direct or indirect method is used to present operating cash flows.

3.2.1. Operating Activities: Direct Method
We first determine how much cash Acme received from its customers, followed by how much cash was paid to suppliers and to employees as well as how much cash was paid for other operating expenses, interest, and income taxes.

3.2.1.1. Cash Received from Customers The income statement for Acme reported revenue of $23,598 for the year ended December 31, 2018. To determine the approximate cash receipts from its customers, it is necessary to adjust this revenue amount by the net change in accounts receivable for the year. If accounts receivable increase during the year, revenue on an accrual basis is higher than cash receipts from customers, and vice versa. For Acme Corporation, accounts receivable increased by $55, so cash received from customers was $23,543, as follows:

Revenue	$23,598
Less: Increase in accounts receivable	(55)
Cash received from customers	**$23,543**

Cash received from customers affects the accounts receivable account as follows:

Beginning accounts receivable	957
Plus revenue	23,598
Minus cash collected from customers	**(23,543)**
Ending accounts receivable	$1,012

The accounts receivable account information can also be presented as follows:

Beginning accounts receivable	$957
Plus revenue	23,598
Minus ending accounts receivable	(1,012)
Cash collected from customers	**$23,543**

EXAMPLE 3   Computing Cash Received from Customers

Blue Bayou, a fictitious advertising company, reported revenues of $50 million, total expenses of $35 million, and net income of $15 million in the most recent year. If accounts receivable decreased by $12 million, how much cash did the company receive from customers?

A. $38 million.
B. $50 million.
C. $62 million.

Solution: C is correct. Revenues of $50 million plus the decrease in accounts receivable of $12 million equals $62 million cash received from customers. The decrease in accounts receivable means that the company received more in cash than the amount of revenue it reported.

"Cash received from customers" is sometimes referred to as "cash collections from customers" or "cash collections."

3.2.1.2. Cash Paid to Suppliers   For Acme, the cash paid to suppliers was $11,900, determined as follows:

Cost of goods sold	$11,456
Plus: Increase in inventory	707
Equals purchases from suppliers	$12,163
Less: Increase in accounts payable	(263)
Cash paid to suppliers	**$11,900**

There are two pieces to this calculation: the amount of inventory purchased and the amount paid for it. To determine purchases from suppliers, cost of goods sold is adjusted for the change in inventory. If inventory increased during the year, then purchases during the year exceeded cost of goods sold, and vice versa. Acme reported cost of goods sold of $11,456 for the year ended December 31, 2018. For Acme Corporation, inventory increased by $707, so purchases from suppliers was $12,163. Purchases from suppliers affect the inventory account, as shown below:

Beginning inventory	$ 3,277
Plus purchases	12,163
Minus cost of goods sold	(11,456)
Ending inventory	$3,984

Acme purchased $12,163 of inventory from suppliers in 2018, but is this the amount of cash that Acme paid to its suppliers during the year? Not necessarily. Acme may not have yet paid for all of these purchases and may yet owe for some of the purchases made this year. In other words, Acme may have paid less cash to its suppliers than the amount of this year's purchases, in which case Acme's liability (accounts payable) will have increased by the difference. Alternatively, Acme may have paid even more to its suppliers than the amount of this year's purchases, in which case Acme's accounts payable will have decreased.

Therefore, once purchases have been determined, cash paid to suppliers can be calculated by adjusting purchases for the change in accounts payable. If the company made all purchases with cash, then accounts payable would not change, and cash outflows would equal purchases. If accounts payable increased during the year, then purchases on an accrual basis would be higher than they would be on a cash basis, and vice versa. In this example, Acme made more purchases than it paid in cash, so the balance in accounts payable increased. For Acme, the cash paid to suppliers was $11,900, determined as follows:

Purchases from suppliers	$12,163
Less: Increase in accounts payable	(263)
Cash paid to suppliers	**$11,900**

The amount of cash paid to suppliers is reflected in the accounts payable account, as shown below:

Beginning accounts payable	$3,325
Plus purchases	12,163
Minus cash paid to suppliers	**(11,900)**
Ending accounts payable	$3,588

EXAMPLE 4   Computing Cash Paid to Suppliers

Orange Beverages Plc., a fictitious manufacturer of tropical drinks, reported cost of goods sold for the year of $100 million. Total assets increased by $55 million, but inventory declined by $6 million. Total liabilities increased by $45 million, but accounts payable decreased by $2 million. How much cash did the company pay to its suppliers during the year?

A. $96 million.
B. $104 million.
C. $108 million.

Solution: A is correct. Cost of goods sold of $100 million less the decrease in inventory of $6 million equals purchases from suppliers of $94 million. The decrease in accounts payable of $2 million means that the company paid $96 million in cash ($94 million plus $2 million).

3.2.1.3. Cash Paid to Employees   To determine the cash paid to employees, it is necessary to adjust salary and wages expense by the net change in salary and wages payable for the year. If salary and wages payable increased during the year, then salary and wages expense on an accrual basis would be higher than the amount of cash paid for this expense, and vice versa. For Acme, salary and wages payable increased by $10, so cash paid for salary and wages was $4,113, as follows:

Salary and wages expense	$4,123
Less: Increase in salary and wages payable	(10)
Cash paid to employees	**$4,113**

The amount of cash paid to employees is reflected in the salary and wages payable account, as shown below:

Beginning salary and wages payable	$ 75
Plus salary and wages expense	4,123
Minus cash paid to employees	**(4,113)**
Ending salary and wages payable	$ 85

3.2.1.4. Cash Paid for Other Operating Expenses   To determine the cash paid for other operating expenses, it is necessary to adjust the other operating expenses amount on the income statement by the net changes in prepaid expenses and accrued expense liabilities for the year. If prepaid expenses increased during the year, other operating expenses on a cash basis would be higher than on an accrual basis, and vice versa. Likewise, if accrued expense liabilities increased during the year, other operating expenses on a cash basis would be lower than on an accrual basis, and vice versa. For Acme Corporation, the amount of cash paid for operating expenses in 2018 was $3,532, as follows:

Other operating expenses	$3,577
Less: Decrease in prepaid expenses	(23)
Less: Increase in other accrued liabilities	(22)
Cash paid for other operating expenses	**$3,532**

EXAMPLE 5   Computing Cash Paid for Other Operating Expenses

Black Ice, a fictitious sportswear manufacturer, reported other operating expenses of $30 million. Prepaid insurance expense increased by $4 million, and accrued utilities payable decreased by $7 million. Insurance and utilities are the only two components of other operating expenses. How much cash did the company pay in other operating expenses?

A. $19 million.
B. $33 million.
C. $41 million.

Solution: C is correct. Other operating expenses of $30 million plus the increase in prepaid insurance expense of $4 million plus the decrease in accrued utilities payable of $7 million equals $41 million.

3.2.1.5. Cash Paid for Interest   The cash paid for interest is included in operating cash flows under US GAAP and may be included in operating or financing cash flows under IFRS. To determine the cash paid for interest, it is necessary to adjust interest expense by the net change in interest payable for the year. If interest payable increases during the year, then interest expense on an accrual basis will be higher than the amount of cash paid for interest, and vice versa. For Acme Corporation, interest payable decreased by $12, and cash paid for interest was $258, as follows:

Interest expense	$246
Plus: Decrease in interest payable	12
Cash paid for interest	**$258**

Alternatively, cash paid for interest may also be determined by an analysis of the interest payable account, as shown below:

Beginning interest payable	$74
Plus interest expense	246
Minus cash paid for interest	**(258)**
Ending interest payable	$62

3.2.1.6. Cash Paid for Income Taxes   To determine the cash paid for income taxes, it is nec-essary to adjust the income tax expense amount on the income statement by the net changes in taxes receivable, taxes payable, and deferred income taxes for the year. If taxes receivable or deferred tax assets increase during the year, income taxes on a cash basis will be higher than on an accrual basis, and vice versa. Likewise, if taxes payable or deferred tax liabilities increase during the year, income tax expense on a cash basis will be lower than on an accrual basis, and vice versa. For Acme Corporation, the amount of cash paid for income taxes in 2018 was $1,134, as follows:

Income tax expense	$1,139
Less: Increase in income tax payable	(5)
Cash paid for income taxes	**$1,134**

3.2.2. Investing Activities

The second and third steps in preparing the cash flow statement are to determine the total cash flows from investing activities and from financing activities. The presentation of this information is identical, regardless of whether the direct or indirect method is used for operating cash flows.

Purchases and sales of equipment were the only investing activities undertaken by Acme in 2018, as evidenced by the fact that the amounts reported for land and buildings were unchanged during the year. An informational note in Exhibit 7 tells us that Acme *purchased* new equipment in 2018 for a total cost of $1,300. However, the amount of equipment shown on Acme's balance sheet increased by only $243 (ending balance of $8,798 minus beginning balance of $8,555); therefore, Acme must have also *sold or otherwise disposed of* some equip-ment during the year. To determine the cash inflow from the sale of equipment, we analyze the equipment and accumulated depreciation accounts as well as the gain on the sale of equipment from Exhibits 6 and 7. Assuming that the entire accumulated depreciation is related to equip-ment, the cash received from sale of equipment is determined as follows.

The historical cost of the equipment sold was $1,057. This amount is determined as follows:

Beginning balance equipment (from balance sheet)	$8,555
Plus equipment purchased (from informational note)	1,300
Minus ending balance equipment (from balance sheet)	(8,798)
Equals historical cost of equipment sold	$1,057

The accumulated depreciation on the equipment sold was $500, determined as follows:

Beginning balance accumulated depreciation (from balance sheet)	$2,891
Plus depreciation expense (from income statement)	1,052
Minus ending balance accumulated depreciation (from balance sheet)	(3,443)
Equals accumulated depreciation on equipment sold	$ 500

The historical cost information, accumulated depreciation information, and information from the income statement about the gain on the sale of equipment can be used to determine the cash received from the sale.

Historical cost of equipment sold (calculated above)	$1,057
Less accumulated depreciation on equipment sold (calculated above)	(500)
Equals book value of equipment sold	$ 557
Plus gain on sale of equipment (from the income statement)	205
Equals cash received from sale of equipment	**$ 762**

EXAMPLE 6   Computing Cash Received from the Sale of Equipment

Copper, Inc., a fictitious brewery and restaurant chain, reported a gain on the sale of equipment of $12 million. In addition, the company's income statement shows depreciation expense of $8 million, and the cash flow statement shows capital expenditure of $15 million, all of which was for the purchase of new equipment.

Balance sheet item	12/31/2018	12/31/2017	Change
Equipment	$100 million	$109 million	$9 million
Accumulated depreciation—equipment	$30 million	$36 million	$6 million

Using the above information from the comparative balance sheets, how much cash did the company receive from the equipment sale?

A. $12 million.
B. $16 million.
C. $18 million.

Solution: B is correct. Selling price (cash inflow) minus book value equals gain or loss on sale; therefore, gain or loss on sale plus book value equals selling price (cash inflow). The amount of gain is given, $12 million. To calculate the book value of the equipment sold, find the historical cost of the equipment and the accumulated depreciation on the equipment.

- Beginning balance of equipment of $100 million plus equipment purchased of $15 million minus ending balance of equipment of $109 million equals historical cost of equipment sold, or $6 million.
- Beginning accumulated depreciation on equipment of $30 million plus depreciation expense for the year of $8 million minus ending balance of accumulated depreciation of $36 million equals accumulated depreciation on the equipment sold, or $2 million.
- Therefore, the book value of the equipment sold was $6 million minus $2 million, or $4 million.
- Because the gain on the sale of equipment was $12 million, the amount of cash received must have been $16 million.

3.2.3. Financing Activities

As with investing activities, the presentation of financing activities is identical, regardless of whether the direct or indirect method is used for operating cash flows.

3.2.3.1. Long-Term Debt and Common Stock   The change in long-term debt, based on the beginning 2018 (ending 2017) and ending 2018 balances in Exhibit 7, was a decrease of $500. Absent other information, this indicates that Acme retired $500 of long-term debt. Retiring long-term debt is a cash outflow relating to financing activities.

Similarly, the change in common stock during 2018 was a decrease of $600. Absent other information, this indicates that Acme repurchased $600 of its common stock. Repurchase of common stock is also a cash outflow related to financing activity.

3.2.3.2. Dividends   Recall the following relationship:

Beginning retained earnings + Net income − Dividends = Ending retained earnings

Based on this relationship, the amount of cash dividends paid in 2018 can be determined from an analysis of retained earnings, as follows:

Beginning balance of retained earnings (from the balance sheet)	$2,876
Plus net income (from the income statement)	2,210
Minus ending balance of retained earnings (from the balance sheet)	(3,966)
Equals dividends paid	**$1,120**

Note that dividends paid are presented in the statement of changes in equity.

3.2.4. Overall Statement of Cash Flows: Direct Method

Exhibit 8 summarizes the information about Acme's operating, investing, and financing cash flows in the statement of cash flows. At the bottom of the statement, the total net change in cash is shown to be a decrease of $152 (from $1,163 to $1,011). This decrease can also be seen on the comparative balance sheet in Exhibit 7. The cash provided by operating activities of $2,606 was adequate to cover the net cash used in investing activities of $538; however, the company's debt repayments, cash payments for dividends, and repurchase of common stock (i.e., its financing activities) of $2,220 resulted in an overall decrease in cash of $152.

EXHIBIT 8   Acme Corporation Cash Flow Statement
(Direct Method) for Year Ended December 31, 2009

Cash flow from operating activities:	
Cash received from customers	$23,543
Cash paid to suppliers	(11,900)
Cash paid to employees	(4,113)
Cash paid for other operating expenses	(3,532)
Cash paid for interest	(258)
Cash paid for income tax	(1,134)
Net cash provided by operating activities	2,606
Cash flow from investing activities:	
Cash received from sale of equipment	762
Cash paid for purchase of equipment	(1,300)
Net cash used for investing activities	(538)
Cash flow from financing activities:	
Cash paid to retire long-term debt	(500)
Cash paid to retire common stock	(600)
Cash paid for dividends	(1,120)
Net cash used for financing activities	(2,220)
Net increase (decrease) in cash	(152)
Cash balance, December 31, 2017	1,163
Cash balance, December 31, 2018	$1,011

3.2.5. Overall Statement of Cash Flows: Indirect Method

Using the alternative approach to reporting cash from operating activities, the indirect method, we will present the same amount of cash provided by operating activities. Under this approach, we reconcile Acme's net income of $2,210 to its operating cash flow of $2,606.

To perform this reconciliation, net income is adjusted for the following: a) any non-operating activities, b) any non-cash expenses, and c) changes in operating working capital items.

The only non-operating activity in Acme's income statement, the sale of equipment, resulted in a gain of $205. This amount is removed from the operating cash flow section; the cash effects of the sale are shown in the investing section.

Acme's only non-cash expense was depreciation expense of $1,052. Under the indirect method, depreciation expense must be added back to net income because it was a non-cash deduction in the calculation of net income.

Changes in working capital accounts include increases and decreases in the current operating asset and liability accounts. The changes in these accounts arise from applying accrual accounting; that is, recognizing revenues when they are earned and expenses when they are incurred instead of when the cash is received or paid. To make the working capital adjustments under the indirect method, any increase in a current operating asset account is subtracted from net income, and a net decrease is added to net income. As described above, the increase in accounts receivable, for example, resulted from Acme recording income statement revenue higher than the amount of cash received from customers; therefore, to reconcile back to operating cash flow, that increase in accounts receivable must be deducted from net income. For current operating liabilities, a net increase is added to net income, and a net decrease is subtracted from net income. As described above, the increase in wages payable, for example, resulted from Acme recording income statement expenses higher than the amount of cash paid to employees.

Exhibit 9 presents a tabulation of the most common types of adjustments that are made to net income when using the indirect method to determine net cash flow from operating activities.

EXHIBIT 9   Adjustments to Net Income Using the Indirect Method

Additions	• Non-cash items
	▪ Depreciation expense of tangible assets
	▪ Amortization expense of intangible assets
	▪ Depletion expense of natural resources
	▪ Amortization of bond discount
	• Non-operating losses
	▪ Loss on sale or write-down of assets
	▪ Loss on retirement of debt
	▪ Loss on investments accounted for under the equity method
	• Increase in deferred income tax liability
	• Changes in working capital resulting from accruing higher amounts for expenses than the amounts of cash payments or lower amounts for revenues than the amounts of cash receipts
	▪ Decrease in current operating assets (e.g., accounts receivable, inventory, and prepaid expenses)
	▪ Increase in current operating liabilities (e.g., accounts payable and accrued expense liabilities)
Subtractions	• Non-cash items (e.g., amortization of bond premium)
	• Non-operating items
	▪ Gain on sale of assets
	▪ Gain on retirement of debt
	▪ Income on investments accounted for under the equity method
	• Decrease in deferred income tax liability
	• Changes in working capital resulting from accruing lower amounts for expenses than for cash payments or higher amounts for revenues than for cash receipts
	▪ Increase in current operating assets (e.g., accounts receivable, inventory, and prepaid expenses)
	▪ Decrease in current operating liabilities (e.g., accounts payable and accrued expense liabilities)

Accordingly, for Acme Corporation, the $55 increase in accounts receivable and the $707 increase in inventory are subtracted from net income, and the $23 decrease in prepaid expenses is added to net income. For Acme's current liabilities, the increases in accounts payable, salary and wage payable, income tax payable, and other accrued liabilities ($263, $10, $5, and $22, respectively) are added to net income, and the $12 decrease in interest payable is subtracted from net income. Exhibit 10 presents the cash flow statement for Acme Corporation under the indirect method by using the information that we have determined from our analysis of the income statement and the comparative balance sheets. Note that the investing and financing sections are identical to the statement of cash flows prepared using the direct method.

EXHIBIT 10   Acme Corporation Cash Flow Statement (Indirect Method) Year Ended December 31, 2018

Cash flow from operating activities:	
Net income	$2,210
Depreciation expense	1,052
Gain on sale of equipment	(205)
Increase in accounts receivable	(55)
Increase in inventory	(707)
Decrease in prepaid expenses	23
Increase in accounts payable	263
Increase in salary and wages payable	10
Decrease in interest payable	(12)
Increase in income tax payable	5
Increase in other accrued liabilities	22
Net cash provided by operating activities	2,606
Cash flow from investing activities:	
Cash received from sale of equipment	762
Cash paid for purchase of equipment	(1,300)
Net cash used for investing activities	(538)
Cash flow from financing activities:	
Cash paid to retire long-term debt	(500)
Cash paid to retire common stock	(600)
Cash paid for dividends	(1,120)
Net cash used for financing activities	(2,220)
Net decrease in cash	(152)
Cash balance, December 31, 2017	1,163
Cash balance, December 31, 2018	$1,011

EXAMPLE 7   Adjusting Net Income to Compute Operating Cash Flow

Based on the following information for Pinkerly Inc., a fictitious company, what are the total adjustments that the company would make to net income in order to derive operating cash flow?

		Year Ended	
Income statement item		12/31/2018	
Net income		$30 million	
Depreciation		$7 million	
Balance sheet item	12/31/2017	12/31/2018	Change
Accounts receivable	$15 million	$30 million	$15 million
Inventory	$16 million	$13 million	($3 million)
Accounts payable	$10 million	$20 million	$10 million

A. Add $5 million.
B. Add $21 million.
C. Subtract $9 million.

Solution: A is correct. To derive operating cash flow, the company would make the following adjustments to net income: add depreciation (a non-cash expense) of $7 million; add the decrease in inventory of $3 million; add the increase in accounts payable of $10 million; and subtract the increase in accounts receivable of $15 million. Total additions of $20 million and total subtractions of $15 million result in net total additions of $5 million.

3.3. Conversion of Cash Flows from the Indirect to the Direct Method

An analyst may desire to review direct-format operating cash flow to review trends in cash receipts and payments (such as cash received from customers or cash paid to suppliers). If a direct-format statement is not available, cash flows from operating activities reported under the indirect method can be converted to the direct method. Accuracy of conversion depends on adjustments using data available in published financial reports. The method described here is sufficiently accurate for most analytical purposes.

The three-step conversion process is demonstrated for Acme Corporation in Exhibit 11. Referring again to Exhibits 6 and 7 for Acme Corporation's income statement and balance sheet information, begin by disaggregating net income of $2,210 into total revenues and total expenses (Step 1). Next, remove any non-operating and non-cash items (Step 2). For Acme, we therefore remove the non-operating gain on the sale of equipment of $205 and the non-cash depreciation expense of $1,052. Then, convert accrual amounts of revenues and expenses to cash flow amounts of receipts and payments by adjusting for changes in working capital accounts (Step 3). The results of these adjustments are the items of information for the direct format of operating cash flows. These line items are shown as the results of Step 3.

EXHIBIT 11   Conversion from the Indirect to the Direct Method

Step 1	Total revenues	$23,803
Aggregate all revenue and all expenses	Total expenses	21,593
	Net income	$2,210
Step 2	Total revenue less noncash item revenues:	
Remove all noncash items from aggregated revenues and expenses, and break out remaining items into relevant cash flow items	($23,803 – $205) =	$23,598
	Revenue	$23,598
	Total expenses less noncash item expenses:	
	($21,593 – $1,052) =	$20,541
	Cost of goods sold	$11,456
	Salary and wage expenses	4,123
	Other operating expenses	3,577
	Interest expense	246
	Income tax expense	1,139
	Total	$20,541
Step 3	Cash received from customers[a]	$23,543
Convert accrual amounts to cash flow amounts by adjusting for working capital changes	Cash paid to suppliers[b]	(11,900)
	Cash paid to employees[c]	(4,113)
	Cash paid for other operating expenses[d]	(3,532)
	Cash paid for interest[e]	(258)
	Cash paid for income tax[f]	(1,134)
	Net cash provided by operating activities	$2,606

Calculations for Step 3:
[a] Revenue of $23,598 less increase in accounts receivable of $55.
[b] Cost of goods sold of $11,456 plus increase in inventory of $707 less increase in accounts payable of $263.
[c] Salary and wage expense of $4,123 less increase in salary and wage payable of $10.
[d] Other operating expenses of $3,577 less decrease in prepaid expenses of $23 less increase in other accrued liabilities of $22.
[e] Interest expense of $246 plus decrease in interest payable of $12.
[f] Income tax expense of $1,139 less increase in income tax payable of $5.

4. CASH FLOW STATEMENT ANALYSIS

The analysis of a company's cash flows can provide useful information for understanding a company's business and earnings and for predicting its future cash flows. This section describes tools and techniques for analyzing the statement of cash flows, including the analysis of sources and uses of cash and cash flow, common-size analysis, and calculation of free cash flow measures and cash flow ratios.

4.1. Evaluation of the Sources and Uses of Cash

Evaluation of the cash flow statement should involve an overall assessment of the sources and uses of cash between the three main categories as well as an assessment of the main drivers of cash flow within each category, as follows:

1. Evaluate where the major sources and uses of cash flow are between operating, investing, and financing activities.
2. Evaluate the primary determinants of operating cash flow.
3. Evaluate the primary determinants of investing cash flow.
4. Evaluate the primary determinants of financing cash flow.

Step 1   The major sources of cash for a company can vary with its stage of growth. For a mature company, it is expected and desirable that operating activities be the primary source of cash flows. Over the long term, a company must generate cash from its operating activities. If operating cash flow were consistently negative, a company would need to borrow money or issue stock (financing activities) to fund the shortfall. Eventually, these providers of capital need to be repaid from operations, or they will no longer be willing to provide capital. Cash generated from operating activities can be used in either investing or financing activities. If the company has good opportunities to grow the business or other investment opportunities, it is desirable to use the cash in investing activities. If the company does not have profitable investment opportunities, the cash should be returned to capital providers, a financing activity. For a new or growth-stage company, operating cash flow may be negative for some period of time as it invests in such assets as inventory and receivables (extending credit to new customers) in order to grow the business. This situation is not sustainable over the long term, so eventually the cash must start to come primarily from operating activities so that capital can be returned to the providers of capital. Lastly, it is desirable that operating cash flows be sufficient to cover capital expenditures (in other words, the company has free cash flow as discussed further in Section 4.3). In summary, major points to consider at this step are:

- What are the major sources and uses of cash flow?
- Is operating cash flow positive and sufficient to cover capital expenditures?

Step 2   Turning to the operating section, the analysts should examine the most significant determinants of operating cash flow. Companies need cash for use in operations (for example, to hold receivables and inventory and to pay employees and suppliers) and receive cash from operating activities (for example, payments from customers). Under the indirect method, the increases and decreases in receivables, inventory, payables, and so on can be examined to determine whether the company is using or generating cash in operations and why. It is also useful to compare operating cash flow with net income. For a mature company, because net income includes non-cash expenses (depreciation and amortization), it is expected and desirable that operating cash flow exceed net income. The relationship between net income and operating cash flow is also an indicator of earnings quality. If a company has large net income but poor operating cash flow, it may be a sign of poor earnings quality. The company may be making aggressive accounting choices to increase net income but not be generating cash for its business. You should also examine the variability of both earnings and cash flow and consider the impact of this variability on the company's risk as well as the ability to forecast future cash flows for valuation purposes. In summary:

- What are the major determinants of operating cash flow?
- Is operating cash flow higher or lower than net income? Why?
- How consistent are operating cash flows?

Step 3   Within the investing section, you should evaluate each line item. Each line item represents either a source or use of cash. This enables you to understand where the cash is being spent (or received). This section will tell you how much cash is being invested for the future in property, plant, and equipment; how much is used to acquire entire companies; and how much is put aside in liquid investments, such as stocks and bonds. It will also tell you how much cash is being raised by selling these types of assets. If the company is making major capital investments, you should consider where the cash is coming from to cover these investments (e.g., is the cash coming from excess operating cash flow or from the financing activities described in Step 4). If assets are being sold, it is important to determine why and to assess the effects on the company.

Step 4   Within the financing section, you should examine each line item to understand whether the company is raising capital or repaying capital, and what the nature of its capital sources are. If the company is borrowing each year, you should consider when repayment may be required. This section will also present dividend payments and repurchases of stock that are alternative means of returning capital to owners. It is important to assess why capital is being raised or repaid.

   We now provide an example of a cash flow statement evaluation.

EXAMPLE 8   Analysis of the Cash Flow Statement

Derek Yee, CFA, is preparing to forecast cash flow for Groupe Danone as an input into his valuation model. He has asked you to evaluate the historical cash flow statement of Groupe Danone, which is presented in Exhibit 12. Groupe Danone prepares its financial statements in conformity with IFRS. Note that Groupe Danone presents the most recent period on the right. Exhibit 13 presents excerpts from Danone's 2017 Registration Document.

   Yee would like answers to the following questions:

- What are the major sources of cash for Groupe Danone?
- What are the major uses of cash for Groupe Danone?
- Is cash flow from operating activities sufficient to cover capital expenditures?
- What is the relationship between net income and cash flow from operating activities?
- What types of financing cash flows does Groupe Danone have?

EXHIBIT 12   Groupe Danone Consolidated Financial Statements Consolidated Statements of Cash Flows (in € Millions)

Years Ended December 31	2016	2017
Net income	1,827	2,563
Share of profits of associates net of dividends received	52	(54)
Depreciation, amortization, and impairment of tangible and intangible assets	786	974
Increases in (reversals of) provisions	51	153
Change in deferred taxes	(65)	(353)
(Gains) losses on disposal of property, plant, and equipment and financial investments	(74)	(284)
Expense related to Group performance shares	24	22
Cost of net financial debt	149	265
Net interest paid	(148)	(186)
Net change in interest income (expense)	—	80
Other components with no cash impact	13	(15)
Cash flows provided by operating activities, before changes in net working capital	**2,615**	**3,085**
(Increase) decrease in inventories	(24)	(122)
(Increase) decrease in trade receivables	(110)	(190)
Increase (decrease) in trade payables	298	145
Changes in other receivables and payables	(127)	40
Change in other working capital requirements	37	(127)
Cash flows provided by (used in) operating activities	**2,652**	**2,958**
Capital expenditure	(925)	(969)
Proceeds from the disposal of property, plant, and equipment	27	45
Net cash outflows on purchases of subsidiaries and financial investments	(66)	(10,949)
Net cash inflows on disposal of subsidiaries and financial investments	110	441
(Increase) decrease in long-term loans and other long-term financial assets	6	(4)
Cash flows provided by (used in) investing activities	**(848)**	**(11,437)**
Increase in capital and additional paid-in capital	46	47
Purchases of treasury stock (net of disposals) and DANONE call options	32	13
Issue of perpetual subordinated debt securities	—	1,245
Interest on perpetual subordinated debt securities	—	—
Dividends paid to Danone shareholders	(985)	(279)
Buyout of non-controlling interests	(295)	(107)
Dividends paid	(94)	(86)
Contribution from non-controlling interests to capital increases	6	1
Transactions with non-controlling interests	(383)	(193)
Net cash flows on hedging derivatives	50	(52)
Bonds issued during the period	11,237	—

(continued)

EXHIBIT 12   (Continued)

Years Ended December 31	2016	2017
Bonds repaid during the period	(638)	(1,487)
Net cash flows from other current and non-current financial debt	(442)	(564)
Net cash flows from short-term investments	(10,531)	9,559
Cash flows provided by (used in) financing activities	**(1,616)**	**8,289**
Effect of exchange rate and other changes	(151)	272
Increase (decrease) in cash and cash equivalents	**38**	**81**
Cash and cash equivalents at beginning of period	519	557
Cash and cash equivalents at end of period	557	638
Supplemental disclosures		
Income tax payments during the year	(891)	(1,116)

Note: the numbers in the consolidated statement of cash flows were derived straight from company filings; some sub-totals may not sum exactly due to rounding by the company.

EXHIBIT 13   Groupe Danone Excerpt from 2017 Registration Statement

Excerpt from Footnote 2 to the financial statements:
. . . On July 7, 2016, Danone announced the signing of an agreement to acquire The WhiteWave Foods Company ("WhiteWave"), the global leader in plant-based foods and beverages and organic produce. The acquisition in cash, for USD 56.25 per share, represented, as of the date of the agreement, a total enterprise value of approximately USD 12.5 billion, including debt and certain other WhiteWave liabilities. . . .

"Acquisition expenses recognized in Danone's consolidated financial statements totaled €51 million before tax, of which €48 million was recognized in 2016 in Other operating income (expense), with the balance recognized in 2017.

"WhiteWave's contribution to 2017 consolidated sales totaled €2.7 billion. Had the transaction been completed on January 1, 2017, the Group's 2017 consolidated sales would have been €25.7 billion, with recurring operating income of €3.6 billion.

"Meanwhile, integration expenses for the period totaled €91 million, recognized under Other operating income (expense). . . .

Excerpt from Overview of Activities:
". . . As part of its transformation plan aimed at ensuring a safe journey to deliver strong, profitable and sustainable growth, Danone set objectives for 2020 that include like-for-like sales growth between 4% and 5% . . . a recurring operating margin of over 16% in 2020. . . . Finally, Danone will continue to focus on growing its free cash flow, which will contribute to financial deleverage with an objective of a ratio of Net debt/EBITDA below 3x in 2020. Danone is committed to reaching a ROIC level around 12% in 2020."

Solution: The major categories of cash flows can be summarized as follows (in € millions):

	2016	2017
Cash flows provided by operating activities	2,615	3,085
Cash flows provided by (used in) investing activities	(848)	(11,437)
Cash flows provided by (used in) financing activities	(1,616)	8,289
Exchange rate effects on cash	(151)	272
Increase in cash	38	81

The primary source of cash for Groupe Danone in 2016 is operating activities. In both 2016 and 2017, there was sufficient operating cash flow to cover usual capital expenditures, and operating cash flow exceeded net income. Evaluating the five prior years [not shown in this Example], you confirm that Danone typically derives most of its cash from operating activities, reports operating cash flow greater than net income, and generates sufficient operating cash flow to cover capital expenditures.

The fact that the primary source of cash is from operations is positive and desirable for a mature company. Additionally, the fact that operating cash flow exceeds net income in both years is a positive sign. Finally, operating cash flows exceed normal capital expenditures, indicating that the company can fund capital expenditures from operations.

In 2017, however, the primary source of cash was financing activities, and the investing section shows significant use of cash for purchase of subsidiaries within investing activities. Footnotes disclose a major acquisition with an aggregate value of €12.5 billion, some of which was funded through proceeds from an earlier bond issuance, which appears as a financing cash flow in the financing section for 2016.

For purposes of Yee's cash flow forecast, the company's targets for free cash flow and debt reduction—as well as disclosures concerning the acquisition's impact on 2017 operating results—are potentially helpful.

4.2. Common-Size Analysis of the Statement of Cash Flows

In common-size analysis of a company's income statement, each income and expense line item is expressed as a percentage of net revenues (net sales). For the common-size balance sheet, each asset, liability, and equity line item is expressed as a percentage of total assets. For the common-size cash flow statement, there are two alternative approaches. The first approach is to express each line item of cash inflow (outflow) as a percentage of total inflows (outflows) of cash, and the second approach is to express each line item as a percentage of net revenue.

Exhibit 14 demonstrates the total cash inflows/total cash outflows method for Acme Corporation. Under this approach, each of the cash inflows is expressed as a percentage of the total cash inflows, whereas each of the cash outflows is expressed as a percentage of the total cash outflows. In Panel A, Acme's common-size statement is based on a cash flow statement using the direct method of presenting operating cash flows. Operating cash inflows and outflows are separately presented on the cash flow statement, and therefore, the common-size cash flow statement shows each of these operating inflows (outflows) as a percentage of total inflows (outflows). In Panel B, Acme's common-size statement is based on a cash flow statement using the indirect method of presenting operating cash flows. When a cash flow statement has been presented using the indirect method, operating cash inflows and outflows are not separately presented; therefore, the common-size cash flow statement shows only the net operating cash flow (net cash provided by or used in operating activities) as a percentage of total inflows or outflows, depending on whether the net amount was a cash inflow or outflow. Because Acme's net operating cash flow is positive, it is shown as a percentage of total inflows.

EXHIBIT 14   Acme Corporation Common-Size Cash Flow Statement Year Ended December 31, 2018

Panel A. Direct Format for Cash Flow

Inflows		Percentage of Total Inflows
Receipts from customers	$23,543	96.86%
Sale of equipment	762	3.14
Total	$24,305	100.00%

Outflows		Percentage of Total Outflows
Payments to suppliers	$11,900	48.66%
Payments to employees	4,113	16.82
Payments for other operating expenses	3,532	14.44
Payments for interest	258	1.05
Payments for income tax	1,134	4.64
Purchase of equipment	1,300	5.32
Retirement of long-term debt	500	2.04
Retirement of common stock	600	2.45
Dividend payments	1,120	4.58
Total	$24,457	100.00%
Net increase (decrease) in cash	($152)	

Panel B. Indirect Format for Cash Flow

Inflows		Percentage of Total Inflows
Net cash provided by operating activities	$2,606	77.38%
Sale of equipment	762	22.62
Total	$3,368	100.00%

Outflows		Percentage of Total Outflows
Purchase of equipment	$1,300	36.93%

EXHIBIT 14   (Continued)

Outflows		Percentage of Total Outflows
Retirement of long-term debt	500	14.20
Retirement of common stock	600	17.05
Dividend payments	1,120	31.82
Total	$3,520	100.00%
Net increase (decrease) in cash	($152)	

Exhibit 15 demonstrates the net revenue common-size cash flow statement for Acme Corporation. Under the net revenue approach, each line item in the cash flow statement is shown as a percentage of net revenue. The common-size statement in this exhibit has been developed based on Acme's cash flow statement using the indirect method for operating cash flows and using net revenue of $23,598 as shown in Exhibit 6. Each line item of the reconciliation between net income and net operating cash flows is expressed as a percentage of net revenue. The common-size format makes it easier to see trends in cash flow rather than just looking at the total amount. This method is also useful to the analyst in forecasting future cash flows because individual items in the common-size statement (e.g., depreciation, fixed capital expenditures, debt borrowing, and repayment) are expressed as a percentage of net revenue. Thus, once the analyst has forecast revenue, the common-size statement provides a basis for forecasting cash flows for those items with an expected relation to net revenue.

EXHIBIT 15   Acme Corporation Common-Size Cash Flow Statement: Indirect Format Year Ended December 31, 2018

		Percentage of Net Revenue
Cash flow from operating activities:		
Net income	$2,210	9.37%
Depreciation expense	1,052	4.46
Gain on sale of equipment	(205)	(0.87)
Increase in accounts receivable	(55)	(0.23)
Increase in inventory	(707)	(3.00)
Decrease in prepaid expenses	23	0.10
Increase in accounts payable	263	1.11
Increase in salary and wage payable	10	0.04
Decrease in interest payable	(12)	(0.05)
Increase in income tax payable	5	0.02
Increase in other accrued liabilities	22	0.09
Net cash provided by operating activities	$2,606	11.04%

(continued)

EXHIBIT 15   (Continued)

		Percentage of Net Revenue
Cash flow from investing activities:		
Cash received from sale of equipment	$ 762	3.23%
Cash paid for purchase of equipment	(1,300)	(5.51)
Net cash used for investing activities	$(538)	(2.28)%
Cash flow from financing activities:		
Cash paid to retire long-term debt	$(500)	(2.12)%
Cash paid to retire common stock	(600)	(2.54)
Cash paid for dividends	(1,120)	(4.75)
Net cash used for financing activities	$(2,220)	(9.41)%
Net decrease in cash	$(152)	(0.64)%

EXAMPLE 9   Analysis of a Common-Size Cash Flow Statement

Andrew Potter is examining an abbreviated common-size cash flow statement for Apple Inc., a multinational technology company. The common-size cash flow statement was prepared by dividing each line item by total net sales for the same year.

Apple Inc. Common Size Statements of Cash Flows as Percentage of Total Net Sales

	12 Months Ended		
	Sep. 30, 2017	Sep. 24, 2016	Sep. 26, 2015
Statement of Cash Flows [Abstract]			
Operating activities:			
Net income	21.1%	21.2%	22.8%
Adjustments to reconcile net income to cash generated by operating activities:			
Depreciation and amortization	4.4%	4.9%	4.8%
Share-based compensation expense	2.1%	2.0%	1.5%
Deferred income tax expense	2.6%	2.3%	0.6%
Other	−0.1%	0.2%	0.2%
Changes in operating assets and liabilities:			
Accounts receivable, net	−0.9%	0.2%	0.2%
Inventories	−1.2%	0.1%	−0.1%
Vendor non-trade receivables	−1.9%	0.0%	−1.6%
Other current and non-current assets	−2.3%	0.5%	−0.1%
Accounts payable	4.2%	0.9%	2.1%

| | 12 Months Ended | | |
	Sep. 30, 2017	Sep. 24, 2016	Sep. 26, 2015
Deferred revenue	−0.3%	−0.7%	0.4%
Other current and non-current liabilities	−0.1%	−0.9%	3.9%
Cash generated by operating activities	27.7%	30.5%	34.8%
Investing activities:			
Purchases of marketable securities	−69.6%	−66.0%	−71.2%
Proceeds from maturities of marketable securities	13.9%	9.9%	6.2%
Proceeds from sales of marketable securities	41.3%	42.0%	46.0%
Payments made in connection with business acquisitions, net	−0.1%	−0.1%	−0.1%
Payments for acquisition of property, plant, and equipment	−5.4%	−5.9%	−4.8%
Payments for acquisition of intangible assets	−0.2%	−0.4%	−0.1%
Payments for strategic investments, net	−0.2%	−0.6%	0.0%
Other	0.1%	−0.1%	0.0%
Cash used in investing activities	−20.3%	−21.3%	−24.1%
Financing activities:			
Proceeds from issuance of common stock	0.2%	0.2%	0.2%
Excess tax benefits from equity awards	0.3%	0.2%	0.3%
Payments for taxes related to net share settlement of equity awards	−0.8%	−0.7%	−0.6%
Payments for dividends and dividend equivalents	5.6%	5.6%	4.9%
Repurchases of common stock	−14.4%	−13.8%	−15.1%
Proceeds from issuance of term debt, net	12.5%	11.6%	—
Repayments of term debt	−1.5%	−1.2%	0.0%
Change in commercial paper, net	1.7%	−0.2%	0.9%
Cash used in financing activities	−7.6%	−9.5%	−7.6%
Increase/(Decrease) in cash and cash equivalents	−0.1%	−0.3%	3.1%

Based on the information in the above exhibit:

1. Discuss the significance of
   A. depreciation and amortization.
   B. capital expenditures.
2. Compare Apple's operating cash flow as a percentage of revenue with Apple's net profit margin.
3. Discuss Apple's use of its positive operating cash flow.

Solution to 1:
A. Apple's depreciation and amortization expense was consistently just less than 5% of total net revenue in 2015 and 2016, declining to 4.4% in 2017.
B. Apple's level of capital expenditures is greater than depreciation and amortization in 2016 and 2017, whereas it was at about the same level as depreciation and amortization in 2015. In 2017 capital expenditures approached 6%. This is an indication that Apple is doing more than replacing property, plant, and equipment, and is expanding those investments. With cash generated from operating activities exceeding 27% of sales in every year, however, Apple has more than enough cash flow from operations to fund these expenditures.

Solution to 2: Apple's operating cash flow as a percentage of sales is much higher than net profit margin in every year. This gap appears to be declining, however, over the three-year period. In 2015 net profit margin was 22.8% while operating cash flow as a percentage of sales was 34.8%. By 2017 the net profit margin declined slightly to 21.1% while the operating cash flow as a percentage of sales declined more to 27.7%. The primary difference appears to have been an increase in the level of receivables and inventory purchases, somewhat offset by an increase in accounts payable.

Solution to 3: Apple has a very strong cash flow statement. Apple generates a large amount of operating cash flow in every year, exceeding net income. This cash flow is used for relatively modest purchases of property, plant, and equipment; substantial purchases of marketable securities (investments); dividend payments; and repurchases of its own stock.

4.3. Free Cash Flow to the Firm and Free Cash Flow to Equity

It was mentioned earlier that it is desirable that operating cash flows be sufficient to cover capital expenditures. The excess of operating cash flow over capital expenditures is known generically as **free cash flow**. For purposes of valuing a company or its equity securities, an analyst may want to determine and use other cash flow measures, such as free cash flow to the firm (FCFF) or free cash flow to equity (FCFE).

FCFF is the cash flow available to the company's suppliers of debt and equity capital after all operating expenses (including income taxes) have been paid and necessary investments in working capital and fixed capital have been made. FCFF can be computed starting with net income as

$$FCFF = NI + NCC + Int(1 - Tax\ rate) - FCInv - WCInv$$

where

NI = Net income
NCC = Non-cash charges (such as depreciation and amortization)
Int = Interest expense
$FCInv$ = Capital expenditures (fixed capital, such as equipment)
$WCInv$ = Working capital expenditures

The reason for adding back interest is that FCFF is the cash flow available to the suppliers of debt capital as well as equity capital. Conveniently, FCFF can also be computed from cash flow from operating activities as

$$FCFF = CFO + Int(1 - Tax\ rate) - FCInv$$

CFO represents cash flow from operating activities under US GAAP or under IFRS where the company has included interest paid in operating activities. If interest paid was included in financing activities, then CFO does not have to be adjusted for $Int(1 - Tax\ rate)$. Under IFRS, if the company has placed interest and dividends received in investing activities, these should be added back to CFO to determine FCFF. Additionally, if dividends paid were subtracted in the operating section, these should be added back in to compute FCFF.

The computation of FCFF for Acme Corporation (based on the data from Exhibits 6, 7, and 8) is as follows:

CFO	$2,606
Plus: Interest paid times (1 – income tax rate)	
{$258 [1 – 0.34[a]]}	170
Less: Net investments in fixed capital	
($1,300 – $762)	(538)
FCFF	$2,238

[a] Income tax rate of 0.34 = (Tax expense ÷ Pretax income) = ($1,139 ÷ $3,349).

FCFE is the cash flow available to the company's common stockholders after all operating expenses and borrowing costs (principal and interest) have been paid and necessary investments in working capital and fixed capital have been made. FCFE can be computed as

$$FCFE = CFO - FCInv + Net\ borrowing$$

When net borrowing is negative, debt repayments exceed receipts of borrowed funds. In this case, FCFE can be expressed as

$$FCFE = CFO - FCInv - Net\ debt\ repayment$$

The computation of FCFE for Acme Corporation (based on the data from Exhibits 6, 7, and 8) is as follows:

CFO	$2,606
Less: Net investments in fixed capital ($1,300 – $762)	(538)
Less: Debt repayment	(500)
FCFE	$1,568

Positive FCFE means that the company has an excess of operating cash flow over amounts needed for capital expenditures and repayment of debt. This cash would be available for distribution to owners.

4.4. Cash Flow Ratios

The statement of cash flows provides information that can be analyzed over time to obtain a better understanding of the past performance of a company and its future prospects. This information can also be effectively used to compare the performance and prospects of different companies in an industry and of different industries. There are several ratios based on cash flow from operating activities that are useful in this analysis. These ratios generally fall into cash flow performance (profitability) ratios and cash flow coverage (solvency) ratios. Exhibit 16 summarizes the calculation and interpretation of some of these ratios.

EXHIBIT 16   Cash Flow Ratios

Performance Ratios	Calculation	What It Measures
Cash flow to revenue	CFO ÷ Net revenue	Operating cash generated per dollar of revenue
Cash return on assets	CFO ÷ Average total assets	Operating cash generated per dollar of asset investment
Cash return on equity	CFO ÷ Average shareholders' equity	Operating cash generated per dollar of owner investment
Cash to income	CFO ÷ Operating income	Cash generating ability of operations
Cash flow per share[a]	(CFO − Preferred dividends) ÷ Number of common shares outstanding	Operating cash flow on a per-share basis
Coverage Ratios	Calculation	What It Measures
Debt coverage	CFO ÷ Total debt	Financial risk and financial leverage
Interest coverage[b]	(CFO + Interest paid + Taxes paid) ÷ Interest paid	Ability to meet interest obligations
Reinvestment	CFO ÷ Cash paid for long-term assets	Ability to acquire assets with operating cash flows
Debt payment	CFO ÷ Cash paid for long-term debt repayment	Ability to pay debts with operating cash flows
Dividend payment	CFO ÷ Dividends paid	Ability to pay dividends with operating cash flows
Investing and financing	CFO ÷ Cash outflows for investing and financing activities	Ability to acquire assets, pay debts, and make distributions to owners

Notes:

[a] If the company reports under IFRS and includes total dividends paid as a use of cash in the operating section, total dividends should be added back to CFO as reported, and then preferred dividends should be subtracted. Recall that CFO reported under US GAAP and IFRS may differ depending on the treatment of interest and dividends, received and paid.

[b] If the company reports under IFRS and included interest paid as a use of cash in the financing section, then interest paid should not be added back to the numerator.

EXAMPLE 10   A Cash Flow Analysis of Comparables

Andrew Potter is comparing the cash-flow-generating ability of Microsoft with that of Apple Inc. He collects information from the companies' annual reports and prepares the following table.

Cash Flow from Operating Activities as a Percentage of Total Net Revenue

	2017 (%)	2016 (%)	2015 (%)
Microsoft	43.9	39.1	31.7
Apple Inc.	27.7	30.5	34.8

As a Percentage of Average Total Assets

	2017 (%)	2016 (%)	2015 (%)
Microsoft	18.2	18.1	17.1
Apple Inc.	18.2	21.5	31.1

What is Potter likely to conclude about the relative cash-flow-generating ability of these two companies?

Solution: On both measures—operating cash flow divided by revenue and operating cash flow divided by assets—both companies have overall strong results. However, Microsoft has higher cash flow from operating activities as a percentage of revenues in both 2016 and 2017. Further, Microsoft has an increasing trend. While Apple had a higher operating cash flow as a percent of revenue in 2015 compared to Microsoft, it has had a declining trend and was below Microsoft in the two more recent years. Microsoft's operating cash flow relative to assets is the same as Apple's in 2016 and relatively stable with a slight increase since 2015. Apple started the three years with a much stronger ratio but saw a declining trend such that its ratio is now at the same level as Microsoft. We should note that this ratio is heavily influenced by substantial investments in financial instruments that Apple has made over the years due to its strong historic cash flow.

5. SUMMARY

The cash flow statement provides important information about a company's cash receipts and cash payments during an accounting period as well as information about a company's operating, investing, and financing activities. Although the income statement provides a measure of a company's success, cash and cash flow are also vital to a company's long-term success. Information on the sources and uses of cash helps creditors, investors, and other statement users evaluate the company's liquidity, solvency, and financial flexibility. Key concepts are as follows:

- Cash flow activities are classified into three categories: operating activities, investing activities, and financing activities. Significant non-cash transaction activities (if present) are reported by using a supplemental disclosure note to the cash flow statement.
- Cash flow statements under IFRS and US GAAP are similar; however, IFRS provide companies with more choices in classifying some cash flow items as operating, investing, or financing activities.
- Companies can use either the direct or the indirect method for reporting their operating cash flow:
  - The direct method discloses operating cash inflows by source (e.g., cash received from customers, cash received from investment income) and operating cash outflows by use (e.g., cash paid to suppliers, cash paid for interest) in the operating activities section of the cash flow statement.
  - The indirect method reconciles net income to operating cash flow by adjusting net income for all non-cash items and the net changes in the operating working capital accounts.
- The cash flow statement is linked to a company's income statement and comparative balance sheets and to data on those statements.
- Although the indirect method is most commonly used by companies, an analyst can generally convert it to an approximation of the direct format by following a simple three-step process.
- An evaluation of a cash flow statement should involve an assessment of the sources and uses of cash and the main drivers of cash flow within each category of activities.
- The analyst can use common-size statement analysis for the cash flow statement. Two approaches to developing the common-size statements are the total cash inflows/total cash outflows method and the percentage of net revenues method.
- The cash flow statement can be used to determine free cash flow to the firm (FCFF) and free cash flow to equity (FCFE).
- The cash flow statement may also be used in financial ratios that measure a company's profitability, performance, and financial strength.

PRACTICE PROBLEMS

1. The three major classifications of activities in a cash flow statement are:
   A. inflows, outflows, and net flows.
   B. operating, investing, and financing.
   C. revenues, expenses, and net income.

2. The sale of a building for cash would be classified as what type of activity on the cash flow statement?
   A. Operating.
   B. Investing.
   C. Financing.

3. Under which section of a manufacturing company's cash flow statement are the following activities reported?

   Item 1: Purchases of securities held for trading

   Item 2: Sales of securities considered cash equivalents

   A. Both items are investing activities.

   B. Both items are operating activities.

   C. Only Item 1 is an investing activity.

4. Which of the following is an example of a financing activity on the cash flow statement under US GAAP?

   A. Payment of interest.

   B. Receipt of dividends.

   C. Payment of dividends.

5. A conversion of a face value $1 million convertible bond for $1 million of common stock would most likely be:

   A. reported as a $1 million investing cash inflow and outflow.

   B. reported as a $1 million financing cash outflow and inflow.

   C. reported as supplementary information to the cash flow statement.

6. A company recently engaged in a non-cash transaction that significantly affected its property, plant, and equipment. The transaction is:

   A. reported under the investing section of the cash flow statement.

   B. reported differently in cash flow from operations under the direct and indirect methods.

   C. disclosed as a separate note or in a supplementary schedule to the cash flow statement.

7. Interest paid is classified as an operating cash flow under:

   A. US GAAP but may be classified as either operating or investing cash flows under IFRS.

   B. IFRS but may be classified as either operating or investing cash flows under US GAAP.

   C. US GAAP but may be classified as either operating or financing cash flows under IFRS.

8. Cash flows from taxes on income must be separately disclosed under:

   A. IFRS only.

   B. US GAAP only.

   C. both IFRS and US GAAP.

9. Which of the following components of the cash flow statement may be prepared under the indirect method under both IFRS and US GAAP?

   A. Operating.

   B. Investing.

   C. Financing.

10. Which of the following is *most likely* to appear in the operating section of a cash flow statement under the indirect method?

    A. Net income.

    B. Cash paid to suppliers.

    C. Cash received from customers.

11. A benefit of using the direct method rather than the indirect method when reporting operating cash flows is that the direct method:
   A. mirrors a forecasting approach.
   B. is easier and less costly.
   C. provides specific information on the sources of operating cash flows.

12. Mabel Corporation (MC) reported accounts receivable of $66 million at the end of its second fiscal quarter. MC had revenues of $72 million for its third fiscal quarter and reported accounts receivable of $55 million at the end of its third fiscal quarter. Based on this information, the amount of cash MC collected from customers during the third fiscal quarter is:
   A. $61 million.
   B. $72 million.
   C. $83 million.

13. When computing net cash flow from operating activities using the indirect method, an addition to net income is *most likely* to occur when there is a:
   A. gain on the sale of an asset.
   B. loss on the retirement of debt.
   C. decrease in a deferred tax liability.

14. Red Road Company, a consulting company, reported total revenues of $100 million, total expenses of $80 million, and net income of $20 million in the most recent year. If accounts receivable increased by $10 million, how much cash did the company receive from customers?
   A. $90 million.
   B. $100 million.
   C. $110 million.

15. In 2018, a company using US GAAP made cash payments of $6 million for salaries, $2 million for interest expense, and $4 million for income taxes. Additional information for the company is provided in the table:

($ millions)	2017	2018
Revenue	42	37
Cost of goods sold	18	16
Inventory	36	40
Accounts receivable	22	19
Accounts payable	14	12

Based only on the information given, the company's operating cash flow for 2018 is *closest to*:
   A. $6 million.
   B. $10 million.
   C. $14 million.

16. Green Glory Corp., a garden supply wholesaler, reported cost of goods sold for the year of $80 million. Total assets increased by $55 million, including an increase of $5 million in inventory. Total liabilities increased by $45 million, including an increase of $2 million in accounts payable. The cash paid by the company to its suppliers is most likely *closest* to:
    A. $73 million.
    B. $77 million.
    C. $83 million.

17. Purple Fleur S.A., a retailer of floral products, reported cost of goods sold for the year of $75 million. Total assets increased by $55 million, but inventory declined by $6 million. Total liabilities increased by $45 million, and accounts payable increased by $2 million. The cash paid by the company to its suppliers is most likely *closest* to:
    A. $67 million.
    B. $79 million.
    C. $83 million.

18. White Flag, a women's clothing manufacturer, reported salaries expense of $20 million. The beginning balance of salaries payable was $3 million, and the ending balance of salaries payable was $1 million. How much cash did the company pay in salaries?
    A. $18 million.
    B. $21 million.
    C. $22 million.

19. An analyst gathered the following information from a company's 2018 financial statements (in $ millions):

Year ended December 31	2017	2018
Net sales	245.8	254.6
Cost of goods sold	168.3	175.9
Accounts receivable	73.2	68.3
Inventory	39.0	47.8
Accounts payable	20.3	22.9

Based only on the information above, the company's 2018 statement of cash flows in the direct format would include amounts (in $ millions) for cash received from customers and cash paid to suppliers, respectively, that are *closest* to:

	Cash Received from Customers	Cash Paid to Suppliers
A.	249.7	169.7
B.	259.5	174.5
C.	259.5	182.1

20. Golden Cumulus Corp., a commodities trading company, reported interest expense of $19 million and taxes of $6 million. Interest payable increased by $3 million, and taxes payable decreased by $4 million over the period. How much cash did the company pay for interest and taxes?
    A. $22 million for interest and $10 million for taxes.
    B. $16 million for interest and $2 million for taxes.
    C. $16 million for interest and $10 million for taxes.

21. An analyst gathered the following information from a company's 2018 financial statements (in $ millions):

Balances as of Year Ended December 31	2017	2018
Retained earnings	120	145
Accounts receivable	38	43
Inventory	45	48
Accounts payable	36	29

In 2018, the company declared and paid cash dividends of $10 million and recorded depreciation expense in the amount of $25 million. The company considers dividends paid a financing activity. The company's 2018 cash flow from operations (in $ millions) was *closest* to
    A. 25.
    B. 45.
    C. 75.

22. Silverago Incorporated, an international metals company, reported a loss on the sale of equipment of $2 million in 2018. In addition, the company's income statement shows depreciation expense of $8 million, and the cash flow statement shows capital expenditure of $10 million, all of which was for the purchase of new equipment. Using the following information from the comparative balance sheets, how much cash did the company receive from the equipment sale?

Balance Sheet Item	12/31/2017	12/31/2018	Change
Equipment	$100 million	$105 million	$5 million
Accumulated depreciation—equipment	$40 million	$46 million	$6 million

    A. $1 million.
    B. $2 million.
    C. $3 million.

23. Jaderong Plinkett Stores reported net income of $25 million. The company has no outstanding debt. Using the following information from the comparative balance sheets (in millions), what should the company report in the financing section of the statement of cash flows in 2018?

Balance Sheet Item	12/31/2017	12/31/2018	Change
Common stock	$100	$102	$ 2
Additional paid-in capital common stock	$100	$140	$40
Retained earnings	$100	$115	$15
Total stockholders' equity	$300	$357	$57

A. Issuance of common stock of $42 million; dividends paid of $10 million.
B. Issuance of common stock of $38 million; dividends paid of $10 million.
C. Issuance of common stock of $42 million; dividends paid of $40 million.

24. Based on the following information for Star Inc., what are the total net adjustments that the company would make to net income in order to derive operating cash flow?

		Year Ended	
Income Statement Item		12/31/2018	
Net income		$20 million	
Depreciation		$ 2 million	
Balance Sheet Item	12/31/2017	12/31/2018	Change
Accounts receivable	$25 million	$22 million	($3 million)
Inventory	$10 million	$14 million	$4 million
Accounts payable	$ 8 million	$13 million	$5 million

A. Add $2 million.
B. Add $6 million.
C. Subtract $6 million.

25. The first step in cash flow statement analysis should be to:
    A. evaluate consistency of cash flows.
    B. determine operating cash flow drivers.
    C. identify the major sources and uses of cash.

26. Which of the following would be valid conclusions from an analysis of the cash flow statement for Telefónica Group presented in Exhibit 3?
    A. The primary use of cash is financing activities.
    B. The primary source of cash is operating activities.
    C. Telefónica classifies dividends paid as an operating activity.

27. The following information is extracted from Sweetfall Incorporated's financial statements.

Income Statement		Balance Sheet Changes	
Revenue	$56,800	Decrease in accounts receivable	$1,324
Cost of goods sold	27,264	Decrease in inventory	501
Other operating expense	562	Increase in prepaid expense	6
Depreciation expense	2,500	Increase in accounts payable	1,063

The amount of cash Sweetfall Inc. paid to suppliers is:
A. $25,700.
B. $26,702.
C. $27,826.

28. Which is an appropriate method of preparing a common-size cash flow statement?
A. Show each item of revenue and expense as a percentage of net revenue.
B. Show each line item on the cash flow statement as a percentage of net revenue.
C. Show each line item on the cash flow statement as a percentage of total cash outflows.

29. Which of the following is an appropriate method of computing free cash flow to the firm?
A. Add operating cash flows to capital expenditures and deduct after-tax interest payments.
B. Add operating cash flows to after-tax interest payments and deduct capital expenditures.
C. Deduct both after-tax interest payments and capital expenditures from operating cash flows.

30. An analyst has calculated a ratio using as the numerator the sum of operating cash flow, interest, and taxes and as the denominator the amount of interest. What is this ratio, what does it measure, and what does it indicate?
A. This ratio is an interest coverage ratio, measuring a company's ability to meet its interest obligations and indicating a company's solvency.
B. This ratio is an effective tax ratio, measuring the amount of a company's operating cash flow used for taxes and indicating a company's efficiency in tax management.
C. This ratio is an operating profitability ratio, measuring the operating cash flow generated accounting for taxes and interest and indicating a company's liquidity.

CHAPTER 6

FINANCIAL ANALYSIS TECHNIQUES

Elaine Henry, CFA

Thomas R. Robinson, CFA

Jan Hendrik van Greuning, CFA

LEARNING OUTCOMES

After completing this chapter, you will be able to do the following:

- describe tools and techniques used in financial analysis, including their uses and limitations;
- classify, calculate, and interpret activity, liquidity, solvency, profitability, and valuation ratios;
- describe relationships among ratios and evaluate a company using ratio analysis;
- demonstrate the application of DuPont analysis of return on equity and calculate and interpret effects of changes in its components;
- calculate and interpret ratios used in equity analysis and credit analysis;
- explain the requirements for segment reporting and calculate and interpret segment ratios;
- describe how ratio analysis and other techniques can be used to model and forecast earnings.

1. INTRODUCTION

Financial analysis tools can be useful in assessing a company's performance and trends in that performance. In essence, an analyst converts data into financial metrics that assist in decision making. Analysts seek to answer such questions as: How successfully has the company performed, relative to its own past performance and relative to its competitors? How is the company likely to perform in the future? Based on expectations about future performance, what is the value of this company or the securities it issues?

A primary source of data is a company's annual report, including the financial statements and notes, and management commentary (operating and financial review or management's discussion and analysis). This chapter focuses on data presented in financial reports prepared under International Financial Reporting Standards (IFRS) and United States generally accepted accounting principles (US GAAP). However, financial reports do not contain all the information needed to perform effective financial analysis. Although financial statements do contain data about the *past* performance of a company (its income and cash flows) as well as its *current* financial condition (assets, liabilities, and owners' equity), such statements do not necessarily provide all the information useful for analysis, nor do they forecast *future* results. The financial analyst must be capable of using financial statements in conjunction with other information to make projections and reach valid conclusions. Accordingly, an analyst typically needs to supplement the information found in a company's financial reports with other information, including information on the economy, industry, comparable companies, and the company itself.

This chapter describes various techniques used to analyze a company's financial statements. Financial analysis of a company may be performed for a variety of reasons, such as valuing equity securities, assessing credit risk, conducting due diligence related to an acquisition, or assessing a subsidiary's performance. This chapter will describe techniques common to any financial analysis and then discuss more specific aspects for the two most common categories: equity analysis and credit analysis.

Equity analysis incorporates an owner's perspective, either for valuation or performance evaluation. Credit analysis incorporates a creditor's (such as a banker or bondholder) perspective. In either case, there is a need to gather and analyze information to make a decision (ownership or credit); the focus of analysis varies because of the differing interests of owners and creditors. Both equity and credit analyses assess the entity's ability to generate and grow earnings, and cash flow, as well as any associated risks. Equity analysis usually places a greater emphasis on growth, whereas credit analysis usually places a greater emphasis on risks. The difference in emphasis reflects the different fundamentals of these types of investments: The value of a company's equity generally increases as the company's earnings and cash flow increase, whereas the value of a company's debt has an upper limit.[1]

The balance of this chapter is organized as follows: Section 2 recaps the framework for financial statements and the place of financial analysis techniques within the framework. Section 3 provides a description of analytical tools and techniques. Section 4 explains how to compute, analyze, and interpret common financial ratios. Sections 5 through 8 explain the use of ratios and other analytical data in equity analysis, credit analysis, segment analysis, and forecasting, respectively. A summary of the key points and practice problems in the CFA Institute multiple-choice format concludes the chapter.

2. THE FINANCIAL ANALYSIS PROCESS

In financial analysis, it is essential to clearly identify and understand the final objective and the steps required to reach that objective. In addition, the analyst needs to know where to find relevant data, how to process and analyze the data (in other words, know the typical questions to address when interpreting data), and how to communicate the analysis and conclusions.

---

[1] The upper limit is equal to the undiscounted sum of the principal and remaining interest payments (i.e., the present value of these contractual payments at a zero percent discount rate).

2.1. The Objectives of the Financial Analysis Process

Because of the variety of reasons for performing financial analysis, the numerous available techniques, and the often substantial amount of data, it is important that the analytical approach be tailored to the specific situation. Prior to beginning any financial analysis, the analyst should clarify the purpose and context, and clearly understand the following:

- What is the purpose of the analysis? What questions will this analysis answer?
- What level of detail will be needed to accomplish this purpose?
- What data are available for the analysis?
- What are the factors or relationships that will influence the analysis?
- What are the analytical limitations, and will these limitations potentially impair the analysis?

Having clarified the purpose and context of the analysis, the analyst can select the set of techniques (e.g., ratios) that will best assist in making a decision. Although there is no single approach to structuring the analysis process, a general framework is set forth in Exhibit 1.[2] The steps in this process were discussed in more detail in an earlier chapter; the primary focus of this chapter is on Phases 3 and 4, processing and analyzing data.

EXHIBIT 1   A Financial Statement Analysis Framework

Phase	Sources of Information	Output
1. Articulate the purpose and context of the analysis.	• The nature of the analyst's function, such as evaluating an equity or debt investment or issuing a credit rating. • Communication with client or supervisor on needs and concerns. • Institutional guidelines related to developing specific work product.	• Statement of the purpose or objective of analysis. • A list (written or unwritten) of specific questions to be answered by the analysis. • Nature and content of report to be provided. • Timetable and budgeted resources for completion.
2. Collect input data.	• Financial statements, other financial data, questionnaires, and industry/economic data. • Discussions with management, suppliers, customers, and competitors. • Company site visits (e.g., to production facilities or retail stores).	• Organized financial statements. • Financial data tables. • Completed questionnaires, if applicable.
3. Process data.	• Data from the previous phase.	• Adjusted financial statements. • Common-size statements. • Ratios and graphs. • Forecasts.
4. Analyze/interpret the processed data.	• Input data as well as processed data.	• Analytical results.

(continued)

---

[2]Components of this framework have been adapted from van Greuning and Bratanovic (2003, p. 300) and Benninga and Sarig (1997, pp. 134–156).

EXHIBIT 1   (Continued)

Phase	Sources of Information	Output
5. Develop and communicate conclusions and recommendations (e.g., with an analysis report).	• Analytical results and previous reports. • Institutional guidelines for published reports.	• Analytical report answering questions posed in Phase 1. • Recommendation regarding the purpose of the analysis, such as whether to make an investment or grant credit.
6. Follow-up.	• Information gathered by periodically repeating above steps as necessary to determine whether changes to holdings or recommendations are necessary.	• Updated reports and recommendations.

2.2. Distinguishing between Computations and Analysis

An effective analysis encompasses both computations and interpretations. A well-reasoned analysis differs from a mere compilation of various pieces of information, computations, tables, and graphs by integrating the data collected into a cohesive whole. Analysis of past performance, for example, should address not only what happened but also why it happened and whether it advanced the company's strategy. Some of the key questions to address include:

• What aspects of performance are critical for this company to successfully compete in this industry?
• How well did the company's performance meet these critical aspects? (Established through computation and comparison with appropriate benchmarks, such as the company's own historical performance or competitors' performance.)
• What were the key causes of this performance, and how does this performance reflect the company's strategy? (Established through analysis.)

If the analysis is forward looking, additional questions include:

• What is the likely impact of an event or trend? (Established through interpretation of analysis.)
• What is the likely response of management to this trend? (Established through evaluation of quality of management and corporate governance.)
• What is the likely impact of trends in the company, industry, and economy on future cash flows? (Established through assessment of corporate strategy and through forecasts.)
• What are the recommendations of the analyst? (Established through interpretation and forecasting of results of analysis.)
• What risks should be highlighted? (Established by an evaluation of major uncertainties in the forecast and in the environment within which the company operates.)

Example 1 demonstrates how a company's financial data can be analyzed in the context of its business strategy and changes in that strategy. An analyst must be able to understand the "why" behind the numbers and ratios, not just what the numbers and ratios are.

EXAMPLE 1   Strategy Reflected in Financial Performance

Apple Inc. engages in the design, manufacture, and sale of computer hardware, mobile devices, operating systems and related products, and services. It also operates retail and online stores. Microsoft develops, licenses, and supports software products, services, and technology devices through a variety of channels including retail stores in recent years. Selected financial data for 2015 through 2017 for these two companies are given below. Apple's fiscal year (FY) ends on the final Saturday in September (for example, FY2017 ended on September 30, 2017). Microsoft's fiscal year ends on June 30 (for example, FY2017 ended on June 30, 2017).

Selected Financial Data for Apple (Dollars in Millions)

Fiscal year	2017	2016	2015
Net sales (or Revenue)	229,234	215,639	233,715
Gross margin	88,186	84,263	93,626
Operating income	61,344	60,024	71,230

Selected Financial Data for Microsoft (Dollars in Millions)*

Fiscal year	2017	2016	2015
Net sales (or Revenue)	89,950	85,320	93,580
Gross margin	55,689	52,540	60,542
Operating income	22,326	20,182	18,161

* Microsoft revenue for 2017 and 2016 were subsequently revised in the company's 2018 10-K report due to changes in revenue recognition and lease accounting standards.

Source: 10-K reports for Apple and Microsoft.

Apple reported a 7.7 percent decrease in net sales from FY2015 to FY2016 and an increase of 6.3 percent from FY2016 to FY2017 for an overall slight decline over the three-year period. Gross margin decreased 10.0 percent from FY2015 to FY2016 and increased 4.7 percent from FY2016 to FY2017. This also represented an overall decline in gross margin over the three-year period. The company's operating income exhibited similar trends.

Microsoft reported an 8.8 percent decrease in net sales from FY2015 to FY2016 and an increase of 5.4 percent from FY2016 to FY2017 for an overall slight decline over the three-year period. Gross margin decreased 13.2 percent from FY2015 to FY2016 and increased 6.0 percent from FY2016 to FY2017. Similar to Apple, this represented an overall decline in gross margin over the three-year period. Microsoft's operating income on the other hand exhibited growth each year and for the three-year period. Overall growth in operating income was 23%.

What caused Microsoft's growth in operating income while Apple and Microsoft had similar negative trends in sales and gross margin? Apple's decline in sales, gross margin, and operating income from FY2015 to FY2016 was caused by declines in iPhone sales and weakness in foreign currencies relative to the US dollar. FY2017 saw a rebound in sales of iPhones, Mac computers, and services offset somewhat by continued weaknesses in foreign currencies. Microsoft similarly had declines in revenue and gross margin from sales of its devices and Windows software in FY2016, as well as negative impacts from foreign currency weakness. Microsoft's increase in revenue and gross margin in FY2017 was driven by the acquisition of LinkedIn, higher sales of Microsoft Office software, and higher sales of cloud services. The driver in the continuous increase in operating income for Microsoft was a large decline over the three-year period in impairment, integration, and restructuring charges. Microsoft recorded a $10 billion charge in FY2015 related to its phone business, and there were further charges of $1.1 billion in FY2016 and $306 million in FY2017. Absent these large write-offs, Microsoft would have had a trend similar to Apple's in operating income over the three-year period.

Analysts often need to communicate the findings of their analysis in a written report. Their reports should communicate how conclusions were reached and why recommendations were made. For example, a report might present the following:

- the purpose of the report, unless it is readily apparent;
- relevant aspects of the business context:
  - economic environment (country/region, macro economy, sector);
  - financial and other infrastructure (accounting, auditing, rating agencies);
  - legal and regulatory environment (and any other material limitations on the company being analyzed);
- evaluation of corporate governance and assessment of management strategy, including the company's competitive advantage(s);
- assessment of financial and operational data, including key assumptions in the analysis; and
- conclusions and recommendations, including limitations of the analysis and risks.

An effective narrative and well supported conclusions and recommendations are normally enhanced by using 3–10 years of data, as well as analytic techniques appropriate to the purpose of the report.

3. ANALYTICAL TOOLS AND TECHNIQUES

The tools and techniques presented in this section facilitate evaluations of company data. Evaluations require comparisons. It is difficult to say that a company's financial performance was "good" without clarifying the basis for comparison. In assessing a company's ability to generate and grow earnings and cash flow, and the risks related to those earnings and cash flows, the analyst draws comparisons to other companies (cross-sectional analysis) and over time (trend or time-series analysis).

For example, an analyst may wish to compare the profitability of companies competing in a global industry. If the companies differ significantly in size and/or report their financial data in different currencies, comparing net income as reported is not useful. Ratios (which express one number in relation to another) and common-size financial statements can remove size as a factor and enable a more relevant comparison. To achieve comparability across companies reporting in different currencies, one approach is to translate all reported numbers into a common currency using exchange rates at the end of a period. Others may prefer to translate reported numbers using the average exchange rates during the period. Alternatively, if the focus is primarily on ratios, comparability can be achieved without translating the currencies.

The analyst may also want to examine comparable performance over time. Again, the nominal currency amounts of sales or net income may not highlight significant changes. To address this challenge, horizontal financial statements (whereby quantities are stated in terms of a selected base year value) can make such changes more apparent. Another obstacle to comparison is differences in fiscal year end. To achieve comparability, one approach is to develop trailing 12 months data, which will be described in a section below. Finally, it should be noted that differences in accounting standards can limit comparability.

EXAMPLE 2   Ratio Analysis

An analyst is examining the profitability of two international companies with large shares of the global personal computer market: Acer Inc. and Lenovo Group Limited. Acer has pursued a strategy of selling its products at affordable prices. In contrast, Lenovo aims to achieve higher selling prices by stressing the high engineering quality of its personal computers for business use. Acer reports in TWD,[3] and Lenovo reports in USD. For Acer, fiscal year end is December 31. For Lenovo, fiscal year end is March 31; thus, FY2017 ended March 31, 2018.

The analyst collects the data shown in Exhibit 2 below. Use this information to answer the following questions:

1. Which company is larger based on the amount of revenue, in USD, reported in fiscal year 2017? For FY2017, assume the relevant, average exchange rate was 30.95 TWD/USD.
2. Which company had the higher revenue growth from FY2016 to FY2017? FY2013 to FY2017?
3. How do the companies compare, based on profitability?

EXHIBIT 2

Acer

TWD Millions	FY2013	FY2014	FY2015	FY2016	FY2017
Revenue	360,132	329,684	263,775	232,724	237,275
Gross profit	22,550	28,942	24,884	23,212	25,361
Net income	(20,519)	1,791	604	(4,901)	2,797

Lenovo

USD Millions	FY2013*	FY2014*	FY2015*	FY2016*	FY2017*
Revenue	38,707	46,296	44,912	43,035	45,350
Gross profit	5,064	6,682	6,624	6,105	6,272
Net income (Loss)	817	837	(145)	530	(127)

* Fiscal years for Lenovo end March 31. Thus FY2017 represents the fiscal year ended March 31, 2018; the same applies respectively for prior years.

---

[3] TWD is the three-letter ISO 4217 currency code for Taiwan New Dollar.

Solution to 1: Lenovo is much larger than Acer based on FY2017 revenues in USD terms. Lenovo's FY2017 revenues of $USD45.35 billion are considerably higher than Acer's USD7.67 million (= TWD 237.275 million/30.95).

Acer: At the assumed average exchange rate of 30.95 TWD/USD, Acer's FY2017 revenues are equivalent to USD7.67 billion (= TWD237.275 billion ÷ 30.95 TWD/USD).

Lenovo: Lenovo's FY2017 revenues totaled USD45.35 billion.

Note: Comparing the size of companies reporting in different currencies requires translating reported numbers into a common currency using exchange rates at some point in time. This solution converts the revenues of Acer to billions of USD using the average exchange rate of the fiscal period. It would be equally informative (and would yield the same conclusion) to convert the revenues of Lenovo to TWD.

Solution to 2: The growth in Lenovo's revenue was much higher than Acer's in the most recent fiscal year and for the five-year period.

	Change in Revenue FY2016 versus FY2017 (%)	Change in Revenue FY2013 to FY2017 (%)
Acer	1.96	(34.11)
Lenovo	5.38	17.16

The table shows two growth metrics. Calculations are illustrated using the revenue data for Acer:

The change in Acer's revenue for FY2016 versus FY2017 is 1.96% percent calculated as (237,275 − 232,724) ÷ 232,724 or equivalently (237,275 ÷ 232,724) − 1. The change in Acer's revenue from FY2013 to FY2017 is a decline of 34.11%.

Solution to 3: Profitability can be assessed by comparing the amount of gross profit to revenue and the amount of net income to revenue. The following table presents these two profitability ratios—**gross profit margin** (gross profit divided by revenue) and **net profit margin** (net income divided by revenue)—for each year.

Acer	FY2013 (%)	FY2014 (%)	FY2015 (%)	FY2016 (%)	FY2017 (%)
Gross profit margin	6.26	8.78	9.43	9.97	10.69
Net profit margin	(5.70)	0.54	0.23	(2.11)	1.18

Lenovo	FY2013 (%)	FY2014 (%)	FY2015 (%)	FY2016 (%)	FY2017 (%)
Gross profit margin	13.08	14.43	14.75	14.19	13.83
Net profit margin	2.11	1.81	(0.32)	1.23	(0.28)

The net profit margins indicate that both companies' profitability is relatively low. Acer's net profit margin is lower than Lenovo's in three out of the five years. Acer's gross profit margin increased each year but remains significantly below that of Lenovo. Lenovo's gross profit margin grew from FY2013 to FY2015 and then declined in FY2016 and FY2017. Overall, Lenovo is the more profitable company, likely attributable to its larger size and commensurate economies of scale. (Lenovo has the largest share of the personal computer market relative to other personal computer companies.)

Section 3.1 describes the tools and techniques of ratio analysis in more detail. Sections 3.2 to 3.4 describe other tools and techniques.

3.1. Ratios

There are many relationships among financial accounts and various expected relationships from one point in time to another. Ratios are a useful way of expressing these relationships. Ratios express one quantity in relation to another (usually as a quotient).

Extensive academic research has examined the importance of ratios in predicting stock returns (Ou and Penman, 1989; Abarbanell and Bushee, 1998) or credit failure (Altman, 1968; Ohlson, 1980; Hopwood et al., 1994). This research has found that financial statement ratios are effective in selecting investments and in predicting financial distress. Practitioners routinely use ratios to derive and communicate the value of companies and securities.

Several aspects of ratio analysis are important to understand. First, the computed ratio is not "the answer." The ratio is an *indicator* of some aspect of a company's performance, telling what happened but not why it happened. For example, an analyst might want to answer the question: Which of two companies was more profitable? As demonstrated in the previous example, the net profit margin, which expresses profit relative to revenue, can provide insight into this question. Net profit margin is calculated by dividing net income by revenue:[4]

$$\frac{\text{Net income}}{\text{Revenue}}$$

Assume Company A has €100,000 of net income and Company B has €200,000 of net income. Company B generated twice as much income as Company A, but was it more profitable? Assume further that Company A has €2,000,000 of revenue, and thus a net profit margin of 5 percent, and Company B has €6,000,000 of revenue, and thus a net profit margin of 3.33 percent. Expressing net income as a percentage of revenue clarifies the relationship: For each €100 of revenue, Company A earns €5 in net income, whereas Company B earns only €3.33 for each €100 of revenue. So, we can now answer the question of which company was more profitable in percentage terms: Company A was more profitable, as indicated by its higher net profit margin of 5 percent. Note that Company A was more *profitable* despite the fact that Company B reported higher absolute amounts of net income and revenue. However, this ratio by itself does not tell us *why* Company A has a higher profit margin. Further analysis is required to determine the reason (perhaps higher relative sales prices or better cost control or lower effective tax rates).

Company size sometimes confers economies of scale, so the absolute amounts of net income and revenue are useful in financial analysis. However, ratios control for the effect of size, which enhances comparisons between companies and over time.

A second important aspect of ratio analysis is that differences in accounting policies (across companies and across time) can distort ratios, and a meaningful comparison may,

---

[4] The term "sales" is often used interchangeably with the term "revenues." Other times it is used to refer to revenues derived from sales of products versus services. The income statement usually reflects "revenues" or "sales" after returns and allowances (e.g., returns of products or discounts offered after a sale to induce the customer to not return a product). Additionally, in some countries, including the United Kingdom and South Africa, the term "turnover" is used in the sense of "revenue."

therefore, involve adjustments to the financial data. Third, not all ratios are necessarily relevant to a particular analysis. The ability to select a relevant ratio or ratios to answer the research question is an analytical skill. Finally, as with financial analysis in general, ratio analysis does not stop with computation; interpretation of the result is essential. In practice, differences in ratios across time and across companies can be subtle, and interpretation is situation specific.

3.1.1. The Universe of Ratios

There are no authoritative bodies specifying exact formulas for computing ratios or providing a standard, comprehensive list of ratios. Formulas and even names of ratios often differ from analyst to analyst or from database to database. The number of different ratios that can be created is practically limitless. There are, however, widely accepted ratios that have been found to be useful. Section 4 of this chapter will focus primarily on these broad classes and commonly accepted definitions of key ratios. However, the analyst should be aware that different ratios may be used in practice and that certain industries have unique ratios tailored to the characteristics of that industry. When faced with an unfamiliar ratio, the analyst can examine the underlying formula to gain insight into what the ratio is measuring. For example, consider the following ratio formula:

$$\frac{\text{Operating income}}{\text{Average total assets}}$$

Never having seen this ratio, an analyst might question whether a result of 12 percent is better than 8 percent. The answer can be found in the ratio itself. The numerator is operating income and the denominator is average total assets, so the ratio can be interpreted as the amount of operating income generated per unit of assets. For every €100 of average total assets, generating €12 of operating income is better than generating €8 of operating income. Furthermore, it is apparent that this particular ratio is an indicator of profitability (and, to a lesser extent, efficiency in use of assets in generating operating profits). When encountering a ratio for the first time, the analyst should evaluate the numerator and denominator to assess what the ratio is attempting to measure and how it should be interpreted. This is demonstrated in Example 3.

EXAMPLE 3   Interpreting a Financial Ratio

A US insurance company reports that its "combined ratio" is determined by dividing losses and expenses incurred by net premiums earned. It reports the following combined ratios:

Fiscal Year	5	4	3	2	1
Combined ratio	90.1%	104.0%	98.5%	104.1%	101.1%

Explain what this ratio is measuring and compare the results reported for each of the years shown in the chart. What other information might an analyst want to review before making any conclusions on this information?

Solution: The combined ratio is a profitability measure. The ratio is explaining how much costs (losses and expenses) were incurred for every dollar of revenue (net premiums earned). The underlying formula indicates that a *lower* value for this ratio is better. The Year 5 ratio of 90.1 percent means that for every dollar of net premiums earned, the costs were $0.901, yielding a gross profit of $0.099. Ratios greater than 100 percent indicate an overall loss. A review of the data indicates that there does not seem to be a consistent trend in this ratio. Profits were achieved in Years 5 and 3. The results for Years 4 and 2 show the most significant costs at approximately 104 percent.

The analyst would want to discuss this data further with management and understand the characteristics of the underlying business. He or she would want to understand why the results are so volatile. The analyst would also want to determine what should be used as a benchmark for this ratio.

The Operating income/Average total assets ratio shown above is one of many versions of the **return on assets (ROA)** ratio. Note that there are other ways of specifying this formula based on how assets are defined. Some financial ratio databases compute ROA using the ending value of assets rather than average assets. In limited cases, one may also see beginning assets in the denominator. Which one is right? It depends on what you are trying to measure and the underlying company trends. If the company has a stable level of assets, the answer will not differ greatly under the three measures of assets (beginning, average, and ending). However, if the assets are growing (or shrinking), the results will differ among the three measures. When assets are growing, operating income divided by ending assets may not make sense because some of the income would have been generated before some assets were purchased, and this would understate the company's performance. Similarly, if beginning assets are used, some of the operating income later in the year may have been generated only because of the addition of assets; therefore, the ratio would overstate the company's performance. Because operating income occurs throughout the period, it generally makes sense to use some average measure of assets. A good general rule is that when an income statement or cash flow statement number is in the numerator of a ratio and a balance sheet number is in the denominator, then an average should be used for the denominator. It is generally not necessary to use averages when only balance sheet numbers are used in both the numerator and denominator because both are determined as of the same date. However, in some instances, even ratios that only use balance sheet data may use averages. For example, **return on equity (ROE)**, which is defined as net income divided by average shareholders' equity, can be decomposed into other ratios, some of which only use balance sheet data. In decomposing ROE into component ratios, if an average is used in one of the component ratios then it should be used in the other component ratios. The decomposition of ROE is discussed further in Section 4.6.2.

If an average is used, judgment is also required about what average should be used. For simplicity, most ratio databases use a simple average of the beginning and end-of-year balance sheet amounts. If the company's business is seasonal so that levels of assets vary by interim period (semiannual or quarterly), then it may be beneficial to take an average over all interim periods, if available. (If the analyst is working within a company and has access to monthly data, this can also be used.)

3.1.2. Value, Purposes, and Limitations of Ratio Analysis

The value of ratio analysis is that it enables a financial analyst to evaluate past performance, assess the current financial position of the company, and gain insights useful for projecting future results. As noted previously, the ratio itself is not "the answer" but is an indicator of some aspect of a company's performance. Financial ratios provide insights into:

- economic relationships within a company that help analysts project earnings and free cash flow;
- a company's financial flexibility, or ability to obtain the cash required to grow and meet its obligations, even if unexpected circumstances develop;
- management's ability;
- changes in the company and/or industry over time; and
- comparability with peer companies or the relevant industry(ies).

There are also limitations to ratio analysis. Factors to consider include:

- *The heterogeneity or homogeneity of a company's operating activities.* Companies may have divisions operating in many different industries. This can make it difficult to find comparable industry ratios to use for comparison purposes.
- *The need to determine whether the results of the ratio analysis are consistent.* One set of ratios may indicate a problem, whereas another set may indicate that the potential problem is only short term in nature.
- *The need to use judgment.* A key issue is whether a ratio for a company is within a reasonable range. Although financial ratios are used to help assess the growth potential and risk of a company, they cannot be used alone to directly value a company or its securities, or to determine its creditworthiness. The entire operation of the company must be examined, and the external economic and industry setting in which it is operating must be considered when interpreting financial ratios.
- *The use of alternative accounting methods.* Companies frequently have latitude when choosing certain accounting methods. Ratios taken from financial statements that employ different accounting choices may not be comparable unless adjustments are made. Some important accounting considerations include the following:
  - FIFO (first in, first out), LIFO (last in, first out), or average cost inventory valuation methods (IFRS does not allow LIFO);
  - Cost or equity methods of accounting for unconsolidated affiliates;
  - Straight line or accelerated methods of depreciation; and
  - Operating or finance lease treatment for lessors (under US GAAP, the type of lease affects classifications of expenses; under IFRS, operating lease treatment for lessors is not applicable).

The expanding use of IFRS and past convergence efforts between IFRS and US GAAP make the financial statements of different companies more comparable and may overcome some of these difficulties. Nonetheless, there will remain accounting choices that the analyst must consider.

3.1.3. Sources of Ratios

Ratios may be computed using data obtained directly from companies' financial statements or from a database such as Bloomberg, Compustat, FactSet, or Thomson Reuters. The information provided by the database may include information as reported in companies' financial statements and ratios calculated based on the information. These databases are popular because they provide easy access to many years of historical data so that trends over time can be examined. They also allow for ratio calculations based on periods other than the company's fiscal year, such as for the trailing 12 months (TTM) or most recent quarter (MRQ).

EXAMPLE 4   Trailing 12 Months

On 15 July, an analyst is examining a company with a fiscal year ending on December 31. Use the following data to calculate the company's trailing 12 month earnings (for the period ended June 30, 2018):

- Earnings for the year ended December 31, 2017: $1,200;
- Earnings for the six months ended June 30, 2017: $550; and
- Earnings for the six months ended June 30, 2018: $750.

Solution: The company's trailing 12 months earnings is $1,400, calculated as $1,200 − $550 + $750.

Analysts should be aware that the underlying formulas for ratios may differ by vendor. The formula used should be obtained from the vendor, and the analyst should determine whether any adjustments are necessary. Furthermore, database providers often exercise judgment when classifying items. For example, operating income may not appear directly on a company's income statement, and the vendor may use judgment to classify income statement items as "operating" or "non-operating." Variation in such judgments would affect any computation involving operating income. It is therefore a good practice to use the same source for data when comparing different companies or when evaluating the historical record of a single company. Analysts should verify the consistency of formulas and data classifications by the data source. Analysts should also be mindful of the judgments made by a vendor in data classifications and refer back to the source financial statements until they are comfortable that the classifications are appropriate.

Collection of financial data from regulatory filings and calculation of ratios can be automated. The eXtensible Business Reporting Language (XBRL) is a mechanism that attaches "smart tags" to financial information (e.g., total assets), so that software can automatically collect the data and perform desired computations. The organization developing XBRL (www.xbrl.org) is an international nonprofit consortium of over 600 members from companies, associations, and agencies, including the International Accounting Standards Board. Many stock exchanges and regulatory agencies around the world now use XBRL for receiving and distributing public financial reports from listed companies.

Analysts can compare a subject company to similar (peer) companies in these databases or use aggregate industry data. For non-public companies, aggregate industry data can be obtained from such sources as Annual Statement Studies by the Risk Management Association or Dun & Bradstreet. These publications typically provide industry data with companies sorted into quartiles. By definition, twenty-five percent of companies' ratios fall within the lowest quartile, 25 percent have ratios between the lower quartile and median value, and so on. Analysts can then determine a company's relative standing in the industry.

3.2. Common-Size Analysis

Common-size analysis involves expressing financial data, including entire financial statements, in relation to a single financial statement item, or base. Items used most frequently as the bases are total assets or revenue. In essence, common-size analysis creates a ratio between every financial statement item and the base item.

Common-size analysis was demonstrated in chapters for the income statement, balance sheet, and cash flow statement. In this section, we present common-size analysis of financial statements in greater detail and include further discussion of their interpretation.

3.2.1. Common-Size Analysis of the Balance Sheet

A vertical[5] common-size balance sheet, prepared by dividing each item on the balance sheet by the same period's total assets and expressing the results as percentages, highlights the composition of the balance sheet. What is the mix of assets being used? How is the company financing itself? How does one company's balance sheet composition compare with that of peer companies, and what are the reasons for any differences?

A horizontal common-size balance sheet, prepared by computing the increase or decrease in percentage terms of each balance sheet item from the prior year or prepared by dividing the quantity of each item by a base year quantity of the item, highlights changes in items. These changes can be compared to expectations. The section on trend analysis below will illustrate a horizontal common-size balance sheet.

Exhibit 3 presents a vertical common-size (partial) balance sheet for a hypothetical company in two time periods. In this example, receivables have increased from 35 percent to 57 percent of total assets, and the ratio has increased by 63 percent from Period 1 to Period 2. What are possible reasons for such an increase? The increase might indicate that the company is making more of its sales on a credit basis rather than a cash basis, perhaps in response to some action taken by a competitor. Alternatively, the increase in receivables as a percentage of assets may have occurred because of a change in another current asset category, for example, a decrease in the level of inventory; the analyst would then need to investigate why that asset category has changed. Another possible reason for the increase in receivables as a percentage of assets is that the company has lowered its credit standards, relaxed its collection procedures, or adopted more aggressive revenue recognition policies. The analyst can turn to other comparisons and ratios (e.g., comparing the rate of growth in accounts receivable with the rate of growth in sales) to help determine which explanation is most likely.

EXHIBIT 3   Vertical Common-Size (Partial) Balance Sheet for a Hypothetical Company

	Period 1 Percent of Total Assets	Period 2 Percent of Total Assets
Cash	25	15
Receivables	35	57
Inventory	35	20
Fixed assets, net of depreciation	5	8
Total assets	100	100

---

[5]The term **vertical analysis** is used to denote a common-size analysis using only one reporting period or one base financial statement, whereas **horizontal analysis** refers to an analysis comparing a specific financial statement with prior or future time periods or to a cross-sectional analysis of one company with another.

3.2.2. Common-Size Analysis of the Income Statement

A vertical common-size income statement divides each income statement item by revenue, or sometimes by total assets (especially in the case of financial institutions). If there are multiple revenue sources, a decomposition of revenue in percentage terms is useful. Exhibit 4 presents a hypothetical company's vertical common-size income statement in two time periods. Revenue is separated into the company's four services, each shown as a percentage of total revenue.

In this example, revenues from Service A have become a far greater percentage of the company's total revenue (30 percent in Period 1 and 45 percent in Period 2). What are possible reasons for and implications of this change in business mix? Did the company make a strategic decision to sell more of Service A, perhaps because it is more profitable? Apparently not, because the company's earnings before interest, taxes, depreciation, and amortization (EBITDA) declined from 53 percent of sales to 45 percent, so other possible explanations should be examined. In addition, we note from the composition of operating expenses that the main reason for this decline in profitability is that salaries and employee benefits have increased from 15 percent to 25 percent of total revenue. Are more highly compensated employees required for Service A? Were higher training costs incurred in order to increase revenues from Service A? If the analyst wants to predict future performance, the causes of these changes must be understood.

In addition, Exhibit 4 shows that the company's income tax as a percentage of sales has declined dramatically (from 15 percent to 8 percent). Furthermore, taxes as a percentage of earnings before tax (EBT) (the effective tax rate, which is usually the more relevant comparison), have decreased from 36 percent (= 15/42) to 24 percent (= 8/34). Is Service A, which in Period 2 is a greater percentage of total revenue, provided in a jurisdiction with lower tax rates? If not, what is the explanation for the change in effective tax rate?

The observations based on Exhibit 4 summarize the issues that can be raised through analysis of the vertical common-size income statement.

EXHIBIT 4   Vertical Common-Size Income Statement for Hypothetical Company

	Period 1 Percent of Total Revenue	Period 2 Percent of Total Revenue
Revenue source: Service A	30	45
Revenue source: Service B	23	20
Revenue source: Service C	30	30
Revenue source: Service D	17	5
Total revenue	**100**	**100**
Operating expenses (excluding depreciation)		
Salaries and employee benefits	15	25
Administrative expenses	22	20
Rent expense	10	10
EBITDA	**53**	**45**
Depreciation and amortization	4	4

(*continued*)

EXHIBIT 4   (Continued)

	Period 1 Percent of Total Revenue	Period 2 Percent of Total Revenue
EBIT	**49**	**41**
Interest paid	7	7
EBT	**42**	**34**
Income tax provision	15	8
Net income	**27**	**26**

EBIT = earnings before interest and tax.

3.2.3. Cross-Sectional Analysis

As noted previously, ratios and common-size statements derive part of their meaning through comparison to some benchmark. **Cross-sectional analysis** (sometimes called "relative analysis") compares a specific metric for one company with the same metric for another company or group of companies, allowing comparisons even though the companies might be of significantly different sizes and/or operate in different currencies. This is illustrated in Exhibit 5.

EXHIBIT 5   Vertical Common-Size (Partial) Balance Sheet for Two Hypothetical Companies

Assets	Company 1 Percent of Total Assets	Company 2 Percent of Total Assets
Cash	38	12
Receivables	33	55
Inventory	27	24
Fixed assets net of depreciation	1	2
Investments	1	7
Total Assets	**100**	**100**

Exhibit 5 presents a vertical common-size (partial) balance sheet for two hypothetical companies at the same point in time. Company 1 is clearly more liquid (liquidity is a function of how quickly assets can be converted into cash) than Company 2, which has only 12 percent of assets available as cash, compared with the highly liquid Company 1, which has 38 percent of assets available as cash. Given that cash is generally a relatively low-yielding asset and thus not a particularly efficient use of excess funds, why does Company 1 hold such a large percentage of total assets in cash? Perhaps the company is preparing for an acquisition, or maintains a large cash position as insulation from a particularly volatile operating environment. Another issue highlighted by the comparison in this example is the relatively high percentage of receivables in Company 2's assets, which may indicate a greater proportion of credit sales, overall changes in asset composition, lower credit or collection standards, or aggressive accounting policies.

3.2.4. Trend Analysis[6]

When looking at financial statements and ratios, trends in the data, whether they are improving or deteriorating, are as important as the current absolute or relative levels. Trend analysis provides important information regarding historical performance and growth and, given a sufficiently long history of accurate seasonal information, can be of great assistance as a planning and forecasting tool for management and analysts.

Exhibit 6A presents a partial balance sheet for a hypothetical company over five periods. The last two columns of the table show the changes for Period 5 compared with Period 4, expressed both in absolute currency (in this case, dollars) and in percentages. A small percentage change could hide a significant currency change and vice versa, prompting the analyst to investigate the reasons despite one of the changes being relatively small. In this example, the largest percentage change was in investments, which decreased by 33.3 percent.[7] However, an examination of the absolute currency amount of changes shows that investments changed by only $2 million, and the more significant change was the $12 million increase in receivables.

Another way to present data covering a period of time is to show each item in relation to the same item in a base year (i.e., a horizontal common-size balance sheet). Exhibits 6B and 6C illustrate alternative presentations of horizontal common-size balance sheets. Exhibit 6B presents the information from the same partial balance sheet as in Exhibit 6A, but indexes each item relative to the same item in Period 1. For example, in Period 2, the company had $29 million cash, which is 74 percent or 0.74 of the amount of cash it had in Period 1. Expressed as an index relative to Period 1, where each item in Period 1 is given a value of 1.00, the value in Period 2 would be 0.74 ($29/$39 = 0.74). In Period 3, the company had $27 million cash, which is 69 percent of the amount of cash it had in Period 1 ($27/$39 = 0.69).

Exhibit 6C presents the percentage change in each item, relative to the previous year. For example, the change in cash from Period 1 to Period 2 was –25.6 percent ($29/$39 – 1 = –0.256), and the change in cash from Period 2 to Period 3 was –6.9 percent ($27/$29 – 1 = –0.069). An analyst will select the horizontal common-size balance that addresses the particular period of interest. Exhibit 6B clearly highlights that in Period 5 compared to Period 1, the company has less than half the amount of cash, four times the amount of investments, and eight times the amount of property, plant, and equipment. Exhibit 6C highlights year-to-year changes: For example, cash has declined in each period. Presenting data this way highlights significant changes. Again, note that a mathematically big change is not necessarily an important change. For example, fixed assets increased 100 percent, that is, doubled between Period 1 and 2; however, as a proportion of total assets, fixed assets increased from 1 percent of total assets to 2 percent of total assets. The company's working capital assets (receivables and inventory) are a far higher proportion of total assets and would likely warrant more attention from an analyst.

An analysis of horizontal common-size balance sheets highlights structural changes that have occurred in a business. Past trends are obviously not necessarily an accurate predictor of the future, especially when the economic or competitive environment changes. An examination

---

[6]In financial statement analysis, the term "trend analysis" usually refers to comparisons across time periods of 3–10 years not involving statistical tools. This differs from the use of the term in the quantitative methods portion of the CFA curriculum, where "trend analysis" refers to statistical methods of measuring patterns in time-series data.

[7]Percentage change is calculated as (Ending value – Beginning value)/Beginning value, or equivalently, (Ending value/Beginning value) – 1.

of past trends is more valuable when the macroeconomic and competitive environments are relatively stable and when the analyst is reviewing a stable or mature business. However, even in less stable contexts, historical analysis can serve as a basis for developing expectations. Understanding of past trends is helpful in assessing whether these trends are likely to continue or if the trend is likely to change direction.

EXHIBIT 6A Partial Balance Sheet for a Hypothetical Company over Five Periods

Assets ($ Millions)	Period					Change 4 to 5 ($ Million)	Change 4 to 5 (Percent)
	1	2	3	4	5		
Cash	39	29	27	19	16	−3	−15.8
Investments	1	7	7	6	4	−2	−33.3
Receivables	44	41	37	67	79	12	17.9
Inventory	15	25	36	25	27	2	8.0
Fixed assets net of depreciation	1	2	6	9	8	−1	−11.1
Total assets	100	104	113	126	134	8	6.3

EXHIBIT 6B Horizontal Common-Size (Partial) Balance Sheet for a Hypothetical Company over Five Periods, with Each Item Expressed Relative to the Same Item in Period One

Assets	Period				
	1	2	3	4	5
Cash	1.00	0.74	0.69	0.49	0.41
Investments	1.00	7.00	7.00	6.00	4.00
Receivables	1.00	0.93	0.84	1.52	1.80
Inventory	1.00	1.67	2.40	1.67	1.80
Fixed assets net of depreciation	1.00	2.00	6.00	9.00	8.00
Total assets	1.00	1.04	1.13	1.26	1.34

EXHIBIT 6C Horizontal Common-Size (Partial) Balance Sheet for a Hypothetical Company over Five Periods, with Percent Change in Each Item Relative to the Prior Period

Assets	Period			
	2 (%)	3 (%)	4 (%)	5 (%)
Cash	−25.6	−6.9	−29.6	−15.8
Investments	600.0	0.0	−14.3	−33.3
Receivables	−6.8	−9.8	81.1	17.9
Inventory	66.7	44.0	−30.6	8.0
Fixed assets net of depreciation	100.0	200.0	50.0	−11.1
Total assets	4.0	8.7	11.5	6.3

One measure of success is for a company to grow at a rate greater than the rate of the overall market in which it operates. Companies that grow slowly may find themselves unable to attract equity capital. Conversely, companies that grow too quickly may find that their administrative and management information systems cannot keep up with the rate of expansion.

3.2.5. Relationships among Financial Statements

Trend data generated by a horizontal common-size analysis can be compared across financial statements. For example, the growth rate of assets for the hypothetical company in Exhibit 6 can be compared with the company's growth in revenue over the same period of time. If revenue is growing more quickly than assets, the company may be increasing its efficiency (i.e., generating more revenue for every dollar invested in assets).

As another example, consider the following year-over-year percentage changes for a hypothetical company:

Revenue	+20%
Net income	+25%
Operating cash flow	−10%
Total assets	+30%

Net income is growing faster than revenue, which indicates increasing profitability. However, the analyst would need to determine whether the faster growth in net income resulted from continuing operations or from non-operating, non-recurring items. In addition, the 10 percent decline in operating cash flow despite increasing revenue and net income clearly warrants further investigation because it could indicate a problem with earnings quality (perhaps aggressive reporting of revenue). Lastly, the fact that assets have grown faster than revenue indicates the company's efficiency may be declining. The analyst should examine the composition of the increase in assets and the reasons for the changes. Example 5 illustrates a historical example of a company where comparisons of trend data from different financial statements were actually indicative of aggressive accounting policies.

EXAMPLE 5   Use of Comparative Growth Information[8]

In July 1996, Sunbeam, a US company, brought in new management to turn the company around. In the following year, 1997, using 1996 as the base, the following was observed based on reported numbers:

Revenue	+19%
Inventory	+58%
Receivables	+38%

It is generally more desirable to observe inventory and receivables growing at a slower (or similar) rate compared to revenue growth. Receivables growing faster than revenue can indicate operational issues, such as lower credit standards or aggressive accounting

---

[8] Adapted from Robinson and Munter (2004, pp. 2–15).

policies for revenue recognition. Similarly, inventory growing faster than revenue can indicate an operational problem with obsolescence or aggressive accounting policies, such as an improper overstatement of inventory to increase profits.

In this case, the explanation lay in aggressive accounting policies. Sunbeam was later charged by the US Securities and Exchange Commission with improperly accelerating the recognition of revenue and engaging in other practices, such as billing customers for inventory prior to shipment.

3.3. The Use of Graphs as an Analytical Tool

Graphs facilitate comparison of performance and financial structure over time, highlighting changes in significant aspects of business operations. In addition, graphs provide the analyst (and management) with a visual overview of risk trends in a business. Graphs may also be used effectively to communicate the analyst's conclusions regarding financial condition and risk management aspects.

Exhibit 7 presents the information from Exhibit 6A in a stacked column format. The graph makes the significant decline in cash and growth in receivables (both in absolute terms and as a percentage of assets) readily apparent. In Exhibit 7, the vertical axis shows US$ millions and the horizontal axis denotes the period.

Choosing the appropriate graph to communicate the most significant conclusions of a financial analysis is a skill. In general, pie graphs are most useful to communicate the composition of a total value (e.g., assets over a limited amount of time, say one or two periods). Line graphs are useful when the focus is on the change in amount for a limited number of items over a relatively longer time period. When the composition and amounts, as well as their change over time, are all important, a stacked column graph can be useful.

EXHIBIT 7   Stacked Column Graph of Asset Composition of Hypothetical Company over Five Periods

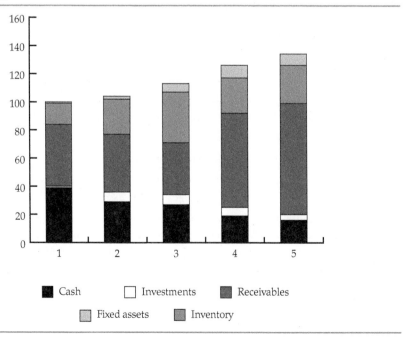

When comparing Period 5 with Period 4, the growth in receivables appears to be within normal bounds; but when comparing Period 5 with earlier periods, the dramatic growth becomes apparent. In the same manner, a simple line graph will also illustrate the growth trends in key financial variables. Exhibit 8 presents the information from Exhibit 6A as a line graph, illustrating the growth of assets of a hypothetical company over five periods. The steady decline in cash, volatile movements of inventory, and dramatic growth of receivables are clearly illustrated. Again, the vertical axis is shown in US$ millions and the horizontal axis denotes periods.

EXHIBIT 8   Line Graph of Growth of Assets of Hypothetical Company over Five Periods

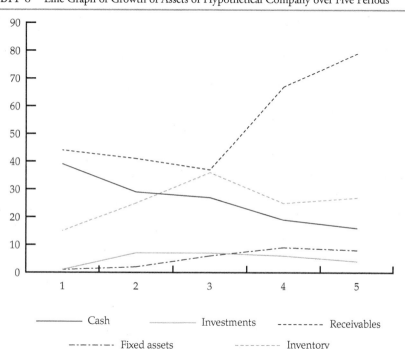

3.4. Regression Analysis

When analyzing the trend in a specific line item or ratio, frequently it is possible simply to visually evaluate the changes. For more complex situations, regression analysis can help identify relationships (or correlation) between variables. For example, a regression analysis could relate a company's sales to GDP over time, providing insight into whether the company is cyclical. In addition, the statistical relationship between sales and GDP could be used as a basis for forecasting sales.

Other examples where regression analysis may be useful include the relationship between a company's sales and inventory over time, or the relationship between hotel occupancy and a company's hotel revenues. In addition to providing a basis for forecasting, regression analysis facilitates identification of items or ratios that are not behaving as expected, given historical statistical relationships.

4. COMMON RATIOS USED IN FINANCIAL ANALYSIS

In the previous section, we focused on ratios resulting from common-size analysis. In this section, we expand the discussion to include other commonly used financial ratios and the broad classes into which they are categorized. There is some overlap with common-size financial statement ratios. For example, a common indicator of profitability is the net profit margin, which is calculated as net income divided by sales. This ratio appears on a vertical common-size income statement. Other ratios involve information from multiple financial statements or even data from outside the financial statements.

Because of the large number of ratios, it is helpful to think about ratios in terms of broad categories based on what aspects of performance a ratio is intended to detect. Financial analysts and data vendors use a variety of categories to classify ratios. The category names and the ratios included in each category can differ. Common ratio categories include activity, liquidity, solvency, profitability, and valuation. These categories are summarized in Exhibit 9. Each category measures a different aspect of the company's business, but all are useful in evaluating a company's overall ability to generate cash flows from operating its business and the associated risks.

EXHIBIT 9   Categories of Financial Ratios

Category	Description
Activity	**Activity ratios** measure how efficiently a company performs day-to-day tasks, such as the collection of receivables and management of inventory.
Liquidity	**Liquidity ratios** measure the company's ability to meet its short-term obligations.
Solvency	**Solvency ratios** measure a company's ability to meet long-term obligations. Subsets of these ratios are also known as "leverage" and "long-term debt" ratios.
Profitability	**Profitability ratios** measure the company's ability to generate profits from its resources (assets).
Valuation	**Valuation ratios** measure the quantity of an asset or flow (e.g., earnings) associated with ownership of a specified claim (e.g., a share or ownership of the enterprise).

These categories are not mutually exclusive; some ratios are useful in measuring multiple aspects of the business. For example, an activity ratio measuring how quickly a company collects accounts receivable is also useful in assessing the company's liquidity because collection of revenues increases cash. Some profitability ratios also reflect the operating efficiency of the business. In summary, analysts appropriately use certain ratios to evaluate multiple aspects of the business. Analysts also need to be aware of variations in industry practice in the calculation of financial ratios. In the text that follows, alternative views on ratio calculations are often provided.

4.1. Interpretation and Context

Financial ratios can only be interpreted in the context of other information, including benchmarks. In general, the financial ratios of a company are compared with those of its major competitors (cross-sectional and trend analysis) and to the company's prior periods (trend analysis). The goal is to understand the underlying causes of divergence between a company's ratios and those of the industry. Even ratios that remain consistent require understanding because consistency can sometimes indicate accounting policies selected to smooth earnings. An analyst should evaluate financial ratios based on the following:

1. *Company goals and strategy*. Actual ratios can be compared with company objectives to determine whether objectives are being attained and whether the results are consistent with the company's strategy.
2. *Industry norms (cross-sectional analysis)*. A company can be compared with others in its industry by relating its financial ratios to industry norms or to a subset of the companies in an industry. When industry norms are used to make judgments, care must be taken because:
   • Many ratios are industry specific, and not all ratios are important to all industries.
   • Companies may have several different lines of business. This will cause aggregate financial ratios to be distorted. It is better to examine industry-specific ratios by lines of business.
   • Differences in accounting methods used by companies can distort financial ratios.
   • Differences in corporate strategies can affect certain financial ratios.
3. *Economic conditions*. For cyclical companies, financial ratios tend to improve when the economy is strong and weaken during recessions. Therefore, financial ratios should be examined in light of the current phase of the business cycle.

The following sections discuss activity, liquidity, solvency, and profitability ratios in turn. Selected valuation ratios are presented later in the section on equity analysis.

4.2. Activity Ratios

Activity ratios are also known as **asset utilization ratios** or **operating efficiency ratios**. This category is intended to measure how well a company manages various activities, particularly how efficiently it manages its various assets. Activity ratios are analyzed as indicators of ongoing operational performance—how effectively assets are used by a company. These ratios reflect the efficient management of both working capital and longer-term assets. As noted, efficiency has a direct impact on liquidity (the ability of a company to meet its short-term obligations), so some activity ratios are also useful in assessing liquidity.

4.2.1. Calculation of Activity Ratios
Exhibit 10 presents the most commonly used activity ratios. The exhibit shows the numerator and denominator of each ratio.

EXHIBIT 10   Definitions of Commonly Used Activity Ratios

Activity Ratios	Numerator	Denominator
Inventory turnover	Cost of sales or cost of goods sold	Average inventory
Days of inventory on hand (DOH)	Number of days in period	Inventory turnover
Receivables turnover	Revenue	Average receivables
Days of sales outstanding (DSO)	Number of days in period	Receivables turnover
Payables turnover	Purchases	Average trade payables
Number of days of payables	Number of days in period	Payables turnover

(continued)

EXHIBIT 10   (Continued)

Activity Ratios	Numerator	Denominator
Working capital turnover	Revenue	Average working capital
Fixed asset turnover	Revenue	Average net fixed assets
Total asset turnover	Revenue	Average total assets

Activity ratios measure how efficiently the company utilizes assets. They generally combine information from the income statement in the numerator with balance sheet items in the denominator. Because the income statement measures what happened *during* a period whereas the balance sheet shows the condition only at the end of the period, average balance sheet data are normally used for consistency. For example, to measure inventory management efficiency, cost of sales or cost of goods sold (from the income statement) is divided by average inventory (from the balance sheet). Most databases, such as Bloomberg and Baseline, use this averaging convention when income statement and balance sheet data are combined. These databases typically average only two points: the beginning of the year and the end of the year. The examples that follow based on annual financial statements illustrate that practice. However, some analysts prefer to average more observations if they are available, especially if the business is seasonal. If a semiannual report is prepared, an average can be taken over three data points (beginning, middle, and end of year). If quarterly data are available, a five-point average can be computed (beginning of year and end of each quarterly period) or a four-point average using the end of each quarterly period. Note that if the company's year ends at a low or high point for inventory for the year, there can still be bias in using three or five data points, because the beginning and end of year occur at the same time of the year and are effectively double counted.

Because cost of goods sold measures the cost of inventory that has been sold, this ratio measures how many times per year the entire inventory was theoretically turned over, or sold. (We say that the entire inventory was "theoretically" sold because in practice companies do not generally sell out their entire inventory.) If, for example, a company's cost of goods sold for a recent year was €120,000 and its average inventory was €10,000, the inventory turnover ratio would be 12. The company theoretically turns over (i.e., sells) its entire inventory 12 times per year (i.e., once a month). (Again, we say "theoretically" because in practice the company likely carries some inventory from one month into another.) Turnover can then be converted to days of inventory on hand (DOH) by dividing inventory turnover into the number of days in the accounting period. In this example, the result is a DOH of 30.42 (365/12), meaning that, on average, the company's inventory was on hand for about 30 days, or, equivalently, the company kept on hand about 30 days' worth of inventory, on average, during the period.

Activity ratios can be computed for any annual or interim period, but care must be taken in the interpretation and comparison across periods. For example, if the same company had cost of goods sold for the first quarter (90 days) of the following year of €35,000 and average inventory of €11,000, the inventory turnover would be 3.18 times. However, this turnover rate is 3.18 times per quarter, which is not directly comparable to the 12 times per year in the preceding year. In this case, we can annualize the quarterly inventory turnover rate by multiplying the quarterly turnover by 4 (12 months/3 months; or by 4.06, using 365 days/90 days) for comparison to the annual turnover rate. So, the quarterly inventory turnover is equivalent to a 12.72 annual inventory turnover (or 12.91 if we annualize the ratio using a 90-day quarter and a 365-day year). To compute the DOH using quarterly data, we can use the quarterly turnover rate and the number of days in the quarter for the numerator—or, we can use the annualized turnover rate and 365 days; either results in DOH of around 28.3, with slight differences due to rounding (90/3.18 = 28.30 and 365/12.91 = 28.27). Another time-related computational detail is that for companies using a 52/53-week annual period and for leap years, the actual days in the year should be used rather than 365.

In some cases, an analyst may want to know how many days of inventory are on hand at the end of the year rather than the average for the year. In this case, it would be appropriate to use the year-end inventory balance in the computation rather than the average. If the company is growing rapidly or if costs are increasing rapidly, analysts should consider using cost of goods sold just for the fourth quarter in this computation because the cost of goods sold of earlier quarters may not be relevant. Example 6 further demonstrates computation of activity ratios using Hong Kong Stock Exchange(HKEX)-listed Lenovo Group Limited.

EXAMPLE 6   Computation of Activity Ratios

An analyst would like to evaluate Lenovo Group's efficiency in collecting its trade accounts receivable during the fiscal year ended March 31, 2018 (FY2017). The analyst gathers the following information from Lenovo's annual and interim reports:

	US$ in Thousands
Trade receivables as of March 31, 2017	4,468,392
Trade receivables as of March 31, 2018	4,972,722
Revenue for year ended March 31, 2018	45,349,943

Calculate Lenovo's receivables turnover and number of days of sales outstanding (DSO) for the fiscal year ended March 31, 2018.

Solution:

$$\text{Receivables turnover} = \text{Revenue/Average receivables}$$
$$= 45,349,943/[(4,468,392 + 4,972,722)/2]$$
$$= 45,349,943/4,720,557$$
$$= 9.6069 \text{ times, or } 9.6 \text{ rounded}$$
$$\text{DSO} = \text{Number of days in period/Receivables turnover}$$
$$= 365/9.6$$
$$= 38.0 \text{ days}$$

On average, it took Lenovo 38 days to collect receivables during the fiscal year ended March 31, 2018.

4.2.2. Interpretation of Activity Ratios

In the following section, we further discuss the activity ratios that were defined in Exhibit 10.

Inventory Turnover and DOH   Inventory turnover lies at the heart of operations for many entities. It indicates the resources tied up in inventory (i.e., the carrying costs) and can, therefore, be used to indicate inventory management effectiveness. A higher inventory turnover ratio implies a shorter period that inventory is held, and thus a lower DOH. In general, inventory turnover and DOH should be benchmarked against industry norms.

A high inventory turnover ratio relative to industry norms might indicate highly effective inventory management. Alternatively, a high inventory turnover ratio (and commensurately low DOH) could possibly indicate the company does not carry adequate inventory, so shortages could potentially hurt revenue. To assess which explanation is more likely, the analyst can compare the company's revenue growth with that of the industry. Slower growth combined with higher inventory turnover could indicate inadequate inventory levels. Revenue growth at or above the industry's growth supports the interpretation that the higher turnover reflects greater inventory management efficiency.

A low inventory turnover ratio (and commensurately high DOH) relative to the rest of the industry could be an indicator of slow-moving inventory, perhaps due to technological obsolescence or a change in fashion. Again, comparing the company's sales growth with the industry can offer insight.

Receivables Turnover and DSO   The number of DSO represents the elapsed time between a sale and cash collection, reflecting how fast the company collects cash from customers to whom it offers credit. Although limiting the numerator to sales made on credit in the receivables turnover would be more appropriate, credit sales information is not always available to analysts; therefore, revenue as reported in the income statement is generally used as an approximation.

A relatively high receivables turnover ratio (and commensurately low DSO) might indicate highly efficient credit and collection. Alternatively, a high receivables turnover ratio could indicate that the company's credit or collection policies are too stringent, suggesting the possibility of sales being lost to competitors offering more lenient terms. A relatively low receivables turnover ratio would typically raise questions about the efficiency of the company's credit and collections procedures. As with inventory management, comparison of the company's sales growth relative to the industry can help the analyst assess whether sales are being lost due to stringent credit policies. In addition, comparing the company's estimates of uncollectible accounts receivable and actual credit losses with past experience and with peer companies can help assess whether low turnover reflects credit management issues. Companies often provide details of receivables aging (how much receivables have been outstanding by age). This can be used along with DSO to understand trends in collection, as demonstrated in Example 7.

EXAMPLE 7   Evaluation of an Activity Ratio

An analyst has computed the average DSO for Lenovo for fiscal years ended March 31, 2018 and 2017:

	FY2017	FY2016
Days of sales outstanding	38.0	37.6

Revenue increased from US$43.035 billion for fiscal year ended March 31, 2017 (FY2016) to US$45.350 billion for fiscal year ended March 31, 2018 (FY2017). The analyst would like to better understand the change in the company's DSO from FY2016 to FY2017 and whether the increase is indicative of any issues with the customers' credit quality. The analyst collects accounts receivable aging information from Lenovo's annual reports and computes the percentage of accounts receivable by days outstanding. This information is presented in Exhibit 11:

EXHIBIT 11

	FY2017		FY2016		FY2015	
	US$000	Percent	US$000	Percent	US$000	Percent
Accounts receivable						
0–30 days	3,046,240	59.95	2,923,083	63.92	3,246,600	71.99
31–60 days	1,169,286	23.01	985,251	21.55	617,199	13.69
61–90 days	320,183	6.30	283,050	6.19	240,470	5.33
Over 90 days	545,629	10.74	381,387	8.34	405,410	8.99
Total	5,081,338	100.00	4,572,771	100.00	4,509,679	100.00
Less: Provision for impairment	−108,616	−2.14	−104,379	−2.28	−106,172	−2.35
Trade receivables, net	4,972,722	97.86	4,468,392	97.72	4,403,507	97.65
Total sales	*45,349,943*		*43,034,731*		*44,912,097*	

Note: Lenovo's footnotes disclose that general trade customers are provided with credit terms ranging from 0 to 120 days.

These data indicate that total accounts receivable increased by about 11.3% in FY2017 versus FY2016, while total sales increased by only 5.4%. Further, the percentage of receivables in all categories older than 30 days has increased over the three-year period, indicating that customers are indeed taking longer to pay. On the other hand, the provision for impairment (estimate of uncollectible accounts) has declined as a percent of total receivables. Considering all this information, the company may be increasing customer financing purposely to drive its sales growth. They also may be underestimating the impairment. This should be investigated further by the analyst.

Payables Turnover and the Number of Days of Payables   The number of days of payables reflects the average number of days the company takes to pay its suppliers, and the payables turnover ratio measures how many times per year the company theoretically pays off all its creditors. For purposes of calculating these ratios, an implicit assumption is that the company makes all its purchases using credit. If the amount of purchases is not directly available, it can be computed as cost of goods sold plus ending inventory less beginning inventory. Alternatively, cost of goods sold is sometimes used as an approximation of purchases.

A payables turnover ratio that is high (low days payable) relative to the industry could indicate that the company is not making full use of available credit facilities; alternatively, it could result from a company taking advantage of early payment discounts. An excessively low turnover ratio (high days payable) could indicate trouble making payments on time, or alternatively, exploitation of lenient supplier terms. This is another example where it is useful to look simultaneously at other ratios. If liquidity ratios indicate that the company has sufficient cash and other short-term assets to pay obligations and yet the days payable ratio is relatively high, the analyst would favor the lenient supplier credit and collection policies as an explanation.

Working Capital Turnover   **Working capital** is defined as current assets minus current liabilities. Working capital turnover indicates how efficiently the company generates revenue with its working capital. For example, a working capital turnover ratio of 4.0 indicates that the company generates €4 of revenue for every €1 of working capital. A high working capital turnover ratio indicates greater efficiency (i.e., the company is generating a high level of revenues relative to working capital). For some companies, working capital can be near zero or negative, rendering this ratio incapable of being interpreted. The following two ratios are more useful in those circumstances.

Fixed Asset Turnover   This ratio measures how efficiently the company generates revenues from its investments in fixed assets. Generally, a higher fixed asset turnover ratio indicates more efficient use of fixed assets in generating revenue. A low ratio can indicate inefficiency, a capital-intensive business environment, or a new business not yet operating at full capacity—in which case the analyst will not be able to link the ratio directly to efficiency. In addition, asset turnover can be affected by factors other than a company's efficiency. The fixed asset turnover ratio would be lower for a company whose assets are newer (and, therefore, less depreciated and so reflected in the financial statements at a higher carrying value) than the ratio for a company with older assets (that are thus more depreciated and so reflected at a lower carrying value). The fixed asset ratio can be erratic because, although revenue may have a steady growth rate, increases in fixed assets may not follow a smooth pattern; so, every year-to-year change in the ratio does not necessarily indicate important changes in the company's efficiency.

Total Asset Turnover   The total asset turnover ratio measures the company's overall ability to generate revenues with a given level of assets. A ratio of 1.20 would indicate that the company is generating €1.20 of revenues for every €1 of average assets. A higher ratio indicates greater efficiency. Because this ratio includes both fixed and current assets, inefficient working capital management can distort overall interpretations. It is therefore helpful to analyze working capital and fixed asset turnover ratios separately.

A low asset turnover ratio can be an indicator of inefficiency or of relative capital intensity of the business. The ratio also reflects strategic decisions by management—for example, the decision whether to use a more labor-intensive (and less capital-intensive) approach to its business or a more capital-intensive (and less labor-intensive) approach.

When interpreting activity ratios, the analysts should examine not only the individual ratios but also the collection of relevant ratios to determine the overall efficiency of a company.

EXAMPLE 8 Evaluation of Activity Ratios

ZZZ Company is a hypothetical manufacturing company. As part of an analysis of management's operating efficiency, an analyst collects the following activity ratios from a data provider:

Ratio	2018	2017	2016	2015
DOH	35.68	40.70	40.47	48.51
DSO	45.07	58.28	51.27	76.98
Total asset turnover	0.36	0.28	0.23	0.22

These ratios indicate that the company has improved on all three measures of activity over the four-year period. The company appears to be managing its inventory more efficiently, is collecting receivables faster, and is generating a higher level of revenues relative to total assets. The overall trend appears good, but thus far, the analyst has only determined *what* happened. A more important question is *why* the ratios improved, because understanding good changes as well as bad ones facilitates judgments about the company's future performance. To answer this question, the analyst examines company financial reports as well as external information about the industry and economy. In examining the annual report, the analyst notes that in the fourth quarter of 2018, the company experienced an "inventory correction" and that the company recorded an allowance for the decline in market value and obsolescence of inventory of about 15 percent of year-end inventory value (compared with about a 6 percent allowance in the prior year). This reduction in the value of inventory accounts for a large portion of the decline in DOH from 40.70 in 2017 to 35.68 in 2018. Management claims that this inventory obsolescence is a short-term issue; analysts can watch DOH in future interim periods to confirm this assertion. In any event, all else being equal, the analyst would likely expect DOH to return to a level closer to 40 days going forward.

More positive interpretations can be drawn from the total asset turnover. The analyst finds that the company's revenues increased more than 35 percent while total assets only increased by about 6 percent. Based on external information about the industry and economy, the analyst attributes the increased revenues both to overall growth in the industry and to the company's increased market share. Management was able to achieve growth in revenues with a comparatively modest increase in assets, leading to an improvement in total asset turnover. Note further that part of the reason for the increase in asset turnover is lower DOH and DSO.

Example 8 demonstrates the evaluation of activity ratios, both narrow (e.g., days of inventory on hand) and broad (e.g., total asset turnover) for a hypothetical manufacturer.

4.3. Liquidity Ratios

Liquidity analysis, which focuses on cash flows, measures a company's ability to meet its short-term obligations. Liquidity measures how quickly assets are converted into cash. Liquidity ratios also measure the ability to pay off short-term obligations. In day-to-day operations, liquidity management is typically achieved through efficient use of assets. In the medium term, liquidity in the non-financial sector is also addressed by managing the structure of liabilities. (See the discussion on the financial sector below.)

The level of liquidity needed differs from one industry to another. A particular company's liquidity position may vary according to the anticipated need for funds at any given time. Judging whether a company has adequate liquidity requires analysis of its historical funding requirements, current liquidity position, anticipated future funding needs, and options for reducing funding needs or attracting additional funds (including actual and potential sources of such funding).

Larger companies are usually better able to control the level and composition of their liabilities than smaller companies. Therefore, they may have more potential funding sources, including public capital and money markets. Greater discretionary access to capital markets also reduces the size of the liquidity buffer needed relative to companies without such access.

Contingent liabilities, such as letters of credit or financial guarantees, can also be relevant when assessing liquidity. The importance of contingent liabilities varies for the non-banking and banking sector. In the non-banking sector, contingent liabilities (usually disclosed in the footnotes to the company's financial statements) represent potential cash outflows and, when appropriate, should be included in an assessment of a company's liquidity. In the banking sector, contingent liabilities represent potentially significant cash outflows that are not dependent on the bank's financial condition. Although outflows in normal market circumstances typically may be low, a general macroeconomic or market crisis can trigger a substantial increase in cash outflows related to contingent liabilities because of the increase in defaults and business bankruptcies that often accompany such events. In addition, such crises are usually characterized by diminished levels of overall liquidity, which can further exacerbate funding shortfalls. Therefore, for the banking sector, the effect of contingent liabilities on liquidity warrants particular attention.

4.3.1. Calculation of Liquidity Ratios

Common liquidity ratios are presented in Exhibit 12. These liquidity ratios reflect a company's position at a point in time and, therefore, typically use data from the ending balance sheet rather than averages. The current, quick, and cash ratios reflect three measures of a company's ability to pay current liabilities. Each uses a progressively stricter definition of liquid assets.

The **defensive interval ratio** measures how long a company can pay its daily cash expenditures using only its existing liquid assets, without additional cash flow coming in. This ratio is similar to the "burn rate" often computed for start-up Internet companies in the late 1990s or for biotechnology companies. The numerator of this ratio includes the same liquid assets used in the quick ratio, and the denominator is an estimate of daily cash expenditures. To obtain daily cash expenditures, the total of cash expenditures for the period is divided by the number of days in the period. Total cash expenditures for a period can be approximated by summing all expenses on the income statement—such as cost of goods sold; selling, general, and administrative expenses; and research and development expenses—and then subtracting any non-cash expenses, such as depreciation and amortization. (Typically, taxes are not included.)

The **cash conversion cycle**, a financial metric not in ratio form, measures the length of time required for a company to go from cash paid (used in its operations) to cash received (as a result of its operations). The cash conversion cycle is sometimes expressed as the length of time funds are tied up in working capital. During this period of time, the company needs to finance its investment in operations through other sources (i.e., through debt or equity).

EXHIBIT 12   Definitions of Commonly Used Liquidity Ratios

Liquidity Ratios	Numerator	Denominator
Current ratio	Current assets	Current liabilities
Quick ratio	Cash + Short-term marketable investments + Receivables	Current liabilities
Cash ratio	Cash + Short-term marketable investments	Current liabilities
Defensive interval ratio	Cash + Short-term marketable investments + Receivables	Daily cash expenditures
Additional Liquidity Measure		
Cash conversion cycle (net operating cycle)	DOH + DSO – Number of days of payables	

4.3.2. Interpretation of Liquidity Ratios

In the following, we discuss the interpretation of the five basic liquidity measures presented in Exhibit 12.

Current Ratio   This ratio expresses current assets in relation to current liabilities. A higher ratio indicates a higher level of liquidity (i.e., a greater ability to meet short-term obligations). A current ratio of 1.0 would indicate that the book value of its current assets exactly equals the book value of its current liabilities.

A lower ratio indicates less liquidity, implying a greater reliance on operating cash flow and outside financing to meet short-term obligations. Liquidity affects the company's capacity to take on debt. The current ratio implicitly assumes that inventories and accounts receivable are indeed liquid (which is presumably not the case when related turnover ratios are low).

Quick Ratio   The quick ratio is more conservative than the current ratio because it includes only the more liquid current assets (sometimes referred to as "quick assets") in relation to current liabilities. Like the current ratio, a higher quick ratio indicates greater liquidity.

The quick ratio reflects the fact that certain current assets—such as prepaid expenses, some taxes, and employee-related prepayments—represent costs of the current period that have been paid in advance and cannot usually be converted back into cash. This ratio also reflects the fact that inventory might not be easily and quickly converted into cash and, furthermore, that a company would probably not be able to sell all of its inventory for an amount equal to its carrying value, especially if it were required to sell the inventory quickly. In situations where inventories are illiquid (as indicated, for example, by low inventory turnover ratios), the quick ratio may be a better indicator of liquidity than is the current ratio.

Cash Ratio   The cash ratio normally represents a reliable measure of an entity's liquidity in a crisis situation. Only highly marketable short-term investments and cash are included. In a general market crisis, the fair value of marketable securities could decrease significantly as a result of market factors, in which case even this ratio might not provide reliable information.

Defensive Interval Ratio   This ratio measures how long the company can continue to pay its expenses from its existing liquid assets without receiving any additional cash inflow. A defensive interval ratio of 50 would indicate that the company can continue to pay its operating expenses for 50 days before running out of quick assets, assuming no additional cash inflows. A higher defensive interval ratio indicates greater liquidity. If a company's defensive interval ratio is very low relative to peer companies or to the company's own history, the analyst would want to ascertain whether there is sufficient cash inflow expected to mitigate the low defensive interval ratio.

Cash Conversion Cycle (Net Operating Cycle) This metric indicates the amount of time that elapses from the point when a company invests in working capital until the point at which the company collects cash. In the typical course of events, a merchandising company acquires inventory on credit, incurring accounts payable. The company then sells that inventory on credit, increasing accounts receivable. Afterwards, it pays out cash to settle its accounts payable, and it collects cash in settlement of its accounts receivable. The time between the outlay of cash and the collection of cash is called the "cash conversion cycle." A shorter cash conversion cycle indicates greater liquidity. A short cash conversion cycle implies that the company only needs to finance its inventory and accounts receivable for a short period of time. A longer cash conversion cycle indicates lower liquidity; it implies that the company must finance its inventory and accounts receivable for a longer period of time, possibly indicating a need for a higher level of capital to fund current assets. Example 9 demonstrates the advantages of a short cash conversion cycle as well as how a company's business strategies are reflected in financial ratios.

EXAMPLE 9   Evaluation of Liquidity Measures

An analyst is evaluating the liquidity of Apple and calculates the number of days of receivables, inventory, and accounts payable, as well as the overall cash conversion cycle, as follows:

	FY2017	FY2016	FY2015
DSO	27	28	27
DOH	9	6	6
Less: Number of days of payables	112	101	86
Equals: Cash conversion cycle	(76)	(67)	(53)

The minimal DOH indicates that Apple maintains lean inventories, which is attributable to key aspects of the company's business model, where manufacturing is outsourced. In isolation, the increase in number of days payable (from 86 days in FY2015 to 112 days in FY2017) might suggest an inability to pay suppliers; however, in Apple's case, the balance sheet indicates that the company has more than $70 billion of cash and short-term investments, which would be more than enough to pay suppliers sooner if Apple chose to do so. Instead, Apple takes advantage of the favorable credit terms granted by its suppliers. The overall effect is a negative cash cycle, a somewhat unusual result. Instead of requiring additional capital to fund working capital as is the case for most companies, Apple has excess cash to invest for over 50 days during that 3-year period (reflected on the balance sheet as short-term investments) on which it is earning, rather than paying, interest.

EXAMPLE 10   Bounds and Context of Financial Measures

The previous example focused on the cash conversion cycle, which many companies identify as a key performance metric. The less positive the number of days in the cash conversion cycle, typically, the better it is considered to be. However, is this always true?

This example considers the following question: If a larger negative number of days in a cash conversion cycle is considered to be a desirable performance metric, does identifying a company with a large negative cash conversion cycle necessarily imply good performance?

Using a historical example, National Datacomputer, a technology company, had a large negative number of days in its cash conversion cycle during the 2005 to 2009 period. In 2008 its cash conversion cycle was 275.5 days.

EXHIBIT 13   National Datacomputer Inc. ($ millions)

Fiscal year	2004	2005	2006	2007	2008	2009
Sales	3.248	2.672	2.045	1.761	1.820	1.723
Cost of goods sold	1.919	1.491	0.898	1.201	1.316	1.228
Receivables, Total	0.281	0.139	0.099	0.076	0.115	0.045
Inventories, Total	0.194	0.176	0.010	0.002	0.000	0.000
Accounts payable	0.223	0.317	0.366	1.423	0.704	0.674
DSO		28.69	21.24	18.14	19.15	16.95
DOH		45.29	37.80	1.82	0.28	0.00
*Less: Number of days of payables**		66.10	138.81	271.85	294.97	204.79
Equals: Cash conversion cycle		7.88	–79.77	–251.89	–275.54	–187.84

*Notes: Calculated using Cost of goods sold as an approximation of purchases. Ending inventories 2008 and 2009 are reported as $0 million; therefore, inventory turnover for 2009 cannot be measured. However, given inventory and average sales per day, DOH in 2009 is 0.00.
Source: Raw data from Compustat. Ratios calculated.

The reason for the negative cash conversion cycle is that the company's accounts payable increased substantially over the period. An increase from approximately 66 days in 2005 to 295 days in 2008 to pay trade creditors is clearly a negative signal. In addition, the company's inventories disappeared, most likely because the company did not have enough cash to purchase new inventory and was unable to get additional credit from its suppliers.

Of course, an analyst would have immediately noted the negative trends in these data, as well as additional data throughout the company's financial statements. In its MD&A, the company clearly reports the risks as follows:

> Because we have historically had losses and only a limited amount of cash has been generated from operations, we have funded our operating activities to date primarily from the sale of securities and from the sale of a product line

in 2009. In order to continue to fund our operations, we may need to raise additional capital, through the sale of securities. We cannot be certain that any such financing will be available on acceptable terms, or at all. Moreover, additional equity financing, if available, would likely be dilutive to the holders of our common stock, and debt financing, if available, would likely involve restrictive covenants and a security interest in all or substantially all of our assets. If we fail to obtain acceptable financing when needed, we may not have sufficient resources to fund our normal operations which would have a material adverse effect on our business.

IF WE ARE UNABLE TO GENERATE ADEQUATE WORKING CAPITAL FROM OPERATIONS OR RAISE ADDITIONAL CAPITAL THERE IS SUBSTANTIAL DOUBT ABOUT THE COMPANY'S ABILITY TO CONTINUE AS A GOING CONCERN. (emphasis added by company).

Source: National Datacomputer Inc., 2009 Form 10-K, page 7.

Subsequently, the company's 2010 Form 10K reported:

"In January 2011, due to our inability to meet our financial obligations and the impending loss of a critical distribution agreement granting us the right to distribute certain products, our secured lenders ("Secured Parties") acting upon an event of default, sold certain of our assets (other than cash and accounts receivable) to Micronet, Ltd. ("Micronet"), an unaffiliated corporation pursuant to the terms of an asset purchase agreement between the Secured Parties and Micronet dated January 10, 2010 (the "Asset Purchase Agreement"). In order to induce Micronet to enter into the agreement, the Company also provided certain representations and warranties regarding certain business matters."

In summary, it is always necessary to consider ratios within bounds of reasonability and to understand the reasons underlying changes in ratios. Ratios must not only be calculated but must also be interpreted by an analyst.

4.4. Solvency Ratios

Solvency refers to a company's ability to fulfill its long-term debt obligations. Assessment of a company's ability to pay its long-term obligations (i.e., to make interest and principal payments) generally includes an in-depth analysis of the components of its financial structure. Solvency ratios provide information regarding the relative amount of debt in the company's capital structure and the adequacy of earnings and cash flow to cover interest expenses and other fixed charges (such as lease or rental payments) as they come due.

Analysts seek to understand a company's use of debt for several main reasons. One reason is that the amount of debt in a company's capital structure is important for assessing the company's risk and return characteristics, specifically its financial leverage. Leverage is a magnifying effect that results from the use of **fixed costs**—costs that stay the same within some range of activity—and can take two forms: operating leverage and financial leverage.

Operating leverage results from the use of fixed costs in conducting the company's business. Operating leverage magnifies the effect of changes in sales on operating income. Profitable companies may use operating leverage because when revenues increase, with operating leverage, their operating income increases at a faster rate. The explanation is that, although **variable costs** will rise proportionally with revenue, fixed costs will not.

When financing a company (i.e., raising capital for it), the use of debt constitutes **financial leverage** because interest payments are essentially fixed financing costs. As a result of interest payments, a given percent change in EBIT results in a larger percent change in earnings before taxes (EBT). Thus, financial leverage tends to magnify the effect of changes in EBIT on returns flowing to equity holders. Assuming that a company can earn more on funds than it pays in interest, the inclusion of some level of debt in a company's capital structure may lower a company's overall cost of capital and increase returns to equity holders. However, a higher level of debt in a company's capital structure increases the risk of default and results in higher borrowing costs for the company to compensate lenders for assuming greater credit risk. Starting with Modigliani and Miller (1958, 1963), a substantial amount of research has focused on determining a company's optimal capital structure, and the subject remains an important one in corporate finance.

In analyzing financial statements, an analyst aims to understand levels and trends in a company's use of financial leverage in relation to past practices and the practices of peer companies. Analysts also need to be aware of the relationship between operating leverage (results from the use of non-current assets with fixed costs) and financial leverage (results from the use of long-term debt with fixed costs). The greater a company's operating leverage, the greater the risk of the operating income stream available to cover debt payments; operating leverage can thus limit a company's capacity to use financial leverage.

A company's relative solvency is fundamental to valuation of its debt securities and its creditworthiness. Finally, understanding a company's use of debt can provide analysts with insight into the company's future business prospects because management's decisions about financing may signal their beliefs about a company's future. For example, the issuance of long-term debt to repurchase common shares may indicate that management believes the market is underestimating the company's prospects and that the shares are undervalued.

4.4.1. Calculation of Solvency Ratios

Solvency ratios are primarily of two types. Debt ratios, the first type, focus on the balance sheet and measure the amount of debt capital relative to equity capital. Coverage ratios, the second type, focus on the income statement and measure the ability of a company to cover its debt payments. These ratios are useful in assessing a company's solvency and, therefore, in evaluating the quality of a company's bonds and other debt obligations.

Exhibit 14 describes commonly used solvency ratios. The first three of the debt ratios presented use total debt in the numerator. The definition of total debt used in these ratios varies among informed analysts and financial data vendors, with some using the total of interest-bearing short-term and long-term debt, excluding liabilities such as accrued expenses and accounts payable. (For calculations in this chapter, we use this definition.) Other analysts use definitions that are more inclusive (e.g., all liabilities) or restrictive (e.g., long-term debt only, in which case the ratio is sometimes qualified as "long-term," as in "long-term debt-to-equity ratio"). If using different definitions of total debt materially changes conclusions about a company's solvency, the reasons for the discrepancies warrant further investigation.

EXHIBIT 14   Definitions of Commonly Used Solvency Ratios

Solvency Ratios	Numerator	Denominator
Debt Ratios		
Debt-to-assets ratio[a]	Total debt[b]	Total assets
Debt-to-capital ratio	Total debt[b]	Total debt[b] + Total shareholders' equity
Debt-to-equity ratio	Total debt[b]	Total shareholders' equity
Financial leverage ratio[c]	Average total assets	Average total equity
Debt-to-EBITDA	Total debt	EBITDA
Coverage Ratios		
Interest coverage	EBIT	Interest payments
Fixed charge coverage	EBIT + Lease payments	Interest payments + Lease payments

[a]"Total debt ratio" is another name sometimes used for this ratio.
[b]In this chapter, total debt is the sum of interest-bearing short-term and long-term debt.
[c] *Average* total assets divided by *average* total equity is used for the purposes of this chapter (in particular, Dupont analysis covered later). In practice, period-end total assets divided by period-end total equity is often used.

4.4.2. Interpretation of Solvency Ratios
In the following, we discuss the interpretation of the basic solvency ratios presented in Exhibit 14.

Debt-to-Assets Ratio   This ratio measures the percentage of total assets financed with debt. For example, a **debt-to-assets ratio** of 0.40 or 40 percent indicates that 40 percent of the company's assets are financed with debt. Generally, higher debt means higher financial risk and thus weaker solvency.

Debt-to-Capital Ratio   The **debt-to-capital ratio** measures the percentage of a company's capital (debt plus equity) represented by debt. As with the previous ratio, a higher ratio generally means higher financial risk and thus indicates weaker solvency.

Debt-to-Equity Ratio   The **debt-to-equity ratio** measures the amount of debt capital relative to equity capital. Interpretation is similar to the preceding two ratios (i.e., a higher ratio indicates weaker solvency). A ratio of 1.0 would indicate equal amounts of debt and equity, which is equivalent to a debt-to-capital ratio of 50 percent. Alternative definitions of this ratio use the market value of stockholders' equity rather than its book value (or use the market values of both stockholders' equity and debt).

Financial Leverage Ratio   This ratio (often called simply the "leverage ratio") measures the amount of total assets supported for each money unit of equity. For example, a value of 3 for this ratio means that each €1 of equity supports €3 of total assets. The higher the **financial leverage ratio**, the more leveraged the company is in the sense of using debt and other liabilities to finance assets. This ratio is often defined in terms of average total assets and average total equity and plays an important role in the DuPont decomposition of return on equity that will be presented in Section 4.6.2.

Debt-to-EBITDA Ratio   This ratio estimates how many years it would take to repay total debt based on earnings before income taxes, depreciation, and amortization (an approximation of operating cash flow).

Interest Coverage   This ratio measures the number of times a company's EBIT could cover its interest payments. Thus, it is sometimes referred to as "times interest earned." A higher **interest coverage** ratio indicates stronger solvency, offering greater assurance that the company can service its debt (i.e., bank debt, bonds, notes) from operating earnings.

Fixed Charge Coverage   This ratio relates fixed charges, or obligations, to the cash flow generated by the company. It measures the number of times a company's earnings (before interest, taxes, and lease payments) can cover the company's interest and lease payments.[9] Similar to the interest coverage ratio, a higher **fixed charge coverage** ratio implies stronger solvency, offering greater assurance that the company can service its debt (i.e., bank debt, bonds, notes, and leases) from normal earnings. The ratio is sometimes used as an indication of the quality of the preferred dividend, with a higher ratio indicating a more secure preferred dividend.

Example 11 demonstrates the use of solvency ratios in evaluating the creditworthiness of a company.

EXAMPLE 11   Evaluation of Solvency Ratios

A credit analyst is evaluating the solvency of Eskom, a South African public utility, based on financial statements for the year ended March 31, 2017. The following data are gathered from the company's 2017 annual report:

South African Rand, millions	2017	2016	2015
Total Assets	710,009	663,170	559,688
Short-Term Debt	18,530	15,688	19,976
Long-Term Debt	336,770	306,970	277,458
Total Liabilities	534,067	480,818	441,269
Total Equity	175,942	182,352	118,419

1. A. Calculate the company's financial leverage ratio for 2016 and 2017.
   B. Interpret the financial leverage ratio calculated in Part A.
2. A. What are the company's debt-to-assets, debt-to-capital, and debt-to-equity ratios for the three years?
   B. Is there any discernable trend over the three years?

---

[9] For computing this ratio, an assumption sometimes made is that one-third of the lease payment amount represents interest on the lease obligation and that the rest is a repayment of principal on the obligation. For this variant of the fixed charge coverage ratio, the numerator is EBIT plus one-third of lease payments, and the denominator is interest payments plus one-third of lease payments.

Solutions to 1: (Amounts are millions of Rand.)

A. For 2017, average total assets were (710,009 + 663,170)/2 = 686,590, and average total equity was (175,942 + 182,352)/2 = 179,147. Thus, financial leverage was 686,590/179,942 = 3.83. For 2016, financial leverage was 4.07.

	2017	2016
Average Assets	686,590	611,429
Average Equity	179,147	150,386
Financial Leverage	3.83	4.07

B. For 2017, every Rand in total equity supported R3.83 in total assets, on average. Financial leverage decreased from 2016 to 2017 on this measure.

Solutions to 2: (Amounts are millions of Rand other than ratios)

A.

	2017	2016	2015
Total Debt	355,300	322,658	297,434
Total Capital	531,242	505,010	415,853
Debt/Assets	50.0%	48.7%	53.1%
Debt/Capital	66.9%	63.9%	71.5%
Debt/Equity	2.02	1.77	2.51

B. On all three metrics, the company's leverage decreased from 2015 to 2016 and increased from 2016 to 2017. For 2016 the decrease in leverage resulted from a conversion of subordinated debt into equity as well as additional issuance of equity. However, in 2017 debt levels increased again relative to assets, capital, and equity, indicating that the company's solvency has weakened. From a creditor's perspective, lower solvency (higher debt) indicates higher risk of default on obligations.

As with all ratio analysis, it is important to consider leverage ratios in a broader context. In general, companies with lower business risk and operations that generate steady cash flows are better positioned to take on more leverage without a commensurate increase in the risk of insolvency. In other words, a higher proportion of debt financing poses less risk of non-payment of interest and debt principal to a company with steady cash flows than to a company with volatile cash flows.

4.5. Profitability Ratios

The ability to generate profit on capital invested is a key determinant of a company's overall value and the value of the securities it issues. Consequently, many equity analysts would consider profitability to be a key focus of their analytical efforts.

Profitability reflects a company's competitive position in the market and, by extension, the quality of its management. The income statement reveals the sources of earnings and the components of revenue and expenses. Earnings can be distributed to shareholders or reinvested in the company. Reinvested earnings enhance solvency and provide a cushion against short-term problems.

4.5.1. Calculation of Profitability Ratios

Profitability ratios measure the return earned by the company during a period. Exhibit 15 provides the definitions of a selection of commonly used profitability ratios. Return-on-sales profitability ratios express various subtotals on the income statement (e.g., gross profit, operating profit, net profit) as a percentage of revenue. Essentially, these ratios constitute part of a common-size income statement discussed earlier. Return on investment profitability ratios measure income relative to assets, equity, or total capital employed by the company. For operating ROA, returns are measured as operating income, that is, prior to deducting interest on debt capital. For ROA and ROE, returns are measured as net income, that is, after deducting interest paid on debt capital. For return on common equity, returns are measured as net income minus preferred dividends (because preferred dividends are a return to preferred equity).

EXHIBIT 15   Definitions of Commonly Used Profitability Ratios

Profitability Ratios	Numerator	Denominator
Return on Sales[a]		
Gross profit margin	Gross profit	Revenue
Operating profit margin	Operating income[b]	Revenue
Pretax margin	EBT (earnings before tax but after interest)	Revenue
Net profit margin	Net income	Revenue
Return on Investment		
Operating ROA	Operating income	Average total assets
ROA	Net income	Average total assets
Return on total capital	EBIT	Average short- and long-term debt and equity
ROE	Net income	Average total equity
Return on common equity	Net income – Preferred dividends	Average common equity

[a] "Sales" is being used as a synonym for "revenue."
[b] Some analysts use EBIT as a shortcut representation of operating income. Note that EBIT, strictly speaking, includes non-operating items such as dividends received and gains and losses on investment securities. Of utmost importance is that the analyst compute ratios consistently, whether comparing different companies or analyzing one company over time.

4.5.2. Interpretation of Profitability Ratios

In the following, we discuss the interpretation of the profitability ratios presented in Exhibit 15. For each of the profitability ratios, a higher ratio indicates greater profitability.

Gross Profit Margin   **Gross profit margin** indicates the percentage of revenue available to cover operating and other expenses and to generate profit. Higher gross profit margin indicates some combination of higher product pricing and lower product costs. The ability to charge a higher price is constrained by competition, so gross profits are affected by (and usually inversely related to) competition. If a product has a competitive advantage (e.g., superior branding, better quality, or exclusive technology), the company is better able to charge more for it. On the cost side, higher gross profit margin can also indicate that a company has a competitive advantage in product costs.

Operating Profit Margin   Operating profit is calculated as gross profit minus operating costs. So, an **operating profit margin** increasing faster than the gross profit margin can indicate improvements in controlling operating costs, such as administrative overheads. In contrast, a declining operating profit margin could be an indicator of deteriorating control over operating costs.

Pretax Margin   Pretax income (also called "earnings before tax" or "EBT") is calculated as operating profit minus interest, and the **pretax margin** is the ratio of pretax income to revenue. The pretax margin reflects the effects on profitability of leverage and other (non-operating) income and expenses. If a company's pretax margin is increasing primarily as a result of increasing amounts of non-operating income, the analyst should evaluate whether this increase reflects a deliberate change in a company's business focus and, therefore, the likelihood that the increase will continue.

Net Profit Margin   Net profit, or net income, is calculated as revenue minus all expenses. Net income includes both recurring and non-recurring components. Generally, the net income used in calculating the net profit margin is adjusted for non-recurring items to offer a better view of a company's potential future profitability.

ROA   ROA measures the return earned by a company on its assets. The higher the ratio, the more income is generated by a given level of assets. Most databases compute this ratio as:

$$\frac{\text{Net income}}{\text{Average total assets}}$$

An issue with this computation is that net income is the return to equity holders, whereas assets are financed by both equity holders and creditors. Interest expense (the return to creditors) has already been subtracted in the numerator. Some analysts, therefore, prefer to add back interest expense in the numerator. In such cases, interest must be adjusted for income taxes because net income is determined after taxes. With this adjustment, the ratio would be computed as:

$$\frac{\text{Net income} + \text{Interest expense}(1 - \text{Tax rate})}{\text{Average total assets}}$$

Alternatively, some analysts elect to compute ROA on a pre-interest and pre-tax basis (operating ROA in Exhibit 15) as:

$$\frac{\text{Operating income or EBIT}}{\text{Average total assets}}$$

In this ROA calculation, returns are measured prior to deducting interest on debt capital (i.e., as operating income or EBIT). This measure reflects the return on all assets invested in the company, whether financed with liabilities, debt, or equity. Whichever form of ROA is chosen, the analyst must use it consistently in comparisons to other companies or time periods.

Return on Total Capital   **Return on total capital** measures the profits a company earns on all of the capital that it employs (short-term debt, long-term debt, and equity). As with operating ROA, returns are measured prior to deducting interest on debt capital (i.e., as operating income or EBIT).

ROE   ROE measures the return earned by a company on its equity capital, including minority equity, preferred equity, and common equity. As noted, return is measured as net income (i.e., interest on debt capital is not included in the return on equity capital). A variation of ROE is return on common equity, which measures the return earned by a company only on its common equity.

Both ROA and ROE are important measures of profitability and will be explored in more detail in section 4.6.2. As with other ratios, profitability ratios should be evaluated individually and as a group to gain an understanding of what is driving profitability (operating versus non-operating activities). Example 12 demonstrates the evaluation of profitability ratios and the use of the management report (sometimes called management's discussion and analysis or management commentary) that accompanies financial statements to explain the trend in ratios.

EXAMPLE 12   Evaluation of Profitability Ratios

Recall from Example 1 that an analysis found that Apple's gross margin declined over the three-year period FY2015 to FY2017. An analyst would like to further explore Apple's profitability using a five-year period. He gathers the following revenue data and calculates the following profitability ratios from information in Apple's annual reports:

Dollars in millions	2017	2016	2015	2014	2013
Sales	229,234	215,639	233,715	182,795	170,910
Gross profit	88,186	84,263	93,626	70,537	64,304
Operating income	61,344	60,024	71,230	52,503	48,999
Pre-tax income	64,089	61,372	72,515	53,483	50,155
Net income	48,351	45,687	53,394	39,510	37,037
Gross profit margin	38.47%	39.08%	40.06%	38.59%	37.62%
Operating income margin	26.76%	27.84%	30.48%	28.72%	28.67%
Pre-tax income	27.96%	28.46%	31.03%	29.26%	29.35%
Net profit margin	21.09%	21.19%	22.85%	21.61%	21.67%

Evaluate the overall trend in Apple's profitability ratios for the five-year period.

Solution: Sales had increased steadily through 2015, dropped in 2016, and rebounded somewhat in 2017. As noted in Example 1, the sales decline in 2016 was related to a decline in iPhone sales and weakness in foreign currencies. Margins also rose from 2013 to 2015 and declined in 2016. However, in spite of the increase in sales in 2017, all margins declined slightly indicating costs were rising faster than sales. In spite of the fluctuations, Apple's bottom line net profit margin was relatively stable over the five-year period.

4.6. Integrated Financial Ratio Analysis

In prior sections, the text presented separately activity, liquidity, solvency, and profitability ratios. Prior to discussing valuation ratios, the following sections demonstrate the importance of examining a variety of financial ratios—not a single ratio or category of ratios in isolation—to ascertain the overall position and performance of a company. Experience shows that the information from one ratio category can be helpful in answering questions raised by another category and that the most accurate overall picture comes from integrating information from all sources. Section 4.6.1 provides some introductory examples of such analysis, and Section 4.6.2 shows how return on equity can be analyzed into components related to profit margin, asset utilization (activity), and financial leverage.

4.6.1. The Overall Ratio Picture: Examples

This section presents two simple illustrations to introduce the use of a variety of ratios to address an analytical task. Example 13 shows how the analysis of a pair of activity ratios resolves an issue concerning a company's liquidity. Example 14 shows that examining the overall ratios of multiple companies can assist an analyst in drawing conclusions about their relative performances.

EXAMPLE 13   A Variety of Ratios

An analyst is evaluating the liquidity of a Canadian manufacturing company and obtains the following liquidity ratios:

Fiscal Year	10	9	8
Current ratio	2.1	1.9	1.6
Quick ratio	0.8	0.9	1.0

The ratios present a contradictory picture of the company's liquidity. Based on the increase in its current ratio from 1.6 to 2.1, the company appears to have strong and improving liquidity; however, based on the decline of the quick ratio from 1.0 to 0.8, its liquidity appears to be deteriorating. Because both ratios have exactly the same denominator, current liabilities, the difference must be the result of changes in some asset that is included in the current ratio but not in the quick ratio (e.g., inventories). The analyst collects the following activity ratios:

DOH	55	45	30	
DSO	24	28	30	

The company's DOH has deteriorated from 30 days to 55 days, meaning that the company is holding increasingly larger amounts of inventory relative to sales. The decrease in DSO implies that the company is collecting receivables faster. If the proceeds from these collections were held as cash, there would be no effect on either the current ratio or the quick ratio. However, if the proceeds from the collections were used to purchase inventory, there would be no effect on the current ratio and a decline in the quick ratio (i.e., the pattern shown in this example). Collectively, the ratios suggest that liquidity is declining and that the company may have an inventory problem that needs to be addressed.

EXAMPLE 14   A Comparison of Two Companies (1)

An analyst collects the information[10] shown in Exhibit 16 for two hypothetical companies:

EXHIBIT 16

	Fiscal Year			
Anson Industries	5	4	3	2
Inventory turnover	76.69	89.09	147.82	187.64
DOH	4.76	4.10	2.47	1.95
Receivables turnover	10.75	9.33	11.14	7.56
DSO	33.95	39.13	32.77	48.29
Accounts payable turnover	4.62	4.36	4.84	4.22
Days payable	78.97	83.77	75.49	86.56
Cash from operations/Total liabilities	31.41%	11.15%	4.04%	8.81%
ROE	5.92%	1.66%	1.62%	−0.62%
ROA	3.70%	1.05%	1.05%	−0.39%
Net profit margin (Net income/Revenue)	3.33%	1.11%	1.13%	−0.47%
Total asset turnover (Revenue/Average assets)	1.11	0.95	0.93	0.84
Leverage (Average assets/Average equity)	1.60	1.58	1.54	1.60

---

[10]Note that ratios are expressed in terms of two decimal places and are rounded. Therefore, expected relationships may not hold perfectly.

Clarence Corporation	Fiscal Year			
	5	4	3	2
Inventory turnover	9.19	9.08	7.52	14.84
DOH	39.73	40.20	48.51	24.59
Receivables turnover	8.35	7.01	6.09	5.16
DSO	43.73	52.03	59.92	70.79
Accounts payable turnover	6.47	6.61	7.66	6.52
Days payable	56.44	55.22	47.64	56.00
Cash from operations/Total liabilities	13.19%	16.39%	15.80%	11.79%
ROE	9.28%	6.82%	–3.63%	–6.75%
ROA	4.64%	3.48%	–1.76%	–3.23%
Net profit margin (Net income/Revenue)	4.38%	3.48%	–1.60%	–2.34%
Total asset turnover (Revenue/Average assets)	1.06	1.00	1.10	1.38
Leverage (Average assets/Average equity)	2.00	1.96	2.06	2.09

Which of the following choices best describes reasonable conclusions an analyst might make about the companies' efficiency?

A. Over the past four years, Anson has shown greater improvement in efficiency than Clarence, as indicated by its total asset turnover ratio increasing from 0.84 to 1.11.

B. In FY5, Anson's DOH of only 4.76 indicated that it was less efficient at inventory management than Clarence, which had DOH of 39.73.

C. In FY5, Clarence's receivables turnover of 8.35 times indicated that it was more efficient at receivables management than Anson, which had receivables turnover of 10.75.

Solution: A is correct. Over the past four years, Anson has shown greater improvement in efficiency than Clarence, as indicated by its total asset turnover ratio increasing from 0.84 to 1.11. Over the same period of time, Clarence's total asset turnover ratio has declined from 1.38 to 1.06. Choices B and C are incorrect because DOH and receivables turnover are misinterpreted.

4.6.2. DuPont Analysis: The Decomposition of ROE

As noted earlier, ROE measures the return a company generates on its equity capital. To understand what drives a company's ROE, a useful technique is to decompose ROE into its component parts. (Decomposition of ROE is sometimes referred to as **DuPont analysis** because it was developed originally at that company.) Decomposing ROE involves expressing the basic ratio (i.e., net income divided by average shareholders' equity) as the product of component ratios. Because each of these component ratios is an indicator of a distinct aspect of a company's performance that affects ROE, the decomposition allows us to evaluate how these different aspects of performance affected the company's profitability as measured by ROE.[11]

---

[11] For purposes of analyzing ROE, this method usually uses average balance sheet factors; however, the math will work out if beginning or ending balances are used throughout. For certain purposes, these alternative methods may be appropriate.

Decomposing ROE is useful in determining the reasons for changes in ROE over time for a given company and for differences in ROE for different companies in a given time period. The information gained can also be used by management to determine which areas they should focus on to improve ROE. This decomposition will also show why a company's overall profitability, measured by ROE, is a function of its efficiency, operating profitability, taxes, and use of financial leverage. DuPont analysis shows the relationship between the various categories of ratios discussed in this chapter and how they all influence the return to the investment of the owners.

Analysts have developed several different methods of decomposing ROE. The decomposition presented here is one of the most commonly used and the one found in popular research databases, such as Bloomberg. Return on equity is calculated as:

$$ROE = \text{Net income/Average shareholders' equity}$$

The decomposition of ROE makes use of simple algebra and illustrates the relationship between ROE and ROA. Expressing ROE as a product of only two of its components, we can write:

$$
\begin{aligned}
ROE &= \frac{\text{Net income}}{\text{Average shareholders' equity}} \\
&= \frac{\text{Net income}}{\text{Average total assets}} \times \frac{\text{Average total assets}}{\text{Average shareholders' equity}}
\end{aligned}
\tag{1a}
$$

which can be interpreted as:

$$ROE = ROA \times \text{Leverage}$$

In other words, ROE is a function of a company's ROA and its use of financial leverage ("leverage" for short, in this discussion). A company can improve its ROE by improving ROA or making more effective use of leverage. Consistent with the definition given earlier, leverage is measured as average total assets divided by average shareholders' equity. If a company had no leverage (no liabilities), its leverage ratio would equal 1.0, and ROE would exactly equal ROA. As a company takes on liabilities, its leverage increases. As long as a company is able to borrow at a rate lower than the marginal rate it can earn investing the borrowed money in its business, the company is making an effective use of leverage, and ROE would increase as leverage increases. If a company's borrowing cost exceeds the marginal rate it can earn on investing in the business, ROE would decline as leverage increased because the effect of borrowing would be to depress ROA.

Using the data from Example 14 for Anson Industries, an analyst can examine the trend in ROE and determine whether the increase from an ROE of –0.625 percent in FY2 to 5.925 percent in FY5 is a function of ROA or the use of leverage:

	ROE	=	ROA	×	Leverage
FY5	5.92%		3.70%		1.60
FY4	1.66%		1.05%		1.58
FY3	1.62%		1.05%		1.54
FY2	–0.62%		–0.39%		1.60

Over the four-year period, the company's leverage factor was relatively stable. The primary reason for the increase in ROE is the increase in profitability measured by ROA.

Just as ROE can be decomposed, the individual components such as ROA can be decomposed. Further decomposing ROA, we can express ROE as a product of three component ratios:

$$\frac{\text{Net income}}{\text{Average shareholders' equity}} = \frac{\text{Net income}}{\text{Revenue}} \times \frac{\text{Revenue}}{\text{Average total assets}}$$
$$\times \frac{\text{Average total assets}}{\text{Average shareholders' equity}} \tag{1b}$$

which can be interpreted as:

$$\text{ROE} = \text{Net profit margin} \times \text{Total asset turnover} \times \text{Leverage}$$

The first term on the right-hand side of this equation is the net profit margin, an indicator of profitability: how much income a company derives per one monetary unit (e.g., euro or dollar) of sales. The second term on the right is the asset turnover ratio, an indicator of efficiency: how much revenue a company generates per one money unit of assets. Note that ROA is decomposed into these two components: net profit margin and total asset turnover. A company's ROA is a function of profitability (net profit margin) and efficiency (total asset turnover). The third term on the right-hand side of Equation 1b is a measure of financial leverage, an indicator of solvency: the total amount of a company's assets relative to its equity capital. This decomposition illustrates that a company's ROE is a function of its net profit margin, its efficiency, and its leverage. Again, using the data from Example 14 for Anson Industries, the analyst can evaluate in more detail the reasons behind the trend in ROE:[12]

	ROE	=	Net profit margin	×	Total asset turnover	×	Leverage
FY5	5.92%		3.33%		1.11		1.60
FY4	1.66%		1.11%		0.95		1.58
FY3	1.62%		1.13%		0.93		1.54
FY2	−0.62%		−0.47%		0.84		1.60

This further decomposition confirms that increases in profitability (measured here as net profit margin) are indeed an important contributor to the increase in ROE over the four-year period. However, Anson's asset turnover has also increased steadily. The increase in ROE is, therefore, a function of improving profitability and improving efficiency. As noted above, ROE decomposition can also be used to compare the ROEs of peer companies, as demonstrated in Example 15.

---

[12] Ratios are expressed in terms of two decimal places and are rounded. Therefore, ROE may not be the exact product of the three ratios.

EXAMPLE 15   A Comparison of Two Companies (2)

Referring to the data for Anson Industries and Clarence Corporation in Example 14, which of the following choices best describes reasonable conclusions an analyst might make about the companies' ROE?

A. Anson's inventory turnover of 76.69 indicates it is more profitable than Clarence.

B. The main driver of Clarence's superior ROE in FY5 is its more efficient use of assets.

C. The main drivers of Clarence's superior ROE in FY5 are its greater use of debt financing and higher net profit margin.

Solution: C is correct. The main driver of Clarence's superior ROE (9.28 percent compared with only 5.92 percent for Anson) in FY5 is its greater use of debt financing (leverage of 2.00 compared with Anson's leverage of 1.60) and higher net profit margin (4.38 percent compared with only 3.33 percent for Anson). A is incorrect because inventory turnover is not a direct indicator of profitability. An increase in inventory turnover may indicate more efficient use of inventory which in turn could affect profitability; however, an increase in inventory turnover would also be observed if a company was selling more goods even if it was not selling those goods at a profit. B is incorrect because Clarence has less efficient use of assets than Anson, indicated by turnover of 1.06 for Clarence compared with Anson's turnover of 1.11.

To separate the effects of taxes and interest, we can further decompose the net profit margin and write:

$$\frac{\text{Net income}}{\text{Average shareholders' equity}} = \frac{\text{Net income}}{\text{EBT}} \times \frac{\text{EBT}}{\text{EBIT}} \times \frac{\text{EBIT}}{\text{Revenue}}$$
$$\times \frac{\text{Revenue}}{\text{Average total assets}} \times \frac{\text{Average total assets}}{\text{Average shareholders' equity}}$$

(1c)

which can be interpreted as:

$$\text{ROE} = \text{Tax burden} \times \text{Interest burden} \times \text{EBIT margin}$$
$$\times \text{Total asset turnover} \times \text{Leverage}$$

This five-way decomposition is the one found in financial databases such as Bloomberg. The first term on the right-hand side of this equation measures the effect of taxes on ROE. Essentially, it reflects one minus the average tax rate, or how much of a company's pretax profits it gets to keep. This can be expressed in decimal or percentage form. So, a 30 percent tax rate would yield a factor of 0.70 or 70 percent. A higher value for the tax burden implies that the company can keep a higher percentage of its pretax profits, indicating a lower tax rate. A decrease in the tax burden ratio implies the opposite (i.e., a higher tax rate leaving the company with less of its pretax profits).

The second term on the right-hand side captures the effect of interest on ROE. Higher borrowing costs reduce ROE. Some analysts prefer to use operating income instead of EBIT for this term and the following term. Either operating income or EBIT is acceptable as long as it is applied consistently. In such a case, the second term would measure both the effect of interest expense and non-operating income on ROE.

The third term on the right-hand side captures the effect of operating margin (if operating income is used in the numerator) or EBIT margin (if EBIT is used) on ROE. In either case, this term primarily measures the effect of operating profitability on ROE.

The fourth term on the right-hand side is again the total asset turnover ratio, an indicator of the overall efficiency of the company (i.e., how much revenue it generates per unit of total assets). The fifth term on the right-hand side is the financial leverage ratio described above—the total amount of a company's assets relative to its equity capital.

This decomposition expresses a company's ROE as a function of its tax rate, interest burden, operating profitability, efficiency, and leverage. An analyst can use this framework to determine what factors are driving a company's ROE. The decomposition of ROE can also be useful in forecasting ROE based upon expected efficiency, profitability, financing activities, and tax rates. The relationship of the individual factors, such as ROA to the overall ROE, can also be expressed in the form of an ROE tree to study the contribution of each of the five factors, as shown in Exhibit 17 for Anson Industries.[13]

Exhibit 17 shows that Anson's ROE of 5.92 percent in FY5 can be decomposed into ROA of 3.70 percent and leverage of 1.60. ROA can further be decomposed into a net profit margin of 3.33 percent and total asset turnover of 1.11. Net profit margin can be decomposed into a tax burden of 0.70 (an average tax rate of 30 percent), an interest burden of 0.90, and an EBIT margin of 5.29 percent. Overall ROE is decomposed into five components.

EXHIBIT 17   DuPont Analysis of Anson Industries' ROE: Fiscal Year 5

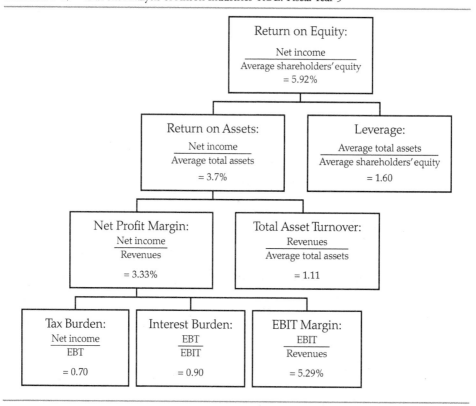

---

[13] Note that a breakdown of net profit margin was not provided in Example 14, but is added here.

Example 16 demonstrates how the five-component decomposition can be used to determine reasons behind the trend in a company's ROE.

EXAMPLE 16   Five-Way Decomposition of ROE

An analyst examining Amsterdam PLC (a hypothetical company) wishes to understand the factors driving the trend in ROE over a four-year period. The analyst obtains and calculates the following data from Amsterdam's annual reports:

	2017	2016	2015	2014
ROE	9.53%	20.78%	26.50%	24.72%
Tax burden	60.50%	52.10%	63.12%	58.96%
Interest burden	97.49%	97.73%	97.86%	97.49%
EBIT margin	7.56%	11.04%	13.98%	13.98%
Asset turnover	0.99	1.71	1.47	1.44
Leverage	2.15	2.17	2.10	2.14

What might the analyst conclude?

Solution: The tax burden measure has varied, with no obvious trend. In the most recent year, 2017, taxes declined as a percentage of pretax profit. (Because the tax burden reflects the relation of after-tax profits to pretax profits, the increase from 52.10 percent in 2016 to 60.50 percent in 2017 indicates that taxes declined as a percentage of pretax profits.) This decline in average tax rates could be a result of lower tax rates from new legislation or revenue in a lower tax jurisdiction. The interest burden has remained fairly constant over the four-year period indicating that the company maintains a fairly constant capital structure. Operating margin (EBIT margin) declined over the period, indicating the company's operations were less profitable. This decline is generally consistent with declines in oil prices in 2017 and declines in refining industry gross margins in 2016 and 2017. The company's efficiency (asset turnover) decreased in 2017. The company's leverage remained constant, consistent with the constant interest burden. Overall, the trend in ROE (declining substantially over the recent years) resulted from decreases in operating profits and a lower asset turnover. Additional research on the causes of these changes is required in order to develop expectations about the company's future performance.

The most detailed decomposition of ROE that we have presented is a five-way decomposition. Nevertheless, an analyst could further decompose individual components of a five-way analysis. For example, EBIT margin (EBIT/Revenue) could be further decomposed into a non-operating component (EBIT/Operating income) and an operating component (Operating income/Revenue). The analyst can also examine which other factors contributed to these five components. For example, an improvement in efficiency (total asset turnover) may have resulted from better management of inventory (DOH) or better collection of receivables (DSO).

5. EQUITY ANALYSIS

One application of financial analysis is to select securities as part of the equity portfolio management process. Analysts are interested in valuing a security to assess its merits for inclusion or retention in a portfolio. The valuation process has several steps, including:

1. understanding the business and the existing financial profile
2. forecasting company performance
3. selecting the appropriate valuation model
4. converting forecasts to a valuation
5. making the investment decision

Financial analysis assists in providing the core information to complete the first two steps of this valuation process: understanding the business and forecasting performance.

Fundamental equity analysis involves evaluating a company's performance and valuing its equity in order to assess its relative attractiveness as an investment. Analysts use a variety of methods to value a company's equity, including valuation ratios (e.g., the price-to-earnings or P/E ratio), discounted cash flow approaches, and residual income approaches (ROE compared with the cost of capital), among others. The following section addresses the first of these approaches—the use of valuation ratios.

5.1. Valuation Ratios

Valuation ratios have long been used in investment decision making. A well known example is the **price to earnings ratio** (P/E ratio)—probably the most widely cited indicator in discussing the value of equity securities—which relates share price to the earnings per share (EPS). Additionally, some analysts use other market multiples, such as price to book value (P/B) and price to cash flow (P/CF). The following sections explore valuation ratios and other quantities related to valuing equities.

5.1.1. Calculation of Valuation Ratios and Related Quantities
Exhibit 18 describes the calculation of some common valuation ratios and related quantities.

EXHIBIT 18   Definitions of Selected Valuation Ratios and Related Quantities

Valuation Ratios	Numerator	Denominator
P/E	Price per share	Earnings per share
P/CF	Price per share	Cash flow per share
P/S	Price per share	Sales per share
P/BV	Price per share	Book value per share

(continued)

EXHIBIT 18   (Continued)

Per-Share Quantities	Numerator	Denominator
Basic EPS	Net income minus preferred dividends	Weighted average number of ordinary shares outstanding
Diluted EPS	Adjusted income available for ordinary shares, reflecting conversion of dilutive securities	Weighted average number of ordinary and potential ordinary shares outstanding
Cash flow per share	Cash flow from operations	Weighted average number of shares outstanding
EBITDA per share	EBITDA	Weighted average number of shares outstanding
Dividends per share	Common dividends declared	Weighted average number of ordinary shares outstanding

Dividend-Related Quantities	Numerator	Denominator
Dividend payout ratio	Common share dividends	Net income attributable to common shares
Retention rate (b)	Net income attributable to common shares – Common share dividends	Net income attributable to common shares
Sustainable growth rate	$b \times$ ROE	

The P/E ratio expresses the relationship between the price per share and the amount of earnings attributable to a single share. In other words, the P/E ratio tells us how much an investor in common stock pays per dollar of earnings.

Because P/E ratios are calculated using net income, the ratios can be sensitive to non-recurring earnings or one-time earnings events. In addition, because net income is generally considered to be more susceptible to manipulation than are cash flows, analysts may use **price to cash flow** as an alternative measure—particularly in situations where earnings quality may be an issue. EBITDA per share, because it is calculated using income before interest, taxes, and depreciation, can be used to eliminate the effect of different levels of fixed asset investment across companies. It facilitates comparison between companies in the same sector but at different stages of infrastructure maturity. **Price to sales** is calculated in a similar manner and is sometimes used as a comparative price metric when a company does not have positive net income.

Another price-based ratio that facilitates useful comparisons of companies' stock prices is **price to book value**, or P/B, which is the ratio of price to book value per share. This ratio is often interpreted as an indicator of market judgment about the relationship between a company's required rate of return and its actual rate of return. Assuming that book values reflect the fair values of the assets, a price to book ratio of one can be interpreted as an indicator that the company's future returns are expected to be exactly equal to the returns required by the market. A ratio greater than one would indicate that the future profitability of the company is expected to exceed the required rate of return, and values of this ratio less than one indicate that the company is not expected to earn excess returns.[14]

---

[14] For more detail on valuation ratios as used in equity analysis, see the curriculum reading "Equity Valuation: Concepts and Basic Tools."

5.1.2. Interpretation of Earnings per Share

Exhibit 18 presented a number of per-share quantities that can be used in valuation ratios. In this section, we discuss the interpretation of one such critical quantity, earnings per share or EPS.[15]

EPS is simply the amount of earnings attributable to each share of common stock. In isolation, EPS does not provide adequate information for comparison of one company with another. For example, assume that two companies have only common stock outstanding and no dilutive securities outstanding. In addition, assume the two companies have identical net income of $10 million, identical book equity of $100 million, and, therefore, identical profitability (10 percent, using ending equity in this case for simplicity). Furthermore, assume that Company A has 100 million weighted average common shares outstanding, whereas Company B has 10 million weighted average common shares outstanding. So, Company A will report EPS of $0.10 per share, and Company B will report EPS of $1 per share. The difference in EPS does not reflect a difference in profitability—the companies have identical profits and profitability. The difference reflects only a different number of common shares outstanding. Analysts should understand in detail the types of EPS information that companies report:

Basic EPS provides information regarding the earnings attributable to each share of common stock.[16] To calculate basic EPS, the weighted average number of shares outstanding during the period is first calculated. The weighted average number of shares consists of the number of ordinary shares outstanding at the beginning of the period, adjusted by those bought back or issued during the period, multiplied by a time-weighting factor.

Accounting standards generally require the disclosure of basic as well as **diluted EPS** (diluted EPS includes the effect of all the company's securities whose conversion or exercise would result in a reduction of basic EPS; dilutive securities include convertible debt, convertible preferred, warrants, and options). Basic EPS and diluted EPS must be shown with equal prominence on the face of the income statement for each class of ordinary share. Disclosure includes the amounts used as the numerators in calculating basic and diluted EPS, and a reconciliation of those amounts to the company's profit or loss for the period. Because both basic and diluted EPS are presented in a company's financial statements, an analyst does not need to calculate these measures for reported financial statements. Understanding the calculations is, however, helpful for situations requiring an analyst to calculate expected future EPS.

To calculate diluted EPS, earnings are adjusted for the after-tax effects assuming conversion, and the following adjustments are made to the weighted number of shares:

- The weighted average number of shares for basic EPS, *plus* those that would be issued on conversion of all potentially dilutive ordinary shares. Potential ordinary shares are treated as dilutive when their conversion would decrease net profit per share from continuing ordinary operations.
- These shares are deemed to have been converted into ordinary shares at the beginning of the period or, if later, at the date of the issue of the shares.

---

[15] For more detail on EPS calculation, see the chapter "Understanding Income Statements."
[16] IAS 33, *Earnings per Share* and FASB ASC Topic 260 [Earnings per Share].

- Options, warrants (and their equivalents), convertible instruments, contingently issuable shares, contracts that can be settled in ordinary shares or cash, purchased options, and written put options should be considered.

5.1.3. Dividend-Related Quantities

In this section, we discuss the interpretation of the dividend-related quantities presented in Exhibit 18. These quantities play a role in some present value models for valuing equities.

Dividend Payout Ratio   The **dividend payout ratio** measures the percentage of earnings that the company pays out as dividends to shareholders. The amount of dividends per share tends to be relatively fixed because any reduction in dividends has been shown to result in a disproportionately large reduction in share price. Because dividend amounts are relatively fixed, the dividend payout ratio tends to fluctuate with earnings. Therefore, conclusions about a company's dividend payout policies should be based on examination of payout over a number of periods. Optimal dividend policy, similar to optimal capital structure, has been examined in academic research and continues to be a topic of significant interest in corporate finance.

Retention Rate   The retention rate, or earnings retention rate, is the complement of the payout ratio or dividend payout ratio (i.e., 1 − payout ratio). Whereas the payout ratio measures the percentage of earnings that a company pays out as dividends, the retention rate is the percentage of earnings that a company retains. (Note that both the payout ratio and retention rate are percentages of earnings. The difference in terminology—"ratio" versus "rate" versus "percentage"—reflects common usage rather than any substantive differences.)

Sustainable Growth Rate   A company's **sustainable growth rate** is viewed as a function of its profitability (measured as ROE) and its ability to finance itself from internally generated funds (measured as the retention rate). The sustainable growth rate is ROE times the retention rate. A higher ROE and a higher retention rate result in a higher sustainable growth rate. This calculation can be used to estimate a company's growth rate, a factor commonly used in equity valuation.

5.2. Industry-Specific Ratios

As stated earlier in this chapter, a universally accepted definition and classification of ratios does not exist. The purpose of ratios is to serve as indicators of important aspects of a company's performance and value. Aspects of performance that are considered important in one industry may be irrelevant in another, and industry-specific ratios reflect these differences. For example, companies in the retail industry may report same-store sales changes because, in the retail industry, it is important to distinguish between growth that results from opening new stores and growth that results from generating more sales at existing stores. Industry-specific metrics can be especially important to the value of equity in early stage industries, where companies are not yet profitable.

In addition, regulated industries—especially in the financial sector—often are required to comply with specific regulatory ratios. For example, the banking sector's liquidity and cash reserve ratios provide an indication of banking liquidity and reflect monetary and regulatory requirements. Banking capital adequacy requirements attempt to relate banks' solvency requirements directly to their specific levels of risk exposure.

Exhibit 19 presents, for illustrative purposes only, some industry-specific and task-specific ratios.[17]

EXHIBIT 19   Definitions of Some Common Industry- and Task-Specific Ratios

Ratio	Numerator	Denominator
Business Risk		
Coefficient of variation of operating income	Standard deviation of operating income	Average operating income
Coefficient of variation of net income	Standard deviation of net income	Average net income
Coefficient of variation of revenues	Standard deviation of revenue	Average revenue

Financial Sector Ratios	Numerator	Denominator
Capital adequacy—banks	Various components of capital	Various measures such as risk-weighted assets, market risk exposure, or level of operational risk assumed
Monetary reserve requirement (Cash reserve ratio)	Reserves held at central bank	Specified deposit liabilities
Liquid asset requirement	Approved "readily marketable" securities	Specified deposit liabilities
Net interest margin	Net interest income	Total interest-earning assets

Retail Ratios	Numerator	Denominator
Same (or comparable) store sales	Average revenue growth year over year for stores open in both periods	Not applicable
Sales per square meter (or square foot)	Revenue	Total retail space in square meters (or square feet)

Service Companies	Numerator	Denominator
Revenue per employee	Revenue	Total number of employees
Net income per employee	Net income	Total number of employees

[17] There are many other industry- and task-specific ratios that are outside the scope of this chapter. Resources such as Standard and Poor's Industry Surveys present useful ratios for each industry. Industry organizations may present useful ratios for the industry or a task specific to the industry.

EXHIBIT 19   (Continued)

Hotel	Numerator	Denominator
Average daily rate	Room revenue	Number of rooms sold
Occupancy rate	Number of rooms sold	Number of rooms available

5.3. Historical Research on Ratios in Equity Analysis

Some ratios may be particularly useful in equity analysis. The end product of equity analysis is often a valuation and investment recommendation. Theoretical valuation models are useful in selecting ratios that would be useful in this process. For example, a company's P/B is theoretically linked to ROE, growth, and the required return. ROE is also a primary determinant of residual income in a residual income valuation model. In both cases, higher ROE relative to the required return denotes a higher valuation. Similarly, profit margin is related to justified price-to-sales (P/S) ratios. Another common valuation method involves forecasts of future cash flows that are discounted back to the present. Trends in ratios can be useful in forecasting future earnings and cash flows (e.g., trends in operating profit margin and collection of customer receivables). Future growth expectations are a key component of all of these valuation models. Trends may be useful in assessing growth prospects (when used in conjunction with overall economic and industry trends). The variability in ratios and common-size data can be useful in assessing risk, an important component of the required rate of return in valuation models. A great deal of academic research has focused on the use of these fundamental ratios in evaluating equity investments.

A classic study, Ou and Penman (1989a and 1989b), found that ratios and common-size metrics generated from accounting data were useful in forecasting earnings and stock returns. Ou and Penman examined 68 such metrics and found that these could be reduced to a more parsimonious list of relevant variables, including percentage changes in a variety of measures such as current ratio, inventory, and sales; gross and pretax margins; and returns on assets and equity. These variables were found to be useful in forecasting earnings and stock returns.

Subsequent studies have also demonstrated the usefulness of ratios in evaluation of equity investments and valuation. Lev and Thiagarajan (1993) examined fundamental financial variables used by analysts to assess whether they are useful in security valuation. They found that fundamental variables add about 70 percent to the explanatory power of earnings alone in predicting excess returns (stock returns in excess of those expected). The fundamental variables they found useful included percentage changes in inventory and receivables relative to sales, gross margin, sales per employee, and the change in bad debts relative to the change in accounts receivable, among others. Abarbanell and Bushee (1997) found some of the same variables useful in predicting future accounting earnings. Abarbanell and Bushee (1998) devised an investment strategy using these same variables and found that they can generate excess returns under this strategy.

Piotroski (2000) used financial ratios to supplement a value investing strategy and found that he could generate significant excess returns. Variables used by Piotroski include ROA, cash flow ROA, change in ROA, change in leverage, change in liquidity, change in gross margin, and change in inventory turnover.

This research shows that in addition to being useful in evaluating the past performance of a company, ratios can be useful in predicting future earnings and equity returns.

6. CREDIT ANALYSIS

Credit risk is the risk of loss caused by a counterparty's or debtor's failure to make a promised payment. For example, credit risk with respect to a bond is the risk that the obligor (the issuer of the bond) may not be able to pay interest and principal according to the terms of the bond indenture (contract). **Credit analysis** is the evaluation of credit risk.

Approaches to credit analysis vary and, as with all financial analysis, depend on the purpose of the analysis and the context in which it is done. Credit analysis for specific types of debt (e.g., acquisition financing and other highly leveraged financing) often involves projections of period-by-period cash flows similar to projections made by equity analysts. Whereas the equity analyst may discount projected cash flows to determine the value of the company's equity, a credit analyst would use the projected cash flows to assess the likelihood of a company complying with its financial covenants in each period and paying interest and principal as due.[18] The analysis would also include expectations about asset sales and refinancing options open to the company.

Credit analysis may relate to the borrower's credit risk in a particular transaction or to its overall creditworthiness. In assessing overall creditworthiness, one general approach is credit scoring, a statistical analysis of the determinants of credit default.

Another general approach to credit analysis is the credit rating process that is used, for example, by credit rating agencies to assess and communicate the probability of default by an issuer on its debt obligations (e.g., commercial paper, notes, and bonds). A credit rating can be either long term or short term and is an indication of the rating agency's opinion of the creditworthiness of a debt issuer with respect to a specific debt security or other obligation. Where a company has no debt outstanding, a rating agency can also provide an issuer credit rating that expresses an opinion of the issuer's overall capacity and willingness to meet its financial obligations. The following sections review research on the use of ratios in credit analysis and the ratios commonly used in credit analysis.

6.1. The Credit Rating Process

The credit rating process involves both the analysis of a company's financial reports as well as a broad assessment of a company's operations. In assigning credit ratings, rating agencies emphasize the importance of the relationship between a company's business risk profile and its financial risk.

For corporate entities, credit ratings typically reflect a combination of qualitative and quantitative factors. Qualitative factors generally include an industry's growth prospects, volatility, technological change, and competitive environment. At the individual company level, qualitative factors may include operational effectiveness, strategy, governance, financial policies, risk management practices, and risk tolerance. In contrast, quantitative factors generally include profitability, leverage, cash flow adequacy, and liquidity.[19]

When analyzing financial ratios, rating agencies normally investigate deviations of ratios from the median ratios of the universe of companies for which such ratios have been calculated and also use the median ratings as an indicator for the ratings grade given to a specific debt

---

[18] Financial covenants are clauses in bond indentures relating to the financial condition of the bond issuer.
[19] Concepts in this paragraph are based on Standard & Poor's *General Criteria: Principles of Credit Ratings* (2011). This represents the last updated version at the time of publication.

issuer. This so-called universe of rated companies frequently changes, and any calculations are obviously affected by economic factors as well as by mergers and acquisitions. International ratings include the influence of country and economic risk factors. Exhibit 20 presents a few key financial ratios used by Standard & Poor's in evaluating industrial companies. Note that before calculating ratios, rating agencies make certain adjustments to reported financials such as adjusting debt to include off-balance sheet debt in a company's total debt.

EXHIBIT 20   Selected Credit Ratios

Credit Ratio	Numerator[a]	Denominator[a]
EBITDA interest coverage	EBITDA[b]	Interest expense, including non-cash interest on conventional debt instruments
FFO[c] (Funds from operations) to debt	FFO	Total debt
Free operating cash flow to debt	CFO[d] (adjusted) minus capital expenditures	Total debt
EBIT margin	EBIT[e]	Total revenues
EBITDA margin	EBITDA	Total revenues
Debt to EBITDA	Total debt	EBITDA
Return on capital	EBIT	Average beginning-of-year and end-of-year capital[f]

[a] Note that both the numerator and the denominator definitions are adjusted from ratio to ratio and may not correspond to the definitions used elsewhere in this chapter.

[b] EBITDA = earnings before interest, taxes, depreciation, and amortization.

[c] FFO = funds from operations, defined as EBITDA minus net interest expense minus current tax expense (plus or minus all applicable adjustments).

[d] CFO = cash flow from operations.

[e] EBIT = earnings before interest and taxes.

[f] Capital = debt plus noncurrent deferred taxes plus equity (plus or minus all applicable adjustments).

Source: Based on data from Standard & Poor's *Corporate Methodology: Ratios and Adjustments* (2013). This represents the last updated version at the time of publication.

6.2. Historical Research on Ratios in Credit Analysis

A great deal of academic and practitioner research has focused on determining which ratios are useful in assessing the credit risk of a company, including the risk of bankruptcy.

One of the earliest studies examined individual ratios to assess their ability to predict failure of a company up to five years in advance. Beaver (1967) found that six ratios could correctly predict company failure one year in advance 90 percent of the time and five years in advance at least 65 percent of the time. The ratios found effective by Beaver were cash flow to total debt, ROA, total debt to total assets, working capital to total assets, the current ratio, and the no-credit interval ratio (the length of time a company could go without borrowing). Altman (1968) and Altman, Haldeman, and Narayanan (1977) found that financial ratios could be combined in an effective model for predicting bankruptcy. Altman's initial work involved creation of a *Z*-score that was able to correctly predict financial distress. The *Z*-score was computed as

$$Z = 1.2 \times (\text{Current assets} - \text{Current liabilities})/\text{Total assets}$$
$$+ 1.4 \times (\text{Retained earnings}/\text{Total assets})$$
$$+ 3.3 \times (\text{EBIT}/\text{Total assets})$$
$$+ 0.6 \times (\text{Market value of stock}/\text{Book value of liabilities})$$
$$+ 1.0 \times (\text{Sales}/\text{Total assets})$$

In his initial study, a Z-score of lower than 1.81 predicted failure, and the model was able to accurately classify 95 percent of companies studied into a failure group or a non-failure group. The original model was designed for manufacturing companies. Subsequent refinements to the models allow for other company types and time periods. Generally, the variables found to be useful in prediction include profitability ratios, coverage ratios, liquidity ratios, capitalization ratios, and earnings variability (Altman 2000).

Similar research has been performed on the ability of ratios to predict bond ratings and bond yields. For example, Ederington, Yawtiz, and Roberts (1987) found that a small number of variables (total assets, interest coverage, leverage, variability of coverage, and subordination status) were effective in explaining bond yields. Similarly, Ederington (1986) found that nine variables in combination could correctly classify more than 70 percent of bond ratings. These variables included ROA, long-term debt to assets, interest coverage, cash flow to debt, variability of coverage and cash flow, total assets, and subordination status. These studies have shown that ratios are effective in evaluating credit risk, bond yields, and bond ratings.

7. BUSINESS AND GEOGRAPHIC SEGMENTS

Analysts often need to evaluate the performance underlying business segments (subsidiary companies, operating units, or simply operations in different geographic areas) to understand in detail the company as a whole. Although companies are not required to provide full financial statements for segments, they are required to provide segment information under both IFRS and US GAAP.[20]

7.1. Segment Reporting Requirements

An operating segment is defined as a component of a company: a) that engages in activities that may generate revenue and create expenses, including a start-up segment that has yet to earn revenues; b) whose results are regularly reviewed by the company's senior management; and c) for which discrete financial information is available.[21] A company must disclose separate information about any operating segment that meets certain quantitative criteria—namely, the segment constitutes 10 percent or more of the combined operating segments' revenue, assets, or profit. (For purposes of determining whether a segment constitutes 10 percent or more of combined profits or losses, the criteria are expressed in terms of the absolute value of the segment's profit or loss as a percentage of the greater of (i) the combined profits of all profitable segments and (ii) the absolute amount of the combined losses of all loss-making segments.) If, after applying these quantitative criteria, the combined revenue from external customers for all reportable segments combined is less than 75 percent of the total company revenue, the company must identify additional reportable segments until the 75 percent level is reached. Small

---

[20] IFRS 8, *Operating Segments* and FASB ASC Topic 280 [Segment Reporting].
[21] IFRS 8, *Operating Segments*, paragraph 5.

segments might be combined as one if they share a substantial number of factors that define a business or geographical segment, or they might be combined with a similar significant reportable segment. Information about operating segments and businesses that are not reportable is combined in an "all other segments" category.

Companies may internally report business results in a variety of ways (e.g., product segments and geographical segments). Companies identify the segments for external reporting purposes considering the definition of an operating segment and using factors such as what information is reported to the board of directors and whether a manager is responsible for each segment. Companies must disclose the factors used to identify reportable segments and the types of products and services sold by each reportable segment.

For each reportable segment, the following should also be disclosed:

- a measure of profit or loss;
- a measure of total assets and liabilities[22] (if these amounts are regularly reviewed by the company's chief decision-making officer);
- segment revenue, distinguishing between revenue to external customers and revenue from other segments;
- interest revenue and interest expense;
- cost of property, plant, and equipment, and intangible assets acquired;
- depreciation and amortization expense;
- other non-cash expenses;
- income tax expense or income; and
- share of the net profit or loss of an investment accounted for under the equity method.

Companies also must provide a reconciliation between the information of reportable segments and the consolidated financial statements in terms of segment revenue, profit or loss, assets, and liabilities.

Another disclosure required is the company's reliance on any single customer. If any single customer represents 10 percent or more of the company's total revenues, the company must disclose that fact. From an analysts' perspective, information about a concentrated customer base can be useful in assessing the risks faced by the company.

7.2. Segment Ratios

Based on the segment information that companies are required to present, a variety of useful ratios can be computed, as shown in Exhibit 21.

EXHIBIT 21   Definitions of Segment Ratios

Segment Ratios	Numerator	Denominator
Segment margin	Segment profit (loss)	Segment revenue
Segment turnover	Segment revenue	Segment assets
Segment ROA	Segment profit (loss)	Segment assets
Segment debt ratio	Segment liabilities	Segment assets

---

[22] IFRS 8 and FASB ASC Topic 280 are largely converged. One notable difference is that US GAAP does not require disclosure of segment liabilities, while IFRS requires disclosure of segment liabilities if that information is regularly provided to the company's "chief operating decision maker."

The segment margin measures the operating profitability of the segment relative to revenues, whereas the segment ROA measures the operating profitability relative to assets. Segment turnover measures the overall efficiency of the segment: how much revenue is generated per unit of assets. The segment debt ratio examines the level of liabilities (hence solvency) of the segment. Example 17 demonstrates the evaluation of segment ratios.

EXAMPLE 17

The Evaluation of Segment Ratios

The information contained in Exhibit 22 relates to the business segments of Groupe Danone for 2016 and 2017 in millions of euro. According to the company's 2017 annual report the company operates in four business segments, which are primarily evaluated on operating income and operating margin and in two geographic segments for which they also provide information on assets deployed.

Evaluate the performance of the segments using the relative proportion of sales of each segment, the segment margins, segment ROA where available, and segment turnover where available.

EXHIBIT 22   Group Danone Segment Disclosures (in € millions)

	2016		2017	
Business Segments	Sales	Recurring Operating Income	Sales	Recurring Operating Income
Fresh Dairy Products – International	8,229	731	8,424	760
Fresh Dairy Products – North America	2,506	351	4,530	556
Specialized Nutrition	6,634	1,419	7,102	1,685
Waters	4,574	521	4,621	541
Group Total	21,944	3,022	24,677	3,542

	2016			2017		
Geographic Segments	Sales	Recurring Operating Income	Non-Current Assets	Sales	Recurring Operating Income	Non-Current Assets
Europe and North America	10,933	1,842	11,532	13,193	2,048	22,517
Rest of World	11,011	1,180	9,307	11,484	1,495	8,433
Group Total	21,944	3,022	20,839	24,677	3,543	30,950

Source: Company's 2017 Annual Report.

Solution:

Business Segments	2016		2017	
	Segment Revenue Percent	Recurring Operating Margin	Segment Revenue Percent	Recurring Operating Margin
Fresh Dairy Products – International	37.5%	8.9%	34.1%	9.0%
Fresh Dairy Products – North America	11.4%	14.0%	18.4%	12.3%
Specialized Nutrition	30.2%	21.4%	28.8%	23.7%
Waters	20.8%	11.4%	18.7%	11.7%
Group Total	100.0%	13.8%	100.0%	14.4%

Business Segments	2017 % change in revenue
Fresh Dairy Products – International	2.4%
Fresh Dairy Products – North America	80.8%
Specialized Nutrition	7.1%
Waters	1.0%
Group Total	12.5%

The business segment analysis shows that the largest proportion of the company's revenues occurs in the Fresh Dairy Products – International segment: 37.5% and 34.1% of the total in 2016 and 2017, respectively. The greatest increase in relative revenue, however, came from the Fresh Dairy Products – North America segment, which grew by 80.8% and increased from 11.4% of total revenues in 2016 to 18.4% of total revenues in 2017. Examination of the company's full annual report reveals that Danone Group acquired a large health-oriented North American food company, Whitewave, in 2017. This caused the shift in the relative proportion of sales. The highest segment operating margin in both years comes from the Specialized Nutrition segment with operating margins of 21.4% in 2016 increasing to 23.7% in 2017. Margins increased slightly in the Fresh Dairy Products – International and Waters segments, while margins declined in Fresh Dairy Products – North America. The latter is likely due to costs associated with the Whitewave acquisition.

Geographic Segments	2016				2017			
	Segment Revenue Percent	Recurring Operating Margin	Segment ROA	Segment Asset Turnover	Segment Revenue Percent	Recurring Operating Margin	Segment ROA	Segment Asset Turnover
Europe and North America	49.8%	16.8%	16.0%	0.9	53.5%	15.5%	9.1%	0.6
Rest of World	50.2%	10.7%	12.7%	1.2	46.5%	13.0%	17.7%	1.4
Group Total	100.0%	13.8%	14.5%	1.1	100.0%	14.4%	11.4%	0.8

As used in this table, ROA refers to operating income divided by ending assets, and Asset Turnover is defined as Revenue divided by non-current assets.

> The geographic segment analysis shows that the company's sales are split roughly evenly between the two geographic segments. Operating margins were higher in the Europe and North America segment in both years but declined from 16.8% in 2016 to 15.5% in 2017, likely in connection with the North American acquisition of White-wave. Operating margins in the rest of the world, however, increased in 2017. Segment return on assets and segment asset turnover declined significantly for the Europe and North America segment in 2017, again largely due to the acquisition of Whitewave. An examination of the annual report disclosures reveals that the large increase in segment assets came from intangible assets (mainly goodwill) recorded in the Whitewave acquisition. In contrast, segment return on assets and turnover improved significantly in the Rest of World segment.

8. MODEL BUILDING AND FORECASTING

Analysts often need to forecast future financial performance. For example, analysts' EPS forecasts and related equity valuations are widely followed by Wall Street. Analysts use data about the economy, industry, and company in arriving at a company's forecast. The results of an analyst's financial analysis, including common-size and ratio analyses, are integral to this process, along with the judgment of the analysts.

Based upon forecasts of growth and expected relationships among the financial statement data, the analyst can build a model (sometimes referred to as an "earnings model") to forecast future performance. In addition to budgets, pro forma financial statements are widely used in financial forecasting within companies, especially for use by senior executives and boards of directors. Last but not least, these budgets and forecasts are also used in presentations to credit analysts and others in obtaining external financing.

For example, based on a revenue forecast, an analyst may budget expenses based on expected common-size data. Forecasts of balance sheet and cash flow statements can be derived from expected ratio data, such as DSO. Forecasts are not limited to a single point estimate but should involve a range of possibilities. This can involve several techniques:

- **Sensitivity analysis**: Also known as "what if" analysis, sensitivity analysis shows the range of possible outcomes as specific assumptions are changed; this could, in turn, influence financing needs or investment in fixed assets.
- **Scenario analysis**: This type of analysis shows the changes in key financial quantities that result from given (economic) events, such as the loss of customers, the loss of a supply source, or a catastrophic event. If the list of events is mutually exclusive and exhaustive, and the events can be assigned probabilities, the analyst can evaluate not only the range of outcomes but also standard statistical measures such as the mean and median value for various quantities of interest.
- **Simulation**: This is computer-generated sensitivity or scenario analysis based on probability models for the factors that drive outcomes. Each event or possible outcome is assigned a probability. Multiple scenarios are then run using the probability factors assigned to the possible values of a variable.

9. SUMMARY

Financial analysis techniques, including common-size financial statements and ratio analysis, are useful in summarizing financial reporting data and evaluating the performance and financial position of a company. The results of financial analysis techniques provide important inputs into security valuation. Key facets of financial analysis include the following:

- Common-size financial statements and financial ratios remove the effect of size, allowing comparisons of a company with peer companies (cross-sectional analysis) and comparison of a company's results over time (trend or time-series analysis).
- Activity ratios measure the efficiency of a company's operations, such as collection of receivables or management of inventory. Major activity ratios include inventory turnover, days of inventory on hand, receivables turnover, days of sales outstanding, payables turnover, number of days of payables, working capital turnover, fixed asset turnover, and total asset turnover.
- Liquidity ratios measure the ability of a company to meet short-term obligations. Major liquidity ratios include the current ratio, quick ratio, cash ratio, and defensive interval ratio.
- Solvency ratios measure the ability of a company to meet long-term obligations. Major solvency ratios include debt ratios (including the debt-to-assets ratio, debt-to-capital ratio, debt-to-equity ratio, and financial leverage ratio) and coverage ratios (including interest coverage and fixed charge coverage).
- Profitability ratios measure the ability of a company to generate profits from revenue and assets. Major profitability ratios include return on sales ratios (including gross profit margin, operating profit margin, pretax margin, and net profit margin) and return on investment ratios (including operating ROA, ROA, return on total capital, ROE, and return on common equity).
- Ratios can also be combined and evaluated as a group to better understand how they fit together and how efficiency and leverage are tied to profitability.
- ROE can be analyzed as the product of the net profit margin, asset turnover, and financial leverage. This decomposition is sometimes referred to as DuPont analysis.
- Valuation ratios express the relation between the market value of a company or its equity (for example, price per share) and some fundamental financial metric (for example, earnings per share).
- Ratio analysis is useful in the selection and valuation of debt and equity securities, and is a part of the credit rating process.
- Ratios can also be computed for business segments to evaluate how units within a business are performing.
- The results of financial analysis provide valuable inputs into forecasts of future earnings and cash flow.

REFERENCES

Abarbanell, J.S., and B. J. Bushee. 1997. "Fundamental Analysis, Future Earnings, and Stock Prices." *Journal of Accounting Research*, vol. 35, no. 1:1–24. doi:10.2307/2491464.

Abarbanell, J.S., and B.J. Bushee. 1998. "Abnormal Returns to a Fundamental Analysis Strategy." *Accounting Review*, vol. 73, no. 1:19–46.

Altman, E. 1968. "Financial Ratios, Discriminant Analysis and the Prediction of Corporate Bankruptcy." *Journal of Finance*, vol. 23, no. 4:589–609. doi:10.2307/2978933.

Altman, E.I. 2013, "Predicting Financial Distress of Companies: Revisiting the Z-Score and Zeta Models," in Prokopczuk, Marcel; Brooks, Chris; Bell, Adrian R., *Handbook of Research Methods and Applications in Empirical Finance*: 428-456.

Altman, E., R. Haldeman, and P. Narayanan. 1977. "Zeta Analysis: A New Model to Identify Bankruptcy Risk of Corporations." *Journal of Banking & Finance*, vol. 1, no. 1. doi:10.1016/0378-4266(77)90017-6.

Beaver, W., 1967. "Financial Ratios as Predictors of Failures." *Empirical Research in Accounting*, selected studies supplement to *Journal of Accounting Research*, 4 (1).

Benninga, Simon Z., and Oded H. Sarig. 1997. *Corporate Finance: A Valuation Approach*. New York: McGraw-Hill Publishing.

Ederington, L.H. 1986. "Why Split Ratings Occur." *Financial Management*, vol. 15, no. 1:37–47. doi:10.2307/3665276.

Ederington, L.H., J.B. Yawitz, and B.E. Robert. 1987. "The Information Content of Bond Ratings." *Journal of Financial Research*, vol. 10, no. 3:211–226.

Lev, B., and S.R. Thiagarajan. 1993. "Fundamental Information Analysis." *Journal of Accounting Research*, vol. 31, no. 2:190–215. doi:10.2307/2491270.

Modigliani, F., and M. Miller. 1958. "The Cost of Capital, Corporation Finance and the Theory of Investment." *American Economic Review*, vol. 48: 261–298.

Modigliani, F., and M. Miller. 1963. "Corporate Income Taxes and the Cost of Capital: A Correction." *American Economic Review*, vol. 53: 433–444.

Ou, J.A., and S.H. Penman. 1989a. "Financial Statement Analysis and the Prediction of Stock Returns." *Journal of Accounting and Economics*, vol. 11, no. 4:295–329. doi:10.1016/0165-4101(89)90017-7.

Ou, J.A., and S.H. Penman. 1989b. "Accounting Measurement, Price-Earnings Ratio, and the Information Content of Security Prices." *Journal of Accounting Research*, vol. 27, no. Supplement: 111–144. doi:10.2307/2491068.

Piotroski, J.D. 2000. "Value Investing: The Use of Historical Financial Statement Information to Separate Winners from Losers." *Journal of Accounting Research*, vol. 38, no. Supplement: 1–41. doi:10.2307/2672906.

Robinson, T., and P. Munter. 2004. "Financial Reporting Quality: Red Flags and Accounting Warning Signs." *Commercial Lending Review*, vol. 19, no. 1:2–15.

van Greuning, H., and S. Brajovic Bratanovic. 2003. *Analyzing and Managing Banking Risk: A Framework for Assessing Corporate Governance and Financial Risk*. Washington, DC: World Bank.

PRACTICE PROBLEMS

1. Comparison of a company's financial results to other peer companies for the same time period is called:
   A. technical analysis.
   B. time-series analysis.
   C. cross-sectional analysis.

2. In order to assess a company's ability to fulfill its long-term obligations, an analyst would *most likely* examine:
   A. activity ratios.
   B. liquidity ratios.
   C. solvency ratios.

3. Which ratio would a company *most likely* use to measure its ability to meet short-term obligations?
   A. Current ratio.
   B. Payables turnover.
   C. Gross profit margin.

4. Which of the following ratios would be *most* useful in determining a company's ability to cover its lease and interest payments?
   A. ROA.
   B. Total asset turnover.
   C. Fixed charge coverage.

5. An analyst is interested in assessing both the efficiency and liquidity of Spherion PLC. The analyst has collected the following data for Spherion:

	FY3	FY2	FY1
Days of inventory on hand	32	34	40
Days sales outstanding	28	25	23
Number of days of payables	40	35	35

   Based on this data, what is the analyst *least likely* to conclude?
   A. Inventory management has contributed to improved liquidity.
   B. Management of payables has contributed to improved liquidity.
   C. Management of receivables has contributed to improved liquidity.

6. An analyst is evaluating the solvency and liquidity of Apex Manufacturing and has collected the following data (in millions of euro):

	FY5 (€)	FY4 (€)	FY3 (€)
Total debt	2,000	1,900	1,750
Total equity	4,000	4,500	5,000

   Which of the following would be the analyst's *most likely* conclusion?
   A. The company is becoming increasingly less solvent, as evidenced by the increase in its debt-to-equity ratio from 0.35 to 0.50 from FY3 to FY5.
   B. The company is becoming less liquid, as evidenced by the increase in its debt-to-equity ratio from 0.35 to 0.50 from FY3 to FY5.
   C. The company is becoming increasingly more liquid, as evidenced by the increase in its debt-to-equity ratio from 0.35 to 0.50 from FY3 to FY5.

7. With regard to the data in Problem 6, what would be the *most* reasonable explanation of the financial data?
   A. The decline in the company's equity results from a decline in the market value of this company's common shares.
   B. The €250 increase in the company's debt from FY3 to FY5 indicates that lenders are viewing the company as increasingly creditworthy.
   C. The decline in the company's equity indicates that the company may be incurring losses, paying dividends greater than income, and/or repurchasing shares.

8. An analyst observes a decrease in a company's inventory turnover. Which of the following would *most likely* explain this trend?
   A. The company installed a new inventory management system, allowing more efficient inventory management.
   B. Due to problems with obsolescent inventory last year, the company wrote off a large amount of its inventory at the beginning of the period.
   C. The company installed a new inventory management system but experienced some operational difficulties resulting in duplicate orders being placed with suppliers.

9. Which of the following would *best* explain an increase in receivables turnover?
   A. The company adopted new credit policies last year and began offering credit to customers with weak credit histories.
   B. Due to problems with an error in its old credit scoring system, the company had accumulated a substantial amount of uncollectible accounts and wrote off a large amount of its receivables.
   C. To match the terms offered by its closest competitor, the company adopted new payment terms now requiring net payment within 30 days rather than 15 days, which had been its previous requirement.

10. Brown Corporation had average days of sales outstanding of 19 days in the most recent fiscal year. Brown wants to improve its credit policies and collection practices, and decrease its collection period in the next fiscal year to match the industry average of 15 days. Credit sales in the most recent fiscal year were $300 million, and Brown expects credit sales to increase to $390 million in the next fiscal year. To achieve Brown's goal of decreasing the collection period, the change in the average accounts receivable balance that must occur is *closest* to:
    A. +$0.41 million.
    B. −$0.41 million.
    C. −$1.22 million.

11. An analyst observes the following data for two companies:

	Company A ($)	Company B ($)
Revenue	4,500	6,000
Net income	50	1,000
Current assets	40,000	60,000
Total assets	100,000	700,000
Current liabilities	10,000	50,000
Total debt	60,000	150,000
Shareholders' equity	30,000	500,000

Which of the following choices *best* describes reasonable conclusions that the analyst might make about the two companies' ability to pay their current and long-term obligations?
   A. Company A's current ratio of 4.0 indicates it is more liquid than Company B, whose current ratio is only 1.2, but Company B is more solvent, as indicated by its lower debt-to-equity ratio.
   B. Company A's current ratio of 0.25 indicates it is less liquid than Company B, whose current ratio is 0.83, and Company A is also less solvent, as indicated by a debt-to-equity ratio of 200 percent compared with Company B's debt-to-equity ratio of only 30 percent.

C. Company A's current ratio of 4.0 indicates it is more liquid than Company B, whose current ratio is only 1.2, and Company A is also more solvent, as indicated by a debt-to-equity ratio of 200 percent compared with Company B's debt-to-equity ratio of only 30 percent.

The following information relates to Questions 12–15

The data in Exhibit 1 appear in the five-year summary of a major international company. A business combination with another major manufacturer took place in FY13.

EXHIBIT 1

	FY10	FY11	FY12	FY13	FY14
Financial statements	GBP m	GBP m	GBP m	GBP m	GBP m
Income statements					
Revenue	4,390	3,624	3,717	8,167	11,366
Profit before interest and taxation (EBIT)	844	700	704	933	1,579
Net interest payable	–80	–54	–98	–163	–188
Taxation	–186	–195	–208	–349	–579
Minorities	–94	–99	–105	–125	–167
Profit for the year	484	352	293	296	645
Balance sheets					
Fixed assets	3,510	3,667	4,758	10,431	11,483
Current asset investments, cash at bank and in hand	316	218	290	561	682
Other current assets	558	514	643	1,258	1,634
Total assets	4,384	4,399	5,691	12,250	13,799
Interest-bearing debt (long term)	–602	–1,053	–1,535	–3,523	–3,707
Other creditors and provisions (current)	–1,223	–1,054	–1,102	–2,377	–3,108
Total liabilities	–1,825	–2,107	–2,637	–5,900	–6,815
Net assets	2,559	2,292	3,054	6,350	6,984
Shareholders' funds	2,161	2,006	2,309	5,572	6,165
Equity minority interests	398	286	745	778	819
Capital employed	2,559	2,292	3,054	6,350	6,984
Cash flow					
Working capital movements	–53	5	71	85	107
Net cash inflow from operating activities	864	859	975	1,568	2,292

12. The company's total assets at year-end FY9 were GBP 3,500 million. Which of the following choices *best* describes reasonable conclusions an analyst might make about the company's efficiency?
    A. Comparing FY14 with FY10, the company's efficiency improved, as indicated by a total asset turnover ratio of 0.86 compared with 0.64.

B. Comparing FY14 with FY10, the company's efficiency deteriorated, as indicated by its current ratio.

C. Comparing FY14 with FY10, the company's efficiency deteriorated due to asset growth faster than turnover revenue growth.

13. Which of the following choices *best* describes reasonable conclusions an analyst might make about the company's solvency?

A. Comparing FY14 with FY10, the company's solvency improved, as indicated by an increase in its debt-to-assets ratio from 0.14 to 0.27.

B. Comparing FY14 with FY10, the company's solvency deteriorated, as indicated by a decrease in interest coverage from 10.6 to 8.4.

C. Comparing FY14 with FY10, the company's solvency improved, as indicated by the growth in its profits to GBP 645 million.

14. Which of the following choices *best* describes reasonable conclusions an analyst might make about the company's liquidity?

A. Comparing FY14 with FY10, the company's liquidity improved, as indicated by an increase in its debt-to-assets ratio from 0.14 to 0.27.

B. Comparing FY14 with FY10, the company's liquidity deteriorated, as indicated by a decrease in interest coverage from 10.6 to 8.4.

C. Comparing FY14 with FY10, the company's liquidity improved, as indicated by an increase in its current ratio from 0.71 to 0.75.

15. Which of the following choices *best* describes reasonable conclusions an analyst might make about the company's profitability?

A. Comparing FY14 with FY10, the company's profitability improved, as indicated by an increase in its debt-to-assets ratio from 0.14 to 0.27.

B. Comparing FY14 with FY10, the company's profitability deteriorated, as indicated by a decrease in its net profit margin from 11.0 percent to 5.7 percent.

C. Comparing FY14 with FY10, the company's profitability improved, as indicated by the growth in its shareholders' equity to GBP 6,165 million.

16. Assuming no changes in other variables, which of the following would decrease ROA?

A. A decrease in the effective tax rate.

B. A decrease in interest expense.

C. An increase in average assets.

17. An analyst compiles the following data for a company:

	FY13	FY14	FY15
ROE	19.8%	20.0%	22.0%
Return on total assets	8.1%	8.0%	7.9%
Total asset turnover	2.0	2.0	2.1

Based only on the information above, the *most* appropriate conclusion is that, over the period FY13 to FY15, the company's:

A. net profit margin and financial leverage have decreased.

B. net profit margin and financial leverage have increased.

C. net profit margin has decreased, but its financial leverage has increased.

18. A decomposition of ROE for Integra SA is as follows:

	FY12	FY11
ROE	18.90%	18.90%
Tax burden	0.70	0.75
Interest burden	0.90	0.90
EBIT margin	10.00%	10.00%
Asset turnover	1.50	1.40
Leverage	2.00	2.00

Which of the following choices *best* describes reasonable conclusions an analyst might make based on this ROE decomposition?

A. Profitability and the liquidity position both improved in FY12.

B. The higher average tax rate in FY12 offset the improvement in profitability, leaving ROE unchanged.

C. The higher average tax rate in FY12 offset the improvement in efficiency, leaving ROE unchanged.

19. A decomposition of ROE for Company A and Company B is as follows:

	Company A		Company B	
	FY15	FY14	FY15	FY14
ROE	26.46%	18.90%	26.33%	18.90%
Tax burden	0.7	0.75	0.75	0.75
Interest burden	0.9	0.9	0.9	0.9
EBIT margin	7.00%	10.00%	13.00%	10.00%
Asset turnover	1.5	1.4	1.5	1.4
Leverage	4	2	2	2

An analyst is *most likely* to conclude that:

A. Company A's ROE is higher than Company B's in FY15, and one explanation consistent with the data is that Company A may have purchased new, more efficient equipment.

B. Company A's ROE is higher than Company B's in FY15, and one explanation consistent with the data is that Company A has made a strategic shift to a product mix with higher profit margins.

C. the difference between the two companies' ROE in FY15 is very small and Company A's ROE remains similar to Company B's ROE mainly due to Company A increasing its financial leverage.

20. What does the P/E ratio measure?

A. The "multiple" that the stock market places on a company's EPS.

B. The relationship between dividends and market prices.

C. The earnings for one common share of stock.

21. A creditor *most likely* would consider a decrease in which of the following ratios to be positive news?
    A. Interest coverage (times interest earned).
    B. Debt-to-total assets.
    C. Return on assets.

22. When developing forecasts, analysts should *most likely*:
    A. develop possibilities relying exclusively on the results of financial analysis.
    B. use the results of financial analysis, analysis of other information, and judgment.
    C. aim to develop extremely precise forecasts using the results of financial analysis.

CHAPTER 7

INVENTORIES

Michael A. Broihahn, CPA, CIA, CFA

LEARNING OUTCOMES

After completing this chapter, you will be able to do the following:

- distinguish between costs included in inventories and costs recognized as expenses in the period in which they are incurred;
- describe different inventory valuation methods (cost formulas);
- calculate and compare cost of sales, gross profit, and ending inventory using different inventory valuation methods and using perpetual and periodic inventory systems;
- calculate and explain how inflation and deflation of inventory costs affect the financial statements and ratios of companies that use different inventory valuation methods;
- explain LIFO reserve and LIFO liquidation, and their effects on financial statements and ratios;
- explain LIFO reserve and LIFO liquidation, and their effects on financial statements and ratios;
- convert a company's reported financial statements from LIFO to FIFO for purposes of comparison;
- describe implications of valuing inventory at net realizable value for financial statements and ratios;
- describe the measurement of inventory at the lower of cost and net realizable value;
- describe the financial statement presentation of and disclosures relating to inventories;
- explain issues that analysts should consider when examining a company's inventory disclosures and other sources of information;
- calculate and compare ratios of companies, including companies that use different inventory methods;
- analyze and compare the financial statements of companies, including companies that use different inventory methods.

1. INTRODUCTION

Merchandising and manufacturing companies generate revenues and profits through the sale of inventory. Further, inventory may represent a significant asset on these companies' balance sheets. Merchandisers (wholesalers and retailers) purchase inventory, ready for sale, from manufacturers and thus account for only one type of inventory—finished goods inventory. Manufacturers, however, purchase raw materials from suppliers and then add value by transforming the raw materials into finished goods. They typically classify inventory into three different categories:[1] raw materials, work in progress,[2] and finished goods. Work-in-progress inventories have started the conversion process from raw materials but are not yet finished goods ready for sale. Manufacturers may report either the separate carrying amounts of their raw materials, work-in-progress, and finished goods inventories on the balance sheet or simply the total inventory amount. If the latter approach is used, the company must then disclose the carrying amounts of its raw materials, work-in-progress, and finished goods inventories in a footnote to the financial statements.

Inventories and cost of sales (cost of goods sold)[3] are significant items in the financial statements of many companies. Comparing the performance of these companies is challenging because of the allowable choices for valuing inventories: Differences in the choice of inventory valuation method can result in significantly different amounts being assigned to inventory and cost of sales. Financial statement analysis would be much easier if all companies used the same inventory valuation method or if inventory price levels remained constant over time. If there was no inflation or deflation with respect to inventory costs and thus unit costs were unchanged, the choice of inventory valuation method would be irrelevant. However, inventory price levels typically do change over time.

International Financial Reporting Standards (IFRS) permit the assignment of inventory costs (costs of goods available for sale) to inventories and cost of sales by three cost formulas: specific identification, first-in, first-out (FIFO), and weighted average cost.[4] US generally accepted accounting principles (US GAAP) allow the same three inventory valuation methods, referred to as cost flow assumptions in US GAAP, but also include a fourth method called last-in, first-out (LIFO).[5] The choice of inventory valuation method affects the allocation of the cost of goods available for sale to ending inventory and cost of sales. Analysts must understand the various inventory valuation methods and the related impact on financial statements and financial ratios in order to evaluate a company's performance over time and relative to industry peers. The company's financial statements and related notes provide important information that the analyst can use in assessing the impact of the choice of inventory valuation method on financial statements and financial ratios.

This chapter is organized as follows: Section 2 discusses the costs that are included in inventory and the costs that are recognized as expenses in the period in which they are incurred. Section 3 describes inventory valuation methods and compares the measurement of ending inventory, cost of sales and gross profit under each method, and when using periodic versus perpetual inventory systems. Section 4 describes the LIFO method, LIFO reserve, and effects of LIFO liquidations, and demonstrates the adjustments required to compare a company that uses LIFO with one that uses FIFO. Section 5 describes the financial statement effects of a change in inventory valuation method. Section 6 discusses the measurement and reporting of inventory when its value changes. Section 7 describes the presentation of inventories on the financial statements and related disclosures, discusses inventory ratios and their interpretation, and shows examples of financial analysis with respect to inventories. A summary and practice problems conclude the chapter.

---

[1] Other classifications are possible. Inventory classifications should be appropriate to the entity.
[2] This category is commonly referred to as *work in process* under US GAAP.
[3] Typically, *cost of sales* is IFRS terminology and *cost of goods sold* is US GAAP terminology.
[4] International Accounting Standard (IAS) 2 [Inventories].
[5] Financial Accounting Standards Board, *Accounting Standards Codification* (FASB ASC) Topic 330 [Inventory].

2. COST OF INVENTORIES

Under IFRS, the costs to include in inventories are "all costs of purchase, costs of conversion, and other costs incurred in bringing the inventories to their present location and condition."[6] The costs of purchase include the purchase price, import and tax-related duties, transport, insurance during transport, handling, and other costs directly attributable to the acquisition of finished goods, materials, and services. Trade discounts, rebates, and similar items reduce the price paid and the costs of purchase. The costs of conversion include costs directly related to the units produced, such as direct labor and fixed and variable overhead costs.[7] Including these product-related costs in inventory (i.e., as an asset) means that they will not be recognized as an expense (i.e., as cost of sales) on the income statement until the inventory is sold. US GAAP provide a similar description of the costs to be included in inventory.[8]

Both IFRS and US GAAP exclude the following costs from inventory: abnormal costs incurred as a result of waste of materials, labor, or other production conversion inputs, any storage costs (unless required as part of the production process), and all administrative overhead and selling costs. These excluded costs are treated as expenses and recognized on the income statement in the period in which they are incurred. Including costs in inventory defers their recognition as an expense on the income statement until the inventory is sold. Therefore, including costs in inventory that should be expensed will overstate profitability on the income statement (because of the inappropriate deferral of cost recognition) and create an overstated inventory value on the balance sheet.

EXAMPLE 1   Treatment of Inventory-Related Costs

Acme Enterprises, a hypothetical company that prepares its financial statements in accordance with IFRS, manufactures tables. In 2018, the factory produced 900,000 finished tables and scrapped 1,000 tables. For the finished tables, raw material costs were €9 million, direct labor conversion costs were €18 million, and production overhead costs were €1.8 million. The 1,000 scrapped tables (attributable to abnormal waste) had a total production cost of €30,000 (€10,000 raw material costs and €20,000 conversion costs; these costs are not included in the €9 million raw material and €19.8 million total conversion costs of the finished tables). During the year, Acme spent €1 million for freight delivery charges on raw materials and €500,000 for storing finished goods inventory. Acme does not have any work-in-progress inventory at the end of the year.

---

[6] International Accounting Standard (IAS) 2 [Inventories].

[7] Fixed production overhead costs (depreciation, factory maintenance, and factory management and administration) represent indirect costs of production that remain relatively constant regardless of the volume of production. Variable production overhead costs are indirect production costs (indirect labor and materials) that vary with the volume of production.

[8] FASB Accounting Standards Codification™ (ASC) Topic 330 [Inventory].

1. What costs should be included in inventory in 2018?
2. What costs should be expensed in 2018?

Solution to 1: Total inventory costs for 2018 are as follows:

Raw materials	€9,000,000
Direct labor	18,000,000
Production overhead	1,800,000
Transportation for raw materials	1,000,000
Total inventory costs	€29,800,000

Solution to 2: Total costs that should be expensed (not included in inventory) are as follows:

Abnormal waste	€30,000
Storage of finished goods inventory	500,000
Total	€530,000

3. INVENTORY VALUATION METHODS

Generally, inventory purchase costs and manufacturing conversion costs change over time. As a result, the allocation of total inventory costs (i.e., cost of goods available for sale) between cost of sales on the income statement and inventory on the balance sheet will vary depending on the inventory valuation method used by the company. As mentioned in the introduction, inventory valuation methods are referred to as cost formulas and cost flow assumptions under IFRS and US GAAP, respectively. If the choice of method results in more cost being allocated to cost of sales and less cost being allocated to inventory than would be the case with other methods, the chosen method will cause, in the current year, reported gross profit, net income, and inventory carrying amount to be lower than if alternative methods had been used. Accounting for inventory, and consequently the allocation of costs, thus has a direct impact on financial statements and their comparability.

Both IFRS and US GAAP allow companies to use the following inventory valuation methods: specific identification; first-in, first-out (FIFO); and weighted average cost. US GAAP allow companies to use an additional method: last-in, first-out (LIFO). A company must use the same inventory valuation method for all items that have a similar nature and use. For items with a different nature or use, a different inventory valuation method can be used.[9] When items are sold, the carrying amount of the inventory is recognized as an expense (cost of sales) according to the cost formula (cost flow assumption) in use.

Specific identification is used for inventory items that are not ordinarily interchangeable, whereas FIFO, weighted average cost, and LIFO are typically used when there are large

---

[9] For example, if a clothing manufacturer produces both a retail line and one-of-a-kind designer garments, the retail line might be valued using FIFO, and the designer garments using specific identification.

numbers of interchangeable items in inventory. Specific identification matches the actual historical costs of the specific inventory items to their physical flow; the costs remain in inventory until the actual identifiable inventory is sold. FIFO, weighted average cost, and LIFO are based on cost flow assumptions. Under these methods, companies must make certain assumptions about which goods are sold and which goods remain in ending inventory. As a result, the allocation of costs to the units sold and to the units in ending inventory can be different from the physical movement of the items.

The choice of inventory valuation method would be largely irrelevant if inventory costs remained constant or relatively constant over time. Given relatively constant prices, the allocation of costs between cost of goods sold and ending inventory would be very similar under each of the four methods. Given changing price levels, however, the choice of inventory valuation method can have a significant impact on the amount of reported cost of sales and inventory. And the reported cost of sales and inventory balances affect other items, such as gross profit, net income, current assets, and total assets.

3.1. Specific Identification

The specific identification method is used for inventory items that are not ordinarily interchangeable and for goods that have been produced and segregated for specific projects. This method is also commonly used for expensive goods that are uniquely identifiable, such as precious gemstones. Under this method, the cost of sales and the cost of ending inventory reflect the actual costs incurred to purchase (or manufacture) the items specifically identified as sold and the items specifically identified as remaining in inventory. Therefore, this method matches the physical flow of the specific items sold and remaining in inventory to their actual cost.

3.2. First-In, First-Out (FIFO)

FIFO assumes that the oldest goods purchased (or manufactured) are sold first and the newest goods purchased (or manufactured) remain in ending inventory. In other words, the first units included in inventory are assumed to be the first units sold from inventory. Therefore, cost of sales reflects the cost of goods in beginning inventory plus the cost of items purchased (or manufactured) earliest in the accounting period, and the value of ending inventory reflects the costs of goods purchased (or manufactured) more recently. In periods of rising prices, the costs assigned to the units in ending inventory are higher than the costs assigned to the units sold. Conversely, in periods of declining prices, the costs assigned to the units in ending inventory are lower than the costs assigned to the units sold.

3.3. Weighted Average Cost

Weighted average cost assigns the average cost of the goods available for sale (beginning inventory plus purchase, conversion, and other costs) during the accounting period to the units that are sold as well as to the units in ending inventory. In an accounting period, the weighted average cost per unit is calculated as the total cost of the units available for sale divided by the total number of units available for sale in the period (Total cost of goods available for sale/Total units available for sale).

3.4. Last-In, First-Out (LIFO)

LIFO is permitted only under US GAAP. This method assumes that the newest goods purchased (or manufactured) are sold first and the oldest goods purchased (or manufactured), including beginning inventory, remain in ending inventory. In other words, the last units included in inventory are assumed to be the first units sold from inventory. Therefore, cost of sales reflects the cost of goods purchased (or manufactured) more recently, and the value of ending inventory reflects the cost of older goods. In periods of rising prices, the costs assigned to the units in ending inventory are lower than the costs assigned to the units sold. Conversely, in periods of declining prices, the costs assigned to the units in ending inventory are higher than the costs assigned to the units sold.

3.5. Calculation of Cost of Sales, Gross Profit, and Ending Inventory

In periods of changing prices, the allocation of total inventory costs (i.e., cost of goods available for sale) between cost of sales on the income statement and inventory on the balance sheet will vary depending on the inventory valuation method used by the company. The following example illustrates how cost of sales, gross profit, and ending inventory differ based on the choice of inventory valuation method.

EXAMPLE 2   Inventory Cost Flow Illustration for the Specific Identification, Weighted Average Cost, FIFO, and LIFO Methods

Global Sales, Inc. (GSI) is a hypothetical Dubai-based distributor of consumer products, including bars of luxury soap. The soap is sold by the kilogram. GSI began operations in 2018, during which it purchased and received initially 100,000 kg of soap at 110 dirham (AED)/kg, then 200,000 kg of soap at 100 AED/kg, and finally 300,000 kg of soap at 90 AED/kg. GSI sold 520,000 kg of soap at 240 AED/kg. GSI stores its soap in its warehouse so that soap from each shipment received is readily identifiable. During 2018, the entire 100,000 kg from the first shipment received, 180,000 kg of the second shipment received, and 240,000 kg of the final shipment received were sent to customers. Answers to the following questions should be rounded to the nearest 1,000 AED.

1. What are the reported cost of sales, gross profit, and ending inventory balances for 2018 under the specific identification method?
2. What are the reported cost of sales, gross profit, and ending inventory balances for 2018 under the weighted average cost method?
3. What are the reported cost of sales, gross profit, and ending inventory balances for 2018 under the FIFO method?
4. What are the reported cost of sales, gross profit, and ending inventory balances for 2018 under the LIFO method?

Solution to 1: Under the specific identification method, the physical flow of the specific inventory items sold is matched to their actual cost.

Sales = 520,000 × 240 = 124,800,000 AED
Cost of sales = (100,000 × 110) + (180,000 × 100) + (240,000 × 90) = 50,600,000 AED
Gross profit = 124,800,000 – 50,600,000 = 74,200,000 AED
Ending inventory = (20,000 × 100) + (60,000 × 90) = 7,400,000 AED

Note that in spite of the segregation of inventory within the warehouse, it would be inappropriate to use specific identification for this inventory of interchangeable items. The use of specific identification could potentially result in earnings manipulation through the shipment decision.

Solution to 2: Under the weighted average cost method, costs are allocated to cost of sales and ending inventory by using a weighted average mix of the actual costs incurred for all inventory items. The weighted average cost per unit is determined by dividing the total cost of goods available for sale by the number of units available for sale.

Weighted average cost = [(100,000 × 110) + (200,000 × 100) + (300,000 × 90)]/
    600,000 = 96.667 AED/kg
Sales = 520,000 × 240 = 124,800,000 AED
Cost of sales = 520,000 × 96.667 = 50,267,000 AED
Gross profit = 124,800,000 – 50,267,000 = 74,533,000 AED
Ending inventory = 80,000 × 96.667 = 7,733,360 AED

Solution to 3: Under the FIFO method, the oldest inventory units acquired are assumed to be the first units sold. Ending inventory, therefore, is assumed to consist of those inventory units most recently acquired.

Sales = 520,000 × 240 = 124,800,000 AED
Cost of sales = (100,000 × 110) + (200,000 × 100) + (220,000 × 90) = 50,800,000 AED
Gross profit = 124,800,000 – 50,800,000 = 74,000,000 AED
Ending inventory = 80,000 × 90 = 7,200,000 AED

Solution to 4: Under the LIFO method, the newest inventory units acquired are assumed to be the first units sold. Ending inventory, therefore, is assumed to consist of the oldest inventory units.

Sales = 520,000 × 240 = 124,800,000 AED
Cost of sales = (20,000 × 110) + (200,000 × 100) + (300,000 × 90) = 49,200,000 AED
Gross profit = 124,800,000 – 49,200,000 = 75,600,000 AED
Ending inventory = 80,000 × 110 = 8,800,000 AED

The following table (in thousands of AED) summarizes the cost of sales, the ending inventory, and the cost of goods available for sale that were calculated for each of the four inventory valuation methods. Note that in the first year of operation, the total cost of goods available for sale is the same under all four methods. Subsequently, the cost of goods available for sale will typically differ because beginning inventories will differ. Also shown is the gross profit figure for each of the four methods. Because the cost of a kg of soap declined over the period, LIFO had the highest ending inventory amount, the lowest cost of sales, and the highest gross profit. FIFO had the lowest ending inventory amount, the highest cost of sales, and the lowest gross profit.

Inventory Valuation Method	Specific ID	Weighted Average Cost	FIFO	LIFO
Cost of sales	50,600	50,267	50,800	49,200
Ending inventory	7,400	7,733	7,200	8,800
Total cost of goods available for sale	58,000	58,000	58,000	58,000
Gross profit	74,200	74,533	74,000	75,600

3.6. Periodic versus Perpetual Inventory Systems

Companies typically record changes to inventory using either a periodic inventory system or a perpetual inventory system. Under a periodic inventory system, inventory values and costs of sales are determined at the end of an accounting period. Purchases are recorded in a purchases account. The total of purchases and beginning inventory is the amount of goods available for sale during the period. The ending inventory amount is subtracted from the goods available for sale to arrive at the cost of sales. The quantity of goods in ending inventory is usually obtained or verified through a physical count of the units in inventory. Under a perpetual inventory system, inventory values and cost of sales are continuously updated to reflect purchases and sales.

Under either system, the allocation of goods available for sale to cost of sales and ending inventory is the same if the inventory valuation method used is either specific identification or FIFO. This is not generally true for the weighted average cost method. Under a periodic inventory system, the amount of cost of goods available for sale allocated to cost of sales and ending inventory may be quite different using the FIFO method compared to the weighted average cost method. Under a perpetual inventory system, inventory values and cost of sales are continuously updated to reflect purchases and sales. As a result, the amount of cost of goods available for sale allocated to cost of sales and ending inventory is similar under the FIFO and weighted average cost methods. Because of lack of disclosure and the dominance of perpetual inventory systems, analysts typically do not make adjustments when comparing a company using the weighted average cost method with a company using the FIFO method.

Using the LIFO method, the periodic and perpetual inventory systems will generally result in different allocations to cost of sales and ending inventory. Under either a perpetual or periodic inventory system, the use of the LIFO method will generally result in significantly different allocations to cost of sales and ending inventory compared to other inventory valuation methods. When inventory costs are increasing and inventory unit levels are stable or increasing, using the LIFO method will result in higher cost of sales and lower inventory carrying amounts than using the FIFO method. The higher cost of sales under LIFO will result in lower gross profit, operating income, income before taxes, and net income. Income tax expense will be lower under LIFO, causing the company's net operating cash flow to be higher. On the balance sheet, the lower inventory carrying amount will result in lower reported current assets, working capital, and total assets. Analysts must carefully assess the financial statement implications of the choice of inventory valuation method when comparing companies that use the LIFO method with companies that use the FIFO method.

Example 3 illustrates the impact of the choice of system under LIFO.

EXAMPLE 3   Perpetual versus Periodic Inventory Systems

If GSI (the company in Example 2) had used a perpetual inventory system, the timing of purchases and sales would affect the amounts of cost of sales and inventory. Below is a record of the purchases, sales, and quantity of inventory on hand after the transaction in 2018.

Date	Purchased	Sold	Inventory on Hand
January 5	100,000 kg at 110 AED/kg		100,000 kg
February 1		80,000 kg at 240 AED/kg	20,000 kg
March 8	200,000 kg at 100 AED/kg		220,000 kg
April 6		100,000 kg at 240 AED/kg	120,000 kg
May 23		60,000 kg at 240 AED/kg	60,000 kg
July 7		40,000 kg at 240 AED/kg	20,000 kg
August 2	300,000 kg at 90 AED/kg		320,000 kg
September 5		70,000 kg at 240 AED/kg	250,000 kg
November 17		90,000 kg at 240 AED/kg	160,000 kg
December 8		80,000 kg at 240 AED/kg	80,000 kg
	Total goods available for sale = 58,000,000 AED	Total sales = 124,800,000 AED	

The amounts for total goods available for sale and sales are the same under either the perpetual or periodic system in this first year of operation. The carrying amount of the ending inventory, however, may differ because the perpetual system will apply LIFO continuously throughout the year. Under the periodic system, it was assumed that the ending inventory was composed of 80,000 units of the oldest inventory, which cost 110 AED/kg.

What are the ending inventory, cost of sales, and gross profit amounts using the perpetual system and the LIFO method? How do these compare with the amounts using the periodic system and the LIFO method, as in Example 2?

Solution: The carrying amounts of the inventory at the different time points using the perpetual inventory system are as follows:

Date	Quantity on Hand	Quantities and Cost	Carrying Amount
January 5	100,000 kg	100,000 kg at 110 AED/kg	11,000,000 AED
February 1	20,000 kg	20,000 kg at 110 AED/kg	2,200,000 AED
March 8	220,000 kg	20,000 kg at 110 AED/kg + 200,000 kg at 100 AED/kg	22,200,000 AED
April 6	120,000 kg	20,000 kg at 110 AED/kg + 100,000 kg at 100 AED/kg	12,200,000 AED
May 23	60,000 kg	20,000 kg at 110 AED/kg + 40,000 kg at 100 AED/kg	6,200,000 AED
July 7	20,000 kg	20,000 kg at 110 AED/kg	2,200,000 AED
August 2	320,000 kg	20,000 kg at 110 AED/kg + 300,000 kg at 90 AED/kg	29,200,000 AED
September 5	250,000 kg	20,000 kg at 110 AED/kg + 230,000 kg at 90 AED/kg	22,900,000 AED
November 17	160,000 kg	20,000 kg at 110 AED/kg + 140,000 kg at 90 AED/kg	14,800,000 AED
December 8	80,000 kg	20,000 kg at 110 AED/kg + 60,000 kg at 90 AED/kg	7,600,000 AED

Perpetual system
Sales = 520,000 × 240 = 124,800,000 AED
Cost of sales = 58,000,000 − 7,600,000 = 50,400,000 AED
Gross profit = 124,800,000 − 50,400,000 = 74,400,000 AED
Ending inventory = 7,600,000 AED

Periodic system from Example 2
Sales = 520,000 × 240 = 124,800,000 AED
Cost of sales = (20,000 × 110) + (200,000 × 100) + (300,000 × 90) = 49,200,000 AED
Gross profit = 124,800,000 − 49,200,000 = 75,600,000 AED
Ending inventory = 80,000 × 110 = 8,800,000 AED

In this example, the ending inventory amount is lower under the perpetual system because only 20,000 kg of the oldest inventory with the highest cost is assumed to remain in inventory. The cost of sales is higher, and the gross profit is lower under the perpetual system compared to the periodic system.

3.7. Comparison of Inventory Valuation Methods

As shown in Example 2, the allocation of the total cost of goods available for sale to cost of sales on the income statement and to ending inventory on the balance sheet varies under the different inventory valuation methods. In an environment of declining inventory unit costs and constant or increasing inventory quantities, FIFO (in comparison with weighted average cost or LIFO) will allocate a higher amount of the total cost of goods available for sale to cost of sales on the income statement and a lower amount to ending inventory on the balance sheet. Accordingly, because cost of sales will be higher under FIFO, a company's gross profit, operating profit, and income before taxes will be lower.

Conversely, in an environment of rising inventory unit costs and constant or increasing inventory quantities, FIFO (in comparison with weighted average cost or LIFO) will allocate a lower amount of the total cost of goods available for sale to cost of sales on the income statement and a higher amount to ending inventory on the balance sheet. Accordingly, because cost of sales will be lower under FIFO, a company's gross profit, operating profit, and income before taxes will be higher.

The carrying amount of inventories under FIFO will more closely reflect current replacement values because inventories are assumed to consist of the most recently purchased items. The cost of sales under LIFO will more closely reflect current replacement value. LIFO ending inventory amounts are typically not reflective of current replacement value because the ending inventory is assumed to be the oldest inventory and costs are allocated accordingly. Example 4 illustrates the different results obtained by using either the FIFO or LIFO methods to account for inventory.

EXAMPLE 4   Impact of Inflation Using LIFO Compared to FIFO

Company L and Company F are identical in all respects except that Company L uses the LIFO method and Company F uses the FIFO method. Each company has been in business for five years and maintains a base inventory of 2,000 units each year. Each year, except the first year, the number of units purchased equaled the number of units sold. Over the five-year period, unit sales increased 10 percent each year, and the unit purchase and selling prices increased at the beginning of each year to reflect inflation of 4 percent per year. In the first year, 20,000 units were sold at a price of $15.00 per unit, and the unit purchase price was $8.00.

1. What were the end of year inventory, sales, cost of sales, and gross profit for each company for each of the five years?
2. Compare the inventory turnover ratios (based on ending inventory carrying amounts) and gross profit margins over the five-year period and between companies.

Solution to 1:

Company L Using LIFO	Year 1	Year 2	Year 3	Year 4	Year 5
Ending inventory[a]	$16,000	$16,000	$16,000	$16,000	$16,000
Sales[b]	$300,000	$343,200	$392,621	$449,158	$513,837

Company L Using LIFO	Year 1	Year 2	Year 3	Year 4	Year 5
Cost of sales[c]	160,000	183,040	209,398	239,551	274,046
Gross profit	$140,000	$160,160	$183,223	$209,607	$239,791

[a] Inventory is unchanged at $16,000 each year (2,000 units × $8). 2,000 of the units acquired in the first year are assumed to remain in inventory.
[b] Sales Year X = $(20,000 \times \$15)(1.10)^{X-1}(1.04)^{X-1}$. The quantity sold increases by 10 percent each year, and the selling price increases by 4 percent each year.
[c] Cost of sales Year X = $(20,000 \times \$8)(1.10)^{X-1}(1.04)^{X-1}$. In Year 1, 20,000 units are sold with a cost of $8. In subsequent years, the number of units purchased equals the number of units sold, and the units sold are assumed to be those purchased in the year. The quantity purchased increases by 10 percent each year, and the purchase price increases by 4 percent each year.

Note that if the company sold more units than it purchased in a year, inventory would decrease. This is referred to as LIFO liquidation. The cost of sales of the units sold in excess of those purchased would reflect the inventory carrying amount. In this example, each unit sold in excess of those purchased would have a cost of sales of $8 and a higher gross profit.

Company F Using FIFO	Year 1	Year 2	Year 3	Year 4	Year 5
Ending inventory[a]	$16,000	$16,640	$17,306	$17,998	$18,718
Sales[b]	$300,000	$343,200	$392,621	$449,158	$513,837
Cost of sales[c]	160,000	182,400	208,732	238,859	273,326
Gross profit	$140,000	$160,800	$183,889	$210,299	$240,511

[a] Ending Inventory Year X = 2,000 units × Cost in Year X = 2,000 units $[\$8 \times (1.04)^{X-1}]$. 2,000 units of the units acquired in Year X are assumed to remain in inventory.
[b] Sales Year X = $(20,000 \times \$15)(1.10)^{X-1}(1.04)^{X-1}$
[c] Cost of sales Year 1 = $160,000 (= 20,000 units × $8). There was no beginning inventory.
Cost of sales Year X (where X ≠ 1) = Beginning inventory plus purchases less ending inventory = (Inventory at Year X–1) + $[(20,000 \times \$8)(1.10)^{X-1}(1.04)^{X-1}]$ – (Inventory at Year X) = 2,000($8) $(1.04)^{X-2}$ + $[(20,000 \times \$8)(1.10)^{X-1}(1.04)^{X-1}]$ – [2,000 ($8)$(1.04)^{X-1}$]
For example, cost of sales Year 2 = 2,000($8) + [(20,000 × $8)(1.10)(1.04)] – [2,000 ($8)(1.04)] = $16,000 + 183,040 – 16,640 = $182,400

Solution to 2:

	Company L					Company F				
Year	1	2	3	4	5	1	2	3	4	5
Inventory turnover	10.0	11.4	13.1	15.0	17.1	10.0	11.0	12.1	13.3	14.6
Gross profit margin (%)	46.7	46.7	46.7	46.7	46.7	46.7	46.9	46.8	46.8	46.8

Inventory turnover ratio = Cost of sales ÷ Ending inventory. The inventory turnover ratio increased each year for both companies because the units sold increased, whereas the units in ending inventory remained unchanged. The increase in the inventory turnover ratio is higher for Company L because Company L's cost of sales is increasing for inflation but the inventory carrying amount is unaffected by inflation. It might appear that a company using the LIFO method manages its inventory more effectively, but this is deceptive. Both companies have identical quantities and prices of purchases and sales and only differ in the inventory valuation method used.

Gross profit margin = Gross profit ÷ Sales. The gross profit margin is stable under LIFO because both sales and cost of sales increase at the same rate of inflation. The gross profit margin is slightly higher under the FIFO method after the first year because a proportion of the cost of sales reflects an older purchase price.

4. THE LIFO METHOD

The potential income tax savings are a benefit of using the LIFO method when inventory costs are increasing. The higher cash flows due to lower income taxes may make the company more valuable because the value of a company is based on the present value of its future cash flows. Under the LIFO method, ending inventory is assumed to consist of those units that have been held the longest. This generally results in ending inventories with carrying amounts lower than current replacement costs because inventory costs typically increase over time. Cost of sales will more closely reflect current replacement costs.

If the purchase prices (purchase costs) or production costs of inventory are increasing, the income statement consequences of using the LIFO method compared to other methods will include higher cost of sales, and lower gross profit, operating profit, income tax expense, and net income. The balance sheet consequences include lower ending inventory, working capital, total assets, retained earnings, and shareholders' equity. The lower income tax paid will result in higher net cash flow from operating activities. Some of the financial ratio effects are a lower current ratio, higher debt-to-equity ratios, and lower profitability ratios.

If the purchase prices or production costs of inventory are decreasing, it is unlikely that a company will use the LIFO method for tax purposes (and therefore for financial reporting purposes due to the LIFO conformity rule) because this will result in lower cost of sales, and higher taxable income and income taxes. However, if the company had elected to use the LIFO method and cannot justify changing the inventory valuation method for tax and financial reporting purposes when inventory costs begin to decrease, the income statement, balance sheet, and ratio effects will be opposite to the effects during a period of increasing costs.

4.1. LIFO Reserve

For companies using the LIFO method, US GAAP requires disclosure, in the notes to the financial statements or on the balance sheet, of the amount of the LIFO reserve. The **LIFO reserve** is the difference between the reported LIFO inventory carrying amount and the inventory amount that would have been reported if the FIFO method had been used (in other words, the FIFO inventory value less the LIFO inventory value). The disclosure provides the information that analysts need to adjust a company's cost of sales (cost of goods sold) and ending inventory balance based on the LIFO method, to the FIFO method.

To compare companies using LIFO with companies not using LIFO, inventory is adjusted by adding the disclosed LIFO reserve to the inventory balance that is reported on the balance sheet. The reported inventory balance, using LIFO, plus the LIFO reserve equals the inventory that would have been reported under FIFO. Cost of sales is adjusted by subtract-ing the increase in the LIFO reserve during the period from the cost of sales amount that is reported on the income statement. If the LIFO reserve has declined during the period,[10] the decrease in the reserve is added to the cost of sales amount that is reported on the income statement. The LIFO reserve disclosure can be used to adjust the financial statements of a US company using the LIFO method to make them comparable with a similar company using the FIFO method.

4.2. LIFO Liquidations

In periods of rising inventory unit costs, the carrying amount of inventory under FIFO will always exceed the carrying amount of inventory under LIFO. The LIFO reserve may increase over time as the result of the increasing difference between the older costs used to value inventory under LIFO and the more recent costs used to value inventory under FIFO. Also, when the number of inventory units manufactured or purchased exceeds the number of units sold, the LIFO reserve may increase as the result of the addition of new LIFO layers (the quantity of inventory units is increasing and each increase in quantity creates a new LIFO layer).

When the number of units sold exceeds the number of units purchased or manufac-tured, the number of units in ending inventory is lower than the number of units in be-ginning inventory, and a company using LIFO will experience a LIFO liquidation (some of the older units held in inventory are assumed to have been sold). If inventory unit costs have been rising from period to period and LIFO liquidation occurs, this will produce an inventory-related increase in gross profits. The increase in gross profits occurs because of the lower inventory carrying amounts of the liquidated units. The lower inventory carrying amounts are used for cost of sales, and the sales are at the current prices. The gross profit on these units is higher than the gross profit that would be recognized using more current costs. These inventory profits caused by a LIFO liquidation, however, are one-time events and are not sustainable.

LIFO liquidations can occur for a variety of reasons. The reduction in inventory levels may be outside of management's control; for example, labor strikes at a supplier may force a company to reduce inventory levels to meet customer demands. In periods of economic recession or when customer demand is declining, a company may choose to reduce existing inventory levels rather than invest in new inventory. Analysts should be aware that manage-ment can potentially manipulate and inflate their company's reported gross profits and net income at critical times by intentionally reducing inventory quantities and liquidating older layers of LIFO inventory (selling some units of beginning inventory). During economic downturns, LIFO liquidation may result in higher gross profit than would otherwise be real-ised. If LIFO layers of inventory are temporarily depleted and not replaced by fiscal year-end, LIFO liquidation will occur resulting in unsustainable higher gross profits. Therefore, it is imperative to review the LIFO reserve footnote disclosures to determine if LIFO liquidation has occurred. A decline in the LIFO reserve from the prior period may be indicative of LIFO liquidation.

---

[10] This typically results from a reduction in inventory units and is referred to as LIFO liquidation. LIFO liquidation is discussed in the next section.

EXAMPLE 5   Inventory Conversion from LIFO to FIFO

Caterpillar Inc. (CAT), based in Peoria, Illinois, USA, is the largest maker of construction and mining equipment, diesel and natural gas engines, and industrial gas turbines in the world. Excerpts from CAT's consolidated financial statements are shown in Exhibits 1 and 2; notes pertaining to CAT's inventories are presented in Exhibit 3. CAT's Management Discussion and Analysis (MD&A) disclosure states that effective income tax rates were 28 percent for 2017 and 36 percent for 2016.

1. What inventory values would CAT report for 2017, 2016, and 2015 if it had used the FIFO method instead of the LIFO method?
2. What amount would CAT's cost of goods sold for 2017 and 2016 be if it had used the FIFO method instead of the LIFO method?
3. What net income (profit) would CAT report for 2017 and 2016 if it had used the FIFO method instead of the LIFO method?
4. By what amount would CAT's 2017 and 2016 net cash flow from operating activities decline if CAT used the FIFO method instead of the LIFO method?
5. What is the cumulative amount of income tax savings that CAT has generated through 2017 by using the LIFO method instead of the FIFO method?
6. What amount would be added to CAT's retained earnings (profit employed in the business) at December 31, 2017 if CAT had used the FIFO method instead of the LIFO method?
7. What would be the change in Cat's cash balance if CAT had used the FIFO method instead of the LIFO method?
8. Calculate and compare the following for 2017 under the LIFO method and the FIFO method: inventory turnover ratio, days of inventory on hand, gross profit margin, net profit margin, return on assets, current ratio, and total liabilities-to-equity ratio.

EXHIBIT 1   Caterpillar Inc. Consolidated Results of Operation (US$ millions)

For the years ended December 31	2017	2016	2015
Sales and revenues:			
Sales of Machinery and Engines	42,676	35,773	44,147
Revenue of Financial Products	2,786	2,764	2,864
Total sales and revenues	45,462	38,537	47,011
Operating costs:			
Cost of goods sold	31,049	28,309	33,546
⋮	⋮	⋮	⋮
Interest expense of Financial Products	646	596	587
⋮	⋮	⋮	⋮
Total operating costs	41,056	38,039	43,226

(continued)

EXHIBIT 1   (Continued)

For the years ended December 31	2017	2016	2015
Operating profit	4,406	498	3,785
Interest expense excluding Financial Products	531	505	507
Other income (expense)	207	146	161
Consolidated profit before taxes	4,082	139	4,439
Provision for income taxes	3,339	192	916
Profit (loss) of consolidated companies	743	(53)	2,523
Equity in profit (loss) of unconsolidated affiliated companies	16	(6)	—
Profit attributable to noncontrolling interests	5	8	11
Profit (loss)	754	(67)	2,512

EXHIBIT 2   Caterpillar Inc. Consolidated Financial Position (US$ millions)

December 31	2017	2016	2015
Assets			
Current assets:			
Cash and short-term investments	8,261	7,168	6,460
⋮	⋮	⋮	⋮
Inventories	10,018	8,614	9,700
Total current assets	36,244	31,967	33,508
⋮	⋮	⋮	⋮
Total assets	76,962	74,704	78,342
Liabilities			
Total current liabilities	26,931	26,132	26,242
⋮	⋮	⋮	⋮
Total liabilities	63,196	61,491	63,457
Stockholders' equity			
Common stock of $1.00 par value:			
Authorized shares: 2,000,000,000			
Issued shares (2017, 2016 and 2015 – 814,894,624) at paid-in amount	5,593	5,277	5,238
Treasury stock (2017 – 217,268,852 shares; 2016 – 228,408,600 shares and 2015 – 232,572,734 shares) at cost	(17,005)	(17,478)	(17,640)
Profit employed in the business	26,301	27,377	29,246
Accumulated other comprehensive income (loss)	(1,192)	(2,039)	(2,035)
Noncontrolling interests	69	76	76
Total stockholders' equity	13,766	13,213	14,885
Total liabilities and stockholders' equity	76,962	74,704	78,342

EXHIBIT 3 Caterpillar Inc. Selected Notes to Consolidated Financial Statements

Note 1. Operations and Summary of Significant Accounting Policies
D. Inventories

Inventories are stated at the lower of cost or net realizable value. Cost is principally determined using the last-in, first-out (LIFO) method. The value of inventories on the LIFO basis represented about 65% of total inventories at December 31, 2017 and about 60% of total inventories at December 31, 2016 and 2015.

If the FIFO (first-in, first-out) method had been in use, inventories would have been $1,924 million, $2,139 million and $2,498 million higher than reported at December 31, 2017, 2016 and 2015, respectively.

Note 7. Inventories

December 31 (millions of dollars)	2017	2016	2015
Raw Materials	2,802	2,102	2,467
Work-in-process	2,254	1,719	1,857
Finished goods	4,761	4,576	5,122
Supplies	261	217	254
Total inventories	10,018	8,614	9,700

We had long-term material purchase obligations of approximately $813 million at December 31, 2017.

Solution to 1:

December 31 (millions of dollars)	2017	2016	2015
Total inventories (LIFO method)	10,018	8,614	9,700
From Note 1. D (LIFO reserve)	1,934	2,139	2,498
Total inventories (FIFO method)	11,952	10,753	12,198

Note that the decrease in the LIFO reserve from 2015–2016 and again from 2016–2017 likely indicates a LIFO liquidation for both 2016 and 2017.

Solution to 2:

December 31 (millions of dollars)	2017	2016
Cost of goods sold (LIFO method)	31,049	28,309
Plus: Decrease in LIFO reserve*	215	359
Cost of goods sold (FIFO method)	31,264	28,668

* From Note 1.D, the decrease in LIFO reserve for 2017 is 215 (1,924 − 2,139) and for 2016 is 359 (2,139 − 2,498).

Solution to 3:

December 31 (millions of dollars)	2017	2016
Net income (loss) (LIFO method)	754	−67
Less: Increase in cost of goods sold (decrease in operating profit)	−215	−359
Tax reduction on decreased operating profit*	60	129
Net income (loss) (FIFO method)	599	−297

* The reduction in taxes on the decreased operating profit are 60 (215 × 28%) for 2017 and 129 (359 × 36%) for 2016.

Solution to 4: The effect on a company's net cash flow from operating activities is limited to the impact of the change on income taxes paid; changes in allocating inventory costs to ending inventory and cost of goods sold does not change any cash flows except income taxes. Consequently, the effect of using FIFO on CAT's net operating cash flow from operating activities would be an increase of $60 million in 2017 and an increase of $129 million in 2016. These are the approximate incremental decreases in income taxes that CAT would have incurred if the FIFO method were used instead of the LIFO method (see solution to 3 above).

Solution to 5: Using the previously mentioned effective tax rates of 28 percent for 2017 and 36 percent for 2016 (as well as for earlier years), the cumulative amount of income tax savings that CAT has generated by using the LIFO method instead of FIFO is approximately $710 million (−215 × 28% + 2,139 × 36%). Note 1.D indicates a LIFO reserve of $2,139 million at the end of 2016 and a decrease in the LIFO reserve of $215 million in 2017. Therefore, under the FIFO method, cumulative gross profits would have been $2,139 million higher as of the end of 2016 and $1,924 million higher as of the end of 2017. The estimated tax savings would be higher (lower) if income tax rates were assumed to be higher (lower).

Solution to 6: The amount that would be added to CAT's retained earnings is $1,214 million (1,924 − 710) or (−215 × 72% + 2,139 × 64%). This represents the cumulative increase in operating profit due to the decrease in cost of goods sold (LIFO reserve of $1,924 million) less the assumed taxes on that profit ($710 million, see solution to 5 above). Some analysts advocate ignoring the tax consequences and suggest simply adjusting inventory and equity by the same amount. They argue that the reported equity of the firm is understated by the difference between the current value of its inventory (approximated by the value under FIFO) and its carrying value (value under LIFO).

Solution to 7: Under the FIFO method, an additional $710 million is assumed to have been incurred for tax expenses. If CAT switched to FIFO, it would have an additional tax liability of $710 million as a consequence of the restatement of financial statements to the FIFO method. This illustrates the significant immediate income tax liabilities that may arise in the year of transition from the LIFO method to the FIFO method. If CAT switched to FIFO for tax purposes, there would be a cash outflow of $710 million for the additional taxes. However, because the company is not actually converting at this point for either tax or reporting purposes, it is appropriate to reflect a deferred tax liability rather than a reduction in cash. In this case for analysis purposes, under FIFO, inventory would increase by $1,924 million, equity by $1,214 million, and non-current liabilities by $710 million.

Solution to 8: CAT's ratios for 2017 under the LIFO and FIFO methods are as follows:

	LIFO	FIFO
Inventory turnover	3.33	2.76
Days of inventory on hand	109.6 days	132.2 days
Gross profit margin	27.24%	26.74%
Net profit margin	1.66%	1.32%
Return on assets	0.99%	0.77%
Current ratio	1.35	1.42
Total liabilities-to-equity ratio	4.59	4.27

Inventory turnover ratio = Cost of goods sold ÷ Average inventory
LIFO = 3.33 = 31,049 ÷ [(10,018 + 8,614) ÷ 2]
FIFO = 2.76 = 31,264 ÷ [(11,942 + 10,753) ÷ 2]

The ratio is higher under LIFO because, given rising inventory costs, cost of goods sold will be higher and inventory carrying amounts will be lower under LIFO. If an analyst made no adjustment for the difference in inventory methods, it might appear that a company using the LIFO method manages its inventory more effectively.

Days of inventory on hand = Number of days in period ÷ Inventory turnover ratio
LIFO = 109.6 days = (365 days ÷ 3.33)
FIFO = 132.2 days = (365 days ÷ 2.76)

Without adjustment, a company using the LIFO method might appear to manage its inventory more effectively. This is primarily the result of the lower inventory carrying amounts under LIFO.

Gross profit margin = Gross profit ÷ Total revenue
LIFO = 27.24 percent = [(42,676 – 31,049) ÷ 42,676]
FIFO = 26.74 percent = [(42,676 – 31,264) ÷ 42,676]

Revenue of financial products is excluded from the calculation of gross profit. Gross profit is sales of machinery and engines less cost of goods sold. The gross profit margin is lower under FIFO because the cost of goods sold is lower from the LIFO reserve reduction.

Net profit margin = Net income ÷ Total revenue
LIFO = 1.66 percent = (754 ÷ 45,462)
FIFO = 1.32 percent = (599 ÷ 45,462]

The net profit margin is higher under LIFO because the cost of goods sold is lower due to the LIFO liquidation. The absolute percentage difference is less than that of the gross profit margin because of lower income taxes on the decreased income reported under FIFO and because net income is divided by total revenue including sales of machinery and engines and revenue of financial products. The company appears to be more profitable under LIFO.

Return on assets = Net income ÷ Average total assets
LIFO = 0.99 percent = 754 ÷ [(76,962 + 74,704) ÷ 2]
FIFO = 0.77 percent = 599 ÷ [(76,962 + 1,924) + (74,704 + 2,139) ÷ 2]

The total assets under FIFO are the LIFO total assets increased by the LIFO reserve. The return on assets is lower under FIFO because of the lower net income due to the higher cost of goods sold as well as higher total assets due to the LIFO reserve adjustment. The company appears to be less profitable under FIFO.

Current ratio = Current assets ÷ Current liabilities
LIFO = 1.35 = (36,244 ÷ 26,931)
FIFO = 1.42 = [(36,244 + 1,924) ÷ 26,931]

The current ratio is lower under LIFO primarily because of lower inventory carrying amount. The company appears to be less liquid under LIFO.

Total liabilities-to-equity ratio = Total liabilities ÷ Total shareholders' equity
LIFO = 4.59 = (63,196 ÷ 13,766)
FIFO = 4.27 = [(63,196 + 710) ÷ (13,766 + 1,214)]

The ratio is higher under LIFO because the addition to retained earnings under FIFO reduces the ratio. The company appears to be more highly leveraged under LIFO.

In summary, the company appears to be more profitable, less liquid, and more highly leveraged under LIFO. Yet, because a company's value is based on the present value of future cash flows, LIFO will increase the company's value because the cash flows are higher in earlier years due to lower taxes. LIFO is primarily used for the tax benefits it provides.

EXAMPLE 6   LIFO Liquidation Illustration

Reliable Fans, Inc. (RF), a hypothetical company, sells high-quality fans and has been in business since 2015. Exhibit 4 provides relevant data and financial statement information about RF's inventory purchases and sales of fan inventory for the years 2015 through 2018. RF uses the LIFO method and a periodic inventory system. What amount of RF's 2018 gross profit is due to LIFO liquidation?

EXHIBIT 4   RF Financial Statement Information under LIFO

	2015	2016	2017	2018
Fans units purchased	12,000	12,000	12,000	12,000
Purchase cost per fan	$100	$105	$110	$115
Fans units sold	10,000	12,000	12,000	13,000
Sales price per fan	$200	$205	$210	$215
LIFO Method				
Beginning inventory	$0	$200,000	$200,000	$200,000
Purchases	1,200,000	1,260,000	1,320,000	1,380,000
Goods available for sale	1,200,000	1,460,000	1,520,000	1,580,000
Ending inventory*	(200,000)	(200,000)	(200,000)	(100,000)
Cost of goods sold	$1,000,000	1,260,000	$1,320,000	$1,480,000
Income Statement				
Sales	$2,000,000	$2,460,000	$2,520,000	$2,795,000
Cost of goods sold	1,000,000	1,260,000	1,320,000	1,480,000
Gross profit	$1,000,000	$1,200,000	$1,200,000	$1,315,000
Balance Sheet				
Inventory	$200,000	$200,000	$200,000	$100,000

* Ending inventory 2015, 2016, and 2017 = (2,000 × $100); Ending inventory 2018 = (1,000 × $100).

Solution: RF's reported gross profit for 2018 is $1,315,000. RF's 2018 gross profit due to LIFO liquidation is $15,000. If RF had purchased 13,000 fans in 2018 rather than 12,000 fans, the cost of goods sold under the LIFO method would have been $1,495,000 (13,000 fans sold at $115.00 purchase cost per fan), and the reported gross profit would have been $1,300,000 ($2,795,000 less $1,495,000). The gross profit due to LIFO liquidation is $15,000 ($1,315,000 reported gross profit less the $1,300,000 gross profit that would have been reported without the LIFO liquidation). The gross profit due to LIFO liquidation may also be determined by multiplying the number of units liquidated times the difference between the replacement cost of the units liquidated and their historical purchase cost. For RF, 1,000 units times $15 ($115 replacement cost per fan less the $100 historical cost per fan) equals the $15,000 gross profit due to LIFO liquidation.

5. INVENTORY METHOD CHANGES

Companies on rare occasion change inventory valuation methods. Under IFRS, a change in method is acceptable only if the change "results in the financial statements providing reliable and more relevant information about the effects of transactions, other events, or conditions on the business entity's financial position, financial performance, or cash flows."[11] If the change is justifiable, then it is applied retrospectively.

---

[11] IAS 8 [Accounting Policies, Changes in Accounting Estimates and Errors].

This means that the change is applied to comparative information for prior periods as far back as is practicable. The cumulative amount of the adjustments relating to periods prior to those presented in the current financial statements is made to the opening balance of each affected component of equity (i.e., retained earnings or comprehensive income) of the earliest period presented. For example, if a company changes its inventory method in 2018 and it presents three years of comparative financial statements (2016, 2017, and 2018) in its annual report, it would retrospectively reflect this change as far back as possible. The change would be reflected in the three years of financial statements presented, the financial statements for 2016 and 2017 would be restated as if the new method had been used in these periods, and the cumulative effect of the change on periods prior to 2016 would be reflected in the 2016 opening balance of each affected component of equity. An exemption to the restatement applies when it is impracticable to determine either the period-specific effects or the cumulative effect of the change.

Under US GAAP, the conditions to make a change in accounting policy and the accounting for a change in inventory policy are similar to IFRS.[12] US GAAP, however, requires companies to thoroughly explain why the newly adopted inventory accounting method is superior and preferable to the old method. If a company decides to change from LIFO to another inventory method, US GAAP requires a retrospective restatement as described above. However, if a company decides to change to the LIFO method, it must do so on a prospective basis, and retrospective adjustments are not made to the financial statements. The carrying amount of inventory under the old method becomes the initial LIFO layer in the year of LIFO adoption.

Analysts should carefully evaluate changes in inventory valuation methods. Although the stated reason for the inventory change may be to better match inventory costs with sales revenue (or some other plausible business explanation), the real underlying (and unstated) purpose may be to reduce income tax expense (if changing to LIFO from FIFO or average cost), or to increase reported profits (if changing from LIFO to FIFO or average cost). As always, the choice of inventory valuation method can have a significant impact on financial statements and the financial ratios that are derived from them. As a consequence, analysts must carefully consider the impact of the change in inventory valuation methods and the differences in inventory valuation methods when comparing a company's performance with that of its industry or its competitors.

6. INVENTORY ADJUSTMENTS

Significant financial risk can result from the holding of inventory. The cost of inventory may not be recoverable due to spoilage, obsolescence, or declines in selling prices. IFRS state that inventories shall be measured (and carried on the balance sheet) at the lower of cost and net realizable value.[13] **Net realizable value** is the estimated selling price in the ordinary course of business less the estimated costs necessary to make the sale and estimated costs to get the inventory in condition for sale. The assessment of net realizable value is typically done item by item or by groups of similar or related items. In the event that the value of

---

[12] FASB ASC Topic 250 [Accounting Changes and Error Corrections].
[13] IAS 2 paragraphs 28–33 [Inventories – Net realizable value].

inventory declines below the carrying amount on the balance sheet, the inventory carrying amount must be written down to its net realizable value[14] and the loss (reduction in value) recognized as an expense on the income statement. This expense may be included as part of cost of sales or reported separately.

In each subsequent period, a new assessment of net realizable value is made. Reversal (limited to the amount of the original write-down) is required for a subsequent increase in value of inventory previously written down. The reversal of any write-down of inventories is recognized as a reduction in cost of sales (reduction in the amount of inventories recognized as an expense).

US GAAP used to specify the lower of cost or market to value inventories.[15] For fiscal years beginning after December 15, 2016, inventories measured using other than LIFO and retail inventory methods are measured at the lower of cost or net realizable value. This is broadly consistent with IFRS with one major difference: US GAAP prohibit the reversal of write-downs. For inventories measured using LIFO and retail inventory methods, market value is defined as current replacement cost subject to upper and lower limits. Market value cannot exceed net realizable value (selling price less reasonably estimated costs of completion and disposal). The lower limit of market value is net realizable value less a normal profit margin. Any write-down to market value or net realizable value reduces the value of the inventory, and the loss in value (expense) is generally reflected in the income statement in cost of goods sold.

An inventory write-down reduces both profit and the carrying amount of inventory on the balance sheet and thus has a negative effect on profitability, liquidity, and solvency ratios. However, activity ratios (for example, inventory turnover and total asset turnover) will be positively affected by a write-down because the asset base (denominator) is reduced. The negative impact on some key ratios, due to the decrease in profit, may result in the reluctance by some companies to record inventory write-downs unless there is strong evidence that the decline in the value of inventory is permanent. This is especially true under US GAAP where reversal of a write-down is prohibited.

IAS 2 [Inventories] does not apply to the inventories of producers of agricultural and forest products and minerals and mineral products, nor to commodity broker–traders. These inventories may be measured at net realizable value (fair value less costs to sell and complete) according to well-established industry practices. If an active market exists for these products, the quoted market price in that market is the appropriate basis for determining the fair value of that asset. If an active market does not exist, a company may use market-determined prices or values (such as the most recent market transaction price) when available for determining fair value. Changes in the value of inventory (increase or decrease) are recognized in profit or loss in the period of the change. US GAAP is similar to IFRS in its treatment of inventories of agricultural and forest products and mineral ores. Mark-to-market inventory accounting is allowed for bullion.

---

[14] Frequently, rather than writing inventory down directly, an inventory valuation allowance account is used. The allowance account is netted with the inventory accounts to arrive at the carrying amount that appears on the balance sheet.

[15] FASB ASC Section 330-10-35 [Inventory – Overall – Subsequent Measurement].

EXAMPLE 7   Accounting for Declines and Recoveries
of Inventory Value

Hatsumei Enterprises, a hypothetical company, manufactures computers and prepares
its financial statements in accordance with IFRS. In 2017, the cost of ending inventory
was €5.2 million but its net realizable value was €4.9 million. The current replacement
cost of the inventory is €4.7 million. This figure exceeds the net realizable value less a
normal profit margin. In 2018, the net realizable value of Hatsumei's inventory was €0.5
million greater than the carrying amount.

1. What was the effect of the write-down on Hatsumei's 2017 financial statements?
   What was the effect of the recovery on Hatsumei's 2018 financial statements?
2. Under US GAAP, if Hatsumei used the LIFO method, what would be the effects
   of the write-down on Hatsumei's 2017 financial statements and of the recovery on
   Hatsumei's 2018 financial statements?
3. What would be the effect of the recovery on Hatsumei's 2018 financial statements if
   Hatsumei's inventory were agricultural products instead of computers?

Solution to 1: For 2017, Hatsumei would write its inventory down to €4.9 million
and record the change in value of €0.3 million as an expense on the income statement.
For 2018, Hatsumei would increase the carrying amount of its inventory and reduce
the cost of sales by €0.3 million (the recovery is limited to the amount of the original
write-down).

Solution to 2: Under US GAAP, for 2017, Hatsumei would write its inventory down to
€4.7 million and typically include the change in value of €0.5 million in cost of goods
sold on the income statement. For 2018, Hatsumei would not reverse the write-down.

Solution to 3: If Hatsumei's inventory were agricultural products instead of computers,
inventory would be measured at net realizable value, and Hatsumei would, therefore,
increase inventory by and record a gain of €0.5 million for 2018.

Analysts should consider the possibility of an inventory write-down because the impact
on a company's financial ratios may be substantial. The potential for inventory write-downs
can be high for companies in industries where technological obsolescence of inventories is a
significant risk. Analysts should carefully evaluate prospective inventory impairments (as well
as other potential asset impairments) and their potential effects on the financial ratios when
debt covenants include financial ratio requirements. The breaching of debt covenants can have
a significant impact on a company.

Companies that use specific identification, weighted average cost, or FIFO methods are
more likely to incur inventory write-downs than companies that use the LIFO method. Under
the LIFO method, the *oldest* costs are reflected in the inventory carrying amount on the balance sheet. Given increasing inventory costs, the inventory carrying amounts under the LIFO
method are already conservatively presented at the oldest and lowest costs. Thus, it is far less
likely that inventory write-downs will occur under LIFO—and if a write-down does occur, it
is likely to be of a lesser magnitude.

EXAMPLE 8   Effect of Inventory Write-Downs on Financial Ratios

The Volvo Group, based in Göteborg, Sweden, is a leading supplier of commercial transport products such as construction equipment, trucks, busses, and drive systems for marine and industrial applications as well as aircraft engine components.[16] Excerpts from Volvo's consolidated financial statements are shown in Exhibits 5 and 6. Notes pertaining to Volvo's inventories are presented in Exhibit 7.

1. What inventory values would Volvo have reported for 2017, 2016, and 2015 if it had no allowance for inventory obsolescence?
2. Assuming that any changes to the allowance for inventory obsolescence are reflected in the cost of sales, what amount would Volvo's cost of sales be for 2017 and 2016 if it had not recorded inventory write-downs in 2017 and 2016?
3. What amount would Volvo's profit (net income) be for 2017 and 2016 if it had not recorded inventory write-downs in 2017 and 2016? Volvo's effective income tax rate was reported as 25 percent for 2017 and 31 percent for 2016.
4. What would Volvo's 2017 profit (net income) have been if it had reversed all past inventory write-downs in 2017? This question is independent of 1, 2, and 3. The effective income tax rate was 25 percent for 2017.
5. Compare the following for 2017 based on the numbers as reported and those assuming no allowance for inventory obsolescence as in questions 1, 2, and 3: inventory turnover ratio, days of inventory on hand, gross profit margin, and net profit margin.
6. CAT (Example 5) has no disclosures indicative of either inventory write-downs or a cumulative allowance for inventory obsolescence in its 2017 financial statements. Provide a conceptual explanation as to why Volvo incurred inventory write-downs for 2017 but CAT did not.

EXHIBIT 5   Volvo Group Consolidated Income Statements (Swedish krona in millions, except per share data)

For the years ended December 31	2017	2016	2015
Net sales	334,748	301,914	312,515
Cost of sales	(254,581)	(231,602)	(240,653)
Gross income	80,167	70,312	71,862
⋮	⋮	⋮	⋮
Operating income	30,327	20,826	23,318
Interest income and similar credits	164	240	257

(continued)

---

[16]The Volvo line of automobiles has not been under the control and management of the Volvo Group since 1999.

EXHIBIT 5   (Continued)

For the years ended December 31	2017	2016	2015
Income expenses and similar charges	(1,852)	(1,847)	(2,366)
Other financial income and expenses	(386)	11	(792)
Income after financial items	28,254	19,230	20,418
Income taxes	(6,971)	(6,008)	(5,320)
Income for the period	21,283	13,223	15,099
Attributable to:			
Equity holders of the parent company	20,981	13,147	15,058
Minority interests	302	76	41
Profit	21,283	13,223	15,099

EXHIBIT 6   Volvo Group Consolidated Balance Sheets (Swedish krona in millions)

December 31	2017	2016	2015
Assets			
Total non-current assets	213,455	218,465	203,478
Current assets:			
Inventories	52,701	48,287	44,390
⋮	⋮	⋮	⋮
Cash and cash equivalents	36,092	23,949	21,048
Total current assets	199,039	180,301	170,687
Total assets	412,494	398,916	374,165
Shareholders' equity and liabilities			
Equity attributable to equity holders of the parent company	107,069	96,061	83,810
Minority interests	1,941	1,703	1,801
Total shareholders' equity	109,011	97,764	85,610
Total non-current provisions	29,147	29,744	26,704
Total non-current liabilities	96,213	104,873	91,814
Total current provisions	10,806	11,333	14,176
Total current liabilities	167,317	155,202	155,860
Total shareholders' equity and liabilities	412,404	398,916	374,165

EXHIBIT 7   Volvo Group Selected Notes to Consolidated Financial Statements

NOTE 17. INVENTORIES
Accounting Policy
Inventories are reported at the lower of cost and net realizable value. The cost is established using the first-in, first-out principle (FIFO) and is based on the standard cost method, including costs for all direct manufacturing expenses and the attributable share of capacity and other related manufacturing-related costs. The standard costs are tested regularly, and adjustments are made based on current conditions. Costs for research and development, selling, administration, and financial expenses are not included. Net realizable value is calculated as the selling price less costs attributable to the sale.

SOURCES OF ESTIMATION UNCERTAINTY
Inventory obsolescence
If the net realizable value is lower than cost, a valuation allowance is established for inventory obsolescence. The total inventory value, net of inventory obsolescence allowance, was: SEK (in millions) 52,701 as of December 2017 and 48,287 as of December 31, 2016.

Inventories

December 31 (millions of Krona)	2017	2016	2015
Finished products	32,304	31,012	27,496
Production materials, etc.	20,397	17,275	16,894
Total	**52,701**	**48,287**	**44,390**

Increase (decrease) in allowance for inventory obsolescence

December 31 (millions of Krona)	2017	2016	2015
Opening balance	3,683	3,624	3,394
Change in allowance for inventory obsolescence charged to income	304	480	675
Scrapping	(391)	(576)	(435)
Translation differences	(116)	177	(29)
Reclassifications, etc.	8	(23)	20
Allowance for inventory obsolescence as of December 31	3,489	3,683	3,624

Solution to 1:

December 31 (Swedish krona in millions)	2017	2016	2015
Total inventories, net	52,701	48,287	44,390
From Note 17. (Allowance for obsolescence)	3,489	3,683	3,624
Total inventories (without allowance)	56,190	51,970	48,014

Solution to 2:

December 31 (Swedish krona in millions)	2017	2016
Cost of sales	254,581	231,602
(Increase) decrease in allowance for obsolescence*	194	(59)
Cost of sales without allowance	254,775	231,543

* From Note 17, the decrease in allowance for obsolescence for 2017 is 194 (3,489 − 3,683), and the increase for 2016 is 59 (3,683 − 3,624).

Solution to 3:

December 31 (Swedish krona in millions)	2017	2016
Profit (net income)	21,283	13,223
Increase (reduction) in cost of sales	(194)	59
Taxes (tax reduction) on operating profit*	49	(18)
Profit (without allowance)	21,138	13,264

* Taxes (tax reductions) on the operating profit are assumed to be 49 (194 × 25%) for 2017 and −18 (−59 × 31%) for 2016.

Solution to 4:

December 31 (Swedish krona in millions)	2017
Profit (net income)	21,283
Reduction in cost of sales (increase in operating profit)	3,489
Taxes on increased operating profit*	−872
Profit (after recovery of previous write-downs)	23,900

* Taxes on the increased operating profit are assumed to be 872 (3,489 × 25%) for 2017.

Solution to 5: The Volvo Group's financial ratios for 2017 with the allowance for inventory obsolescence and without the allowance for inventory obsolescence are as follows:

	With Allowance (As Reported)	Without Allowance (Adjusted)
Inventory turnover ratio	5.04	4.71
Days of inventory on hand	72.4	77.5
Gross profit margin	23.95%	23.89%
Net profit margin	6.36%	6.31%

Inventory turnover ratio = Cost of sales ÷ Average inventory
With allowance (as reported) = 5.04 = 254,581 ÷ [(52,701 + 48,287) ÷ 2]
Without allowance (adjusted) = 4.71 = 254,775 ÷ [(56,190 + 51,970) ÷ 2]

Inventory turnover is higher based on the numbers as reported because inventory carrying amounts will be lower with an allowance for inventory obsolescence. The company might appear to manage its inventory more efficiently when it has inventory write-downs.

Days of inventory on hand = Number of days in period ÷ Inventory turnover ratio
With allowance (as reported) = 72.4 days = (365 days ÷ 5.04)
Without allowance (adjusted) = 77.5 days = (365 days ÷ 4.71)

Days of inventory on hand are lower based on the numbers as reported because the inventory turnover is higher. A company with inventory write-downs might appear to manage its inventory more effectively. This is primarily the result of the lower inventory carrying amounts.

Gross profit margin = Gross income ÷ Net sales
With allowance (as reported) = 23.95 percent = (80,167 ÷ 334,748)
Without allowance (adjusted) = 23.89 percent = [(80,167 − 194) ÷ 334,748]

In this instance, the gross profit margin is slightly higher with inventory write-downs because the cost of sales is lower (due to the reduction in the allowance for inventory obsolescence). This assumes that inventory write-downs (and inventory write-down recoveries) are reported as part of cost of sales.

Net profit margin = Profit ÷ Net sales
With allowance (as reported) = 6.36 percent = (21,283 ÷ 334,748)
Without allowance (adjusted) = 6.31 percent = (21,138 ÷ 334,748)

In this instance, the net profit margin is higher with inventory write-downs because the cost of sales is lower (due to the reduction in the allowance for inventory obsolescence). The absolute percentage difference is less than that of the gross profit margin because of the income tax reduction on the decreased income without write-downs.

The profitability ratios (gross profit margin and net profit margin) for Volvo Group would have been slightly lower for 2017 if the company had not recorded inventory write-downs. The activity ratio (inventory turnover ratio) would appear less attractive without the write-downs. The inventory turnover ratio is slightly better (higher) with inventory write-downs because inventory write-downs decrease the average inventory (denominator), making inventory management appear more efficient with write-downs.

Solution to 6: CAT uses the LIFO method whereas Volvo uses the FIFO method. Given increasing inventory costs, companies that use the FIFO inventory method are far more likely to incur inventory write-downs than those companies that use the LIFO method. This is because under the LIFO method, the inventory carrying amounts reflect the *oldest* costs and therefore the *lowest* costs given increasing inventory costs. Because inventory carrying amounts under the LIFO method are already conservatively presented, it is less likely that inventory write-downs will occur.

7. EVALUATION OF INVENTORY MANAGEMENT

The choice of inventory valuation method impacts the financial statements. The financial statement items impacted include cost of sales, gross profit, net income, inventories, current assets, and total assets. Therefore, the choice of inventory valuation method also affects financial ratios that contain these items. Ratios such as current ratio, return on assets, gross profit margin, and inventory turnover are impacted. As a consequence, analysts must carefully consider inventory valuation method differences when evaluating a company's performance over time or when comparing its performance with the performance of the industry or industry competitors. Additionally, the financial statement items and ratios may be impacted by adjustments of inventory carrying amounts to net realizable value or current replacement cost.

7.1. Presentation and Disclosure

Disclosures are useful when analyzing a company. IFRS require the following financial statement disclosures concerning inventory:

a. the accounting policies adopted in measuring inventories, including the cost formula (inventory valuation method) used;
b. the total carrying amount of inventories and the carrying amount in classifications (for example, merchandise, raw materials, production supplies, work in progress, and finished goods) appropriate to the entity;
c. the carrying amount of inventories carried at fair value less costs to sell;
d. the amount of inventories recognized as an expense during the period (cost of sales);
e. the amount of any write-down of inventories recognized as an expense in the period;
f. the amount of any reversal of any write-down that is recognized as a reduction in cost of sales in the period;
g. the circumstances or events that led to the reversal of a write-down of inventories; and
h. the carrying amount of inventories pledged as security for liabilities.

Inventory-related disclosures under US GAAP are very similar to the disclosures above, except that requirements (f) and (g) are not relevant because US GAAP do not permit the reversal of prior-year inventory write-downs. US GAAP also require disclosure of significant estimates applicable to inventories and of any material amount of income resulting from the liquidation of LIFO inventory.

7.2. Inventory Ratios

Three ratios often used to evaluate the efficiency and effectiveness of inventory management are **inventory turnover, days of inventory on hand**, and **gross profit margin**.[17] These ratios are directly impacted by a company's choice of inventory valuation method. Analysts should be aware, however, that many other ratios are also affected by the choice of inventory valuation method, although less directly. These include the current ratio, because inventory is a component of current assets; the return-on-assets ratio, because cost of sales is a key component in deriving net income and inventory is a component of total assets; and even the debt-to-equity ratio, because the cumulative measured net income from the inception of a business is an aggregate component of retained earnings.

The inventory turnover ratio measures the number of times during the year a company sells (i.e., turns over) its inventory. The higher the turnover ratio, the more times that inventory is sold during the year and the lower the relative investment of resources in inventory. Days

---

[17] *Days of inventory on hand* is also referred to as *days in inventory* and *average inventory days outstanding*.

of inventory on hand can be calculated as days in the period divided by inventory turnover. Thus, inventory turnover and days of inventory on hand are inversely related. It may be that inventory turnover, however, is calculated using average inventory in the year whereas days of inventory on hand is based on the ending inventory amount. In general, inventory turnover and the number of days of inventory on hand should be benchmarked against industry norms and compared across years.

A high inventory turnover ratio and a low number of days of inventory on hand might indicate highly effective inventory management. Alternatively, a high inventory ratio and a low number of days of inventory on hand could indicate that the company does not carry an adequate amount of inventory or that the company has written down inventory values. Inventory shortages could potentially result in lost sales or production problems in the case of the raw materials inventory of a manufacturer. To assess which explanation is more likely, analysts can compare the company's inventory turnover and sales growth rate with those of the industry and review financial statement disclosures. Slower growth combined with higher inventory turnover could indicate inadequate inventory levels. Write-downs of inventory could reflect poor inventory management. Minimal write-downs and sales growth rates at or above the industry's growth rates would support the interpretation that the higher turnover reflects greater efficiency in managing inventory.

A low inventory turnover ratio and a high number of days of inventory on hand relative to industry norms could be an indicator of slow-moving or obsolete inventory. Again, comparing the company's sales growth across years and with the industry and reviewing financial statement disclosures can provide additional insight.

The gross profit margin, the ratio of gross profit to sales, indicates the percentage of sales being contributed to net income as opposed to covering the cost of sales. Firms in highly competitive industries generally have lower gross profit margins than firms in industries with fewer competitors. A company's gross profit margin may be a function of its type of product. A company selling luxury products will generally have higher gross profit margins than a company selling staple products. The inventory turnover of the company selling luxury products, however, is likely to be much lower than the inventory turnover of the company selling staple products.

7.3. Financial Analysis Illustrations

IFRS and US GAAP require companies to disclose, either on the balance sheet or in the notes to the financial statements, the carrying amounts of inventories in classifications suitable to the company. For manufacturing companies, these classifications might include production supplies, raw materials, work in progress, and finished goods. For a retailer, these classifications might include significant categories of merchandise or the grouping of inventories with similar attributes. These disclosures may provide signals about a company's future sales and profits.

For example, a significant increase (attributable to increases in unit volume rather than increases in unit cost) in raw materials and/or work-in-progress inventories may signal that the company expects an increase in demand for its products. This suggests an anticipated increase in sales and profit. However, a substantial increase in finished goods inventories while raw materials and work-in-progress inventories are declining may signal a decrease in demand for the company's products and hence lower future sales and profit. This may also signal a potential future write down of finished goods inventory. Irrespective of the signal, an analyst should thoroughly investigate the underlying reasons for any significant changes in a company's raw materials, work-in-progress, and finished goods inventories.

Analysts also should compare the growth rate of a company's sales to the growth rate of its finished goods inventories, because this could also provide a signal about future sales and profits. For example, if the growth of inventories is greater than the growth of sales, this could indicate a decline in demand and a decrease in future earnings. The company may have to lower (mark down) the selling price of its products to reduce its inventory balances, or it may have to write down the value of its inventory because of obsolescence, both of which would negatively affect profits. Besides the potential for mark-downs or write-downs, having too much inventory on hand or the wrong type of inventory can have a negative financial effect on a company because it increases inventory-related expenses such as insurance, storage costs, and taxes. In addition, it means that the company has less cash and working capital available to use for other purposes.

Inventory write-downs may have a substantial impact on a company's activity, profitability, liquidity, and solvency ratios. It is critical for the analyst to be aware of industry trends toward product obsolescence and to analyze the financial ratios for their sensitivity to potential inventory impairment. Companies can minimize the impact of inventory write-downs by better matching their inventory composition and growth with prospective customer demand. To obtain additional information about a company's inventory and its future sales, a variety of sources of information are available. Analysts should consider the Management Discussion and Analysis (MD&A) or similar sections of the company's financial reports, industry-related news and publications, and industry economic data.

When conducting comparisons, differences in the choice of inventory valuation method can significantly affect the comparability of financial ratios between companies. A restatement from the LIFO method to the FIFO method is critical to make a valid comparison with companies using a method other than the LIFO method, such as those companies reporting under IFRS. Analysts should seek out as much information as feasible when analyzing the performance of companies.

EXAMPLE 9   Comparative Illustration

1. Using CAT's LIFO numbers as reported and FIFO adjusted numbers (Example 5) and Volvo's numbers as reported (Example 8), compare the following for 2017: inventory turnover ratio, days of inventory on hand, gross profit margin, net profit margin, return on assets, current ratio, total liabilities-to-equity ratio, and return on equity. For the current ratio, include current provisions as part of current liabilities. For the total liabilities-to-equity ratio, include provisions in total liabilities.

2. How much do inventories represent as a component of total assets for CAT using LIFO numbers as reported and FIFO adjusted numbers, and for Volvo using reported numbers in 2017 and 2016? Discuss any changes that would concern an analyst.

3. Using the reported numbers, compare the 2016 and 2017 growth rates of CAT and Volvo for sales, finished goods inventory, and inventories other than finished goods.

Solution to 1: The comparisons between Caterpillar and Volvo for 2017 are as follows:

	CAT (LIFO)	CAT (FIFO)	Volvo
Inventory turnover ratio	3.33	2.76	5.04
Days of inventory on hand	109.6 days	132.2 days	72.4 days
Gross profit margin	27.24%	26.74%	23.95%
Net profit margin	1.66%	1.32%	6.36%
Return on assets[a]	0.99%	0.77%	5.25%
Current ratio[b]	1.35	1.42	1.12
Total liabilities-to-equity ratio[c]	4.59	4.27	2.78
Return on equity[d]	5.59%	4.05%	20.59%

Calculations for ratios previously calculated (see Examples 5 and 8) are not shown again.
[a]Return on assets = Net income ÷ Average total assets
    Volvo = 5.25 percent = 21,283 ÷ [(412,494 + 398,916) ÷ 2]
[b]Current ratio = Current assets ÷ Current liabilities
    Volvo = 1.12 = [199,039 ÷ (10,806 + 167,317)]
The question indicates to include current provisions in current liabilities.
[c]Total liabilities-to-equity ratio = Total liabilities ÷ Total shareholders' equity
    Volvo = 2.78 = [(29,147 + 96,213 + 10,806 + 167,317) ÷ 109,011]
The question indicates to include provisions in total liabilities.
[d]Return on equity = Net income ÷ Average shareholders' equity
CAT (LIFO) = 5.59 percent = 754 ÷ [(13,766 + 13,213) ÷ 2]
CAT (FIFO) = 4.05 percent = 599 ÷ {[(13,766 + 1,924 − 710) + (13,213 + 2,139 − 770)] ÷ 2}
Volvo = 20.59 percent = 21,283 ÷ [(109,011 + 97,764) ÷ 2]

Comparing CAT (FIFO) and Volvo, it appears that Volvo manages its inventory more effectively. It has higher inventory turnover and fewer days of inventory on hand. Volvo appears to have superior profitability based on net profit margin. A primary reason for CAT's low profitability in 2017 was due to a substantial increase in the provision for income taxes. An analyst would likely further investigate CAT's increase in provision for income taxes, as well as other reported numbers, rather than reaching a conclusion based on ratios alone (in other words, try to identify the underlying causes of changes or differences in ratios).

Solution to 2: The 2017 and 2016 inventory to total assets ratios for CAT using LIFO and adjusted to FIFO and for Volvo as reported, are as follows:

	CAT (LIFO)	CAT (FIFO)	Volvo
2017	13.02%	15.28%	12.78%
2016	11.53%	14.14%	12.10%

Inventory to total assets

CAT (LIFO) 2017 = 13.02 percent = 10,018 ÷ 76,962
CAT (LIFO) 2016 = 11.53 percent = 8,614 ÷ 74,704
CAT (FIFO) 2017 = 15.28 percent = 11,942 ÷ (76,962 + 1,924 − 710)

CAT (FIFO) 2016 = 14.14 percent = 10,753 ÷ (74,704 + 2,139 – 770)
Volvo 2017 = 12.78 percent = 52,701 ÷ 412,494
Volvo 2016 = 12.10 percent = 48,287 ÷ 398,916

Based on the numbers as reported, CAT appears to have a similar percentage of assets tied up in inventory as Volvo. However, when CAT's inventory is adjusted to FIFO, it has a higher percentage of its assets tied up in inventory than Volvo.

The increase in inventory as a percentage of total assets is cause for some concern. Higher inventory typically results in higher maintenance costs (for example, storage and financing costs). A build-up of slow moving or obsolete inventories may result in future inventory write-downs. In Volvo's Note 17, the breakdown by inventory classification shows a significant increase in the inventory of production materials. Volvo may be planning on increasing production of more finished goods inventory (which has also increased). Looking at CAT's Note 7, all classifications of inventory seem to be increasing, and because these are valued using the LIFO method, there is some cause for concern. The company must be increasing inventory quantities and adding new LIFO layers.

Solution to 3: CAT's and Volvo's 2017 and 2016 growth rates for sales ("Sales of machinery and engines" for CAT and "Net sales" for Volvo), finished goods, and inventories other than finished goods" are as follows:

2017	CAT	Volvo
Sales	19.3%	10.9%
Finished goods	4.0%	4.2%
Inventories other than finished goods	30.2%	18.1%

2016	CAT	Volvo
Sales	–19.0%	–3.4%
Finished goods	–10.7%	12.8%
Inventories other than finished goods	–11.8%	2.3%

Growth rate = (Value for year – Value for previous year)/Value for previous year

2017 CAT

Sales = 19.3 percent = (42,676 – 35,773) ÷ 35,773
Finished goods = 4.0 percent = (4,761 – 4,576) ÷ 4,576
Inventories other than finished goods = 30.2 percent = [(2,802 + 2,254 + 201) – (2,102 + 1,719 + 217)] ÷ (2,102 + 1,719 + 217)

2017 Volvo

Sales = 10.9 percent = (334,748 – 301,914) ÷ 301,914
Finished products = 4.2 percent = (32,304 – 31,012) ÷ 31,012
Inventories other than finished products =18.1 percent = (20,397 – 17,275) ÷ 17,275

2016 CAT

Sales = –19.0 percent = (35,773 – 44,147) ÷ 44,147
Finished goods = –10.7 percent = (4,576 – 5,122) ÷ 5,122
Inventories other than finished goods = –11.8 percent = [(2,102 + 1,719 + 217)
    – (2,467 + 1,857 + 254)] ÷ (2,467 + 1,857 + 254)

2016 Volvo

Sales = – 3.4 percent = (301,914 – 312,515) ÷ 312,515
Finished products = 12.8 percent = (31,012 – 27,496) ÷ 27,496
Inventories other than finished products = 2.3 percent = (17,275 – 16,894) ÷ 16,894

For both companies, the growth rates in finished goods inventory exceeds the growth rate in sales; this could be indicative of accumulating excess inventory. Volvo's growth rate in finished goods compared to its growth rate in sales is significantly higher, but the lower growth rates in finished goods inventory for CAT are potentially a result of using the LIFO method versus the FIFO method. It appears Volvo is aware that an issue exists and is planning on cutting back production given the relatively small increase in inventories other than finished products. Regardless, an analyst should do further investigation before reaching any conclusion about a company's future prospects for sales and profit.

EXAMPLE 10   Single Company Illustration

Selected excerpts from the consolidated financial statements and notes to consolidated financial statements for Jollof Inc., a hypothetical telecommunications company providing networking and communications solutions, are presented in Exhibits 8, 9, and 10. Exhibit 8 contains excerpts from the consolidated income statements, and Exhibit 9 contains excerpts from the consolidated balance sheets. Exhibit 10 contains excerpts from three of the notes to consolidated financial statements.

Note 1 (a) discloses that Jollof's finished goods inventories and work in progress are valued at the lower of cost or net realizable value. Note 2 (a) discloses that the impact of inventory and work in progress write-downs on Jollof's income before tax was a net reduction of €239 million in 2017, a net reduction of €156 million in 2016, and a net reduction of €65 million in 2015.[18] The inventory impairment loss amounts steadily increased from 2015 to 2017 and are included as a component, (additions)/reversals, of Jollof's change in valuation allowance as disclosed in Note 3 (b) from Exhibit 10. Observe also that Jollof discloses its valuation allowance at December 31, 2017, 2016, and 2015 in Note 3 (b) and details on the allocation of the allowance are included in Note 19 (a). The €549 million valuation allowance is the total of a €528 million allowance for inventories and a €21 million allowance for work in progress on construction contracts.

---

[18]This reduction is often referred to as a *charge*. An accounting charge is the recognition of a loss or expense. In this case, the charge is attributable to the impairment of assets.

Finally, observe that the €1,845 million net value for inventories (excluding construction contracts) at December 31, 2017 in Note 19 (a) reconciles with the balance sheet amount for inventories and work in progress, net, on December 31, 2017, as presented in Exhibit 9.

The inventory valuation allowance represents the total amount of inventory write-downs taken for the inventory reported on the balance sheet (which is measured at the lower of cost or net realizable value). Therefore, an analyst can determine the historical cost of the company's inventory by adding the inventory valuation allowance to the reported inventory carrying amount on the balance sheet. The valuation allowance increased in magnitude and as a percentage of gross inventory values from 2015 to 2017.

EXHIBIT 8   Alcatel-Lucent Consolidated Income Statements (€ millions)

For years ended December 31	2017	2016	2015
Revenues	14,267	14,945	10,317
Cost of sales	(9,400)	(10,150)	(6,900)
Gross profit	4,867	4,795	3,417
Administrative and selling expenses	(2,598)	(2,908)	(1,605)
Research and development costs	(2,316)	(2,481)	(1,235)
Income from operating activities before restructuring costs, impairment of assets, gain/(loss) on disposal of consolidated entities, and post-retirement benefit plan amendments	(47)	(594)	577
Restructuring costs	(472)	(719)	(594)
Impairment of assets	(3,969)	(2,473)	(118)
Gain/(loss) on disposal of consolidated entities	(6)	—	13
Post-retirement benefit plan amendments	39	217	—
Income (loss) from operating activities	(4,455)	(3,569)	(122)
⋮	⋮	⋮	⋮
Income (loss) from continuing operations	(4,373)	(3,433)	(184)
Income (loss) from discontinued operations	28	512	133
Net income (loss)	(4,345)	(2,921)	51

EXHIBIT 9   Alcatel-Lucent Consolidated Balance Sheets (€ millions)

December 31	2017	2016	2015
⋮	⋮	⋮	⋮
Total non-current assets	10,703	16,913	21,559
Inventories and work in progress, net	1,845	1,877	1,898
Amounts due from customers on construction contracts	416	591	517
Trade receivables and related accounts, net	3,637	3,497	3,257
Advances and progress payments	83	92	73
⋮	⋮	⋮	⋮

Total current assets	12,238	11,504	13,629
Total assets	22,941	28,417	35,188
⋮	⋮	⋮	⋮
Retained earnings, fair value, and other reserves	(7,409)	(3,210)	(2,890)
⋮	⋮	⋮	⋮
Total shareholders' equity	4,388	9,830	13,711
Pensions, retirement indemnities, and other post-retirement benefits	4,038	3,735	4,577
Bonds and notes issued, long-term	3,302	3,794	4,117
Other long-term debt	56	40	123
Deferred tax liabilities	968	1,593	2,170
Other non-current liabilities	372	307	232
Total non-current liabilities	8,736	9,471	11,219
Provisions	2,036	2,155	1,987
Current portion of long-term debt	921	406	975
Customers' deposits and advances	780	711	654
Amounts due to customers on construction contracts	158	342	229
Trade payables and related accounts	3,840	3,792	3,383
Liabilities related to disposal groups held for sale	—	—	1,349
Current income tax liabilities	155	59	55
Other current liabilities	1,926	1,651	1,625
Total current liabilities	9,817	9,117	10,257
Total liabilities and shareholders' equity	22,941	28,417	35,188

EXHIBIT 10   Jollof Inc. Selected Notes to Consolidated Financial Statements

Note 1. Summary of Significant Accounting Policies
(a) Inventories and work in progress

Inventories and work in progress are valued at the lower of cost (including indirect production costs where applicable) or net realizable value.[19] Net realizable value is the estimated sales revenue for a normal period of activity less expected completion and selling costs.

Note 2. Principal uncertainties regarding the use of estimates
(a) Valuation allowance for inventories and work in progress

Inventories and work in progress are measured at the lower of cost or net realizable value. Valuation allowances for inventories and work in progress are calculated based on an analysis of foreseeable changes in demand, technology, or the market, in order to determine obsolete or excess inventories and work in progress.

(continued)

---

[19] *Cost* approximates cost on a first-in, first-out basis.

EXHIBIT 10   (Continued)

The valuation allowances are accounted for in cost of sales or in restructuring costs, depending on the nature of the amounts concerned.

	December 31		
(€ millions)	2017	2016	2015
Valuation allowance for inventories and work in progress on construction contracts	(549)	(432)	318
Impact of inventory and work in progress write-downs on income (loss) before income tax related reduction of goodwill and discounted operations	(239)	(156)	(65)

Note 3. Inventories and work in progress

(a) Analysis of net value

(€ millions)	2017	2016	2015
Raw materials and goods	545	474	455
Work in progress excluding construction contracts	816	805	632
Finished goods	1,011	995	1,109
Gross value (excluding construction contracts)	2,373	2,274	2,196
Valuation allowance	(528)	(396)	(298)
Net value (excluding construction contracts)	1,845	1,877	1,898
Work in progress on construction contracts, gross*	184	228	291
Valuation allowance	(21)	(35)	(19)
Work in progress on construction contracts, net	163	193	272
Total, net	2,008	2,071	2,170

* Included in the amounts due from/to construction contracts.

(b) Change in valuation allowance

(€ millions)	2017	2016	2015
At January 1	(432)	(318)	(355)
(Additions)/reversals	(239)	(156)	(65)
Utilization	58	32	45
Changes in consolidation group	—	—	45
Net effect of exchange rate changes and other changes	63	10	12
At December 31	(549)	(432)	(318)

Rounding differences may result in totals that are slightly different from the sum and from corresponding numbers in the note.

1. Calculate Jollof's inventory turnover, number of days of inventory on hand, gross profit margin, current ratio, debt-to-equity ratio, and return on total assets for 2017 and 2016 based on the numbers reported. Use an average for inventory and total asset amounts and year-end numbers for other ratio items. For debt, include only bonds and notes issued, long-term; other long-term debt; and current portion of long-term debt.
2. Based on the answer to Question 1, comment on the changes from 2016 to 2017.

EXHIBIT 10   (Continued)

3. If Jollof had used the weighted average cost method instead of the FIFO method during 2017, 2016, and 2015, what would be the effect on Jollof's reported cost of sales and inventory carrying amounts? What would be the directional impact on the financial ratios that were calculated for Jollof in Question 1?

Solution to 1: The financial ratios are as follows:

	2017	2016
Inventory turnover ratio	5.05	5.38
Number of days of inventory on hand	72.3 days	67.8 days
Gross profit margin	34.1%	32.1%
Current ratio	1.25	1.26
Debt-to-equity ratio	0.98	0.43
Return on total assets	−16.9%	−9.2%

Inventory turnover ratio = Cost of sales ÷ Average inventory
2017 inventory turnover ratio = 5.05 = 9,400 ÷ [(1,845 + 1,877) ÷ 2]
2016 inventory turnover ratio = 5.38 = 10,150 ÷ [(1,877 + 1,898) ÷ 2]

Number of days of inventory = 365 days ÷ Inventory turnover ratio
2017 number of days of inventory = 72.3 days = 365 days ÷ 5.05
2016 number of days of inventory = 67.8 days = 365 days ÷ 5.38

Gross profit margin = Gross profit ÷ Total revenue
2017 gross profit margin = 34.1% = 4,867 ÷ 14,267
2016 gross profit margin = 32.1% = 4,795 ÷ 14,945

Current ratio = Current assets ÷ Current liabilities
2017 current ratio = 1.25 = 12,238 ÷ 9,817
2016 current ratio = 1.26 = 11,504 ÷ 9,117

Debt-to-equity ratio = Total debt ÷ Total shareholders' equity
2017 debt-to-equity ratio = 0.98 = (3,302 + 56 + 921) ÷ 4,388
2016 debt-to-equity ratio = 0.43 = (3,794 + 40 + 406) ÷ 9,830

Return on assets = Net income ÷ Average total assets
2017 return on assets = −16.9% = −4,345 ÷ [(22,941 + 28,417) ÷ 2]
2016 return on assets = −9.2% = −2,921 ÷ [(28,417 + 35,188) ÷ 2]

Solution to 2: From 2016 to 2017, the inventory turnover ratio declined, and the number of days of inventory increased by 4.5 days. Jollof appears to be managing inventory less efficiently. The gross profit margin improved by 2.0 percent, from 32.1 percent in 2016 to 34.1 percent in 2017. The current ratio is relatively unchanged from 2016 to 2017. The debt-to-equity ratio has risen significantly in 2017 compared to 2016.

(continued)

EXHIBIT 10   (Continued)

Although Jollofn's total debt has been relatively stable during this time period, the company's equity has been declining rapidly because of the cumulative effect of its net losses on retained earnings.

The return on assets is negative and deteriorated in 2017 compared to 2016. A larger net loss and lower total assets in 2017 resulted in a higher negative return on assets. The analyst should investigate the underlying reasons for the sharp decline in Jollof's return on assets. From Exhibit 8, it is apparent that Jollof's gross profit margins were insufficient to cover the administrative and selling expenses, and research and development costs in 2016 and 2017. Large restructuring costs and asset impairment losses contributed to the loss from operating activities in both 2016 and 2017.

Solution to 3: If inventory replacement costs were increasing during 2015, 2016, and 2017 (and inventory quantity levels were stable or increasing), Jollof's cost of sales would have been higher, and its gross profit margin would have been lower under the weighted average cost inventory method than what was reported under the FIFO method (assuming no inventory write-downs that would otherwise neutralize the differences between the inventory valuation methods). FIFO allocates the oldest inventory costs to cost of sales; the reported cost of sales would be lower under FIFO given increasing inventory costs. Inventory carrying amounts would be higher under the FIFO method than under the weighted average cost method because the more recently purchased inventory items would be included in inventory at their higher costs (again assuming no inventory write-downs that would otherwise neutralize the differences between the inventory valuation methods). Consequently, Jollof's reported gross profit, net income, and retained earnings would also be higher for those years under the FIFO method.

The effects on ratios are as follows:

- The inventory turnover ratios would all be higher under the weighted average cost method because the numerator (cost of sales) would be higher and the denominator (inventory) would be lower than what was reported by Jollof under the FIFO method.
- The number of days of inventory would be lower under the weighted average cost method because the inventory turnover ratios would be higher.
- The gross profit margin ratios would all be lower under the weighted average cost method because cost of sales would be higher under the weighted average cost method than under the FIFO method.
- The current ratios would all be lower under the weighted average cost method because inventory carrying values would be lower than under the FIFO method (current liabilities would be the same under both methods).
- The return-on-assets ratios would all be lower under the weighted average cost method because the incremental profit added to the numerator (net income) has a greater impact than the incremental increase to the denominator (total assets). By way of example, assume that a company has €3 million in net income and €100 million in total assets using the weighted average cost method. If the company reports another €1 million in net income by using FIFO instead of weighted average cost, it would

EXHIBIT 10   (Continued)

then also report an additional €1 million in total assets (after tax). Based on this example, the return on assets is 3.00 percent (€3/€100) under the weighted average cost method and 3.96 percent (€4/€101) under the FIFO method.
- The debt-to-equity ratios would all be higher under the weighted average cost method because retained earnings would be lower than under the FIFO method (again assuming no inventory write-downs that would otherwise neutralize the differences between the inventory valuation methods).

Conversely, if inventory replacement costs were decreasing during 2015, 2016, and 2017 (and inventory quantity levels were stable or increasing), Jollof's cost of sales would have been lower, and its gross profit and inventory would have been higher under the weighted average cost method than were reported under the FIFO method (assuming no inventory write-downs that would otherwise neutralize the differences between the inventory valuation methods). As a result, the ratio assessment that was performed above would result in directly opposite conclusions.

8. SUMMARY

The choice of inventory valuation method (cost formula or cost flow assumption) can have a potentially significant impact on inventory carrying amounts and cost of sales. These in turn impact other financial statement items, such as current assets, total assets, gross profit, and net income. The financial statements and accompanying notes provide important information about a company's inventory accounting policies that the analyst needs to correctly assess financial performance and compare it with that of other companies. Key concepts in this chapter are as follows:

- Inventories are a major factor in the analysis of merchandising and manufacturing companies. Such companies generate their sales and profits through inventory transactions on a regular basis. An important consideration in determining profits for these companies is measuring the cost of sales when inventories are sold.
- The total cost of inventories comprises all costs of purchase, costs of conversion, and other costs incurred in bringing the inventories to their present location and condition. Storage costs of finished inventory and abnormal costs due to waste are typically treated as expenses in the period in which they occurred.
- The allowable inventory valuation methods implicitly involve different assumptions about cost flows. The choice of inventory valuation method determines how the cost of goods available for sale during the period is allocated between inventory and cost of sales.
- IFRS allow three inventory valuation methods (cost formulas): first-in, first-out (FIFO); weighted average cost; and specific identification. The specific identification method is used for inventories of items that are not ordinarily interchangeable and for goods or services produced and segregated for specific projects. US GAAP allow the three methods above plus the last-in, first-out (LIFO) method. The LIFO method is widely used in the United States for both tax and financial reporting purposes because of potential income tax savings.

- The choice of inventory method affects the financial statements and any financial ratios that are based on them. As a consequence, the analyst must carefully consider inventory valuation method differences when evaluating a company's performance over time or in comparison to industry data or industry competitors.
- A company must use the same cost formula for all inventories having a similar nature and use to the entity.
- The inventory accounting system (perpetual or periodic) may result in different values for cost of sales and ending inventory when the weighted average cost or LIFO inventory valuation method is used.
- Under US GAAP, companies that use the LIFO method must disclose in their financial notes the amount of the LIFO reserve or the amount that would have been reported in inventory if the FIFO method had been used. This information can be used to adjust reported LIFO inventory and cost of goods sold balances to the FIFO method for comparison purposes.
- LIFO liquidation occurs when the number of units in ending inventory declines from the number of units that were present at the beginning of the year. If inventory unit costs have generally risen from year to year, this will produce an inventory-related increase in gross profits.
- Consistency of inventory costing is required under both IFRS and US GAAP. If a company changes an accounting policy, the change must be justifiable and applied retrospectively to the financial statements. An exception to the retrospective restatement is when a company reporting under US GAAP changes to the LIFO method.
- Under IFRS, inventories are measured at the lower of cost and net realizable value. Net realizable value is the estimated selling price in the ordinary course of business less the estimated costs necessary to make the sale. Under US GAAP, inventories are measured at the lower of cost, market value, or net realizable value depending upon the inventory method used. Market value is defined as current replacement cost subject to an upper limit of net realizable value and a lower limit of net realizable value less a normal profit margin. Reversals of previous write-downs are permissible under IFRS but not under US GAAP.
- Reversals of inventory write-downs may occur under IFRS but are not allowed under US GAAP.
- Changes in the carrying amounts within inventory classifications (such as raw materials, work-in-process, and finished goods) may provide signals about a company's future sales and profits. Relevant information with respect to inventory management and future sales may be found in the Management Discussion and Analysis or similar items within the annual or quarterly reports, industry news and publications, and industry economic data.
- The inventory turnover ratio, number of days of inventory ratio, and gross profit margin ratio are useful in evaluating the management of a company's inventory.
- Inventory management may have a substantial impact on a company's activity, profitability, liquidity, and solvency ratios. It is critical for the analyst to be aware of industry trends and management's intentions.
- Financial statement disclosures provide information regarding the accounting policies adopted in measuring inventories, the principal uncertainties regarding the use of estimates related to inventories, and details of the inventory carrying amounts and costs. This information can greatly assist analysts in their evaluation of a company's inventory management.

PRACTICE PROBLEMS

1. Inventory cost is *least likely* to include:
   A. production-related storage costs.
   B. costs incurred as a result of normal waste of materials.
   C. transportation costs of shipping inventory to customers.

2. Mustard Seed PLC adheres to IFRS. It recently purchased inventory for €100 million and spent €5 million for storage prior to selling the goods. The amount it charged to inventory expense (€ millions) was *closest* to:
   A. €95.
   B. €100.
   C. €105.

3. Carrying inventory at a value above its historical cost would *most likely* be permitted if:
   A. the inventory was held by a producer of agricultural products.
   B. financial statements were prepared using US GAAP.
   C. the change resulted from a reversal of a previous write-down.

The following information relates to Questions 4 and 5.

A retail company is comparing different approaches to valuing inventory. The company has one product that it sells for $50.

EXHIBIT 1   Units Purchased and Sold (first quarter)

Date	Units Purchased	Purchase Price	Units Sold	Selling Price	Inventory Units on Hand
Jan 2	1,000	$20.00			1,000
Jan 17			500	$50.00	500
Feb 16	1,000	$18.00			1,500
Mar 3			1,200	$50.00	300
Mar 13	1,000	$17.00			1,300
Mar 23			500	$50.00	800
End of quarter totals:	3,000	$55,000	2,200	$110,000	

EXHIBIT 2   Comparison of Inventory Methods and Models

End of Quarter Valuations

March 31	Perpetual LIFO	Periodic LIFO	Perpetual FIFO
Sales	$110,000	$110,000	$110,000
Ending inventory		$16,000	$13,600
Cost of goods sold		$39,000	$41,400
Gross profit		$71,000	$68,600
Inventory turnover ratio	279%		

Note: LIFO is last in, first out and FIFO is first in, first out.

4. What is the value of ending inventory for the first quarter if the company uses a perpetual LIFO inventory valuation method?
   A. $14,500.
   B. $15,000.
   C. $16,000.

5. Which inventory accounting method results in the lowest inventory turnover ratio for the first quarter?
   A. Periodic LIFO.
   B. Perpetual LIFO.
   C. Perpetual FIFO.

6. During periods of rising inventory unit costs, a company using the FIFO method rather than the LIFO method will report a lower:
   A. current ratio.
   B. inventory turnover.
   C. gross profit margin.

7. LIFO reserve is *most likely* to increase when inventory unit:
   A. costs are increasing.
   B. costs are decreasing.
   C. levels are decreasing.

8. If inventory unit costs are increasing from period-to-period, a LIFO liquidation is *most likely* to result in an increase in:
   A. gross profit.
   B. LIFO reserve.
   C. inventory carrying amounts.

9. A company using the LIFO method reports the following in £:

	2018	2017
Cost of goods sold (COGS)	50,800	48,500
Ending inventories	10,550	10,000
LIFO reserve	4,320	2,600

Cost of goods sold for 2018 under the FIFO method is *closest* to:
   A. £48,530.
   B. £49,080.
   C. £52,520.

10. Eric's Used Book Store prepares its financial statements in accordance with IFRS. Inventory was purchased for £1 million and later marked down to £550,000. One of the books, however, was later discovered to be a rare collectible item, and the inventory is now worth an estimated £3 million. The inventory is *most likely* reported on the balance sheet at:
    A. £550,000.
    B. £1,000,000.
    C. £3,000,000.

11. Fernando's Pasta purchased inventory and later wrote it down. The current net realizable value is higher than the value when written down. Fernando's inventory balance will *most likely* be:
    A. higher if it complies with IFRS.
    B. higher if it complies with US GAAP.
    C. the same under US GAAP and IFRS.

12. A write down of the value of inventory to its net realizable value will have a positive effect on the:
    A. balance sheet.
    B. income statement.
    C. inventory turnover ratio.

For Questions 13–24, assume the companies use a periodic inventory system.

13. Cinnamon Corp. started business in 2017 and uses the weighted average cost method. During 2017, it purchased 45,000 units of inventory at €10 each and sold 40,000 units for €20 each. In 2018, it purchased another 50,000 units at €11 each and sold 45,000 units for €22 each. Its 2018 cost of sales (€ thousands) was *closest* to:
    A. €490.
    B. €491.
    C. €495.

14. Zimt AG started business in 2017 and uses the FIFO method. During 2017, it purchased 45,000 units of inventory at €10 each and sold 40,000 units for €20 each. In 2018, it purchased another 50,000 units at €11 each and sold 45,000 units for €22 each. Its 2018 ending inventory balance (€ thousands) was *closest* to:
    A. €105.
    B. €109.
    C. €110.

15. Zimt AG uses the FIFO method, and Nutmeg Inc. uses the LIFO method. Compared to the cost of replacing the inventory, during periods of rising prices, the cost of sales reported by:
    A. Zimt is too low.
    B. Nutmeg is too low.
    C. Nutmeg is too high.

16. Zimt AG uses the FIFO method, and Nutmeg Inc. uses the LIFO method. Compared to the cost of replacing the inventory, during periods of rising prices the ending inventory balance reported by:
    A. Zimt is too high.
    B. Nutmeg is too low.
    C. Nutmeg is too high.

17. Like many technology companies, TechnoTools operates in an environment of declining prices. Its reported profits will tend to be *highest* if it accounts for inventory using the:
    A. FIFO method.
    B. LIFO method.
    C. weighted average cost method.

18. Compared to using the weighted average cost method to account for inventory, during a period in which prices are generally rising, the current ratio of a company using the FIFO method would *most likely* be:
    A. lower.
    B. higher.
    C. dependent upon the interaction with accounts payable.

19. Zimt AG wrote down the value of its inventory in 2017 and reversed the write-down in 2018. Compared to the ratios that would have been calculated if the write-down had never occurred, Zimt's reported 2017:
    A. current ratio was too high.
    B. gross margin was too high.
    C. inventory turnover was too high.

20. Zimt AG wrote down the value of its inventory in 2017 and reversed the write-down in 2018. Compared to the results the company would have reported if the write-down had never occurred, Zimt's reported 2018:
    A. profit was overstated.
    B. cash flow from operations was overstated.
    C. year-end inventory balance was overstated.

21. Compared to a company that uses the FIFO method, during periods of rising prices a company that uses the LIFO method will *most likely* appear more:
    A. liquid.
    B. efficient.
    C. profitable.

22. Nutmeg, Inc. uses the LIFO method to account for inventory. During years in which inventory unit costs are generally rising and in which the company purchases more inventory than it sells to customers, its reported gross profit margin will *most likely* be:
    A. lower than it would be if the company used the FIFO method.
    B. higher than it would be if the company used the FIFO method.
    C. about the same as it would be if the company used the FIFO method.

23. Compared to using the FIFO method to account for inventory, during periods of rising prices, a company using the LIFO method is *most likely* to report higher:
    A. net income.
    B. cost of sales.
    C. income taxes.

24. Carey Company adheres to US GAAP, whereas Jonathan Company adheres to IFRS. It is *least likely* that:
    A. Carey has reversed an inventory write-down.
    B. Jonathan has reversed an inventory write-down.
    C. Jonathan and Carey both use the FIFO inventory accounting method.

25. Company A adheres to US GAAP, and Company B adheres to IFRS. Which of the following is *most likely* to be disclosed on the financial statements of both companies?
    A. Any material income resulting from the liquidation of LIFO inventory.
    B. The amount of inventories recognized as an expense during the period.
    C. The circumstances that led to the reversal of a write down of inventories.

26. Which of the following *most likely* signals that a manufacturing company expects demand for its product to increase?
    A. Finished goods inventory growth rate higher than the sales growth rate.
    B. Higher unit volumes of work in progress and raw material inventories.
    C. Substantially higher finished goods, with lower raw materials and work-in-process.

27. Compared with a company that uses the FIFO method, during a period of rising unit inventory costs, a company using the LIFO method will *most likely* appear more:
    A. liquid.
    B. efficient.
    C. profitable.

28. In a period of declining inventory unit costs and constant or increasing inventory quantities, which inventory method is *most likely* to result in a higher debt-to-equity ratio?
    A. LIFO.
    B. FIFO.
    C. Weighted average cost.

The following information relates to Questions 29–36

Hans Annan, CFA, a food and beverage analyst, is reviewing Century Chocolate's inventory policies as part of his evaluation of the company. Century Chocolate, based in Switzerland, manufactures chocolate products and purchases and resells other confectionery products to complement its chocolate line. Annan visited Century Chocolate's manufacturing facility last year. He learned that cacao beans, imported from Brazil, represent the most significant raw material and that the work-in-progress inventory consists primarily of three items: roasted cacao beans, a thick paste produced from the beans (called chocolate liquor), and a sweetened mixture that needs to be "conched" to produce chocolate. On the tour, Annan learned that the conching process ranges from a few hours for lower-quality products to six days for the highest-quality chocolates. While there, Annan saw the facility's climate-controlled area where manufactured finished products (cocoa and chocolate) and purchased finished goods are stored prior to shipment to customers. After touring the facility, Annan had a discussion with Century Chocolate's CFO regarding the types of costs that were included in each inventory category.

Annan has asked his assistant, Joanna Kern, to gather some preliminary information regarding Century Chocolate's financial statements and inventories. He also asked Kern to calculate the inventory turnover ratios for Century Chocolate and another chocolate manufacturer for the most recent five years. Annan does not know Century Chocolate's most direct competitor, so he asks Kern to do some research and select the most appropriate company for the ratio comparison.

Kern reports back that Century Chocolate prepares its financial statements in accordance with IFRS. She tells Annan that the policy footnote states that raw materials and purchased finished goods are valued at purchase cost whereas work in progress and manufactured finished goods are valued at production cost. Raw material inventories and purchased finished goods are accounted for using the FIFO (first-in, first-out) method, and the weighted average cost method is used for other inventories. An allowance is established when the net realizable value of any inventory item is lower than the value calculated above.

Kern provides Annan with the selected financial statements and inventory data for Century Chocolate shown in Exhibits 1 through 5. The ratio exhibit Kern prepared compares Century Chocolate's inventory turnover ratios to those of Gordon's Goodies, a US-based company. Annan returns the exhibit and tells Kern to select a different competitor that reports using

IFRS rather than US GAAP. During this initial review, Annan asks Kern why she has not indicated whether Century Chocolate uses a perpetual or a periodic inventory system. Kern replies that she learned that Century Chocolate uses a perpetual system but did not include this information in her report because inventory values would be the same under either a perpetual or periodic inventory system. Annan tells Kern she is wrong and directs her to research the matter.

While Kern is revising her analysis, Annan reviews the most recent month's Cocoa Market Review from the International Cocoa Organization. He is drawn to the statement that "the ICCO daily price, averaging prices in both futures markets, reached a 29-year high in US$ terms and a 23-year high in SDRs terms (the SDR unit comprises a basket of major currencies used in international trade: US$, euro, pound sterling and yen)." Annan makes a note that he will need to factor the potential continuation of this trend into his analysis.

EXHIBIT 1   Century Chocolate Income Statements (CHF Millions)

For Years Ended December 31	2018	2017
Sales	95,290	93,248
Cost of sales	–41,043	–39,047
Marketing, administration, and other expenses	–35,318	–42,481
Profit before taxes	**18,929**	**11,720**
Taxes	–3,283	–2,962
Profit for the period	**15,646**	**8,758**

EXHIBIT 2   Century Chocolate Balance Sheets (CHF Millions)

December 31	2018	2017
Cash, cash equivalents, and short-term investments	6,190	8,252
Trade receivables and related accounts, net	11,654	12,910
Inventories, net	8,100	7,039
Other current assets	2,709	2,812
Total current assets	**28,653**	**31,013**
Property, plant, and equipment, net	18,291	19,130
Other non-current assets	45,144	49,875
Total assets	**92,088**	**100,018**
Trade and other payables	10,931	12,299
Other current liabilities	17,873	25,265
Total current liabilities	**28,804**	**37,564**
Non-current liabilities	15,672	14,963
Total liabilities	**44,476**	**52,527**
Equity		
Share capital	332	341
Retained earnings and other reserves	47,280	47,150
Total equity	**47,612**	**47,491**
Total liabilities and shareholders' equity	**92,088**	**100,018**

EXHIBIT 3   Century Chocolate Supplementary Footnote Disclosures: Inventories (CHF Millions)

December 31	2018	2017
Raw Materials	2,154	1,585
Work in Progress	1,061	1,027
Finished Goods	5,116	4,665
Total inventories before allowance	8,331	7,277
Allowance for write-downs to net realizable value	–231	–238
Total inventories net of allowance	8,100	7,039

EXHIBIT 4   Century Chocolate Inventory Record for Purchased Lemon Drops

Date		Cartons	Per Unit Amount (CHF)
	Beginning inventory	100	22
Feb. 4, 09	Purchase	40	25
Apr. 3, 09	Sale	50	32
Jul. 23, 09	Purchase	70	30
Aug. 16, 09	Sale	100	32
Sep. 9, 09	Sale	35	32
Nov. 15, 09	Purchase	100	28

EXHIBIT 5   Century Chocolate Net Realizable Value Information for Black Licorice Jelly Beans

	2018	2017
FIFO cost of inventory at December 31 (CHF)	314,890	374,870
Ending inventory at December 31 (Kilograms)	77,750	92,560
Cost per unit (CHF)	4.05	4.05
Net Realizable Value (CHF per Kilograms)	4.20	3.95

29. The costs *least likely* to be included by the CFO as inventory are:
    A. storage costs for the chocolate liquor.
    B. excise taxes paid to the government of Brazil for the cacao beans.
    C. storage costs for chocolate and purchased finished goods awaiting shipment to customers.

30. What is the *most likely* justification for Century Chocolate's choice of inventory valuation method for its purchased finished goods?
    A. It is the preferred method under IFRS.
    B. It allocates the same per unit cost to both cost of sales and inventory.
    C. Ending inventory reflects the cost of goods purchased most recently.

31. In Kern's comparative ratio analysis, the 2018 inventory turnover ratio for Century Chocolate is *closest* to:
    A. 5.07.
    B. 5.42.
    C. 5.55.

32. The *most accurate* statement regarding Annan's reasoning for requiring Kern to select a competitor that reports under IFRS for comparative purposes is that under US GAAP:
   A. fair values are used to value inventory.
   B. the LIFO method is permitted to value inventory.
   C. the specific identification method is permitted to value inventory.

33. Annan's statement regarding the perpetual and periodic inventory systems is most significant when which of the following costing systems is used?
   A. LIFO.
   B. FIFO.
   C. Specific identification.

34. Using the inventory record for purchased lemon drops shown in Exhibit 4, the cost of sales for 2018 will be *closest* to:
   A. CHF 3,550.
   B. CHF 4,550.
   C. CHF 4,850.

35. Ignoring any tax effect, the 2018 net realizable value reassessment for the black licorice jelly beans will *most likely* result in:
   A. an increase in gross profit of CHF 7,775.
   B. an increase in gross profit of CHF 11,670.
   C. no impact on cost of sales because under IFRS, write-downs cannot be reversed.

36. If the trend noted in the ICCO report continues and Century Chocolate plans to maintain constant or increasing inventory quantities, the *most likely* impact on Century Chocolate's financial statements related to its raw materials inventory will be:
   A. a cost of sales that more closely reflects current replacement values.
   B. a higher allocation of the total cost of goods available for sale to cost of sales.
   C. a higher allocation of the total cost of goods available for sale to ending inventory.

The following information relates to Questions 37–42

John Martinson, CFA, is an equity analyst with a large pension fund. His supervisor, Linda Packard, asks him to write a report on Karp Inc. Karp prepares its financial statements in accordance with US GAAP. Packard is particularly interested in the effects of the company's use of the LIFO method to account for its inventory. For this purpose, Martinson collects the financial data presented in Exhibits 1 and 2.

EXHIBIT 1   Balance Sheet Information (US$ Millions)

As of December 31	2018	2017
Cash and cash equivalents	172	157
Accounts receivable	626	458
Inventories	620	539
Other current assets	125	65
Total current assets	1,543	1,219
Property and equipment, net	3,035	2,972
Total assets	4,578	4,191

EXHIBIT 1   (Continued)

As of December 31	2018	2017
Total current liabilities	1,495	1,395
Long-term debt	644	604
Total liabilities	2,139	1,999
Common stock and paid in capital	1,652	1,652
Retained earnings	787	540
Total shareholders' equity	2,439	2,192
Total liabilities and shareholders' equity	4,578	4,191

EXHIBIT 2   Income Statement Information (US$ Millions)

For the Year Ended December 31	2018	2017
Sales	4,346	4,161
Cost of goods sold	2,211	2,147
Depreciation and amortization expense	139	119
Selling, general, and administrative expense	1,656	1,637
Interest expense	31	18
Income tax expense	62	48
Net income	247	192

Martinson finds the following information in the notes to the financial statements:

- The LIFO reserves as of December 31, 2018 and 2017 are $155 million and $117 million respectively, and
- The effective income tax rate applicable to Karp for 2018 and earlier periods is 20 percent.

37. If Karp had used FIFO instead of LIFO, the amount of inventory reported as of 31 December 2018 would have been *closest* to:
    A. $465 million.
    B. $658 million.
    C. $775 million.

38. If Karp had used FIFO instead of LIFO, the amount of cost of goods sold reported by Karp for the year ended 31 December 2018 would have been *closest* to:
    A. $2,056 million.
    B. $2,173 million.
    C. $2,249 million.

39. If Karp had used FIFO instead of LIFO, its reported net income for the year ended 31 December 2018 would have been higher by an amount *closest to*:
    A. $30 million.
    B. $38 million.
    C. $155 million.

40. If Karp had used FIFO instead of LIFO, Karp's retained earnings as of 31 December 2018 would have been higher by an amount *closest to*:
    A. $117 million.
    B. $124 million.
    C. $155 million.

41. If Karp had used FIFO instead of LIFO, which of the following ratios computed as of 31 December 2018 would *most likely* have been lower?
    A. Cash ratio.
    B. Current ratio.
    C. Gross profit margin.

42. If Karp had used FIFO instead of LIFO, its debt to equity ratio computed as of 31 December 2018 would have:
    A. increased.
    B. decreased.
    C. remained unchanged.

The following information relates to Questions 43–48

Robert Groff, an equity analyst, is preparing a report on Crux Corp. As part of his report, Groff makes a comparative financial analysis between Crux and its two main competitors, Rolby Corp. and Mikko Inc. Crux and Mikko report under US GAAP, and Rolby reports under IFRS.

Groff gathers information on Crux, Rolby, and Mikko. The relevant financial information he compiles is in Exhibit 1. Some information on the industry is in Exhibit 2.

EXHIBIT 1   Selected Financial Information (US$ Millions)

	Crux	Rolby	Mikko
Inventory valuation method	LIFO	FIFO	LIFO
From the Balance Sheets			
As of December 31, 2018			
Inventory, gross	480	620	510
Valuation allowance	20	25	14
Inventory, net	460	595	496
Total debt	1,122	850	732
Total shareholders' equity	2,543	2,403	2,091
As of December 31, 2017			
Inventory, gross	465	602	401
Valuation allowance	23	15	12
Inventory, net	442	587	389
From the Income Statements			
Year Ended December 31, 2018			
Revenues	4,609	5,442	3,503
Cost of goods sold[a]	3,120	3,782	2,550
Net income	229	327	205
[a]Charges included in cost of goods sold for inventory write-downs*	13	15	15

* This does not match the change in the inventory valuation allowance because the valuation allowance is reduced to reflect the valuation allowance attached to items sold and increased for additional necessary write-downs.

LIFO Reserve

As of December 31, 2018	55	0	77
As of December 31, 2017	72	0	50
As of December 31, 2016	96	0	43

Tax Rate

Effective tax rate	30%	30%	30%

EXHIBIT 2   Industry Information

	2018	2017	2016
Raw materials price index	112	105	100
Finished goods price index	114	106	100

To compare the financial performance of the three companies, Groff decides to convert LIFO figures into FIFO figures, and adjust figures to assume no valuation allowance is recognized by any company.

After reading Groff's draft report, his supervisor, Rachel Borghi, asks him the following questions:

Question 1   Which company's gross profit margin would best reflect current costs of the industry?

Question 2   Would Rolby's valuation method show a higher gross profit margin than Crux's under an inflationary, a deflationary, or a stable price scenario?

Question 3   Which group of ratios usually appears more favorable with an inventory write-down?

43. Crux's inventory turnover ratio computed as of December 31, 2018, after the adjustments suggested by Groff, is *closest* to:
    A. 5.67.
    B. 5.83.
    C. 6.13.

44. Rolby's net profit margin for the year ended December 31, 2018, after the adjustments suggested by Groff, is *closest* to:
    A. 6.01%.
    B. 6.20%.
    C. 6.28%.

45. Compared with its unadjusted debt-to-equity ratio, Mikko's debt-to-equity ratio as of December 31, 2018, after the adjustments suggested by Groff, is:
    A. lower.
    B. higher.
    C. the same.

46. The *best* answer to Borghi's Question 1 is:
    A. Crux's.
    B. Rolby's.
    C. Mikko's.

47. The *best* answer to Borghi's Question 2 is:
    A. Stable.
    B. Inflationary.
    C. Deflationary.

48. The *best* answer to Borghi's Question 3 is:
    A. Activity ratios.
    B. Solvency ratios.
    C. Profitability ratios.

The following information relates to Questions 49–55

ZP Corporation is a (hypothetical) multinational corporation headquartered in Japan that trades on numerous stock exchanges. ZP prepares its consolidated financial statements in accordance with US GAAP. Excerpts from ZP's 2018 annual report are shown in Exhibits 1–3.

EXHIBIT 1   Consolidated Balance Sheets (¥ Millions)

December 31	2017	2018
Current Assets		
Cash and cash equivalents	¥542,849	¥814,760
⋮	⋮	⋮
Inventories	608,572	486,465
⋮	⋮	⋮
Total current assets	4,028,742	3,766,309
⋮	⋮	⋮
Total assets	**¥10,819,440**	**¥9,687,346**
⋮	⋮	⋮
Total current liabilities	¥3,980,247	¥3,529,765
⋮	⋮	⋮
Total long-term liabilities	2,663,795	2,624,002
Minority interest in consolidated subsidiaries	218,889	179,843
Total shareholders' equity	3,956,509	3,353,736
Total liabilities and shareholders' equity	**¥10,819,440**	**¥9,687,346**

EXHIBIT 2   Consolidated Statements of Income (¥ Millions)

For the years ended December 31	2016	2017	2018
Net revenues			
Sales of products	¥7,556,699	¥8,273,503	¥6,391,240
Financing operations	425,998	489,577	451,950
	7,982,697	8,763,080	6,843,190
Cost and expenses			
Cost of products sold	6,118,742	6,817,446	5,822,805
Cost of financing operations	290,713	356,005	329,128
Selling, general and administrative	827,005	832,837	844,927
⋮	⋮	⋮	⋮
Operating income (loss)	746,237	756,792	−153,670
⋮	⋮	⋮	⋮
Net income	¥548,011	¥572,626	−¥145,646

EXHIBIT 3   Selected Disclosures in the 2018 Annual Report

Management's Discussion and Analysis of Financial Condition and Results of Operations
Cost reduction efforts were offset by increased prices of raw materials, other production materials and parts. . . . Inventories decreased during fiscal 2009 by ¥122.1 billion, or 20.1%, to ¥486.5 billion. This reflects the impacts of decreased sales volumes and fluctuations in foreign currency translation rates.

Management & Corporate Information
Risk Factors
Industry and Business Risks
The worldwide market for our products is highly competitive. ZP faces intense competition from other manufacturers in the respective markets in which it operates. Competition has intensified due to the worldwide deterioration in economic conditions. In addition, competition is likely to further intensify because of continuing globalization, possibly resulting in industry reorganization. Factors affecting competition include product quality and features, the amount of time required for innovation and development, pricing, reliability, safety, economy in use, customer service, and financing terms. Increased competition may lead to lower unit sales and excess production capacity and excess inventory. This may result in a further downward price pressure.

ZP's ability to adequately respond to the recent rapid changes in the industry and to maintain its competitiveness will be fundamental to its future success in maintaining and expanding its market share in existing and new markets.

Notes to Consolidated Financial Statements
2. Summary of significant accounting policies:
Inventories. Inventories are valued at cost, not in excess of market. Cost is determined on the "average-cost" basis, except for the cost of finished products carried by certain subsidiary companies, which is determined on a "last-in, first-out" ("LIFO") basis. Inventories valued on the LIFO basis totaled ¥94,578 million and ¥50,037 million at December 31, 2017 and 2018, respectively. Had the "first-in, first-out" basis been used for those companies using the LIFO basis, inventories would have been ¥10,120 million and ¥19,660 million higher than reported at December 31, 2017 and 2018, respectively.

9. Inventories:
Inventories consist of the following:

December 31 (¥ Millions)	2017	2018
Finished goods	¥ 403,856	¥ 291,977
Raw materials	99,869	85,966
Work in process	79,979	83,890
Supplies and other	24,868	24,632
	¥ 608,572	¥ 486,465

49. The MD&A indicated that the prices of raw material, other production materials, and parts increased. Based on the inventory valuation methods described in Note 2, which inventory classification would *least accurately* reflect current prices?
    A. Raw materials.
    B. Finished goods.
    C. Work in process.

50. The 2017 inventory value as reported on the 2018 Annual Report if the company had used the FIFO inventory valuation method instead of the LIFO inventory valuation method for a portion of its inventory would be *closest* to:
    A. ¥104,698 million.
    B. ¥506,125 million.
    C. ¥618,692 million.

51. If ZP had prepared its financial statement in accordance with IFRS, the inventory turnover ratio (using average inventory) for 2018 would be:
    A. lower.
    B. higher.
    C. the same.

52. Inventory levels decreased from 2017 to 2018 for all of the following reasons *except*:
    A. LIFO liquidation.
    B. decreased sales volume.
    C. fluctuations in foreign currency translation rates.

53. Which observation is *most likely* a result of looking only at the information reported in Note 9?
    A. Increased competition has led to lower unit sales.
    B. There have been significant price increases in supplies.
    C. Management expects a further downturn in sales during 2010.

54. Note 2 indicates that, "Inventories valued on the LIFO basis totaled ¥94,578 million and ¥50,037 million at December 31, 2017 and 2018, respectively." Based on this, the LIFO reserve should *most likely*:
    A. increase.
    B. decrease.
    C. remain the same.

55. The Industry and Business Risk excerpt states that, "Increased competition may lead to lower unit sales and excess production capacity and excess inventory. This may result in a further downward price pressure." The downward price pressure could lead to inventory that is valued above current market prices or net realizable value. Any write-downs of inventory are *least likely* to have a significant effect on the inventory valued using:
    A. weighted average cost.
    B. first-in, first-out (FIFO).
    C. last-in, first-out (LIFO).

CHAPTER **8**

LONG-LIVED ASSETS

Elaine Henry, PhD, CFA
Elizabeth A. Gordon, PhD, MBA, CPA

LEARNING OUTCOMES

After completing this chapter, you will be able to do the following:

- distinguish between costs that are capitalized and costs that are expensed in the period in which they are incurred;
- compare the financial reporting of the following types of intangible assets: purchased, internally developed, acquired in a business combination;
- explain and evaluate how capitalizing versus expensing costs in the period in which they are incurred affects financial statements and ratios;
- describe the different depreciation methods for property, plant, and equipment and calculate depreciation expense;
- describe how the choice of depreciation method and assumptions concerning useful life and residual value affect depreciation expense, financial statements, and ratios;
- describe the different amortization methods for intangible assets with finite lives and calculate amortization expense;
- describe how the choice of amortization method and assumptions concerning useful life and residual value affect amortization expense, financial statements, and ratios;
- describe the revaluation model;
- explain the impairment of property, plant, and equipment and intangible assets;
- explain the derecognition of property, plant, and equipment and intangible assets;
- explain and evaluate how impairment, revaluation, and derecognition of property, plant, and equipment and intangible assets affect financial statements and ratios;
- describe the financial statement presentation of, and disclosures relating to, property, plant, and equipment and intangible assets;
- analyze and interpret financial statement disclosures regarding property, plant, and equipment and intangible assets;
- compare the financial reporting of investment property with that of property, plant, and equipment.

1. INTRODUCTION

Long-lived assets, also referred to as non-current assets or long-term assets, are assets that are expected to provide economic benefits over a future period of time, typically greater than one year.[1] Long-lived assets may be tangible, intangible, or financial assets. Examples of long-lived tangible assets, typically referred to as **property, plant, and equipment** and sometimes as fixed assets, include land, buildings, furniture and fixtures, machinery and equipment, and vehicles; examples of long-lived **intangible assets** (assets lacking physical substance) include patents and trademarks; and examples of long-lived financial assets include investments in equity or debt securities issued by other entities. The scope of this chapter is limited to long-lived tangible and intangible assets (hereafter, referred to for simplicity as long-lived assets).

The first issue in accounting for a long-lived asset is determining its cost at acquisition. The second issue is how to allocate the cost to expense over time. The costs of most long-lived assets are capitalized and then allocated as expenses in the profit or loss (income) statement over the period of time during which they are expected to provide economic benefits. The two main types of long-lived assets with costs that are typically *not* allocated over time are land, which is not depreciated, and those intangible assets with indefinite useful lives. Additional issues that arise are the treatment of subsequent costs incurred related to the asset, the use of the cost model versus the revaluation model, unexpected declines in the value of the asset, classification of the asset with respect to intent (for example, held for use or held for sale), and the derecognition of the asset.

This chapter is organised as follows. Section 2 describes and illustrates accounting for the acquisition of long-lived assets, with particular attention to the impact of capitalizing versus expensing expenditures. Section 3 describes the allocation of the costs of long-lived assets over their useful lives. Section 4 discusses the revaluation model that is based on changes in the fair value of an asset. Section 5 covers the concepts of impairment (unexpected decline in the value of an asset). Section 6 describes accounting for the derecognition of long-lived assets. Section 7 describes financial statement presentation, disclosures, and analysis of long-lived assets. Section 8 discusses differences in financial reporting of investment property compared with property, plant, and equipment. A summary is followed by practice problems.

2. ACQUISITION OF LONG-LIVED ASSETS

Upon acquisition, property, plant, and equipment (tangible assets with an economic life of longer than one year and intended to be held for the company's own use) are recorded on the balance sheet at cost, which is typically the same as their fair value.[2] Accounting for an intangible asset depends on how the asset is acquired. If several assets are acquired as part of a group, the purchase price is allocated to each asset on the basis of its fair value. An asset's cost potentially includes expenditures additional to the purchase price.

---

[1] In some industries, inventory is held longer than one year but is nonetheless reported as a current asset.
[2] Fair value is defined in International Financial Reporting Standards (IFRS) and under US generally accepted accounting principles (US GAAP) in the Financial Accounting Standards Board (FASB) Accounting Standards Codification (ASC) as "the price that would be received to sell an asset or paid to transfer a liability in an orderly transaction between market participants at the measurement date." [IFRS 13 and FASB ASC Topic 820]

A key concept in accounting for expenditures related to long-lived assets is whether and when such expenditures are capitalized (i.e., included in the asset shown on the balance sheet) versus expensed (i.e., treated as an expense of the period on the income statement). After examining the specific treatment of certain expenditures, we will consider the general financial statement impact of capitalizing versus expensing and two analytical issues related to the decision—namely, the effects on an individual company's trend analysis and on comparability across companies.

2.1. Property, Plant, and Equipment

This section primarily discusses the accounting treatment for the acquisition of long-lived tangible assets (property, plant, and equipment) through purchase. Assets can be acquired by methods other than purchase.[3] When an asset is exchanged for another asset, the asset acquired is recorded at fair value if reliable measures of fair value exist. Fair value is the fair value of the asset given up unless the fair value of the asset acquired is more clearly evident. If there is no reliable measure of fair value, the acquired asset is measured at the carrying amount of the asset given up. In this case, the carrying amount of the assets is unchanged, and no gain or loss is reported.

Typically, accounting for the exchange involves removing the carrying amount of the asset given up, adding a fair value for the asset acquired, and reporting any difference between the carrying amount and the fair value as a gain or loss. A gain would be reported when the fair value used for the newly acquired asset exceeds the carrying amount of the asset given up. A loss would be reported when the fair value used for the newly acquired asset is less than the carrying amount of the asset given up.

When property, plant, or equipment is purchased, the buyer records the asset at cost. In addition to the purchase price, the buyer also includes, as part of the cost of an asset, all the expenditures necessary to get the asset ready for its intended use. For example, freight costs borne by the purchaser to get the asset to the purchaser's place of business and special installation and testing costs required to make the asset usable are included in the total cost of the asset.

Subsequent expenditures related to long-lived assets are included as part of the recorded value of the assets on the balance sheet (i.e., capitalized) if they are expected to provide benefits beyond one year in the future and are expensed if they are not expected to provide benefits in future periods. Expenditures that extend the original life of the asset are typically capitalized. Example 1 illustrates the difference between costs that are capitalized and costs that are expensed in a period.

EXAMPLE 1   Acquisition of PPE

Assume a (hypothetical) company, Trofferini S.A., incurred the following expenditures to purchase a towel and tissue roll machine: €10,900 purchase price including taxes, €200 for delivery of the machine, €300 for installation and testing of the machine, and €100 to train staff on maintaining the machine. In addition, the company paid a

---

[3] IAS 16 *Property, Plant and Equipment*, paragraphs 24–26 [Measurement of Cost]; IAS 38 *Intangible Assets*, paragraphs 45–47 [Exchange of Assets]; and FASB ASC Section 845-10-30 [Nonmonetary Transactions – Overall – Initial Measurement].

construction team €350 to reinforce the factory floor and ceiling joists to accommodate the machine's weight. The company also paid €1,500 to repair the factory roof (a repair expected to extend the useful life of the factory by five years) and €1,000 to have the exterior of the factory and adjoining offices repainted for maintenance reasons. The repainting neither extends the life of factory and offices nor improves their usability.

1. Which of these expenditures will be capitalized and which will be expensed?
2. How will the treatment of these expenditures affect the company's financial statements?

Solution to 1: The company will capitalize as part of the cost of the machine all costs that are necessary to get the new machine ready for its intended use: €10,900 purchase price, €200 for delivery, €300 for installation and testing, and €350 to reinforce the factory floor and ceiling joists to accommodate the machine's weight (which was necessary to use the machine and does not increase the value of the factory). The €100 to train staff is not necessary to get the asset ready for its intended use and will be expensed.

The company will capitalize the expenditure of €1,500 to repair the factory roof because the repair is expected to extend the useful life of the factory. The company will expense the €1,000 to have the exterior of the factory and adjoining offices repainted because the painting does not extend the life or alter the productive capacity of the buildings.

Solution to 2: The costs related to the machine that are capitalized—€10,900 purchase price, €200 for delivery, €300 for installation and testing, and €350 to prepare the factory—will increase the carrying amount of the machine asset as shown on the balance sheet and will be included as investing cash outflows. The item related to the factory that is capitalized—the €1,500 roof repair—will increase the carrying amount of the factory asset as shown on the balance sheet and is an investing cash outflow. The expenditures of €100 to train staff and €1,000 to paint are expensed in the period and will reduce the amount of income reported on the company's income statement (and thus reduce retained earnings on the balance sheet) and the operating cash flow.

Example 1 describes capitalizing versus expensing in the context of purchasing property, plant, and equipment. When a company constructs an asset (or acquires an asset that requires a long period of time to get ready for its intended use), borrowing costs incurred directly related to the construction are generally capitalized. Constructing a building, whether for sale (in which case, the building is classified as inventory) or for the company's own use (in which case, the building is classified as a long-lived asset), typically requires a substantial amount of time. To finance construction, any borrowing costs incurred prior to the asset being ready for its intended use are capitalized as part of the cost of the asset. The company determines the interest rate to use on the basis of its existing borrowings or, if applicable, on a borrowing specifically incurred for constructing the asset. If a company takes out a loan specifically to construct a building, the interest cost on that loan during the time of construction would be capitalized as part of the building's cost. Under IFRS, but not under US GAAP, income earned on temporarily investing the borrowed monies decreases the amount of borrowing costs eligible for capitalization.

Thus, a company's interest costs for a period are included either on the balance sheet (to the extent they are capitalized as part of an asset) or on the income statement (to the extent they are expensed). If the interest expenditure is incurred in connection with constructing an asset for the company's own use, the capitalized interest appears on the balance sheet as a part of the relevant long-lived asset (i.e., property, plant, and equipment). The capitalized interest is expensed over time as the property is depreciated and is thus part of subsequent years' depreciation expense rather than interest expense of the current period. If the interest expenditure is incurred in connection with constructing an asset to sell (for example, by a home builder), the capitalized interest appears on the company's balance sheet as part of inventory. The capitalized interest is expensed as part of the cost of goods sold when the asset is sold. Interest payments made prior to completion of construction that are capitalized are classified as an investing cash outflow. Expensed interest may be classified as an operating or financing cash outflow under IFRS and is classified as an operating cash outflow under US GAAP.

EXAMPLE 2   Capitalized Borrowing Costs

BILDA S.A., a hypothetical company, borrows €1,000,000 at an interest rate of 10 percent per year on January 1, 2010 to finance the construction of a factory that will have a useful life of 40 years. Construction is completed after two years, during which time the company earns €20,000 by temporarily investing the loan proceeds.

1. What is the amount of interest that will be capitalized under IFRS, and how would that amount differ from the amount that would be capitalized under US GAAP?
2. Where will the capitalized borrowing cost appear on the company's financial statements?

Solution to 1: The total amount of interest paid on the loan during construction is €200,000 (= €1,000,000 × 10% × 2 years). Under IFRS, the amount of borrowing cost eligible for capitalization is reduced by the €20,000 interest income from temporarily investing the loan proceeds, so the amount to be capitalized is €180,000. Under US GAAP, the amount to be capitalized is €200,000.

Solution to 2: The capitalized borrowing costs will appear on the company's balance sheet as a component of property, plant, and equipment. In the years prior to completion of construction, the interest paid will appear on the statement of cash flows as an investment activity. Over time, as the property is depreciated, the capitalized interest component is part of subsequent years' depreciation expense on the company's income statement.

2.2. Intangible Assets

Intangible assets are assets lacking physical substance. Intangible assets include items that involve exclusive rights, such as patents, copyrights, trademarks, and franchises. Under IFRS, identifiable intangible assets must meet three definitional criteria. They must be (1) identifiable (either capable of being separated from the entity or arising from contractual or legal rights),

(2) under the control of the company, and (3) expected to generate future economic benefits. In addition, two recognition criteria must be met: (1) It is probable that the expected future economic benefits of the asset will flow to the company, and (2) the cost of the asset can be reliably measured. Goodwill, which is not considered an identifiable intangible asset,[4] arises when one company purchases another and the acquisition price exceeds the fair value of the net identifiable assets (both the tangible assets and the identifiable intangible assets, minus liabilities) acquired.

Accounting for an intangible asset depends on how it is acquired. The following sections describe accounting for intangible assets obtained in three ways: purchased in situations other than business combinations, developed internally, and acquired in business combinations.

2.2.1. Intangible Assets Purchased in Situations Other than Business Combinations

Intangible assets purchased in situations other than business combinations, such as buying a patent, are treated at acquisition the same as long-lived tangible assets; they are recorded at their fair value when acquired, which is assumed to be equivalent to the purchase price. If several intangible assets are acquired as part of a group, the purchase price is allocated to each asset on the basis of its fair value.

In deciding how to treat individual intangible assets for analytical purposes, analysts are particularly aware that companies must use a substantial amount of judgment and numerous assumptions to determine the fair value of individual intangible assets. For analysis, therefore, understanding the types of intangible assets acquired can often be more useful than focusing on the values assigned to the individual assets. In other words, an analyst would typically be more interested in understanding what assets a company acquired (for example, franchise rights) than in the precise portion of the purchase price a company allocated to each asset. Understanding the types of assets a company acquires can offer insights into the company's strategic direction and future operating potential.

2.2.2. Intangible Assets Developed Internally

In contrast with the treatment of construction costs of tangible assets, the costs to internally develop intangible assets are generally expensed when incurred. There are some situations, however, in which the costs incurred to internally develop an intangible asset are capitalized. The general analytical issues related to the capitalizing-versus-expensing decision apply here—namely, comparability across companies and the effect on an individual company's trend analysis.

The general requirement that costs to internally develop intangible assets be expensed should be compared with capitalizing the cost of acquiring intangible assets in situations other than business combinations. Because costs associated with internally developing intangible assets are usually expensed, a company that has internally developed such intangible assets as patents, copyrights, or brands through expenditures on R&D or advertising will recognize a lower amount of assets than a company that has obtained intangible assets through external purchase. In addition, on the statement of cash flows, costs of internally developing intangible assets are classified as operating cash outflows whereas costs of acquiring intangible assets are classified as investing cash outflows. Differences in strategy (developing versus acquiring intangible assets) can thus impact financial ratios.

---

[4] The IFRS definition of an intangible asset as an "identifiable non-monetary asset without physical substance" applies to intangible assets not specifically dealt with in standards other than IAS 38. The definition of intangible assets under US GAAP—"assets (other than financial assets) that lack physical substance"—includes goodwill in the definition of an intangible asset.

IFRS require that expenditures on research (or during the research phase of an internal project) be expensed rather than capitalized as an intangible asset.[5] Research is defined as "original and planned investigation undertaken with the prospect of gaining new scientific or technical knowledge and understanding."[6] The "research phase of an internal project" refers to the period during which a company cannot demonstrate that an intangible asset is being created—for example, the search for alternative materials or systems to use in a production process. In contrast with the treatment of research-phase expenditures, IFRS allow companies to recognize an intangible asset arising from development expenditures (or the development phase of an internal project) if certain criteria are met, including a demonstration of the technical feasibility of completing the intangible asset and the intent to use or sell the asset. Development is defined as "the application of research findings or other knowledge to a plan or design for the production of new or substantially improved materials, devices, products, processes, systems or services before the start of commercial production or use."[7]

Generally, US GAAP require that both research and development costs be expensed as incurred but require capitalization of certain costs related to software development.[8] Costs incurred to develop a software product for sale are expensed until the product's technological feasibility is established and are capitalized thereafter. Similarly, companies' expense costs related to the development of software for internal use until it is probable that the project will be completed and that the software will be used as intended. Thereafter, development costs are capitalized. The probability that the project will be completed is easier to demonstrate than is technological feasibility. The capitalized costs, related directly to developing software for sale or internal use, include the costs of employees who help build and test the software. The treatment of software development costs under US GAAP is similar to the treatment of all costs of internally developed intangible assets under IFRS.

EXAMPLE 3   Software Development Costs

Assume REH AG, a hypothetical company, incurs expenditures of €1,000 per month during the fiscal year ended December 31, 2019 to develop software for internal use. Under IFRS, the company must treat the expenditures as an expense until the software meets the criteria for recognition as an intangible asset, after which time the expenditures can be capitalized as an intangible asset.

1. What is the accounting impact of the company being able to demonstrate that the software met the criteria for recognition as an intangible asset on February 1 versus December 1?
2. How would the treatment of expenditures differ if the company reported under US GAAP and it had established in 2018 that the project was likely to be completed and the software used to perform the function intended?

---

[5] IAS 38 *Intangible Assets*.
[6] IAS 38 *Intangible Assets*, paragraph 8 [Definitions].
[7] IAS 38 *Intangible Assets*, paragraph 8 [Definitions].
[8] FASB ASC Section 350-40-25 [Intangibles—Goodwill and Other–Internal-Use Software–Recognition] and FASB ASC Section 985-20-25 [Software – Costs of Software to be Sold, Leased, or Marketed – Recognition] specify US GAAP accounting for software development costs for software for internal use and for software to be sold, respectively.

Solution to 1: If the company is able to demonstrate that the software met the criteria for recognition as an intangible asset on 1 February, the company would recognize the €1,000 expended in January as an expense on the income statement for the fiscal year ended December 31, 2019. The other €11,000 of expenditures would be recognized as an intangible asset (on the balance sheet). Alternatively, if the company is not able to demonstrate that the software met the criteria for recognition as an intangible asset until December 1, the company would recognize the €11,000 expended in January through November as an expense on the income statement for the fiscal year ended December 31, 2019, with the other €1,000 of expenditures recognized as an intangible asset.

Solution to 2: Under US GAAP, the company would capitalize the entire €12,000 spent to develop software for internal use.

2.2.3. Intangible Assets Acquired in a Business Combination

When one company acquires another company, the transaction is accounted for using the **acquisition method** of accounting.[9] Under the acquisition method, the company identified as the acquirer allocates the purchase price to each asset acquired (and each liability assumed) on the basis of its fair value. If the purchase price exceeds the sum of the amounts that can be allocated to individual identifiable assets and liabilities, the excess is recorded as goodwill. Goodwill cannot be identified separately from the business as a whole.

Under IFRS, the acquired individual assets include identifiable intangible assets that meet the definitional and recognition criteria.[10] Otherwise, if the item is acquired in a business combination and cannot be recognized as a tangible or identifiable intangible asset, it is recognized as goodwill. Under US GAAP, there are two criteria to judge whether an intangible asset acquired in a business combination should be recognized separately from goodwill: The asset must be either an item arising from contractual or legal rights or an item that can be separated from the acquired company. Examples of intangible assets treated separately from goodwill include the intangible assets previously mentioned that involve exclusive rights (patents, copyrights, franchises, licenses), as well as such items as internet domain names and video and audiovisual materials.

Exhibit 1 describes how AB InBev allocated the $103 billion purchase consideration in its 2016 acquisition of SABMiller Group. The combined company was renamed Anheuser-Busch InBev SA/NV. The majority of the intangible asset valuation relates to brands with indefinite life ($19.9 billion of the $20.0 billion total). Of $63.0 billion total assets acquired, assets to be divested were valued at $24.8 billion, and assets to be held for were valued at $38.2 billion. In total, intangible assets represent 52 percent of the total assets to be held for use. In addition, $74.1 billion of goodwill was recognized in the transaction.

[9] Both IFRS and US GAAP require the use of the acquisition method in accounting for business combinations (IFRS 3 and FASB ASC Section 805).
[10] As previously described, the definitional criteria are identifiability, control by the company, and expected future benefits. The recognition criteria are probable flows of the expected economic benefits to the company and measurability.

EXHIBIT 1   Acquisition of Intangible Assets through a Business Combination

Excerpt from the 2016 annual report of AB InBev:

"On 10 October 2016, AB InBev announced the ... successful completion of the business combination with the former SABMiller Group ("SAB").

"The transaction resulted in 74.1 billion US dollar of goodwill provisionally allocated primarily to the businesses in Colombia, Ecuador, Peru, Australia, South Africa and other African, Asia Pacific and Latin American countries. The factors that contributed to the recognition of goodwill include the acquisition of an assembled workforce and the premiums paid for cost synergies expected to be achieved in SABMiller. Management's assessment of the future economic benefits supporting recognition of this goodwill is in part based on expected savings through the implementation of AB InBev best practices such as, among others, a zero based budgeting program and initiatives that are expected to bring greater efficiency and standardization, generate cost savings and maximize purchasing power. Goodwill also arises due to the recognition of deferred tax liabilities in relation to the preliminary fair value adjustments on acquired intangible assets for which the amortization does not qualify as a tax deductible expense. None of the goodwill recognized is deductible for tax purposes.

"The majority of the intangible asset valuation relates to brands with indefinite life, valued for a total amount of 19.9 billion US dollar. The valuation of the brands with indefinite life is based on a series of factors, including the brand history, the operating plan and the countries in which the brands are sold. The fair value of brands was estimated by applying a combination of known valuation methodologies, such as the royalty relief and excess earnings valuation approaches.

"The intangibles with an indefinite life mainly include the Castle and Carling brand families in Africa, the Aguila and Poker brand families in Colombia, the Cristal and Pilsner brand families in Ecuador, and the Carlton brand family in Australia.

"Assets held for sale were recognized in relation to the divestiture of SABMiller's interests in the MillerCoors LLC joint venture and certain of SABMiller's portfolio of Miller brands outside of the U.S. to Molson Coors Brewing company; the divestiture of SABMiller's European premium brands to Asahi Group Holdings, Ltd and the divestiture of SABMiller's interest in China Resources Snow Breweries Ltd. to China Resources Beer (Holdings) Co. Ltd. ...." [Excerpt]

The following is a summary of the provisional allocation of AB InBev's purchase price of SABMiller:

Assets	$ million
Property, plant and equipment	9,060
Intangible assets	20,040
Investment in associates	4,386
Inventories	977
Trade and other receivables	1,257
Cash and cash equivalents	1,410
Assets held for sale	24,805
All other assets	*1,087*

(continued)

EXHIBIT 1   (Continued)

Assets	$ million
Total assets	*63,022*
Total liabilities	*−27,769*
Net identified assets and liabilities	**35,253**
Non-controlling interests	−6,200
Goodwill on acquisition	**74,083**
Purchase consideration	**103,136**

Table is excerpted from the company's 2016 Annual Report. Portions of detail are omitted, and subtotals are shown in italics.

Source: AB InBev 2016 Annual Report, pp. 82-85.

2.3. Capitalizing versus Expensing: Impact on Financial Statements and Ratios

This section discusses the implications for financial statements and ratios of capitalizing versus expensing costs in the period in which they are incurred. We first summarize the general financial statement impact of capitalizing versus expensing and two analytical issues related to the decision—namely the effect on an individual company's trend analysis and on comparability across companies.

In the period of the expenditure, an expenditure that is capitalized increases the amount of assets on the balance sheet and appears as an investing cash outflow on the statement of cash flows. After initial recognition, a company allocates the capitalized amount over the asset's useful life as depreciation or amortization expense (except assets that are not depreciated, i.e., land, or amortized. e.g., intangible assets with indefinite lives). This expense reduces net income on the income statement and reduces the value of the asset on the balance sheet. Depreciation and amortization are non-cash expenses and therefore, apart from their effect on taxable income and taxes payable, have no impact on the cash flow statement. In the section of the statement of cash flows that reconciles net income to operating cash flow, depreciation and amortization expenses are added back to net income.

Alternatively, an expenditure that is expensed reduces net income by the after-tax amount of the expenditure in the period it is made. No asset is recorded on the balance sheet and thus no depreciation or amortization occurs in subsequent periods. The lower amount of net income is reflected in lower retained earnings on the balance sheet. An expenditure that is expensed appears as an operating cash outflow in the period it is made. There is no effect on the financial statements of subsequent periods.

Example 4 illustrates the impact on the financial statements of capitalizing versus expensing an expenditure.

EXAMPLE 4   General Financial Statement Impact of Capitalizing Versus Expensing

Assume two identical (hypothetical) companies, CAP Inc. (CAP) and NOW Inc. (NOW), start with €1,000 cash and €1,000 common stock. Each year the companies recognize total revenues of €1,500 cash and make cash expenditures, excluding an equipment purchase, of €500. At the beginning of operations, each company pays €900 to purchase equipment. CAP estimates the equipment will have a useful life of three years and an estimated salvage value of €0 at the end of the three years. NOW estimates a much shorter useful life and expenses the equipment immediately. The companies have no other assets and make no other asset purchases during the three-year period. Assume the companies pay no dividends, earn zero interest on cash balances, have a tax rate of 30 percent, and use the same accounting method for financial and tax purposes.

The left side of Exhibit 2 shows CAP's financial statements; i.e., with the expenditure capitalized and depreciated at €300 per year based on the straight-line method of depreciation (€900 cost minus €0 salvage value equals €900, divided by a three-year life equals €300 per year). The right side of the exhibit shows NOW's financial statements, with the entire €900 expenditure treated as an expense in the first year. All amounts are in euro.

EXHIBIT 2   Capitalizing versus Expensing

CAP Inc.				NOW Inc.			
Capitalize €900 as asset and depreciate				Expense €900 immediately			
For Year	1	2	3	For Year	1	2	3
Revenue	1,500	1,500	1,500	Revenue	1,500	1,500	1,500
Cash expenses	500	500	500	Cash expenses	1,400	500	500
Depreciation	300	300	300	Depreciation	0	0	0
Income before tax	700	700	700	Income before tax	100	1,000	1,000
Tax at 30%	210	210	210	Tax at 30%	30	300	300
Net income	490	490	490	Net income	70	700	700
Cash from operations	790	790	790	Cash from operations	70	700	700
Cash used in investing	(900)	0	0	Cash used in investing	0	0	0
Total change in cash	(110)	790	790	Total change in cash	70	700	700

As of	Time 0	End of Year 1	End of Year 2	End of Year 3	Time	Time 0	End of Year 1	End of Year 2	End of Year 3
Cash	1,000	890	1,680	2,470	Cash	1,000	1,070	1,770	2,470
PP & E (net)	—	600	300	—	PP & E (net)	—	—	—	—
Total Assets	1,000	1,490	1,980	2,470	Total Assets	1,000	1,070	1,770	2,470

(*continued*)

EXHIBIT 2   (Continued)

As of	Time 0	End of Year 1	End of Year 2	End of Year 3	Time	Time 0	End of Year 1	End of Year 2	End of Year 3
Retained earnings	0	490	980	1,470	Retained earnings	0	70	770	1,470
Common stock	1,000	1,000	1,000	1,000	Common stock	1,000	1,000	1,000	1,000
Total shareholders' equity	1,000	1,490	1,980	2,470	Total shareholders' equity	1,000	1,070	1,770	2,470

1. Which company reports higher net income over the three years? Total cash flow? Cash from operations?
2. Based on ROE and net profit margin, how does the profitability of the two companies compare?
3. Why does NOW report change in cash of €70 in Year 1, while CAP reports total change in cash of (€110)?

Solution to 1: Neither company reports higher total net income or cash flow over the three years. The sum of net income over the three years is identical (€1,470 total) whether the €900 is capitalized or expensed. Also, the sum of the change in cash (€1,470 total) is identical under either scenario. CAP reports higher cash from operations by an amount of €900 because, under the capitalization scenario, the €900 purchase is treated as an investing cash flow.

Note: Because the companies use the same accounting method for both financial and taxable income, absent the assumption of zero interest on cash balances, expensing the €900 would have resulted in higher income and cash flow for NOW because the lower taxes paid in the first year (€30 versus €210) would have allowed NOW to earn interest income on the tax savings.

Solution to 2: In general, Ending shareholders' equity = Beginning shareholders' equity + Net income + Other comprehensive income − Dividends + Net capital contributions from shareholders. Because the companies in this example do not have other comprehensive income, did not pay dividends, and reported no capital contributions from shareholders, Ending retained earnings = Beginning retained earnings + Net income, and Ending shareholders' equity = Beginning shareholders' equity + Net income.

ROE is calculated as Net income divided by Average shareholders' equity, and Net profit margin is calculated as Net income divided by Total revenue. For example, CAP had Year 1 ROE of 39 percent (€490/[(€1,000 + €1,490)/2]), and Year 1 net profit margin of 33 percent (€490/€1,500).

CAP Inc.				NOW Inc.			
Capitalize €900 as asset and depreciate				Expense €900 immediately			
For year	1	2	3	For year	1	2	3
ROE	39%	28%	22%	ROE	7%	49%	33%
Net profit margin	33%	33%	33%	Net profit margin	5%	47%	47%

As shown, compared to expensing, capitalizing results in higher profitability ratios (ROE and net profit margin) in the first year, and lower profitability ratios in subsequent years. For example, CAP's Year 1 ROE of 39 percent was higher than NOW's Year 1 ROE of 7 percent, but in Years 2 and 3, NOW reports superior profitability.

Note also that NOW's superior growth in net income between Year 1 and Year 2 is not attributable to superior performance compared to CAP but rather to the accounting decision to recognize the expense sooner than CAP. In general, all else equal, accounting decisions that result in recognizing expenses sooner will give the appearance of greater subsequent growth. Comparison of the growth of the two companies' net incomes without an awareness of the difference in accounting methods would be misleading. As a corollary, NOW's income and profitability exhibit greater volatility across the three years, not because of more volatile performance but rather because of the different accounting decision.

Solution to 3: NOW reports an increase in cash of €70 in Year 1, while CAP reports a decrease in cash of €110 because NOW's taxes were €180 lower than CAP's taxes (€30 versus €210).

Note that this problem assumes the accounting method used by each company for its tax purposes is identical to the accounting method used by the company for its financial reporting. In many countries, companies are allowed to use different depreciation methods for financial reporting and taxes, which may give rise to deferred taxes.

As shown, discretion regarding whether to expense or capitalize expenditures can impede comparability across companies. Example 4 assumes the companies purchase a single asset in one year. Because the sum of net income over the three-year period is identical whether the asset is capitalized or expensed, it illustrates that although capitalizing results in higher profitability compared to expensing in the first year, it results in lower profitability in the subsequent years. Conversely, expensing results in lower profitability in the first year but higher profitability in later years, indicating a favorable trend.

Similarly, shareholders' equity for a company that capitalizes the expenditure will be higher in the early years because the initially higher profits result in initially higher retained earnings. Example 4 assumes the companies purchase a single asset in one year and report identical amounts of total net income over the three-year period, so shareholders' equity (and retained earnings) for the firm that expenses will be identical to shareholders' equity (and retained earnings) for the capitalizing firm at the end of the three-year period.

Although Example 4 shows companies purchasing an asset only in the first year, if a company continues to purchase similar or increasing amounts of assets each year, the profitability-enhancing effect of capitalizing continues if the amount of the expenditures in a period continues to be more than the depreciation expense. Example 5 illustrates this point.

EXAMPLE 5 Impact of Capitalizing Versus Expensing for Ongoing Purchases

A company buys a £300 computer in Year 1 and capitalizes the expenditure. The computer has a useful life of three years and an expected salvage value of £0, so the annual depreciation expense using the straight-line method is £100 per year. Compared to expensing the entire £300 immediately, the company's pre-tax profit in Year 1 is £200 greater.

1. Assume that the company continues to buy an identical computer each year at the same price. If the company uses the same accounting treatment for each of the computers, when does the profit-enhancing effect of capitalizing versus expensing end?
2. If the company buys another identical computer in Year 4, using the same accounting treatment as the prior years, what is the effect on Year 4 profits of capitalizing versus expensing these expenditures?

Solution to 1: The profit-enhancing effect of capitalizing versus expensing would end in Year 3. In Year 3, the depreciation expense on each of the three computers bought in Years 1, 2, and 3 would total £300 (£100 + £100 + £100). Therefore, the total depreciation expense for Year 3 will be exactly equal to the capital expenditure in Year 3. The expense in Year 3 would be £300, regardless of whether the company capitalized or expensed the annual computer purchases.

Solution to 2: There is no impact on Year 4 profits. As in the previous year, the depreciation expense on each of the three computers bought in Years 2, 3, and 4 would total £300 (£100 + £100 + £100). Therefore, the total depreciation expense for Year 4 will be exactly equal to the capital expenditure in Year 4. Pre-tax profits would be reduced by £300, regardless of whether the company capitalized or expensed the annual computer purchases.

Compared to expensing an expenditure, capitalizing the expenditure typically results in greater amounts reported as cash from operations. Capitalized expenditures are typically treated as an investment cash outflow whereas expenses reduce operating cash flows. Because cash flow from operating activities is an important consideration in some valuation models, companies may try to maximize reported cash flow from operations by capitalizing expenditures that should be expensed. Valuation models that use free cash flow will consider not only operating cash flows but also investing cash flows. Analysts should be alert to evidence of companies manipulating reported cash flow from operations by capitalizing expenditures that should be expensed.

In summary, holding all else constant, capitalizing an expenditure enhances current profitability and increases reported cash flow from operations. The profitability-enhancing effect of capitalizing continues so long as capital expenditures exceed the depreciation expense. Profitability-enhancing motivations for decisions to capitalize should be considered when analyzing performance. For example, a company may choose to capitalize more expenditures (within the allowable bounds of accounting standards) to achieve earnings targets for a given period. Expensing a cost in the period reduces current period profits but enhances future profitability and thus enhances the profit trend. Profit trend-enhancing motivations should also be considered when analyzing performance. If the company is in a reporting environment that requires identical accounting methods for financial reporting and taxes (unlike the United States, which permits companies to use depreciation methods for reporting purposes that differ from the depreciation method required by tax purposes), then expensing will have a more favorable cash flow impact because paying lower taxes in an earlier period creates an opportunity to earn interest income on the cash saved.

In contrast with the relatively simple examples above, it is generally neither possible nor desirable to identify individual instances involving discretion about whether to capitalize or expense expenditures. An analyst can, however, typically identify significant items of expenditure treated differently across companies. The items of expenditure giving rise to the most relevant differences across companies will vary by industry. This cross-industry variation is apparent in the following discussion of the capitalization of expenditures.

2.4. Capitalization of Interest Costs

As noted above, companies generally must capitalize interest costs associated with acquiring or constructing an asset that requires a long period of time to get ready for its intended use.[11]

As a consequence of this accounting treatment, a company's interest costs for a period can appear either on the balance sheet (to the extent they are capitalized) or on the income statement (to the extent they are expensed).

If the interest expenditure is incurred in connection with constructing an asset for the company's own use, the capitalized interest appears on the balance sheet as a part of the relevant long-lived asset. The capitalized interest is expensed over time as the property is depreciated—and is thus part of depreciation expense rather than interest expense. If the interest expenditure is incurred in connection with constructing an asset to sell, for example by a real estate construction company, the capitalized interest appears on the company's balance sheet as part of inventory. The capitalized interest is then expensed as part of the cost of sales when the asset is sold.

The treatment of capitalized interest poses certain issues that analysts should consider. First, capitalized interest appears as part of investing cash outflows, whereas expensed interest typically reduces operating cash flow. US GAAP reporting companies are required to categorize interest in operating cash flow, and IFRS reporting companies can categorize interest in operating, investing, or financing cash flows. Although the treatment is consistent with accounting standards, an analyst may want to examine the impact on reported cash flows. Second, interest coverage ratios are solvency indicators measuring the extent to which a company's earnings (or cash flow) in a period covered its interest costs. To provide a true picture of a company's interest coverage, the entire amount of interest expenditure, both the capitalized portion and the expensed portion, should be used in calculating interest coverage ratios. Additionally, if a company is depreciating interest that it capitalized in a previous period, income should be adjusted to eliminate the effect of that depreciation. Example 6 illustrates the calculations.

EXAMPLE 6   Effect of Capitalized Interest Costs on Coverage Ratios and Cash Flow

---

Melco Resorts & Entertainment Limited (NASDAQ: MLCO), a Hong Kong SAR based casino company that is listed on the NASDAQ stock exchange and prepares financial reports under US GAAP, disclosed the following information in one of the footnotes to

---

[11] IAS 23 [Borrowing Costs] and FASB ASC Subtopic 835-20 [Interest – Capitalization of Interest] specify respectively IFRS and US GAAP for capitalization of interest costs. Although the standards are not completely converged, the standards are in general agreement.

its 2017 financial statements: "Interest and amortization of deferred financing costs associated with major development and construction projects is capitalized and included in the cost of the project. . . . Total interest expenses incurred amounted to $267,065, $252,600, and $253,168, of which $37,483, $29,033, and $134,838 were capitalized during the years ended December 31, 2017, 2016, and 2015, respectively. Amortization of deferred financing costs of $26,182, $48,345, and $38,511, net of amortization capitalized of nil, nil, and $5,458, were recorded during the years ended December 31, 2017, 2016, and 2015, respectively." (Form 20-F filed 12 April 2018). Cash payments for deferred financing costs were reported in cash flows from financing activities.

EXHIBIT 3   Melco Resorts & Entertainment Limited Selected Data, as Reported (Dollars in thousands)

	2017	2016	2015
EBIT (from income statement)	544,865	298,663	58,553
Interest expense (from income statement)	229,582	223,567	118,330
Capitalized interest (from footnote)	37,483	29,033	134,838
Amortization of deferred financing costs (from footnote)	26,182	48,345	38,511
Net cash provided by operating activities	1,162,500	1,158,128	522,026
Net cash from (used) in investing activities	(410,226)	280,604	(469,656)
Net cash from (used) in financing activities	(1,046,041)	(1,339,717)	(29,688)

Notes: EBIT represents "Income (Loss) Before Income Tax" plus "Interest expenses, net of capitalized interest" from the income statement.

1. Calculate and interpret Melco's interest coverage ratio with and without capitalized interest.
2. Calculate Melco's percentage change in operating cash flow from 2016 to 2017. Assuming the financial reporting does not affect reporting for income taxes, what were the effects of capitalized interest on operating and investing cash flows?

Solution to 1: Interest coverage ratios with and without capitalized interest were as follows:

For 2017

2.37 ($544,865 ÷ $229,582) without adjusting for capitalized interest; and
2.14 [($544,865 + $26,182) ÷ ($229,582 + $37,483)] including an adjustment
    to EBIT for depreciation of previously capitalized interest and an adjustment
    to interest expense for the amount of interest capitalized in 2017.

For 2016

1.34 ($298,663÷ $223,567) without adjusting for capitalized interest; and
1.37 [($298,663 + $48,345) ÷ ($223,567 + $29,033)] including an adjustment
    to EBIT for depreciation of previously capitalized interest and an adjustment
    to interest expense for the amount of interest capitalized in 2016.

For 2015

0.49 ($58,533÷ $118,330) without adjusting for capitalized interest; and
0.36 [($58,533 + $33,053) ÷ ($118,330+ $134,838)] including an adjustment to
    EBIT for depreciation of previously capitalized interest and an adjustment to
    interest expense for the amount of interest capitalized in 2015.

The above calculations indicate that Melco's interest coverage improved in 2017 compared to the previous two years. In both 2017 and 2015, the coverage ratio is lower when adjusted for capitalized interest.

Solution to 2: If the interest had been expensed rather than capitalized, operating cash flows would have been lower in all three years. On an adjusted basis, but not on an unadjusted basis, the company's operating cash flow declined in 2017 compared to 2016. On an unadjusted basis, for 2017 compared with 2016, Melco's operating cash flow increased by 0.4 percent in 2017 [($1,162,500 ÷ $1,158,128) − 1]. Including adjustments to expense all interest costs, Melco's operating cash flow also decreased by 0.4 percent in 2017 {[($1,162,500 − $37,483) ÷ ($1,158,128 − $29,033)] − 1}.

If the interest had been expensed rather than capitalized, financing cash flows would have been higher in all three years.

The treatment of capitalized interest raises issues for consideration by an analyst. First, capitalized interest appears as part of investing cash outflows, whereas expensed interest reduces operating or financing cash flow under IFRS and operating cash flow under US GAAP. An analyst may want to examine the impact on reported cash flows of interest expenditures when comparing companies. Second, interest coverage ratios are solvency indicators measuring the extent to which a company's earnings (or cash flow) in a period covered its interest costs. To provide a true picture of a company's interest coverage, the entire amount of interest, both the capitalized portion and the expensed portion, should be used in calculating interest coverage ratios.

Generally, including capitalized interest in the calculation of interest coverage ratios provides a better assessment of a company's solvency. In assigning credit ratings, rating agencies include capitalized interest in coverage ratios. For example, Standard & Poor's calculates the EBIT interest coverage ratio as EBIT divided by gross interest (defined as interest prior to deductions for capitalized interest or interest income).

Maintaining a minimum interest coverage ratio is a financial covenant often included in lending agreements, e.g., bank loans and bond indentures. The definition of the coverage ratio can be found in the company's credit agreement. The definition is relevant because treatment of capitalized interest in calculating coverage ratios would affect an assessment of how close a company's actual ratios are to the levels specified by its financial covenants and thus the probability of breaching those covenants.

2.5. Capitalization of Internal Development Costs

As noted above, accounting standards require companies to capitalize software development costs after a product's feasibility is established. Despite this requirement, judgment in determining feasibility means that companies' capitalization practices may differ. For example, as illustrated in Exhibit 4, Microsoft judges product feasibility to be established very shortly before manufacturing begins and, therefore, effectively expenses—rather than capitalizes—research and development costs.

EXHIBIT 4   Disclosure on Software Development Costs

Excerpt from Management's Discussion and Analysis (MD&A) of Microsoft Corporation, Application of Critical Accounting Policies, Research and Development Costs:

> "Costs incurred internally in researching and developing a computer software product are charged to expense until technological feasibility has been established for the product. Once technological feasibility is established, all software costs are capitalized until the product is available for general release to customers. Judgment is required in determining when technological feasibility of a product is established. We have determined that technological feasibility for our software products is reached after all high-risk development issues have been resolved through coding and testing. Generally, this occurs shortly before the products are released to production. The amortization of these costs is included in cost of revenue over the estimated life of the products."

Source: Microsoft Corporation Annual Report on Form 10-K 2017, p. 45.

Expensing rather than capitalizing development costs results in lower net income in the current period. Expensing rather than capitalizing will continue to result in lower net income so long as the amount of the current-period development expenses is higher than the amortization expense that would have resulted from amortising prior periods' capitalized development costs—the typical situation when a company's development costs are increasing. On the statement of cash flows, expensing rather than capitalizing development costs results in lower net operating cash flows and higher net investing cash flows. This is because the development costs are reflected as operating cash outflows rather than investing cash outflows.

In comparing the financial performance of a company that expenses most or all software development costs, such as Microsoft, with another company that capitalizes software development costs, adjustments can be made to make the two comparable. For the company that capitalizes software development costs, an analyst can adjust (a) the income statement to include software development costs as an expense and to exclude amortization of prior years' software development costs; (b) the balance sheet to exclude capitalized software (decrease assets and equity); and (c) the statement of cash flows to decrease operating cash flows and decrease cash used in investing by the amount of the current period development costs. Any ratios that include income, long-lived assets, or cash flow from operations—such as return on equity—will also be affected.

EXAMPLE 7   Software Development Costs

You are working on a project involving the analysis of JHH Software, a (hypothetical) software development company that established technical feasibility for its first product in 2017. Part of your analysis involves computing certain market-based ratios, which you will use to compare JHH to another company that expenses all of its software development expenditures. Relevant data and excerpts from the company's annual report are included in Exhibit 5.

EXHIBIT 5   JHH SOFTWARE (Dollars in Thousands, Except Per-Share Amounts)

CONSOLIDATED STATEMENT OF EARNINGS—abbreviated			
For year ended December 31:	2018	2017	2016
Total revenue	$91,424	$91,134	$96,293
Total operating expenses	78,107	78,908	85,624
Operating income	13,317	12,226	10,669
Provision for income taxes	3,825	4,232	3,172
Net income	$9,492	$7,994	$7,479
Earnings per share (EPS)	$1.40	$0.82	$0.68

STATEMENT OF CASH FLOWS—abbreviated			
For year ended December 31:	2018	2017	2016
Net cash provided by operating activities	$15,007	$14,874	$15,266
Net cash used in investing activities*	(11,549)	(4,423)	(5,346)
Net cash used in financing activities	(8,003)	(7,936)	(7,157)
Net change in cash and cash equivalents	($4,545)	$2,515	$2,763
*Includes software development expenses of and includes	($6,000)	($4,000)	($2,000)
capital expenditures of	($2,000)	($1,600)	($1,200)

Additional information:			
For year ended December 31:	2018	2017	2016
Market value of outstanding debt	0	0	0
Amortization of capitalized software development expenses	($2,000)	($667)	0
Depreciation expense	($2,200)	($1,440)	($1,320)
Market price per share of common stock	$42	$26	$17
Shares of common stock outstanding (thousands)	6,780	9,765	10,999

Footnote disclosure of accounting policy for software development:
Expenses that are related to the conceptual formulation and design of software products are expensed to research and development as incurred. The company capitalizes expenses that are incurred to produce the finished product after technological feasibility has been established.

1. Compute the following ratios for JHH based on the reported financial statements for fiscal year ended December 31, 2018, with no adjustments. Next, determine the approximate impact on these ratios if the company had expensed rather than capitalized its investments in software. (Assume the financial reporting does not affect reporting for income taxes. There would be no change in the effective tax rate.)
   A. P/E: Price/Earnings per share
   B. P/CFO: Price/Operating cash flow per share

C. EV/EBITDA: Enterprise value/EBITDA, where enterprise value is defined as the total market value of all sources of a company's financing, including equity and debt, and EBITDA is earnings before interest, taxes, depreciation, and amortization.

2. Interpret the changes in the ratios.

Solution to 1: (Dollars are in thousands, except per-share amounts.) JHH's 2019 ratios are presented in the following table:

	Ratios	As reported	As adjusted
A.	P/E ratio	30.0	42.9
B.	P/CFO	19.0	31.6
C.	EV/EBITDA	16.3	24.7

A. Based on the information as reported, the P/E ratio was 30.0 ($42 ÷ $1.40). Based on EPS adjusted to expense software development costs, the P/E ratio was 42.9 ($42 ÷ $0.98).
   - Price: Assuming that the market value of the company's equity is based on its fundamentals, the price per share is $42, regardless of a difference in accounting.
   - EPS: As reported, EPS was $1.40. Adjusted EPS was $0.98. Expensing software development costs would have reduced JHH's 2018 operating income by $6,000, but the company would have reported no amortization of prior years' software costs, which would have increased operating income by $2,000. The net change of $4,000 would have reduced operating income from the reported $13,317 to $9,317. The effective tax rate for 2018 ($3,825 ÷ $13,317) is 28.72%, and using this effective tax rate would give an adjusted net income of $6,641 [$9,317 × (1 − 0.2872)], compared to $9,492 before the adjustment. The EPS would therefore be reduced from the reported $1.40 to $0.98 (adjusted net income of $6,641 divided by 6,780 shares).

B. Based on information as reported, the P/CFO was 19.0 ($42 ÷ $2.21). Based on CFO adjusted to expense software development costs, the P/CFO was 31.6 ($42 ÷ $1.33).
   - Price: Assuming that the market value of the company's equity is based on its fundamentals, the price per share is $42, regardless of a difference in accounting.
   - CFO per share, as reported, was $2.21 (total operating cash flows $15,007 ÷ 6,780 shares).
   - CFO per share, as adjusted, was $1.33. The company's $6,000 expenditure on software development costs was reported as a cash outflow from investing activities, so expensing those costs would reduce cash from operating activities by $6,000, from the reported $15,007 to $9,007. Dividing adjusted total operating cash flow of $9,007 by 6,780 shares results in cash flow per share of $1.33.

C. Based on information as reported, the EV/EBITDA was 16.3 ($284,760 ÷ $17,517). Based on EBITDA adjusted to expense software development costs, the EV/EBITDA was 24.7 ($284,760 ÷ $11,517).
   - Enterprise Value: Enterprise value is the sum of the market value of the company's equity and debt. JHH has no debt, and therefore the enterprise value

is equal to the market value of its equity. The market value of its equity is
$284,760 ($42 per share × 6,780 shares).
- EBITDA, as reported, was $17,517 (earnings before interest and taxes of
$13,317 plus $2,200 depreciation plus $2,000 amortization).
- EBITDA, adjusted for expensing software development costs by the inclusion
of $6,000 development expense and the exclusion of $2,000 amortization of
prior expense, would be $11,517 (earnings before interest and taxes of $9,317
plus $2,200 depreciation plus $0 amortization).

Solution to 2: Expensing software development costs would decrease historical profits,
operating cash flow, and EBITDA, and would thus increase all market multiples. So
JHH's stock would appear more expensive if it expensed rather than capitalized the
software development costs.

If the unadjusted market-based ratios were used in the comparison of JHH to
its competitor that expenses all software development expenditures, then JHH might
appear to be under-priced when the difference is solely related to accounting factors.
JHH's adjusted market-based ratios provide a better basis for comparison.

For the company in Example 7, current period software development expenditures exceed
the amortization of prior periods' capitalized software development expenditures. As a result,
expensing rather than capitalizing software development costs would have the effect of lowering income. If, however, software development expenditures slowed such that current expenditures were lower than the amortization of prior periods' capitalized software development
expenditures, then expensing software development costs would have the effect of increasing
income relative to capitalizing it.

This section illustrated how decisions about capitalizing versus expensing impact financial
statements and ratios. Earlier expensing lowers current profits but enhances trends, whereas
capitalizing now and expensing later enhances current profits. Having described the accounting for acquisition of long-lived assets, we now turn to the topic of measuring long-lived assets
in subsequent periods.

3. DEPRECIATION AND AMORTIZATION OF LONG-LIVED ASSETS

Under the cost model of reporting long-lived assets, which is permitted under IFRS and
required under US GAAP, the capitalized costs of long-lived tangible assets (other than land,
which is not depreciated) and intangible assets with finite useful lives are allocated to subsequent periods as depreciation and amortization expenses. Depreciation and amortization are
effectively the same concept, with the term depreciation referring to the process of allocating
tangible assets' costs and the term amortization referring to the process of allocating intangible
assets' costs.[12] The alternative model of reporting long-lived assets is the **revaluation model**,
which is permitted under IFRS but not under US GAAP. Under the revaluation model, a

---

[12]Depletion is the term applied to a similar concept for natural resources; costs associated with those
resources are allocated to a period on the basis of the usage or extraction of those resources.

company reports the long-lived asset at fair value rather than at acquisition cost (historical cost) less accumulated depreciation or amortization, as in the cost model.

An asset's carrying amount is the amount at which the asset is reported on the balance sheet. Under the cost model, at any point in time, the carrying amount (also called carrying value or net book value) of a long-lived asset is equal to its historical cost minus the amount of depreciation or amortization that has been accumulated since the asset's purchase (assuming that the asset has not been impaired, a topic which will be addressed in Section 5). Companies may present on the balance sheet the total net amount of property, plant, and equipment and the total net amount of intangible assets. However, more detail is disclosed in the notes to financial statements. The details disclosed typically include the acquisition costs, the depreciation and amortization expenses, the accumulated depreciation and amortization amounts, the depreciation and amortization methods used, and information on the assumptions used to depreciate and amortize long-lived assets.

3.1. Depreciation Methods and Calculation of Depreciation Expense

Depreciation methods include the **straight-line method**, in which the cost of an asset is allocated to expense evenly over its useful life; **accelerated methods**, in which the allocation of cost is greater in earlier years; and the **units-of-production method**, in which the allocation of cost corresponds to the actual use of an asset in a particular period. The choice of depreciation method affects the amounts reported on the financial statements, including the amounts for reported assets and operating and net income. This, in turn, affects a variety of financial ratios, including fixed asset turnover, total asset turnover, operating profit margin, operating return on assets, and return on assets.

Using the straight-line method, depreciation expense is calculated as depreciable cost divided by estimated useful life and is the same for each period. Depreciable cost is the historical cost of the tangible asset minus the estimated residual (salvage) value.[13] A commonly used accelerated method is the declining balance method, in which the amount of depreciation expense for a period is calculated as some percentage of the carrying amount (i.e., cost net of accumulated depreciation at the beginning of the period). When an accelerated method is used, depreciable cost is not used to calculate the depreciation expense but the carrying amount should not be reduced below the estimated residual value. In the units-of-production method, the amount of depreciation expense for a period is based on the proportion of the asset's production during the period compared with the total estimated productive capacity of the asset over its useful life. The depreciation expense is calculated as depreciable cost times production in the period divided by estimated productive capacity over the life of the asset. Equivalently, the company may estimate a depreciation cost per unit (depreciable cost divided by estimated productive capacity) and calculate depreciation expense as depreciation cost per unit times production in the period. Regardless of the depreciation method used, the carrying amount of the asset is not reduced below the estimated residual value. Example 8 provides an example of these depreciation methods.

---

[13] The residual value is the estimated amount that an entity will obtain from disposal of the asset at the end of its useful life.

EXAMPLE 8   Alternative Depreciation Methods

You are analyzing three hypothetical companies: EVEN-LI Co., SOONER Inc., and AZUSED Co. At the beginning of Year 1, each company buys an identical piece of box manufacturing equipment for $2,300 and has the same assumptions about useful life, estimated residual value, and productive capacity. The annual production of each company is the same, but each company uses a different method of depreciation. As disclosed in each company's notes to the financial statements, each company's depreciation method, assumptions, and production are as follows:

Depreciation method
- EVEN-LI Co.: straight-line method
- SOONER Inc.: double-declining balance method (the rate applied to the carrying amount is double the depreciation rate for the straight-line method)
- AZUSED Co.: units-of-production method

Assumptions and production
- Estimated residual value: $100
- Estimated useful life: 4 years
- Total estimated productive capacity: 800 boxes
- Production in each of the four years: 200 boxes in the first year, 300 in the second year, 200 in the third year, and 100 in the fourth year

1. Using the following template for each company, record its beginning and ending net book value (carrying amount), end-of-year accumulated depreciation, and annual depreciation expense for the box manufacturing equipment.

Template:

	Beginning Net Book Value	Depreciation Expense	Accumulated Depreciation	Ending Net Book Value
Year 1				
Year 2				
Year 3				
Year 4				

2. Explain the significant differences in the timing of the recognition of the depreciation expense.
3. For each company, assume that sales, earnings before interest, taxes, depreciation, and amortization, and assets other than the box manufacturing equipment are as shown in the following table. Calculate the total asset turnover ratio, the operating profit margin, and the operating return on assets for each company for each of the four years. Discuss the ratios, comparing results within and across companies.

	Sales	Earnings before Interest, Taxes, Depreciation, and Amortization	Carrying Amount of Total Assets, Excluding the Box Manufacturing Equipment, at Year End*
Year 1	$300,000	$36,000	$30,000
Year 2	320,000	38,400	32,000
Year 3	340,000	40,800	34,000
Year 4	360,000	43,200	36,000

*Assume that total assets at the beginning of Year 1, *including* the box manufacturing equipment, had a value of $30,300. Assume that depreciation expense on assets other than the box manufacturing equipment totaled $1,000 per year.

Solution to 1: For *each* company, the following information applies: Beginning net book value in Year 1 equals the purchase price of $2,300; accumulated year-end depreciation equals the balance from the previous year plus the current year's depreciation expense; ending net book value (carrying amount) equals original cost minus accumulated year-end depreciation (which is the same as beginning net book value minus depreciation expense); and beginning net book value in Years 2, 3, and 4 equals the ending net book value of the prior year. The following text and filled-in templates describe how depreciation *expense* is calculated for each company.

EVEN-LI Co. uses the straight-line method, so depreciation expense in each year equals $550, which is calculated as ($2,300 original cost − $100 residual value)/4 years. The net book value at the end of Year 4 is the estimated residual value of $100.

EVEN-LI Co.	Beginning Net Book Value	Depreciation Expense	Accumulated Year-End Depreciation	Ending Net Book Value
Year 1	$2,300	$550	$550	$1,750
Year 2	1,750	550	1,100	1,200
Year 3	1,200	550	1,650	650
Year 4	650	550	2,200	100

SOONER Inc. uses the double-declining balance method. The depreciation rate for the double-declining balance method is double the depreciation rate for the straight-line method. The depreciation rate under the straight-line method is 25 percent (100 percent divided by 4 years). Thus, the depreciation rate for the double-declining balance method is 50 percent (2 times 25 percent). The depreciation expense for the first year is $1,150 (50 percent of $2,300). Note that under this method, the depreciation rate of 50 percent is applied to the carrying amount (net book value) of the asset, without adjustment for expected residual value. Because the carrying amount of the asset is not depreciated below its estimated residual value, however, the depreciation expense in the final year of depreciation decreases the ending net book value (carrying amount) to the estimated residual value.

SOONER Inc.	Beginning Net Book Value	Depreciation Expense	Accumulated Year-End Depreciation	Ending Net Book Value
Year 1	$2,300	$1,150	$1,150	$1,150
Year 2	1,150	575	1,725	575
Year 3	575	288	2,013	287
Year 4	287	187	2,200	100

Another common approach (not required in this question) is to use an accelerated method, such as the double-declining method, for some period (a year or more) and then to change to the straight-line method for the remaining life of the asset. If SOONER had used the double-declining method for the first year and then switched to the straight-line method for Years 2, 3, and 4, the depreciation expense would be $350 [($1,150 − $100 estimated residual value)/3 years] a year for Years 2, 3, and 4. The results for SOONER under this alternative approach are shown below.

SOONER Inc.	Beginning Net Book Value	Depreciation Expense	Accumulated Year-End Depreciation	Ending Net Book Value
Year 1	$2,300	$1,150	$1,150	$1,150
Year 2	1,150	350	1,500	800
Year 3	800	350	1,850	450
Year 4	450	350	2,200	100

AZUSED Co. uses the units-of-production method. Dividing the equipment's total depreciable cost by its total productive capacity gives a cost per unit of $2.75, calculated as ($2,300 original cost − $100 residual value)/800. The depreciation expense recognized each year is the number of units produced times $2.75. For Year 1, the amount of depreciation expense is $550 (200 units times $2.75). For Year 2, the amount is $825 (300 units times $2.75). For Year 3, the amount is $550. For Year 4, the amount is $275.

AZUSED Co.	Beginning Net Book Value	Depreciation Expense	Accumulated Year-End Depreciation	Ending Net Book Value
Year 1	$2,300	$550	$550	$1,750
Year 2	1,750	825	1,375	925
Year 3	925	550	1,925	375
Year 4	375	275	2,200	100

Solution to 2: All three methods result in the same total amount of accumulated depreciation over the life of the equipment. The significant differences are simply in the timing of the recognition of the depreciation expense. The straight-line method recognizes the expense evenly, the accelerated method recognizes most of the expense in the first year, and the units-of-production method recognizes the expense on the basis of production (or use of the asset). Under all three methods, the ending net book value is $100.

Solution to 3:

Total asset turnover ratio = Total revenue ÷ Average total assets

Operating profit margin = Earnings before interest and taxes ÷ Total revenue

Operating return on assets = Earnings before interest and taxes ÷ Average total assets

Ratios are shown in the table below, and details of the calculations for Years 1 and 2 are described after discussion of the ratios.

	EVEN-LI Co.			SOONER Inc.			AZUSED Co.		
Ratio*	AT	PM (%)	ROA (%)	AT	PM (%)	ROA (%)	AT	PM (%)	ROA (%)
Year 1	9.67	11.48	111.04	9.76	11.28	110.17	9.67	11.48	111.04
Year 2	9.85	11.52	113.47	10.04	11.51	115.57	9.90	11.43	113.10
Year 3	10.02	11.54	115.70	10.17	11.62	118.21	10.10	11.54	116.64
Year 4	10.18	11.57	117.74	10.23	11.67	119.42	10.22	11.65	118.98

*AT = Total asset turnover ratio. PM = Operating profit margin. ROA = Operating return on assets.

For all companies, the asset turnover ratio increased over time because sales grew at a faster rate than that of the assets. SOONER had consistently higher asset turnover ratios than the other two companies, however, because higher depreciation expense in the earlier periods decreased its average total assets. In addition, the higher depreciation in earlier periods resulted in SOONER having lower operating profit margin and operating ROA in the first year and higher operating profit margin and operating ROA in the later periods. SOONER appears to be more efficiently run, on the basis of its higher asset turnover and greater increases in profit margin and ROA over time; however, these comparisons reflect differences in the companies' choice of depreciation method. In addition, an analyst might question the sustainability of the extremely high ROAs for all three companies because such high profitability levels would probably attract new competitors, which would likely put downward pressure on the ratios.

EVEN-LI Co.
Year 1:

Total asset turnover ratio = 300,000/[(30,300 + 30,000 + 1,750)/2]
      = 300,000/31,025 = 9.67
Operating profit margin = (36,000 − 1,000 − 550)/300,000
      = 34,450/300,000 = 11.48%
Operating ROA = 34,450/31,025 = 111.04%

Year 2:

Total asset turnover ratio = 320,000/[(30,000 + 1,750 + 32,000 + 1,200)/2]
      = 320,000/32,475 = 9.85

Operating profit margin = (38,400 − 1,000 − 550)/320,000
    = 36,850/320,000 = 11.52%
Operating ROA = 36,850/32,475 = 113.47%

SOONER Inc.
Year 1:

Total asset turnover ratio = 300,000/[(30,300 + 30,000 + 1,150)/2]
    = 300,000/30,725 = 9.76
Operating profit margin = (36,000 − 1,000 − 1,150)/300,000
    = 33,850/300,000 = 11.28%
Operating ROA = 33,850/30,725 = 110.17%

Year 2:

Total asset turnover ratio = 320,000/[(30,000 + 1,150 + 32,000 + 575)/2]
    = 320,000/31,862.50 = 10.04
Operating profit margin = (38,400 − 1,000 − 575)/320,000
    = 36,825/320,000 = 11.51%
Operating ROA = 36,825/31,862.50 = 115.57%

AZUSED Co.
Year 1:

Total asset turnover ratio = 300,000/[(30,300 + 30,000 + 1,750)/2]
    = 300,000/31,025 = 9.67
Operating profit margin = (36,000 − 1,000 − 550)/300,000
    = 34,450/300,000 = 11.48%
Operating ROA = 34,450/31,025 = 111.04%

Year 2:

Total asset turnover ratio = 320,000/[(30,000 + 1,750 + 32,000 + 925)/2]
    = 320,000/32,337.50 = 9.90
Operating profit margin = (38,400 − 1,000 − 825)/320,000
    = 36,575/320,000 = 11.43%
Operating ROA = 36,575/32,337.50 = 113.10%

In many countries, a company must use the same depreciation methods for both financial and tax reporting. In other countries, including the United States, a company need not use the same depreciation method for financial reporting and taxes. As a result of using different depreciation methods for financial and tax reporting, pre-tax income on the income statement and taxable income on the tax return may differ. Thus, the amount of tax expense computed on the basis of pre-tax income and the amount of taxes actually owed on the basis of taxable income may differ. Although these differences eventually reverse because the total depreciation is the same regardless of the timing of its recognition in financial statements versus on tax returns, during the period of the difference, the balance sheet will show what is known as deferred taxes. For instance, if a company uses straight-line depreciation for financial reporting and an accelerated depreciation method for tax purposes, the company's financial statements will report lower depreciation expense and higher pre-tax income in the first year, compared with the amount of depreciation expense and taxable income in its tax reporting. (Compare the depreciation expense in Year 1 for EVEN-LI Co. and SOONER Inc. in the previous example.) Tax expense calculated on the basis of the financial statements' pre-tax income will be higher than taxes payable on the basis of taxable income; the difference between the two amounts represents a deferred tax liability. The deferred tax liability will be reduced as the difference reverses (i.e., when depreciation for financial reporting is higher than the depreciation for tax purposes) and the income tax is paid.

Significant estimates required for calculating depreciation include the useful life of the asset (or its total lifetime productive capacity) and its expected residual value at the end of that useful life. A longer useful life and higher expected residual value decrease the amount of annual depreciation expense relative to a shorter useful life and lower expected residual value. Companies should review their estimates periodically to ensure they remain reasonable. IFRS require companies to review estimates annually.

Although no significant differences exist between IFRS and US GAAP with respect to the definition of depreciation and the acceptable depreciation methods, IFRS require companies to use a component method of depreciation.[14] Companies are required to separately depreciate the significant components of an asset (parts of an item with a cost that is significant in relation to the total cost and/or with different useful lives) and thus require additional estimates for the various components. For instance, it may be appropriate to depreciate separately the engine, frame, and interior furnishings of an aircraft. Under US GAAP, the component method of depreciation is allowed but is seldom used in practice.[15] Example 9 illustrates depreciating components of an asset.

EXAMPLE 9   Illustration of Depreciating Components of an Asset

CUTITUP Co., a hypothetical company, purchases a milling machine, a type of machine used for shaping metal, at a total cost of $10,000. $2,000 was estimated to represent the cost of the rotating cutter, a significant component of the machine. The company expects the machine to have a useful life of eight years and a residual value of $3,000 and that the rotating cutter will need to be replaced every two years. Assume the entire residual value is attributable to the milling machine itself, and assume the company uses straight-line depreciation for all assets.

1. How much depreciation expense would the company report in Year 1 if it uses the component method of depreciation, and how much depreciation expense would the company report in Year 1 if it does not use the component method?
2. Assuming a new cutter with an estimated two-year useful life is purchased at the end of Year 2 for $2,000, what depreciation expenses would the company report in Year 3 if it uses the component method and if it does not use the component method?

---

[14] IAS 16 *Property, Plant and Equipment*, paragraphs 43–47 [Depreciation].
[15] According to KPMG's *IFRS Compared to US GAAP*, December 2017, kpmg.com.

3. Assuming replacement of the cutter every two years at a price of $2,000, what is the total depreciation expense over the eight years if the company uses the component method compared with the total depreciation expense if the company does not use the component method?

4. How many different items must the company estimate in the first year to compute depreciation expense for the milling machine if it uses the component method, and how does this compare with what would be required if it does not use the component method?

Solution to 1: Depreciation expense in Year 1 under the component method would be $1,625. For the portion of the machine excluding the cutter, the depreciable base is total cost minus the cost attributable to the cutter minus the estimated residual value = $10,000 − $2,000 − $3,000 = $5,000. Depreciation expense for the machine excluding the cutter in the first year equals $625 (depreciable cost divided by the useful life of the machine = $5,000/8 years). For the cutter, the depreciation expense equals $1,000 (depreciable cost divided by the useful life of the cutter = $2,000/2 years). Thus, the total depreciation expense for Year 1 under the component method is $1,625 (the sum of the depreciation expenses of the two components = $625 + $1,000). Depreciation expense in Year 2 would also be $1,625.

If the company does not use the component method, depreciation expense in Year 1 is $875 (the depreciable cost of the total milling machine divided by its useful life = [$10,000 − $3,000]/8 years). Depreciation expense in Year 2 would also be $875.

Solution to 2: Assuming that at the end of Year 2, the company purchases a new cutter for $2,000 with an estimated two-year life, under the component method, the depreciation expense in Year 3 will remain at $1,625. If the company does not use the component method and purchases a new cutter with an estimated two-year life for $2,000 at the end of Year 2, the depreciation expense in Year 3 will be $1,875 [$875 + ($2,000/2) = $875 + $1,000].

Solution to 3: Over the eight years, assuming replacement of the cutters every two years at a price of $2,000, the total depreciation expense will be $13,000 [$1,625 × 8 years] when the component method is used. When the component method is not used, the total depreciation expense will also be $13,000 [$875 × 2 years + $1,875 × 6 years]. This amount equals the total expenditures of $16,000 [$10,000 + 3 cutters × $2,000] less the residual value of $3,000.

Solution to 4: The following table summarizes the estimates required in the first year to compute depreciation expense if the company does or does not use the component method:

Estimate	Required using component method?	Required if not using component method?
Useful life of milling machine	Yes	Yes
Residual value of milling machine	Yes	Yes
Portion of machine cost attributable to cutter	Yes	No
Portion of residual value attributable to cutter	Yes	No
Useful life of cutter	Yes	No

Total depreciation expense may be allocated between the cost of sales and other expenses. Within the income statement, depreciation expense of assets used in production is usually allocated to the cost of sales, and the depreciation expense of assets not used in production may be allocated to some other expense category. For instance, depreciation expense may be allocated to selling, general, and administrative expenses if depreciable assets are used in those functional areas. Notes to the financial statements sometimes disclose information regarding which income statement line items include depreciation expense, although the exact amount of detail disclosed by individual companies varies.

3.2. Amortization Methods and Calculation of Amortization Expense

Amortization is similar in concept to depreciation. The term amortization applies to intangible assets, and the term depreciation applies to tangible assets. Both terms refer to the process of allocating the cost of an asset over the asset's useful life. Only those intangible assets assumed to have finite useful lives are amortized over their useful lives, following the pattern in which the benefits are used up. Acceptable amortization methods are the same as the methods acceptable for depreciation. Assets assumed to have an indefinite useful life (in other words, without a finite useful life) are not amortized. An intangible asset is considered to have an indefinite useful life when there is "no foreseeable limit to the period over which the asset is expected to generate net cash inflows" for the company.[16]

Intangible assets with finite useful lives include an acquired customer list expected to provide benefits to a direct-mail marketing company for two to three years, an acquired patent or copyright with a specific expiration date, an acquired license with a specific expiration date and no right to renew the license, and an acquired trademark for a product that a company plans to phase out over a specific number of years. Examples of intangible assets with indefinite useful lives include an acquired license that, although it has a specific expiration date, can be renewed at little or no cost and an acquired trademark that, although it has a specific expiration, can be renewed at a minimal cost and relates to a product that a company plans to continue selling for the foreseeable future.

As with depreciation for a tangible asset, the calculation of amortization for an intangible asset requires the original amount at which the intangible asset is recognized and estimates of the length of its useful life and its residual value at the end of its useful life. Useful lives are estimated on the basis of the expected use of the asset, considering any factors that may limit the life of the asset, such as legal, regulatory, contractual, competitive, or economic factors.

EXAMPLE 10   Amortization Expense

IAS 38 *Intangible Assets* provides illustrative examples regarding the accounting for intangible assets, including the following:

> A direct-mail marketing company acquires a customer list and expects that it will be able to derive benefit from the information on the list for at least one year, but no more than three years. The customer list would be amortized over management's best estimate of its useful

---

[16] IAS 38 *Intangible Assets*, paragraph 88.

life, say 18 months. Although the direct-mail marketing company may intend to add customer names and other information to the list in the future, the expected benefits of the acquired customer list relate only to the customers on that list at the date it was acquired.

In this example, in what ways would management's decisions and estimates affect the company's financial statements?

Solution: Because the acquired customer list is expected to generate future economic benefits for a period greater than one year, the cost of the list should be capitalized and not expensed. The acquired customer list is determined to not have an indefinite life and must be amortized. Management must estimate the useful life of the customer list and must select an amortization method. In this example, the list appears to have no residual value. Both the amortization method and the estimated useful life affect the amount of the amortization expense in each period. A shorter estimated useful life, compared with a longer estimated useful life, results in a higher amortization expense each year over a shorter period, but the *total* accumulated amortization expense over the life of the intangible asset is unaffected by the estimate of the useful life. Similarly, the total accumulated amortization expense over the life of the intangible asset is unaffected by the choice of amortization method. The amortization expense per period depends on the amortization method. If the straight-line method is used, the amortization expense is the same for each year of useful life. If an accelerated method is used, the amortization expense will be higher in earlier years.

4. THE REVALUATION MODEL

The revaluation model is an alternative to the cost model for the periodic valuation and reporting of long-lived assets. IFRS permit the use of either the revaluation model or the cost model, but the revaluation model is not allowed under US GAAP. Revaluation changes the carrying amounts of classes of long-lived assets to fair value (the fair value must be measured reliably). Under the cost model, carrying amounts are historical costs less accumulated depreciation or amortization. Under the revaluation model, carrying amounts are the fair values at the date of revaluation less any subsequent accumulated depreciation or amortization.

IFRS allow companies to value long-lived assets either under a cost model at historical cost minus accumulated depreciation or amortization or under a revaluation model at fair value. In contrast, US accounting standards require that the cost model be used. A key difference between the two models is that the cost model allows only decreases in the values of long-lived assets compared with historical costs but the revaluation model may result in increases in the values of long-lived assets to amounts greater than historical costs.

IFRS allow a company to use the cost model for some classes of assets and the revaluation model for others, but the company must apply the same model to all assets within a particular class of assets and must revalue all items within a class to avoid selective revaluation. Examples of different classes of assets include land, land and buildings, machinery, motor vehicles, furniture and fixtures, and office equipment. The revaluation model may be used for classes of intangible assets but only if an active market for the assets exists, because the revaluation model may only be used if the fair values of the assets can be measured reliably. For practical purposes, the revaluation model is rarely used for either tangible or intangible assets, but its use is especially rare for intangible assets.

Under the revaluation model, whether an asset revaluation affects earnings depends on whether the revaluation initially increases or decreases an asset class's carrying amount. If a revaluation initially decreases the carrying amount of the asset class, the decrease is recognized in profit or loss. Later, if the carrying amount of the asset class increases, the increase is recognized in profit or loss to the extent that it reverses a revaluation decrease of the same asset class previously recognized in profit or loss. Any increase in excess of the reversal amount will not be recognized in the income statement but will be recorded directly to equity in a revaluation surplus account. An upward revaluation is treated the same as the amount in excess of the reversal amount. In other words, if a revaluation initially increases the carrying amount of the asset class, the increase in the carrying amount of the asset class bypasses the income statement and goes directly to equity under the heading of revaluation surplus. Any subsequent decrease in the asset's value first decreases the revaluation surplus and then goes to income. When an asset is retired or disposed of, any related amount of revaluation surplus included in equity is transferred directly to retained earnings.

Asset revaluations offer several considerations for financial statement analyses. First, an increase in the carrying amount of depreciable long-lived assets increases total assets and shareholders' equity, so asset revaluations that increase the carrying amount of an asset can be used to reduce reported leverage. Defining leverage as average total assets divided by average shareholders' equity, increasing both the numerator (assets) and denominator (equity) by the same amount leads to a decline in the ratio. (Mathematically, when a ratio is greater than one, as in this case, an increase in both the numerator and the denominator by the same amount leads to a decline in the ratio.) Therefore, the leverage motivation for the revaluation should be considered in analysis. For example, a company may revalue assets up if it is seeking new capital or approaching leverage limitations set by financial covenants.

Second, assets revaluations that decrease the carrying amount of the assets reduce net income. In the year of the revaluation, profitability measures such as return on assets and return on equity decline. However, because total assets and shareholders' equity are also lower, the company may appear more profitable in future years. Additionally, reversals of downward revaluations also go through income, thus increasing earnings. Managers can then opportunistically time the reversals to manage earnings and increase income. Third, asset revaluations that increase the carrying amount of an asset initially increase depreciation expense, total assets, and shareholders' equity. Therefore, profitability measures, such as return on assets and return on equity, would decline. Although upward asset revaluations also generally decrease income (through higher depreciation expense), the increase in the value of the long-lived asset is presumably based on increases in the operating capacity of the asset, which will likely be evidenced in increased future revenues.

Finally, an analyst should consider who did the appraisal—that is, an independent external appraiser or management—and how often revaluations are made. Appraisals of the fair value of long-lived assets involve considerable judgment and discretion. Presumably, appraisals of assets from independent external sources are more reliable. How often assets are revalued can provide an indicator of whether their reported value continues to be representative of their fair values.

The next two examples illustrate revaluation of long-lived assets under IFRS.

EXAMPLE 11   Revaluation Resulting in an Increase in Carrying Amount Followed by Subsequent Revaluation Resulting in a Decrease in Carrying Amount

UPFIRST, a hypothetical manufacturing company, has elected to use the revaluation model for its machinery. Assume for simplicity that the company owns a single machine, which it purchased for €10,000 on the first day of its fiscal period, and that the measurement date occurs simultaneously with the company's fiscal period end.

1. At the end of the first fiscal period after acquisition, assume the fair value of the machine is determined to be €11,000. How will the company's financial statements reflect the asset?
2. At the end of the second fiscal period after acquisition, assume the fair value of the machine is determined to be €7,500. How will the company's financial statements reflect the asset?

Solution to 1: At the end of the first fiscal period, the company's balance sheet will show the asset at a value of €11,000. The €1,000 increase in the value of the asset will appear in other comprehensive income and be accumulated in equity under the heading of revaluation surplus.

Solution to 2: At the end of the second fiscal period, the company's balance sheet will show the asset at a value of €7,500. The total decrease in the carrying amount of the asset is €3,500 (€11,000 − €7,500). Of the €3,500 decrease, the first €1,000 will reduce the amount previously accumulated in equity under the heading of revaluation surplus. The other €2,500 will be shown as a loss on the income statement.

EXAMPLE 12   Revaluation Resulting in a Decrease in Asset's Carrying Amount Followed by Subsequent Revaluation Resulting in an Increase in Asset's Carrying Amount

DOWNFIRST, a hypothetical manufacturing company, has elected to use the revaluation model for its machinery. Assume for simplicity that the company owns a single machine, which it purchased for €10,000 on the first day of its fiscal period, and that the measurement date occurs simultaneously with the company's fiscal period end.

1. At the end of the first fiscal period after acquisition, assume the fair value of the machine is determined to be €7,500. How will the company's financial statements reflect the asset?
2. At the end of the second fiscal period after acquisition, assume the fair value of the machine is determined to be €11,000. How will the company's financial statements reflect the asset?

Solution to 1: At the end of the first fiscal period, the company's balance sheet will show the asset at a value of €7,500. The €2,500 decrease in the value of the asset will appear as a loss on the company's income statement.

Solution to 2: At the end of the second fiscal period, the company's balance sheet will show the asset at a value of €11,000. The total increase in the carrying amount of the asset is an increase of €3,500 (€11,000 − €7,500). Of the €3,500 increase, the first €2,500 reverses a previously reported loss and will be reported as a gain on the income statement. The other €1,000 will bypass profit or loss and be reported as other comprehensive income and be accumulated in equity under the heading of revaluation surplus.

Exhibit 6 provides two examples of disclosures concerning the revaluation model. The first disclosure is an excerpt from the 2006 annual report of KPN, a Dutch telecommunications and multimedia company. The report was produced at a time during which any IFRS-reporting company with a US stock exchange listing was required to explain differences between its reporting under IFRS and its reporting if it had used US GAAP.[17] One of these differences, as previously noted, is that US GAAP do not allow revaluation of fixed assets held for use. KPN's disclosure states that the company elected to report a class of fixed assets (cables) at fair value and explained that under US GAAP, using the cost model, the value of the asset class would have been €350 million lower. The second disclosure is an excerpt from the 2017 annual report of Avianca Holdings S.A., a Latin American airline that reports under IFRS and uses the revaluation model for one component of its fixed assets.

EXHIBIT 6   Impact of Revaluation

1. Excerpt from the annual report of Koninklijke KPN N.V. explaining certain differences between IFRS and US GAAP regarding "Deemed cost fixed assets":

   KPN elected the exemption to revalue certain of its fixed assets upon the transition to IFRS to fair value and to use this fair value as their deemed cost. KPN applied the depreciated replacement cost method to determine this fair value. The revalued assets pertain to certain cables, which form part of property, plant, and equipment. Under US GAAP, this revaluation is not allowed and therefore results in a reconciling item. As a result, the value of these assets as of December 31, 2006 under US GAAP is EUR 350 million lower (2005: EUR 415 million; 2004: EUR 487 million) than under IFRS.

Source: KPN's Form 20-F, p. 168, filed March 1, 2007.

---

[17] On November 15, 2007, the SEC approved rule amendments under which financial statements from foreign private issuers in the United States will be accepted without reconciliation to US GAAP if the financial statements are prepared in accordance with IFRS as issued by the International Accounting Standards Board. The rule took effect for the 2007 fiscal year. As a result, companies such as KPN no longer need to provide reconciliations to US GAAP.

EXHIBIT 6   (Continued)

2. The 2017 annual report of Avianca Holdings S.A. and Subsidiaries shows $58.4 million of "Revaluation and Other Reserves" as a component of Equity on its balance sheet and $31.0 million in Other Comprehensive Income for the current year's "Revaluation of Administrative Property." The relevant footnote disclosure explains:

> "Administrative property in Bogota, Medellín, El Salvador, and San Jose is recorded at fair value less accumulated depreciation on buildings and impairment losses recognized at the date of revaluation. Valuations are performed with sufficient frequency to ensure that the fair value of a revalued asset does not differ materially from its carrying amount. A revaluation reserve is recorded in other comprehensive income and credited to the asset revaluation reserve in equity. However, to the extent that it reverses a revaluation deficit of the same asset previously recognized in profit or loss, the increase is recognized in profit and loss. A revaluation deficit is recognized in the income statement, except to the extent that it offsets an existing surplus on the same asset recognized in the asset revaluation reserve. Upon disposal, any revaluation reserve relating to the particular asset being sold is transferred to retained earnings.

Source: AVIANCA HOLDINGS S.A. Form 20-F filed May 1, 2018.

Clearly, the use of the revaluation model as opposed to the cost model can have a significant impact on the financial statements of companies. This has potential consequences for comparing financial performance using financial ratios of companies that use different models.

5. IMPAIRMENT OF ASSETS

In contrast with depreciation and amortization charges, which serve to allocate the depreciable cost of a long-lived asset over its useful life, impairment charges reflect an unanticipated decline in the value of an asset. Both IFRS and US GAAP require companies to write down the carrying amount of impaired assets. Impairment reversals for identifiable, long-lived assets are permitted under IFRS but typically not under US GAAP.

An asset is considered to be impaired when its carrying amount exceeds its recoverable amount. Although IFRS and US GAAP define recoverability differently (as described below), in general, impairment losses are recognized when the asset's carrying amount is not recoverable. The following paragraphs describe accounting for impairment for different categories of assets.

5.1. Impairment of Property, Plant, and Equipment

Accounting standards do not require that property, plant, and equipment be tested annually for impairment. Rather, at the end of each reporting period (generally, a fiscal year), a company assesses whether there are indications of asset impairment. If there is no indication of impairment, the asset is not tested for impairment. If there is an indication of impairment, such as evidence of obsolescence, decline in demand for products, or technological advancements, the recoverable amount of the asset should be measured in order to test for impairment. For property, plant, and equipment, impairment losses are recognized when the asset's carrying amount is not recoverable; the carrying amount is more than the recoverable amount. The amount of the impairment loss will reduce the carrying amount of the asset on the balance sheet and will reduce net income on the income statement. The impairment loss is a non-cash item and will not affect cash from operations.

IFRS and US GAAP differ somewhat both in the guidelines for determining that impairment has occurred and in the measurement of an impairment loss. Under IAS 36, an impairment loss is measured as the excess of carrying amount over the recoverable amount of the asset. The recoverable amount of an asset is defined as "the higher of its fair value less costs to sell and its value in use." Value in use is based on the present value of expected future cash flows. Under US GAAP, assessing recoverability is separate from measuring the impairment loss. The carrying amount of an asset "group" is considered not recoverable when it exceeds the undiscounted expected future cash flows of the group. If the asset's carrying amount is considered not recoverable, the impairment loss is measured as the difference between the asset's fair value and carrying amount.

EXAMPLE 13   Impairment of Property, Plant, and Equipment

Sussex, a hypothetical manufacturing company in the United Kingdom, has a machine it uses to produce a single product. The demand for the product has declined substantially since the introduction of a competing product. The company has assembled the following information with respect to the machine:

Carrying amount	£18,000
Undiscounted expected future cash flows	£19,000
Present value of expected future cash flows	£16,000
Fair value if sold	£17,000
Costs to sell	£2,000

1. Under IFRS, what would the company report for the machine?
2. Under US GAAP, what would the company report for the machine?

Solution to 1: Under IFRS, the company would compare the carrying amount (£18,000) with the higher of its fair value less costs to sell (£15,000) and its value in use (£16,000). The carrying amount exceeds the value in use, the higher of the two amounts, by £2,000. The machine would be written down to the recoverable amount of £16,000, and a loss of £2,000 would be reported in the income statement. The carrying amount of the machine is now £16,000. A new depreciation schedule based on the carrying amount of £16,000 would be developed.

Solution to 2: Under US GAAP, the carrying amount (£18,000) is compared with the undiscounted expected future cash flows (£19,000). The carrying amount is less than the undiscounted expected future cash flows, so the carrying amount is considered recoverable. The machine would continue to be carried at £18,000, and no loss would be reported.

In Example 13, a write down in the value of a piece of property, plant, and equipment occurred under IFRS but not under US GAAP. In Example 14, a write down occurs under both IFRS and US GAAP.

EXAMPLE 14   Impairment of Property, Plant, and Equipment

Essex, a hypothetical manufacturing company, has a machine it uses to produce a single product. The demand for the product has declined substantially since the introduction of a competing product. The company has assembled the following information with respect to the machine:

Carrying amount	£18,000
Undiscounted expected future cash flows	£16,000
Present value of expected future cash flows	£14,000
Fair value if sold	£10,000
Costs to sell	£2,000

1. Under IFRS, what would the company report for the machine?
2. Under US GAAP, what would the company report for the machine?

Solution to 1: Under IFRS, the company would compare the carrying amount (£18,000) with the higher of its fair value less costs to sell (£8,000) and its value in use (£14,000). The carrying amount exceeds the value in use, the higher of the two amounts, by £4,000. The machine would be written down to the recoverable amount of £14,000, and a loss of £4,000 would be reported in the income statement. The carrying amount of the machine is now £14,000. A new depreciation schedule based on the carrying amount of £14,000 would be developed.

Solution to 2: Under US GAAP, the carrying amount (£18,000) is compared with the undiscounted expected future cash flows (£16,000). The carrying amount exceeds the undiscounted expected future cash flows, so the carrying amount is considered not recoverable. The machine would be written down to fair value of £10,000, and a loss of £8,000 would be reported in the income statement. The carrying amount of the machine is now £10,000. A new depreciation schedule based on the carrying amount of £10,000 would be developed.

Example 14 shows that the write down to value in use under IFRS can be less than the write down to fair value under US GAAP. The difference in recognition of impairment losses is ultimately reflected in difference in book value of equity.

5.2. Impairment of Intangible Assets with a Finite Life

Intangible assets with a finite life are amortized (carrying amount decreases over time) and may become impaired. As is the case with property, plant, and equipment, the assets are not tested annually for impairment. Instead, they are tested only when significant events suggest the need to test. The company assesses at the end of each reporting period whether a significant event suggesting the need to test for impairment has occurred. Examples of such events include a significant decrease in the market price or a significant adverse change in legal or economic factors. Impairment accounting for intangible assets with a finite life is essentially the same as for tangible assets; the amount of the impairment loss will reduce the carrying amount of the asset on the balance sheet and will reduce net income on the income statement.

5.3. Impairment of Intangibles with Indefinite Lives

Intangible assets with indefinite lives are not amortized. Instead, they are carried on the balance sheet at historical cost but are tested at least annually for impairment. Impairment exists when the carrying amount exceeds its fair value.

5.4. Impairment of Long-Lived Assets Held for Sale

A long-lived (non-current) asset is reclassified as held for sale rather than held for use when management's intent is to sell it and its sale is highly probable. (Additionally, accounting standards require that the asset must be available for immediate sale in its present condition.)[18] For instance, assume a building is no longer needed by a company and management's intent is to sell it, if the transaction meets the accounting criteria, the building is reclassified from property, plant, and equipment to non-current assets held for sale. At the time of reclassification, assets previously held for use are tested for impairment. If the carrying amount at the time of reclassification exceeds the fair value less costs to sell, an impairment loss is recognized, and the asset is written down to fair value less costs to sell. Long-lived assets held for sale cease to be depreciated or amortized.

5.5. Reversals of Impairments of Long-Lived Assets

After an asset has been deemed impaired and an impairment loss has been reported, the asset's recoverable amount could potentially increase. For instance, a lawsuit appeal may successfully challenge a patent infringement by another company, with the result that a patent previously written down has a higher recoverable amount. IFRS permit impairment losses to be reversed if the recoverable amount of an asset increases regardless of whether the asset is classified as held for use or held for sale. Note that IFRS permit the reversal of impairment losses only. IFRS do not permit the revaluation to the recoverable amount if the recoverable amount exceeds the previous carrying amount. Under US GAAP, the accounting for reversals of impairments depends on whether the asset is classified as held for use or held for sale.[19] Under US GAAP, once an impairment loss has been recognized for assets held for use, it cannot be reversed. In other words, once the value of an asset held for use has been decreased by an impairment charge, it cannot be increased. For assets held for sale, if the fair value increases after an impairment loss, the loss can be reversed.

6. DERECOGNITION

A company derecognizes an asset (i.e., removes it from the financial statements) when the asset is disposed of or is expected to provide no future benefits from either use or disposal. A company may dispose of a long-lived operating asset by selling it, exchanging it, abandoning it, or

---

[18] IFRS 5 *Non-current Assets Held for Sale and Discontinued Operations.*
[19] FASB ASC Section 360-10-35 [Property, Plant, and Equipment – Overall – Subsequent Measurement].

distributing it to existing shareholders. As previously described, non-current assets that management intends to sell or to distribute to existing shareholders and which meet the accounting criteria (immediately available for sale in current condition and the sale is highly probable) are reclassified as non-current assets held for sale.

6.1. Sale of Long-Lived Assets

The gain or loss on the sale of long-lived assets is computed as the sales proceeds minus the carrying amount of the asset at the time of sale. An asset's carrying amount is typically the net book value (i.e., the historical cost minus accumulated depreciation), unless the asset's carrying amount has been changed to reflect impairment and/or revaluation, as previously discussed.

EXAMPLE 15   Calculation of Gain or Loss on the Sale of Long-Lived Assets

Moussilauke Diners Inc., a hypothetical company, as a result of revamping its menus to focus on healthier food items, sells 450 used pizza ovens and reports a gain on the sale of $1.2 million. The ovens had a carrying amount of $1.9 million (original cost of $5.1 million less $3.2 million of accumulated depreciation). At what price did Moussilauke sell the ovens?

A. $0.7 million.
B. $3.1 million.
C. $6.3 million.

Solution: B is correct. The ovens had a carrying amount of $1.9 million, and Moussilauke recognized a gain of $1.2 million. Therefore, Moussilauke sold the ovens at a price of $3.1 million. The gain on the sale of $1.2 million is the selling price of $3.1 million minus the carrying amount of $1.9 million. Ignoring taxes, the cash flow from the sale is $3.1 million, which would appear as a cash inflow from investing.

A gain or loss on the sale of an asset is disclosed on the income statement, either as a component of other gains and losses or in a separate line item when the amount is material. A company typically discloses further detail about the sale in the management discussion and analysis and/or financial statement footnotes. In addition, a statement of cash flows prepared using the indirect method adjusts net income to remove any gain or loss on the sale from operating cash flow and to include the amount of proceeds from the sale in cash from investing activities. Recall that the indirect method of the statement of cash flows begins with net income and makes all adjustments to arrive at cash from operations, including removal of gains or losses from non-operating activities.

6.2. Long-Lived Assets Disposed of Other than by a Sale

Long-lived assets to be disposed of other than by a sale (e.g., abandoned, exchanged for another asset, or distributed to owners in a spin-off) are classified as held for use until disposal or until they meet the criteria to be classified as held for sale or held for distribution.[20] Thus, the long-lived assets continue to be depreciated and tested for impairment, unless their carrying amount is zero, as required for other long-lived assets owned by the company.

When an asset is retired or abandoned, the accounting is similar to a sale, except that the company does not record cash proceeds. Assets are reduced by the carrying amount of the asset at the time of retirement or abandonment, and a loss equal to the asset's carrying amount is recorded.

When an asset is exchanged, accounting for the exchange typically involves removing the carrying amount of the asset given up, adding a fair value for the asset acquired, and reporting any difference between the carrying amount and the fair value as a gain or loss. The fair value used is the fair value of the asset given up unless the fair value of the asset acquired is more clearly evident. If no reliable measure of fair value exists, the acquired asset is measured at the carrying amount of the asset given up. A gain is reported when the fair value used for the newly acquired asset exceeds the carrying amount of the asset given up. A loss is reported when the fair value used for the newly acquired asset is less than the carrying amount of the asset given up. If the acquired asset is valued at the carrying amount of the asset given up because no reliable measure of fair value exists, no gain or loss is reported.

When a spin-off occurs, typically, an entire cash generating unit of a company with all its assets is spun off. As an illustration of a spin-off, Fiat Chrysler Automobiles (FCA) spun off its ownership of Ferrari in 2016. Prior to the spinoff, FCA had sold 10 percent of its ownership of Ferrari in an IPO and recognized an increase in Shareholders' equity of € 873 million (the difference between the consideration it received in the IPO of € 866 million and the carrying amount of the equity interest sold of € 7 million.) In contrast, the spin-off, in which FCA distributed its ownership in Ferrari to the existing FCA shareholders, did not result in any gain or loss.

FCA's spinoff was completed on January 3, 2016, with each FCA shareholder receiving one common share of Ferrari N.V. for every ten common shares of FCA. In its financial statements for the prior fiscal year, FCA shows the assets and liabilities of Ferrari as held for distribution. Specifically, its balance sheet includes € 3,650 million Assets Held for Distribution as a component of current assets and € 3,584 million Liabilities Held for Distribution. Exhibit 7 includes excerpts from the company's December 31, 2015 annual report.

EXHIBIT 7   Fiat Chrysler Automobiles (FCA) Excerpts from Notes to the Consolidated Financial Statements—2015 Annual Report

Ferrari Spin-off and Discontinued Operations

"As the spin-off of Ferrari N.V. became highly probable with the aforementioned shareholders' approval and since it was available for immediate distribution at that date, the Ferrari segment met the criteria to be classified as a disposal group held

---

[20] In a spin-off, shareholders of the parent company receive a proportional number of shares in a new, separate entity.

EXHIBIT 7   (Continued)

for distribution to owners and a discontinued operation pursuant to IFRS 5 – *Non-current Assets Held for Sale and Discontinued Operations.*"

The following assets and liabilities of the Ferrari segment were classified as held for distribution at December 31, 2015:

	At December 31, 2015
Assets classified as held for distribution	(€ million)
Goodwill	786
Other intangible assets	297
Property, plant, and equipment	627
Other non-current assets	134
Receivables from financing activities	1,176
Cash and cash equivalents	182
Other current assets	448
Total Assets held for distribution	**3,650**
Liabilities classified as held for distribution	
Provisions	224
Debt	2,256
Other current liabilities	624
Trade payables	480
Total Liabilities held for distribution	**3,584**

Source: Fiat Chrysler Automobiles (FCA)'s Form 20-F for the year ending December 31, 2015.

7. PRESENTATION AND DISCLOSURES

Under IFRS, for each class of property, plant, and equipment, a company must disclose the measurement bases, the depreciation method, the useful lives (or, equivalently, the depreciation rate) used, the gross carrying amount, and the accumulated depreciation at the beginning and end of the period, and a reconciliation of the carrying amount at the beginning and end of the period.[21] In addition, disclosures of restrictions on title and pledges as security of property, plant, and equipment and contractual agreements to acquire property, plant, and equipment are required. If the revaluation model is used, the date of revaluation, details of how the fair value was obtained, the carrying amount under the cost model, and the revaluation surplus must be disclosed.

The disclosure requirements under US GAAP are less exhaustive.[22] A company must disclose the depreciation expense for the period, the balances of major classes of depreciable assets, accumulated depreciation by major classes or in total, and a general description of the

---

[21] IAS 16 *Property, Plant and Equipment*, paragraphs 73–79 [Disclosure].
[22] FASB ASC Section 360-10-50 [Property, Plant, and Equipment – Overall – Disclosure].

depreciation method(s) used in computing depreciation expense with respect to the major classes of depreciable assets.

Under IFRS, for each class of intangible assets, a company must disclose whether the useful lives are indefinite or finite. If finite, for each class of intangible asset, a company must disclose the useful lives (or, equivalently, the amortization rate) used, the amortization methods used, the gross carrying amount and the accumulated amortization at the beginning and end of the period, where amortization is included on the income statement, and a reconciliation of the carrying amount at the beginning and end of the period.[23] If an asset has an indefinite life, the company must disclose the carrying amount of the asset and why it is considered to have an indefinite life. Similar to property, plant, and equipment, disclosures of restrictions on title and pledges as security of intangible assets and contractual agreements to acquire intangible assets are required. If the revaluation model is used, the date of revaluation, details of how the fair value was obtained, the carrying amount under the cost model, and the revaluation surplus must be disclosed.

Under US GAAP, companies are required to disclose the gross carrying amounts and accumulated amortization in total and by major class of intangible assets, the aggregate amortization expense for the period, and the estimated amortization expense for the next five fiscal years.[24]

The disclosures related to impairment losses also differ under IFRS and US GAAP. Under IFRS, a company must disclose for each class of assets the amounts of impairment losses and reversals of impairment losses recognized in the period and where those are recognized on the financial statements.[25] The company must also disclose in aggregate the main classes of assets affected by impairment losses and reversals of impairment losses and the main events and circumstances leading to recognition of these impairment losses and reversals of impairment losses. Under US GAAP, there is no reversal of impairment losses for assets held for use. The company must disclose a description of the impaired asset, what led to the impairment, the method of determining fair value, the amount of the impairment loss, and where the loss is recognized on the financial statements.[26]

Disclosures about long-lived assets appear throughout the financial statements: in the balance sheet, the income statement, the statement of cash flows, and the notes. The balance sheet reports the carrying value of the asset. For the income statement, depreciation expense may or may not appear as a separate line item. Under IFRS, whether the income statement discloses depreciation expense separately depends on whether the company is using a 'nature of expense' method or a 'function of expense' method. Under the nature of expense method, a company aggregates expenses "according to their nature (for example, depreciation, purchases of materials, transport costs, employee benefits and advertising costs), and does not reallocate them among functions within the entity."[27] Under the function of expense method, a company classifies expenses according to the function, for example, as part of cost of sales or of SG&A (selling, general, and administrative expenses). At a minimum, a company using the function of expense method must disclose cost of sales, but the other line items vary.

---

[23] IAS 38 *Intangible Assets*, paragraphs 118–128 [Disclosure].

[24] FASB ASC Section 350-30-50 [Intangibles – General – Disclosure].

[25] IAS 36 *Impairment of Assets*, paragraphs 126–137 [Disclosure].

[26] FASB ASC Section 360-10-50 [Property, Plant, and Equipment – Overall – Disclosure] and FASB ASC Section 350-30-50 [Intangibles – General – Disclosure].

[27] IAS 1 paragraph 102.

The statement of cash flows reflects acquisitions and disposals of fixed assets in the investing section. In addition, when prepared using the indirect method, the statement of cash flows typically shows depreciation expense (or depreciation plus amortization) as a line item in the adjustments of net income to cash flow from operations. The notes to the financial statements describe the company's accounting method(s), the range of estimated useful lives, historical cost by main category of fixed asset, accumulated depreciation, and annual depreciation expense.

To illustrate financial statement presentation and disclosures, the following example provides excerpts relating to intangible assets and property, plant, and equipment from the annual report of Orange SA for the year ended December 31, 2017.

EXAMPLE 16   Financial Statement Presentation and Disclosures for Long-Lived Assets

Exhibits 8, 9, and 10 include excerpts from the annual report for the year ended December 31, 2017 of Orange SA, an international telecommunications company based in France.

EXHIBIT 8   Orange SA
Excerpts from the 2017 Consolidated Financial Statements
(Note that only selected line items/data are shown for illustrative purposes)

	Excerpt from Consolidated income statement EUR (€) € in Millions		
	12 Months Ended		
	Dec. 31, 2017	Dec. 31, 2016	Dec. 31, 2015
Revenues	€41,096	€40,918	€40,236
...	...	...	...
Depreciation and amortization	(6,846)	(6,728)	(6,465)
...	...	...	...
Impairment of goodwill	(20)	(772)	
Impairment of fixed assets	(190)	(207)	(38)
...	...	...	...
Operating income	4,917	4,077	4,742
...	...	...	...
Consolidated net income of continuing operations	2,114	1,010	2,510
Consolidated net income of discontinued operations (EE)	29	2,253	448
Consolidated net income	**2,143**	**3,263**	**2,958**
Net income attributable to owners of the parent company	1,906	2,935	2,652
Non-controlling interests	€237	€328	€306

Excerpt from the Consolidated statement of financial position EUR (€) € in Millions			
Assets	Dec. 31, 2017	Dec. 31, 2016	Dec. 31, 2015
Goodwill	€27,095	€27,156	€27,071
Other intangible assets	14,339	14,602	14,327
Property, plant and equipment	26,665	25,912	25,123
...	...	...	...
Total non-current assets	74,035	74,819	71,330
...	...	...	...
Total current assets	20,679	19,849	14,312
Assets held for sale			5,788
Total assets	**94,714**	**94,668**	**91,430**
Equity and liabilities			
...	...	...	...
Total equity	32,942	33,174	33,267
...	...	...	...
Total non-current liabilities	32,736	35,590	36,537
...	...	...	...
Total current liabilities	29,036	25,904	21,626
Total equity and liabilities	**94,714**	**94,668**	**91,430**

EXHIBIT 9   Orange

Excerpts from the 2017 Notes to the Consolidated Financial Statements

Excerpt from Note 7.2 Goodwill

[Excerpt] Reconciliation of Changes in Goodwill (€ in Millions)

	12 Months Ended		
	Dec. 31, 2017	Dec. 31, 2016	Dec. 31, 2015
Gross Value in the opening balance	€32,689	€32,606	€30,271
Acquisitions	38	904	2,333
Disposals	0	(6)	(69)
Translation adjustment	(40)	(815)	73
Reclassifications and other items	0	0	(2)
Reclassification to assets held for sale	0	0	0
Gross Value in Closing Balance	32,687	32,689	32,606
Accumulated Impairment losses in the opening balance	(5,533)	(5,535)	(5,487)
Impairment	(20)	(772)	0
Disposals	0	0	0
Translation adjustment	(39)	774	(48)
Reclassifications and other items	0	0	0
Reclassification to assets held for sale	0	0	0
Accumulated Impairment losses in the closing balance	€(5,592)	€(5,533)	€(5,535)
Net book value of goodwill	**27,095**	**27,156**	**27,071**

Excerpt* from Note 7.3 Key assumptions used to determine recoverable amounts as of December 31, 2017

The parameters used for the determination of recoverable amount of the main consolidated operations are set forth below:

	France	Spain	Poland	Belgium	Romania
Perpetuity growth rate	0.8%	1.5%	1.0%	0.5%	2.3%
Post-tax discount rate	5.5%	8.6%	8.3%	6.8%	8.8%

Excerpt* from Note 7.4 Sensitivity of recoverable amounts as of December 31, 2017

The level of sensitivity presented allows readers of the financial statements to estimate the impact in their own assessment.

(in billions of euros)	France	Spain	Poland	Belgium	Romania
Decrease by 1% in perpetuity growth rate	10.4	1.6	0.6	0.3	0.3
An increase by 1% in post-tax discount rate	11.4	2.0	0.6	0.3	0.3

* Table extracted presents only selected assumptions and selected countries.

The company's annual report provides more detail.

Goodwill is not amortized. It is tested for impairment at least annually and more frequently when there is an indication that it may be impaired.... These tests are performed at the level of each Cash Generating Unit (CGU) (or group of CGUs).... To determine whether an impairment loss should be recognized, the carrying value of the assets and liabilities of the CGUs or groups of CGUs is compared to recoverable amount, for which Orange uses mostly the value in use.... Value in use is the present value of the future expected cash flows. Cash flow projections are based on economic and regulatory assumptions, license renewal assumptions and forecast trading and investment activity drawn up by the Group's management....

Excerpt from Note 8.3 Other intangible assets – Net book value

	December 31		
(in millions of euros)	2017	2016	2015
Telecommunications licenses	6,233	6,440	5,842
Orange brand	3,133	3,133	3,133
Other brands	88	102	137
Customer bases	555	703	729
Software	3,946	3,781	3,815
Other intangible assets	384	443	671
Total	€14,339	€14,602	€14,327

Excerpt from Note 8.4 Property, plant and equipment – Net book value

	December 31		
(in millions of euros)	2017	2016	2015
Land and buildings	2,535	2,661	2,733
Network and terminals	22,880	21,984	21,194
IT equipment	802	784	787
Other property, plant and equipment	448	483	409
Total	€26,665	€25,912	€25,123

EXHIBIT 10   Orange
Excerpt from the 2017 Analysis of the Group's financial position and earnings

"Orange group operating income stood at 4,077 million euros in 2016, compared with 4,742 million euros in 2015 on a historical basis, a drop of 14.0% or 665 million euros. This drop on a historical basis was largely attributable to:

- the recognition, in 2016, of 772 million euros in impairment loss of goodwill ... and 207 million euros in impairment loss of fixed assets ... primarily relating to:
  - Poland for 507 million euros. This impairment loss mainly reflects a decline in competitiveness in the ADSL market, a deterioration in revenue assumptions in the mobile market and an increase in the post-tax discount rate due to the downgrading of the country's sovereign rating by the rating agencies,
  - Egypt for 232 million euros. This impairment loss reflects the financial terms of the 4G license awarded in 2016, the sharp depreciation of the Egyptian pound and increased political and economic uncertainty,
  - in the Congo (DRC), for 109 million euros. This impairment loss reflects political and economic uncertainty, a decline in purchasing power with a knock-on effect on the consumption of telecommunications products and services and an increased regulatory burden (particularly connected with the implementation of customer identification),
  - Cameroon for 90 million euros. This impairment loss reflects a decline in voice revenues following the surge in messaging services and in VoIP of Over-The-Top (OTT) providers and heightened competition in the mobile market,
  - and Niger for 26 million euros;
- and the 263 million euro increase in depreciation and amortization...

1. What proportion of Orange's total assets as of December 31, 2017, is represented by goodwill and other intangible assets?
2. What is the largest component of the company's impairment losses during the year ending December 2016?
3. The company discloses that it determines whether an impairment loss should be recognized by comparing the carrying value of a unit's assets and liabilities to the "recoverable amount" for which the company uses mostly the value in use. How does the company determine value in use?
4. By what amount would the estimated recoverable value of the company's operations in France, Spain, Poland, Belgium, and Romania change if the company decreased

its estimate of the perpetuity growth rate by 1%? By what amount would the estimated recoverable value of these operations change if the company increased its
estimate of the post-tax discount rate by 1%?

5. What are the largest components of other intangible assets as of December 31,
    2017? What is the largest component of property, plant, and equipment as of De-
    cember 31, 2017?

Solution to 1: As of December 31, 2017, goodwill represents 28% (= 27,095 ÷ 97,714)
of Orange's total assets. Other intangible assets represent 15% (= 14,339 ÷ 97,714).
Data are from the company's balance sheet in Exhibit 8.

Solution to 2: The largest component of the € 772 impairment loss on goodwill and the
€ 207 million impairment loss of fixed assets related to a € 507 million loss in Poland.
The company attributed the loss to a decline in the competitiveness of the market for its
ADSL technology, a reduction in revenue assumptions, and an increase in the discount
rate resulting from the downgrading of the country's debt rating. From Exhibit 10.

  [The company's financial statements define ADSL (Asymmetrical Digital Subscriber Line) as a "broadband data transmission technology on the traditional telephone network. It enables broadband data transmission (first and foremost Internet
access) via twisted paired copper cable (the most common type of telephone line found
in buildings)."]

Solution to 3: The company determines value in use – which it uses as a unit's assets
and liabilities "recoverable amount" in impairment testing – as the present value of
the future expected cash flows. The cash flow projections are based on management's
assumptions. From Note 7.4 in Exhibit 9.

Solution to 4: If the company decreased its estimate of the perpetuity growth rate by
1%, the estimated recoverable value of the company's operations in France, Spain, Poland, Belgium, and Romania would change by €13.2 billion (=10.4 + 1.6 + 0.6 + 0.3
+ 0.3). A decrease in estimated growth decreases the present value of the cash flows. If
the company increased its estimate of the post-tax discount rate by 1%, the estimated
recoverable value of these operations would change by €14.6 billion (=11.4 + 2.0 + 0.6
+ 0.3 + 0.3). An increase in the discount rate decreases the present value of cash flows.
Data are from Note 7.4 in Exhibit 9.

Solution to 5: The largest components of other intangible assets as of December 31,
2017, are telecommunications licenses, software, and the Orange brand, reported at
€6,233 million, €3,946 million, and €3,133 million, respectively. The largest component of property, plant, and equipment as of December 31, 2017, is network and termi-
nals (€22,880 million.) Data are from Note 8.3 and 8.4 in Exhibit 9.

  Note that the exhibits in the previous example contain relatively brief excerpts from the
company's disclosures. The complete text of the disclosures concerning the company's non-
current assets spans numerous different footnotes, some of which are several pages long.
Overall, an analyst can use the disclosures to understand a company's investments in tangible

and intangible assets, how those investments changed during a reporting period, how those changes affected current performance, and what those changes might indicate about future performance.

Ratios used in analyzing fixed assets include the fixed asset turnover ratio and several asset age ratios. The fixed asset turnover ratio (total revenue divided by average net fixed assets) reflects the relationship between total revenues and investment in PPE. The higher this ratio, the higher the amount of sales a company is able to generate with a given amount of investment in fixed assets. A higher asset turnover ratio is often interpreted as an indicator of greater efficiency.

Asset age ratios generally rely on the relationship between historical cost and depreciation. Under the revaluation model (permitted under IFRS but not US GAAP), the relationship between carrying amount, accumulated depreciation, and depreciation expense will differ when the carrying amount differs significantly from the depreciated historical cost. Therefore, the following discussion of asset age ratios applies primarily to PPE reported under the cost model.

Asset age and remaining useful life, two asset age ratios, are important indicators of a company's need to reinvest in productive capacity. The older the assets and the shorter the remaining life, the more a company may need to reinvest to maintain productive capacity. The average age of a company's asset base can be estimated as accumulated depreciation divided by depreciation expense. The average remaining life of a company's asset base can be estimated as net PPE divided by depreciation expense. These estimates simply reflect the following relationships for assets accounted for on a historical cost basis: total historical cost minus accumulated depreciation equals net PPE; and, under straight-line depreciation, total historical cost less salvage value divided by estimated useful life equals annual depreciation expense. Equivalently, total historical cost less salvage value divided by annual depreciation expense equals estimated useful life. Assuming straight-line depreciation and no salvage value (for simplicity), we have the following:

Estimated total useful life	=	Time elapsed since purchase (Age)	+	Estimated remaining life
Historical cost ÷ annual depreciation expense	=	Estimated total useful life		
Historical cost	=	Accumulated depreciation	+	Net PPE

Equivalently,

Estimated total useful life	=	Estimated age of equipment	+	Estimated remaining life
Historical cost ÷ annual depreciation expense	=	Accumulated depreciation ÷ annual depreciation expense	+	Net PPE ÷ annual depreciation expense

The application of these estimates can be illustrated by a hypothetical example of a company with a single depreciable asset. Assume the asset initially cost $100, had an estimated useful life of 10 years, and an estimated salvage value of $0. Each year, the company records a depreciation expense of $10, so accumulated depreciation will equal $10 times the number of years since the asset was acquired (when the asset is 7 years old, accumulated depreciation will be $70). Equivalently, the age of the asset will equal accumulated depreciation divided by the annual depreciation expense.

In practice, such estimates are difficult to make with great precision. Companies use depreciation methods other than the straight-line method and have numerous assets with varying useful lives and salvage values, including some assets that are fully depreciated, so this approach produces an estimate only. Moreover, fixed asset disclosures are often quite general. Consequently, these estimates may be primarily useful to identify areas for further investigation.

One further measure compares a company's current reinvestment in productive capacity. Comparing annual capital expenditures to annual depreciation expense provides an indication of whether productive capacity is being maintained. It is a very general indicator of the rate at which a company is replacing its PPE relative to the rate at which PPE is being depreciated.

EXAMPLE 17   Using Fixed Asset Disclosure to Compare Companies' Fixed Asset Turnover and Average Age of Depreciable Assets

You are analyzing the property, plant, and equipment of three international telecommunications companies:

1. Orange SA, which we discussed previously, has been listed on Euronext Paris (symbol ORA) and on the New York Stock Exchange (symbol ORAN) since 1997. At December 31, 2017, the French government retained 22.95% of the share capital.
2. BCE Inc., Canada's largest communications company, provides wireless, wireline, Internet, TV, and business communications across Canada. BCE's shares are publicly traded on the Toronto Stock Exchange and on the New York Stock Exchange (TSX, NYSE: BCE).
3. Verizon Communications Inc. is a US-based global provider of communications, information, and entertainment products and services to consumers, businesses, and governmental agencies. Verizon's shares are listed on the New York Stock Exchange and the NASDAQ Global Select Market (symbol VZ).

Exhibit 11 presents selected information from the companies' financial statements.

EXHIBIT 11

	Orange	BCE Inc	Verizon
Currency, Millions of:	Euro €	Canadian $	US $
Historical cost total PPE, end of year	€97,092	$69,230	$246,498
Accumulated depreciation, end of year	70,427	45,197	157,930
Net PPE, end of year	26,665	24,033	88,568
Net PPE, beginning of year	25,912	22,346	84,751
Revenues	41,096	22,719	126,034
Annual depreciation expense	4,708	3,037	14,741
Capital expenditure	5,677	4,149	17,247
Land included in PPE	Not separated	Not separated	806
Accounting standards	IFRS	IFRS	US GAAP
PPE measurement	Historical cost	Historical cost	Historical cost
Depreciation method	Straight-line	Straight-line	Straight-line

Sources: Companies' 2017 Annual Financial Reports.

1. Based on the above data for each company, estimate the total useful life, age, and remaining useful life of PPE.
2. Interpret the estimates. What items might affect comparisons across these companies?
3. How does each company's 2017 depreciation expense compare to its capital expenditures for the year?
4. Calculate and compare fixed asset turnover for each company.

Solution to 1: The following table presents the estimated total useful life, estimated age, and estimated remaining useful life of PPE for each of the companies.

Estimates	Orange	BCE Inc	Verizon
Estimated total useful life (years)	20.6	22.8	16.7
Estimated age (years)	15.0	14.9	10.7
Estimated remaining life (years)	5.7	7.9	6.0

The computations are demonstrated using Verizon's data ($ millions). The estimated total useful life of PPE is total historical cost of PPE of $246,498 divided by annual depreciation expense of $14,741, giving 16.7 years. Estimated age and estimated remaining life are obtained by dividing accumulated depreciation of $157,930 and net PPE of $88,568 by the annual depreciation expense of $14,741, giving 10.7 years and 6.0 years, respectively.

Ideally, the estimates of asset lives illustrated in this example should exclude land, which is not depreciable, when the information is available; however, both Orange and BCE report Land and Buildings as a combined amount. We will use Verizon, for which land appeared to be disclosed separately in the above table, to illustrate the estimates with adjusting for land. As an illustration of the calculations to exclude land, excluding Verizon's land would give an estimated total useful life for the non-land PPE of 16.7 years [(total cost €246,498 minus land cost of $806) divided by annual depreciation expense of €14,741 million]. The estimate is essentially unchanged from the estimate including land because land represents such a small component of Verizon's PPE.

Solution to 2: The estimated total useful life suggests that Orange and BCE depreciate PPE over a much longer period than Verizon: 20.6 and 22.8 years for Orange and BCE, respectively, versus 16.7 years for Verizon.

The estimated age of the equipment suggests that Verizon has the newest PPE with an estimated age of 10.7 years. Additionally, the estimates suggest that around 73 percent of Orange's assets' useful lives have passed (15.0 years ÷ 20.6 years, or equivalently, €70,427 million ÷ €97,092 million). In comparison, around 65 and 64 percent of the useful lives of the PPE of BCE and Verizon, respectively, have passed.

Items that can affect comparisons across the companies include business differences, such as differences in composition of the companies' operations and differences in acquisition and divestiture activity. This result can be compared, to an extent, to the useful lives and asset mix disclosed in the companies' footnotes; however, differences in disclosures, e.g. in the categories of assets disclosed, can affect comparisons.

Solution to 3: All three companies' capital expenditure exceeds its depreciation expense. Rounding to the nearest 10%, capital expenditure as a percentage of depreciation is 120 percent for Orange, 140 percent for BCE, and 120 percent for Verizon. All three companies are replacing PPE at a faster rate than the PPE is being depreciated, consistent with the companies' somewhat older asset base.

Solution to 4: Fixed asset turnover is calculated as total revenues divided by average net PPE. Orange's fixed asset turnover is 1.6 (= 41,096/((26,665 + 25,912)/2). BCE's fixed asset turnover is 1.0, and Verizon's fixed asset turnover is 1.5.

Orange's and Verizon's higher levels of fixed asset turnover indicate these companies, compared to BCE, are able to generate more sales per unit of investment in fixed assets.

8. INVESTMENT PROPERTY

Investment property is defined under IFRS as property that is owned (or, in some cases, leased under a **finance lease**) for the purpose of earning rentals or capital appreciation or both.[28] An example of investment property is a building owned by a company and leased out to tenants. In contrast, other long-lived tangible assets (i.e., property considered to be property, plant, and equipment) are owner-occupied properties used for producing the company's goods and services or for housing the company's administrative activities. Investment properties do not include long-lived tangible assets held for sale in the ordinary course of business. For example, the houses and property owned by a housing construction company are considered to be its inventory.

Under IFRS, companies are allowed to value investment properties using either a cost model or a fair value model. The cost model is identical to the cost model used for property, plant, and equipment. If the cost model is used, the fair value of investment property must be disclosed.[29] The fair value model, however, differs from the revaluation model used for property, plant, and equipment. Under the revaluation model, whether an asset revaluation affects net income depends on whether the revaluation initially increases or decreases the carrying amount of the asset. In contrast, under the fair value model, all changes in the fair value of the asset affect net income. To use the fair value model, a company must be able to reliably determine the property's fair value on a continuing basis.

Example 18 presents an excerpt from the annual report of a property company reporting under IFRS.

---

[28] IAS 40 *Investment Property* prescribes the accounting treatment for investment property.
[29] Ibid., paragraph 32.

EXAMPLE 18   Financial Statement Presentation and Disclosures
for Long-Lived Assets

The following exhibit presents information and excerpts from the annual report for
the year ended December 31, 2017 of intu properties plc, a property company headquartered in London that owns, develops, and manages shopping centres in the United
Kingdom and Spain. Its common stock is listed in London and Johannesburg.

EXHIBIT 12   Information and excerpts from the Annual Report of intu properties plc
(Currency in £ millions)

Financial Information

Financial Statement	Item Label	Amount 2017	Amount 2016
Balance Sheet	Investment and development property	9,179.4	9,212.1
Balance Sheet	Plant and equipment	12.2	7.6
Balance Sheet	Total assets	10,794.5	10,369.2
Income Statement	Net rental income	423.4	406.1
Income Statement	Revaluation of investment and development property	30.8	(78.0)

Excerpt from Note 2 Accounting policies
Investment and development property

Investment and development property is owned or leased by the Group and
held for long-term rental income and capital appreciation.

The Group has elected to use the fair value model. Properties are initially recognized at cost and subsequently revalued at the balance sheet date
to fair value as determined by professionally qualified external valuers on the
basis of market value with the exception of certain development land where
an assessment of fair value may be made internally. External valuations are
received for significant development land once required planning permissions
are obtained. The cost of investment and development property includes
capitalized interest and other directly attributable outgoings incurred during
development. Interest is capitalized on the basis of the average interest rate on
the relevant debt outstanding. Interest ceases to be capitalized on the date of
practical completion.

Gains or losses arising from changes in the fair value of investment and
development property are recognized in the income statement. Depreciation
is not provided in respect of investment and development property. Gains or
losses arising on the sale of investment and development property are recognized when the significant risks and rewards of ownership have been transferred to the buyer. The gain or loss recognized is the proceeds received less
the carrying value of the property and costs directly associated with the sale.

Plant and equipment

Plant and equipment consists of vehicles, fixtures, fittings and other equipment. Plant and equipment is stated at cost less accumulated depreciation and any accumulated impairment losses. Depreciation is charged to the income statement on a straight-line basis over an asset's estimated useful life up to a maximum of five years.

Excerpt from Note 14 Investment and development property

The market value of investment and development property at December 31, 2017 includes £8,831.9 million (December 31, 2016: £9,088.6 million) in respect of investment property and £376.5 million (December 31, 2016: £153.2 million) in respect of development property.... All the Group's significant investment and development property relates to prime shopping centres which are of a similar nature and share characteristics and risks....

Valuation methodology

The fair value of the Group's investment and development property at December 31, 2017 was determined by independent external valuers.... Fair values for investment properties are calculated using the present value income approach.... The key driver of the property valuations is the terms of the leases in place at the valuation date. These determine the majority of the cash flow profile of the property for a number of years and therefore form the base of the valuation...

1. How do the assets included in the balance sheet line item "Investment and development property" differ from the assets included in the balance sheet line item "Plant and equipment"?
2. How does the valuation model used by the company for its investment and development property differ from the valuation model used for its plant and equipment?
3. How does accounting for depreciation differ for investment and development property versus plant and equipment?
4. Do the revaluation gains and losses on investment and development properties indicate that the properties have been sold?

Solution to 1: The assets included in the balance sheet line item "Investment and development property" are shopping centers, which the company holds for long-term rental income and capital appreciation. In 2017, the company reported net rental income of £423.4 million. The balance sheet line item "Plant and equipment" includes vehicles, fixtures, fittings, and other equipment used by the company in its operations.

Solution to 2: The valuation model used by the company for its investment and development property is the fair value model, in which properties are initially recognized at cost and subsequently revalued and shown on the balance sheet at fair value. All changes in the fair value of the asset affect net income. The company employs external valuation experts to determine the fair value, which is based on expected future cash flow from rental income.

The valuation model used for its plant and equipment is the historical cost model in which properties are shown on the balance sheet at cost minus accumulated depreciation and any impairment losses.

Solution to 3: Depreciation in accounting refers to the allocation of the cost of a long-lived asset over its useful life. No depreciation is recorded for investment and development property. Depreciation expense for plant and equipment is calculated on a straight-line basis over the asset's estimated useful life.

Solution to 4: No. The revaluation gains and losses on investment properties arise from changes in the fair value of properties that are owned by the company. The company reported a revaluation gain of £30.8 million in 2017 and a revaluation loss of £78.0 million in 2016.

Sales of property would have resulted in a gain or loss on disposal, calculated as the proceeds minus the carrying value of the property and related selling costs.

In general, a company must apply its chosen model (cost or fair value) to all of its investment property. If a company chooses the fair value model for its investment property, it must continue to use the fair value model until it disposes of the property or changes its use such that it is no longer considered investment property (e.g., it becomes owner-occupied property or part of inventory). The company must continue to use the fair value model for that property even if transactions on comparable properties, used to estimate fair value, become less frequent.

Certain valuation issues arise when a company changes the use of property such that it moves from being an investment property to owner-occupied property or part of inventory. If a company's chosen model for investment property is the cost model, such transfers do not change the carrying amount of the property transferred. If a company's chosen model is the fair value model, transfers from investment property to owner-occupied property or to inventory are made at fair value. In other words, the property's fair value at the time of transfer is considered to be its cost for ongoing accounting for the property. If a company's chosen model for investment property is the fair value model and it transfers a property from owner-occupied to investment property, the change in measurement of the property from depreciated cost to fair value is treated like a revaluation. If a company's chosen model is the fair value model and it transfers a property from inventory to investment property, any difference between the inventory carrying amount and the property's fair value at the time of transfer is recognized as profit or loss.

Investment property appears as a separate line item on the balance sheet. Companies are required to disclose whether they use the fair value model or the cost model for their investment property. If the company uses the fair value model, it must make additional disclosures about how it determines fair value and must provide reconciliation between the beginning and ending carrying amounts of investment property. If the company uses the cost model, it must make additional disclosures similar to those for property, plant, and equipment—for example, the depreciation method and useful lives must be disclosed. In addition, if the company uses the cost model, it must also disclose the fair value of investment property.

Under US GAAP, there is no specific definition of investment property. Most operating companies and real estate companies in the United States that hold investment-type property use the historical cost model.

9. SUMMARY

Understanding the reporting of long-lived assets at inception requires distinguishing between expenditures that are capitalized (i.e., reported as long-lived assets) and those that are expensed. Once a long-lived asset is recognized, it is reported under the cost model at its historical cost less accumulated depreciation (amortization) and less any impairment or under the revaluation model at its fair value. IFRS permit the use of either the cost model or the revaluation model, whereas US GAAP require the use of the cost model. Most companies reporting under IFRS use the cost model. The choice of different methods to depreciate (amortize) long-lived assets can create challenges for analysts comparing companies.

Key points include the following:

- Expenditures related to long-lived assets are capitalized as part of the cost of assets if they are expected to provide future benefits, typically beyond one year. Otherwise, expenditures related to long-lived assets are expensed as incurred.
- Although capitalizing expenditures, rather than expensing them, results in higher reported profitability in the initial year, it results in lower profitability in subsequent years; however, if a company continues to purchase similar or increasing amounts of assets each year, the profitability-enhancing effect of capitalization continues.
- Capitalizing an expenditure rather than expensing it results in a greater amount reported as cash from operations because capitalized expenditures are classified as an investing cash outflow rather than an operating cash outflow.
- Companies must capitalize interest costs associated with acquiring or constructing an asset that requires a long period of time to prepare for its intended use.
- Including capitalized interest in the calculation of interest coverage ratios provides a better assessment of a company's solvency.
- IFRS require research costs be expensed but allow all development costs (not only software development costs) to be capitalized under certain conditions. Generally, US accounting standards require that research and development costs be expensed; however, certain costs related to software development are required to be capitalized.
- When one company acquires another company, the transaction is accounted for using the acquisition method of accounting in which the company identified as the acquirer allocates the purchase price to each asset acquired (and each liability assumed) on the basis of its fair value. Under acquisition accounting, if the purchase price of an acquisition exceeds the sum of the amounts that can be allocated to individual identifiable assets and liabilities, the excess is recorded as goodwill.
- The capitalized costs of long-lived tangible assets and of intangible assets with finite useful lives are allocated to expense in subsequent periods over their useful lives. For tangible assets, this process is referred to as depreciation, and for intangible assets, it is referred to as amortization.
- Long-lived tangible assets and intangible assets with finite useful lives are reviewed for impairment whenever changes in events or circumstances indicate that the carrying amount of an asset may not be recoverable.

- Intangible assets with an indefinite useful life are not amortized but are reviewed for impairment annually.
- Impairment disclosures can provide useful information about a company's expected cash flows.
- Methods of calculating depreciation or amortization expense include the straight-line method, in which the cost of an asset is allocated to expense in equal amounts each year over its useful life; accelerated methods, in which the allocation of cost is greater in earlier years; and the units-of-production method, in which the allocation of cost corresponds to the actual use of an asset in a particular period.
- Estimates required for depreciation and amortization calculations include the useful life of the equipment (or its total lifetime productive capacity) and its expected residual value at the end of that useful life. A longer useful life and higher expected residual value result in a smaller amount of annual depreciation relative to a shorter useful life and lower expected residual value.
- IFRS permit the use of either the cost model or the revaluation model for the valuation and reporting of long-lived assets, but the revaluation model is not allowed under US GAAP.
- Under the revaluation model, carrying amounts are the fair values at the date of revaluation less any subsequent accumulated depreciation or amortization.
- In contrast with depreciation and amortization charges, which serve to allocate the cost of a long-lived asset over its useful life, impairment charges reflect an unexpected decline in the fair value of an asset to an amount lower than its carrying amount.
- IFRS permit impairment losses to be reversed, with the reversal reported in profit. US GAAP do not permit the reversal of impairment losses.
- The gain or loss on the sale of long-lived assets is computed as the sales proceeds minus the carrying amount of the asset at the time of sale.
- Estimates of average age and remaining useful life of a company's assets reflect the relationship between assets accounted for on a historical cost basis and depreciation amounts.
- The average remaining useful life of a company's assets can be estimated as net PPE divided by depreciation expense, although the accounting useful life may not necessarily correspond to the economic useful life.
- Long-lived assets reclassified as held for sale cease to be depreciated or amortized. Long-lived assets to be disposed of other than by a sale (e.g., by abandonment, exchange for another asset, or distribution to owners in a spin-off) are classified as held for use until disposal. Thus, they continue to be depreciated and tested for impairment.
- Investment property is defined as property that is owned (or, in some cases, leased under a finance lease) for the purpose of earning rentals, capital appreciation, or both.
- Under IFRS, companies are allowed to value investment properties using either a cost model or a fair value model. The cost model is identical to the cost model used for property, plant, and equipment, but the fair value model differs from the revaluation model used for property, plant, and equipment. Unlike the revaluation model, under the fair value model, all changes in the fair value of investment property affect net income.
- Under US GAAP, investment properties are generally measured using the cost model.

PRACTICE PROBLEMS

1. JOOVI Inc. has recently purchased and installed a new machine for its manufacturing plant. The company incurred the following costs:

Purchase price	$12,980
Freight and insurance	$1,200
Installation	$700
Testing	$100
Maintenance staff training costs	$500

The total cost of the machine to be shown on JOOVI's balance sheet is *closest* to:

A. $14,180.
B. $14,980.
C. $15,480.

2. Which costs incurred with the purchase of property and equipment are expensed?
A. Delivery charges.
B. Installation and testing.
C. Training required to use the property and equipment.

3. When constructing an asset for sale, directly related borrowing costs are *most likely*:
A. expensed as incurred.
B. capitalized as part of inventory.
C. capitalized as part of property, plant, and equipment.

4. BAURU, S.A., a Brazilian corporation, borrows capital from a local bank to finance the construction of its manufacturing plant. The loan has the following conditions:

Borrowing date	January 1, 2009
Amount borrowed	500 million Brazilian real (BRL)
Annual interest rate	14 percent
Term of the loan	3 years
Payment method	Annual payment of interest only. Principal amortization is due at the end of the loan term.

The construction of the plant takes two years, during which time BAURU earned BRL 10 million by temporarily investing the loan proceeds. Which of the following is the amount of interest related to the plant construction (in BRL million) that can be capitalized in BAURU's balance sheet?
A. 130.
B. 140.
C. 210.

5. After analyzing the financial statements and footnotes of a company that follows IFRS, an analyst identified the following intangible assets:
   - product patent expiring in 40 years;
   - copyright with no expiration date; and
   - goodwill acquired 2 years ago in a business combination.

   Which of these assets is an intangible asset with a finite useful life?

	Product Patent	Copyright	Goodwill
A	Yes	Yes	No
B	Yes	No	No
C	No	Yes	Yes

6. Intangible assets with finite useful lives *mostly* differ from intangible assets with infinite useful lives with respect to accounting treatment of:
   A. revaluation.
   B. impairment.
   C. amortization.

7. Costs incurred for intangible assets are generally expensed when they are:
   A. internally developed.
   B. individually acquired.
   C. acquired in a business combination.

8. Under US GAAP, when assets are acquired in a business combination, goodwill *most likely* arises from:
   A. contractual or legal rights.
   B. assets that can be separated from the acquired company.
   C. assets that are neither tangible nor identifiable intangible assets.

9. All else equal, in the fiscal year when long-lived equipment is purchased:
   A. depreciation expense increases.
   B. cash from operations decreases.
   C. net income is reduced by the amount of the purchase.

10. Companies X and Z have the same beginning-of-the-year book value of equity and the same tax rate. The companies have identical transactions throughout the year and report all transactions similarly except for one. Both companies acquire a £300,000 printer with a three-year useful life and a salvage value of £0 on January 1 of the new year. Company X capitalizes the printer and depreciates it on a straight-line basis, and Company Z expenses the printer. The following year-end information is gathered for Company X.

	Company X As of December 31
Ending shareholders' equity	£10,000,000
Tax rate	25%
Dividends	£0.00
Net income	£750,000

Based on the information given, Company Z's return on equity using year-end equity will be *closest* to:
A. 5.4%.
B. 6.1%.
C. 7.5%.

11. A financial analyst is studying the income statement effect of two alternative depreciation methods for a recently acquired piece of equipment. She gathers the following information about the equipment's expected production life and use:

	Year 1	Year 2	Year 3	Year 4	Year 5	Total
Units of production	2,000	2,000	2,000	2,000	2,500	10,500

Compared with the units-of-production method of depreciation, if the company uses the straight-line method to depreciate the equipment, its net income in Year 1 will *most likely* be:
A. lower.
B. higher.
C. the same.

12. A company purchases a piece of equipment for €1,500. The equipment is expected to have a useful life of five years and no residual value. In the first year of use, the units of production are expected to be 15% of the equipment's lifetime production capacity and the equipment is expected to generate €1,500 of revenue and incur €500 of cash expenses.

The depreciation method yielding the lowest operating profit on the equipment in the first year of use is:
A. straight line.
B. units of production.
C. double-declining balance.

13. Juan Martinez, CFO of VIRMIN, S.A., is selecting the depreciation method to use for a new machine. The machine has an expected useful life of six years. Production is expected to be relatively low initially but to increase over time. The method chosen for tax reporting must be the same as the method used for financial reporting. If Martinez wants to minimize tax payments in the first year of the machine's life, which of the following depreciation methods is Martinez *most likely* to use?
A. Straight-line method.
B. Units-of-production method.
C. Double-declining balance method.

The following information relates to Questions 14–15

Miguel Rodriguez of MARIO S.A., an Uruguayan corporation, is computing the depreciation expense of a piece of manufacturing equipment for the fiscal year ended December 31, 2009.

The equipment was acquired on January 1, 2009. Rodriguez gathers the following information (currency in Uruguayan pesos, UYP):

Cost of the equipment	UYP 1,200,000
Estimated residual value	UYP 200,000
Expected useful life	8 years
Total productive capacity	800,000 units
Production in FY 2009	135,000 units
Expected production for the next 7 years	95,000 units each year

14. If MARIO uses the straight-line method, the amount of depreciation expense on MARIO's income statement related to the manufacturing equipment is *closest* to:
    A. 125,000.
    B. 150,000.
    C. 168,750.

15. If MARIO uses the units-of-production method, the amount of depreciation expense (in UYP) on MARIO's income statement related to the manufacturing equipment is *closest* to:
    A. 118,750.
    B. 168,750.
    C. 202,500.

---

16. Which of the following amortization methods is *most likely* to evenly distribute the cost of an intangible asset over its useful life?
    A. Straight-line method.
    B. Units-of-production method.
    C. Double-declining balance method.

17. Which of the following will cause a company to show a lower amount of amortization of intangible assets in the first year after acquisition?
    A. A higher residual value.
    B. A higher amortization rate.
    C. A shorter useful life.

18. A company purchases equipment for $200,000 with a five-year useful life and salvage value of zero. It uses the double-declining balance method of depreciation for two years, then shifts to straight-line depreciation at the beginning of Year 3. Compared with annual depreciation expense under the double-declining balance method, the resulting annual depreciation expense in Year 4 is:
    A. smaller.
    B. the same.
    C. greater.

19. An analyst in the finance department of BOOLDO S.A., a French corporation, is computing the amortization of a customer list, an intangible asset, for the fiscal year ended December 31, 2009. She gathers the following information about the asset:

Acquisition cost	€2,300,000
Acquisition date	January 1, 2008
Expected residual value at time of acquisition	€500,000

The customer list is expected to result in extra sales for three years after acquisition. The present value of these expected extra sales exceeds the cost of the list.

If the analyst uses the straight-line method, the amount of accumulated amortization related to the customer list as of December 31, 2009 is *closest* to:

A. €600,000.
B. €1,200,000.
C. €1,533,333.

20. A financial analyst is analyzing the amortization of a product patent acquired by MAKETTI S.p.A., an Italian corporation. He gathers the following information about the patent:

Acquisition cost	€5,800,000
Acquisition date	January 1, 2009
Patent expiration date	December 31, 2015
Total plant capacity of patented product	40,000 units per year
Production of patented product in fiscal year ended December 31, 2009	20,000 units
Expected production of patented product during life of the patent	175,000 units

If the analyst uses the units-of-production method, the amortization expense on the patent for fiscal year 2009 is *closest* to:

A. €414,286.
B. €662,857.
C. €828,571.

21. A company acquires a patent with an expiration date in six years for ¥100 million. The company assumes that the patent will generate economic benefits that will decline over time and decides to amortize the patent using the double-declining balance method. The annual amortization expense in Year 4 is closest to:

A. ¥6.6 million.
B. ¥9.9 million.
C. ¥19.8 million.

22. A company is comparing straight-line and double-declining balance amortization methods for a non-renewable six-year license, acquired for €600,000. The difference between the Year 4 ending net book values using the two methods is *closest to*:

A. €81,400.
B. €118,600.
C. €200,000.

23. MARU S.A. de C.V., a Mexican corporation that follows IFRS, has elected to use the revaluation model for its property, plant, and equipment. One of MARU's machines was purchased for 2,500,000 Mexican pesos (MXN) at the beginning of the fiscal year ended March 31, 2010. As of March 31, 2010, the machine has a fair value of MXN 3,000,000. Should MARU show a profit for the revaluation of the machine?
   A. Yes.
   B. No, because this revaluation is recorded directly in equity.
   C. No, because value increases resulting from revaluation can never be recognized as a profit.

24. An analyst is studying the impairment of the manufacturing equipment of WLP Corp., a UK-based corporation that follows IFRS. He gathers the following information about the equipment:

Fair value	£16,800,000
Costs to sell	£800,000
Value in use	£14,500,000
Net carrying amount	£19,100,000

The amount of the impairment loss on WLP Corp.'s income statement related to its manufacturing equipment is *closest* to:
   A. £2,300,000.
   B. £3,100,000.
   C. £4,600,000.

25. Under IFRS, an impairment loss on a property, plant, and equipment asset is measured as the excess of the carrying amount over the asset's:
   A. fair value.
   B. recoverable amount.
   C. undiscounted expected future cash flows.

26. A financial analyst at BETTO S.A. is analyzing the result of the sale of a vehicle for 85,000 Argentine pesos (ARP) on December 31, 2009. The analyst compiles the following information about the vehicle:

Acquisition cost of the vehicle	ARP 100,000
Acquisition date	January 1, 2007
Estimated residual value at acquisition date	ARP 10,000
Expected useful life	9 years
Depreciation method	Straight-line

The result of the sale of the vehicle is *most likely*:
   A. a loss of ARP 15,000.
   B. a gain of ARP 15,000.
   C. a gain of ARP 18,333.

27. CROCO S.p.A sells an intangible asset with a historical acquisition cost of €12 million and an accumulated depreciation of €2 million and reports a loss on the sale of €3.2 million. Which of the following amounts is *most likely* the sale price of the asset?
    A. €6.8 million.
    B. €8.8 million.
    C. €13.2 million.

28. The impairment of intangible assets with finite lives affects:
    A. the balance sheet but not the income statement.
    B. the income statement but not the balance sheet.
    C. both the balance sheet and the income statement.

29. The gain or loss on a sale of a long-lived asset to which the revaluation model has been applied is *most likely* calculated using sales proceeds less:
    A. carrying amount.
    B. carrying amount adjusted for impairment.
    C. historical cost net of accumulated depreciation.

30. According to IFRS, all of the following pieces of information about property, plant, and equipment must be disclosed in a company's financial statements and footnotes *except for*:
    A. useful lives.
    B. acquisition dates.
    C. amount of disposals.

31. According to IFRS, all of the following pieces of information about intangible assets must be disclosed in a company's financial statements and footnotes *except for*:
    A. fair value.
    B. impairment loss.
    C. amortization rate.

32. Which of the following is a required financial statement disclosure for long-lived intangible assets under US GAAP?
    A. The useful lives of assets.
    B. The reversal of impairment losses.
    C. Estimated amortization expense for the next five fiscal years.

33. Which of the following characteristics is *most likely* to differentiate investment property from property, plant, and equipment?
    A. It is tangible.
    B. It earns rent.
    C. It is long-lived.

34. If a company uses the fair value model to value investment property, changes in the fair value of the asset are *least likely* to affect:
    A. net income.
    B. net operating income.
    C. other comprehensive income.

35. Investment property is *most likely* to:
    A. earn rent.
    B. be held for resale.
    C. be used in the production of goods and services.

36. A company is *most likely* to:
    A. use a fair value model for some investment property and a cost model for other invest-ment property.
    B. change from the fair value model when transactions on comparable properties become less frequent.
    C. change from the fair value model when the company transfers investment property to property, plant, and equipment.

37. Under the revaluation model for property, plant, and equipment and the fair model for investment property:
    A. fair value of the asset must be able to be measured reliably.
    B. net income is affected by all changes in the fair value of the asset.
    C. net income is never affected if the asset increases in value from its carrying amount.

38. Under IFRS, what must be disclosed under the cost model of valuation for investment properties?
    A. Useful lives.
    B. The method for determining fair value.
    C. Reconciliation between beginning and ending carrying amounts of investment property.

The following information relates to Questions 39–42

Melanie Hart, CFA, is a transportation analyst. Hart has been asked to write a research report on Altai Mountain Rail Company (AMRC). Like other companies in the railroad industry, AMRC's operations are capital intensive, with significant investments in such long-lived tangi-ble assets as property, plant, and equipment. In November of 2008, AMRC's board of directors hired a new team to manage the company. In reviewing the company's 2009 annual report, Hart is concerned about some of the accounting choices that the new management has made. These choices differ from those of the previous management and from common industry prac-tice. Hart has highlighted the following statements from the company's annual report:

Statement 1   "In 2009, AMRC spent significant amounts on track replacement and sim-ilar improvements. AMRC expensed rather than capitalized a significant proportion of these expenditures."

Statement 2   "AMRC uses the straight-line method of depreciation for both financial and tax reporting purposes to account for plant and equipment."

Statement 3   "In 2009, AMRC recognized an impairment loss of €50 million on a fleet of locomotives. The impairment loss was reported as 'other income' in the income statement and reduced the carrying amount of the assets on the balance sheet."

Exhibits 1 and 2 contain AMRC's 2009 consolidated income statement and balance sheet. AMRC prepares its financial statements in accordance with International Financial Reporting Standards.

EXHIBIT 1   Consolidated Statement of Income

For the Years Ended December 31	2009 € Millions	2009 % Revenues	2008 € Millions	2008 % Revenues
Operating revenues	2,600	100.0	2,300	100.0
Operating expenses				
Depreciation	(200)	(7.7)	(190)	(8.3)
Other operating expense	(1,590)	(61.1)	(1,515)	(65.9)
Total operating expenses	(1,790)	(68.8)	(1,705)	(74.2)
Operating income	810	31.2	595	25.8
Other income	(50)	(1.9)	—	0.0
Interest expense	(73)	(2.8)	(69)	(3.0)
Income before taxes	687	26.5	526	22.8
Income taxes	(272)	(10.5)	(198)	(8.6)
Net income	415	16	328	14.2

EXHIBIT 2   Consolidated Balance Sheet

As of December 31	2009 € Millions	2009 % Assets	2008 € Millions	2008 % Assets
Assets				
Current assets	500	9.4	450	8.5
Property & equipment:				
Land	700	13.1	700	13.2
Plant & equipment	6,000	112.1	5,800	109.4
Total property & equipment	6,700	125.2	6,500	122.6
Accumulated depreciation	(1,850)	(34.6)	(1,650)	(31.1)
Net property & equipment	4,850	90.6	4,850	91.5
Total assets	5,350	100.0	5,300	100.0
Liabilities and Shareholders' Equity				
Current liabilities	480	9.0	430	8.1
Long-term debt	1,030	19.3	1,080	20.4
Other long-term provisions and liabilities	1,240	23.1	1,440	27.2
Total liabilities	2,750	51.4	2,950	55.7
Shareholders' equity				
Common stock and paid-in-surplus	760	14.2	760	14.3
Retained earnings	1,888	35.5	1,600	30.2
Other comprehensive losses	(48)	(0.9)	(10)	(0.2)
Total shareholders' equity	2,600	48.6	2,350	44.3
Total liabilities & shareholders' equity	5,350	100.0	5,300	100.0

39. With respect to Statement 1, which of the following is the *most likely* effect of management's decision to expense rather than capitalize these expenditures?
    A. 2009 net profit margin is higher than if the expenditures had been capitalized.
    B. 2009 total asset turnover is lower than if the expenditures had been capitalized.
    C. Future profit growth will be higher than if the expenditures had been capitalized.

40. With respect to Statement 2, what would be the *most likely* effect in 2010 if AMRC were to switch to an accelerated depreciation method for both financial and tax reporting?
    A. Net profit margin would increase.
    B. Total asset turnover would decrease.
    C. Cash flow from operating activities would increase.

41. With respect to Statement 3, what is the *most likely* effect of the impairment loss?
    A. Net income in years prior to 2009 was likely understated.
    B. Net profit margins in years after 2009 will likely exceed the 2009 net profit margin.
    C. Cash flow from operating activities in 2009 was likely lower due to the impairment loss.

42. Based on Exhibits 1 and 2, the *best estimate* of the average remaining useful life of the company's plant and equipment at the end of 2009 is:
    A. 20.75 years.
    B. 24.25 years.
    C. 30.00 years.

The following information relates to Questions 43–48

Brian Jordan is interviewing for a junior equity analyst position at Orion Investment Advisors. As part of the interview process, Mary Benn, Orion's Director of Research, provides Jordan with information about two hypothetical companies, Alpha and Beta, and asks him to comment on the information on their financial statements and ratios. Both companies prepare their financial statements in accordance with International Financial Reporting Standards (IFRS) and are identical in all respects except for their accounting choices.

Jordan is told that at the beginning of the current fiscal year, both companies purchased a major new computer system and began building new manufacturing plants for their own use. Alpha capitalized, and Beta expensed the cost of the computer system; Alpha capitalized and Beta expensed the interest costs associated with the construction of the manufacturing plants.

Benn asks Jordan, "What was the impact of these decisions on each company's current fiscal year financial statements and ratios?"

Jordan responds, "Alpha's decision to capitalize the cost of its new computer system instead of expensing it results in lower net income, lower total assets, and higher cash flow from operating activities in the current fiscal year. Alpha's decision to capitalize its interest costs instead of expensing them results in a lower fixed asset turnover ratio and a higher interest coverage ratio."

Jordan is told that Alpha uses the straight-line depreciation method and Beta uses an accelerated depreciation method; both companies estimate the same useful lives for long-lived assets. Many companies in their industry use the units-of-production method.

Benn asks Jordan, "What are the financial statement implications of each depreciation method, and how do you determine a company's need to reinvest in its productive capacity?"

Jordan replies, "All other things being equal, the straight-line depreciation method results in the least variability of net profit margin over time, while an accelerated depreciation method results in a declining trend in net profit margin over time. The units-of-production can result in a net profit margin trend that is quite variable. I use a three-step approach to estimate a company's need to reinvest in its productive capacity. First, I estimate the average age of the assets by dividing net property, plant, and equipment by annual depreciation expense. Second, I estimate the average remaining useful life of the assets by dividing accumulated depreciation by depreciation expense. Third, I add the estimates of the average remaining useful life and the average age of the assets in order to determine the total useful life."

Jordan is told that at the end of the current fiscal year, Alpha revalued a manufacturing plant; this increased its reported carrying amount by 15 percent. There was no previous downward revaluation of the plant. Beta recorded an impairment loss on a manufacturing plant; this reduced its carrying by 10 percent.

Benn asks Jordan "What was the impact of these decisions on each company's current fiscal year financial ratios?"

Jordan responds, "Beta's impairment loss increases its debt to total assets and fixed asset turnover ratios, and lowers its cash flow from operating activities. Alpha's revaluation increases its debt to capital and return on assets ratios, and reduces its return on equity."

At the end of the interview, Benn thanks Jordan for his time and states that a hiring decision will be made shortly.

43. Jordan's response about the financial statement impact of Alpha's decision to capitalize the cost of its new computer system is most likely *correct* with respect to:
    A. lower net income.
    B. lower total assets.
    C. higher cash flow from operating activities.

44. Jordan's response about the ratio impact of Alpha's decision to capitalize interest costs is most likely *correct* with respect to the:
    A. interest coverage ratio.
    B. fixed asset turnover ratio.
    C. interest coverage and fixed asset turnover ratios.

45. Jordan's response about the impact of the different depreciation methods on net profit margin is most likely *incorrect* with respect to:
    A. accelerated depreciation.
    B. straight-line depreciation.
    C. units-of-production depreciation.

46. Jordan's response about his approach to estimating a company's need to reinvest in its productive capacity is most likely *correct* regarding:
    A. estimating the average age of the asset base.
    B. estimating the total useful life of the asset base.
    C. estimating the average remaining useful life of the asset base.

47. Jordan's response about the effect of Beta's impairment loss is most likely *incorrect* with respect to the impact on its:
    A. debt to total assets.
    B. fixed asset turnover.
    C. cash flow from operating activities.

48. Jordan's response about the effect of Alpha's revaluation is most likely *correct* with respect to the impact on its:
    A. return on equity.
    B. return on assets.
    C. debt to capital ratio.

CHAPTER 9

INCOME TAXES

Elbie Louw, PhD, CFA, CIPM
Michael A. Broihahn, CPA, CIA, CFA

LEARNING OUTCOMES

After completing this chapter, you will be able to do the following:

- describe the differences between accounting profit and taxable income, and define key terms, including deferred tax assets, deferred tax liabilities, valuation allowance, taxes payable, and income tax expense;
- explain how deferred tax liabilities and assets are created and the factors that determine how a company's deferred tax liabilities and assets should be treated for the purposes of financial analysis;
- calculate the tax base of a company's assets and liabilities;
- calculate income tax expense, income taxes payable, deferred tax assets, and deferred tax liabilities, and calculate and interpret the adjustment to the financial statements related to a change in the income tax rate;
- evaluate the effect of tax rate changes on a company's financial statements and ratios;
- distinguish between temporary and permanent differences in pre-tax accounting income and taxable income;
- describe the valuation allowance for deferred tax assets—when it is required and what effect it has on financial statements;
- explain recognition and measurement of current and deferred tax items;
- analyze disclosures relating to deferred tax items and the effective tax rate reconciliation, and explain how information included in these disclosures affects a company's financial statements and financial ratios;
- identify the key provisions of and differences between income tax accounting under International Financial Reporting Standards (IFRS) and US generally accepted accounting principles (GAAP).

1. INTRODUCTION

For those companies reporting under International Financial Reporting Standards (IFRS), IAS 12 [Income Taxes] covers accounting for a company's income taxes and the reporting of deferred taxes. For those companies reporting under United States generally accepted accounting principles (US GAAP), FASB ASC Topic 740 [Income Taxes] is the primary source for information on accounting for income taxes. Although IFRS and US GAAP follow similar conventions on many income tax issues, there are some key differences that will be discussed in the chapter.

Differences between how and when transactions are recognized for financial reporting purposes relative to tax reporting can give rise to differences in tax expense and related tax assets and liabilities. To reconcile these differences, companies that report under either IFRS or US GAAP create a provision on the balance sheet called deferred tax assets or deferred tax liabilities, depending on the nature of the situation.

Deferred tax assets or liabilities usually arise when accounting standards and tax authorities recognize the timing of revenues and expenses at different times. Because timing differences such as these will eventually reverse over time, they are called "temporary differences." Deferred tax assets represent taxes that have been recognized for tax reporting purposes (or often the carrying forward of losses from previous periods) but have not yet been recognized on the income statement prepared for financial reporting purposes. Deferred tax liabilities represent tax expense that has appeared on the income statement for financial reporting purposes, but has not yet become payable under tax regulations.

This chapter provides a primer on the basics of income tax accounting and reporting. The chapter is organized as follows. Section 2 describes the differences between taxable income and accounting profit. Section 3 explains the determination of tax base, which relates to the valuation of assets and liabilities for tax purposes. Section 4 discusses several types of timing differences between the recognition of taxable and accounting profit. Section 5 examines unused tax losses and tax credits. Section 6 describes the recognition and measurement of current and deferred tax. Section 7 discusses the disclosure and presentation of income tax information on companies' financial statements and illustrates its practical implications for financial analysis. Section 8 provides an overview of the similarities and differences for income-tax reporting between IFRS and US GAAP. A summary of the key points and practice problems in the CFA Institute multiple-choice format conclude the chapter.

2. DIFFERENCES BETWEEN ACCOUNTING PROFIT AND TAXABLE INCOME

A company's **accounting profit** is reported on its income statement in accordance with prevailing accounting standards. Accounting profit (also referred to as income before taxes or pretax income) does not include a provision for income tax expense.[1] A company's **taxable income** is the portion of its income that is subject to income taxes under the tax laws of its jurisdiction. Because of different guidelines for how income is reported on a company's financial statements and how it is measured for income tax purposes, accounting profit and taxable income may differ.

---

[1] As defined under IAS 12, paragraph 5.

A company's taxable income is the basis for its **income tax payable** (a liability) or recoverable (an asset), which is calculated on the basis of the company's tax rate and appears on its balance sheet. A company's **tax expense**, or tax benefit in the case of a recovery, appears on its income statement and is an aggregate of its income tax payable (or recoverable in the case of a tax benefit) and any changes in deferred tax assets and liabilities.

When a company's taxable income is greater than its accounting profit, then its income taxes payable will be higher than what would have otherwise been the case had the income taxes been determined based on accounting profit. **Deferred tax assets**, which appear on the balance sheet, arise when an excess amount is paid for income taxes (taxable income higher than accounting profit) and the company expects to recover the difference during the course of future operations. Actual income taxes payable will thus exceed the financial accounting income tax expense (which is reported on the income statement and is determined based on accounting profit). Related to deferred tax assets is a **valuation allowance**, which is a reserve created against deferred tax assets. The valuation allowance is based on the likelihood of realizing the deferred tax assets in future accounting periods. **Deferred tax liabilities**, which also appear on the balance sheet, arise when a deficit amount is paid for income taxes and the company expects to eliminate the deficit over the course of future operations. In this case, financial accounting income tax expense exceeds income taxes payable.

Income tax paid in a period is the actual amount paid for income taxes (not a provision, but the actual cash outflow). The income tax paid may be less than the income tax expense because of payments in prior periods or refunds received in the current period. Income tax paid reduces the income tax payable, which is carried on the balance sheet as a liability.

The **tax base** of an asset or liability is the amount at which the asset or liability is valued for tax purposes, whereas the **carrying amount** is the amount at which the asset or liability is valued according to accounting principles.[2] Differences between the tax base and the carrying amount also result in differences between accounting profit and taxable income. These differences can carry through to future periods. For example, a **tax loss carry forward** occurs when a company experiences a loss in the current period that may be used to reduce future taxable income. The company's tax expense on its income statement must not only reflect the taxes payable based on taxable income, but also the effect of these differences.

2.1. Current Tax Assets and Liabilities

A company's current tax liability is the amount payable in taxes and is based on current taxable income. If the company expects to receive a refund for some portion previously paid in taxes, the amount recoverable is referred to as a current tax asset. The current tax liability or asset may, however, differ from what the liability would have been if it was based on accounting profit rather than taxable income for the period. Differences in accounting profit and taxable income are the result of the application of different rules. Such differences between accounting profit and taxable income can occur in several ways, including:

• Revenues and expenses may be recognized in one period for accounting purposes and a different period for tax purposes;

---

[2]The terms "tax base" and "tax basis" are interchangeable. "Tax basis" is more commonly used in the United States. Similarly, "carrying amount" and "book value" refer to the same concept.

- Specific revenues and expenses may be either recognized for accounting purposes and not for tax purposes; or not recognized for accounting purposes but recognized for tax purposes;
- The carrying amount and tax base of assets and/or liabilities may differ;
- The deductibility of gains and losses of assets and liabilities may vary for accounting and income tax purposes;
- Subject to tax rules, tax losses of prior years might be used to reduce taxable income in later years, resulting in differences in accounting and taxable income (tax loss carryforward); and
- Adjustments of reported financial data from prior years might not be recognized equally for accounting and tax purposes or might be recognized in different periods.

2.2. Deferred Tax Assets and Liabilities

Deferred tax assets represent taxes that have been paid (or often the carrying forward of losses from previous periods) but have not yet been recognized on the income statement. Deferred tax liabilities occur when financial accounting income tax expense is greater than regulatory income tax expense. Deferred tax assets and liabilities usually arise when accounting standards and tax authorities recognize the timing of taxes due at different times; for example, when a company uses accelerated depreciation when reporting to the tax authority (to increase expense and lower tax payments in the early years) but uses the straight-line method on the financial statements. Although not similar in treatment on a year-to-year basis (e.g., depreciation of 5 percent on a straight-line basis may be permitted for accounting purposes whereas 10 percent is allowed for tax purposes) over the life of the asset, both approaches allow for the total cost of the asset to be depreciated (or amortized). Because these timing differences will eventually reverse or self-correct over the course of the asset's depreciable life, they are called "temporary differences."

Any deferred tax asset or liability is based on temporary differences that result in an excess or a deficit amount paid for taxes, which the company expects to recover from future operations. Because taxes will be recoverable or payable at a future date, it is only a temporary difference, and a deferred tax asset or liability is created. Changes in the deferred tax asset or liability on the balance sheet reflect the difference between the amounts recognized in the previous period and the current period. The changes in deferred tax assets and liabilities are added to income tax payable to determine the company's income tax expense (or credit) as it is reported on the income statement.

At the end of each fiscal year, deferred tax assets and liabilities are recalculated by comparing the tax bases and carrying amounts of the balance sheet items. Identified temporary differences should be assessed on whether the difference will result in future economic benefits. For example, Pinto Construction (a hypothetical company) depreciates equipment on a straight-line basis of 10 percent per year. The tax authorities allow depreciation of 15 percent per year. At the end of the fiscal year, the carrying amount of the equipment for accounting purposes would be greater than the tax base of the equipment thus resulting in a temporary difference. A deferred tax item may only be created if it is not doubtful that the company will realize economic benefits in the future. In our example, the equipment is used in the core business of Pinto Construction. If the company is a going concern and stable, there should be no doubt that future economic benefits will result from the equipment, and it would be appropriate to create the deferred tax item.

Should it be doubtful that future economic benefits will be realized from a temporary difference (such as Pinto Construction being under liquidation), the temporary difference will not lead to the creation of a deferred tax asset or liability. If a deferred tax asset or liability resulted in the past, but the criteria of economic benefits are not met on the current balance sheet date, then, under IFRS, an existing deferred tax asset or liability related to the item will be reversed. Under US GAAP, a valuation allowance is established. In assessing future economic benefits, much is left to the discretion of the auditor in assessing the temporary differences and the issue of future economic benefits.

EXAMPLE 1

The following information pertains to a hypothetical company, Reston Partners:

Reston Partners Consolidated Income Statement			
Period Ending March 31 (£ Millions)	Year 3	Year 2	Year 1
Revenue	£40,000	£30,000	£25,000
Other net gains	2,000	0	0
Changes in inventories of finished goods and work in progress	400	180	200
Raw materials and consumables used	(5,700)	(4,000)	(8,000)
Depreciation expense	(2,000)	(2,000)	(2,000)
Other expenses	(6,000)	(5,900)	(4,500)
Interest expense	(2,000)	(3,000)	(6,000)
Profit before tax	£26,700	£15,280	£4,700

The financial performance and accounting profit of Reston Partners on this income statement is based on accounting principles appropriate for the jurisdiction in which Reston Partners operates. The principles used to calculate accounting profit (profit before tax in the example above) may differ from the principles applied for tax purposes (the calculation of taxable income). For illustrative purposes, however, assume that all income and expenses on the income statement are treated identically for tax and accounting purposes *except* depreciation.

The depreciation is related to equipment owned by Reston Partners. For simplicity, assume that the equipment was purchased at the beginning of Year 1. Depreciation should thus be calculated and expensed for the full year. Assume that accounting standards permit equipment to be depreciated on a straight-line basis over a 10-year period, whereas the tax standards in the jurisdiction specify that equipment should be depreciated on a straight-line basis over a 7-year period. For simplicity, assume a salvage value of £0 at the end of the equipment's useful life. Both methods will result in the full depreciation of the asset over the respective tax or accounting life.

The equipment was originally purchased for £20,000. In accordance with accounting standards, over the next 10 years the company will recognize annual depreciation of £2,000 (£20,000 ÷ 10) as an expense on its income statement and for the determination of accounting profit. For tax purposes, however, the company will recognize £2,857 (£20,000 ÷ 7) in depreciation each year. Each fiscal year the depreciation expense related to the use of the equipment will, therefore, differ for tax and accounting purposes (tax base vs. carrying amount), resulting in a difference between accounting profit and taxable income.

The previous income statement reflects accounting profit (depreciation at £2,000 per year). The following table shows the taxable income for each fiscal year.

Taxable Income (£ Millions)	Year 3	Year 2	Year 1
Revenue	£40,000	£30,000	£25,000
Other net gains	2,000	0	0
Changes in inventories of finished goods and work in progress	400	180	200
Raw materials and consumables used	(5,700)	(4,000)	(8,000)
Depreciation expense	(2,857)	(2,857)	(2,857)
Other expenses	(6,000)	(5,900)	(4,500)
Interest expense	(2,000)	(3,000)	(6,000)
Taxable income	£25,843	£14,423	£3,843

The carrying amount and tax base for the equipment are as follows:

(£ Millions)	Year 3	Year 2	Year 1
Equipment value for accounting purposes (*carrying amount*) (depreciation of £2,000/year)	£14,000	£16,000	£18,000
Equipment value for tax purposes (*tax base*) (depreciation of £2,857/year)	£11,429	£14,286	£17,143
Difference	£2,571	£1,714	£857

At each balance sheet date, the tax base and carrying amount of all assets and liabilities must be determined. The income tax payable by Reston Partners will be based on the taxable income of each fiscal year. If a tax rate of 30 percent is assumed, then the income taxes payable for Year 1, Year 2, and Year 3 are £1,153 (30% × 3,843), £4,327 (30% × 14,423), and £7,753 (30% × 25,843).

Remember, though, that if the tax obligation is calculated based on accounting profits, it will differ because of the differences between the tax base and the carrying amount of equipment. The difference in each fiscal year is reflected in the table above. In each fiscal year the carrying amount of the equipment exceeds its tax base. For tax purposes, therefore, the asset tax base is less than its carrying value under financial accounting principles. The difference results in a deferred tax liability.

(£ Millions)	Year 3	Year 2	Year 1
Deferred tax liability	£771	£514	£257

(Difference between tax base and carrying amount) × tax rate

Year 1: £(18,000 − 17,143) × 30% = 257

Year 2: £(16,000 − 14,286) × 30% = 514

Year 3: £(14,000 − 11,429) × 30% = 771

The comparison of the tax base and carrying amount of equipment shows what the deferred tax liability should be on a particular balance sheet date. In each fiscal year, only the change in the deferred tax liability should be included in the calculation of the income tax expense reported on the income statement prepared for accounting purposes.

On the income statement, the company's income tax expense will be the sum of change in the deferred tax liability and the income tax payable.

(£ Millions)	Year 3	Year 2	Year 1
Income tax payable (based on tax accounting)	£7,753	£4,327	£1,153
Change in deferred tax liability	257	257	257
Income tax (based on financial accounting)	£8,010	£4,584	£1,410

Note that because the different treatment of depreciation is a temporary difference, the income tax on the income statement is 30 percent of the accounting profit, although only a part is income tax payable, and the rest is a deferred tax liability.

The consolidated income statement of Reston Partners including income tax is presented as follows:

Reston Partners Consolidated Income Statement			
Period Ending March 31 (£ Millions)	Year 3	Year 2	Year 1
Revenue	£40,000	£30,000	£25,000
Other net gains	2,000	0	0
Changes in inventories of finished goods and work in progress	400	180	200
Raw materials and consumables used	(5,700)	(4,000)	(8,000)
Depreciation expense	(2,000)	(2,000)	(2,000)
Other expenses	(6,000)	(5,900)	(4,500)
Interest expense	(2,000)	(3,000)	(6,000)
Profit before tax	£26,700	£15,280	£4,700
Income tax	(8,010)	(4,584)	(1,410)
Profit after tax	£18,690	£10,696	£3,290

Any amount paid to the tax authorities will reduce the liability for income tax payable and be reflected on the statement of cash flows of the company.

3. DETERMINING THE TAX BASE OF ASSETS AND LIABILITIES

As mentioned in Section 2, temporary differences arise from a difference in the tax base and carrying amount of assets and liabilities. The tax base of an asset or liability is the amount attributed to the asset or liability for tax purposes, whereas the carrying amount is based on accounting principles. Such a difference is considered temporary if it is expected that the taxes will be recovered or payable at a future date.

3.1. Determining the Tax Base of an Asset

The tax base of an asset is the amount that will be deductible for tax purposes in future periods as the economic benefits become realized and the company recovers the carrying amount of the asset.

For example, our previously mentioned Reston Partners (from Example 1) depreciates equipment on a straight-line basis at a rate of 10 percent per year. The tax authorities allow depreciation of approximately 15 percent per year. At the end of the fiscal year, the carrying amount of equipment for accounting purposes is greater than the asset tax base thus resulting in a temporary difference.

EXAMPLE 2   Determining the Tax Base of an Asset

The following information pertains to Entiguan Sports, a hypothetical developer of products used to treat sports-related injuries. (The treatment of items for accounting and tax purposes is based on hypothetical accounting and tax standards and is not specific to a particular jurisdiction.) Calculate the tax base and carrying amount for each item.

1. *Dividends receivable*: On its balance sheet, Entiguan Sports reports dividends of €1 million receivable from a subsidiary. Assume that dividends are not taxable.
2. *Development costs*: Entiguan Sports capitalized development costs of €3 million during the year. Entiguan amortized €500,000 of this amount during the year. For tax purposes amortization of 25 percent per year is allowed.
3. *Research costs*: Entiguan incurred €500,000 in research costs, which were all expensed in the current fiscal year for financial reporting purposes. Assume that applicable tax legislation requires research costs to be expensed over a four-year period rather than all in one year.
4. *Accounts receivable*: Included on the income statement of Entiguan Sports is a pro-vision for doubtful debt of €125,000. The accounts receivable amount reflected on the balance sheet, after taking the provision into account, amounts to €1,500,000. The tax authorities allow a deduction of 25 percent of the gross amount for doubtful debt.

Solutions:

	Carrying Amount (€)	Tax Base (€)	Temporary Difference (€)
1. Dividends receivable	1,000,000	1,000,000	0
2. Development costs	2,500,000	2,250,000	250,000
3. Research costs	0	375,000	(375,000)
4. Accounts receivable	1,500,000	1,218,750	281,250

Comments:

1. *Dividends receivable*: Although the dividends received are economic benefits from the subsidiary, we are assuming that dividends are not taxable. Therefore, the carrying amount equals the tax base for dividends receivable.

2. *Development costs*: First, we assume that development costs will generate economic benefits for Entiguan Sports. Therefore, it may be included as an asset on the balance sheet for the purposes of this example. Second, the amortization allowed by the tax authorities exceeds the amortization accounted for based on accounting rules. Therefore, the carrying amount of the asset exceeds its tax base. The carrying amount is (€3,000,000 − €500,000) = €2,500,000 whereas the tax base is [€3,000,000 − (25% × €3,000,000)] = €2,250,000.

3. *Research costs*: We assume that research costs will result in future economic benefits for the company. If this were not the case, creation of a deferred tax asset or liability would not be allowed. The tax base of research costs exceeds their carrying amount. The carrying amount is €0 because the full amount has been expensed for financial reporting purposes in the year in which it was incurred. Therefore, there would not have been a balance sheet item "Research costs" for tax purposes, and only a proportion may be deducted in the current fiscal year. The tax base of the asset is (€500,000 − €500,000/4) = €375,000.

4. *Accounts receivable*: The economic benefits that should have been received from accounts receivable have already been included in revenues included in the calculation of the taxable income when the sales occurred. Because the receipt of a portion of the accounts receivable is doubtful, the provision is allowed. The provision, based on tax legislation, results in a greater amount allowed in the current fiscal year than would be the case under accounting principles. This results in the tax base of accounts receivable being lower than its carrying amount. Note that the example specifically states that the balance sheet amount for accounts receivable after the provision for accounting purposes amounts to €1,500,000. Therefore, accounts receivable before any provision was €1,500,000 + €125,000 = €1,625,000. The tax base is calculated as (€1,500,000 + €125,000) − [25% × (€1,500,000 + €125,000)] = €1,218,750.

3.2. Determining the Tax Base of a Liability

The tax base of a liability is the carrying amount of the liability less any amounts that will be deductible for tax purposes in the future. With respect to payments from customers received in advance of providing the goods and services, the tax base of such a liability is the carrying amount less any amount of the revenue that will not be taxable in future. Keep in mind the following fundamental principle: In general, a company will recognize a deferred tax asset or liability when recovery/settlement of the carrying amount will affect future tax payments by either increasing or reducing the taxable profit. Remember, an analyst is not only evaluating the difference between the carrying amount and the tax base, but the relevance of that difference on future profits and losses, and thus by implication future taxes.

IFRS offers specific guidelines with regard to revenue received in advance: IAS 12 states that the tax base is the carrying amount less any amount of the revenue that will not be taxed at a future date. Under US GAAP, an analysis of the tax base would result in a similar outcome. The tax legislation within the jurisdiction will determine the amount recognized on the income statement and whether the liability (revenue received in advance) will have a tax base greater than zero. This will depend on how tax legislation recognizes revenue received in advance.

EXAMPLE 3   Determining the Tax Base of a Liability

The following information pertains to the hypothetical company Entiguan Sports for the fiscal year-end. The treatment of items for accounting and tax purposes is based on fictitious accounting and tax standards and is not specific to a particular jurisdiction. Calculate the tax base and carrying amount for each item.

1. *Donations*: Entiguan Sports made donations of €100,000 in the current fiscal year. The donations were expensed for financial reporting purposes, but are not tax deductible based on applicable tax legislation.
2. *Interest received in advance*: Entiguan Sports received in advance interest of €300,000. The interest is taxed because tax authorities recognize the interest to accrue to the company (part of taxable income) on the date of receipt.
3. *Rent received in advance*: Entiguan recognized €10 million for rent received in advance from a lessee for an unused warehouse building. Rent received in advance is deferred for accounting purposes but taxed on a cash basis.
4. *Loan*: Entiguan Sports secured a long-term loan for €550,000 in the current fiscal year. Interest is charged at 13.5 percent per annum and is payable at the end of each fiscal year.

Solutions:

	Carrying Amount (€)	Tax Base (€)	Temporary Difference (€)
1. Donations	0	0	0
2. Interest received in advance	300,000	0	(300,000)
3. Rent received in advance	10,000,000	0	(10,000,000)
4. Loan (capital)	550,000	550,000	0
Interest paid	0	0	0

Comments:

1. *Donations*: The amount of €100,000 was immediately expensed on Entiguan's income statement; therefore, the carrying amount is €0. Tax legislation does not allow donations to be deducted for tax purposes, so the tax base of the donations equals the carrying amount. Note that while the carrying amount and tax base are the same, the difference in the treatment of donations for accounting and tax purposes (expensed for accounting purposes, but not deductible for tax purposes) represents a permanent difference (a difference that will not be reversed in future). Permanent and temporary differences are elaborated on in Section 4, and it will refer to this particular case with an expanded explanation.

2. *Interest received in advance*: Based on the information provided, for tax purposes, interest is deemed to accrue to the company on the date of receipt. For tax purposes, it is thus irrelevant whether it is for the current or a future accounting period; it must be included in taxable income in the financial year received. Interest received in advance is, for accounting purposes, though, included in the financial period in which it is deemed to have been earned. For this reason, the interest income received in advance is a balance sheet liability. It was not included on the income statement because the income relates to a future financial year. Because the full €300,000 is included in taxable income in the current fiscal year, the tax base is €300,000 − 300,000 = €0. Note that although interest received in advance and rent received in advance are both taxed, the timing depends on how the particular item is treated in tax legislation.

3. *Rent received in advance*: The result is similar to interest received in advance. The carrying amount of rent received in advance would be €10,000,000 while the tax base is €0.

4. *Loan*: Repayment of the loan has no tax implications. The repayment of the capital amount does not constitute an income or expense. The interest paid is included as an expense in the calculation of taxable income as well as accounting income. Therefore, the tax base and carrying amount is €0. For clarity, the interest paid that would be included on the income statement for the year amounts to 13.5% × €550,000 = €74,250 if the loan was acquired at the beginning of the current fiscal year.

3.3. Changes in Income Tax Rates

The measurement of deferred tax assets and liabilities is based on current tax law. But if there are subsequent changes in tax laws or new income tax rates, existing deferred tax assets and liabilities must be adjusted for the effects of these changes. The resulting effects of the changes are also included in determining accounting profit in the period of change.

When income tax rates change, the deferred tax assets and liabilities are adjusted to the new tax rate. If income tax rates increase, deferred taxes (that is, the deferred tax assets and liabilities) will also increase. Likewise, if income tax rates decrease, deferred taxes will decrease. A decrease in tax rates decreases deferred tax liabilities, which reduces future tax payments to the taxing authorities. A decrease in tax rates will also decrease deferred tax assets, which reduces their value toward the offset of future tax payments to the taxing authorities.

To illustrate the effect of a change in tax rate, consider Example 1 again. In that illustration, the timing difference that led to the recognition of a deferred tax liability for Reston Partners was attributable to differences in the method of depreciation and the related effects on the accounting carrying value and the asset tax base. The relevant information is restated below.

The carrying amount and tax base for the equipment is:

(£ Millions)	Year 3	Year 2	Year 1
Equipment value for accounting purposes (*carrying amount*) (depreciation of £2,000/year)	£14,000	£16,000	£18,000
Equipment value for tax purposes (*tax base*) (depreciation of £2,857/year)	£11,429	£14,286	£17,143
Difference	£2,571	£1,714	£857

At a 30 percent income tax rate, the deferred tax liability was then determined as follows:

(£ Millions)	Year 3	Year 2	Year 1
Deferred tax liability	£771	£514	£257
(Difference between tax base and carrying amount)			
Year 1: £(18,000 − 17,143) × 30% = £257			
Year 2: £(16,000 − 14,286) × 30% = £514			
Year 3: £(14,000 − 11,429) × 30% = £771			

For this illustration, assume that the taxing authority has changed the income tax rate to 25 percent for Year 3. Although the difference between the carrying amount and the tax base of the depreciable asset are the same, the deferred tax liability for 2017 will be £643 (instead of £771 or a reduction of £128 in the liability). 2017: £(14,000 − 11,429) × 25% = £643.

Reston Partners' provision for income tax expense is also affected by the change in tax rates. Taxable income for Year 3 will now be taxed at a rate of 25 percent. The benefit of the Year 3 accelerated depreciation tax shield is now only £214 (£857 × 25%) instead of the previous £257 (a reduction of £43). In addition, the reduction in the beginning carrying value of the deferred tax liability for Year 3 (the year of change) further reduces the income tax expense for Year 3. The reduction in income tax expense attributable to the change in tax rate is £86. Year 3: (30% − 25%) × £1,714 = £86. Note that these two components together account for the reduction in the deferred tax liability (£43 + £86 = £129).

As may be seen from this discussion, changes in the income tax rate have an effect on a company's deferred tax asset and liability carrying values as well as an effect on the measurement of income tax expense in the year of change. The analyst must thus note that proposed changes in tax law can have a quantifiable effect on these accounts (and any related financial ratios that are derived from them) if the proposed changes are subsequently enacted into law.

4. TEMPORARY AND PERMANENT DIFFERENCES BETWEEN TAXABLE AND ACCOUNTING PROFIT

Temporary differences arise from a difference between the tax base and the carrying amount of assets and liabilities. The creation of a deferred tax asset or liability from a temporary difference is only possible if the difference reverses itself at some future date and to such an extent that the balance sheet item is expected to create future economic benefits for the company. IFRS and US GAAP both prescribe the balance sheet liability method for recognition of deferred tax. This balance sheet method focuses on the recognition of a deferred tax asset or liability should there be a temporary difference between the carrying amount and tax base of balance sheet items.[3]

---

[3] Previously, IAS 12 required recognition of deferred tax based on the deferred method (also known as the income statement method), which focused on timing differences. Timing differences are differences in the recognition of income and expenses for accounting and tax purposes that originate in one period and will reverse in a future period. Given the definition of timing differences, all timing differences are temporary differences, such as the different treatment of depreciation for tax and accounting purposes (although the timing is different with regard to the allowed depreciation for tax and accounting purposes, the asset will eventually be fully depreciated).

Permanent differences are differences between tax and financial reporting of revenue (expenses) that *will not* be reversed at some future date. Because they will not be reversed at a future date, these differences do not give rise to deferred tax. These items typically include

- Income or expense items not allowed by tax legislation, and
- Tax credits for some expenditures that directly reduce taxes.

Because no deferred tax item is created for permanent differences, all permanent differences result in a difference between the company's effective tax rate and statutory tax rate. The effective tax rate is also influenced by different statutory taxes should an entity conduct business in more than one tax jurisdiction. The formula for the reported effective tax rate is thus equal to:

Reported effective tax rate = Income tax expense ÷ Pretax income (accounting profit)

The net change in deferred tax during a reporting period is the difference between the balance of the deferred tax asset or liability for the current period and the balance of the previous period.

4.1. Taxable Temporary Differences

Temporary differences are further divided into two categories, namely, taxable temporary differences and deductible temporary differences. **Taxable temporary differences** are temporary differences that result in a taxable amount in a future period when determining the taxable profit as the balance sheet item is recovered or settled. Taxable temporary differences result in a deferred tax liability when the carrying amount of an asset exceeds its tax base and, in the case of a liability, when the tax base of the liability exceeds its carrying amount.

Under US GAAP, a deferred tax asset or liability is not recognized for unamortizable goodwill. Under IFRS, a deferred tax account is not recognized for goodwill arising in a business combination. Since goodwill is a residual, the recognition of a deferred tax liability would increase the carrying amount of goodwill. Discounting deferred tax assets or liabilities is generally not allowed for temporary differences related to business combinations as it is for other temporary differences.

IFRS provides an exemption (that is, deferred tax is not provided on the temporary difference) for the initial recognition of an asset or liability in a transaction that: a) is not a business combination (e.g., joint ventures, branches and unconsolidated investments); and b) affects neither accounting profit nor taxable profit at the time of the transaction. US GAAP does not provide an exemption for these circumstances.

As a simple example of a temporary difference with no recognition of deferred tax liability, assume that a holding company of various leisure-related businesses and holiday resorts buys an interest in a hotel in the current financial year. The goodwill related to the transaction will be recognized on the financial statements, but the related tax liability will not, as it relates to the initial recognition of goodwill.

4.2. Deductible Temporary Differences

Deductible temporary differences are temporary differences that result in a reduction or deduction of taxable income in a future period when the balance sheet item is recovered or settled. Deductible temporary differences result in a deferred tax asset when the tax base of an asset exceeds its carrying amount and, in the case of a liability, when the carrying amount of the liability exceeds its tax base. The recognition of a deferred tax asset is only allowed to the extent there is a reasonable expectation of future profits against which the asset or liability (that gave rise to the deferred tax asset) can be recovered or settled.

To determine the probability of sufficient future profits for utilization, one must consider the following: 1) sufficient taxable temporary differences must exist that are related to the same tax authority and the same taxable entity; and 2) the taxable temporary differences that are expected to reverse in the same periods as expected for the reversal of the deductible temporary differences.

As with deferred tax liabilities, IFRS states that deferred tax assets should not be recognized in cases that would arise from the initial recognition of an asset or liability in transactions that are not a business combination and when, at the time of the transaction, there is no impact on either accounting or taxable profit. Subsequent to initial recognition under IFRS and US GAAP, any deferred tax assets that arise from investments in subsidiaries, branches, associates, and interests in joint ventures are recognized as a deferred tax asset.

IFRS and US GAAP allow the creation of a deferred tax asset in the case of tax losses and tax credits. These two unique situations will be further elaborated on in Section 6. IAS 12 *does not* allow the creation of a deferred tax asset arising from negative goodwill. Negative goodwill arises when the amount that an entity pays for an interest in a business is less than the net fair market value of the portion of assets and liabilities of the acquired company, based on the interest of the entity.

4.3. Examples of Taxable and Deductible Temporary Differences

Exhibit 1 summarizes how differences between the tax bases and carrying amounts of assets and liabilities give rise to deferred tax assets or deferred tax liabilities.

EXHIBIT 1   Treatment of Temporary Differences

Balance Sheet Item	Carrying Amount vs. Tax Base	Results in Deferred Tax Asset/Liability
Asset	Carrying amount > tax base	Deferred tax liability
Asset	Carrying amount < tax base	Deferred tax asset
Liability	Carrying amount > tax base	Deferred tax asset
Liability	Carrying amount < tax base	Deferred tax liability

EXAMPLE 4   Taxable and Deductible Temporary Differences

Examples 2 and 3 illustrated how to calculate the tax base of assets and liabilities, respectively. Based on the information provided in Examples 2 and 3, indicate whether the difference in the tax base and carrying amount of the assets and liabilities are temporary or permanent differences and whether a deferred tax asset or liability will be recognized based on the difference identified.

Solution to Example 2:

	Carrying Amount (€)	Tax Base (€)	Temporary Difference (€)	Will Result in Deferred Tax Asset/Liability
1. Dividends receivable	1,000,000	1,000,000	0	*N/A*
2. Development costs	2,500,000	2,250,000	250,000	*Deferred tax liability*
3. Research costs	0	375,000	(375,000)	*Deferred tax asset*
4. Accounts receivable	1,500,000	1,218,750	281,250	*Deferred tax liability*

Example 2 included comments on the calculation of the carrying amount and tax base of the assets.

1. *Dividends receivable*: As a result of non-taxability, the carrying amount equals the tax base of dividends receivable. This constitutes a permanent difference and will not result in the recognition of any deferred tax asset or liability. A temporary difference constitutes a difference that will, at some future date, be reversed. Although the timing of recognition is different for tax and accounting purposes, in the end the full carrying amount will be expensed/recognized as income. A permanent difference will never be reversed. Based on tax legislation, dividends from a subsidiary are not recognized as income. Therefore, no amount will be reflected as dividend income when calculating the taxable income, and the tax base of dividends receivable must be the total amount received, namely €1,000,000. The taxable income and accounting profit will permanently differ with the amount of dividends receivable, even on future financial statements as an effect on the retained earnings reflected on the balance sheet.

2. *Development costs*: The difference between the carrying amount and tax base is a temporary difference that, in the future, will reverse. In this fiscal year, it will result in a deferred tax liability.

3. *Research costs*: The difference between the carrying amount and tax base is a temporary difference that results in a deferred tax asset. Remember the explanation in Section 2 for deferred tax assets—a deferred tax asset arises because of an excess amount paid for taxes (when taxable income is greater than accounting profit), which is expected to be recovered from future operations. Based on accounting principles, the full amount was deducted resulting in a lower accounting profit, while the taxable income by implication, should be greater because of the lower amount expensed.

4. *Accounts receivable*: The difference between the carrying amount and tax base of the asset is a temporary difference that will result in a deferred tax liability.

Solution to Example 3:

	Carrying Amount (€)	Tax Base (€)	Temporary Difference (€)	Will Result in Deferred Tax Asset/Liability
1. Donations	0	0	0	*N/A*
2. Interest received in advance	300,000	0	(300,000)	*Deferred tax asset*
3. Rent received in advance	10,000,000	0	(10,000,000)	*Deferred tax asset*
4. Loan (capital)	550,000	550,000	0	*N/A*
Interest paid	0	0	0	*N/A*

Example 3 included extensive comments on the calculation of the carrying amount and tax base of the liabilities.

1. *Donations*: It was assumed that tax legislation does not allow donations to be deducted for tax purposes. No temporary difference results from donations, and thus a deferred tax asset or liability will not be recognized. This constitutes a permanent difference.
2. *Interest received in advance*: Interest received in advance results in a temporary difference that gives rise to a deferred tax asset. A deferred tax asset arises because of an excess amount paid for taxes (when taxable income is greater than accounting profit), which is expected to be recovered from future operations.
3. *Rent received in advance*: The difference between the carrying amount and tax base is a temporary difference that leads to the recognition of a deferred tax asset.
4. *Loan*: There are no temporary differences as a result of the loan or interest paid, and thus no deferred tax item is recognized.

4.4. Temporary Differences at Initial Recognition of Assets and Liabilities

In some situations the carrying amount and tax base of a balance sheet item may vary at initial recognition. For example, a company may deduct a government grant from the initial carrying amount of an asset or liability that appears on the balance sheet. For tax purposes, such grants may not be deducted when determining the tax base of the balance sheet item. In such circumstances, the carrying amount of the asset or liability will be lower than its tax base. Differences in the tax base of an asset or liability as a result of the circumstances described above may not be recognized as deferred tax assets or liabilities.

For example, a government may offer grants to Small, Medium, and Micro Enterprises (SMME) in an attempt to assist these entrepreneurs in their endeavors that contribute to the country's GDP and job creation. Assume that a particular grant is offered for infrastructure needs (office furniture, property, plant, and equipment, etc.). In these circumstances, although the carrying amount will be lower than the tax base of the asset, the related deferred tax may not be recognized. As mentioned earlier, deferred tax assets and liabilities should not be recognized in cases that would arise from the initial recognition of an asset or liability in transactions that are not a business combination and when, at the time of the transaction, there is no impact on either accounting or taxable profit.

A deferred tax liability will also not be recognized at the initial recognition of goodwill. Although goodwill may be treated differently across tax jurisdictions, which may lead to differences in the carrying amount and tax base of goodwill, IAS 12 does not allow the recognition of such a deferred tax liability. Any impairment that an entity should, for accounting purposes, impose on goodwill will again result in a temporary difference between its carrying amount and tax base. Any impairment that an entity should, for accounting purposes, impose on goodwill and if part of the goodwill is related to the initial recognition, that part of the difference in tax base and carrying amount should not result in any deferred taxation because the initial deferred tax liability was not recognized. Any future differences between the carrying amount and tax base as a result of amortization and the deductibility of a portion of goodwill constitute a temporary difference for which provision should be made.

4.5. Business Combinations and Deferred Taxes

The fair value of assets and liabilities acquired in a business combination is determined on the acquisition date and may differ from the previous carrying amount. It is highly probable that the values of acquired intangible assets, including goodwill, would differ from their carrying amounts. This temporary difference will affect deferred taxes as well as the amount of goodwill recognized as a result of the acquisition.

4.6. Investments in Subsidiaries, Branches, Associates, and Interests in Joint Ventures

Investments in subsidiaries, branches, associates, and interests in joint ventures may lead to temporary differences on the consolidated versus the parent's financial statements. The related deferred tax liabilities as a result of temporary differences will be recognized unless both of the following criteria are satisfied:

- The parent is in a position to control the timing of the future reversal of the temporary difference, and
- It is probable that the temporary difference will not reverse in the future.

With respect to deferred tax assets related to subsidiaries, branches, and associates and interests, deferred tax assets will only be recognized if the following criteria are satisfied:

- The temporary difference will reverse in the future, and
- Sufficient taxable profits exist against which the temporary difference can be used.

5. UNUSED TAX LOSSES AND TAX CREDITS

IAS 12 allows the recognition of unused tax losses and tax credits only to the extent that it is probable that in the future there will be taxable income against which the unused tax losses and credits can be applied. Under US GAAP, a deferred tax asset is recognized in full but is then reduced by a valuation allowance if it is more likely than not that some or all of the deferred tax asset will not be realized. The same requirements for creation of a deferred tax asset as a result of deductible temporary differences also apply to unused tax losses and tax credits. The existence of tax losses may indicate that the entity cannot reasonably be expected to generate sufficient future taxable income. All other things held constant, the greater the history of tax losses, the greater the concern regarding the company's ability to generate future taxable profits.

Should there be concerns about the company's future profitability, then the deferred tax asset may not be recognized until it is realized. When assessing the probability that sufficient taxable profit will be generated in the future, the following criteria can serve as a guide:

- If there is uncertainty as to the probability of future taxable profits, a deferred tax asset as a result of unused tax losses or tax credits is only recognized to the extent of the available taxable temporary differences;
- Assess the probability that the entity will in fact generate future taxable profits before the unused tax losses and/or credits expire pursuant to tax rules regarding the carry forward of the unused tax losses;

- Verify that the above is with the same tax authority and based on the same taxable entity;
- Determine whether the past tax losses were a result of specific circumstances that are unlikely to be repeated; and
- Discover if tax planning opportunities are available to the entity that will result in future profits. These may include changes in tax legislation that is phased in over more than one financial period to the benefit of the entity.

It is imperative that the timing of taxable and deductible temporary differences also be considered before creating a deferred tax asset based on unused tax credits.

6. RECOGNITION AND MEASUREMENT OF CURRENT AND DEFERRED TAX

Current taxes payable or recoverable from tax authorities are based on the applicable tax rates at the balance sheet date. Deferred taxes should be measured at the tax rate that is expected to apply when the asset is realized or the liability settled. With respect to the income tax for a current or prior period not yet paid, it is recognized as a tax liability until paid. Any amount paid in excess of any tax obligation is recognized as an asset. The income tax paid in excess or owed to tax authorities is separate from deferred taxes on the company's balance sheet.

When measuring deferred taxes in a jurisdiction, there are different forms of taxation such as income tax, capital gains tax (any capital gains made), or secondary tax on companies (tax payable on the dividends that a company declares) and possibly different tax bases for a balance sheet item (as in the case of government grants influencing the tax base of an asset such as property). In assessing which tax laws should apply, it is dependent on how the related asset or liability will be settled. It would be prudent to use the tax rate and tax base that is consistent with how it is expected that the tax base will be recovered or settled.

Although deferred tax assets and liabilities are related to temporary differences expected to be recovered or settled at some future date, neither are discounted to present value in determining the amounts to be booked. Both must be adjusted for changes in tax rates.

Deferred taxes as well as income taxes should always be recognized on the income statement of an entity unless it pertains to:

- Taxes or deferred taxes charged directly to equity, or
- A possible provision for deferred taxes relates to a business combination.

The carrying amount of the deferred tax assets and liabilities should also be assessed. The carrying amounts may change even though there may have been no change in temporary differences during the period evaluated. This can result from:

- Changes in tax rates;
- Reassessments of the recoverability of deferred tax assets; or
- Changes in the expectations for how an asset will be recovered and what influences the deferred tax asset or liability.

All unrecognized deferred tax assets and liabilities must be reassessed at the balance sheet date and measured against the criteria of probable future economic benefits. If such a deferred asset is likely to be recovered, it may be appropriate to recognize the related deferred tax asset.

Different jurisdictions have different requirements for determining tax obligations that can range from different forms of taxation to different tax rates based on taxable income. When comparing financial statements of entities that conduct business in different jurisdictions subject to different tax legislation, the analyst should be cautious in reaching conclusions because of the potentially complex tax rules that may apply.

6.1. Recognition of a Valuation Allowance

Deferred tax assets must be assessed at each balance sheet date. If there is any doubt whether the deferral will be recovered, then the carrying amount should be reduced to the expected recoverable amount. Should circumstances subsequently change and suggest the future will lead to recovery of the deferral, the reduction may be reversed.

Under US GAAP, deferred tax assets are reduced by creating a valuation allowance. Establishing a valuation allowance reduces the deferred tax asset and income in the period in which the allowance is established. Should circumstances change to such an extent that a deferred tax asset valuation allowance may be reduced, the reversal will increase the deferred tax asset and operating income. Because of the subjective judgment involved, an analyst should carefully scrutinize any such changes.

6.2. Recognition of Current and Deferred Tax Charged Directly to Equity

In general, IFRS and US GAAP require that the recognition of deferred tax liabilities and current income tax should be treated similarly to the asset or liability that gave rise to the deferred tax liability or income tax based on accounting treatment. Should an item that gives rise to a deferred tax liability be taken directly to equity, the same should hold true for the resulting deferred tax.

The following are examples of such items:

- Revaluation of property, plant, and equipment (revaluations are not permissible under US GAAP);
- Long-term investments at fair value;
- Changes in accounting policies;
- Errors corrected against the opening balance of retained earnings;
- Initial recognition of an equity component related to complex financial instruments; and
- Exchange rate differences arising from the currency translation procedures for foreign operations.

Whenever it is determined that a deferred tax liability will not be reversed, an adjustment should be made to the liability. The deferred tax liability will be reduced, and the amount by which it is reduced should be taken directly to equity. Any deferred taxes related to a business combination must also be recognized in equity.

Depending on the items that gave rise to the deferred tax liabilities, an analyst should exercise judgment regarding whether the taxes should be included with deferred tax liabilities or whether it should be taken directly to equity. It may be more appropriate simply to ignore deferred taxes.

EXAMPLE 5   Taxes Charged Directly to Equity

The following information pertains to Khaleej Company (a hypothetical company). A building owned by Khaleej Company was originally purchased for €1,000,000 on January 1, 20x1. For accounting purposes, buildings are depreciated at 5 percent a year on a straight-line basis, and depreciation for tax purposes is 10 percent a year on a straight-line basis. On the first day of 20x3, the building is revalued at €1,200,000. It is estimated that the remaining useful life of the building from the date of revaluation is 20 years. *Important*: For tax purposes the revaluation of the building is not recognized.

Based on the information provided, the following illustrates the difference in treatment of the building for accounting and tax purposes.

	Carrying Amount of Building	Tax Base of Building
Balance on January 1, 20x1	€1,000,000	€1,000,000
Depreciation 20x1	(50,000)	(100,000)
Balance on December 31, 20x1	€950,000	€900,000
Depreciation 20x2	(50,000)	(100,000)
Balance on December 31, 20x2	€900,000	€800,000
Revaluation on January 1, 20x3	300,000	n/a
Balance on January 1, 20x3	€1,200,000	€800,000
Depreciation 20x3	(60,000)	(100,000)
Balance on December 31, 20x3	€1,140,000	€700,000
Accumulated depreciation		
Balance on January 1, 20x1	€0	€0
Depreciation 20x1	50,000	100,000
Balance on December 31, 20x1	€50,000	€100,000
Depreciation 20x2	50,000	100,000
Balance on December 31, 20x2	€100,000	€200,000
Revaluation at January 1, 20x3	(100,000)	n/a
Balance on January 1, 20x3	€0	€200,000
Depreciation 20x3	60,000	100,000
Balance on November 30, 20x3	€60,000	€300,000

	Carrying Amount	Tax Base
On December 31, 20x1	€950,000	€900,000
On December 31, 20x2	€900,000	€800,000
On December 31, 20x3	€1,140,000	€700,000

December 31, 20x1: On December 31, 20x1, different treatments for depreciation expense result in a temporary difference that gives rise to a deferred tax liability. The difference in the tax base and carrying amount of the building was a result of different depreciation amounts for tax and accounting purposes. Depreciation appears on the income statement. For this reason the deferred tax liability will also be reflected on the income statement. If we assume that the applicable tax rate in 20x1 was 40 percent, then the resulting deferred tax liability will be 40% × (€950,000 − €900,000) = €20,000.

December 31, 20x2: As of December 31, 20x2, the carrying amount of the building remains greater than the tax base. The temporary difference again gives rise to a deferred tax liability. Again, assuming the applicable tax rate to be 40 percent, the deferred tax liability from the building is 40% × (€900,000 − €800,000) = €40,000.

December 31, 20x3: On December 31, *20x3*, the carrying amount of the building again exceeds the tax base. This is not the result of disposals or additions, but is a result of the revaluation at the beginning of the *20x3* fiscal year and the different rates of depreciation. The deferred tax liability would seem to be 40% × (€1,140,000 − €700,000) = €176,000, *but* the treatment is different than it was for the 20x1 and 20x2. In 20x3, revaluation of the building gave rise to a balance sheet equity account, namely "Revaluation Surplus" in the amount of €300,000, which is not recognized for tax purposes.

The deferred tax liability would usually have been calculated as follows:

	20x3	20x2	20x1
Deferred tax liability (closing balance at end of fiscal year)	€176,000	€40,000	€20,000
(Difference between tax base and carrying amount)			
20x1: €(950,000 − 900,000) × 40% = 20,000			
20x2: €(900,000 − 800,000) × 40% = 40,000			
20x3: €(1,140,000 − 700,000) × 40% = 176,000			

The change in the deferred tax liability in 20x1 is €20,000, in 20x2: €20,000 (€40,000 − €20,000) and, it would seem, in 20x3: €136,000 (€176,000 − €40,000). In 20x3, although it would seem that the balance for deferred tax liability should be €176,000, the revaluation is not recognized for tax purposes. Only the portion of the difference between the tax base and carrying amount that is not a result of the revaluation is recognized as giving rise to a deferred tax liability.

The effect of the revaluation surplus and the associated tax effects are accounted for in a direct adjustment to equity. The revaluation surplus is reduced by the tax provision associated with the excess of the fair value over the carry value, and it affects retained earnings (€300,000 × 40% = €120,000).

The deferred tax liability that should be reflected on the balance sheet is thus not €176,000 but only €56,000 (€176,000 − €120,000). Given the balance of deferred tax liability at the beginning of the 20x3 fiscal year in the amount of €40,000, the change in the deferred tax liability is only €56,000 − €40,000 = €16,000.

In the future, at the end of each year, an amount equal to the depreciation as a result of the revaluation minus the deferred tax effect will be transferred from the revaluation reserve to retained earnings. In 20x3 this will amount to a portion of depreciation resulting from the revaluation, €15,000 (€300,000 ÷ 20), minus the deferred tax effect of €6,000 (€15,000 × 40%), thus €9,000.

7. PRESENTATION AND DISCLOSURE

We will discuss the presentation and disclosure of income tax related information by way of example. The Consolidated Statements of Operations (Income Statements) and Consolidated Balance Sheets for Micron Technology (MU), a global technology company based in the US, are provided in Exhibits 2 and 3, respectively. Exhibit 4 provides the income tax note disclosures for MU for the 2015, 2016, and 2017 fiscal years.

MU's income tax provision (i.e., income tax expense) for fiscal year 2017 is $114 million (see Exhibit 2). The income tax note disclosure in Exhibit 4 reconciles how the income tax provision was determined beginning with MU's reported income before taxes (shown in Exhibit 4 as $5,196 million for fiscal year 2017). The note disclosure then denotes the income tax provision for 2017 that is current ($153 million), which is then offset by the deferred tax benefit for foreign taxes ($39 million), for a net income tax provision of $114 million. Exhibit 4 further shows a reconciliation of how the income tax provision was derived from the US federal statutory rate. Many public companies comply with this required disclosure by displaying the information in percentage terms, but MU has elected to provide the disclosure in absolute dollar amounts. From this knowledge, for 2017 we can see that the dollar amount shown for US federal income tax provision at the statutory rate ($1,819 million) was determined by multiplying MU's income before taxes by the 35 percent US federal statutory rate ($5,196 × 0.35 = $1,819).

In addition, the note disclosure in Exhibit 4 provides detailed information about the derivation of the deferred tax assets ($766 million for 2017) and deferred tax liabilities ($17 million for 2017). These deferred tax assets are shown separately on MU's consolidated balance sheet for fiscal year 2017 with noncurrent assets (see Exhibit 3), while the deferred tax liabilities are included in other noncurrent liabilities (also see Exhibit 3).

EXHIBIT 2   Micron Technology, Inc. Consolidated Statements of Operations (Amounts in US$ Millions except Per Share)

For the Year Ended	Aug. 31, 2017	Sep. 1, 2016	Sep. 3, 2015
Net sales	20,322	$12,399	$16,192
Cost of goods sold	11,886	9,894	10,977
Gross margin	8,436	2,505	5,215
Selling, general and administrative	743	659	719
Research and development	1,824	1,617	1,540
Restructure and asset impairments	18	67	3
Other operating (income) expense, net	(17)	(6)	(45)
Operating income	5,868	168	2,998
Interest income (expense), net	(560)	(395)	(336)
Other non-operating income (expense), net	(112)	(54)	(53)
Income tax (provision) benefit	(114)	(19)	(157)
Equity in net income (loss) of equity method investees	8	25	447

EXHIBIT 2   (Continued)

For the Year Ended	Aug. 31, 2017	Sep. 1, 2016	Sep. 3, 2015
Net income (loss) attributable to noncontrolling interests	(1)	(1)	—
Net income (loss) attributable to Micron	$5,089	$(276)	$2,899
Earnings (loss) per share:			
Basic	$4.67	$(0.27)	$2.71
Diluted	$4.41	$(0.27)	$2.47
Number of shares used in per share calculations:			
Basic	1,089	1,036	1,070
Diluted	1,154	1,036	1,170

EXHIBIT 3   Micron Technology, Inc. Consolidated Balance Sheets (Amounts in US$ Millions)

As of	Aug. 31, 2017	Sep. 1, 2016
Assets		
Cash and equivalents	$5,109	$4,140
Short-term investments	319	258
Receivables	3,759	2,068
Inventories	3,123	2,889
Other current assets	147	140
Total current assets	12,457	9,495
Long-term marketable investments	617	414
Property, plant, and equipment, net	19,431	14,686
Equity method investments	16	1,364
Intangible assets, net	387	464
Deferred tax assets	766	657
Other noncurrent assets	1,662	460
Total assets	$35,336	$27,540
Liabilities and shareholders' equity		
Accounts payable and accrued expenses	$3,664	$3,879
Deferred income	408	200
Current debt	1,262	756
Total current liabilities	5,334	4,835
Long-term debt	9,872	9,154
Other noncurrent liabilities	639	623
Total liabilities	15,845	14,612

(continued)

EXHIBIT 3 (Continued)

As of	Aug. 31, 2017	Sep. 1, 2016
Redeemable convertible notes	21	—
Micron shareholder's equity		
Common stock of $0.10 par value, 3,000 shares authorized, 1,116 shares issued and 1,112 shares outstanding (1,094 issued and 1,040 outstanding as of September 1, 2016)	112	109
Additional capital	8,287	7,736
Retained earnings	10,260	5,299
Treasury stock, 4 shares held (54 as of September 1, 2016)	(67)	(1,029)
Accumulated other comprehensive income (loss)	29	(35)
Total Micron shareholders' equity	18,621	12,080
Noncontrolling interests in subsidiaries	849	848
Total equity	19,470	12,928
Total liabilities and shareholders' equity	35,336	$27,540

EXHIBIT 4 Micron Technology, Inc. Income Taxes Note to the Consolidated Financial Statements

Income (loss) before taxes and the income tax (provision) benefit consisted of the following:

(in US$ Millions)	2017	2016	2015
Income (loss) before income taxes, net income (loss) attributable to noncontrolling interests, and equity in net income (loss) of equity method investees			
Foreign	$5,252	$(353)	$2,431
US	(56)	72	178
	$5,196	$(281)	$2,609
Income tax (provision) benefit:			
Current:			
Foreign	$(152)	$(27)	$(93)
State	(1)	(1)	(1)
US federal	—	—	6
	(153)	(28)	(88)
Deferred:			
US federal	—	39	15
State	—	2	1
Foreign	39	(32)	(85)
	39	9	(69)
Income tax (provision)	$(114)	$(19)	$(157)

The company's income tax (provision) computed using the US federal statutory rate and the company's income tax (provision) benefit is reconciled as follows:

(US$ Millions)	2017	2016	2015
US federal income tax (provision) benefit at statutory rate	$(1,819)	$98	$(913)
Foreign tax rate differential	1,571	(300)	515
Change in valuation allowance	64	63	260
Change in unrecognized tax benefits	12	52	(118)
Tax credits	66	48	53
Noncontrolling investment transactions	—	—	57
Other	(8)	20	(11)
Income tax (provision) benefit	(114)	$(19)	$(157)

State taxes reflect investment tax credits of $233 million as at August 31, 2017. Deferred income taxes reflect the net tax effects of temporary differences between the bases of assets and liabilities for financial reporting and income tax purposes. The company's deferred tax assets and liabilities consist of the following as of the end of the periods shown below:

(US$ Millions)	2017	2016
Deferred tax assets:		
Net operating loss and tax credit carryforwards	$3,426	$3,014
Accrued salaries, wages, and benefits	211	142
Other accrued liabilities	59	76
Other	86	65
Gross deferred assets	3,782	3,297
Less valuation allowance	(2,321)	(2,107)
Deferred tax assets, net of valuation allowance	1,461	1,190
Deferred tax liabilities:		
Debt discount	(145)	(170)
Property, plant, and equipment	(300)	(135)
Unremitted earnings on certain subsidiaries	(123)	(121)
Product and process technology	(85)	(81)
Other	(59)	(28)
Deferred tax liabilities	(712)	(535)
Net deferred tax assets	$749	$655
Reported as:		
Current deferred tax assets (included in other current assets)	$—	$—
Deferred tax assets	766	657

(US$ Millions)	2017	2016
Current deferred tax liabilities (included in accounts payable and accrued expenses)	—	
Deferred tax liabilities (included in other noncurrent liabilities)	(17)	(2)
Net deferred tax assets	$749	$655

The company has a valuation allowance against substantially all of its US net deferred tax assets. As of August 31, 2017, the company had aggregate US tax net operating loss carryforwards of $3.88 billion and unused US tax credit carryforwards of $416 million. The company also has unused state tax net operating loss carryforwards of $1.95 billion and unused state tax credits of $233 million. The net operating loss carryforwards and the tax credit carryforwards expire between 2018 to 2037.

The changes in valuation allowance of $64 million and $63 million in 2017 and 2016, respectively, are primarily a result of uncertainties of realizing certain US and foreign net operating losses and certain tax credit carryforwards.

Provision has been made for deferred taxes on undistributed earnings of non-US subsidiaries to the extent that dividend payments from such companies are expected to result in additional tax liability. Remaining undistributed earnings of $12.91 billion as of August 31, 2017 have been indefinitely reinvested. Determination of the amount of unrecognized deferred tax liability on these unremitted earnings is not practicable.

EXAMPLE 6   Financial Analysis Example

Use the financial statement information and disclosures provided by MU in Exhibits 2, 3, and 4 to answer the following questions:

1. MU discloses a valuation allowance of $2,321 million (see Exhibit 4) against gross deferred assets of $3,782 million in 2017. Does the existence of this valuation allowance have any implications concerning MU's future earnings prospects?
2. How would MU's deferred tax assets and deferred tax liabilities be affected if the federal statutory tax rate was changed to 21 percent?
3. How would reported earnings have been affected if MU were not using a valuation allowance?
4. How would MU's $3.88 billion in net operating loss carryforwards in 2017 (see Exhibit 4) affect the valuation that an acquiring company would be willing to offer?
5. Under what circumstances should the analyst consider MU's deferred tax liability as debt or as equity? Under what circumstances should the analyst exclude MU's deferred tax liability from both debt and equity when calculating the debt-to-equity ratio?

Solution to 1: According to Exhibit 4, MU's deferred tax assets expire gradually until 2037 (2018 to 2037 for the net operating loss carryforwards and the tax credit carryforwards).

Because the company is still relatively young, it is likely that most of these expirations occur toward the end of that period. Because cumulative US tax net operating loss carryforwards total $3.88 billion, the valuation allowance could imply that MU is not reasonably expected to earn $3.88 billion over the next 20 years. However, as we can see in Exhibit 2, MU earned a profit for 2017 and 2015, thereby showing that the allowance could be adjusted downward if the company continues to generate profits in the future, and making it more likely than not that the deferred tax asset would be recognized.

Solution to 2: MU's total deferred tax assets exceed total deferred tax liabilities by $749 million. A change in the federal statutory tax rate to 21 percent from the current rate of 35 percent would make these net deferred assets less valuable. Also, because it is possible that the deferred tax asset valuation allowance could be adjusted downward in the future (see discussion to solution 1), the impact could be far greater in magnitude.

Solution to 3: The disclosure in Exhibit 4 shows that the increase in the valuation allowance increased the income tax provision as reported on the income statement by $64 million in 2017. Additional potential reductions in the valuation allowance could similarly reduce reported income taxes (actual income taxes would not be affected by a valuation allowance established for financial reporting) in future years (see discussion to solution 1).

Solution to 4: If an acquiring company is profitable, it may be able to use MU's tax loss carryforwards to offset its own tax liabilities. The value to an acquirer would be the present value of the carryforwards, based on the acquirer's tax rate and expected timing of realization. The higher the acquiring company's tax rate, and the more profitable the acquirer, the sooner it would be able to benefit. Therefore, an acquirer with a high current tax rate would theoretically be willing to pay more than an acquirer with a lower tax rate.

Solution to 5: The analyst should classify the deferred tax liability as debt if the liability is expected to reverse with subsequent tax payment. If the liability is not expected to reverse, there is no expectation of a cash outflow, and the liability should be treated as equity. By way of example, future company losses may preclude the payment of any income taxes, or changes in tax laws could result in taxes that are never paid. The deferred tax liability should be excluded from both debt and equity when both the amounts and timing of tax payments resulting from the reversals of temporary differences are uncertain.

8. COMPARISON OF IFRS AND US GAAP

As mentioned earlier, though IFRS and US GAAP follow similar conventions on many tax issues, there are some notable differences. Exhibit 5 summarizes many of the key similarities and differences between IFRS and US GAAP. Though both frameworks require a provision for deferred taxes, there are differences in the methodologies.

EXHIBIT 5   Deferred Income Tax Issues IFRS and US GAAP Methodology Similarities
and Differences

IFRS	US GAAP
Introduction	
The objective in accounting for income taxes is to recognize the amount of taxes currently payable or refundable and deferred taxes. Income tax expense is the current tax expense (or recovery) plus the period change in deferred taxes (net of tax arising from a business combination or recorded outside profit or loss).	Similar to IFRS.
Unpaid taxes for current and prior periods are recognized as a liability, and an asset is recognised if the amount already paid exceeds the amount due. A prior tax loss benefit used to recover previous period current tax is also an asset.	The approach to calculating current taxes is similar to IFRS with some exceptions, such as the treatment of taxes on the elimination of intercompany profits.
In general, deferred taxes are recognized using an asset and liability approach which focuses on temporary differences arising between the tax base of an asset or liability and its carrying amount in the statement of financial position. Deferred taxes are recognized for the future tax consequences of events that have been recognized in an entity's financial statements or tax returns.	US GAAP also follows an asset and liability approach to calculating deferred taxes, although there are some differences in the application relative to IFRS.
Deferred taxes are not recognized for: • The initial recognition of goodwill • The initial recognition of an asset or liability in a non-business combination transaction and where accounting profit or taxable profit (tax loss) is not affected • Taxable temporary differences from investments in subsidiaries/branches/associates, and interests in joint ventures in which the parent etc. is able to control the timing of the reversal of the temporary difference, and it is probable that the temporary difference will not reverse in the foreseeable future	Deferred taxes are not recognized for: • Goodwill for which amortization is not deductible for tax purposes • Unlike IFRS, US GAAP does not have a similar exception • An excess of the amount for the financial reporting over the tax basis of an investment in a foreign subsidiary or a foreign corporate joint venture that is essentially permanent in duration, unless it becomes apparent that those temporary differences will reverse in the foreseeable future. Unlike IFRS, this exception does not apply to domestic subsidiaries and corporate joint venture and investments in equity investees.
	Unlike IFRS, recognition of deferred taxes is prohibited for differences that are remeasured from the local currency into the functional currency using historical exchange rates and that result from changes in exchange rates or indexing for tax purposes.
Deferred taxes should be recognized for the difference between the carrying amount determined by using the historical exchange rate and the relevant tax base, which may have been affected by exchange rate changes or tax indexing.	

EXHIBIT 5   (Continued)

IFRS	US GAAP
Recognition and measurement	
Current tax liabilities and assets for the current and prior periods are measured at amounts expected to be paid to (recovered from) the taxation authorities based on tax rates (and tax laws) that have been enacted or substantially enacted by the end of the reporting period.	Similar to IFRS. Measurement of current and deferred tax assets and liabilities is based on enacted tax law. Deferred tax assets and liabilities are measured using enacted tax rate(s) expected to apply to taxable income in periods in which deferred tax is expected to be settled or realized. Unlike IFRS, use of substantially enacted tax rates is not permitted.
Deferred tax assets are measured at the tax rates that are expected to apply when the asset is realized or the liability is settled, based on tax rates (and tax laws) that have been enacted or substantively enacted by the end of the reporting period.	
Deferred tax assets are recognized to the extent that it is probable (more likely than not) that taxable profit will be available to utilize the deductible temporary difference or carryforward of unused tax losses or tax credits. End of reporting period reviews may reduce the carrying amount if sufficient taxable profit is no longer probable such as to allow the utilization benefit of all or part of that deferred tax asset, and any such reduction is reversed if it subsequently becomes probable again.	Unlike IFRS, deferred tax assets are recognized in full and reduced by a valuation allowance if it is more likely than not that some portion or all of the deferred tax assets will not be realized.
Current and deferred taxes are recognized outside profit or loss if the tax relates to items that are recognized, in the same or a different period, in other comprehensive income (OCI), or directly to equity.	Similar to IFRS, the tax effects of certain items occurring during the year are charged or credited directly to OCI or to related components of shareholders' equity.
Deferred tax assets and liabilities are not discounted.	Similar to IFRS.
Presentation and disclosure	
Deferred tax assets and liabilities are offset if the entity has a legally enforceable right to offset current tax assets against current tax liabilities and the deferred tax assets and deferred tax liabilities relate to income taxes levied by the same taxing authority on either the same taxable entity, or different taxable entities that intend either to settle current tax assets and liabilities on a net basis or to simultaneously realize/settle the asset/liability.	All deferred taxes are offset and presented as a single amount.
Deferred tax assets and liabilities are presented as separate line items in the statement of financial position. If a classified statement of financial position is used, deferred taxes are classified as noncurrent.	Deferred tax assets and deferred tax liabilities are presented as noncurrent in a classified statement of financial position, which aligns with IFRS.

(continued)

EXHIBIT 5   (Continued)

IFRS	US GAAP
All entities must disclose an explanation of the relationship between tax expense and accounting profit using either or both of the following formats: • A numerical reconciliation between tax expense (income) and the product of accounting profit multiplied by the applicable tax rate(s) including disclosure of the basis on which the applicable rate is computed. • A numerical reconciliation between the average effective tax rate and the applicable tax rate, including disclosure of the basis on which the applicable tax rate is computed.	Public companies must disclose a reconciliation using percentages or dollar amounts of the reported amount of income tax expense attributable to continuing operations for the year to that amount of income tax expense that would result from applying domestic federal statutory tax rates to pretax income from continuing operations. Nonpublic enterprises must disclose the nature of significant reconciling items but may omit a numerical reconciliation.

Sources: IFRS: IAS 12 and 32. US GAAP: ASC 740. "Comparison between US GAAP and IFRS Standards," Section 5.3 Taxation, Grant Thornton, April 2017. "IFRS and US GAAP: similarities and differences", PricewaterhouseCoopers LLC, 2018.

9. SUMMARY

Income taxes are a significant category of expense for profitable companies. Analyzing income tax expenses is often difficult for the analyst because there are many permanent and temporary timing differences between the accounting that is used for income tax reporting and the accounting that is used for financial reporting on company financial statements. The financial statements and notes to the financial statements of a company provide important information that the analyst needs to assess financial performance and to compare a company's financial performance with other companies. Key concepts in this chapter are as follows:

- Differences between the recognition of revenue and expenses for tax and accounting purposes may result in taxable income differing from accounting profit. The discrepancy is a result of different treatments of certain income and expenditure items.
- The tax base of an asset is the amount that will be deductible for tax purposes as an expense in the calculation of taxable income as the company expenses the tax basis of the asset. If the economic benefit will not be taxable, the tax base of the asset will be equal to the carrying amount of the asset.
- The tax base of a liability is the carrying amount of the liability less any amounts that will be deductible for tax purposes in the future. With respect to revenue received in advance, the tax base of such a liability is the carrying amount less any amount of the revenue that will not be taxable in the future.
- Temporary differences arise from recognition of differences in the tax base and carrying amount of assets and liabilities. The creation of a deferred tax asset or liability as a result of a temporary difference will only be allowed if the difference reverses itself at some future date

and to the extent that it is expected that the balance sheet item will create future economic benefits for the company.

- Permanent differences result in a difference in tax and financial reporting of revenue (expenses) that will not be reversed at some future date. Because it will not be reversed at a future date, these differences do not constitute temporary differences and do not give rise to a deferred tax asset or liability.
- Current taxes payable or recoverable are based on the applicable tax rates on the balance sheet date of an entity; in contrast, deferred taxes should be measured at the tax rate that is expected to apply when the asset is realized or the liability settled.
- All unrecognized deferred tax assets and liabilities must be reassessed on the appropriate balance sheet date and measured against their probable future economic benefit.
- Deferred tax assets must be assessed for their prospective recoverability. If it is probable that they will not be recovered at all or partly, the carrying amount should be reduced. Under US GAAP, this is done through the use of a valuation allowance.

PRACTICE PROBLEMS

1. Using the straight-line method of depreciation for reporting purposes and accelerated depreciation for tax purposes would *most likely* result in a:
   A. valuation allowance.
   B. deferred tax asset.
   C. temporary difference.
2. In early 2018 Sanborn Company must pay the tax authority €37,000 on the income it earned in 2017. This amount was recorded on the company's December 31, 2017 financial statements as:
   A. taxes payable.
   B. income tax expense.
   C. a deferred tax liability.
3. Income tax expense reported on a company's income statement equals taxes payable, plus the net increase in:
   A. deferred tax assets and deferred tax liabilities.
   B. deferred tax assets, less the net increase in deferred tax liabilities.
   C. deferred tax liabilities, less the net increase in deferred tax assets.
4. Analysts should treat deferred tax liabilities that are expected to reverse as:
   A. equity.
   B. liabilities.
   C. neither liabilities nor equity.
5. Deferred tax liabilities should be treated as equity when:
   A. they are not expected to reverse.
   B. the timing of tax payments is uncertain.
   C. the amount of tax payments is uncertain.

6. When both the timing and amount of tax payments are uncertain, analysts should treat deferred tax liabilities as:
   A. equity.
   B. liabilities.
   C. neither liabilities nor equity.

7. When accounting standards require recognition of an expense that is not permitted under tax laws, the result is a:
   A. deferred tax liability.
   B. temporary difference.
   C. permanent difference.

8. When certain expenditures result in tax credits that directly reduce taxes, the company will *most likely* record:
   A. a deferred tax asset.
   B. a deferred tax liability.
   C. no deferred tax asset or liability.

9. When accounting standards require an asset to be expensed immediately but tax rules require the item to be capitalized and amortized, the company will *most likely* record:
   A. a deferred tax asset.
   B. a deferred tax liability.
   C. no deferred tax asset or liability.

10. A company incurs a capital expenditure that may be amortized over five years for accounting purposes, but over four years for tax purposes. The company will *most likely* record:
    A. a deferred tax asset.
    B. a deferred tax liability.
    C. no deferred tax asset or liability.

11. A company receives advance payments from customers that are immediately taxable but will not be recognized for accounting purposes until the company fulfills its obligation. The company will *most likely* record:
    A. a deferred tax asset.
    B. a deferred tax liability.
    C. no deferred tax asset or liability.

The following information relates to Questions 12–14

Note I
Income Taxes

The components of earnings before income taxes are as follows ($ thousands):

	Year 3	Year 2	Year 1
Earnings before income taxes:			
United States	$88,157	$75,658	$59,973
Foreign	116,704	113,509	94,760
Total	$204,861	$189,167	$154,733

The components of the provision for income taxes are as follows ($ thousands):

	Year 3	Year 2	Year 1
Income taxes			
Current:			
Federal	$30,632	$22,031	$18,959
Foreign	28,140	27,961	22,263
	$58,772	$49,992	$41,222
Deferred:			
Federal	($4,752)	$5,138	$2,336
Foreign	124	1,730	621
	(4,628)	6,868	2,957
Total	$54,144	$56,860	$44,179

12. In Year 3, the company's US GAAP income statement recorded a provision for income taxes *closest* to:
    A. $30,632.
    B. $54,144.
    C. $58,772.
13. The company's effective tax rate was *highest* in:
    A. Year 1.
    B. Year 2.
    C. Year 3.
14. Compared to the company's effective tax rate on US income, its effective tax rate on foreign income was:
    A. lower in each year presented.
    B. higher in each year presented.
    C. higher in some periods and lower in others.

15. Zimt AG presents its financial statements in accordance with US GAAP. In Year 3, Zimt discloses a valuation allowance of $1,101 against total deferred tax assets of $19,201. In Year 2, Zimt disclosed a valuation allowance of $1,325 against total deferred tax assets of $17,325. The change in the valuation allowance most likely indicates that Zimt's:
    A. deferred tax liabilities were reduced in Year 3.
    B. expectations of future earning power has increased.
    C. expectations of future earning power has decreased.
16. Cinnamon, Inc. recorded a total deferred tax asset in Year 3 of $12,301, offset by a $12,301 valuation allowance. Cinnamon *most likely*:
    A. fully utilized the deferred tax asset in Year 3.
    B. has an equal amount of deferred tax assets and deferred tax liabilities.
    C. expects not to earn any taxable income before the deferred tax asset expires.

The following information relates to Questions 17–19

The tax effects of temporary differences that give rise to deferred tax assets and liabilities are as follows ($ thousands):

	Year 3	Year 2
Deferred tax assets:		
Accrued expenses	$8,613	$7,927
Tax credit and net operating loss carryforwards	2,288	2,554
LIFO and inventory reserves	5,286	4,327
Other	2,664	2,109
Deferred tax assets	18,851	16,917
Valuation allowance	(1,245)	(1,360)
Net deferred tax assets	$17,606	$15,557
Deferred tax liabilities:		
Depreciation and amortization	$(27,338)	$(29,313)
Compensation and retirement plans	(3,831)	(8,963)
Other	(1,470)	(764)
Deferred tax liabilities	(32,639)	(39,040)
Net deferred tax liability	$(15,033)	$(23,483)

17. A reduction in the statutory tax rate would *most likely* benefit the company's:
    A. income statement and balance sheet.
    B. income statement but not the balance sheet.
    C. balance sheet but not the income statement.
18. If the valuation allowance had been the same in Year 3 as it was in Year 2, the company would have reported $115 *higher*:
    A. net income.
    B. deferred tax assets.
    C. income tax expense.
19. Compared to the provision for income taxes in Year 3, the company's cash tax payments were:
    A. lower.
    B. higher.
    C. the same.

The following information relates to Questions 20–22

A company's provision for income taxes resulted in effective tax rates attributable to loss from continuing operations before cumulative effect of change in accounting principles that varied from the statutory federal income tax rate of 34 percent, as summarized in the table below.

Year Ended 30 June	Year 3	Year 2	Year 1
Expected federal income tax expense (benefit) from continuing operations at 34 percent	($112,000)	$768,000	$685,000
Expenses not deductible for income tax purposes	357,000	32,000	51,000
State income taxes, net of federal benefit	132,000	22,000	100,000
Change in valuation allowance for deferred tax assets	(150,000)	(766,000)	(754,000)
Income tax expense	$227,000	$56,000	$82,000

20. In Year 3, the company's net income (loss) was *closest* to:
    A. ($217,000).
    B. ($329,000).
    C. ($556,000).
21. The $357,000 adjustment in Year 3 *most likely* resulted in:
    A. an increase in deferred tax assets.
    B. an increase in deferred tax liabilities.
    C. no change to deferred tax assets and liabilities.
22. Over the three years presented, changes in the valuation allowance for deferred tax assets were *most likely* indicative of:
    A. decreased prospects for future profitability.
    B. increased prospects for future profitability.
    C. assets being carried at a higher value than their tax base.

CHAPTER **10**

NON-CURRENT (LONG-TERM) LIABILITIES

Elizabeth A. Gordon, PhD, MBA, CPA

Elaine Henry, PhD, CFA

LEARNING OUTCOMES

After completing this chapter, you will be able to do the following:

- determine the initial recognition, initial measurement, and subsequent measurement of bonds;
- describe the effective interest method and calculate interest expense, amortization of bond discounts/premiums, and interest payments;
- explain the derecognition of debt;
- describe the role of debt covenants in protecting creditors;
- describe the financial statement presentation of and disclosures relating to debt;
- explain motivations for leasing assets instead of purchasing them;
- explain the financial reporting of leases from a lessee's perspective;
- explain the financial reporting of leases from a lessor's perspective;
- compare the presentation and disclosure of defined contribution and defined benefit pension plans;
- calculate and interpret leverage and coverage ratios.

1. INTRODUCTION

A non-current liability (long-term liability) broadly represents a probable sacrifice of economic benefits in periods generally greater than one year in the future. Common types of **non-current liabilities** reported in a company's financial statements include long-term debt (e.g., bonds payable, long-term notes payable), leases, pension liabilities, and deferred tax liabilities. This chapter focuses on bonds payable, leases, and pension liabilities.

    This chapter is organised as follows. Section 2 describes and illustrates the accounting for long-term bonds, including the issuance of bonds, the recording of interest expense and interest payments, the amortization of any discount or premium, the derecognition of debt, and the disclosure of information about debt financings. In discussing the financial statement effects and analyses of these issues, we focus on solvency and coverage ratios. Section 3 discusses leases, including benefits of leasing and accounting for leases by both lessees and lessors. Section 4 provides an introduction to pension accounting and the resulting non-current liabilities. Section 5 discusses the use of leverage and coverage ratios in evaluating solvency. Section 6 concludes and summarizes the chapter.

2. BONDS PAYABLE

This section discusses accounting for bonds payable—a common form of long-term debt. In some contexts (e.g., some government debt obligations), the word "bond" is used only for a debt security with a maturity of 10 years or longer; "note" refers to a debt security with a maturity between 2 and 10 years; and "bill" refers to a debt security with a maturity of less than 2 years. In this chapter, we use the terms bond and note interchangeably because the accounting treatments of bonds payable and long-term notes payable are similar. In the following sections, we discuss bond issuance (initial recognition and measurement); bond amortization, interest expense, and interest payments; market rates and fair value (subsequent measurement); repayment of bonds, including retirements and redemptions (derecognition); and other issues concerning disclosures related to debt. We also discuss debt covenants.

2.1. Accounting for Bond Issuance

Bonds are contractual promises made by a company (or other borrowing entity) to pay cash in the future to its lenders (i.e., bondholders) in exchange for receiving cash in the present. The terms of a bond contract are contained in a document called an indenture. The cash or sales proceeds received by a company when it issues bonds are based on the value (price) of the bonds at the time of issue; the price at the time of issue is determined as the present value of the future cash payments promised by the company in the bond agreement.

Ordinarily, bonds contain promises of two types of future cash payments: 1) the face value of the bonds, and 2) periodic interest payments. The **face value** of the bonds is the amount of cash payable by the company to the bondholders when the bonds mature. The face value is also referred to as the principal, par value, stated value, or maturity value. The date of maturity of the bonds (the date on which the face value is paid to bondholders) is stated in the bond contract and typically is a number of years in the future. Periodic interest payments are made based on the interest rate promised in the bond contract applied to the bonds' face value. The interest rate promised in the contract, which is the rate used to calculate the periodic interest payments, is referred to as the **coupon rate**, nominal rate, or stated rate. Similarly, the periodic interest payment is referred to as the coupon payment or simply the coupon. For fixed-rate bonds (the primary focus of our discussion here), the coupon rate remains unchanged throughout the life of the bonds. The frequency with which interest payments are made is also stated in the bond contract. For example, bonds paying interest semi-annually will make two interest payments per year.[1]

---

[1] Interest rates are stated on an annual basis regardless of the frequency of payment.

The future cash payments are discounted to the present to arrive at the market value of the bonds. The **market rate of interest** is the rate demanded by purchasers of the bonds given the risks associated with future cash payment obligations of the particular bond issue. The market rate of interest at the time of issue often differs from the coupon rate because of interest rate fluctuations that occur between the time the issuer establishes the coupon rate and the day the bonds are actually available to investors. If the market rate of interest when the bonds are issued equals the coupon rate, the market value (price) of the bonds will equal the face value of the bonds. Thus, ignoring issuance costs, the issuing company will receive sales proceeds (cash) equal to the face value of the bonds. When a bond is issued at a price equal to its face value, the bond is said to have been issued at par.

If the coupon rate when the bonds are issued is higher than the market rate, the market value of the bonds—and thus the amount of cash the company receives—will be higher than the face value of the bonds. In other words, the bonds will sell at a premium to face value because they are offering an attractive coupon rate compared to current market rates. If the coupon rate is lower than the market rate, the market value and thus the sale proceeds from the bonds will be less than the face value of the bonds; the bond will sell at a discount to face value. The market rate at the time of issuance is the **effective interest rate** or borrowing rate that the company incurs on the debt. The effective interest rate is the discount rate that equates the present value of the two types of promised future cash payments to their selling price. For the issuing company, interest expense reported for the bonds in the financial statements is based on the effective interest rate.

On the issuing company's statement of cash flows, the cash received (sales proceeds) from issuing bonds is reported as a financing cash inflow. On the issuing company's balance sheet at the time of issue, bonds payable normally are measured and reported at the sales proceeds. In other words, the bonds payable are initially reported at the face value of the bonds minus any discount, or plus any premium.

Using a three-step approach, Examples 1 and 2 illustrate accounting for bonds issued at face value and then accounting for bonds issued at a discount to face value. Accounting for bonds issued at a premium involves steps similar to the steps followed in the examples below. For simplicity, these examples assume a flat interest rate yield curve (i.e., that the market rate of interest is the same for each period). More-precise bond valuations use the interest rate applicable to each time period in which a payment of interest or principal occurs.

EXAMPLE 1   Bonds Issued at Face Value

Debond Corp. (a hypothetical company) issues £1,000,000 worth of five-year bonds, dated January 1, 2018, when the market interest rate on bonds of comparable risk and terms is 5 percent per annum. The bonds pay 5 percent interest annually on December 31. What are the sales proceeds of the bonds when issued, and how is the issuance reflected in the financial statements?

Solution: Calculating the value of the bonds at issuance and thus the sales proceeds involves three steps: 1) identifying key features of the bonds and the market interest rate, 2) determining future cash outflows, and 3) discounting the future cash flows to the present.

First, identify key features of the bonds and the market interest rate necessary to determine sales proceeds:

Face value (principal):	£1,000,000
Time to maturity:	5 years
Coupon rate:	5%
Market rate at issuance:	5%
Frequency of interest payments:	annual
Interest payment:	£50,000 Each annual interest payment is the face value times the coupon rate (£1,000,000 × 5%). If interest is paid other than annually, adjust the interest rate to match the interest payment period (e.g., divide the annual coupon rate by two for semi-annual interest payments).

Second, determine future cash outflows. Debond will pay bondholders £1,000,000 when the bonds mature in five years. On December 31 of each year until the bonds mature, Debond will make an interest payment of £50,000.

Third, sum the present value[2] of the future payments of interest and principal to obtain the value of the bonds and thus the sales proceeds from issuing the bonds. In this example, the sum is £1,000,000 = (£216,474 + £783,526).

Date	Interest Payment	Present Value at Market Rate (5%)	Face Value Payment	Present Value at Market Rate (5%)	Total Present Value
December 31, 2018	£50,000	£47,619			
December 31, 2019	50,000	45,352			
December 31, 2020	50,000	43,192			
December 31, 2021	50,000	41,135			
December 31, 2022	50,000	39,176	£1,000,000	£783,526	
Total		£216,474		£783,526	£1,000,000
					Sales Proceeds

The sales proceeds of the bonds when issued are £1,000,000. There is no discount or premium because these bonds are issued at face value. The issuance is reflected on the balance sheet as an increase of cash and an increase in a long-term liability, bonds payable, of £1,000,000. The issuance is reflected in the statement of cash flows as a financing cash inflow of £1,000,000.

[2] Alternative ways to calculate the present value include 1) to treat the five annual interest payments as an annuity and use the formula for finding the present value of an annuity and then add the present value of the principal payment, or 2) to use a financial calculator to calculate the total present value.

The price of bonds is often expressed as a percentage of face value. For example, the price of bonds issued at par, as in Example 1, is 100 (i.e., 100 percent of face value). In Example 2, in which bonds are issued at a discount, the price is 95.79 (i.e., 95.79 percent of face value).

EXAMPLE 2   Bonds Issued at a Discount

Debond Corp. issues £1,000,000 worth of five-year bonds, dated January 1, 2018, when the market interest rate on bonds of comparable risk and terms is 6 percent. The bonds pay 5 percent interest annually on December 31. What are the sales proceeds of the bonds when issued, and how is the issuance reflected in the financial statements?

Solution: The key features of the bonds and the market interest rate are:

Face value (principal):	£1,000,000	
Time to maturity:	5 years	
Coupon rate:	5%	
Market rate at issuance:	6%	
Frequency of interest payments:	annual	
Interest payment:	£50,000	Each annual interest payment is the face value times the coupon rate (£1,000,000 × 5%).

The future cash outflows (interest payments and face value payment), the present value of the future cash outflows, and the total present value are:

Date	Interest Payment	Present Value at Market Rate (6%)	Face Value Payment	Present Value at Market Rate (6%)	Total Present Value
December 31, 2018	£50,000	£47,170			
December 31, 2019	50,000	44,500			
December 31, 2020	50,000	41,981			
December 31, 2021	50,000	39,605			
December 31, 2022	50,000	37,363	£1,000,000	£747,258	
Total		£210,618		£747,258	£957,876
					Sales Proceeds

The sales proceeds of the bonds when issued are £957,876. The bonds sell at a discount of £42,124 = (£1,000,000 − £957,876) because the market rate when the bonds are issued (6 percent) is greater than the bonds' coupon rate (5 percent). The issuance is reflected on the balance sheet as an increase of cash and an increase in a long-term liability, bonds payable, of £957,876. The bonds payable is composed of the face value of £1,000,000 minus a discount of £42,124. The issuance is reflected in the statement of cash flows as a financing cash inflow of £957,876.

In Example 2, the bonds were issued at a discount to face value because the bonds' coupon rate of 5 percent was less than the market rate. Bonds are issued at a premium to face value when the bonds' coupon rate exceeds the market rate.

Bonds issued with a coupon rate of zero (zero-coupon bonds) are always issued at a discount to face value. The value of zero-coupon bonds is based on the present value of the principal payment only because there are no periodic interest payments.

Such issuance costs as printing, legal fees, commissions, and other types of charges are costs incurred when bonds are issued. Under International Financial Reporting Standards (IFRS), all debt issuance costs are included in the measurement of the liability, bonds payable. Under US generally accepted accounting principles (US GAAP), companies generally used to show these debt issuance costs as an asset (a deferred charge), which was amortized on a straight-line basis to the relevant expense (e.g., legal fees) over the life of the bonds. Under US GAAP, debt issuance costs are deducted from the related debt liability. Companies reporting under US GAAP may still report debt issuance costs for lines of credit as an asset because the SEC indicated that it would not object to this treatment. Under IFRS and US GAAP, cash outflows related to bond issuance costs are included in the financing section of the statement of cash flows, usually netted against bond proceeds.

2.2. Accounting for Bond Amortization, Interest Expense, and Interest Payments

In this section, we discuss accounting and reporting for bonds after they are issued. Most companies maintain the historical cost (sales proceeds) of the bonds after issuance, and they amortize any discount or premium over the life of the bond. The amount reported on the balance sheet for bonds is thus the historical cost plus or minus the cumulative amortization, which is referred to as amortized cost. Companies also have the option to report the bonds at their current fair values.

The rationale for reporting the bonds at amortized historical cost is the company's intention to retain the debt until it matures. Therefore, changes in the underlying economic value of the debt are not relevant from the issuing company's perspective. From an investor's perspective, however, analysis of a company's underlying economic liabilities and solvency is more difficult when debt is reported at amortized historical cost. The rest of this section illustrates accounting and reporting of bonds at amortized historical cost. Section 2.3 discusses the alternative of reporting bonds at fair value.

Companies initially report bonds as a liability on their balance sheet at the amount of the sales proceeds net of issuance costs under both IFRS and US GAAP, ignoring any bond issuance costs. The amount at which bonds are reported on the company's balance sheet is referred to as the carrying amount, carrying value, book value, or net book value. If the bonds are issued at par, the initial carrying amount will be identical to the face value, and usually the carrying amount will not change over the life of the bonds.[3] For bonds issued at face value, the amount of periodic interest *expense* will be the same as the amount of periodic interest *payment* to bondholders.

If, however, the market rate differs from the bonds' coupon rate at issuance such that the bonds are issued at a premium or discount, the premium or discount is amortized systematically over the life of the bonds as a component of interest expense. For bonds issued at a premium to face value, the carrying amount of the bonds is initially greater than the face value. As the premium is amortized, the carrying amount (amortized cost) of the bonds will decrease to the face value. The reported interest expense will be less than the coupon payment. For bonds issued at a discount to face value, the carrying amount of the bonds is initially less than the face value. As the discount is amortized, the carrying amount (amortized cost) of the bonds will increase to the face value. The reported interest expense will be higher than the coupon payment.

The accounting treatment for bonds issued at a discount reflects the fact that the company essentially paid some of its borrowing costs at issuance by selling its bonds at a discount. Rather than there being an actual cash transfer in the future, this "payment" was made in the form of accepting less than the face value for the bonds at the date of issuance. The remaining borrowing cost occurs as a cash interest payment to investors each period. The total interest expense reflects both components of the borrowing cost: the periodic interest payments plus the amortization of the discount. The accounting treatment for bonds issued at a premium reflects the fact that the company essentially received a reduction on its borrowing costs at issuance by selling its bonds at a premium. Rather than there being an actual reduced cash transfer in the future, this "reduction" was made in the form of receiving more than face value for the bonds at the date of issuance. The total interest expense reflects both components of the borrowing cost: the periodic interest payments less the amortization of the premium. When the bonds mature, the carrying amount will be equal to the face value regardless of whether the bonds were issued at face value, a discount, or a premium.

Two methods for amortizing the premium or discount of bonds that were issued at a price other than par are the effective interest rate method and the straight-line method. The effective interest rate method is required under IFRS and preferred under US GAAP because it better reflects the economic substance of the transaction. The effective interest rate method applies the market rate in effect when the bonds were issued (historical market rate or effective interest rate) to the current amortized cost (carrying amount) of the bonds to obtain interest expense for the period. The difference between the interest expense (based on the effective interest rate and amortized cost) and the interest payment (based on the coupon rate and face value) is the **amortization** of the discount or premium. The straight-line method of amortization evenly amortizes the premium or discount over the life of the bond, similar to straight-line depreciation on long-lived assets. Under either method, as the bond approaches maturity, the amortized cost approaches face value.

Example 3 illustrates both methods of amortization for bonds issued at a discount. Example 4 shows amortization for bonds issued at a premium.

---

[3] If a company reports debt at fair value, rather than amortized cost, the carrying value may change.

EXAMPLE 3 Amortizing a Bond Discount

Debond Corp. issues £1,000,000 face value of five-year bonds, dated January 1, 2017, when the market interest rate is 6 percent. The sales proceeds are £957,876. The bonds pay 5 percent interest annually on December 31.

1. What is the interest *payment* on the bonds each year?
2. What amount of interest *expense* on the bonds would be reported in 2017 and 2018 using the effective interest rate method?
3. Determine the reported value of the bonds (i.e., the carrying amount) at December 31, 2017 and 2018, assuming the effective interest rate method is used to amortize the discount.
4. What amount of interest expense on the bonds would be reported under the straight-line method of amortizing the discount?

Solution to 1: The interest payment equals £50,000 annually (£1,000,000 × 5%).

Solution to 2: The sales proceeds of £957,876 are less than the face value of £1,000,000; the bonds were issued at a discount of £42,124. The bonds are initially reported as a long-term liability, bonds payable, of £957,876, which comprises the face value of £1,000,000 minus a discount of £42,124. The discount is amortized over time, ultimately, increasing the carrying amount (amortized cost) to face value.

Under the effective interest rate method, interest expense on the bonds is calculated as the bonds' carrying amount times the market rate in effect when the bonds are issued (effective interest rate). For 2017, interest expense is £57,473 = (£957,876 × 6%). The amount of the discount amortized in 2017 is the difference between the interest expense of £57,473 and the interest payment of £50,000 (i.e., £7,473). The bonds' carrying amount increases by the discount amortization; at December 31, 2017, the bonds' carrying amount is £965,349 (beginning balance of £957,876 plus £7,473 discount amortization). At this point, the carrying amount reflects a remaining unamortized discount of £34,651 (£42,124 discount at issuance minus £7,473 amortized).

For 2018, interest expense is £57,921 = (£965,349 × 6%), the carrying amount of the bonds on January 1, 2018 times the effective interest rate. The amount of the discount amortized in 2018 is the difference between the interest expense of £57,921 and the interest payment of £50,000 (i.e., £7,921). At December 31, 2018, the bonds' carrying amount is £973,270 (beginning balance of £965,349 plus £7,921 discount amortization).

The following table illustrates interest expense, discount amortization, and carrying amount (amortized cost) over the life of the bonds.

Year	Carrying Amount (beginning of year)	Interest Expense (at effective interest rate of 6%)	Interest Payment (at coupon rate of 5%)	Amortization of Discount	Carrying Amount (end of year)
	(a)	(b)	(c)	(d)	(e)
2017	£957,876	£57,473	£50,000	£7,473	£965,349
2018	965,349	57,921	50,000	7,921	973,270
2019	973,270	58,396	50,000	8,396	981,666
2020	981,666	58,900	50,000	8,900	990,566
2021	990,566	59,434	50,000	9,434	1,000,000
Total		£292,124	£250,000	£42,124	

Solution to 3: The carrying amounts of the bonds at December 31, 2017 and 2018 are £965,349 and £973,270, respectively. Observe that the carrying amount of the bonds issued at a discount increases over the life of the bonds. At maturity, December 31, 2021, the carrying amount of the bonds equals the face value of the bonds. The carrying amount of the bonds will be reduced to zero when the principal payment is made.

Solution to 4: Under the straight-line method, the discount (or premium) is evenly amortized over the life of the bonds. In this example, the £42,124 discount would be amortized by £8,424.80 (£42,124 divided by 5 years) each year under the straight-line method. So, the annual interest expense under the straight-line method would be £58,424.80 (£50,000 plus £8,424.80).

The accounting and reporting for zero-coupon bonds is similar to the example above except that no interest payments are made; thus, the amount of interest expense each year is the same as the amount of the discount amortization for the year.

EXAMPLE 4   Amortizing a Bond Premium

Prembond Corp. issues £1,000,000 face value of five-year bonds, dated January 1, 2017, when the market interest rate is 4 percent. The sales proceeds are £1,044,518. The bonds pay 5 percent interest annually on December 31.

1. What is the interest *payment* on the bonds each year?
2. What amount of interest *expense* on the bonds would be reported in 2017 and 2018 using the effective interest rate method?
3. Determine the reported value of the bonds (i.e., the carrying amount) at December 31, 2017 and 2018, assuming the effective interest rate method is used to amortize the premium.

4. What amount of interest expense on the bonds would be reported under the straight-line method of amortizing the premium?

Solution to 1: The interest payment equals £50,000 annually (£1,000,000 × 5%).

Solution to 2: The sales proceeds of £1,044,518 are more than the face value of £1,000,000; the bonds were issued at a premium of £44,518. The bonds are initially reported as a long-term liability, bonds payable, of £1,044,518, which comprises the face value of £1,000,000 plus a premium of £44,518. The premium is amortized over time, ultimately decreasing the carrying amount (amortized cost) to face value.

Under the effective interest rate method, interest expense on the bonds is calculated as the bonds' carrying amount times the market rate in effect when the bonds are issued (effective interest rate). For 2017, interest expense is £41,781 = (£1,044,518 × 4%). The amount of the premium amortized in 2017 is the difference between the interest expense of £41,781 and the interest payment of £50,000 (i.e., £8,219). The bonds' carrying amount decreases by the premium amortization; at December 31, 2017, the bonds' carrying amount is £1,036,299 (beginning balance of £1,044,518 less £8,219 premium amortization). At this point, the carrying amount reflects a remaining unamortized premium of £36,299 (£44,518 premium at issuance minus £8,219 amortized).

For 2018, interest expense is £41,452 = (£1,036,299 × 4%). The amount of the premium amortized in 2011 is the difference between the interest expense of £41,452 and the interest payment of £50,000 (i.e., £8,548). At December 31, 2018, the bonds' carrying amount is £1,027,751 (beginning balance of £1,036,299 less £8,548 premium amortization).

The following table illustrates interest expense, premium amortization, and carrying amount (amortized cost) over the life of the bonds.

Year	Carrying Amount (beginning of year)	Interest Expense (at effective interest rate of 4%)	Interest Payment (at coupon rate of 5%)	Amortization of Premium	Carrying Amount (end of year)
	(a)	(b)	(c)	(d)	(e)
2017	£1,044,518	£41,781	£50,000	£8,219	£1,036,299
2018	1,036,299	41,452	50,000	8,548	1,027,751
2019	1,027,751	41,110	50,000	8,890	1,018,861
2020	1,018,861	40,754	50,000	9,246	1,009,615
2021	1,009,615	40,385	50,000	9,615	1,000,000
Total				£44,518	

Solution to 3: The carrying amounts of the bonds at December 31, 2017 and 2018 are £1,036,299 and £1,027,751, respectively. Observe that the carrying amount of the bonds issued at a premium decreases over the life of the bonds. At maturity, December 31, 2021, the carrying amount of the bonds equals the face value of the bonds. The carrying amount of the bonds will be reduced to zero when the principal payment is made.

Solution to 4: Under the straight-line method, the premium is evenly amortized over the life of the bonds. In this example, the £44,518 premium would be amortized by £8,903.64 (£44,518 divided by 5 years) each year under the straight-line method. So, the annual interest expense under the straight-line method would be £41,096.36 (£50,000 less £8,903.64).

The reporting of interest payments on the statement of cash flows can differ under IFRS and US GAAP. Under IFRS, interest payments on bonds can be included as an outflow in either the operating section or the financing section of the statement of cash flows. US GAAP requires interest payments on bonds to be included as an operating cash outflow. (Some financial statement users consider the placement of interest payments in the operating section to be inconsistent with the placement of bond issue proceeds in the financing section of the statement of cash flows.) Typically, cash interest paid is not shown directly on the statement of cash flows, but companies are required to disclose interest paid separately.

Amortization of a discount (premium) is a non-cash item and thus, apart from its effect on pretax income, has no effect on cash flow. In the section of the statement of cash flows that reconciles net income to operating cash flow, amortization of a discount (premium) is added back to (subtracted from) net income.

2.3. Current Market Rates and Fair Value Reporting Option

Reporting bonds at amortized historical costs (historical cost plus or minus the cumulative amortization) reflects the market rate at the time the bonds were *issued* (i.e., historical market rate or effective interest rate). As market interest rates change, the bonds' carrying amount diverges from the bonds' fair market value. When market interest rates decline, the fair value of a bond with a fixed coupon rate increases. As a result, a company's economic liabilities may be higher than its reported debt based on amortized historical cost. Conversely, when market interest rates increase, the fair value of a bond with a fixed coupon rate decreases, and the company's economic liability may be lower than its reported debt. Using financial statement amounts based on amortized cost may underestimate (or overestimate) a company's debt-to-total-capital ratio and similar leverage ratios.

Companies have the option to report financial liabilities at fair value. Financial liabilities reported at fair value are designated as financial liabilities at fair value through profit or loss under IFRS, or, equivalently under US GAAP, as liabilities under the fair value option. Even if a company does not opt to report financial liabilities at fair value, the availability of fair value information in the financial statements has increased. IFRS and US GAAP require fair value disclosures in the financial statements unless the carrying amount approximates fair value or the fair value cannot be reliably measured.[4]

A company electing to measure a liability at fair value will report decreases in the liability's fair value as income and increases in the liability's fair value as losses. Because changes in a liability's fair value can result from changes in market rates and/or changes in the credit quality of the issuing company, accounting standards require companies to present separately the portion

---

[4] IFRS (IAS 32, IFRS 7, IFRS 9) and US GAAP (FASB ASC 820 and 825).

of the change resulting from changes in their own credit risk. Specifically, the company will report the portion of the change in value attributable to changes in their credit risk in other comprehensive income. Only the portion of the change in value not attributable to changes in their credit risk will be recognised in profit or loss.[5]

As of the end of 2018, few companies have selected the option to report financial liabilities at fair value. Those that have are primarily companies in the financial sector. Reporting standards for financial investments and derivatives already required these companies to report a significant portion of their assets at fair values. Measuring financial liabilities at other than fair value, when financial assets are measured at fair value, results in earnings volatility. This volatility is the result of using different bases of measurement for financial assets and financial liabilities. Furthermore, when a liability is related to a specific asset, using different measurement bases creates an accounting mismatch. Goldman Sachs elected to account for some financial liabilities at fair value under the fair value option. In its fiscal year 2017 10-K filing (page 136), Goldman explains this choice:

"The primary reasons for electing the fair value option are to:

- Reflect economic events in earnings on a timely basis;
- Mitigate volatility in earnings from using different measurement attributes (e.g., transfers of financial instruments owned accounted for as financings are recorded at fair value, whereas the related secured financing would be recorded on an accrual basis absent electing the fair value option); and
- Address simplification and cost-benefit considerations (e.g., accounting for hybrid financial instruments at fair value in their entirety versus bifurcation of embedded derivatives and hedge accounting for debt hosts)."

Most companies, as required under IFRS and US GAAP, disclose the fair values of financial liabilities. The primary exception to the disclosure occurs when fair value cannot be reliably measured. Example 5 illustrates ING Group's fair value disclosures, including the fair values of long-term debt.

EXAMPLE 5   Fair Value Disclosures of Debt and Financial Instruments

ING Group 2017 Form 20-F

ING Group [Condensed] Balance Sheet as of December 31, 2017 and 2016 [Liabilities Only]

Amounts in billions of euros	2017	2016
Deposits from banks	36.8	32.0
Customer deposits	539.8	522.9
Financial liabilities at fair value through profit or loss	87.2	99.0

---

[5]IFRS 9, US GAAP (FASB ASC 825 and ASU 2016-01).

Other liabilities	18.9	20.1
Debt securities in issue/subordinated loans	112.1	120.4
Total liabilities	**794.8**	**794.4**

The following are excerpts from the footnotes to ING Group's financial statements.

Excerpt from Note 1 Accounting Policies

Financial assets and liabilities at fair value through profit or loss

... Financial liabilities at fair value through profit or loss comprise the following sub-categories: trading liabilities, non-trading derivatives, and other financial liabilities designated at fair value through profit or loss by management. Trading liabilities include equity securities, debt securities, funds on deposit, and derivatives.

A financial asset or financial liability is classified at fair value through profit or loss if acquired principally for the purpose of selling in the short term or if designated by management as such. Management will designate a financial asset or a financial liability as such only if this eliminates a measurement inconsistency or if the related assets and liabilities are managed on a fair value basis....

Financial liabilities at amortized cost

Financial liabilities at amortized cost include the following sub-categories: preference shares classified as debt, debt securities in issue, subordinated loans, and deposits from banks and customer deposits.

Financial liabilities at amortized cost are recognised initially at their issue proceeds (fair value of consideration received) net of transaction costs incurred. Liabilities in this category are subsequently stated at amortized cost; any difference between proceeds, net of transaction costs, and the redemption value is recognized in the statement of profit or loss over the period of the liability using the effective interest method....

Excerpt from Note 16 Debt securities in issue

Debt securities in issue relate to debentures and other issued debt securities with either fixed interest rates or interest rates based on floating interest rate levels, such as certificates of deposit and accepted bills issued by ING Group, except for subordinated items. Debt securities in issue do not include debt securities presented as Financial liabilities at fair value through profit or loss.

Excerpt from Note 37 Fair value of assets and liabilities

Fair Value of Financial Liabilities as of December 31, 2017 and 2016

Amounts in millions of euros	Estimated Fair Value		Statement of Financial Position Value	
	2017	2016	2017	2016
Financial liabilities				
Deposits from banks	36,868	32,352	36,821	31,964
Customer deposits	540,547	523,850	539,828	522,908
Financial liabilities at fair value through profit or loss				
• trading liabilities	73,596	83,167	73,596	83,167
• non-trading derivatives	2,331	3,541	2,331	3,541
• designated as at fair value through profit or loss	11,215	12,266	11,215	12,266
Other liabilities	14,488	15,247	14,488	15,247
Debt securities in issue	96,736	103,559	96,086	103,234
Subordinated loans	16,457	17,253	15,968	17,223
	792,238	**791,235**	**790,333**	**789,550**

Use the condensed balance sheet and excerpts from the notes to ING Group's financial statements shown above to address the following questions:

1. As of December 31, 2017, what proportion of the amount of liabilities on ING Group's balance sheet is reported at fair value through profit or loss?
2. As of December 31, 2017 and 2016, what is the percent difference between the carrying amount and fair value of the debt securities that are shown on ING Group's balance sheet at amortized cost?

Solution to 1: Of ING Group's total €794.8 billion liabilities, 11 percent (= €87.2 billion/€794.8 billion) are reported at fair value through profit or loss.

Solution to 2: ING's debt securities that are shown on the balance sheet at amortized cost appear in the line labeled "Debt securities in issue". Note 1 states that "Debt securities in issue" are reported at amortized cost. Note 16 indicates that this line item relates to debentures and other issued debt securities, and thus we exclude subordinated loans and deposits from banks and customer deposits in this case (there are no preference shares classified as debt listed in the Note 37 excerpt).

According to the above excerpt from Note 37, in each year the fair value of ING's debt securities is slightly higher than its carrying amount. The difference is 0.7% [= (96,736/96,086) − 1] on December 31, 2017 and 0.3% [= (103,559/103,234) − 1] on December 31, 2016.

2.4. Derecognition of Debt

Once bonds are issued, a company may leave the bonds outstanding until maturity or redeem the bonds before maturity either by calling the bonds (if the bond issue includes a call provision) or by purchasing the bonds in the open market. If the bonds remain outstanding until the maturity date, the company pays bondholders the face value of the bonds at maturity. The discount or premium on the bonds would be fully amortized at maturity; the carrying amount would equal face value. Upon repayment, the bonds payable account is reduced by the carrying amount at maturity (face value) of the bonds, and cash is reduced by an equal amount. Repayment of the bonds appears in the statement of cash flows as a financing cash outflow.

If a company decides to redeem bonds before maturity and thus extinguish the liability early, the bonds payable account is reduced by the carrying amount of the redeemed bonds. The difference between the cash required to redeem the bonds and the carrying amount of the bonds is a gain or loss on the extinguishment of debt. Under IFRS, debt issuance costs are included in the measurement of the liability and are thus part of its carrying amount. Under US GAAP, debt issuance costs are accounted for separately from bonds payable and are amortized over the life of the bonds. Any unamortized debt issuance costs must be written off at the time of redemption and included in the gain or loss on debt extinguishment.

For example, a company reporting under IFRS has a £10 million bond issuance with a carrying amount equal to its face value and five years remaining until maturity. The company redeems the bonds at a call price of 103. The redemption cost is £10.3 million (= £10 million × 103%). The company's loss on redemption would be £300 thousand (£10 million carrying amount minus £10.3 million cash paid to redeem the callable bonds).

A gain or loss on the extinguishment of debt is reported on the income statement, in a separate line item, when the amount is material. A company typically discloses further detail about the extinguishment in the management discussion and analysis (MD&A) and/or notes to the financial statements.[6] In addition, in a statement of cash flows prepared using the indirect method, net income is adjusted to remove any gain or loss on the extinguishment of debt from operating cash flows, and the cash paid to redeem the bonds is classified as cash used for financing activities. (Recall that the indirect method of the statement of cash flows begins with net income and makes necessary adjustments to arrive at cash from operations, including removal of gains or losses from non-operating activities.)

To illustrate the financial statement impact of the extinguishment of debt, consider the notes payable repurchase in Example 6 below.

EXAMPLE 6   Debt Extinguishment Disclosure

The following excerpts are from the 2018 annual report of Monte Rock Inc. (a hypothetical company). In its statement of cash flows, the company uses the indirect method to reconcile net income with net cash (used in) provided by operations.

---

[6]We use the term MD&A generally to refer to any management commentary provided on a company's financial condition, changes in financial condition, and results of operations. In the United States, the Securities and Exchange Commission (SEC) requires a management discussion and analysis for companies listed on US public markets. Reporting requirements for such a commentary as the SEC-required MD&A vary across exchanges, but some are similar to the SEC requirements. The IASB issued an IFRS Practice Statement, "Management Commentary," in December 2010 to guide all companies reporting under IFRS.

Excerpt from Consolidated Statements of Income
For the years ended December 31, 2018, 2017, and 2016

	2018	2017	2016
Revenues:			
⋮	⋮	⋮	⋮
Total revenues	104,908,900	112,416,800	96,879,000
⋮	⋮	⋮	⋮
Total operating expenses	100,279,900	96,140,600	71,018,900
Income from operations	4,629,000	16,276,200	25,860,100
Other income (expense):			
⋮	⋮	⋮	⋮
Gain on debt extinguishment	2,345,000	—	—
⋮	⋮	⋮	⋮
Total other income (expense), net	11,236,100	(14,257,000)	(7,085,800)
Net income	$15,865,100	$2,019,200	$18,774,300

Excerpt from Consolidated Statements of Cash Flows
For the years ended December 31, 2018, 2017, and 2016

	2018	2017	2016
CASH FLOWS FROM OPERATING ACTIVITIES:			
Net Income	$15,865,100	$2,019,200	$18,774,300
Adjustments to reconcile net income to net cash (used in) provided by operating activities:			
⋮	⋮	⋮	⋮
Gain on debt extinguishment	(2,345,000)	—	—
⋮	⋮	⋮	⋮
Total adjustments	(16,636,000)	38,842,400	19,815,800
Net cash (used in) provided by operating activities	(770,900)	40,861,600	38,590,100
⋮	⋮	⋮	⋮

CASH FLOWS FROM FINANCING ACTIVITIES:			
Payments for debt financing costs	(294,000)	(1,526,500)	(1,481,500)
⋮	⋮	⋮	⋮
Purchase of debt securities	(2,155,000)	—	(5,000,000)
⋮	⋮	⋮	⋮
Payments of unsecured debt	—	(31,402,960)	(1,356,000)

Excerpt from NOTE 8: BONDS PAYABLE

   On December 12, 2014, the Company issued $25 million of unsecured bonds.... Interest on the bonds is equal to Libor plus 4%, payable quarterly in arrears.... During the 4th quarter of 2018, the Company repurchased the unsecured bonds with a face value of $4.5 million and realized a $2.3 million gain.

1. The balance in bonds payable was reduced at redemption by:
   A. $2,155,000.
   B. $2,345,000.
   C. $4,500,000.
2. How much cash did the Company pay to redeem the bonds?
   A. $2,155,000.
   B. $2,345,000.
   C. $4,500,000.

Solution to 1: C is correct. The bonds payable is reduced at redemption by the carrying amount of the bonds redeemed. The cash paid to extinguish the bonds plus the gain on redemption equals the carrying amount of the bonds. The carrying amount of the bonds was $4,500,000. In this case, the carrying amount equals the face value. The company recognized a gain of $2,345,000 when it extinguished the debt of $4,500,000 by paying only $2,155,000.

Solution to 2: A is correct. As shown in the Statement of Cash flow, the company paid $2,155,000 to redeem the bonds. The company recognized a gain of $2,345,000 when it extinguished the debt of $4,500,000 by paying only $2,155,000.

2.5. Debt Covenants

Borrowing agreements (the bond indenture) often include restrictions called covenants that protect creditors by restricting activities of the borrower. Debt covenants benefit borrowers to the extent that they lower the risk to the creditors and thus reduce the cost of borrowing.

Affirmative covenants restrict the borrower's activities by requiring certain actions. For instance, covenants may require that the borrower maintain certain ratios above a specified amount or perform regular maintenance on real assets used as collateral. Negative covenants require that the borrower not take certain actions. These covenants may restrict the borrower's ability to invest, pay dividends, or make other operating and strategic decisions that might adversely affect the company's ability to pay interest and principal.

Common covenants include limitations on how borrowed monies can be used, maintenance of collateral pledged as security (if any), restrictions on future borrowings, and requirements that limit dividends. Covenants may also specify minimum acceptable levels of financial ratios, such as debt-to-equity ratio, current ratio, or interest coverage.

When a company violates a debt covenant, it is a breach of contract. Depending on the severity of the breach and the terms of the contract, lenders may choose to waive the covenant, be entitled to a penalty payment or higher interest rate, renegotiate, or call for payment of the debt. Bond contracts typically require that the decision to call for immediate repayment be made, on behalf of all the bondholders, by holders of some minimum percentage of the principal amount of the bond issue.

Example 7 illustrates common disclosures related to debt covenants included in financial statement disclosures (notes to the financial statements).

EXAMPLE 7　　Illustration of Debt Covenant Disclosures

The following excerpts are from the 2017 Form 20-F filing of TORM plc, a tanker company that describes itself as one of the world's largest carriers of refined oil products. TORM plc was established in 2016 following the restructuring of TORM A/S.

The following excerpt is from the Risk Factors section of TORM's fiscal year 2017 Form 20-F.

> "Our current debt facilities impose restrictions on our financial and operational flexibility. Our debt facilities impose, and any future debt facility may impose, covenants and other operating and financial restrictions on our ability to, among other things, pay dividends, charter-in vessels, incur additional debt, sell vessels or refrain from procuring the timely release of arrested vessels. Our debt facilities require us to maintain various financial ratios, including a specified minimum liquidity requirement, a minimum equity requirement and a collateral maintenance requirement. Our ability to comply with these restrictions and covenants is dependent on our future performance and our ability to operate our fleet and may be affected by events beyond our control, including fluctuating vessel values. We may therefore need to seek permission from our lenders in order to engage in certain corporate actions.
>
> … As of December 31, 2017, we were in compliance with the financial covenants contained in our debt facilities.

The following excerpt is from the Liquidity and Capital Resources section in TORM's fiscal year 2017 Form 20-F.

The DSF [Danish Ship Finance] Facility contains, among others, the following financial and other covenants:

- Loan-to-value. If at any time the aggregate market value of the vessels and the value of any additional security is less than 133% of the loan amount less amounts on credit in the deposit accounts and reserve account and the value of any additional security, the borrower and guarantors shall, within 30 days of a written request, post additional security or prepay the loan to reduce the excess to zero.
- Free Liquidity. Minimum unencumbered cash and cash equivalents ... of the higher of $75 million and 5% of our total debt, of which $40 million is required to be unencumbered cash and cash equivalents.
- Equity Ratio. The ratio of market value adjusted shareholders' equity to total market value adjusted assets shall be at least 25%.
- Dividends. We are restricted from making any distributions, including payment of dividends and repayments of shareholders loans, except....

1. Which of the covenants described in the above excerpts are affirmative covenants?
2. Based on the excerpt above, what are the potential consequences of breaching the loan covenants?

Solution to 1: Examples of affirmative covenants in the above excerpts are from TORM's disclosure about the DSF Facility and include: the requirement for TORM to maintain a loan-to-value relationship such that the assets securing the loan (the vessels) are 133% of the loan amount; the requirement for TORM to maintain "free liquidity" (i.e., a minimum level of cash and cash equivalents); and the requirement that the equity ratio be at least 25%. These covenants require the issuer to do something. The dividend covenant requiring that TORM not take certain actions (i.e., not pay dividends unless certain conditions are met) is a negative covenant. In addition, the excerpt from Risk Factors describes other negative covenants in TORM's debt facilities including restrictions on chartering-in vessels, incurring additional debt, or selling vessels.

Solution to 2: A breach of a loan covenant by TORM—an event of default—may result in the entire amount of its debt becoming due.

2.6. Presentation and Disclosure of Long-Term Debt

The non-current (long-term) liabilities section of the balance sheet usually includes a single line item of the total amount of a company's long-term debt due after one year, with the portion of long-term debt due in the next 12 months shown as a current liability. Notes to the financial statements provide more information on the types and nature of a company's debt. These note disclosures can be used to determine the amount and timing of future cash outflows. The notes generally include stated and effective interest rates, maturity dates, restrictions imposed by creditors (covenants), and collateral pledged (if any). The amount of scheduled debt repayments for the next five years also is shown in the notes.

Example 8 contains an excerpt from the 2017 Form 10-K of Johnson & Johnson (J&J), a US manufacturer of health care products.

EXAMPLE 8   Illustration of Long-Term Debt Disclosures

Exhibit 1 is an excerpt from Note 7 of Johnson & Johnson's 2017 annual report that illustrates financial statement disclosures for long-term debt, including type and nature of long-term debt, carrying amounts, effective interest rates, and required payments over the next five years. Johnson & Johnson reports its debt at amortized cost.

EXHIBIT 1   Johnson & Johnson Borrowings

The components of long-term debt are as follows:

(Dollars in Millions)	2017	Effective Rate %	2016	Effective Rate %
5.55% Debentures due 2017	$—	—	$1,000	5.55
1.125% Notes due 2017	—	—	699	1.15
5.15% Debentures due 2018	900	5.18	899	5.18
1.65% Notes due 2018	597	1.70	600	1.70
4.75% Notes due 2019 (1B Euro 1.1947)[2]/(1B Euro 1.0449)[3]	1,192	5.83	1,041	5.83
1.875% Notes due 2019	496	1.93	499	1.93
0.89% Notes due 2019	300	1.75	299	1.20
1.125% Notes due 2019	699	1.13	699	1.13
3% Zero Coupon Convertible Subordinated Debentures due 2020	60	3.00	84	3.00
2.95% Debentures due 2020	547	3.15	546	3.15
[PORTIONS OMITTED]				
Subtotal	**32,174**	**3.19**[1]	**24,146**	**3.33**[1]
Less current portion	1,499		1,704	
Total long-term debt	**$30,675**		**$22,442**	

[1] Weighted average effective rate.
[2] Translation rate at December 31, 2017.
[3] Translation rate at January 1, 2017.

"Fair value of the long-term debt was estimated using market prices, which were corroborated by quoted broker prices and significant other observable inputs.

"The Company has access to substantial sources of funds at numerous banks worldwide. In September 2017, the Company secured a new 364-day Credit Facility. Total credit available to the Company approximates $10 billion, which expires on September 13, 2018. Interest charged on borrowings under the credit line agreements is based on either bids provided by banks, the prime rate or London Interbank Offered Rates (Libor), plus applicable margins. Commitment fees under the agreements are not material.... Throughout 2017, the Company continued to have access to liquidity through the commercial paper market. Short-term borrowings and the current portion of long-term debt amounted to approximately $3.9 billion at the end of 2017, of which $2.3 billion was borrowed under the Commercial Paper Program, $1.5 billion is the current portion of the long term debt, and the remainder principally represents local borrowing by international subsidiaries...."

Aggregate maturities of long-term obligations commencing in 2018 are (dollars in millions):

2018	2019	2020	2021	2022	After 2022
$1,499	2,752	1,105	1,797	2,189	22,832

Use the information in Exhibit 1 to answer the following questions:

1. Why are the effective interest rates unchanged from 2016 to 2017 for most of the borrowings listed?
2. Why does the carrying amount of the "1.125% Notes due 2019" remain the same in 2016 and 2017?
3. Why is the carrying amount of the "4.75% Notes due 2019" higher in 2017 than in 2016?

Solution to 1: The effective rate typically refers to the market rate at which the bonds are issued and typically does not change from year to year.

Solution to 2: The carrying amount of the "1.125% Notes due 2019" remains the same because the effective interest rate at which the debentures were issued (1.13%) is approximately the same as the coupon rate indicating that the notes were issued approximately at par. Thus, there would be no amortization of a premium or discount to affect the carrying amount of the notes, and assuming no repurchases, the carrying amount would not change.

Solution to 3: The notes are denominated in euros, with a face value of €1 billion. The dollar/euro translation exchange rate at the end of 2017 was higher than the exchange rate at the end of 2016 (1.1947 versus 1.0449). That increase explains part of the increase in carrying value. In addition, the effective interest rate of 5.83 % is higher than the 4.75 % coupon rate – implying that the notes were issued at a discount. Thus, the increase in the carrying amount of the notes also reflects the amortization of the issuance discount.

In this chapter, we focus on accounting for simple debt contracts. Debt contracts can take on additional features, which lead to more complexity. For instance, convertible debt and debt with warrants are more complex instruments that have both debt and equity features. Convertible debt gives the debt holder the option to exchange the debt for equity. Bonds issued with warrants give holders the right to purchase shares of the issuer's common stock at a specific price, similar to stock options. Issuance of bonds with warrants is more common by non-US companies. Example 9 provides an example of a financial statement disclosure of bonds with warrants.

EXAMPLE 9   Financial Statement Disclosure of Bonds with Warrants

The following describes a company's issuance of convertible bonds with warrants.

> On 1 February 2018, the Company issued convertible bonds with stock war-
> rants due 2024 with an aggregate principal amount of RMB 30 billion (the
> "Bonds with Warrants"). The Bonds with Warrants with fixed interest rate of
> 0.8% per annum and interest payable annually, were issued at par value of
> RMB 100. Each lot of the Bonds with Warrants, comprising ten Bonds with
> Warrants are entitled to warrants (the "Warrants") to subscribe 50.5 shares of
> the Company during the 5 trading days prior to March 3, 2020 at an initial
> exercise price of RMB 19.68 per share, subject to adjustment for, amongst
> other things, cash dividends, subdivision or consolidation of shares, bonus
> issues, rights issues, capital distribution, change of control and other events
> which have a dilutive effect on the issued share capital of the Company.

If all warrants were exercised, how many shares would be subscribed for?

Solution: 1,515,000,000 shares would be subscribed for [aggregate principal amount
divided by par value of a lot times shares subscribed per lot = (RMB 30,000,000,000/
RMB 1,000) × 50.5 shares].

In addition to disclosures in the notes to the financial statements, an MD&A commonly
provides other information about a company's capital resources, including debt financing and
off-balance-sheet financing. In the MD&A, management often provides a qualitative discussion on any material trends, favorable or unfavorable, in capital resources and indicates any
expected material changes in their mix and relative cost. Additional quantitative information
is typically provided, including schedules summarizing a company's contractual obligations
(e.g., bond payables) and other commitments (e.g., lines of credit and guarantees) in total and
over the next five years.

3. LEASES

A lease is a contract between the owner of an asset (the **lessor**) and another party seeking use
of the asset (the **lessee**). As part of the lease, the lessor grants the right to use the asset to the
lessee. The right to use the asset can be for a long period, such as 20 years, or a much shorter
period such as a month. In exchange for the right to use the asset, the lessee makes periodic
lease payments to the lessor. A lease, then, is a form of financing that enables the lessee to purchase the *use* of the leased asset.

There are several advantages to leasing an asset compared to purchasing it. Leases can
provide a lessee with less costly financing, usually require little, if any, down payment, and are
often at fixed interest rates. The negotiated lease contract may contain less restrictive provisions
than other forms of borrowing. A lease can also reduce the lessee's exposure to risks of obsolescence, residual value, and disposition to the lessee because the lessee does not own the asset.

3.1. Lessee accounting

Accounting for leases changed significantly under both IFRS and US GAAP.[7] Prior to the introduction of these standards, many lessees used then-acceptable "off-balance sheet" leasing structures. Under the previous rules, if leases were classified as operating leases, companies were not required to report the asset and liability related to the lease; instead, for this type of lease, companies were only required to report the periodic lease payment as an expense. Analysts typically adjusted the amount of companies' reported debt, either by taking the present value of future lease payments or, as a short cut, multiplying the annual lease payment by 8.

Under the revised reporting standards under IFRS and US GAAP, a lessee must recognize an asset and a lease liability at inception of each of its leases (with an exception for short-term leases). The lessee reports a "right-of-use" ("ROU") asset and a lease liability, calculated essentially as the present value of fixed lease payments, on its balance sheet.

After the lease inception, a lessee's treatment of leases differs for IFRS and US GAAP. Under IFRS, after inception, the lessee records depreciation expense on the right-of-use asset, recognizes interest expense on the lease liability, and reduces the balance of the lease liability for the portion of the lease payment that represents repayment of the lease liability. In effect, the lease treatment is similar to having purchased a long-term asset, financed by a long-term interest-bearing liability.

Under US GAAP, lessee accounting after inception depends whether the lessee categorizes a lease as a finance lease or an operating lease. A **finance lease** is similar to purchasing an asset while an **operating lease** is similar to renting an asset. Criteria for categorizing a lease as a finance lease include indicators that the benefits and risks of owning the leased asset have been transferred to the lessee.[8] (Note that this categorization does not affect the requirement for recognition of the asset and lease liability at inception.) A lessee's accounting for a finance lease under US GAAP is the same as described above for leases under IFRS: after inception, the lessee records depreciation expense on the right-of-use asset, recognizes interest expense on the lease liability, and reduces the balance of the lease liability for the portion of the lease payment that represents repayment of the lease liability. For an operating lease after inception, under US GAAP, the lessee recognizes a single lease expense, which is a straight-line allocation of the cost of the lease over its term.

Exceptions exist for short-term leases (those with a lease term less than one year) and, under IFRS, for leases where the leased asset is low in value. When these exceptions apply, the lessee is not required to recognize an asset and liability and instead records lease payments as an expense when paid.

When comparing an IFRS-reporting company to a US GAAP-reporting company, an analyst should be aware that the effects of a lease on the companies' income statements and statement of cash flows—even if the terms of the leases are identical—will differ. The most

---

[7] IFRS 16 [Leases] was issued in January 2016 and is effective beginning January 1, 2019. FASB ASC Topic 842 [Leases] was issued February 2016 as ASU 2016 – 02 and is effective for fiscal years beginning after December 15, 2018. Previous accounting standards did not require a lessee to report an asset and liability for Operating Leases.

[8] A lessee classifies a lease as a finance lease if any of the following criteria are met: 1) transfers ownership of the asset to the lessee, 2) includes a bargain purchase option, 3) covers a period of time that is a major part of the asset's useful life, 4) involves lease payments that equal or exceed the asset's fair value, or 5) involves an asset that is so specialized that it will have no alternative use to the lessor after the lease ends.

important difference between lessee accounting under IFRS and US GAAP is that IFRS has a single category of leases. On the income statement, every lease that an IFRS-reporting company records as a right-of-use asset and a lease liability at inception will result in a subsequent division of lease payments between depreciation expense and interest expense. Conversely, under US GAAP, a lessee reports depreciation expense and interest expense separately only in the case of finance leases. For operating leases, the lessee reports a single lease expense. On the statement of cash flows, IFRS allows companies to classify interest paid within operating, investing, or financing activities. Unlike IFRS, US GAAP requires companies to classify interest paid as an operating activity.

EXAMPLE 10   Lessee Accounting

An analyst is comparing the financial performance of two companies—one of which reports under IFRS and the other under US GAAP. Both companies extensively lease buildings and equipment in their operations. Assuming the companies enter into an identical long-term contract to lease an identical asset, which of the following metrics is *most* likely to differ because of differences in the companies' accounting standards? *(Assume that the leased asset would not qualify for the "low value" reporting exception under IFRS.)*

A. Total assets.
B. Total liabilities.
C. Operating cash flows.

Solution: The answer is C. C is correct because IFRS requires interest to be reported separately for all leases and further permits companies to classify interest paid within operating, investing, or financing activities on the statement of cash flows. A and B are incorrect because at inception, both total assets and total liabilities are unlikely to differ because both IFRS and US GAAP require lessees to record a right-of-use asset and a lease liability for leases with a term longer than one year.

3.2. Lessor accounting

Under IFRS, a lessor classifies each lease as either a finance lease or an operating lease. For a finance lease, at inception, the lessor derecognizes the underlying leased asset and recognizes a lease asset comprising the lease receivable and relevant residual value. In addition, if the lessor is a manufacturer or dealer, the lessor recognizes revenue equal to the value of the leased asset, cost of goods sold equal to the carrying value of the leased asset, and selling profit or loss equal to the revenue minus the cost of goods sold. Subsequently for a finance lease, the lessor recognizes finance income over the lease term. For an operating lease, the lessor recognizes lease receipts as income and recognizes related costs, including deprecation of the leased asset, as expenses.

Under US GAAP, a lessor classifies a lease in one of three categories: sales-type, operating, or direct financing. The lessor's classification uses the same criteria that a lessee uses in determining whether the benefits and risks of owning the leased asset have been transferred to the lessee. If any of these criteria are met, the lessor will categorize the lease as a sales-type lease, assuming that collection of the future lease payments is probable.

If none of the criteria indicating that the benefits and risks of owning the leased asset have been transferred to the lessee or if collection of the future lease payments is not reasonably assured, the lessor is viewed as effectively continuing to own the leased asset and therefore does not recognize any selling profit at lease inception. In this case, the lessor will classify a lease as either an operating lease or a **direct financing lease**. Lessor accounting for an operating lease under US GAAP is similar to IFRS: over the lease term, the lessor recognizes lease receipts as income and recognizes related costs, including deprecation of the leased asset, as expenses.

A direct financing lease applies when a lease doesn't meet the ownership-transfer criteria to be considered a sale-type lease but yet results in the lessor relying on future lease receipts to recover the asset's cost. A financing lease is a type of lease transaction that "effectively converts the lessor's risk arising from ownership of the underlying asset (that is, asset risk) into credit risk.[9] A lease is considered a direct financing lease under US GAAP if the lease contract provides for a third-party guaranteed residual value, which, combined with the future lease payments by the lessee will equal or exceed the fair value of the leased asset.

Although the differences between IFRS and US GAAP for lessor accounting are not as significant as the differences for lessee accounting, it is nonetheless useful for an analyst to be aware of how the categorization differences can affect companies' financial statements. Because IFRS does not include a distinction between **sales-type leases** and direct financing leases, an IFRS-reporting lessor will recognize selling profit at the beginning of all leases that are not classified as operating leases. In contrast, a US-GAAP reporting lessor will recognize selling profit only on sales-type leases at the beginning of the lease term.

EXHIBIT 2   Summary of Financial Statement Impact of Leases on the Lessee and Lessor

	Balance Sheet	Income Statement	Statement of Cash Flows
Lessee			
All IFRS leases, and US GAAP finance leases	Recognize "right-of-use" (ROU) asset and lease liability	Report depreciation expense on ROU asset	Reduction of lease liability is a financing cash outflow
		Report interest expense on lease liability	Interest portion of lease payment is either an operating or financing cash outflow under IFRS and an operating cash outflow under US GAAP
US GAAP operating leases	Recognize "right-of-use" (ROU) asset and lease liability	Report single lease expense (a straight-line allocation of lease cost)	Entire cash payment is an operating cash outflow
Exceptions: short-term leases and, under IFRS, leases where leased asset is low value	No effect	Report rent expense	Rent payment is operating cash outflow

(continued)

---

[9]FASB Accounting Standard Update ASU 2016-02 Leases (Topic 842) Section C – Background Information and Basis for Conclusions.

EXHIBIT 2   (Continued)

	Balance Sheet	Income Statement	Statement of Cash Flows
Lessor			
IFRS and US GAAP operating leases	Retain asset on balance sheet	Report lease income	Lease payments received are an operating cash inflow
		Report depreciation expense on leased asset	
IFRS finance leases and US GAAP sales-type leases	Remove leased asset from balance sheet	Report interest revenue on lease receivable	Interest portion of lease payment received is either an operating or investing cash inflow under IFRS
	Recognize lease asset (lease receivable and residual)	If applicable, report revenue, cost of goods sold, and selling profit	and an operating cash inflow under US GAAP.
			Receipt of lease principal is an investing cash inflow[a]
US GAAP direct financing leases	Remove leased asset from balance sheet	Report interest revenue on lease receivable	Interest portion of lease payment received is an operating cash inflow under US GAAP
	Recognise lease receivable		Receipt of lease principal is an investing cash inflow[a]

[a] If providing leases is part of a company's normal business activity, the cash flows related to the leases are classified as operating cash.

4. INTRODUCTION TO PENSIONS AND OTHER POST-EMPLOYMENT BENEFITS

Pensions and other post-employment benefits give rise to non-current liabilities reported by many companies. Companies may offer various types of benefits to their employees following retirement, such as pension plans, health care plans, medical insurance, and life insurance. Pension plans often are the most significant post-employment benefits provided to retired employees.

The accounting and reporting for pension plans depends on the type of pension plan offered. Two common types of pension plans are **defined contribution pension plans** and **defined benefit pension plans**. Under a defined-contribution plan, a company contributes an agreed-upon (defined) amount into the plan. The agreed-upon amount is the pension expense. The amount the company contributes to the plan is treated as an operating cash outflow. The only impact on assets and liabilities is a decrease in cash, although if some portion of the agreed-upon amount has not been paid by fiscal year-end, a liability would be recognised on the balance sheet. Because the amount of the contribution is defined and the company has no further obligation once the contribution has been made, accounting for a defined-contribution plan is fairly straightforward.

Accounting for a defined-benefit plan is more complicated. Under a defined-benefit plan, a company makes promises of future benefits to be paid to the employee during retirement.

For example, a company could promise an employee annual pension payments equal to 70 percent of his final salary at retirement until death. Estimating the eventual amount of the obligation arising from that promise requires the company to make many assumptions, such as the employee's expected salary at retirement and the number of years the employee is expected to live beyond retirement. The company estimates the future amounts to be paid and discounts the future estimated amounts to a present value (using a rate reflective of a high-quality corporate bond yield) to determine the pension obligation. The discount rate used to determine the pension obligation significantly affects the amount of the pension obligation. The pension obligation is allocated over the employee's employment as part of pension expense.

Most defined-benefit pension plans are funded through a separate legal entity, typically a pension trust fund. A company makes payments into the pension fund, and retirees are paid from the fund. The payments that a company makes into the fund are invested until they are needed to pay the retirees. If the fair value of the fund's assets is higher than the present value of the estimated pension obligation, the plan has a surplus, and the company's balance sheet will reflect a net pension asset.[10] Conversely, if the present value of the estimated pension obligation exceeds the fund's assets, the plan has a deficit, and the company's balance sheet will reflect a net pension liability.[11] Thus, a company reports either a net pension asset or a net pension liability. Each period, the change in the net pension asset or liability is recognized either in profit or loss or in other comprehensive income.

Under IFRS, the change in the net pension asset or liability each period is viewed as having three general components. Two of the components of this change are recognized as pension expense in profit and loss: (1) employees' service costs, and (2) the net interest expense or income accrued on the beginning net pension asset or liability. The service cost during the period for an employee is the present value of the increase in the pension benefit earned by the employee as a result of providing one more year of service. The service cost also includes past service costs, which are changes in the present value of the estimated pension obligation related to employees' service in prior periods, such as might arise from changes in the plan. The net interest expense or income represents the change in value of the net defined benefit pension asset or liability and is calculated as the net pension asset or liability multiplied by the discount rate used in estimating the present value of the pension obligation. The third component of the change in the net pension asset or liability during a period —"remeasurements"— is recognized in other comprehensive income. Remeasurements are not amortized into profit or loss over time.

Remeasurements include (a) actuarial gains and losses and (b) the actual return on plan assets less any return included in the net interest expense or income. Actuarial gains and losses can occur when changes are made to the assumptions on which a company bases its estimated pension obligation (e.g., employee turnover, mortality rates, retirement ages, compensation increases). The actual return on plan assets includes interest, dividends, and other income derived from the plan assets, including realized and unrealized gains or losses. The actual return typically differs from the amount included in the net interest expense or income, which is calculated using a rate reflective of a high-quality corporate bond yield; plan assets are typically allocated across various asset classes, including equity as well as bonds.

---

[10] The amount of any reported net pension asset is capped at the amount of any expected future economic benefits to the company from the plan; this cap is referred to as the asset ceiling.

[11] The description of accounting for pensions presented in this chapter corresponds to the June 2011 version of IAS 19 *Employee Benefits*, which took effect on January 1, 2013. Both IFRS and US GAAP require companies to present the amount of net pension liability or asset on the balance sheet.

Under US GAAP, the change in net pension asset or liability each period is viewed as having five components, some of which are recognized in profit and loss in the period incurred, and some of which are recognized in other comprehensive income and amortized into profit and loss over time. The three components recognized in profit and loss in the period incurred are (1) employees' service costs for the period, (2) interest expense accrued on the beginning pension obligation, and (3) expected return on plan assets, which is a reduction in the amount of expense recognized. The other two components are past service costs and actuarial gains and losses. Past service costs are recognized in other comprehensive income in the period in which they arise and then subsequently amortized into pension expense over the future service period of the employees covered by the plan. Actuarial gains and losses are typically also recognized in other comprehensive income in the period in which they occur and then amortized into pension expense over time. In effect, this treatment allows companies to "smooth" the effects on pension expense over time for these latter two components. US GAAP do permit companies to immediately recognize actuarial gains and losses in profit and loss.

Similar to other forms of employee compensation for a manufacturing company, the pension expense related to production employees is added to inventory and expensed through cost of sales (cost of goods sold). For employees not involved directly in the production process, the pension expense is included with salaries and other administrative expenses. Therefore, pension expense is not directly reported on the income statement. Rather, extensive disclosures are included in the notes to the financial statements.

Example 11 presents excerpts from the balance sheet and pension-related disclosures in BT Group plc's Annual Report for the year ended March 31, 2018.

EXAMPLE 11   BT Group plc: Excerpt from Balance Sheets

Below is an excerpt of BT Group plc's balance sheet from the annual report for the year ended March 31, 2018. BT reports under IFRS.

Non-current liabilities, GBP million	Mar. 31, 2018	Mar. 31, 2017	Mar. 31, 2016
Loans and other borrowings	11,994	10,081	11,025
Derivative financial instruments	787	869	863
Retirement benefit obligations	6,371	9,088	6,382
Other payables	1,326	1,298	1,106
Deferred tax liabilities	1,340	1,240	1,262
Provisions	452	536	565
Non-current liabilities	22,270	23,112	21,203

Pension-Related Disclosures
The following are excerpts of pension-related disclosures from BT Group plc's 2018 Annual Report.

Extract from Note 3 "Summary of Significant Accounting Policies"

Retirement benefits

The group's net obligation in respect of defined benefit pension plans is the present value of the defined benefit obligation less the fair value of the plan assets.

The calculation of the obligation is performed by a qualified actuary using the projected unit credit method and key actuarial assumptions at the balance sheet date.

The income statement expense is allocated between an operating charge and net finance income or expense. The operating charge reflects the increase in the defined benefit obligation resulting from the pension benefit earned by active employees in the current period, the costs of administering the plans and any past service costs/credits such as those arising from curtailments or settlements. The net finance income or expense reflects the interest on the net retirement benefit obligations recognized in the group balance sheet, based on the discount rate at the start of the year. Actuarial gains and losses are recognized in full in the period in which they occur and are presented in the group statement of comprehensive income.

The group also operates defined contribution pension plans and the income statement expense represents the contributions payable for the year.

Extract from Note 20 "Retirement Benefit Plans" Information on Defined Benefit Pension Plans

£m	2018	2017	2016
Present value of liabilities	**57,327**	60,200	50,350
Fair value of plan assets	**50,956**	51,112	43,968

Use information in the excerpts to answer the following questions:

1. What type(s) of pension plans does BT have?
2. What proportion of BT's total non-current liabilities are related to its retirement benefit obligations?
3. Describe how BT's retirement benefit obligation is calculated.

Solution to 1: Note 3 "Summary of Significant Accounting Policies" indicates that the company has both defined contribution and defined benefit pension plans.

Solution to 2: Retirement benefit obligations represent 29%, 39%, and 30% of BT's total non-current liabilities for the years 2018, 2017, and 2016. Using 2018 to illustrate, £6,371/£22,270 = 29%. (£ million)

Solution to 3: Note 3 "Summary of Significant Accounting Policies" indicates that BT's Retirement benefit obligation is calculated as the present value of the defined benefit obligation minus the fair value of the plan assets.

Using data from Note 20 "Retirement Benefit Plans" the retirement benefit obligation for each year can be calculated. Using 2018 to illustrate, £57,327 - £50,956 = £6,371 (£ million).

5. EVALUATING SOLVENCY: LEVERAGE AND COVERAGE RATIOS

Solvency refers to a company's ability to meet its long-term debt obligations, including both principal and interest payments. In evaluating a company's solvency, ratio analyses can provide information about the relative amount of debt in the company's capital structure and the adequacy of earnings and cash flow to cover interest expense and other fixed charges (such as lease or rental payments) as they come due. Ratios are useful to evaluate a company's performance over time compared to the performance of other companies and industry norms. Ratio analysis has the advantage of allowing the comparison of companies regardless of their size and reporting currency.

The two primary types of solvency ratios are leverage ratios and coverage ratios. Leverage ratios focus on the balance sheet and measure the extent to which a company uses liabilities rather than equity to finance its assets. Coverage ratios focus on the income statement and cash flows, and measure the ability of a company to cover its debt-related payments.

Exhibit 3 describes the two types of commonly used solvency ratios. The first three leverage ratios use total debt in the numerator.[12] The *debt-to-assets ratio* expresses the percentage of total assets financed with debt. Generally, the higher the ratio, the higher the financial risk and thus the weaker the solvency. The *debt-to-capital ratio* measures the percentage of a company's total capital (debt plus equity) financed through debt. The *debt-to-equity ratio* measures the amount of debt financing relative to equity financing. A *debt-to-equity ratio* of 1.0 indicates equal amounts of debt and equity, which is the same as a debt-to-capital ratio of 50 percent. Interpretations of these ratios are similar. Higher debt-to-capital or debt-to-equity ratios imply weaker solvency. A caveat must be made when comparing debt ratios of companies in different countries. Within certain countries, companies historically have obtained more capital from debt than equity financing, so debt ratios tend to be higher for companies in these countries.

EXHIBIT 3   Definitions of Commonly Used Solvency Ratios

Solvency Ratios	Numerator	Denominator
Leverage ratios		
Debt-to-assets ratio	Total debt[a]	Total assets
Debt-to-capital ratio	Total debt[a]	Total debt[a] + Total shareholders' equity
Debt-to-equity ratio	Total debt[a]	Total shareholders' equity
Financial leverage ratio	Average total assets	Average shareholders' equity
Coverage ratios		
Interest coverage ratio	EBIT[b]	Interest payments
Fixed charge coverage ratio	EBIT[b] + lease payments	Interest payments + lease payments

[a] In this chapter, debt is defined as the sum of interest-bearing short-term and long-term debt.
[b] EBIT is earnings before interest and taxes.

---

[12] For calculations in this chapter, total debt is the sum of interest-bearing short-term and long-term debt, excluding non-interest-bearing liabilities, such as accrued expenses, accounts payable, and deferred income taxes. This definition of total debt differs from other definitions that are more inclusive (e.g., all liabilities) or more restrictive (e.g., long-term debt only). If the use of different definitions of total debt materially changes conclusions about a company's solvency, the reasons for the discrepancies should be further investigated.

The *financial leverage ratio* (also called the 'leverage ratio' or 'equity multiplier') measures the amount of total assets supported by one money unit of equity. For example, a value of 4 for this ratio means that each €1 of equity supports €4 of total assets. The higher the financial leverage ratio, the more leveraged the company in the sense of using debt and other liabilities to finance assets. This ratio often is defined in terms of average total assets and average total equity and plays an important role in the DuPont decomposition of return on equity.[13]

The *interest coverage ratio* measures the number of times a company's EBIT could cover its interest payments. A higher interest coverage ratio indicates stronger solvency, offering greater assurance that the company can service its debt from operating earnings. The *fixed charge coverage ratio* relates fixed financing charges, or obligations, to the cash flow generated by the company. It measures the number of times a company's earnings (before interest, taxes, and lease payments) can cover the company's interest and lease payments.

Example 12 demonstrates the use of solvency ratios in evaluating the creditworthiness of a company.

EXAMPLE 12   Evaluating Solvency Ratios

A credit analyst is evaluating and comparing the solvency of two companies—BT Group plc (BT) and Telefonica S A (Telefonica). The following data are gathered from the companies' fiscal 2017 annual reports (line item titles may vary between the two companies):

	BT Group plc (£ millions)		Telefonica S A (€ millions)	
	Mar-31-18	Mar-31-17	Dec-31-17	Dec-31-16
Short-term borrowings	2,281	2,632	9,414	14,749
Long-term debt	11,994	10,081	46,332	45,612
Total shareholders' equity	10,304	8,335	26,618	28,385
Total assets	42,759	42,372	115,066	123,641
EBIT*	3,381	3,167	6,791	5,469
Interest expense	776	817	3,363	4,476

* Operating profit (or operating income) is used as a proxy for EBIT for both companies.

Use the above information to answer the following questions:

1. With regard to leverage ratios of BT and Telefonica:
   A. What are each company's debt-to-assets, debt-to-capital, and debt-to-equity ratios for 2017 and 2016?
   B. Comment on any changes in the calculated leverage ratios from year-to-year for each company.
   C. Comment on the calculated leverage ratios of BT Group plc compared to Telefonica SA.

---

[13] The basic DuPont decomposition is: Return on Equity = Net income/Average shareholders' equity = (Sales/Average total assets) × (Net income/Sales) × (Average total assets/Average shareholders' equity).

2. With regard to coverage ratios of BT and Telefonica:
    A. What is each company's interest coverage ratio for 2017 and 2016?
    B. Comment on any changes in the interest coverage ratio from year to year for each company.
    C. Comment on the interest coverage ratio of BT Group plc compared to Telefonica SA.

Solution to 1:
A. The debt-to-assets, debt-to-capital, and debt-to-equity ratios are as follows, with supporting calculations from each company's most recent year demonstrated below.

	BT Group plc		Telefonica S A	
	Mar-31-18	Mar-31-17	Dec-31-17	Dec-31-16
Debt-to-assets	33.4%	30.0%	48.4%	48.8%
Debt-to-capital	58.1%	60.4%	67.7%	68.0%
Debt-to-equity	1.39	1.53	2.09	2.13

	BT Group plc	Telefonica S A
	Mar-31-18	*Dec-31-17*
Debt-to-assets	33.4% = (2,281 + 11,994)/42,759	48.4% = (9,414 + 46,332)/115,066
Debt-to-capital	58.1% = (2,281 + 11,994)/(2,281 + 11,994 + 10,304)	67.7% = (9,414 + 46,332)/(9,414 + 46,332 + 26,618)
Debt-to-equity	1.39 = (2,281 + 11,994)/10,304	2.09 = (9,414 + 46,332)/26,618

B. BT's debt-to-assets ratio increased, while its debt-to-capital and debt-to-equity ratios both decreased. The decrease in BT's debt-to-capital and debt-to-equity ratios resulted primarily from the company's increase in total equity and indicate stronger solvency. In addition, we observe that BT decreased its short-term borrowings and increased its long-term debt.

    Telefonica's leverage ratios appear fairly similar, albeit slightly lower, for 2017 compared to 2016. Similar to BT, it appears that Telefonica shifted away from short borrowings to long-term debt in 2017.
C. In both years, all three of BT's leverage ratios were lower than Telefonica's. Based on these ratios, this may imply higher solvency of BT relative to Telefonica.

Solution to 2:
A. The interest coverage ratios are as follows, with supporting calculations from each company's most recent year demonstrated below.

	BT Group plc		Telefonica S A	
	Mar-31-18	Mar-31-17	Dec-31-17	Dec-31-16
Interest coverage ratio	4.36	3.88	2.02	1.22

	BT Group plc	Telefonica S A
	Mar-31-18	Dec-31-17
Interest coverage ratio	4.36 = 3,381/776	2.02 = 6,791/3,363

B. Both companies' interest coverage ratios increased from 2017 to 2018, indicating an improvement in solvency, consistent with the conclusions drawn from the companies' ratios in question 1. Both companies have sufficient operating earnings to cover interest payments.

C. BT's ability to cover interest payments is greater than Telefonica's, although both companies have sufficient operating earnings to service its interest payments. This comparison indicates that BT has greater financial strength than Telefonica, which is also consistent with the conclusions drawn from a comparison of the companies' ratios in question 1.

6. SUMMARY

Non-current liabilities arise from different sources of financing and different types of creditors. Bonds are a common source of financing from debt markets. Key points in accounting and reporting of non-current liabilities include the following:

- The sales proceeds of a bond issue are determined by discounting future cash payments using the market rate of interest at the time of issuance (effective interest rate). The reported interest expense on bonds is based on the effective interest rate.
- Future cash payments on bonds usually include periodic interest payments (made at the stated interest rate or coupon rate) and the principal amount at maturity.
- When the market rate of interest equals the coupon rate for the bonds, the bonds will sell at par (i.e., at a price equal to the face value). When the market rate of interest is higher than the bonds' coupon rate, the bonds will sell at a discount. When the market rate of interest is lower than the bonds' coupon rate, the bonds will sell at a premium.
- An issuer amortizes any issuance discount or premium on bonds over the life of the bonds.
- If a company redeems bonds before maturity, it reports a gain or loss on debt extinguishment computed as the net carrying amount of the bonds (including bond issuance costs under IFRS) less the amount required to redeem the bonds.
- Debt covenants impose restrictions on borrowers, such as limitations on future borrowing or requirements to maintain a minimum debt-to-equity ratio.
- The carrying amount of bonds is typically the amortized historical cost, which can differ from their fair value.
- Companies are required to disclose the fair value of financial liabilities, including debt. Although permitted to do so, few companies opt to report debt at fair values on the balance sheet.

- Beginning with fiscal year 2019, lessees report a right-of-use asset and a lease liability for all leases longer than one year. An exception under IFRS exists for leases when the underlying asset is of low value.
  - Subsequent to lease inception, the lessee's income statement will include both a depreciation expense on the right-of-use asset and an interest expense on the lease liability for all leases under IFRS and, under US GAAP for finance leases.
  - For lessee accounting, the distinction between finance leases and operating leases exists in US GAAP but not in IFRS. For operating leases under US GAAP, the lessee's income statement will show a single lease expense.
  - Under IFRS, a lessor classifies each lease as either a finance lease or an operating lease. A lease is classified as a finance lease if it "transfers substantially all the risks and rewards incidental to ownership of an underlying asset" and otherwise as an operating lease. For finance leases, but not for operating leases, the lessor derecognizes the underlying leased asset, and recognizes a lease receivable, and recognizes selling profit where applicable. For operating leases, the lessor does not derecognize the underlying asset and recognizes lease receipts as income.
  - Under US GAAP, a lessor classifies a lease in one of three categories: sales-type, direct financing, or operating. The lessor's classification and accounting for operating leases under US GAAP is similar to that under IFRS. For both sales-type and direct financing leases, the lessor derecognizes the underlying asset and recognizes a lease receivable; however, the lessor recognizes selling profit only if the lease is considered a sales-type lease.
- Two types of pension plans are defined contribution plans and defined benefits plans. In a defined contribution plan, the amount of contribution into the plan is specified (i.e., defined), and the amount of pension that is ultimately paid by the plan (received by the retiree) depends on the performance of the plan's assets. In a defined benefit plan, the amount of pension that is ultimately paid by the plan (received by the retiree) is defined, usually according to a benefit formula.
- Under a defined contribution pension plan, the cash payment made into the plan is recognised as pension expense.
- Under both IFRS and US GAAP, companies must report the difference between the defined benefit pension obligation and the pension assets as an asset or liability on the balance sheet. An underfunded defined benefit pension plan is shown as a non-current liability.
- Under IFRS, the change in the defined benefit plan net asset or liability is recognized as a cost of the period, with two components of the change (service cost and net interest expense or income) recognized in profit and loss and one component (remeasurements) of the change recognized in other comprehensive income.
- Under US GAAP, the change in the defined benefit plan net asset or liability is also recognised as a cost of the period with three components of the change (current service costs, interest expense on the beginning pension obligation, and expected return on plan assets) recognized in profit and loss and two components (past service costs and actuarial gains and losses) typically recognized in other comprehensive income.
- Solvency refers to a company's ability to meet its long-term debt obligations.
- In evaluating solvency, leverage ratios focus on the balance sheet and measure the amount of debt financing relative to equity financing.
- In evaluating solvency, coverage ratios focus on the income statement and cash flows and measure the ability of a company to cover its interest payments.

PRACTICE PROBLEMS

1. A company issues €1 million of bonds at face value. When the bonds are issued, the company will record a:
   A. cash inflow from investing activities.
   B. cash inflow from financing activities.
   C. cash inflow from operating activities.

2. At the time of issue of 4.50% coupon bonds, the effective interest rate was 5.00%. The bonds were *most likely* issued at:
   A. par.
   B. a discount.
   C. a premium.

3. Oil Exploration LLC paid $45,000 in printing, legal fees, commissions, and other costs associated with its recent bond issue. It is *most likely* to record these costs on its financial statements as:
   A. an asset under US GAAP and reduction of the carrying value of the debt under IFRS.
   B. a liability under US GAAP and reduction of the carrying value of the debt under IFRS.
   C. a cash outflow from investing activities under both US GAAP and IFRS.

4. A company issues $1,000,000 face value of 10-year bonds on January 1, 2015 when the market interest rate on bonds of comparable risk and terms is 5%. The bonds pay 6% interest annually on December 31. At the time of issue, the bonds payable reflected on the balance sheet is *closest* to:
   A. $926,399.
   B. $1,000,000.
   C. $1,077,217.

5. Midland Brands issues three-year bonds dated January 1, 2015 with a face value of $5,000,000. The market interest rate on bonds of comparable risk and term is 3%. If the bonds pay 2.5% annually on December 31, bonds payable when issued are most likely reported as *closest* to:
   A. $4,929,285.
   B. $5,000,000.
   C. $5,071,401.

6. A firm issues a bond with a coupon rate of 5.00% when the market interest rate is 5.50% on bonds of comparable risk and terms. One year later, the market interest rate increases to 6.00%. Based on this information, the effective interest rate is:
   A. 5.00%.
   B. 5.50%.
   C. 6.00%.

7. On January 1, 2010, Elegant Fragrances Company issues £1,000,000 face value, five-year bonds with annual interest payments of £55,000 to be paid each December 31. The market interest rate is 6.0 percent. Using the effective interest rate method of amortization, Elegant Fragrances is *most likely* to record:

   A. an interest expense of £55,000 on its 2010 income statement.

   B. a liability of £982,674 on the December 31, 2010 balance sheet.

   C. a £58,736 cash outflow from operating activity on the 2010 statement of cash flows.

8. Consolidated Enterprises issues €10 million face value, five-year bonds with a coupon rate of 6.5 percent. At the time of issuance, the market interest rate is 6.0 percent. Using the effective interest rate method of amortization, the carrying value after one year will be *closest* to:

   A. €10.17 million.

   B. €10.21 million.

   C. €10.28 million.

9. A company issues €10,000,000 face value of 10-year bonds dated January 1, 2015 when the market interest rate on bonds of comparable risk and terms is 6%. The bonds pay 7% interest annually on December 31. Based on the effective interest rate method, the interest expense on December 31, 2015 is *closest* to:

   A. €644,161.

   B. €700,000.

   C. €751,521.

10. A company issues $30,000,000 face value of five-year bonds dated January 1, 2015 when the market interest rate on bonds of comparable risk and terms is 5%. The bonds pay 4% interest annually on December 31. Based on the effective interest rate method, the carrying amount of the bonds on December 31, 2015 is *closest* to:

   A. $28,466,099.

   B. $28,800,000.

   C. $28,936,215.

11. Lesp Industries issues five-year bonds dated January 1, 2015 with a face value of $2,000,000 and 3% coupon rate paid annually on December 31. The market interest rate on bonds of comparable risk and term is 4%. The sales proceeds of the bonds are $1,910,964. Under the effective interest rate method, the interest expense in 2017 is *closest* to:

   A. $77,096.

   B. $77,780.

   C. $77,807.

12. For a bond issued at a premium, using the effective interest rate method, the:

   A. carrying amount increases each year.

   B. amortization of the premium increases each year.

   C. premium is evenly amortized over the life of the bond.

13. Comte Industries issues $3,000,000 worth of three-year bonds dated January 1, 2015. The bonds pay interest of 5.5% annually on December 31. The market interest rate on bonds of comparable risk and term is 5%. The sales proceeds of the bonds are $3,040,849. Under the straight-line method, the interest expense in the first year is *closest* to:

   A. $150,000.

   B. $151,384.

   C. $152,042.

14. The management of Bank EZ repurchases its own bonds in the open market. They pay €6.5 million for bonds with a face value of €10.0 million and a carrying value of €9.8 million. The bank will *most likely* report:
   A. other comprehensive income of €3.3 million.
   B. other comprehensive income of €3.5 million.
   C. a gain of €3.3 million on the income statement.

15. A company redeems $1,000,000 face value bonds with a carrying value of $990,000. If the call price is 104 the company will:
   A. reduce bonds payable by $1,000,000.
   B. recognize a loss on the extinguishment of debt of $50,000.
   C. recognize a gain on the extinguishment of debt of $10,000.

16. Innovative Inventions, Inc. needs to raise €10 million. If the company chooses to issue zero-coupon bonds, its debt-to-equity ratio will *most likely*:
   A. rise as the maturity date approaches.
   B. decline as the maturity date approaches.
   C. remain constant throughout the life of the bond.

17. Fairmont Golf issued fixed rate debt when interest rates were 6 percent. Rates have since risen to 7 percent. Using only the carrying amount (based on historical cost) reported on the balance sheet to analyze the company's financial position would *most likely* cause an analyst to:
   A. overestimate Fairmont's economic liabilities.
   B. underestimate Fairmont's economic liabilities.
   C. underestimate Fairmont's interest coverage ratio.

18. Which of the following is an example of an affirmative debt covenant? The borrower is:
   A. prohibited from entering into mergers.
   B. prevented from issuing excessive additional debt.
   C. required to perform regular maintenance on equipment pledged as collateral.

19. Debt covenants are *least likely* to place restrictions on the issuer's ability to:
   A. pay dividends.
   B. issue additional debt.
   C. issue additional equity.

20. Regarding a company's debt obligations, which of the following is *most likely* presented on the balance sheet?
   A. Effective interest rate.
   B. Maturity dates for debt obligations.
   C. The portion of long-term debt due in the next 12 months.

21. Compared to using a finance lease, a lessee that makes use of an operating lease will *most likely* report higher:
   A. debt.
   B. rent expense.
   C. cash flow from operating activity.

22. Which of the following is *most likely* a lessee's disclosure about operating leases?
    A. Lease liabilities.
    B. Future obligations by maturity.
    C. Net carrying amounts of leased assets.

23. For a lessor, the leased asset appears on the balance sheet and continues to be depreciated when the lease is classified as:
    A. a sales-type lease.
    B. an operating lease.
    C. a financing lease.

24. Under US GAAP, a lessor's reported revenues at lease inception will be *highest* if the lease is classified as:
    A. a sales-type lease.
    B. an operating lease.
    C. a direct financing lease.

25. A lessor will record interest income if a lease is classified as:
    A. a capital lease.
    B. an operating lease.
    C. either a capital or an operating lease.

26. Compared with a finance lease, an operating lease:
    A. is similar to renting an asset.
    B. is equivalent to the purchase of an asset.
    C. term is for the majority of the economic life of the asset.

27. Under US GAAP, which of the following would require the lessee to classify a lease as a capital lease?
    A. The term is 60% of the useful life of the asset.
    B. The lease contains an option to purchase the asset at fair value.
    C. The present value of the lease payments is 95% of the fair value.

28. A lessee that enters into a finance lease will report the:
    A. lease payable on its balance sheet.
    B. full lease payment on its income statement.
    C. full lease payment as an operating cash flow.

29. A company enters into a finance lease agreement to acquire the use of an asset for three years with lease payments of €19,000,000 starting next year. The leased asset has a fair market value of €49,000,000, and the present value of the lease payments is €47,250,188. Based on this information, the value of the lease payable reported on the company's balance sheet is *closest* to:
    A. €47,250,188.
    B. €49,000,000.
    C. €57,000,000.

30. Which of the following *best* describes reporting and disclosure requirements for a company that enters into an operating lease as the lessee? The operating lease obligation is:
    A. reported as a receivable on the balance sheet.
    B. disclosed in notes to the financial statements.
    C. reported as a component of debt on the balance sheet.

31. Cavalier Copper Mines has $840 million in total liabilities and $520 million in shareholders' equity. It discloses operating lease commitments over the next five years with a present value of $100 million. If the lease commitments are treated as debt, the debt-to-total-capital ratio is *closest* to:
    A. 0.58.
    B. 0.62.
    C. 0.64.

32. The following presents selected financial information for a company:

	$ Millions
Short-term borrowing	4,231
Current portion of long-term interest-bearing debt	29
Long-term interest-bearing debt	925
Average shareholders' equity	18,752
Average total assets	45,981

The financial leverage ratio is *closest* to:
    A. 0.113.
    B. 0.277.
    C. 2.452.

33. An analyst evaluating three industrial companies calculates the following ratios:

	Company A	Company B	Company C
Debt-to-Equity	23.5%	22.5%	52.5%
Interest Coverage	15.6	49.5	45.5

The company with both the lowest financial leverage and the greatest ability to meet interest payments is:
    A. Company A.
    B. Company B.
    C. Company C.

34. An analyst evaluating a company's solvency gathers the following information:

	$ Millions
Short-term interest-bearing debt	1,258
Long-term interest-bearing debt	321
Total shareholder's equity	4,285
Total assets	8,750
EBIT	2,504
Interest payments	52

The company's debt-to-assets ratio is *closest* to:
A. 0.18.
B. 0.27.
C. 0.37.

35. Penben Corporation has a defined benefit pension plan. At December 31, its pension obligation is €10 million, and pension assets are €9 million. Under either IFRS or US GAAP, the reporting on the balance sheet would be *closest* to which of the following?
A. €10 million is shown as a liability, and €9 million appears as an asset.
B. €1 million is shown as a net pension obligation.
C. Pension assets and obligations are not required to be shown on the balance sheet but only disclosed in footnotes.

36. The following information is associated with a company that offers its employees a defined benefit plan:

Fair value of fund's assets	$1,500,000,000
Estimated pension obligations	$2,600,000,000
Present value of estimated pension obligations	$1,200,000,000

Based on this information, the company's balance sheet will present a net pension:
A. asset of $300,000,000.
B. asset of $1,400,000,000.
C. liability of $1,100,000,000.

CHAPTER **11**

FINANCIAL REPORTING QUALITY

Jack T. Ciesielski, CPA, CFA
Elaine Henry, PhD, CFA
Thomas I. Selling, PhD, CPA

LEARNING OUTCOMES

After completing this chapter, you will be able to do the following:

- distinguish between financial reporting quality and quality of reported results (including quality of earnings, cash flow, and balance sheet items);
- describe a spectrum for assessing financial reporting quality;
- distinguish between conservative and aggressive accounting;
- describe motivations that might cause management to issue financial reports that are not high quality;
- describe conditions that are conducive to issuing low-quality, or even fraudulent, financial reports;
- describe mechanisms that determine financial reporting quality and the potential limitations of those mechanisms;
- describe presentation choices, including non-GAAP measures, that could be used to influence an analyst's opinion;
- describe accounting methods (choices and estimates) that could be used to manage earnings, cash flow, and balance sheet items;
- describe accounting warning signs and methods for detecting manipulation of information in financial reports.

1. INTRODUCTION

Ideally, analysts would always have access to financial reports that are based on sound financial reporting standards, such as those from the International Accounting Standards Board (IASB) and the Financial Accounting Standards Board (FASB), and are free from manipulation. But, in practice, the quality of financial reports can vary greatly. High-quality financial reporting provides information that is useful to analysts in assessing a company's performance and prospects. Low-quality financial reporting contains inaccurate, misleading, or incomplete information.

Extreme lapses in financial reporting quality have given rise to high-profile scandals that resulted not only in investor losses but also in reduced confidence in the financial system. Financial statement users who were able to accurately assess financial reporting quality were better positioned to avoid losses. These lapses illustrate the challenges analysts face as well as the potential costs of failing to recognize practices that result in misleading or inaccurate financial reports.[1] Examples of misreporting can provide an analyst with insight into various signals that may indicate poor-quality financial reports.

This chapter addresses *financial reporting quality*, which pertains to the quality of information in financial reports, including disclosures in notes. High-quality reporting provides decision-useful information, which is relevant and faithfully represents the economic reality of the company's activities during the reporting period as well as the company's financial condition at the end of the period. A separate but interrelated attribute of quality is *quality of reported results* or *earnings quality*, which pertains to the earnings and cash generated by the company's actual economic activities and the resulting financial condition. The term "earnings quality" is commonly used in practice and will be used broadly to encompass the quality of earnings, cash flow, and/or balance sheet items. High-quality earnings result from activities that a company will likely be able to sustain in the future and provide a sufficient return on the company's investment. The concepts of earnings quality and financial reporting quality are interrelated because a correct assessment of earnings quality is possible only when there is some basic level of financial reporting quality. Beyond this basic level, as the quality of reporting increases, the ability of financial statement users to correctly assess earnings quality and to develop expectations for future performance arguably also increases.

Section 2 provides a conceptual overview of reporting quality. Section 3 discusses motivations that might cause, and conditions that might enable, management to issue financial reports that are not high quality and mechanisms that aim to provide discipline to financial reporting quality. Section 4 describes choices made by management that can affect financial reporting quality—presentation choices, accounting methods, and estimates—as well as warning signs of poor-quality financial reporting.

2. CONCEPTUAL OVERVIEW

As indicated in the introduction, financial reporting quality and results or earnings quality are interrelated attributes of quality. Exhibit 1 illustrates this interrelationship and its implications.

---

[1] In this chapter, the examples of misleading or inaccurate financial reports occurred in prior years—*not* because there are no current examples of questionable financial reporting, but rather because it has been conclusively resolved that misreporting occurred in the historical examples.

EXHIBIT 1   Relationships between Financial Reporting Quality and Earnings Quality

		Financial Reporting Quality	
		Low	High
Earnings (Results) Quality	High	LOW financial reporting quality impedes assessment of earnings quality and impedes valuation.	HIGH financial reporting quality enables assessment. HIGH earnings quality increases company value.
	Low		HIGH financial reporting quality enables assessment. LOW earnings quality decreases company value.

As can be seen in Exhibit 1, if financial reporting quality is low, the information provided is of little use in assessing the company's performance, and thus in making investment and other decisions.

Financial reporting quality varies across companies. High-quality reports contain information that is relevant, complete, neutral, and free from error. The lowest-quality reports contain information that is pure fabrication. Earnings (results) quality can range from high and sustainable to low and unsustainable. Providers of resources prefer high and sustainable earnings. Combining the two measures of quality—financial reporting and earnings—the overall quality of financial reports from a user perspective can be thought of as spanning a continuum from the highest to the lowest. Exhibit 2 presents a quality spectrum that provides a basis for evaluating better versus poorer quality reports. This spectrum ranges from reports that are of high financial reporting quality and reflect high and sustainable earnings quality to reports that are not useful because of poor financial reporting quality.

EXHIBIT 2   Quality Spectrum of Financial Reports

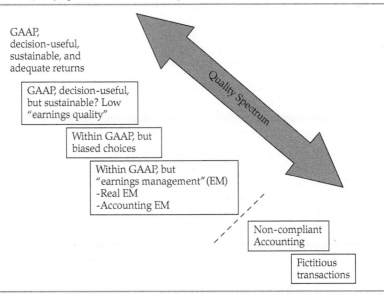

2.1. GAAP, Decision-Useful, Sustainable, and Adequate Returns

At the top of the spectrum, labeled in Exhibit 2 as "GAAP, decision-useful, sustainable, and adequate returns," are high-quality reports that provide useful information about high-quality earnings.

- High-quality financial reports conform to the generally accepted accounting principles (GAAP) of the jurisdiction, such as International Financial Reporting Standards (IFRS), US GAAP, or other home-country GAAP. The exhibit uses the term GAAP to refer generically to the accounting standards accepted in a company's jurisdiction.
- In addition to conforming to GAAP, high-quality financial reports also embody the characteristics of decision-useful information such as those defined in the *Conceptual Framework*.[2] Recall that the fundamental characteristics of useful information are relevance and faithful representation. Relevant information is defined as information that can affect a decision and encompasses the notion of materiality. (Information is considered material if "omitting it or misstating it could influence decisions that users make on the basis of the financial information of a specific reporting entity."[3]) Faithful representation of economic events is complete, neutral, and free from error.

  The *Conceptual Framework* also enumerates enhancing characteristics of useful information: comparability, verifiability, timeliness, and understandability. Of course, the desirable characteristics for financial information require trade-offs. For example, financial reports must balance the aim of providing information that is produced quickly enough to be timely and thus relevant, and yet not so quickly that errors occur. Financial reports must balance the aim of providing information that is complete but not so exhaustive that immaterial information is included. High-quality information results when these and other tradeoffs are made in an unbiased, skillful manner.
- High-quality earnings indicate an adequate level of return on investment and derive from activities that a company will likely be able to sustain in the future. An adequate level of return on investment exceeds the cost of the investment and also equals or exceeds the expected return. Sustainable activities and sustainable earnings are those expected to recur in the future. Sustainable earnings that provide a high return on investment contribute to higher valuation of a company and its securities.

2.2. GAAP, Decision-Useful, but Sustainable?

The next level down in Exhibit 2, "GAAP, decision-useful, but sustainable?" refers to circumstances in which high-quality reporting provides useful information, but that information reflects results or earnings that are not sustainable (lower earnings quality). The earnings may

---

[2] The characteristics of decision-useful information are identical under IFRS and US GAAP. In September 2010, the IASB adopted the *Conceptual Framework for Financial Reporting* in place of the *Framework for the Preparation and Presentation of Financial Statements* (1989). The *Conceptual Framework* represents the partial completion of a joint convergence project between the IASB and FASB on an updated framework. The *Conceptual Framework* (2010) contains two updated chapters: "The Objective of Financial Reporting" and "Qualitative Characteristics of Useful Financial Information." The remainder of the material in the *Conceptual Framework* is from the *Framework* (1989) and will be updated as the project is completed. Also in September 2010, the FASB issued Concepts Statement 8, "Conceptual Framework for Financial Reporting," to replace Concepts Statements 1 and 2.

[3] Text from conceptual frameworks referenced in Note 4.

not be sustainable because the company cannot expect earnings that generate the same level of return on investment in the future or because the earnings, although replicable, will not generate sufficient return on investment to sustain the company. Earnings quality is low in both cases. Reporting can be high quality even when the economic reality being depicted is not of high quality. For example, consider a company that generates a loss, or earnings that do not provide an adequate return on investment, or earnings that resulted from non-recurring activities. The relatively undesirable economic reality could nonetheless be depicted in financial reporting that provides high-quality, decision-useful information.

Exhibit 3 presents an excerpt from the fiscal year 2014 first-quarter results of Toyota Motor Corporation, a Japanese automobile company. As highlighted by a *Wall Street Journal* article,[4] the company sold fewer cars but reported an 88% increase in operating profits compared with the prior year, primarily because of the change in exchange rates. The weaker yen benefited Toyota both because the company manufactures more cars in Japan (compared with its competitors) and because the company sells a significant number of cars outside of Japan. Exchange rate weakening is a less sustainable source of profits than manufacturing and selling cars. In summary, this example is a case of high-quality financial reporting coupled with lower earnings quality.

EXHIBIT 3   Excerpt from Toyota Motor Corporation's Consolidated Financial Results for FY2014 First Quarter Ending June 30, 2013

Consolidated vehicle unit sales in Japan and overseas decreased by 37 thousand units, or 1.6%, to 2,232 thousand units in FY2014 first quarter (the three months ended June 30, 2013) compared with FY2013 first quarter (the three months ended June 30, 2012). Vehicle unit sales in Japan decreased by 51 thousand units, or 8.8%, to 526 thousand units in FY2014 first quarter compared with FY2013 first quarter. Meanwhile, overseas vehicle unit sales increased by 14 thousand units, or 0.8%, to 1,706 thousand units in FY2014 first quarter compared with FY2013 first quarter.

As for the results of operations, net revenues increased by 753.7 billion yen, or 13.7%, to 6,255.3 billion yen in FY2014 first quarter compared with FY2013 first quarter, and operating income increased by 310.2 billion yen, or 87.9%, to 663.3 billion yen in FY2014 first quarter compared with FY2013 first quarter. The factors contributing to an increase in operating income were the effects of changes in exchange rates of 260.0 billion yen, cost reduction efforts of 70.0 billion yen, marketing efforts of 30.0 billion yen and other factors of 10.2 billion yen. On the other hand, the factors contributing to a decrease in operating income were the increase in expenses and others of 60.0 billion yen.

2.3. Biased Accounting Choices

The next level down in the spectrum in Exhibit 2 is "Within GAAP, but biased choices." Biased choices result in financial reports that do not faithfully represent the economic substance of what is being reported. The problem with bias in financial reporting, as with other deficiencies in reporting quality, is that it impedes an investor's ability to correctly assess a company's past performance, to accurately forecast future performance, and thus to appropriately value the company.

Choices are deemed to be "aggressive" if they increase a company's reported performance and financial position in the period under review. The choice can increase the amount of revenues, earnings, and/or operating cash flow reported for the period, or decrease expenses, and/or reduce the level of debt reported on the balance sheet. Aggressive choices may lead to a

---

[4] Back (2013).

reduction in the company's reported performance and in its financial position in later periods. In contrast, choices are deemed "conservative" if they decrease a company's performance and financial position in the reporting period. This can include lowering the reported revenues, earnings, and/or operating cash flow reported or increasing expenses, or recording a higher level of debt on the balance sheet. Conservative choices may lead to a rise in the company's reported performance and financial position in later periods.

Another type of bias is understatement of earnings volatility, so-called earnings "smoothing." Earnings smoothing can result from conservative choices to understate earnings in periods when a company's operations are performing well, building up (often hidden) reserves that allow aggressive choices in periods when its operations are struggling.

Biased choices can be made not only in the context of reported amounts but also in the context of how information is presented. For example, companies can disclose information transparently, which facilitates analysis, or they can disclose it in a manner that aims to obscure unfavorable and/or emphasize favorable information.

EXAMPLE 1 Quality of Financial Reports

PACCAR Inc. designs, manufactures, and distributes trucks and related aftermarket parts that are sold worldwide under the Kenworth, Peterbilt, and DAF nameplates. In 2013, the US SEC charged PACCAR for various accounting deficiencies that "clouded their financial reporting to investors in the midst of the financial crisis." The SEC complaint cites the company's 2009 segment reporting. Exhibit 4A presents an excerpt from the notes to PACCAR's financial statements, and Exhibit 4B presents an excerpt from the management's discussion and analysis (MD&A) of PACCAR's annual report.

EXHIBIT 4A   Excerpt from Notes to PACCAR's 2009 Financial Statements

S. SEGMENT AND RELATED INFORMATION
PACCAR operates in two principal segments, Truck and Financial Services.
The Truck segment includes the manufacture of trucks and the distribution of related aftermarket parts, both of which are sold through a network of independent dealers. . . .
The Financial Services segment is composed of finance and leasing products and services provided to truck customers and dealers . . . Included in All Other is PACCAR's industrial winch manufacturing business. Also within this category are other sales, income and expenses not attributable to a reportable segment, including a portion of corporate expense.

Business Segment Data ($ millions)

	2009	2008	2007
Income before Income Taxes			
Truck	$25.9	$1,156.5	$1,352.8
All other	42.2	6.0	32.0
	68.1	1,162.5	1,384.8
Financial services	84.6	216.9	284.1
Investment income	22.3	84.6	95.4
	$175.0	$1,464.0	$1,764.3

EXHIBIT 4B   Excerpt from MD&A of PACCAR's 2009 Annual Report

Net sales and revenues and gross margins for truck units and aftermarket parts are provided below. The aftermarket parts gross margin includes direct revenues and costs, but excludes certain truck segment costs.

	2009	2008	% Change
Net Sales and Revenues			
Trucks	$5,103.30	$11,281.30	−55
Aftermarket parts	1,890.70	2,266.10	−17
	$6,994.00	$13,547.40	−48
Gross Margin			
Trucks	−$46.6	$1,141.70	−104
Aftermarket parts	625.7	795.20	−21
	$579.1	$1,936.90	−70

1. Based on the segment data excerpted from the notes to the financial statements, was PACCAR's truck segment profitable in 2009?
2. Based on the data about the truck's gross margin presented in the MD&A, was PACCAR's truck segment profitable in 2009?
3. What is the main difference between the note presentation and the MD&A presentation?
4. The SEC complaint stated that "PACCAR failed to report the operating results of its aftermarket parts business separately from its truck sales business as required under segment reporting requirements, which are in place to ensure that investors gain the same insight into a company as its executives." Is the PACCAR situation an example of issues with financial reporting quality, earnings quality, or both?

Solution to 1: Yes, the segment data presented in the note to the financial statements indicates that the Truck segment earned $25.9 million in 2009.

Solution to 2: No, the segment data presented in the MD&A indicates that the Truck segment had a negative gross margin.

Solution to 3: The main difference between the note presentation and the MD&A presentation is that the aftermarket parts business is combined with the trucks business in the notes but separated in the MD&A. Although the data are not exactly comparable in the two disclosures (because the note shows income before taxes and the MD&A shows gross profit), the two disclosures present a different picture of PACCAR's profits from truck sales.

Solution to 4: The PACCAR situation appears to be an example of issues with both financial reporting quality and earnings quality. The substantial decrease in truck sales and the negative gross margin reflect poor earnings quality. The failure to disclose clear segment information is an instance of poor financial reporting quality.

While choices exist within GAAP for the presentation of a desired economic picture, non-GAAP reporting adds yet another dimension of management discretion. Non-GAAP reporting of financial metrics not in compliance with generally accepted accounting principles such as US GAAP and IFRS includes both financial metrics and operating metrics.[5] Non-GAAP financial metrics relate directly to the financial statements. A common non-GAAP financial metric is "non-GAAP earnings," which are created by companies "that adjust standards-compliant earnings to *exclude items required* by accounting standards or to *include items not permitted* by accounting standards" (Ciesielski and Henry, 2017). In contrast, non-GAAP operating metrics do not relate directly to the financial statements and include metrics that are typically industry-driven, such as subscriber numbers, active users, and occupancy rates.

Non-GAAP financial reporting has become increasingly common, presenting challenges to analysts. An important challenge is that non-GAAP financial reporting diminishes comparability across financial statements. The adjustments that companies make to create non-GAAP earnings, for example, are generally ad hoc and thus differ significantly. When evaluating non-GAAP metrics, investors must decide the extent to which specific adjustments should be incorporated into their analyses and forecasts.[6]

Another challenge arises from differences in terminology. Non-GAAP earnings are sometimes referred to as underlying earnings, adjusted earnings, recurring earnings, core earnings, or similar. Exhibit 5 provides an example from Jaguar Land Rover Automotive plc (JLR), a subsidiary of Tata Motors Ltd. The company prepares its financial reports under IFRS. The exhibit is an excerpt from JLR's 2016/17 annual report and uses the term "alternative performance measures." Exhibit 6 is from Tata Motors Ltd's Form 6-K filed with the US SEC, containing supplemental information regarding JLR and using the term "non-IFRS Financial Measures." The information in the two exhibits is essentially identical, but the terminology and formatting differ.

EXHIBIT 5

JLR's 2016/17 Annual Report: Footnote 3 [Excerpt]
3) ALTERNATIVE PERFORMANCE MEASURES
Many companies use alternative performance measures (APMs) to provide helpful additional information for users of their financial statements, telling a clearer story of how the business has performed over the period. . . . These measures exclude certain items that are included in comparable statutory measures. . . .

---

[5] The term "non-GAAP" refers generally to all metrics that are non-compliant with generally accepted accounting principles and thus includes "non-IFRS" metrics.
[6] A survey of non-GAAP earnings in the S&P 500 is presented in Ciesielski and Henry (2017). Some observers even recommend that investors shift their focus from a company's earnings to a company's "strategic assets" and the contribution of these assets to its competitive edge (Gu and Lev, 2017).

EXHIBIT 5   (Continued)

Reconciliations between these alternative performance measures and statutory reported measures are shown below.

EBIT AND EBITDA (£m)

Year ended Match 31	2017
EBITDA	**2,955**
Depreciation and amortization	–1,656
Share of profit/(loss) of equity accounted investments	159
EBIT	**1,458**
Foreign exchange (loss)/gain on derivatives	–11
Unrealized gain/(loss) on commodities	148
Foreign exchange loss on loans	–101
Finance income	33
Finance expense (net)	–68
Exceptional item	151
Profit before tax	**1,610**

EXHIBIT 6

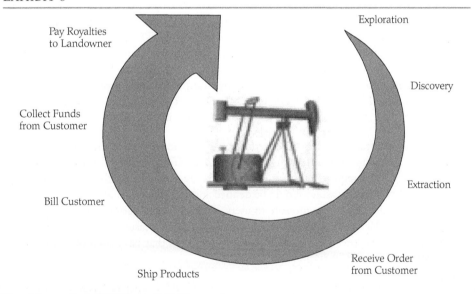

Tata Motors Ltd. SEC Form 6-K [Excerpt]

Non-IFRS Financial Measures

This Report includes references to certain non-IFRS measures, including EBITDA, EBIT . . . [These measures] and related ratios should not be considered in isolation and are not measures of JLR's financial performance or liquidity under IFRS and should not be considered as an alternative to profit or loss for the period or any other performance measures derived in accordance with IFRS or as an alternative to cash flow from operating, investing or financing activities or any other measure of JLR's liquidity derived in accordance with IFRS. . . . In addition, EBITDA, EBIT . . . as defined, may not be comparable to other similarly titled measures used by other companies.

(continued)

EXHIBIT 6   (Continued)

Exhibit 1 to Form 6-K Supplemental Information Regarding the Jaguar and Land Rover Business of Tata Motors Limited [Excerpt]
The reconciliation of JLR's EBIT and EBITDA to profit for the period line item is:

Fiscal year ended March 31, 2017	£m
Profit for the period	1,272
Add back taxation	338
Add/(less) back exceptional charge/(credit)	−151
Add back/(less) foreign exchange (gains)/loss – financing	101
Add back/(less) foreign exchange (gains)/loss – derivatives	11
Add back/(less) unrealized commodity losses/(gains) – unrealized derivatives	−148
Less finance income	−33
Add back finance expense (net)	68
EBIT	**1,458**
Add back depreciation and amortization	1,656
Add/(less) back share of loss/(profit) from equity accounted investees	−159
EBITDA	**2,955**

Management emphasis on non-GAAP financial measures to deflect attention from less-than-desirable GAAP financial results is an example of an aggressive presentation choice. Since 2003, if a company uses a non-GAAP financial measure[7] in an SEC filing, it is required to display the most directly comparable GAAP measure with equal prominence and to provide a reconciliation between the non-GAAP measure and the equivalent GAAP measure. In other words, a company is not allowed to give more prominence to a non-GAAP financial measure in an SEC filing.

Similarly, the IFRS Practice Statement "Management Commentary," issued December 2010, requires disclosures when non-IFRS measures are included in financial reports:

> If information from the financial statements has been adjusted for inclusion in management commentary, that fact should be disclosed. If financial performance measures that are not required or defined by IFRSs are included within management commentary, those measures should be defined and explained, including an explanation of the relevance of the measure to users. When financial performance measures are derived or drawn from the financial statements, those measures should be reconciled to measures presented in the financial statements that have been prepared in accordance with IFRSs. (Page 17)

The reconciliation between as-reported measures (GAAP financial measures presented in the financial statements) and as-adjusted measures (non-GAAP financial measures presented in places other than the financial statements) can provide important information.

The European Securities and Markets Authority (ESMA) published guidelines in October 2015 *(ESMA Guidelines on Alternative Performance Measures)* covering such points as the definition of APMs, reconciliation to GAAP, explanation of the metrics' relevance, and consistency over time. We discuss ESMA in more detail later in this chapter.

---

[7] Non-domestic private issuers can file financial statements prepared in accordance with IFRS without reconciliation to US GAAP. The SEC recognizes US GAAP and IFRS as GAAP.

EXAMPLE 2   Presentation of Non-GAAP Financial Measures

ConvaTec Group PLC (ConvaTec), a global medical products manufacturer, raised $1.8 billion via an initial public offering (IPO) on the London Stock Exchange in 2016. The company had been purchased by private equity firms from Bristol-Myers Squibb in 2008 for $4.1 billion. Exhibit 7 presents excerpts from the company's regulatory filing at the London Stock Exchange announcing its full year 2016 results.

EXHIBIT 7   Excerpt from ConvaTec's Press Release for Full Year 2016 Results

Headline: "Strong results, delivering on strategy"

CEO Review [Excerpt]

At constant currency, revenue grew 4% to $1,688 million and adjusted EBITDA was $508 million, up 6.5% at constant currency. . . .

   [Footnote] Constant currency growth 'CER' is calculated by restating 2016 results using 2015 foreign exchange rates for the relevant period.

Consolidated Statement of Profit or Loss for the year ended December 31, 2016 ($ m)

	2016	2015
Revenue	1,688.3	1,650.4
Cost of goods sold	−821.0	−799.9
Gross profit	867.3	850.5
Selling and distribution expenses	−357.0	−346.7
General and administrative expenses	−318.2	−233.1
Research and development expenses	−38.1	−40.3
Operating profit	154.0	230.4
Finance costs	−271.4	−303.6
Other expense, net	−8.4	−37.1
Loss before income taxes	−125.8	−110.3
Income tax (expense) benefit	−77.0	16.9
Net loss	−202.8	−93.4

Non-IFRS Financial Information [Excerpt]

This release contains certain financial measures that are not defined or recognized under IFRS. These measures are referred to as "Adjusted" measures. . . . These measures are not measurements of financial performance or liquidity under IFRS and should not replace measures of liquidity or operating profit that are derived in accordance with IFRS.

Reconciliation to adjusted earnings [Excerpt]

2016	Reported	(a)	(b)	(c)	(d)	(e)	(f)	(g)	Adjusted
Revenue	1,688.3	—	—	—	—	—	—	—	1,688.3
. . .									
Operating profit	**154.0**	**155.1**	**30.9**	**11.7**	**0.8**	**—**	**90.2**	**29.5**	**472.2**
. . .									
(Loss) profit before income taxes	−125.8	155.1	30.9	11.7	0.8	37.6	90.2	29.5	230.0
Income tax expense[h]	−77.0								−51.2
Net (loss) profit	−202.8								178.8

(a) Represents an adjustment to exclude (i) acquisition-related amortization expense . . . (ii) accelerated depreciation . . . related to the closure of certain manufacturing facilities, and (iii) impairment charges and assets write offs related to property, plant and equipment and intangible assets. . . .
(b) Represents restructuring costs and other related costs. . . .
(c) Represents remediation costs which include regulatory compliance costs related to FDA activities, IT enhancement costs, and professional service fees associated with activities that were undertaken in respect of the Group's compliance function and to strengthen its control environment within finance.
(d) Represents costs primarily related to (i) corporate development activities and (ii) a settlement of ordinary course multi-year patent-related litigations in 2015. . . .
(e) Represents adjustments to exclude (i) loss on extinguishment of debt and write off of deferred financing fees . . . and (ii) foreign exchange related transactions.
(f) Represents an adjustment to exclude (i) share-based compensation expense . . . arising from pre-IPO employee equity grants and (ii) pre-IPO ownership structure related costs, including management fees to Nordic Capital and Avista (refer to Note 6 Related Party Transactions for further information).
(g) Represents IPO related costs, primary advisory fees.
(h) Adjusted income tax expense/benefit is income tax (expense) benefit net of tax adjustments.

Adjusted EBITDA [Excerpt]

Adjusted EBITDA is defined as Adjusted EBIT . . . further adjusted to exclude (i) software and R&D amortization, (ii) depreciation and (iii) post-IPO share-based compensation.

The following table reconciles the Group's Adjusted EBIT to Adjusted EBITDA.

	2016 ($m)
Adjusted EBIT	472.2
Software and R&D amortization	6.7
Depreciation	27.9
Post-IPO share-based compensation	0.8
Adjusted EBITDA	507.6

1. Based on the information provided, explain the differences between the following two disclosures contained in Convatec's press release:
   A. The CEO Review of 2016 results, at the beginning of the release, states that "revenue grew 4% to $1,688 million."
   B. ConvaTec's Consolidated Statement of Profit or Loss shows 2016 revenues of $1,688.3 million and 2015 revenues of $1,650.4 million.
2. Based on the information provided, explain the differences between the following two disclosures contained in ConvaTecs's earnings release:
   A. The CEO Review of 2016 results states that "adjusted EBITDA was $508 million, up 6.5% at constant currency."
   B. ConvaTec's Consolidated Statement of Profit or Loss shows 2016 net loss of $202.8 million and 2015 net loss of $93.4 million.

Solution to 1: The amount of revenue reported on the company's income statement conforms to International Financial Reporting Standards (IFRS). Using the amounts from the income statement, the company's total revenue increased by 2.3 % (= $1,688.3/$1,650.4 − 1). The revenue growth rate of 4% in the CEO review is a non-IFRS measure, calculated on a "constant currency" basis, which the footnote describes as a comparison using 2016 revenues restated at 2015 foreign exchange rates.

Solution to 2: The amounts reported on the company's income statement conform to IFRS. Using amounts from the income statement, the company reported a loss in 2016 of $202.8 million, which was more than twice as large a loss as the $93.4 million loss reported in 2015. Also referring to the income statement, the company reported 2016 operating profit (referred to elsewhere as EBIT) of $154.0 million, a decline of 33.2% from the $230.4 million operating profit reported in 2016.

In contrast, the "Adjusted EBITDA" amount highlighted in the CEO Review is neither defined nor recognized under IFRS. It is a non-IFRS measure. To create the Adjusted EBITDA, the company first begins with EBIT (called Operating profit in excerpts II and III) of $154.0 and creates Adjusted EBIT ($472.2 million) by adding back 8 different expenses that IFRS requires the company to recognize. These adjustments are listed beneath the first tabular reconciliation in Items a through g. After developing Adjusted EBIT, the company creates Adjusted EBITDA ($507.6 million) by adding back a further 3 different expenses that IFRS requires the company to recognize.

Overall, there are three key differences between Disclosures A and B: (1) Most importantly, disclosure A refers to a non-IFRS metric rather than an IFRS-compliant metric; (2) Disclosure A refers to operating profit, which was positive, rather than to net income, which was negative; and (3) Disclosure A highlights a positive economic outcome—i.e., an increase, on a currency adjusted basis. An analyst should be aware of the alternative means by which earnings announcements can paint a positive picture of companies' results.

Often, poor reporting quality occurs simultaneously with poor earnings quality; for example, aggressive accounting choices are made to obscure poor performance. It is also possible, of course, for poor reporting quality to occur with high-quality earnings. Although a company with good performance would not require aggressive accounting choices to obscure poor performance, it might nonetheless produce poor-quality reports for other reasons. A company with good performance might be unable to produce high-quality reports because of inadequate internal systems.

Another scenario in which poor reporting quality might occur simultaneously with high quality earnings is that a company with good performance might deliberately produce reports based on "conservative" rather than aggressive accounting choices—that is, choices that make current performance look worse. One motivation might be to avoid unwanted political attention. Another motivation could arise in a period in which management had already exceeded targets before the end of the period and thus made conservative accounting choices that would delay reporting profits until the following period (so-called "hidden reserves"). Similar motivations might also contribute to accounting choices that create the appearance that the trajectory of future results would appear more attractive. For example, a company might make choices to accelerate losses in the first year of an acquisition or the first year of a new CEO's tenure so that the trajectory of future results would appear more attractive.

Overall, *unbiased* financial reporting is the ideal. Some investors may prefer conservative choices rather than aggressive ones, however, because a positive surprise is easier to tolerate than a negative surprise. Biased reporting, whether conservative or aggressive, adversely affects a user's ability to assess a company.

The quality spectrum considers the more intuitive situation in which less-than-desired underlying economics are the central motivation for poor reporting quality. In addition, it is necessary to have some degree of reporting quality in order to evaluate earnings quality. Proceeding down the spectrum, therefore, the concepts of reporting quality and earnings quality become progressively less distinguishable.

2.3.1. Within GAAP, but "Earnings Management"

The next level down on the spectrum in Exhibit 2 is labeled "Within GAAP, but 'earnings management.'" The term "earnings management" is defined here as making intentional choices that create biased financial reports.[8] The distinction between earnings management and biased choices is subtle and, primarily, a matter of intent. Earnings management represents "deliberate actions to influence reported earnings and their interpretation" (Ronen and Yaari, 2008). Earnings can be "managed" upward (increased) by taking *real* actions, such as deferring research and development (R&D) expenses into the next reporting period. Alternatively, earnings can be increased by *accounting* choices, such as changing accounting estimates. For example, the amount of estimated product returns, bad debt expense, or asset impairment could be decreased to create higher earnings. Because it is difficult to determine intent, we include earnings management under the biased choices discussion.

2.4. Departures from GAAP

The next levels down on the spectrum in Exhibit 2 mark departures from GAAP. Financial reporting that departs from GAAP can generally be considered low quality. In such situations, earnings quality is likely difficult or impossible to assess because comparisons with earlier periods and/or other entities cannot be made. An example of improper accounting was Enron (accounting issues revealed in 2001), whose inappropriate use of off-balance-sheet structures and other complex transactions resulted in vastly understated indebtedness as well as overstated profits and operating cash flow. Another notorious example of improper accounting was WorldCom (accounting issues discovered in 2002), a company that by improperly capitalizing certain expenditures dramatically understated its expenses and thus overstated its profits. More recently, New Century Financial (accounting issues revealed in 2007) issued billions of dollars of subprime mortgages and improperly reserved only minimal amounts for loan repurchase losses. Each of these companies subsequently filed for bankruptcy.

In the 1980s, Polly Peck International (PPI) reported currency losses, incurred in the normal course of operations, directly through equity rather than in its profit and loss statements. In the 1990s, Sunbeam improperly reported revenues from "bill-and-hold" sales and also manipulated the timing of expenses in an effort to falsely portray outstanding performance of its then-new chief executive.

At the bottom of the quality spectrum, fabricated reports portray fictitious events, either to fraudulently obtain investments by misrepresenting the company's performance and/or to obscure fraudulent misappropriation of the company's assets. Examples of fraudulent reporting

---

[8]Various definitions have appeared in academic research. Closest to the discussion here is Schipper (1989), which uses the term "earnings management" to mean "'disclosure management' in the sense of a purposeful intervention in the external financial reporting process, with the intent of obtaining some private gain (as opposed to, say, merely facilitating the neutral operation of the process)."

are unfortunately easy to find, although they were not necessarily easy to identify at the time. In the 1970s, Equity Funding Corp. created fictitious revenues and even fictitious policy-holders. In the 1980s, Crazy Eddie's reported fictitious inventory as well as fictitious revenues supported by fake invoices. In 2004, Parmalat reported fictitious bank balances.

EXAMPLE 3   Spectrum for Assessing Quality of Financial Reports

Jake Lake, a financial analyst, has identified several items in the financial reports of several (hypothetical) companies. Describe each of these items in the context of the financial reporting quality spectrum.

1. ABC Co.'s 2018 earnings totaled $233 million, including a $100 million gain from selling one of its less profitable divisions. ABC's earnings for the prior three years totaled $120 million, $107 million, and $111 million. The company's financial reports are extremely clear and detailed, and the company's earnings announcement highlights the one-time nature of the $100 million gain.
2. DEF Co. discloses that in 2018, it changed the depreciable life of its equipment from 3 years to 15 years. Equipment represents a substantial component of the company's assets. The company's disclosures indicate that the change is permissible under the accounting standards of its jurisdiction but provide only limited explanation of the change.
3. GHI Co.'s R&D expenditures for the past five years have been approximately 3% of sales. In 2018, the company significantly reduced its R&D expenditures. Without the reduction in R&D expenditures, the company would have reported a loss. No explanation is disclosed.

Solution to 1: ABC's 2018 total earnings quality can be viewed as low because nearly half of the earnings are derived from a non-sustainable activity, namely the sale of a division. ABC's 2018 quality of earnings from continuing operations may be high because the amounts are fairly consistent from year to year, although an analyst would undertake further analysis to confirm earnings quality. In general, a user of financial reports should look beyond the bottom-line net income. The description provided suggests that the company's reporting quality is high; the reports are clear and detailed, and the one-time nature of the $100 million gain is highlighted.

Solution to 2: DEF's accounting choice appears to be within permissible accounting standards, but its effect is to substantially lower depreciation expense and thus to increase earnings for the year. The quality of reported earnings is questionable. Although the new level of earnings may be sustainable, similar increases in earnings for future periods might not be achievable, because increasing earnings solely by changing accounting estimates is likely not sustainable. In addition, the description provided suggests that the company's reporting quality is low because it offers only a limited explanation for the change.

Solution to 3: GHI's operational choice to reduce its R&D may reflect real earnings management because the change enabled the company to avoid reporting a loss. In addition, the description provided suggests that the company's reporting quality is low because it does not offer an explanation for the change.

2.5. Differentiate between Conservative and Aggressive Accounting

This section returns to the implications of conservative and aggressive accounting choices. As mentioned earlier, *unbiased* financial reporting is the ideal. But some investors may prefer or be perceived to prefer conservative rather than aggressive accounting choices because a positive surprise is acceptable. In contrast, management may make, or be perceived to make, aggressive accounting choices because they increase the company's reported performance and financial position.

Aggressive accounting choices in the period under review may decrease the company's reported performance and financial position in later periods, which creates a sustainability issue. Conservative choices do not typically create a sustainability issue because they decrease the company's reported performance and financial position, and may increase them in later periods. In terms of establishing expectations for the future, however, financial reporting that is relevant and faithfully representative is the most useful.

A common presumption is that financial reports are typically biased upward, but that is not always the case. Although accounting standards ideally promote unbiased financial reporting, some accounting standards may specifically require a conservative treatment of a transaction or an event. Also, managers may choose to take a conservative approach when applying standards. It is important that an analyst consider the possibility of conservative choices and their effects.

At its most extreme, conservatism follows accounting practices that "anticipate no profit, but anticipate all losses" (Bliss, 1924). But in general, conservatism means that revenues may be recognized once a verifiable and legally enforceable receivable has been generated and that losses need not be recognized until it becomes "probable" that an actual loss will be incurred. Conservatism is not an absolute but is characterized by degrees, such as "the accountant's tendency to require a higher degree of verification to recognize good news as gains than to recognize bad news as losses" (Basu, 1997). From this perspective, "verification" (e.g., physical existence of inventories, evidence of costs incurred or to be incurred, or establishment of rights and obligations on legal grounds) drives the degree of conservatism. For recognition of revenues, a higher degree of verification would be required than for expenses.

2.5.1. Conservatism in Accounting Standards

The *Conceptual Framework* supports neutrality of information: "A neutral depiction is without bias in the selection or presentation of financial information."[9] Neutrality—lack of upward or downward bias—is considered a desirable characteristic of financial reporting. Conservatism directly conflicts with the characteristic of neutrality because the asymmetric nature of conservatism leads to bias in measuring assets and liabilities—and ultimately, earnings.

Despite efforts to support neutrality in financial reporting, many conservatively biased standards remain. Standards across jurisdictions may differ on the extent of conservatism embedded within them. An analyst should be aware of the implications of accounting standards for the financial reports.

An example is the different treatment by IFRS and US GAAP of the impairment of long-lived assets.[10] Both IFRS and US GAAP specify an impairment analysis protocol that begins with an assessment of whether recent events indicate that the economic benefit from

---

[9] IASB and FASB, *The Conceptual Framework for Financial Reporting* (2010): QC 14.
[10] See IAS 36 and FASB ASC Section 360-10-35.

an individual or group of long-lived assets may be less than its carrying amount(s). From that point on, however, the two regimes diverge:

- Under IFRS, if the "recoverable amount" (the higher of fair value less costs to sell and value in use) is less than the carrying amount, then an impairment charge will be recorded.
- Under US GAAP, an impairment charge will be recorded only when the sum of the undiscounted future cash flows expected to be derived from the asset(s) is less than the carrying amount(s). If the undiscounted future cash flows are less than the carrying amount, the asset is written down to fair value.

To illustrate the difference in application, assume that a factory is the unit of account eligible for impairment testing. Its carrying amount is $10,000,000; "fair value" and "recoverable amount" are both $6,000,000; and the undiscounted future net cash flows associated with the factory total $10,000,000. Under IFRS, an impairment charge of $4,000,000 would be recorded; but under US GAAP, no impairment charge would be recognized.

Thus, on its face, IFRS would be regarded as more conservative than US GAAP because impairment losses would normally be recognized earlier under IFRS than under US GAAP. But, taking the analysis one step further, such a broad generalization may not hold up. For example, if an asset is impaired under both IFRS and US GAAP and the asset's value in use exceeds its fair value, the impairment loss under US GAAP will be greater. Also, IFRS permits the recognition of recoveries of the recoverable amount in subsequent periods if evidence indicates that the recoverable amount has subsequently increased. In contrast, US GAAP prohibits the subsequent write-up of an asset after an impairment charge has been taken; it would recognize the asset's increased value only when the asset is ultimately sold.

Common examples of conservatism in accounting standards include the following:

- *Research costs*. Because the future benefit of research costs is uncertain at the time the costs are incurred, both US GAAP and IFRS require immediate expensing instead of capitalization.
- *Litigation losses*. When it becomes "probable" that a cost will be incurred, both US GAAP and IFRS require expense recognition, even though a legal liability may not be incurred until a future date.
- *Insurance recoverables*. Generally, a company that receives payment on an insurance claim may not recognize a receivable until the insurance company acknowledges the validity of the claimed amount.

Watts (2003) reviews empirical studies of conservatism, and identifies four potential benefits of conservatism:

- Given asymmetrical information, conservatism may protect the contracting parties with less information and greater risk. This protection is necessary because the contracting party may be at a disadvantage. For example, corporations that access debt markets have limited liability, and lenders thus have limited recourse to recover their losses from shareholders. As another example, executives who receive earnings-based bonuses might not be subject to having those bonuses "clawed back" if earnings are subsequently discovered to be overstated.
- Conservatism reduces the possibility of litigation and, by extension, litigation costs. Rarely, if ever, is a company sued because it understated good news or overstated bad news.
- Conservative rules may protect the interests of regulators and politicians by reducing the possibility that fault will be found with them if companies overstate earnings or assets.

- In many tax jurisdictions, financial and tax reporting rules are linked. For example, in Germany and Japan, only deductions taken against reported income can be deducted against taxable income. Hence, companies can reduce the present value of their tax payments by electing conservative accounting policies for certain types of events.

Analysts should consider possible conservative and aggressive biases and their consequences when examining financial reports. Current-period financial reports may be unbiased, upward biased through aggressive accounting choices, downward biased through conservative accounting choices, or biased through a combination of conservative and aggressive accounting choices.

2.5.2. Bias in the Application of Accounting Standards

Any application of accounting standards, whether the standard itself is neutral or not, often requires significant amounts of judgment. Characterizing the application of an accounting standard as conservative or aggressive is more a matter of intent rather than definition.

Careful analysis of disclosures, facts, and circumstances contributes to making an accurate inference of intent. Management seeking to manipulate earnings may take a longer view by sacrificing short-term profitability in order to ensure higher profits in later periods. One example of biased accounting in the guise of conservatism is the so-called "big bath" restructuring charges. Both US GAAP and IFRS provide for accrual of future costs associated with restructurings, and these costs are often associated with and presented along with asset impairments. But in some instances, companies use the accounting provisions to estimate "big" losses in the period under review so that performance in future periods will appear better. Having observed numerous instances of manipulative practices in the late 1990s, in which US companies set up opportunities to report higher profits in future periods that were not connected with performance in those periods, the SEC staff issued rules that narrowed the circumstances under which costs can be categorized as part of a "non-recurring" restructuring event and enhanced the transparency surrounding restructuring charges and asset impairments.[11]

A similar manifestation of "big bath" accounting is often referred to as "cookie jar reserve accounting." Both US GAAP and IFRS require accruals of estimates of future non-payments of loans. In his 1998 speech "The 'Numbers Game,'" SEC chair Arthur Levitt expressed the general concern that corporations were overstating loans and other forms of loss allowances for the purpose of smoothing income over time.[12] In 2003, the SEC issued interpretive guidance that essentially requires a company to provide a separate section in management's discussion and analysis (MD&A) titled "Critical Accounting Estimates."[13] If the effects of subjective estimates and judgments of highly uncertain matters are material to stakeholders (investors, customers, suppliers, and other users of the financial statements), disclosures of their nature and exposure to uncertainty should be made in the MD&A. This requirement is in addition to required disclosures in the notes to the financial statements.

---

[11] SEC, "Restructuring and Impairment Charges," Staff Accounting Bulletin (SAB) No. 100 (1999): www.sec.gov/interps/account/sab100.htm.

[12] Arthur Levitt, "The 'Numbers Game,'" Remarks given at NYU Center for Law and Business (September 28, 1998): www.sec.gov/news/speech/speecharchive/1998/spch220.txt.

[13] SEC, "Commission Guidance Regarding Management's Discussion and Analysis of Financial Condition and Results of Operations," Financial Reporting Release (FRR) No. 72 (2003): www.sec.gov/rules/interp/33-8350.htm.

3. CONTEXT FOR ASSESSING FINANCIAL REPORTING QUALITY

In assessing financial reporting quality, it is useful to consider whether a company's managers may be motivated to issue financial reports that are not high quality. If motivation exists, an analyst should consider whether the reporting environment is conducive to managers' misreporting. It is important to consider mechanisms within the reporting environment that discipline financial reporting quality, such as the regulatory regime.

3.1. Motivations

Managers may be motivated to issue financial reports that are not high quality to mask poor performance, such as loss of market share or lower profitability than competitors. Lewis (2012) stated, "A firm experiencing performance problems, particularly those it considers transient, may induce a response that inflates current earnings numbers in exchange for lower future earnings."

- Even when there is no need to mask poor performance, managers frequently have incentives to meet or beat market expectations as reflected in analysts' forecasts and/or management's own forecasts. Exceeding forecasts typically increases the stock price, if only temporarily. Additionally, exceeding forecasts can increase management compensation that is linked to increases in stock price or to reported earnings. Graham, Harvey, and Rajgopal (2005) found that the CFOs they surveyed view earnings as the most important financial metric to financial markets. Achieving (or exceeding) particular benchmarks, including prior-year earnings and analysts' forecasts, is very important. The authors examined a variety of motivations for why managers might "exercise accounting discretion to achieve some desirable earnings goal." Motivations to meet earnings benchmarks include equity market effects (for example, building credibility with market participants and positively affecting stock price) and trade effects (for example, enhancing reputation with customers and suppliers). Equity market effects are the most powerful incentives, but trade effects are important, particularly for smaller companies.
- Career concerns and incentive compensation may motivate accounting choices. For example, managers might be concerned that working for a company that performs poorly will limit their future career opportunities or that they will not receive a bonus based on exceeding a particular earnings target. In both cases, management might be motivated to make accounting choices to increase earnings. In a period of marginally poor performance, a manager might accelerate or inflate revenues and/or delay or under report expenses. Conversely, in a period of strong performance, a manager might delay revenue recognition or accelerate expense recognition to increase the probability of exceeding the next period's targets (i.e., to "bank" some earnings for the next period). The surveyed managers indicated a greater concern with career implications of reported results than with incentive compensation implications.

Avoiding debt covenant violations can motivate managers to inflate earnings. Graham, Harvey, and Rajgopal's survey indicates that avoidance of bond covenant violation is important to highly leveraged and unprofitable companies but relatively unimportant overall.

3.2. Conditions Conducive to Issuing Low-Quality Financial Reports

As discussed, deviations from a neutral presentation of financial results could be driven by management choices or by a jurisdiction's financial reporting standards. Ultimately, a decision to issue low-quality, or even fraudulent, financial reports is made by an individual or individuals. Why individuals make such choices is not always immediately apparent. For example, why would the newly appointed CEO of Sunbeam, who already had a net worth of more than $100 million, commit accounting fraud by improperly reporting revenues from "bill-and-hold" sales and manipulating the timing of expenses, rather than admit to lower-than-expected financial results?

Typically, three conditions exist when low-quality financial reports are issued: opportunity, motivation, and rationalization. Opportunity can be the result of internal conditions, such as poor internal controls or an ineffective board of directors, or external conditions, such as accounting standards that provide scope for divergent choices or minimal consequences for an inappropriate choice. Motivation can result from pressure to meet some criteria for personal reasons, such as a bonus, or corporate reasons, such as concern about financing in the future. Rationalization is important because if an individual is concerned about a choice, he or she needs to be able to justify it to him- or herself.

Former Enron CFO Andrew Fastow, speaking at the 2013 Association of Certified Fraud Examiners Annual Fraud Conference, indicated that he knew at the time he was doing something wrong but followed procedure to justify his decision (Pavlo, 2013). He made sure to get management and board approval, as well as legal and accounting opinions, and to include appropriate disclosures. The incentive and corporate culture was to create earnings rather than focus on long-term value. Clearly, as reflected in his prison sentence, he did something that was not only wrong but illegal.

3.3. Mechanisms That Discipline Financial Reporting Quality

Markets potentially discipline financial reporting quality. Companies and nations compete for capital, and the cost of capital is a function of perceived risk—including the risk that a company's financial statements will skew investors' expectations. Thus, in the absence of other conflicting economic incentives, a company seeking to minimize its long-term cost of capital should aim to provide high-quality financial reports. In addition to markets, other mechanisms that discipline financial reporting quality include market regulatory authorities, auditors, and private contracts.

3.3.1. Market Regulatory Authorities

Companies seeking to minimize the cost of capital should maximize reporting quality, but as discussed earlier, conflicting incentives often exist. For this reason, national regulations, and the regulators that establish and enforce rules, can play a significant role in financial reporting quality. Many of the world's securities regulators are members of the International Organization of Securities Commissions (IOSCO). IOSCO is recognized as the "global standard setter for the securities sector" although it does not actually set standards but rather establishes objectives and principles to guide securities and capital market regulation. IOSCO's membership includes more than 120 securities regulators and 80 other securities market participants, such as stock exchanges.[14]

One member of IOSCO is ESMA, an independent EU authority with a mission to "enhance the protection of investors and reinforce stable and well-functioning financial markets in the European Union."[15] ESMA organizes financial reporting enforcement activities

[14]Visit www.iosco.org for more information.
[15]Text from ESMA's mission statement on their website: www.esma.europa.eu.

through a forum consisting of European enforcers from European Economic Area countries. Direct supervision and enforcement activities are performed at the national level. For example, the Financial Conduct Authority (FCA) is the IOSCO member with primary responsibility for securities regulation in the United Kingdom. ESMA reported that European enforcers examined the interim and/or annual financial statements of 1,141 issuers in 2017, which in turn led to enforcement actions for 328 issuers with the following outcomes: 12 required reissuances of financial statements, 71 public corrective notes, and 245 required corrections in future financial statements.[16]

Another member of IOSCO is the US regulatory authority, the Securities and Exchange Commission. The SEC is responsible for overseeing approximately 9,100 US public companies (along with investment advisers, broker/dealers, securities exchanges, and other entities) and reviews the disclosures of these companies at least once every three years with the aim of improving information available to investors and potentially uncovering possible violations of securities laws.[17] In 2017, the SEC reported that it had filed 754 total and 446 standalone enforcement actions, about 20% of which concerned issuer reporting/accounting and auditing.[18]

Examples of regulatory bodies in Asia include the Financial Services Agency in Japan, the China Securities Regulatory Commission, and the Securities and Exchange Board of India. Examples of regulatory bodies in South America include the Comisión Nacional de Valores in Argentina, Comissão de Valores Mobiliários in Brazil, and Superintendencia de Valores y Seguros in Chile. A full list of IOSCO members can be found on the organization's website.

Typical features of a regulatory regime that most directly affect financial reporting quality include the following:

- *Registration requirements.* Market regulators typically require publicly traded companies to register securities before offering the securities for sale to the public. A registration document typically contains current financial statements, other relevant information about the risks and prospects of the company issuing the securities, and information about the securities being offered.
- *Disclosure requirements.* Market regulators typically require publicly traded companies to make public periodic reports, including financial reports and management comments. Standard-setting bodies, such as the IASB and FASB, are typically private sector, self-regulated organizations with board members who are experienced accountants, auditors, users of financial statements, and academics. Regulatory authorities, such as the Accounting and Corporate Regulatory Authority in Singapore, the Securities and Exchange Commission in the United States, the Securities and Exchange Commission in Brazil, and the Financial Reporting Council in the United Kingdom, have the legal authority to enforce financial reporting requirements and exert other controls over entities that participate in the capital markets within their jurisdiction. In other words, *generally*, standard-setting bodies set the standards, and regulatory authorities recognize and

---

[16] ESMA, "Enforcement and Regulatory Activities of Accounting Enforcers in 2017," ESMA32-63-424, European Securities and Markets Authority (April 3, 2018): www.esma.europa.eu.

[17] SEC, "FY2013 Congressional Justification," Securities and Exchange Commission (February 2012): www.sec.gov/about/secfy13congbudgjust.pdf.

[18] SEC, Securities and Exchange Commission Division of Enforcement Annual Report, "A Look Back at Fiscal Year 2017" www.sec.gov/report.

enforce those standards. Without the recognition of standards by regulatory authorities, the private-sector standard-setting bodies would have no authority. Regulators often retain the legal authority to establish financial reporting standards in their jurisdiction and can overrule the private-sector standard-setting bodies.

- *Auditing requirements.* Market regulators typically require companies' financial statements to be accompanied by an audit opinion attesting that the financial statements conform to the relevant set of accounting standards. Some regulators, such as the SEC in the United States, require an additional audit opinion attesting to the effectiveness of the company's internal controls over financial reporting.

- *Management commentaries.* Regulations typically require publicly traded companies' financial reports to include statements by management. For example, the FCA in the United Kingdom requires a management report containing "(1) a fair review of the issuer's business; and (2) a description of the principal risks and uncertainties facing the issuer" (Disclosure Guidance and Transparency Rules sourcebook).

- *Responsibility statements.* Regulations typically require a statement from the person or persons responsible for the company's filings. Such statements require the responsible individuals to explicitly acknowledge responsibility and to attest to the correctness of the financial reports. Some regulators, such as the SEC in the United States, require formal certifications that carry specific legal penalties for false certifications.

- *Regulatory review of filings.* Regulators typically undertake a review process to ensure that the rules have been followed. The review process typically covers all initial registrations and a sample of subsequent periodic financial reports.

- *Enforcement mechanisms.* Regulators are granted various powers to enforce the securities market rules. Such powers can include assessing fines, suspending or permanently barring market participants, and bringing criminal prosecutions. Public announcements of disciplinary actions are also a type of enforcement mechanism.

In summary, market regulatory authorities play a central role in encouraging high-quality financial reporting.

3.3.2. Auditors

As noted, regulatory authorities typically require that publicly traded companies' financial statements be audited by an independent auditor. Private companies also obtain audit opinions for their financial statements, either voluntarily or because audit reports are required by an outside party, such as providers of debt or equity capital.

Audit opinions provide financial statement users with some assurance that the information complies with the relevant set of accounting standards and presents the company's information fairly. Exhibits 8, 9, 10, and 11 provide excerpts from the independent auditors' reports for GlaxoSmithKline plc, Alibaba Group Holding Limited, Apple Inc., and Tata Motors Limited, respectively. For each company, the auditor issued an unqualified opinion on the financial statements, indicating that the financial statements present fairly the company's performance in accordance with relevant standards. (Note: The term "unqualified opinion" means that the opinion did not include any qualifications or exceptions; the term is synonymous with the less formal term "clean opinion." Unqualified opinions are the most common.) Other items in the audit reports reflect the specific requirements of the company's regulatory regime. For example, the audit report for GlaxoSmithKline spans nine pages and includes opinions on the company's financial statements as well as the Strategic Report and the Directors' Report. This audit report also includes disclosures about "Key audit matters," in accordance with International Standards on Auditing (ISAs) issued by the International Auditing and Assurance Standards Board (IAASB) in 2015 and effective for periods ending on or after December 15, 2016.

EXHIBIT 8   Excerpts from Audit Opinion of PricewaterhouseCoopers LLP from the 2017 Annual Report *(pages 149–157)* of GlaxoSmithKline plc

In our opinion, GlaxoSmithKline plc's Group financial statements (the "financial statements"):

- give a true and fair view of the state of the Group's affairs as at December 31, 2017 and of its profit and cash flows for the year then ended;
- have been properly prepared in accordance with International Financial Reporting Standards ("IFRSs") as adopted by the European Union; and
- have been prepared in accordance with the requirements of the Companies Act 2006 and Article 4 of the IAS Regulation.

. . .

In our opinion, the Group financial statements have been properly prepared in accordance with IFRSs as issued by the IASB.

. . .

Key audit matters

Key audit matters are those matters that, in the auditors' professional judgement, were of most significance in the audit of the financial statements of the current period and include the most significant assessed risks of material misstatement (whether or not due to fraud) identified by the auditors, including those which had the greatest effect on: the overall audit strategy; the allocation of resources in the audit; and directing the efforts of the engagement team. These matters, and any comments we make on the results of our procedures thereon, were addressed in the context of our audit of the financial statements as a whole, and in forming our opinion thereon, and we do not provide a separate opinion on these matters. This is not a complete list of all risks identified by our audit.

. . .

In our opinion, based on the work undertaken in the course of the audit, the information given in the Strategic Report and Directors' Report for the year ended December 31, 2017 is consistent with the financial statements and has been prepared in accordance with applicable legal requirements.

EXHIBIT 9   Excerpts from Audit Opinion of PricewaterhouseCoopers Hong Kong, SAR from the Annual Report *(SEC Form 20-F, Pages F-2 and F-3)* of Alibaba Group Holding Limited for the year ended March 31, 2018

In our opinion, the consolidated financial statements referred to above present fairly, in all material respects, the financial position of the Company as of March 31, 2017 and 2018, and the results of their operations and their cash flows for each of the three years in the period ended March 31, 2018 in conformity with accounting principles generally accepted in the United States of America. Also in our opinion, the Company maintained, in all material respects, effective internal control over financial reporting as of March 31, 2018, based on criteria established in Internal Control — Integrated Framework (2013) issued by the COSO.

EXHIBIT 10 Excerpt from Audit Opinion of Ernst & Young from the Annual Report (*SEC Form 10-K, pages 70 and 71*) of Apple Inc. for the year ended September 30, 2017

[From the Financial Statement Opinion]
    We have audited the accompanying consolidated balance sheets of Apple Inc. as of September 30, 2017 and September 24, 2016, and the related consolidated statements of operations, comprehensive income, shareholders' equity and cash flows for each of the three years in the period ended September 30, 2017.

. . .

In our opinion, the financial statements referred to above present fairly, in all material respects, the consolidated financial position of Apple Inc. at September 30, 2017 and September 24, 2016, and the consolidated results of its operations and its cash flows for each of the three years in the period ended September 30, 2017, in conformity with U.S. generally accepted accounting principles.

. . .

We also have audited, in accordance with the standards of the Public Company Accounting Oversight Board (United States), Apple Inc.'s internal control over financial reporting as of September 30, 2017, based on criteria established in Internal Control – Integrated Framework issued by the Committee of Sponsoring Organizations of the Treadway Commission (2013 framework) and our report dated November 3, 2017 expressed an unqualified opinion thereon.

[From the Internal Controls Opinion]
    We have audited Apple Inc.'s internal control over financial reporting as of September 30, 2017, based on criteria established in Internal Control – Integrated Framework issued by the Committee of Sponsoring Organizations of the Treadway Commission (2013 framework) ("the COSO criteria").

. . .

In our opinion, Apple Inc. maintained, in all material respects, effective internal control over financial reporting as of September 30, 2017, based on the COSO criteria.
    We also have audited, in accordance with the standards of the Public Company Accounting Oversight Board (United States), the 2017 consolidated financial statements of Apple Inc. and our report dated November 3, 2017 expressed an unqualified opinion thereon.

EXHIBIT 11 Excerpt from Audit Opinion of KPMG Mumbai, India from the Annual Report (*SEC Form 20-F, pages F2 to F4*) of Tata Motors Limited for the year ended March 31, 2018

Opinion on the Consolidated Financial Statements
We have audited the accompanying consolidated balance sheet of Tata Motors Limited and its subsidiaries (the "Company") as of March 31, 2018, the related consolidated income statement, statement of comprehensive income, statement of cash flows, and statement of changes in equity for the year ended March 31, 2018, and the related notes and financial statement schedule 1 (collectively, the consolidated financial statements).
    In our opinion, the consolidated financial statements present fairly, in all material respects, the financial position of the Company as of March 31, 2018, and the results of its operations and its cash flows for the year ended March 31, 2018, in conformity with the International Financial Reporting Standards as issued by the International Accounting Standards Board ("IFRS").

EXHIBIT 11   (Continued)

We also have audited, in accordance with the standards of the Public Company Account-ing Oversight Board (United States) (PCAOB), the Company's internal control over financial reporting as of March 31, 2018, based on criteria established in *Internal Control – Integrated Framework (2013)* issued by the Committee of Sponsoring Organizations of the Treadway Commission, and our report dated July, 31, 2018 expressed an adverse opinion on the effec-tiveness of the Company's internal control over financial reporting.

· · ·

Opinion on Internal Control Over Financial Reporting
We have audited Tata Motors Limited's and subsidiaries' (the Company) internal control over financial reporting as of March 31, 2018, based on criteria established in Internal Control – Integrated Framework (2013) issued by the Committee of Sponsoring Organizations of the Treadway Commission. In our opinion, because of the effect of the material weakness described below, on the achievement of the objectives of the control criteria, the Company has not maintained effective internal control over financial reporting as of March 31, 2018, based on criteria established in *Internal Control – Integrated Framework (2013)* issued by the Committee of Sponsoring Organizations of the Treadway Commission.

· · ·

A material weakness is a deficiency, or a combination of deficiencies, in internal control over fi-nancial reporting, such that there is a reasonable possibility that a material misstatement of the company's annual or interim financial statements will not be prevented or detected on a timely basis. A material weakness related to inappropriate system access restrictions at a third party logistics provider has been identified and included in management's assessment. The material weakness was considered in determining the nature, timing, and extent of audit tests applied in our audit of the 2018 consolidated financial statements, and this report does not affect our report on those consolidated financial statements.

The excerpts for Alibaba, Apple, and Tata Motors show the auditors' opinions on the compa-nies' financial statements and additionally the SEC-required opinions on the effectiveness of the companies' internal controls because these companies are listed in the United States. For Alibaba, a single report includes both unqualified opinions: (i) the financial statements present fairly the financial position, results of operations, and cash flows . . . in conformity with US GAAP; and (ii) the company maintained effective control over financial reporting. For Apple, the first report includes the unqualified opinion on the financial statements, and the second report includes the unqualified opinion on the company's effective internal controls. For Tata Motors, the first report includes the unqualified opinion that the financial statements present the company's position and results fairly in accordance with IFRS. (The SEC permits non-US companies to report using US GAAP, IFRS as issued by the IASB, or home-country GAAP.) However, the second report includes an *adverse* opinion on the effectiveness of the company's internal controls: "In our opinion, because of the effect of the material weakness . . . the company has not maintained effective internal con-trol." The report explains that the material weakness involved a third party's inappropriate access to the company's systems. The report further states that although the material weakness resulted in ineffective internal controls, it did not affect the audit opinion on the financial statements. Else-where in Tata Motors' annual report (not shown in the excerpt), the company discloses that the weakness did not result in a financial misstatement and that it has undertaken remedial measures.

Although audit opinions provide discipline for financial reporting quality, inherent lim-itations exist. First, an audit opinion is based on a review of information prepared by the company. If a company deliberately intends to deceive its auditor, a review of information might not uncover misstatements. Second, an audit is based on sampling, and the sample might not reveal misstatements. Third, an "expectations gap" may exist between the auditor's role and the public's expectation of auditors. An audit is not typically intended to detect fraud; it is intended to provide assurance that the financial reports are fairly presented. Finally, the company being audited pays the audit fees, often established through a competitive process. This situation could provide an auditor with an incentive to show leniency to the company being audited, particularly if the auditor's firm provides additional services to the company.

3.3.3. Private Contracting

Aspects of private contracts, such as loan agreements or investment contracts, can serve as mechanisms to discipline financial reporting quality. Many parties that have a contractual arrangement with a company have an incentive to monitor that company's performance and to ensure that the company's financial reports are high quality. For example, loan agreements often contain loan covenants, which create specifically tailored financial reporting requirements that are legally binding for the issuer. As noted earlier, avoidance of debt covenant violation is a potential motivation for managers to inflate earnings. As another example, an investment contract could contain provisions giving investors the option to recover all or part of their investment if certain financial triggers occur. Such provisions could motivate the investee's managers to manipulate reported results to avoid the financial triggers.

Because the financial reports prepared by the investees or borrowers directly affect the contractual outcomes—potentially creating a motivation for misreporting—investors and lenders are motivated to monitor financial reports and to ensure that they are high quality.

EXAMPLE 4   Financial Reporting Manipulation: Motivations and Disciplining Mechanisms

For each of the following two scenarios, identify (1) factors that might motivate the company's managers to manipulate reported financial amounts and (2) applicable mechanisms that could discipline financial reporting quality.

1. ABC Co. is a private company. Bank NTBig has made a loan to ABC Co. ABC is required to maintain a minimum 2.0 interest coverage ratio. In its most recent financial reports, ABC reported earnings before interest and taxes of $1,200 and interest expense of $600. In the report's notes, the company discloses that it changed the estimated useful life of its property, plant, and equipment during the year. Depreciation was approximately $150 lower as a result of this change in estimate.
2. DEF Co. is a publicly traded company. For the most recent quarter, the average of analysts' forecasts for earnings per share was $2.50. In its quarterly earnings announcement, DEF reported net income of $3,458,780. The number of common shares outstanding was 1,378,000. DEF's main product is a hardware device that includes a free two-year service contract in the selling price. Based on management estimates, the company allocates a portion of revenues to the hardware device, which it recognizes immediately, and a portion to the service contract, which it defers and

recognizes over the two years of the contract. Based on the disclosures, a higher percentage of revenue was allocated to hardware than in the past, with an estimated after-tax impact on net income of $27,000.

Solution to 1: The need to maintain a minimum interest coverage ratio of 2.0 might motivate ABC's managers to manipulate reported financial amounts. The company's coverage ratio based on the reported amounts is exactly equal to 2.0. If ABC's managers had not changed the estimated useful life of the property, plant, and equipment, the coverage ratio would have fallen below the required level.

EBIT, as reported	$1,200
Impact on depreciation expense of changed assumptions about useful life	150
EBIT, as adjusted	$1,050
Interest expense	$600
Coverage ratio, as reported	2.00
Coverage ratio, as adjusted	1.75

The potential disciplining mechanisms include the auditors, who will assess the reasonableness of the depreciable lives estimates. In addition, the lenders will carefully scrutinize the change in estimate because the company only barely achieved the minimum coverage ratio and would not have achieved the minimum without the change in accounting estimate.

Solution to 2: The desire to meet or exceed the average of analysts' forecasts for earnings per share might motivate DEF Co.'s managers to manipulate reported financial amounts. As illustrated in the following calculations, the impact of allocating a greater portion of revenue to hardware enabled the company to exceed analysts' earnings per share forecasts by $0.01.

Net income, as reported	$3,458,780
Impact on gross profit of changed revenue recognition, net of tax	27,000
Net income, as adjusted	$3,431,780
Weighted average number of shares	1,378,000
Earnings per share, as reported	$2.51
Earnings per share, as adjusted	$2.49

The potential disciplining mechanisms include the auditors, market regulators, financial analysts, and financial journalists.

4. DETECTION OF FINANCIAL REPORTING QUALITY ISSUES

Choices in the application of accounting standards abound, which is perhaps one reason why accounting literature and texts are so voluminous. Compounding the complexity, measurement often depends on estimates of economic phenomena. Two estimates might be justifiable, but they may have significantly different effects on the company's financial statements. As discussed earlier, the choice of a particular estimate may depend on the motivations of the reporting company's managers. With many choices available, and the inherent flexibility of estimates in the accounting process, managers have many tools for managing and meeting analysts' expectations through financial reporting.

An understanding of the choices that companies make in financial reporting is fundamental to evaluating the overall quality—both financial reporting and earnings quality—of the reports produced. Choices exist both in how information is presented (financial reporting quality) and in how financial results are calculated (earnings quality). Choices in presentation (financial reporting quality) may be fairly transparent to investors. Choices in the calculation of financial results (earnings quality), however, are more difficult to discern because they can be deeply embedded in the construction of reported financial results.

The availability of accounting choices enables managers to affect the reporting of financial results. Some choices increase performance and financial position in the reporting period (aggressive choices), and others increase them in later periods (conservative choices). A manager that wants to increase performance and financial position in the reporting period could:

- Recognize revenue prematurely;
- Use non-recurring transactions to increase profits;
- Defer expenses to later periods;
- Measure and report assets at higher values; and/or
- Measure and report liabilities at lower values.

A manager that wants to increase performance and financial position in a later period could:

- Defer current income to a later period (save income for a "rainy day"); and/or
- Recognize future expenses in a current period, setting the table for improving future performance.

The following sections describe some of the potential choices for how information is presented and how accounting elements [assets, liabilities, owners' equity, revenue and gains (income), and expenses and losses] are recognized, measured, and reported. In addition to choices within GAAP, companies may prepare fraudulent reports. For example, these reports may include non-existent revenue or assets. Section 4 concludes with some of the warning signs that can indicate poor-quality financial reports.

4.1. Presentation Choices

The technology boom of the 1990s and the internet bubble of the early 2000s featured companies, popular with investors, that often shared the same characteristic: They could not generate enough current earnings to justify their stock prices using the traditional price-to-earnings ratio (P/E) approaches to valuation. Many investors chose to explain these apparent anomalies by rationalizing that the old focus on profits and traditional valuation approaches no longer applied to such companies. Strange new metrics for determining operating performance emerged. Website operators spoke of the "eyeballs" they had captured in a quarter, or the "stickiness" of their websites for web surfers' visits. Various versions of "pro forma earnings"— that is, "non-GAAP earnings measures"—became a financial reporting staple of the era.

Many technology companies were accomplished practitioners of pro forma reporting, but they were not the first to use it. In the early 1990s, downsizing of large companies was a commonplace event, and massive restructuring charges obscured the operating performance at many established companies. For example, as it learned to cope in a world that embraced the personal computer rather than mainframe computing, International Business Machines (IBM) reported massive restructuring charges in 1991, 1992, and 1993: $3.7 billion, $11.6 billion, and $8.9 billion, respectively. IBM was not alone. Sears incurred $2.7 billion of restructuring charges in 1993, and AT&T reported restructuring charges of $7.7 billion in 1995. These events were not isolated; restructuring charges were a standard quarterly reporting event. To counter perceptions that their operations were floundering, and supposedly to assist investors in evaluating operating performance, companies often sanitized earnings releases by excluding restructuring charges in pro forma measures of financial performance.

Accounting principles for reporting business combinations also played a role in boosting the popularity of pro forma earnings. Before 2001, acquisitions of one company by another often resulted in goodwill amortization charges that made subsequent earnings reports look weak. Complicating matters, there were two accounting methods for recording acquisitions: pooling-of-interests and purchase methods. The now-extinct pooling-of-interests treatment was difficult for companies to achieve because of the many restrictive criteria for its use, but it was greatly desired because it did not result in goodwill amortization charges. In the technology boom period, acquisitions were common and many were reported as purchases, with consequential goodwill amortization dragging down earnings for as long as 40 years under the then-existing rules. Acquisitive companies reporting under purchase accounting standards perceived themselves to be at a reporting disadvantage compared with companies able to apply pooling-of-interests. They responded by presenting earnings adjusted for the exclusion of amortization of intangible assets and goodwill.

Because investors try to make intercompany comparisons on a consistent basis, earnings before interest, taxes, depreciation, and amortization has become an extremely popular performance measure. EBITDA is widely viewed as eliminating noisy reporting signals. That noise may be introduced by different accounting methods among companies for depreciation, amortization of intangible assets, and restructuring charges. Companies may construct and report their own version of EBITDA, sometimes referring to it as "adjusted EBITDA," by adding to the list of items to exclude from net income. Items that analysts might encounter include the following:

- Rental payments for operating leases, resulting in EBITDAR (earnings before interest, taxes, depreciation, amortization, and rentals);
- Equity-based compensation, usually justified on the grounds that it is a non-cash expense;
- Acquisition-related charges;
- Impairment charges for goodwill or other intangible assets;
- Impairment charges for long-lived assets;
- Litigation costs; and
- Loss/gain on debt extinguishments.

Among other incentives for the spread of non-GAAP earnings measures are loan covenants. Lenders may make demands on a borrowing company that require achieving and maintaining performance criteria that use GAAP net income as a starting point but arrive at a measure suitable to the lender. The company may use this measure as its preferred non-GAAP metric in earnings releases, and also when describing its liquidity or solvency situation in the management commentary (called management discussion and analysis in the United States).

As mentioned earlier, if a company uses a non-GAAP financial measure in an SEC filing, it must display the most directly comparable GAAP measure with equal prominence and provide a reconciliation between the two. Management must explain why it believes that the non-GAAP financial measure provides useful information regarding the company's financial condition and operations. Management must also disclose additional purposes, if material, for which it uses the non-GAAP financial measures.

Similarly, IFRS requires a definition and explanation of any non-IFRS measures included in financial reports, including why the measure is potentially relevant to users. Management must provide reconciliations of non-IFRS measures with IFRS measures. There is a concern that management may use non-GAAP measures to distract attention from GAAP measures.

The SEC intended that the definition of non-GAAP financial measures would capture all measures with the effect of depicting either:

- a measure of performance that differs from that presented in the financial statements, such as income or loss before taxes or net income or loss, as calculated in accordance with GAAP; or
- a measure of liquidity that differs from cash flow or cash flow from operations computed in accordance with GAAP.[19]

The SEC prohibits the exclusion of charges or liabilities requiring cash settlement from any non-GAAP liquidity measures, other than EBIT and EBITDA. Also prohibited is the calculation of a non-GAAP performance measure intended to eliminate or smooth items tagged as non-recurring, infrequent, or unusual when such items are very likely to occur again. The SEC views the period within two years of either before or after the reporting date as the relevant time frame for considering whether a charge or gain is a recurring item. Example 5 describes a case of misuse and misreporting of non-GAAP measures.

EXAMPLE 5   Misuse and Misreporting of Non-GAAP Measures

Groupon is an online discount merchant. In the company's initial S-1 registration statement in 2011, then-CEO Andrew Mason gave prospective investors an up-front warning in a section entitled "We don't measure ourselves in conventional ways," which described Groupon's adjusted consolidated segment operating income (adjusted CSOI) measure. Exhibit 12 provides excerpts from a section entitled "Non-GAAP Financial

---

[19] SEC, "Final Rule: Conditions for Use of Non-GAAP Financial Measures," Securities and Exchange Commission (www.sec.gov/rules/final/33-8176.htm).

Measures," which offered a more detailed explanation. Exhibit 13, also from the initial registration statement, shows a reconciliation of CSOI to the most comparable US GAAP measure. In its review, the SEC took the position that online marketing expenses were a recurring cost of business. Groupon responded that the marketing costs were similar to acquisition costs, not recurring costs, and that "we'll ramp down marketing just as fast as we ramped it up, reducing the customer acquisition part of our marketing expenses" as time passes.[20]

Eventually, and after much negative publicity, Groupon changed its non-GAAP measure. Exhibit 14 shows an excerpt from the final prospectus filed in November, after the SEC's review. Use the three exhibits to answer the questions that follow.

EXHIBIT 12   Groupon's "Non-GAAP Financial Measures"

Disclosures from June S-1 Filing

Adjusted CSOI is operating income of our two segments, North America and International, adjusted for online marketing expense, acquisition-related costs and stock-based compensation expense. Online marketing expense primarily represents the cost to acquire new subscribers and is dictated by the amount of growth we wish to pursue. Acquisition-related costs are non-recurring non-cash items related to certain of our acquisitions. Stock-based compensation expense is a non-cash item. We consider Adjusted CSOI to be an important measure of the performance of our business as it excludes expenses that are non-cash or otherwise not indicative of future operating expenses. We believe it is important to view Adjusted CSOI as a complement to our entire consolidated statements of operations.

Our use of Adjusted CSOI has limitations as an analytical tool, and you should not consider this measure in isolation or as a substitute for analysis of our results as reported under GAAP. Some of these limitations are:

- Adjusted CSOI does not reflect the significant cash investments that we currently are making to acquire new subscribers;
- Adjusted CSOI does not reflect the potentially dilutive impact of issuing equity-based compensation to our management team and employees or in connection with acquisitions;
- Adjusted CSOI does not reflect any interest expense or the cash requirements necessary to service interest or principal payments on any indebtedness that we may incur;
- Adjusted CSOI does not reflect any foreign exchange gains and losses;
- Adjusted CSOI does not reflect any tax payments that we might make, which would represent a reduction in cash available to us;
- Adjusted CSOI does not reflect changes in, or cash requirements for, our working capital needs; and
- Other companies, including companies in our industry, may calculate Adjusted CSOI differently or may use other financial measures to evaluate their profitability, which reduces the usefulness of it as a comparative measure.

---

[20] Correspondence between Groupon and SEC, filed in EDGAR on September 16, 2011.

Because of these limitations, Adjusted CSOI should not be considered as a measure of discretionary cash available to us to invest in the growth of our business. When evaluating our performance, you should consider Adjusted CSOI alongside other financial performance measures, including various cash flow metrics, net loss and our other GAAP results.

EXHIBIT 13   Groupon's "Adjusted CSOI"

Excerpt from June S-1 Filing
The following is a reconciliation of CSOI to the most comparable US GAAP measure, "loss from operations," for the years ended December 31, 2008, 2009, and 2010 and the three months ended March 31, 2010 and 2011:

	Year Ended December 31			Three Months Ended March 31	
(in $ thousands)	2008	2009	2010	2010	2011
(Loss) Income from operations	(1,632)	(1,077)	(420,344)	8,571	(117,148)
Adjustments:					
Online marketing	162	4,446	241,546	3,904	179,903
Stock-based compensation	24	115	36,168	116	18,864
Acquisition-related	—	—	203,183	—	—
Total adjustments	186	4,561	480,897	4,020	198,767
Adjusted CSOI	(1,446)	3,484	60,553	12,591	81,619

EXHIBIT 14   Groupon's "CSOI"

Excerpt from Revised S-1 Filing
The following is a reconciliation of CSOI to the most comparable US GAAP measure, "loss from operations," for the years ended December 31, 2008, 2009, and 2010 and the nine months ended September 30, 2010 and 2011:

	Year Ended December 31			Nine Months Ended September 30	
(in $ thousands)	2008	2009	2010	2010	2011
Loss from operations	(1,632)	(1,077)	(420,344)	(84,215)	(218,414)
Adjustments:					
Stock-based compensation	24	115	36,168	8,739	60,922
Acquisition-related	—	—	203,183	37,844	(4,793)
Total adjustments	24	115	239,351	46,583	56,129
CSOI	(1,608)	(962)	(180,993)	(37,632)	(162,285)

1. What cautions did Groupon include along with its description of the "Adjusted CSOI" metric?
2. Groupon excludes "online marketing" from "Adjusted CSOI." How does the exclusion of this expense compare with the SEC's limits on non-GAAP performance measures?

3. In the first quarter of 2011, what was the effect of excluding online marketing expenses on the calculation of "Adjusted CSOI"?

4. For 2010, how did results under the revised non-GAAP metric compare with the originally reported metric?

Solution to 1: Groupon cautioned that the "Adjusted CSOI" metric should not be considered in isolation, should not be considered as a substitute for analysis using GAAP results, and "should not be considered a measure of discretionary cash flow." The company lists numerous limitations, primarily citing items that adjusted CSOI did not reflect.

Solution to 2: The SEC specifies that non-GAAP measures should not eliminate items tagged as non-recurring, infrequent, or unusual when such items may be very likely to occur again. Because the online marketing expense occurred in every period reported and is likely to occur again, exclusion of this item appears contrary to SEC requirements.

Solution to 3: As shown in Exhibit 13, in the first quarter of 2011, the exclusion of the online marketing expense was enough to swing the company from a net loss under US GAAP reporting to a profit—at least, a profit as defined by adjusted CSOI. Using adjusted CSOI as a performance measure, the company showed results that were 35% higher for the first *quarter* of 2011 compared with the entire previous *year*.

Solution to 4: As shown in Exhibit 14, the revised metric is now called "CSOI" and no longer refers to "Adjusted CSOI." For 2010, results under the revised non-GAAP metric, which includes online marketing costs, shows a loss of $180,993,000 instead of a profit of $60,553,000.

In the case described in Example 5, Groupon changed its reporting and corrected the non-GAAP metric that the SEC had identified as misleading. In other cases, the SEC has pursued enforcement actions against companies for reporting misleading non-GAAP information. One such action was brought in 2009 against SafeNet Inc., where the SEC charged the company with improperly classifying ordinary operating expenses as non-recurring. This related to the integration of an acquired company and exclusion of the expenses from non-GAAP earnings in order to exceed earnings targets. A second action was brought by the SEC in 2017 against MDC Partners Inc. ("MDCA") for improper reconciliation of a non-GAAP measure and for improperly displaying the non-GAAP measure with greater prominence in its earnings releases. The case was brought after the company agreed to follow the rules but then failed to do so, as evidenced by the remark in the SEC's action: "Despite agreeing to comply with non-GAAP financial measure disclosure rules in December 2012 correspondence with the [SEC's] Division of Corporation Finance, MDCA continued to violate those rules for six quarters . . ." Exhibit 15 presents the headline and sub-headings for one of MDC Partners' earnings announcements that was the subject of the enforcement action.

EXHIBIT 15   MDC Partners Inc. Press Release [Excerpt]

SEC Form 8-K filed April 24, 2014

This excerpt shows the headline, sub-heads, and lead sentence of the company's press release announcing periodic earnings.

MDC PARTNERS INC. REPORTS RECORD RESULTS FOR THE THREE MONTHS ENDED MARCH 31, 2014

ORGANIC REVENUE GROWTH OF 8.3%, EBITDA GROWTH OF 18.1% AND 90 BASIS POINTS OF MARGIN IMPROVEMENT

FREE CASH FLOW GROWTH OF 34.0%

INCREASED 2014 GUIDANCE IMPLIES YEAR-OVER-YEAR EBITDA GROWTH OF +13.5% TO +16.1%, MARGIN IMPROVEMENT OF 60 TO 70 BASIS POINTS, AND FREE CASH FLOW GROWTH OF +15.8% TO +20.2%

FIRST QUARTER HIGHLIGHTS:

- Revenue increased to $292.6 million from $265.6 million, an increase of 10.1%
- Organic revenue increased 8.3%
- EBITDA increased to $36.4 million from $30.8 million, an increase of 18.1%
- EBITDA margin increased 90 basis points to 12.5% from 11.6%
- Free Cash Flow increased to $20.6 million from $15.4 million, an increase of 34.0%
- Net New Business wins totaled $24.4 million

NEW YORK, NY (April 24, 2014) – MDC Partners Inc. (NASDAQ: MDCA; TSX: MDZ.A) today announced financial results for the three months ended March 31, 2014.
. . .

In general, management may choose to construct non-GAAP financial measures not only to help investors better understand the company's performance but also to paint a more flattering picture of its performance. In some cases, management may attempt to present non-GAAP measures in a way that diverts attention from the standards-compliant financial information that it is required to present.

4.2. Accounting Choices and Estimates

Choices do not necessarily involve complex accounting standards. Something as simple as the shipping terms for goods delivered to customers can have a profound effect on the timing of revenue. On the last day of the first quarter, suppose a company ships $10,000 of goods to a customer on the terms "free on board (FOB) shipping point," arriving the next day. This shipping term means that the customer takes title to the goods, and bears the risk of loss, at the time the goods leave the seller's loading dock. Barring any issues with collectability of the receivable, or a likelihood of a return, the seller would be able to recognize revenue on the sale along with the associated profit. That revenue and profit would be recognized in the first quarter of the year. Change the point at which the goods' title transfers to the customer to "FOB destination" and the revenue pattern will be completely different. Under these terms, the title—and risk of loss—transfers to the customer when the goods arrive at their destination, which is the customer's address. The seller cannot recognize the sale and profit until the shipment arrives the following day, which is the start of a new accounting period.

A simple change in shipping terms can make the difference between revenue and profits in the reporting period or postponing them until the next period. Shipping terms can also influence management behavior. To "make the numbers," managers might push product out the door prematurely under FOB shipping point arrangements in order to reflect as much revenue as possible in the reporting period. Alternatively, in the case of an over-abundance of orders, the company could run the risk of exceeding analysts' consensus estimates by a large margin. Management might be uncomfortable with this situation because investors might extrapolate too much from one reporting period in which expectations were exceeded. Management might want to prevent investors from becoming too optimistic and, if possible, delay revenue recognition until the next quarter. This result could be accomplished by fulfilling customer orders by initiating delivery on the last day of the quarter, with shipping terms set as FOB destination. By doing so, title would transfer in the next accounting period. Another possibility in this scenario is that if the customers insisted on FOB shipping point terms, the selling company could simply delay shipment until after the close of the quarter.

This illustration also highlights a difficult distinction for investors to make. A company may use accounting as a tool to aggressively promote earnings growth—as in the example with the premature shipment of goods with FOB shipping point terms—but it may be aggressively managing the business flow by slacking off on shipping goods when business is "too good," as in the second example. In either case, a desired management outcome is obtained by a simple change in shipping terms. Yet, many investors might be inclined to say that the second example is a conservative kind of earnings management and accept it, even though it artificially masks the actual economic activity that occurred at the time.

4.2.1. How Accounting Choices and Estimates Affect Earnings and Balance Sheets
Assumptions about inventory cost flows provide another example of how accounting choices can affect financial reporting. Companies may assume that their purchases of inventory items are sold to customers on a first-in-first-out (FIFO) basis, with the result that the remaining inventory reflects the most recent costs. Alternatively, they may assume that their purchases of inventory items are sold to customers on a weighted-average cost basis. Example 6 makes the point that merely choosing a cost flow assumption can affect profitability.

EXAMPLE 6   Effect of Cost Flow Assumption

A company starts operations with no inventory at the beginning of a fiscal year and makes purchases of a good for resale five times during the period at increasing prices. Each purchase is for the same number of units of the good. The purchases, and the cost of goods available for sale, appear in the following table. Notice that the price per unit has increased by 140% by the end of the period.

	Units	Price	Cost
Purchase 1	5	$100	$500
Purchase 2	5	150	750
Purchase 3	5	180	900
Purchase 4	5	200	1,000
Purchase 5	5	240	1,200
Cost of goods available for sale			$4,350

During the period, the company sells, at $250 each, all of the goods purchased except for five of them. Although the ending inventory consists of five units, the cost attached to those units can vary greatly.

1. What are the ending inventory and cost of goods sold if the company uses the FIFO method of inventory costing?
2. What are the ending inventory and cost of goods sold if the company uses the weighted-average method of inventory costing?
3. Compare cost of goods sold and gross profit calculated under the two methods.

Solution to 1: The ending inventory and cost of goods sold if the company uses the FIFO method of inventory costing are $1,200 and $3,150.

Solution to 2: The ending inventory and cost of goods sold if the company uses the weighted-average method of inventory costing are $870 and $3,480.

Solution to 3: The following table shows how the choice of inventory costing methods—FIFO versus weighted average—affects the cost of goods sold and gross profit.

Cost Flow Assumption	FIFO	Weighted Average
Cost of goods available for sale	$4,350	$4,350
Ending inventory (5 units)	(1,200)	(870)
Cost of goods sold	$3,150	$3,480
Sales	$5,000	$5,000
Cost of goods sold	3,150	3,480
Gross profit	$1,850	$1,520
Gross profit margin	37.0%	30.4%

Note: Average inventory cost is calculated as Cost of goods available for sale/Units purchased = $4,350/25 = $174. There are five units in ending inventory, yielding an inventory value of $870.

Depending on which cost flow assumption the company uses, the end-of-period inventory is either $870 (under the weighted-average method) or $1,200 (under FIFO). The choice of method results in a difference of $330 in gross profit and 6.6% in gross profit margin.

The previous example is simplified and extreme for purposes of illustration clarity, but the point is important: Management's choice among acceptable inventory assumptions and methods affects profit. The selection of an inventory costing method is a policy decision, and companies cannot arbitrarily switch from one method to another. The selection does matter to profitability, however, and it also matters to the balance sheet.

In periods of changing prices, the FIFO cost assumption will provide a more current picture of ending inventory value, because the most recent purchases will remain in inventory. The balance sheet will be more relevant to investors. Under the weighted-average cost assumption, however, the balance sheet will display a blend of old and new costs. During inflationary periods, the value of the inventory will be understated: The company will not be able to replenish its inventory at the value shown. At the same time, the weighted-average inventory cost method ensures that the more current costs are shown in cost of sales, making the income statement more relevant than under the FIFO assumption. Trade-offs exist, and investors should be aware of how accounting choices affect financial reports. High-quality financial reporting provides users with sufficient information to assess the effects of accounting choices.

Estimates abound in financial reporting because of the use of accrual accounting, which attempts to show the effects of all economic events on a company during a particular period. Accrual accounting stands in contrast to cash basis accounting, which shows only the cash transactions conducted by a company. Although a high degree of certainty exists with reporting only cash transactions, much information is hidden. For instance, a company with growing revenues that makes the majority of its sales on credit would be understating its revenues for each period if it reported only cash transactions. On an accrual basis, revenues reflect all transactions that occurred, whether they transacted on a cash basis or credit-extended basis. Estimates enter the process because some facts related to events occurring in a particular period might not yet be known. Estimates can be well grounded in reality and applied to present a complete picture of the events affecting a company, or they can be management tools for achieving a desired financial picture.

To illustrate how estimates can affect financial reporting, consider sales made on credit. A company sells $1,000,000 of merchandise on credit and records the sale just before year end. Under accrual accounting, that amount is included in revenues and accounts receivable. The company's managers know from experience that they will never collect every dollar of the accounts receivable. Past experience is that, on average, only 97% of accounts receivable is collected. The company would estimate an amount of the uncollectible accounts at the time the sales occur and record an uncollectible accounts expense of $30,000, lowering earnings. The other side of the entry would be to establish an allowance for uncollectible accounts of $30,000. This allowance would be a contra asset account, presented as an offset to accounts receivable. The accounts receivable, net of the allowance for uncollectible accounts, would be stated at $970,000, which is the amount of cash the company ultimately expects to receive. If cash-basis accounting had been used, no revenues or accounts receivable would have been reported even though sales of merchandise had occurred. Accrual accounting, which contains estimates about future events, provides a much fuller picture of what transpired in the period than pure cash-basis accounting.

Yet, accrual accounting poses temptations to managers to manage the numbers, rather than to manage the business. Suppose a company's managers realize that the company will not meet analysts' consensus estimates in a particular quarter, and further, their bonus pay is dependent on reaching specified earnings targets. By offering special payment terms, or discounts, the managers may induce customers to take delivery of products that they would normally not order, so they could ship the products on FOB shipping point terms and recognize the revenues in the current quarter. They could even be so bold as to ship the goods under those terms even if the customer did not order them, in the hope that the customer would keep them or, at worst, return them in the next accounting period. Their aim would be to move the product off the company's property with FOB shipping point terms.

To further improve earnings in order to meet the consensus estimates, the company's managers might revise their estimate of the uncollectible accounts. The company's collection history shows a typical non-collection rate of 3% of sales, but the managers might rationalize the use of a 2% non-collection rate. This change will reduce the allowance for uncollectible accounts and the expense reported for the period. The managers might be able to justify the reduction on the grounds that the sales occurred in a part of the country that was experiencing an improved economic outlook, or that the company's collection history had been biased by the inclusion of a prolonged period of economic downturn. Whatever the justification, it would be hard to prove that the new estimate was completely right or wrong until time had passed. Because proof of the reliability of estimates is rarely available at the time the estimate is recorded, managers have a readily available means for manipulating earnings at their discretion.

ConAgra Foods Inc. provides an example of how the allowance for uncollectible accounts may be manipulated to manage earnings.[21] A subsidiary, called United Agri-Products (UAP), engaged in several improper accounting practices, one of them being the understatement of uncollectible accounts expense for several years. Exhibit 16 presents an excerpt from the SEC's Accounting and Auditing Enforcement Release.

EXHIBIT 16   SEC's Accounting and Auditing Enforcement Release Regarding United Agri-Products

---

. . . Generally, UAP's policy required that accounts which were past due between 90 days and one year should be reserved at 50%, and accounts over one year past due were to be reserved at 100%.

. . . In FY 1999 and continuing through FY 2000, UAP had substantial bad debt problems. In FY 2000, certain former UAP senior executives were informed that UAP needed to record an additional $50 million of bad debt expense. Certain former UAP senior executives were aware that in FY 1999 the size of the bad debt at certain IOCs had been substantial enough that it could have negatively impacted those IOC's ability to achieve PBT (profits before taxes) targets. In addition, just prior to the end of UAP's FY 2000, the former UAP COO (chief operating officer), in the presence of other UAP employees, ordered that UAP's bad debt reserve be reduced by $7 million in order to assist the Company in meeting its PBT target for the fiscal year.

. . . At the end of FY 2000, former UAP senior executives reported financial results to ConAgra which they knew, or were reckless in not knowing, overstated UAP's income before income taxes because UAP had failed to record sufficient bad debt expense. The misconduct with respect to bad debt expense caused ConAgra to overstate its reported income before income taxes by $7 million, or 1.13%, in FY 2000. At the Agricultural Products' segment level, the misconduct caused that segment's reported operating profit to be overstated by 5.05%.

Deferred-tax assets provide a similar example of choices in estimates affecting the earnings outcome. Deferred-tax assets may arise when a company reports a net operating loss under tax accounting rules. A company may record a deferred-tax asset based on the expectation that losses in the reporting period will offset expected future profits and reduce the company's future income tax liability. Accounting standards require that the deferred tax asset be reduced by a "valuation allowance" to account for the possibility that the company will be unable to generate enough profit to use all of the available tax benefits.[22]

Assume a company loses €1 billion in 2012, generating a net operating loss of the same amount for tax purposes. The company's income tax rate is 25%, and it will be able to apply the net operating loss to its taxable income for the next 10 years. The net operating loss results in a deferred tax asset with a nominal value of €250 million (25% × €1,000,000,000). Initial recognition would result in a deferred tax asset of €250 million and a credit to deferred tax expense of €250 million.

---

[21] Accounting and Auditing Enforcement Release No. 2542, "SEC v. James Charles Blue, Randy Cook, and Victor Campbell,) United States District Court for the District of Colorado, Civ. Action No. 07-CV-00095 REB-MEH (January 17, 2007).
[22] See Accounting Standards Codification 740-10-30-16 to 25, "Establishment of a Valuation Allowance for Deferred Tax Assets."

The company must address the question of whether or not the €250 million will ever be completely applied to future income. It may be experiencing increased competition and other circumstances that resulted in the €1 billion loss, and it may be unreasonable to assume it will have taxable income against which to apply the loss. In fact, the company's managers might believe it is reasonable to assume only that it will survive for five years, and with marginal profitability. The €250 million deferred tax asset is thus overstated if no valuation allowance is recorded to offset it.

The managers believe that only €100 million of the net operating losses will actually be applied to the company's taxable income. That belief implies that only €25 million of the tax benefits will ever be realized. The deferred tax assets reported on the balance sheet should not exceed this amount. The company should record a valuation allowance of €225 million, which would offset the deferred tax asset balance of €250 million, resulting in a net deferred tax asset balance of €25 million. There would also be a €225 million credit to the deferred tax provision. It is important to understand that the valuation allowance should be revised whenever facts and circumstances change.

The ultimate value of the deferred tax asset is driven by management's outlook for the future—and that outlook may be influenced by other factors. If the company needs to stay in compliance with debt covenants and needs every euro of value that can be justified by the outlook, its managers may take a more optimistic view of the future and keep the valuation allowance artificially low (in other words, the net deferred tax asset high).

PowerLinx Inc. provides an example of how over-optimism about the realizability of a deferred tax asset can lead to misstated financial reports. PowerLinx was a maker of security video cameras, underwater cameras, and accessories. Aside from fraudulently reporting 90% of its fiscal year 2000 revenue, PowerLinx had problems with valuation of its deferred tax assets. Exhibit 17 provides an excerpt from the SEC's Accounting and Auditing Enforcement Release with emphasis added.[23]

EXHIBIT 17   SEC's Accounting and Auditing Enforcement Release Regarding PowerLinx

PowerLinx improperly recorded on its fiscal year 2000 balance sheet a deferred tax asset of $1,439,322 without any valuation allowance. The tax asset was material, representing *almost forty percent of PowerLinx's total assets* of $3,841,944. PowerLinx also recorded deferred tax assets of $180,613, $72,907, and $44,921, respectively, in its financial statements for the first three quarters of 2000.

PowerLinx did not have a proper basis for recording the deferred tax assets. The company had accumulated significant losses in 2000 and had no historical operating basis from which to conclude that it would be profitable in future years. Underwater camera sales had declined significantly and the company had devoted most of its resources to developing its SecureView product. The sole basis for PowerLinx's "expectation" of future profitability was the purported $9 million backlog of SecureView orders, which management assumed would generate taxable income; however, this purported backlog, which predated Bauer's hiring, did not reflect actual demand for SecureView cameras and, consequently, was not a reasonable or reliable indicator of future profitability.

Another example of misstated financial results caused by improper reflection of the realizability of a deferred tax asset occurred with Hampton Roads Bankshares Inc. ("HRBS"), a commercial bank with deteriorating loan portfolio quality and commensurate losses in the years following the financial crisis. The company reported a deferred tax asset related to its loan

(continued)

---

[23] Accounting and Auditing Enforcement Release No. 2448, "In the Matter of Douglas R. Bauer, Respondent," SEC (27 June 2006): www.sec.gov/litigation/admin/2006/34-54049.pdf.

EXHIBIT 17   (Continued)

losses; however, it did not establish a valuation allowance against its deferred tax asset. This decision was based on dubious projections indicating that the company would earn the necessary future taxable income "to fully utilize the [deferred tax asset] DTA over the applicable carry-forward period."[24] Over time, it became clear that the earnings projections were not realistic, and ultimately the company restated its financial results to include a valuation allowance against almost the entire deferred tax asset. Exhibit 18 presents an excerpt from the company's amended Form 10-Q/A containing the restatement.

EXHIBIT 18   Hampton Roads Bankshares, Inc. Form 10-Q/A filed August 13, 2010 [Excerpt from footnotes]

NOTE B – RESTATEMENT OF CONSOLIDATED FINANCIAL STATEMENTS

Subsequent to filing the Company's annual report on Form 10-K for the year ended December 31, 2009 and its Form 10-Q for the three months ended March 31, 2010 the Company determined that a valuation allowance on its deferred tax assets should be recognized as of December 31, 2009. The Company decided to establish a valuation allowance against the deferred tax asset because it is uncertain when it will realize this asset.

Accordingly, the December 31, 2009 consolidated balance sheet and the March 31, 2010 consolidated financial statements have been restated to account for this determination. The effect of this change in the consolidated financial statements was as follows (in thousands, except per share amounts).

Consolidated Balance Sheet at March 31, 2010

	As Reported	Adjustment	As Restated
Deferred tax assets, net	$70,323	$(70,323)	—
Total assets	3,016,470	(70,323)	$2,946,147
Retained earnings deficit	(158,621)	(70,323)	(228,944)
Total shareholder's equity	156,509	(70,323)	86,186
Total Liabilities and shareholders' equity	3,016,470	(70,323)	2,946,147

Consolidated Balance Sheet at December 31, 2009

	As Reported	Adjustment	As Restated
Deferred tax assets, net	$56,380	$(55,983)	$397
Total assets	2,975,559	(55,983)	2,919,576
Retained earnings deficit	(132,465)	(55,983)	(188,488)
Total shareholder's equity	180,996	(55,983)	125,013
Total Liabilities and shareholders' equity	2,975,559	(55,983)	2,919,576

Another example of how choices and estimates can affect reported results lies in the selection of a depreciation method for allocating the cost of long-lived assets to accounting periods subsequent to their acquisition. A company's managers may choose to depreciate long-lived

---

[24] Accounting and Auditing Enforcement Release No. 3600, "In the Matter of Hampton Roads Bankshares Inc., Respondent," SEC (December 5, 2014) https://www.sec.gov/litigation/admin/2014/34-73750.pdf.

assets (1) on a straight-line basis, with each year bearing the same amount of depreciation expense; (2) using an accelerated method, with greater depreciation expense recognition in the earlier part of an asset's life; or (3) using an activity-based depreciation method, which allocates depreciation expense based on units of use or production. Depreciation expense is affected by another set of choices and estimates regarding the salvage value of the assets being depreciated. A salvage value of zero will always increase depreciation expense under any method compared with the choice of a non-zero salvage value.

Assume a company invests $1,000,000 in manufacturing equipment and expects it to have a useful economic life of 10 years. During its expected life, the equipment will produce 400,000 units of product, or $2.50 depreciation expense per unit produced. When it is disposed of at the end of its expected life, the company's managers expect to realize no value for the equipment. The following table shows the differences in the three alternative methods of depreciation: straight-line, accelerated on a double-declining balance basis, and units-of-production method, with no salvage value assumed at the end of the equipment's life.

Year	Straight-Line Method Depreciation Expense	Double-Declining Balance Method			Units-of-Production Method		
		Balance	Declining Balance Rate[1]	Depreciation Expense	Units Produced	Depreciation Rate/Unit	Depreciation Expense
1	$100,000	$1,000,000	20%	$200,000	90,000	$2.50	$225,000
2	100,000	800,000	20%	160,000	80,000	$2.50	200,000
3	100,000	640,000	20%	128,000	70,000	$2.50	175,000
4	100,000	512,000	20%	102,400	60,000	$2.50	150,000
5	100,000	409,600	20%	81,920	50,000	$2.50	125,000
6	100,000	327,680	20%	65,536	10,000	$2.50	25,000
7	100,000	262,144	20%	52,429	10,000	$2.50	25,000
8	100,000	209,715	20%	41,943	10,000	$2.50	25,000
9	100,000	167,772	20%	33,554	10,000	$2.50	25,000
10	100,000	134,218	20%	26,844	10,000	$2.50	25,000
Total	$1,000,000			$892,626	400,000		$1,000,000

[1]Declining balance rate of 20% calculated as 10-year life being equivalent to 10% annual depreciation rate, multiplied by 2 = 20%.

The straight-line method allocates the cost of the equipment evenly to all 10 years of the equipment's life. The double-declining balance method will have a higher allocation of cost to the earlier years of the equipment's life. As its name implies, the depreciation expense will decline in each succeeding year because it is based on a fixed rate applied to a declining balance. The rate used was double the straight-line rate, but it could have been any other rate that the company's managers believed was representative of the way the actual equipment depreciation occurred. Notice that the double-declining balance method also results in an incomplete depreciation of the machine at the end of 10 years; a balance of $107,374 (= $1,000,000 − $892,626) remains at the end of the expected life, which will result in a loss upon the retirement of the equipment if the company's expectation of zero salvage value turns out to be correct. Some companies may choose to depreciate the equipment to its expected salvage, zero in this case, in its final year of use. Some companies may use a policy of switching to straight-line depreciation after the mid-life of its depreciable assets in order to fully depreciate them. That particular pattern is coincidentally displayed in the units-of-production example, in which the equipment is used most heavily in the earliest part of its useful life, and then levels off to much less utilization in the second half of the expected life.

Exhibit 19 shows the different expense allocation patterns of the methods over the same life. Each will affect earnings differently.

EXHIBIT 19   Expense Allocation Patterns of Different Depreciation Methods

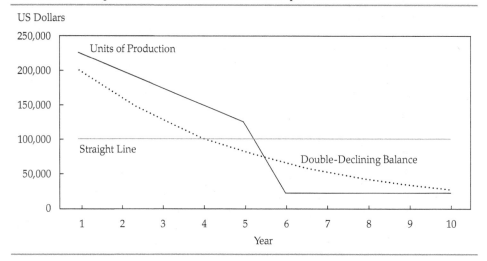

The company's managers could justify any of these methods. Each might fairly represent the way the equipment will be consumed over its expected economic life, which is a subjective estimate itself. The choices of methods and lives can profoundly affect reported income. These choices are not proven right or wrong until far into the future—but managers must estimate their effects in the present.

Exhibit 20 shows the effects of the three different methods on operating profit and operating profit margins, assuming that the production output of the equipment generates revenues of $500,000 each year and $200,000 of cash operating expenses are incurred, leaving $300,000 of operating profit before depreciation expense.

EXHIBIT 20   Effects of Depreciation Methods on Operating Profit

	Straight Line		
Year	Depreciation	Operating Profit	Operating Profit Margin
1	$100,000	$200,000	40.0%
2	100,000	200,000	40.0%
3	100,000	200,000	40.0%
4	100,000	200,000	40.0%
5	100,000	200,000	40.0%
6	100,000	200,000	40.0%
7	100,000	200,000	40.0%
8	100,000	200,000	40.0%
9	100,000	200,000	40.0%
10	100,000	200,000	40.0%

EXHIBIT 20   (Continued)

| Year | Double Declining Balance | | |
	Depreciation	Operating Profit	Operating Profit Margin
1	$200,000	$100,000	20.0%
2	160,000	140,000	28.0%
3	128,000	172,000	34.4%
4	102,400	197,600	39.5%
5	81,920	218,080	43.6%
6	65,536	234,464	46.9%
7	52,429	247,571	49.5%
8	41,943	258,057	51.6%
9	33,554	266,446	53.3%
10	134,218*	165,782	33.2%

| Year | Units of Production | | |
	Depreciation	Operating Profit	Operating Profit Margin
1	$225,000	$75,000	15.0%
2	200,000	100,000	20.0%
3	175,000	125,000	25.0%
4	150,000	150,000	30.0%
5	125,000	175,000	35.0%
6	25,000	275,000	55.0%
7	25,000	275,000	55.0%
8	25,000	275,000	55.0%
9	25,000	275,000	55.0%
10	25,000	275,000	55.0%

*Includes $107,374 of undepreciated basis, treated as depreciation expense in final year of service.

The straight-line method shows consistent operating profit margins, and the other two methods show varying degrees of increasing operating profit margins as the depreciation expense decreases over time.

The example above shows the differences among alternative methods, but even more depreciation expense variation is possible by changing estimated lives and assumptions about salvage value. For instance, change the expected life assumption to 5 years from 10 and add an expectation that the equipment will have a 10% salvage value at the end of its expected life. Exhibit 21 shows the revised depreciation calculations. Notice that under the double-declining balance method, the depreciation rate is applied to the gross cost, unlike the other two methods. The straight-line method and the units-of-production method subtract the salvage value from the cost before depreciation expense is calculated. Also note that the assumption about the usage of the equipment is revised so that it is depreciated only to its salvage value of $100,000 by the end of its estimated life. The total depreciation under each method is $900,000.

EXHIBIT 21   Depreciation Calculations for Each Method in Changed Scenario

	Straight-Line Method	Double-Declining Balance Method			Units-of-Production Method		
Year	Depreciation Expense	Balance	Declining Balance Rate[1]	Depreciation Expense	Units Produced	Depreciation Rate/Unit	Depreciation Expense
1	$180,000	$1,000,000	40%	$400,000	100,000	$2.25	$225,000
2	180,000	600,000	40%	240,000	90,000	$2.25	202,500
3	180,000	360,000	40%	144,000	80,000	$2.25	180,000
4	180,000	216,000	40%	86,400	70,000	$2.25	157,500
5	180,000	129,600	40%	29,600[2]	60,000	$2.25	135,000
Total	$900,000			$900,000	400,000		$900,000

[1] Declining balance rate of 40% calculated as 5-year life being equivalent to 20% annual depreciation rate, multiplied by 2 = 40%.
[2] Depreciation calculated as $29,600 instead of 40% × $129,600. Rote application of the declining-balance rate would have resulted in $51,840 of expense, which would have depreciated the asset below salvage value.

Exhibit 22 shows the different expense allocation patterns of the methods over the five-year expected life, and assuming a 10% salvage value. Although each method is distinctly different in the timing of the cost allocation over time, the variation is less pronounced than over the longer life used in the previous example.

EXHIBIT 22   Expense Allocation Patterns of Depreciation Methods in Changed Scenario

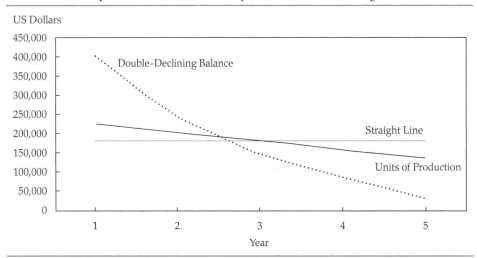

One of the clearest examples of how choices affect both the balance sheet and income statement can be found in capitalization practices. In classifying a payment made, management must determine whether the payment will benefit only the current period—making it an expense—or whether it will benefit future periods, leading to classification as a cost to be capitalized as an asset. This management judgment embodies an implicit forecast of how the item acquired by the payment will be used, or not used, in the future.

That judgment can be biased by the powerful effect a capitalization policy can have on earnings. Every amount capitalized on the balance sheet as a building, an item of inventory, a deferred cost, or any "other asset" is an amount that does not get recognized as an expense in the reporting period.

A real-life example can be found in the case of WorldCom Inc., a telecom concern that grew rapidly in the late 1990s. Much of WorldCom's financial reporting was eventually found to be fraudulent. An important part of the misreporting centered on its treatment of what is known in the telecom industry as "line costs." These are the costs of carrying a voice call or data transmission from its starting point to its ending point, and they represented WorldCom's largest expense. WorldCom's chief financial officer decided to capitalize such costs instead of treating them as an operating expense. As a consequence, from the second quarter of 1999 through the first quarter of 2002, WorldCom increased its operating income by $7 billion. In three of the five quarters in which the improper line cost capitalization took place, WorldCom would have recognized pre-tax losses instead of profits.[25]

Similarly, acquisitions are an area in which managers must exercise judgment. An allocation of the purchase price must be made to all of the different assets acquired based on their fair values, and those fair values are not always objectively verifiable. Management may have to make its own estimate of fair values for assets acquired, and it may be biased towards a low estimate for the values of depreciable assets in order to depress future depreciation expense. Another benefit to keeping depreciable asset values low is that the amount of the purchase price that cannot be allocated to specific assets is classified as goodwill, which is neither depreciated nor amortized in future reporting periods.

Goodwill reporting has choices of its own. Although goodwill has no effect on future earnings when unimpaired, annual testing of its fair value may reveal that the excess of price paid over the fair value of assets may not be recoverable, which should lead to a write-down of goodwill. The estimation process for the fair value of goodwill may depend heavily on projections of future performance. Those projections may be biased upward in order to avoid a goodwill write-down.

4.2.2. How Choices Affect the Cash Flow Statement

The cash flow statement consists of three sections: the operating section, which shows the cash generated or used by operations; the investing section, which shows cash used for investments or provided by their disposal; and the financing section, which shows transactions attributable to financing activities.

The operating section is closely scrutinized by investors. Many of them consider it a reality check on reported earnings, on the grounds that earnings attributable to accrual accounting only and unsupported by actual cash flows may indicate earnings manipulation. Such investors believe that amounts shown for cash generated by operations is more insulated from managerial manipulation than the income statement. Cash generated by operations can be managed to an extent, however.

The operating section of the cash flow statement can be shown either under the direct method or the indirect method. Under the direct method, "entities are encouraged to report

---

[25] See Report of Investigation by the Special Investigative Committee of the Board of Directors of World-Com, Inc., by Dennis R. Beresford, Nicholas deB. Katzenbach, & C.B. Rogers, Jr.PP 9-11: www.sec.gov/Archives/edgar/data/723527/000093176303001862/dex991.htm.

major classes of gross cash receipts and gross cash payments and their arithmetic sum—the net cash flow from operating activities."[26] In practice, companies rarely use the direct method. Instead, they use the indirect method, which shows a reconciliation of net income to cash provided by operations. The reconciliation shows the non-cash items affecting net income along with changes in working capital accounts affecting cash from operations. Exhibit 23 provides an example of the indirect presentation method.

EXHIBIT 23   Indirect Presentation Method

Cash Flows from Operating Activities ($ millions)	2018
Net income	$3,000
Adjustments to reconcile net income to net cash provided by operating activities:	
Provision for doubtful receivables	10
Provision for depreciation and amortization	1,000
Goodwill impairment charges	35
Share-based compensation expense	100
Provision for deferred income taxes	200
Changes in assets and liabilities:	
Trade, notes, and financing receivables related to sales	(2,000)
Inventories	(1,500)
Accounts payable	1,200
Accrued income taxes payable/receivable	(80)
Retirement benefits	90
Other	(250)
Net cash provided by operating activities	$1,805

Whether the indirect method or direct method is used, simple choices exist for managers to improve the *appearance* of cash flow provided by operations without actually improving it. One such choice is in the area of accounts payable management, shaded in Exhibit 23. Assume that the accounts payable balance is $5,200 million at the end of the period, an increase of $1,200 million from its previous year-end balance of $4,000 million. The $1,200 million increase in accounts payable matched increased expenses and/or assets but did not require cash. If the company's managers had further delayed paying creditors $500 million until the day *after* the balance sheet date, they could have increased the cash provided by operating activities by $500 million. If the managers believe that cash generated from operations is a metric of focus for investors, they can impress them with artificially strong cash flow by simply stretching the accounts payable credit period.

What might alert investors to such machinations? They need to examine the composition of the operations section of the cash flow statement—if they do not, then *nothing* will ever alert them. Studying changes in the working capital can reveal unusual patterns that may indicate manipulation of the cash provided by operations.

Another practice that might lead an investor to question the quality of cash provided by operations is to compare a company's cash generation with an industry-wide level or with the cash operating performance of one or more similar competitors. Cash generation performance

---

[26] Accounting Standards Codification Section 230-10-45-25, "Reporting Operating, Investing, and Financing Activities." The direct method and indirect method are similar in IFRS, as addressed in IAS 7, Paragraph 18.

can be measured several ways. One way is to compare the relationship between cash generated by operations and net income. Cash generated by operations in excess of net income signifies better quality of earnings, whereas a chronic excess of net income over cash generated by operations should be a cause for concern; it may signal the use of accounting methods to simply raise net income instead of depicting financial reality. Another way to measure cash generation performance is to compare cash generated by operations with debt service, capital expenditures, and dividends (if any). When there is a wide variance between the company's cash generation performance and that of its benchmarks, investors should seek an explanation and carefully examine the changes in working capital accounts.

Because investors may focus on cash from operations as an important metric, managers may resort to managing the working capital accounts as described in order to present the most favorable picture. But there are other ways to do this. A company may misclassify operating uses of cash into either the investing or financing sections of the cash flow statement, which enhances the appearance of cash generated by operating activities.

Dynegy Inc. provides an example of manipulation of cash from operations through clever construction of contracts and assistance from an unconsolidated special purpose entity named ABG Gas Supply LLC (ABG). In April 2001, Dynegy entered into a contract for the purchase of natural gas from ABG. According to the contract, Dynegy would purchase gas at *below-market* rates from ABG for nine months and sell it at the current market rate. The nine-month term coincided with Dynegy's 2001 year-end and would result in gains backed by cash flows. Dynegy also agreed to buy gas at *above-market* rates from ABG for the following 51 months and sell it at the current market rate. The contract was reported at its fair value at the end of fiscal year 2001. It had no effect on net income for the year. The earlier portion of the contract resulted in a gain, supported by $300 million of cash flow, but the latter portion of the contract resulted in non-cash losses that offset the profit. The mark-to-market rules required the recognition of both gains and losses from all parts of the contract, and hence the net effect on earnings was zero.

In April 2002, a *Wall Street Journal* article exposed the chicanery, thanks to leaked documents. The SEC required Dynegy to restate the cash flow statement by reclassifying $300 million from the operating section of the cash flow statement to the financing section, on the grounds that Dynegy had used ABG as a conduit to effectively borrow $300 million from Citigroup. The bank had extended credit to ABG, which it used to finance its losses on the contract (Lee, 2012).

Another area of flexibility in cash flow reporting is found in the area of interest capitalization, which creates differences between total interest payments and total interest costs.[27] Assume a company incurs total interest cost of $30,000, composed of $3,000 of discount amortization and $27,000 of interest payments. Of the $30,000, two-thirds of it ($20,000) is expensed; the remaining third ($10,000) is capitalized as plant assets. If the company uses the same interest expense/capitalization proportions to allocate the interest payments between operating and investing activities, then it will report $18,000 (2/3 × $27,000) as an operating outflow and $9,000 (1/3 × $27,000) as an investing outflow. The company might also choose to offset the entire $3,000 of non-cash discount amortization against the $20,000 treated as expense, resulting in an operating outflow as low as $17,000, or as much as $20,000 if it allocated all of the non-cash discount amortization to interest capitalized as investing activities. Similarly, the investing outflow could be as much as $10,000 or as little as $7,000, depending on the treatment of the non-cash discount amortization. There are choices within the choices,

---

[27] See Nurnberg and Largay (1998) and Nurnberg (2006).

all in areas where investors believe choices do not even exist. Nurnberg and Largay (1998) note that companies apparently favor the method that reports the lowest operating outflow, presumably to maximize reported cash from operations.

Investors and analysts need to be aware that presentation choices permitted in IAS 7, "Statement of Cash Flows," offer flexibility in classification of certain items in the cash flow statement. This flexibility can drastically change the results in the operating section of the cash flow statement. An excerpt from IAS 7, Paragraphs 33 and 34, provides the background:

> 33. Interest paid and interest and dividends received are usually classified as operating cash flows for a financial institution. However, there is no consensus on the classification of these cash flows for other entities. Interest paid and interest and dividends received may be classified as operating cash flows because they enter into the determination of profit or loss. *Alternatively, interest paid and interest and dividends received may be classified as financing cash flows and investing cash flows respectively, because they are costs of obtaining financial resources or returns on investments.*
>
> 34. Dividends paid may be classified as a financing cash flow because they are a cost of obtaining financial resources. *Alternatively, dividends paid may be classified as a component of cash flows from operating activities in order to assist users to determine the ability of an entity to pay dividends out of operating cash flows.* [Emphasis added.]

By allowing a choice of operating or financing for the placement of interest and dividends received or paid, IAS 7 gives a company's managers the opportunities to select the presentation that gives the best-looking picture of operating performance. An example is Norse Energy Corp. ASA, a Norwegian gas explorer and producer, which changed its classifications of interest paid and interest received in 2007 (Gordon, Henry, Jorgensen, and Linthicum, 2017). Interest paid was switched to financing instead of decreasing cash generated from operations. Norse Energy also switched its classification of interest received to investing from operating cash flow. The net effect of these changes was to report positive, rather than negative, operating cash flows in both 2007 and 2008. With these simple changes, the company could also change the perception of its operations. The cash flow statement formerly presented the appearance of a company with operations that used more cash than it generated, and it possibly raised questions about the sustainability of operations. After the revision, the operating section of the cash flow statement depicted a much more viable operation.

Exhibit 24 shows the net effect of the reclassifications on Norse Energy's cash flows.

EXHIBIT 24   Reclassification of Cash Flows (amounts in $ millions)

	As Reported (following 2007 reclassification)		Adjustments (if no reclassification)*		Pro-forma (if no reclassification)	
	2008	2007	2008	2007	2008	2007
Operating	**$5.30**	**$2.80**	**($13.70)**	**($14.40)**	**($8.40)**	**($11.60)**
Investing	$0.90	($56.80)	($9.00)	($3.50)	($8.10)	($60.30)
Financing	($16.60)	$34.50	$22.70	$17.90	$6.10	$52.40
Total	($10.40)	($19.50)	$0	$0	($10.40)	($19.50)

*The adjustments reverse the addition of interest received to investing and instead add it to operating. The adjustments also reverse the deduction of interest paid from financing and instead subtract it from operating.

4.2.3. Choices That Affect Financial Reporting

Exhibit 25 summarizes some of the areas where choices can be made that affect financial reports.

EXHIBIT 25   Areas Where Choices and Estimates Affect Financial Reporting

Area of Choice/ Estimate	Analyst Concerns
Revenue recognition	• How is revenue recognized: upon shipment or upon delivery of goods? • Is the company engaging in "channel stuffing"—the practice of overloading a distribution channel with more product than it is normally capable of selling? This can be accomplished by inducing customers to buy more through unusual discounts, the threat of near-term price increases, or both—or simply by shipping goods that were not ordered. These transactions may be corrected in a subsequent period and may result in restated results. Are accounts receivable relative to revenues abnormally high relative to the company's history or to its peers? If so, channel stuffing may have occurred. • Is there unusual activity in the allowance for sales returns relative to past history? • Does the company's days sales outstanding show any collection issues that might indicate shipment of unneeded or unwanted goods to customers? • Does the company engage in "bill-and-hold" transactions? This is when a customer purchases goods but requests that they remain with the seller until a later date. This kind of transaction makes it possible for a seller to manufacture fictitious sales by declaring end-of-period inventory as "sold but held," with a minimum of effort and phony documentation. • Does the company use rebates as part of its marketing approach? If so, how significantly do the estimates of rebate fulfillment affect net revenues, and have any unusual breaks with history occurred? • Does the company separate its revenue arrangements into multiple deliverables of goods or services? This area is one of great revenue recognition flexibility, and also one that provides little visibility to investors. They simply cannot examine a company's arrangements and decide for themselves whether revenue has been properly allocated to different components of a contract. If a company uses multiple deliverable arrangements with its customers as a routine matter, investors might be more sensitive to revenue reporting risks. In seeking a comfort level, they might ask the following questions: Does the company explain adequately how it determines the different allocations of deliverables and how revenue is recognized on each one? Do deferred revenues result? If not, does it seem reasonable that there are no deferred revenues for this kind of arrangement? Are there unusual trends in revenues and receivables, particularly with regard to cash conversion? If an investor is not satisfied with the answers to these questions, he or she might be more comfortable with other investment choices.
Long-lived assets: Depreciation policies	• Do the estimated life spans of the associated assets make sense, or are they unusually low compared with others in the same industry? • Have there been changes in depreciable lives that have a positive effect on current earnings? • Do recent asset write-downs indicate that company policy on asset lives might need to be reconsidered?

(continued)

EXHIBIT 25   (Continued)

Area of Choice/ Estimate	Analyst Concerns
Intangibles: Capitalization policies	• Does the company capitalize expenditures related to intangibles, such as software? Does its balance sheet show any R&D capitalized as a result of acquisitions? Or, if the company is an IFRS filer, has it capitalized any internally generated development costs? • How do the company's capitalization policies compare with the competition? • Are amortization policies reasonable?
Allowance for doubtful accounts/loan loss reserves	• Are additions to such allowances lower or higher than in the past? • Does the collection experience justify any difference from historical provisioning? • Is there a possibility that any lowering of the allowance may be the result of industry difficulties along with the difficulty of meeting earnings expectations?
Inventory cost methods	• Does the company use a costing method that produces fair reporting results in view of its environment? How do its inventory methods compare with others in its industry? Are there differences that will make comparisons uneven if there are unusual changes in inflation? • Does the company use reserves for obsolescence in its inventory valuation? If so, are they subject to unusual fluctuations that might indicate adjusting them to arrive at a specified earnings result? • If a company reports under US GAAP and uses last-in-first-out (LIFO) inventory accounting, does LIFO liquidation (the assumed sale of old, lower-cost layers of inventory) occur through inventory reduction programs? This inventory reduction may generate earnings without supporting cash flow, and management may intentionally reduce the layers to produce specific earnings benefits.
Tax asset valuation accounts	• Tax assets, if present, must be stated at the value at which management expects to realize them, and an allowance must be set up to restate tax assets to the level expected to eventually be converted into cash. Determining the allowance involves an estimate of future operations and tax payments. Does the amount of the valuation allowance seem reasonable, overly optimistic, or overly pessimistic? • Are there contradictions between the management commentary and the allowance level, or the tax note and the allowance level? There cannot be an optimistic management commentary and a fully reserved tax asset, or vice versa. One of them has to be wrong. • Look for changes in the tax asset valuation account. It may be 100% reserved at first, and then "optimism" increases whenever an earnings boost is needed. Lowering the reserve decreases tax expense and increases net income.
Goodwill	• Companies must annually assess goodwill balances for impairment on a qualitative basis. If further testing appears necessary, it is based on estimates of the fair value of the reporting units (US GAAP issuers), or cash-generating units (IFRS issuers), associated with goodwill balances. The tests are based on subjective estimates, including future cash flows and the employment of discount rates. • Do the disclosures on goodwill testing suggest that the exercise was skewed to avoid impairment charges?

EXHIBIT 25   (Continued)

Area of Choice/ Estimate	Analyst Concerns
Warranty reserves	• Have additions to the reserves been reduced, perhaps to make earnings targets? Examine the trend in the charges of actual costs against the reserves: Do they support or contradict the warranty provisioning activity? Do the actual costs charged against the reserve give the analyst any indication about the quality of the products sold?
Related-party transactions	• Is the company engaged in transactions that disproportionately benefit members of management? Does one company have control over another's destiny through supply contracts or other dealings? • Do extensive dealings take place with *non-public* companies that are under management control? If so, those companies could absorb losses (through supply arrangements that are unfavorable to them, for example) in order to make the public company's performance look good. This scenario may provide opportunities for an owner to cash out.

The most important lesson is that choices exist among accounting methods and estimates, and an analyst needs a working knowledge of them in order to understand whether management may have made choices to achieve a desired result.

4.3. Warning Signs

The choices management makes to achieve desired results leave a trail, like tracks in sand or snow. The evidence, or warning signs, of information manipulation in financial reports is directly linked to the basic means of manipulation: biased revenue recognition and biased expense recognition. The bias may relate to timing and/or location of recognition. An example of the timing issue is that a company may choose to defer expenses by capitalizing them. Regarding location, it may recognize a loss in other comprehensive income or directly through equity, rather than through the profit and loss statement. The alert investor or analyst should do the following to find warning signs.

1) Pay attention to revenue.   The single largest number on the income statement is revenue, and revenue recognition is a recurring source of accounting manipulation and even outright fraud. Answering the question, "Is revenue higher or lower than the previous comparable period?" is not sufficient. Many analytical procedures can be routinely performed to identify warning signals of malfeasance:

• *Examine the accounting policies note for a company's revenue recognition policies.*
  • Consider whether the policies make it easier to prematurely recognize revenue, such as recognizing revenue immediately upon shipment of goods, or if the company uses bill-and-hold arrangements whereby a sale is recognized before goods are actually shipped to the customer.
  • Barter transactions may exist, which can be difficult to value properly.
  • Rebate programs involve many estimates, including forecasts of the amount of rebates that will ultimately be incurred, which can have significant effects on revenue recognition.

- Multiple-deliverable arrangements of goods and services are common, but clarity about the timing of revenue recognition for each item or service delivered is necessary for the investor to be comfortable with the reporting of revenues.

Although none of these decisions necessarily violates accounting standards, each involves significant judgement and warrants close attention if other warning signs are present.

- *Look at revenue relationships.* Compare a company's revenue growth with its primary competitors or its industry peer group.
  - If a company's revenue growth is out of line with its competitors, its industry, or the economy, the investor or analyst needs to understand the reasons for the outperformance. It may be a result of superior management or products and services, but not all management is superior, nor are the products and services of their companies. Revenue quality might be suspect, and the investor should take additional analytical steps.
  - Compare accounts receivable with revenues over several years.
    - Examine the trend to determine whether receivables are increasing as a percentage of total revenues. If so, a company might be engaging in channel-stuffing activities, or worse, recording fictitious sales transactions.
    - Calculate receivables turnover for several years:
      - Examine the trend for unusual changes and seek an explanation if they exist.
      - Compare a company's days sales outstanding (DSO) or receivables turnover with that of relevant competitors or an industry peer group and determine whether the company is an outlier.

An increase in DSO or decrease in receivables turnover could suggest that some revenues are recorded prematurely or are even fictitious, or that the allowance for doubtful accounts is insufficient.

  - Examine asset turnover. If a company's managers make poor asset allocation choices, revenues may not be sufficient to justify the investment. Be particularly alert when asset allocation choices involve acquisitions of entire companies. If post-acquisition revenue generation is weak, managers might reach for revenue growth anywhere it can be found. That reach for growth might result in accounting abuses.

    Revenues, divided by total assets, indicate the productivity of assets in generating revenues. If the company's asset turnover is continually declining, or lagging the asset turnover of competitors or the industry, it may portend future asset write-downs, particularly in the goodwill balances of acquisitive companies.

2) Pay attention to signals from inventories.   Although inventory is not a component of every company's asset base, its presence creates an opportunity for accounting manipulation.

- *Look at inventory relationships.* Because revenues involve items sold from inventory, the kind of examination an investor should perform on inventory is similar to that for revenues.
  - Compare growth in inventories with competitors and industry benchmarks. If a company's inventory growth is out of line with its peers, without any concurrent sales growth, then it may be simply the result of poor inventory management—an operational inefficiency that might affect an investor's view of a company. It may also signal obsolescence problems in the company's inventory that have not yet been recognized through markdowns to the inventory's net realizable value. Reported gross and net profits could be overstated because of overstated inventory.
  - Calculate the inventory turnover ratio. This ratio is the cost of sales divided by the average ending inventory. Declining inventory turnover could also suggest obsolescence problems that should be recognized.

- Companies reporting under US GAAP may use LIFO inventory cost flow assumptions. When this assumption is part of the accounting policies, and a company operates in an inflationary environment, investors should note whether old, low-cost inventory costs have been passed through current earnings and artificially improved gross, operating, and net profits.

3) Pay attention to capitalization policies and deferred costs.   In a study of enforcement actions over a five-year period, the SEC found that improper revenue recognition was the most prevalent accounting issue.[28] Suppression of expenses was the next most prevalent problem noted. As the earlier discussion of WorldCom showed, improper capitalization practices can result in a significant misstatement of financial results.

- *Examine the company's accounting policy note for its capitalization policy for long-term assets, including interest costs, and for its handling of other deferred costs.* Compare the company's policy with the industry practice. If the company is the only one capitalizing certain costs while other industry participants treat them as expenses, a red flag is raised. If an outlier company of this type is encountered, it would be useful to cross-check such a company's asset turnover and profitability margins with others in its industry. An investor might expect such a company to be more profitable than its competitors, but the investor might also have lower confidence in the quality of the reported numbers.

4) Pay attention to the relationship of cash flow and net income.   Net income propels stock prices, but cash flow pays bills. Management can manipulate either one, but sooner or later, net income must be realized in cash if a company is to remain viable. When net income is higher than cash provided by operations, one possibility is that aggressive accrual accounting policies have shifted current expenses to later periods. Increasing earnings in the presence of declining cash generated by operations might signal accounting irregularities.

- *Construct a time series of cash generated by operations divided by net income.* If the ratio is consistently below 1.0 or has declined repeatedly, there may be problems in the company's accrual accounts.

5) Other potential warnings signs.   Other areas that might suggest the need for further analysis include the following:

- *Depreciation methods and useful lives.* As discussed earlier, selection of depreciation methods and useful lives can greatly influence profitability. An investor should compare a company's policies with those of its peers to determine whether it is particularly lenient in its effects on earnings. Investors should likewise compare the length of depreciable lives used by a company with those used by its peers.
- *Fourth-quarter surprises.* An investor should be suspicious of possible earnings management if a company routinely disappoints investors with poor earnings or overachieves in the fourth quarter of the year when no seasonality exists in the business. The company may be over- or under-reporting profits in the first three quarters of the year.
- *Presence of related-party transactions.* Related-party transactions often arise when a company's founders are still very active in managing the company, with much of their wealth tied to

---

[28]SEC, "Report Pursuant to Section 704 of the Sarbanes–Oxley Act of 2002" (www.sec.gov/news/studies/sox704report.pdf): 5–6.

the company's fortunes. They may be more biased in their view of a company's performance because it relates directly to their own wealth and reputations, and they may be able to transact business with the company in ways that may not be detected. For instance, they may purchase unsellable inventory from the company for disposal in another company of their own in order to avoid markdowns.

- *Non-operating income or one-time sales included in revenue.* To disguise weakening revenue growth, or just to enhance revenue growth, a company might classify non-operating income items into revenues or fail to clarify the nature of revenues. In the first quarter of 1997, Sunbeam Corporation included one-time disposal of product lines in sales without indicating that such non-recurring sales were included in revenues. This inclusion gave investors a false impression of the company's sustainable revenue-generating capability.
- *Classification of expenses as "non-recurring."* To make operating performance look more attractive, managers might carve out "special items" in the income statement. Particularly when these items appear period after period, equity investors might find their interests best served by not accepting the carve-out of serial "special items" and instead focusing on the net income line in evaluating performance over long periods.
- *Gross/operating margins out of line with competitors or industry.* This disparity is an ambivalent warning sign. It might signal superior management ability. But it might also signal the presence of accounting manipulations to add a veneer of superior management ability to the company's reputation. Only the compilation and examination of other warning signals will enable an investor or analyst to decide which signal is being given.

Warning signals are just that: signals, not indisputable declarations of accounting manipulation guilt. Investors and analysts need to evaluate them cohesively, not on an isolated basis. When an investor finds a number of these signals, the investee company should be viewed with caution or even discarded in favor of alternatives.

Furthermore, as discussed earlier, context is important in judging the value of warning signals. A few examples of facts and circumstances to be aware of are as follows.

- *Younger companies with an unblemished record of meeting growth projections.* It is plausible, especially for a younger company with new and popular product offerings, to generate above-average returns for a period of time. But, as demand dissipates, products mature, and competitors challenge for market share, management may seek to extend its recent record of rapid growth in sales and profitability by unconventional means. At this point, the "earnings games" begin: aggressive estimates, drawing down "cookie jar" reserves, selling assets for accounting gains, taking on excess leverage, or entering into financial transactions with no apparent business purpose other than financial statement "window dressing."
- *Management has adopted a minimalist approach to disclosure.* Confidence in accounting quality depends on disclosure. If management does not seem to take seriously its obligation to provide information, one needs to be concerned. For example, for a large company, management might claim that it has only one reportable segment, or its commentary might be similar from period to period. A plausible explanation for minimalist disclosure policies could be that management is protecting investors' interests by withholding valuable information from competitors. But, this is not necessarily the case. For example, after Sony Corporation acquired CBS Records and Columbia Pictures, it incurred substantial losses for a number of years. Yet, Sony chose to hide its negative trends and doubtful future prospects by aggregating the results within a much larger "Entertainment Division." In 1998, after Sony ultimately wrote off much of the goodwill associated with these ill-fated acquisitions,

the SEC sanctioned Sony and its CFO for failing to separately discuss them in MD&A in a balanced manner.[29]

- *Management fixation on earnings reports.* Beware of companies whose management appears to be fixated on reported earnings, sometimes to the detriment of attending to real drivers of value. Indicators of excessive earnings fixation include the aggressive use of non-GAAP measures of performance, special items, or non-recurring charges. Another indicator of earnings fixation is highly decentralized operations in which division managers' compensation packages are heavily weighted toward the attainment of reported earnings or non-GAAP measures of performance.

Company Culture A company's culture is an intangible that investors should bear in mind when they are evaluating financial statements for the possibility of accounting manipulation. A management's highly competitive mentality may serve investors well when the company conducts business (assuming that actions taken are not unethical, illegal, or harmfully myopic), but that kind of thinking should not extend to communications with the owners of the company: the shareholders. That mentality can lead to the kind of accounting gamesmanship seen in the early part of the century. In examining financial statements for warning signs of manipulation, the investor should consider whether that mindset exists in the preparation of the financial statements.

One notable example of the mindset comes from one of the most recognized corporate names in the world, General Electric. In the mid-1980s, GE acquired Kidder Peabody, and it was ultimately determined that much of the earnings that Kidder had reported were bogus. As a consequence, GE would announce within two days that it would take a non-cash write-off of $350 million. Here is how former CEO/Chair Jack Welsh described the ensuing meeting with senior management in his memoir, *Straight from the Gut*:

> "The response of our business leaders to the crisis was typical of the GE *culture* [emphasis added]. Even though the books had closed on the quarter, many immediately offered to pitch in to cover the Kidder gap. Some said they could find an extra $10 million, $20 million, and even $30 million from their businesses to offset the surprise. Though it was too late, their willingness to help was a dramatic contrast to the excuses I had been hearing from the Kidder people." (p. 225)

It appears that the corporate governance apparatus fostered a GE culture that extended the concept of teamwork to the point of "sharing" profits to win one for the team as a whole, which is incompatible with the concept of neutral financial reporting. Although research is not conclusive on this question, it may also be worth considering that predisposition to earnings manipulation is more likely to be present when the CEO and board chair are one and the same, or when the audit committee of the board essentially serves at the pleasure of the CEO and lacks financial reporting sophistication. Finally, one could discuss whether the financial reporting environment today would reward or penalize a CEO who openly endorsed a view that he could legitimately exercise financial reporting discretion—albeit within limits—for the purpose of artificially smoothing earnings.

Restructuring and/or impairment charges. At times, a company's stock price has been observed to rise after it recognized a "big bath" charge to reported earnings. The conventional wisdom

---

[29] Accounting and Auditing Enforcement Release No. 1061, "In the Matter of Sony Corporation and Sumio Sano, Respondents," SEC (August 5, 1998).

explaining the stock price rise is that accounting recognition signals something positive: that management is now ready to part with the lagging portion of a company, so as to redirect its attention and talents to more-profitable activities. Consequently, the earnings charge should be disregarded for being solely related to past events.

The analyst should also consider, however, that the events leading ultimately to the big bath on the financial statements did not happen overnight, even though the accounting for those events occurs at a subsequent point. Management may want to communicate that the accounting adjustments reflect the company's new path, but the restructuring charge also indicates that the old path of reported earnings was not real. In particular, expenses reported in prior years were very likely understated—even assuming that no improper financial statement manipulation had occurred. To extrapolate historical earnings trends, an analyst should consider making pro forma analytical adjustments to prior years' earnings to reflect a reasonable division of the latest period's restructuring and impairment charges.

Management has a merger and acquisition orientation. Tyco International Ltd. acquired more than 700 companies from 1996 to 2002. Even assuming the best of intentions regarding financial reporting, a growth-at-any-cost corporate culture poses a severe challenge to operational and financial reporting controls. In Tyco's case, the SEC found that it consistently and fraudulently understated assets acquired (lowering future depreciation and amortization charges) and overstated liabilities assumed (avoiding expense recognition and potentially increasing earnings in future periods).[30]

5. SUMMARY

Financial reporting quality varies across companies. The ability to assess the quality of a company's financial reporting is an important skill for analysts. Indications of low-quality financial reporting can prompt an analyst to maintain heightened skepticism when reading a company's reports, to review disclosures critically when undertaking financial statement analysis, and to incorporate appropriate adjustments in assessments of past performance and forecasts of future performance.

- Financial reporting quality can be thought of as spanning a continuum from the highest (containing information that is relevant, correct, complete, and unbiased) to the lowest (containing information that is not just biased or incomplete but possibly pure fabrication).
- *Reporting quality*, the focus of this chapter, pertains to the information disclosed. High-quality reporting represents the economic reality of the company's activities during the reporting period and the company's financial condition at the end of the period.
- *Results quality* (commonly referred to as earnings quality) pertains to the earnings and cash generated by the company's actual economic activities and the resulting financial condition, relative to expectations of current and future financial performance. Quality earnings are regarded as being sustainable, providing a sound platform for forecasts.

---

[30] Accounting and Auditing Enforcement Release No. 2414, "SEC Brings Settled Charges Against Tyco International Ltd. Alleging Billion Dollar Accounting Fraud," SEC (April 17, 2006): www.sec.gov/litigation/litreleases/2006/lr19657.htm.

- An aspect of financial reporting quality is the degree to which accounting choices are conservative or aggressive. "Aggressive" typically refers to choices that aim to enhance the company's reported performance and financial position by inflating the amount of revenues, earnings, and/or operating cash flow reported in the period; or by decreasing expenses for the period and/or the amount of debt reported on the balance sheet.
- Conservatism in financial reports can result from either (1) accounting standards that specifically require a conservative treatment of a transaction or an event or (2) judgments made by managers when applying accounting standards that result in conservative results.
- Managers may be motivated to issue less-than-high-quality financial reports in order to mask poor performance, to boost the stock price, to increase personal compensation, and/or to avoid violation of debt covenants.
- Conditions that are conducive to the issuance of low-quality financial reports include a cultural environment that result in fewer or less transparent financial disclosures, book/tax conformity that shifts emphasis toward legal compliance and away from fair presentation, and limited capital markets regulation.
- Mechanisms that discipline financial reporting quality include the free market and incentives for companies to minimize cost of capital, auditors, contract provisions specifically tailored to penalize misreporting, and enforcement by regulatory entities.
- Pro forma earnings (also commonly referred to as non-GAAP or non-IFRS earnings) adjust earnings as reported on the income statement. Pro forma earnings that exclude negative items are a hallmark of aggressive presentation choices.
- Companies are required to make additional disclosures when presenting any non-GAAP or non-IFRS metric.
- Managers' considerable flexibility in choosing their companies' accounting policies and in formulating estimates provides opportunities for aggressive accounting.
- Examples of accounting choices that affect earnings and balance sheets include inventory cost flow assumptions, estimates of uncollectible accounts receivable, estimated realizability of deferred tax assets, depreciation method, estimated salvage value of depreciable assets, and estimated useful life of depreciable assets.
- Cash from operations is a metric of interest to investors that can be enhanced by operating choices, such as stretching accounts payable, and potentially by classification choices.

REFERENCES

Back, Aaron. 2013. "Toyota, What a Difference the Yen Makes." *Wall Street Journal* (4 August 2013).

Basu, Sudipta. 1997. "The Conservatism Principle and the Asymmetric Timeliness of Earnings." *Journal of Accounting and Economics*, vol. 24, no. 1 (December): 3–37.

Bliss, James Harris. 1924. *Management through Accounts*. New York: Ronald Press Company.

Ciesielski, Jack T, and Elaine Henry. 2017. "Accounting's Tower of Babel: Key Considerations in Assessing Non-GAAP Earnings." *Financial Analysts Journal*, vol. 73, no. 2 : 34–50.

Dichev, Ilia, John Graham, Campbell Harvey, and Shivaram Rajgopal. 2013. "Earnings Quality: Evidence from the Field." *Journal of Accounting and Economics*, vol. 56, issues 2–3 : 1–33.

Dichev, Ilia, John Graham, Campbell Harvey, and Shiva Rajgopal. 2016. "The Misrepresentation of Earnings." *Financial Analysts Journal*, vol. 72, issue 1 : 22–35.

Ernst & Young. 2013. *Navigating Today's Complex Business Risks*. Europe, Middle East, India and Africa Fraud Survey 2013 (May): www.ey.com/Publication/vwLUAssets/Navigating_todays_complex_business_risks/$FILE/Navigating_todays_complex_business_risks.pdf.

Ernst & Young Global Limited. 2016. *Corporate misconduct — individual consequences.* 14th Global Fraud Survey. www.ey.com/gl/en/services/assurance/fraud-investigation---dispute-services/ey-global-fraud-survey-2016.

Gordon, Elizabeth, Elaine Henry, Bjorn Jorgensen, and Cheryl Linthicum. 2017. "Flexibility in Cash-Flow Classification under IFRS: Determinants and Consequences." *Review of Accounting Studies*, vol. 22, no. 2 : 839–872.

Graham, John, Campbell Harvey, and Shiva Rajgopal. 2005. "The Economic Implications of Corporate Financial Reporting." *Journal of Accounting and Economics*, vol. 40, no. 1 (December): 3–73.

Lewis, Craig M. 2012. "Risk Modeling at the SEC: The Accounting Quality Model" Speech, the Financial Executives International Committee on Finance and Information Technology (13 December): www.sec.gov/news/speech/2012/spch121312cml.htm.

Nurnberg, H. 2006. "Perspectives on the Cash Flow Statement under FASB Statement No. 95." Center for Excellence in Accounting and Security Analysis Occasional Paper Series. Columbia Business School.

Nurnberg, H., and J. Largay. 1998. "Interest Payments in the Cash Flow Statement." *Accounting Horizons*, vol. 12, no. 4 (December): 407–418.

Pavlo, Walter. 2013. "Fmr Enron CFO Andrew Fastow Speaks At ACFE Annual Conference," *Forbes* (26 June): www.forbes.com/sites/walterpavlo/2013/06/26/fmr-enron-cfo-andrew-fastow-speaks-at-acfe-annual-conference/.

Ronen, Joshua, and Varda Yaari. 2008. *Earnings Management: Emerging Insights in Theory, Practice, and Research.* New York: Springer.

Schipper, Katherine. 1989. "Commentary on Earnings Management." *Accounting Horizons*, vol. 3, no. 4 (December): 91–102.

Watts, Ross. 2003. "Conservatism in Accounting Part I: Explanations and Implications." *Accounting Horizons*, vol. 17, no. 3 (September): 207–221.

PRACTICE PROBLEMS

1. In contrast to earnings quality, financial reporting quality *most likely* pertains to:
   A. sustainable earnings.
   B. relevant information.
   C. adequate return on investment.

2. The information provided by a low-quality financial report will *most likely*:
   A. decrease company value.
   B. indicate earnings are not sustainable.
   C. impede the assessment of earnings quality.

3. To properly assess a company's past performance, an analyst requires:
   A. high earnings quality.
   B. high financial reporting quality.
   C. both high earnings quality and high financial reporting quality.

4. Low quality earnings *most likely* reflect:
   A. low-quality financial reporting.
   B. company activities which are unsustainable.
   C. information that does not faithfully represent company activities.

5. Earnings that result from non-recurring activities *most likely* indicate:
   A. lower-quality earnings.
   B. biased accounting choices.
   C. lower-quality financial reporting.

6. Which attribute of financial reports would *most likely* be evaluated as optimal in the financial reporting spectrum?
   A. Conservative accounting choices
   B. Sustainable and adequate returns
   C. Emphasized pro forma earnings measures

7. Financial reports of the lowest level of quality reflect:
   A. fictitious events.
   B. biased accounting choices.
   C. accounting that is non-compliant with GAAP.

8. When earnings are increased by deferring research and development (R&D) investments until the next reporting period, this choice is considered:
   A. non-compliant accounting.
   B. earnings management as a result of a real action.
   C. earnings management as a result of an accounting choice.

9. A high-quality financial report may reflect:
   A. earnings smoothing.
   B. low earnings quality.
   C. understatement of asset impairment.

10. If a particular accounting choice is considered aggressive in nature, then the financial performance for the reporting period would *most likely*:
    A. be neutral.
    B. exhibit an upward bias.
    C. exhibit a downward bias.

11. Which of the following is *most likely* to reflect conservative accounting choices?
    A. Decreased reported earnings in later periods
    B. Increased reported earnings in the period under review
    C. Increased debt reported on the balance sheet at the end of the current period

12. Which of the following is *most likely* to be considered a potential benefit of accounting conservatism?
    A. A reduction in litigation costs
    B. Less biased financial reporting
    C. An increase in current period reported performance

13. Which of the following statements *most likely* describes a situation that would motivate a manager to issue low-quality financial reports?
    A. The manager's compensation is tied to stock price performance.
    B. The manager has increased the market share of products significantly.
    C. The manager has brought the company's profitability to a level higher than competitors.

14. Which of the following concerns would *most likely* motivate a manager to make conservative accounting choices?
    A. Attention to future career opportunities
    B. Expected weakening in the business environment
    C. Debt covenant violation risk in the current period

15. Which of the following conditions *best* explains why a company's manager would obtain legal, accounting, and board level approval prior to issuing low-quality financial reports?
    A. Motivation
    B. Opportunity
    C. Rationalization

16. A company is experiencing a period of strong financial performance. In order to increase the likelihood of exceeding analysts' earnings forecasts in the next reporting period, the company would *most likely* undertake accounting choices for the period under review that:
    A. inflate reported revenue.
    B. delay expense recognition.
    C. accelerate expense recognition.

17. Which of the following situations represents a motivation, rather than an opportunity, to issue low-quality financial reports?
    A. Poor internal controls
    B. Search for a personal bonus
    C. Inattentive board of directors

18. Which of the following situations will *most likely* motivate managers to inflate reported earnings?
    A. Possibility of bond covenant violation
    B. Earnings in excess of analysts' forecasts
    C. Earnings that are greater than the previous year

19. Which of the following *best* describes an opportunity for management to issue low-quality financial reports?
    A. Ineffective board of directors
    B. Pressure to achieve some performance level
    C. Corporate concerns about financing in the future

20. An audit opinion of a company's financial reports is *most likely* intended to:
    A. detect fraud.
    B. reveal misstatements.
    C. assure that financial information is presented fairly.

21. If a company uses a non-GAAP financial measure in an SEC filing, then the company must:
    A. give more prominence to the non-GAAP measure if it is used in earnings releases.
    B. provide a reconciliation of the non-GAAP measure and equivalent GAAP measure.
    C. exclude charges requiring cash settlement from any non-GAAP liquidity measures.

22. A company wishing to increase earnings in the reporting period may choose to:
    A. decrease the useful life of depreciable assets.
    B. lower estimates of uncollectible accounts receivables.
    C. classify a purchase as an expense rather than a capital expenditure.

23. Bias in revenue recognition would *least likely* be suspected if:
    A. the firm engages in barter transactions.
    B. reported revenue is higher than the previous quarter.
    C. revenue is recognized before goods are shipped to customers.

24. Which technique *most likely* increases the cash flow provided by operations?
    A. Stretching the accounts payable credit period
    B. Applying all non-cash discount amortization against interest capitalized
    C. Shifting classification of interest paid from financing to operating cash flows

25. Which of the following is an indication that a company may be recognizing revenue prematurely? Relative to its competitors, the company's:
    A. asset turnover is decreasing.
    B. receivables turnover is increasing.
    C. days sales outstanding is increasing.

26. Which of the following would *most likely* signal that a company may be using aggressive accrual accounting policies to shift current expenses to later periods? Over the last five-year period, the ratio of cash flow to net income has:
    A. increased each year.
    B. decreased each year.
    C. fluctuated from year to year.

27. An analyst reviewing a firm with a large reported restructuring charge to earnings should:
    A. view expenses reported in prior years as overstated.
    B. disregard it because it is solely related to past events.
    C. consider making pro forma adjustments to prior years' earnings.

CHAPTER 12

APPLICATIONS OF FINANCIAL STATEMENT ANALYSIS

Thomas R. Robinson, PhD, CFA
Jan Hendrik van Greuning, DCom, CFA
Elaine Henry, PhD, CFA
Michael A. Broihahn, CPA, CIA, CFA

LEARNING OUTCOMES

After completing this chapter, you will be able to do the following:

- evaluate a company's past financial performance and explain how a company's strategy is reflected in past financial performance;
- forecast a company's future net income and cash flow;
- describe the role of financial statement analysis in assessing the credit quality of a potential debt investment;
- describe the use of financial statement analysis in screening for potential equity investments;
- explain appropriate analyst adjustments to a company's financial statements to facilitate comparison with another company.

1. INTRODUCTION

This chapter presents several important applications of financial statement analysis. Among the issues we will address are the following:

- What are the key questions to address in evaluating a company's past financial performance?
- How can an analyst approach forecasting a company's future net income and cash flow?
- How can financial statement analysis be used to evaluate the credit quality of a potential fixed-income investment?

- How can financial statement analysis be used to screen for potential equity investments?
- How can differences in accounting methods affect financial ratio comparisons between companies, and what are some adjustments analysts make to reported financials to facilitate comparability among companies?

The chapter "Financial Statement Analysis: An Introduction" described a framework for conducting financial statement analysis. Consistent with that framework, prior to undertaking any analysis, an analyst should explore the purpose and context of the analysis. The purpose and context guide further decisions about the approach, the tools, the data sources, and the format in which to report results of the analysis, and also suggest which aspects of the analysis are most important. Having identified the purpose and context, the analyst should then be able to formulate the key questions that the analysis must address. The questions will suggest the data the analyst needs to collect to objectively address the questions. The analyst then processes and analyzes the data to answer these questions. Conclusions and decisions based on the analysis are communicated in a format appropriate to the context, and follow-up is undertaken as required. Although this chapter will not formally present applications as a series of steps, the process just described is generally applicable.

Section 2 of this chapter describes the use of financial statement analysis to evaluate a company's past financial performance, and Section 3 describes basic approaches to projecting a company's future financial performance. Section 4 presents the use of financial statement analysis in assessing the credit quality of a potential debt investment. Section 5 concludes the survey of applications by describing the use of financial statement analysis in screening for potential equity investments. Analysts often encounter situations in which they must make adjustments to a company's reported financial results to increase their accuracy or comparability with the financials of other companies. Section 6 illustrates several common types of analyst adjustments. Section 7 presents a summary, and practice problems in the CFA Institute multiple-choice format conclude the chapter.

2. APPLICATION: EVALUATING PAST FINANCIAL PERFORMANCE

Analysts examine a company's past financial performance for a number of reasons. Cross-sectional analysis of financial performance facilitates understanding of the comparability of companies for a market-based valuation.[1] Analysis of a company's historical performance over time can provide a basis for a forward-looking analysis of the company. Both cross-sectional and trend analysis can provide information for evaluating the quality and performance of a company's management.

An evaluation of a company's past performance addresses not only *what* happened (i.e., how the company performed) but also *why* it happened—the causes behind the performance and how the performance reflects the company's strategy. Evaluative judgments assess whether the performance is better or worse than a relevant benchmark, such as the company's own

[1]Pinto et al. (2010) describe market-based valuation as using price multiples—ratios of a stock's market price to some measure of value per share (e.g., price-to-earnings ratios). Although the valuation method may be used independently of an analysis of a company's past financial performance, such an analysis may provide reasons for differences in companies' price multiples.

historical performance, a competitor's performance, or market expectations. Some key analytical questions include the following:

- How and why have corporate measures of profitability, efficiency, liquidity, and solvency changed over the periods being analyzed?
- How do the level and trend in a company's profitability, efficiency, liquidity, and solvency compare with the corresponding results of other companies in the same industry? What factors explain any differences?
- What aspects of performance are critical for a company to successfully compete in its industry, and how did the company perform relative to those critical performance aspects?
- What are the company's business model and strategy, and how did they influence the company's performance as reflected in, for example, its sales growth, efficiency, and profitability?

Data available to answer these questions include the company's (and its competitors') financial statements, materials from the company's investor relations department, corporate press releases, and non-financial-statement regulatory filings, such as proxies. Useful data also include industry information (e.g., from industry surveys, trade publications, and government sources), consumer information (e.g., from consumer satisfaction surveys), and information that is gathered by the analyst firsthand (e.g., through on-site visits). Processing the data typically involves creating common-size financial statements, calculating financial ratios, and reviewing or calculating industry-specific metrics. Example 1 illustrates the effects of strategy on performance and the use of basic economic reasoning in interpreting results.

EXAMPLE 1   A Change in Products Reflected in Financial Performance

Apple Inc. is a company that has evolved and adapted over time. In its 1994 Prospectus filed with the US SEC, Apple identified itself as "one of the world's leading personal computer technology companies." At that time, most of its revenue was generated by computer sales. In the prospectus, however, Apple stated, "The Company's strategy is to expand its market share in the personal computing industry while developing and expanding into new related business such as Personal Interactive Electronics and Apple Business Systems." Over time, products other than computers became significant generators of revenue and profit.

In 2005, an article in *Barron's* said, "In the last year, the iPod has become Apple's best-selling product, bringing in a third of revenues for the Cupertino, Calif. firm... Little noticed by these iPod zealots, however is a looming threat... Wireless phone companies are teaming up with the music industry to make most mobile phones into music players" (*Barron's* 27 June 2005, p. 19). The threat noted by *Barron's* was not unnoticed or ignored by Apple.

In June 2007, Apple itself entered the mobile phone market with the launch of the original iPhone, followed in June 2008 by the second-generation iPhone 3G (a handheld device combining the features of a mobile phone, an iPod, and an internet connection device). Soon after, the company launched the iTunes App Store, which allows users to download third-party applications onto their iPhones. As noted in a 2009 *Business Week* article, Apple "is the world's largest music distributor, having passed Wal-Mart Stores in early 2008. Apple sells around 90% of song downloads and 75% of digital music players in the United States" (*Business Week*, September 28, 2009, p. 34). Product innovations continue as evidenced by the introduction of the iPad in January 2010.

In analyzing the historical performance of Apple in 2018, an analyst might refer to the information presented in Exhibit 1, which shows sales, profitability, sales by product line, and product mix.

EXHIBIT 1 (dollars in millions)

Sales and Profitability	2017	2016	2015	2014	2013	2012	2011	2010
Sales	229,234	215,639	233,715	182,795	170,910	156,608	108,249	65,225
Cost of goods sold	141,048	131,376	140,089	112,258	106,606	87,846	64,431	39,541
Gross profit	88,186	84,263	93,626	70,537	64,304	68,762	43,818	25,684
Gross margin	38.5%	39.1%	40.1%	38.6%	37.6%	43.9%	40.5%	39.4%
Net sales by product								
Mac	25,850	22,831	25,471	24,079	21,483	23,221	21,783	25,850
iPhone and related	141,319	136,700	155,041	101,991	91,279	78,692	45,998	141,319
iPad and related	19,222	20,628	23,227	30,283	31,980	30,945	19,168	19,222
Services	29,980	24,348	19,909	18,063	16,051	12,890	9,373	29,980
Other (includes iPod)	12,863	11,132	10,067	8,379	10,117	10,760	11,927	12,863
Total	229,234	215,639	233,715	182,795	170,910	156,508	108,249	65,225
Net sales % by product								
Mac	11.3%	10.6%	10.9%	13.2%	12.6%	14.8%	20.1%	26.8%
iPhone and related	61.6%	63.4%	66.3%	55.8%	53.4%	50.3%	42.5%	38.6%
iPad and related	8.4%	9.6%	9.9%	16.6%	18.7%	19.8%	17.7%	7.6%
Services	13.1%	11.3%	8.5%	9.9%	9.4%	8.2%	8.7%	15.5%
Other (includes iPod)	5.6%	5.2%	4.3%	4.6%	5.9%	6.9%	11.0%	11.5%
Total	100.0%	100.0%	100.0%	100.0%	100.0%	100.0%	100.0%	100.0%

Source: Apple 10-K filings.

Using the information provided, address the following:

1.   How have sales and gross margin changed over time?
2.   How has the company's product mix changed since the introduction of the iPad in 2010, and what might this change suggest for an analyst in evaluating Apple's profitability over time and its ability to maintain that profitability?

Solution to 1: Since 2010 total sales have increased from $65 billion to $229 billion. This represents an annualized growth rate of almost 20%. There was only one year that did not have sales growth in dollars (2016). Gross margin has ranged from 37.6% to 43.9%. Gross margin increased from 2010, when the iPad was introduced, through 2012, when it reached its peak. Gross margin then declined in 2013 and trended upward through 2015. There were modest declines in gross margin after 2015.

Solution to 2: When the iPad was introduced in 2010 it received a significant share of the product mix, rising to 17.7% in 2011, the first full year after introduction. The iPad's product mix share approached a 20% share in 2012 and then declined slightly for two years before a larger decline down to a relatively stable product mix share of around 9%. This could be explained by reaching fairly widespread adoption. The iPhone also gained significant product mix share, rising steadily from 38.6% in 2010 to 66.3% in 2015. Share declined slightly since 2015 but still remains the largest of Apple's product segments at more than 60%. Sales of their original product, the Mac, have declined from more than 25% of sales to around 10%. Services have changed significantly but have shown a steady increase in recent years, most likely due to Apple's music and other media subscription plans. Initially a blockbuster product, the iPod is now included in "other," and this is the largest driver of the decline in that category over time.

Apple had a history of introducing new products every few years, but in recent years the company has not created new product categories. Instead the company has periodically introduced new models of iPads and iPhones. The recent decline in margins is attributable in part to the lack of new products and services and highlights the importance of product innovation to Apple in maintaining historically healthy margins.

In calculating and interpreting financial statement ratios, an analyst needs to be aware of the potential impact on the financial statements and related ratios of companies reporting under different accounting standards, such as international financial reporting standards (IFRS), US generally accepted accounting principles (US GAAP), or other home-country GAAP. Furthermore, even within a given set of accounting standards, companies still have discretion to choose among acceptable methods. A company also may make different assumptions and estimates even when applying the same method as another company. Therefore, making selected adjustments to a company's financial statement data may be useful to facilitate comparisons with other companies or with the industry overall. Examples of such analyst adjustments will be discussed in Section 6.

Non-US companies that use any acceptable body of accounting standards (other than IFRS or US GAAP) and file with the US SEC (because their shares or depositary receipts based on their shares trade in the United States) are required to reconcile their net income and shareholders' equity accounts to US GAAP. Note that in 2007, the SEC eliminated the reconciliation requirement for non-US companies using IFRS and filing with the SEC, however companies may still voluntarily provide this information for comparison purposes.

In general, because the reconciliation data are no longer required by the SEC, we cannot always determine whether differences in net income, equity, and thus ROE also exist between IFRS and the companies' home-country GAAP (including US GAAP).

Comparison of the levels and trends in a company's performance provide information about *how* the company performed. The company's management presents its view about causes underlying its performance in the management commentary or management discussion and analysis (MD&A) section of its annual report and during periodic conference calls with analysts and investors. To gain additional understanding of the causes underlying a company's performance, an analyst can review industry information or seek information from additional sources, such as consumer surveys.

The results of an analysis of past performance provide a basis for reaching conclusions and making recommendations. For example, an analysis undertaken as the basis for a forward-looking study might conclude that a company's future performance is or is not likely to reflect continuation of recent historical trends. As another example, an analysis to support a market-based valuation of a company might focus on whether the company's profitability and growth outlook, which is better (worse) than the peer group median, justifies its relatively high (low) valuation. This analysis would consider market multiples, such as price-to-earnings ratio (P/E), price-to-book ratio, and total invested capital to EBITDA (earnings before interest, taxes, depreciation, and amortization).[2] As another example, an analysis undertaken as part of an evaluation of the management of two companies might result in conclusions about whether one company has grown as fast as another company, or as fast as the industry overall, and whether each company has maintained profitability while growing.

3. APPLICATION: PROJECTING FUTURE FINANCIAL PERFORMANCE

Projections of future financial performance are used in determining the value of a company or its equity component. Projections of future financial performance are also used in credit analysis—particularly in project finance or acquisition finance—to determine whether a company's cash flows will be adequate to pay the interest and principal on its debt and to evaluate whether a company will likely remain in compliance with its financial covenants.

Sources of data for analysts' projections include some or all of the following: the company's projections, the company's previous financial statements, industry structure and outlook, and macroeconomic forecasts.

Evaluating a company's past performance may provide a basis for forward-looking analyses. An evaluation of a company's business and economic environment and its history may persuade the analyst that historical information constitutes a valid basis for such analyses and that the analyst's projections may be based on the continuance of past trends, perhaps with some adjustments. Alternatively, in the case of a major acquisition or divestiture, for a start-up company, or for a company operating in a volatile industry, past performance may be less relevant to future performance.

---

[2]**Total invested capital** is the sum of market value of common equity, book value of preferred equity, and face value of debt.

Projections of a company's near-term performance may be used as an input to market-based valuation or relative valuation (i.e., valuation based on price multiples). Such projections may involve projecting next year's sales and using the common-size income statement to project major expense items or particular margins on sales (e.g., gross profit margin or operating profit margin). These calculations will then lead to the development of an income measure for a valuation calculation, such as net income, earnings per share (EPS), or EBITDA. More complex projections of a company's future performance involve developing a more detailed analysis of the components of performance for multiple periods—for example, projections of sales and gross margin by product line, projection of operating expenses based on historical patterns, and projection of interest expense based on requisite debt funding, interest rates, and applicable taxes. Furthermore, a projection should include sensitivity analyses applied to the major assumptions.

3.1. Projecting Performance: An Input to Market-Based Valuation

One application of financial statement analysis involves projecting a company's near-term performance as an input to market-based valuation. For example, an analyst might project a company's sales and profit margin to estimate EPS and then apply a projected P/E to establish a target price for the company's stock.

Analysts often take a top-down approach to projecting a company's sales.[3] First, industry sales are projected on the basis of their historical relationship with some macroeconomic indicator, such as growth in real gross domestic product (GDP). In researching the automobile industry, for example, the analyst may find that the industry's annual domestic unit car sales (number of cars sold in domestic markets) bears a relationship to annual changes in real GDP. Regression analysis is often used to establish the parameters of such relationships. Other factors in projecting sales may include consumer income or tastes, technological developments, and the availability of substitute products or services. After industry sales are projected, a company's market share is projected. Company-level market share projections may be based on historical market share and a forward-looking assessment of the company's competitive position. The company's sales are then estimated as its projected market share multiplied by projected total industry sales.

After developing a sales forecast for a company, an analyst can choose among various methods for forecasting income and cash flow. An analyst must decide on the level of detail to consider in developing forecasts. For example, separate forecasts may be made for individual expense items or for more aggregated expense items, such as total operating expenses. Rather than stating a forecast in terms of expenses, the forecast might be stated in terms of a forecasted profit margin (gross, operating, or net). The net profit margin, in contrast to the gross or operating profit margins, is affected by financial leverage and tax rates, which are subject to managerial and legal/regulatory revisions; therefore, historical data may sometimes be more relevant for projecting gross or operating profit margins than for projecting net profit margins. Whatever the margin used, the forecasted amount of profit for a given period is the product of the forecasted amount of sales and the forecast of the selected profit margin.

As Example 2 illustrates, for relatively mature companies operating in non-volatile product markets, historical information on operating profit margins can provide a useful starting point for forecasting future operating profits (at least over short forecasting horizons). Historical operating profit margins are typically less reliable for projecting future margins for a new or relatively volatile business or one with significant fixed costs (which can magnify the volatility of operating margins).

---

[3]The discussion in this paragraph is indebted to Benninga and Sarig (1997).

EXAMPLE 2   Using Historical Operating Profit Margins to Forecast Operating Profit

One approach to projecting operating profit is to determine a company's average operating profit margin over the previous several years and apply that margin to a forecast of the company's sales. Use the following information on three companies to answer Questions 1 and 2 below:

- Johnson & Johnson (JNJ). This US health care conglomerate, founded in 1887, had 2017 sales of around $76.5 billion from its three main businesses: pharmaceuticals, medical devices and diagnostics, and consumer products.
- BHP Billiton (BHP). This company, with group headquarters in Australia and secondary headquarters in London, is the world's largest natural resources company, reporting revenue of approximately US$38.3 billion for the fiscal year ended June 2017. The company mines, processes, and markets coal, copper, nickel, iron, bauxite, and silver and also has substantial petroleum operations.
- Baidu. This Chinese company, which was established in 2000 and went public on NASDAQ in 2005, is the leading Chinese language search engine. The company's revenues for 2017 were 84.8 billion renminbi (RMB), an increase of 20 percent from 2016 and almost 4 times the revenue in 2012.
  1. For each of the three companies, state and justify whether the suggested forecasting method (applying the average operating profit over the previous several years to a forecast of sales) would be a reasonable starting point for projecting future operating profit.
  2. Assume that the 2017 forecast of sales was perfect and, therefore, equal to the realized sales by the company in 2017. Compare the forecast of 2017 operating profit, using an average of the previous five years' operating profit margins, with the actual 2017 operating profit reported by the company given the following additional information:
- JNJ: For the five years prior to 2017, JNJ's average operating profit margin was approximately 25.6 percent. The company's actual operating profit for 2017 was $18.2 billion.
- BHP: For the four years prior to the year ending June 2017, BHP's average operating profit margin was approximately 24.0 percent. The company's actual operating profit for the year ended June 2017 was US$11.8 billion.
- Baidu: Over the four years prior to 2017, Baidu's average operating profit margin was approximately 28.5 percent. The company's actual operating profit for 2017 was RMB15.7 billion.

Using the additional information given, state and justify whether actual results support the usefulness of the stable operating margin assumption.

Solution to 1:

   JNJ. Because JNJ is an established company with diversified operations in relatively stable businesses, the suggested approach to projecting the company's operating profit would be a reasonable starting point.

BHP. Because commodity prices tend to be volatile and the mining industry is relatively capital intensive, the suggested approach to projecting BHP's operating profit would probably not be a useful starting point.

Baidu. Compared to the other two companies, Baidu has a more limited operating history and remains in a period of rapid growth. These aspects about the company suggests that the broad approach to projecting operating profit would not be a useful starting point for Baidu.

Solution to 2:

JNJ. JNJ's actual operating profit margin for 2017 was 23.8 percent ($18.2 billion divided by sales of $76.5 billion), which is a little less than the company's five-year average operating profit margin of approximately 25.6 percent.

BHP. BHP's actual operating profit margin for the year ended June 2017 was 30.8 percent ($11.8 billion divided by sales of $38.3 billion). If the company's average profit margin of 24.0 percent had been applied to perfectly forecasted sales, the forecasted operating profit would have been approximately US$9.2 billion, around 22 percent lower than actual operating profit.

Baidu. Baidu's actual operating profit margin for 2017 was 18.5 percent (RMB15.7 billion divided by sales of RMB84.8 billion). If the average profit margin of 28.5 percent had been applied to perfectly forecasted sales, the forecasted operating profit would have been approximately RMB24.2 billion, or around 54 percent higher than Baidu's actual operating profit.

Although prior years' profit margins can provide a useful starting point in projections for companies with relatively stable business, the underlying data should, nonetheless, be examined to identify items that are not likely to occur again in the following year(s). Such non-recurring (i.e., transitory) items should be removed from computations of any profit amount or profit margin that will be used in projections. Example 3 illustrates this principle.

EXAMPLE 3   Issues in Forecasting

Following are excerpts from the 2017 annual report of Textron, a global aircraft, defense and industrial company.

Textron Consolidated Statements of Operations for each of the years in the three-year period ended December 31

(In millions, except per share data)	2017	2016	2015
Revenues			
Manufacturing revenues	$14,129	$13,710	$13,340
Finance revenues	69	78	83
Total revenues	14,198	13,788	13,423
Costs, expenses and other			

(continued)

(Continued)

(In millions, except per share data)	2017	2016	2015
Cost of sales	11,795	11,311	10,979
Selling and administrative expense	1,337	1,304	1,304
Interest expense	174	174	169
Special charges	130	123	—
Total costs, expenses and other	13,436	12,912	12,452
Income from continuing operations before income taxes	762	876	971
Income tax expense	456	33	273
Income from continuing operations	306	843	698
Income (loss) from discontinued operations, net of income taxes*	1	119	(1)
Net income	307	962	697

Footnotes: 2017 Note 12 Special Charges

In 2016, we initiated a plan to restructure and realign our businesses by implementing head-count reductions, facility consolidations and other actions in order to improve overall operating efficiency across Textron. Under this plan, Textron Systems discontinued production of its sensor-fuzed weapon product within its Weapons and Sensors operating unit, we combined our Jacobsen business with the Textron Specialized Vehicles business by consolidating facilities and general and administrative functions, and we reduced headcount at Textron Aviation, as well as other businesses and corporate functions. In December 2017, we decided to take additional restructuring actions to further consolidate operating facilities and streamline product lines, primarily within the Bell, Textron Systems and Industrial segments, which resulted in additional special charges of $45 million in the fourth quarter of 2017. We recorded total special charges of $213 million since the inception of the 2016 plan, which included $97 million of severance costs, $84 million of asset impairments and $32 million in contract terminations and other costs. Of these amounts, $83 million was incurred at Textron Systems, $63 million at Textron Aviation, $38 million at Industrial, $28 million at Bell and $1 million at Corporate. The total headcount reduction under this plan is expected to be approximately 2,100 positions, representing 5% of our workforce.

In connection with the acquisition of Arctic Cat, as discussed in Note 2, we initiated a restructuring plan in the first quarter of 2017 to integrate this business into our Textron Specialized Vehicles business within the Industrial segment and reduce operating redundancies and maximize efficiencies. Under the Arctic Cat plan, we recorded restructuring charges of $28 million in 2017, which included $19 million of severance costs, largely related to change-of-control provisions, and $9 million of contract termination and other costs. In addition, we recorded $12 million of acquisition-related integration and transaction costs in 2017.

2016 Financial Statement General Footnote

*Income from discontinued operations, net of income taxes for the year ended December 31, 2016 primarily includes the settlement of a U.S. federal income tax audit. See Note 13 to the Consolidated Financial Statements for additional information.

2016 Note 13 Income Taxes

The provision for income taxes for 2016 included a benefit of $319 million to reflect the settlement with the U.S. Internal Revenue Service Office of Appeals for our 1998 to 2008 tax years, which resulted in a $206 million benefit attributable to continuing operations and $113 million attributable to discontinued operations.

Source: Textron annual reports.

Discussion:

Results of discontinued operations and restructuring charges should generally not be included when assessing past performance or when forecasting future net income. For purposes of evaluating the company's ongoing operating and net profit margins, the special charges related to restructuring and the special tax benefit related to discontinued operations should be removed. For example, the company's operating margin for 2017 including special charges would be 5.4% ($762 million/$14,198 million). Excluding special charges, the operating margin would be 6.3% ($762 million + $130 million)/$14,198 million. Similarly, the net profit margin would be determined by eliminating the income from discontinued operations, particularly for 2016.

In general, when earnings projections are used as a foundation for market-based valuations, an analyst will make appropriate allowance for transitory components of past earnings. Occasionally, an analyst will observe that a company takes special charges virtually every year. In such cases, they are not transitory and should not be removed in evaluating past and future margins.

3.2. Projecting Multiple-Period Performance

Projections of future financial performance over multiple periods are needed in valuation models that estimate the value of a company or its equity by discounting future cash flows. The value of a company or its equity developed in this way can then be compared with its current market price as a basis for investment decisions.

Projections of future performance are also used for credit analysis. These projections are important in assessing a borrower's ability to repay interest and principal of debt obligations. Investment recommendations depend on the needs and objectives of the client and on an evaluation of the risk of the investment relative to its expected return—both of which are a function of the terms of the debt obligation itself as well as financial market conditions. Terms of the debt obligation include amount, interest rate, maturity, financial covenants, and collateral.

Example 4 presents an elementary illustration of net income and cash flow forecasting to illustrate a format for analysis and some basic principles. In Example 4, assumptions are shown first; then, the period-by-period abbreviated financial statement resulting from the assumptions is shown.

Depending on the use of the forecast, an analyst may choose to compute further, more specific cash flow metrics. For example, free cash flow to equity, which is used in discounted cash flow approaches to equity valuation, can be estimated as net income adjusted for non-cash items, minus investment in net working capital and in net fixed assets, plus net borrowing.

EXAMPLE 4   Basic Example of Financial Forecasting

Assume a company is formed with $100 of equity capital, all of which is immediately invested in working capital. Assumptions are as follows:

Dividends	Non-dividend-paying
First-year sales	$100
Sales growth	10% per year
Cost of goods sold/Sales	20%
Operating expense/Sales	70%
Interest income rate	5%
Tax rate	30%
Working capital as percent of sales	90%

Based on this information, forecast the company's net income and cash flow for five years.

Solution: Exhibit 2 shows the net income forecasts in Line 7 and cash flow forecasts ("Change in cash") in Line 18.

EXHIBIT 2   Basic Financial Forecasting

	Time Period					
	0	1	2	3	4	5
(1) Sales		100.0	110.0	121.0	133.1	146.4
(2) Cost of goods sold		(20.0)	(22.0)	(24.2)	(26.6)	(29.3)
(3) Operating expenses		(70.0)	(77.0)	(84.7)	(93.2)	(102.5)
(4) Interest income		0.0	0.9	0.8	0.8	0.7
(5) Income before tax		10.0	11.9	12.9	14.1	15.3
(6) Taxes		(3.0)	(3.6)	(3.9)	(4.2)	(4.6)
(7) Net income		7.0	8.3	9.0	9.9	10.7
(8) Cash/Borrowing	0.0	17.0	16.3	15.4	14.4	13.1
(9) Working capital (non-cash)	100.0	90.0	99.0	108.9	119.8	131.8
(10) Total assets	100.0	107.0	115.3	124.3	134.2	144.9
(11) Liabilities	0.0	0.0	0.0	0.0	0.0	0.0
(12) Equity	100.0	107.0	115.3	124.3	134.2	144.9
(13) Total liabilities + Equity	100.0	107.0	115.3	124.3	134.2	144.9
(14) Net income		7.0	8.3	9.0	9.9	10.7
(15) Plus: Non-cash items		0.0	0.0	0.0	0.0	0.0

EXHIBIT 2   (Continued)

			Time Period			
	0	1	2	3	4	5
(16) Less: Investment in working capital		−10.0	9.0	9.9	10.9	12.0
(17) Less: Investment in fixed capital		0.0	0.0	0.0	0.0	0.0
(18) Change in cash		17.0	−0.7	−0.9	−1.0	−1.3
(19) Beginning cash		0.0	17.0	16.3	15.4	14.4
(20) Ending cash		17.0	16.3	15.4	14.4	13.1

Exhibit 2 indicates that at time 0, the company is formed with $100 of equity capital (Line 12). All of the company's capital is assumed to be immediately invested in working capital (Line 9). In future periods, because it is assumed that no dividends are paid, book equity increases each year by the amount of net income (Line 14). Future periods' required working capital (Line 9) is assumed to be 90 percent of annual sales (Line 1). Sales are assumed to be $100 in the first period and to grow at a constant rate of 10 percent per year (Line 1). The cost of goods sold is assumed to be constant at 20 percent of sales (Line 2), so the gross profit margin is 80 percent. Operating expenses are assumed to be 70 percent of sales each year (Line 3). Interest income (Line 4) is calculated as 5 percent of the beginning balance of cash/borrowing or the ending balance of the previous period (Line 8) and is an income item when there is a cash balance, as in this example. (If available cash is inadequate to cover required cash outflows, the shortfall is presumed to be covered by borrowing. This borrowing would be shown as a negative balance on Line 8 and an associated interest expense on Line 4. Alternatively, a forecast can be presented with separate lines for cash and borrowing.) Taxes of 30 percent are deducted to obtain net income (Line 7).

To calculate each period's cash flow, begin with net income (Line 7 = Line 14), add back any noncash items, such as depreciation (Line 15), deduct investment in working capital in the period or change in working capital over the period (Line 16), and deduct investment in fixed capital in the period (Line 17).[4] In this simple example, we are assuming that the company does not invest in any fixed capital (long-term assets) but, rather, rents furnished office space. Therefore, there is no depreciation and noncash items are zero. Each period's change in cash (Line 18) is added to the beginning cash balance (Line 19) to obtain the ending cash balance (Line 20 = Line 8).

Example 4 is simplified to demonstrate some principles of forecasting. In practice, each aspect of a forecast presents a range of challenges. Sales forecasts may be very detailed, with separate forecasts for each year of each product line, each geographical area, and/or each business segment. Sales forecasts may be based on past results (for relatively stable businesses),

---

[4] Working capital represents funds that must be invested in the daily operations of a business to, for example, carry inventory and accounts receivable. The term "investment" in this context means "addition to" or "increase in." The "investment in fixed capital" is also referred to as "capital expenditure" ("capex").

management forecasts, industry studies, and/or macroeconomic forecasts. Similarly, gross profit margins may be based on past results or forecasted relationships and may be detailed. Expenses other than cost of goods sold may be broken down into more detailed line items, each of which may be forecasted on the basis of its relationship with sales (if variable) or on the basis of its historical levels. Working capital requirements may be estimated as a proportion of the amount of sales (as in Example 4) or the change in sales or as a compilation of specific forecasts for inventory, receivables, and payables. Most forecasts will involve some investment in fixed assets, in which case, depreciation amounts affect taxable income and net income but not cash flow. Example 4 makes the simplifying assumption that interest is paid on the beginning-of-year cash balance.

Example 4 develops a series of point estimates for future net income and cash flow. In practice, forecasting generally includes an analysis of the risk in forecasts—in this case, an assessment of the impact on income and cash flow if the realized values of variables differ significantly from the assumptions used in the base case or if actual sales are much different from forecasts. Quantifying the risk in forecasts requires an analysis of the economics of the company's businesses and expense structure and the potential impact of events affecting the company, the industry, and the economy in general. When that investigation is completed, the analyst can use scenario analysis or Monte Carlo simulation to assess risk. Scenario analysis involves specifying assumptions that differ from those used as the base-case assumptions. In Example 4, the projections of net income and cash flow could be recast in a more pessimistic scenario, with assumptions changed to reflect slower sales growth and higher costs. A Monte Carlo simulation involves specifying probability distributions of values for variables and random sampling from those distributions. In the analysis in Example 4, the projections would be repeatedly recast with the selected values for the drivers of net income and cash flow, thus permitting the analyst to evaluate a range of possible results and the probability of simulating the possible actual outcomes.

An understanding of financial statements and ratios can enable an analyst to make more detailed projections of income statement, balance sheet, and cash flow statement items. For example, an analyst may collect information on normal inventory and receivables turnover and use this information to forecast accounts receivable, inventory, and cash flows based on sales projections rather than use a composite working capital investment assumption, as in Example 4.

As the analyst makes detailed forecasts, he or she must ensure that the forecasts are consistent with each other. For instance, in Example 5, the analyst's forecast concerning days of sales outstanding (which is an estimate of the average time to collect payment from sales made on credit) should flow from a model of the company that yields a forecast of the change in the average accounts receivable balance. Otherwise, predicted days of sales outstanding and accounts receivable will not be mutually consistent.

EXAMPLE 5   Consistency of Forecasts

Brown Corporation, a hypothetical company, had an average days-of-sales-outstanding (DSO) period of 19 days in 2017. An analyst thinks that Brown's DSO will decline in 2018 (because of expected improvements in the company's collections department) to match the industry average of 15 days. Total sales (all on credit) in 2017 were $300 million, and Brown expects total sales (all on credit) to increase to $320 million in 2018.

> To achieve the lower DSO, the change in the average accounts receivable balance from 2017 to 2018 that must occur is *closest* to:
>
>   A. –$3.51 million.
>   B. –$2.46 million.
>   C. $2.46 million.
>   D. $3.51 million.
>
> *Solution:* B is correct. The first step is to calculate accounts receivable turnover from the DSO collection period. Receivable turnover equals 365/19 (DSO) = 19.2 for 2017 and 365/15 = 24.3 in 2018. Next, the analyst uses the fact that the average accounts receivable balance equals sales/receivable turnover to conclude that for 2017, average accounts receivable was $300,000,000/19.2 = $15,625,000 and for 2018, it must equal $320,000,000/24.3 = $13,168,724. The difference is a reduction in receivables of $2,456,276.

The next section illustrates the application of financial statement analysis to credit risk analysis.

4. APPLICATION: ASSESSING CREDIT RISK

Credit risk is the risk of loss caused by a counterparty's or debtor's failure to make a promised payment. For example, credit risk with respect to a bond is the risk that the obligor (the issuer of the bond) will not be able to pay interest and/or principal according to the terms of the bond indenture (contract). **Credit analysis** is the evaluation of credit risk. Credit analysis may relate to the credit risk of an obligor in a particular transaction or to an obligor's overall creditworthiness.

In assessing an obligor's overall creditworthiness, one general approach is credit scoring, a statistical analysis of the determinants of credit default. Credit analysis for specific types of debt (e.g., acquisition financing and other highly leveraged financing) typically involves projections of period-by-period cash flows.

Whatever the techniques adopted, the analytical focus of credit analysis is on debt-paying ability. Unlike payments to equity investors, payments to debt investors are limited by the agreed contractual interest. If a company experiences financial success, its debt becomes less risky but its success does not increase the amount of payments to its debtholders. In contrast, if a company experiences financial distress, it may be unable to pay interest and principal on its debt obligations. Thus, credit analysis has a special concern with the sensitivity of debt-paying ability to adverse events and economic conditions—cases in which the creditor's promised returns may be most at risk. Because those returns are generally paid in cash, credit analysis usually focuses on cash flow rather than accrual income. Typically, credit analysts use return measures related to operating cash flow because it represents cash generated internally, which is available to pay creditors.

These themes are reflected in Example 6, which illustrates Moody's application of four quantitative factors in the credit analysis of the aerospace and defense industry.[5] These factors include

1. scale,
2. business profile,

---

[5]The information in this paragraph and in Example 7 are based upon the "Rating Methodology: Aerospace and Defense Industry" (Moody's, 2018).

3. leverage and coverage, and
4. financial policy.

   "Scale" relates to a company's sensitivity to adverse events, adverse economic conditions, and other factors—such as market leadership, purchasing power with suppliers, and access to capital markets—that may affect debt-paying ability. "Business profile" represents a company's competitive position, stability of revenues, product and geographic diversity, growth prospects, and the stability and volatility of cash flows. "Leverage and coverage" reflects a company's "financial flexibility" and viability. Finally, "financial policy" relates to a company's financial risk tolerance and its capital structure.

EXAMPLE 6   Moody's Evaluation of Quantifiable Rating Factors for the Aerospace and Defense Industry

Moody's considers four broad rating factors for the aerospace and defense industry: scale; business profile, leverage and coverage; and financial policy. A company's ratings for each of these factors are weighted and aggregated in determining the overall credit rating assigned. The broad factors, the sub-factors, and weightings are as follows:

Broad Factor	Sub-factors	Sub-factor Weighting (%)	Broad Factor Weighting (%)
Scale	Total revenue	10	25
	Operating profit	15	
Business profile	Competitive position	10	20
	Expected revenue stability	10	
Leverage and coverage	Debt/EBITDA	10	35
	Retained cash flow[a]/Net debt	15	
	EBIT/Interest	10	
Financial policy	Financial policy	20	20
Total		100	100

[a]Retained cash flow is defined by Moody's as cash flow before working capital and after dividends.

   Why might the leverage and coverage factor be weighted higher compared to the other rating factors?

Solution: The level of debt relative to earnings and cash flow is a critical factor in assessing creditworthiness. Higher levels of debt for a company typically result in a higher risk in meeting interest and principal payments on its debt obligations.

A point to note regarding Example 6 is that the rating factors and the metrics used to represent each can vary by industry group.

Analyses of a company's historical and projected financial statements are an integral part of the credit evaluation process. Moody's and other rating agencies compute a variety of ratios in assessing creditworthiness. A comparison of a company's ratios with the ratios of its peers is informative in evaluating relative creditworthiness, as demonstrated in Example 7.

EXAMPLE 7   Peer Comparison of Ratios

A credit analyst is assessing the efficiency and leverage of two aerospace and defense companies based on certain sub-factors identified by Moody's in Example 7. The analyst collects the information from the companies' annual reports and calculates the following ratios:

	Company 1	Company 2
Debt/EBITDA	9.3	4.1
Retained cash flow/Net debt	2.6%	9.6%
EBIT/Interest	5.7	8.2

Based solely on the data given, which company is more likely to be assigned a higher credit rating, and why?

Solution: The ratio comparisons are all in favor of Company 2, which has a lower level of debt relative to EBITDA, higher retained cash flow to net debt, and higher interest coverage. Based only on the data given, Company 2 is likely to be assigned a higher credit rating.

In calculating credit ratios, such as those presented in Example 8, analysts typically make certain adjustments to reported financial statements. We describe some common adjustments later in the chapter.

Financial statement analysis, especially financial ratio analysis, can also be an important tool in selecting equity investments, as discussed in the next section.

5. APPLICATION: SCREENING FOR POTENTIAL EQUITY INVESTMENTS

Ratios constructed from financial statement data and market data are often used to screen for potential equity investments. **Screening** is the application of a set of criteria to reduce a set of potential investments to a smaller set having certain desired characteristics. Criteria involving financial ratios generally involve comparing one or more ratios with some pre-specified target or cutoff values.

A security selection approach incorporating financial ratios may be applied whether the investor uses top-down analysis or bottom-up analysis. **Top-down analysis** involves identifying attractive geographical segments and/or industry segments, from which the investor chooses the most attractive investments. **Bottom-up analysis** involves selection of specific investments from all companies within a specified investment universe. Regardless of the direction, screening for potential equity investments aims to identify companies that meet specific criteria. An analysis of this type may be used as the basis for directly forming a portfolio, or it may be undertaken as a preliminary part of a more thorough analysis of potential investment targets.

Fundamental to this type of analysis are decisions about which metrics to use as screens, how many metrics to include, what values of those metrics to use as cutoff points, and what weighting to give each metric. Metrics may include not only financial ratios but also characteristics such as market capitalization or membership as a component security in a specified index. Exhibit 3 presents a hypothetical example of a simple stock screen based on the following criteria: a valuation ratio (P/E) less than a specified value, a solvency ratio measuring financial leverage (total liabilities/total assets) not exceeding a specified value, positive operating margin, and dividend yield (dividends per share divided by price per share) greater than a specified value. Exhibit 3 shows the results of applying the screen in August 2018 to a set of 6,406 US companies with market capitalization greater than $100 million, which compose a hypothetical equity manager's investment universe.

EXHIBIT 3   Example of a Stock Screen

Criterion	Stocks Meeting Criterion	
	Number	Percent of Total
Market capitalization > $100 million	4,357	68.01%
P/E < 15	1,104	17.23%
Total liabilities/Total assets ≤ 0.9	61	0.95%
Operating income/Sales > 0	3,509	54.78%
Dividend yield > 0.5%	2,391	37.32%
Meeting all five criteria simultaneously	17	0.27%

Source for data: http://google.com/finance/.

Several points about the screen in Exhibit 3 are consistent with many screens used in practice:

- Some criteria serve as checks on the results from applying other criteria. In this hypothetical example, the second criterion selects stocks that appear relatively cheaply valued. The stocks might be cheap for a good reason, however, such as poor profitability or excessive financial leverage. So, the requirement for net income to be positive serves as a check on profitability, and the limitation on financial leverage serves as a check on financial risk. Of course, financial ratios or other statistics cannot generally control for exposure to certain other types of risk (e.g., risk related to regulatory developments or technological innovation).

- If all the criteria were completely independent of each other, the set of stocks meeting all four criteria would be 2, equal to 6,406 times 0.023 percent—the product of the fraction of stocks satisfying the four criteria individually (i.e., $0.6801 \times 0.1723 \times 0.0095 \times 0.5478 = 0.2723$, or 0.023 percent). As the screen illustrates, criteria are often not independent, and the result is that more securities pass the screening than if criteria were independent. In this example, 17 of the securities pass all five screens simultaneously. For an example of the lack of independence, we note that dividend-paying status is probably positively correlated with the ability to generate positive operating margin. If stocks that pass one test tend to also pass another, few are eliminated after the application of the second test.
- The results of screens can sometimes be relatively concentrated in a subset of the sectors represented in the benchmark. The financial leverage criterion in Exhibit 3 would exclude banking stocks, for example. What constitutes a high or low value of a measure of a financial characteristic can be sensitive to the industry in which a company operates.

Screens can be used by both **growth investors** (focused on investing in high-earnings-growth companies), **value investors** (focused on paying a relatively low share price in relation to earnings or assets per share), and **market-oriented investors** (an intermediate grouping of investors whose investment disciplines cannot be clearly categorized as value or growth). Growth screens would typically feature criteria related to earnings growth and/or momentum. Value screens, as a rule, feature criteria setting upper limits for the value of one or more valuation ratios. Market-oriented screens would not strongly emphasize valuation or growth criteria. The use of screens involving financial ratios may be most common among value investors.

An analyst may want to evaluate how a portfolio based on a particular screen would have performed historically. For this purpose, the analyst uses a process known as "back-testing." **Back-testing** applies the portfolio selection rules to historical data and calculates what returns would have been earned if a particular strategy had been used. The relevance of back-testing to investment success in practice, however, may be limited. Haugen and Baker (1996) described some of these limitations:

- Survivorship bias: If the database used in back-testing eliminates companies that cease to exist because of a bankruptcy or merger, then the remaining companies collectively will appear to have performed better.
- Look-ahead bias: If a database includes financial data updated for restatements (where companies have restated previously issued financial statements to correct errors or reflect changes in accounting principles), then there is a mismatch between what investors would have actually known at the time of the investment decision and the information used in the back-testing.
- Data-snooping bias: If researchers build a model on the basis of previous researchers' findings, then use the same database to test that model, they are not actually testing the model's predictive ability. When each step is backward looking, the same rules may or may not produce similar results in the future. The predictive ability of the model's rules can validly be tested only by using future data. One academic study has argued that the apparent ability of value strategies to generate excess returns is largely explainable as the result of collective data snooping (Conrad, Cooper, and Kaul, 2003).

EXAMPLE 8   Ratio-Based Screening for Potential Equity Investments

Below are two alternative strategies under consideration by an investment firm:

Strategy A: Invest in stocks that are components of a global equity index, have a ROE above the median ROE of all stocks in the index, and have a P/E less than the median P/E.

Strategy B: Invest in stocks that are components of a broad-based US equity index, have a ratio of price to operating cash flow in the lowest quartile of companies in the index, and have shown increases in sales for at least the past three years.

Both strategies were developed with the use of back-testing.

1. How would you characterize the two strategies?
2. What concerns might you have about using such strategies?

Solution to 1: Strategy A appears to aim for global diversification and combines a requirement for high relative profitability with a traditional measure of value (low P/E). Strategy B focuses on both large and small companies in a single market and apparently aims to identify companies that are growing and have a lower price multiple based on cash flow from operations.

Solution to 2: The use of *any* approach to investment decisions depends on the objectives and risk profile of the investor. With that crucial consideration in mind, we note that ratio-based benchmarks may be an efficient way to screen for potential equity investments. In screening, however, many questions arise.

   First, unintentional selections can be made if criteria are not specified carefully. For example, Strategy A might unintentionally select a loss-making company with negative shareholders' equity because negative net income divided by negative shareholders' equity arithmetically results in a positive ROE. Strategy B might unintentionally select a company with negative operating cash flow because price to operating cash flow will be negative and thus very low in the ranking. In both cases, the analyst can add additional screening criteria to avoid unintentional selections; these additional criteria could include requiring positive shareholders' equity in Strategy A and requiring positive operating cash flow in Strategy B.

   Second, the inputs to ratio analysis are derived from financial statements, and companies may differ in the financial standards they apply (e.g., IFRS versus US GAAP), the specific accounting method(s) they choose within those allowed by the reporting standards, and/or the estimates made in applying an accounting method.

   Third, back-testing may not provide a reliable indication of future performance because of survivorship bias, look-ahead bias, or data-snooping bias. Also, as suggested by finance theory and by common sense, the past is not necessarily indicative of the future.

   Fourth, implementation decisions can dramatically affect returns. For example, decisions about frequency and timing of portfolio re-evaluation and changes affect transaction costs and taxes paid out of the portfolio.

6. ANALYST ADJUSTMENTS TO REPORTED FINANCIALS

When comparing companies that use different accounting methods or estimate key accounting inputs in different ways, analysts frequently adjust a company's financials. In this section, we first provide a framework for considering potential analyst adjustments to facilitate such comparisons and then provide examples of such adjustments. In practice, required adjustments vary widely. The examples presented here are not intended to be comprehensive but, rather, to illustrate the use of adjustments to facilitate a meaningful comparison.

6.1. A Framework for Analyst Adjustments

In this discussion of potential analyst adjustments to a company's financial statements, we use a framework focused on the *balance sheet*. Because the financial statements are interrelated, however, adjustments to items reported on one statement may also be reflected in adjustments to items on another financial statement. For example, an analyst adjustment to inventory on the balance sheet affects cost of goods sold on the income statement (and thus also affects net income and, subsequently, the retained earnings account on the balance sheet).

Regardless of the particular order in which an analyst considers the items that may require adjustment for comparability, the following aspects are appropriate:

* *Importance (materiality)*. Is an adjustment to this item likely to affect the conclusions? In other words, does it matter? For example, in an industry where companies require minimal inventory, does it matter that two companies use different inventory accounting methods?
* *Body of standards*. Is there a difference in the body of standards being used (US GAAP versus IFRS)? If so, in which areas is the difference likely to affect a comparison?
* *Methods*. Is there a difference in accounting methods used by the companies being compared?
* *Estimates*. Is there a difference in important estimates used by the companies being compared?

The following sections illustrate analyst adjustments—first, those relating to the asset side of the balance sheet and then those relating to the liability side.

6.2. Analyst Adjustments Related to Investments

Accounting for investments in the debt and equity securities of other companies (other than investments accounted for under the equity method and investments in consolidated subsidiaries) depends on management's intention (i.e., whether to actively trade the securities, make them available for sale, or in the case of debt securities, hold them to maturity). When securities are classified as "financial assets measured at fair value through profit or loss" (similar to "trading" securities in US GAAP), unrealized gains and losses are reported in the income statement. When securities are classified as "financial assets measured at fair value through other comprehensive income" (similar to "available-for-sale" securities in US GAAP), unrealized gains and losses are not reported in the income statement and, instead, are recognized in equity. If two otherwise comparable companies have significant differences in the classification of investments, analyst adjustments may be useful to facilitate comparison.

6.3. Analyst Adjustments Related to Inventory

With inventory, adjustments may be required for different accounting methods. As described in previous chapters, a company's decision about inventory method will affect the value of inventory shown on the balance sheet as well as the value of inventory that is sold (cost of goods sold). If a company not reporting under IFRS[6] uses LIFO (last-in, first-out) and another uses FIFO (first-in, first-out), comparability of the financial results of the two companies will suffer. Companies that use the LIFO method, must also, however, disclose the value of their inventory under the FIFO method. To recast inventory values for a company using LIFO reporting on a FIFO basis, the analyst adds the ending balance of the LIFO reserve to the ending value of inventory under LIFO accounting. To adjust cost of goods sold to a FIFO basis, the analyst subtracts the change in the LIFO reserve from the reported cost of goods sold under LIFO accounting. Example 9 illustrates the use of a disclosure of the value of inventory under the FIFO method to make a more consistent comparison of the current ratios of two companies reporting in different methods.

EXAMPLE 9 Adjustment for a Company Using LIFO Accounting for Inventories

An analyst is comparing the financial performance of LP Technology Corporation (LP Tech), a hypothetical company, with the financial performance of a similar company that uses IFRS for reporting. The company reporting under IFRS uses the FIFO method of inventory accounting. Therefore, the analyst converts LP Tech's results to a comparable basis. Exhibit 4 provides balance sheet information on LP Tech.

EXHIBIT 4   Data for LP Technology Corporation

	June 30	
	2018	2017
Total current assets	820.2	749.7
Total current liabilities	218.1	198.5

NOTE 6. INVENTORIES

Inventories consist of the following ($ millions):

	June 30	
	2018	2017
Raw materials	$30.7	$29.5
Work in process	109.1	90.8
Finished goods	63.8	65.1
	$203.6	$185.4

---

[6]IAS No. 2 does not permit the use of LIFO.

If the first-in, first-out method of inventory had been used instead of the LIFO method, inventories would have been $331.8 and $305.8 million higher as of June 30, 2018 and 2017, respectively.

1. Based on the information in Exhibit 4, calculate LP Tech's current ratio under FIFO and LIFO for 2017 and 2018.
2. LP Tech makes the following disclosure in the risk section of its MD&A. Assuming an effective tax rate of 35 percent, estimate the impact on LPTC's tax liability.

> **"We value most of our inventory using the LIFO method, which could be repealed resulting in adverse effects on our cash flows and financial condition.**
>
> The cost of our inventories is primarily determined using the Last-In First-Out ("LIFO") method. Under the LIFO inventory valuation method, changes in the cost of raw materials and production activities are recognized in cost of sales in the current period even though these materials and other costs may have been incurred at significantly different values due to the length of time of our production cycle. Generally in a period of rising prices, LIFO recognizes higher costs of goods sold, which both reduces current income and assigns a lower value to the year-end inventory. Recent proposals have been initiated aimed at repealing the election to use the LIFO method for income tax purposes. According to these proposals, generally taxpayers that currently use the LIFO method would be required to revalue their LIFO inventory to its first-in, first-out ("FIFO") value. As of June 30, 2018, if the FIFO method of inventory had been used instead of the LIFO method, our inventories would have been about $332 million higher. This increase in inventory would result in a one time increase in taxable income which would be taken into account ratably over the first taxable year and the following several taxable years. The repeal of LIFO could result in a substantial tax liability which could adversely impact our cash flows and financial condition."

3. LP Tech reported cash flow from operations of $115.2 million for the year ended 30 June 2018. In comparison with the company's operating cash flow, how significant is the additional potential tax liability?

Solution to 1: The calculations of LP Tech's current ratio (current assets divided by current liabilities) are as follows:

	2018	2017
I. Current ratio (unadjusted)		
Total current assets	$820.2	$749.7
Total current liabilities	$218.1	$198.5
Current ratio (unadjusted)	3.8	3.8

(continued)

(Continued)

	2018	2017
II. Current ratio (adjusted)		
Total current assets	$820.2	$749.7
Adjust inventory to FIFO, add:	331.8	305.8
Total current assets (adjusted)	$1,152	$1,056
Total current liabilities	218.1	198.5
Current ratio (adjusted)	5.3	5.3

To adjust the LIFO inventory to FIFO, add the excess amounts of FIFO cost over LIFO cost to LIFO inventory and increase current assets by an equal amount. The effect of adjusting inventory on the current ratio is to increase the current ratio from 3.8 to 5.3 in both 2017 and 2018. LP Tech has greater liquidity according to the adjusted current ratio.

Solution to 2: Assuming an effective tax rate of 35 percent, we find the total increase in LP Tech's tax liability to be $116.1 million (0.35 × $331.8 million).

Solution to 3: The additional tax liability would be greater than the entire amount of the company's cash flow from operations of $115.2 million; the additional tax liability would be apportioned, however, over several years.

In summary, the information disclosed by companies that use LIFO allows an analyst to calculate the value of the company's inventory as if the company were using the FIFO method. If the LIFO method is used for a substantial part of a company's inventory and the LIFO reserve is large relative to reported inventory, however, the adjustment to a FIFO basis can be important for comparison of the LIFO-reporting company with a company that uses the FIFO method of inventory valuation. Example 10 illustrates a case in which such an adjustment would have a major impact on an analyst's conclusions.

EXAMPLE 10   Analyst Adjustment to Inventory Value for Comparability in a Current Ratio Comparison

Company A reports under IFRS and uses the FIFO method of inventory accounting. Company B reports under US GAAP and uses the LIFO method. Exhibit 5 gives data pertaining to current assets, LIFO reserves, and current liabilities of these companies.

EXHIBIT 5   Data for Companies Accounting for Inventory on Different Bases

	Company A (FIFO)	Company B (LIFO)
Current assets (includes inventory)	$300,000	$80,000
LIFO reserve	NA	$20,000
Current liabilities	$150,000	$45,000

NA = not applicable.

Based on the data given in Exhibit 5, compare the liquidity of the two companies as measured by the current ratio.

Solution: Company A's current ratio is 2.0. Based on unadjusted balance sheet data, Company B's current ratio is 1.78. Company A's higher current ratio indicates that Company A appears to be more liquid than Company B; however, the use of unadjusted data for Company B is not appropriate for making comparisons with Company A.

After adjusting Company B's inventory to a comparable basis (i.e., to a FIFO basis), the conclusion changes. The following table summarizes the results when Company B's inventory is left on a LIFO basis and when it is placed on a FIFO basis for comparability with Company A.

	Company A (FIFO)	Company B Unadjusted (LIFO basis)	Company B Adjusted (FIFO basis)
Current assets (includes inventory)	$300,000	$80,000	$100,000
Current liabilities	$150,000	$45,000	$45,000
Current ratio	2.00	1.78	2.22

When both companies' inventories are stated on a FIFO basis, Company B appears to be the more liquid, as indicated by its current ratio of 2.22 versus Company A's ratio of 2.00.

The adjustment to place Company B's inventory on a FIFO basis was significant because Company B was assumed to use LIFO for its entire inventory and its inventory reserve was $20,000/$80,000 = 0.25, or 25 percent of its reported inventory.

As mentioned earlier, an analyst can also adjust the cost of goods sold for a company using LIFO to a FIFO basis by subtracting the change in the amount of the LIFO reserve from cost of goods sold. Such an adjustment would be appropriate for making profitability comparisons with a company reporting on a FIFO basis and is important to make when the impact of the adjustment would be material.

6.4. Analyst Adjustments Related to Property, Plant, and Equipment

Management generally has considerable discretion in determination of depreciation expense. Depreciation expense affects the values of reported net income and reported net fixed assets. Analysts often consider management's choices related to depreciation as a qualitative factor in evaluating the quality of a company's financial reporting, and in some cases, analysts may adjust reported depreciation expense for a specific analytical purpose.

The amount of depreciation expense depends on both the accounting method and the estimates used in the calculations. Companies can use the straight-line method, an accelerated method, or a usage method to depreciate fixed assets (other than land). The straight-line method reports an equal amount of depreciation expense each period, and the expense is computed as the depreciable cost divided by the estimated useful life of the asset (when acquired, an asset's depreciable cost is calculated as its total cost minus its estimated salvage value). Accelerated methods depreciate the asset more quickly; they apportion a greater amount of the depreciable cost to depreciation expense in the earlier periods. Usage-based methods depreciate an asset in proportion to its usage. In addition to selecting a depreciation method, companies must estimate an asset's salvage value and useful life to compute depreciation.

Disclosures required for depreciation often do not facilitate specific adjustments, so comparisons of companies concerning their decisions in depreciating assets are often qualitative and general. The accounts that are associated with depreciation include the balance sheet accounts for gross property, plant, and equipment (PPE) and accumulated depreciation; the income statement amount for depreciation expense; and the statement of cash flows disclosure of capital expenditure (capex) and asset disposals. The relationships among these items can reveal various pieces of information. Note, however, that PPE typically includes a mix of assets with different depreciable lives and salvage values, so the items in the following list reflect general relationships in the total pool of assets.

- Accumulated depreciation divided by gross PPE, from the balance sheet, suggests how much of the useful life of the company's overall asset base has passed.
- Accumulated depreciation divided by depreciation expense suggests how many years' worth of depreciation expense have already been recognized (i.e., the average age of the asset base).
- Net PPE (net of accumulated depreciation) divided by depreciation expense is an approximate indicator of how many years of useful life remain for the company's overall asset base.
- Gross PPE divided by depreciation expense suggests the average life of the assets at installation.
- Capex divided by the sum of gross PPE plus capex can suggest what percentage of the asset base is being renewed through new capital investment.
- Capex in relation to asset disposal provides information on growth of the asset base.

As Example 11 shows, these relationships can be evaluated for companies in an industry to suggest differences in their strategies for asset utilization or areas for further investigation.

EXAMPLE 11   Differences in Depreciation

An analyst is evaluating the financial statements of two companies in the same industry. The companies have similar strategies with respect to the use of equipment in manufacturing their products. The following information is provided (amounts in millions):

	Company A	Company B
Net PPE	$1,200	$750
Depreciation expense	$120	$50

1. Based on the information given, estimate the average remaining useful lives of the asset bases of Company A and Company B.

2. Suppose that, based on a physical inspection of the companies' plants and other industry information, the analyst believes that the actual remaining useful lives of Company A's and Company B's assets are roughly equal at 10 years. Based only on the facts given, what might the analyst conclude about Company B's reported net income?

Solution to 1: The estimated average remaining useful life of Company A's asset base is 10 years (calculated as net PPE divided by depreciation expense, or $1,200/$120 = 10$ years). For Company B, the average remaining useful life of the asset base appears to be far longer, 15 years ($750/$50$).

Solution to 2: If 10 years were used to calculate Company B's depreciation expense, the expense would be $75 million (i.e., $25 million higher than reported) and higher depreciation expense would decrease net income. The analyst might conclude that Company B's reported net income reflects relatively more aggressive accounting estimates than estimates reflected in Company A's reported net income.

6.5. Analyst Adjustments Related to Goodwill

Goodwill arises when one company purchases another for a price that exceeds the fair value of the net identifiable assets acquired. Net identifiable assets include current assets, fixed assets, and certain intangible assets that have value and meet recognition criteria under accounting standards. A broad range of intangible assets might require valuation in the context of a business combination—for example, brands, technology, and customer lists. Goodwill is recorded as an asset and essentially represents the difference between the purchase price and the net identifiable assets. For example, assume ParentCo purchases TargetCo for a purchase price of $400 million and the fair value of TargetCo's identifiable assets is $300 million (which includes the fair values of current assets, fixed assets, and a recognized brand). ParentCo will record total assets of $400 million consisting of $300 million in identifiable assets (including the fair value of the brand) and $100 million of goodwill. The goodwill is tested annually for impairment and if the value of the goodwill is determined to be impaired, ParentCo will then reduce the amount of the asset and report a write-off resulting from impairment.

One of the conceptual difficulties with goodwill arises in comparative financial statement analysis. Consider, for example, two hypothetical US companies, one of which has grown by making an acquisition and the other of which has grown internally. Assume that the economic value of the two companies is identical: Each has an identically valuable branded product, well-trained workforce, and proprietary technology. The company that has grown by acquisition will have recorded the transaction to acquire the target company and its underlying net assets on the basis of the total consideration paid for the acquisition. The company that has grown internally will have done so by incurring expenditures for advertising, staff training, and research, all of which are expensed as incurred under US GAAP. Given the immediate expensing, the value of the internally generated assets is not capitalized onto the balance sheet and is thus not directly reflected on the company's balance sheet (revenues, income, and cash flows should reflect the benefits derived from the investment in the intangible assets). Ratios based on asset values and/or income, including profitability ratios (such as ROA) and market value to book value (MV/BV),[7] will generally differ for the two companies because of differences in the accounting values of assets and income related to acquired intangibles and goodwill, although, by assumption, the economic value of the companies is identical.

EXAMPLE 12   Ratio Comparisons for Goodwill

Miano Marseglia is an analyst who is evaluating the relative valuation of two securities brokerage companies: TD Ameritrade Holding Corporation (AMTD) and the Charles Schwab Corporation (SCHW). As one part of an overall analysis, Marseglia would like to see how the two companies compare with each other and with the industry based on market value to book value. Because both companies are large players in the industry, Marseglia expects them to sell at a higher MV/BV than the financial services sector median of 2.2. He collects the following data on the two companies.

	SCHW	AMTD
Market capitalization on August 30, 2018 (market price per share times the number of shares outstanding)	$68,620	$33,247
Total shareholders' equity (as of June 30, 2018 for both companies)	$20,097	$7,936
Goodwill	$1,227	$4,198
Other intangible assets	$93	$1,363

Marseglia computes the MV/BV for the companies as follows:

SCHW $68,620/$20,097 = 3.4
AMTD $33,247/$7,936 = 4.2

As expected, each company appears to be selling at a premium to the sector median MV/BV of 2.2. The companies have similar MV/BVs (i.e., they are somewhat equally valued relative to the book value of shareholders' equity). Marseglia is concerned, however, because he notes that AMTD has significant amounts of goodwill and acquired intangible assets. He wonders what the relative value would be if the MV/BV were computed after adjusting book value, first, to remove goodwill and, second, to remove all intangible assets. Book value reduced by all intangible assets (including goodwill) is known as "tangible book value."

1. Compute the MV/BV adjusted for goodwill and the price/tangible book value for each company.
2. Which company appears to be a better value based *solely* on this data? (Note that the MV/BV is only one part of a broader analysis. Much more evidence related to

---

[7]MV/BV equals the total market value of the stock (the market capitalization) divided by total stockholders' equity. It is also referred to as the price-to-book ratio because it can also be calculated as price per share divided by stockholders' equity per share.

the valuations and the comparability of the companies would be required to reach a conclusion about whether one company is a better value.)

Solution to 1:

	($ millions)	
	SCHW	AMTD
Total stockholders' equity	$20,097	$7,936
Less: Goodwill	$1,227	$4,198
Book value, adjusted	$18,870	$3,738
Adjusted MV/BV	**3.6**	**8.9**

	($ millions)	
	SCHW	AMTD
Total stockholders' equity	$20,097	$7,936
Less: Goodwill	$1,227	$4,198
Less: Other intangible assets	$93	$1,363
Tangible book value	$18,777	$2,375
MV/tangible book value	**3.7**	**14.0**

Solution to 2:
After adjusting for goodwill, SCHW appears to be selling for a much lower price relative to book value than does AMTD (3.6 versus 8.9) after adjusting for goodwill. The difference is more extreme after adjusting for other intangibles.

7. SUMMARY

This chapter described selected applications of financial statement analysis, including the evaluation of past financial performance, the projection of future financial performance, the assessment of credit risk, and the screening of potential equity investments. In addition, the chapter introduced analyst adjustments to reported financials. In all cases, the analyst needs to have a good understanding of the financial reporting standards under which the financial statements were prepared. Because standards evolve over time, analysts must stay current in order to make good investment decisions.

The main points in the chapter are as follows:

- Evaluating a company's historical performance addresses not only what happened but also the causes behind the company's performance and how the performance reflects the company's strategy.
- The projection of a company's future net income and cash flow often begins with a top-down sales forecast in which the analyst forecasts industry sales and the company's market share. By projecting profit margins or expenses and the level of investment in working and fixed capital needed to support projected sales, the analyst can forecast net income and cash flow.

- Projections of future performance are needed for discounted cash flow valuation of equity and are often needed in credit analysis to assess a borrower's ability to repay interest and principal of a debt obligation.
- Credit analysis uses financial statement analysis to evaluate credit-relevant factors, including tolerance for leverage, operational stability, and margin stability.
- When ratios constructed from financial statement data and market data are used to screen for potential equity investments, fundamental decisions include which metrics to use as screens, how many metrics to include, what values of those metrics to use as cutoff points, and what weighting to give each metric.
- Analyst adjustments to a company's reported financial statements are sometimes necessary (e.g., when comparing companies that use different accounting methods or assumptions). Adjustments can include those related to investments; inventory; property, plant, and equipment; and goodwill.

REFERENCES

Benninga, Simon Z., and Oded H. Sarig. 1997. *Corporate Finance: A Valuation Approach*. New York: McGraw-Hill Publishing.
Conrad, J., M. Cooper, and G. Kaul. 2003. "Value versus Glamour." *Journal of Finance*, vol. 58, no. 5: 1969–1996.
Haugen, R.A., and N.L. Baker. 1996. "Commonality in the Determinants of Expected Stock Returns." *Journal of Financial Economics*, vol. 41, no. 3 : 401–439.

PRACTICE PROBLEMS

1. Projecting profit margins into the future on the basis of past results would be *most* reliable when the company:
   A. is in the commodities business.
   B. operates in a single business segment.
   C. is a large, diversified company operating in mature industries.

2. Galambos Corporation had an average receivables collection period of 19 days in 2003. Galambos has stated that it wants to decrease its collection period in 2004 to match the industry average of 15 days. Credit sales in 2003 were $300 million, and analysts expect credit sales to increase to $400 million in 2004. To achieve the company's goal of decreasing the collection period, the change in the average accounts receivable balance from 2003 to 2004 that must occur is *closest* to:
   A. –$420,000.
   B. $420,000.
   C. $836,000.

3. Credit analysts are likely to consider which of the following in making a rating recommendation?
   A. Business risk but not financial risk
   B. Financial risk but not business risk
   C. Both business risk and financial risk

4. When screening for potential equity investments based on return on equity, to control risk, an analyst would be *most likely* to include a criterion that requires:
   A. positive net income.
   B. negative net income.
   C. negative shareholders' equity.

5. One concern when screening for stocks with low price-to-earnings ratios is that companies with low P/Es may be financially weak. What criterion might an analyst include to avoid inadvertently selecting weak companies?
   A. Net income less than zero
   B. Debt-to-total assets ratio below a certain cutoff point
   C. Current-year sales growth lower than prior-year sales growth

6. When a database eliminates companies that cease to exist because of a merger or bankruptcy, this can result in:
   A. look-ahead bias.
   B. back-testing bias.
   C. survivorship bias.

7. In a comprehensive financial analysis, financial statements should be:
   A. used as reported without adjustment.
   B. adjusted after completing ratio analysis.
   C. adjusted for differences in accounting standards, such as international financial reporting standards and US generally accepted accounting principles.

8. When comparing a US company that uses the last in, first out (LIFO) method of inventory with companies that prepare their financial statements under international financial reporting standards (IFRS), analysts should be aware that according to IFRS, the LIFO method of inventory:
   A. is never acceptable.
   B. is always acceptable.
   C. is acceptable when applied to finished goods inventory only.

9. An analyst is evaluating the balance sheet of a US company that uses last in, first out (LIFO) accounting for inventory. The analyst collects the following data:

	Dec. 31, 2005	Dec. 31, 2006
Inventory reported on balance sheet	$500,000	$600,000
LIFO reserve	$50,000	$70,000
Average tax rate	30%	30%

   After adjusting the amounts to convert to the first in, first out (FIFO) method, inventory at December 31, 2006 would be *closest* to:
   A. $600,000.
   B. $620,000.
   C. $670,000.

10. An analyst gathered the following data for a company ($ millions):

	Dec. 31, 2000	Dec. 31, 2001
Gross investment in fixed assets	$2.8	$2.8
Accumulated depreciation	$1.2	$1.6

The average age and average depreciable life of the company's fixed assets at the end of 2001 are *closest* to:

	Average Age	Average Depreciable Life
A.	1.75 years	7 years
B.	1.75 years	14 years
C.	4.00 years	7 years

11. To compute tangible book value, an analyst would:
    A. add goodwill to stockholders' equity.
    B. add all intangible assets to stockholders' equity.
    C. subtract all intangible assets from stockholders' equity.

12. Which of the following is an off-balance-sheet financing technique? The use of:
    A. capital leases.
    B. operating leases.
    C. the last in, first out inventory method.

13. To better evaluate the solvency of a company, an analyst would *most likely* add to total liabilities:
    A. the present value of future capital lease payments.
    B. the total amount of future operating lease payments.
    C. the present value of future operating lease payments.

CHAPTER 13

INTERCORPORATE INVESTMENTS

Susan Perry Williams, CPA, CMA, PhD

LEARNING OUTCOMES

After completing this chapter, you will be able to do the following:

- describe the classification, measurement, and disclosure under International Financial Reporting Standards (IFRS) for 1) investments in financial assets, 2) investments in associates, 3) joint ventures, 4) business combinations, and 5) special purpose and variable interest entities;
- distinguish between IFRS and US GAAP in the classification, measurement, and disclosure of investments in financial assets, investments in associates, joint ventures, business combinations, and special purpose and variable interest entities;
- analyze how different methods used to account for intercorporate investments affect financial statements and ratios.

1. INTRODUCTION

Intercorporate investments (investments in other companies) can have a significant impact on an investing company's financial performance and position. Companies invest in the debt and equity securities of other companies to diversify their asset base, enter new markets, obtain competitive advantages, deploy excess cash, and achieve additional profitability. Debt securities include commercial paper, corporate and government bonds and notes, redeemable preferred stock, and asset-backed securities. Equity securities include common stock and non-redeemable preferred stock. The percentage of equity ownership a company acquires in an investee depends on the resources available, the ability to acquire the shares, and the desired level of influence or control.

The International Accounting Standards Board (IASB) and the US Financial Accounting Standards Board (FASB) worked to reduce differences in accounting standards that apply to the classification, measurement, and disclosure of intercorporate investments. The resulting standards have improved the relevance, transparency, and comparability of information provided in financial statements.

Complete convergence between IFRS accounting standards and US GAAP did not occur for accounting for financial instruments, and some differences still exist. The terminology used in this chapter is IFRS-oriented. US GAAP may not use identical terminology, but in most cases the terminology is similar.

This chapter is organized as follows: Section 2 explains the basic categorization of corporate investments. Section 3 describes reporting under IFRS 9, the IASB standard for financial instruments. Section 4 describes equity method reporting for investments in associates where significant influence can exist including the reporting for joint ventures, a type of investment where control is shared. Section 5 describes reporting for business combinations, the parent/subsidiary relationship, and variable interest and special purpose entities. A summary concludes the chapter.

2. BASIC CORPORATE INVESTMENT CATEGORIES

In general, investments in marketable debt and equity securities can be categorized as 1) investments in financial assets in which the investor has no significant influence or control over the operations of the investee, 2) investments in associates in which the investor can exert significant influence (but not control) over the investee, 3) joint ventures where control is shared by two or more entities, and 4) business combinations, including investments in subsidiaries, in which the investor obtains a controlling interest over the investee The distinction between investments in financial assets, investments in associates, and business combinations is based on the degree of influence or control rather than purely on the percent holding. However, lack of influence is generally presumed when the investor holds less than a 20% equity interest, significant influence is generally presumed between 20% and 50%, and control is presumed when the percentage of ownership exceeds 50%.

The following excerpt from Note 2 to the Financial Statements in the 2017 Annual Report of GlaxoSmithKline, a British pharmaceutical and healthcare company, illustrates the categorization and disclosure in practice:

> Entities over which the Group has the power to direct the relevant activities so as to affect the returns to the Group, generally through control over the financial and operating policies, are accounted for as subsidiaries.
>
> Where the Group has the ability to exercise joint control over, and rights to the net assets of, entities, the entities are accounted for as joint ventures. Where the Group has the ability to exercise joint control over an arrangement, but has rights to specified assets and obligations for specified liabilities of the arrangement, the arrangement is accounted for as a joint operation. Where the Group has the ability to exercise significant influence over entities, they are accounted for as associates. The results and assets and liabilities of associates and joint ventures are incorporated into the consolidated financial statements using the equity method of accounting. The Group's rights to assets, liabilities, revenue and expenses of joint operations are included in the consolidated financial statements in accordance with those rights and obligations.

A summary of the financial reporting and relevant standards for various types of corporate investment is presented in Exhibit 1 (the headings in Exhibit 1 use the terminology of IFRS;

US GAAP categorizes intercorporate investments similarly but not identically). The reader should be alert to the fact that value measurement and/or the treatment of changes in value can vary depending on the classification and whether IFRS or US GAAP is used. The alternative treatments are discussed in greater depth later in this chapter.

EXHIBIT 1   Summary of Accounting Treatments for Investments

	In Financial Assets	In Associates	Business Combinations	In Joint Ventures
Influence	Not significant	Significant	Controlling	Shared control
Typical percentage interest	Usually < 20%	Usually 20% to 50%	Usually > 50% or other indications of control	
US GAAP[b]	FASB ASC Topic 320	FASB ASC Topic 323	FASB ASC Topics 805 and 810	FASB ASC Topic 323
Financial Reporting	Classified as: • Fair value through profit or loss • Fair value through other comprehensive income • Amortized cost	Equity method	Consolidation	IFRS: Equity method
Applicable IFRS[a]	IFRS 9	IAS 28	IAS 27 IFRS 3 IFRS 10	IFRS 11 IFRS 12 IAS 28
US GAAP[b]	FASB ASC Topic 320	FASB ASC Topic 323	FASB ASC Topics 805 and 810	FASB ASC Topic 323

[a] IFRS 9 Financial Instruments; IAS 28 Investments in Associates; IAS 27 Separate Financial Statements; IFRS 3 Business Combinations; IFRS 10 Consolidated Financial Statements; IFRS 11 Joint Arrangements; IFRS 12, Disclosure of Interests in Other Entities.
[b] FASB ASC Topic 320 [Investments–Debt and Equity Securities]; FASB ASC Topic 323 [Investments–Equity Method and Joint Ventures]; FASB ASC Topics 805 [Business Combinations] and 810 [Consolidations].

3. INVESTMENTS IN FINANCIAL ASSETS: IFRS 9

Both IASB and FASB developed revised standards for financial investments. The IASB issued the first phase of their project dealing with classification and measurement of financial instruments by including relevant chapters in IFRS 9, *Financial Instruments*. IFRS 9, which replaces IAS 39, became effective for annual periods on January 1, 2018. The FASB's guidance relating to the accounting for investments in financial instruments is contained in ASC 825, *Financial Instruments*, which has been updated several times, with the standard being effective for periods after December 15, 2017. The resulting US GAAP guidance has many consistencies with IFRS requirements, but there are also some differences.

IFRS 9 is based on an approach that considers the contractual characteristics of cash flows as well as the management of the financial assets. The portfolio approach of the previous standard (i.e., designation of held for trading, available-for-sale, and held-to-maturity) is no longer appropriate, and the terms *available-for-sale* and *held-to-maturity* no longer appear in

IFRS 9. Another key change in IFRS 9, compared with IAS 39, relates to the approach to loan impairment. In particular, companies are required to migrate from an incurred loss model to an expected credit loss model. This results in companies evaluating not only historical and current information about loan performance, but also forward-looking information.[1]

The criteria for using amortized cost are similar to those of the IAS 39 "management intent to hold-to-maturity" classification. Specifically, to be measured at amortized cost, financial assets must meet two criteria:[2]

1. A business model test:[3] The financial assets are being held to collect contractual cash flows; and
2. A cash flow characteristic test: The contractual cash flows are solely payments of principal and interest on principal.

3.1. Classification and Measurement

IFRS 9 divides all financial assets into two classifications—those measured at amortized cost and those measured at fair value. Under this approach, there are three different categories of measurement:

- Amortized cost
- Fair value through profit or loss (FVPL) or
- Fair Value through other comprehensive income (FVOCI).

All financial assets are measured at fair value when initially acquired (which will generally be equal to the cost basis on the date of acquisition). Subsequently, financial assets are measured at either fair value or amortized cost. Financial assets that meet the two criteria above are generally measured at amortized cost. If the financial asset meets the criteria above but may be sold, a "hold-to-collect and sell" business model, it may be measured at fair value through other comprehensive income (FVOCI). However, management may choose the "fair value through profit or loss" (FVPL) option to avoid an accounting mismatch.[4] An "accounting mismatch" refers to an inconsistency resulting from different measurement bases for assets and liabilities, i.e., some are measured at amortized cost and some at fair value. Debt instruments are measured at amortized cost, fair value through other comprehensive income (FVOCI), or fair value through profit or loss (FVPL) depending upon the business model.

Equity instruments are measured at FVPL or at FVOCI; they are not eligible for measurement at amortized cost. Equity investments held-for-trading must be measured at FVPL. Other equity investments can be measured at FVPL or FVOCI; however, the choice is irrevocable. If the entity uses the FVOCI option, only the dividend income is recognized in profit or loss. Furthermore, the requirements for reclassifying gains or losses recognized in other comprehensive income are different for debt and equity instruments.

---

[1] Under US GAAP, requirements for assessing credit impairment are included in ASC 326, which is effective for most public companies beginning January 1, 2020.
[2] IFRS 9, paragraph 4.1.2.
[3] A business model refers to how an entity manages its financial assets in order to generate cash flows – by collecting contractual cash flows, selling financial assets or both. (IFRS 9 Financial Instruments, Project Summary, July 2014)
[4] IFRS 9, paragraph 4.1.5.

EXHIBIT 2   Financial Assets Classification and Measurement Model, IFRS 9

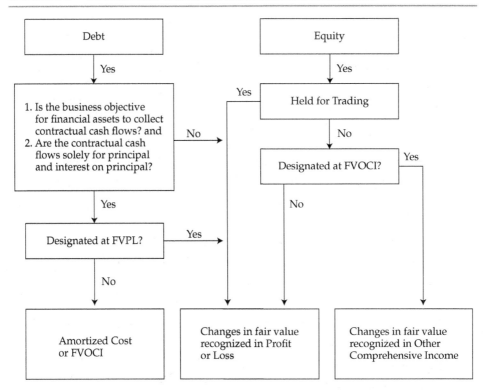

Financial assets that are derivatives are measured at fair value through profit or loss (except for hedging instruments). Embedded derivatives are not separated from the hybrid contract if the asset falls within the scope of this standard and the asset as a whole is measured at FVPL.

Exhibit 3 contains an excerpt from the 2017 Deutsche Bank financial statements that describes how financial assets and financial liabilities are determined, measured, and recognized on its financial statements.

EXHIBIT 3   Excerpt from Deutsche Bank's 2017 Financial Statements

FINANCIAL ASSETS

IFRS 9 requires that an entity's business model and a financial instrument's contractual cash flows will determine its classification and measurement in the financial statements. Upon initial recognition each financial asset will be classified as either fair value through profit or loss ('FVTPL'), amortized cost, or fair value through Other Comprehensive Income ('FVOCI'). As the requirements under IFRS 9 are different than the assessments under the existing IAS 39 rules, there will be some differences from the classification and measurement of financial assets under IAS 39, including whether to elect the fair value option on certain assets. The classification and measurement of financial liabilities remain largely unchanged under IFRS 9 from current requirements.

In 2015, the Group made an initial determination of business models and assessed the contractual cash flow characteristics of the financial assets within such business models to determine the potential classification and measurement changes as a result of IFRS 9. As a result of the

(continued)

EXHIBIT 3   (Continued)

initial analysis performed, in 2016 the Group identified a population of financial assets which are to be measured at either amortized cost or fair value through other comprehensive income, which will be subject to the IFRS 9 impairment rules. In 2017, the Group updated its business model assessments and completed outstanding classification decisions. On initial recognition of an equity investment not held for trading, the Group may on an investment-by-investment basis, irrevocably elect to present subsequent fair value changes in OCI. The Group has not made any such elections. Where issued debt liabilities are designated at fair value, the fair value movements attributable to an entity's own credit risk will be recognized in Other Comprehensive Income rather than in the Statement of Income. The standard also allows the Group the option to elect to apply early the presentation of fair value movements of an entity's credit risk in Other Comprehensive Income prior to adopting IFRS 9 in full. The Group did not early adopt this requirement

3.2. Reclassification of Investments

Under IFRS 9, the reclassification of equity instruments is not permitted because an entity's initial classification of FVPL and FVOCI is irrevocable. Reclassification of debt instruments is only permitted if the business model for the financial assets (objective for holding the financial assets) has changed in a way that significantly affects operations. Changes to the business model will require judgment and are expected to be very infrequent.

When reclassification is deemed appropriate, there is no restatement of prior periods at the reclassification date. For example, if the financial asset is reclassified from amortized cost to FVPL, the asset is then measured at fair value with any gain or loss immediately recognized in profit or loss. If the financial asset is reclassified from FVPL to amortized cost, the fair value at the reclassification date becomes the carrying amount.

In summary, the major changes made by IFRS 9 are:

- A business model approach to classification of debt instruments.
- Three classifications for financial assets:
  - fair value through profit or loss (FVPL),
  - fair value through other comprehensive income (FVOCI), and
  - amortized cost.
- Reclassifications of debt instruments are permitted only when the business model changes. The choice to measure equity investments at FVOCI or FVPL is irrevocable.
- A redesign of the provisioning models for financial assets, financial guarantees, loan commitments, and lease receivables. The new standard moves the recognition criteria from an "incurred loss" model to an "expected loss" model. Under the new criteria, there is an earlier recognition of impairment—12 month expected losses for performing assets and lifetime expected losses for non-performing assets, to be captured upfront.[5]

Analysts typically evaluate performance separately for operating and investing activities. Analysis of operating performance should exclude items related to investing activities such as interest income, dividends, and realized and unrealized gains and losses. For comparative purposes, analysts should exclude non-operating assets in the determination of return on net operating assets. IFRS and US GAAP[6] require disclosure of fair value of each class of investment in

---

[5] IFRS 9, paragraphs 5.5.4, 5.5.5, 5.5.15, 5.5.16.
[6] IFRS 7 Financial Instruments: Disclosures and FASB ASC Section 320-10-50 [Investments–Debt and Equity Securities–Overall–Disclosure].

financial assets. Using market values and adjusting pro forma financial statements for consistency improves assessments of performance ratios across companies.

4. INVESTMENTS IN ASSOCIATES AND JOINT VENTURES

Under both IFRS and US GAAP, when a company (investor) holds 20 to 50% of the voting rights of an associate (investee), either directly or indirectly (i.e., through subsidiaries), it is presumed that the company has (or can exercise) significant influence, but not control, over the investee's business activities.[7] Conversely, if the investor holds, directly or indirectly, less than 20% of the voting power of the associate (investee), it is presumed that the investor cannot exercise significant influence, unless such influence can be demonstrated. IAS 28 (IFRS) and FASB ASC Topic 323 (US GAAP) apply to most investments in which an investor has significant influence; they also provide guidance on accounting for investments in associates using the equity method.[8] These standards note that significant influence may be evidenced by

- representation on the board of directors;
- participation in the policy-making process;
- material transactions between the investor and the investee;
- interchange of managerial personnel; or
- technological dependency.

The ability to exert significant influence means that the financial and operating performance of the investee is partly influenced by management decisions and operational skills of the investor. The equity method of accounting for the investment reflects the economic reality of this relationship and provides a more objective basis for reporting investment income.

Joint ventures—ventures undertaken and controlled by two or more parties—can be a convenient way to enter foreign markets, conduct specialized activities, and engage in risky projects. They can be organized in a variety of different forms and structures. Some joint ventures are primarily contractual relationships, whereas others have common ownership of assets. They can be partnerships, limited liability companies (corporations), or other legal forms (unincorporated associations, for example). IFRS identify the following common characteristics of joint ventures: 1) A contractual arrangement exists between two or more venturers, and 2) the contractual arrangement establishes joint control. Both IFRS and US GAAP[9] require the equity method of accounting for joint ventures.[10]

Only under rare circumstances will joint ventures be allowed to use proportionate consolidation under IFRS and US GAAP. On the venturer's financial statements, proportionate

---

[7] The determination of significant influence under IFRS also includes currently exercisable or convertible warrants, call options, or convertible securities that the investor owns, which give it additional voting power or reduce another party's voting power over the financial and operating policies of the investee. Under US GAAP, the determination of an investor's voting stock interest is based only on the voting shares outstanding at the time of the purchase. The existence and effect of securities with potential voting rights are not considered.

[8] IAS 28 Investments in Associates and Joint Ventures and FASB ASC Topic 323 [Investments–Equity Method and Joint Ventures].

[9] Under US GAAP, ASC 323-10 provides guidance on the application of the equity method of accounting.

[10] IFRS 11, Joint Arrangements classifies joint arrangements as either a joint operation or a joint venture. Joint ventures are arrangements wherein parties with joint control have rights to the net assets of the arrangement. Joint ventures are required to use equity method under IAS 28.

consolidation requires the venturer's share of the assets, liabilities, income, and expenses of the joint venture to be combined or shown on a line-by-line basis with similar items under its sole control. In contrast, the equity method results in a single line item (equity in income of the joint venture) on the income statement and a single line item (investment in joint venture) on the balance sheet.

Because the single line item on the income statement under the equity method reflects the net effect of the sales and expenses of the joint venture, the total income recognized is identical under the two methods. In addition, because the single line item on the balance sheet item (investment in joint venture) under the equity method reflects the investors' share of the net assets of the joint venture, the total net assets of the investor is identical under both methods. There can be significant differences, however, in ratio analysis between the two methods because of the differential effects on values for total assets, liabilities, sales, expenses, etc.

4.1. Equity Method of Accounting: Basic Principles

Under the equity method of accounting, the equity investment is initially recorded on the investor's balance sheet at cost. In subsequent periods, the carrying amount of the investment is adjusted to recognize the investor's proportionate share of the investee's earnings or losses, and these earnings or losses are reported in income. Dividends or other distributions received from the investee are treated as a return of capital and reduce the carrying amount of the investment and are not reported in the investor's profit or loss. The equity method is often referred to as "one-line consolidation" because the investor's proportionate ownership interest in the assets and liabilities of the investee is disclosed as a single line item (net assets) on its balance sheet, and the investor's share of the revenues and expenses of the investee is disclosed as a single line item on its income statement. (Contrast these disclosures with the disclosures on consolidated statements in Section 6.) Equity method investments are classified as non-current assets on the balance sheet. The investor's share of the profit or loss of equity method investments, and the carrying amount of those investments, must be separately disclosed on the income statement and balance sheet.

EXAMPLE 1   Equity Method: Balance in Investment Account

Branch (a fictitious company) purchases a 20% interest in Williams (a fictitious company) for €200,000 on January 1, 2016. Williams reports income and dividends as follows:

	Income	Dividends
2016	€200,000	€50,000
2017	300,000	100,000
2018	400,000	200,000
	€900,000	€350,000

Calculate the investment in Williams that appears on Branch's balance sheet as of the end of 2018.

Solution: Investment in Williams at December 31, 2018:

Initial cost	€200,000	
Equity income 2016	€40,000	= (20% of €200,000 Income)
Dividends received 2016	(€10,000)	= (20% of €50,000 Dividends)
Equity income 2017	€60,000	= (20% of €300,000 Income)
Dividends received 2017	(€20,000)	= (20% of €100,000 Dividends)
Equity income 2018	€80,000	= (20% of €400,000 Income)
Dividends received 2018	(€40,000)	= (20% of €200,000 Dividends)
Balance-Equity Investment	€310,000	= [€200,000 + 20% × (€900,000 – €350,000)]

This simple example implicitly assumes that the purchase price equals the purchased equity (20%) in the book value of Williams' net assets. Sections 5.2 and 5.3 will cover the more typical case in which the purchase price does not equal the proportionate share of the book value of the investee's net assets.

Using the equity method, the investor includes its share of the investee's profit and losses on the income statement. The equity investment is carried at cost, plus its share of post-acquisition income, less dividends received. The recorded investment value can decline as a result of investee losses or a permanent decline in the investee's market value (see Section 5.5 for treatment of impairments). If the investment value is reduced to zero, the investor usually discontinues the equity method and does not record further losses. If the investee subsequently reports profits, the equity method is resumed after the investor's share of the profits equals the share of losses not recognized during the suspension of the equity method. Exhibit 4 contains excerpts from Deutsche Bank's 2017 annual report that describes its accounting treatment for investments in associates.

EXHIBIT 4   Excerpt from Deutsche Bank 2017 Annual Report

[From Note 01] ASSOCIATES

An associate is an entity in which the Group has significant influence, but not a controlling interest, over the operating and financial management policy decisions of the entity. Significant influence is generally presumed when the Group holds between 20 % and 50 % of the voting rights. The existence and effect of potential voting rights that are currently exercisable or convertible are considered in assessing whether the Group has significant influence. Among the other factors that are considered in determining whether the Group has significant influence are representation on the board of directors (supervisory board in the case of German stock corporations) and material intercompany transactions. The existence of these factors could require the application of the equity method of accounting for a particular investment even though the Group's investment is less than 20 % of the voting stock.

Investments in associates are accounted for under the equity method of accounting. The Group's share of the results of associates is adjusted to conform to the accounting policies of the Group and is reported in the Consolidated Statement of Income as Net income (loss) from equity method investments. The Group's share in the associate's profits and losses resulting from intercompany sales is eliminated on consolidation.

(continued)

EXHIBIT 4   (Continued)

If the Group previously held an equity interest in an entity (for example, as available for sale) and subsequently gained significant influence, the previously held equity interest is remeasured to fair value and any gain or loss is recognized in the Consolidated Statement of Income. Any amounts previously recognized in other comprehensive income associated with the equity interest would be reclassified to the Consolidated Statement of Income at the date the Group gains significant influence, as if the Group had disposed of the previously held equity interest.

Under the equity method of accounting, the Group's investments in associates and jointly controlled entities are initially recorded at cost including any directly related transaction costs incurred in acquiring the associate, and subsequently increased (or decreased) to reflect both the Group's pro-rata share of the post-acquisition net income (or loss) of the associate or jointly controlled entity and other movements included directly in the equity of the associate or jointly controlled entity. Goodwill arising on the acquisition of an associate or a jointly controlled entity is included in the carrying value of the investment (net of any accumulated impairment loss). As goodwill is not reported separately it is not specifically tested for impairment. Rather, the entire equity method investment is tested for impairment at each balance sheet date.

If there is objective evidence of impairment, an impairment test is performed by comparing the investment's recoverable amount, which is the higher of its value in use and fair value less costs to sell, with its carrying amount. An impairment loss recognized in prior periods is only reversed if there has been a change in the estimates used to determine the in-vestment's recoverable amount since the last impairment loss was recognized. If this is the case the carrying amount of the investment is increased to its higher recoverable amount. The increased carrying amount of the investment in associate attributable to a reversal of an impairment loss shall not exceed the carrying amount that would have been determined had no impairment loss been recognized for the investment in prior years.

At the date that the Group ceases to have significant influence over the associate or jointly controlled entity the Group recognizes a gain or loss on the disposal of the equity method in-vestment equal to the difference between the sum of the fair value of any retained investment and the proceeds from disposing of the associate and the carrying amount of the investment. Amounts recognized in prior periods in other comprehensive income in relation to the associate are accounted for on the same basis as would have been required if the investee had directly disposed of the related assets or liabilities.

[From Note 17] EQUITY METHOD INVESTMENTS

Investments in associates and jointly controlled entities are accounted for using the equity method of accounting.

The Group holds interests in 77 (2016: 92) associates and 13 (2016: 14) jointly controlled entities. There are no individually material investments in associates and joint ventures.

Aggregated financial information on the Group's share in associates and joint ventures that are individually immaterial (in €m)	Dec 31, 2017	Dec 31, 2016
Carrying amount of all associated that are individually immaterial to the Group	866	1,027
Aggregated amount of the Group's share of profit (loss) from continuing operations	141	183
Aggregated amount of the Group's share of post-tax profit (loss) from discontinued operations	0	0
Aggregated amount of the Group's share of other comprehensive income	(36)	11
Aggregated amount of the Group's share of total comprehensive income	105	194

It is interesting to note the explanations for the treatment of associates when the ownership percentage is less than 20% or is greater than 50%. The equity method reflects the strength of the relationship between the investor and its associates. In the instances where the percentage ownership is less than 20%, Deutsche Bank uses the equity method because it has significant influence over these associates' operating and financial policies either through its representation on their boards of directors and/or other measures. The equity method provides a more objective basis for reporting investment income than the accounting treatment for investments in financial assets because the investor can potentially influence the timing of dividend distributions.

4.2. Investment Costs That Exceed the Book Value of the Investee

The cost (purchase price) to acquire shares of an investee is often greater than the book value of those shares. This is because, among other things, many of the investee's assets and liabilities reflect historical cost rather than fair value. IFRS allow a company to measure its property, plant, and equipment using either historical cost or fair value (less accumulated depreciation).[11] US GAAP, however, require the use of historical cost (less accumulated depreciation) to measure property, plant, and equipment.[12]

When the cost of the investment exceeds the investor's proportionate share of the book value of the investee's (associate's) net identifiable tangible and intangible assets (e.g., inventory, property, plant and equipment, trademarks, patents), the difference is first allocated to specific assets (or categories of assets) using fair values. These differences are then amortized to the investor's proportionate share of the investee's profit or loss over the economic lives of the assets whose fair values exceeded book values. It should be noted that the allocation is not recorded formally; what appears initially in the investment account on the balance sheet of the investor is the cost. Over time, as the differences are amortized, the balance in the investment account will come closer to representing the ownership percentage of the book value of the net assets of the associate.

IFRS and US GAAP both treat the difference between the cost of the acquisition and investor's share of the fair value of the net identifiable assets as goodwill. Therefore, any remaining difference between the acquisition cost and the fair value of net identifiable assets that cannot be allocated to specific assets is treated as goodwill and is not amortized. Instead, it is reviewed for impairment on a regular basis, and written down for any identified impairment. Goodwill, however, is included in the carrying amount of the investment, because investment is reported as a single line item on the investor's balance sheet.[13]

---

[11] After initial recognition, an entity can choose to use either a cost model or a revaluation model to measure its property, plant, and equipment. Under the revaluation model, property, plant, and equipment whose fair value can be measured reliably can be carried at a revalued amount. This revalued amount is its fair value at the date of the revaluation less any subsequent accumulated depreciation

[12] Successful companies should be able to generate, through the productive use of assets, economic value in excess of the resale value of the assets themselves. Therefore, investors may be willing to pay a premium in anticipation of future benefits. These benefits could be a result of general market conditions, the investor's ability to exert significant influence on the investee, or other synergies.

[13] If the investor's share of the fair value of the associate's net assets (identifiable assets, liabilities, and contingent liabilities) is greater than the cost of the investment, the difference is excluded from the carrying amount of the investment and instead included as income in the determination of the investor's share of the associate's profit or loss in the period in which the investment is acquired.

EXAMPLE 2   Equity Method Investment in Excess of Book Value

Blake Co. and Brown Co. are two hypothetical companies. Assume that Blake Co. acquires 30% of the outstanding shares of Brown Co. At the acquisition date, book values and fair values of Brown's recorded assets and liabilities are as follows:

	Book Value	Fair Value
Current assets	€10,000	€10,000
Plant and equipment	190,000	220,000
Land	120,000	140,000
	€320,000	€370,000
Liabilities	100,000	100,000
Net assets	€220,000	€270,000

Blake Co. believes the value of Brown Co. is higher than the fair value of its identifiable net assets. They offer €100,000 for a 30% interest in Brown, which represents a €34,000 excess purchase price. The difference between the fair value and book value of the net identifiable assets is €50,000 (€270,000 – 220,000). Based on Blake Co.'s 30% ownership, €15,000 of the excess purchase price is attributable to the net identifiable assets, and the residual is attributable to goodwill. Calculate goodwill.

Solution:

Purchase price	€100,000
30% of book value of Brown (30% × €220,000)	66,000
Excess purchase price	€34,000
Attributable to net assets	
Plant and equipment (30% × €30,000)	€9,000
Land (30% × €20,000)	6,000
Goodwill (residual)	19,000
	€34,000

As illustrated above, goodwill is the residual excess not allocated to identifiable assets or liabilities. The investment is carried as a non-current asset on Blake's book as a single line item (Investment in Brown, €100,000) on the acquisition date.

4.3. Amortization of Excess Purchase Price

The excess purchase price allocated to the assets and liabilities is accounted for in a manner that is consistent with the accounting treatment for the specific asset or liability to which it is assigned. Amounts allocated to assets and liabilities that are expensed (such as inventory) or periodically depreciated or amortized (plant, property, and intangible assets) must be treated in a similar manner. These allocated amounts are not reflected on the financial statements of the investee (associate), and the investee's income statement will not reflect the necessary periodic adjustments. Therefore, the investor must directly record these adjustment effects by reducing the carrying amount of the investment on its balance sheet and by reducing the investee's profit recognized on its income statement. Amounts allocated to assets or liabilities that are not systematically amortized (e.g., land) will continue to be reported at their fair value as of the date the investment was acquired. As stated previously, goodwill is included in the carrying amount of the investment instead of being separately recognized. It is not amortized because it is considered to have an indefinite life.

Using the previous example and assuming a 10-year useful life for plant, property, and equipment and using straight-line depreciation, the annual amortization is as follows:

Account	Excess Price (€)	Useful Life	Amortization/Year (€)
Plant and equipment	9,000	10 years	900
Land	6,000	Indefinite	0
Goodwill	19,000	Indefinite	0

Annual amortization would reduce the investor's share of the investee's reported income (equity income) and the balance in the investment account by €900 for each year over the 10-year period.

EXAMPLE 3   Equity Method Investments with Goodwill

On January 1, 2018, Parker Company acquired 30% of Prince Inc. common shares for the cash price of €500,000 (both companies are fictitious). It is determined that Parker has the ability to exert significant influence on Prince's financial and operating decisions. The following information concerning Prince's assets and liabilities on January 1, 2018 is provided:

Prince, Inc.

	Book Value	Fair Value	Difference
Current assets	€100,000	€100,000	€0
Plant and equipment	1,900,000	2,200,000	300,000
	€2,000,000	€2,300,000	€300,000
Liabilities	800,000	800,000	0
Net assets	€1,200,000	€1,500,000	€300,000

The plant and equipment are depreciated on a straight-line basis and have 10 years of remaining life. Prince reports net income for 2011 of €100,000 and pays dividends of €50,000. Calculate the following:

1. Goodwill included in the purchase price.
2. Investment in associate (Prince) at the end of 2018.

Solution to 1:

Purchase price	€500,000
Acquired equity in book value of Prince's net assets (30% × €1,200,000)	360,000
Excess purchase price	€140,000
Attributable to plant and equipment (30% × €300,000)	(90,000)
Goodwill (residual)	€50,000

Solution to 2: Investment in associate

Purchase price	€500,000
Parker's share of Prince's net income (30% × €100,000)	30,000
Dividends received (30% of €50,000)	(15,000)
Amortization of excess purchase price attributable to plant and equipment (€90,000 ÷ 10 years)	(9,000)
December 31, 2018 balance in investment in Prince	€506,000

An alternate way to look at the balance in the investment account is that it reflects the basic valuation principle of the equity method. At any point in time, the investment account balance equals the investor's (Parker) proportionate share of the net equity (net assets at book value) of the investee (Prince) plus the unamortized balance of the original excess purchase price. Applying this principle to this example:

2018 Beginning net assets =	€1,200,000
Plus: Net income	100,000
Less: Dividends	(50,000)
2018 Ending net assets	€1,250,000
Parker's proportionate share of Prince's recorded net assets (30% × €1,250,000)	€375,000
Unamortized excess purchase price (€140,000 – 9,000)	131,000
Investment in Prince	€506,000

Note that the unamortized excess purchase price is a cost incurred by Parker, not Prince. Therefore, the total amount is included in the investment account balance.

4.4 Fair Value Option

Both IFRS and US GAAP give the investor the option to account for their equity method investment at fair value.[14] Under US GAAP, this option is available to all entities; however, under IFRS, its use is restricted to venture capital organizations, mutual funds, unit trusts, and similar entities, including investment-linked insurance funds.

Both standards require that the election to use the fair value option occur at the time of initial recognition and is irrevocable. Subsequent to initial recognition, the investment is reported at fair value with unrealized gains and losses arising from changes in fair value as well as any interest and dividends received included in the investor's profit or loss (income). Under the fair value method, the investment account on the investor's balance sheet does not reflect

---

[14] IFRS 9 Financial Instruments. FASB ASC Section 825-10-25 [Financial Instruments–Overall–Recognition].

the investor's proportionate share of the investee's profit or loss, dividends, or other distributions. In addition, the excess of cost over the fair value of the investee's identifiable net assets is not amortized, nor is goodwill created.

4.5. Impairment

Both IFRS and US GAAP require periodic reviews of equity method investments for impairment. If the fair value of the investment is below its carrying value and this decline is deemed to be other than temporary, an impairment loss must be recognized.

Under IFRS, there must be objective evidence of impairment as a result of one or more (loss) events that occurred after the initial recognition of the investment, and that loss event has an impact on the investment's future cash flows, which can be reliably estimated. Because goodwill is included in the carrying amount of the investment and is not separately recognized, it is not separately tested for impairment. Instead, the entire carrying amount of the investment is tested for impairment by comparing its recoverable amount with its carrying amount.[15] The impairment loss is recognized on the income statement, and the carrying amount of the investment on the balance sheet is either reduced directly or through the use of an allowance account.

US GAAP takes a different approach. If the fair value of the investment declines below its carrying value *and* the decline is determined to be permanent, US GAAP[16] requires an impairment loss to be recognized on the income statement and the carrying value of the investment on the balance sheet is reduced to its fair value.

Both IFRS and US GAAP prohibit the reversal of impairment losses even if the fair value later increases.

Section 6.4.4 of this chapter discusses impairment tests for the goodwill attributed to a controlling investment (consolidated subsidiary). Note the distinction between the disaggregated goodwill impairment test for consolidated statements and the impairment test of the total fair value of equity method investments.

4.6. Transactions with Associates

Because an investor company can influence the terms and timing of transactions with its associates, profits from such transactions cannot be realized until confirmed through use or sale to third parties. Accordingly, the investor company's share of any unrealized profit must be deferred by reducing the amount recorded under the equity method. In the subsequent period(s) when this deferred profit is considered confirmed, it is added to the equity income. At that time, the equity income is again based on the recorded values in the associate's accounts.

Transactions between the two affiliates may be **upstream** (associate to investor) or **downstream** (investor to associate). In an upstream sale, the profit on the intercompany transaction is recorded on the associate's income (profit or loss) statement. The investor's share of the unrealized profit is thus included in equity income on the investor's income statement.

---

[15] Recoverable amount is the higher of "value in use" or net selling price. Value in use is equal to the present value of estimated future cash flows expected to arise from the continuing use of an asset and from its disposal at the end of its useful life. Net selling price is equal to fair value less cost to sell.

[16] FASB ASC Section 323-10-35 [Investments–Equity Method and Joint Ventures–Overall–Subsequent Measurement].

In a downstream sale, the profit is recorded on the investor's income statement. Both IFRS and US GAAP require that the unearned profits be eliminated to the extent of the investor's interest in the associate.[17] The result is an adjustment to equity income on the investor's income statement.

EXAMPLE 4   Equity Method with Sale of Inventory: Upstream Sale

On January 1, 2018, Wicker Company acquired a 25% interest in Foxworth Company (both companies are fictitious) for €1,000,000 and used the equity method to account for its investment. The book value of Foxworth's net assets on that date was €3,800,000. An analysis of fair values revealed that all fair values of assets and liabilities were equal to book values except for a building. The building was undervalued by €40,000 and has a 20-year remaining life. The company used straight-line depreciation for the building. Foxworth paid €3,200 in dividends in 2018. During 2018, Foxworth reported net income of €20,000. During the year, Foxworth sold inventory to Wicker. At the end of the year, there was €8,000 profit from the upstream sale in Foxworth's net income. The inventory sold to Wicker by Foxworth had not been sold to an outside party.

1. Calculate the equity income to be reported as a line item on Wicker's 2018 income statement.
2. Calculate the balance in the investment in Foxworth to be reported on the December 31, 2018 balance sheet.

Purchase price	€1,000,000
Acquired equity in book value of Foxworth's net assets (25% × €3,800,000)	950,000
Excess purchase price	€50,000
Attributable to:	
Building (25% × €40,000)	€10,000
Goodwill (residual)	40,000
	€50,000

Solution to 1: Equity Income

Wicker's share of Foxworth's reported income (25% × €20,000)	€5,000
Amortization of excess purchase price attributable to building, (€10,000 ÷ 20)	(500)
Unrealized profit (25% × €8,000)	(2,000)
Equity income 2018	€2,500

---

[17] IAS 28 Investments in Associates and Joint Ventures; FASB ASC Topic 323 [Investments–Equity Method and Joint Ventures].

Solution to 2: Investment in Foxworth:

Purchase price	€1,000,000
Equity income 2018	2,500
Dividends received (25% × €3,200)	(800)
Investment in Foxworth, Dec 31, 2018	€1,001,700
Composition of investment account:	
Wicker's proportionate share of Foxworth's net equity (net assets at book value) [25% × (€3,800,000 + (20,000 – 8,000) – 3,200)]	€952,200
Unamortized excess purchase price (€50,000 – 500)	49,500
	€1,001,700

EXAMPLE 5   Equity Method with Sale of Inventory: Downstream Sale

Jones Company owns 25% of Jason Company (both fictitious companies) and appropriately applies the equity method of accounting. Amortization of excess purchase price, related to undervalued assets at the time of the investment, is €8,000 per year. During 2017 Jones sold €96,000 of inventory to Jason for €160,000. Jason resold €120,000 of this inventory during 2017. The remainder was sold in 2018. Jason reports income from its operations of €800,000 in 2017 and €820,000 in 2018.

1. Calculate the equity income to be reported as a line item on Jones's 2017 income statement.
2. Calculate the equity income to be reported as a line item on Jones's 2018 income statement.

Solution to 1: Equity Income 2017

Jones's share of Jason's reported income (25% × €800,000)	€200,000
Amortization of excess purchase price	(8,000)
Unrealized profit (25% × €16,000)	(4,000)
Equity income 2017	€188,000

Jones's profit on the sale to Jason = €160,000 – 96,000 = €64,000
Jason sells 75% (€120,000/160,000) of the goods purchased from Jones; 25% is unsold.
Total unrealized profit = €64,000 × 25% = €16,000
Jones's share of the unrealized profit = €16,000 × 25% = €4,000
Alternative approach:
    Jones's profit margin on sale to Jason: 40% (€64,000/€160,000)
    Jason's inventory of Jones's goods at December 31, 2017: €40,000
    Jones's profit margin on this was 40% × 40,000 = €16,000
    Jones's share of profit on unsold goods = €16,000 × 25% = €4,000

Solution to 2: Equity Income 2018

Jones's share of Jason's reported income (25% × €820,000)	€205,000
Amortization of excess purchase price	(8,000)
Realized profit (25% × €16,000)	4,000
Equity income 2018	€201,000

Jason sells the remaining 25% of the goods purchased from Jones.

4.7. Disclosure

The notes to the financial statements are an integral part of the information necessary for investors. Both IFRS and US GAAP require disclosure about the assets, liabilities, and results of equity method investments. For example, in their 2017 annual report, within its note titled "Principles of Consolidation," Deutsche Bank reports that:

> Investments in associates are accounted for under the equity method of accounting. The Group's share of the results of associates is adjusted to conform to the accounting policies of the Group and is reported in the Consolidated Statement of Income as Net income (loss) from equity method investments. The Group's share in the associate's profits and losses resulting from intercompany sales is eliminated on consolidation.
>
> If the Group previously held an equity interest in an entity (for example, as available for sale) and subsequently gained significant influence, the previously held equity interest is remeasured to fair value and any gain or loss is recognized in the Consolidated Statement of Income. Any amounts previously recognized in other comprehensive income associated with the equity interest would be reclassified to the Consolidated Statement of Income at the date the Group gains significant influence, as if the Group had disposed of the previously held equity interest.
>
> Under the equity method of accounting, the Group's investments in associates and jointly controlled entities are initially recorded at cost including any directly related transaction costs incurred in acquiring the associate, and subsequently increased (or decreased) to reflect both the Group's pro-rata share of the post-acquisition net income (or loss) of the associate or jointly controlled entity and other movements included directly in the equity of the associate or jointly controlled entity. Goodwill arising on the acquisition of an associate or a jointly controlled entity is included in the carrying value of the investment (net of any accumulated impairment loss). As goodwill is not reported separately it is not specifically tested for impairment. Rather, the entire equity method investment is tested for impairment at each balance sheet date.

For practical reasons, associated companies' results are sometimes included in the investor's accounts with a certain time lag, normally not more than one quarter. Dividends from associated companies are not included in investor income because it would be a double counting. Applying the equity method recognizes the investor's full share of the associate's income. Dividends received involve exchanging a portion of equity interest for cash. In the consolidated balance sheet, the book value of shareholdings in associated companies is increased by the investor's share of the company's net income and reduced by amortization of surplus values and the amount of dividends received.

4.8. Issues for Analysts

Equity method accounting presents several challenges for analysis. First, analysts should question whether the equity method is appropriate. For example, an investor holding 19% of an associate may in fact exert significant influence but may attempt to avoid using the equity method to avoid reporting associate losses. On the other hand, an investor holding 25% of an associate may be unable to exert significant influence and may be unable to access cash flows, and yet may prefer the equity method to capture associate income.

Second, the investment account represents the investor's percentage ownership in the net assets of the investee company through "one-line consolidation." There can be significant assets and liabilities of the investee that are not reflected on the investor's balance sheet, which will significantly affect debt ratios. Net margin ratios could be overstated because income for the associate is included in investor net income but is not specifically included in sales. An investor may actually control the investee with less than 50% ownership but prefer the financial results using the equity method. Careful analysis can reveal financial performance driven by accounting structure.

Finally, the analyst must consider the quality of the equity method earnings. The equity method assumes that a percentage of each dollar earned by the investee company is earned by the investor (i.e., a fraction of the dollar equal to the fraction of the company owned), even if cash is not received. Analysts should, therefore, consider potential restrictions on dividend cash flows (the statement of cash flows).

5. BUSINESS COMBINATIONS

Business combinations (controlling interest investments) involve the combination of two or more entities into a larger economic entity. Business combinations are typically motivated by expectations of added value through synergies, including potential for increased revenues, elimination of duplicate costs, tax advantages, coordination of the production process, and efficiency gains in the management of assets.[18]

Under IFRS, there is no distinction among business combinations based on the resulting structure of the larger economic entity. For all business combinations, one of the parties to the business combination is identified as the acquirer. Under US GAAP, an acquirer is identified, but the business combinations are categorized as merger, acquisition, or consolidation based on the legal structure after the combination. Each of these types of business combinations has distinctive characteristics that are described in Exhibit 5. Features of variable interest and special purpose entities are also described in Exhibit 5 because these are additional instances where control is exerted by another entity. Under both IFRS and US GAAP, business combinations are accounted for using the *acquisition method*.

EXHIBIT 5   Types of Business Combinations

Merger

The distinctive feature of a merger is that only one of the entities remains in existence. One hundred percent of the target is absorbed into the acquiring company. Company A may issue common stock, preferred stock, bonds, or pay cash to acquire the net assets. The net assets of

(continued)

---

[18]IFRS 3, *Business Combinations*, revised in 2008 and FASB ASC Topic 805 [*Business Combinations*] provide guidance on business combinations.

EXHIBIT 5   (Continued)

Company B are transferred to Company A. Company B ceases to exist and Company A is the
only entity that remains.

$$\text{Company A} + \text{Company B} = \text{Company A}$$

Acquisition

The distinctive feature of an acquisition is the legal continuity of the entities. Each entity continues operations but is connected through a parent–subsidiary relationship. Each entity is an individual that maintains separate financial records, but the parent (the acquirer) provides consolidated financial statements in each reporting period. Unlike a merger or consolidation, the acquiring
company does not need to acquire 100% of the target. In fact, in some cases, it may acquire less
than 50% and still exert control. If the acquiring company acquires less than 100%, non-controlling (minority) shareholders' interests are reported on the consolidated financial statements.

$$\text{Company A} + \text{Company B} = (\text{Company A} + \text{Company B})$$

Consolidation

The distinctive feature of a consolidation is that a new legal entity is formed and none of the
predecessor entities remain in existence. A new entity is created to take over the net assets of
Company A and Company B. Company A and Company B cease to exist and Company C is
the only entity that remains.

$$\text{Company A} + \text{Company B} = \text{Company C}$$

Special Purpose or Variable Interest Entities

The distinctive feature of a special purpose (variable interest) entity is that control is not
usually based on voting control, because equity investors do not have a sufficient amount
at risk for the entity to finance its activities without additional subordinated financial
support. Furthermore, the equity investors may lack a controlling financial interest. The
sponsoring company usually creates a special purpose entity (SPE) for a narrowly defined
purpose. IFRS require consolidation if the substance of the relationship indicates control
by the sponsor.

Under IFRS 10, *Consolidated Financial Statements* and SIC-12, *Consolidation-Special Purpose Entities*, the definition of control extends to a broad range of activities. The control concept
requires judgment and evaluation of relevant factors to determine whether control exists. Control is present when 1) the investor has the ability to exert influence on the financial and operating policy of the entity; and 2) is exposed, or has rights, to variable returns from its involvement
with the investee. Consolidation criteria apply to all entities that meet the definition of control.

US GAAP uses a two-component consolidation model that includes both a variable
interest component and a voting interest (control) component. Under the variable interest
component, US GAAP[19] requires the primary beneficiary of a variable interest entity (VIE) to
consolidate the VIE regardless of its voting interests (if any) in the VIE or its decision-making
authority. The primary beneficiary is defined as the party that will absorb the majority of the
VIE's expected losses, receive the majority of the VIE's expected residual returns, or both.

In the past, business combinations could be accounted for either as a purchase transaction
or as a uniting (or pooling) of interests. However, the use of the pooling accounting method

---

[19] FASB ASC Topic 810 [Consolidation].

for acquisitions is no longer permitted, and IFRS and US GAAP now require that all business combinations be accounted for in a similar manner. The *acquisition method* developed by the IASB and the FASB replaces the purchase method, and substantially reduces any differences between IFRS and US GAAP for business combinations.[20]

5.1. Acquisition Method

IFRS and US GAAP require the acquisition method of accounting for business combinations, although both have a few specific exemptions.

Under this approach, the fair value of the consideration given by the acquiring company is the appropriate measurement for acquisitions and also includes the acquisition-date fair value of any contingent consideration. Direct costs of the business combination, such as professional and legal fees, valuation experts, and consultants, are expensed as incurred.

The acquisition method (which replaced the purchase method) addresses three major accounting issues that often arise in business combinations and the preparation of consolidated (combined) financial statements:

- The recognition and measurement of the assets and liabilities of the combined entity;
- The initial recognition and subsequent accounting for goodwill; and
- The recognition and measurement of any non-controlling interest.

5.1.1. Recognition and Measurement of Identifiable Assets and Liabilities

IFRS and US GAAP require that the acquirer measure the identifiable tangible and intangible assets and liabilities of the acquiree (acquired entity) at fair value as of the date of the acquisition. The acquirer must also recognize any assets and liabilities that the acquiree had not previously recognized as assets and liabilities in its financial statements. For example, identifiable intangible assets (for example, brand names, patents, technology) that the acquiree developed internally would be recognized by the acquirer.

5.1.2. Recognition and Measurement of Contingent Liabilities[21]

On the acquisition date, the acquirer must recognize any contingent liability assumed in the acquisition if 1) it is a present obligation that arises from past events, and 2) it can be measured reliably. Costs that the acquirer expects (but is not obliged) to incur, however, are not recognized as liabilities as of the acquisition date. Instead, the acquirer recognizes these costs in future periods as they are incurred. For example, expected restructuring costs arising from exiting an acquiree's business will be recognized in the period in which they are incurred.

There is a difference between IFRS and US GAAP with regard to treatment of contingent liabilities. IFRS include contingent liabilities if their fair values can be reliably measured. US GAAP includes only those contingent liabilities that are probable and can be reasonably estimated.

5.1.3. Recognition and Measurement of Indemnification Assets

On the acquisition date, the acquirer must recognize an indemnification asset if the seller (acquiree) contractually indemnifies the acquirer for the outcome of a contingency or an uncertainty related to all or part of a specific asset or liability of the acquiree. The seller may also indemnify the acquirer against losses above a specified amount on a liability arising from a

---

[20] IFRS 10, Consolidated Financial Statements; IFRS 3, Business Combinations; FASB ASC Topic 805 [Business Combinations]; FASB ASC Topic 810 [Consolidations].

[21] A contingent liability must be recognized even if it is not probable that an outflow of resources or economic benefits will be used to settle the obligation.

particular contingency. For example, the seller guarantees that an acquired contingent liability will not exceed a specified amount. In this situation, the acquirer recognizes an indemnification asset at the same time it recognizes the indemnified liability, with both measured on the same basis. If the indemnification relates to an asset or a liability that is recognized at the acquisition date and measured at its acquisition date fair value, the acquirer will also recognize the indemnification asset at the acquisition date at its acquisition date fair value.

5.1.4. Recognition and Measurement of Financial Assets and Liabilities

At the acquisition date, identifiable assets and liabilities acquired are classified in accordance with IFRS (or US GAAP) standards. The acquirer reclassifies the financial assets and liabilities of the acquiree based on the contractual terms, economic conditions, and the acquirer's operating or accounting policies, as they exist at the acquisition date.

5.1.5. Recognition and Measurement of Goodwill

IFRS allows two options for recognizing goodwill at the transaction date. The goodwill option is on a transaction-by-transaction basis. "Partial goodwill" is measured as the fair value of the acquisition (fair value of consideration given) less the acquirer's share of the fair value of all identifiable tangible and intangible assets, liabilities, and contingent liabilities acquired. "Full goodwill" is measured as the fair value of the entity as a whole less the fair value of all identifiable tangible and intangible assets, liabilities, and contingent liabilities. US GAAP views the entity as a whole and requires full goodwill.[22]

Because goodwill is considered to have an indefinite life, it is not amortized. Instead, it is tested for impairment annually or more frequently if events or circumstances indicate that goodwill might be impaired.

EXAMPLE 6   Recognition and Measurement of Goodwill

Acquirer contributes $800,000 for an 80% interest in Acquiree. The identifiable net assets have a fair value of $900,000. The fair value of the entire entity is determined to be $1 million.

	IFRS Partial Goodwill
Fair value of consideration	$800,000
80% of Fair value of identifiable net assets	720,000
Goodwill recognized	$80,000

	IFRS and US GAAP Full Goodwill
Fair value of entity	$1,000,000
Fair value of identifiable assets	900,000
Goodwill recognized	$100,000

---

[22] FASB ASC Topic 805 [Business Combinations].

5.1.6. Recognition and Measurement when Acquisition Price Is Less than Fair Value
Occasionally, a company faces adverse circumstances such that its market value drops below the fair value of its net assets. In an acquisition of such a company, where the purchase price is less than the fair value of the target's (acquiree's) net assets, the acquisition is considered to be a "bargain purchase" acquisition. IFRS and US GAAP require the difference between the fair value of the acquired net assets and the purchase price to be recognized immediately as a gain in profit or loss. Any contingent consideration must be measured and recognized at fair value at the time of the business combination. Any subsequent changes in value of the contingent consideration are recognized in profit or loss.

5.2. Impact of the Acquisition Method on Financial Statements, Post-Acquisition

Example 7 shows the consolidated balance sheet of an acquiring company after the acquisition.

EXAMPLE 7   Acquisition Method Post-Combination Balance Sheet

Franklin Company, a hypothetical company, acquired 100% of the outstanding shares of Jefferson, Inc. (another fictitious company) by issuing 1,000,000 shares of its €1 par common stock (€15 market value). Immediately before the transaction, the two companies compiled the following information:

	Franklin Book Value (000)	Jefferson Book Value (000)	Jefferson Fair Value (000)
Cash and receivables	€10,000	€300	€300
Inventory	12,000	1,700	3,000
PP&E (net)	27,000	2,500	4,500
	€49,000	€4,500	€7,800
Current payables	8,000	600	600
Long-term debt	16,000	2,000	1,800
	24,000	2,600	2,400
Net assets	€25,000	€1,900	€5,400
Shareholders' equity:			
Capital stock (€1 par)	€5,000	€400	
Additional paid in capital	6,000	700	
Retained earnings	€14,000	€800	

Jefferson has no identifiable intangible assets. Show the balances in the post-combination balance sheet using the acquisition method.

Solution: Under the acquisition method, the purchase price allocation would be as follows:

Fair value of the stock issued (1,000,000 shares at market value of €15)	€15,000,000
Book value of Jefferson's net assets	1,900,000
Excess purchase price	€13,100,000
Fair value of the stock issued	€15,000,000
Fair value allocated to identifiable net assets	5,400,000
Goodwill	€9,600,000

Allocation of excess purchase price (based on the differences between fair values and book values):

Inventory	€1,300,000
PP&E (net)	2,000,000
Long-term debt	200,000
Goodwill	9,600,000
	€13,100,000

Both IFRS and US GAAP record the fair value of the acquisition at the market value of the stock issued, or €15,000,000. In this case, the purchase price exceeds the book value of Jefferson's net assets by €13,100,000. Inventory, PP&E (net), and long-term debt are adjusted to fair values. The excess of the purchase price over the fair value of identifiable net assets results in goodwill recognition of €9,600,000.

The post-combination balance sheet of the combined entity would appear as follows:

Franklin Consolidated Balance Sheet (Acquisition Method) (000)	
Cash and receivables	€10,300
Inventory	15,000
PP&E (net)	31,500
Goodwill	9,600
Total assets	€66,400
Current payables	€8,600
Long-term debt	17,800
Total liabilities	€26,400
Capital stock (€1 par)	€6,000
Additional paid in capital	20,000
Retained earnings	14,000
Total stockholders' equity	€40,000
Total liabilities and stockholders' equity	€66,400

Assets and liabilities are combined using book values of Franklin plus fair values for the assets and liabilities acquired from Jefferson. For example, the book value of Franklin's inventory (€12,000,000) is added to the fair value of inventory acquired from Jefferson (€3,000,000) for a combined inventory of €15,000,000. Long-term debt has a book value of €16,000,000 on Franklin's pre-acquisition statements, and Jefferson's fair value of debt is €1,800,000. The combined long-term debt is recorded as €17,800,000.

Franklin's post-merger financial statement reflects in stockholders' equity the stock issued by Franklin to acquire Jefferson. Franklin issues stock with a par value of €1,000,000; however, the stock is measured at fair value under both IFRS and US GAAP. Therefore, the consideration exchanged is 1,000,000 shares at market value of €15, or €15,000,000. Prior to the transaction, Franklin had 5,000,000 shares of €1 par stock outstanding (€5,000,000). The combined entity reflects the Franklin capital stock outstanding of €6,000,000 (€5,000,000 plus the additional 1,000,000 shares of €1 par stock issued to effect the transaction). Franklin's additional paid in capital of €6,000,000 is increased by the €14,000,000 additional paid in capital from the issuance of the 1,000,000 shares (€15,000,000 less par value of €1,000,000) for a total of €20,000,000. At the acquisition date, only the acquirer's retained earnings are carried to the combined entity. Earnings of the target are included on the consolidated income statement and retained earnings only in post-acquisition periods.

In the periods subsequent to the business combination, the financial statements continue to be affected by the acquisition method. Net income reflects the performance of the combined entity. Under the acquisition method, amortization/depreciation is based on historical cost of Franklin's assets and the fair value of Jefferson's assets. Using Example 7, as Jefferson's acquired inventory is sold, the cost of goods sold would be €1,300,000 higher and depreciation on PP&E would be €2,000,000 higher over the life of the asset than if the companies had not combined.

5.3. The Consolidation Process

Consolidated financial statements combine the separate financial statements for distinct legal entities, the parent and its subsidiaries, as if they were one economic unit. Consolidation combines the assets, liabilities, revenues, and expenses of subsidiaries with the parent company. Transactions between the parent and subsidiary (intercompany transactions) are eliminated to avoid double counting and premature income recognition. Consolidated statements are presumed to be more meaningful in terms of representational faithfulness. It is important for the analyst to consider the differences in IFRS and US GAAP, valuation bases, and other factors that could impair the validity of comparative analyses.

5.3.1. Business Combination with Less than 100% Acquisition

The acquirer purchases 100% of the equity of the target company in a transaction structured as a merger or consolidation. For a transaction structured as an acquisition, however, the acquirer does not have to purchase 100% of the equity of the target in order to achieve control. The acquiring company may purchase less than 100% of the target because it may be constrained by resources or it may be unable to acquire all the outstanding shares. As a result, both the acquirer and the target remain separate legal entities. Both IFRS and US GAAP presume a company has control if it owns more than 50% of the voting shares of an entity. In this case, the acquiring company is viewed as the parent, and the target company is viewed as the subsidiary. Both the parent and the subsidiary typically prepare their own financial records, but the parent also prepares consolidated financial statements at each reporting period. The consolidated financial statements are the primary source of information for investors and analysts.

5.3.2. Non-controlling (Minority) Interests: Balance Sheet

A non-controlling (minority) interest is the portion of the subsidiary's equity (residual interest) that is held by third parties (i.e., not owned by the parent). Non-controlling interests are created when the parent acquires less than a 100% controlling interest in a subsidiary. IFRS and US GAAP have similar treatment for how non-controlling interests are classified.[23] Non-controlling interests in consolidated subsidiaries are presented on the consolidated balance sheet as a separate component of stockholders' equity. IFRS and US GAAP differ, however, on the measurement of non-controlling interests. Under IFRS, the parent can measure the non-controlling interest at either its fair value (full goodwill method) or at the non-controlling interest's proportionate share of the acquiree's identifiable net assets (partial goodwill method). Under US GAAP, the parent must use the full goodwill method and measure the non-controlling interest at fair value.

Example 8 illustrates the differences in reporting requirements.

EXAMPLE 8 Non-controlling Asset Valuation

On January 1, 2018, the hypothetical Parent Co. acquired 90% of the outstanding shares of the hypothetical Subsidiary Co. in exchange for shares of Parent Co.'s no par common stock with a fair value of €180,000. The fair market value of the subsidiary's shares on the date of the exchange was €200,000. Below is selected financial information from the two companies immediately prior to the exchange of shares (before the parent recorded the acquisition):

	Parent Book Value	Subsidiary Book Value	Fair Value
Cash and receivables	€40,000	€15,000	€15,000
Inventory	125,000	80,000	80,000
PP&E (net)	235,000	95,000	155,000
	€400,000	€190,000	€250,000
Payables	55,000	20,000	20,000
Long-term debt	120,000	70,000	70,000
	175,000	90,000	90,000
Net assets	€225,000	€100,000	€160,000
Shareholders' equity:			
Capital stock (no par)	€87,000	€34,000	
Retained earnings	€138,000	€66,000	

---

[23] IFRS 10, Consolidated Financial Statements and FASB ASC Topic 810 [Consolidation].

1. Calculate the value of PP&E (net) on the consolidated balance sheet under both IFRS and US GAAP.
2. Calculate the value of goodwill and the value of the non-controlling interest at the acquisition date under the full goodwill method.
3. Calculate the value of goodwill and the value of the non-controlling interest at the acquisition date under the partial goodwill method.

Solution to 1: Relative to fair value, the PP&E of the subsidiary is understated by €60,000. Under the acquisition method (IFRS and US GAAP), as long as the parent has control over the subsidiary (i.e., regardless of whether the parent had purchased 51% or 100% of the subsidiary's stock), it would include 100% of the subsidiary's assets and liabilities at fair value on the consolidated balance sheet. Therefore, PP&E on the consolidated balance sheet would be valued at €390,000.

Solution to 2: Under the full goodwill method (mandatory under US GAAP and optional under IFRS), goodwill on the consolidated balance sheet would be the difference between the total fair value of the subsidiary and the fair value of the subsidiary's identifiable net assets.

Fair value of the subsidiary	€200,000
Fair value of subsidiary's identifiable net assets	160,000
Goodwill	€40,000

The value of the non-controlling interest is equal to the non-controlling interest's proportionate share of the subsidiary's fair value. The non-controlling interest's proportionate share of the subsidiary is 10% and the fair value of the subsidiary is €200,000 on the acquisition date. Under the full goodwill method, the value of the non-controlling interest would be €20,000 (10% × €200,000).

Solution to 3: Under the partial goodwill method (IFRS only), goodwill on the parent's consolidated balance sheet would be €36,000, the difference between the purchase price and the parent's proportionate share of the subsidiary's identifiable assets.

Acquisition price	€180,000
90% of fair value	144,000
Goodwill	€36,000

The value of the non-controlling interest is equal to the non-controlling interest's proportionate share of the fair value of the subsidiary's identifiable net assets. The non-controlling interest's proportionate share is 10%, and the fair value of the subsidiary's identifiable net assets on the acquisition date is €160,000. Under the partial goodwill method, the value of the non-controlling interest would be €16,000 (10% × €160,000).

Regardless of which method is used, goodwill is not amortized under either IFRS or US GAAP but it is tested for impairment at least annually.

For comparative purposes, the following is the balance sheet at the acquisition date under the full goodwill and partial goodwill methods.

Comparative Consolidated Balance Sheet at Acquisition Date: Acquisition Method

	Full Goodwill	Partial Goodwill
Cash and receivables	€55,000	€55,000
Inventory	205,000	205,000
PP&E (net)	390,000	390,000
Goodwill	40,000	36,000
Total assets	€690,000	€686,000
Payables	€75,000	€75,000
Long-term debt	190,000	190,000
Total liabilities	€265,000	€265,000
Shareholders' equity:		
Noncontrolling interests	€20,000	€16,000
Capital stock (no par)	€267,000	€267,000
Retained earnings	138,000	138,000
Total equity	€425,000	€421,000
Total liabilities and shareholders' equity	€690,000	€686,000

5.3.3. Non-controlling (Minority) Interests: Income Statement

On the income statement, non-controlling (minority) interests are presented as a line item reflecting the allocation of profit or loss for the period. Intercompany transactions, if any, are eliminated in full.

Using assumed data consistent with the facts in Example 8, the amounts included for the subsidiary in the consolidated income statements under IFRS and US GAAP are presented below:

	Full Goodwill	Partial Goodwill
Sales	€250,000	€250,000
Cost of goods sold	137,500	137,500
Interest expense	10,000	10,000
Depreciation expense	39,000	39,000
Income from continuing operations	€63,500	€63,500
Non-controlling interest (10%)	(6,350)	(6,350)
Consolidated net income to parent's shareholders	€57,150	€57,150

Income to the parent's shareholders is €57,150 using either method. This is because the fair value of the PP&E is allocated to non-controlling shareholders as well as to the controlling shareholders under the full goodwill and the partial goodwill methods. Therefore, the non-controlling interests will share in the adjustment for excess depreciation resulting from the €60,000 increase in PP&E. Because depreciation expense is the same under both methods, it results in identical net income to all shareholders, whichever method is used to recognize goodwill and to measure the non-controlling interest.

Although net income to parent's shareholders is the same, the impact on ratios would be different because total assets and stockholders' equity would differ.

Impact on Ratios

	Full Goodwill (%)	Partial Goodwill (%)
Return on assets	8.28	8.33
Return on equity	13.45	13.57

Over time, the value of the subsidiary will change as a result of net income and changes in equity. As a result, the value of the non-controlling interest on the parent's consolidated balance sheet will also change.

5.3.4. Goodwill Impairment

Although goodwill is not amortized, it must be tested for impairment at least annually or more frequently if events or changes in circumstances indicate that it might be impaired. If it is probable that some or all of the goodwill will not be recovered through the profitable operations of the combined entity, it should be partially or fully written off by charging it to an expense. Once written down, goodwill cannot be later restored.

IFRS and US GAAP differ on the definition of the levels at which goodwill is assigned and how goodwill is tested for impairment.

Under IFRS, at the time of acquisition, the total amount of goodwill recognized is allocated to each of the acquirer's cash-generating units that will benefit from the expected synergies resulting from the combination with the target. A cash-generating unit represents the lowest level within the combined entity at which goodwill is monitored for impairment purposes.[24] Goodwill impairment testing is then conducted under a one-step approach. The recoverable amount of a cash-generating unit is calculated and compared with the carrying value of the cash-generating unit.[25] An impairment loss is recognized if the recoverable amount of the cash-generating unit is less than its carrying value. The impairment loss (the difference between these two amounts) is first applied to the goodwill that has been allocated to the cash-generating unit. Once this has been reduced to zero, the remaining amount of the loss is then allocated to all of the other non-cash assets in the unit on a pro rata basis.

Under US GAAP, at the time of acquisition, the total amount of goodwill recognized is allocated to each of the acquirer's reporting units. A reporting unit is an operating segment or component of an operating segment that is one level below the operating segment as a whole. Goodwill impairment testing is then conducted under a two-step approach: identification of impairment and then measurement of the loss. First, the carrying amount of the reporting unit (including goodwill) is compared to its fair value. If the carrying value of the reporting unit exceeds its fair value, potential impairment has been identified. The second step is then performed to measure the amount of the impairment loss. The amount of the impairment loss is the difference between the implied fair value of the reporting unit's goodwill and its carrying

---

[24] A cash-generating unit is the smallest identifiable group of assets that generates cash inflows that are largely independent of the cash inflows from other assets or groups of assets.

[25] The recoverable amount of a cash-generating unit is the higher of net selling price (i.e., fair value less costs to sell) and its value in use. Value in use is the present value of the future cash flows expected to be derived from the cash-generating unit. The carrying value of a cash-generating unit is equal to the carrying value of the unit's assets and liabilities including the goodwill that has been allocated to that unit.

amount. The implied fair value of goodwill is determined in the same manner as in a business combination (it is the difference between the fair value of the reporting unit and the fair value of the reporting unit's assets and liabilities). The impairment loss is applied to the goodwill that has been allocated to the reporting unit. After the goodwill of the reporting unit has been eliminated, no other adjustments are made automatically to the carrying values of any of the reporting unit's other assets or liabilities. However, it may be prudent to test other asset values for recoverability and possible impairment.

Under both IFRS and US GAAP, the impairment loss is recorded as a separate line item in the consolidated income statement.

EXAMPLE 9   Goodwill Impairment: IFRS

The cash-generating unit of a French company has a carrying value of €1,400,000, which includes €300,000 of allocated goodwill. The recoverable amount of the cash-generating unit is determined to be €1,300,000, and the estimated fair value of its identifiable net assets is €1,200,000. Calculate the impairment loss.

Solution:

Recoverable amount of unit	€1,300,000
Carrying amount of unit	1,400,000
Impairment loss	€100,000

The impairment loss of €100,000 is reported on the income statement, and the goodwill allocated to the cash-generating unit would be reduced by €100,000 to €200,000.

If the recoverable amount of the cash-generating unit had been €800,000 instead of €1,300,000, the impairment loss recognized would be €600,000. This would first be absorbed by the goodwill allocated to the unit (€300,000). Once this has been reduced to zero, the remaining amount of the impairment loss (€300,000) would then be allocated on a pro rata basis to the other non-cash assets within the unit.

EXAMPLE 10   Goodwill Impairment: US GAAP

A reporting unit of a US corporation (e.g., a division) has a fair value of $1,300,000 and a carrying value of $1,400,000 that includes recorded goodwill of $300,000. The estimated fair value of the identifiable net assets of the reporting unit at the impairment test date is $1,200,000. Calculate the impairment loss.

Solution:

Step 1 – Determination of an Impairment Loss
Because the fair value of the reporting unit is less than its carrying book value, a potential impairment loss has been identified.

Fair value of unit: $1,300,000 < $1,400,000

Step 2 – Measurement of the Impairment Loss

Fair value of reporting unit	$1,300,000
Less: net assets	1,200,000
Implied goodwill	$100,000
Current carrying value of goodwill	$300,000
Less: implied goodwill	100,000
Impairment loss	$200,000

The impairment loss of $200,000 is reported on the income statement, and the goodwill allocated to the reporting unit would be reduced by $200,000 to $100,000.

If the fair value of the reporting unit was $800,000 (instead of $1,300,000), the implied goodwill would be a negative $400,000. In this case, the maximum amount of the impairment loss recognized would be $300,000, the carrying amount of goodwill.

5.4. Financial Statement Presentation Subsequent to the Business Combination

The presentation of consolidated financial statements is similar under IFRS and US GAAP. For example, selected financial statements for GlaxoSmithKline are shown in Exhibits 6 and 7. GlaxoSmithKline is a leading pharmaceutical company headquartered in the United Kingdom.

The consolidated balance sheet in Exhibit 6 combines the operations of GlaxoSmith-Kline and its subsidiaries. The analyst can observe that in 2017 GlaxoSmithKline had investments in financial assets (other investments of £918,000,000 and liquid investments of £78,000,000), and investments in associates and joint ventures of £183,000,000. In 2017 GlaxoSmithKline did not acquire any additional companies, however, it made a number of small business disposals during the year for a net cash consideration of £342,000,000, including contingent consideration receivable of £86,000,000. In addition, during 2017 GlaxoSmithKline made a cash investment of £15,000,000 in associates and disposed of two associated for a cash consideration of £198,000,000.[26] The decrease in goodwill on the balance sheet reflects exchange adjustments recognized by GlaxoSmithKline due to the weakness of the functional currency of the parent (pound sterling). Note that GlaxoSmithKline has £6,172,000 in contingent consideration liabilities, which relate to future events such as development milestones or sales performance for acquired companies. Of the £6 billion total contingent liability, £1,076,000 is expected to be paid within one year in respect of the Novartis Vaccines business, which reached its sales milestone. The remaining contingent consideration relates to the acquisition of the Shionogi-ViiV Healthcare joint venture and Novartis Vaccines are expected to be paid over a number of years.[27] The analyst can also note that GlaxoSmithKline is the parent company in a less than 100% acquisition. The minority interest of £3,557,000,000 in the equity section is the portion of the combined entity that accrues to non-controlling shareholders.

---

[26] Note 38: Acquisitions and Disposals, GlaxoSmithKline financial statements 2017.

[27] The notes state that the amount included in the balance sheet is the present value of the expected contingent consideration payments, which have been discounted using a rate of 8.5%.

EXHIBIT 6   GlaxoSmithKline Consolidated Balance Sheet at December 31, 2017

	Notes	2017 £m	2016 £m
Non-current assets			
Property, plant and equipment	17	**10,860**	10,808
Goodwill	18	**5,734**	5,965
Other intangible assets	19	**17,562**	18,776
Investments in associates and joint ventures	20	**183**	263
Other investments	21	**918**	985
Deferred tax assets	14	**3,796**	4,374
Derivative financial instruments	42	**8**	–
Other non-current assets	22	**1,413**	1,199
Total non-current assets		**40,474**	42,370
Current assets			
Inventories	23	**5,557**	5,102
Current tax recoverable	14	**258**	226
Trade and other receivables	24	**6,000**	6,026
Derivative financial instruments	42	**68**	156
Liquid investments	31	**78**	89
Cash and cash equivalents	25	**3,833**	4,897
Assets held for sale	26	**113**	215
Total current assets		**15,907**	16,711
Total assets		**56,381**	59,081
Current liabilities			
Short-term borrowings	31	**(2,825)**	(4,129)
Contingent consideration liabilities	39	**(1,076)**	(561)
Trade and other payables	27	(20,970)	(11,964)
Derivative financial instruments	42	(74)	(194)
Current tax payable	14	**(995)**	(1,305)
Short-term provisions	29	**(629)**	(848)
Total current liabilities		**(26,569)**	(19,001)
Non-current liabilities			
Long-term borrowings	31	**(14,264)**	(14,661)
Corporation tax payable	14	**(411)**	–
Deferred tax liabilities	14	**(1,396)**	(1,934)
Pensions and other post-employment benefits	28	**(3,539)**	(4,090)
Other provisions	29	**(636)**	(652)
Contingent consideration liabilities	39	**(5,096)**	(5,335)
Other non-current liabilities	30	**(981)**	(8,445)
Total non-current liabilities		**(26,323)**	(35,117)
Total liabilities		**(52,892)**	(54,118)
Net assets		**3,489**	4,963
Equity			
Share capital	33	**1,343**	1,342
Share premium account	33	**3,019**	2,954
Retained earnings	34	**(6,477)**	(5,392)

EXHIBIT 6   (Continued)

	Notes	2017 £m	2016 £m
Other reserves	34	**2,047**	2,220
Shareholders' equity		**(68)**	1,124
Non-controlling interests		**3,557**	3,839
Total equity		**3,489**	4,963

The consolidated income statement for GlaxoSmithKline is presented in Exhibit 7. IFRS and US GAAP have similar formats for consolidated income statements. Each line item (e.g., turnover [sales], cost of sales, etc.) includes 100% of the parent and the subsidiary transactions after eliminating any **upstream** (subsidiary sells to parent) or **downstream** (parent sells to subsidiary) intercompany transactions. The portion of income accruing to non-controlling shareholders is presented as a separate line item on the consolidated income statement. Note that net income would be the same under IFRS and US GAAP.[28] The analyst will need to make adjustments for any analysis comparing specific line items that might differ between IFRS and US GAAP.

EXHIBIT 7   GlaxoSmithKline Consolidated Income Statement for the Year Ended December 31, 2017

	Notes	2017 Total £m	2016 £m	2015 £m
Turnover	6	**30,186**	27,889	23,923
Cost of sales		**(10,342)**	(9,290)	(8,853)
Gross profit		**19,844**	18,599	15,070
Selling, general and administration		**(9,672)**	(9,366)	(9,232)
Research and development		**(4,476)**	(3,628)	(3,560)
Royalty income		**356**	398	329
Other operating income	7	**(1,965)**	(3,405)	7,715
Operating profit	8	**4,087**	2,598	10,322
Finance income	11	**65**	72	104
Finance costs	12	**(734)**	(736)	(757)
Profit on disposal of interests in associates		**95**	–	843
Share of after tax profits of associates and joint ventures	13	**13**	5	14
Profit before taxation		**3,525**	1,939	10,526
Taxation	14	**(1,356)**	(877)	(2,154)
Profit after taxation for the year		**2,169**	1,062	8,372
Profit/(loss) attributable to non-controlling interests		**637**	150	(50)
Profit attributable to shareholders		**1,532**	912	8,472
		2,169	1,062	8,372
Basic earnings per share (pence)	15	**31.4p**	18.8p	174.3p
Diluted earnings per share (pence)	**15**	**31.0p**	18.6p	172.3p

---

[28] It is possible, however, for differences to arise through the application of different accounting rules (e.g., valuation of fixed assets).

5.5. Variable Interest and Special Purpose Entities

Special purpose entities (SPEs) are enterprises that are created to accommodate specific needs of the sponsoring entity.[29] The sponsoring entity (on whose behalf the SPE is created) frequently transfers assets to the SPE, obtains the right to use assets held by the SPE, or performs services for the SPE, while other parties (capital providers) provide funding to the SPE. SPEs can be a legitimate financing mechanism for a company to segregate certain activities and thereby reduce risk. SPEs may take the form of a limited liability company (corporation), trust, partnership, or unincorporated entity. They are often created with legal arrangements that impose strict and sometimes permanent limits on the decision-making powers of their governing board or management.

Beneficial interest in an SPE may take the form of a debt instrument, an equity instrument, a participation right, or a residual interest in a lease. Some beneficial interests may simply provide the holder with a fixed or stated rate of return, while beneficial interests give the holder the rights or the access to future economic benefits of the SPE's activities. In most cases, the creator/sponsor of the entity retains a significant beneficial interest in the SPE even though it may own little or none of the SPE's voting equity.

In the past, sponsors were able to avoid consolidating SPEs on their financial statements because they did not have "control" (i.e., own a majority of the voting interest) of the SPE. SPEs were structured so that the sponsoring company had financial control over their assets or operating activities, while third parties held the majority of the voting interest in the SPE.

These outside equity participants often funded their investments in the SPE with debt that was either directly or indirectly guaranteed by the sponsoring companies. The sponsoring companies, in turn, were able to avoid the disclosure of many of these guarantees as well as their economic significance. In addition, many sponsoring companies created SPEs to facilitate the transfer of assets and liabilities from their own balance sheets. As a result, they were able to recognize large amounts of revenue and gains, because these transactions were accounted for as sales. By avoiding consolidation, sponsoring companies did not have to report the assets and the liabilities of the SPE; financial performance as measured by the unconsolidated financial statements was potentially misleading. The benefit to the sponsoring company was improved asset turnover, lower operating and financial leverage metrics, and higher profitability.

Enron, for example, used SPEs to obtain off-balance sheet financing and artificially improve its financial performance. Its subsequent collapse was partly attributable to its guarantee of the debt of the SPEs it had created.

To address the accounting issues arising from the misuse and abuse of SPEs, the IASB and the FASB worked to improve the consolidation models to take into account financial arrangements where parties other than the holders of the majority of the voting interests exercise financial control over another entity. IFRS 10, *Consolidated Financial Statements*, revised the definition of control to encompass many special purpose entities. Special purpose entities involved in a structured financial transaction will require an evaluation of the purpose, design, and risks.

In developing new accounting standards to address this consolidation issue, the FASB used the more general term variable interest entity (VIE) to more broadly define an entity that

---

[29] The term "special purpose entity" is used by IFRS and "variable interest entity" and "special purpose entity" is used by US GAAP.

is financially controlled by one or more parties that do not hold a majority voting interest. Therefore, under US GAAP, a VIE includes other entities besides SPEs. FASB ASC Topic 810 [*Consolidation*] provides guidance for US GAAP, which classifies special purpose entities as variable interest entities if:

1. total equity at risk is insufficient to finance activities without financial support from other parties, or
2. equity investors lack any one of the following:
   a. the ability to make decisions;
   b. the obligation to absorb losses; or
   c. the right to receive returns.

Common examples of variable interests are entities created to lease real estate or other property, entities created for the securitization of financial assets, or entities created for research and development activity.

Under FASB ASC Topic 810 [*Consolidation*], the primary beneficiary of a VIE must consolidate it as a subsidiary regardless of how much of an equity investment the beneficiary has in the VIE. The primary beneficiary (which is often the sponsor) is the entity that is expected to absorb the majority of the VIE's expected losses, receive the majority of the VIE's residual returns, or both. If one entity will absorb a majority of the VIE's expected losses and another unrelated entity will receive a majority of the VIE's expected residual returns, the entity absorbing a majority of the losses must consolidate the VIE. If there are non-controlling interests in the VIE, these would also be shown in the consolidated balance sheet and consolidated income statement of the primary beneficiary. ASC Topic 810 also requires entities to disclose information about their relationships with VIEs, even if they are not considered the primary beneficiary.

5.5.1. Securitization of Assets

Example 11 shows the effects of securitizing assets on companies' balance sheets.

EXAMPLE 11   Receivables Securitization

Odena, a (fictional) Italian auto manufacturer, wants to raise €55M in capital by borrowing against its financial receivables. To accomplish this objective, Odena can choose between two alternatives:

Alternative 1   Borrow directly against the receivables; or

Alternative 2   Create a special purpose entity, invest €5M in the SPE, have the SPE borrow €55M, and then use the funds to purchase €60M of receivables from Odena.

Using the financial statement information provided below, describe the effect of each alternative on Odena, assuming that Odena meets the definition of control and will consolidate the SPE.

Odena Balance Sheet

Cash	€30,000,000
Accounts receivable	60,000,000
Other assets	40,000,000
Total assets	€130,000,000
Current liabilities	€27,000,000
Noncurrent liabilities	20,000,000
Total liabilities	€47,000,000
Shareholder equity	€83,000,000
Total liabilities and equity	€130,000,000

Alternative 1: Odena's cash will increase by €55M (to €85M) and its debt will increase by €55M (to €75M). Its sales and net income will not change.

Odena: Alternative 1 Balance Sheet

Cash	€85,000,000
Accounts receivable	60,000,000
Other assets	40,000,000
Total assets	€185,000,000
Current liabilities	€27,000,000
Noncurrent liabilities	75,000,000
Total liabilities	€102,000,000
Shareholder equity	€83,000,000
Total liabilities and equity	€185,000,000

Alternative 2: Odena's accounts receivable will decrease by €60M and its cash will increase by €55 (it invests €5M in cash in the SPE). However, if Odena is able to sell the receivables to the SPE for more than their carrying value (for example, €65), it would also report a gain on the sale in its profit and loss. Equally important, the SPE may be able to borrow the funds at a lower rate than Odena, since they are bankruptcy remote from Odena (i.e., out of reach of Odena's creditors), and the lenders to the SPE are the claimants on its assets (i.e., the purchased receivables).

SPE Balance Sheet

Accounts receivable	€60,000,000
Total assets	€60,000,000
Long-term debt	€55,000,000
Equity	5,000,000
Total liabilities and equity	€60,000,000

Because Odena consolidates the SPE, its financial balance sheet would look like the following:

Odena: Alternative 2 Consolidated Balance Sheet

Cash	€85,000,000
Accounts receivable	60,000,000
Other assets	40,000,000
Total assets	€185,000,000
Current liabilities	€27,000,000
Noncurrent liabilities	75,000,000
Total liabilities	€102,000,000
Shareholder equity	€83,000,000
Total liabilities and equity	€185,000,000

Therefore, the consolidated balance sheet of Odena would look exactly the same as if it borrowed directly against the receivables. In addition, as a result of the consolidation, the transfer (sale) of the receivables to the SPE would be reversed along with any gain Odena recognized on the sale.

5.6. Additional Issues in Business Combinations That Impair Comparability

Accounting for business combinations is a complex topic. In addition to the basics covered so far in this reading, we briefly mention some of the more common issues that impair comparability between IFRS and US GAAP.

5.6.1. Contingent Assets and Liabilities

Under IFRS, the cost of an acquisition is allocated to the fair value of assets, liabilities, and contingent liabilities. Contingent liabilities are recorded separately as part of the cost allocation process, provided that their fair values can be measured reliably. Subsequently, the contingent liability is measured at the higher of the amount initially recognized or the best estimate of the amount required to settle. As mentioned previously, GlaxoSmithKline had approximately £6 billion in contingent liabilities in relation to a number of purchases for the year ended December 31, 2017, with the notes to the financial statements further stating that the £6 billion was the expected value of the contingent consideration payments, discounted at an appropriate discount rate. Contingent assets are not recognized under IFRS.

Under US GAAP, contractual contingent assets and liabilities are recognized and recorded at their fair values at the time of acquisition. Non-contractual contingent assets and liabilities must also be recognized and recorded only if it is "more likely than not" they meet the definition of an asset or a liability at the acquisition date. Subsequently, a contingent liability is measured at the higher of the amount initially recognized or the best estimate of the amount of the loss. A contingent asset, however, is measured at the lower of the acquisition date fair value or the best estimate of the future settlement amount.

5.6.2. Contingent Consideration

Contingent consideration may be negotiated as part of the acquisition price. For example, the acquiring company (parent) may agree to pay additional money to the acquiree's (subsidiary's) former shareholders if certain agreed upon events occur. These can include achieving specified sales or profit levels for the acquiree and/or the combined entity. Under both IFRS and US GAAP, contingent consideration is initially measured at fair value. IFRS and US GAAP classify contingent consideration as an asset, liability, or equity. In subsequent periods, changes in the fair value of liabilities (and assets, in the case of US GAAP) are recognized in the consolidated income statement. Both IFRS and US GAAP do not remeasure equity classified contingent consideration; instead, settlement is accounted for within equity.

5.6.3. In-Process R&D

IFRS and US GAAP recognize in-process research and development acquired in a business combination as a separate intangible asset and measure it at fair value (if it can be measured reliably). In subsequent periods, this research and development is subject to amortization if successfully completed (a marketable product results) or to impairment if no product results or if the product is not technically and/or financially viable.

5.6.4. Restructuring Costs

IFRS and US GAAP do not recognize restructuring costs that are associated with the business combination as part of the cost of the acquisition. Instead, they are recognized as an expense in the periods the restructuring costs are incurred.

6. SUMMARY

Intercompany investments play a significant role in business activities and create significant challenges for the analyst in assessing company performance. Investments in other companies can take five basic forms: investments in financial assets, investments in associates, joint ventures, business combinations, and investments in special purpose and variable interest entities. Key concepts are as follows:

- Investments in financial assets are those in which the investor has no significant influence. They can be measured and reported as
  - fair value through profit or loss;
  - fair value through other comprehensive income; or
  - amortized cost.
  IFRS and US GAAP treat investments in financial assets in a similar manner.
- Investments in associates and joint ventures are those in which the investor has significant influence, but not control, over the investee's business activities. Because the investor can exert significant influence over financial and operating policy decisions, IFRS and US GAAP require the equity method of accounting because it provides a more objective basis for reporting investment income.
- The equity method requires the investor to recognize income as earned rather than when dividends are received.
- The equity investment is carried at cost, plus its share of post-acquisition income (after adjustments) less dividends received.
- The equity investment is reported as a single line item on the balance sheet and on the income statement.

- IFRS and US GAAP accounting standards require the use of the acquisition method to account for business combinations. Fair value of the consideration given is the appropriate measurement for identifiable assets and liabilities acquired in the business combination.
- Goodwill is the difference between the acquisition value and the fair value of the target's identifiable net tangible and intangible assets. Because it is considered to have an indefinite life, it is not amortized. Instead, it is evaluated at least annually for impairment. Impairment losses are reported on the income statement. IFRS use a one-step approach to determine and measure the impairment loss, whereas US GAAP uses a two-step approach.
- If the acquiring company acquires less than 100%, non-controlling (minority) shareholders' interests are reported on the consolidated financial statements. IFRS allows the non-controlling interest to be measured at either its fair value (full goodwill) or at the non-controlling interest's proportionate share of the acquiree's identifiable net assets (partial goodwill). US GAAP requires the non-controlling interest to be measured at fair value (full goodwill).
- Consolidated financial statements are prepared in each reporting period.
- Special purpose entities (SPEs) and variable interest entities (VIEs) are required to be consolidated by the entity which is expected to absorb the majority of the expected losses or receive the majority of expected residual benefits.

PRACTICE PROBLEMS

The following information relates to Questions 1–5

Cinnamon, Inc. is a diversified manufacturing company headquartered in the United Kingdom. It complies with IFRS. In 2017, Cinnamon held a 19 percent passive equity ownership interest in Cambridge Processing. In December 2017, Cinnamon announced that it would be increasing its ownership interest to 50 percent effective January 1, 2018 through a cash purchase. Cinnamon and Cambridge have no intercompany transactions.

Peter Lubbock, an analyst following both Cinnamon and Cambridge, is curious how the increased stake will affect Cinnamon's consolidated financial statements. He asks Cinnamon's CFO how the company will account for the investment, and is told that the decision has not yet been made. Lubbock decides to use his existing forecasts for both companies' financial statements to compare the outcomes of alternative accounting treatments.

Lubbock assembles abbreviated financial statement data for Cinnamon (Exhibit 1) and Cambridge (Exhibit 2) for this purpose.

EXHIBIT 1   Selected Financial Statement Information for
Cinnamon, Inc. (£ Millions)

Year ending December 31	2017	2018*
Revenue	1,400	1,575
Operating income	126	142
Net income	62	69
December 31	2017	2018*
Total assets	1,170	1,317
Shareholders' equity	616	685

*Estimates made prior to announcement of increased stake in Cambridge.

EXHIBIT 2   Selected Financial Statement Information for
Cambridge Processing (£ Millions)

Year ending December 31	**20**17	2018*
Revenue	1,000	1,100
Operating income	80	88
Net income	40	44
Dividends paid	20	22
December 31	2017	2018*
Total assets	800	836
Shareholders' equity	440	462

*Estimates made prior to announcement of increased stake by Cinnamon.

1. In 2018, if Cinnamon is deemed to have control over Cambridge, it will *most likely* account for its investment in Cambridge using:
   A. the equity method.
   B. the acquisition method.
   C. proportionate consolidation.

2. At December 31, 2018, Cinnamon's total shareholders' equity on its balance sheet would *most likely* be:
   A. highest if Cinnamon is deemed to have control of Cambridge.
   B. independent of the accounting method used for the investment in Cambridge.
   C. highest if Cinnamon is deemed to have significant influence over Cambridge.

3. In 2018, Cinnamon's net profit margin would be *highest* if:
   A. it is deemed to have control of Cambridge.
   B. it had not increased its stake in Cambridge.
   C. it is deemed to have significant influence over Cambridge.

4. At December 31, 2018, assuming control and recognition of goodwill, Cinnamon's reported debt to equity ratio will *most likely* be highest if it accounts for its investment in Cambridge using the:
   A. equity method.
   B. full goodwill method.
   C. partial goodwill method.

5. Compared to Cinnamon's operating margin in 2017, if it is deemed to have control of Cambridge, its operating margin in 2018 will *most likely* be:
   A. lower.
   B. higher.
   C. the same.

The following information relates to Questions 6–10

Zimt, AG is a consumer products manufacturer headquartered in Austria. It complies with IFRS. In 2017, Zimt held a 10 percent passive stake in Oxbow Limited. In December 2017, Zimt announced that it would be increasing its ownership to 50 percent effective January 1, 2018.

Franz Gelblum, an analyst following both Zimt and Oxbow, is curious how the increased stake will affect Zimt's consolidated financial statements. Because Gelblum is uncertain how the company will account for the increased stake, he uses his existing forecasts for both companies' financial statements to compare various alternative outcomes.

Gelblum gathers abbreviated financial statement data for Zimt (Exhibit 1) and Oxbow (Exhibit 2) for this purpose.

EXHIBIT 1   Selected Financial Statement Estimates for Zimt AG (€ Millions)

Year ending December 31	2017	2018*
Revenue	1,500	1,700
Operating income	135	153
Net income	66	75
31 December	2017	2018*
Total assets	1,254	1,421
Shareholders' equity	660	735

*Estimates made prior to announcement of increased stake in Oxbow.

EXHIBIT 2   Selected Financial Statement Estimates for Oxbow Limited (€ Millions)

Year ending December 31	2017	2018*
Revenue	1,200	1,350
Operating income	120	135
Net income	60	68
Dividends paid	20	22
December 31	2017	2018*
Total assets	1,200	1,283
Shareholders' equity	660	706

*Estimates made prior to announcement of increased stake by Zimt.

6. At December 31, 2018, Zimt's total assets balance would *most likely* be:
   A. highest if Zimt is deemed to have control of Oxbow.
   B. highest if Zimt is deemed to have significant influence over Oxbow.
   C. unaffected by the accounting method used for the investment in Oxbow.

7. Based on Gelblum's estimates, if Zimt is deemed to have significant influence over Oxbow, its 2018 net income (in € millions) would be *closest* to:
   A. €75.
   B. €109.
   C. €143.

8. Based on Gelblum's estimates, if Zimt is deemed to have joint control of Oxbow, and Zimt uses the proportionate consolidation method, its December 31, 2018 total liabilities (in € millions) will *most likely* be *closest* to:
   A. €686.
   B. €975.
   C. €1,263.

9. Based on Gelblum's estimates, if Zimt is deemed to have control over Oxbow, its 2018 consolidated sales (in € millions) will be *closest* to:
   A. €1,700.
   B. €2,375.
   C. €3,050.

10. Based on Gelblum's estimates, Zimt's net income in 2018 will *most likely* be:
    A. highest if Zimt is deemed to have control of Oxbow.
    B. highest if Zimt is deemed to have significant influence over Oxbow.
    C. independent of the accounting method used for the investment in Oxbow.

The following information relates to Questions 11–16

Burton Howard, CFA, is an equity analyst with Maplewood Securities. Howard is preparing a research report on Confabulated Materials, SA, a publicly traded company based in France that complies with IFRS 9. As part of his analysis, Howard has assembled data gathered from the financial statement footnotes of Confabulated's 2018 Annual Report and from discussions with company management. Howard is concerned about the effect of this information on Confabulated's future earnings.

Information about Confabulated's investment portfolio for the years ended December 31, 2017 and 2018 is presented in Exhibit 1. As part of his research, Howard is considering the possible effect on reported income of Confabulated's accounting classification for fixed income investments.

EXHIBIT 1   Confabulated's Investment Portfolio (€ Thousands)

Characteristic	Bugle AG	Cathay Corp	Dumas SA
Classification	FVPL	FVOCI	Amortized cost
Cost*	€25,000	€40,000	€50,000
Market value, December 31, 2017	29,000	38,000	54,000
Market value, December 31, 2018	28,000	37,000	55,000

* All securities were acquired at par value.

In addition, Confabulated's annual report discusses a transaction under which receivables were securitized through a special purpose entity (SPE) for Confabulated's benefit.

11. The balance sheet carrying value of Confabulated's investment portfolio (in € thousands) at December 31, 2018 is *closest* to:
    A. 112,000.
    B. 115,000.
    C. 118,000.

12. The balance sheet carrying value of Confabulated's investment portfolio at December 31, 2018 would have been higher if which of the securities had been reclassified as FVPL security?
    A. Bugle.
    B. Cathay.
    C. Dumas.

13. Compared to Confabulated's reported interest income in 2018, if Dumas had been classified as FVPL, the interest income would have been:
    A. lower.
    B. the same.
    C. higher.

14. Compared to Confabulated's reported earnings before taxes in 2018, if Dumas had been classified as a FVPL security, the earnings before taxes (in € thousands) would have been:
    A. the same.
    B. €1,000 lower.
    C. €3,000 higher.

15. Confabulated's reported interest income would be lower if the cost was the same but the par value (in € thousands) of:
    A. Bugle was €28,000.
    B. Cathay was €37,000.
    C. Dumas was €55,000.

16. Confabulated's special purpose entity is *most likely* to be:
    A. held off-balance sheet.
    B. consolidated on Confabulated's financial statements.
    C. consolidated on Confabulated's financial statements only if it is a "qualifying SPE."

The following information relates to Questions 17–22

BetterCare Hospitals, Inc. operates a chain of hospitals throughout the United States. The company has been expanding by acquiring local hospitals. Its largest acquisition, that of State-wide Medical, was made in 2001 under the pooling of interests method. BetterCare complies with US GAAP.

BetterCare is currently forming a 50/50 joint venture with Supreme Healthcare under which the companies will share control of several hospitals. BetterCare plans to use the equity method to account for the joint venture. Supreme Healthcare complies with IFRS and will use the proportionate consolidation method to account for the joint venture.

Erik Ohalin is an equity analyst who covers both companies. He has estimated the joint venture's financial information for 2018 in order to prepare his estimates of each company's earnings and financial performance. This information is presented in Exhibit 1.

EXHIBIT 1   Selected Financial Statement
Forecasts for Joint Venture ($ Millions)

Year ending December 31	2018
Revenue	1,430
Operating income	128
Net income	62
December 31	2018
Total assets	1,500
Shareholders' equity	740

Supreme Healthcare recently announced it had formed a special purpose entity through which it plans to sell up to $100 million of its accounts receivable. Supreme Healthcare has no voting interest in the SPE, but it is expected to absorb any losses that it may incur. Ohalin wants to estimate the impact this will have on Supreme Healthcare's consolidated financial statements.

17. Compared to accounting principles currently in use, the pooling method BetterCare used for its Statewide Medical acquisition has *most likely* caused its reported:
   A. revenue to be higher.
   B. total equity to be lower.
   C. total assets to be higher.

18. Based on Ohalin's estimates, the amount of joint venture revenue (in $ millions) included on BetterCare's consolidated 2018 financial statements should be *closest* to:
   A. $0.
   B. $715.
   C. $1,430.

19. Based on Ohalin's estimates, the amount of joint venture net income included on the consolidated financial statements of each venturer will *most likely* be:
   A. higher for BetterCare.
   B. higher for Supreme Healthcare.
   C. the same for both BetterCare and Supreme Healthcare.

20. Based on Ohalin's estimates, the amount of the joint venture's December 31, 2018 total assets (in $ millions) that will be included on Supreme Healthcare's consolidated financial statements will be *closest* to:
   A. $0.
   B. $750.
   C. $1,500.

21. Based on Ohalin's estimates, the amount of joint venture shareholders' equity at December 31, 2018 included on the consolidated financial statements of each venturer will *most likely* be:
   A. higher for BetterCare.
   B. higher for Supreme Healthcare.
   C. the same for both BetterCare and Supreme Healthcare.

22. If Supreme Healthcare sells its receivables to the SPE, its consolidated financial results will *most likely* show:
    A. a higher revenue for 2018.
    B. the same cash balance at December 31, 2018.
    C. the same accounts receivable balance at December 31, 2018.

The following information relates to Questions 23–28

Percy Byron, CFA, is an equity analyst with a UK-based investment firm. One firm Byron follows is NinMount PLC, a UK-based company. On December 31, 2008, NinMount paid £320 million to purchase a 50 percent stake in Boswell Company. The excess of the purchase price over the fair value of Boswell's net assets was attributable to previously unrecorded licenses. These licenses were estimated to have an economic life of six years. The fair value of Boswell's assets and liabilities other than licenses was equal to their recorded book values. NinMount and Boswell both use the pound sterling as their reporting currency and prepare their financial statements in accordance with IFRS.

Byron is concerned whether the investment should affect his "buy" rating on NinMount common stock. He knows NinMount could choose one of several accounting methods to report the results of its investment, but NinMount has not announced which method it will use. Byron forecasts that both companies' 2019 financial results (excluding any merger accounting adjustments) will be identical to those of 2018.

NinMount's and Boswell's condensed income statements for the year ended December 31, 2018, and condensed balance sheets at December 31, 2018, are presented in Exhibits 1 and 2, respectively.

EXHIBIT 1   NinMount PLC and Boswell Company Income Statements for the Year Ended December 31, 2018 (£ millions)

	NinMount	Boswell
Net sales	950	510
Cost of goods sold	(495)	(305)
Selling expenses	(50)	(15)
Administrative expenses	(136)	(49)
Depreciation & amortization expense	(102)	(92)
Interest expense	(42)	(32)
Income before taxes	125	17
Income tax expense	(50)	(7)
Net income	75	10

EXHIBIT 2   NinMount PLC and Boswell Company Balance Sheets at December 31, 2018
(£ millions)

	NinMount	Boswell
Cash	50	20
Receivables—net	70	45
Inventory	130	75
Total current assets	250	140
Property, plant, & equipment—net	1,570	930
Investment in Boswell	320	—
Total assets	2,140	1,070
Current liabilities	110	90
Long-term debt	600	400
Total liabilities	710	490
Common stock	850	535
Retained earnings	580	45
Total equity	1,430	580
Total liabilities and equity	2,140	1,070

Note: Balance sheets reflect the purchase price paid by NinMount, but do not yet consider the impact of the accounting method choice.

23. NinMount's current ratio on December 31, 2018 *most likely* will be highest if the results of the acquisition are reported using:
    A. the equity method.
    B. consolidation with full goodwill.
    C. consolidation with partial goodwill.

24. NinMount's long-term debt to equity ratio on December 31, 2018 *most likely* will be lowest if the results of the acquisition are reported using:
    A. the equity method.
    B. consolidation with full goodwill.
    C. consolidation with partial goodwill.

25. Based on Byron's forecast, if NinMount deems it has acquired control of Boswell, Nin-Mount's consolidated 2019 depreciation and amortization expense (in £ millions) will be *closest* to:
    A. 102.
    B. 148.
    C. 204.

26. Based on Byron's forecast, NinMount's net profit margin for 2019 *most likely* will be highest if the results of the acquisition are reported using:
    A. the equity method.
    B. consolidation with full goodwill.
    C. consolidation with partial goodwill.

27. Based on Byron's forecast, NinMount's 2019 return on beginning equity *most likely* will be the same under:
    A. either of the consolidations, but different under the equity method.
    B. the equity method, consolidation with full goodwill, and consolidation with partial goodwill.
    C. none of the equity method, consolidation with full goodwill, or consolidation with partial goodwill.

28. Based on Byron's forecast, NinMount's 2019 total asset turnover ratio on beginning assets under the equity method is *most likely*:
    A. lower than if the results are reported using consolidation.
    B. the same as if the results are reported using consolidation.
    C. higher than if the results are reported using consolidation.

The following information relates to Questions 29–36

John Thronen is an analyst in the research department of an international securities firm. He is preparing a research report on Topmaker, Inc., a publicly traded company that complies with IFRS.

On January 1, 2018, Topmaker invested $11 million in Blanca Co. debt securities (with a 5.0% stated coupon on par value, and interest payable each December 31). The par value of the securities is $10 million, and the market interest rate in effect when the bonds were purchased was 4.0%. Topmaker designates the investment as amortized cost. As of December 31, 2018, the fair value of the securities is $12 million.

Blanca Co. wants to raise $40 million in capital by borrowing against its financial receivables. Blanca plans to create a special-purpose entity (SPE), invest $10 million in the SPE, have the SPE borrow $40 million, and then use the funds to purchase $50 million of receivables from Blanca. Blanca meets the definition of control and plans to consolidate the SPE. Blanca's balance sheet is presented in Exhibit 1.

EXHIBIT 1   Blanca Co. Balance Sheet at December 31, 2018 ($ millions)

Cash	20	Current liabilities	25
Accounts receivable	50	Noncurrent liabilities	30
Other assets	30	Shareholders' equity	45
Total assets	**100**	**Total liabilities and equity**	**100**

Also on January 1, 2018, Topmaker acquired a 15% equity interest with voting power in Rainer Co. for $300 million. Topmaker has representation on Rainer's board of directors and participates in Rainer's policymaking process. Thronen believes that Topmaker underestimated the goodwill and balance sheet value of its investment account in Rainer. To estimate these figures, Thronen gathers selected financial information for Rainer as of December 31, 2018 in Exhibit 2. The plant and equipment are depreciated on a straight-line basis and have 10 years of remaining life.

EXHIBIT 2   Selected Financial Data for Rainer Co., Year
Ending December 31, 2018 ($ millions)

	Book Value	Fair Value
Revenue	1,740	N/A
Net income	360	N/A
Dividends paid	220	N/A
Plant and equipment	2,900	3,160
Total assets	3,170	3,430
Liabilities	1,830	1,830
Net assets	1,340	1,600

During 2018, Rainer sold $60 million in inventory to Topmaker for $80 million. In 2019, Topmaker resold the entire inventory to a third party.

Thronen is concerned about possible goodwill impairment resulting from expected changes in the industry effective at the end of 2019. He calculates the impairment loss based on the projected consolidated balance sheet data shown in Exhibit 3, assuming that the cash-generating unit and reporting unit of Topmaker are the same.

EXHIBIT 3   Selected Financial Data for Topmaker, Inc., Estimated Year
Ending December 31, 2019 ($ millions)

Carrying value of cash-generating unit/reporting unit	15,200
Recoverable amount of cash-generating unit/reporting unit	14,900
Fair value of reporting unit	14,800
Identifiable net assets	14,400
Goodwill	520

Finally, Topmaker announces its plan to increase its ownership interest in Rainer to 80% effective January 1, 2020. It will account for the investment in Rainer using the partial goodwill method. Thronen estimates that the fair market value of the Rainer's shares on the expected date of exchange is $2 billion, with the identifiable assets valued at $1.5 billion.

29. The carrying value reported on the balance sheet of Topmaker's investment in Blanca's debt securities at December 31, 2018 is:
    A. $10,940,000.
    B. $11,000,000.
    C. $12,000,000.

30. Based on Exhibit 1 and Blanca's plans to borrow against its financial receivables, the consolidated balance sheet will show total assets of:
    A. $50,000,000.
    B. $140,000,000.
    C. $150,000,000.

31. Topmaker's influence on Rainer's business activities can be *best* described as:
    A. significant.
    B. controlling.
    C. shared control.

32. Based on Exhibit 2, the goodwill included in Topmaker's purchase of Rainer is:
    A. $21 million.
    B. $60 million.
    C. $99 million.

33. Based on Exhibit 2, the carrying value of Topmaker's investment in Rainer at the end of 2018 is *closest* to:
    A. $282 million.
    B. $317 million.
    C. $321 million.

34. Which of the following statements regarding the sale of inventory by Rainer to Topmaker is correct?
    A. The sale represents a downstream sale.
    B. Topmaker's unrealized profits are initially deferred.
    C. Profits will decline on Topmaker's 2018 income statement.

35. Based on Exhibit 3, Topmaker's impairment loss under IFRS is:
    A. $120 million.
    B. $300 million.
    C. $400 million.

36. The value of the minority interest at the acquisition date of January 1, 2020 is:
    A. $300 million.
    B. $400 million.
    C. $500 million.

CHAPTER 14

EMPLOYEE COMPENSATION: POST-EMPLOYMENT AND SHARE-BASED

Elaine Henry, PhD, CFA
Elizabeth A. Gordon, PhD, MBA, CPA

LEARNING OUTCOMES

After completing this chapter, you will be able to do the following:

- describe the types of post-employment benefit plans and implications for financial reports;
- explain and calculate measures of a defined benefit pension obligation (i.e., present value of the defined benefit obligation and projected benefit obligation) and net pension liability (or asset);
- describe the components of a company's defined benefit pension costs;
- explain and calculate the effect of a defined benefit plan's assumptions on the defined benefit obligation and periodic pension cost;
- explain and calculate how adjusting for items of pension and other post-employment benefits that are reported in the notes to the financial statements affects financial statements and ratios;
- interpret pension plan note disclosures including cash flow related information;
- explain issues associated with accounting for share-based compensation;
- explain how accounting for stock grants and stock options affects financial statements, and the importance of companies' assumptions in valuing these grants and options.

1. INTRODUCTION

This chapter covers two complex aspects of employee compensation: post-employment (retirement) benefits and share-based compensation. Retirement benefits include pensions and other post-employment benefits, such as health insurance. Examples of share-based compensation are stock options and stock grants.

A common issue underlying both of these aspects of employee compensation is the difficulty in measuring the value of the compensation. One factor contributing to the difficulty is that employees earn the benefits in the periods that they provide service but typically receive the benefits in future periods, so measurement requires a significant number of assumptions.

This chapter provides an overview of the methods companies use to estimate and measure the benefits they provide to their employees and how this information is reported in financial statements. There has been some convergence between International Financial Reporting Standards (IFRS) and US generally accepted accounting principles (US GAAP) in the measurement and accounting treatment for pensions, other post-employment benefits, and share-based compensation, but some differences remain. Although this chapter focuses on IFRS as the basis for discussion, instances where US GAAP significantly differ are discussed.

The chapter is organized as follows: Section 2 addresses pensions and other post-employment benefits, and Section 3 covers share-based compensation with a primary focus on the accounting for and analysis of stock options. A summary and practice problems conclude the chapter.

2. PENSIONS AND OTHER POST-EMPLOYMENT BENEFITS

This section discusses the accounting and reporting of pensions and other post-employment benefits by the companies that provide these benefits (accounting and reporting by pension and other retirement funds are not covered in this chapter). Under IFRS, IAS 19, *Employee Benefits*, provides the principal source of guidance in accounting for pensions and other post-employment benefits.[1] Under US GAAP, the guidance is spread across several sections of the FASB Codification.[2]

The discussion begins with an overview of the types of benefits and measurement issues involved, including the accounting treatment for defined contribution plans. It then continues with financial statement reporting of pension plans and other post-employment benefits, including an overview of critical assumptions used to value these benefits. The section concludes with a discussion of evaluating defined benefit pension plans and other post-employment benefit disclosures.

2.1. Types of Post-Employment Benefit Plans

Companies may offer various types of benefits to their employees following retirement, including pension plans, health care plans, medical insurance, and life insurance. Some of these benefits involve payments in the current period, but many are promises of future benefits. The objectives of accounting for employee benefits is to measure the cost associated with providing these benefits and to recognize these costs in the sponsoring company's financial statements

---

[1] This chapter describes IFRS requirements contained in IAS 19 as updated in June 2011 and effective beginning January 2013.

[2] Guidance on pension and other post-employment benefits is included in FASB ASC Topic 712 [Compensation-Nonretirement Postemployment Benefits], FASB ASC Topic 715 [Compensation-Retirement Benefits], FASB ASC Topic 960 [Plan Accounting-Defined Benefit Pension Plans], and FASB ASC Topic 965 [Plan Accounting-Health and Welfare Benefit Plans].

during the employees' periods of service. Complexity arises because the sponsoring company must make assumptions to estimate the value of future benefits. The assumptions required to estimate and recognize these future benefits can have a significant impact on the company's reported performance and financial position. In addition, differences in assumptions can reduce comparability across companies.

Pension plans, as well as other post-employment benefits, may be either defined contribution plans or defined benefit plans. Under **defined contribution pension plans**, specific (or agreed-upon) contributions are made to an employee's pension plan. The agreed upon amount is the pension expense. Typically, in a defined contribution (DC) pension plan, an individual account is established for each participating employee. The accounts are generally invested through a financial intermediary, such as an investment management company or an insurance company. The employees and the employer may each contribute to the plan. After the employer makes its agreed-upon contribution to the plan on behalf of an employee— generally in the same period in which the employee provides the service—the employer has no obligation to make payments beyond this amount. The future value of the plan's assets depends on the performance of the investments within the plan. Any gains or losses related to those investments accrue to the employee. Therefore, in DC pension plans, the employee bears the risk that plan assets will not be sufficient to meet future needs. The impact on the company's financial statements of DC pension plans is easily assessed because the company has no obligations beyond the required contributions.

In contrast to DC pension plans, **defined benefit pension plans** are essentially promises by the employer to pay a defined amount of pension in the future. As part of total compensation, the employee works in the current period in exchange for a pension to be paid after retirement. In a defined benefit (DB) pension plan, the amount of pension benefit to be provided is defined, usually by reference to age, years of service, compensation, etc. For example, a DB pension plan may provide for the retiree to be paid, annually until death, an amount equal to 1 percent of the final year's salary times the number of years of service. The future pension payments represent a liability or obligation of the employer (i.e., the sponsoring company). To measure this obligation, the employer must make various actuarial assumptions (employee turnover, average retirement age, life expectancy after retirement) and computations. It is important for an analyst to evaluate such assumptions for their reasonableness and to analyze the impact of these assumptions on the financial reports of the company.

Under IFRS and US GAAP, all plans for pensions and other post-employment benefits other than those explicitly structured as DC plans are classified as DB plans.[3] DB plans include both formal plans and those informal arrangements that create a constructive obligation by the employer to its employees.[4] The employer must estimate the total cost of the benefits promised and then allocate these costs to the periods in which the employees provide service. This estimation and allocation further increases the complexity of pension reporting because the timing of cash flows (contributions into the plan and payments from the plan) can differ

---

[3] Multi-employer plans are an exception under IFRS. These are plans to which many different employers contribute on behalf of their employees, such as an industry association pension plan. For multi-employer plans, the employer accounts for its proportionate share of the plan. If, however, the employer does not have sufficient information from the plan administrator to meet the reporting requirement for a defined benefit plan, IFRS allow the employer to account for the plan as if it were a defined contribution plan.

[4] For example, a company has a constructive obligation if the benefits it promises are not linked solely to the amount of its contributions or if it indirectly or directly guarantees a specified return on pension assets.

significantly from the timing of accrual-basis reporting. Accrual-basis reporting is based on when the services are rendered and the benefits are earned.

Most DB pension plans are funded through a separate legal entity, typically a pension trust, and the assets of the trust are used to make the payments to retirees. The sponsoring company is responsible for making contributions to the plan. The company also must ensure that there are sufficient assets in the plan to pay the ultimate benefits promised to plan participants. Regulatory requirements usually specify minimum funding levels for DB pension plans, but those requirements vary by country. The funded status of a pension plan—overfunded or underfunded—refers to whether the amount of assets in the pension trust is greater than or less than the estimated liability. If the amount of assets in the DB pension trust exceeds the present value of the estimated liability, the DB pension plan is said to be overfunded; conversely, if the amount of assets in the pension trust is less than the estimated liability, the plan is said to be underfunded. Because the company has promised a defined amount of benefit to the employees, it is obligated to make those pension payments when they are due regardless of whether the pension plan assets generate sufficient returns to provide the benefits. In other words, the company bears the investment risk. Many companies are reducing the use of DB pension plans because of this risk.

Similar to DB pension plans, **other post-employment benefits** (OPB) are promises by the company to pay benefits in the future, such as life insurance premiums and all or part of health care insurance for its retirees. OPB are typically classified as DB plans, with accounting treatment similar to DB pension plans. However, the complexity in reporting for OPB may be even greater than for DB pension plans because of the need to estimate future increases in costs, such as health care, over a long time horizon. Unlike DB pension plans, however, companies may not be required by regulation to fund an OPB in advance to the same degree as DB pension plans. This is partly because governments, through some means, often insure DB pension plans but not OPB, partly because OPB may represent a much smaller financial liability, and partly because OPB are often easier to eliminate should the costs become burdensome. It is important that an analyst determine what OPB are offered by a company and the obligation they represent.

Types of post-employment benefits offered by employers differ across countries. For instance, in countries where government-sponsored universal health care plans exist (such as Germany, France, Canada, Brazil, Mexico, New Zealand, South Africa, India, Israel, Bhutan, and Singapore), companies are less likely to provide post-retirement health care benefits to employees. The extent to which companies offer DC or DB pension plans also varies by country.

Exhibit 1 summarizes these three types of post-employment benefits.

EXHIBIT 1   Types of Post-Employment Benefits

Type of Benefit	Amount of Post-Employment Benefit to Employee	Obligation of Sponsoring Company	Sponsoring Company's Pre-funding of its Future Obligation
Defined contribution pension plan	Amount of future benefit is not defined. Actual future benefit will depend on investment performance of plan assets. Investment risk is borne by employee.	Amount of the company's obligation (contribution) is defined in each period. The contribution, if any, is typically made on a periodic basis with no additional future obligation.	Not applicable.

EXHIBIT 1   (Continued)

Type of Benefit	Amount of Post-Employment Benefit to Employee	Obligation of Sponsoring Company	Sponsoring Company's Pre-funding of its Future Obligation
Defined benefit pension plan	Amount of future benefit is defined, based on the plan's formula (often a function of length of service and final year's compensation). Investment risk is borne by company.	Amount of the future obligation, based on the plan's formula, must be estimated in the current period.	Companies typically pre-fund the DB plans by contributing funds to a pension trust. Regulatory requirements to pre-fund vary by country.
Other post-employment benefits (e.g., retirees' health care)	Amount of future benefit depends on plan specifications and type of benefit.	Eventual benefits are specified. The amount of the future obligation must be estimated in the current period.	Companies typically do not pre-fund other post-employment benefit obligations.

The following sections provide additional detail on how DB pension plan liabilities and periodic costs are measured, the financial statement impact of reporting pension and other post-employment benefits, and how disclosures in the notes to the financial statements can be used to gain insights about the underlying economics of a company's defined benefit plans. Section 2.2 describes how a DB pension plan's obligation is estimated and the key inputs into and assumptions behind the estimate. Section 2.3 describes financial statement reporting of pension and OPB plans and demonstrates the calculation of defined benefit obligations and current costs and the effects of assumptions. Section 2.4 describes disclosures in financial reports about pension and OPB plans. These include disclosures about assumptions that can be useful in analyzing and comparing pension and OPB plans within and among companies.

2.2. Measuring a Defined Benefit Pension Plan's Obligations

Both IFRS and US GAAP measure the **pension obligation** as the present value of future benefits earned by employees for service provided to date. The obligation is called the present value of the defined benefit obligation (PVDBO) under IFRS and the projected benefit obligation (PBO) under US GAAP.[5] This measure is defined as "the present value, without deducting any plan assets, of expected future payments required to settle the obligation arising from employee

---

[5] In addition to the projected benefit obligation, US GAAP identify two other measures of the pension liability. The **vested benefit obligation** (VBO) is the "actuarial present value of vested benefits" (FASB ASC Glossary). The **accumulated benefit obligation** (ABO) is "the actuarial present value of benefits (whether vested or non-vested) attributed, generally by the pension benefit formula, to employee service rendered before a specified date and based on employee service and compensation (if applicable) before that date. The accumulated benefit obligation differs from the projected benefit obligation in that it includes no assumption about future compensation levels" (FASB ASC Glossary). Both the vested benefit obligation and the accumulated benefit obligation are based on the amounts promised as a result of an employee's service up to a specific date. Thus, both of these measures will be less than the projected benefit obligation (VBO < ABO < PBO).

service in the current and prior periods" under IFRS and "the actuarial present value as of a date of all benefits attributed by the pension benefit formula to employee service rendered prior to that date" under US GAAP. In the remainder of this chapter, the term "pension obligation" will be used to generically refer to PVDBO and PBO.

In determining the pension obligation, a company estimates the future benefits it will pay. To estimate the future benefits, the company must make a number of assumptions[6] such as future compensation increases and levels, discount rates, and expected vesting. For instance, an estimate of future compensation is made if the pension benefit formula is based on future compensation levels (examples include pay-related, final-pay, final-average-pay, or career-average-pay plans). The expected annual increase in compensation over the employee service period can have a significant impact on the defined benefit obligation. The determination of the benefit obligation implicitly assumes that the company will continue to operate in the future (the "going concern assumption") and recognizes that benefits will increase with future compensation increases.

Another key assumption is the discount rate—the interest rate used to calculate the present value of the future benefits. This rate is based on current rates of return on high-quality corporate bonds (or government bonds in the absence of a deep market in corporate bonds) with currency and durations consistent with the currency and durations of the benefits.

Under both DB and DC pension plans, the benefits that employees earn may be conditional on remaining with the company for a specified period of time. "Vesting" refers to a provision in pensions plans whereby an employee gains rights to future benefits only after meeting certain criteria, such as a pre-specified number of years of service. If the employee leaves the company before meeting the criteria, he or she may be entitled to none or a portion of the benefits earned up until that point. However, once the employee has met the vesting requirements, he or she is entitled to receive the benefits earned in prior periods (i.e., once the employee has become vested, benefits are not forfeited if the employee leaves the company). In measuring the defined benefit obligation, the company considers the probability that some employees may not satisfy the vesting requirements (i.e., may leave before the vesting period) and uses this probability to calculate the current service cost and the present value of the obligation. Current service cost is the increase in the present value of a defined benefit obligation as a result of employee service in the current period. Current service cost is not the only cause of change in the present value of a defined benefit obligation.

The estimates and assumptions about future salary increases, the discount rate, and the expected vesting can change. Of course, any changes in these estimates and assumptions will change the estimated pension obligation. If the changes increase the obligation, the increase is referred to as an actuarial loss. If the changes decrease the obligation, the change is referred to as an actuarial gain. Section 2.3.3 further discusses estimates and assumptions and the effect on the pension obligation and expense.

2.3. Financial Statement Reporting of Pension Plans and Other Post-Employment Benefits

Sections 2.3.1 to 2.3.3 describe how pension plans and other post-employment benefits are reported in the financial statements of the sponsoring company and how assumptions affect the amounts reported. Disclosures related to pensions plans and OPB are described in Section 2.4.

---

[6] These assumptions are referred to as "actuarial assumptions." Thus, losses or gains due to changes in these assumptions, or due to differences between these assumptions and what actually occurs, are referred to as "actuarial gains or losses."

2.3.1. Defined Contribution Pension Plans

The accounting treatment for defined contribution pension plans is relatively simple. From a financial statement perspective, the employer's obligation for contributions into the plan, if any, is recorded as an expense on the income statement. Because the employer's obligation is limited to a defined amount that typically equals its contribution, no significant pension-related liability accrues on the balance sheet. An accrual (current liability) is recognized at the end of the reporting period only for any unpaid contributions.

2.3.2. Defined Benefit Pension Plans

The accounting treatment for defined benefit pension plans is more complex, primarily because of the complexities of measuring the pension obligation and expense.

2.3.2.1. Balance Sheet Presentation   Both IFRS and US GAAP require a pension plan's funded status to be reported on the balance sheet. The funded status is determined by netting the pension obligation against the fair value of the pension plan assets. If the pension obligation exceeds the pension plan assets, the plan has a deficit. If the plan assets exceed the pension obligation, the plan has a surplus. Summarizing this information in equation form gives

Funded status = Fair value of the plan assets − PV of the Defined benefit obligation

If the plan has a deficit, an amount equal to the net underfunded pension obligation is reported on the balance sheet as a net pension liability. If the plan has a surplus, an asset equal to the overfunded pension obligation is reported on the balance sheet as a net pension asset (except that the amount of reported assets is subject to a ceiling defined as the present value of future economic benefits, such as refunds from the plan or reductions of future contributions). Disclosures in the notes provide additional information about the net pension liability or asset reported on the balance sheet.

EXAMPLE 1   Determination of Amounts to be Reported on the Balance Sheet

The following information pertains to two hypothetical companies' defined benefit pension plans as of December 31, 2010:

- For company ABC, the present value of the company's defined benefit obligation is €6,723 and the fair value of the pension plan's assets is €4,880.
- For company DEF, the present value of the company's defined benefit obligation is €5,485 and the fair value of the pension plan assets is €5,998. In addition, the present value of available future refunds and reductions in future contributions is €326.

Calculate the amount each company would report as a pension asset or liability on its 2010 balance sheet.

Solution: Company ABC would report the full underfunded status of its pension plan (i.e., the amount by which the present value of the defined benefit obligation exceeds the fair value of plan assets) as a liability. Specifically, the company would report a pension liability of €1,843.

Present value of defined benefit obligation	€6,723
Fair value of plan assets	(4,880)
Net pension liability	€1,843

Company DEF's pension plan is overfunded by €513, which is the amount by which the fair value of the plan's assets exceed the defined benefit obligation (€5,998 – €5,485). However, when a company has a surplus in a defined benefit plan, the amount of asset that can be reported is the lower of the surplus and the asset ceiling (the present value of future economic benefits, such as refunds from the plan or reductions of future contributions). In this case, the asset ceiling is given as €326, so the amount of company DEF's reported net pension asset would be limited to €326.

2.3.2.2. Periodic Pension Cost   The periodic cost of a company's DB pension plan is the change in the net pension liability or asset adjusted for the employer's contributions. Each period, the periodic pension cost is recognized in profit or loss (P&L) and/or in other comprehensive income (OCI). (In some cases, amounts of pension costs may qualify for inclusion as part of the costs of such assets as inventories and thus be included in P&L as part of cost of goods sold when those inventories are later sold. The focus here is on the amounts not capitalized.) IFRS and US GAAP differ in the way that the periodic pension cost is divided between P&L and OCI.

Under IFRS, the periodic pension cost is viewed as having three components, two of which are recognized in P&L and one of which is recognized in OCI.

1. *Service costs.* The first component of periodic pension cost is service cost. Current service cost is the amount by which a company's pension obligation increases as a result of employees' service in the current period. Past service cost is the amount by which a company's pension obligation relating to employees' service in prior periods changes as a result of plan amendments or a plan curtailment.[7] Under IFRS, service costs (including both current service costs and past service costs) are recognized as an expense in P&L.

2. *Net interest expense/income.* The second component of periodic pension cost is net interest expense or income, which we will refer to as "net interest expense/income." Net interest expense/income is calculated by multiplying the net pension liability or net pension asset by the discount rate used in determining the present value of the pension liability. A net interest expense represents the financing cost of deferring payments related to the plan, and a net interest income represents the financing income from prepaying amounts related to the plan. Under IFRS, the net interest expense/income is recognized in P&L.

---

[7] A curtailment occurs when there is a significant reduction by the entity either in the number of employees covered by a plan or in benefits.

3. *Remeasurement.* The third component of periodic pension cost is remeasurement of the net pension liability or asset. Remeasurement includes (a) actuarial gains and losses and (b) any differences between the actual return on plan assets and the amount included in the net interest expense/income calculation. Under IFRS, remeasurement amounts are recognized in OCI. Remeasurement amounts are not subsequently amortized to P&L.

Similar to IFRS, under US GAAP current service cost is recognized in P&L. However, under US GAAP, past service costs are reported in OCI in the period in which the change giving rise to the cost occurs. In subsequent periods, these past service costs are amortized to P&L over the average service lives of the affected employees.

Also similar to IFRS, under US GAAP the periodic pension cost for P&L includes interest expense on pension obligations (which increases the amount of the periodic cost) and returns on the pension plan assets (which reduce the amount of the periodic cost). Unlike IFRS, however, under US GAAP, the two components are not presented net. Also, under US GAAP, returns on plan assets included in the P&L recognition of pension costs (pension expense) use an expected return rather than the actual return. (Under IFRS, returns on plan assets included in the P&L recognition of pension costs (pension expense) use the discount rate as the expected return.) Thus, under US GAAP, differences between the expected return and the actual return on plan assets represent another source of actuarial gains or losses. As noted, actuarial gains and losses can also result from changes in the actuarial assumptions used in determining the benefit obligation. Under US GAAP, all actuarial gains and losses are included in the net pension liability or net pension asset and can be reported either in P&L or in OCI. Typically, companies report actuarial gains and losses in OCI and recognize gains and losses in P&L only when certain conditions are met under a so-called corridor approach.

Under the corridor approach, the net cumulative unrecognized actuarial gains and losses at the beginning of the reporting period are compared with the defined benefit obligation and the fair value of plan assets at the beginning of the period. If the cumulative amount of unrecognized actuarial gains and losses becomes too large (i.e., exceeds 10 percent of the greater of the defined benefit obligation or the fair value of plan assets), then the excess is amortized over the expected average remaining working lives of the employees participating in the plan and is included as a component of periodic pension cost in P&L. The term "corridor" refers to the 10 percent range, and only amounts in excess of the corridor must be amortized.

To illustrate the corridor approach, assume that the beginning balance of the defined benefit obligation is $5,000,000, the beginning balance of fair value of plan assets is $4,850,000, and the beginning balance of unrecognized actuarial losses is $610,000. The expected average remaining working lives of the plan employees is 10 years. In this scenario, the corridor is $500,000, which is 10 percent of the defined benefit obligation (selected as the greater of the defined benefit obligation or the fair value of plan assets). Because the balance of unrecognized actuarial losses exceeds the $500,000 corridor, amortization is required. The amount of the amortization is $11,000, which is the excess of the unrecognized actuarial loss over the corridor divided by the expected average remaining working lives of the plan employees [($610,000 − $500,000) ÷ 10 years]. Actuarial gains or losses can also be amortized more quickly than under the corridor method; companies may use a faster recognition method, provided the company applies the method of amortization to both gains and losses consistently in all periods presented.

To summarize, under IFRS, the periodic pension costs recognized in P&L include service costs (both current and past) and net interest expense/income. The periodic pension costs recognized in OCI include remeasurements that comprise net return on plan assets and actuarial gains and losses. Under US GAAP, the periodic pension costs recognized in P&L include current service costs, interest expense on plan liabilities, expected returns on plan assets (which is a reduction of the cost), the amortization of past service costs, and actuarial gains and losses to the extent not reported in OCI. The components of a company's defined benefit periodic pension costs are summarized in Exhibit 2.

EXHIBIT 2   Components of a Company's Defined Benefit Pension Periodic Costs

IFRS Component	IFRS Recognition	US GAAP Component	US GAAP Recognition
Service costs	Recognized in P&L.	Current service costs	Recognized in P&L.
		Past service costs	Recognized in OCI and subsequently amortized to P&L over the service life of employees.
Net interest income/expense	Recognized in P&L as the following amount: Net pension liability or asset × interest rate[a]	Interest expense on pension obligation	Recognized in P&L.
		Expected return on plan assets	Recognized in P&L as the following amount: Plan assets × expected return.
Remeasurements: Net return on plan assets and actuarial gains and losses	Recognized in OCI and not subsequently amortized to P&L. • Net return on plan assets = Actual return − (Plan assets × Interest rate). • Actuarial gains and losses = Changes in a company's pension obligation arising from changes in actuarial assumptions.	Actuarial gains and losses including differences between the actual and expected returns on plan assets	Recognized immediately in P&L or, more commonly, recognized in OCI and subsequently amortized to P&L using the corridor or faster recognition method.[b] • Difference between expected and actual return on assets = Actual return − (Plan assets × Expected return). • Actuarial gains and losses = Changes in a company's pension obligation arising from changes in actuarial assumptions.

[a] The interest rate used is equal to the discount rate used to measure the pension liability (the yield on high-quality corporate bonds.)
[b] If the cumulative amount of unrecognized actuarial gains and losses exceeds 10 percent of the greater of the value of the plan assets or of the present value of the DB obligation (under US GAAP, the projected benefit obligation), the difference must be amortized over the service lives of the employees.

Reporting the Periodic Pension Cost. As noted above, some amounts of pension costs may qualify for capitalization as part of the costs of self-constructed assets, such as inventories. Pension costs included in inventories would thus be recognized in P&L as part of cost of goods sold when those inventories are sold. For pension costs that are not capitalized, IFRS do not specify where companies present the various components of periodic pension cost beyond differentiating between components included in P&L and in OCI. In contrast, for pension costs that are not capitalized, US GAAP require all components of periodic pension cost that are recognized in P&L to be aggregated and presented as a net amount within the same line item on the income statement. Both IFRS and US GAAP require total periodic pension cost to be disclosed in the notes to the financial statements.

2.3.3. More on the Effect of Assumptions and Actuarial Gains and Losses on Pension and Other Post-Employment Benefits Costs

As noted, a company's pension obligation for a DB pension plan is based on many estimates and assumptions. The amount of future pension payments requires assumptions about employee turnover, length of service, and rate of increase in compensation levels. The length of time the pension payments will be made requires assumptions about employees' life expectancy post-employment. Finally, the present value of these future payments requires assumptions about the appropriate discount rate (which is used as the rate at which interest expense or income will subsequently accrue on the net pension liability or asset).

Changes in any of the assumptions will increase or decrease the pension obligation. An increase in pension obligation resulting from changes in actuarial assumptions is considered an actuarial loss, and a decrease is considered an actuarial gain. The estimate of a company's pension liability also affects several components of periodic pension costs, apart from actuarial gains and losses. First, the service cost component of annual pension cost is essentially the amount by which the pension liability increases as a result of the employees' service during the year. Second, the interest expense component of annual pension cost is based on the amount of the liability. Third, the past service cost component of annual pension cost is the amount by which the pension liability increases because of changes to the plan.

Estimates related to plan assets can also affect annual pension cost reported in P&L (pension expense), primarily under US GAAP. Because a company's periodic pension cost reported in P&L under US GAAP includes the *expected* return on pension assets rather than the actual return, the assumptions about the expected return on plan assets can have a significant impact. Also, the expected return on plan assets requires estimating in which future period the benefits will be paid. As noted above, a divergence of actual returns on pension assets from expected returns results in an actuarial gain or loss.

Understanding the effect of assumptions on the estimated pension obligation and on periodic pension costs is important both for interpreting a company's financial statements and for evaluating whether a company's assumptions appear relatively conservative or aggressive.

The projected unit credit method is the IFRS approach to measuring the DB obligation. Under the projected unit credit method, each period of service (e.g., year of employment) gives rise to an additional unit of benefit to which the employee is entitled at retirement. In other words, for each period in which an employee provides service, they earn a portion of the post-employment benefits that the company has promised to pay. An equivalent way of thinking about this is that the amount of eventual benefit increases with each additional year of service. The employer measures each unit of service as it is earned to determine the amount of benefits it is obligated to pay in future reporting periods.

The objective of the projected unit credit method is to allocate the entire expected retirement costs (benefits) for an employee over the employee's service periods. The defined benefit obligation represents the actuarial present value of all units of benefit (credit) to which the employee is entitled (i.e., those that the employee has earned) as a result of prior and current periods of service. This obligation is based on actuarial assumptions about demographic variables, such as employee turnover and life expectancy, and on estimates of financial variables, such as future inflation and the discount rate. If the pension benefit formula is based on employees' future compensation levels, then the unit of benefit earned each period will reflect this estimate.

Under both IFRS and US GAAP, the assumed rate of increase in compensation—the expected annual increase in compensation over the employee service period—can have a significant impact on the defined benefit obligation. Another key assumption is the discount rate used to calculate the present value of the future benefits. It represents the rate at which the defined benefit obligation could be effectively settled. This rate is based on current rates of return on high quality corporate bonds with durations consistent with the durations of the benefit.

The following example illustrates the calculation of the defined benefit pension obligation and current service costs, using the projected unit credit method, for an individual employee under four different scenarios. Interest on the opening obligation also increases the obligation and is part of current costs. The fourth scenario is used to demonstrate the impact on a company's pension obligation of changes in certain key estimates. Examples 2 and 3 focus on the pension obligation. The change in pension obligation over the period is included in the calculation of pension expense (pension cost reported in P&L).

EXAMPLE 2   Calculation of Defined Benefit Pension Obligation for an Individual Employee

The following information applies to each of the four scenarios. Assume that a (hypothetical) company establishes a DB pension plan. The employee has a salary in the coming year of €50,000 and is expected to work five more years before retiring. The assumed discount rate is 6 percent, and the assumed annual compensation increase is 4.75 percent. For simplicity, assume that there are no changes in actuarial assumptions, all compensation increases are awarded on the first day of the service year, and no additional adjustments are made to reflect the possibility that the employee may leave the company at an earlier date.

Current salary	€50,000.00
Years until retirement	5
Annual compensation increases	4.75%
Discount rate	6.00%
Final year's estimated salary[a]	€60,198.56

[a] Final year's estimated salary = Current year's salary × $[(1 + \text{Annual compensation increase})^{\text{Years until retirement} - 1}]$.

At the end of Year 1, the final year's estimated salary = €50,000 × $[(1 + 0.0475)^4]$ = €60,198.56, assuming that the employee's salary increases by 4.75 percent each year.

With no change in assumption about the rate of increase in compensation or the date of retirement, the estimate of the final year's salary will remain unchanged.

At the end of Year 2, assuming the employee's salary actually increased by 4.75 percent, the final year's estimated salary = €52,375 × [(1 + 0.0475)^3] = €60,198.56.

Scenario 1: Benefit is paid as a lump sum amount upon retirement.
The plan will pay a lump sum pension benefit equal to 1.5 percent of the employee's final salary for each year of service beyond the date of establishment. The lump sum payment to be paid upon retirement = (Final salary × Benefit formula) × Years of service = (€60,198.56 × 0.015) × 5 = €4,514.89.

$$\text{Annual unit credit (benefit) per service year} = \text{Value at retirement/}$$
$$\text{Years of service} = €4,514.89/5 = €902.98.$$

If the discount rate (the interest rate at which the defined benefit obligation could be effectively settled) is assumed to be 0 percent, the amount of annual unit credit per service year is the amount of the company's annual obligation and the closing obligation each year is simply the annual unit credit multiplied by the number of past and current years of service. However, because the assumed discount rate must be based on the yield on high-quality corporate bonds and will thus not equal 0 percent, the future obligation resulting from current and prior service is discounted to determine the value of the obligation at any point in time.

The following table shows how the obligation builds up for this employee.

Year	1	2	3	4	5
Estimated annual salary	€50,000.00	€52,375.00	€54,862.81	€57,468.80	€60,198.56
Benefits attributed to:					
Prior years[a]	€0.00	€902.98	€1,805.96	€2,708.94	€3,611.92
Current year[b]	902.98	902.98	902.98	902.98	902.97*
Total benefits earned	€902.98	€1,805.96	€2,708.94	€3,611.92	€4,514.89
Opening obligation[c]	€0.00	€715.24	€1,516.31	€2,410.94	€3,407.47
Interest cost at 6 percent[d]	0.00	42.91	90.98	144.66	204.45
Current service costs[e]	715.24	758.16	803.65	851.87	902.97
Closing obligation[f]	€715.24	€1,516.31	€2,410.94	€3,407.47	€4,514.89

*Final amounts may differ slightly to compensate for rounding in earlier years.
[a]The benefit attributed to prior years = Annual unit credit × Years of prior service.

For Year 2, €902.98 × 1 = €902.98.
For Year 3, €902.98 × 2 = €1,805.96.

[b]The benefit attributed to current year = Annual unit credit based on benefit formula = Final year's estimated salary × Benefit formula = Value at retirement date/Years of service = (€60,198.56 × 1.5%) = €4,514.89/5 = €902.98.

[c] The opening obligation is the closing obligation at the end of the previous year, but can also be viewed as the present value of benefits earned in prior years:

Benefits earned in prior years/$[(1 + \text{Discount rate})^{\text{Years until retirement}}]$.
Opening obligation Year 1 = €0.
Opening obligation Year 2 = €902.98/$[(1 + 0.06)^4]$ = €715.24.
Opening obligation Year 3 = €1,805.96/$[(1 + 0.06)^3]$ = €1,516.32.

[d] The interest cost is the increase in the present value of the defined benefit obligation due to the passage of time:

Interest cost = Opening obligation × Discount rate.
For Year 2 = €715.24 × 0.06 = €42.91.
For Year 3 = €1,516.32 × 0.06 = €90.98.

[e] Current service costs are the present value of annual unit credits earned in the current period:

Annual unit credit/$[(1 + \text{Discount rate})^{\text{Years until retirement}}]$.
For Year 1 = €902.98/$[(1 + 0.06)^4]$ = €715.24.
For Year 2 = €902.98/$[(1 + 0.06)^3]$ = €758.16.

Note: Given no change in actuarial assumptions and estimates of financial growth, the current service costs in any year (except the first) are the previous year's current service costs increased by the discount rate; the current service costs increase with the passage of time.

[f] The closing obligation is the opening obligation plus the interest cost and the current service costs but can also be viewed as the present value of benefits earned in prior and current years. There is a slight difference due to rounding.

Total benefits earned/$[(1 + \text{Discount rate})^{\text{Years until retirement}}]$.
Closing obligation Year 1 = €902.98/$[(1 + 0.06)^4]$ = €715.24.
Closing obligation Year 2 = €1,805.96/$[(1 + 0.06)^3]$ = €1,516.32.
Closing obligation Year 3 = €2,708.94/$[(1 + 0.06)^2]$ = €2,410.95.

Note: Assuming no past service costs or actuarial gains/losses, the closing obligation less the fair value of the plan assets represents both the funded status of the plan and the net pension liability/asset. The change in obligation is the amount of expense for pensions on the income statement.

Scenario 2: Prior years of service, and benefit paid as a lump sum upon retirement.
The plan will pay a lump sum pension benefit equal to 1.5 percent of the employee's final salary for each year of service beyond the date of establishment. In addition, at the time the pension plan is established, the employee is given credit for 10 years of prior service with immediate vesting. The lump sum payment to be paid upon retirement = (Final salary × Benefit formula) × Years of service = (€60,198.56 × 0.015) × 15 = €13,544.68.

Annual unit credit = Value at retirement date/Years of service =
€13,544.68/15 = €902.98.

The following table shows how the obligation builds up for this employee.

Year	1	2	3	4	5
Benefits attributed to:					
Prior years[a]	€9,029.78	€9,932.76	€10,835.74	€11,738.72	€12,641.70
Current years	902.98	902.98	902.98	902.98	902.98
Total benefits earned	€9,932.76	€10,835.74	€11,738.72	€12,641.70	€13,544.68

Year	1	2	3	4	5
Opening obligation[b]	€6,747.58	€7,867.67	€9,097.89	€10,447.41	€11,926.13
Interest at 6 percent	404.85	472.06	545.87	626.85	715.57
Current service costs	715.24	758.16	803.65	851.87	902.98
Closing obligation	€7,867.67	€9,097.89	€10,447.41	€11,926.13	€13,544.68

[a] Benefits attributed to prior years of service = Annual unit credit × Years of prior service. At beginning of Year 1 = (€60,198.56 × 0.015) × 10 = €9,029.78.
[b] Opening obligation is the present value of the benefits attributed to prior years = Benefits attributed to prior years/(1 + Discount rate)$^{\text{Number of years to retirement}}$.

At beginning of Year 1 = €9,029.78/$(1.06)^5$ = €6,747.58. This is treated as past service costs in Year 1 because there was no previous recognition and there is immediate vesting.

Scenario 3: Employee to receive benefit payments for 20 years (no prior years of service).

Years of receiving pension = 20.

Estimated annual payment (end of year) for each of the 20 years = (Estimated final salary × Benefit formula) × Years of service = (€60,198.56 × 0.015) × 5 = €4,514.89.
Value at the end of Year 5 (retirement date) of the estimated future payments = PV of €4,514.89 for 20 years at 6 percent = €51,785.46.[8]

Annual unit credit = Value at retirement date/Years of service = €51,785.46/5 = €10,357.09.

Year	1	2	3	4	5
Benefit attributed to:					
Prior years	€0.00	€10,357.09	€20,714.18	€31,071.27	€41,428.36
Current year	10,357.09	10,357.09	10,357.09	10,357.09	10,357.10
Total benefits earned	€10,357.09	€20,714.18	€31,071.27	€41,428.36	€51,785.46
Opening obligation	€0.00	€8,203.79	€17,392.03	€27,653.32	€39,083.36
Interest at 6 percent	0.00	492.23	1,043.52	1,659.20	2,345.00
Current service costs	8,203.79	8,696.01	9,217.77	9,770.84	10,357.10
Closing obligation	€8,203.79	€17,392.03	€27,653.32	€39,083.36	€51,785.46

In this scenario, the pension obligation at the end of Year 3 is €27,653.32 and the portion of pension expense (pension costs reported in P&L) attributable to interest

[8] This is a simplification of the valuation process for illustrative purposes. For example, the actuarial valuation would use mortality rates, not just assumed life expectancy. Additionally, annualizing the present value of an ordinary annuity probably understates the liability because the actual benefit payments are usually made monthly or bi-weekly rather than annually.

and current service costs for Year 3 is €10,261.29 (= €1,043.52 + €9,217.77). The total pension expense would include other items such as a reduction for return on plan assets.

Scenario 4: Employee to receive benefit payments for 20 years and is given credit for 10 years of prior service with immediate vesting.

$$\text{Estimated annual payment (end of year) for each of the 20 years} =$$
$$(\text{Estimated final salary} \times \text{Benefit formula}) \times \text{Years of service} =$$
$$(€60,198.56 \times 0.015) \times (10 + 5) = €13,544.68.$$

Value at the end of Year 5 (retirement date) of the estimated future payments = PV of €13,544.68 for 20 years at 6 percent = €155,356.41.

$$\text{Annual unit credit} = \text{Value at retirement date/Years of service} =$$
$$€155,356.41/15 = €10,357.09.$$

Year	1	2	3	4	5
Benefit attributed to:					
Prior years	€103,570.94	€113,928.03	€124,285.12	€134,642.21	€144,999.30
Current year	10,357.09	10,357.09	10,357.09	10,357.09	10,357.11
Total benefits earned	€113,928.03	€124,285.12	€134,642.21	€144,999.30	€155,356.41
Opening obligation[a]	€77,394.23	€90,241.67	€104,352.18	€119,831.08	€136,791.79
Interest at 6 percent	4,643.65	5,414.50	6,261.13	7,189.87	8,207.51
Current service costs	8,203.79	8,696.01	9,217.77	9,770.84	10,357.11
Closing obligation	€90,241.67	€104,352.18	€119,831.08	€136,791.79	€155,356.41

[a]This is treated as past service costs in Year 1 because there was no previous recognition and there is immediate vesting.

EXAMPLE 3   The Effect of a Change in Assumptions

Based on Scenario 4 of Example 2 (10 years of prior service and the employee receives benefits for 20 years after retirement):

1. What is the effect on the Year 1 closing pension obligation of a 100 basis point increase in the assumed discount rate—that is, from 6 percent to 7 percent? What is the effect on pension cost in Year 1?
2. What is the effect on the Year 1 closing pension obligation of a 100 basis point increase in the assumed annual compensation increase—that is, from 4.75 percent to 5.75 percent? Assume this is independent of the change in Question 1.

Solution to 1:
The estimated final salary and the estimated annual payments after retirement are unchanged at €60,198.56 and €13,544.68, respectively. However, the value at the retirement date is changed. Value at the end of Year 5 (retirement date) of the estimated future payments = PV of €13,544.68 for 20 years at 7 percent = €143,492.53. Annual unit credit = Value at retirement date/Years of service = €143,492.53/15 = €9,566.17.

Year	1
Benefit attributed to:	
Prior years	€95,661.69
Current year	9,566.17
Total benefits earned	€105,227.86
Opening obligation[a]	€68,205.46
Interest at 7 percent	4,774.38
Current service costs	7,297.99
Closing obligation	€80,277.83

[a]Opening obligation = Benefit attributed to prior years discounted for the remaining time to retirement at the assumed discount rate = $95,661.69/(1 + 0.07)^5$.

A 100 basis point increase in the assumed discount rate (from 6 percent to 7 percent) will *decrease* the Year 1 closing pension obligation by €90,241.67 – €80,277.83 = €9,963.84. The Year 1 pension cost declined from €12,847.44 (= 4,643.65 + 8,203.79) to €12,072.37 (= 4,774.38 + 7,297.99). The change in the interest component is a function of the decline in the opening obligation (which will decrease the interest component) and the increased discount rate (which will increase the interest component). In this case, the increase in the discount rate dominated and the interest component increased. The current service costs and the opening obligation both declined because of the increase in the discount rate.

Solution to 2:
The estimated final salary is [€50,000 × [(1 + 0.0575)⁴] = €62,530.44. Estimated annual payment for each of the 20 years = (Estimated final salary × Benefit formula) × Years of service = (€62,530.44 × 0.015) × (10 + 5) = €14,069.35. Value at the end of Year 5 (retirement date) of the estimated future payments = PV of €14,069.35 for 20 years at 6 percent = €161,374.33. Annual unit credit = Value at retirement date/Years of service = €161,374.33/15 = €10,758.29.

Year	1
Benefit attributed to:	
Prior years	€107,582.89
Current year	10,758.29
Total benefits earned	€118,341.18

(continued)

Year	1
Opening obligation	€80,392.19
Interest at 6 percent	4,823.53
Current service costs	8,521.57
Closing obligation	€93,737.29

A 100 basis point increase in the assumed annual compensation increase (from 4.75 percent to 5.75 percent) will *increase* the pension obligation by €93,737.29 − €90,241.67 = €3,495.62.

Example 3 illustrates that an increase in the assumed discount rate will *decrease* a company's pension obligation. In the Solution to 1, there is a slight increase in the interest component of the pension obligation and periodic pension cost (from €4,643.65 in Scenario 4 of Example 2 to €4,774.38 in Example 3). Depending on the pattern and duration of the annual benefits being projected, however, it is possible that the amount of the interest component could decrease because the decrease in the opening obligation may more than offset the effect of the increase in the discount rate.

Example 3 also illustrates that an increase in the assumed rate of annual compensation increase will *increase* a company's pension obligation when the pension formula is based on the final year's salary. In addition, a higher assumed rate of annual compensation increase will increase the service components and the interest component of a company's periodic pension cost because of an increased annual unit credit and the resulting increased obligation. An increase in life expectancy also will increase the pension obligation unless the promised pension payments are independent of life expectancy—for example, paid as a lump sum or over a fixed period.

Finally, under US GAAP, because the expected return on plan assets reduces periodic pension costs reported in P&L, a higher expected return will decrease pension cost reported in P&L (pension expense). Exhibit 3 summarizes the impact of some key estimates on the balance sheet and the periodic pension cost.

EXHIBIT 3   Impact of Key DB Pension Assumptions on Balance Sheet and Periodic Costs

Assumption	Impact of Assumption on Balance Sheet	Impact of Assumption on Periodic Cost
Higher discount rate.	Lower obligation.	Periodic pension costs will typically be lower because of lower opening obligation and lower service costs.
Higher rate of compensation increase.	Higher obligation.	Higher service costs.
Higher expected return on plan assets.	No effect, because fair value of plan assets is used on balance sheet.	Not applicable for IFRS. Lower periodic pension expense under US GAAP.

Accounting for other post-employment benefits also requires assumptions and estimates. For example, assumed trends in health care costs are an important component of estimating costs of post-employment health care plans. A higher assumed medical expense inflation rate will result in a higher post-employment medical obligation. Companies also estimate various patterns of health care cost trend rates—for example, higher in the near term but becoming lower after some point in time. For post-employment health plans, an increase in the assumed inflationary trends in health care costs or an increase in life expectancy will increase the obligation and associated periodic expense of these plans.

The sections above have explained how the amounts to be reported on the balance sheet are calculated, how the various components of periodic pension cost are reflected in income, and how changes in assumptions can affect pension-related amounts. The next section evaluates disclosures of pension and other post-employment benefits, including disclosures about key assumptions.

2.4. Disclosures of Pension and Other Post-Employment Benefits

Several aspects of the accounting for pensions and other post-employment benefits described above can affect comparative financial analysis using ratios based on financial statements.

- Differences in key assumptions can affect comparisons across companies.
- Amounts disclosed in the balance sheet are net amounts (plan liabilities minus plan assets). Adjustments to incorporate gross amounts would change certain financial ratios.
- Periodic pension costs recognized in P&L (pension expense) may not be comparable. IFRS and US GAAP differ in their provisions about costs recognized in P&L versus in OCI.
- Reporting of periodic pension costs in P&L may not be comparable. Under US GAAP, all of the components of pension costs in P&L are reported in operating expense on the income statement even though some of the components are of a financial nature (specifically, interest expense and the expected return on assets). However, under IFRS, the components of periodic pension costs in P&L can be included in various line items.
- Cash flow information may not be comparable. Under IFRS, some portion of the amount of contributions might be treated as a financing activity rather than an operating activity; under US GAAP, the contribution is treated as an operating activity.

Information related to pensions can be obtained from various portions of the financial statement note disclosures, and appropriate analytical adjustments can be made. In the following sections, we examine pension plan note disclosures and highlight analytical issues related to each of the points listed above.

2.4.1. Assumptions

Companies disclose their assumptions about discount rates, expected compensation increases, medical expense inflation, and—for US GAAP companies—expected return on plan assets. Comparing these assumptions over time and across companies provides a basis to assess any conservative or aggressive biases. Some companies also disclose the effects of a change in their assumptions.

Exhibit 4 presents the assumed discount rates (Panel A) and assumed annual compensation increases (Panel B) to estimate pension obligations for four companies operating in the automotive and equipment manufacturing sector. Fiat S.p.A. (an Italy-based company) and the Volvo Group[9] (a Sweden-based company) use IFRS. General Motors and Ford Motor Company are US-based companies that use US GAAP. All of these companies have both US and non-US defined benefit pension plans, which facilitates comparison.

EXHIBIT 4

Panel A. Assumed discount rates used to estimate pension obligations (percent)					
	2009	2008	2007	2006	2005
Fiat S.p.A. (Italy)	5.02	5.10	4.70	3.98	3.53
The Volvo Group (Sweden)	4.00	4.50	4.50	4.00	4.00
General Motors (non-US plans)	5.31	6.22	5.72	4.76	4.72
Ford Motor Company (non-US plans)	5.93	5.58	5.58	4.91	4.58
Fiat S.p.A. (US plans)	5.50	5.10	5.80	5.80	5.50
The Volvo Group (US plans)	4.00–5.75	5.75–6.25	5.75–6.25	5.50	5.75
General Motors (US plans)	5.52	6.27	6.35	5.90	5.70
Ford Motor Company (US plans)	6.50	6.25	6.25	5.86	5.61

Panel B. Assumed annual compensation increases used to estimate pension obligations (percent)					
	2009	2008	2007	2006	2005
Fiat S.p.A. (Italy)	4.02	4.65	4.60	3.65	2.58
The Volvo Group (Sweden)	3.00	3.50	3.20	3.20	3.20
General Motors (non-US plans)	3.23	3.59	3.60	3.00	3.10
Ford Motor Company (non-US plans)	3.13	3.21	3.21	3.30	3.44
Fiat S.p.A. (US plans)*	na	na	na	na	na
The Volvo Group (US plans)	3.00	3.50	3.50	3.50	3.50
General Motors (US plans)	3.94	5.00	5.25	5.00	4.90
Ford Motor Company (US plans)	3.80	3.80	3.80	3.80	4.00

* In the United States, Fiat has obligations to former employees under DB pension plans but no longer offers DB plans. As a result, annual compensation increases are not applicable (na).

---

[9] The Volvo Group primarily manufactures trucks, buses, construction equipment, and engines and engine components for boats, industry, and aircraft. The Volvo car division was sold to Ford Motor Company in 1999, and Ford sold Volvo Car Corporation to the Zhejiang Geely Holding Group in 2010.

The assumed discount rates used to estimate pension obligations are generally based on the market interest rates of high-quality corporate fixed-income investments with a maturity profile similar to the timing of a company's future pension payments. The trend in discount rates across the companies (in both their non-US plans and US plans) is generally similar. In the non-US plans, discount rates increased from 2005 to 2008 and then decreased in 2009 except for Ford, which increased discount rates in 2009. In the US plans, discount rates increased from 2005 to 2007 and held steady or decreased in 2008. In 2009, Fiat and Ford's discount rates increased while Volvo and GM's discount rates decreased. Ford had the highest assumed discount rates for both its non-US and US plans in 2009. Recall that a higher discount rate assumption results in a lower estimated pension obligation. Therefore, the use of a higher discount rate compared with its peers may indicate a less conservative bias.

Explanations for differences in the level of the assumed discount rates, apart from bias, are differences in the regions/countries involved and differences in the timing of obligations (for example, differences in the percentage of employees covered by the DB pension plan that are at or near retirement). In this example, the difference in regions/countries might explain the difference in rates used for the non-US plans but would not explain the difference in the rates shown for the companies' US plans. The timing of obligations under the companies' DB pension plans likely varies, so the relevant market interest rates selected as the discount rate will vary accordingly. Because the timing of the pension obligations is not disclosed, differences in timing cannot be ruled out as an explanation for differences in discount rates.

An important consideration is whether the assumptions are internally consistent. For example, do the company's assumed discount rates and assumed compensation increases reflect a consistent view of inflation? For Volvo, both the assumed discount rates and the assumed annual compensation increases (for both its non-US and US plans) are lower than those of the other companies, so the assumptions appear internally consistent. The assumptions are consistent with plans located in lower-inflation regions. Recall that a lower rate of compensation increase results in a lower estimated pension obligation.

In Ford's US and non-US pension plans, the assumed discount rate is increasing and the assumed rate of compensation increase is decreasing or holding steady in 2009. Each of these will reduce the pension obligation. Therefore, holding all else equal, Ford's pension liability is decreasing because of the higher assumed discount rate and the reduced assumed rate of compensation increase.

Another relevant assumption—for US GAAP companies but not for IFRS companies— is the expected return on pension plan assets. Under US GAAP, a higher expected return on plan assets lowers the periodic pension cost. (Of course, a higher expected return on plan assets presumably reflects riskier investments, so it would not be advisable for a company to simply invest in riskier investments to reduce periodic pension expense.) Because companies are also required to disclose the target asset allocation for their pension plan assets, analysts can assess reasonableness of those assumptions by comparing companies' assumed expected return on plan assets in the context of the plans' asset allocation. For example, a higher expected return is consistent with a greater proportion of plan assets being allocated to riskier asset classes.

Companies with other post-employment benefits also disclose information about these benefits, including assumptions made to estimate the obligation and expense. For example, companies with post-employment health care plans disclose assumptions about increases in health care costs. The assumptions are typically that the inflation rate in health care costs will taper off to some lower, constant rate at some year in the future. That future inflation rate is known as the ultimate health care trend rate. Holding all else equal, each of the following assumptions would result in a higher benefit obligation and a higher periodic cost:

- A higher assumed near-term increase in health care costs,
- A higher assumed ultimate health care cost trend rate, and
- A later year in which the ultimate health care cost trend rate is assumed to be reached.

Conversely, holding all else equal, each of the following assumptions would result in a lower benefit obligation and a lower periodic cost:

- A lower assumed near-term increase in health care costs,
- A lower assumed ultimate health care cost trend rate, and
- An earlier year in which the ultimate health care cost trend rate is assumed to be reached.

Example 4 examines two companies' assumptions about trends in US health care costs.

EXAMPLE 4   Comparison of Assumptions about Trends in US Health Care Costs

In addition to disclosing assumptions about health care costs, companies also disclose information on the sensitivity of the measurements of both the obligation and the periodic cost to changes in those assumptions. Exhibit 5 presents information obtained from the notes to the financial statements for CNH Global N.V. (a Dutch manufacturer of construction and mining equipment) and Caterpillar Inc. (a US manufacturer of construction and mining equipment, engines, and turbines). Each company has US employees for whom they provide post-employment health care benefits.

Panel A shows the companies' assumptions about health care costs and the amounts each reported for post-employment health care benefit plans. For example, CNH assumes that the initial year's (2010) increase in health care costs will be 9 percent, and this rate of increase will decline to 5 percent over the next seven years to 2017. Caterpillar assumes a lower initial-year increase of 7 percent and a decline to the ultimate health care cost trend rate of 5 percent in 2016.

Panel B shows the effect of a 100 basis point increase or decrease in the assumed health care cost trend rates. A 1 percentage point increase in the assumed health care cost trend rates would increase Caterpillar's 2009 service and interest cost component of the other post-employment benefit costs by $23 million and the related obligation by $220 million. A 1 percentage point increase in the assumed health care cost trend rates would increase CNH Global's 2009 service and interest cost component of the other post-employment benefit costs by $8 million and the related obligation by $106 million.

EXHIBIT 5   Post-Employment Health Care Plan Disclosures

Panel A. Assumptions and Reported Amounts for US Post-Employment
Health Care Benefit Plans

	Assumptions about Health Care Costs			Amounts Reported for Other Post-Employment Benefits ($ Millions)	
	Initial Health Care Cost Trend Rate 2010	Ultimate Health Care Cost Trend Rate	Year Ultimate Trend Rate Attained	Accumulated Benefit Obligation Year-End 2009	Periodic Expense for Benefits for 2009
CNH Global N.V.	9.0%	5%	2017	$1,152	$65
Caterpillar Inc.	7.0%	5%	2016	$4,537	$287

Panel B. Effect of 1 Percentage Point Increase (Decrease) in Assumed Health Care Cost
Trend Rates on 2009 Total Accumulated Post-Employment Benefit Obligations and Periodic
Expense

	1 Percentage Point Increase	1 Percentage Point Decrease
CNH Global N.V.	+$106 million (Obligation) +$8 million (Expense)	−$90 million (Obligation) −$6 million (Expense)
Caterpillar Inc.	+$220 million (Obligation) +$23 million (Expense)	−$186 million (Obligation) −$20 million (Expense)

Sources: Caterpillar information is from the company's Form 10-K filed February 19, 2010, Note 14 (pages A-36 and A-42). CNH Global information is from the company's 2009 Form 20-F, Note 12 (pages F-41, F-43, and F-45).

Based on the information in Exhibit 5, answer the following questions:

1. Which company's assumptions about health care costs appear less conservative?
2. What would be the effect of adjusting the post-employment benefit obligation and the periodic post-employment benefit expense of the less conservative company for a 1 percentage point increase in health care cost trend rates? Does this make the two companies more comparable?
3. What would be the change in each company's 2009 ratio of debt to equity assuming a 1 percentage point increase in the health care cost trend rate? Assume the change would have no impact on taxes. Total liabilities and total equity at December 31, 2009 are given below.

At December 31, 2009 (US$ millions)	CNH Global N.V.	Caterpillar Inc.
Total liabilities	$16,398	$50,738
Total equity	$6,810	$8,823

Solution to 1:

Caterpillar's assumptions about health care costs appear less conservative (the assumptions will result in lower health care costs) than CNH's. Caterpillar's initial assumed health care cost increase of 7 percent is significantly lower than CNH's assumed 9 percent. Further, Caterpillar assumes that the ultimate health care cost trend rate of 5 percent will be reached a year earlier than assumed by CNH.

Solution to 2:

The sensitivity disclosures indicate that a 1 percentage point increase in the assumed health care cost trend rate would increase Caterpillar's post-employment benefit obligation by $220 million and its periodic cost by $23 million. However, Caterpillar's initial health care cost trend rate is 2 percentage points lower than CNH's. Therefore, the impact of a 1 percentage point change for Caterpillar multiplied by 2 provides an approximation of the adjustment required for comparability to CNH. Note, however, that the sensitivity of the pension obligation and expense to a change of more than 1 percentage point in the assumed health care cost trend rate cannot be assumed to be exactly linear, so this adjustment is only an approximation. Further, there may be justifiable differences in the assumptions based on the location of their US operations.

Solution to 3:

A 1 percentage point increase in the health care cost trend rate increases CNH's ratio of debt to equity by about 2 percent, from 2.41 to 2.46. A 1 percentage point increase in the health care cost trend rate increases Caterpillar's ratio of debt to equity by about 3 percent, from 5.75 to 5.92.

CNH Global N.V. ($ millions)	Reported	Adjustment for 1 percentage point increase in health care cost trend rate	Adjusted
Total liabilities	$16,398	+ $106	$16,504
Total equity	$6,810	– $106	$6,704
Ratio of debt to equity	2.41		2.46

Caterpillar Inc. ($ millions)	Reported	Adjustment for 1 percentage point increase in health care cost trend rate	Adjusted
Total liabilities	$50,738	+ $220	$50,958
Total equity	$8,823	– $220	$8,603
Ratio of debt to equity	5.75		5.92

This section has explored the use of pension and other post-employment benefit disclosures to assess a company's assumptions and explore how the assumptions can affect comparisons across companies. The following sections describe the use of disclosures to further analyze a company's pension and other post-employment benefits.

2.4.2. Net Pension Liability (or Asset)

Under both IFRS and US GAAP standards, the amount disclosed in the balance sheet is a net amount. Analysts can use information from the notes to adjust a company's assets and liabilities for the gross amount of the benefit plan assets and the gross amount of the benefit plan liabilities. An argument for making such adjustments is that they reflect the underlying economic liabilities and assets of a company; however, it should be recognized that actual consolidation is precluded by laws protecting a pension or other benefit plan as a separate legal entity.

At a minimum, an analyst will compare the gross benefit obligation (i.e., the benefit obligation without deducting related plan assets) with the sponsoring company's total assets, including the gross amount of the benefit plan assets, shareholders' equity, and earnings. Although presumably infrequent in practice, if the gross benefit obligation is large relative to these items, a small change in the pension liability can have a significant financial impact on the sponsoring company.

2.4.3. Total Periodic Pension Costs

The total periodic cost of a company's DB pension plan is the change in the net pension liability or asset—excluding the effect of the employer's periodic contribution into the plan. To illustrate this point, assume a company has a completely new DB pension plan. At inception, the net pension liability equals $0 ($0 plan assets minus $0 obligations). In the first period, the plan obligation increases by $500 because of service costs. If the employer makes no contribution to the plan, then the net pension liability would increase to $500 ($0 plan assets minus $500 obligations) and the periodic service costs would be exactly equal to that change. If, however, the employer contributes $500 to the plan in that period, then the net pension liability would remain at $0 ($500 plan assets minus $500 obligations). In this situation, although the change in net pension liability is $0, the periodic pension cost is $500.

Thus, the total periodic pension cost in a given period is calculated by summing the periodic components of cost or, alternatively, by adjusting the change in the net pension liability or asset for the amount of employer contributions. The relationship between the periodic pension cost and the plan's funded status can be expressed as Periodic pension cost = Ending funded status – Employer contributions – Beginning funded status.[10]

Note that, unlike employer contributions into the plan's assets, the payment of cash out of a DB plan to a retiree does not affect the net pension liability or asset. Payment of cash out of a DB plan to a retiree reduces plan assets and plan obligations in an equal amount.

2.4.4. Periodic Pension Costs Recognized in P&L vs. OCI

Each period, the components of periodic pension cost—other than any amounts that qualify for capitalization as part of the costs of such assets as inventories—are recognized either in P&L (an expense) or in OCI. To understand the total pension cost of the period, an analyst should thus consider the amounts shown both in P&L and in OCI.

IFRS and US GAAP differ in their provisions about which periodic pension costs are recognized in P&L versus in OCI. These differences can be relevant to an analyst in comparing the reported profitability of companies that use different sets of standards. Under IFRS,

---

[10]Note that a net pension liability is treated as a negative funded status in this relationship.

P&L for the period includes both current and past service costs; in contrast, under US GAAP, P&L for the period includes only current service costs (and any amortization of past service costs.) Under IFRS, P&L incorporates a return on plan assets set equal to the discount rate used in estimating the pension obligation; in contrast, under US GAAP, P&L incorporates an expected return on plan assets. Under US GAAP, P&L may show the impact of amortizing actuarial gains or losses that were recognized in previous periods' OCI. Under IFRS, P&L would not show any similar impact because amortizing amounts from OCI into P&L is not permitted.

An analyst comparing an IFRS-reporting company with a US GAAP–reporting company could adjust the reported amounts of P&L to achieve comparability. For example, the analyst could adjust the US GAAP company's P&L to make it similar to an IFRS company by including past service costs arising during the period, excluding amortization of past service costs arising in previous periods, and including an amount of return on plan assets at the discount rate rather than the expected rate. Alternatively, the analyst could use comprehensive income (net income from P&L plus OCI) as the basis for comparison.

2.4.5. Classification of Periodic Pension Costs Recognized in P&L

Amounts of periodic pension costs recognized in P&L (pension expense) are generally treated as operating expenses. An issue with the reported periodic pension expense is that conceptually the components of this expense could be classified as operating and/or non-operating expenses. It can be argued that only the current service cost component is an operating expense, whereas the interest component and asset returns component are both non-operating. The interest expense component of pension expense is conceptually similar to the interest expense on any of the company's other liabilities. The pension liability is essentially equivalent to borrowing from employees, and the interest expense of that borrowing can be considered a financing cost. Similarly, the return on pension plan assets is conceptually similar to returns on any of the company's other financial assets. These classification issues apply equally to OPB costs.

To better reflect a company's operating performance, an adjustment can be made to operating income by adding back the full amount of pensions costs reported in the P&L (pension expense) and then subtracting only the service costs (or the total of service costs and settlements and curtailments). Note that this adjustment excludes from operating income the amortization of past service costs and the amortization of net actuarial gains and losses. This adjustment also eliminates the interest expense component and the return on plan assets component from the company's operating income. The interest expense component would be added to the company's interest expense, and the return on plan assets would be treated as non-operating income.

In addition to adjusting for the classification of different components of pension costs, an adjustment can be made to incorporate the *actual return* on plan assets. Recall that under IFRS, the net interest expense/income calculation effectively includes a return on plan assets calculated using the discount rate used to determine the present value of the pension liability and any difference from the actual return is shown as a component of OCI. Under US GAAP, the *expected* return on plan assets is included as a component of periodic pension cost in P&L and any difference between the actual and expected return is shown as a component of OCI. Under either set of standards, an adjustment can incorporate the actual return. This adjustment changes net income and potentially introduces earnings volatility. The reclassification of interest expense would not change net income. Example 5 illustrates adjustments to operating and non-operating incomes.

EXAMPLE 5   Adjusting Periodic Costs Expensed to P&L and Reclassifying Components between Operating and Non-Operating Income

SABMiller plc is a UK-based company that brews and distributes beer and other beverages. The following information was taken from the company's 2010 Annual Report. Note that in 2010, IFRS required the use of expected return on plan assets, similar to US GAAP. All amounts are in millions of US dollars.

Summary information from the Consolidated Income Statement
For the year ended March 31, 2010

Revenue	$18,020
Net operating expenses	(15,401)
Operating profit	2,619
Interest payable and similar charges*	(879)
Interest receivable and similar income*	316
Share of post-tax results of associates	873
Profit before taxation	$2,929

* *Note*: This is the terminology used in the income statement. The solution to question 2 below uses *interest expense* and *interest and investment income*.

Excerpt from Note 31: Pensions and post-retirement benefits

	Pension	OPB	Total
Current service costs	$(8)	$(3)	$(11)
Interest costs	(29)	(10)	(39)
Expected return on plan assets	14		14
Total	$(23)	$(13)	$(36)
Actual return (loss) on plan assets	$47		

(Components of the amount recognized in net operating expenses for pension and other post-retirement benefits.)

Based on the information above,

1. Adjust pre-tax income for the actual rather than expected return on plan assets.
2. Adjust the individual line items on the company's income statement to re-classify the components of the pension and other post-retirement benefits expense as operating expense, interest expense, or interest income.

Solution to 1: The total amount of periodic pension cost reported in P&L as an expense is $23. If the actual return on plan assets of $47 is used instead of the expected return on plan assets, the total P&L expense (income) will be $(10) [(= 8 + 29 − 47) or (= 23 + 14 − 47)]. Use of the actual rather than expected return on plan assets provides an estimate of the economic expense (income) for the pension. Profit before taxation adjusted for actual rather than expected return on plan assets will be higher by $33 ($47 − $14) and will total $2,962.

Solution to 2: All adjustments are summarized below.

	Reported	Adjustments	Adjusted
Revenue	$18,020		$18,020
Net operating expenses	−15,401	+ 36 − 11[a]	−15,376
Operating profit	2,619		2,644
Interest expense	−879	− 39[b]	−918
Interest and investment income	316	+ 47[c]	363
Share of post-tax results of associates	873		873
Profit before taxation	$2,929	$33	$2,962

[a]Operating income is adjusted to include only the current service costs. The $36 total of pension and OPB expenses are excluded from operating expenses, and only the $11 current service cost component is included in operating expenses.
[b]The $39 interest cost component is reclassified as interest expense.
[c]The *actual* return on plan assets is added as investment income.

2.4.6. Cash Flow Information

For a sponsoring company, the cash flow impact of pension and other post-employment benefits is the amount of contributions that the company makes to fund the plan—or for plans without funding requirements, the amount of benefits paid. The amount of contributions a company makes to fund a pension or other post-employment benefit plan is partially determined by the regulations of the countries in which the company operates. In the United States, for example, the amount of contributions to DB pension plans is governed by ERISA (the Employee Retirement and Income Security Act) and depends on the funded status of the plan. Companies may choose to make contributions in excess of those required by regulation.

   If a sponsoring company's periodic contributions to a plan exceed the total pension costs of the period, the excess can be viewed from an economic perspective as a reduction of the pension obligation. The contribution covers not only the pension obligation arising in the current period but also the pension obligations of another period. Such a contribution would be similar in concept to making a principal payment on a loan in excess of the scheduled principal payment. Conversely, a periodic contribution that is less than the total pension cost of the period can be viewed as a source of financing. Where the amounts of benefit obligations are material, an analyst may choose to adjust the cash flows that a company presents in its statement of cash flows. Example 6 describes such an adjustment.

EXAMPLE 6   Adjusting Cash Flow

Vassiliki Doukas is analyzing the cash flow statement of a hypothetical company, Geo-Race plc, as part of a valuation. Doukas suggests to her colleague, Dimitri Krontiras, that the difference between the company's contributions to the pension plan and the total pension costs incurred during a period is similar to a form of borrowing or a repayment of borrowing, depending on the direction of the difference; this affects the company's reported cash from operating activities and cash from financing activities. Based on information from the company's 2009 annual report (currency in £ millions), she determines that the company's total pension cost was £437; however, the company also disclosed that it made a contribution of £504. GeoRace reported cash inflow from operating activities of £6,161 and cash outflow from financing activities of £1,741. The company's effective tax rate was 28.7 percent.

Use the information provided to answer the following questions:

1. How did the company's 2009 contribution to the pension plan compare with the total pension cost for the year?
2. How would cash from operating activities and financing activities be adjusted to illustrate Doukas' interpretation of the difference between the company's contribution and the total pension cost?

Solution to 1: The company's contribution to the pension plan in 2009 was £504, which was £67 more than the total pension cost of £437. The £67 difference is approximately £48 on an after-tax basis, using the effective tax rate of 28.7 percent.

Total pension costs	£437	
Company's contribution	£504	
Amount by which the sponsoring company's contribution exceeds total pension cost (pre-tax)	£67	
Tax rate	28.7%	
After-tax amount by which the sponsoring company's contribution exceeds total pension cost	£48	[= £67 × (1 − 0.2870)]

Solution to 2: The company's contribution to the pension plan in 2009 was £67 (£48 after tax) greater than the 2009 total pension cost. Interpreting the excess contribution as similar to a repayment of borrowing (financing use of funds) rather than as an operating cash flow would increase the company's cash outflow from financing activities by £48, from £1,741 to £1,789, and increase the cash inflow from operations by £48, from £6,161 to £6,209.

3. SHARE-BASED COMPENSATION

In this section, we provide an overview of executive compensation other than pension plans and other post-retirement benefits, focusing on share-based compensation. First, we briefly discuss common components of executive compensation packages, their objectives, and advantages and disadvantages of share-based compensation. The discussion of share-based compensation then moves to accounting for and reporting of stock grants and stock options. The explanation includes a discussion of fair value accounting, the choice of valuation models, the assumptions used, common disclosures, and important dates in measuring and reporting compensation expense.

Employee compensation packages are structured to achieve varied objectives, including satisfying employees' needs for liquidity, retaining employees, and motivating employees. Common components of employee compensation packages are salary, bonuses, non-monetary benefits, and share-based compensation.[11] The salary component provides for the liquidity needs of an employee. Bonuses, generally in the form of cash, motivate and reward employees for short- or long-term performance or goal achievement by linking pay to performance. Non-monetary benefits, such as medical care, housing, and cars, may be provided to facilitate employees performing their jobs. Salary, bonuses, and non-monetary benefits are short-term employee benefits.

Share-based compensation is intended to align employees' interests with those of the shareholders and is typically a form of deferred compensation. Both IFRS and US GAAP[12] require a company to disclose in their annual report key elements of management compensation. Regulators may require additional disclosure. The disclosures enable analysts to understand the nature and extent of compensation, including the share-based payment arrangements that existed during the reporting period. Below are examples of descriptions of the components and objectives of executive compensation programs for companies that report under IFRS and under US GAAP. Exhibit 6 shows excerpts of the disclosure for the executive compensation program of SABMiller plc; SABMiller plc reports under IFRS and includes a nine-page remuneration report as part of its annual report.

EXHIBIT 6

Excerpts from Remuneration Report of SABMiller plc

...On balance, the committee concluded that its policy of agreeing a total remuneration package for each executive director comprising an annual base salary, a short-term incentive in the form of an annual cash bonus, long-term incentives through participation in share incentive plans, pension contributions, other usual security and health benefits, and benefits in kind, continued to be appropriate....

The committee's policy continues to be to ensure that executive directors and members of the executive committee are rewarded for their contribution to the group's operating and financial performance at levels which take account of industry, market and country benchmarks, and that their remuneration is appropriate to their scale of responsibility and performance, and will attract, motivate and retain individuals of the necessary calibre. The committee takes account of the need to be competitive in the different parts of the world in which the company operates....

(continued)

---

[11] An extensive overview of different employee compensation mechanisms can be found in Lynch and Perry (2003).

[12] IAS 24 *Related Party Disclosures*, paragraph 17; FASB ASC Section 718-10-50 [Compensation-Stock Compensation-Overall-Disclosure].

EXHIBIT 6   (Continued)

> The committee considers that alignment with shareholders' interests and linkage to SABMiller's long-term strategic goals is best achieved through a twin focus on earnings per share and, from 2010 onwards, additional value created for shareholders, and a blend of absolute and relative performance.

Source: SABMiller plc, Annual Report 2010.

In the United States, similar disclosures are required in a company's proxy statement that is filed with the SEC. Exhibit 7 shows the disclosure of American Eagle Outfitters, Inc.'s executive compensation program, including a description of the key elements and objectives.

EXHIBIT 7   Excerpts from Executive Compensation Disclosures of American Eagle Outfitters, Inc.

Compensation Program Elements

Our executive compensation program is designed to place a sizeable amount of pay at risk for all executives and this philosophy is intended to cultivate a pay-for-performance environment. Our executive compensation plan design has six key elements:

- Base Salary
- Annual Incentive Bonus
- Long-term Incentive Cash Plan—in place for the Chief Executive Officer and Vice Chairman, Executive Creative Director only
- Restricted Stock ("RS")—issued as Units ("RSUs") and Awards ("RSAs")
- Performance Shares ("PS")
- Non-Qualified Stock Options ("NSOs")

Two of the elements (Annual Incentive Bonus and LTICP) were entirely "at risk" based on the Company's performance in Fiscal 2009 and were subject to forfeiture if the Company did not achieve threshold performance goals. Performance Shares are entirely "at risk" and subject to forfeiture if the Company does not achieve threshold performance goals by the close of Fiscal 2011, as described below. At threshold performance, the CEO's total annual compensation declines by 46% relative to target performance. The NEO's total annual compensation declines by an average of 33% relative to target performance. Company performance below threshold levels results in forfeiture of all elements of direct compensation other than base salary, RSUs and NSOs. NSOs provide compensation only to the extent that vesting requirements are satisfied and our share price appreciates.

We strategically allocate compensation between short-term and long-term components and between cash and equity in order to maximize executive performance and retention. Long-term compensation and equity awards comprise an increasingly larger proportion of total compensation as position level increases. The portion of total pay attributable to long-term incentive cash and equity compensation increases at successively higher levels of management. This philosophy ensures that executive compensation closely aligns with changes in stockholder value and achievement of performance objectives while also ensuring that executives are held accountable for results relative to position level.

Source: American Eagle Outfitters, Inc. Proxy Statement (Form Def 14A) filed April 26, 2010.

Share-based compensation, in addition to theoretically aligning the interests of employees (management) with shareholders, has the advantage of potentially requiring no cash outlay.[13] Share-based compensation arrangements can take a variety of forms, including those that are equity-settled and those that are cash-settled. However, share-based compensation is treated as an expense and thus as a reduction of earnings even when no cash changes hands. In addition to decreasing earnings through compensation expense, stock options have the potential to dilute earnings per share.

Although share-based compensation is generally viewed as motivating employees and aligning managers' interests with those of the shareholders, there are several disadvantages of share-based compensation. One disadvantage is that the recipient of the share-based compensation may have limited influence over the company's market value (consider the scenario of overall market decline), so share-based compensation does not necessarily provide the desired incentives. Another disadvantage is that the increased ownership may lead managers to be risk averse. In other words, fearing a large market value decline (and loss in individual wealth), managers may seek less risky (and less profitable) projects. An opposite effect, excessive risk taking, can also occur with the awarding of options. Because options have skewed payouts that reward excessive risk taking, managers may seek more risky projects. Finally, when share-based compensation is granted to employees, existing shareholders' ownership is diluted.

For financial reporting, a company reports compensation expense during the period in which employees earn that compensation. Accounting for cash salary payments and cash bonuses is relatively straightforward. When the employee has earned the salary or bonus, an expense is recorded. Typically, compensation expense for managers is reported in sales, general, and administrative expenses on the income statement.

Share-based compensation is more varied and includes such items as stock, stock options, stock appreciation rights, and phantom shares. By granting shares or share options in addition to other compensation, companies are paying additional compensation for services rendered by employees. Under both IFRS and US GAAP, companies use the fair value of the share-based compensation granted to measure the value of the employees' services for purposes of reporting compensation expense. However, the specifics of the accounting depend on the type of share-based compensation given to the employee. Under both IFRS and US GAAP, the usual disclosures required for share-based compensation include (1) the nature and extent of share-based compensation arrangements during the period, (2) how the fair value of a share-based compensation arrangement was determined, and (3) the effect of share-based compensation on the company's income for the period and on its financial position.

Two common forms of equity-settled share-based compensation, stock grants and stock options, are discussed below.

3.1. Stock Grants

A company can grant stock to employees outright, with restrictions, or contingent on performance. For an outright stock grant, compensation expense is reported on the basis of the fair value of the stock on the grant date—generally the market value at grant date. Compensation expense is allocated over the period benefited by the employee's service, referred to as the

---

[13] Although issuing employee stock options requires no initial cash outlay, the company implicitly forgoes issuing new shares of stock at the then-current market price (and receiving cash) when the options are exercised.

service period. The employee service period is presumed to be the current period unless there are some specific requirements, such as three years service in the future, before the employee is vested (has the right to receive the compensation).

Another type of stock award is a restricted stock, which requires the employee to return ownership of those shares to the company if certain conditions are not met. Common restrictions include the requirements that employees remain with the company for a specified period or that certain performance goals are met. Compensation expense for restricted stock grants is measured as the fair value (usually market value) of the shares issued at the grant date. This compensation expense is allocated over the employee service period.

Shares granted contingent on meeting performance goals are called performance shares. The amount of the grant is usually determined by performance measures other than the change in stock price, such as accounting earnings or return on assets. Basing the grant on accounting performance addresses employees' potential concerns that the stock price is beyond their control and thus should not form the basis for compensation. However, performance shares can potentially have the unintended impact of providing incentives to manipulate accounting numbers. Compensation expense is equal to the fair value (usually market value) of the shares issued at the grant date. This compensation expense is allocated over the employee service period.

3.2. Stock Options

Like stock grants, compensation expense related to option grants is reported at fair value under both IFRS and US GAAP. Both require that fair value be estimated using an appropriate valuation model.

Whereas the fair value of stock grants is usually based on the market value at the date of the grant, the fair value of option grants must be estimated. Companies cannot rely on market prices of options to measure the fair value of employee stock options because features of employee stock options typically differ from traded options. To measure the fair value of employee stock options, therefore, companies must use a valuation model. The choice of valuation or option pricing model is one of the critical elements in estimating fair value. Several models are commonly used, such as the Black–Scholes option pricing model or a binomial model. Accounting standards do not prescribe a particular model. Generally, though, the valuation method should (1) be consistent with fair value measurement, (2) be based on established principles of financial economic theory, and (3) reflect all substantive characteristics of the award.

Once a valuation model is selected, a company must determine the inputs to the model, typically including exercise price, stock price volatility, estimated life of each award, estimated number of options that will be forfeited, dividend yield, and the risk-free rate of interest.[14] Some inputs, such as the exercise price, are known at the time of the grant. Other critical inputs are highly subjective—such as stock price volatility or the estimated life of stock options—and can greatly change the estimated fair value and thus compensation expense. Higher volatility, a longer estimated life, and a higher risk-free interest rate increase the estimated fair value, whereas a higher assumed dividend yield decreases the estimated fair value.

Combining different assumptions with alternative valuation models can significantly affect the fair value of employee stock options. Following is an excerpt from GlaxoSmithKline, plc explaining the assumptions and model used in valuing its stock options. (Although not

---

[14]The estimated life of an option award incorporates such assumptions as employee turnover and is usually shorter than the expiration period.

discussed in the disclosure, from 2007 to 2009 the trends of decreasing interest rates, lower share price, and increasing dividend yield would decrease estimated fair values and thus lower option expense. In contrast, the trend of increasing volatility would increase the estimated fair values.)

EXHIBIT 8   Assumptions Used in Stock Option Pricing Models: Excerpts from Financial Statements of GlaxoSmithKline, plc

Note 42—Employee share schemes *[excerpt]*

Option pricing

For the purposes of valuing options and awards to arrive at the share based payment charge, the Black–Scholes option pricing model has been used. The assumptions used in the model for 2007, 2008 and 2009 are as follows:

	2009	2008	2007
Risk-free interest rate	1.4%–2.9%	1.3%–4.8%	4.7%–5.3%
Dividend yield	5.20%	4.80%	4.00%
Volatility	23%–29%	19%–24%	17%–25%
Expected lives of options granted under:			
Share option schemes	5 years	5 years	5 years
Savings-related share option and share award schemes	3–4 years	3 years	3 years
Weighted average share price for grants in the year:			
Ordinary Shares	£11.72	£11.59	£14.41
ADS*	$33.73	$45.02	$57.59

* American Depositary Shares

Volatility is determined based on the three and five year share price history where appropriate. The fair value of performance share plan grants take into account market conditions. Expected lives of options were determined based on weighted average historic exercises of options.

Source: GlaxoSmithKline Annual Report 2009.

In accounting for stock options, there are several important dates, including the grant date, the vesting date, the exercise date, and the expiration date. The **grant date** is the day that options are granted to employees. The **service period** is usually the period between the grant date and the vesting date.

The **vesting date** is the date that employees can first exercise the stock options. The vesting can be immediate or over a future period. If the share-based payments vest immediately (i.e., no further period of service is required), then expense is recognized on the grant date. If the share-based awards do not vest until a specified service period is completed, compensation expense is recognized and allocated over the service period. If the share-based awards are conditional upon the achievement of a performance condition or a market condition (i.e., a target share price), then compensation expense is recognized over the estimated service period. The **exercise date** is the date when employees actually exercise the options and convert them to stock. If the options go unexercised, they may expire at some pre-determined future date, commonly 5 or 10 years from the grant date.

The grant date is also usually the date that compensation expense is measured if both the number of shares and the option price are known. If facts affecting the value of options granted depend on events after the grant date, then compensation expense is measured at the exercise date. In the example below, Coca Cola, Inc. reported, in the 2009 Form 10-K, $241 million of compensation expense from option grants.

EXAMPLE 7   Disclosure of Stock Options' Current Compensation Expense, Vesting, and Future Compensation Expense

Using information from Coca Cola, Inc.'s Note 9 to financial statements, given below, determine the following:

1. Total compensation expense relating to options already granted that will be recognized in future years as options vest.
2. Approximate compensation expense in 2010 and 2011 relating to options already granted.

Excerpts from Note 9: Stock Compensation Plans in the Notes to Financial Statements of Coca Cola, Inc.
    NOTE 9: STOCK COMPENSATION PLANS
    Our Company grants stock options and restricted stock awards to certain employees of the Company. Total stock-based compensation expense was approximately $241 million in 2009, $266 million in 2008 and $313 million in 2007 and was included as a component of selling, general and administrative expenses in our consolidated statements of income. The total income tax benefit recognized in our consolidated statements of income for share-based compensation arrangements was approximately $68 million, $72 million and $91 million for 2009, 2008 and 2007, respectively.
    As of December 31, 2009, we had approximately $335 million of total unrecognized compensation cost related to nonvested share-based compensation arrangements granted under our plans. This cost is expected to be recognized over a weighted-average period of 1.7 years as stock-based compensation expense. This expected cost does not include the impact of any future stock-based compensation awards.

Source: Coca Cola, Inc. Form 10-K filed 26 February 2010.

Solution to 1: Coca Cola, Inc. discloses that unrecognized compensation expense relating to stock options already granted but not yet vested totals $335 million.

Solution to 2: The options already granted will vest over the next 1.7 years. Compensation expense related to stock options already granted will be $197 million ($335/1.7 years) in 2010 and $138 million in 2011 ($335 total less $197 expensed in 2010). New options granted in the future will likely raise the total reported compensation expense.

As the option expense is recognized over the relevant vesting period, the impact on the financial statements is to ultimately reduce retained earnings (as with any other expense). The offsetting entry is an increase in paid-in capital. Thus, the recognition of option expense has no net impact on total equity.

3.3. Other Types of Share-Based Compensation

Both stock grants and stock options allow the employee to obtain direct ownership in the company. Other types of share-based compensation, such as stock appreciation rights (SARs) or phantom stock, compensate an employee on the basis of changes in the value of shares without requiring the employee to hold the shares. These are referred to as cash-settled share-based compensation. With SARs, an employee's compensation is based on increases in a company's share price. Like other forms of share-based compensation, SARs serve to motivate employees and align their interests with shareholders. The following are two additional advantages of SARs:

- The potential for risk aversion is limited because employees have limited downside risk and unlimited upside potential similar to employee stock options, and
- Shareholder ownership is not diluted.

Similar to other share-based compensation, SARs are valued at fair value and compensation expense is allocated over the service period of the employee. While phantom share plans are similar to other types of share-based compensation, they differ somewhat because compensation is based on the performance of hypothetical stock rather than the company's actual stock. Unlike SARs, phantom shares can be used by private companies or business units within a company that are not publicly traded or by highly illiquid companies.

4. SUMMARY

This chapter discussed two different forms of employee compensation: post-employment benefits and share-based compensation. Although different, the two are similar in that they are forms of compensation outside of the standard salary arrangements. They also involve complex valuation, accounting, and reporting issues. Although IFRS and US GAAP are converging on accounting and reporting, it is important to note that differences in a country's social system, laws, and regulations can result in differences in a company's pension and share-based compensation plans that may be reflected in the company's earnings and financial reports.

Key points include the following:

- Defined contribution pension plans specify (define) only the amount of contribution to the plan; the eventual amount of the pension benefit to the employee will depend on the value of an employee's plan assets at the time of retirement.
- Balance sheet reporting is less analytically relevant for defined contribution plans because companies make contributions to defined contribution plans as the expense arises and thus no liabilities accrue for that type of plan.
- Defined benefit pension plans specify (define) the amount of the pension benefit, often determined by a plan formula, under which the eventual amount of the benefit to the employee is a function of length of service and final salary.

- Defined benefit pension plan obligations are funded by the sponsoring company contributing assets to a pension trust, a separate legal entity. Differences exist in countries' regulatory requirements for companies to fund defined benefit pension plan obligations.
- Both IFRS and US GAAP require companies to report on their balance sheet a pension liability or asset equal to the projected benefit obligation minus the fair value of plan assets. The amount of a pension asset that can be reported is subject to a ceiling.
- Under IFRS, the components of periodic pension cost are recognized as follows: Service cost is recognized in P&L, net interest income/expense is recognized in P&L, and remeasurements are recognized in OCI and are not amortized to future P&L.
- Under US GAAP, the components of periodic pension cost recognized in P&L include current service costs, interest expense on the pension obligation, and expected returns on plan assets (which reduces the cost). Other components of periodic pension cost—including past service costs, actuarial gains and losses, and differences between expected and actual returns on plan assets—are recognized in OCI and amortized to future P&L.
- Estimates of the future obligation under defined benefit pension plans and other post-employment benefits are sensitive to numerous assumptions, including discount rates, assumed annual compensation increases, expected return on plan assets, and assumed health care cost inflation.
- Employee compensation packages are structured to fulfill varied objectives, including satisfying employees' needs for liquidity, retaining employees, and providing incentives to employees.
- Common components of employee compensation packages are salary, bonuses, and share-based compensation.
- Share-based compensation serves to align employees' interests with those of the shareholders. It includes stocks and stock options.
- Share-based compensation has the advantage of requiring no current-period cash outlays.
- Share-based compensation expense is reported at fair value under IFRS and US GAAP.
- The valuation technique, or option pricing model, that a company uses is an important choice in determining fair value and is disclosed.
- Key assumptions and input into option pricing models include such items as exercise price, stock price volatility, estimated life of each award, estimated number of options that will be forfeited, dividend yield, and the risk-free rate of interest. Certain assumptions are highly subjective, such as stock price volatility or the expected life of stock options, and can greatly change the estimated fair value and thus compensation expense.

REFERENCE

Lynch, L.J., and S.E. Perry. 2003. "An Overview of Management Compensation." *Journal of Accounting Education*, vol. 21, no. 1 (1st Quarter): 43–60. doi:10.1016/S0748-5751(02)00034-9

PRACTICE PROBLEMS

The following information relates to Questions 1–7

Kensington plc, a hypothetical company based in the United Kingdom, offers its employees a defined benefit pension plan. Kensington complies with IFRS. The assumed discount rate that the company used in estimating the present value of its pension obligations was 5.48 percent. Information on Kensington's retirement plans is presented in Exhibit 1.

EXHIBIT 1   Kensington plc Defined Benefit Pension Plan

(in millions)	2010
Components of periodic benefit cost	
Service cost	£228
Net interest (income) expense	273
Remeasurements	–18
Periodic pension cost	£483
Change in benefit obligation	
Benefit obligations at beginning of year	£28,416
Service cost	228
Interest cost	1,557
Benefits paid	–1,322
Actuarial gain or loss	0
Benefit obligations at end of year	£28,879
Change in plan assets	
Fair value of plan assets at beginning of year	£23,432
Actual return on plan assets	1,302
Employer contributions	693
Benefits paid	–1,322
Fair value of plan assets at end of year	£24,105
Funded status at beginning of year	–£4,984
Funded status at end of year	–£4,774

1. At year-end 2010, £28,879 million represents:
   A. the funded status of the plan.
   B. the defined benefit obligation.
   C. the fair value of the plan's assets.

2. For the year 2010, the net interest expense of £273 represents the interest cost on the:
   A. ending benefit obligation.
   B. beginning benefit obligation.
   C. beginning net pension obligation.

3. For the year 2010, the remeasurement component of Kensington's periodic pension cost represents:
   A. the change in the net pension obligation.
   B. actuarial gains and losses on the pension obligation.
   C. actual return on plan assets minus the amount of return on plan assets included in the net interest expense.

4. Which of the following is *closest* to the actual rate of return on beginning plan assets and the rate of return on beginning plan assets that is included in the interest income/expense calculation?
   A. The actual rate of return was 5.56 percent, and the rate included in interest income/expense was 5.48 percent.
   B. The actual rate of return was 1.17 percent, and the rate included in interest income/expense was 5.48 percent.
   C. Both the actual rate of return and the rate included in interest income/expense were 5.48 percent.

5. Which component of Kensington's periodic pension cost would be shown in OCI rather than P&L?
   A. Service cost
   B. Net interest (income) expense
   C. Remeasurements

6. The relationship between the periodic pension cost and the plan's funded status is *best* expressed in which of the following?
   A. Periodic pension cost of –£483 = Ending funded status of –£4,774 – Employer contributions of £693 – Beginning funded status of –£4,984.
   B. Periodic pension cost of £1,322 = Benefits paid of £1,322.
   C. Periodic pension cost of £210 = Ending funded status of –£4,774 – Beginning funded status of –£4,984.

7. An adjustment to Kensington's statement of cash flows to reclassify the company's excess contribution for 2010 would *most likely* entail reclassifying £210 million (excluding income tax effects) as an outflow related to:
   A. investing activities rather than operating activities.
   B. financing activities rather than operating activities.
   C. operating activities rather than financing activities.

The following information relates to Questions 8–12

XYZ SA, a hypothetical company, offers its employees a defined benefit pension plan. Information on XYZ's retirement plans is presented in Exhibit 2. It also grants stock options to executives. Exhibit 3 contains information on the volatility assumptions used to value stock options.

EXHIBIT 2   XYZ SA Retirement Plan Information 2009

Employer contributions	1,000
Current service costs	200
Past service costs	120
Discount rate used to estimate plan liabilities	7.00%
Benefit obligation at beginning of year	42,000
Benefit obligation at end of year	41,720
Actuarial loss due to increase in plan obligation	460
Plan assets at beginning of year	39,000
Plan assets at end of year	38,700
Actual return on plan assets	2,700
Expected rate of return on plan assets	8.00%

EXHIBIT 3   XYZ SA Volatility Assumptions Used to Value Stock
Option Grants

Grant Year	Weighted Average Expected Volatility
2009 valuation assumptions	
2005–2009	21.50%
2008 valuation assumptions	
2004–2008	23.00%

8. The total periodic pension cost is *closest* to:
    A. 320.
    B. 1,020.
    C. 1,320.

9. The amount of periodic pension cost that would be reported in P&L under IFRS is *closest* to:
    A. 20.
    B. 530.
    C. 1,020.

10. Assuming the company chooses not to immediately recognize the actuarial loss and assuming there is no amortization of past service costs or actuarial gains and losses, the amount of periodic pension cost that would be reported in P&L under US GAAP is *closest* to:
    A. 20.
    B. 59.
    C. 530.

11. Under IFRS, the amount of periodic pension cost that would be reported in OCI is *closest* to:
    A. 20.
    B. 490.
    C. 1,020.

12. Compared to 2009 net income as reported, if XYZ had used the same volatility assumption for its 2009 option grants that it had used in 2008, its 2009 net income would have been:
    A. lower.
    B. higher.
    C. the same.

The following information relates to Questions 13–18

Stereo Warehouse is a US retailer that offers employees a defined benefit pension plan and stock options as part of its compensation package. Stereo Warehouse prepares its financial statements in accordance with US GAAP.

Peter Friedland, CFA, is an equity analyst concerned with earnings quality. He is particularly interested in whether the discretionary assumptions the company is making regarding compensation plans are contributing to the recent earnings growth at Stereo Warehouse. He gathers information from the company's regulatory filings regarding the pension plan assumptions in Exhibit 4 and the assumptions related to option valuation in Exhibit 5.

EXHIBIT 4   Assumptions Used for Stereo Warehouse Defined Benefit Plan

	2009	2008	2007
Expected long-term rate of return on plan assets	6.06%	6.14%	6.79%
Discount rate	4.85	4.94	5.38
Estimated future salary increases	4.00	4.44	4.25
Inflation	3.00	2.72	2.45

EXHIBIT 5   Option Valuation Assumptions

	2009	2008	2007
Risk-free rate	4.6%	3.8%	2.4%
Expected life	5.0 yrs	4.5 yrs	5.0 yrs
Dividend yield	1.0%	0.0%	0.0%
Expected volatility	29%	31%	35%

13. Compared to the 2009 reported financial statements, if Stereo Warehouse had used the same expected long-term rate of return on plan assets assumption in 2009 as it used in 2007, its year-end 2009 pension obligation would *most likely* have been:
    A. lower.
    B. higher.
    C. the same.

14. Compared to the reported 2009 financial statements, if Stereo Warehouse had used the same discount rate as it used in 2007, it would have *most likely* reported lower:
    A. net income.
    B. total liabilities.
    C. cash flow from operating activities.

15. Compared to the assumptions Stereo Warehouse used to compute its periodic pension cost in 2008, earnings in 2009 were *most favorably* affected by the change in the:
    A. discount rate.
    B. estimated future salary increases.
    C. expected long-term rate of return on plan assets.

16. Compared to the pension assumptions Stereo Warehouse used in 2008, which of the following pairs of assumptions used in 2009 is *most likely* internally inconsistent?
    A. Estimated future salary increases, inflation
    B. Discount rate, estimated future salary increases
    C. Expected long-term rate of return on plan assets, discount rate

17. Compared to the reported 2009 financial statements, if Stereo Warehouse had used the 2007 volatility assumption to value its employee stock options, it would have *most likely* reported higher:
    A. net income.
    B. compensation expense.
    C. deferred compensation liability.

18. Compared to the assumptions Stereo Warehouse used to value stock options in 2008, earnings in 2009 were most favorably affected by the change in the:
    A. expected life.
    B. risk-free rate.
    C. dividend yield.

The following information relates to Questions 19–25

The board of directors at Sallie-Kwan Industrials (SKI), a publicly traded company, is meeting with various committees following the release of audited financial statements prepared in accordance with IFRS. The finance committee (FC) is next on the agenda to review retirement benefits funding and make recommendations to the board.

SKI's three retirement benefit plans are described as follows:

Plan A

- Benefit: Annual payments for life equal to 1% of the employee's final salary for each year of service beyond the date of the plan's establishment
- The employer makes regular contributions to the plan in order to meet the future obligation
- Closed to new participants; benefits accrue for existing participants
- Fair value of assets: €5.98 billion
- Present value of obligation: €4.80 billion
- Present value of reductions in future contributions: €1.50 billion
- Ten-year vesting schedule; 70% of the participants are fully vested

Plan B

- Benefit: Discretionary retirement withdrawals; amounts depend on the plan's investment performance
- Employer makes its agreed-upon contribution to the plan on behalf of the employee in the same period during which the employee provides the service; SKI is current on this obligation
- The employee may also contribute to the plan during employment years
- Available to all employees after one year of service; 80% of the employees are fully vested

Plan C

- Benefit: Medical, prescription drug, and dental coverage for the retiree, spouse, and dependents under age 18
- 80% funded
- Available to all employees on day one of service

The FC chair reviews Plan A's funded status and the amount recorded on the balance sheet with the board, explaining that the current service cost change from last quarter has primarily resulted from a higher percentage of employees that are expected to leave before the full vesting period.

A board member inquires how Plan A's periodic pension costs affect SKI's operating performance. The FC chair reviews the adjustments needed to account for individual pension components that are considered operating costs and those considered non-operating costs, when calculating profit before taxation. Note 16 in the income statement lists the following:

current service costs of €40 million, interest costs of €263 million, expected return on plan assets of €299 million, and actual return on plan assets of €205 million.

Next, the FC chairman presents the following case study data to illustrate SKI's current pension obligation for an average fully vested participant in Plan A with 10 years of prior service:

- Current annual salary: €100,000
- Years to retirement: 17
- Retirement life expectancy: 20 years
- Current plan assumptions:
  - Annual compensation increase: 6%
  - Discount rate: 4%
  - Compensation increases are awarded on the first day of the service year; no adjustments are made to reflect the possibility that the employee may leave the firm at an earlier date.

A discussion ensues regarding the effect on the pension obligation, for an average participant, of changing Plan A's annual compensation increase to 5%.

Lastly, the FC chair recommends that the board consider modifying some key assumptions affecting Plan A in response to recent market trends. The chair also reviews how these changes will alter SKI's plan obligation.

Recommendation 1: Change the assumed discount rate to 5%.
Recommendation 2: Increase the retirement life expectancy assumption by eight years.
Recommendation 3: Reduce investment risk by decreasing the expected return to 3%.

19. The participant bears the greatest amount of investment risk under which plan?
    A. Plan A
    B. Plan B
    C. Plan C

20. The plan for which the amount of SKI's financial obligation is defined in the current period with no obligation for future retirement benefits is:
    A. Plan A.
    B. Plan B.
    C. Plan C.

21. For Plan A, SKI should report a net pension:
    A. asset of €1.50 billion.
    B. asset of €1.18 billion.
    C. liability of €1.18 billion.

22. Based on the FC chair's explanation about the current service cost change, the present value of Plan A's obligation:
    A. decreased.
    B. stayed the same.
    C. increased.

23. Based on Note 16, after reclassifying pension components to reflect economic income or expense, the net adjustment to profit before taxation is:
    A. −€205 million.
    B. −€94 million.
    C. +€129 million.

24. Based on the case study illustration and the effect of changing the annual compensation rate, the annual unit credit for the average participant would decrease by an amount *closest* to:
    A. €4,349.
    B. €4,858.
    C. €5,446.

25. All else being equal, which of the following FC recommendations will increase the plan's obligation?
    A. Recommendation 1
    B. Recommendation 2
    C. Recommendation 3

The following information relates to Questions 26–32

Natalie Holmstead, a senior portfolio manager, works with Daniel Rickards, a junior analyst. Together they are evaluating the financial statements of Company XYZ (XYZ) with a focus on post-employment benefits. XYZ has a defined benefit pension plan and prepares financial statements according to IFRS requirements.

Rickards calculates the current service cost for a single employee's defined benefit pension obligation using the projected unit credit method. The employee is expected to work for 7 years before retiring and has 15 years of vested service. Rickards assumes a discount rate of 4.00% and a lump sum value of the employee's benefit at retirement of $393,949.

Next, Holmstead and Rickards discuss the present value of the defined benefit obligation (PVDBO). Rickards makes the following statements to clarify his understanding:

Statement 1   An increase in the PVDBO will result in an actuarial loss for the company.
Statement 2   The PVDBO measures the present value of future benefits earned by plan participants and includes plan assets.
Statement 3   The company should use the expected long-term rate of return on plan assets as the discount rate to calculate the PVDBO.

XYZ's pension plan offers benefits based on the employee's final year's salary. Rickards calculates the PVDBO as of the end of the current period, based on the information presented in Exhibit 1.

EXHIBIT 1   Select XYZ Defined Benefit Pension Plan Data

	Current Period	Prior Period
Assumed future compensation growth rate	2.5%	3.0%
Plan assets (in $ millions)	3,108	
Net pension liability (in $ millions)	525	
Present value of reductions of future contributions (in $ millions)	48	

Rickards adjusts the balance sheet and cash flow statement information presented in Exhibit 2 to better reflect the economic nature of certain items related to the pension plan.

EXHIBIT 2   Select XYZ Balance Sheet and
Cash Flow Data (in $ millions)

Item	Current Period
Total assets	24,130
Total liabilities	17,560
Total equity	6,570
Total pension cost	96
Pension contribution	66
Financing cash flow	2,323
Operating cash flow	–1,087
Effective tax rate	30%

Finally, Rickards examines the data in Exhibit 3 and calculates the effect of a 100-basis-point increase in health care inflation on XYZ's debt-to-equity ratio.

EXHIBIT 3   Sensitivity of Accumulated Post-Employment Benefit Obligations to Changes in Assumed Health Care Inflation (in $ millions)

Item	100-bp Increase	100-bp Decrease
Benefit obligation change	$93	–$76
Benefit expense change	$12	–$10

26. The current service cost is *closest* to:
    A. $14,152.
    B. $15,758.
    C. $17,907.

27. Which of Rickards's statements about the PVDBO is correct?
    A. Statement 1
    B. Statement 2
    C. Statement 3

28. Based on Exhibit 1, the PVDBO is *closest* to:
    A. $3,585 million.
    B. $3,633 million.
    C. $3,681 million.

29. Based on Exhibit 1 and the method XYZ uses to link pension benefits to salaries, the change in the compensation growth rate compared with the prior period will *most likely* result in:
    A. lower periodic pension cost.
    B. no change in the periodic pension cost.
    C. higher periodic pension cost.

30. Based on the change in the assumed future compensation growth rate presented in Exhibit 1, which of the following pension cost components is affected?
    A. Service cost
    B. Remeasurement
    C. Net interest expense/income

31. Based on Exhibit 2, Rickards should adjust the operating and financing cash flows by:
    A. $21 million.
    B. $30 million.
    C. $96 million.

32. Based on Exhibits 2 and 3, as well as Holmstead's assumption about future health care inflation, the debt-to-equity ratio calculated by Rickards for XYZ should be *closest* to:
    A. 2.69.
    B. 2.71.
    C. 2.73.

CHAPTER 15

MULTINATIONAL OPERATIONS

Timothy S. Doupnik, PhD

Elaine Henry, PhD, CFA

LEARNING OUTCOMES

After completing this chapter, you will be able to do the following:

- distinguish among presentation (reporting) currency, functional currency, and local currency;
- describe foreign currency transaction exposure, including accounting for and disclosures about foreign currency transaction gains and losses;
- analyze how changes in exchange rates affect the translated sales of the subsidiary and parent company;
- compare the current rate method and the temporal method, evaluate how each affects the parent company's balance sheet and income statement, and determine which method is appropriate in various scenarios;
- calculate the translation effects and evaluate the translation of a subsidiary's balance sheet and income statement into the parent company's presentation currency;
- analyze how the current rate method and the temporal method affect financial statements and ratios;
- analyze how alternative translation methods for subsidiaries operating in hyperinflationary economies affect financial statements and ratios;
- describe how multinational operations affect a company's effective tax rate;
- explain how changes in the components of sales affect the sustainability of sales growth;
- analyze how currency fluctuations potentially affect financial results, given a company's countries of operation.

1. INTRODUCTION

According to the World Trade Organization, merchandise exports worldwide were nearly US$15 trillion in 2010.[1] The amount of worldwide merchandise exports in 2010 was more than twice the amount in 2003 (US$7.4 trillion) and more than four times the amount in 1993 (US$3.7 trillion). The top five exporting countries in 2010, in order, were China, the United States, Germany, Japan, and the Netherlands. In the United States alone, 293,131 companies were identified as exporters in 2010, but only 2.2% of those companies were large (more than 500 employees).[2] The vast majority of US companies with export activity were small or medium-sized entities.

The point illustrated by these statistics is that many companies engage in transactions that cross national borders. The parties to these transactions must agree on the currency in which to settle the transaction. Generally, this will be the currency of either the buyer or the seller. Exporters that receive payment in foreign currency and allow the purchaser time to pay must carry a foreign currency receivable on their books. Conversely, importers that agree to pay in foreign currency will have a foreign currency account payable. To be able to include them in the total amount of accounts receivable (payable) reported on the balance sheet, these foreign currency denominated accounts receivable (payable) must be translated into the currency in which the exporter (importer) keeps its books and presents financial statements.

The prices at which foreign currencies can be purchased or sold are called foreign exchange rates. Because foreign exchange rates fluctuate over time, the value of foreign currency payables and receivables also fluctuates. The major accounting issue related to foreign currency transactions is how to reflect the changes in value for foreign currency payables and receivables in the financial statements.

Many companies have operations located in foreign countries. For example, the Swiss food products company Nestlé SA reports that it has factories in 83 countries and a presence in almost every country in the world. US-based Procter & Gamble's annual filing discloses more than 400 subsidiaries located in more than 80 countries around the world. Foreign subsidiaries are generally required to keep accounting records in the currency of the country in which they are located. To prepare consolidated financial statements, the parent company must translate the foreign currency financial statements of its foreign subsidiaries into its own currency. Nestlé, for example, must translate the assets and liabilities its various foreign subsidiaries carry in foreign currency into Swiss francs to be able to consolidate those amounts with the Swiss franc assets and liabilities located in Switzerland.

A multinational company like Nestlé is likely to have two types of foreign currency activities that require special accounting treatment. Most multinationals (1) engage in transactions that are denominated in a foreign currency and (2) invest in foreign subsidiaries that keep their books in a foreign currency. To prepare consolidated financial statements, a multinational company must translate the foreign currency amounts related to both types of international activities into the currency in which the company presents its financial statements.

This chapter presents the accounting for foreign currency transactions and the translation of foreign currency financial statements. The conceptual issues related to these

---

[1] World Trade Organization, *International Trade Statistics 2011*, Table 14, page 21.
[2] US Census Bureau, Department of Commerce. *A Profile of US Importing and Exporting Companies, 2009–2010*. Released April 12, 2012.

EXAMPLE 1   Accounting for Foreign Currency Transactions with
Settlement before the Balance Sheet Date

FinnCo purchases goods from its Mexican supplier on November 1, 20X1; the purchase
price is 100,000 Mexican pesos. Credit terms allow payment in 45 days, and FinnCo
makes payment of 100,000 pesos on December 15, 20X1. FinnCo's functional and
presentation currency is the euro. Spot exchange rates between the euro (EUR) and
Mexican peso (MXN) are as follows:

November 1, 20X1   MXN1 = EUR0.0684

December 15, 20X1   MXN1 = EUR0.0703

FinnCo's fiscal year end is December 31. How will FinnCo account for this foreign currency transaction, and what effect will it have on the 20X1 financial statements?

Solution: The euro value of the Mexican peso account payable on November 1, 20X1
was EUR6,840 (MXN100,000 × EUR0.0684). FinnCo could have paid for its inventory on November 1 by converting 6,840 euro into 100,000 Mexican pesos. Instead, the company purchases 100,000 Mexican pesos on December 15, 20X1, when
the value of the peso has increased to EUR0.0703. Thus, FinnCo pays 7,030 euro
to purchase 100,000 Mexican pesos. The net result is a loss of 190 euro (EUR7,030
– EUR6,840).

   Although the cash outflow to acquire the inventory is EUR7,030, the cost
included in the inventory account is only EUR6,840. This cost represents the amount
that FinnCo could have paid if it had not waited 45 days to settle its account. By
deferring payment, and because the Mexican peso increased in value between the
transaction date and settlement date, FinnCo has to pay an additional 190 euro.
The company will report a foreign exchange loss of EUR190 in its net income in
20X1. This is a realized loss because FinnCo actually spent an additional 190 euro
to purchase its inventory. The net effect on the financial statements, in EUR, can be
seen as follows:

Balance Sheet				Income Statement	
Assets		= Liabilities +	Stockholders' Equity		Revenues and Gains	Expenses and Losses
Cash	−7,030		Retained			Foreign
Inventory	+6,840		earnings	−190		exchange loss −190
	−190					

2.1.2. Accounting for Foreign Currency Transactions with Intervening Balance Sheet Dates
Another important issue related to the accounting for foreign currency transactions is what, if
anything, should be done if a balance sheet date falls between the initial transaction date and
the settlement date. For foreign currency transactions whose settlement dates fall in subsequent accounting periods, both IFRS and US GAAP require adjustments to reflect intervening

changes in currency exchange rates. Foreign currency transaction gains and losses are reported on the income statement, creating one of the few situations in which accounting rules allow, indeed require, companies to include (recognize) a gain or loss in income before it has been realized.

Subsequent foreign currency transaction gains and losses are recognized from the balance sheet date through the date the transaction is settled. Adding together foreign currency transaction gains and losses for both accounting periods (transaction initiation to balance sheet date and balance sheet date to transaction settlement) produces an amount equal to the actual realized gain or loss on the foreign currency transaction.

EXAMPLE 2   Accounting for Foreign Currency Transaction with Intervening Balance Sheet Date

FinnCo sells goods to a customer in the United Kingdom for £10,000 on November 15, 20X1, with payment to be received in British pounds on January 15, 20X2. FinnCo's functional and presentation currency is the euro. Spot exchange rates between the euro (€) and British pound (£) are as follows:

November 15, 20X1	£1 = €1.460
December 31, 20X1	£1 = €1.480
January 15, 20X2	£1 = €1.475

FinnCo's fiscal year end is December 31. How will FinnCo account for this foreign currency transaction, and what effect will it have on the 20X1 and 20X2 financial statements?

Solution: The euro value of the British pound account receivable at each of the three relevant dates is determined as follows:

		Account Receivable (£10,000)	
Date	€/£ Exchange Rate	Euro Value	Change in Euro Value
15 Nov 20X1	€1.460	14,600	N/A
31 Dec 20X1	€1.480	14,800	+ 200
15 Jan 20X2	€1.475	14,750	− 50

A change in the euro value of the British pound receivable from November 15 to December 31 would be recognized as a foreign currency transaction gain or loss on FinnCo's 20X1 income statement. In this case, the increase in the value of the British pound results in a transaction gain of €200 [£10,000 × (€1.48 − €1.46)]. Note that the gain recognized in 20X1 income is unrealized, and remember that this is one of few situations in which companies include an unrealized gain in income.

Any change in the exchange rate between the euro and British pound that occurs from the balance sheet date (December 31, 20X1) to the transaction settlement date (January 15, 20X2) will also result in a foreign currency transaction gain or loss. In our example, the British pound weakened slightly against the euro during this period, resulting in an exchange rate of €1.475/ £1 on January 15, 20X2. The £10,000 account receivable now has a value of €14,750, which is a decrease of €50 from December 31, 20X1. FinnCo will recognize a foreign currency transaction loss on January 15, 20X2 of €50 that will be included in the company's calculation of net income for the first quarter of 20X2.

From the transaction date to the settlement date, the British pound has increased in value by €0.015 (€1.475 – €1.460), which generates a realized foreign currency transaction gain of €150. A gain of €200 was recognized in 20X1 and a loss of €50 is recognized in 20X2. Over the two-month period, the net gain recognized in the financial statements is equal to the actual realized gain on the foreign currency transaction.

In Example 2, FinnCo's British pound account receivable resulted in a net foreign currency transaction gain because the British pound strengthened (increased) in value between the transaction date and the settlement date. In this case, FinnCo has an asset exposure to foreign exchange risk. This asset exposure benefited the company because the foreign currency strengthened. If FinnCo instead had a British pound account payable, a liability exposure would have existed. The euro value of the British pound account payable would have increased as the British pound strengthened, and FinnCo would have recognized a foreign currency transaction loss as a result.

Whether a change in exchange rate results in a foreign currency transaction gain or loss (measured in local currency) depends on (1) the nature of the exposure to foreign exchange risk (asset or liability) and (2) the direction of change in the value of the foreign currency (strengthens or weakens).

		Foreign Currency	
Transaction	Type of Exposure	Strengthens	Weakens
Export sale	Asset (account receivable)	Gain	Loss
Import purchase	Liability (account payable)	Loss	Gain

A foreign currency receivable arising from an export sale creates an asset exposure to foreign exchange risk. If the foreign currency strengthens, the receivable increases in value in terms of the company's functional currency and a foreign currency transaction gain arises. The company will be able to convert the foreign currency when received into more units of functional currency because the foreign currency has strengthened. Conversely, if the foreign currency weakens, the foreign currency receivable loses value in terms of the functional currency and a loss results.

A foreign currency payable resulting from an import purchase creates a liability exposure to foreign exchange risk. If the foreign currency strengthens, the payable increases in value in terms of the company's functional currency and a foreign currency transaction loss arises. The company must spend more units of functional currency to be able to settle the foreign currency liability because the foreign currency has strengthened. Conversely, if the foreign currency weakens, the foreign currency payable loses value in terms of the functional currency and a gain exists.

2.2. Analytical Issues

Both IFRS and US GAAP require foreign currency transaction gains and losses to be reported in net income (even if the gains and losses have not yet been realized), but neither standard indicates where on the income statement these gains and losses should be placed. The two most common treatments are either (1) as a component of other operating income/expense or (2) as a component of non-operating income/expense, in some cases as a part of net financing cost. The calculation of operating profit margin is affected by where foreign currency transaction gains or losses are placed on the income statement.

EXAMPLE 3   Placement of Foreign Currency Transaction Gains/Losses on the Income Statement—Effect on Operating Profit

Assume that FinnCo had the following income statement information in both 20X1 and 20X2, excluding a foreign currency transaction gain of €200 in 20X1 and a transaction loss of €50 in 20X2.

	20X1	20X2
Revenues	€20,000	€20,000
Cost of goods sold	12,000	12,000
Other operating expenses, net	5,000	5,000
Non-operating expenses, net	1,200	1,200

FinnCo is deciding between two alternatives for the treatment of foreign currency transaction gains and losses. Alternative 1 calls for the reporting of foreign currency transaction gains/losses as part of "Other operating expenses, net." Under Alternative 2, the company would report this information as part of "Non-operating expenses, net."

FinnCo's fiscal year end is December 31. How will Alternatives 1 and 2 affect the company's gross profit margin, operating profit margin, and net profit margin for 20X1? For 20X2?

Solution: Remember that a gain would serve to reduce expenses, whereas a loss would increase expenses.

20X1—Transaction Gain of €200		
	Alternative 1	Alternative 2
Revenues	€20,000	€20,000
Cost of goods sold	(12,000)	(12,000)
Gross profit	8,000	8,000
Other operating expenses, net	(4,800) incl. gain	(5,000)
Operating profit	3,200	3,000
Non-operating expenses, net	(1,200)	(1,000) incl. gain
Net profit	€ 2,000	€ 2,000

Profit margins in 20X1 under the two alternatives can be calculated as follows:

	Alternative 1	Alternative 2
Gross profit margin	€8,000/€20,000 = 40.0%	€8,000/€20,000 = 40.0%
Operating profit margin	3,200/20,000 = 16.0%	3,000/20,000 = 15.0%
Net profit margin	2,000/20,000 = 10.0%	2,000/20,000 = 10.0%

20X2—Transaction Loss of €50		
	Alternative 1	Alternative 2
Revenues	€20,000	€20,000
Cost of goods sold	(12,000)	(12,000)
Gross profit	8,000	8,000
Other operating expenses, net	(5,050) incl. loss	(5,000)
Operating profit	2,950	3,000
Non-operating expenses, net	(1,200)	(1,250) incl. loss
Net profit	€ 1,750	€ 1,750

Profit margins in 20X2 under the two alternatives can be calculated as follows:

	Alternative 1	Alternative 2
Gross profit margin	€8,000/€20,000 = 40.0%	€8,000/€20,000 = 40.0%
Operating profit margin	2,950/20,000 = 14.75%	3,000/20,000 = 15.0%
Net profit margin	1,750/20,000 = 8.75%	1,750/20,000 = 8.75%

Gross profit and net profit are unaffected, but operating profit differs under the two alternatives. In 20X1, the operating profit margin is larger under Alternative 1, which includes the transaction gain as part of "Other operating expenses, net." In 20X2, Alternative 1 results in a smaller operating profit margin than Alternative 2. Alternative 2 has the same operating profit margin in both periods. Because exchange rates do not fluctuate by the same amount or in the same direction from one accounting period to the next, Alternative 1 will cause greater volatility in operating profit and operating profit margin over time.

Because accounting standards do not provide guidance on the placement of foreign currency transaction gains and losses on the income statement, companies are free to choose among the alternatives. Two companies in the same industry could choose different alternatives, which would distort the direct comparison of operating profit and operating profit margins between those companies.

A second issue that should be of interest to analysts relates to the fact that unrealized foreign currency transaction gains and losses are included in net income when the balance sheet date falls between the transaction and settlement dates. The implicit assumption underlying this accounting requirement is that the unrealized gain or loss as of the balance sheet date reflects the company's ultimate net gain or loss. In reality, though, the ultimate net gain or loss may vary dramatically because of the possibility for changes in trend and volatility of currency prices.

This effect was seen in the previous hypothetical Example 2 with FinnCo. Using given currency exchange rate data shows that the real-world effect can also be quite dramatic. Assume that a French company purchased goods from a Canadian supplier on December 1, 20X1, with payment of 100,000 Canadian dollars (C$) to be made on May 15, 20X2. Actual exchange rates between the Canadian dollar and euro (€) during the period December 1, 20X1 and May 15, 20X2, the euro value of the Canadian dollar account payable, and the foreign currency transaction gain or loss are shown below:

| | | Account Payable (C$100,000) | |
	€/C$	€ Value	Change in € Value (Gain/Loss)
Dec. 1, X1	0.7285	72,850	N/A
Dec. 31, X1	0.7571	75,710	2,860 loss
Mar. 31, X2	0.7517	75,170	540 gain
May 15, X2	0.7753	77,530	2,360 loss

As the Canadian dollar strengthened against the euro in late 20X1, the French company would have recorded a foreign currency transaction loss of €2,860 in the fourth quarter of 20X1. The Canadian dollar reversed course by weakening over the first three months of 20X2, resulting in a transaction gain of €540 in the first quarter, and then strengthened against the euro in the second quarter of 20X2, resulting in a transaction loss of €2,360. At the time payment is made on May 15, 20X2, the French company realizes a net foreign currency transaction loss of €4,680 (€77,530 – €72,850).

2.3. Disclosures Related to Foreign Currency Transaction Gains and Losses

Because accounting rules allow companies to choose where they present foreign currency transaction gains and losses on the income statement, it is useful for companies to disclose both the amount of transaction gain or loss that is included in income and the presentation alternative they have selected. IFRS require disclosure of "the amount of exchange differences recognized in profit or loss," and US GAAP require disclosure of "the aggregate transaction gain or loss included in determining net income for the period," but neither standard specifically requires disclosure of the line item in which these gains and losses are located.

Exhibit 1 provides disclosures from BASF AG's 2011 annual report that the German company made related to foreign currency transaction gains and losses. Exhibit 2 presents similar disclosures found in the Netherlands-based Heineken NV's 2011 Annual Report. Both companies use IFRS to prepare their consolidated financial statements.

BASF's income statement in Exhibit 1 does not include a separate line item for foreign currency gains and losses. From Note 6 in Exhibit 1, an analyst can determine that BASF has chosen to include "Income from foreign currency and hedging transactions" in "Other operating income." Of the total amount of €2,008 million reported as "Other operating income" in 2011, €170 million is attributable to foreign currency and hedging transaction income. It is not possible to determine from BASF's financial statements whether or not these gains were realized in 2011, and any unrealized gain reported in 2011 income might or might not be realized in 2012.

Note 7 in Exhibit 1 indicates that "Expenses from foreign currency and hedging transactions as well as market valuation" in 2011 were €399 million, making up 15% of Other operating expenses. Combining foreign currency transaction gains and losses results in a net loss of €229 million, which is equal to 2.55% of BASF's "Income before taxes and minority interests."

EXHIBIT 1   Excerpts from BASF AG's 2011 Annual Report Related to Foreign Currency Transactions

Consolidated Statements of Income Million €	Explanation in Notes	2011	2010
Sales	(4)	73,497	63,873
Cost of sales		(53,986)	(45,310)
Gross profit on sales		**19,511**	**18,563**
Selling expenses		(7,323)	(6,700)
General and administrative expenses		(1,315)	(1,138)
Research and development expenses		(1,605)	(1,492)
Other operating income	(6)	2,008	1,140
Other operating expenses	(7)	(2,690)	(2,612)
Income from operations	(4)	**8,586**	**7,761**
(detail omitted)			
Financial result	(8)	**384**	**(388)**
Income before taxes and minority interests		**8,970**	**7,373**
Income taxes	(9)	(2,367)	(2,299)
Income before minority interests		**6,603**	**5,074**
Minority interests	(10)	(415)	(517)
Net income		**6,188**	**4,557**

Notes:

1. Summary of Accounting Policies

   Foreign currency transactions: The cost of assets acquired in foreign currencies and revenues from sales in foreign currencies are recorded at the exchange rate on the date of the transaction. Foreign currency receivables and liabilities are valued at the exchange rates on the balance sheet date.

6. Other Operating Income

Million €	2011	2010
Reversal and adjustment of provisions	170	244
Revenue from miscellaneous revenue-generating activities	207	142
Income from foreign currency and hedging transactions	170	136
Income from the translation of financial statements in foreign currencies	42	76
Gains on the disposal of property, plant and equipment and divestitures	666	101
Reversals of impairments of property, plant and equipment	—	40
Gains on the reversal of allowance for doubtful business-related receivables	77	36
Other	676	365
	2,008	1,140

(continued)

EXHIBIT 1 (Continued)

Income from foreign currency and hedging transactions concerned foreign currency transactions, the measurement at fair value of receivables and payables in foreign currencies, as well as currency derivatives and other hedging transactions.

7. Other Operating Expenses

Million €	2011	2010
Restructuring measures	233	276
Environmental protection and safety measures, costs of demolition and removal, and planning expenses related to capital expenditures that are not subject to mandatory capitalization	203	98
Valuation adjustments on tangible and intangible assets	366	247
Costs from miscellaneous revenue-generating activities	220	180
Expenses from foreign currency and hedging transactions as well as market valuation	399	601
Losses from the translation of the financial statements in foreign currencies	56	63
Losses from the disposal of property, plant and equipment and divestitures	40	24
Oil and gas exploration expenses	184	190
Expenses from additions to allowances for business-related receivables	124	107
Expenses from the use of inventories measured at market value and the derecognition of obsolete inventory	233	188
Other	632	638
	2,690	2,612

Expenses from foreign currency and hedging transactions as well as market valuation concern foreign currency translations of receivables and payables as well as changes in the fair value of currency derivatives and other hedging transactions.

In Exhibit 2, Heineken's Note 2, Basis of Preparation, part (c) explicitly states that the euro is the company's functional currency. Note 3(b)*(i)* indicates that monetary assets and liabilities denominated in foreign currencies at the balance sheet date are translated to the functional currency and that foreign currency differences arising on the translation (i.e., translation gains and losses) are recognized on the income statement. Note 3(r) discloses that foreign currency gains and losses are included on a net basis in the other net finance income and expenses. Note 12, "Net finance income and expense," shows that a net foreign exchange loss of €107 million existed in 2011 and a net gain of €61 million arose in 2010. The net foreign currency transaction gain in 2010 amounted to 3.1% of Heineken's profit before income tax that year, and the net translation loss in 2011 represented 5.3% of the company's profit before income tax in that year. Note 12 also shows gains and losses related to changes in the fair value of derivatives, some of which related to foreign currency derivatives.

EXHIBIT 2   Excerpts from Heineken NV's 2011 Annual Report Related to Foreign Currency
Transactions

Consolidated Income Statement for the Year Ended December 31, in Millions of EUR	Note	2011	2010
Revenue	5	**17,123**	**16,133**
Other income	8	**64**	**239**
Raw materials, consumables, and services	9	(10,966)	(10,291)
Personnel expenses	10	(2,838)	(2,665)
Amortization, depreciation, and impairments	11	(1,168)	(1,118)
Total expenses		**(14,972)**	**(14,074)**
Results from operating activities		**2,215**	**2,298**
Interest income	12	70	100
Interest expenses	12	(494)	(590)
Other net finance income/(expenses)	12	(6)	(19)
Net finance expenses		**(430)**	**(509)**
Share of profit of associates and joint ventures and impairments thereof (net of income tax)	16	240	193
Profit before income tax		**2,025**	**1,982**
Income tax expenses	13	(465)	(403)
Profit		**1,560**	**1,579**
Attributable to:			
Equity holders of the Company (net profit)		1,430	1,447
Minority interest		130	132
Profit		**1,560**	**1,579**

Notes:
2. Basis of preparation
    c. Functional and presentation currency
        These consolidated financial statements are presented in euro, which is the Company's functional currency. All financial information presented in euro has been rounded to the nearest million unless stated otherwise.
3. Significant accounting policies
    b. Foreign currency
        i. Foreign currency transactions
            Transactions in foreign currencies are translated to the respective functional currencies of Heineken entities at the exchange rates at the dates of the transactions. Monetary assets and liabilities denominated in foreign currencies at the reporting date are retranslated to the functional currency at the exchange rate at that date. . . . Foreign currency differences arising on retranslation are recognized in profit or loss, except for differences arising on the retranslation of available-for-sale (equity) investments and foreign currency differences

(continued)

EXHIBIT 2   (Continued)

arising on the retranslation of a financial liability designated as a hedge of a net investment, which are recognized in other comprehensive income.[4]

r.   Interest income, interest expenses and other net finance income and expenses
    . . . Foreign currency gains and losses are reported on a net basis in the other net finance income and expenses.

12.   Net finance income and expense

Recognized in profit or loss

In millions of EUR	2011	2010
Interest income	**70**	**100**
Interest expenses	**(494)**	**(590)**
Dividend income on available-for-sale investments	2	1
Dividend income on investments held for trading	11	7
Net gain/(loss) on disposal of available-for-sale investments	1	—
Net change in fair value of derivatives	96	(75)
Net foreign exchange gain/(loss)	(107)	61
Impairment losses on available-for-sale investments	—	(3)
Unwinding discount on provisions	(7)	(7)
Other net financial income/(expenses)	(2)	(3)
Other net finance income/(expenses)	**(6)**	**(19)**
Net finance income/(expenses)	**(430)**	**(509)**

Disclosures related to foreign currency are commonly found both in the Management Discussion & Analysis (MD&A) and the Notes to Financial Statements sections of an annual report. In applying US GAAP to account for its foreign currency transactions, Yahoo! Inc. reported the following in the Quantitative and Qualitative Disclosures about Market Risk section of its 2011 annual report:

Our exposure to foreign currency transaction gains and losses is the result of assets and liabilities, (including inter-company transactions) that are denominated in currencies other than the relevant entity's functional currency . . . . We may enter into derivative instruments, such as foreign currency forward contracts or other instruments to minimize the short-term foreign currency fluctuations on such assets and liabilities. The gains and losses on the forward contracts may not offset any or more than a portion of the transaction gains and losses on certain foreign currency receivables, investments and payables recognized in earnings. Transaction gains and losses on these foreign exchange contracts are recognized each period in other income, net included on the consolidated statements of income. During the years ended December 31, 2011, 2010, and 2009, we recorded net realized and unrealized foreign currency transaction gains of $9 million and $13 million, and a transaction loss of $1 million, respectively.

---

[4]Note that this excerpt uses "retranslation" in the same way that "translation" is used throughout the rest of this chapter. The translation of currency for foreign subsidiaries will be covered in the next section.

Yahoo!'s disclosure clearly explains that both realized and unrealized foreign currency transaction gains and losses are reflected in income, specifically as a part of non-operating activities. The net foreign currency transaction gain in 2011 of $9 million represented only 1.1% of the company's pretax income ($827.5 million) for the year.

Some companies may choose not to disclose either the location or the amount of their foreign currency transaction gains and losses, presumably because the amounts involved are immaterial. There are several reasons why the amount of transaction gains and losses can be immaterial for a company:

1. The company engages in a limited number of foreign currency transactions that involve relatively small amounts of foreign currency.
2. The exchange rates between the company's functional currency and the foreign currencies in which it has transactions tend to be relatively stable.
3. Gains on some foreign currency transactions are naturally offset by losses on other transactions, such that the net gain or loss is immaterial. For example, if a US company sells goods to a customer in Canada with payment in Canadian dollars to be received in 90 days and at the same time purchases goods from a supplier in Canada with payment to be made in Canadian dollars in 90 days, any loss that arises on the Canadian dollar receivable due to a weakening in the value of the Canadian dollar will be exactly offset by a gain of equal amount on the Canadian dollar payable.
4. The company engages in foreign currency hedging activities to offset the foreign exchange gains and losses that arise from foreign currency transactions. Hedging foreign exchange risk is a common practice for many companies engaged in foreign currency transactions.

The two most common types of hedging instruments used to minimize foreign exchange transaction risk are foreign currency forward contracts and foreign currency options. Nokia Corporation describes its foreign exchange risk management approach in its 2011 Form 20-F annual report in Note 34, Risk Management. An excerpt from that note follows:

> Nokia operates globally and is thus exposed to foreign exchange risk arising from various currencies. Foreign currency denominated assets and liabilities together with foreign currency denominated cash flows from highly probable or probable purchases and sales contribute to foreign exchange exposure. These transaction exposures are managed against various local currencies because of Nokia's substantial production and sales outside the Euro zone.
>
> According to the foreign exchange policy guidelines of the Group, which remains the same as in the previous year, material transaction foreign exchange exposures are hedged unless hedging would be uneconomical due to market liquidity and/or hedging cost. Exposures are defined using nominal values of the transactions. Exposures are mainly hedged with derivative financial instruments such as forward foreign exchange contracts and foreign exchange options. The majority of financial instruments hedging foreign exchange risk have duration of less than a year. The Group does not hedge forecasted foreign currency cash flows beyond two years.

Elsewhere in its annual report, Nokia provides additional disclosures about the currencies to which it has exposure and the accounting for different types of hedges. The company also summarizes the effect of material exchange rate movements. For example, the 4.2% appreciation of the US dollar in 2011 had a positive effect on net sales expressed in euro (40% of Nokia's net sales are in US dollars or currencies closely following the US dollar) and a negative effect on product cost (60% of Nokia's components are sourced in US dollars); this resulted in a slightly negative effect on operating profit.

3. TRANSLATION OF FOREIGN CURRENCY FINANCIAL STATEMENTS

Many companies have operations in foreign countries. Most operations located in foreign countries keep their accounting records and prepare financial statements in the local currency. For example, the US subsidiary of German automaker BMW AG keeps its books in US dollars. IFRS and US GAAP require parent companies to prepare consolidated financial statements in which the assets, liabilities, revenues, and expenses of both domestic and foreign subsidiaries are added to those of the parent company. To prepare worldwide consolidated statements, parent companies must translate the foreign currency financial statements of their foreign subsidiaries into the parent company's presentation currency. BMW AG, for example, must translate both the US dollar financial statements of its US subsidiary and the South African rand financial statements of its South African subsidiary into euro to consolidate these foreign operations. If, for example, the US dollar and South African rand appreciate against the euro over the course of a given year, the amount of sales translated into euro will be greater than if the subsidiary's currencies weaken against the euro.

IFRS and US GAAP have similar rules for the translation of foreign currency financial statements. To fully understand the results from applying these rules, however, several conceptual issues must first be examined.

3.1. Translation Conceptual Issues

In translating foreign currency financial statements into the parent company's presentation currency, two questions must be addressed:

1. What is the appropriate exchange rate to use in translating each financial statement item?
2. How should the translation adjustment that inherently arises from the translation process be reflected in the consolidated financial statements? In other words, how is the balance sheet brought back into balance?

These issues and the basic concepts underlying the translation of financial statements are demonstrated through the following example.

Spanco is a hypothetical Spain-based company that uses the euro as its presentation currency. Spanco establishes a wholly owned subsidiary, Amerco, in the United States on December 31, 20X1 by investing €10,000 when the exchange rate between the euro and the US dollar is €1 = US$1. The equity investment of €10,000 is physically converted into US$10,000 to begin operations. In addition, Amerco borrows US$5,000 from local banks on December 31, 20X1. Amerco purchases inventory that costs US$12,000 on

December 31, 20X1 and retains US$3,000 in cash. Amerco's balance sheet at December 31, 20X1 thus appears as follows:

Amerco Balance Sheet, December 31, 20X1 (in US Dollars)			
Cash	$3,000	Notes payable	$5,000
Inventory	12,000	Common stock	10,000
Total	$15,000	Total	$15,000

To prepare a consolidated balance sheet in euro as of December 31, 20X1, Spanco must translate all of the US dollar balances on Amerco's balance sheet at the €1 = US$1 exchange rate. The translation worksheet as of December 31, 20X1 is as follows:

Translation Worksheet for Amerco, December 31, 20X1			
	USD	Exchange Rate (€)	EUR
Cash	$3,000	1.00	€ 3,000
Inventory	12,000	1.00	12,000
Total	$15,000		€15,000
Notes payable	5,000	1.00	5,000
Common stock	10,000	1.00	10,000
Total	$15,000		€15,000

By translating each US dollar balance at the same exchange rate (€1.00), Amerco's translated balance sheet in euro reflects an equal amount of total assets and total liabilities plus equity and remains in balance.

During the first quarter of 20X2, Amerco engages in no transactions. During that period, however, the US dollar weakens against the euro such that the exchange rate on March 31, 20X2 is €0.80 = US$1.

To prepare a consolidated balance sheet at the end of the first quarter of 20X2, Spanco now must choose between the current exchange rate of €0.80 and the historical exchange rate of €1.00 to translate Amerco's balance sheet amounts into euro. The original investment made by Spanco of €10,000 is a historical fact, so the company wants to translate Amerco's common stock in such a way that it continues to reflect this amount. This goal is achieved by translating common stock of US$10,000 into euro using the historical exchange rate of €1 = US$1.

Two approaches for translating the foreign subsidiary's assets and liabilities are as follows:

1. All assets and liabilities are translated at the **current exchange rate** (the spot exchange rate on the balance sheet date).
2. Only **monetary assets and liabilities** are translated at the current exchange rate; **non-monetary assets and liabilities** are translated at **historical exchange rates** (the exchange rates that existed when the assets and liabilities were acquired). Monetary items are cash and receivables (payables) that are to be received (paid) in a fixed number of currency units. Non-monetary assets include inventory, fixed assets, and intangibles, and non-monetary liabilities include deferred revenue.

These two different approaches are demonstrated and the results analyzed in turn.

3.1.1 All Assets and Liabilities Are Translated at the Current Exchange Rate

The translation worksheet on March 31, 20X2, in which all assets and liabilities are translated at the current exchange rate (€0.80), is as follows:

Translation Worksheet for Amerco, March 31, 20X2

	US Dollar	Exchange Rate (€)	Euro	Change in Euro Value since Dec 31, 20X1
Cash	$3,000	0.80 C	€2,400	−€600
Inventory	12,000	0.80 C	9,600	−2,400
Total	$15,000		€12,000	−€3,000
Notes payable	5,000	0.80 C	4,000	−1,000
Common stock	10,000	1.00 H	10,000	0
Subtotal	$15,000		14,000	−1,000
Translation adjustment			(2,000)	−2,000
Total			€12,000	−€3,000

Note: C = current exchange rate; H = historical exchange rate

By translating all assets at the lower current exchange rate, total assets are written down from December 31, 20X1 to March 31, 20X2 in terms of their euro value by €3,000. Liabilities are written down by €1,000. To keep the euro translated balance sheet in balance, a *negative* translation adjustment of €2,000 is created and included in stockholders' equity on the consolidated balance sheet.

Those foreign currency balance sheet accounts that are translated using the current exchange rate are revalued in terms of the parent's functional currency. This process is very similar to the revaluation of foreign currency receivables and payables related to foreign currency transactions. The net translation adjustment that results from translating individual assets and liabilities at the current exchange rate can be viewed as the *net* foreign currency translation gain or loss caused by a change in the exchange rate:

(€600)	loss on cash
(€2,400)	loss on inventory
€1,000	gain on notes payable
(€2,000)	net translation loss

The negative translation adjustment (net translation loss) does not result in a cash outflow of €2,000 for Spanco and thus is unrealized. The loss could be realized, however, if Spanco were to sell Amerco at its book value of US$10,000. The proceeds from the sale would be converted into euro at €0.80 per US$1, resulting in a cash inflow of €8,000. Because Spanco originally invested €10,000 in its US operation, a *realized* loss of €2,000 would result.

The second conceptual issue related to the translation of foreign currency financial statements is whether the unrealized net translation loss should be included in the determination of consolidated net income currently or deferred in the stockholders' equity section of the consolidated balance sheet until the loss is realized through sale of the foreign subsidiary. There is some debate as to which of these two treatments is most appropriate. This issue is discussed in more detail after considering the second approach for translating assets and liabilities.

3.1.2. Only Monetary Assets and Monetary Liabilities Are Translated at the Current Exchange Rate

Now assume only monetary assets and monetary liabilities are translated at the current exchange rate. The worksheet at March 31, 20X2, in which only monetary assets and liabilities are translated at the current exchange rate (€0.80), is as follows:

Translation Worksheet for Amerco, March 31, 20X2

	US Dollar	Exchange Rate (€)	Euro	Change in Euro Value since Dec 31, 20X1
Cash	$3,000	0.80 C	€2,400	−€600
Inventory	12,000	1.00 H	12,000	0
Total	$15,000		€14,400	−€600
Notes payable	5,000	0.80 C	4,000	−1,000
Common stock	10,000	1.00 H	10,000	0
Subtotal	$15,000		14,000	−1,000
Translation adjustment			400	400
Total			€14,400	−€600

Note: C = current exchange rate; H = historical exchange rate

Using this approach, cash is written down by €600 but inventory continues to be carried at its euro historical cost of €12,000. Notes payable is written down by €1,000. To keep the balance sheet in balance, a positive translation adjustment of €400 must be included in stockholders' equity. The translation adjustment reflects the *net* translation gain or loss related to monetary items only:

(€600)	loss on cash
€1,000	gain on notes payable
€400	net translation gain

The positive translation adjustment (net translation gain) also is *unrealized*. The gain could be *realized*, however, if:

1. The subsidiary uses its cash (US$3,000) to pay as much of its liabilities as possible, and
2. The parent sends enough euro to the subsidiary to pay its remaining liabilities (US$5,000 − US$3,000 = US$2,000). As of December 31, 20X1, at the €1.00 per US$1 exchange rate, Spanco will have sent €2,000 to Amerco to pay liabilities of US$2,000. On March 31, 20X2, given the €0.80 per US$1 exchange rate, the parent needs to send only €1,600 to pay US$2,000 of liabilities. As a result, Spanco would enjoy a foreign exchange gain of €400.

The second conceptual issue again arises under this approach. Should the unrealized foreign exchange gain be recognized in current period net income or deferred on the balance sheet as a separate component of stockholders' equity? The answer to this question, as provided by IFRS and US GAAP, is described in Section 3.2, Translation Methods.

3.1.3. Balance Sheet Exposure

Those assets and liabilities translated at the *current* exchange rate are revalued from balance sheet to balance sheet in terms of the parent company's presentation currency. These items are said to be *exposed* to translation adjustment. Balance sheet items translated at *historical* exchange rates do not change in parent currency value and therefore are not exposed to translation adjustment. Exposure to translation adjustment is referred to as balance sheet translation exposure, or accounting exposure.

A foreign operation will have a **net asset balance sheet exposure** when assets translated at the current exchange rate are greater than liabilities translated at the current exchange rate. A **net liability balance sheet exposure** exists when liabilities translated at the current exchange rate are greater than assets translated at the current exchange rate. Another way to think about the issue is to realize that there is a net asset balance sheet exposure when exposed assets are greater than exposed liabilities and a net liability balance sheet exposure when exposed liabilities are greater than exposed assets. The sign (positive or negative) of the current period's translation adjustment is a function of two factors: (1) the nature of the balance sheet exposure (asset or liability) and (2) the direction of change in the exchange rate (strengthens or weakens). The relationship between exchange rate fluctuations, balance sheet exposure, and the current period's translation adjustment can be summarized as follows:

Balance Sheet	Foreign Currency (FC)	
Exposure	Strengthens	Weakens
Net asset	Positive translation adjustment	Negative translation adjustment
Net liability	Negative translation adjustment	Positive translation adjustment

These relationships are the same as those summarized in Section 2.2 with respect to foreign currency transaction gains and losses. In reference to the example in Section 3.1.2, for instance, the amount of exposed assets (the US$3,000 cash) was less than the amount of exposed liabilities (US$5,000 of notes payable), implying a net liability exposure. Further, in the example the foreign currency (US$) weakened, resulting in a positive translation adjustment.

The combination of balance sheet exposure and direction of exchange rate change determines whether the current period's translation adjustment will be positive or negative. After the initial period of operations, a cumulative translation adjustment is required to keep the translated balance sheet in balance. The cumulative translation adjustment will be the sum of the translation adjustments that arise over successive accounting periods. For example, assume that Spanco translates all of Amerco's assets and liabilities using the current exchange rate (a net asset balance sheet exposure exists), which, because of a weakening US dollar in the first quarter of 20X2, resulted in a negative translation adjustment of €2,000 on March 31, 20X2 (as shown in Section 3.1.1). Assume further that in the second quarter of 20X2, the US dollar strengthens against the euro and there still is a net asset balance sheet exposure, which results in a *positive* translation adjustment of €500 for that quarter. Although the current period translation adjustment for the second quarter of 20X2 is positive, the cumulative translation adjustment as of June 30, 20X2 still will be negative, but the amount now will be only €1,500.

3.2. Translation Methods

The two approaches to translating foreign currency financial statements described in the previous section are known as (1) the **current rate method** (all assets and liabilities are translated at the current exchange rate), and (2) the **monetary/non-monetary method** (only monetary assets and liabilities are translated at the current exchange rate). A variation of the monetary/non-monetary method requires not only monetary assets and liabilities but also non-monetary assets and liabilities that are measured at their current value on the balance sheet date to be translated at the current exchange rate. This variation of the monetary/non-monetary method sometimes is referred to as the **temporal method**.

The basic idea underlying the temporal method is that assets and liabilities should be translated in such a way that the measurement basis (either current value or historical cost) in the foreign currency is preserved after translating to the parent's presentation currency. To achieve this objective, assets and liabilities carried on the foreign currency balance sheet at a current value should be translated at the current exchange rate, and assets and liabilities carried on the foreign currency balance sheet at historical costs should be translated at historical exchange rates. Although neither the IASB nor the FASB specifically refer to translation methods by name, the procedures specified by IFRS and US GAAP for translating foreign currency financial statements essentially require the use of either the current rate or the temporal method.

Which method is appropriate for an individual foreign entity depends on that entity's functional currency. As noted earlier, the functional currency is the currency of the primary economic environment in which an entity operates. A foreign entity's functional currency can be either the parent's presentation currency or another currency, typically the currency of the country in which the foreign entity is located. Exhibit 3 lists the factors that IFRS indicate should be considered in determining a foreign entity's functional currency. Although not identical, US GAAP provide similar indicators for determining a foreign entity's functional currency.

When the functional currency indicators listed in Exhibit 3 are mixed and the functional currency is not obvious, IFRS indicate that management should use its best judgment in determining the functional currency. In this case, however, indicators 1 and 2 should be given priority over indicators 3 through 9.

EXHIBIT 3   Factors Considered in Determining the Functional Currency

---

In accordance with IFRS, the following factors should be considered in determining an entity's functional currency:

1. The currency that mainly influences sales prices for goods and services.
2. The currency of the country whose competitive forces and regulations mainly determine the sales price of its goods and services.
3. The currency that mainly influences labor, material, and other costs of providing goods and services.
4. The currency in which funds from financing activities are generated.
5. The currency in which receipts from operating activities are usually retained.

(continued)

EXHIBIT 3   (Continued)

Additional factors to consider in determining whether the foreign entity's functional currency is the same as the parent's functional currency are

6. Whether the activities of the foreign operation are an extension of the parent's or are carried out with a significant amount of autonomy.
7. Whether transactions with the parent are a large or a small proportion of the foreign entity's activities.
8. Whether cash flows generated by the foreign operation directly affect the cash flow of the parent and are available to be remitted to the parent.
9. Whether operating cash flows generated by the foreign operation are sufficient to service existing and normally expected debt or whether the foreign entity will need funds from the parent to service its debt.

The following three steps outline the functional currency approach required by accounting standards in translating foreign currency financial statements into the parent company's presentation currency:

1. Identify the functional currency of the foreign entity.
2. Translate foreign currency balances into the foreign entity's functional currency.
3. Use the current exchange rate to translate the foreign entity's functional currency balances into the parent's presentation currency, if they are different.

To illustrate how this approach is applied, consider a US parent company with a Mexican subsidiary that keeps its accounting records in Mexican pesos. Assume that the vast majority of the subsidiary's transactions are carried out in Mexican pesos, but it also has an account payable in Guatemalan quetzals. In applying the three steps, the US parent company first determines that the Mexican peso is the functional currency of the Mexican subsidiary. Second, the Mexican subsidiary translates its foreign currency balances (i.e., the Guatemalan quetzal account payable), into Mexican pesos using the current exchange rate. In step 3, the Mexican peso financial statements (including the translated account payable) are translated into US dollars using the current rate method.

Now assume, alternatively, that the primary operating currency of the Mexican subsidiary is the US dollar, which thus is identified as the Mexican subsidiary's functional currency. In that case, in addition to the Guatemalan quetzal account payable, all of the subsidiary's accounts that are denominated in Mexican pesos also are considered to be foreign currency balances (because they are not denominated in the subsidiary's functional currency, which is the US dollar). Along with the Guatemalan quetzal balance, each of the Mexican peso balances must be translated into US dollars as if the subsidiary kept its books in US dollars. Assets and liabilities carried at current value in Mexican pesos are translated into US dollars using the current exchange rate, and assets and liabilities carried at historical cost in Mexican pesos are translated into US dollars using historical exchange rates. After completing this step, the Mexican subsidiary's financial statements are stated in terms of US dollars, which is both the subsidiary's functional currency and the parent's presentation currency. As a result, there is no need to apply step 3.

The following two sections describe the procedures to be followed in applying the functional currency approach in more detail.

3.2.1. Foreign Currency Is the Functional Currency

In most cases, a foreign entity will operate primarily in the currency of the country where it is located, which will differ from the currency in which the parent company presents its financial statements. For example, the Japanese subsidiary of a French parent company is likely to have the Japanese yen as its functional currency, whereas the French parent company must prepare consolidated financial statements in euro. When a foreign entity has a functional currency that differs from the parent's presentation currency, the foreign entity's foreign currency financial statements are translated into the parent's presentation currency using the following procedures:

1. All assets and liabilities are translated at the current exchange rate at the balance sheet date.
2. Stockholders' equity accounts are translated at historical exchange rates.
3. Revenues and expenses are translated at the exchange rate that existed when the transactions took place. For practical reasons, a rate that approximates the exchange rates at the dates of the transactions, such as an average exchange rate, may be used.

These procedures essentially describe the *current rate method*.

When the current rate method is used, the cumulative translation adjustment needed to keep the translated balance sheet in balance is reported as a separate component of stockholders' equity.

The basic concept underlying the current rate method is that the entire investment in a foreign entity is exposed to translation gain or loss. Therefore, all assets and all liabilities must be revalued at each successive balance sheet date. The net translation gain or loss that results from this procedure is unrealized, however, and will be realized only when the entity is sold. In the meantime, the unrealized translation gain or loss that accumulates over time is deferred on the balance sheet as a separate component of stockholders' equity. When a specific foreign entity is sold, the cumulative translation adjustment related to that entity is reported as a realized gain or loss in net income.

The current rate method results in a net asset balance sheet exposure (except in the rare case in which an entity has negative stockholders' equity):

Items Translated at Current Exchange Rate

Total assets > Total liabilities → Net asset balance sheet exposure

When the foreign currency increases in value (i.e., strengthens), application of the current rate method results in an increase in the positive cumulative translation adjustment (or a decrease in the negative cumulative translation adjustment) reflected in stockholders' equity. When the foreign currency decreases in value (i.e., weakens), the current rate method results in a decrease in the positive cumulative translation adjustment (or an increase in the negative cumulative translation adjustment) in stockholders' equity.

3.2.2. Parent's Presentation Currency Is the Functional Currency

In some cases, a foreign entity might have the parent's presentation currency as its functional currency. For example, a Germany-based manufacturer might have a 100%-owned distribution subsidiary in Switzerland that primarily uses the euro in its day-to-day operations and thus has the euro as its functional currency. As a Swiss company, however, the subsidiary is required to record its transactions and keep its books in Swiss francs. In that situation, the subsidiary's Swiss franc financial statements must be translated into euro as if the subsidiary's transactions had originally been recorded in euro. US GAAP refer to this process as *remeasurement*. IFRS do not refer to this process as remeasurement but instead describe this situation as "reporting foreign currency transactions in the functional currency." To achieve the objective of translating to the parent's presentation currency as if the subsidiary's transactions had been recorded in that currency, the following procedures are used:

1. a. Monetary assets and liabilities are translated at the current exchange rate.
   b. Non-monetary assets and liabilities measured at historical cost are translated at historical exchange rates.
   c. Non-monetary assets and liabilities measured at current value are translated at the exchange rate at the date when the current value was determined.
2. Stockholders' equity accounts are translated at historical exchange rates.
3. a. Revenues and expenses, other than those expenses related to non-monetary assets (as explained in 3.b. below), are translated at the exchange rate that existed when the transactions took place (for practical reasons, average rates may be used).
   b. Expenses related to non-monetary assets, such as cost of goods sold (inventory), depreciation (fixed assets), and amortization (intangible assets), are translated at the exchange rates used to translate the related assets.

These procedures essentially describe the *temporal method*.

Under the temporal method, companies must keep record of the exchange rates that exist when non-monetary assets (inventory, prepaid expenses, fixed assets, and intangible assets) are acquired, because these assets (normally measured at historical cost) are translated at historical exchange rates. Keeping track of the historical exchange rates for these assets is not necessary under the current rate method. Translating these assets (and their related expenses) at historical exchange rates complicates application of the temporal method.

The historical exchange rates used to translate inventory (and cost of goods sold) under the temporal method will differ depending on the cost flow assumption—first in, first out (FIFO); last in, first out (LIFO); or average cost—used to account for inventory. Ending inventory reported on the balance sheet is translated at the exchange rate that existed when the inventory's acquisition is assumed to have occurred. If FIFO is used, ending inventory is assumed to be composed of the most recently acquired items and thus inventory will be translated at relatively recent exchange rates. If LIFO is used, ending inventory is assumed to consist of older items and thus inventory will be translated at older exchange rates. The weighted-average exchange rate for the year is used when inventory is carried at weighted-average cost. Similarly, cost of goods sold is translated using the exchange rates that existed when the inventory items assumed to have been sold during the year (using FIFO or LIFO) were acquired. If weighted-average cost is used to account for inventory, cost of goods sold will be translated at the weighted-average exchange rate for the year.

Under both international and US accounting standards, when the temporal method is used, the translation adjustment needed to keep the translated balance sheet in balance is reported as a gain or loss in net income. US GAAP refer to these as *remeasurement* gains and losses. The basic assumption underlying the recognition of a translation gain or loss in income relates to timing. Specifically, if the foreign entity primarily uses the parent company's currency in its day-to-day operations, then the foreign entity's monetary items that are denominated in a foreign currency generate translation gains and losses that will be realized in the near future and thus should be reflected in current net income.

The temporal method generates either a net asset or a net liability balance sheet exposure, depending on whether assets translated at the current exchange rate—that is, monetary assets and non-monetary assets measured on the balance sheet date at current value (exposed assets)—are greater than or less than liabilities translated at the current exchange rate—that is, monetary liabilities and non-monetary liabilities measured on the balance sheet date at current value (exposed liabilities):

Items Translated at Current Exchange Rate

Exposed assets > Exposed liabilities → Net asset balance sheet exposure

Exposed assets < Exposed liabilities → Net liability balance sheet exposure

Most liabilities are monetary liabilities. Only cash and receivables are monetary assets, and non-monetary assets generally are measured at their historical cost. As a result, liabilities translated at the current exchange rate (exposed liabilities) often exceed assets translated at the current exchange rate (exposed assets), which results in a net liability balance sheet exposure when the temporal method is applied.

3.2.3. Translation of Retained Earnings

Stockholders' equity accounts are translated at historical exchange rates under both the current rate and the temporal methods. This approach creates somewhat of a problem in translating retained earnings (R/E), which are the accumulation of previous years' income less dividends over the life of the company. At the end of the first year of operations, foreign currency (FC) retained earnings are translated into the parent's currency (PC) as follows:

Net income in FC	[Translated according to the method used to translate the income statement]	= Net income in PC
$\dfrac{-\text{ Dividends in FC}}{\text{R/E in FC}}$ × Exchange rate when dividends declared =		$\dfrac{-\text{ Dividends in PC}}{\text{R/E in PC}}$

Retained earnings in parent currency at the end of the first year become the beginning retained earnings in parent currency for the second year, and the translated retained earnings in the second year (and subsequent years) are then calculated in the following manner:

Beginning R/E in FC	[From last year's translation]	→ Beginning R/E in PC
+ Net income in FC	[Translated according to method used to translate the income statement]	= + Net income in PC
− Dividends in FC × Exchange rate when dividends declared =		− Dividends in PC
Ending R/E in FC		Ending R/E in PC

Exhibit 4 summarizes the translation rules as discussed in Sections 3.2.1, 3.2.2, and 3.2.3.

EXHIBIT 4   Rules for the Translation of a Foreign Subsidiary's Foreign Currency Financial
Statements into the Parent's Presentation Currency under IFRS and US GAAP

| | Foreign Subsidiary's Functional Currency | |
| | Foreign Currency | Parent's Presentation Currency |
Translation method:	Current Rate Method	Temporal Method
Exchange rate at which financial statement items are translated from the foreign subsidiary's bookkeeping currency to the parent's presentation currency:		
Assets		
Monetary, such as cash and receivables	Current rate	Current rate
Non-monetary		
• measured at current value (e.g., marketable securities and inventory measured at market value under the lower of cost or market rule)	Current rate	Current rate
• measured at historical costs, (e.g., inventory measured at cost under the lower of cost or market rule; property, plant & equipment; and intangible assets)	Current rate	Historical rates
Liabilities		
Monetary, such as accounts payable, accrued expenses, long-term debt, and deferred income taxes	Current rate	Current rate
Non-monetary		
• measured at current value	Current rate	Current rate
• not measured at current value, such as deferred revenue	Current rate	Historical rates
Equity		
Other than retained earnings	Historical rates	Historical rates
Retained earnings	Beginning balance plus translated net income less dividends translated at historical rate	Beginning balance plus translated net income less dividends translated at historical rate
Revenues	Average rate	Average rate
Expenses		
Most expenses	Average rate	Average rate
Expenses related to assets translated at historical exchange rate, such as cost of goods sold, depreciation, and amortization	Average rate	Historical rates
Treatment of the translation adjustment in the parent's consolidated financial statements	Accumulated as a separate component of equity	Included as gain or loss in net income

3.2.4. Highly Inflationary Economies

When a foreign entity is located in a highly inflationary economy, the entity's functional currency is irrelevant in determining how to translate its foreign currency financial statements into the parent's presentation currency. IFRS require that the foreign entity's financial statements first be restated for local inflation using the procedures outlined in IAS 29, "Financial Reporting in Hyperinflationary Economies." Then, the inflation-restated foreign currency financial statements are translated into the parent's presentation currency using the current exchange rate.

US GAAP require a very different approach for translating the foreign currency financial statements of foreign entities located in highly inflationary economies. US GAAP do not allow restatement for inflation but instead require the foreign entity's financial statements to be remeasured as if the functional currency were the reporting currency (i.e., the temporal method).

US GAAP define a highly inflationary economy as one in which the cumulative three-year inflation rate exceeds 100% (but note that the definition should be applied with judgment, particularly because the trend of inflation can be as important as the absolute rate). A cumulative three-year inflation rate of 100% equates to an average of approximately 26% per year. IAS 21 does not provide a specific definition of high inflation, but IAS 29 indicates that a cumulative inflation rate approaching or exceeding 100% over three years would be an indicator of hyperinflation. If a country in which a foreign entity is located ceases to be classified as highly inflationary, the functional currency of that entity must be identified to determine the appropriate method for translating the entity's financial statements.

The FASB initially proposed that companies restate for inflation and then translate the financial statements, but this approach met with stiff resistance from US multinational corporations. Requiring the temporal method ensures that companies avoid a "disappearing plant problem" that exists when the current rate method is used in a country with high inflation. In a highly inflationary economy, as the local currency loses purchasing power within the country, it also tends to weaken in value in relation to other currencies. Translating the historical cost of assets such as land and buildings at progressively weaker exchange rates causes these assets to slowly disappear from the parent company's consolidated financial statements. Example 4 demonstrates the effect of three different translation approaches when books are kept in the currency of a highly inflationary economy. Example 4 pertains to Turkey in the period 2000 to 2002, when it was recognized as one of the few highly inflationary countries. Turkey is no longer viewed as having a highly inflationary economy. (In 2010, the International Practices Task Force of the Center for Audit Quality SEC Regulations Committee indicated that Venezuela had met the thresholds for being considered highly inflationary.)

EXAMPLE 4   Foreign Currency Translation in a Highly Inflationary Economy

---

Turkey was one of the few remaining highly inflationary countries at the beginning of the 21st century. Annual inflation rates and selected exchange rates between the Turkish lira (TL) and US dollar during the 2000–2002 period were as follows:

Date	Exchange Rates	Year	Inflation Rate (%)
Jan 1, 2000	TL542,700 = US$1		
Dec 31, 2000	TL670,800 = US$1	2000	38
Dec 31, 2001	TL1,474,525 = US$1	2001	69
Dec 31, 2002	TL1,669,000 = US$1	2002	45

Assume that a US-based company established a subsidiary in Turkey on January 1, 2000. The US parent sent the subsidiary US$1,000 on January 1, 2000 to purchase a piece of land at a cost of TL542,700,000 (TL542,700/US$ × US$1,000 = TL542,700,000). Assuming no other assets or liabilities, what are the annual and cumulative translation gains or losses that would be reported under each of three possible translation approaches?

Solution:

Approach 1: Translate Using the Current Rate Method
The historical cost of the land is translated at the current exchange rate, which results in a new translated amount at each balance sheet date.

Date	Carrying Value	Current Exchange Rate	Translated Amount in US$	Annual Translation Gain (Loss)	Cumulative Translation Gain (Loss)
Jan 1, 2000	TL542,700,000	542,700	$1,000	N/A	N/A
Dec 31, 2000	542,700,000	670,800	809	($191)	($191)
Dec 31, 2001	542,700,000	1,474,525	368	(441)	(632)
Dec 31, 2002	542,700,000	1,669,000	325	(43)	(675)

At the end of three years, land that was originally purchased with US$1,000 would be reflected on the parent's consolidated balance sheet at US$325 (and remember that land is not a depreciable asset). A cumulative translation loss of US$675 would be reported as a separate component of stockholders' equity on December 31, 2002. Because this method accounts for adjustments in exchange rates but does not account for likely changes in the local currency values of assets, it does a poor job of accurately reflecting the economic reality of situations such as the one in our example. That is the major reason this approach is not acceptable under either IFRS or US GAAP.

Approach 2: Translate Using the Temporal Method (US GAAP ASC 830)
The historical cost of land is translated using the historical exchange rate, which results in the same translated amount at each balance sheet date.

Date	Carrying Value	Historical Exchange Rate	Translated Amount in US$	Annual Translation Gain (Loss)	Cumulative Translation Gain (Loss)
Jan 1, 2000	TL542,700,000	542,700	$1,000	N/A	N/A
Dec 31, 2000	542,700,000	542,700	1,000	N/A	N/A
Dec 31, 2001	542,700,000	542,700	1,000	N/A	N/A
Dec 31, 2002	542,700,000	542,700	1,000	N/A	N/A

Under this approach, land continues to be reported on the parent's consolidated balance sheet at its original cost of US$1,000 each year. There is no translation gain or loss related to balance sheet items translated at historical exchange rates. This approach is required by US GAAP and ensures that non-monetary assets do not disappear from the translated balance sheet.

Approach 3: Restate for Inflation/Translate Using Current Exchange Rate (IAS 21)
The historical cost of the land is restated for inflation, and then the inflation-adjusted historical cost is translated using the current exchange rate.

Date	Inflation Rate (%)	Restated Carrying Value	Current Exchange Rate	Translated Amount in US$	Annual Translation Gain (Loss)	Cumulative Translation Gain (Loss)
Jan 1, 00		TL542,700,000	542,700	$1,000	N/A	N/A
Dec 31, 00	38	748,926,000	670,800	1,116	$116	$116
Dec 31, 01	69	1,265,684,940	1,474,525	858	(258)	(142)
Dec 31, 02	45	1,835,243,163	1,669,000	1,100	242	100

Under this approach, land is reported on the parent's December 31, 2002 consolidated balance sheet at US$1,100 with a cumulative, unrealized gain of US$100. Although the cumulative translation gain on December 31, 2002 is unrealized, it could have been realized if (1) the land had appreciated in TL value by the rate of local inflation, (2) the Turkish subsidiary sold the land for TL1,835,243,163, and (3) the sale proceeds were converted into US$1,100 at the current exchange rate on December 31, 2002.

This approach is required by IAS 21. It is the approach that, apart from doing an appraisal, perhaps best represents economic reality, in the sense that it reflects both the likely change in the local currency value of the land as well as the actual change in the exchange rate.

3.3. Illustration of Translation Methods (Excluding Hyperinflationary Economies)

To demonstrate the procedures required in translating foreign currency financial statements (excluding hyperinflationary economies), assume that Interco is a Europe-based company that has the euro as its presentation currency. On January 1, 20X1, Interco establishes a wholly owned subsidiary in Canada, Canadaco. In addition to Interco making an equity investment in Canadaco, a long-term note payable to a Canadian bank was negotiated to purchase property and equipment. The subsidiary begins operations with the following balance sheet in Canadian dollars (C$):

Canadaco Balance Sheet, January 1, 20X1

Assets

Cash	C$1,500,000
Property and equipment	3,000,000
	C$4,500,000

Liabilities and Equity

Long-term note payable	C$3,000,000
Capital stock	1,500,000
	C$4,500,000

Canadaco purchases and sells inventory in 20X1, generating net income of C$1,180,000, out of which C$350,000 in dividends are paid. The company's income statement and statement of retained earnings for 20X1 and balance sheet at December 31, 20X1 follow:

Canadaco Income Statement and Statement of Retained Earnings, 20X1

Sales	C$12,000,000
Cost of sales	(9,000,000)
Selling expenses	(750,000)
Depreciation expense	(300,000)
Interest expense	(270,000)
Income tax	(500,000)
Net income	C$1,180,000
Less: Dividends, Dec 1, 20X1	(350,000)
Retained earnings, Dec 31, 20X1	C$830,000

Canadaco Balance Sheet, December 31, 20X1

Assets		Liabilities and Equity	
Cash	C$980,000	Accounts payable	C$450,000
Accounts receivable	900,000	Total current liabilities	450,000
Inventory	1,200,000	Long-term notes payable	3,000,000
Total current assets	C$3,080,000	Total liabilities	C$3,450,000
Property and equipment	3,000,000	Capital stock	1,500,000
Less: accumulated depreciation	(300,000)	Retained earnings	830,000
Total	C$5,780,000	Total	C$5,780,000

Inventory is measured at historical cost on a FIFO basis.

To translate Canadaco's Canadian dollar financial statements into euro for consolidation purposes, the following exchange rate information was gathered:

Date	€ per C$
January 1, 20X1	0.70
Average, 20X1	0.75
Weighted-average rate when inventory was acquired	0.74
December 1, 20X1 when dividends were declared	0.78
December 31, 20X1	0.80

During 20X1, the Canadian dollar strengthened steadily against the euro from an exchange rate of €0.70 at the beginning of the year to €0.80 at year-end.

The translation worksheet that follows shows Canadaco's translated financial statements under each of the two translation methods. Assume first that Canadaco's functional currency is the Canadian dollar, and thus the current rate method must be used. The Canadian dollar income statement and statement of retained earnings are translated first. Income statement items for 20X1 are translated at the average exchange rate for 20X1 (€0.75), and dividends are translated at the exchange rate that existed when they were declared (€0.78). The ending balance in retained earnings as of December 31, 20X1 of €612,000 is transferred to the Canadian dollar balance sheet. The remaining balance sheet accounts are then translated. Assets and liabilities are translated at the current exchange rate on the balance sheet date of December 31, 20X1 (€0.80), and the capital stock account is translated at the historical exchange rate (€0.70) that existed on the date that Interco made the capital contribution. A positive translation adjustment of €202,000 is needed as a balancing amount, which is reported in the stockholders' equity section of the balance sheet.

If instead Interco determines that Canadaco's functional currency is the euro (the parent's presentation currency), the temporal method must be applied as shown in the far right columns of the table. The differences in procedure from the current rate method are that inventory, property, and equipment (and accumulated depreciation), as well as their related expenses (cost of goods sold and depreciation), are translated at the historical exchange rates that existed when the assets were acquired: €0.70 in the case of property and equipment, and €0.74 for inventory. The balance sheet is translated first, with €472,000 determined as the amount of retained earnings needed to keep the balance sheet in balance. This amount is transferred to the income statement and statement of retained earnings as the ending balance in retained earnings as of December 31, 20X1. Income statement items then are translated, with cost of goods sold and depreciation expense being translated at historical exchange rates. A negative translation adjustment of €245,000 is determined as the amount needed to arrive at the ending balance in retained earnings of €472,000, and this adjustment is reported as a translation loss on the income statement.

The positive translation adjustment under the current rate method can be explained by the facts that Canadaco has a net asset balance sheet exposure (total assets exceed total liabilities) during 20X1 and the Canadian dollar strengthened against the euro. The negative translation adjustment (translation loss) under the temporal method is explained by the fact that Canadaco has a net liability balance sheet exposure under this method (because the amount of exposed liabilities [accounts payable plus notes payable] exceeds the amount of exposed assets [cash plus receivables]) during 20X1 when the Canadian dollar strengthened against the euro.

Canadaco Income Statement and Statement of Retained Earnings, 20X1

Canadaco's Functional Currency Is:		Local Currency (C$)		Parent's Currency (€)	
		Current Rate		Temporal	
	C$	Exch. Rate	€	Exch. Rate	€
Sales	12,000,000	0.75 A	9,000,000	0.75 A	9,000,000
Cost of goods sold	(9,000,000)	0.75 A	(6,750,000)	0.74 H	(6,660,000)
Selling expenses	(750,000)	0.75 A	(562,500)	0.75 A	(562,500)
Depreciation expense	(300,000)	0.75 A	(225,000)	0.70 H	(210,000)
Interest expense	(270,000)	0.75 A	(202,500)	0.75 A	(202,500)
Income tax	(500,000)	0.75 A	(375,000)	0.75 A	(375,000)
Income before trans. gain (loss)	1,180,000		885,000		990,000
Translation gain (loss)	N/A		N/A	to balance	(245,000)
Net income	1,180,000		885,000		745,000
Less: Dividends, 12/1/20X1	(350,000)	0.78 H	(273,000)	0.78 H	(273,000)
Retained earnings, 12/31/20X1	830,000		612,000	from B/S	472,000

Note: C = current exchange rate; A = average-for-the-year exchange rate; H = historical exchange rate

Canadaco Balance Sheet, December 31, 20X1

Canadaco's Functional Currency Is:		Local Currency (C$)		Parent's Currency (€)	
		Current Rate		Temporal	
	C$	Exch. Rate	€	Exch. Rate	€
Assets					
Cash	980,000	0.80 C	784,000	0.80 C	784,000
Accounts receivable	900,000	0.80 C	720,000	0.80 C	720,000
Inventory	1,200,000	0.80 C	960,000	0.74 H	888,000
Total current assets	3,080,000		2,464,000		2,392,000
Property and equipment	3,000,000	0.80 C	2,400,000	0.70 H	2,100,000
Less: accumulated depreciation	(300,000)	0.80 C	(240,000)	0.70 H	(210,000)
Total assets	5,780,000		4,624,000		4,282,000
Liabilities and Equity					
Accounts payable	450,000	0.80 C	360,000	0.80 C	360,000
Total current liabilities	450,000		360,000		360,000
Long-term notes payable	3,000,000	0.80 C	2,400,000	0.80 C	2,400,000
Total liabilities	3,450,000		2,760,000		2,760,000
Capital stock	1,500,000	0.70 H	1,050,000	0.70 H	1,050,000
Retained earnings	830,000	from I/S	612,000	to balance	472,000
Translation adjustment	N/A	to balance	202,000		N/A
Total	5,780,000		4,624,000		4,282,000

Note: C = current exchange rate; A = average-for-the-year exchange rate; H = historical exchange rate

3.4. Translation Analytical Issues

The two different translation methods used to translate Canadaco's Canadian dollar financial statements into euro result in very different amounts to be included in Interco's consolidated financial statements. The chart below summarizes some of these differences:

Canadaco's Functional Currency Is:	Local Currency (C$)	Parent's Currency (€)	
	Translation Method		
Item	Current Rate (€)	Temporal (€)	Difference (%)
Sales	9,000,000	9,000,000	0.0
Net income	885,000	745,000	+18.8
Income before translation gain (loss)	885,000	990,000	−10.6
Total assets	4,624,000	4,282,000	+8.0
Total equity	1,864,000	1,522,000	+22.5

In this particular case, the current rate method results in a significantly larger net income than the temporal method. This result occurs because under the current rate method, the translation adjustment is not included in the calculation of income. If the translation loss were excluded from net income, the temporal method would result in a significantly larger amount of net income. The combination of smaller net income under the temporal method and a positive translation adjustment reported on the balance sheet under the current rate method results in a much larger amount of total equity under the current rate method. Total assets also are larger under the current rate method because all assets are translated at the current exchange rate, which is higher than the historical exchange rates at which inventory and fixed assets are translated under the temporal method.

To examine the effects of translation on the underlying relationships that exist in Canadaco's Canadian dollar financial statements, several significant ratios are calculated from the original Canadian dollar financial statements and the translated (euro) financial statements and are presented in the table below.

Canadaco's Functional Currency Is:	C$	*Local Currency (C$)* Current Rate (€)	*Parent's Currency (€)* Temporal (€)
Current ratio	6.84	6.84	6.64
Current assets	$= \dfrac{3,080,000}{450,000}$	$= \dfrac{2,464,000}{360,000}$	$= \dfrac{2,392,000}{360,000}$
Current liabilities			
Debt-to-assets ratio	0.52	0.52	0.56
Total debt	$= \dfrac{3,000,000}{5,780,000}$	$= \dfrac{2,400,000}{4,624,000}$	$= \dfrac{2,400,000}{4,282,000}$
Total assets			
Debt-to-equity ratio	1.29	1.29	1.58
Total debt	$= \dfrac{3,000,000}{2,330,000}$	$= \dfrac{2,400,000}{1,864,000}$	$= \dfrac{2,400,000}{1,522,000}$
Total equity			
Interest coverage	7.22	7.22	7.74
EBIT	$= \dfrac{1,950,000}{270,000}$	$= \dfrac{1,462,500}{202,500}$	$= \dfrac{1,567,500}{202,500}$
Interest payments			
Gross profit margin	0.25	0.25	0.26
Gross profit	$= \dfrac{3,000,000}{12,000,000}$	$= \dfrac{2,250,000}{9,000,000}$	$= \dfrac{2,340,000}{9,000,000}$
Sales			
Operating profit margin	0.16	0.16	0.17
Operating profit	$= \dfrac{1,950,000}{12,000,000}$	$= \dfrac{1,462,500}{9,000,000}$	$= \dfrac{1,567,500}{9,000,000}$
Sales			
Net profit margin	0.10	0.10	0.08
Net income	$= \dfrac{1,180,000}{12,000,000}$	$= \dfrac{885,000}{9,000,000}$	$= \dfrac{745,000}{9,000,000}$
Sales			
Receivables turnover	13.33	12.50	12.50
Sales	$= \dfrac{12,000,000}{900,000}$	$= \dfrac{9,000,000}{720,000}$	$= \dfrac{9,000,000}{720,000}$
Accounts receivable			
Inventory turnover	7.50	7.03	7.50
Cost of goods sold	$= \dfrac{9,000,000}{1,200,000}$	$= \dfrac{6,750,000}{960,000}$	$= \dfrac{6,660,000}{888,000}$
Inventory			
Fixed asset turnover	4.44	4.17	4.76

(continued)

(Continued)

Canadaco's Functional Currency Is:		C$	Local Currency (C$) Current Rate (€)	Parent's Currency (€) Temporal (€)
Sales	=	12,000,000	= 9,000,000	= 9,000,000
Property & equipment (net)		2,700,000	2,160,000	1,890,000
Return on assets		0.20	0.19	0.17
Net income	=	1,180,000	= 885,000	= 745,000
Total assets		5,780,000	4,624,000	4,282,000
Return on equity		0.51	0.47	0.49
Net income	=	1,180,000	= 885,000	= 745,000
Total equity		2,330,000	1,864,000	1,522,000

Comparing the current rate method (€) and temporal method (€) columns in the above table shows that financial ratios calculated from Canadaco's translated financial statements (in €) differ significantly depending on which method of translation is used. Of the ratios presented, only receivables turnover is the same under both translation methods. This is the only ratio presented in which there is no difference in the type of exchange rate used to translate the items that comprise the numerator and the denominator. Sales are translated at the average exchange rate and receivables are translated at the current exchange rate under both methods. For each of the other ratios, at least one of the items included in either the numerator or the denominator is translated at a different type of rate (current, average, or historical) under the temporal method than under the current rate method. For example, the current ratio has a different value under the two translation methods because inventory is translated at the current exchange rate under the current rate method and at the historical exchange rate under the temporal method. In this case, because the euro/Canadian dollar exchange rate on December 31, 20X1 (€0.80) is higher than the historical exchange rate when the inventory was acquired (€0.74), the current ratio is larger under the current rate method of translation.

Comparing the ratios in the Canadian dollar and current rate method (euro) columns of the above table shows that many of the underlying relationships that exist in Canadaco's Canadian dollar financial statements are preserved when the current rate method of translation is used (i.e., the ratio calculated from the Canadian dollar and euro translated amounts is the same). The current ratio, the leverage ratios (debt-to-assets and debt-to-equity ratios), the interest coverage ratio, and the profit margins (gross profit margin, operating profit margin, and net profit margin) are the same in the Canadian dollar and current rate method (euro) columns of the above table. This result occurs because each of the ratios is calculated using information from either the balance sheet or the income statement, but not both. Those ratios that compare amounts from the balance sheet with amounts from the income statement (e.g., turnover and return ratios) are different. In this particular case, each of the turnover and return ratios is larger when calculated from the Canadian dollar amounts than when calculated using the current rate (euro) amounts. The underlying Canadian dollar relationships are distorted when translated using the current rate method because the balance sheet amounts are translated using the current exchange rate while revenues and expenses are translated using the average exchange rate. (These distortions would not occur if revenues and expenses also were translated at the current exchange rate.)

Comparing the ratios in the Canadian dollar and temporal method (euro) columns of the table shows that translation using the temporal method distorts all of the underlying relationships that exist in the Canadian dollar financial statements, except inventory turnover. Moreover, it is not possible to generalize the direction of the distortion across ratios. In Canadaco's case, using the temporal method results in a larger gross profit margin and operating profit margin but a smaller net profit margin as compared with the values of these ratios calculated from the original Canadian dollar amounts. Similarly, receivables turnover is smaller, inventory turnover is the same, and fixed asset turnover is larger when calculated from the translated amounts.

In translating Canadaco's Canadian dollar financial statements into euro, the temporal method results in a smaller amount of net income than the current rate method only because IFRS and US GAAP require the resulting translation loss to be included in net income when the temporal method is used. The translation loss arises because the Canadian dollar strengthened against the euro and Canadaco has a larger amount of liabilities translated at the current exchange rate (monetary liabilities) than it has assets translated at the current exchange rate (monetary assets). If Canadaco had a net monetary asset exposure (i.e., if monetary assets exceeded monetary liabilities), a translation gain would arise and net income under the temporal method (including the translation gain) would be greater than under the current rate method. Example 5 demonstrates how different types of balance sheet exposure under the temporal method can affect translated net income.

EXAMPLE 5   Effects of Different Balance Sheet Exposures under the Temporal Method *(Canadaco's functional currency is the parent's functional currency)*

Canadaco begins operations on January 1, 20X1, with cash of C$1,500,000 and property and equipment of C$3,000,000. In Case A, Canadaco finances the acquisition of property and equipment with a long-term note payable and begins operations with net monetary liabilities of C$1,500,000 (C$3,000,000 long-term note payable less C$1,500,000 cash). In Case B, Canadaco finances the acquisition of property and equipment with capital stock and begins operations with net monetary assets of C$1,500,000. To isolate the effect that balance sheet exposure has on net income under the temporal method, assume that Canadaco continues to have C$270,000 in interest expense in Case B, even though there is no debt financing. This assumption is inconsistent with reality, but it allows us to more clearly see the effect of balance sheet exposure on net income. The only difference between Case A and Case B is the net monetary asset/liability position of the company, as shown in the following table:

Canadaco Balance Sheet, January 1, 20X1

	Case A	Case B
Assets		
Cash	C$1,500,000	C$1,500,000
Property and equipment	3,000,000	3,000,000
	C$4,500,000	C$4,500,000

(continued)

(Continued)

	Case A	Case B
Liabilities and Equity		
Long-term note payable	C$3,000,000	C$0
Capital stock	1,500,000	4,500,000
	C$4,500,000	C$4,500,000

Canadaco purchases and sells inventory in 20X1, generating net income of C$1,180,000, out of which dividends of C$350,000 are paid. The company has total assets of C$5,780,000 as of December 31, 20X1. Canadaco's functional currency is determined to be the euro (the parent's presentation currency), and the company's Canadian dollar financial statements are translated into euro using the temporal method. Relevant exchange rates are as follows:

Date	€ per C$
January 1, 20X1	0.70
Average, 20X1	0.75
Weighted-average rate when inventory was acquired	0.74
December 1, 20X1 when dividends were declared	0.78
December 31, 20X1	0.80

What effect does the nature of Canadaco's net monetary asset or liability position have on the euro translated amounts?

Solution: Translation of Canadaco's December 31, 20X1 balance sheet under the temporal method in Case A and Case B is shown in the following table:

Canadaco Balance Sheet on December 31, 20X1 under the Temporal Method

	Case A: Net Monetary Liabilities			Case B: Net Monetary Assets		
	C$	Exch. Rate	€	C$	Exch. Rate	€
Assets						
Cash	980,000	0.80 C	784,000	980,000	0.80 C	784,000
Accounts receivable	900,000	0.80 C	720,000	900,000	0.80 C	720,000
Inventory	1,200,000	0.74 H	888,000	1,200,000	0.74 H	888,000
Total current assets	3,080,000		2,392,000	3,080,000		2,392,000
Property and equipment	3,000,000	0.70 H	2,100,000	3,000,000	0.70 H	2,100,000
Less: accum. deprec.	(300,000)	0.70 H	(210,000)	(300,000)	0.70 H	(210,000)
Total assets	5,780,000		4,282,000	5,780,000		4,282,000
Liabilities and Equity						
Accounts payable	450,000	0.80 C	360,000	450,000	0.80 C	360,000
Total current liabilities	450,000		360,000	450,000		360,000
Long-term notes payable	3,000,000	0.80 C	2,400,000	0		0
Total liabilities	3,450,000		2,760,000	450,000		360,000

(Continued)

	Case A: Net Monetary Liabilities			Case B: Net Monetary Assets		
	C$	Exch. Rate	€	C$	Exch. Rate	€
Capital stock	1,500,000	0.70 H	1,050,000	4,500,000	0.70 H	3,150,000
Retained earnings	830,000		472,000	830,000		772,000
Total	5,780,000		4,282,000	5,780,000		4,282,000

Note: C = current exchange rate; A = average-for-the-year exchange rate; H = historical exchange rate.

To keep the balance sheet in balance, retained earnings must be €472,000 in Case A (net monetary liability exposure) and €772,000 in Case B (net monetary asset exposure). The difference in retained earnings of €300,000 is equal to the translation loss that results from holding a Canadian dollar–denominated note payable during a period in which the Canadian dollar strengthens against the euro. This difference is determined by multiplying the amount of long-term note payable in Case A by the change in exchange rate during the year [C$3,000,000 × (€0.80 − €0.70) = €300,000]. Notes payable are exposed to foreign exchange risk under the temporal method, whereas capital stock is not. Canadaco could avoid the €300,000 translation loss related to long-term debt by financing the acquisition of property and equipment with equity rather than debt.

Translation of Canadaco's 20X1 income statement and statement of retained earnings under the temporal method for Case A and Case B is shown in the following table:

Canadaco Income Statement and Statement of Retained Earnings for 20X1 under the Temporal Method

	Case A: Net Monetary Liabilities			Case B: Net Monetary Assets		
	C$	Exch. Rate	€	C$	Exch. Rate	€
Sales	12,000,000	0.75 A	9,000,000	12,000,000	0.75 A	9,000,000
Cost of goods sold	(9,000,000)	0.74 H	(6,660,000)	(9,000,000)	0.74 H	(6,660,000)
Selling expenses	(750,000)	0.75 A	(562,500)	(750,000)	0.75 A	(562,500)
Depreciation expense	(300,000)	0.70 H	(210,000)	(300,000)	0.70 H	(210,000)
Interest expense	(270,000)	0.75 A	(202,500)	(270,000)	0.75 A	(202,500)
Income tax	(500,000)	0.75 A	(375,000)	(500,000)	0.75 A	(375,000)
Income before translation gain (loss)	1,180,000		990,000	1,180,000		990,000
Translation gain (loss)	N/A		(245,000)	N/A		55,000
Net income	1,180,000		745,000	1,180,000		1,045,000
Less: Dividends on December 1, 20X1	(350,000)	0.78 H	(273,000)	(350,000)	0.78 H	(273,000)
Retained earnings on December 31, 20X1	830,000		472,000	830,000		772,000

Note: C = current exchange rate; A = average-for-the-year exchange rate; H = historical exchange rate.

Income before translation gain (loss) is the same in both cases. To obtain the amount of retained earnings needed to keep the balance sheet in balance, a translation loss of €245,000 must be subtracted from net income in Case A (net monetary liabilities), whereas a translation gain of €55,000 must be added to net income in Case B (net monetary assets). The difference in net income between the two cases is €300,000, which equals the translation loss related to the long-term note payable.

When using the temporal method, companies can manage their exposure to translation gain (loss) more easily than when using the current rate method. If a company can manage the balance sheet of a foreign subsidiary such that monetary assets equal monetary liabilities, no balance sheet exposure exists. Elimination of balance sheet exposure under the current rate method occurs only when total assets equal total liabilities. This equality is difficult to achieve because it requires the foreign subsidiary to have no stockholders' equity.

For Canadaco, in 20X1, applying the current rate method results in larger euro amounts of total assets and total equity being reported in the consolidated financial statements than would result from applying the temporal method. The direction of these differences between the two translation methods is determined by the direction of change in the exchange rate between the Canadian dollar and the euro. For example, total exposed assets are greater under the current rate method because all assets are translated at the current exchange rate. The current exchange rate at December 31, 20X1 is greater than the exchange rates that existed when the non-monetary assets were acquired, which is the translation rate for these assets under the temporal method. Therefore, the current rate method results in a larger amount of total assets because the Canadian dollar strengthened against the euro. The current rate method would result in a smaller amount of total assets than the temporal method if the Canadian dollar had weakened against the euro.

Applying the current rate method also results in a much larger amount of stockholders' equity than the temporal method. A positive translation adjustment arises under the current rate method, which is included in equity, whereas a translation loss reduces total equity (through retained earnings) under the temporal method.

Example 6 shows the effect that the direction of change in the exchange rate has on the translated amounts. Canadaco's Canadian dollar financial statements are translated into euro, first assuming no change in the exchange rate during 20X1, and then assuming the Canadian dollar strengthens and weakens against the euro. Using the current rate method to translate the foreign currency financial statements into the parent's presentation currency, the foreign currency strengthening increases the revenues, income, assets, liabilities, and total equity reported on the parent company's consolidated financial statements. Likewise, smaller amounts of revenues, income, assets, liabilities, and total equity will be reported if the foreign currency weakens against the parent's presentation currency.

When the temporal method is used to translate foreign currency financial statements, foreign currency strengthening still increases revenues, assets, and liabilities reported in the parent's consolidated financial statements. Net income and stockholders' equity, however, translate into smaller amounts (assuming that the foreign subsidiary has a net monetary liability position) because of the translation loss. The opposite results are obtained when the foreign currency weakens against the parent's presentation currency.

EXAMPLE 6   Effect of Direction of Change in the Exchange Rate on Translated Amounts

Canadaco's Canadian dollar (C$) financial statements are translated into euro (€) under three scenarios: (1) the Canadian dollar remains stable against the euro, (2) the Canadian dollar strengthens against the euro, and (3) the Canadian dollar weakens against the euro. Relevant exchange rates are as follows:

	€ per C$		
Date	Stable	Strengthens	Weakens
January 1, 20X1	0.70	0.70	0.70
Average, 20X1	0.70	0.75	0.65
Weighted-average rate when inventory was acquired	0.70	0.74	0.66
Rate when dividends were declared	0.70	0.78	0.62
December 31, 20X1	0.70	0.80	0.60

What amounts will be reported on the parent's consolidated financial statements under the three different exchange rate assumptions if Canadaco's Canadian dollar financial statements are translated using the:

1. current rate method?
2. temporal method?

Solution to 1: Current Rate Method: Using the current rate method, Canadaco's Canadian dollar financial statements would be translated into euro as follows under the three different exchange rate assumptions:

Canadaco Income Statement and Statement of Retained Earnings for 20X1 under the Current Rate Method

		C$ Stable		C$ Strengthens		C$ Weakens	
	C$	Exch. Rate	€	Exch. Rate	€	Exch. Rate	€
Sales	12,000,000	0.70	8,400,000	0.75 A	9,000,000	0.65 A	7,800,000
Cost of goods sold	(9,000,000)	0.70	(6,300,000)	0.75 A	(6,750,000)	0.65 A	(5,850,000)
Selling expenses	(750,000)	0.70	(525,000)	0.75 A	(562,500)	0.65 A	(487,500)
Deprec. expense	(300,000)	0.70	(210,000)	0.75 A	(225,000)	0.65 A	(195,000)
Interest expense	(270,000)	0.70	(189,000)	0.75 A	(202,500)	0.65 A	(175,500)
Income tax	(500,000)	0.70	(350,000)	0.75 A	(375,000)	0.65 A	(325,000)

(continued)

(Continued)

	C$	C$ Stable		C$ Strengthens		C$ Weakens	
		Exch. Rate	€	Exch. Rate	€	Exch. Rate	€
Net income	1,180,000		826,000		885,000		767,000
Less:							
Dividends	(350,000)	0.70	(245,000)	0.78 H	(273,000)	0.62 H	(217,000)
Retained earnings	830,000		581,000		612,000		550,000

Note: C = current (period-end) exchange rate; A = average-for-the-year exchange rate; H = historical exchange rate.

Compared with the translated amount of sales and net income under a stable Canadian dollar, a stronger Canadian dollar results in a larger amount of sales and net income being reported in the consolidated income statement. A weaker Canadian dollar results in a smaller amount of sales and net income being reported in consolidated net income.

Canadaco Balance Sheet on December 31, 20X1 under the Current Rate Method

	C$	C$ Stable		C$ Strengthens		C$ Weakens	
		Exch. Rate	€	Exch. Rate	€	Exch. Rate	€
Assets							
Cash	980,000	0.70	686,000	0.80 C	784,000	0.60 C	588,000
Accounts receivable	900,000	0.70	630,000	0.80 C	720,000	0.60 C	540,000
Inventory	1,200,000	0.70	840,000	0.80 C	960,000	0.60 C	720,000
Total current assets	3,080,000		2,156,000		2,464,000		1,848,000
Property and equipment	3,000,000	0.70	2,100,000	0.80 C	2,400,000	0.60 C	1,800,000
Less: accum. deprec.	(300,000)	0.70	(210,000)	0.80 C	(240,000)	0.60 C	(180,000)
Total assets	5,780,000		4,046,000		4,624,000		3,468,000
Liabilities and Equity							
Accounts payable	450,000	0.70	315,000	0.80 C	360,000	0.60 C	270,000
Total current liabilities	450,000		315,000		360,000		270,000
Long-term notes pay	3,000,000	0.70	2,100,000	0.80 C	2,400,000	0.60 C	1,800,000
Total liabilities	3,450,000		2,415,000		2,760,000		2,070,000

(Continued)

	C$	C$ Stable		C$ Strengthens		C$ Weakens	
		Exch. Rate	€	Exch. Rate	€	Exch. Rate	€
Capital stock	1,500,000	0.70	1,050,000	0.70 H	1,050,000	0.70 H	1,050,000
Retained earnings	830,000		581,000		612,000		550,000
Translation adjustment	N/A		0		202,000		(202,000)
Total equity	2,330,000		1,631,000		1,864,000		1,398,000
Total	5,780,000		4,046,000		4,624,000		3,468,000

Note: C = current (period-end) exchange rate; A = average-for-the-year exchange rate; H = historical exchange rate.

The translation adjustment is zero when the Canadian dollar remains stable for the year; it is positive when the Canadian dollar strengthens and negative when the Canadian dollar weakens. Compared with the amounts that would appear in the euro consolidated balance sheet under a stable Canadian dollar assumption, a stronger Canadian dollar results in a larger amount of assets, liabilities, and equity being reported on the consolidated balance sheet, and a weaker Canadian dollar results in a smaller amount of assets, liabilities, and equity being reported on the consolidated balance sheet.

Solution to 2:   Temporal Method: Using the temporal method, Canadaco's financial statements would be translated into euro as follows under the three different exchange rate scenarios:

Canadaco Balance Sheet on December 31, 20X1

		Temporal Method					
		C$ Stable		C$ Strengthens		C$ Weakens	
	C$	Exch. Rate	€	Exch. Rate	€	Exch. Rate	€
Assets							
Cash	980,000	0.70	686,000	0.80 C	784,000	0.60 C	588,000
Accounts receivable	900,000	0.70	630,000	0.80 C	720,000	0.60 C	540,000
Inventory	1,200,000	0.70	840,000	0.74 H	888,000	0.66 H	792,000
Total current assets	3,080,000		2,156,000		2,392,000		1,920,000
Property and equipment	3,000,000	0.70	2,100,000	0.70 H	2,100,000	0.70 H	2,100,000
Less: accum. deprec.	(300,000)	0.70	(210,000)	0.70 H	(210,000)	0.70 H	(210,000)
Total assets	5,780,000		4,046,000		4,282,000		3,810,000

(continued)

(Continued)

		Temporal Method					
		C$ Stable		C$ Strengthens		C$ Weakens	
	C$	Exch. Rate	€	Exch. Rate	€	Exch. Rate	€
Liabilities and Equity							
Accounts payable	450,000	0.70	315,000	0.80 C	360,000	0.60 C	270,000
Total current liabilities	450,000		315,000		360,000		270,000
Long-term notes pay	3,000,000	0.70	2,100,000	0.80 C	2,400,000	0.60 C	1,800,000
Total liabilities	3,450,000		2,415,000		2,760,000		2,070,000
Capital stock	1,500,000	0.70	1,050,000	0.70 H	1,050,000	0.70 H	1,050,000
Retained earnings	830,000		581,000		472,000		690,000
Total equity	2,330,000		1,631,000		1,522,000		1,740,000
Total	5,780,000		4,046,000		4,282,000		3,810,000

Note: C = current (period-end) exchange rate; A = average-for-the-year exchange rate; H = historical exchange rate.

Compared with the stable Canadian dollar scenario, a stronger Canadian dollar results in a larger amount of assets and liabilities but a smaller amount of equity reported on the consolidated balance sheet. A weaker Canadian dollar results in a smaller amount of assets and liabilities but a larger amount of equity reported on the consolidated balance sheet.

Canadaco Income Statement and Statement of Retained Earnings for 2008 under the Temporal Method

		C$ Stable		C$ Strengthens		C$ Weakens	
	C$	Exch. Rate	€	Exch. Rate	€	Exch. Rate	€
Sales	12,000,000	0.70	8,400,000	0.75 A	9,000,000	0.65 A	7,800,000
Cost of sales	(9,000,000)	0.70	(6,300,000)	0.74 H	(6,660,000)	0.66 H	(5,940,000)
Selling expenses	(750,000)	0.70	(525,000)	0.75 A	(562,500)	0.65 A	(487,500)
Depreciation expense	(300,000)	0.70	(210,000)	0.70 H	(210,000)	0.70 H	(210,000)

(Continued)

	C$	C$ Stable		C$ Strengthens		C$ Weakens	
		Exch. Rate	€	Exch. Rate	€	Exch. Rate	€
Interest expense	(270,000)	0.70	(189,000)	0.75 A	(202,500)	0.65 A	(175,500)
Income tax	(500,000)	0.70	(350,000)	0.75 A	(375,000)	0.65 A	(325,000)
Income before translation gain (loss)	1,180,000		826,000		990,000		662,000
Translation gain (loss)	N/A		0		(245,000)		245,000
Net income	1,180,000		826,000		745,000		907,000
Less: Dividends	(350,000)	0.70	(245,000)	0.78 H	(273,000)	0.62 H	(217,000)
Retained earnings	830,000		581,000		472,000		690,000

Note: C = current (period-end) exchange rate; A = average-for-the-year exchange rate; H = historical exchange rate.

No translation gain or loss exists when the Canadian dollar remains stable during the year. Because the subsidiary has a net monetary liability exposure to changes in the exchange rate, a stronger Canadian dollar results in a translation loss and a weaker Canadian dollar results in a translation gain. Compared with a stable Canadian dollar, a stronger Canadian dollar results in a larger amount of sales and a smaller amount of net income reported on the consolidated income statement. This difference in direction results from the translation loss that is included in net income. (As demonstrated in Example 5, a translation gain would have resulted if the subsidiary had a net monetary asset exposure.) A weaker Canadian dollar results in a smaller amount of sales but a larger amount of net income than if the Canadian dollar had remained stable.

Exhibit 5 summarizes the relationships illustrated in Examples 5 and 6, focusing on the typical effect that a strengthening or weakening of the foreign currency has on financial statement amounts compared with what the amounts would be if the foreign currency were to remain stable.

EXHIBIT 5   Effect of Currency Exchange Rate Movement on Financial Statements

	Temporal Method, Net Monetary Liability Exposure	Temporal Method, Net Monetary Asset Exposure	Current Rate Method
Foreign currency strengthens relative to parent's presentation currency	↑ Revenues ↑ Assets ↑ Liabilities ↓ Net income ↓ Shareholders' equity Translation loss	↑ Revenues ↑ Assets ↑ Liabilities ↑ Net income ↑ Shareholders' equity Translation gain	↑ Revenues ↑ Assets ↑ Liabilities ↑ Net income ↑ Shareholders' equity Positive translation adjustment
Foreign currency weakens relative to parent's presentation currency	↓ Revenues ↓ Assets ↓ Liabilities ↑ Net income ↑ Shareholders' equity Translation gain	↓ Revenues ↓ Assets ↓ Liabilities ↓ Net income ↓ Shareholders' equity Translation loss	↓ Revenues ↓ Assets ↓ Liabilities ↓ Net income ↓ Shareholders' equity Negative translation adjustment

3.5. Translation when a Foreign Subsidiary Operates in a Hyperinflationary Economy

As noted earlier, IFRS and US GAAP differ substantially in their approach to translating the foreign currency financial statements of foreign entities operating in the currency of a hyperinflationary economy. US GAAP simply require the foreign currency financial statements of such an entity to be translated as if the parent's currency is the functional currency (i.e., the temporal method must be used with the resulting translation gain or loss reported in net income). IFRS require the foreign currency financial statements first to be restated for inflation using the procedures of IAS 29, and then the inflation-adjusted financial statements are translated using the current exchange rate.

IAS 29 requires the following procedures in adjusting financial statements for inflation:

Balance Sheet

• Monetary assets and monetary liabilities are not restated because they are already expressed in terms of the monetary unit current at the balance sheet date. Monetary items consist of cash, receivables, and payables.
• Non-monetary assets and non-monetary liabilities are restated for changes in the general purchasing power of the monetary unit. Most non-monetary items are carried at historical cost. In these cases, the restated cost is determined by applying to the historical cost the change in the general price index from the date of acquisition to the balance sheet date. Some non-monetary items are carried at revalued amounts; for example, property, plant, and equipment revalued according to the allowed alternative treatment in IAS 16, "Property, Plant and Equipment." These items are restated from the date of revaluation.
• All components of stockholders' equity are restated by applying the change in the general price level from the beginning of the period or, if later, from the date of contribution to the balance sheet date.

Income Statement

- All income statement items are restated by applying the change in the general price index from the dates when the items were originally recorded to the balance sheet date.
- The net gain or loss in purchasing power that arises from holding monetary assets and monetary liabilities during a period of inflation is included in net income.

The procedures for adjusting financial statements for inflation are similar in concept to the procedures followed when using the temporal method for translation. By restating non-monetary assets and liabilities along with stockholders' equity in terms of the general price level at the balance sheet date, these items are carried at their historical amount of purchasing power. Only the monetary items, which are not restated for inflation, are exposed to inflation risk. The effect of that exposure is reflected through the purchasing power gain or loss on the net monetary asset or liability position.

Holding cash and receivables during a period of inflation results in a **purchasing power loss**, whereas holding payables during inflation results in a **purchasing power gain**. This relationship can be demonstrated through the following examples.

Assume that the general price index (GPI) on January 1, 20X1 is 100; that is, a representative basket of goods and services can be purchased on that date for $100. At the end of 20X1, the same basket of goods and services costs $120; thus, the country has experienced an inflation rate of 20% [($120 – $100) ÷ $100]. Cash of $100 can be used to acquire one basket of goods on January 1, 20X1. One year later, however, when the GPI stands at 120, the same $100 in cash can now purchase only 83.3% of a basket of goods and services. At the end of 20X1, it now takes $120 to purchase the same amount as $100 could purchase at the beginning of the year. The difference between the amount of cash needed to purchase one market basket at year end ($120) and the amount actually held ($100) results in a purchasing power loss of $20 from holding cash of $100 during the year.

Borrowing money during a period of inflation increases purchasing power. Assume that a company expects to receive $120 in cash at the end of 20X1. If it waits until the cash is received, the company will be able to purchase exactly 1.0 basket of goods and services when the GPI stands at 120. If instead, the company borrows $120 on January 1, 20X1 when the GPI is 100, it can acquire 1.2 baskets of goods and services. This transaction results in a purchasing power gain of $20. Of course, there is an interest cost associated with the borrowing that offsets a portion of this gain.

A net purchasing power gain will arise when a company holds a greater amount of monetary liabilities than monetary assets, and a net purchasing power loss will result when the opposite situation exists. As such, purchasing power gains and losses are analogous to the translation gains and losses that arise when the currency is weakening in value and the temporal method of translation is applied.

Although the procedures required by IFRS and US GAAP for translating the foreign currency financial statements in high-inflation countries are fundamentally different, the results, in a rare occurrence, can be very similar. Indeed, if the exchange rate between two currencies changes by exactly the same percentage as the change in the general price index in the highly inflationary country, then the two methodologies produce the same results. Example 7 demonstrates this scenario.

EXAMPLE 7   Translation of Foreign Currency Financial Statements of a Foreign Entity Operating in a High Inflation Country

ABC Company formed a subsidiary in a foreign country on January 1, 20X1, through a combination of debt and equity financing. The foreign subsidiary acquired land on January 1, 20X1, which it rents to a local farmer. The foreign subsidiary's financial statements for its first year of operations, in foreign currency units (FC), are as follows:

Foreign Subsidiary Income Statement

(in FC)	20X1
Rent revenue	1,000
Interest expense	(250)
Net income	750

Foreign Subsidiary Balance Sheets

(in FC)	Jan 1, 20X1	Dec 31, 20X1
Cash	1,000	1,750
Land	9,000	9,000
Total	10,000	10,750
Note payable (5%)	5,000	5,000
Capital stock	5,000	5,000
Retained earnings	0	750
Total	10,000	10,750

The foreign country experienced significant inflation in 20X1, especially in the second half of the year. The general price index during the year was as follows:

January 1, 20X1	100
Average, 20X1	125
December 31, 20X1	200

The inflation rate in 20X1 was 100%, and the foreign country clearly meets the definition of a highly inflationary economy.

As a result of the high inflation rate in the foreign country, the FC weakened substantially during the year relative to other currencies. Relevant exchange rates between ABC's presentation currency (US dollars) and the FC during 20X1 were as follows:

	US$ per FC
January 1, 20X1	1.00
Average, 20X1	0.80
December 31, 20X1	0.50

What amounts will ABC Company include in its consolidated financial statements for the year ended December 31, 20X1 related to this foreign subsidiary?

Solution: Assuming that ABC Company wishes to prepare its consolidated financial statements in accordance with IFRS, the foreign subsidiary's 20X1 financial statements will be restated for local inflation and then translated into ABC's presentation currency using the current exchange rate as follows:

	FC	Restatement Factor	Inflation-Adjusted FC	Exch. Rate	US$
Cash	1,750	200/200	1,750	0.50	875
Land	9,000	200/100	18,000	0.50	9,000
Total	10,750		19,750		9,875
Note payable	5,000	200/200	5,000	0.50	2,500
Capital stock	5,000	200/100	10,000	0.50	5,000
Retained earnings	750		4,750	0.50	2,375
Total	10,750		19,750		9,875
Revenues	1,000	200/125	1,600	0.50	800
Interest expense	(250)	200/125	(400)	0.50	(200)
Subtotal	750		1,200		600
Purchasing power gain/loss			3,550	0.50	1,775
Net income			4,750		2,375

All financial statement items are restated to the GPI at December 31, 20X1. The net purchasing power gain of FC3,550 can be explained as follows:

Gain from holding note payable	FC5,000 × (200 − 100)/100 =	FC5,000
Loss from holding beginning balance in cash	−1,000 × (200 − 100)/100 =	(1,000)
Loss from increase in cash during the year	−750 × (200 − 125)/125 =	(450)
Net purchasing power gain (loss)		FC3,550

Note that all inflation-adjusted FC amounts are translated at the current exchange rate, and thus no translation adjustment is needed.

Now assume alternatively that ABC Company wishes to comply with US GAAP in preparing its consolidated financial statements. In that case, the foreign subsidiary's FC financial statements are translated into US dollars using the temporal method, with the resulting translation gain/loss reported in net income, as follows:

	FC	Exch. Rate	US$
Cash	1,750	0.50 C	875
Land	9,000	1.00 H	9,000
Total	10,750		9,875

(continued)

(Continued)

	FC	Exch. Rate	US$
Note payable	5,000	0.50 C	2,500
Capital stock	5,000	1.00 H	5,000
Retained earnings	750		2,375
Total	10,750		9,875
Revenues	1,000	0.80 A	800
Interest expense	(250)	0.80 A	(200)
Subtotal	750		600
Translation gain*			1,775
Net income			2,375

* The dividend is US$0 and the increase in retained earnings is US$2,375 (from the balance sheet); so, net income is US$2,375, and thus the translation gain is US$1,775.

Note: C = current (period-end) exchange rate; A = average-for-the-year exchange rate; H = historical exchange rate

Application of the temporal method as required by US GAAP in this situation results in exactly the same US dollar amounts as were obtained under the restate/translate approach required by IFRS. The equivalence of results under the two approaches exists because of the exact one-to-one inverse relationship between the change in the foreign country's GPI and the change in the dollar value of the FC, as predicted by the theory of purchasing power parity. The GPI doubled and the FC lost half its purchasing power, which caused the FC to lose half its value in dollar terms. To the extent that this relationship does not hold, and it rarely ever does, the two different methodologies will generate different translated amounts. For example, if the December 31, 20X1 exchange rate had adjusted to only US$0.60 per FC1 (rather than US$0.50 per FC1), then translated net income would have been US$2,050 under US GAAP and US$2,850 under IFRS.

3.6. Companies Use Both Translation Methods at the Same Time

Under both IFRS and US GAAP, a multinational corporation may need to use both the current rate and the temporal methods of translation at a single point in time. This situation will apply when some foreign subsidiaries have a foreign currency as their functional currency (and therefore are translated using the current rate method) and other foreign subsidiaries have the parent's currency as their functional currency (and therefore are translated using the temporal method). As a result, a multinational corporation's consolidated financial statements can reflect simultaneously both a net translation gain or loss that is included in the determination of net income (from foreign subsidiaries translated using the temporal method) and a separate cumulative translation adjustment reported on the balance sheet in stockholders' equity (from foreign subsidiaries translated using the current rate method).

Exxon Mobil Corporation is an example of a company that has a mixture of foreign currency and parent currency functional currency subsidiaries, as evidenced by the following excerpt from its 2011 annual report, Note 1 Summary of Accounting Policies:

Foreign Currency Translation. The Corporation selects the functional reporting currency for its international subsidiaries based on the currency of the primary economic environment in which each subsidiary operates. Downstream and Chemical operations primarily use the local currency. However, the US dollar is used in countries with a history of high inflation (primarily in Latin America) and Singapore, which predominantly sells into the US dollar export market. Upstream operations which are relatively self-contained and integrated within a particular country, such as Canada, the United Kingdom, Norway and continental Europe, use the local currency. Some upstream operations, primarily in Asia and Africa, use the US dollar because they predominantly sell crude and natural gas production into US dollar–denominated markets. For all operations, gains or losses from remeasuring foreign currency transactions into the functional currency are included in income.

Because of the judgment involved in determining the functional currency of foreign operations, two companies operating in the same industry might apply this judgment differently. For example, although Exxon Mobil has identified the local currency as the functional currency for many of its international subsidiaries, Chevron Corporation has designated the US dollar as the functional currency for substantially all of its overseas operations, as indicated in its 2011 annual report, Note 1 Summary of Significant Accounting Policies:

Currency Translation. The US dollar is the functional currency for substantially all of the company's consolidated operations and those of its equity affiliates. For those operations, all gains and losses from currency remeasurement are included in current period income. The cumulative translation effects for those few entities, both consolidated and affiliated, using functional currencies other than the US dollar are included in "Currency translation adjustment" on the Consolidated Statement of Equity.

Evaluating net income reported by Exxon Mobil against net income reported by Chevron presents a comparability problem. This problem can be partially resolved by adding the translation adjustments reported in stockholders' equity to net income for both companies. The feasibility of this solution depends on the level of detail disclosed by multinational corporations with respect to the translation of foreign currency financial statements.

3.7. Disclosures Related to Translation Methods

Both IFRS and US GAAP require two types of disclosures related to foreign currency translation:

1. the amount of exchange differences recognized in net income, and
2. the amount of cumulative translation adjustment classified in a separate component of equity, along with a reconciliation of the amount of cumulative translation adjustment at the beginning and end of the period.

US GAAP also specifically require disclosure of the amount of translation adjustment transferred from stockholders' equity and included in current net income as a result of the disposal of a foreign entity.

The amount of exchange differences recognized in net income consists of

- foreign currency *transaction* gains and losses, and
- *translation* gains and losses resulting from application of the temporal method.

Neither IFRS nor US GAAP require disclosure of the two separate amounts that constitute the total exchange difference recognized in net income, and most companies do not provide disclosure at that level of detail. However, BASF AG (shown earlier in Exhibit 1) is an exception. Note 6 in BASF's annual report separately discloses gains from foreign currency and hedging transactions and gains from translation of financial statements, both of which are included in the line item "Other Operating Income" on the income statement, as shown below:

6 Other Operating Income

Million €	2011	2010
Reversal and adjustment of provisions	170	244
Revenue from miscellaneous revenue-generating activities	207	142
Income from foreign currency and hedging transactions	170	136
Income from the translation of financial statements in foreign currencies	42	76
Gains on the disposal of property, plant and equipment and divestitures	666	101
Reversals of impairments of property, plant and equipment	—	40
Gains on the reversal of allowance for doubtful business-related receivables	77	36
Other	676	365
	2,008	1,140

The company provides a similar level of detail in Note 7 related to "Other Operating Expenses."

Disclosures related to foreign currency translation are commonly found in both the MD&A and the Notes to Financial Statements sections of an annual report. Example 8 uses the foreign currency translation–related disclosures made in 2011 by Yahoo! Inc.

EXAMPLE 8 Disclosures Related to Foreign Currency Translation: Yahoo! Inc. 2011 Annual Report

Yahoo! Inc. is a US-based digital media company that reports in US dollars and prepares financial statements in accordance with US GAAP.

The stockholders' equity section of Yahoo!'s consolidated balance sheets includes the following line items:

	December 31	
(in thousands)	2010	2011
Common stock	$1,306	$1,242
Additional paid-in capital	10,109,913	9,825,899
Treasury stock	—	(416,237)
Retained earnings	1,942,656	2,432,294
Accumulated other comprehensive income (loss)	504,254	697,869
Total Yahoo! Inc. stockholders' equity	12,558,129	12,541,067

The consolidated statement of stockholders' equity provides detail on the components comprising "Accumulated other comprehensive income." The relevant portion of that statement appears below:

	Years Ended December 31		
	2009	2010	2011
Accumulated other comprehensive income			
Balance, beginning of year	120,276	369,236	504,254
Net change in unrealized gains/losses on available-for-sale securities, net of tax	(1,936)	3,813	(16,272)
Foreign currency translation adjustments, net of tax	250,896	131,205	209,887
Balance, end of year	369,236	504,254	697,869

Yahoo! reported the following net income in 2010 and 2011, as shown on the consolidated statement of income:

	2010	2011	% Change
Net income	$1,244,628	$1,062,699	–14.6%

Yahoo!'s disclosures for its three geographic segments are disclosed in a note to the financial statements. Revenue (excluding total acquisition costs) and direct segment operating costs are shown below:

	2009	2010	2011
Revenue ex-TAC by segment:			
Americas	3,656,752	3,467,850	3,142,879
EMEA	390,456	368,884	407,467
Asia Pacific	635,281	751,495	830,482
Total revenue ex-TAC	4,682,489	4,588,229	4,380,828
Direct costs by segment:			
Americas	620,690	568,017	560,016
EMEA	115,778	118,954	135,266
Asia Pacific	138,739	146,657	194,394

In the MD&A section of the 2011 annual report, Yahoo! describes the source of its translation exposure:

Translation Exposure

We are also exposed to foreign exchange rate fluctuations as we convert the financial statements of our foreign subsidiaries and our investments in equity interests into US dollars in consolidation. If there is a change in foreign currency exchange rates, the conversion of the foreign subsidiaries' financial statements into US dollars results in a gain or loss which is recorded as a component of accumulated other comprehensive income which is part of stockholders' equity.

Revenue ex-TAC (total acquisition costs) and related expenses generated from our international subsidiaries are generally denominated in the currencies of the local countries. The statements of income of our international operations are translated into US dollars at exchange rates indicative of market rates during each applicable period. To the extent the US dollar strengthens against foreign currencies, the translation of these foreign currency-denominated transactions results in reduced consolidated revenue and operating expenses. Conversely, our consolidated revenue and operating expenses will increase if the US dollar weakens against foreign currencies. Using the foreign currency exchange rates from the year ended December 31, 2010, revenue ex-TAC for the Americas segment for the year ended December 31, 2011 would have been lower than we reported by $6 million, revenue ex-TAC for the EMEA segment would have been lower than we reported by $16 million, and revenue ex-TAC for the Asia Pacific segment would have been lower than we reported by $59 million. Using the foreign currency exchange rates from the year ended December 31, 2010, direct costs for the Americas segment for the year ended December 31, 2011 would have been lower than we reported by $2 million, direct costs for the EMEA segment would have been lower than we reported by $5 million, and direct costs for the Asia Pacific segment would have been lower than we reported by $15 million.

Using the information above, address the following questions:

1. By how much did accumulated other comprehensive income change during the year ended December 31, 2011? Where can this information be found?
2. How much foreign currency translation adjustment was included in other comprehensive income for the year ended December 31, 2011? How does such an adjustment arise?
3. If foreign currency translation adjustment had been included in net income (rather than in other comprehensive income), how would the 2010/2011 change in income have been affected?
4. From what perspective does Yahoo! describe its foreign currency risk?
5. What percentage of total revenue ex-TAC was generated by the Asia-Pacific segment for the year ended December 31, 2011? What would this percentage have been if there had been no change in foreign currency exchange rates during the year?

Solutions:
1. Accumulated other comprehensive income increased by $193,615 thousand (from $504,254 thousand beginning balance to $697,869 thousand at the end of the year). This information can be found in two places: the stockholders' equity section of the balance sheet and the consolidated statement of stockholders' equity.
2. The amount of foreign currency translation adjustment included in other comprehensive income for 2011 was $209,887 thousand. The foreign currency translation adjustment arises from applying the current rate method to translate the foreign currency functional currency financial statements of foreign subsidiaries. Assuming that Yahoo!'s foreign subsidiaries have positive net assets, the positive translation

adjustment in 2011 results from a strengthening in foreign currencies (weakening in the US dollar).

3. If foreign currency translation adjustment had been included in net income (rather than other comprehensive income), the percentage decrease in reported net income from 2010 to 2011 of 14.6% would have been smaller (7.5%).

	2010	2011	% Change
Net income	$1,244,628	$1,062,699	−14.6%
Foreign currency translation adjustment	131,205	209,887	
	$1,375,833	$1,272,586	−7.5%

4. Yahoo! describes its foreign currency risk from the perspective of how the US dollar fluctuates against foreign currencies because the dollar is the reporting currency. If the US dollar strengthens, then foreign currencies must weaken, which will result in reduced revenues, expenses, and income from foreign operations.

5. The Asia-Pacific segment represented 19.0% of total revenue ex-TAC. Information from the MD&A disclosure can be used to determine that if there had been no change in foreign currency exchange rates during the year, the segment would have represented a slightly lower percentage of total revenue (17.9%).

	2011, as reported			2011, if no change in exchange rates	
Revenue ex-TAC by segment:					
Americas	3,142,879	71.7%	6,000	3,136,879	73.0%
EMEA	407,467	9.3%	16,000	391,467	9.1%
Asia Pacific	830,482	19.0%	59,000	771,482	17.9%
Total revenue ex-TAC	4,380,828	100.0%		4,299,828	100.0%

As noted in the previous section, because of the judgment involved in determining the functional currency of foreign operations, two companies operating in the same industry might use different predominant translation methods. As a result, income reported by these companies may not be directly comparable. Exxon Mobil Corporation and Chevron Corporation, both operating in the petroleum industry, are an example of two companies for which this is the case. Whereas Chevron has identified the US dollar as the functional currency for substantially all of its foreign subsidiaries, Exxon Mobil indicates that its downstream and chemical operations, as well as some of its upstream operations, primarily use the local currency as the functional currency. As a result, Chevron primarily uses the temporal method with translation gains and losses included in income, while Exxon Mobil uses the current rate method to a much greater extent, with the resulting translation adjustments excluded from income. To make the income of these two companies more comparable, an analyst can use the disclosures related to translation adjustments to include these as gains and losses in determining an adjusted amount of income. Example 9 demonstrates this process for Exxon Mobil and Chevron.

EXAMPLE 9   Comparing Net Income for Exxon Mobil Corporation
and Chevron Corporation

Exxon Mobil Corporation uses the current rate method to translate the foreign currency
financial statements of a substantial number of its foreign subsidiaries and includes the
resulting translation adjustments in the "Accumulated other non-owner changes in equity" line item in the stockholders' equity section of the consolidated balance sheet. Detail
on the items composing "Accumulated other non-owner changes in equity," including
"Foreign exchange translation adjustment," is provided in the consolidated statement of
shareholders' equity.

    Chevron Corporation uses the temporal method to translate the foreign currency
financial statements of substantially all of its foreign subsidiaries. For those few entities
using functional currencies other than the US dollar, however, the current rate method
is used and the resulting translation adjustments are included in the "Accumulated other
comprehensive loss" component of stockholders' equity. The consolidated statement of
stockholders' equity provides detail on the changes in the component of stockholders'
equity, including a "Currency translation adjustment."

    Combining net income from the income statement and the change in the cumu-
lative translation adjustment account from the statement of stockholders' equity, an
adjusted net income in which translation adjustments are treated as gains and losses can
be calculated for each company, as shown in the following table (amounts in millions
of US dollars):

Exxon Mobil	2011	2010	2009
Reported net income	42,206	31,398	19,658
Translation adjustment	(867)	1,034	3,629
Adjusted net income	41,339	32,432	23,287

Chevron	2011	2010	2009
Reported net income	27,008	19,136	10,563
Translation adjustment	17	6	60
Adjusted net income	27,025	19,142	10,623

    The direction, positive or negative, of the translation adjustment is the same for
both companies in 2009 and 2010 but not in 2011. Overall, Exxon Mobil has significantly larger translation adjustments than Chevron because Exxon Mobil designates
the local currency as functional currency for a substantially larger portion of its foreign
operations.

    A comparison of the relative amounts of net income generated by the two compa-
nies is different depending on whether reported net income or adjusted net income is
used. Exxon Mobil's reported net income in 2009 is 1.90 times larger than Chevron's,
whereas its adjusted net income is 2.2 times larger, as shown in the following table.

	2011	2010	2009
Exxon Mobil reported net income/ Chevron reported net income	1.6	1.6	1.9
Exxon Mobil adjusted net income/ Chevron adjusted net income	1.5	1.7	2.2

Including translation adjustments as gains and losses in the measurement of an adjusted net income provides a more comparable basis for evaluating the profitability of two companies that use different predominant translation methods. Bringing the translation adjustments into the calculation of adjusted net income still might not provide truly comparable measures, however, because of the varying effect that the different translation methods have on reported net income.

Some analysts believe that all non-owner changes in stockholders' equity, such as translation adjustments, should be included in the determination of net income. This approach is referred to as clean-surplus accounting, as opposed to dirty-surplus accounting, in which some income items are reported as part of stockholders' equity rather than as gains and losses on the income statement. One of the dirty-surplus items found in both IFRS and US GAAP financial statements is the translation adjustment that arises when a foreign currency is determined to be the functional currency of a foreign subsidiary. Disclosures made in accordance with IFRS and US GAAP provide analysts with the detail needed to calculate net income on a clean-surplus basis. In fact, both sets of standards now require companies to prepare a statement of comprehensive income in which unrealized gains and losses that have been deferred in stockholders' equity are included in a measure of comprehensive income.

4. MULTINATIONAL OPERATIONS AND A COMPANY'S EFFECTIVE TAX RATE

In general, multinational companies incur income taxes in the country in which the profit is earned. Transfer prices, the prices that related companies charge on intercompany transactions, affect the allocation of profit between the companies. An entity with operations in multiple countries with different tax rates could aim to set transfer prices such that a higher portion of its profit is allocated to lower tax rate jurisdictions. Countries have established various laws and practices to prevent aggressive transfer pricing practices. Transfer pricing has been defined as "the system of laws and practices used by countries to ensure that goods, services and intellectual property transferred between related companies are appropriately priced, based on market conditions, such that profits are correctly reflected in each jurisdiction."[5] Also, most countries are party to tax treaties that prevent double-taxation of corporate profits by granting a credit for taxes paid to another country.

Whether and when a company also pays income taxes in its home country depends on the specific tax regime. In the United States, for example, multinational companies are liable only for a residual tax on foreign income, after applying a credit for foreign taxes paid on that same income. The effect of the tax credit is that the multinational company owes taxes on the

---

[5]TP Analytics. http://www.tpanalytics.com.

foreign income only to the extent that the US corporate tax rate exceeds the foreign rate of tax on that income. In addition, much of the foreign income earned by US multinationals is not taxed until it is repatriated.[6]

An analyst can obtain information about the effect of multinational operations from companies' disclosure on effective tax rates. Accounting standards require companies to provide an explanation of the relationship between tax expense and accounting profit. The explanation is presented as a reconciliation between the average effective tax rate (tax expense divided by pretax accounting profits) and the relevant statutory rate. The purpose of this disclosure is to enable users of financial statements to understand whether the relationship between tax expense and accounting profit in a particular fiscal period is unusual and to understand the significant factors—including the effect of foreign taxes—that could affect that relationship in the future.[7] Changes in the effective tax rate impact of foreign taxes could be caused by changes in the applicable tax rates and/or changes in the mix of profits earned in different jurisdictions.

EXAMPLE 10

Below are excerpts from the effective tax rate reconciliation disclosures by two companies: Heineken N.V., a Dutch brewer, and Colgate Palmolive, a US consumer products company. Use the disclosures to answer the following questions:

1. Which company's home country has a lower statutory tax rate?
2. What was the impact of multinational operations on each company's 2011 effective tax rate?
3. Changes in the tax rate impact of multinational operations can often be explained by changes of profit mix between countries with higher or lower marginal tax rates. What do Heineken's disclosures suggest about the geographic mix of its 2011 profit?

Heineken N.V. Annual Report 2011
Notes to the consolidated financial statements
13. Income tax expense (excerpt)

Reconciliation of the effective tax rate

In millions of EUR	2011	2010
Profit before income tax	2,025	1,982
Share of net profit of associates and joint ventures and impairments thereof	(240)	(193)
Profit before income tax excluding share of profit of associates and joint ventures (inclusive impairments thereof)	**1,785**	1,789

[6] United States Government Accountability Office (GAO) Report GAO-08-950. *US Multinational Corporations: Effective Tax Rates Are Correlated with Where Income Is Reported.* August 2008.
[7] International Accounting Standard 12 *Income Taxes*, ¶84.

(Continued)

	%	2011	%	2010
Income tax using the Company's domestic tax rate	25.0	446	25.5	456
Effect of tax rates in foreign jurisdictions	3.5	62	1.9	34
Effect of non-deductible expenses	3.2	58	4	72
Effect of tax incentives and exempt income	(6.0)	−107	−8.2	−146
Recognition of previously unrecognized temporary differences	(0.5)	−9	−0.1	−2
Utilisation or recognition of previously unrecognized tax losses	(0.3)	−5	−1.2	−21
Unrecognized current year tax losses	1.0	18	0.8	15
Effect of changes in tax rate	0.1	1	0.2	3
Withholding taxes	1.5	26	1.4	25
Under/(over) provided in prior years	(1.5)	−27	−2.3	−42
Other reconciling items	0.1	2	0.5	9
	26.1	**465**	22.5	403

COLGATE-PALMOLIVE COMPANY Annual Report 2011
Notes to Consolidated Financial Statements
10. Income Taxes (excerpt)

The difference between the statutory US federal income tax rate and the Company's global effective tax rate as reflected in the Consolidated Statements of Income is as follows:

Percentage of income before income taxes	2011	2010	2009
Tax at United States statutory rate	35.0%	35.0%	35.0%
State income taxes, net of federal benefit	0.4	1.1	0.5
Earnings taxed at other than United States statutory rate	(1.7)	(4.6)	(2.5)
Venezuela hyperinflationary transition charge	—	2.8	—
Other, net	(1.1)	(1.7)	(0.8)
Effective tax rate	32.6%	32.6%	32.2%

Solution to 1: Heineken's home country tax rate (25.0% in 2011) is lower than Colgate Palmolive's home country tax rate (35.0%).

Solution to 2: The line item labeled "Effect of tax rates in foreign jurisdictions" indicates that multinational operations increased Heineken's effective tax rate by 3.5 percentage points. The line item labeled "Earnings taxed at other than United States statutory rate" indicates that multinational operations lowered Colgate Palmolive's effective tax rate by 1.7 percentage points in 2011.

Solution to 3: Multinational operations increased Heineken's effective tax rate by 3.5 percentage points in 2011 but only 1.9 percentage points in 2010. This greater impact in 2011 could indicate that Heineken's profit mix in 2011 shifted to countries with higher marginal tax rates. (The change could also indicate that the marginal tax rates increased in the countries in which Heineken earns profits.)

5. ADDITIONAL DISCLOSURES ON THE EFFECTS OF FOREIGN CURRENCY

We turn now to the question of how an analyst can use multinational companies' disclosures to better understand the effects of foreign currency.

5.1. Disclosures Related to Sales Growth

Companies often make important disclosures about foreign currency effect on sales growth in the MD&A. Additional disclosures are also often made in financial presentations to the analyst community.

For a multinational company, sales growth is driven not only by changes in volume and price but also by changes in the exchange rates between the reporting currency and the currency in which sales are made. Arguably, growth in sales that comes from changes in volume or price is more sustainable than growth in sales that comes from changes in exchange rates. Further, management arguably has greater control over growth in sales resulting from greater volume or higher price than from changes in exchange rates. Thus, an analyst will consider the foreign currency effect on sales growth both for forecasting future performance and for evaluating a management team's historical performance.

Companies often include disclosures about the effect of exchange rates on sales growth in the MD&A. Such disclosures may also appear in other financial reports, such as company presentations to investors or earnings announcements. Exhibit 6 provides an example of disclosure from the MD&A, and Example 11 illustrates even more detailed disclosure from a company's report to analysts.

EXHIBIT 6

General Mills' 2011 annual report includes the following disclosures about the components of net sales growth in its international segment. The first excerpt is from the MD&A, and the second is from a supplementary schedule reconciling non-GAAP measures. Although the overall effect on international net sales growth was minimal "flat," the geographic detail provided in the supplementary schedule shows that the effects varied widely by region.

Excerpt from MD&A

Components of International Net Sales Growth

	Fiscal 2011 vs. 2010	Fiscal 2010 vs. 2009
Contributions from volume growth[a]	6 pts	Flat
Net price realization and mix	1 pt	3 pts
Foreign currency exchange	Flat	1 pt
Net sales growth	7 pts	4 pts

[a]Measured in tons based on the stated weight of our product shipments.

Excerpt from Supplementary Schedule on Non-GAAP Measures

International Segment and Region Sales Growth Rates Excluding Impact of Foreign Exchange

	Fiscal Year 2011		
	Percentage Change in Net Sales as Reported	Impact of Foreign Currency Exchange	Percentage Change in Net Sales on Constant Currency Basis
Europe	5%	–2%	7%
Canada	8	5	3
Asia/Pacific	14	5	9
Latin America	–5	–16	11
Total International Segment	7%	Flat	7%

EXAMPLE 11

Use the information disclosed in Procter & Gamble Company's CAGNY [Consumer Analyst Group of New York] conference slides to answer the following questions:

1. Why does the company present "organic sales growth"?
2. On average, for the four quarters beginning October 2008 and ending September 2009, how did changes in foreign exchange rates affect P&G's reported sales growth?

The Procter & Gamble Company
2012 CAGNY CONFERENCE SLIDES
  Reg G Reconciliation of Non-GAAP measures
  In accordance with the SEC's Regulation G, the following provides definitions of the non-GAAP measures used in the earnings call and slides with the reconciliation to the most closely related GAAP measure.

1. *Organic Sales Growth:*
   Organic sales growth is a non-GAAP measure of sales growth excluding the impacts of acquisitions, divestitures and foreign exchange from year-over-year comparisons. We believe this provides investors with a more complete understanding of underlying sales trends by providing sales growth on a consistent basis. "Organic sales" is also one of the measures used to evaluate senior management and is a factor in

determining their at-risk compensation. The reconciliation of reported sales growth to organic sales is as follows:

Total P&G	Net Sales Growth	Foreign Exchange Impact	Acquisition/ Divestiture Impact	Organic Sales Growth
JAS 06	27%	–1%	–20%	6%
OND 06	8%	–3%	0%	5%
JFM07	8%	–2%	0%	6%
AMJ07	8%	–3%	0%	5%
JAS07	8%	–3%	0%	5%
OND07	9%	–5%	1%	5%
JFM08	9%	–5%	1%	5%
AMJ08	10%	–6%	1%	5%
JAS08	9%	–5%	1%	5%
Average–JAS 06–JAS 08	11%	–4%	–2%	5%
OND08	–3%	5%	0%	2%
JFM09	–8%	9%	0%	1%
AMJ09	–11%	9%	1%	–1%
JAS09	–6%	7%	1%	2%
Average–OND 08–JAS 09	–7%	8%	0%	1%
OND09	6%	–2%	1%	5%
JFM010	7%	–3%	0%	4%
AMJ010	5%	–1%	0%	4%
JAS010	2%	3%	–1%	4%
OND010	2%	2%	–1%	3%
JFM011	5%	–1%	0%	4%
AMJ011	10%	–5%	0%	5%
JAS011	9%	–5%	0%	4%
OND011	4%	0%	0%	4%
Average–OND 09–OND 11	5%	–1%	0%	4%
JFM 12 (Estimate)	0% to 2%	3%	0%	3% to 5%
AMJ 12(Estimate)	–1% to 2%	5% to 4%	0%	4% to 6%

Solution to 1: According to its disclosures, Procter & Gamble presents "organic sales growth" because the company believes it provides investors with a better understanding of underlying sales trends and because it is one of the measures used for management evaluation and compensation.

Solution to 2: The average effect of foreign exchange changes during the period was negative: Although organic sales grew by 1%, the company reported net sales growth of –7% as a result of a negative 8% foreign exchange effect. In other words, if no foreign exchange effect had occurred, reported sales growth and organic sales growth would have been equal, both at 1%.

5.2. Disclosures Related to Major Sources of Foreign Exchange Risk

Disclosures about the effects of currency fluctuations often include sensitivity analyses. For example, a company might describe the major sources of foreign exchange risk given its countries of operations and then disclose the profit impact of a given change in exchange rates.

Exhibit 7 includes two excerpts from the 2011 BMW AG annual report. The first excerpt, from the management report, describes the source of the company's currency risks and its approach to measuring and managing those risks. The second excerpt, from the additional disclosures section of the notes, presents the results of the company's sensitivity analysis.

EXHIBIT 7

Excerpts from 2011 BMW AG Annual Report

Excerpt from the management report describing the source of the company's currency risks and its approach to measuring and managing those risks:

"The sale of vehicles outside the euro zone gives rise to exchange risks. Three currencies (the Chinese renminbi, the US dollar and the British pound) accounted for approximately two-thirds of the BMW Group's foreign currency exposures in 2011. We employ cash-flow-at-risk models and scenario analyses to measure exchange rate risks. These tools provide information which serves as the basis for decision-making in the area of currency management.

"We manage currency risks both at a strategic (medium and long term) and at an operating level (short and medium term). In the medium and long term, foreign exchange risks are managed by "natural hedging", in other words by increasing the volume of purchases denominated in foreign currency or increasing the volume of local production. In this context, the expansion of the plant in Spartanburg, USA, and the new plant under construction in Tiexi* at the Shenyang site in China are helping to reduce foreign exchange risks in two major sales markets. For operating purposes (short and medium term), currency risks are hedged on the financial markets. Hedging transactions are entered into only with financial partners of good credit standing. Counterparty risk management procedures are carried out continuously to monitor the creditworthiness of those partners."

Excerpt, from the additional disclosures section of the notes, presenting the results of the company's sensitivity analysis risks:

"The BMW Group measures currency risk using a cash-flow-at-risk model. The starting point for analyzing currency risk with this model is the identification of forecast foreign currency transactions or "exposures". At the end of the reporting period, the principal exposures for the coming year were as follows:

in € million	31.12.2011	31.12.2010
Euro/Chinese Renminbi	7,114	6,256
Euro/US Dollar	4,281	3,888
Euro/British Pound	3,266	3,056
Euro/Japanese Yen	1,334	1,086

"In the next stage, these exposures are compared to all hedges that are in place. The net cash flow surplus represents an uncovered risk position. The cash-flow-at-risk approach involves allocating the impact of potential exchange rate fluctuations to operating cash flows on the basis of probability distributions. Volatilities and correlations serve as input factors to assess the relevant probability distributions.

(continued)

EXHIBIT 7   (Continued)

"The potential negative impact on earnings for the current period is computed on the basis of current market prices and exposures to a confidence level of 95% and a holding period of up to one year for each currency. Aggregation of these results creates a risk reduction effect due to correlations between the various portfolios.

"The following table shows the potential negative impact for the BMW Group—measured on the basis of the cash-flow-at-risk approach—attributable at the balance sheet date to unfavorable changes in exchange rates for the principal currencies."

in € million	12.31.2011	12.31.2011
Euro/Chinese Renminbi	180	265
Euro/US Dollar	121	103
Euro/British Pound	182	184
Euro/Japanese Yen	23	30

The level of detail varies in companies' disclosures about sensitivity of earnings to foreign currency fluctuations, with some companies providing information on the range of possible values of foreign exchange rates. An analyst can use sensitivity analysis disclosures in conjunction with his or her own forecast of exchange rates when developing forecasts of profit and cash flow. When detailed disclosures are provided, the analyst can explicitly incorporate foreign exchange impact. Alternatively, in the absence of detailed disclosures, the analyst can incorporate the sensitivity analysis when calibrating the downside risks to base-case profit and cash flow forecasts.

6. SUMMARY

The translation of foreign currency amounts is an important accounting issue for companies with multinational operations. Foreign exchange rate fluctuations cause the functional currency values of foreign currency assets and liabilities resulting from foreign currency transactions as well as from foreign subsidiaries to change over time. These changes in value give rise to foreign exchange differences that companies' financial statements must reflect. Determining how to measure these foreign exchange differences and whether to include them in the calculation of net income are the major issues in accounting for multinational operations.

- The local currency is the national currency of the country where an entity is located. The functional currency is the currency of the primary economic environment in which an entity operates. Normally, the local currency is an entity's functional currency. For accounting purposes, any currency other than an entity's functional currency is a foreign currency for that entity. The currency in which financial statement amounts are presented is known as the presentation currency. In most cases, the presentation currency will be the same as the local currency.
- When an export sale (import purchase) on an account is denominated in a foreign currency, the sales revenue (inventory) and foreign currency account receivable (account payable) are translated into the seller's (buyer's) functional currency using the exchange rate on the transaction date. Any change in the functional currency value of the foreign currency account receivable (account payable) that occurs between the transaction date and the settlement date is recognized as a foreign currency transaction gain or loss in net income.

- If a balance sheet date falls between the transaction date and the settlement date, the foreign currency account receivable (account payable) is translated at the exchange rate at the balance sheet date. The change in the functional currency value of the foreign currency account receivable (account payable) is recognized as a foreign currency transaction gain or loss in income. Analysts should understand that these gains and losses are unrealized at the time they are recognized and might or might not be realized when the transactions are settled.

- A foreign currency transaction gain arises when an entity has a foreign currency receivable and the foreign currency strengthens or it has a foreign currency payable and the foreign currency weakens. A foreign currency transaction loss arises when an entity has a foreign currency receivable and the foreign currency weakens or it has a foreign currency payable and the foreign currency strengthens.

- Companies must disclose the net foreign currency gain or loss included in income. They may choose to report foreign currency transaction gains and losses as a component of operating income or as a component of non-operating income. If two companies choose to report foreign currency transaction gains and losses differently, operating profit and operating profit margin might not be directly comparable between the two companies.

- To prepare consolidated financial statements, foreign currency financial statements of foreign operations must be translated into the parent company's presentation currency. The major conceptual issues related to this translation process are, What is the appropriate exchange rate for translating each financial statement item, and how should the resulting translation adjustment be reflected in the consolidated financial statements? Two different translation methods are used worldwide.

- Under the current rate method, assets and liabilities are translated at the current exchange rate, equity items are translated at historical exchange rates, and revenues and expenses are translated at the exchange rate that existed when the underlying transaction occurred. For practical reasons, an average exchange rate is often used to translate income items.

- Under the temporal method, monetary assets (and non-monetary assets measured at current value) and monetary liabilities (and non-monetary liabilities measured at current value) are translated at the current exchange rate. Non-monetary assets and liabilities not measured at current value and equity items are translated at historical exchange rates. Revenues and expenses, other than those expenses related to non-monetary assets, are translated at the exchange rate that existed when the underlying transaction occurred. Expenses related to non-monetary assets are translated at the exchange rates used for the related assets.

- Under both IFRS and US GAAP, the functional currency of a foreign operation determines the method to be used in translating its foreign currency financial statements into the parent's presentation currency and whether the resulting translation adjustment is recognized in income or as a separate component of equity.

- The foreign currency financial statements of a foreign operation that has a foreign currency as its functional currency are translated using the current rate method, and the translation adjustment is accumulated as a separate component of equity. The cumulative translation adjustment related to a specific foreign entity is transferred to net income when that entity is sold or otherwise disposed of. The balance sheet risk exposure associated with the current rate method is equal to the foreign subsidiary's net asset position.

- The foreign currency financial statements of a foreign operation that has the parent's presentation currency as its functional currency are translated using the temporal method, and the translation adjustment is included as a gain or loss in income. US GAAP refer to this process as remeasurement. The balance sheet exposure associated with the temporal method is equal to the foreign subsidiary's net monetary asset/liability position (adjusted for non-monetary items measured at current value).

- IFRS and US GAAP differ with respect to the translation of foreign currency financial statements of foreign operations located in a highly inflationary country. Under IFRS, the foreign currency statements are first restated for local inflation and then translated using the current exchange rate. Under US GAAP, the foreign currency financial statements are translated using the temporal method, with no restatement for inflation.
- Applying different translation methods for a given foreign operation can result in very different amounts reported in the parent's consolidated financial statements.
- Companies must disclose the total amount of translation gain or loss reported in income and the amount of translation adjustment included in a separate component of stockholders' equity. Companies are not required to separately disclose the component of translation gain or loss arising from foreign currency transactions and the component arising from application of the temporal method.
- Disclosures related to translation adjustments reported in equity can be used to include these as gains and losses in determining an adjusted amount of income following a clean-surplus approach to income measurement.
- Foreign currency translation rules are well established in both IFRS and US GAAP. Fortunately, except for the treatment of foreign operations located in highly inflationary countries, the two sets of standards have no major differences in this area. The ability to understand the impact of foreign currency translation on the financial results of a company using IFRS should apply equally well in the analysis of financial statements prepared in accordance with US GAAP.
- An analyst can obtain information about the tax impact of multinational operations from companies' disclosure on effective tax rates.
- For a multinational company, sales growth is driven not only by changes in volume and price but also by changes in the exchange rates between the reporting currency and the currency in which sales are made. Arguably, growth in sales that comes from changes in volume or price is more sustainable than growth in sales that comes from changes in exchange rates.

PRACTICE PROBLEMS

The following information relates to Questions 1–6

Pedro Ruiz is an analyst for a credit rating agency. One of the companies he follows, Eurexim SA, is based in France and complies with International Financial Reporting Standards (IFRS). Ruiz has learned that Eurexim used EUR220 million of its own cash and borrowed an equal amount to open a subsidiary in Ukraine. The funds were converted into hryvnia (UAH) on December 31, 20X1 at an exchange rate of EUR1.00 = UAH6.70 and used to purchase UAH1,500 million in fixed assets and UAH300 million of inventories.

Ruiz is concerned about the effect that the subsidiary's results might have on Eurexim's consolidated financial statements. He calls Eurexim's Chief Financial Officer, but learns little. Eurexim is not willing to share sales forecasts and has not even made a determination as to the subsidiary's functional currency.

Absent more useful information, Ruiz decides to explore various scenarios to determine the potential impact on Eurexim's consolidated financial statements. Ukraine is not currently in a hyperinflationary environment, but Ruiz is concerned that this situation could change. Ruiz also believes the euro will appreciate against the hryvnia for the foreseeable future.

1. If Ukraine's economy becomes highly inflationary, Eurexim will *most likely* translate inventory by:
   A. restating for inflation and using the temporal method.
   B. restating for inflation and using the current exchange rate.
   C. using the temporal method with no restatement for inflation.

2. Given Ruiz's belief about the direction of exchange rates, Eurexim's gross profit margin would be *highest* if it accounts for the Ukraine subsidiary's inventory using:
   A. FIFO and the temporal method.
   B. FIFO and the current rate method.
   C. weighted-average cost and the temporal method.

3. If the euro is chosen as the Ukraine subsidiary's functional currency, Eurexim will translate its fixed assets using the:
   A. average rate for the reporting period.
   B. rate in effect when the assets were purchased.
   C. rate in effect at the end of the reporting period.

4. If the euro is chosen as the Ukraine subsidiary's functional currency, Eurexim will translate its accounts receivable using the:
   A. rate in effect at the transaction date.
   B. average rate for the reporting period.
   C. rate in effect at the end of the reporting period.

5. If the hryvnia is chosen as the Ukraine subsidiary's functional currency, Eurexim will translate its inventory using the:
   A. average rate for the reporting period.
   B. rate in effect at the end of the reporting period.
   C. rate in effect at the time the inventory was purchased.

6. Based on the information available and Ruiz's expectations regarding exchange rates, if the hryvnia is chosen as the Ukraine subsidiary's functional currency, Eurexim will *most likely* report:
   A. an addition to the cumulative translation adjustment.
   B. a translation gain or loss as a component of net income.
   C. a subtraction from the cumulative translation adjustment.

The following information relates to Questions 7–12

Consolidated Motors is a US-based corporation that sells mechanical engines and components used by electric utilities. Its Canadian subsidiary, Consol-Can, operates solely in Canada. It was created on December 31, 20X1, and Consolidated Motors determined at that time that it should use the US dollar as its functional currency.

Chief Financial Officer Monica Templeton was asked to explain to the board of directors how exchange rates affect the financial statements of both Consol-Can and the consolidated financial statements of Consolidated Motors. For the presentation, Templeton collects Consol-Can's balance sheets for the years ended 20X1 and 20X2 (Exhibit 1), as well as relevant exchange rate information (Exhibit 2).

EXHIBIT 1   Consol-Can Condensed Balance Sheet for Fiscal Years Ending December 31 (C$ millions)

Account	20X2	20X1
Cash	135	167
Accounts receivable	98	—
Inventory	77	30
Fixed assets	100	100
Accumulated depreciation	(10)	—
Total assets	400	297
Accounts payable	77	22
Long-term debt	175	175
Common stock	100	100
Retained earnings	48	—
Total liabilities and shareholders' equity	400	297

EXHIBIT 2   Exchange Rate Information

	US$/C$
Rate on December 31, 20X1	0.86
Average rate in 20X2	0.92
Weighted-average rate for inventory purchases	0.92
Rate on December 31, 20X2	0.95

Templeton explains that Consol-Can uses the FIFO inventory accounting method and that purchases of C$300 million and the sell-through of that inventory occurred evenly throughout 20X2. Her presentation includes reporting the translated amounts in US dollars for each item, as well as associated translation-related gains and losses. The board responds with several questions.

- Would there be a reason to change the functional currency to the Canadian dollar?
- Would there be any translation effects for Consolidated Motors if the functional currency for Consol-Can were changed to the Canadian dollar?
- Would a change in the functional currency have any impact on financial statement ratios for the parent company?
- What would be the balance sheet exposure to translation effects if the functional currency were changed?

7. After translating Consol-Can's inventory and long-term debt into the parent company's currency (US$), the amounts reported on Consolidated Motor's financial statements on December 31, 20X2 would be *closest* to (in millions):
   A. $71 for inventory and $161 for long-term debt.
   B. $71 for inventory and $166 for long-term debt.
   C. $73 for inventory and $166 for long-term debt.

8. After translating Consol-Can's December 31, 20X2 balance sheet into the parent company's currency (US$), the translated value of retained earnings will be *closest* to:
   A. $41 million.
   B. $44 million.
   C. $46 million.

9. In response to the board's first question, Templeton would *most likely* reply that such a change would be justified if:
   A. the inflation rate in the United States became hyperinflationary.
   B. management wanted to flow more of the gains through net income.
   C. Consol-Can were making autonomous decisions about operations, investing, and financing.

10. In response to the board's second question, Templeton should reply that if the change is made, the consolidated financial statements for Consolidated Motors would begin to recognize:
    A. realized gains and losses on monetary assets and liabilities.
    B. realized gains and losses on non-monetary assets and liabilities.
    C. unrealized gains and losses on non-monetary assets and liabilities.

11. In response to the board's third question, Templeton should note that the change will *most likely* affect:
    A. the cash ratio.
    B. fixed asset turnover.
    C. receivables turnover.

12. In response to the board's fourth question, the balance sheet exposure (in C$ millions) would be *closest* to:
    A. −19.
    B. 148.
    C. 400.

The following information relates to Questions 13–18

Romulus Corp. is a US-based company that prepares its financial statements in accordance with US GAAP. Romulus Corp. has two European subsidiaries: Julius and Augustus. Anthony Marks, CFA, is an analyst trying to forecast Romulus's 20X2 results. Marks has prepared separate forecasts for both Julius and Augustus, as well as for Romulus's other operations (prior to consolidating the results.) He is now considering the impact of currency translation on the results of both the subsidiaries and the parent company's consolidated financials. His research has provided the following insights:

- The results for Julius will be translated into US dollars using the current rate method.
- The results for Augustus will be translated into US dollars using the temporal method.
- Both Julius and Augustus use the FIFO method to account for inventory.
- Julius had year-end 20X1 inventory of €340 million. Marks believes Julius will report €2,300 in sales and €1,400 in cost of sales in 20X2.

Marks also forecasts the 20X2 year-end balance sheet for Julius (Exhibit 1). Data and forecasts related to euro/dollar exchange rates are presented in Exhibit 2.

EXHIBIT 1   Forecasted Balance Sheet Data for Julius,
December 31, 20X2 (€ millions)

Cash	50
Accounts receivable	100
Inventory	700
Fixed assets	1,450
Total assets	2,300
Liabilities	700
Common stock	1,500
Retained earnings	100
Total liabilities and shareholder equity	2,300

EXHIBIT 2   Exchange Rates ($/€)

December 31, 20X1	1.47
December 31, 20X2	1.61
20X2 average	1.54
Rate when fixed assets were acquired	1.25
Rate when 20X1 inventory was acquired	1.39
Rate when 20X2 inventory was acquired	1.49

13. Based on the translation method being used for Julius, the subsidiary is *most likely:*
   A. a sales outlet for Romulus's products.
   B. a self-contained, independent operating entity.
   C. using the US dollar as its functional currency.

14. To account for its foreign operations, Romulus has *most likely* designated the euro as the functional currency for:
   A. Julius only.
   B. Augustus only.
   C. both Julius and Augustus.

15. When Romulus consolidates the results of Julius, any unrealized exchange rate holding gains on monetary assets should be:
   A. reported as part of operating income.
   B. reported as a non-operating item on the income statement.
   C. reported directly to equity as part of the cumulative translation adjustment.

16. When Marks translates his forecasted balance sheet for Julius into US dollars, total assets as of December 31, 20X2 (dollars in millions) will be *closest* to:
   A. $1,429.
   B. $2,392.
   C. $3,703.

17. When Marks converts his forecasted income statement data for Julius into US dollars, the 20X2 gross profit margin will be *closest* to:
    A. 39.1%.
    B. 40.9%.
    C. 44.6%.

18. Relative to the gross margins the subsidiaries report in local currency, Romulus's consolidated gross margin *most likely*:
    A. will not be distorted by currency translations.
    B. would be distorted if Augustus were using the same translation method as Julius.
    C. will be distorted because of the translation and inventory accounting methods Augustus is using.

The following information relates to Questions 19–24

Redline Products, Inc. is a US-based multinational with subsidiaries around the world. One such subsidiary, Acceletron, operates in Singapore, which has seen mild but not excessive rates of inflation. Acceletron was acquired in 2000 and has never paid a dividend. It records inventory using the FIFO method.

Chief Financial Officer Margot Villiers was asked by Redline's board of directors to explain how the functional currency selection and other accounting choices affect Redline's consolidated financial statements. Villiers gathers Acceletron's financial statements denominated in Singapore dollars (SGD) in Exhibit 1 and the US dollar/Singapore dollar exchange rates in Exhibit 2. She does not intend to identify the functional currency actually in use but rather to use Acceletron as an example of how the choice of functional currency affects the consolidated statements.

EXHIBIT 1   Selected Financial Data for Acceletron, December 31, 2007 (SGD millions)

Cash	SGD125
Accounts receivable	230
Inventory	500
Fixed assets	1,640
Accumulated depreciation	(205)
Total assets	SGD2,290
Accounts payable	185
Long-term debt	200
Common stock	620
Retained earnings	1,285
Total liabilities and equity	2,290
Total revenues	SGD4,800
Net income	SGD450

EXHIBIT 2   Exchange Rates Applicable to Acceletron

Exchange Rate in Effect at Specific Times	USD per SGD
Rate when first SGD1 billion of fixed assets were acquired	0.568
Rate when remaining SGD640 million of fixed assets were acquired	0.606
Rate when long-term debt was issued	0.588
December 31, 2006	0.649
Weighted-average rate when inventory was acquired	0.654
Average rate in 2007	0.662
December 31, 2007	0.671

19. Compared with using the Singapore dollar as Acceletron's functional currency for 2007, if the US dollar were the functional currency, it is *most likely* that Redline's consolidated:
   A. inventories will be higher.
   B. receivable turnover will be lower.
   C. fixed asset turnover will be higher.

20. If the US dollar were chosen as the functional currency for Acceletron in 2007, Redline could reduce its balance sheet exposure to exchange rates by:
   A. selling SGD30 million of fixed assets for cash.
   B. issuing SGD30 million of long-term debt to buy fixed assets.
   C. issuing SGD30 million in short-term debt to purchase marketable securities.

21. Redline's consolidated gross profit margin for 2007 would be *highest* if Acceletron accounted for inventory using:
   A. FIFO, and its functional currency were the US dollar.
   B. LIFO, and its functional currency were the US dollar.
   C. FIFO, and its functional currency were the Singapore dollar.

22. If the current rate method is used to translate Acceletron's financial statements into US dollars, Redline's consolidated financial statements will *most likely* include Acceletron's:
   A. USD3,178 million in revenues.
   B. USD118 million in long-term debt.
   C. negative translation adjustment to shareholder equity.

23. If Acceletron's financial statements are translated into US dollars using the temporal method, Redline's consolidated financial statements will *most likely* include Acceletron's:
   A. USD336 million in inventory.
   B. USD956 million in fixed assets.
   C. USD152 million in accounts receivable.

24. When translating Acceletron's financial statements into US dollars, Redline is *least likely* to use an exchange rate of USD per SGD:
   A. 0.671.
   B. 0.588.
   C. 0.654.

The following information relates to Questions 25–33

Adrienne Yu is an analyst with an international bank. She analyzes Ambleu S.A. ("Ambleu"), a multinational corporation, for a client presentation. Ambleu complies with IFRS, and its presentation currency is the Norvoltian krone (NVK). Ambleu's two subsidiaries, Ngcorp and Cendaró, have different functional currencies: Ngcorp uses the Bindiar franc (FB) and Cendaró uses the Crenland guinea (CRG).

Yu first analyzes the following three transactions to assess foreign currency transaction exposure:

Transaction 1:	Cendaró sells goods to a non-domestic customer that pays in dollars on the purchase date.
Transaction 2:	Ngcorp obtains a loan in Bindiar francs on June 1, 2016 from a European bank with the Norvoltian krone as its presentation currency.
Transaction 3:	Ambleu imports inventory from Bindiar under 45-day credit terms, and the payment is to be denominated in Bindiar francs.

Yu then reviews Transactions 2 and 3. She determines the method that Ambleu would use to translate Transaction 2 into its December 31, 2016 consolidated financial statements. While analyzing Transaction 3, Yu notes that Ambleu purchased inventory on June 1, 2016 for FB27,000/ton. Ambleu pays for the inventory on July 15, 2016. Exhibit 1 presents selected economic data for Bindiar and Crenland.

EXHIBIT 1   Selected Economic Data for Bindiar and Crenland

Date	Spot FB/NVK Exchange Rate	Bindiar Inflation Rate (%)	Spot CRG/ NVK Exchange Rate	Crenland Inflation Rate (%)	Crenland GPI
Dec 31, 2015	—	—	5.6780	—	100.0
Jun 1, 2016	4.1779	—	—	—	—
Jul 15, 2016	4.1790	—	—	—	—
Dec 31, 2016	4.2374	3.1	8.6702	40.6	140.6
Average 2016	4.3450	—	—	—	—
Dec 31, 2017	4.3729	2.1	14.4810	62.3	228.2
Average 2017	4.3618	—	11.5823	—	186.2

Prior to reviewing the 2016 and 2017 consolidated financial statements of Ambleu, Yu meets with her supervisor, who asks Yu the following two questions:

Question 1:	Would a foreign currency translation loss reduce Ambleu's net sales growth?
Question 2:	According to IFRS, what disclosures should be included relating to Ambleu's treatment of foreign currency translation for Ngcorp?

To complete her assignment, Yu analyzes selected information and notes from Ambleu's 2016 and 2017 consolidated financial statements, presented in Exhibit 2.

EXHIBIT 2   Selected Information and Notes from Consolidated Financial Statements of Ambleu S.A. (in NVK millions)

Income Statement	2017	2016	Balance Sheet	2017	2016
Revenue [1]	1,069	1,034	Cash [3]	467	425
Profit before tax	294	269	Intangibles [4]	575	570
Income tax expense [2]	–96	–94	—	—	—
Net profit	198	175	—	—	—

Note 1: Cendaro's revenue for 2017 is CRG125.23 million.

Note 2:

Reconciliation of Income Tax Expense	2017 (in NVK millions)	2016 (in NVK millions)
Income tax at Ambleu's domestic tax rate	102	92
Effect of tax rates on non-domestic jurisdictions	–14	–9
Unrecognized current year tax losses	8	11
Income tax expense	96	94

Note 3: The parent company transferred NVK15 million to Cendaró on January 1, 2016 to purchase a patent from a competitor for CRG85.17 million.

Note 4: The 2016 consolidated balance sheet includes Ngcorp's total intangible assets of NVK3 million, which were added to Ngcorp's balance sheet on July 15, 2016.

25. Which transaction would generate foreign currency transaction exposure for Ambleu?
    A. Transaction 1
    B. Transaction 2
    C. Transaction 3

26. Yu's determination regarding Transaction 2 should be based on the currency of the:
    A. loan.
    B. bank.
    C. borrower.

27. Based on Exhibit 1, what is the foreign exchange gain resulting from Transaction 3 on the December 31, 2016 financial statements?
    A. NVK1.70 per ton
    B. NVK90.75 per ton
    C. NVK248.54 per ton

28. What is the *best* response to Question 1?
    A. Yes
    B. No, because it would reduce organic sales growth
    C. No, because it would reduce net price realization and mix

29. Based on Exhibit 1, the *best* response to Question 2 is that Ambleu should disclose:
    A. a restatement for local inflation.
    B. that assets carried at historical cost are translated at historical rates.
    C. the amount of foreign exchange differences included in net income.

30. Based on Exhibit 1 and Note 1 in Exhibit 2, the amount that Ambleu should include in its December 31, 2017 revenue from Cendaró is *closest* to:
    A. NVK10.60 million.
    B. NVK13.25 million.
    C. NVK19.73 million.

31. Based on Exhibit 2 and Note 2, the change in Ambleu's consolidated income tax rate from 2016 to 2017 *most likely* resulted from a:
    A. decrease in Ambleu's domestic tax rate.
    B. more profitable business mix in its subsidiaries.
    C. stronger Norvoltian krone relative to the currencies of its subsidiaries.

32. Based on Exhibit 1 and Note 3 in Exhibit 2, the cumulative translation loss recognized by Ambleu related to the patent purchase on the December 31, 2017 financial statements is *closest* to:
    A. NVK0.39 million.
    B. NVK1.58 million
    C. NVK9.12 million.

33. Based on Exhibit 1 and Note 4 in Exhibit 2, the total intangible assets on Ngcorp's balance sheet as of December 31, 2016 are *closest* to:
    A. ₣B12.54 million.
    B. ₣B12.71 million.
    C. ₣B13.04 million.

The following information relates to Questions 34–40

Triofind, Inc. (Triofind), based in the country of Norvolt, provides wireless services to various countries, including Norvolt, Borliand, Abuelio, and Certait. The company's presentation currency is the Norvolt euro (NER), and Triofind complies with IFRS. Triofind has two wholly owned subsidiaries, located in Borliand and Abuelio. The Borliand subsidiary (Triofind-B) was established on June 30, 2016, by Triofind both investing NER1,000,000, which was converted into Borliand dollars (BRD), and borrowing an additional BRD500,000.

Marie Janssen, a financial analyst in Triofind's Norvolt headquarters office, translates Triofind-B's financial statements using the temporal method. Non-monetary assets are measured at cost under the lower of cost or market rule. Spot BRD/NER exchange rates are presented in Exhibit 1, and the balance sheet for Triofind-B is presented in Exhibit 2.

EXHIBIT 1   Spot BRD/NER Exchange Rates

Date	BRD per NER
June 30, 2016	1.15
Weighted-average rate when inventory was acquired (2016)	1.19
December 31, 2016	1.20
Weighted-average rate when inventory was acquired (2017)	1.18
June 30, 2017	1.17

EXHIBIT 2   Triofind-B Balance Sheet for 2016 and 2017 (BRD)

Assets	December 31, 2016	June 30, 2017	Liabilities and Stockholders' Equity	December 31, 2016	June 30, 2017
Cash	900,000	1,350,000	Notes payable	500,000	500,000
Inventory	750,000	500,000	Common stock	1,150,000	1,150,000
			Retained earnings		200,000
Total	1,650,000	1,850,000	Total	1,650,000	1,850,000

Janssen next analyzes Triofind's Abuelio subsidiary (Triofind-A), which uses the current rate method to translate its results into Norvolt euros. Triofind-A, which prices its goods in Abuelio pesos (ABP), sells mobile phones to a customer in Certait on May 31, 2017 and receives payment of 1 million Certait rand (CRD) on July 31, 2017.

On May 31, 2017, Triofind-A also received NER50,000 from Triofind and used the funds to purchase a new warehouse in Abuelio. Janssen translates the financial statements of Triofind-A as of July 31, 2017 and must determine the appropriate value for the warehouse in Triofind's presentation currency. She observes that the cumulative Abuelio inflation rate exceeded 100% from 2015 to 2017. Spot exchange rates and inflation data are presented in Exhibit 3.

EXHIBIT 3   Spot Exchange Rates and Inflation Data for Triofind-A

Date	NER per CRD	NER per ABP	Abuelio Monthly Inflation Rate (%)
May 31, 2017	0.2667	0.0496	—
June 30, 2017	0.2703	0.0388	25
July 31, 2017	0.2632	0.0312	22

Janssen gathers corporate tax rate data and company disclosure information to include in Triofind's annual report. She determines that the corporate tax rates for Abuelio, Norvolt, and Borliand are 35%, 34%, and 0%, respectively, and that Norvolt exempts the non-domestic income of multinationals from taxation. Triofind-B constitutes 25% of Triofind's net income, and Triofind-A constitutes 15%. Janssen also gathers data on components of net sales growth in different countries, presented in Exhibit 4.

EXHIBIT 4   Components of Net Sales Growth (%) Fiscal Year 2017

Country	Contribution from Volume Growth	Contribution from Price Growth	Foreign Currency Exchange	Net Sales Growth
Abuelio	7	6	−2	11
Borliand	4	5	4	13
Norvolt	7	3	—	10

34. Based on Exhibits 1 and 2 and Janssen's translation method, total assets for Triofind-B translated into Triofind's presentation currency as of December 31, 2016 are *closest* to:
   A. NER1,375,000.
   B. NER1,380,252.
   C. NER1,434,783.

35. Based on Exhibits 1 and 2, the translation adjustment for Triofind-B's liabilities into Triofind's presentation currency for the six months ended December 31, 2016 is:
   A. negative.
   B. zero.
   C. positive.

36. Based on Exhibits 1 and 2 and Janssen's translation method, retained earnings for Triofind-B translated into Triofind's presentation currency as of June 30, 2017 are *closest* to:
   A. NER150,225.
   B. NER170,940.
   C. NER172,414.

37. The functional currency for Triofind-A's sale of mobile phones to a customer in Certait is the:
    A. Certait real.
    B. Norvolt euro.
    C. Abuelio peso.

38. Based on Exhibit 3, the value of the new warehouse in Abuelio on Triofind's balance sheet as of July 31, 2017 is *closest* to:
    A. NER31,452.
    B. NER47,964.
    C. NER50,000.

39. Relative to its domestic tax rate, Triofind's effective tax rate is *most likely*:
    A. lower.
    B. the same.
    C. higher.

40. Based on Exhibit 4, the country with the highest sustainable sales growth is:
    A. Norvolt.
    B. Abuelio.
    C. Borliand.

CHAPTER 16

ANALYSIS OF FINANCIAL INSTITUTIONS

Jack T. Ciesielski, CPA, CFA
Elaine Henry, PhD, CFA

LEARNING OUTCOMES

After completing this chapter, you will be able to do the following:

- describe how financial institutions differ from other companies;
- describe key aspects of financial regulations of financial institutions;
- explain the CAMELS (capital adequacy, asset quality, management, earnings, liquidity, and sensitivity) approach to analyzing a bank, including key ratios and its limitations;
- describe other factors to consider in analyzing a bank;
- analyze a bank based on financial statements and other factors;
- describe key ratios and other factors to consider in analyzing an insurance company.

1. INTRODUCTION

Financial institutions provide a wide range of financial products and services. They serve as intermediaries between providers and recipients of capital, facilitate asset and risk management, and execute transactions involving cash, securities, and other financial assets.

Given the diversity of financial services, it is unsurprising that numerous types of financial institutions exist. Types of financial institutions include deposit-taking, loan-making institutions (referred to as *banks* in this chapter), investment banks, credit card companies, brokers, dealers, exchanges, clearing houses, depositories, investment managers, financial advisers, and insurance companies. In many situations, overlap of services exists across types of institutions. For example, banks not only take deposits and make loans but also may undertake investment management and other securities-related activities and may offer such products as derivatives, which are effectively insurance against adverse effects of movements in the interest rate, equity, and foreign currency markets. As another example of overlap, life insurance companies not only provide mortality-related insurance products but also offer savings vehicles. This chapter focuses primarily on two types of financial institutions: banks (broadly defined as deposit-taking, loan-making institutions) and insurance companies.

Section 2 explains what makes financial institutions different from other types of companies, such as manufacturers or merchandisers. Section 3 discusses how to analyze a bank. Section 4 focuses on analyzing insurance companies. A summary of key points concludes the chapter.

2. WHAT MAKES FINANCIAL INSTITUTIONS DIFFERENT?

A distinctive feature of financial institutions—in particular, banks—is their systemic importance, which means that their smooth functioning is essential to the overall health of an economy. The most fundamental role of banks is to serve as intermediaries, accepting deposits from capital providers and providing capital via loans to borrowers. Their role as intermediaries between and among providers and recipients of capital creates financial inter-linkages across all types of entities, including households, banks, corporations, and governments. The network of inter-linkages across entities means that the failure of one bank will negatively affect other financial and non-financial entities. The larger the bank and the more widespread its inter-linkages, the greater its potential impact on the entire financial system. If an extremely large bank were to fail, the negative impact of its failure could spread and potentially result in the failure of the entire financial system.

Systemic risk has been defined as "a risk of disruption to financial services that is (i) caused by an impairment of all or parts of the financial system and (ii) has the potential to have serious negative consequences for the economy as a whole. Fundamental to the definition is the notion of contagion across the economy from a disruption or failure in a financial institution, market or instrument. All types of financial intermediaries, markets and infrastructure can potentially be systemically important to some degree."[1] The problem of systemic risk (the risk of failure of the financial system as a result of the failure of a major financial institution) has emerged as an issue in many countries around the world in the aftermath of the 2008 global financial crisis. *Financial contagion* is a situation in which financial shocks spread from their place or sector of origin to other locales or sectors. Globally, a faltering economy may infect other, healthier economies.

Because of their systemic importance, financial institutions' activities are heavily regulated. Regulations attempt to constrain excessive risk taking that could cause an entity to fail. Regulations address various aspects of a financial institution's operations, including the amount of capital that must be maintained, the minimum liquidity, and the riskiness of assets.

The liabilities of most banks are made up primarily of deposits. For example, as of December 2016, deposits constituted over 80% of the total liabilities of domestically chartered commercial banks in the United States.[2] The failure of a bank to honor its deposits could have negative consequences across the economy. Even the expectation that a bank might not be able to honor its deposits could cause depositors to withdraw their money from the bank, and a large sudden withdrawal of deposits (a bank run) could cause an actual failure and financial

---

[1] "Guidance to Assess the Systemic Importance of Financial Institutions, Markets and Instruments: Initial Considerations," report to the G–20 finance ministers and central bank governors, prepared by the staff of the International Monetary Fund and the Bank for International Settlements and the secretariat of the Financial Stability Board (October 2009): https://www.imf.org/external/np/g20/pdf/100109.pdf.

[2] "Assets and Liabilities of Commercial Banks in the United States - H.8," Federal Reserve statistical release (https://www.federalreserve.gov).

contagion across the economy. Therefore, deposits are often insured (up to a stated limit) by the government of the country in which the bank operates.

Another distinctive feature of financial institutions is that their assets are predominantly financial assets, such as loans and securities. In contrast, the assets of most non-financial companies are predominantly tangible assets. Financial assets create direct exposure to a different variety of risks, including credit risks, liquidity risks, market risks, and interest rate risks. Unlike many tangible assets, financial assets are often measured at fair market value for financial reporting.

This chapter focuses on the financial analysis of banks and insurers (property and casualty insurers and life and health insurers). There are many other types of financial institutions, including different types of depository institutions. Some of these other financial institutions are described briefly in Exhibit 1. Note that the list in Exhibit 1 includes types of entities that an analyst may evaluate for potential investment and, therefore, excludes supra-national organizations. Typically, supra-national entities are formed by member countries to focus on lending activities in support of specific missions. For example, the World Bank—whose mission is to reduce poverty and support development globally—comprises 189 member countries and provides loans and grants through the International Bank for Reconstruction and Development and the International Development Association.[3] Other prominent examples of supra-national entities are the Asian Development and Asian Infrastructure Investment Bank.

EXHIBIT 1   A Sampling of Financial Institutions

The list that follows is illustrative only and should not be viewed as comprehensive. The list is organized by primary activity, but many service overlaps exist. Additionally, the structure of financial service providers differs across countries, and state ownership of financial institutions is more common in some countries.

Institutions That Provide Basic Banking Services

- **Commercial banks.** This term generally refers to institutions whose business focuses on classic banking services, such as taking deposits, making loans, and facilitating payment transactions. Historically, regulation in some countries, such as the United States and France, created distinctions between commercial banking activities (e.g., deposit taking and loan making), insurance activities, and investment banking activities, such as securities underwriting, trading, and investing. In general, this distinction has been declining. For example, in France, regulations beginning in the mid-1980s eliminated many restrictions on banks' allowable types of activities, and in the United States, a 1999 law granted commercial banks the ability to undertake broad-based securities and insurance activities.[4] Germany's universal banks provide commercial banking, investment banking, insurance, and other financial and non-financial services, and Spain's leading commercial banks are "dominant in cross-selling mutual funds to their retail clients."[5] Japanese banks are permitted to engage in a range of activities including equity ownership in non-financial corporations (within limits) that strengthens their role in corporate governance beyond that typical of a creditor.[6]

(continued)

---

[3] www.worldbank.org.

[4] Berger, Allen N., Phillip Molyneux, and John O.S. Wilson, *The Oxford Handbook of Banking* (Oxford, UK: Oxford University Press, 2009).

[5] Berger et al., *The Oxford Handbook of Banking*.

[6] Berger et al., *The Oxford Handbook of Banking*.

EXHIBIT 1   (Continued)

- **Credit unions, cooperative and mutual banks.** These are depository institutions that function like banks and offer many of the same services as banks. They are owned by their members, rather than being publicly traded like many banks. Another difference from commercial banks is that these institutions are organized as non-profits and, therefore, do not pay income taxes.
- **Specialized financial service providers.**
  - **Building societies** and **savings and loan associations** are depository institutions that specialize in financing long-term residential mortgages.
  - **Mortgage banks** originate, sell, and service mortgages and are usually active participants in the securitization markets.
  - **Trust banks (Japan)** are commercial banks, and because their deposits are in the form of "money trusts" (typically with three- to five-year terms and one-year minimums), they can make long-term commercial loans and securities investments. Japan also has city banks (universal banks), regional banks, second regional banks, and Shinkin banks and credit cooperatives (which provide commercial banking services to their members—smaller enterprises and individuals).[7]
  - **Online payment companies**, such as Paypal (United States), Alipay (China), and other non-bank online payment companies, have expanded rapidly and continue to broaden service offerings.

Intermediaries within the Investment Industry
Within this category, services offered by different entities are particularly varied. A few of these are described briefly below.

- *Managers of pooled investment vehicles, such as open-end mutual funds, closed-end funds, and exchange-traded funds.* These financial institutions pool money from investors and buy and sell securities and other assets. The investors share ownership in the investment vehicle. Pooled investment vehicles, as required by regulation, disclose their investment policies, deposit and redemption procedures, fees and expenses, past performance statistics, and other information.
- *Hedge funds.* These funds also pool investors' money and invest it. They tend to follow more complex strategies; be less transparent, less liquid, and less regulated; and have higher fees and higher minimum investment amounts than open-end mutual funds, closed-end funds, and exchange-traded funds.
- *Brokers and dealers.* These firms facilitate trade in securities, earning a commission or spread on the trades.

Insurers
- **Property and casualty (P&C) insurance companies** provide protection against adverse events related to autos, homes, or commercial activities.
- **Life and health (L&H) insurers** provide mortality- and health-related insurance products. Life insurance companies also provide savings products.
- **Reinsurance companies** sell insurance to insurers. Rather than paying policyholder claims directly, they reimburse insurance companies for claims paid.[8]

---

[7] Berger et al., *The Oxford Handbook of Banking*.
[8] Insurance Information Institute (www.iii.org).

2.1. Global Organizations

With respect to global systemic risk, important differences exist between the banking and insurance sectors.[9] Unlike banks, the overall insurance market has a smaller proportion of cross-border business, although the reinsurance business is largely international. The international aspect of the reinsurance business increases the importance of the insurance sector to the global financial system: Reinsurers may be an international link to financial institutions domiciled in different parts of the world, thereby increasing systemic vulnerability. Another important difference is that insurance companies' foreign branches are generally required to hold assets in a jurisdiction that are adequate to cover the related policy liabilities in that jurisdiction.

Aside from minimizing systemic risk, other reasons for the establishment of global and regional regulatory bodies include the harmonization and globalization of regulatory rules, standards, and oversight. Consistency of standards and regulations helps minimize regulatory arbitrage (whereby multinational companies capitalize on differences in jurisdictions' regulatory systems in order to avoid unfavorable regulation) around the world.

One of the most important global organizations focused on financial stability is the Basel Committee on Banking Supervision, which was established in 1974 and is a standing committee hosted and supported by the Bank for International Settlements. Members of the Basel Committee include central banks and entities responsible for supervising banks. The list of members of the Basel Committee in Exhibit 2 illustrates the range of entities involved with supervising banking activity in different countries and jurisdictions.

The Basel Committee developed the international regulatory framework for banks known as Basel III, which is the enhanced framework succeeding Basel I and Basel II. The purposes of the measures contained in Basel III are the following: "to improve the banking sector's ability to absorb shocks arising from financial and economic stress, whatever the source, improve risk management and governance, and strengthen banks' transparency and disclosures."[10]

Three important highlights of Basel III are the minimum capital requirement, minimum liquidity, and stable funding. First, Basel III specifies the minimum percentage of its risk-weighted assets that a bank must fund with equity capital. This minimum capital requirement prevents a bank from assuming so much financial leverage that it is unable to withstand loan losses (asset write-downs). Second, Basel III specifies that a bank must hold enough high-quality liquid assets to cover its liquidity needs in a 30-day liquidity stress scenario. This minimum liquidity requirement ensures that a bank would have enough cash to cover a partial loss of funding sources (e.g., customers' deposits, other borrowings) or a cash outflow resulting from off-balance-sheet funding commitments. Third, Basel III requires a bank to have a minimum amount of stable funding relative to the bank's liquidity needs over a one-year horizon. Stability of funding is based on the tenor of deposits (e.g., longer-term deposits are more stable than shorter-term deposits) and the type of depositor (e.g., funds from consumers' deposits are considered more stable than funds raised in the interbank markets).

---

[9]"Core Principles: Cross-Sectoral Comparison," report by the Joint Forum (Basel Committee on Banking Supervision, International Organization of Securities Commissions, and International Association of Insurance Supervisors; November 2001): https://www.iaisweb.org/page/supervisory-material/joint-forum//file/34300/core-principles-cross-sectoral-comparison.

[10]www.bis.org.

EXHIBIT 2   Members of the Basel Committee as of July 2017

Country/Jurisdiction	Institutional Representative
Argentina	Central Bank of Argentina
Australia	Reserve Bank of Australia Australian Prudential Regulation Authority
Belgium	National Bank of Belgium
Brazil	Central Bank of Brazil
Canada	Bank of Canada Office of the Superintendent of Financial Institutions
Chinese mainland	People's Bank of China China Banking Regulatory Commission
European Union	European Central Bank European Central Bank Single Supervisory Mechanism
France	Bank of France Prudential Supervision and Resolution Authority
Germany	Deutsche Bundesbank (Central Bank of Germany) Federal Financial Supervisory Authority (BaFin)
Hong Kong SAR	Hong Kong Monetary Authority
India	Reserve Bank of India
Indonesia	Bank Indonesia Indonesia Financial Services Authority
Italy	Bank of Italy
Japan	Bank of Japan Financial Services Agency
Korea	Bank of Korea Financial Supervisory Service
Luxembourg	Surveillance Commission for the Financial Sector
Mexico	Bank of Mexico Comisión Nacional Bancaria y de Valores (National Banking and Securities Commission)
Netherlands	Netherlands Bank
Russia	Central Bank of the Russian Federation
Saudi Arabia	Saudi Arabian Monetary Agency
Singapore	Monetary Authority of Singapore
South Africa	South African Reserve Bank
Spain	Bank of Spain
Sweden	Sveriges Riksbank (Central Bank of Sweden) Finansinspektionen (Financial Supervisory Authority)
Switzerland	Swiss National Bank Swiss Financial Market Supervisory Authority FINMA
Turkey	Central Bank of the Republic of Turkey Banking Regulation and Supervision Agency
United Kingdom	Bank of England Prudential Regulation Authority
United States	Board of Governors of the Federal Reserve System Federal Reserve Bank of New York Office of the Comptroller of the Currency Federal Deposit Insurance Corporation

Observers

Country/Jurisdiction	Institutional Representative
Chile	Central Bank of Chile
	Banking and Financial Institutions Supervisory Agency
Malaysia	Central Bank of Malaysia
United Arab Emirates	Central Bank of the United Arab Emirates

Source: www.bis.org.

As a result of preventing banks from assuming excessive financial leverage, Basel III has prompted banks to focus on asset quality, hold capital against other types of risk (such as operational risk), and develop improved risk assessment processes. Basel III also presents fundamental changes regarding the quality and composition of the capital base of financial institutions. It has improved the ability of their capital base to sustain losses, so these are confined to the financial institutions' capital investors and are not transmitted to depositors, taxpayers, or other institutions in the financial system, thereby reducing risk of contagion.

Having developed the regulatory framework, the Basel Committee monitors the adoption and implementation of Basel III by member jurisdictions.

A number of other important organizations are involved in international cooperation in the area of financial stability. Some of these international organizations are described briefly below.

- The Financial Stability Board includes representatives from supervisory and regulatory authorities for the G–20 members plus Hong Kong SAR, Singapore, Spain, and Switzerland. Its overall goal is to strengthen financial stability. It aims to identify systemic risk in the financial sector and coordinate actions that jurisdictional authorities can take to address the risks.
- The International Association of Deposit Insurers' objective is to "enhance the effectiveness of deposit insurance systems."
- The International Association of Insurance Supervisors (IAIS) includes representatives from insurance regulators and supervisors from most countries around the world. Its overall goal is to promote effective supervision of the insurance industry globally.
- The International Organization of Securities Commissions (IOSCO) includes representatives from the regulators of the securities markets of various countries and jurisdictions. Its overall goals include maintaining fair and efficient securities markets.

The latter two organizations are part of a Joint Forum with the Basel Committee. The Joint Forum comprises representatives from the Basel Committee, IAIS, and IOSCO and works on issues common to the banking, insurance, and securities sectors.

2.2. Individual Jurisdictions' Regulatory Authorities

The global organizations described in the previous section aim to foster financial stability by working with individual jurisdictions' regulatory authorities. It is the individual jurisdictions' regulatory bodies that have authority over specific aspects of a financial institution's operations.

Globally, there are many regulators with overlapping and differing responsibilities over financial institutions; the global network of regulators and the resulting regulations are complex.

Although there is some overlap between member institutions in the Basel Committee and other global organizations mentioned in the previous section, specific membership varies. For example, the 83 member organizations of the International Association of Deposit Insurers include some institutions that are Basel Committee members, such as the US Federal Deposit Insurance Corporation (FDIC), and some that are not Basel Committee members, such as the Singapore Deposit Insurance Corporation Ltd. and Germany's Bundesverband deutscher Banken (Deposit Protection Fund). In some countries, the same regulatory body oversees both banking and insurance—for example, Japan's Financial Services Agency. And in other countries, there is a separate regulatory body for insurance companies—for example, the US National Association of Insurance Commissioners (NAIC) and the China Insurance Regulatory Commission.

As a financial institution's operations expand globally, compliance requirements increase. One of the most global financial institutions, HSBC Holdings, discloses that their operations are "regulated and supervised by approximately 400 different central banks and other regulatory authorities in those jurisdictions in which we have offices, branches or subsidiaries. These authorities impose a variety of requirements and controls."[11]

3. ANALYZING A BANK

In this section, the term "bank" is used in its general sense and applies to entities whose primary business activities are taking deposits and making loans. This section first describes an approach widely used as a starting point to analyze a bank, known as CAMELS, and follows with a description of additional factors to consider when analyzing a bank. The section concludes with a case study analysis of a real bank.

3.1. The CAMELS Approach

"CAMELS" is an acronym for the six components of a widely used bank rating approach originally developed in the United States.[12] The six components are Capital adequacy, Asset quality, Management capabilities, Earnings sufficiency, Liquidity position, and Sensitivity to market risk.

A bank examiner using the CAMELS approach to evaluate a bank conducts an analysis and assigns a numerical rating of 1 through 5 to each component. A rating of 1 represents the best rating, showing the best practices in risk management and performance and generating the least concern for regulators. A rating of 5 is the worst rating, showing the poorest performance and risk management practices and generating the highest degree of regulatory concern.[13]

---

[11] HSBC Holdings Form 20-F (December 31, 2016).

[12] Information on the evolution of risk assessment can be found in "Supervisory Risk Assessment and Early Warning Systems," Ranjana Sahajwala and Paul Van den Bergh, Basel Committee on Banking Supervision Working Paper No. 4 (December 2000). Further information about the CAMELS rating system can be found in the FDIC's description of the Uniform Financial Institutions Rating System at www.fdic.gov.

[13] Sahajwala and Van den Bergh, "Supervisory Risk Assessment and Early Warning Systems."

After the components are rated, a composite rating for the entire bank is constructed from the component ratings. This is not a simple arithmetic mean of the six component ratings: Each component is weighted by the examiner performing the study. The examiner's judgment will affect the weighting accorded to each component's rating. Two examiners could evaluate the same bank on a CAMELS basis and even assign the same ratings to each component and yet arrive at different composite ratings for the entire bank.

Although the CAMELS system was developed as a tool for bank examiners, it provides a useful framework for other purposes, such as equity or debt investment analysis of banks. The following sections discuss each component of the rating system.

3.1.1. Capital Adequacy

It is important for a bank (as with any company) to have adequate capital so that potential losses can be absorbed without causing the bank to become financially weak or even insolvent. Losses reduce the amount of a bank's retained earnings, which is one component of capital. Large enough losses could even result in insolvency. A strong capital position lowers the probability of insolvency and bolsters public confidence in the bank.

Capital adequacy for banks is described in terms of the proportion of the bank's assets funded with capital. For purposes of determining capital adequacy, a bank's assets are adjusted based on their risk, with riskier assets requiring a higher weighting. The risk weightings are specified by individual countries' regulators, and these regulators typically take Basel III into consideration. The risk adjustment results in an amount for risk-weighted assets to use when determining the amount of capital required to fund those assets. For example, cash has a risk weighting of zero, so cash is not included in the risk-weighted assets. As a result, no capital is required to fund cash. Corporate loans have a risk weighting of 100%, and certain risky assets, such as loans on high-volatility commercial real estate and loans that are more than 90 days past due, have a weighting greater than 100%. As a simple example, consider a hypothetical bank with three assets: $10 in cash, $1,000 in performing loans, and $10 in non-performing loans. The bank's risk-weighted assets (RWAs) would equal ($10 × 0%) + ($1,000 × 100%) + ($10 × 150%) = $1,015. Also, off-balance-sheet exposures are assigned risk weights and included in the risk-weighted assets.

For purposes of determining a bank's capital and its capital adequacy, a bank's capital is classified into hierarchical tiers. The most important of these tiers is Common Equity Tier 1 Capital. According to the FDIC:

> Basel III capital standards emphasize common equity tier 1 capital as the predominant form of bank capital. Common equity tier 1 capital is widely recognized as the most loss-absorbing form of capital, as it is permanent and places shareholders' funds at risk of loss in the event of insolvency. Moreover, Basel III strengthens minimum capital ratio requirements and risk-weighting definitions, increases Prompt Corrective Action (PCA) thresholds, establishes a capital conservation buffer, and provides a mechanism to mandate counter-cyclical capital buffers.[14]

---

[14] FDIC, "Risk Management Manual of Examination Policies," Section 2.1 (www.fdic.gov). For a comprehensive description of capital tiers under Basel III, refer to "Basel III: A global regulatory framework for more resilient banks and banking systems" (pp. 13–27), available at www.bis.org.

Common Equity Tier 1 Capital includes common stock, issuance surplus related to common stock, retained earnings, accumulated other comprehensive income, and certain adjustments including the deduction of intangible assets and deferred tax assets. Other Tier 1 Capital includes other types of instruments issued by the bank that meet certain criteria. The criteria require, for example, that the instruments be subordinate to such obligations as deposits and other debt obligations, not have a fixed maturity, and not have any type of payment of dividends or interest that is not totally at the discretion of the bank. Tier 2 Capital includes instruments that are subordinate to depositors and to general creditors of the bank, have an original minimum maturity of five years, and meet certain other requirements.

The minimum capital requirements set forth in Basel III are described here because they are global. However, it is the individual countries' regulators who have authority to establish the minimum capital requirements for institutions within their jurisdiction.

- Common Equity Tier 1 Capital must be at least 4.5% of risk-weighted assets.
- Total Tier 1 Capital must be at least 6.0% of risk-weighted assets.
- Total Capital (Tier 1 Capital plus Tier 2 Capital) must be at least 8.0% of risk-weighted assets.[15]

EXAMPLE 1 Capital Position

Exhibit 3 presents an excerpt from an annual report disclosure by HSBC Holdings plc about its capital position. The excerpt shows the group's capital ratios, amount of capital by tier, and risk-weighted assets by type.

EXHIBIT 3   Excerpt from Annual Report Disclosure of HSBC Holdings plc

Capital Ratios		
	At Dec. 31	
	2016 (%)	2015 (%)
Common equity tier 1 ratio	13.6	11.9
Tier 1 ratio	16.1	13.9
Total capital ratio	20.1	17.2

Total Regulatory Capital and Risk-Weighted Assets		
	At Dec. 31	
	2016 ($m)	2015 ($m)
Regulatory capital		
Common equity tier 1 capital	116,552	130,863
Additional tier 1 capital	21,470	22,440
Tier 2 capital	34,336	36,530
Total regulatory capital	172,358	189,833
Risk-weighted assets	857,181	1,102,995

---

[15] www.bis.org.

Risk-Weighted Assets (RWAs) by Risk Types		
	RWAs ($bn)	Capital required* ($bn)
Credit risk	655.7	52.5
Counterparty credit risk	62.0	5.0
Market risk	41.5	3.3
Operational risk	98.0	7.8
At 31 Dec 2016	857.2	68.6

*"Capital required" represents the Pillar 1 capital charge at 8% of RWAs.

Source: HSBC Holdings plc Annual Report and Accounts 2016 (p. 127).

1. Based on Exhibit 3, did HSBC's capital ratios strengthen or weaken in 2016?
2. Based on Exhibit 3, what was the primary reason for the change in HSBC's capital ratios in 2016?

Solution to 1: HSBC's capital ratios strengthened in 2016. Its Common Equity Tier 1 ratio increased from 11.9% of RWAs to 13.6% of RWAs. Its Tier 1 ratio also increased from 13.9% to 16.1%, and its Total Capital Ratio increased from 17.2% to 20.1%.

Solution to 2: The primary reason for the change in HSBC's capital ratios in 2016 was a reduction in the amount of risk-weighted assets. Total risk-weighted assets declined from $1,102,995 million to $857,181 million.

3.1.2. Asset Quality

Asset quality pertains to the amount of existing and potential credit risk associated with a bank's assets, focusing primarily on financial assets. The concept of asset quality extends beyond the composition of a bank's assets and encompasses the strength of the overall risk management processes by which the assets are generated and managed.

Loans typically constitute the largest portion of a bank's assets. Asset quality for loans reported on the balance sheet depends on the creditworthiness of the borrowers and the corresponding adequacy of adjustments for expected loan losses. Loans are measured at amortized cost and are shown on the balance sheet net of allowances for loan losses.

Investments in securities issued by other entities, often another significant portion of a bank's assets, are measured differently, depending on how the security is categorized. Specifically, under International Financial Reporting Standards (IFRS),[16] financial assets are classified in one of three categories, depending on the company's business model for

---

[16] IFRS 9 *Financial Instruments*, issued July 2014 and effective beginning January 2018.

managing the asset and on the contractual cash flows of the asset. The financial asset's category specifies how it is subsequently measured (either amortized cost or fair value) and, for those measured based on fair value, how any changes in value are reported—either through other comprehensive income (OCI) or through profit and loss (PL). The three categories for financial assets are (1) measured at amortized cost, (2) measured at fair value through other comprehensive income (FVOCI), and (3) measured at fair value through profit and loss (FVTPL).

In contrast to IFRS, US GAAP require all equity investments "(except those accounted for under the equity method of accounting or those that result in consolidation of the investee) to be measured at fair value with changes in fair value recognized in net income."[17] Another exception to fair value measurement is that an equity investment without a readily determinable fair value can be measured at cost minus impairment. Thus, under US GAAP, the three categories used to classify and measure investments apply *only to debt securities*: held to maturity (measured at amortized cost), trading (measured at fair value through net income), and available for sale (measured at fair value through other comprehensive income).

The following example addresses asset quality from the perspective of overall asset composition. The example includes the asset portion of a bank's balance sheet. In practice, terminology used by different entities can vary, and an analyst should refer to the footnotes for further detail on a line item. Here, two comments can be helpful in interpreting the line items in the example. First, when determining the total amount of bank loans, two line items are clearly relevant: "Loans and advances to banks" and "Loans and advances to customers." In addition, note that "Reverse repurchase agreements" are a form of collateralized loan made by a bank to a client. In a repurchase agreement, a borrower (i.e., a bank client) sells a financial asset to a lender (i.e., a bank) and commits to repurchase the financial asset for a fixed price at a future date. The difference between the selling price and the higher repurchase price effectively constitutes interest on the borrowing. The borrower describes the transaction as a "repurchase agreement," and the lender describes the transaction as a "reverse repurchase agreement."[18] Second, the term "assets held for sale" is related to discontinued operations and specifically refers to long-term assets whose value is driven mainly by their intended disposition rather than their continued use.[19] This term should not be confused with the securities-related term "available for sale" (described above).

---

[17] Accounting Standards Update 2016-01 *Financial Instruments—Overall* (Subtopic 825-10) *Recognition and Measurement of Financial Assets and Financial Liabilities.* This Accounting Standards Update was issued in January 2016 and is effective for public business entities for fiscal years beginning after December 15, 2017.

[18] The Office of Financial Research (part of the US Department of the Treasury) estimates that the size of the repurchase ("repo") market is $3.5 trillion.

[19] IFRS 5 *Non-Current Assets Held for Sale and Discontinued Operations.*

EXAMPLE 2   Asset Quality: Composition of Assets

Exhibit 4 presents the asset portion of the balance sheet of HSBC Holdings, which is prepared according to IFRS.

EXHIBIT 4   Excerpt from Consolidated Balance Sheet

HSBC Holdings plc
Consolidated Balance Sheet [Excerpt]
at December 31

Assets	2016 $m	2015 $m
Cash and balances at central banks	128,009	98,934
Items in the course of collection from other banks	5,003	5,768
Hong Kong Government certificates of indebtedness	31,228	28,410
Trading assets	235,125	224,837
Financial assets designated at fair value	24,756	23,852
Derivatives	290,872	288,476
Loans and advances to banks	88,126	90,401
Loans and advances to customers	861,504	924,454
Reverse repurchase agreements, non-trading	160,974	146,255
Financial investments	436,797	428,955
Assets held for sale	4,389	43,900
Prepayments, accrued income, and other assets	59,520	54,398
Current tax assets	1,145	1,221
Interests in associates and joint ventures	20,029	19,139
Goodwill and intangible assets	21,346	24,605
Deferred tax assets	6,163	6,051
Total assets at Dec. 31	**2,374,986**	2,409,656

Source: HSBC Holdings plc Annual Report and Accounts 2016.

1. The following items are the most liquid: Cash and balances at central banks, Items in the course of collection from other banks, and Hong Kong Government certificates of indebtedness. What proportion of HSBC's total assets was invested in these liquid assets in 2015? In 2016? Did HSBC's balance sheet liquidity decrease or increase in 2016?
2. How did the percentage of investments to total assets change from 2015 to 2016? (Include trading assets, financial assets designated at fair value, and financial investments as investments.)
3. What proportion of HSBC's assets are loans? (As noted, the banks' loans include "Loans and advances to banks" and "Loans and advances to customers." In addition, "Reverse repurchase agreements" are a form of collateralized loan.)

Solution to 1: HSBC's balance sheet liquidity increased in 2016.

In 2015, the proportion of HSBC's balance sheet invested in highly liquid assets was 5.5%

[($98,934 + $5,768 + $28,410)/$2,409,656 = 5.5%].

In 2016, the proportion of HSBC's balance sheet invested in highly liquid assets was 6.9%

[($128,009 + $5,003 + $31,228)/$2,374,986 = 6.9%].

Solution to 2: The percentage of investments on HSBC's balance sheet increased in 2016.

In 2015, the percentage of investments to total assets was 28.1%

[($224,837 + $23,852 + $428,955)/$2,409,656 = 28.1%].

In 2016, the percentage of investments to total assets was 29.3%

[($235,125 + $24,756 + $436,797)/$2,374,986 = 29.3%].

Solution to 3: In 2015, loans represented 48.2% [($90,401 + $924,454 + $146,255)/ $2,409,656 = 48.2%] of HSBC's total assets, and in 2016, loans represented 46.8% [($88,126 + $861,504 + $160,974)/$2,374,986 = 46.8%] of HSBC's total assets.

The next example addresses asset quality from the perspective of credit quality. Assessment of credit risk is of course fundamental to banks' decisions about loans—the largest category of a banks' assets. As noted, investments in securities often constitute a significant portion of a bank's assets, and those activities also involve credit risk. Further, a bank's trading activities—including off-balance-sheet trading activities—create exposure to counterparty credit risk. Off-balance-sheet obligations such as guarantees, unused committed credit lines, and letters of credit represent potential assets (as well as potential liabilities) to the bank and thus involve credit risk. In addition to credit risk, other factors, such as liquidity, can also affect the value and marketability of a bank's assets. Diversification of credit risk exposure (and avoiding credit concentration) across the entire asset base—loans and investments—and among counterparties is an important aspect of asset quality.

EXAMPLE 3   Credit Quality of Assets

Exhibit 5 presents an excerpt from an annual report disclosure by HSBC Holdings plc about the credit quality of its financial instruments. The exhibit shows the distribution of financial instruments by credit quality.

Financial instruments included in the exhibit correspond to total amounts for some line items of assets listed on the balance sheet and to partial amounts for line items on the balance sheet where only a portion of the asset involves exposure to credit risk. Total amounts are included for the following balance sheet items: Cash and balances at central banks; Items in the course of collection from other banks; Hong Kong Government certificates of indebtedness; Derivatives; Loans and advances to banks; Loans and advances to customers; and Reverse repurchase agreements, non-trading. Partial amounts are included for the following balance sheet items: Trading assets; Financial assets designated at fair value; Financial investments; Assets held for sale; and Prepayments, accrued income, and other assets.

EXHIBIT 5   Excerpt from Annual Report Disclosure of HSBC Holdings plc

		At 31 Dec. 2016 ($m)	At 31 Dec. 2015 ($m)
Neither past due nor impaired	Strong credit quality	$1,579,517	$1,553,830
	Good credit quality	$313,707	$331,141
	Satisfactory credit quality	$263,995	$293,178
	Sub-standard credit quality	$26,094	$26,199
	Past due but not impaired	$9,028	$13,030
	Impaired	$20,510	$28,058
	Total gross amount	$2,212,851	$2,245,436
	Impairment allowances	$(8,100)	$(11,027)
	Total	$2,204,751	$2,234,409

Source: HSBC Holdings plc Annual Report and Accounts 2016 (pp. 88–89).

1. Based on Exhibit 5, did the credit quality of HSBC's financial instruments improve or deteriorate in 2016? Specifically, how did the proportion of assets invested in strong credit quality instruments change from year to year?
2. Based on Exhibit 5, does the change in HSBC's impairment allowances in 2016 reflect the change in the credit quality of financial instruments (specifically the amount of impaired assets)?

SOLUTIONS EXHIBIT

		At Dec. 31 2016	At Dec. 31 2015	
		Percentage of total gross amount	Percentage of total gross amount	Percentage change in dollar amount
Neither past due nor impaired	Strong credit quality	71.4%	69.2%	1.7%
	Good credit quality	14.2%	14.7%	**–5.3%**
	Satisfactory credit quality	11.9%	13.1%	**–10.0%**
	Sub-standard credit quality	1.2%	1.2%	**–0.4%**
	Past due but not impaired	0.4%	0.6%	**–30.7%**
	Impaired	0.9%	1.2%	**–26.9%**
	Total gross amount	100.0%	100.0%	**–1.5%**
	Impairment allowances	**–0.4%**	**–0.5%**	**–26.5%**

Solution to 1: Based on Exhibit 5, the credit quality of HSBC's financial instruments improved in 2016. As shown in the Solutions Exhibit, the percentage of total investment assets invested in strong credit quality instruments rose from 69.2% in 2015 to 71.4% in 2016 [$1,553,830/$2,245,436 = 69.2%; $1,579,517/$2,212,851 = 71.4%].

Solution to 2: Yes. Based on Exhibit 5, the change in HSBC's impairment allowances in 2016 reflects the change in the credit quality of financial instruments. In general, it is expected that the amount of impairment allowances will be related to the amount of impaired assets. The 26.5% decrease in the amount of HSBC's impairment allowances in 2016 corresponds to the 26.9% decrease in impaired assets. As a corollary, the amount of impairment allowances as a percentage of impaired assets remained roughly constant in both years ($11,027/$28,058 = 39.3% for 2015 and $8,100/$20,510 = 39.5% for 2016).

3.1.3. Management Capabilities

Many of the attributes of effective management of financial institutions are the same as those for other types of entities. Effective management involves successfully identifying and exploiting appropriate profit opportunities while simultaneously managing risk. For all types of entities, compliance with laws and regulations is essential. A strong governance structure—with an independent board that avoids excessive compensation or self-dealing—is also critically important. Sound internal controls, transparent management communication, and financial reporting quality are indicators of management effectiveness. Across all entities, overall performance is ultimately the most reliable indicator of management effectiveness.

For financial institutions, a particularly important aspect of management capability is the ability to identify and control risk, including credit risk, market risk, operating risk, legal risk, and other risks. Directors of banks set overall guidance on risk exposure levels and appropriate implementation policies and provide oversight of bank management. Banks' senior managers must develop and implement effective procedures for measuring and monitoring risks consistent with that guidance.

3.1.4. Earnings

As with any entity, financial institutions should ideally generate an amount of earnings to provide an adequate return on capital to their capital providers and specifically to reward their stockholders through capital appreciation and/or distribution of the earnings. Further, all companies' earnings should ideally be high quality and trending upward. In general, high-quality earnings mean that accounting estimates are unbiased and the earnings are derived from sustainable rather than non-recurring items.

For banks, one important area involving significant estimates is loan impairment allowances. In estimating losses on the loan portfolio collectively, statistical analysis of historical loan losses can provide a basis for an estimation, but statistical analysis based on past data must be supplemented with management judgement about the potential for deviation in future. In estimating losses on individual loans, assessments are required concerning the likelihood of the borrower's default or bankruptcy and the value of any collateral. HSBC describes the complexity of estimating loan impairment allowances as follows: "The exercise of judgement requires the use of assumptions which are highly subjective and very sensitive to the risk factors, in particular to changes in economic and credit conditions across a large number of geographical areas. Many of the factors have a high degree of interdependency and there is no single factor to which our loan impairment allowances as a whole are sensitive."[20]

Banks also must use estimates in valuing some financial assets and liabilities that must be measured at fair value. When fair value of an investment is based on observable market prices,

---

[20] HSBC Holdings plc Annual Report and Accounts 2016, page 199: www.hsbc.com/investor-relations/ group-results-and-reporting/annual-report.

valuation requires little judgment. However, when fair values cannot be based on observable market prices, judgment is required.

Under both IFRS and US GAAP, fair value measurements of financial assets and liabilities are categorized on the basis of the type of inputs used to establish the fair value. Both sets of standards use the concept of a *fair value hierarchy*.[21] The three "levels" of the fair value hierarchy pertain to the observability of the inputs used to establish the fair value.

- Level 1 inputs are quoted prices for identical financial assets or liabilities in active markets.
- Level 2 inputs are observable but are not the quoted prices for identical financial instruments in active markets. Level 2 inputs include quoted prices for similar financial instruments in active markets, quoted prices for identical financial instruments in markets that are not active, and observable data such as interest rates, yield curves, credit spreads, and implied volatility. The inputs are used in a model to determine the fair value of the financial instrument.
- Level 3 inputs are unobservable. The fair value of a financial instrument is based on a model (or models) and unobservable inputs. Financial modeling, by its very nature, contains subjective estimates that are unobservable and will differ from one modeler to another. For example, a financial instrument's value might be based on an option-pricing model employing an unobservable and subjective estimate of the instrument's market volatility. Another example is that a financial instrument's value might be based on estimated future cash flows, discounted to a present value. Neither the estimated future cash flows nor the discount rate can be observed objectively, because they depend on the determinations made by the modeler.

In practice, the "Level 1, 2, 3" fair value terminology can also refer to the valuation approach used. A Level 3 valuation technique is one that relies on one or more significant inputs that are unobservable. For example, as noted, a company might value a private equity investment using a model of estimated future cash flows.

Also, in practice, the "Level 1, 2, 3" terminology can refer to the assets or liabilities being valued using a given level of input. For example, investments can be referred to as "Level 1," "Level 2," or "Level 3" investments depending on whether their fair value is determined based on observable market prices for the exact instrument, observable market inputs for similar investments, or unobservable inputs, respectively.

Other areas involving significant estimates are common to non-financial and financial companies. Judging whether goodwill impairment exists requires estimating future cash flows of a business unit. Deciding to recognize a deferred tax asset relies on making assumptions about the probability of future taxes. Determining whether and how much of a liability to recognize in connection with contingencies (e.g., litigation) typically depends on professional expert advice but nonetheless requires some management judgment.

Regarding sustainability of a bank's earnings, it is important to examine the composition of earnings. Banks' earnings typically comprise (a) net interest income (the difference between interest earned on loans minus interest paid on the deposits supporting those loans), (b) service income, and (c) trading income. Of these three general sources, trading income is typically the most volatile. Thus, a greater proportion of net interest income and service income is typically more sustainable than trading income. In addition, lower volatility within net interest income is desirable: Highly volatile net interest income could indicate excessive interest rate risk exposure.

---

[21] Refer to IFRS 13 *Fair Value Measurement* and Financial Accounting Standards Board ASC 820 *Fair Value Measurement*.

EXAMPLE 4   Composition of Earnings

An analyst has gathered the information in Exhibit 6 to evaluate how important each source of income is to HSBC.

EXHIBIT 6   Five-Year Summary of HSBC's Total Operating Income

	2016 ($m)	2015 ($m)	2014 ($m)	2013 ($m)	2012 ($m)
Net interest income	**$29,813**	$32,531	$34,705	$35,539	$37,672
Net fee income	**$12,777**	$14,705	$15,957	$16,434	$16,430
Net trading income	**$9,452**	$8,723	$6,760	$8,690	$7,091
Net income/(expense) from financial instruments designated at fair value	**($2,666)**	$1,532	$2,473	$768	($2,226)
Gains less losses from financial investments	**$1,385**	$2,068	$1,335	$2,012	$1,189
Dividend income	**$95**	$123	$311	$322	$221
Net insurance premium income	**$9,951**	$10,355	$11,921	$11,940	$13,044
Gains on disposal of US branch network, US cards business, and Ping An Insurance (Group) Company of China, Ltd.	—	—	—	—	$7,024
Other operating income/(expense)	**($971)**	$1,055	$1,131	$2,632	$2,100
Total operating income	**$59,836**	$71,092	$74,593	$78,337	$82,545

Source: HSBC Holdings plc Annual Report and Accounts 2016 (p. 31).

1. Based on Exhibit 6, what is HSBC's primary source of operating income, and what proportion of total operating income was earned from this source in 2016?
2. Based on Exhibit 6, what proportion of total operating income did HSBC earn from trading income in 2016?
3. Based on Exhibit 6, describe the trend in HSBC's operating income.

Solution to 1: HSBC's primary source of operating income is net interest income. In 2016, 49.8% ($29,813/$59,836 = 49.8%) of total operating income was earned from net interest income in 2016.

Solution to 2: In 2016, HSBC earned 15.8% ($9,452/$59,836 = 15.8%) of total operating income from trading activities.

Solution to 3: From 2012 to 2016, HSBC's operating income declined each year. The composition of operating income was fairly constant from 2012 to 2015, with around 46% from net interest income and 21% from fee income.

EXHIBIT 7   Five-Year Summary of HSBC's Total Operating Income: Common-Size Statement

	2016	2015	2014	2013	2012
	As a Percentage of Total Operating Income				
Net interest income	49.8%	45.8%	46.5%	45.4%	45.6%
Net fee income	21.4%	20.7%	21.4%	21.0%	19.9%
Net trading income	15.8%	12.3%	9.1%	11.1%	8.6%
Net income/(expense) from financial instruments designated at fair value	−4.5%	2.2%	3.3%	1.0%	−2.7%
Gains less losses from financial investments	2.3%	2.9%	1.8%	2.6%	1.4%
Dividend income	0.2%	0.2%	0.4%	0.4%	0.3%
Net insurance premium income	16.6%	14.6%	16.0%	15.2%	15.8%
Gains on disposal of US branch network, US cards business, and Ping An Insurance (Group) Company of China, Ltd.	—	—	—	—	8.5%
Other operating income/(expense)	−1.6%	1.5%	1.5%	3.4%	2.5%
Total operating income	100.0%	100.0%	100.0%	100.0%	100.0%

3.1.5. Liquidity Position

Adequate liquidity is essential for any type of entity. Banks' systemic importance increases the importance of adequate liquidity. If a non-bank entity's insufficient liquidity prevents it from paying a current liability, the impact would primarily affect the entity's own supply chain. In contrast, because deposits constitute the primary component of a bank's current liabilities, the impact of a bank's failure to honor a current liability could affect an entire economy. Deposits in most banks are insured up to some specified amount by government insurers; thus, liquidity is a key focus of regulators.

The Basel III Regulatory Framework[22] cites the sudden illiquidity accompanying the financial crisis of 2008 as a main motivation for the introduction of a global liquidity standard. Because of the sudden pressures on liquidity at the inception of the financial crisis, some banks experienced difficulties, despite having an adequate capital base. Basel III thus introduced two minimum liquidity standards, both to be phased in over subsequent years.

- The Liquidity Coverage Ratio (LCR) is expressed as the minimum percentage of a bank's expected cash outflows that must be held in highly liquid assets. For this ratio, the expected cash outflows (the denominator) are the bank's anticipated one-month liquidity needs in a stress scenario, and the highly liquid assets (the numerator) include only those that are easily convertible into cash. The standards set a target minimum of 100%.
- The Net Stable Funding Ratio (NSFR) is expressed as the minimum percentage of a bank's *required* stable funding that must be sourced from *available* stable funding. For

---

[22] Basel Committee on Banking Supervision, "Basel III: A Global Regulatory Framework For More Resilient Banks and Banking System": www.bis.org/publ/bcbs189.pdf.

this ratio, required stable funding (the denominator) is a function of the composition and maturity of a bank's asset base, whereas available stable funding (the numerator) is a function of the composition and maturity of a bank's funding sources (i.e., capital and deposits and other liabilities). Under Basel III, the available stable funding is determined by assigning a bank's capital and liabilities to one of five categories presented in Exhibit 8, shown below. The amount assigned to each category is then multiplied by an available stable funding (ASF) factor, and the total available stable funding is the sum of the weighted amounts.[23]

EXHIBIT 8   Categories of Available Stable Funding

ASF Factor	Components of ASF Category
100%	• Total regulatory capital (excluding Tier 2 instruments with residual maturity of less than one year) • Other capital instruments and liabilities with effective residual maturity of one year or more
95%	• Stable non-maturity (demand) deposits and term deposits with residual maturity of less than one year provided by retail and small business customers
90%	• Less stable non-maturity deposits and term deposits with residual maturity of less than one year provided by retail and small business customers
50%	• Funding with residual maturity of less than one year provided by non-financial corporate customers • Operational deposits • Funding with residual maturity of less than one year from sovereigns, public sector entities, and multilateral and national development banks • Other funding with residual maturity between six months and less than one year not included in the above categories, including funding provided by central banks and financial institutions
0%	• All other liabilities and equity not included in the above categories, including liabilities without a stated maturity (with a specific treatment for deferred tax liabilities and minority interests) • Net Stable Funding Ratio derivative liabilities net of Net Stable Funding Ratio derivative assets if Net Stable Funding Ratio derivative liabilities are greater than Net Stable Funding Ratio derivative assets • "Trade date" payables arising from purchases of financial instruments, foreign currencies, and commodities

The rationale for the Net Stable Funding Ratio is that it relates the liquidity needs of the financial institution's assets to the liquidity provided by the funding sources. With assets, for example, loans with long-dated maturities require stable funding whereas highly liquid assets do not. With funding sources, long-dated deposits and other liabilities are considered more stable than short-dated liabilities, and deposits from retail customers are considered more stable than deposits with the same maturity from other counterparties. The standards set a target minimum of greater than 100%.

---

[23] Basel Committee on Banking Supervision, "Basel III: The Net Stable Funding Ratio" (October 2014, p. 3): www.bis.org/bcbs/publ/d295.pdf. Exhibit 8 is adapted from page 6 of this document.

Among the several liquidity-monitoring metrics described in Basel III,[24] two are discussed here: concentration of funding and contractual maturity mismatch. Concentration of funding refers to the proportion of funding that is obtained from a single source. Excessive concentration of funding exposes a bank to the risk that a single funding source could be withdrawn.

Contractual maturity mismatch refers to the maturity dates of a bank's assets compared to the maturity dates of a bank's funding sources. In a normal yield curve environment, where long-term interest rates are higher than short-term rates, a bank can maximize its net interest income—all else equal—by borrowing short term and lending long term. In doing so, the bank would minimize the interest paid to its depositors and maximize interest earned on its loan assets. In excess, however, such maturity mismatches expose the bank to liquidity risk if the bank needs to return cash on its maturing deposits prior to the time that it receives cash repayment of loans from its borrowers. Monitoring maturity mismatch is thus an important tool in liquidity risk management.

EXAMPLE 5

The following excerpts from HSBC's annual report explain the bank's approach to management of its liquidity and funding risk. The disclosures state that the group's principal operating entities were within the risk tolerance levels established by the board for the Liquidity Coverage Ratio, the Net Stable Funding Ratio, depositor concentration, and term funding maturity concentration.

EXHIBIT 9   Liquidity Disclosure—Excerpts from HSBC's Annual Report

The management of liquidity and funding is primarily undertaken locally (by country) in our operating entities in compliance with the Group's LFRF [liquidity and funding risk management framework], and with practices and limits set by the GMB [Group Management Board] through the RMM [Risk Management Meeting of the Group Management Board] and approved by the Board. Our general policy is that each defined operating entity should be self-sufficient in funding its own activities. Where transactions exist between operating entities, they are reflected symmetrically in both entities.

As part of our asset, liability and capital management structure, we have established asset and liability committees ("ALCO") at Group level, in the regions and in operating entities. . . . The primary responsibility for managing liquidity and funding within the Group's framework and risk appetite resides with the local operating entities' ALCOs, Holdings ALCO and the RMM. . . .

The Liquidity Coverage Ratio ("LCR") aims to ensure that a bank has sufficient unencumbered high-quality liquid assets ("HQLA") to meet its liquidity needs in a 30-calendar-day liquidity stress scenario. HQLA consist of cash or assets that can be converted into cash at little or no loss of value in markets. We reported a Group European Commission ("EC") LCR at December 31, 2016 of 136% (December 31, 2015: 116%) to the PRA [UK Prudential Regulation Authority]. . . . At December 31, 2016,

(continued)

---

[24] Basel Committee on Banking Supervision, "Basel III: A Global Regulatory Framework For More Resilient Banks and Banking System": www.bis.org/publ/bcbs189.pdf.

EXHIBIT 9   (Continued)

all the Group's principal operating entities were within the LCR risk tolerance level established by the Board. . . . The liquidity position of the Group can also be represented by the stand-alone ratios of each of our principal operating entities. . . .

The Net Stable Funding Ratio ("NSFR") requires institutions to maintain sufficient stable funding relative to required stable funding, and reflects a bank's long-term funding profile (funding with a term of more than a year). It is designed to complement the LCR. At December 31, 2016, the Group's principal operating entities were within the NSFR risk tolerance level established by the Board and applicable under the LFRF.

The LCR and NSFR metrics assume a stressed outflow based on a portfolio of depositors within each deposit segment. The validity of these assumptions is challenged if the portfolio of depositors is not large enough to avoid depositor concentration. Operating entities are exposed to term re-financing concentration risk if the current maturity profile results in future maturities being overly concentrated in any defined period. At December 31, 2016, all principal operating entities were within the risk tolerance levels set for depositor concentration and term funding maturity concentration. These risk tolerances were established by the Board. . . .

[The table below displays the following liquidity metrics for HSBC's principal operating entities: individual LCR on an EC LCR basis and NSFR.]

| | Operating Entities' Liquidity Measures | | |
| | LCR | | NSFR |
	Dec. 16 (%)	Dec. 15 (%)	Dec. 16 (%)
HSBC UK liquidity group	123	107	116
The Hongkong and Shanghai Banking Corporation, Hong Kong Branch	185	150	157
The Hongkong and Shanghai Banking Corporation, Singapore Branch	154	189	112
HSBC Bank USA	130	116	120
HSBC France	122	127	120
Hang Seng Bank	218	199	162
HSBC Canada	142	142	139
HSBC Bank China	253	183	49
HSBC Middle East, UAE Branch	241		141
HSBC Mexico	177		128
HSBC Private Bank	178		155

Source: HSBC Holdings plc Annual Report and Accounts 2016 (pp. 108, 143, and 144).

1. Based on the exhibit, in 2016, which of HSBC's operating entities had the highest level of liquid assets relative to its liquidity needs in a stress scenario?
2. Based on the exhibit, which of HSBC's operating entities had the most stable funding relative to its required need for stable funding?

3. Based on the exhibit, which of HSBC's operating entities is the furthest away from achieving the Basel III target for NSFR?

Solution to 1: Based on the exhibit, HSBC Bank China had the highest level of liquid assets relative to its liquidity needs in a stress scenario. Its 2016 LCR of 253% is higher than that of any of the other HSBC entities.

Solution to 2: Based on the exhibit, Hang Seng Bank had the most stable funding relative to its required need for stable funding. Its 2016 NSFR of 162% is higher than that of any of the other HSBC entities.

Solution to 3: Based on the exhibit, HSBC Bank China is the furthest away from achieving the Basel III standard of NSFR greater than 100%. Its NSFR of 49% is lower than that of any of the other HSBC entities. (It is possible that these metrics result from RMB capital controls in China or jurisdictional issues; however, the example does not provide sufficient information to confirm the reason.)

3.1.6. Sensitivity to Market Risk

Almost every entity has some exposure to changes in interest rates, exchange rates, equity prices, or commodity prices. Every company in the United States, for example, is required to provide quantitative and qualitative disclosures in annual filings about exposure to market risk. The nature of banks' operations generally makes sensitivity of earnings to market risks a particularly important consideration for analysts. Mismatches in the maturity, repricing frequency, reference rates, or currency of banks' loans and deposits create exposure to market movements. Further, exposure to risk arises not only from loans and deposits on a bank's balance sheet but also from off-balance-sheet exposures, including, for example, guarantees or derivatives positions linked to interest rates, exchange rates, equities, or commodities. It is important to understand how an adverse change in any of these markets would affect a bank's earnings. It is also important to evaluate the strength of a bank's ability to manage market risks.

Banks disclose information about the sensitivity of earnings to different market conditions—namely, the earnings impact of a shift up or down in some market. Consider a bank's sensitivity to interest rate risk. Even in a purely hypothetical situation of a bank with assets and liabilities that are identical in terms of interest rates, maturity, and frequency of repricing, an increase in interest rates would cause the bank's net interest income to increase. This would occur simply because banks have more assets than liabilities. In reality, of course, the terms of a bank's assets and liabilities differ. Generally, the yield on a bank's loan assets is presumed to be higher than the rate it must pay its depositors, particularly consumer deposits. With respect to term structure, in a typical yield curve environment, longer-dated assets would have a higher yield *ceteris paribus* than shorter-dated funding sources, but another aspect of interest rate sensitivity is repricing frequency. For example, having assets with greater repricing frequency than liabilities would benefit earnings in a rising interest rate scenario. In sum, many structural factors affect interest rate sensitivity.

The following example includes an interest rate sensitivity disclosure showing the earnings impact of an upward and downward shift in interest rates. Disclosures such as these reflect the existing structure of a bank's assets and liabilities.

772 International Financial Statement Analysis

EXAMPLE 6   Market Risk

The following excerpts from HSBC's annual report explain the bank's approach to monitoring its market risk and illustrates one of the tools used by the bank: sensitivity analysis.

EXHIBIT 10   Excerpt from HSBC's Annual Report

Our objective is to manage and control market risk exposures while maintaining a market profile consistent with our risk appetite. We use a range of tools to monitor and limit market risk exposures including sensitivity analysis, value at risk and stress testing.

The following table sets out the assessed impact on our base case projected net interest income ("NII") for 2016 (excluding insurance) of a series of four quarterly parallel shocks of 25 basis points to the current market-implied path of interest rates worldwide at the beginning of each quarter from January 1, 2017. . . .

The sensitivities shown represent our assessment as to the change in expected base case net interest income under the two rate scenarios, assuming that all other non-interest rate risk variables remain constant, and there are no management actions. . . .

We expect NII to rise in the rising rate scenario and fall in the falling rate scenario. This is due to a structural mismatch between our assets and liabilities (on balance we would expect our assets to reprice more quickly, and to a greater extent, than our liabilities).

Net Interest Income Sensitivity (Audited)

	US dollar bloc ($m)	Rest of Americas bloc ($m)	Hong Kong dollar bloc ($m)	Rest of Asia bloc ($m)	Sterling bloc ($m)	Euro bloc ($m)	Total ($m)
Change in 2016 net interest income arising from a shift in yield curves of:							
+25 basis points at the beginning of each quarter	605	47	504	280	61	212	1,709
−25 basis points at the beginning of each quarter	−1,024	−41	−797	−292	−261	9	−2,406

Source: HSBC Holdings plc Annual Report and Accounts 2016 (pp. 78 and 117).

1. Based on the exhibit, by how much would HSBC's planned net interest income decrease if the yield curves shifted downward by 25 basis points at the beginning of each quarter for four quarters?
2. If a decrease in interest rates would hurt the earnings of banks such as HSBC, why would central banks lower interest rates so significantly following the financial crisis in order to prop up the financial sector?

Solution to 1: HSBC's planned net interest income would decrease by $2,406 million if the yield curves shifted downward by 25 basis points at the beginning of each quarter.

> *Solution to 2:* An interest rate sensitivity table such as the one presented by HSBC is a static presentation and thus assumes that the relation between the structure of assets and liabilities in place at the time would remain stationary. Following the financial crisis, the central banks' actions reduced interest rates at which banks could borrow (effectively, to near zero), while the rates that banks were able to charge their loan customers were—while still low—far higher than their borrowing costs. Further, the central banks' actions were not intended solely to prop up banks' earnings but also to provide liquidity and stimulus to the overall economy.

As described in the example, another tool that HSBC uses to measure and monitor market risk is value at risk (VaR). Recall that VaR is a way to estimate the amount of potential loss based on simulations that incorporate historical pricing information. HSBC estimates its VaR using a 99% confidence level, a one-day holding period, and two prior years of pricing data on foreign exchange rates, interest rates, equity prices, commodity prices, and associated volatilities.

3.2. Other Factors Relevant to Analysis of a Bank

While the CAMELS approach to assessing bank soundness is fairly comprehensive, there are important bank-specific attributes that it does not completely address. There are also important attributes not addressed by the CAMELS approach that apply to both banks and other types of companies.

3.2.1. Banking-Specific Analytical Considerations Not Addressed by CAMELS

The CAMELS acronym is useful as a composite of major factors, but it is neither comprehensive nor comprehensively integrated. Also, the ordering of the factors does not signify importance. For example, strong capital (the "C") and strong liquidity (the "L") are equally important in the Basel III standards.[25]

The following bank attributes are either unaddressed or not fully addressed by a CAMELS analysis:

- **Government support.** Governments do not normally strive to save a company or even an entire industry that may be facing failure. In capitalist societies, failure is the unfortunate occasional by-product of risk taking with capital, and bankruptcy laws and courts serve to administer the results of failed capital allocation. The banking industry is different from other industries, however, regarding government support. It is in a government's interest to have a healthy banking system because a nation's economy is affected by banks' lending activity, and a nation's central bank needs a healthy banking system for the effective transmission of monetary policy. A healthy banking system also facilitates commerce by providing adequate payment processing and instilling depositor confidence in the safekeeping of their deposits.

   Government agencies monitor the health of banks in the entire system and will close banks that might fail or will arrange mergers with healthy ones able to absorb them. This

---

[25] Basel Committee on Banking Supervision, "Basel III: A Global Regulatory Framework For More Resilient Banks and Banking System" (December 2010, p. 8, item B.34): www.bis.org/publ/bcbs189.pdf.

pruning activity addresses issues with banks that might otherwise weaken the banking system if left unattended. Alternatively, governments may directly assist banks to keep them afloat rather than closing them or arranging for mergers with healthier banks. Visible examples of both assisting and pruning activities occurred during the financial crisis of 2008. For example, the US Treasury created the Troubled Asset Relief Program (TARP) to purchase loans held by banks and to provide equity injections to the banks. During the same period, the Treasury also arranged numerous mergers among banking giants, leading to even bigger banking giants.

CAMELS analysis will not provide an assessment of government support, but an investor can qualitatively assess whether a bank will enjoy the support of the government in times of economic distress. The following are factors to consider:

- *Size of the bank.* Is the bank large enough to bring damage to a significant part of the economy in the event of its failure? Is it "too big to fail"?
- *Status of the country's banking system.* Is the nation's banking system healthy enough to handle a particular bank's failure? Rather than force the banking system to cope with the failure of a particular bank, would it be a better solution for the government to intervene with taxpayer funds to support it? The global financial crisis of 2008–2009 led the US Federal Reserve to develop the concept of SIFIs: systemically important financial institutions, ones that would pose a significant risk to the economy in the event of a failure. Such institutions have been the target of an increased degree of regulation in the post-crisis era.
- **Government ownership.** Public ownership of banks may include a strong ownership representation by the government of their home country. Government ownership may exist for several reasons. A "development" view of government ownership incorporates a belief that government ownership aids financial development of the banks, leading to broad economic growth. A more pessimistic view is that a nation's banking system is not strong enough to stand on its own and attract large amounts of capital, because of low ethical standards within the industry or a lack of confidence in the banking system among the nation's public at large—an important source of funds for any bank.[26]

  Whatever the reason may be for a government's ownership stake in a bank, its presence adds another dimension of security for a bank investor. A government that owns a stake in a bank is likely to intervene on the bank's behalf in the event of economic distress. Conversely, a government that plans to reduce its ownership stake in a bank may directly reduce that dimension of security; however, that may not always be the case. During the global financial crisis of 2008–2009, some governments became reluctant owners of banks, which were ultimately supported by taxpayer funding. When government ownership of such banks was reduced after the crisis ended, markets viewed the reduction as a signal of renewed strength.
- **Mission of banking entity.** Not all banks share the same mission. For example, community banks primarily serve the needs of the immediate community in which they operate. That community's welfare could be driven by an economy based on farming, mining, or oil or could depend on a single large manufacturing entity. The fortunes of the banks and their borrowers and depositors would depend on economic factors that affect the primary industry or employer. Contrast that situation with a global banking entity absorbing deposits from all around the world while investing globally as well. The global bank is more diversified against a single risk than any community bank.

---

[26] Rafael La Porta, Florencio Lopez-de-Silanes, and Andrei Shleifer, "Government Ownership of Banks," NBER Working Paper No. 7620 (March 2000).

The mission of the bank and the economics of its constituents will affect the way the bank manages its assets and liabilities. That is a qualitative assessment that the bank investor needs to make, and it is not addressed by a CAMELS analysis.

- **Corporate culture.** A bank's culture may be very risk averse and cautious and make only loans perceived to be low risk, or alternatively, it may be risk seeking and willing to take risk in pursuit of high returns on investment. Or a bank's culture may be somewhere in the middle of those two extremes. An overly cautious culture may be too risk averse to provide adequate returns to shareholders for taking on the risk of ownership. A highly risk-hungry culture may lead to boom and bust results and volatility. Differences in the cultural environment are particularly important for banks operating in multiple countries, where there may be a disconnect between corporate culture and national culture.

   A bank investor can qualitatively assess a bank's cultural environment by considering factors such as these:

   - Has the bank generated recent losses resulting from a narrowly focused investment strategy, such as a large, outsized exposure to a particularly risky country or area of the economy?
   - Has the bank restated its financial statements owing to financial reporting internal control failures?
   - Does the bank award above-average equity-based compensation to its top managers, possibly incentivizing risk-taking behavior and short-termism?
   - What does the bank's experience with loss reserves say about its culture? Has it frequently been slow to provide for losses, only to record large asset write-downs later?

3.2.2. Analytical Considerations Not Addressed by CAMELS That Are Also Relevant for Any Company

There are other factors relevant to the analysis of a bank—and to any kind of company—that are not covered by the CAMELS approach. The following factors merit consideration by debt and equity investors in banks as well as investors in non-banking entities:

- **Competitive environment.** A bank's competitive position, relative to its peers, may affect how it allocates capital and assesses risks; it may also affect the aforementioned cultural mindset. A regional bank may have a near-monopolistic hold on a particular region and not take very many risks beyond maintaining its grip. A global bank may be affected by the actions of other global banks. Managers of a global bank may not be satisfied with following the lead of other banks and may pursue ambitious goals of growing market share at all costs and with little regard for risks, or they may be content with more profitable but slower growth. It depends on how the bank's managers perceive their competitive position and how they will react to the perception.
- **Off-balance-sheet items.** Off-balance-sheet assets and liabilities pose a risk to entities and their investors if they should unexpectedly drain resources. The global financial crisis of 2008–2009 was hastened by the Lehman Brothers bankruptcy, and the opacity of their involvement with such financial instruments as credit derivatives prevented concise pre-crisis analysis of the risks they shouldered. However difficult to examine, off-balance-sheet exposures need consideration whenever one analyzes a bank or financial institution.

   Not all off-balance-sheet items involve exotic or highly engineered financial instruments. Operating leases are a low-risk example of off-balance-sheet liabilities: They are not a recognized liability of a company, yet they provide a creditor with a claim on a company's future cash flows. Fortunately, visibility into such future obligations is easily accessed by investors in the lease footnotes.

A financial institution analyst should be alert to the existence in the financial statements of an accounting construct known as variable interest entities, or VIEs. Variable interest entities are a form of "special-purpose entity" usually formed solely for one purpose: perhaps to hold only certain assets or assets that may be financed with specific debt instruments. Before the accounting for variable interest entities was developed, companies sometimes used outside parties to take a majority ownership stake in the special-purpose entity, ensuring that they would not have to consolidate the special-purpose entity's assets and liabilities. The accounting standard setters developed the VIE model to capture the consolidation of such special-purpose entities. By meeting generalized criteria for consolidation apart from clearly defined equity ownership tests, a company that is the primary beneficiary of a VIE's existence may be required to consolidate the VIE's financial statements with its own, even if it has no equity ownership in it. Yet a variable interest entity may also result in off-balance-sheet assets and liabilities for a bank if the bank has an interest in the VIE but is not required to consolidate it. If the VIE is not consolidated with the bank, its existence and certain financial information must be disclosed. Those non-consolidated VIEs should be of interest to investors: The reasons given for non-consolidation should be examined for reasonableness, and the implications to the bank of various scenarios affecting the VIE should be considered.

Benefit plans are another "off-balance-sheet" item for investors to examine. Although these are not completely off-balance-sheet items because the net benefit plan assets or obligations appear on the balance sheet, the economics that drive them are different from the bank's business. Shortfalls in assets due to market performance can cause rapid increases in required contributions to plans. Interest rate decreases, which drive plan obligations higher, can also cause rapid cash drains for required contributions to plans. Bank investors should examine benefits plan footnotes to determine the degree of risk posed by such plans.

One particular off-balance-sheet item that is found in financial companies only—sometimes in banks—is assets under management (AUM). Banks may have trust departments that generate management fees based on the assets under management. Those assets belong to the clients and are not consolidated with a bank's balance sheet accounts, yet they drive the returns of the bank. If such returns are material to a bank's results, the bank investor should be concerned with the size and growth or decline in assets under management.

- **Segment information.** Banks may be organized in different lines of business. They can be organized according to domestic and foreign markets; they can be organized along consumer or industrial lines of business; they may offer financial services, such as leasing or market making in securities; and they may have related businesses that are not strictly banking driven, such as trust operations. Regardless of the lines of business a bank (or any other company) may pursue, segment information should illustrate the information used by the chief operating decision maker in the entity. That information can help the investor decide whether capital is being allocated well within the bank's internally competing operations.

- **Currency exposure.** Although it may not be a problem for smaller, regional banks that operate in a single currency, floating currency exchange rates can create problems for global banks. Banks may finance and lend in a variety of currencies, resulting in foreign currency transaction exposure. Large banks may actively trade in foreign currencies and actively hedge using foreign exchange derivatives, leading to unforeseen gains or losses when world events affect currencies unexpectedly; not all banks may be successful currency traders. Global banks face the same balance sheet translation issues that affect other multinational corporations. When a bank's home currency strengthens against the functional currencies of its foreign subsidiaries, the translation of balance sheet accounts at the end of an accounting period may lead to currency translation adjustments that can reduce capital.

• **Risk factors.** Investors should review the risk factors presented in a company's annual filing. Sometimes derided as a mere list of worst-case scenarios created by a company's legal counsel, the risk factors section of a company's filing can also fill gaps in an investor's knowledge about legal and regulatory issues that might not otherwise be uncovered.

• **Basel III disclosures.** The Basel III requirements include extensive disclosures that complement the minimum risk-based capital requirements and other quantitative requirements with the goal of promoting market discipline by providing useful regulatory information to investors and other interested parties on a consistent, comparable basis.[27]

3.3. An Illustration of the CAMELS Approach to Analysis of a Bank

This section illustrates the CAMELS approach using Citigroup's financial statements as an example. The CAMELS approach is based on the evidence gathered by the analyst in assessing each CAMELS component, and this evidence will vary from investor to investor. Some aspects of the CAMELS approach will matter more to certain investors than others: An equity investor may be far more concerned with earnings and earnings quality than with capital adequacy. A fixed-income investor might be far more concerned with capital adequacy and liquidity than earnings. The interests of each type of investor will determine what kind of analysis they perform to assess each CAMELS component. The following example of Citigroup is not intended to show all possible analyses.

It should also be understood that although the CAMELS approach entails quantitative aspects, it is not a wholly formulaic approach to analyzing a bank. An analyst's judgment and discretion also matter greatly in the application of the CAMELS approach. Judgment and discretion figure into the kind of testing done by an investor to gather evidence for the various CAMELS components, and judgment and discretion also figure into the rating of the various CAMELS components once the evidence has been reviewed.

The following sections present examples of the relevant information for each component and conclude with a summary assessment. In each case, the summary assessment includes a rating, where a rating of 1 is the highest and a rating of 5 is the lowest.

3.3.1. Capital Adequacy

As noted above, capital adequacy relates to the proportion of a bank's assets funded by capital, with the assets accorded varying risk weightings. Not only are assets stratified into risk classes, but the bank capital funding those assets is also stratified into tiers: Common Equity Tier 1 Capital, Total Tier 1 Capital, and Tier 2 Capital.

Common Equity Tier 1 Capital includes common stock, issuance surplus related to common stock, retained earnings, accumulated other comprehensive income, and certain adjustments, including the deduction of intangible assets and deferred tax assets.

Exhibit 11 shows the calculation of Citigroup's Common Equity Tier 1 Capital, Risk-Weighted Assets, and Common Equity Tier 1 Capital Ratio at the end of 2016 and 2015. Citigroup's ratio is well within the required limits in both years. The ratio declined slightly in 2016, from 14.60% to 14.35%. The decline in the ratio is mostly attributable to the increase in deferred tax assets disallowed in the computation of Common Equity Tier 1 Capital.

---

[27] Basel Committee on Banking Supervision, "Standards: Revised Pillar 3 Disclosure Requirements" (January 2015, p. 3): https://www.bis.org/bcbs/publ/d309.pdf.

EXHIBIT 11 Components of Citigroup Common Equity Tier 1 Capital under Current Regulatory Standards (Basel III Advanced Approaches with Transition Arrangements)

(In millions of dollars)	Dec. 31, 2016	Dec. 31, 2015
Citigroup common stockholders' equity	$206,051	$205,286
Add: Qualifying non-controlling interests	259	369
Regulatory capital adjustments and deductions:		
Less: Net unrealized gains (losses) on securities available for sale (AFS), net of tax	(320)	(544)
Less: Defined benefit plan liability adjustment, net of tax	(2,066)	(3,070)
Less: Accumulated net unrealized losses on cash flow hedges, net of tax (4)	(560)	(617)
Less: Cumulative unrealized net gain (loss) related to changes in fair value of financial liabilities attributable to own creditworthiness, net of tax	(37)	176
Less: Intangible assets:		
Goodwill, net of related deferred tax liabilities	20,858	21,980
Identifiable intangible assets other than mortgage servicing rights (MSRs), net of related deferred tax liabilities	2,926	1,434
Less: Defined benefit pension plan net assets	514	318
Less: Deferred tax assets (DTAs) arising from net operating loss, foreign tax credit, and general business credit carry-forwards	12,802	9,464
Less: Excess over 10%/15% limitations for other DTAs, certain common stock investments, and mortgage servicing rights	4,815	2,652
Total Common Equity Tier 1 Capital	$167,378	$173,862
Risk-Weighted Assets under Current Regulatory Standards:		
Credit risk	$773,483	$791,036
Market risk	64,006	74,817
Operational risk	329,275	325,000
Total risk-weighted assets	$1,166,764	$1,190,853
Common Equity Tier 1 Capital Ratio (Tier 1 Capital/ Total risk-weighted assets)	**14.35%**	**14.60%**
Stated minimum Common Equity Tier 1 Capital Ratio	4.50%	4.50%

Total Tier 1 Capital includes other instruments issued by the bank that meet certain criteria based on their subordination to deposit and other debt obligations, bear no fixed maturity, and carry no requirement to pay dividends or interest without full discretion of the bank. Preferred stocks can be constructed to meet these criteria.

Exhibit 12 shows the calculation of Citigroup's Total Tier 1 Capital and Total Tier 1 Capital Ratio at the end of 2016 and 2015. Again, Citigroup's ratio is well within the required limits in both years. The ratio improved in 2016, from 14.81% to 15.29%. The increase in this ratio is mostly attributable to additional perpetual preferred stock qualifying for inclusion in 2016 and the decrease in the amount of deferred tax assets disallowed in the computation of Total Tier 1 Capital.

EXHIBIT 12   Components of Citigroup Total Tier 1 Capital under Current Regulatory Standards (Basel III Advanced Approaches with Transition Arrangements)

(In millions of dollars)	Dec. 31, 2016	Dec. 31, 2015
Common Equity Tier 1 Capital (from Exhibit 11)	$167,378	$173,862
Additional Tier 1 Capital:		
Qualifying perpetual preferred stock	19,069	16,571
Qualifying trust preferred securities	1,371	1,707
Qualifying non-controlling interests	17	12
Regulatory capital adjustments and deductions:		
Less: Cumulative unrealized net gain (loss) related to changes in fair value of financial liabilities attributable to own creditworthiness, net of tax	(24)	265
Less: Defined benefit pension plan net assets	343	476
Less: DTAs arising from net operating loss, foreign tax credit and general business credit carry-forwards	8,535	14,195
Less: Permitted ownership interests in covered funds	533	567
Less: Minimum regulatory capital requirements of insurance underwriting subsidiaries	61	229
Total additional Tier 1 Capital	$11,009	$2,558
Total Tier 1 Capital (Common Equity Tier 1 Capital + Additional Tier 1 Capital)	$178,387	$176,420
Total risk-weighted assets (from Exhibit 11)	$1,166,764	$1,190,853
Tier 1 Capital Ratio	**15.29%**	**14.81%**
Minimum Tier 1 Capital Ratio	6.00%	6.00%

Tier 2 Capital includes, on a limited basis, portions of the allowance for loan and lease losses and other instruments that are subordinate to depositors and general creditors. Exhibit 13 shows the calculation of Citigroup's Tier 2 Capital and Total Capital Ratio at the end of 2016 and 2015. Consistent with the Common Equity Tier 1 Capital Ratio and the Total Tier 1 Capital Ratio, the 2016 Total Capital Ratio far exceeds the minimum requirement. The Total Capital Ratio improved from the 2015 level, from 16.69% to 17.33%. The improvement was mostly due to the increase in Total Tier 1 Capital and the amount of qualifying subordinated debt.

In summary, Citigroup's capital adequacy at the end of 2016 appears to be solidly positive. For each of the three chief capital ratios, the company has exceeded the minimum levels required for being considered to be a well-capitalized bank. A rating of 1 could be justified by their ratios, which far exceeded the minimum levels.

EXHIBIT 13   Components of Citigroup Tier 2 Capital under Current Regulatory Standards (Basel III Advanced Approaches with Transition Arrangements)

(In millions of dollars)	Dec. 31, 2016	Dec. 31, 2015
Total Tier 1 Capital (Common Equity Tier 1 Capital + Additional Tier 1 Capital)	$178,387	$176,420
Qualifying subordinated debt	22,818	21,370
Qualifying trust preferred securities	317	0
Qualifying non-controlling interests	22	17
Excess of eligible credit reserves over expected credit losses	660	1,163
Regulatory capital adjustments and deductions:		
Add: Unrealized gains on AFS equity exposures includable in Tier 2 Capital	3	5
Less: Minimum regulatory capital requirements of insurance underwriting subsidiaries	61	229
Total Tier 2 Capital	$23,759	$22,326
Total Capital (Tier 1 Capital + Tier 2 Capital)	$202,146	$198,746
Total risk-weighted assets	$1,166,764	$1,190,853
Total Capital Ratio	**17.33%**	**16.69%**
Minimum Capital Ratio	**8.00%**	**8.00%**

3.3.2. Asset Quality

Asset quality matters greatly to a bank. As financial intermediaries in an economy, banks owe their existence to the creation of loans. If a bank's credit policies are unsound, its capital base can be quickly eroded during economic downturns, creating strains on the bank's liquidity and its ability to generate earnings. Creating new loans becomes problematic.

A portion of bank assets are held in highly liquid financial instruments, such as cash, deposits held at other banks, and instruments that may convert into cash in a very short time frame, such as repurchase agreements and some receivables. These are not highly risky assets.

Increasing in riskiness are the investments made by the bank in financial instruments with cash deemed to be in excess of operating needs. Under US GAAP and IFRS, these investments may be classified as available-for-sale investments, which are reported at fair value, or held-to-maturity investments, which are reported at their amortized cost unless an impairment occurs. While these investments are riskier than the liquid securities and reflect an investment decision made by management, their value is quite transparent and their reported value reflects their realizability in cash—although it takes more analytical effort to make that assertion for held-to-maturity securities.

The riskiest, and often the largest, asset classes are the loans underwritten by the bank. Loans embody credit risk and the judgment of management in extending credit to customers. The underwriting risks and the management judgments in assessing them are reflected in the allowance for loan losses. It is here that the analyst faces some of the most difficult assessments in understanding the quality of banking assets and is at a disadvantage, because some information simply is unavailable to an analyst (or investor). Conversely, an examiner for a supervisory regulator has the ability to see the bank from the inside and assess the soundness of loan (and investment) policies and procedures. An examiner may also review the construction and workings of internal control procedures and may be able to examine how exceptions to credit policies are being handled.[28]

Although the analyst is interested in all of those inner workings, he/she can be concerned only with circumstantial evidence that the credit policies are sound and are being maintained. That circumstantial evidence can be found in the financial statements, but it is not completely obvious from merely looking at a balance sheet. There are ways to find evidence of asset quality, as will be shown with Citigroup. Exhibit 14 shows the asset side of Citigroup's balance sheet on a condensed basis at the end of 2016 and 2015.

EXHIBIT 14   Citigroup Asset Composition, December 31, 2016 and 2015

| | December 31, 2016 | | December 31, 2015 | |
(In millions of dollars)	$	% Total Assets	$	% Total Assets
Liquid assets:				
Cash and due from banks	$23,043	*1.3%*	$20,900	*1.2%*
Deposits with banks	137,451	*7.7%*	112,197	*6.5%*
Federal funds sold and securities borrowed or purchased under resale agreements	236,813	*13.2%*	219,675	*12.7%*
Brokerage receivables	28,887	*1.6%*	27,683	*1.6%*
Trading account assets	243,925	*13.6%*	241,215	*13.9%*
Total liquid assets	670,119	*37.4%*	621,670	*35.9%*
Investments:				
Available-for-sale	299,424	*16.7%*	299,136	*17.3%*
Held-to-maturity	45,667	*2.5%*	36,215	*2.1%*
Non-marketable equity securities	8,213	*0.5%*	7,604	*0.4%*
Total investments	353,304	*19.7%*	342,955	*19.8%*
Loans:				
Consumer	325,366	*18.2%*	325,785	*18.8%*
Corporate	299,003	*16.7%*	291,832	*16.9%*
Loans, net of unearned income	624,369	*34.9%*	617,617	*35.7%*
Allowance for loan losses	(12,060)	*–0.7%*	(12,626)	*–0.7%*
Total loans, net	612,309	*34.2%*	604,991	*35.0%*
Goodwill	21,659	*1.2%*	22,349	*1.3%*
Intangible assets (other than MSRs)	5,114	*0.3%*	3,721	*0.2%*
Mortgage servicing rights (MSRs)	1,564	*0.1%*	1,781	*0.1%*
Other assets	128,008	*7.1%*	133,743	*7.7%*
Total assets	$1,792,077	*100.0%*	$1,731,210	*100.0%*

Observations from the composition of the assets:

- Citigroup's liquid assets are the largest single group of all, at 37.4% in 2016, and slightly greater than the year before, indicating greater liquidity.

---

[28] See Section 3.1 of the FDIC's "RMS Manual of Examination Policies," available at https://www.fdic.gov/regulations/safety/manual/section3-1.pdf.

- The proportion of investments to total assets of 19.7% is practically unchanged from 2015; the majority of the investments are available-for-sale securities reported at fair value.
- Consumer and corporate loans are the highest-risk assets and in both years amount to more than one-third of all assets. They are the second largest class of assets after the liquid assets.

In assessing asset quality, an analyst would want to focus on the riskiest assets in the mix: the investments and the loans. He or she would want to determine that the investments, while transparent in value, represent sound investment decisions and that the loans result from similarly reasoned underwriting policies. The analyst would want assurance that the stated amount of loans is collectible and that the allowance for loan losses is reasonably stated.

First, take a look at the investments. Exhibit 15 shows Citigroup's available-for-sale securities by class at the end of 2016. Exhibit 15 was extracted from Note 13 of the 2016 10-K, which showed the amortized cost by investment instrument, gross unrealized gains, gross unrealized losses, and fair value as stated in the balance sheet. Added to the table were the gross unrealized gains and losses expressed as a percentage of amortized cost, which is the amount invested.

EXHIBIT 15 Citigroup Available-for-Sale (AFS) Securities at December 31, 2016

| | | | | | % of Cost: | |
| | | Gross Unrealized | | Fair | Gross Unrealized | |
(In millions of dollars)	Amortized Cost	Gains	Losses	Value	Gains	Losses
Debt securities AFS						
Mortgage-backed securities:						
US government-sponsored agency guaranteed	$38,663	$248	$506	$38,405	0.6%	1.3%
Prime	2	—	—	2	—	—
Alt-A	43	7	—	50	16.3%	—
Non-US residential	3,852	13	7	3,858	0.3%	0.2%
Commercial	357	2	1	358	0.6%	0.3%
Total mortgage-backed securities	$42,917	$270	$514	$42,673	0.6%	1.2%
US Treasury and federal agency securities						
US Treasury	$113,606	$629	$452	$113,783	0.6%	0.4%
Agency obligations	9,952	21	85	9,888	0.2%	0.9%
Total US Treasury and federal agency securities	$123,558	$650	$537	$123,671	0.5%	0.4%
State and municipal	$10,797	$80	$757	$10,120	0.7%	**7.0%**
Foreign government	98,112	590	554	98,148	0.6%	0.6%
Corporate	17,195	105	176	17,124	0.6%	1.0%
Asset-backed securities	6,810	6	22	6,794	0.1%	0.3%
Other debt securities	503	—	—	503	0.0%	0.0%
Total debt securities AFS	$299,892	$1,701	$2,560	$299,033	0.6%	0.9%
Marketable equity securities AFS	$377	$20	$6	$391	5.3%	1.6%
Total securities AFS	$300,269	$1,721	$2,566	$299,424	0.6%	0.9%

The fair value ($299,424 million) is less than the amortized cost ($300,269 million) in the aggregate, and the net difference is $845 million; the largest contributor to that loss is the state and municipal obligations, with a $757 million loss. At a 7% loss in value, those were the only securities to generate losses greater than 2%.

Observations from the AFS securities valuation table:

- Although Citigroup has not generated a net winning strategy with its available-for-sale investments, its losses do not suggest reckless abandon.
- In future years, new US GAAP standards will eliminate the AFS classification for marketable equity securities. They will still be measured at fair value, just as they were measured at year end 2016. Starting in 2018, however, the gains and losses resulting from remeasurement will be shown directly in the income statement instead of being recorded in other comprehensive income. As of December 31, 2016, Citigroup's unrealized gains on its AFS equity investments exceeded its unrealized losses. Based on market values at that point in time, the reclassification would benefit the group's income.

A closer look at the gross unrealized losses is possible, because Note 13 also contains a simple aging of the losses: It shows how much of the $2.566 billion of unrealized losses are less than 12 months old and how much of the losses are 12 months old or older, by category. The longer a loss position exists, the greater the possibility that a security is impaired on an "other-than-temporary" basis. It would be unusual for losses to exist for long periods of time and then suddenly reverse.

The aging for the losses in Citigroup's available-for-sale securities is shown in Exhibit 16. Observations from the aging of AFS unrealized losses table:

- A slight majority (54%) of the losses are less than 12 months old, making them of less concern than the rest.
- Of the $1.172 billion of gross unrealized losses 12 months old or older, 60% ($702 million) are related to state and municipal securities, which raises a concern that the largest class of losses may in fact become realized.

EXHIBIT 16   Citigroup Aging of Unrealized Losses on Available-for-Sale Securities at December 31, 2016

	Less than 12 months		12 months or longer		Total	
(In millions of dollars)	Fair value	Gross unrealized losses	Fair value	Gross unrealized losses	Fair value	Gross unrealized losses
Mortgage-backed securities						
US government-sponsored agency sponsored	$23,534	$436	$2,236	$70	$25,770	$506
Prime	1	—	—	—	1	—
Non-US residential	486	—	1,276	7	1,762	7
Commercial	75	1	58	—	133	1
Total mortgage-backed securities	$24,096	$437	$3,570	$77	$27,666	$514

(continued)

EXHIBIT 16   (Continued)

(In millions of dollars)	Less than 12 months		12 months or longer		Total	
	Fair value	Gross unrealized losses	Fair value	Gross unrealized losses	Fair value	Gross unrealized losses
US Treasury and federal agency securities						
US Treasury	$44,342	$445	$1,335	$7	$45,677	$452
Agency obligations	6,552	83	250	2	6,802	85
Total US Treasury and federal agency securities	$50,894	$528	$1,585	$9	$52,479	$537
State and municipal	$1,616	$55	$3,116	$702	$4,732	$757
Foreign government	38,226	243	8,973	311	47,199	554
Corporate	7,011	129	1,877	47	8,888	176
Asset-backed securities	411	—	3,213	22	3,624	22
Other debt securities	5	—	—	—	5	—
Marketable equity securities AFS	19	2	24	4	43	6
Total securities AFS	$122,278	$1,394	$22,358	$1,172	$144,636	$2,566

A similar analysis can be done for the held-to-maturity (HTM) securities. Even though they represent a much smaller proportion of total assets, they still provide evidence of the manager's investment acumen. The result of the HTM securities review of the losses and aging of the losses is consistent with the results of the available-for-sale securities review. Though not presented in exhibits because of space limitations, Citigroup's unrealized losses on its HTM securities totaled $457 million, which is 1.3% of the amount invested. Of that $457 million loss in value, 82% ($373 million) stemmed from held-to-maturity securities that were showing losses older than 12 months, of which $180 million related to state and municipal securities.

Observations on the HTM securities:

- The losses on the HTM securities are much less in dollar amount than the losses on the AFS securities, and although they are minor in percentage terms of a loss, they are troubling because of their age. Problem assets do not usually improve with age, and the fact that the bulk of the losses on the HTM securities are older than 12 months may indicate management reluctance to report economic reality.
- Because HTM securities are reported at amortized cost on the balance sheet, the classification obscures the fair value of the securities. The age of the securities generating the losses indicates that there may be more severe impairment than already recognized. The analysis of the HTM securities reinforces the observations noted in the analysis of the available-for-sale securities review.

Investment assets are not as significant in amount or as risky as the loans. The analyst wants to determine that the loans are the result of a sound credit policy and will be realized over their term. This cannot be determined without analyzing the allowance for loan losses. As was seen in Exhibit 14, **allowance for loan losses** is a balance sheet account; it is a contra asset account to loans. (It is analogous to an account common for non-financial institutions, allowance for bad debts, which is a contra asset account to accounts receivable.) **Provision for loan losses** is an income statement expense account that increases the amount of the allowance for loan losses. Actual loan losses (i.e., charge-offs—net of recoveries) reduce the amount of the allowance for loan losses.

The allowance for loan losses matters greatly to understanding loan quality, because total loans minus the allowance for loan losses represents the expected value of the loans. A bank's balance sheet will typically show the total amount of loans, the amount of allowance for loan losses, and the net amount. Importantly, the allowance for loan losses is discretionary by its very nature. Underestimating the allowance for loan losses would overstate the amounts reported for assets and net income. Almost every bank will disclose allowances for loan losses among its most critical accounting estimates.

To effectively assess the adequacy of the allowance for loan losses, an analyst can examine measures that involve less management discretion. Net charge-offs of loans are less discretionary indicators of loan quality than the allowance for loan losses but have the disadvantage of being a confirming event: The loan has already turned out to be a non-performing asset. Another disadvantage is that net charge-offs can be used in good times to pack away earnings to be brought into earnings later through recoveries of charge-offs. Non-performing loans are another measure that can help in assessing adequacy of the allowance for loan losses. Non-performing (i.e., non-accrual) loans are loans that are not currently paying their contractual amounts due, making them a more objective measure of the quality of loans in the portfolio.

Three ratios are helpful in assessing the quality of the allowance for loan losses:

- The ratio of the allowance for loan losses to non-performing loans
- The ratio of the allowance for loan losses to net loan charge-offs
- The ratio of the provision for loan losses to net loan charge-offs

In each ratio, a discretionary measure (such as the allowance for loan losses or provision for loan losses) is compared to a more objective measure.[29] In the case of Citigroup, the loans and the allowance for loan losses are stratified between consumer loans and corporate loans. Because the types of loan customers differ greatly, the analysis of each should be performed separately. Exhibit 17 shows the variables required to compute the ratios for the last five years, selected from the management discussion and analysis of the relevant 10-Ks, and the resulting ratios.

EXHIBIT 17   Citigroup's Loan Loss Analysis Data at December 31

(In millions of dollars)	2016	2015	2014	2013	2012
Data for Calculating Allowance for Loan Loss Ratios					
Allowance for loan losses:					
Consumer	$9,358	$9,835	$13,547	$16,974	$22,585
Corporate	$2,702	$2,791	$2,447	$2,674	$2,870

(continued)

---

[29] For more discussion on the analysis of the allowance of loan loss reserves, see Stephen G. Ryan, *Financial Instruments and Institutions: Accounting and Disclosure Rules* (Hoboken, NJ: Wiley, 2002): 100–105.

EXHIBIT 17   (Continued)

(In millions of dollars)	2016	2015	2014	2013	2012
Provision for loan losses:					
Consumer	$6,323	$6,228	$6,695	$7,587	$10,312
Corporate	$426	$880	$133	$17	$146
Charge-offs:					
Consumer	$7,644	$8,692	$10,650	$12,400	$16,365
Corporate	$578	$349	$458	$369	$640
Recoveries:					
Consumer	$1,594	$1,634	$1,975	$2,138	$2,357
Corporate	$67	$105	$160	$168	$417
Net charge-offs:					
Consumer	$6,050	$7,058	$8,675	$10,262	$14,008
Corporate	$511	$244	$298	$201	$223
Non-accrual loans:					
Consumer	$3,158	$3,658	$5,905	$7,045	$9,136
Corporate	$2,421	$1,596	$1,202	$1,958	$2,394
Allowance for Loan Loss Ratios					
Allowance for loan losses to non-accrual loans:					
Consumer	2.96	2.69	2.29	2.41	2.47
Corporate	1.12	1.75	2.04	1.37	1.20
Allowance for loan losses to net loan charge-offs:					
Consumer	1.55	1.39	1.56	1.65	1.61
Corporate	5.29	11.44	8.21	13.30	12.87
Provision for loan losses to net loan charge-offs:					
Consumer	1.05	0.88	0.77	0.74	0.74
Corporate	0.83	3.61	0.45	0.08	0.65

Observations on the allowance for loan losses to non-accrual loans, which are loans that have experienced some non-payment from borrowers:

- For the consumer loans, the 2016 ratio of 2.96 is the highest level in the last five years, and this ratio has been increasing in the last two years. It indicates that the allowance (a discretionary amount) is increasing faster than the actual non-accrual loans, lending confidence to analysts that the allowance is being built in advance of loans turning out poorly.
- For the corporate loans, the 2016 ratio of 1.12 is less definitive. It might be expected that the ratio would be more volatile than for the consumer business because the corporate lending business is not homogeneous, and specific credits and their failures could cause spikes in the ratio. Still, the allowance has declined in each of the last three years, and in 2016, it is at its

lowest point in five years. This arouses concern that the allowance for loan losses may be a thin layer of protection against future losses.

Observations on the allowance for loan losses to net loan charge-offs:

- For the consumer loans, the 2016 ratio of 1.55 shows improvement from 2015 and indicates that there is a cushion between the allowance and the net loan charge-offs that has remained fairly constant over the last five years.
- For the corporate loans, the 2016 ratio of 5.29 shows an ample cushion between the allowance and the net loan charge-offs, although it declined greatly from 2015 and is much lower than at any time in the last five years.

Observations on the provision for loan losses to net loan charge-offs:

- The provision for loan losses is the amount added to the allowance each year, and one should expect that the provision correlates to the amount of net loan charge-offs.
- For the consumer loans, the 2016 ratio is the first ratio in five years where the provision exceeded the net loan charge-offs, and although it had been lower in the previous four years, the proportion of the provision to charge-offs had been increasing in the last three years. This indicates that the bank had become more conservative in its provisioning.
- For the corporate loans, the 2016 ratio significantly decreased from the previous year, and the ratio has been less than 1.0 in four of the last five years. This indicates that the provision for corporate loans has trailed the actual net charge-off experience. The large addition in 2015 gives the appearance of an urgent "catch-up" adjustment.

In summary, Citigroup's asset quality at the end of 2016 was mixed. The policies for investments appear to be fairly conservative, but the age of some of the investments with unrealized losses indicates a possible denial of impairment. With regard to loan quality, the ratio analysis of the allowance for loan losses suggests that the consumer loans appear to be well reserved, but the same ratio analysis for the corporate loans does not generate the same degree of comfort. A rating of 2.5—near the midpoint of the rating scale—could be assigned to the asset quality based on the mixed signals from the evidence.

3.3.3. Management Capabilities

External investors can observe only circumstantial evidence of management's quality. Some circumstantial evidence can be found through a review of the proxy statement.

Observations based on a review of Citigroup's 2016 proxy:

- Citigroup aims for two-thirds board representation of independent members, whereas the New York Stock Exchange requires only a majority of independent members.
- Citigroup has a separate CEO and chairman, often viewed as a good governance practice that avoids conflicts of interest. The positions have been separate since 2009.
- Citigroup's Risk Management Committee met frequently in 2016—14 times—providing evidence of attention to one of the most critical parts of a banking operation. Furthermore, the Risk Management Committee created a subcommittee in 2016 to provide oversight of data governance, data quality, and data integrity, and the subcommittee met seven times in 2016.

Although these are good practices, they do not constitute evidence of strong management capabilities. Rather, they provide evidence that an environment exists where strong management quality is permitted to flourish.

With a company as large as Citigroup, it is difficult to avoid related-party transactions. For example, BlackRock and Vanguard beneficially owned 5% or more of the outstanding shares of Citigroup's common stock as of December 31, 2016; during 2016, the company's subsidiaries provided ordinary course lending, trading, and other financial services to BlackRock and Vanguard. The proxy states that the transactions were on an arm's-length basis and contain customary terms that are substantially the terms of comparable transactions with unrelated third parties. Other related-party transactions exist and are discussed in the 10-K, but they are routine for a company of this size.

In terms of operational risk, evidence of the board's influence on management can be found in the unqualified opinion of Citigroup's auditor on the effectiveness of the system of internal controls. This is evidence of a minimally satisfactory environment in which management should operate and not a clear signal of management competence. A qualified (or negative) opinion on the effectiveness of internal controls would be especially concerning for an investor.

In summary, although the board may be solidly constructed and appears to exert adequate control over the managers, the net performance of the company also speaks to the quality of management and directors. The asset quality, discussed above, was not overwhelmingly positive and detracts from the overall view of management quality. A rating of 2 could be assigned to management capabilities.

3.3.4. Earnings

Earnings ideally should be of high quality, and an indication of high-quality earnings is sustainability. Earnings are more sustainable if they are not dependent on the possibly opportunistic fine-tuning of discretionary estimates and not reliant on either non-recurring items or volatile sources of revenues.

As discussed above, allowance for loan losses and provisions for loan losses are estimated amounts that allow for management discretion. The provision for loan losses can have profound effects on the profitability of a bank in any single year and over long periods of time. Exhibit 18 shows the five-year change in Citigroup's pretax income through 2016 and the corresponding change in the consolidated total provisions for credit (i.e., loan loss reserves plus provisions for policyholder benefits and claims and unfunded lending commitments) drawn from the five-year selected financial data from the 2016 and 2015 10-Ks.

EXHIBIT 18   Historical Pretax Income and Total Provisions for Credit Losses

(In millions of dollars)	5-Year Net Change:	2016	2015	2014	2013	2012	2011
Pretax income		$21,477	$24,826	$14,701	$19,802	$8,165	$15,096
Change in pretax income	$6,381	($3,349)	$10,125	($5,101)	$11,637	($6,931)	—
Total provisions for credit losses		$6,982	$7,913	$7,467	$8,514	$11,329	$12,359
Change in total provisions for credit losses	($5,377)	($931)	$446	($1,047)	($2,815)	($1,030)	—
Net difference	$1,004						

Observations on the provisions for credit losses:

- 2013 was the only year in which pretax income increased from the previous year while the total provisions for credit losses decreased. The $2.815 billion decrease in the credit loss provisions drove 24% of the increase.
- In 2016, 2014, and 2012, the pretax income declined from the previous year. The declines would have been more severe if they had not been buffered by decreases in the total provisions for credit losses in each year.
- Over the five-year span, the change in the total credit loss provisions contributed to improving the pretax earnings in four of the years. The only exception was 2015, when the total provisions increased only negligibly compared to the size of the decreases in the other years.
- On a longer-term basis, the five-year net change in the total provisions accounted for 84% of the net change in pretax income—an indication that not much profit growth happened elsewhere.

Another indicator of sustainability is the degree to which trading income is part of a bank's revenue stream. Trading income tends to be volatile and not necessarily sustainable. Higher-quality income would be net interest income and fee-based income: These provide sustainable, returning streams of income. An analyst should examine the composition of a bank's revenue stream to determine whether it is growing and to identify the drivers of growth or decline. The five-year summary of Citigroup's revenue stream, drawn from the five-year selected financial data from the 2016 and 2015 10-Ks, is shown in Exhibit 19.

EXHIBIT 19   Five-Year Summary of Composition of Citigroup's Revenue

(In millions of dollars)	2016	2015	2014	2013	2012
Net interest revenue	$45,104	$46,630	$47,993	$46,793	$46,686
Principal transactions (trading income)	7,585	6,008	6,698	7,302	4,980
All other non-interest revenue	17,186	23,716	22,528	22,629	17,864
Revenues, net of interest expense	$69,875	$76,354	$77,219	$76,724	$69,530
Percent attributable to trading income	10.9%	7.9%	8.7%	9.5%	7.2%
Percent of total:					
Net interest revenue	64.5%	61.1%	62.2%	61.0%	67.1%
All other non-interest revenue	24.6%	31.1%	29.2%	29.5%	25.7%

Observations on revenue composition:

- 2016 total revenues are almost unchanged from 2012 levels.
- At 10.9% of total revenues in 2016, trading income has been trending upward as a proportion of revenues in the last five years. Instead of increasing its sustainable, non-volatile revenues, Citigroup's principal transactions/trading income is moving in the opposite direction—increasing in absolute dollars and in relative importance.
- In 2016, all other non-interest revenue is at its lowest representative level since 2012.
- The net interest income level improved in 2016 but is still lower than it was in 2012.

A bank's net interest revenue (also referred to as *net interest margin* or *spread*) results from the management of interest earned on loans and other interest-bearing assets and the management of interest paid on deposits and other interest-bearing liabilities. Banks may create value through maturity transformation: They can borrow money on shorter terms than the terms for lending to customers. Although this can create value by lending for long terms at a higher rate than their short-term funding costs, it can also destroy value if the markets for short-term funding experience a dislocation or the yield curve unexpectedly inverts. Therefore, a bank's risk management practices, including its diversification practices, are integral to the maturity transformation process.

Analyzing the net interest margin can provide an investor with a view of a bank management's activity and effectiveness in this area. To continue the example with Citigroup, the next two exhibits show the average balances (average volume column) for Citigroup's balance sheet accounts. Exhibit 20 shows Citigroup's assets, as well as interest revenue and interest margin (average interest rate) earned on those assets. Exhibit 21 shows the company's average liabilities, the interest expense and average interest cost of those liabilities, and its equity accounts. It also includes the company's net interest revenue (net interest margin) at the bottom.

EXHIBIT 20   Citigroup's Average Balances and Interest Rates—Assets

In millions of dollars,	Average Volume			Interest Revenue			% Average Rate		
except rates	2016	2015	2014	2016	2015	2014	2016	2015	2014
Assets									
Deposits with banks	$131,925	$133,853	$161,741	$971	$727	$959	**0.74%**	0.54%	0.59%
Federal funds sold and securities borrowed or purchased under agreements to resell									
In US offices	$147,734	$150,340	$153,703	$1,483	$1,215	$1,034	**1.00%**	0.81%	0.67%
In offices outside the United States	85,142	84,013	101,184	1,060	1,301	1,332	**1.24**	1.55	1.32
Total	$232,876	$234,353	$254,887	$2,543	$2,516	$2,366	**1.09%**	1.07%	0.93%
Trading account assets									
In US offices	$103,610	$113,475	$113,716	$3,791	$3,945	$3,471	**3.66%**	3.48%	3.05%
In offices outside the United States	94,603	96,333	113,563	2,095	2,140	2,540	**2.21**	2.22	2.24
Total	$198,213	$209,808	$227,279	$5,886	$6,085	$6,011	**2.97%**	2.90%	2.64%
Investments									
In US offices									
Taxable	$225,764	$214,683	$188,909	$3,980	$3,812	$3,285	**1.76%**	1.78%	1.74%
Exempt from US income tax	19,079	20,034	20,383	693	443	626	**3.63**	2.21	3.07
In offices outside the United States	106,159	102,374	113,182	3,157	3,071	3,627	**2.97**	3.00	3.20
Total	$351,002	$337,091	$322,474	$7,830	$7,326	$7,538	**2.23%**	2.17%	2.34%

EXHIBIT 20   (Continued)

In millions of dollars, except rates	Average Volume			Interest Revenue			% Average Rate		
	2016	2015	2014	2016	2015	2014	2016	2015	2014
Loans (net of unearned income)									
In US offices	**$360,957**	$354,434	$361,773	**$24,240**	$25,082	$26,076	**6.72%**	7.08%	7.21%
In offices outside the United States	**262,715**	273,064	296,666	**15,578**	15,465	18,723	**5.93**	5.66	6.31
Total	**$623,672**	$627,498	$658,439	**$39,818**	$40,547	$44,799	**6.38%**	6.46%	6.80%
Other interest-earning assets	**$56,398**	$63,209	$48,954	**$1,029**	$1,839	$507	**1.82%**	2.91%	1.04%
Total interest-earning assets	**$1,594,086**	$1,605,812	$1,673,774	**$58,077**	$59,040	$62,180	**3.64%**	3.68%	3.71%
Non-interest-earning assets	**$214,642**	$218,025	$223,141						
Total assets	**$1,808,728**	$1,823,837	$1,896,915						

Observations from Citigroup's average assets table:

- The overall interest margin declined slightly in 2016, from 3.68% to 3.64%. One reason is due to changes occurring within the loans, which are the single largest category of assets. Citigroup sold its OneMain Financial subsidiary at the end of 2015, which was engaged in US consumer installment lending and is a high-yielding loan business. That disposal pressured the interest income earned from US offices, decreasing the earned interest rate from 7.08% in 2015 to 6.72% in 2016.
- Average loans in US offices increased to $360,957 million in 2016 from $354,434 million in 2015, despite the OneMain disposal, because of the mid-2016 acquisition of Costco's credit card portfolio, which was insufficient to offset the OneMain interest income.
- Average loans in offices outside the United States decreased to $262,715 million in 2016 from $273,064 million in 2015, partly because Citigroup disposed of its retail banking and credit cards businesses in Japan in the fourth quarter of 2015.
- Although Citigroup realized better interest income from its trading account assets in 2016, earning 2.97% compared to 2.90% in 2015, it allocated less capital to trading and earned less absolute interest income from the trading account assets.
- Despite lower capital committed to deposits with banks ($131,925 million in 2016 compared to $133,853 million in 2015), the higher realized interest margin increased Citigroup's overall interest income. The same is true for its tax-exempt investments in US offices.

EXHIBIT 21   Citigroup's Average Balances and Interest Rates—Liabilities, Equity, and Net Interest Revenue

In millions of dollars, except rates	Average Volume			Interest Expense			% Average Rate		
	2016	2015	2014	2016	2015	2014	2016	2015	2014
Liabilities									
Deposits in US offices	**$288,817**	$273,135	$292,062	**$1,630**	$1,291	$1,432	**0.56%**	0.47%	0.49%
In offices outside the United States	**429,608**	425,086	465,135	**3,670**	3,761	4,260	**0.85**	0.88	0.92
Total	**$718,425**	$698,221	$757,197	**$5,300**	$5,052	$5,692	**0.74%**	0.72%	0.75%
Federal funds purchased and securities loaned or sold under agreements to purchase									
In US offices	**$100,472**	$108,320	$102,672	**$1,024**	$614	$657	**1.02%**	0.57%	0.64%
In offices outside the United States	**57,588**	66,130	88,080	**888**	998	1,238	**1.54**	1.51	1.41
Total	**$158,060**	$174,450	$190,752	**$1,912**	$1,612	$1,895	**1.21%**	0.92%	0.99%
Trading account liabilities									
In US offices	**$29,481**	$24,711	$29,263	**$242**	$107	$74	**0.82%**	0.43%	0.25%
In offices outside the United States	**44,669**	45,252	47,904	**168**	110	94	**0.38**	0.24	0.20
Total	**$74,150**	$69,963	$77,167	**$410**	$217	$168	**0.55%**	0.31%	0.22%
Short-term borrowings									
In US offices	**$61,015**	$64,973	$77,967	**$202**	$224	$161	**0.33%**	0.34%	0.21%
In offices outside the United States	**19,184**	50,803	40,282	**275**	299	419	**1.43**	0.59	1.04
Total	**$80,199**	$115,776	$118,249	**$477**	$523	$580	**0.59%**	0.45%	0.49%
Long-term debt									
In US offices	**$175,342**	$182,347	$191,364	**$4,179**	$4,308	$5,093	**2.38%**	2.36%	2.66%
In offices outside the United States	**6,426**	7,642	7,346	**233**	209	262	**3.63**	2.73	3.57
Total	**$181,768**	$189,989	$198,710	**$4,412**	$4,517	$5,355	**2.43%**	2.38%	2.69%
Total interest-bearing liabilities	**$1,212,602**	$1,248,399	$1,342,075	**$12,511**	$11,921	$13,690	**1.03%**	0.95%	1.02%
Demand deposits									
In US offices	**$38,120**	$26,144	$26,227						
Other non-interest-bearing liabilities	**328,822**	330,104	316,061						
Total liabilities	**$1,579,544**	$1,604,647	$1,684,363						

EXHIBIT 21   (Continued)

In millions of dollars, except rates	Average Volume			Interest Expense			% Average Rate		
	2016	2015	2014	2016	2015	2014	2016	2015	2014
Citigroup stockholders' equity	**$228,065**	$217,875	$210,863						
Non-controlling interest	**1,119**	1,315	1,689						
Total equity	**$229,184**	$219,190	$212,552						
Total liabilities and stockholders' equity	**$1,808,728**	$1,823,837	$1,896,915						
Net interest revenue as a percentage of average interest-earning assets									
In US offices	**$859,311**	$923,309	$953,394	**$27,929**	$28,495	$27,496	**3.25%**	3.09%	2.88%
In offices outside the United States	**734,775**	682,503	720,380	**17,637**	18,624	20,994	**2.40**	2.73	2.91
Total	**$1,594,086**	$1,605,812	$1,673,774	**$45,566**	$47,119	$48,490	**2.86%**	2.93%	2.90%

Observations from Exhibit 21:

• Citigroup's cost of funding its assets increased in every category of liability in 2016. That attribute was even more pronounced in offices outside the United States, with the exception of deposit liabilities.
• This difference between US and non-US asset and liability performance extends to the net interest revenue as a percentage of average interest-earning assets, shown at the bottom of the table. Although the net interest margin improved to 3.25% in 2016 from 3.09% in 2015 for assets in US offices, it declined significantly for assets in offices outside the United States, from 2.73% in 2015 to 2.40% in 2016. The net interest margin in offices outside the United States has been declining consistently since 2014, when the US dollar began strengthening. Citigroup has been experiencing negative foreign currency translation impacts since then.
• An investor might exercise increased caution when observing management's future actions in making foreign investments. These results do not provide assurance that all capital is well allocated overseas or that currency risk is adequately managed. The lower returns might also be due to macroeconomic factors, such as lower yield curves (and even negative rates) overseas, creating fewer profitable opportunities. An investor should factor those possibilities into his or her consideration.

Analyzing the net interest income resulting from average interest-bearing asset and liability balances can be useful for analyzing what happened within a bank for a given period but not necessarily useful for projecting future earnings. The interest earned or paid on an average balance for a given period may have no bearing on what a bank may actually earn or pay in the next period. End-of-period balances of balance sheet components and their associated interest rates may make a better starting point for projecting future earnings than the average balance information.

In summary, the quality of Citigroup's earnings is not exceedingly high. The fact that the decreases in the provision for loan losses has driven 84% of the pretax earnings increases over the last five years does nothing to relieve quality concerns, nor does the increase in trading income over the last five years instill more confidence in the earnings quality. The analysis of the net interest income shows declining net interest income margin over the last three years, largely attributable to the non-US offices. A rating of 3 could be justified for earnings quality.

A Brief Overview of Accounting for Derivatives

Accounting rules for derivatives are extensive. The following points are a very brief summary of this complex topic and are generally applicable to both IFRS and US GAAP.

- At inception, many derivatives contracts do not give rise to an asset or liability on the balance sheet or to a gain or loss on the income statement. For example, an interest rate swap contract can involve the exchange of future cash flows with equivalent present value. Thus, at inception, the only accounting record required for every derivatives contract is a disclosure of the notional amount of the contract. This disclosure appears in the notes to the financial statements.
- Measurement of the mark-to-market value of a derivatives contract creates an asset or liability and subsequently increases or decreases the value of the asset or liability.
- Changes in the value of the asset or liability are recorded either as part of profit and loss on the income statement or as part of comprehensive income, depending on the classification.
- Derivative instruments may be classified as a hedge of a cash flow, a hedge of a fair value, or a hedge of a net investment in a foreign subsidiary. Classification of a derivatives contract as a hedge requires substantiating its correlation with the risk being hedged. If a derivatives contract is classified as a hedge, changes in its value are recorded as part of comprehensive income and will be recognized in net income over the life of the hedged transaction.
- If a derivatives contract fails classification as a hedge and is instead a free-standing derivative instrument, changes in its fair value are reported as income or expense in the income statement at each reporting period. The immediate recognition of a gain or loss in earnings, instead of reporting it in other comprehensive income, can lead to unexpected volatility of earnings and missed earnings targets. Depending on the nature of the derivative transaction, a secondary effect of a contract's failure to qualify as a hedge may also require additional posting of collateral or cash.

3.3.5. Liquidity Position

A bank's liquidity is an extremely important matter for its own well-being in times of financial stress. Given the interdependence of banks, through such transactions as interbank deposits and acting as counterparties in derivative transactions, a bank's liquidity also matters for the well-being of other banks—and possibly an entire economy.

Capital alone is not sufficient to assure liquidity; there must be enough capital available in cash or near-cash for the meeting of obligations. The Basel III Regulatory Framework introduced two liquidity standards to provide assurance that capital would be adequately liquid for meeting obligations under stressful conditions.

The first is the Liquidity Coverage Ratio, which is the minimum percentage of a bank's expected cash outflows to be held in highly liquid assets. Expected net cash outflows are the bank's anticipated 30-day liquidity needs in a stress scenario, and the highly liquid assets include only those of high quality and immediately convertible into cash. Expected net cash outflows are calculated by applying prescribed outflow factors to various liability categories, with any available offsets by inflows from assets maturing within the 30-day stress period. Additionally, banks must include an add-on amount to account for possible maturity mismatches between contractual cash outflows and inflows during the 30-day period to arrive at total net outflows. The minimum LCR threshold is 100%; anything less would indicate an inability to meet the liquidity needs. Exhibit 22 shows the components of Citigroup's LCR at December 31, 2016, September 30, 2016, and December 31, 2015.

EXHIBIT 22   Citigroup's Liquidity Coverage Ratio

(In billions of dollars)	Dec. 31, 2016	Sep. 30, 2016	Dec. 31, 2015
High-quality liquid assets	$403.7	$403.8	$389.2
Net outflows	332.5	335.3	344.4
HQLA in excess of net outflows	$71.2	$68.5	$44.8
Liquidity Coverage Ratio	121%	120%	113%

Observations from the Liquidity Coverage Ratio:

- Citigroup's Liquidity Coverage Ratio has improved in the last two years.
- Citigroup's 2016 LCR indicates it can withstand cash outflows that are 21% higher than its 30-day liquidity needs in a stress scenario or, equivalently, it can withstand a stress level volume of cash outflows for 36.3 days (121% times 30 days). Either way, the LCR indicates adequate liquidity even in the absence of any (likely) remedial management steps in an actual stress event.

The second Basel III liquidity standard is the Net Stable Funding Ratio: a minimum percentage of required stable funding that must be sourced from available stable funding. Required stable funding depends on the composition and maturity of a bank's asset base; available stable funding is a function of the composition and maturity of a bank's funding sources (capital and liabilities). The Net Stable Funding Ratio is a kind of inverted Liquidity Coverage Ratio. Where the Liquidity Coverage Ratio evaluates short-term liquidity, the Net Stable Funding Ratio is a measure of the available stable funding to cover funding of longer-term, less liquid assets, such as loans. Highly liquid assets do not enter the calculation of the Net Stable Funding Ratio. As with the Liquidity Coverage Ratio, a ratio of 100% is the minimum acceptable threshold.

The Net Stable Funding Ratio is not yet a required Basel III standard as of the end of 2016; final rules are expected in 2017. Still, a rough calculation may be made, without the various weightings for components of both available and required stable funding that will be part of the final rules. Exhibit 23 shows one possible calculation of a Net Stable Funding Ratio, based on Citigroup's consolidated balance sheet amounts at December 31, 2016, September 30, 2016, and December 31, 2015. The calculation divides the estimated, unweighted amount of available stable funding by the estimated required amount of stable funding.

EXHIBIT 23   Citigroup's Net Stable Funding Ratio

(In billions of dollars)	Dec. 31, 2016	Sep. 30, 2016	Dec. 31, 2015
Available stable funding:			
Total deposits	$929.4	$940.3	$907.9
Long-term debt	206.2	209.1	201.3
Common equity	205.9	212.3	205.1
Total available stable funding	$1,341.5	$1,361.6	$1,314.3
Required stable funding:			
Total investments	$353.3	$354.9	$343.0
Total loans, net	612.3	626.0	605.0
Goodwill	21.7	22.5	22.3
Intangible assets (other than MSRs)	5.1	5.4	3.7
Mortgage servicing rights (MSRs)	1.6	1.3	1.8
Other assets	128.0	116.5	133.7
Total required stable funding	$1,122.0	$1,126.6	$1,109.5
Net Stable Funding Ratio	120%	121%	118%

Observations on the approximated Net Stable Funding Ratio:

- Citigroup's Net Stable Funding Ratio, as calculated, has stayed relatively stable since the end of 2015, and the available stable funding is well above the minimum required funding needed.

In summary, Citigroup's liquidity position is very good, based on its Liquidity Coverage and Net Stable Funding Ratios. A rating of 1 is justifiable based on the results of the two ratios.

3.3.6. Sensitivity to Market Risk

Bank assets and liabilities are constantly subject to market risk, which impacts their earnings performance and liquidity. Analysts need to understand how adverse changes in interest rates, exchange rates, and other market factors can affect a bank's earnings and balance sheet.

Required disclosures in banks' financial statements make it possible to assess various sensitivities. The value at risk disclosure is helpful for assessing a bank's exposure to market factors. VaR statistics can be effective indicators of trends in intra-company risk taking; because of differences in calculation assumptions across companies, VaR is not as useful for assessing risk-taking activities between different companies.

Using a 99% confidence level, Citigroup estimates the value at risk of a potential decline in the value of a position or a portfolio under normal market conditions for an assumed single-day holding period. Citigroup uses a Monte Carlo simulation VaR model to capture material risk sensitivities of various asset classes/risk types. Citigroup's VaR includes positions that are measured at fair value but excludes investment securities classified as AFS or HTM. Exhibit 24 is an excerpt from Citigroup's 2016 VaR disclosure.

EXHIBIT 24 Citigroup Year-End and Average Trading VaR and Trading and Credit Portfolio VaR

(In millions of dollars)	12/31/16	2016 Average	12/31/15	2015 Average
Interest rate	$37	$35	$37	$44
Credit spread	63	62	56	69
Covariance adjustment [1]	(17)	(28)	(25)	(26)
Fully diversified interest rate and credit spread	$83	$69	$68	$87
Foreign exchange	32	24	27	34
Equity	13	14	17	17
Commodity	27	21	17	19
Covariance adjustment [1]	(70)	(58)	(53)	(65)
Total trading VaR—all market risk factors, including general and specific risk (excluding credit portfolios) [2]	$85	$70	$76	$92
Specific risk-only component [3]	$3	$7	$11	$6
Total trading VaR—general market risk factors only (excluding credit portfolios) [2]	$82	$63	$65	$86
Incremental impact of the credit portfolio [4]	$20	$22	$22	$25
Total trading and credit portfolio VaR	$105	$92	$98	$117
VaR Effects on Earnings & Capital:				
Total trading and credit portfolio VAR	$105	$92	$98	$117
Net income from continuing operations	$15,033		$17,386	
Common equity	$205,867		$205,139	
Total VaR as % of:				
Net income from continuing operations	0.7%	0.6%	0.6%	0.7%
Common equity	0.1%	0.0%	0.0%	0.1%

Notes:
1. Covariance adjustment reflects the fact that the risks within each and across risk types are not perfectly correlated and, consequently, the total VaR on a given day will be lower than the sum of the VARs relating to each individual risk type.
2. The total trading VaR includes mark-to-market and certain fair value option trading positions except for certain hedges. Available-for-sale and accrual exposures are not included.
3. The specific risk-only component represents the level of equity and fixed income issuer-specific risk embedded in VAR.
4. The credit portfolio is composed of mark-to-market positions associated with non-trading business units.

Observations from the VaR table:

- Citigroup's average trading VaR declined in 2016 to $70 million from $92 million in the previous year, mainly owing to changes in interest rate exposures from mark-to-market hedging activity.
- Average trading and credit portfolio VaR also declined in 2016 to $92 million from $117 million in the previous year.
- Although total trading and credit portfolio VaR increased at year end 2016 to $105 million, compared to $98 million at year end 2015, the magnitude of this worst-case single-day VaR is still less than 1% of net income from continuing operations in both years, on either an end-of-period basis (0.7%) or an average basis (0.6%). The magnitude is even more minor compared to equity, representing 0.1% on the end-of-period basis and less than 0.1% on average.
- Importantly, Citigroup's VaR is a single-day measure of market shocks that can affect a company. Market dislocations can linger for days, weeks, and even longer. Although VaR is useful for measuring the effects of very short-term shocks, it does not address the effects of longer-term market impacts.

Another useful disclosure in Citigroup's 10-K focuses on the estimated sensitivity of Citigroup's capital ratios to numerator changes of $100 million in Common Equity Tier 1 Capital, Tier 1 Capital, and Total Capital and changes of $1 billion in risk-weighted assets at the end of 2016. These sensitivities consider only a single change to either a component of capital or risk-weighted assets; an event affecting more than one factor at a time may have a far greater impact than Citigroup's estimate. Exhibit 25 shows an excerpt of the sensitivity table, along with the actual ratios calculated at the end of 2016.

EXHIBIT 25   Citigroup Capital Ratio Estimated Sensitivities at December 31, 2016

(In basis points)	Common Equity Tier 1 Capital Ratio		Tier 1 Capital Ratio		Total Capital Ratio	
	Impact of $100 Million Change in Common Equity Tier 1 Capital	Impact of $1 Billion Change in Risk-Weighted Assets	Impact of $100 Million Change in Tier 1 Capital	Impact of $1 Billion Change in Risk-Weighted Assets	Impact of $100 Million Change in Total Capital	Impact of $1 Billion Change in Risk-Weighted Assets
Citigroup						
Advanced Approach	0.90	1.20	0.90	1.30	0.90	1.50
Standardized Approach	0.90	1.30	0.90	1.40	0.90	1.70
Actual capital ratio	14.35%	14.35%	15.29%	15.29%	17.33%	17.33%
Minimum capital ratio	4.50%	4.50%	6.00%	6.00%	8.00%	8.00%

From Citigroup's description of its risk-based capital ratios, p. 33 of 2016 10-K: "Total risk-weighted assets under the Advanced Approaches, which are primarily models based, include credit, market, and operational risk-weighted assets. Conversely, the Standardized Approach excludes operational risk-weighted assets and generally applies prescribed supervisory risk weights to broad categories of credit risk exposures. As a result, credit risk-weighted assets calculated under the Advanced Approaches are more risk sensitive than those calculated under the Standardized Approach. Market risk-weighted assets are derived on a generally consistent basis under both approaches."

Observations from the capital ratio sensitivity table:

• Regardless of the calculation (advanced or standardized approach), the effect of a $100 million change in capital or a $1 billion change in risk-weighted assets is practically nil compared to the actual capital ratios calculated at year end.
• At the same time, these are static measures of sensitivity and adjust for only one impact at a time.

In summary, Citigroup's sensitivity to market impacts appears to be controlled and provides circumstantial evidence of effective risk management. Based on the evidence, Citigroup could be justifiably rated at 1 for its management of sensitivities.

3.3.7. Overall CAMELS Assessment

After each CAMELS component has been analyzed and rated, the overall CAMELS assessment can be completed. One approach to consolidating CAMELS components on an entity basis would be to simply add all the components' ratings. A bank earning the best CAMELS rating, a rating of 1, for each component would have a total score of 6, and a bank that received the worst ratings would have a composite CAMELS score of 30. To translate the score into the corresponding composite CAMELS rating, the score could be divided by 6. This approach arrives at an arithmetic mean rating as the composite rating for the bank. Note that if each component receives the same rating, the weighting of the components is irrelevant. The arithmetic mean approach, however, fails to take into account the fact that some components of the CAMELS approach are more important to some analysts than others, as discussed in Section 3.3. Depending on the focus of the analysis, the analyst-weighted composite CAMELS score and rating could be quite different from the unweighted score and arithmetic mean of the ratings.

Exhibit 26 presents the calculation of Citigroup's overall CAMELS score from the point of view of an equity analyst who places twice as much value on asset quality and earnings than on the other CAMELS components.

EXHIBIT 26   Citigroup Overall CAMELS Score

	Rating	Weighting	Weighted Rating
Capital adequacy	1.0	1	1.00
Asset quality	2.5	2	5.00
Management	2.0	1	2.00
Earnings	3.0	2	6.00
Liquidity	1.0	1	1.00
Sensitivity	1.0	1	1.00
Total score	**10.5**	**8**	**16.00**
Converted to CAMELS rating (score divided by 6)	**1.75**		**2.00**

Note that without the weighting, which helps the analyst quantify his or her priorities, Citigroup has an overall CAMELS rating of 1.75—not perfect, but indicating a bank that is generally showing strong performance and risk management. Once the ratings are weighted, however, the composite score is 2.00 (16/8 = 2.00). The weighted score indicates a slightly higher degree of flaws that management may need to address.

4. ANALYZING AN INSURANCE COMPANY

Insurance companies provide protection against adverse events. Insurance companies earn revenues from **premiums** (amounts paid by the purchaser of insurance products) and from investment income earned on the **float** (amounts collected as premium and not yet paid out as benefits). Insurance companies are typically categorized as property and casualty (P&C) or life and health (L&H). The products of the two types of insurance companies differ in contract duration and variability of claims.[30] P&C insurers' policies are usually short term, and the final cost will usually be known within a year of occurrence of an insured event, whereas L&H insurers' policies are usually longer term. P&C insurers' claims are more variable and "lumpier" because they arise from accidents and other unpredictable events, whereas L&H insurers' claims are more predictable because they correlate closely with relatively stable actuarially based mortality rates when applied to large populations.

For both types of insurance companies, important areas for analysis include business profile, earnings characteristics, investment returns, liquidity, and capitalization. In addition, for P&C companies, analysis of reserves and the combined ratio, an indicator of overall underwriting profitability, are important.

Some countries, including, for example, the United States, require insurance companies to prepare financial reports according to statutory accounting rules, which differ from US GAAP and IFRS, and have a greater focus on solvency.[31] This section discusses analysis based on US GAAP and IFRS financial reports. A discussion of P&C insurers is followed by a discussion of L&H insurers.

4.1. Property and Casualty Insurance Companies

Property and casualty (P&C) insurers provide risk management services to their insured parties. For the price of an insurance premium, they protect the insured parties against losses many times greater than the premiums paid. Premiums are collected at the outset of the insurance contract, creating a float period between their receipt and the time of any payout to the insured party for losses. During the float period, the insurance company will invest the premiums, providing another income stream apart from the underwriting results. In addition to being risk managers, insurance companies also act as investment companies.

Exhibit 27 displays the revenue composition for Travelers Companies, Inc. The net investment income is the second-highest revenue source, after premiums earned, and is significant relative to total revenues.

---

[30] Refer to the Insurance Information Institute's website: www.iii.org.

[31] In the United States, the National Association of Insurance Commissioners (NAIC) has developed a system of analytical tools (i.e., ratios and guideline values) for solvency monitoring, known as the NAIC Insurance Regulatory Information System (IRIS). Ratios in IRIS are based on statutory accounting reports.

EXHIBIT 27   Travelers Companies, Inc., Revenues Composition

(For the year ended December 31, in millions)	2016		2015		2014	
Premiums	**$24,534**	*88.8%*	$23,874	*89.0%*	$23,713	*87.3%*
Net investment income	**2,302**	*8.3%*	2,379	*8.9%*	2,787	*10.3%*
Fee income	**458**	*1.7%*	460	*1.7%*	450	*1.7%*
Net realized investment gains	**68**	*0.2%*	3	*0.0%*	79	*0.3%*
Other revenues	**263**	*1.0%*	99	*0.4%*	145	*0.5%*
Total revenues	**$27,625**	*100.0%*	$26,815	*100.0%*	$27,174	*100.0%*

Property and casualty insurers try to minimize their payouts to insured parties by exercising care in the underwriting process and charging an adequate price for the risk that they will bear. They may try to diversify the risks they accept by not concentrating excessively on one kind of policy, market, or customer type. They may also diversify their risk by transferring policies, in whole or in part, to reinsurers. Reinsurers deal only with risks insured by other insurers; they do not originate primary policies.

Property and casualty insurance companies differ from life insurance companies in that the length of their duty to perform is comparatively short. Policies are often offered on an annual basis, and the event being covered is often known with certainty during the policy period—fire or weather events, for example. Insured events can also take much longer to emerge: For instance, environmental harm occurring during the policy period may not be obvious until well after the expiration of the policy period.

4.1.1. Operations: Products and Distribution

Property insurance policies protect against loss or damage to property—buildings, automobiles, environmental damage, and other tangible objects of value. The events causing loss or damage vary and determine the kind of policy in force. Events may be attributed to accidents, fire, theft, or catastrophe. Casualty insurance, sometimes called *liability insurance*, protects against a legal liability related to an insured event. Casualty insurance covers the liability to a third party, such as passengers, employees, or bystanders. A single insured event may contain both property and casualty losses: For instance, an automobile accident may result in both the loss of the automobile and injury to passengers. Such policies may be referred to as *multiple peril policies*.

Property and casualty insurance may be considered as personal lines or commercial lines, depending on the customer; some products may be sold in both lines. Types of property and casualty insurance include automobile property and liability policies (an example of both personal and commercial lines selling the same product), homeowners' insurance, workers' compensation, marine insurance, and reinsurance.

There are two methods of distributing insurance: direct writing and agency writing. Direct writers of insurance have their own sales and marketing staff. Direct writers also may sell insurance policies via the internet; through direct response channels, such as mail; and through groups with a shared interest or bond, such as membership in a profession. Agency writers use independent agents, exclusive agents, and insurance brokers to sell policies.

4.1.2. Earnings Characteristics

In the macro view, the property and casualty insurance business is cyclical. It is a price-sensitive business, with many competitors unafraid to cut prices to obtain market share. According to A.M. Best, a US insurance rating agency, there are approximately 1,200 property and casualty groups in the United States, comprising approximately 2,650 property and casualty companies. Of those groups, the top 150 accounted for approximately 92% of the consolidated industry's total net written premiums in 2015. Once the price cutting drives out profitability, creating a "soft" pricing market for insurance premiums, the insurers reach an uncomfortably depleted level of capital. Competition lessens and underwriting standards tighten, creating a "hard" pricing market. Consequently, premiums rise and the insurers return to more reasonable levels of profitability. The increase in profitability once again attracts more entrants into the market, and the cycle repeats.

In the micro view, there are operating cost considerations that affect insurer profitability apart from the "softness" or "hardness" of the insurance market, depending on the method of distribution. Direct writers have higher fixed costs because of the in-house nature of their distribution method: The sales and marketing staff are salaried employees. Agency writers do not have this fixed cost; instead, the commissions paid to agents and brokers are a variable cost.

The underwriting cycle is driven largely by the expenses of the participants. When the industry's combined ratio—the total insurance expenses divided by the net premiums earned—is low, it indicates a hard insurance market, attracting new entrants who cut prices and push the cycle downward. The effect can be seen in the denominator of the combined ratio: The lower prices for premiums decreases the total net premiums earned, and the combined ratio increases, indicating a soft market. Competitors leave the market, either because they want to forgo unprofitable underwriting or because of their own failure.

For a single insurance company, a combined ratio higher than 100% indicates an underwriting loss. In the United States, Statutory Accounting Practices define the combined ratio as the sum of two ratios, using statutory financial statements: an underwriting loss ratio and an expense ratio. The underwriting loss ratio—losses [= claims paid plus (ending loss reserves minus beginning loss reserves)] divided by net premiums earned—is an indicator of the quality of a company's underwriting activities. Underwriting activities include decisions on whether to accept an application for insurance coverage and decisions on the premiums charged for any coverage extended. The expense ratio (underwriting expenses, including sales commissions and related employee expenses, divided by net premiums written) is an indicator of the efficiency of a company's operations in acquiring and managing underwriting business. For financial disclosures, companies sometimes report modified versions of the combined ratio. For example, the combined ratio reported by Travelers calculates the expense ratio with net earned premiums in the denominator, which is consistent with US GAAP.[32] Other companies may make different presentations.

P&C insurers' investment income is not as volatile as their operating income, because the investments are relatively low-return, low-risk holdings, as we will discuss in the next section.

One critical expense for property and casualty insurers results from the management of their loss reserves. Proper estimation of liabilities is essential to the pricing of policies. Underestimation of loss reserves may lead to undercharging for risks assumed. Development

---

[32] The Travelers Companies, Inc., Form 10-K for the year ended December 31, 2016 (p. 36).

of the loss reserves is based on historical information, yet the process also incorporates estimates about future losses. It is a material account that is subject to management discretion, and its improper estimation can have consequences for the property and casualty insurer. If the loss reserves and the annual adjustments to them are too optimistic, the pricing of the insurance policies may be insufficient for the risk being borne by the insurer and insolvency may ensue. Another problematic attribute of the loss reserves is the fact that the longer the insurer's obligation runs, the more difficult it can be to estimate the loss reserve properly. For example, insurance policies covering asbestos liabilities written long before courts began awarding more generous payouts have been problematic for insurers. Their current experience is far different from what they expected when they issued the policies, and the rapid growth in the award sizes made it difficult to properly estimate the associated loss reserves.

Exhibit 28 shows the roll-forward schedule of activity in Travelers Companies' loss reserve balances, drawn from the insurance claims footnote in its 2016 financial statements. It provides a high-level view of the way the components affect the balance sheet and the income statement and offers insights into the way a property and casualty insurance company manages its assumed risks. The roll-forward activity is denominated in terms of the reserves, net of reinsurance recoverables expected to reduce Travelers' ultimate liability. The beginning and ending balances are shown at their gross amounts, reduced by the reinsurance recoverables to arrive at the net reserves.

EXHIBIT 28   Travelers Companies, Inc., Loss Reserve Balances and Activity

(At and for the year ended December 31, in millions)	2016	2015	2014
Gross claims and claim adjustment expense reserves at beginning of year	$48,272	$49,824	$50,865
Less reinsurance recoverables on unpaid losses	(8,449)	(8,788)	(9,280)
Net reserves at beginning of year	39,823	41,036	41,585
Estimated claims and claim adjustment expenses for claims arising in the current year	15,675	14,471	14,688
Estimated decrease in claims and claim adjustment expenses for claims arising in prior years	(680)	(817)	(885)
Total increases	14,995	13,654	13,803
Claims and claim adjustment expense payments for claims arising in:			
Current year	(6,220)	(5,725)	(5,895)
Prior years	(8,576)	(8,749)	(8,171)
Total payments	(14,796)	(14,474)	(14,066)
Acquisition	—	2	—
Unrealized foreign exchange gain	(74)	(395)	(286)
Net reserves at end of year	39,948	39,823	41,036
Plus reinsurance recoverables on unpaid losses	7,981	8,449	8,788
Gross claims and claim adjustment expense reserves at end of year	$47,929	$48,272	$49,824

(continued)

EXHIBIT 28   (Continued)

(At and for the year ended December 31, in millions)	2016	2015	2014
Reinsurance at end of year:			
Reinsurance recoverables on unpaid losses	$7,981	$8,449	$8,788
Gross claims and claim adjustment expense reserves at end of year	$47,929	$48,272	$49,824
Percentage of claims and claim adjustment expense reserves covered by reinsurance	16.7%	17.5%	17.6%
Revisions' effect on income before income taxes:			
Downward revisions of claims and claim adjustment expenses for claims arising in prior years	$680	$817	$885
Income before income taxes	$4,053	$4,740	$5,089
Percentage of contributions of downward revisions to income before income taxes	16.8%	17.2%	17.4%

Observations from Exhibit 28:

- The 2016 claims paid of $6,220 million is 39.7% of the estimated claims and claim adjustments of $15,675 million, indicating that a major part of Travelers Companies' liability exposure is fairly short term. The two prior years show a similar exposure term.
- The company employs significant levels of reinsurance to control its risk exposure. In reinsurance, one insurance company transfers, or cedes, a portion of its risk to another insurer (the "reinsurer") for a premium. The ceding company expects to recover its losses from the reinsurer. As the table shows, Travelers has been ceding between 16.7% and 17.6% of its gross loss reserves to reinsurers.
- The total increases in loss reserves, net of decreases in claims and claim adjustment expenses for prior years' claims, affect the income statement more than any other expense. In 2016, the $14,995 million of total increases in loss reserves represented 63.6% of the $23,572 million of total claims and expenses in the income statement (which is not presented here because of space limitations).
- The company decreased its prior years' estimates of claims by $680 million in 2016, $817 million in 2015, and $885 million in 2014. Downward revisions indicate that a company is estimating its initial recognized reserves conservatively, but aggressive revisions may also be a tool for manipulating earnings. Travelers Companies' downward revisions may appear minor in comparison to the total increases, but they have a profound effect on income before taxes. This effect is shown in the bottom of the exhibit: Downward revisions of prior years' estimates contributed 16.8% to income before income taxes in 2016, 17.2% in 2015, and 17.4% in 2014.

Depending on the ratios used, the ratios of insurers' profitability may distinguish between net premiums written and net premiums earned. Net premiums written are an insurer's direct premiums written, net of any such premiums ceded to other insurers. Premiums are usually billed in advance—for example, twice per year—and they are earned over the period of coverage provided by the insurance policy. Only the net premiums written that are earned over a relevant accounting period—for example, quarterly—are considered to be the net premiums earned.

Useful ratios in analyzing property and casualty insurance companies' profitability include the following:

- *Loss and loss adjustment expense ratio = (Loss expense + Loss adjustment expense)/Net premiums earned.* This ratio indicates the degree of success an underwriter has achieved in estimating the risks insured. The lower the ratio, the greater the success.
- *Underwriting expense ratio = Underwriting expense/Net premiums written.* This ratio measures the efficiency of money spent in obtaining new premiums. A lower ratio indicates higher success.
- *Combined ratio = Loss and loss adjustment expense ratio + Underwriting expense ratio.* This ratio indicates the overall efficiency of an underwriting operation. A combined ratio of less than 100 is considered efficient.
- *Dividends to policyholders (shareholders) ratio = Dividends to policyholders (shareholders)/Net premiums earned.* This ratio is a measure of liquidity, in that it relates the cash outflow of dividends to the premiums earned in the same period.
- *Combined ratio after dividends = Combined ratio + Dividends to policyholders (shareholders) ratio.* This ratio is a stricter measure of efficiency than the ordinary combined ratio, in that it takes into account the cash satisfaction of policyholders or shareholders after consideration of the total underwriting efforts. Dividends are discretionary cash outlays, and factoring them into the combined ratio presents a fuller description of total cash requirements.[33]

Exhibit 29 displays the calculation of these ratios for a group of property and casualty insurers based on their 2016 financial reports. Notice the wide variation in the results. Markel Corp. performed the best (combined ratio of 89%), and Hartford Financial Services Group performed relatively poorly (combined ratio of 131%). The high loss and loss adjustment expense ratio (82.2%) and underwriting expense ratio (48.8%) suggest its underwriting business requires additional management attention. A review of the three ratios related to operations shows that Travelers ranks as the median with respect to loss and loss adjustment expense ratio and below median for underwriting expense and combined ratios. This finding indicates that Travelers' operations are in the better-performing half of this group. After taking into account the dividend distribution policy in the combined ratio after dividends to policyholders (shareholders), Travelers' overall performance remains in the better-performing half of the group.

EXHIBIT 29   2016 Ratios Calculated for Selected Property and Casualty Insurers

($ millions)	Travelers Companies	Hartford Financial Services Group	W. R. Berkley Corp.	CNA Financial Corp.	Markel Corp.
Loss and loss adjustment expense ratio:					
Loss expense and loss adjustment expense	$15,070	$11,351	$3,846	$5,270	$2,051
Net premiums earned	$24,534	$13,811	$6,293	$6,924	$3,866

(continued)

---

[33] "Annual Report on the Insurance Industry," Federal Insurance Office, US Department of the Treasury (September 2015), available at www.treasury.gov.

EXHIBIT 29   (Continued)

($ millions)	Travelers Companies	Hartford Financial Services Group	W. R. Berkley Corp.	CNA Financial Corp.	Markel Corp.
Loss and loss adjustment expense ratio	**61.4%**	**82.2%**	**61.1%**	**76.1%**	**53.1%**
Underwriting expense ratio:					
Underwriting expense	$8,139	$5,156	$2,396	$2,787	$1,437
Net premiums written	$24,958	$10,568	$6,424	$6,988	$4,001
Underwriting expense ratio	**32.6%**	**48.8%**	**37.3%**	**39.9%**	**35.9%**
Combined ratio:					
Loss and loss adjustment expense ratio	61.4%	82.2%	61.1%	76.1%	53.0%
Underwriting expense ratio	32.6%	48.8%	37.3%	39.9%	35.9%
Combined ratio	**94.0%**	**131.0%**	**98.4%**	**116.0%**	**89.0%**
Dividends to policyholders (shareholders) ratio:					
Dividends to policyholders (shareholders)	$757	$334	$184	$813	$0
Net premiums earned	$24,534	$13,811	$6,293	$6,924	$3,866
Dividends to policyholders (shareholders) ratio	**3.1%**	**2.4%**	**2.9%**	**11.7%**	**0.0%**
Combined ratio after dividends:					
Combined ratio	94.0%	131.0%	98.4%	116.0%	89.0%
Dividends to policyholders (shareholders) ratio	3.1%	2.4%	2.9%	11.7%	0.0%
Combined ratio after dividends	**97.1%**	**133.4%**	**101.3%**	**127.7%**	**89.0%**

4.1.3. Investment Returns

Property and casualty insurance companies face much uncertainty in the risks they insure, and their business is enormously competitive when insurance pricing moves into its "hard" stage. To counteract the environment of uncertainty, property and casualty insurers conservatively invest the collected premiums. They typically favor steady-return, low-risk assets, while shunning low-liquidity investments.

An illustration is found in Exhibit 30, which is the investment portion of the assets shown in the Travelers Companies' 2016 balance sheet. Investments represent 70% of total assets in 2016 and 2015. In both years, approximately 86% of the total investment portfolio is composed of fixed-maturity investments, and nearly another 7% of investments are short-term securities, which can be considered proxies for cash. Equity securities are only 1% of investments in both years, and real estate is also a very minor component of investments in both years.

EXHIBIT 30   The Travelers Companies, Inc., Portfolio Composition, 2016 and 2015

(At December 31, $ millions)	2016		2015	
Fixed maturities, available for sale, at fair value (amortized cost $59,650 and $58,878)	$60,515	85.9%	$60,658	86.1%
Equity securities, available for sale, at fair value (cost $504 and $528)	732	1.0%	705	1.0%
Real estate investments	928	1.3%	989	1.4%
Short-term securities	4,865	6.9%	4,671	6.6%
Other investments	3,448	4.9%	3,447	4.9%
Total investments	$70,488	100.0%	$70,470	100.0%

As with any kind of company, the concentrations of assets merit attention. When considering the investments of a property and casualty insurer, the concentration of investments by type, maturity, credit quality, industry, or geographic location or within single issuers should be evaluated.

Investment performance can be estimated by dividing total investment income by invested assets (cash and investments). This metric can also be calculated on two different bases, by using investment income with and without unrealized capital gains, thus showing the relative importance of unrealized capital gains to the total investment income.

Given that property and casualty insurance companies stand ready to meet obligations for policy payouts, liquidity is a priority in the selection of assets. It will be addressed further in the following section.

4.1.4. Liquidity

The uncertainty of the payouts involved in the property and casualty business requires a high degree of liquidity so loss obligations can be met. Because the investments are typically low-risk, steady-return types of financial instruments, their nature is typically liquid. An analysis of the portfolio investments should take into account overall quality of the investments and the ease with which the investments can be converted into cash without affecting their value.

Evidence of the investment liquidity can be found by examining their status in the hierarchy of fair value reporting. Level 1 reported values are based on readily available prices for securities traded in liquid markets and thus indicate the most liquid of securities. Level 2 reported values are based on less liquid conditions: Prices for such securities are not available from a liquid market and may be inferred from similar securities trading in an active market. Thus, these securities are likely to be less liquid than those reported as Level 1 securities. Finally, Level 3 reported values are based on models and assumptions because there is no active market for the securities, implying illiquidity.

Exhibit 31 shows the fair value hierarchy for investment securities held by the Travelers Companies at December 31, 2016.

EXHIBIT 31   The Travelers Companies, Inc., Portfolio Composition by Fair Value Hierarchy

(at December 31, 2016, in millions)	Total	Level 1	Level 2	Level 3
Fixed maturities:				
US Treasury securities and obligations of US government and government agencies and authorities	$2,035	$2,035	$0	$0
Obligations of states, municipalities, and political subdivisions	31,910	—	31,898	12
Debt securities issued by foreign governments	1,662	—	1,662	—
Mortgage-backed securities, collateralized mortgage obligations, and pass-through securities obligations	1,708	—	1,704	4
All other corporate bonds	23,107	—	22,939	168
Redeemable preferred stock	93	3	90	—
Total fixed maturities	$60,515	$2,038	$58,293	$184
% of security class	*100.0%*	*3.4%*	*96.3%*	*0.3%*
Equity securities:				
Public common stock	$603	$603	$0	$0
Non-redeemable preferred stock	129	51	78	—
Total equity securities	$732	$654	$78	$0
% of security class	*100.0%*	*89.3%*	*10.7%*	*0.0%*

Travelers has very little of its portfolio invested in Level 1 assets—only 4.4% [($2,038 + $654)/($60,515 + $732) = 4.4%] on a combined fixed-income securities and equity securities basis. The majority is classified as Level 2 assets, implying less liquidity than Level 1, yet not implying illiquidity. The fair value footnote from the 10-K provides some assurance that the Level 2 assets are not illiquid (underline added by authors):

The Company utilized a pricing service to estimate fair value measurements for approximately 98% of its fixed maturities at both December 31, 2016 and 2015. The pricing service utilizes market quotations for fixed maturity securities that have quoted prices in active markets. Since fixed maturities other than US Treasury securities generally do not trade on a daily basis, the pricing service prepares estimates of fair value measurements for these securities using its proprietary pricing applications, which include available relevant market information, benchmark curves, benchmarking of like securities, sector groupings and matrix pricing.

Additionally, the pricing service uses an Option Adjusted Spread model to develop prepayment and interest rate scenarios. The pricing service evaluates each asset class based on relevant market information, relevant credit information, perceived market movements and sector news. The market inputs utilized in the pricing evaluation, listed in the approximate order of priority, include: benchmark yields, reported trades, broker/dealer quotes, issuer spreads, two-sided markets, benchmark securities, bids, offers, reference data, and industry and economic events. The extent of the use of each market input depends on the asset class and the market conditions. Depending on the security, the priority of the use of inputs may change or some market inputs may not be relevant. For some securities, additional inputs may be necessary.

The information does not provide an investor with absolute assurance of constant liquidity for the investments; instead, it provides persuasive evidence that the reported values are fair. The fact that the pricing service considers market information relating to liquidity (reported trades, broker/dealer quotes, issuer spreads, two-sided markets) in developing its price estimates increases an investor's confidence that the recognized values would reflect the prices Travelers might achieve if it liquidated the securities at year end 2016.

4.1.5. Capitalization

Unlike the banking sector, where international risk-based capital standards have existed since 1988, as of mid-2016, no such global standard exists for the insurance sector (although the IAIS has expressed a commitment to developing a risk-based global insurance capital standard).[34] The standard is expected to include a target minimum capital adequacy ratio. The ratio will be calculated as the amount of qualifying capital divided by the amount of risk-based capital required.

Although no risk-based global insurance capital standard exists, capital standards do exist in various jurisdictions. For example, in Europe, the EU adopted the "Solvency II regime" in 2014, which (among other provisions) establishes minimum capital requirements such that if an insurer falls below the requirements, the supervisory entity in the relevant country will be required to intervene.[35] In the United States, the NAIC risk-based capital requirements, begun in the 1990s, establish a minimum amount of capital an insurer must have, based on its size and risk profile.[36] Under the NAIC regime, the formula for minimum risk-based capital for P&C insurers takes into account asset risk, credit risk, underwriting risk, and other relevant risks.

4.2. Life and Health Insurance Companies

Life and health insurance companies generate revenue from collecting premiums by selling life and health insurance policies—and for many firms, by providing investment products and services. Investment income is the other primary source of revenues.

4.2.1. Operations: Products and Distribution

The types of life insurance products vary widely, with some solely providing a benefit upon the death of the insured and others providing a savings vehicle. In the simplest types of life insurance, a premium is paid for coverage and when the insured dies, the beneficiary receives payment. For example, a term life policy provides a benefit if the insured dies within the fixed term of the contract but expires without value if the insured is still living at the end of the term. In other types of life insurance, the policy both provides a benefit upon the death of the insured and serves as a savings vehicle. Life insurance companies may also offer such investment products as annuities, with fixed payments or variable payments linked to market returns.

Health-related insurance products vary primarily by the type of coverage. Some products cover specific medical expenses and treatments, and others provide income payments if the policyholder is injured or becomes ill.

---

[34] See https://www.iaisweb.org/page/supervisory-material/insurance-capital-standard//file/61723/ics-frequently-asked-questions-updated-29-july-2016.

[35] See http://europa.eu/rapid/press-release_MEMO-15-3120_en.htm.

[36] See www.naic.org/cipr_topics/topic_risk_based_capital.htm.

L&H companies sell their products either directly to consumers via electronic media or through agents. The agents may be either employees of the company, exclusive agents, or independent agents. Distribution via independent agents is more expensive for the insurance company but offers the benefits of minimizing fixed costs and increasing flexibility to pursue growth opportunities.[37]

It is helpful to understand the source of a company's revenue and any changes over time. Diversification reduces risks. L&H companies can be diversified across revenue sources, product offerings, geographic coverage, distribution channels, and investment assets.

EXAMPLE 7   Revenue Diversification

Exhibits 32 and 33 present selected income statement information for Aegon N.V. and MetLife, Inc., respectively.

EXHIBIT 32   Selected Consolidated Income Statement Information: Aegon N.V.

(In EUR millions)	2016	2015	2014	2013	2012
Amounts based upon IFRS					
Premium income	23,453	22,925	19,864	19,939	19,049
Investment income	7,788	8,525	8,148	7,909	8,413
Fees, commissions, other	2,414	2,452	2,145	1,957	1,865
Total revenues	33,655	33,902	30,157	29,805	29,327

EXHIBIT 33   Selected Income Statement Information: MetLife, Inc.

Years Ended December 31	2016	2015	2014	2013	2012
(In $ millions)					
Premiums	$39,153	$38,545	$39,067	$37,674	$37,975
Investment income, including derivatives gains	13,358	19,916	22,273	19,154	19,713
Universal life and investment-type product policy fees, and other	10,965	11,490	11,976	11,371	10,462
Total revenues	$63,476	$69,951	$73,316	$68,199	$68,150

Notes: To create comparability in this illustration, the above exhibit combines certain line items from MetLife's income statement. The company's audited financial statements should be used for purposes other than this example.

1. Based on the data for 2016 in Exhibits 32 and 33, compare the companies' diversification across revenue sources.
2. Based on the data in Exhibits 32 and 33, describe the trends in each company's diversification across revenue sources, with specific reference to premium income.

---

[37] D. Nissim, "Analysis and Valuation of Insurance Companies," Columbia Business School Center for Excellence in Accounting and Security Analysis (November 2010).

SOLUTIONS EXHIBIT

Aegon N.V. Data In Exhibit 32

As percentage of total revenues	2016	2015	2014	2013	2012
Premium income	69.7%	67.6%	65.9%	66.9%	65.0%
Investment income	23.1%	25.1%	27.0%	26.5%	28.7%
Fees, commissions, other	7.2%	7.2%	7.1%	6.6%	6.4%

YOY percent change	2016	2015	2014	2013
Premium income	2.3%	15.4%	–0.4%	4.7%
Investment income	–8.6%	4.6%	3.0%	–6.0%
Fees, commissions, other	–1.5%	14.3%	9.6%	4.9%

MetLife, Inc., Data in Exhibit 33

As percentage of total revenues	2016	2015	2014	2013	2012
Premiums	61.7%	55.1%	53.3%	55.2%	55.7%
Investment income, including derivatives gains	21.0%	28.5%	30.4%	28.1%	28.9%
Universal life and investment-type product policy fees, and other	17.3%	16.4%	16.3%	16.7%	15.4%
YOY percent change					
Premiums	1.6%	–1.3%	3.7%	–0.8%	
Investment income, including derivatives gains	–32.9%	–10.6%	16.3%	–2.8%	
Universal life and investment-type product policy fees, and other	–4.6%	–4.1%	5.3%	8.7%	

Solution to 1: MetLife appears to have greater diversification across revenue sources because it generates only about 62% of total revenues from premiums, compared to nearly 70% for Aegon. It should be noted that premium income can be a more stable source of revenue, and thus greater diversification of revenues should be considered along with potentially greater variability in revenues.

Solution to 2: For both companies, the percentage of total revenues earned from premiums is greater in 2016 than in any of the previous four years. For Aegon, the increase in the proportion of revenue from premiums resulted in part from significant growth in premium income (15.4% in 2015) as well as a decline in investment income (–8.6%) in 2016. For MetLife, the increase in the proportion of revenue from premiums resulted primarily from the decline in investment income in 2015 and 2016 (–10.6% and –32.9%, respectively).

4.2.2. Earnings Characteristics

The major components of L&H insurers' expenses are for benefit payments to policyholders under life insurance, other types of insurance policies, annuity contracts, and other types of contracts. Some types of insurance products that accumulate a cash value include provisions for the policyholder to cancel the contract before its contractual maturity and receive the accumulated cash value. Such early cancellation is known as a contract surrender. Contract surrenders may result in additional expenses for L&H insurers.

Similar to P&C insurers, L&H insures' earnings reflect a number of accounting items that require a significant amount of judgement and estimates. L&H companies must estimate future policyholder benefits and claims based on actuarial assumptions (e.g., about life expectancy). The amounts expensed in a given period are affected by both policyholder benefits actually paid and interest on the estimated liability for future policyholder benefit. As another example of the importance of estimates, L&H companies capitalize the costs of acquiring new and renewal insurance business, which are then amortized on the basis of actual and expected future profits from that business. Another area where accounting judgement can significantly affect L&H companies' earnings—securities valuation—is discussed in the following section on investment returns.

Some general profitability measures can be applied to L&H companies, such as, for example, return on assets (ROA), return on equity (ROE), growth and volatility of capital, and book value per share. Other common profitability measures include pre- and post-tax operating margin (operating profit as a percentage of total revenues) and pre- and post-tax operating return on assets and return on equity.[38] However, most analysis goes beyond these general measures because of the complexity of L&H companies' earnings. Given the possibility of operational distortion and the importance of accounting estimates to L&H companies' reported earnings, a variety of earnings metrics specific to the insurance sector are helpful in providing a good understanding of performance. For example, the profitability ratios used by A.M. Best include (1) total benefits paid as a percentage of net premiums written and deposits and (2) commissions and expenses incurred as a percentage of net premiums written and deposits.[39]

Exhibit 34 shows return on average equity and pretax operating return on average equity for the US L&H sector and MetLife, Inc. In 2011, MetLife had a higher return on average equity than the industry average and a similar pretax operating return on average equity. After 2011, MetLife has not performed as well as the industry on these two measures. Further investigation into causes of the differences between MetLife and the industry and into the reason why the pretax operating return on average equity and return on average equity were similar for MetLife in 2014 and 2015 is needed.

EXHIBIT 34   Return on Equity—US L&H Sector and MetLife, Inc.

	2011	2012	2013	2014	2015	2016
US L&H Sector Return on Average Equity	4.70%	12.60%	12.90%	11.00%	11.20%	na*
US L&H Sector Pretax Operating Return on Average Equity	9.10%	18.70%	19.10%	14.30%	15.10%	na

---

[38] "Annual Report on the Insurance Industry," Federal Insurance Office, US Department of the Treasury (September 2016), available at www.treasury.gov.
[39] A.M. Best is a widely known rating agency for insurance companies. "Best's Credit Rating Methodology: Global Life and Non-Life Insurance Edition" (April 28, 2016) is available at www3.ambest.com/ambv/ratingmethodology/openpdf.aspx?ubcr=1&ri=1011.

EXHIBIT 34   (Continued)

	2011	2012	2013	2014	2015	2016
MetLife, Inc., Return on Average Equity (Source: 10-K)	12.20%	2.00%	5.40%	9.40%	7.50%	1.00%
MetLife, Inc., Pretax Operating Return on Average Equity (Calculated)	9.00%	9.30%	9.90%	9.80%	7.80%	7.50%

*not available

Source for Sector Data: "Annual Report on the Insurance Industry," Federal Insurance Office (September 2016).

L&H companies' earnings can also be distorted by the accounting treatment of certain items. For example, mismatches between the valuation approach for assets and liabilities can introduce distortion when interest rate changes occur. In some cases, significant distortions to reported earnings have occurred because companies' assets are reported on the basis of current market values whereas liabilities are reported at fixed historical costs, which reflect assumptions in place at the time the liabilities were booked.[40]

4.2.3. Investment Returns

Investment returns are an important source of income for L&H companies. Key aspects in evaluating L&H companies' investment activities include diversification, investment performance, and interest rate risk. Liquidity of the portfolio is also relevant for L&H companies and is discussed in the following section.

Investment diversification begins with an assessment of allocation across asset classes and an evaluation of how the allocation corresponds to the insurer's liabilities to policyholders. Compared to P&C companies, L&H companies' relative predictability of claims generally allows them to more often seek the higher returns offered by riskier investments. However, higher-yielding assets, such as equity or real estate investments, experience greater fluctuations in valuation than investments in debt. The insurance industry has also faced investment return challenges from the low-interest rate environment of the last 10 years. It has been harder to earn an adequate risk-adjusted return on financial assets because the low interest rates have limited the available opportunities. Overall, asset concentrations by type, maturity, low credit quality, industry, or geographic location or within single issuers can be a concern, particularly to rating agencies.[41]

Investment performance of L&H companies, as with any investment portfolio's performance, can be measured broadly as the amount of investment income divided by the amount of invested assets (cash and investments). The measure can use investment income plus realized gains (losses) with and without unrealized capital gains (losses). In addition, a common metric for evaluating interest rate risk of L&H companies is the comparison of the duration of the company's assets with the duration of its liabilities.

---

[40] See, for example, Alistair Gray, "MetLife Loss Raises Accounting 'Noise' Concerns," *Financial Times* (February 16, 2017).

[41] Standard & Poor's, "Standard & Poor's Insurance Ratings Criteria: Life Edition" (2004): www .lifecriteria.standardandpoors.com. Note that Standard & Poor's makes ongoing updates to its ratings criteria.

EXAMPLE 8   Investment Portfolio

Exhibit 35 presents information on the investment portfolio of AIA Group. AIA's portfolio of financial investments constitutes 82% of its total assets (and 84% including investment properties).

EXHIBIT 35   AIA Group Limited Investment Portfolio

	Nov-30-16		Nov-30-15	
	US$m	% Total	US$m	% Total
Loans and deposits	7,062	4.6%	7,211	5.1%
Debt securities	113,618	73.3%	104,640	73.3%
Equity securities	30,211	19.5%	27,159	19.0%
Derivative financial instruments	107	0.1%	73	0.1%
Total financial investments	150,998	97.5%	139,083	97.4%
Investment property	3,910	2.5%	3,659	2.6%
Total	154,908	100.0%	142,742	100.0%

AIA Group Limited Investment Income

	Nov-30-16
Investment Returns	US$m
Interest income	$5,290
Dividend income	654
Rental income	140
Investment income	6,084
Gains and losses	1,471
Total investment return	$7,555

Of the $1,471 million in gains and losses, approximately $127 million was related to debt securities.

1. Based on the information in Exhibit 35, describe AIA's investment allocation in 2016 and changes from the prior year.
2. Based on the information in Exhibit 35, estimate the return on average fixed-income assets. (For the purposes of this question, consider loans and deposits and debt securities as a single class of assets—namely, fixed-income assets.)

Solution to 1: The portfolio, which is mainly invested in debt securities, shows a very small shift from loans and deposits to equity securities in 2016.

Solution to 2: The return (in $ millions) can be estimated as Investment income on fixed-income securities divided by Average investment in fixed-income securities.

The Investment income on fixed-income securities equals Interest income plus Gains on debt securities = \$5,290 + \$127 = \$5,417.

The average amounts invested in loans and deposits and debt securities was [(\$7,062 + \$113,618) + (\$7,211 + \$104,640)]/2 = \$232,531/2 = \$116,265.5.

Therefore, the estimated return on the fixed-income investments was 4.7% (calculated as \$5,417/\$116,265.5).

4.2.4. Liquidity

An L&H company's requirements for liquidity are driven by its liabilities to creditors and, primarily, its liabilities to policyholders, including both benefits and policy surrenders. Historically, liquidity was less important to life insurers because of the long-term nature of traditional life insurance products; however, liquidity has become more important to life insurers as new products have been introduced.[42] An L&H company's sources of liquidity include its operating cash flow and the liquidity of its investment assets. An analysis of liquidity includes a review of the overall liquidity of the investment portfolio. Such investments as non-investment-grade bonds and equity real estate are typically less liquid than investment-grade fixed-income investments.[43]

In general, liquidity measures compare the amount of the company's more liquid assets, such as cash and marketable securities, to the amount of its near-term liabilities. Other liquidity measures—for example, the liquidity model used by Standard & Poor's—compare the amount of the company's assets (individually adjusted for assumptions about ready convertibility to cash) with the amount of the company's obligations (individually adjusted for assumptions about potential for withdrawals).[44] The adjusted amounts are calculated under both normal market conditions and stress. The typical "current ratio" is not directly applicable to L&H companies because their balance sheets often do not include the classifications "current" and "non-current."

4.2.5. Capitalization

As noted with P&C insurers, L&H companies are not guided by a global risk-based capital standard. Various jurisdictions do, however, have standards specifying the amount of capital an insurer must have based on its risk profile. If an insurer's capital falls below the minimum requirement, generally, a supervisory authority intervenes.

Differences between the P&C and L&H businesses are reflected in differences in the risk-based capital requirement. For example, because L&H claims are considered more predictable than those of P&C insurers, L&H insurers do not need as high an equity cushion and can have lower capital requirements.[45] Another difference between the factors considered in establishing minimum capital requirements for L&H companies is that many life insurance products create material exposure to interest rate risk. Accordingly, the calculation of risk-based capital for an L&H company incorporates interest rate risk.[46]

---

[42] "Insurance Regulatory Information Systems (IRIS) Manual: IRIS Ratios Manual for Property/Casualty, Life/Accident & Health, and Fraternal—2016 Edition," National Association of Insurance Commissioners (2016): www.naic.org/prod_serv/UIR-ZB-16_UIR_2016.pdf.

[43] Standard & Poor's Liquidity Model for US and Canadian Life Insurers.

[44] "Annual Report on the Insurance Industry," Federal Insurance Office, US Department of the Treasury (September 2016).

[45] Nissim, "Analysis and Valuation of Insurance Companies."

[46] See www.naic.org/cipr_topics/topic_risk_based_capital.htm.

5. SUMMARY

- Financial institutions' systemic importance results in heavy regulation of their activities.
- Systemic risk refers to the risk of impairment in some part of the financial system that then has the potential to spread throughout other parts of the financial system and thereby to negatively affect the entire economy.
- The Basel Committee, a standing committee of the Bank for International Settlements, includes representatives from central banks and bank supervisors from around the world.
- The Basel Committee's international regulatory framework for banks includes minimum capital requirements, minimum liquidity requirements, and stable funding requirements.
- Among the international organizations that focus on financial stability are the Financial Stability Board, the International Association of Insurance Supervisors, the International Association of Deposit Insurers, and the International Organization of Securities Commissions.
- Another distinctive feature of financial institutions (compared to manufacturing or merchandising companies) is that their productive assets are predominantly financial assets, such as loans and securities, creating greater direct exposures to a variety of risks, such as credit risk, liquidity risk, market risk, and interest rate risk. In general, the values of their assets are relatively close to fair market values.
- A widely used approach to analyzing a bank, CAMELS, considers a bank's **C**apital adequacy, **A**sset quality, **M**anagement capabilities, **E**arnings sufficiency, **L**iquidity position, and **S**ensitivity to market risk.
- "**C**apital adequacy," described in terms of the proportion of the bank's assets that is funded with capital, indicates that a bank has enough capital to absorb potential losses without severely damaging its financial position.
- "**A**sset quality" includes the concept of quality of the bank's assets—credit quality and diversification—and the concept of overall sound risk management.
- "**M**anagement capabilities" refers to the bank management's ability to identify and exploit appropriate business opportunities and to simultaneously manage associated risks.
- "**E**arnings" refers to the bank's return on capital relative to cost of capital and also includes the concept of earnings quality.
- "**L**iquidity" refers to the amount of liquid assets held by the bank relative to its near-term expected cash flows. Under Basel III, liquidity also refers to the stability of the bank's funding sources.
- "**S**ensitivity to market risk" pertains to how adverse changes in markets (including interest rate, exchange rate, equity, and commodity markets) could affect the bank's earnings and capital position.
- In addition to the CAMELS components, important attributes deserving analysts' attention include government support, the banking entity's mission, corporate culture and competitive environment, off-balance-sheet items, segment information, currency exposure, and risk disclosures.
- Insurance companies are typically categorized as property and casualty (P&C) or life and health (L&H).
- Insurance companies earn revenues from premiums (amounts paid by the purchaser of insurance products) and from investment income earned on the float (amounts collected as premiums and not yet paid out as benefits).
- P&C insurers' policies are usually short term, and the final cost will usually be known within a year of a covered event, whereas L&H insurers' policies are usually longer term. P&C insurers' claims are more variable, whereas L&H insurers' claims are more predictable.

- For both types of insurance companies, important areas for analysis include business profile, earnings characteristics, investment returns, liquidity, and capitalization. In addition, analysis of P&C companies' profitability includes analysis of loss reserves and the combined ratio.

PRACTICE PROBLEMS

The following information relates to Questions 1–7

Viktoria Smith is a recently hired junior analyst at Aries Investments. Smith and her supervisor, Ingrid Johansson, meet to discuss some of the firm's investments in banks and insurance companies.

Johansson asks Smith to explain why the evaluation of banks is different from the evaluation of non-financial companies. Smith tells Johansson the following:

Statement 1:   As intermediaries, banks are more likely to be systemically important than non-financial companies.

Statement 2:   The assets of banks mostly consist of deposits, which are exposed to different risks than the tangible assets of non-financial companies.

Smith and Johansson also discuss key aspects of financial regulations, particularly the framework of Basel III. Johansson tells Smith:

"Basel III specifies the minimum percentage of its risk-weighted assets that a bank must fund with equity. This requirement of Basel III prevents a bank from assuming so much financial leverage that it is unable to withstand loan losses or asset write-downs."

Johansson tells Smith that she uses the CAMELS approach to evaluate banks, even though it has some limitations. To evaluate P&C insurance companies, Johansson tells Smith that she places emphasis on the efficiency of spending on obtaining new premiums. Johansson and Smith discuss differences between P&C and L&H insurance companies. Smith notes the following differences:

Difference 1:   L&H insurers' claims are more predictable than P&C insurers' claims.

Difference 2:   P&C insurers' policies are usually short term, whereas L&H insurers' policies are usually longer term.

Difference 3:   Relative to L&H insurers, P&C insurers often have lower capital requirements and can also seek higher returns offered by riskier investments.

Johansson asks Smith to review key performance ratios for three P&C insurers in which Aries is invested. The ratios are presented in Exhibit 1.

EXHIBIT 1   Key Performance Ratios for Selected P&C Insurers

	Insurer A	Insurer B	Insurer C
Loss and loss adjustment expense ratio	68.8%	65.9%	64.1%
Underwriting expense ratio	33.7%	37.8%	32.9%
Combined ratio	102.5%	103.7%	97.0%

Johansson also asks Smith to review key performance ratios for ABC Bank, a bank in which Aries is invested. The ratios are presented in Exhibit 2.

EXHIBIT 2   Key Performance Ratios for ABC Bank*

	2017	2016	2015
Common equity Tier 1 capital ratio	10.7%	11.5%	12.1%
Tier 1 capital ratio	11.5%	12.6%	13.4%
Total capital ratio	14.9%	14.8%	14.9%
Liquidity coverage ratio	123.6%	121.4%	119.1%
Net stable funding ratio	114.9%	113.2%	112.7%
Total trading VaR (all market risk factors)	$11	$13	$15
Total trading and credit portfolio VaR	$15	$18	$21

*Note: VaR amounts are in millions and are based on a 99% confidence interval and a single-day holding period.

1. Which of Smith's statements regarding banks is correct?
   A. Only Statement 1
   B. Only Statement 2
   C. Both Statement 1 and Statement 2

2. The aspect of the Basel III framework that Johansson describes to Smith relates to minimum:
   A. capital requirements.
   B. liquidity requirements.
   C. amounts of stable funding requirements.

3. One limitation of the approach used by Johansson to evaluate banks is that it fails to address a bank's:
   A. sensitivity to market risk.
   B. management capabilities.
   C. competitive environment.

4. The best indicator of the operations of a P&C insurance company emphasized by Johansson when evaluating P&C insurance companies is the:
   A. combined ratio.
   B. underwriting loss ratio.
   C. underwriting expense ratio.

5. Which of the differences between P&C insurers and L&H insurers noted by Smith is *incorrect*?
   A. Difference 1
   B. Difference 2
   C. Difference 3

6. Based on Exhibit 1, Smith should conclude that the insurer with the most efficient underwriting operation is:
   A. Insurer A.
   B. Insurer B.
   C. Insurer C.

7. Based on Exhibit 2, Smith and Johansson should conclude that over the past three years, ABC Bank's:
   A. liquidity position has declined.
   B. capital adequacy has improved.
   C. sensitivity to market risk has improved.

The following information relates to Questions 8–14

Ivan Paulinic, an analyst at a large wealth management firm, meets with his supervisor to discuss adding financial institution equity securities to client portfolios. Paulinic focuses on Vermillion Insurance (Vermillion), a property and casualty company, and Cobalt Life Insurance (Cobalt). To evaluate Vermillion further, Paulinic compiles the information presented in Exhibit 1.

EXHIBIT 1   Select Financial Ratios for Vermillion Insurance

Ratio	2017	2016
Loss and loss adjustment expense	59.1%	61.3%
Underwriting expense	36.3%	35.8%
Combined	95.4%	97.1%
Dividend	2.8%	2.6%

In addition to the insurance companies, Paulinic gathers data on three national banks that meet initial selection criteria but require further review. This information is shown in Exhibits 2, 3, and 4.

EXHIBIT 2   Select Balance Sheet Data for National Banks—Trading: Contribution to Total Revenues

Bank	2017	2013	2009	2005
N-bank	4.2%	7.0%	10.1%	8.9%
R-bank	8.3%	9.1%	17.0%	7.9%
T-bank	5.0%	5.0%	11.9%	6.8%

Focusing on N-bank and T-bank, Paulinic prepares the following data.

EXHIBIT 3   2017 Select Data for N-bank and T-bank

	N-bank		T-bank	
	2017	2016	2017	2016
Average daily trading VaR ($ millions)	11.3	12.6	21.4	20.5
Annual trading revenue/average daily trading VaR	160×	134×	80×	80×

Paulinic investigates R-bank's risk management practices with respect to the use of credit derivatives to enhance earnings, following the 2008 financial crisis. Exhibit 4 displays R-bank's exposure over the last decade to credit derivatives not classified as hedges.

EXHIBIT 4   R-bank's Exposure to Freestanding Credit Derivatives

Credit Derivative Balances	2017	2012	2007
Notional amount ($ billions)	13.4	15.5	305.1

All of the national banks under consideration primarily make long-term loans and source a significant portion of their funding from retail deposits. Paulinic and the rest of the research team note that the central bank is unwinding a long period of monetary easing as evidenced by two recent increases in the overnight funding rate. Paulinic informs his supervisor that:

Statement 1:   Given the recently reported stronger-than-anticipated macroeconomic data, there is an imminent risk that the yield curve will invert.

Statement 2:   N-bank is very active in the 30-day reverse repurchase agreement market during times when the bank experiences significant increases in retail deposits.

8. Paulinic's analysis of the two insurance companies *most likely* indicates that:
   A. Cobalt has more-predictable claims than Vermillion.
   B. Cobalt has a higher capital requirement than Vermillion.
   C. Vermillion's calculated risk-based capital is more sensitive than Cobalt's to interest rate risk.

9. Based only on the information in Exhibit 1, in 2017 Vermillion *most likely*:
   A. experienced a decrease in overall efficiency.
   B. improved its ability to estimate insured risks.
   C. was more efficient in obtaining new premiums.

10. Based only on Exhibit 2, which of the following statements is correct?
   A. The quality of earnings for R-bank was the highest in 2009.
   B. Relative to the other banks, N-bank has the highest quality of earnings in 2017.
   C. Trading represented a sustainable revenue source for T-bank between 2005 and 2013.

11. Based only on Exhibit 3, Paulinic should conclude that:
   A. trading activities are riskier at T-bank than N-bank.
   B. trading revenue per unit of risk has improved more at N-bank than T-bank.
   C. compared with duration, the metric used is a better measure of interest rate risk.

12. Based only on Exhibit 4, R-bank's use of credit derivatives since 2007 *most likely*:
   A. increased posted collateral.
   B. decreased the volatility of earnings from trading activities.
   C. indicates consistent correlations among the relevant risks taken.

13. Based on Statement 1, the net interest margin for the three banks' *most likely* will:
   A. decrease.
   B. remain unchanged.
   C. increase.

14. Based on Statement 2, the financial ratio *most* directly affected is the:
   A. Tier 2 capital ratio.
   B. net stable funding ratio.
   C. liquidity coverage ratio.

The following information relates to Questions 15–20

Judith Yoo is a financial sector analyst writing an industry report. In the report, Yoo discusses the relative global systemic risk across industries, referencing Industry A (international property and casualty insurance), Industry B (credit unions), and Industry C (global commercial banks).

Part of Yoo's analysis focuses on Company XYZ, a global commercial bank, and its CAMELS rating, risk management practices, and performance. First, Yoo considers the firm's capital adequacy as measured by the key capital ratios (common equity Tier 1 capital, total Tier 1 capital, and total capital) in Exhibit 1.

EXHIBIT 1   Company XYZ: Excerpt from Annual Report Disclosure

At December 31 Regulatory capital	2017 $m	2016 $m	2015 $m
Common equity Tier 1 capital	146,424	142,367	137,100
Additional Tier 1 capital	22,639	20,443	17,600
Tier 2 capital	22,456	27,564	38,200
Total regulatory capital	191,519	190,374	192,900
Risk-weighted assets (RWAs) by risk type			
Credit risk	960,763	989,639	968,600
Market risk	44,100	36,910	49,600
Operational risk	293,825	256,300	224,300
Total RWAs	1,298,688	1,282,849	1,242,500

Yoo turns her attention to Company XYZ's asset quality using the information in Exhibit 2.

EXHIBIT 2   Company XYZ: Asset Composition

At December 31	2017 $m	2016 $m	2015 $m
Total liquid assets	361,164	354,056	356,255
Investments	434,256	367,158	332,461
Consumer loans	456,957	450,576	447,493
Commercial loans	499,647	452,983	403,058
Goodwill	26,693	26,529	25,705
Other assets	151,737	144,210	121,780
Total assets	1,930,454	1,795,512	1,686,752

To assess Company XYZ's risk management practices, Yoo reviews the consumer loan credit quality profile in Exhibit 3 and the loan loss analysis in Exhibit 4.

EXHIBIT 3   Company XYZ: Consumer Loan Profile by Credit Quality

At December 31	2017 $m	2016 $m	2015 $m
Strong credit quality	338,948	327,345	320,340
Good credit quality	52,649	54,515	54,050
Satisfactory credit quality	51,124	55,311	56,409
Substandard credit quality	23,696	24,893	27,525
Past due but not impaired	2,823	2,314	2,058
Impaired	8,804	9,345	10,235
Total gross amount	478,044	473,723	470,617
Impairment allowances	−5,500	−4,500	−4,000
Total	472,544	469,223	466,617

EXHIBIT 4   Company XYZ: Loan Loss Analysis Data

At December 31	2017 $m	2016 $m	2015 $m
Consumer loans			
Allowance for loan losses	11,000	11,500	13,000
Provision for loan losses	3,000	2,000	1,300
Charge-offs	3,759	3,643	4,007
Recoveries	1,299	1,138	1,106
Net charge-offs	2,460	2,505	2,901
Commercial loans			
Allowance for loan losses	1,540	1,012	169
Provision for loan losses	1,100	442	95
Charge-offs	1,488	811	717
Recoveries	428	424	673
Net charge-offs	1,060	387	44

Finally, Yoo notes the following supplementary information from Company XYZ's annual report:

- Competition in the commercial loan space has become increasingly fierce, leading XYZ managers to pursue higher-risk strategies to increase market share.
- The net benefit plan obligation has steadily decreased during the last three years.
- Company XYZ awards above-average equity-based compensation to its top managers.

15. Which of the following industries *most likely* has the highest level of global systemic risk?
    A. Industry A
    B. Industry B
    C. Industry C

16. Based on Exhibit 1, Company XYZ's capital adequacy over the last three years, as measured by the three key capital ratios, signals conditions that are:
    A. mixed.
    B. declining.
    C. improving.

17. Based only on Exhibit 2, asset composition from 2015 to 2017 indicates:
    A. declining liquidity.
    B. increasing risk based on the proportion of total loans to total assets.
    C. decreasing risk based on the proportion of investments to total assets.

18. Based on Exhibit 3, the trend in impairment allowances is reflective of the changes in:
    A. impaired assets.
    B. strong credit quality assets.
    C. past due but not impaired assets.

19. Based on Exhibit 4, a loan loss analysis for the last three years indicates that:
    A. Company XYZ has become less conservative in its provisioning for consumer loans.
    B. the provision for commercial loan losses has trailed the actual net charge-off experience.
    C. the cushion between the allowance and the net commercial loan charge-offs has declined.

20. Which of the following supplemental factors is consistent with a favorable assessment of Company XYZ's financial outlook?
    A. Competitive environment
    B. Net benefit plan obligation
    C. Equity-based compensation policy

CHAPTER 17

EVALUATING QUALITY OF FINANCIAL REPORTS

Jack T. Ciesielski, CPA, CFA
Elaine Henry, PhD, CFA
Thomas I. Selling, PhD, CPA

LEARNING OUTCOMES

After completing this chapter, you will be able to do the following:

- demonstrate the use of a conceptual framework for assessing the quality of a company's financial reports;
- explain potential problems that affect the quality of financial reports;
- describe how to evaluate the quality of a company's financial reports;
- evaluate the quality of a company's financial reports;
- describe the concept of sustainable (persistent) earnings;
- describe indicators of earnings quality;
- explain mean reversion in earnings and how the accruals component of earnings affects the speed of mean reversion;
- evaluate the earnings quality of a company;
- describe indicators of cash flow quality;
- evaluate the cash flow quality of a company;
- describe indicators of balance sheet quality;
- evaluate the balance sheet quality of a company;
- describe sources of information about risk.

1. INTRODUCTION

The ability to assess the quality of reported financial information can be a valuable skill. An analyst or investor who can recognize high-quality financial reporting can have greater confidence in analysis based on those financial reports and the resulting investment decisions. Similarly, an analyst or investor who can recognize poor financial reporting quality early—before deficiencies become widely known—is more likely to make profitable investment decisions or to reduce or even avoid losses.

An example of early recognition of an ultimate financial disaster is James Chanos's short position in Enron in November 2000 (Chanos 2002)—more than a year before Enron filed for bankruptcy protection (in December 2001). Despite Enron's high profile and reputation,[1] Chanos had a negative view of Enron based on both quantitative and qualitative factors. Chanos noted that Enron's return on capital was both lower than comparable companies' return on capital and lower than the company's own cost of capital. Qualitative factors contributing to Chanos's view included the company's aggressive revenue recognition policy, its complex and difficult-to-understand disclosures on related-party transactions, and one-time earnings-boosting gains. Later events that substantiated Chanos's perspective included sales of the company's stock by insiders and the resignation of senior executives.

Another example of early recognition of eventual financial troubles is June 2001 reports by analyst Enitan Adebonojo. These reports highlighted questionable accounting by Royal Ahold, a European food retailer. The questionable accounting included "claiming profits of acquired firms as 'organic growth,' booking capital gains from sale-and-leaseback deals as profit, and keeping billions in debt off its balance sheet."[2] In 2003, Royal Ahold announced that it had significantly overstated its profits in the prior two years. The CEO and CFO resigned, various regulators announced investigations, and Royal Ahold's market value dropped significantly.

This chapter focuses on reporting quality and the interrelated attribute of results quality. *Reporting quality* pertains to the information disclosed in financial reports. High-quality reporting provides decision-useful information—information that is relevant and faithfully represents the economic reality of the company's activities during the reporting period and the company's financial condition at the end of the period. A separate, but interrelated, attribute of quality is *results* or *earnings quality*, which pertains to the earnings and cash generated by the company's actual economic activities and the resulting financial condition relative to expectations of current and future financial performance. Note that the term "earnings quality" is more commonly used in practice than "results quality," so throughout this chapter, earnings quality is used broadly to encompass the quality of earnings, cash flow, and/or balance sheet items.

High-quality earnings reflect an adequate level of return on investment and are derived from activities that a company will likely be able to sustain in the future. Thus, high-quality earnings increase the value of a company more than low-quality earnings. When reported earnings are described as being high quality, it means that the company's underlying economic performance was good (i.e., value enhancing), and it also implies that the company had high reporting quality (i.e., that the information that the company calculated and disclosed was a good reflection of the economic reality).

Earnings can be termed "low quality" either because the reported information properly represents genuinely bad performance or because the reported information misrepresents economic reality. In theory, a company could have low-quality earnings while simultaneously having high reporting quality. Consider a company with low-quality earnings—for example,

---

[1] In October 2000, Enron was named in the top 25 on *Fortune* magazine's list of the World's Most Admired Companies.
[2] "Ahold: Europe's Enron," *The Economist*, (February 27, 2003).

one whose only source of earnings in a period is a one-off settlement of a lawsuit without which the company would have reported huge losses. The company could nonetheless have high reporting quality if it calculated its results properly and provided decision-useful information. Although it is theoretically possible that a company could have low-quality earnings while simultaneously having high reporting quality, experiencing poor financial performance can motivate the company's management to misreport.

This chapter begins in Section 2 with a description of a conceptual framework for and potential problems with financial reporting quality. This is followed in Section 3 with a discussion of how to evaluate financial reporting quality. Sections 4, 5, and 6 focus on the quality of reported earnings, cash flows, and balance sheets, respectively. Section 7 covers sources of information about risk. A summary and practice problems in the CFA Institute item set format complete the chapter.

2. QUALITY OF FINANCIAL REPORTS

This section reviews a conceptual framework for assessing the quality of financial reports and then outlines potential problems that affect the quality of financial reports.

2.1. Conceptual Framework for Assessing the Quality of Financial Reports

As indicated in the introduction, financial reporting quality and results or earnings quality are related attributes of quality. Exhibit 1 illustrates this relationship and its implications. Low financial reporting quality can make it difficult or impossible to assess a company's results, and as a result, it is difficult to make investment and other decisions, such as lending and extending credit to the company.

EXHIBIT 1   Relationships between Financial Reporting Quality and Earnings Quality

		Financial Reporting Quality	
		Low	High
	High	LOW financial reporting quality impedes assessment of earnings quality and impedes valuation.	HIGH financial <u>reporting</u> quality enables assessment. HIGH <u>earnings</u> quality increases company value.
Earnings (Results) Quality	Low		HIGH financial <u>reporting</u> quality enables assessment. LOW <u>earnings</u> quality decreases company value.

Financial reporting quality varies across companies. Financial reports can range from those that contain relevant and faithfully representational information to those that contain information that is pure fabrication. Earnings (results) quality can range from high and sustainable to low and unsustainable. The presence of high-quality financial reporting is a necessary condition for enabling investors to evaluate results quality. High-quality financial reporting alone is an insufficient condition to ensure the presence of high-quality results, but the existence of high-quality financial reporting allows the investor to make such an assessment.

Combining the two aspects of quality—financial reporting and earnings—the overall quality of financial reports from a user perspective can be thought of as spanning a continuum from the highest to the lowest. Exhibit 2 presents a spectrum that provides a basis for evaluating better versus poorer quality reports.

EXHIBIT 2   Quality Spectrum of Financial Reports

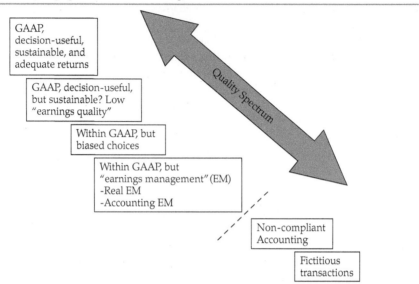

Essentially, the analyst needs to consider two basic questions:

1. Are the financial reports GAAP-compliant and decision-useful?
2. Are the results (earnings) of high quality? In other words, do they provide an adequate level of return, and are they sustainable?

These two questions provide a basic conceptual framework to assess the quality of a company's financial reports and to locate the company's financial reports along the quality spectrum. At the top of the spectrum, labeled in Exhibit 2 as "GAAP, decision-useful, sustainable, and adequate returns" are high-quality reports that provide decision-useful information about high-quality earnings. "GAAP" refers generically to the generally accepted accounting principles or the accepted accounting standards of the jurisdiction under which the company reports. Examples of GAAP are International Financial Reporting Standards (IFRS), US GAAP, and other home-country accounting standards. *Decision-useful* information embodies the characteristics of relevance and faithful representation.[3] High-quality earnings provide an *adequate level of return* on investment (i.e., a return equal to or in excess of the cost of capital) and are sustainable. *Sustainable* indicates that the earnings are derived from activities that a company will likely be able to sustain in the future. Sustainable earnings that provide a high return on investment contribute to a higher valuation of a company and its securities.

---

[3] These characteristics are from the *Conceptual Framework for Financial Reporting* (IASB 2010). The characteristics of decision-useful information are identical under IFRS and US GAAP. Relevant information is defined as information that can affect a decision and encompasses the notion of materiality. Faithful representation of economic events is complete, neutral, and free from error. The *Framework* also identifies enhancing characteristics of useful information: comparability, verifiability, timeliness, and understandability. High-quality information results when necessary trade-offs among these characteristics are made in an unbiased, skillful manner.

Any deviation from the highest point on the quality spectrum can be assessed in terms of the two-question conceptual framework. For example, a company that provides GAAP-compliant, decision-useful information about low-quality earnings (they can be of low quality because they do not provide an adequate level of return and/or they are not sustainable) would appear lower on the quality spectrum. Even lower on the spectrum would be companies that provide GAAP-compliant information, which is less decision-useful because of biased choices.

Biased accounting choices result in financial reports that do not faithfully represent economic phenomena. Biased choices can be made not only in the context of reported amounts but also in the context of how information is presented. For example, companies can disclose information transparently and in a manner that facilitates analysis, or they can disclose information in a manner that aims to obscure unfavorable information and/or to emphasize favorable information.

The problem with bias in accounting choices, as with other deficiencies in financial reporting quality, is that it impedes an investor's ability to correctly assess a company's past performance, to accurately forecast future performance, and thus to appropriately value the company. Choices are deemed to be "aggressive" if they increase the company's reported performance and financial position in the current period. Aggressive choices may decrease the company's reported performance and financial position in later periods. In contrast, choices are deemed to be "conservative" if they decrease the company's reported performance and financial position in the current period. Conservative choices may increase the company's reported performance and financial position in later periods.

Another type of bias is "earnings management." An example of this bias is earnings "smoothing" to understate earnings volatility relative to the volatility if earnings were faithfully represented. Earnings volatility is decreased by understating earnings in periods when a company's operations are performing well and overstating in periods when the company's operations are struggling.

The next levels down on the spectrum mark a departure from GAAP. Financial reports that depart from GAAP can generally be considered low quality; they are of poor financial reporting quality and cannot be relied on to assess earnings quality. The lowest-quality financial reports portray fictitious transactions or omit actual transactions; such financial reports are fabrications.

2.2. Potential Problems that Affect the Quality of Financial Reports

The basic choices that give rise to potential problems with quality of financial reports include reported amounts and timing of recognition and classification. Remember that even GAAP-compliant financial reports can diverge from economic reality if GAAP allows for biased choices. In addition to GAAP-compliant choices, a financial statement preparer may choose to present fraudulent reports. This choice represents a divergence from GAAP and economic reality.

2.2.1. Reported Amounts and Timing of Recognition

The choice of the reported amount and timing of recognition may focus on a single financial statement element (assets, liabilities, owners' equity, revenue and gains [income], or expenses and losses). However, this choice may affect other elements and more than one financial statement because financial statements are interrelated.[4] It is useful to think of the impact of

---

[4]Depending on management's motivation, poor-quality financial reports may either overstate or understate results. Fraudulent financial reports almost always overstate results.

accounting choices in terms of the basic accounting equation (Assets = Liabilities + Equity). This equation can be restated as Assets − Liabilities = Equity, which is also equivalent to Net Assets = Equity. Choices related to income statement elements will affect the balance sheet through equity, and if equity is affected, then another balance sheet element(s) has to be affected or the balance sheet will not balance.

Following are some examples of choices—accounting choices that comply with GAAP, accounting choices that depart from GAAP, and operating choices—and their effects in the current period:

- Aggressive, premature, and fictitious revenue recognition results in overstated income and thus overstated equity. Assets, usually accounts receivable, are also overstated.
- Conservative revenue recognition, such as deferred recognition of revenue, results in understated net income, understated equity, and understated assets.
- Omission and delayed recognition of expenses results in understated expenses and overstated income, overstated equity, overstated assets, and/or understated liabilities. An understatement of bad debt expense results in overstated accounts receivable. Understated depreciation or amortization expense results in the overstatement of the related long-lived asset. Understated interest, taxes, or other expenses result in the understatement of the related liability: accrued interest payable, taxes payable, or other payable.
- Understatement of contingent liabilities is associated with overstated equity resulting from understated expenses and overstated income or overstated other comprehensive income.
- Overstatement of financial assets and understatement of financial liabilities, reported at fair value, are associated with overstated equity resulting from overstated unrealized gains or understated unrealized losses.
- Cash flow from operations may be increased by deferring payments on payables, accelerating payments from customers, deferring purchases of inventory, and deferring other expenditures related to operations, such as maintenance and research.

Example 1 describes events and choices at Satyam Computer Services Limited, which resulted in the issuance of fraudulent reports.

EXAMPLE 1   Fictitious Reports

Satyam Computer Services Limited
Satyam Computer Services Limited, an Indian information technology company, was founded in 1987 and grew rapidly by providing business process outsourcing (BPO) on a global basis. In 2007, its CEO, Ramalinga Raju, was named "Entrepreneur of the Year" by Ernst & Young, and in 2008, the World Council for Corporate Governance recognized the company for "global excellence in corporate accountability." In 2009, the CEO submitted a letter of resignation that outlined a massive financial fraud at the company. The company's decline was so rapid and significant that it came to be referred to as "India's Enron."

In late 2008, the World Bank terminated its relationship with the company after finding that Satyam gave kickbacks to bank staff and billed for services that were not provided. These initial revelations of wrongdoing had the effect of putting the company under increased scrutiny. Among other misconduct, the CEO eventually admitted that he created fictitious bank statements to inflate cash and to show interest income. The CEO also created fake salary accounts and took the money paid to those "employees." The company's head of internal auditing created fictitious customer accounts and invoices to inflate revenues.[5]

The external auditors did not independently verify much of the information provided by the company. Even when bank confirmations, which were sent to them directly as opposed to indirectly through Satyam, contained significantly different balances than those reported by Satyam, they did not follow up.

1. Based on the information provided, characterize Satyam's financial reports, with reference to the quality spectrum of financial reports.
2. Explain each of the following misconducts with reference to the basic accounting equation:
   A. Transactions with World Bank
   B. Fictitious interest income
   C. CEO's embezzlement
   D. Fictitious revenue
3. Based on the information provided, what documents were falsified to support the misconducts listed in Question 2?

Solution to 1: Based on the information provided, Satyam's financial reports were of the lowest quality. They clearly are at the bottom of the quality spectrum of financial reports: reports based on fictitious information.

Solution to 2: The effects on the basic accounting equation of the different acts of misconduct are as follows:

A. Upon billing for fictitious services, the company would increase an asset, such as accounts receivable, and a revenue account, such as service revenues. The kickbacks to the customer's staff, if recorded, would increase an expense account, such as commissions paid, and increase a liability, such as commissions payable, or decrease an asset, such as cash. The net effect of this misconduct is the overstatement of income, net assets, and equity.

B. Fictitious interest income would result in overstated income; overstated assets, such as cash and interest receivable; and overstated equity. These overstatements were hidden by falsifying revenue and cash balances.

C. The embezzlement by creating fictitious employees would increase an expense account, such as wages and salaries, and decrease the asset, cash. The resulting understatement of income and equity was offset by a real but fraudulent decrease in cash, which was hidden by falsifying revenue and cash balances.

D. Fictitious revenues would result in overstated revenues and income; overstated assets, such as cash and accounts receivable; and overstated equity.

---

[5] See Bhasin (2012) for more information.

Solution to 3: Based on the information provided, the documents that were falsified include

- invoices to the World Bank for services that were not provided,
- bank statements,
- employee records, and
- customer accounts and invoices.

The falsified documents were intended to mislead the external auditors.

An astute reader of financial statements may have identified a potential problem at Satyam by comparing the growth in revenue with the growth in assets on its balance sheet, such as short-term and long-term trade receivables and unbilled revenue. Long-term trade receivables and unbilled revenue accounts may have raised questions. Also, there was an account separate from cash, investments in bank deposits, which may have raised questions. However, fraudulent reports that are well constructed can be very challenging to identify.

2.2.2. Classification

Choices with respect to reported amounts and timing of recognition typically affect more than one financial element, financial statement, and financial period. Classification choices typically affect one financial statement and relate to how an item is classified within a particular financial statement. The balance sheet, the statement of comprehensive income, or the cash flow statement may be the primary focus of the choice.

With respect to the balance sheet, the concern may be to make the balance sheet ratios more attractive or to hide an issue. For example, a company may focus on accounts receivable because it wants to hide liquidity or revenue collection issues. Choices include removing the accounts receivable from the balance sheet by selling them externally or transferring them to a controlled entity, converting them to notes receivable, or reclassifying them within the balance sheet, such as by reporting them as long-term receivables. Although these amounts remain on the balance sheet as receivables of some sort, a result of their reclassification is a lower accounts receivable balance. This could imply to investors that a collection has taken place and also might favorably skew receivables measures, such as days' sales outstanding and receivables turnover.

In the 2003 Merck Annual Report, Merck & Co. reclassified a portion of its inventory to "Other assets," a long-term asset. This reclassification affects the balance sheet and financial ratios as demonstrated in Example 2.

EXAMPLE 2   Balance Sheet Reclassifications

Merck & Co., Inc. and Subsidiaries
In the 2002 Annual Report, inventory was reported at $3,411.8 million. In the 2003 Annual Report, the 2002 inventory value was reported at $2,964.3 million and $447.5 million of inventory was included in other assets. This information was contained in Note 6 to the financial statements, reproduced in Exhibit 3.

EXHIBIT 3   Note 6 to Consolidated Financial Statements

6. Inventories
Inventories at December 31 consisted of:

($ in millions)	2003	2002
Finished goods	$552.5	$1,262.3
Raw materials and work in process	2,309.8	2,073.8
Supplies	90.5	75.7
Total (approximate current cost)	$2,952.8	$3,411.8
Reduction to LIFO cost	—	—
	$2,952.8	$3,411.8
Recognized as:		
Inventories	$2,554.7	$2,964.3
Other assets	398.1	447.5

Inventories valued under the LIFO method comprised approximately 51% and 39% of inventories at December 31, 2003 and 2002, respectively. Amounts recognized as Other assets consist of inventories held in preparation for product launches and not expected to be sold within one year. The reduction in finished goods is primarily attributable to the spin-off of Medco Health in 2003.

1. The reclassification of a portion of inventory to other assets will *most likely* result in the days of inventory on hand:
   A. decreasing.
   B. staying the same.
   C. increasing.
2. As a result of the reclassification of a portion of inventory to other assets, the current ratio will *most likely*:
   A. decrease.
   B. stay the same.
   C. increase.

Solution to 1: A is correct. The number of days of inventory on hand calculated using the reported inventory number will most likely decrease because the amount of inventory relative to cost of goods sold will decrease.

Solution to 2: A is correct. The current ratio will decrease because current assets will decrease and current liabilities will stay the same.

From Exhibit 3, notice that the reclassification is described in the sentence, "Amounts recognized as Other assets consist of inventories held in preparation for product launches and not expected to be sold within one year." The reasoning behind the reclassification's explanation is logical: Current assets include assets to be consumed or converted into cash in a company's operating cycle, which is usually one year. The inventory items associated with product launches beyond one year are more appropriately classified as "other assets." Yet, the change in classification poses analytical problems. Inventory turnover is a key indicator of efficiency in managing inventory levels and is calculated as cost of sales divided by average inventory. Although the inventory turnover can be calculated for 2003, it cannot be calculated on a consistent basis for 2002, or any year before then, because the amount of inventory that would have been classified as "other assets" in those periods is not disclosed. An investor has to recognize that a time-series comparison of Merck's inventory turnover is going to produce an inconsistent history because of the lack of consistent information.

The classification of revenues between operating and non-operating may help the user to determine sustainability of a company's earnings, but the classification has potential for misuse by a company. The classification of revenues as being derived from core, continuing operations could mislead financial statement users into considering inflated amounts of income as being sustainable. Similarly, the classification of expenses as non-operating could mislead financial statement users into considering inflated amounts of income as being sustainable. In non-GAAP metrics reported outside of the financial statements, the classification of income-reducing items as non-recurring could also mislead financial statement users into considering inflated amounts of income as being sustainable.

Classifications that result in an item being reported in other comprehensive income rather than on the income statement can affect analysis and comparison. For example, if two otherwise identical companies classify investments differently, net income may differ because the change in value of the investments may flow through net income for one company and through other comprehensive income for the other company.

Classification issues also arise specifically with the statement of cash flows for which management may have incentives to maximize the amount of cash flows that are classified as "operating." Management may be motivated to classify activities, such as the sale of long-term assets, as operating activities rather than investing activities. Operating activities are part of the day-to-day functioning of a company, such as selling inventory or providing services. For most companies, the sale of property or other long-term assets are not operating activities, and including them in operating activities overstates the company's ability to generate cash from its operations. Management may capitalize rather than expense operating expenditures. As a result, the outflow may be classified as an investing activity rather than an operating activity.

Exhibit 4 presents a selection of potential issues, possible actions, and warning signs of possible deviations from high-quality financial reports, some of which will be specifically discussed in later sections of this chapter. The warning signs may be visible in the financial statements themselves, in the notes to the financial statements, or in ratios calculated by the analyst that are assessed over time or compared with those of peer companies. Frequently, the chosen actions bias net income upward. However, a new management or management of a company in financial difficulty may be motivated to bias current income downward to enhance future periods.

EXHIBIT 4   Accounting Warning Signs

Potential Issues	Possible Actions/Choices	Warning Signs

• Overstatement or non-sustainability of operating income and/or net income
  ▪ Overstated or accelerated revenue recognition
  ▪ Understated expenses
  ▪ Misclassification of revenue, gains, expenses, or losses
	• Contingent sales with right of return, "channel stuffing" (the practice of inducing customers to order products they would otherwise not order or order at a later date through generous terms), "bill and hold" sales (encouraging customers to order goods and retain them on seller's premises)	• Growth in revenue higher than that of industry or peers
		• Increases in discounts to and returns from customers
		• Higher growth rate in receivables than revenue
		• Large proportion of revenue in final quarter of year for a non-seasonal business
		• Cash flow from operations is much lower than operating income

EXHIBIT 4   (Continued)

Potential Issues	Possible Actions/Choices	Warning Signs
	• Fictitious (fraudulent) revenue • Capitalizing expenditures as assets • Classifying non-operating income or gains as part of operations • Classifying ordinary expenses as non-recurring or non-operating • Reporting gains through net income and losses through other comprehensive income	• Inconsistency over time in the items included in operating revenues and operating expenses • Increases in operating margin • Aggressive accounting assumptions, such as long, depreciable lives • Losses in non-operating income or other comprehensive income and gains in operating income or net income • Compensation largely tied to financial results

• Misstatement of balance sheet items (may affect income statement)
  ▪ Over- or understatement of assets
  ▪ Over- or understatement of liabilities
  ▪ Misclassification of assets and/or liabilities
	• Choice of models and model inputs to measure fair value
	• Classification from current to non-current
	• Over- or understating reserves and allowances
	• Understating identifiable assets and overstating goodwill
		• Models and model inputs that bias fair value measures
		• Inconsistency in model inputs when measuring fair value of assets compared with that of liabilities
		• Typical current assets, such as accounts receivable and inventory, included in non-current assets
		• Allowances and reserves that fluctuate over time or are not comparable with peers
		• High goodwill value relative to total assets
		• Use of special purpose vehicles
		• Large changes in deferred tax assets and liabilities
		• Significant off-balance-sheet liabilities

• Overstatement of cash flow from operations	• Managing activities to affect cash flow from operations • Misclassifying cash flows to positively affect cash flow from operations	• Increase in accounts payable and decrease in accounts receivable and inventory • Capitalized expenditures in investing activities • Sales and leaseback • Increases in bank overdrafts

2.2.3. Quality Issues and Mergers and Acquisitions

Quality issues with respect to financial reports often arise in connection with mergers and acquisitions. Mergers and acquisitions provide opportunities and motivations to manage financial results. For accounting purposes, the business combination is accounted for using the acquisition method, and one company is identified as the acquirer. The financial results of the combined companies are reported on a consolidated basis.

Companies with faltering cash-generating ability may be motivated to acquire other companies to increase cash flow from operations. The acquisition will be reported in the investing cash flows if paid in cash, or not even appear on the cash flow statement if paid for with equity. The consolidated cash flow from operations will include the cash flow of the acquired company, effectively concealing the acquirer's own cash flow problems. Such an acquisition can provide a one-time boost to cash from operations that may or may not be sustainable. There are no required post-acquisition "with and without acquisitions" disclosures, making it impossible for investors to reliably assess whether or not the acquirer's cash flow problems are worsening.

A potential acquisition may create an incentive for a company to report using aggressive choices or even misreport. For example, an acquirer's managers may be motivated to make choices to increase earnings to make an acquisition on more favorable terms. Evidence indicates that acquirers making an acquisition for stock may manipulate their reported earnings prior to the acquisition to inflate the value of shares being used to pay for the acquisition (Erickson and Wang 1999). Similarly, the target company's managers may be motivated to make choices to increase earnings to secure a more favorable price for their company. As another example, the acquiring managers may try to manipulate earnings upward after an acquisition if they want to positively influence investors' opinion of the acquisition.[6]

In other cases, misreporting can be an incentive to make an acquisition. Acquisitions complicate a company's financial statements and thus can conceal previous accounting misstatements. Some evidence indicates that companies engaged in intentional misreporting (specifically, companies that were subsequently accused of accounting fraud by the US SEC) are more likely than non-misreporting companies to make an acquisition. They are also more likely to acquire a company that would reduce the comparability and consistency of their financial statements, such as by targeting companies that have less public information and less similar operations (Erickson, Heitzman, and Zhang 2012).

There are also opportunities to make choices that affect the initial consolidated balance sheet and consolidated income statements in the future. When a business combination occurs, the acquirer must measure and recognize identifiable assets acquired and liabilities assumed at their fair values as of the acquisition date. These may include assets and liabilities that the acquired company had not previously recognized as assets and liabilities in its financial statements. For example, identifiable intangible assets that the acquired company developed internally and some contingent liabilities would be recognized by the acquirer. The excess of the purchase price over the recognized value of the identified assets acquired and liabilities assumed is reported as goodwill. Unlike other long-lived assets, goodwill is not amortized; however, it is subject to impairment testing. Because goodwill is not amortized, unless appropriate impairment charges are recorded, the capitalized goodwill amount continues indefinitely.

The default accounting treatment for goodwill—no future amortization expense—provides an incentive to acquirers to understate the value of amortizable intangibles when recording an acquisition. Being a residual amount, more of the value of an acquisition will thus be classified as goodwill, with its future earnings-friendly accounting treatment. That bias may result in postponement of the recognition of an uneconomic acquisition until impairment charges on the goodwill are recorded, which may be long after the acquisition. Managements may be willing to take this chance because they may be able to convince analysts and investors that a goodwill impairment charge is a non-recurring, non-cash charge—something that many will overlook. Nevertheless, the presence of goodwill should make an investor more inquisitive about a company's record in recognizing impairments and should

---

[6] Findings consistent with this possibility are presented in Bens, Goodman, and Neamtiu (2012).

also motivate an investor to evaluate a company's impairment testing process for goodwill. Fair value measurement, except in the case of assets and liabilities with quoted prices in active markets for identical assets or liabilities, presents an opportunity for the acquirer's management to exercise judgment and affect reported values. For example, they could understate fair value of assets to avoid future charges to expense. Understating the fair value of assets will result in a higher goodwill amount. In the absence of impairment of goodwill, there will be no charges associated with the goodwill. Many analysts question whether reported goodwill reflects economic reality.

2.2.4. Financial Reporting that Diverges from Economic Reality Despite Compliance with Accounting Rules

Certain accounting standards may give rise to financial reporting that an analyst may find less useful because he or she does not view it as reflective of economic reality. Examples 3 and 4 illustrate these types of situations. When possible, an analyst should adjust the reported information to better reflect his or her view of economic reality. If an adjustment is not possible because the relevant data are not disclosed, an analyst can instead make a qualitative assessment of the effect.

Example 3 describes one of the earlier cases of creative consolidation accounting that raised the need for an in-depth consideration of consolidation accounting and the related issue of control. Many entities are governed by the votes of shareholders under which the majority rules. However, exceptions may exist and both US GAAP and IFRS have endeavored to create regimes under which consolidation is required when it is appropriate to depict economic substance.

EXAMPLE 3   Treatment of Variable Interest (Special Purpose) Entities

SEC enforcement action regarding the financial statements of Digilog, Inc.

In order to develop and introduce a new product, Digilog created a separate business entity, DBS, that was capitalized with $10 million of convertible debt issued to Digilog. Upon conversion, Digilog would end up owning nearly 100% of DBS. Initially, owners' equity of DBS consisted of a few thousand dollars of common stock issued to DBS's manager.

During the first two years of DBS's operations, Digilog did not consolidate DBS; it argued that DBS was controlled by its manager, who owned 100% of the outstanding common shares. Even though DBS generated substantial losses over its first two years of existence, Digilog reported interest income on its investment in the convertible debt. After two years, when DBS started to generate profits, Digilog exercised its conversion option and consolidated from that point forward.

Although DBS had been set up as an "independent" corporation, the SEC took the position that the contractual and operating relationships between the two companies were such that they should have been viewed as constituting a single enterprise for financial reporting purposes. The defendants in the enforcement action, Digilog's auditors, consented to a settlement. The settlement included the opinion by the SEC that consolidation would have provided a user of the financial statements with the most meaningful presentation in accordance with GAAP—even though no specific GAAP at that time directly addressed Digilog's "creative" accounting solution.

Eventually, after many more years of debate, and in the wake of the Enron scandal, which also involved abuse of subsequent consolidation rules, the concept of a "variable interest entity" (VIE) was created. A key aspect is control for consolidation purposes; even in the absence of voting control, consolidation is necessary if the investor has the ability to exert influence on the financial and operating policy of the entity and is exposed, or has rights, to variable returns from its investment in the entity. Although the term VIE is not employed by IFRS, its provisions are similar.

Given the facts above and the consolidation rules for a variable interest entity, Digilog is *most likely* to try to argue that it does not need to consolidate DBS because:

A. Digilog does not have voting control.

B. Digilog's interest income from DBS is not variable.

C. DBS's manager has operational and financial control.

Solution: C is correct. Digilog is most likely to assert that operational and financial control rest with DBS's manager. However, the assertion is not likely to be accepted because the manager's investment is a few thousand dollars compared with $10 million by Digilog. Simply not having voting control is not sufficient to avoid consolidation. Digilog is exposed to variable returns because of possible losses and the convertibility option.

Example 4 considers asset impairments and restructuring charges and their implications.

EXAMPLE 4   Asset Impairments and Restructuring Charges

Two related topics that almost always require special consideration on the part of analysts are asset impairments and restructuring charges. Asset impairments are write-downs of assets required when circumstances indicate that the carrying amount of an asset is excessive compared with the expected future benefits.

The term "restructuring charge" is used under IFRS to indicate a sale or termination of a line of business, closure of business locations, changes in management structure, and/or a fundamental reorganization. All of these events could also give rise to the recognition of a liability (e.g., a commitment to make employee severance payments or to make a payment to settle a lease).

On April 25, 2013, Fuji Electric Co., Ltd, a Japanese company reporting under the GAAP of its home country, announced an impairment loss on land, buildings, structures, and leased assets employed in its "solar cell and module business" in the amount of ¥6.5 billion (Fuji Electric 2013). The entire loss was recorded in its 2012 fiscal year (ending March 31). Assets and net income were reduced by ¥6.5 billion.

Elan Corporation, plc, a biotechnology company headquartered in Ireland, reported US$42.4 million in restructuring and other costs incurred during fiscal year

2012 related to its decision to close a research facility in San Francisco, with the loss of around 200 jobs, and to shift much of its operations back to Ireland because of changing business conditions. Some of these costs were associated with the obligation to make current and deferred employee severance payments (Leuty 2012).[7]

Recognizing an impairment loss and restructuring charges in a single period, although consistent with most GAAP, is *most likely* to overstate:

A. prior periods' net incomes.

B. current period's net income.

C. future periods' net incomes.

Solution: A is correct. The impairment and the restructuring were likely the result of past activities and should be taken into account when evaluating past net incomes. The current period's net income, unless the impairment or restructuring is expected to be repeated, is understated. Future period net income may be overstated if reversals occur, but such behavior is not likely. Charging the entire impairment loss and restructuring charge in the current period are examples of conservative accounting principles.

An analyst would likely consider it probable that the events giving rise to Fuji Electric's impairment loss (evidently, declining activity and future prospects for its solar business) had actually occurred over a longer period than that single year. Similarly, an analyst might view the restructuring charge at Elan as relating to previous periods.

When faced with a restructuring charge, an impairment charge, or a combination of the two, an analyst should consider whether similar events occur regularly enough such that they should be factored into estimates of permanent earnings, or whether they should be regarded as one-off items that provide little information about the future earnings of the remaining activities of the company. If it is the former, then the analyst should attempt to "normalize" earnings by essentially spreading the current restructuring/impairment charge(s) over past periods as well as the current period. If an item is truly one-off—say, the financial effects of a natural disaster—then the analyst is justified in "normalizing" earnings by excluding the item from earnings. This process will require a significant amount of judgment, best informed by knowledge of the underlying facts and circumstances.

Items that are commonly encountered by analysts include the following:

- Revisions to ongoing estimates, such as the remaining economic lives of assets, may lead an analyst to question whether an earlier change in estimate would have been more appropriate.
- Sudden increases to allowances and reserves could call into question whether the prior estimates resulted in overstatement of prior periods' earnings instead of an unbiased picture of economic reality.
- Large accruals for losses (e.g., environmental or litigation-related liabilities) suggest that prior periods' earnings may have been overstated because of the failure to accrue losses earlier.

---

[7] See also Elan Corporation, plc, Form 20-F, filed February 12, 2013.

Management may use items such as reserves and allowances to manage or smooth earnings. The application of accounting standards illustrated in Examples 3 and 4 results in financial statements that may not reflect economic reality. Accounting standards may result in some economic assets and liabilities not being reflected in the financial statements. An example is research and development (R&D) expense. Accounting standards do not permit the capitalization of expenditures for R&D expense, yet R&D produces assets that, in turn, produce future benefits. Accounting standards prohibit R&D's capitalization because of the difficulty in assessing which expenditures will actually produce future benefits and which expenditures will produce nothing. Accounting standards may also result in some information being reported in other comprehensive income rather than through net income. For example, classifying marketable securities as "available for sale" will result in their changes in fair value being reported in other comprehensive income. Contrast that reporting result against that for marketable securities classified as "trading": Their changes in fair value are reported in net income.

No basis of accounting can be expected to recognize all of the economic assets and liabilities for an entity. Consequently, figuring out what *is not* reported can be challenging. One frequently encountered example of an unrecognized asset is a company's sales order backlog. Under most GAAP, revenue is not recognized (and an asset is not created) until services have been performed and other criteria have been met. However, in certain industries, particularly large-scale manufacturing, such as airplane manufacturing, the order backlog can be a significant unrecognized asset. When the amount of backlog is significant, it is typically discussed in the management commentary, and an analyst can use this information to adjust reported amounts and to prepare forecasts.

Another dilemma for analysts is judging whether an item presented in other comprehensive income (OCI) should be included in their analysis as net income. Examples of items presented in OCI include the following:

- unrealized holding gains and losses on certain investments in equity securities,
- unrealized holding gains (and subsequent losses) on items of property and equipment for which the "revaluation option" is elected (IFRS only),
- effects on owners' equity resulting from the translation of the foreign currency-denominated financial statements of a foreign operation to the reporting currency of the consolidated entity,
- certain changes to net pension liability or asset, and
- gains and losses on derivative financial instruments (and certain foreign currency-denominated non-derivative financial instruments) accounted for as a hedge of future cash flows.

When an analyst decides that a significant item presented in OCI should be included in net income, the analyst can adjust reported and forecasted amounts accordingly.

3. EVALUATING THE QUALITY OF FINANCIAL REPORTS

Prior to beginning any financial analysis, an analyst should clarify the purpose and context and clearly understand the following:

- What is the purpose of the analysis? What questions will this analysis answer?
- What level of detail will be needed to accomplish this purpose?

- What data are available for the analysis?
- What are the factors or relationships that will influence the analysis?
- What are the analytical limitations, and will these limitations potentially impair the analysis?

In the context of evaluating the quality of financial reports, an analyst is attempting to answer two basic questions:

1. Are the financial reports GAAP-compliant and decision-useful?
2. Are the results (earnings) of high quality? Do they provide an adequate level of return, and are they sustainable?

General steps, which fit within the general framework just mentioned, are discussed first. Following these steps may help an analyst evaluate the quality of financial reports (answering the two basic questions). Then, quantitative tools for evaluating the quality of financial reports are discussed.

3.1. General Steps to Evaluate the Quality of Financial Reports

It is important to note that the steps presented here are meant to serve as a general guideline only. An analyst may choose to add steps, emphasize or deemphasize steps, or alter the order of the steps. Companies are unique, and variation in specific analytical projects will require specific approaches.

1. Develop an understanding of the company and its industry. Understanding the economic activities of a company provides a basis for understanding why particular accounting principles may be appropriate and why particular financial metrics matter. Understanding the accounting principles used by a company *and* its competitors provides a basis for understanding what constitutes the norm—and to assess whether a company's treatment is appropriate.
2. Learn about management. Evaluate whether the company's management has any particular incentives to misreport. Review disclosures about compensation and insider transactions, especially insiders' sales of the company's stock. Review the disclosures concerning related-party transactions.
3. Identify significant accounting areas, especially those in which management judgment or an unusual accounting rule is a significant determinant of reported financial performance.
4. Make comparisons:
   A. Compare the company's financial statements and significant disclosures in the current year's report with the financial statements and significant disclosures in the prior year's report. Are there major differences in line items or in key disclosures, such as risk disclosures, segment disclosures, classification of specific expense, or revenue items? Are the reasons for the changes apparent?
   B. Compare the company's accounting policies with those of its closest competitors. Are there significant differences? If so, what is the directional effect of the differences?
   C. Using ratio analysis, compare the company's performance with that of its closest competitors.
5. Check for warnings signs of possible issues with the quality of the financial reports. For example,
   - declining receivables turnover could suggest that some revenues are fictitious or recorded prematurely or that the allowance for doubtful accounts is insufficient;

- declining inventory turnover could suggest obsolescence problems that should be recognized; and
- net income greater than cash provided by operations could suggest that aggressive accrual accounting policies have shifted current expenses to later periods.

6. For firms operating in multiple segments by geography or product—particularly multinational firms—consider whether inventory, sales, and expenses have been shifted to make it appear that a company is positively exposed to a geographic region or product segment that the investment community considers to be a desirable growth area. An analyst may suspect that this shift is occurring if the segment is showing strong performance while the consolidated results remain static or worsen.

7. Use appropriate quantitative tools to assess the likelihood of misreporting.

The first six steps listed describe a qualitative approach to evaluating the quality of financial reports. In addition to the qualitative approach, quantitative tools have been developed to help in evaluating financial reports.

3.2. Quantitative Tools to Assess the Likelihood of Misreporting

This section describes some tools for assessing the likelihood of misreporting (Step 7 above). If the likelihood of misreporting appears high, an analyst should take special care in analyzing, including qualitatively analyzing, the financial reports of the company.

3.2.1. Beneish Model

Messod D. Beneish and colleagues conducted studies to identify quantitative indicators of earnings manipulation and to develop a model to assess the likelihood of misreporting (Beneish 1999; Beneish, Lee, and Nichols 2013). The following is the Beneish model and its variables. After the description of each variable, an intuitive explanation of why it is included is given.

The probability of manipulation (M-score) is estimated using a probit model:[8]

$$M\text{-score} = -4.84 + 0.920 \text{ (DSR)} + 0.528 \text{ (GMI)} + 0.404 \text{ (AQI)} + 0.892 \text{ (SGI)} + 0.115 \text{ (DEPI)} - 0.172 \text{ (SGAI)} + 4.679 \text{ (Accruals)} - 0.327 \text{ (LEVI)}$$

where

M-score = Score indicating probability of earnings manipulation

DSR (days sales receivable index) = (Receivables$_t$/Sales$_t$)/(Receivables$_{t-1}$/Sales$_{t-1}$).

Changes in the relationship between receivables and sales could indicate inappropriate revenue recognition.

GMI (gross margin index) = Gross margin$_{t-1}$/Gross margin$_t$.

Deterioration in margins could predispose companies to manipulate earnings.

---

[8]Variables that are statistically significant in the empirical results of Beneish (1999) include the days sales receivable index, gross margin index, asset quality index, sales growth index, and accruals.

AQI (asset quality index) = $[1 - (PPE_t + CA_t)/TA_t]/[1 - (PPE_{t-1} + CA_{t-1})/TA_{t-1}]$, where PPE is property, plant, and equipment; CA is current assets; and TA is total assets.

> *Change in the percentage of assets other than in PPE and CA could indicate excessive expenditure capitalization.*

SGI (sales growth index) = $Sales_t/Sales_{t-1}$.

> *Managing the perception of continuing growth and capital needs from actual growth could predispose companies to manipulate sales and earnings.*

DEPI (depreciation index) = $Depreciation\ rate_{t-1}/Depreciation\ rate_t$, where Depreciation rate = Depreciation/(Depreciation + PPE).

> *Declining depreciation rates could indicate understated depreciation as a means of manipulating earnings.*

SGAI (sales, general, and administrative expenses index) = $(SGA_t /Sales_t)/(SGA_{t-1}/Sales_{t-1})$.

> *An increase in fixed SGA expenses suggests decreasing administrative and marketing efficiency, which could predispose companies to manipulate earnings.*

Accruals = (Income before extraordinary items[9] − Cash from operations)/Total assets.

> *Higher accruals can indicate earnings manipulation.*

LEVI (leverage index) = $Leverage_t/Leverage_{t-1}$, where Leverage is calculated as the ratio of debt to assets.

> *Increasing leverage could predispose companies to manipulate earnings.*

The *M*-score in the Beneish model is a normally distributed random variable with a mean of 0 and a standard deviation of 1.0. Consequently, the probability of earnings manipulation indicated by the model can be calculated by using the cumulative probabilities for a standard normal distribution or the NORMSDIST function in Excel. For example, *M*-scores of −1.49 and −1.78 indicate that the probability of earnings manipulation is 6.8% and 3.8%, respectively. Higher *M*-scores (i.e., less negative numbers) indicate an increased probability of earnings manipulation. The probability is given by the amount in the left side of the distribution.

The use of the *M*-score to classify companies as potential manipulators depends on the relative cost of Type I errors (incorrectly classifying a manipulator company as a non-manipulator) and Type II errors (incorrectly classifying a non-manipulator as a manipulator). The cutoff value for classification minimizes the cost of misclassification. Beneish considered that the likely relevant cutoff for investors is a probability of earnings manipulation of 3.8% (an *M*-score exceeding −1.78).[10] Example 5 shows an application of the Beneish model.

---

[9] US GAAP for fiscal periods beginning after December 15, 2015, will no longer include the concept of extraordinary items.

[10] See Beneish (1999) for an explanation and derivation of the cutoff values. Beneish et al. (2013) use an *M*-score exceeding −1.78 as the cutoff value.

EXAMPLE 5   Application of the Beneish Model

Exhibit 5 presents the variables and Beneish's *M*-Score for XYZ Corporation (a hypothetical company).

EXHIBIT 5   XYZ Corporation *M*-Score

	Value of Variable	Coefficient from Beneish Model	Calculations
DSR	1.300	0.920	1.196
GMI	1.100	0.528	0.581
AQI	0.800	0.404	0.323
SGI	1.100	0.892	0.981
DEPI	1.100	0.115	0.127
SGAI	0.600	−0.172	−0.103
Accruals	0.150	4.679	0.702
LEVI	0.600	−0.327	−0.196
Intercept			−4.840
M-score			−1.231
Probability of manipulation			10.93%

1. Would the results of the Beneish model lead an analyst, using a −1.78 *M*-score as the cutoff, to flag XYZ as a likely manipulator?
2. The values of DSR, GMI, SGI, and DEPI are all greater than one. In the Beneish model, what does this indicate for each variable?

Solution to 1: Yes, the model could be expected to lead an analyst to flag XYZ as a likely manipulator. The *M*-score is higher than the cutoff of −1.78, indicating a higher-than-acceptable probability of manipulation. For XYZ Corporation, the model estimates the probability of manipulation as 10.93%. Although the classification of companies as manipulators depends on the relative cost of Type I errors and Type II errors, the value of 10.93% greatly exceeds the cutoff of 3.8% that Beneish identified as the relevant cutoff.

Solution to 2: Indications are as follows:

A. The value greater than one for DSR indicates that receivables as a percentage of sales have increased; this change may be an indicator of inappropriate revenue recognition. XYZ may have shipped goods prematurely and recognized revenues belonging in later periods. Alternatively, it may be caused by customers with deteriorating credit-paying ability—still a problem for the analyst of XYZ.

B. The value greater than one for GMI indicates that gross margins were higher last year; deteriorating margins could predispose companies to manipulate earnings.

C. The value greater than one for SGI indicates positive sales growth relative to the previous year. Companies could be predisposed to manipulate earnings to manage perceptions of continuing growth and also to obtain capital needed to support growth.

D. The value greater than one for DEPI indicates that the depreciation rate was higher in the prior year; a declining depreciation rate can indicate manipulated earnings.

3.2.2. Other Quantitative Models

Researchers have examined numerous factors that contribute to assessing the probability that a company is engaged in accounting manipulation. Variables that have been found useful for detecting misstatement include accruals quality; deferred taxes; auditor change; market-to-book value; whether the company is publicly listed and traded; growth rate differences between financial and non-financial variables, such as number of patents, employees, and products; and aspects of corporate governance and incentive compensation.[11]

3.2.3. Limitations of Quantitative Models

Accounting is a partial representation of economic reality. Consequently, financial models based on accounting numbers are only capable of establishing associations between variables. The underlying cause and effect can only be determined by a deeper analysis of actions themselves—perhaps through interviews, surveys, or investigations by financial regulators with enforcement powers.

An additional concern is that earnings manipulators are just as aware as analysts of the power of quantitative models to screen for possible cases of earnings manipulation. It is not surprising to learn, therefore, that Beneish et al.'s 2013 study found that the predictive power of the Beneish model is declining over time. Undoubtedly, many managers have learned to test the detectability of earnings manipulation tactics by using the model to anticipate analysts' perceptions. Thus, as useful as the Beneish model may be, the search for more powerful analytical tools continues. It is necessary for analysts to use qualitative, not just quantitative, means to assess quality.

4. EARNINGS QUALITY

This section first discusses indicators of earnings quality and then describes how to evaluate the earnings quality of a company. Analytical tools related to identifying very poor earnings/results quality, such as quantitative approaches to assessing the probability of bankruptcy, are also discussed.

4.1. Indicators of Earnings Quality

In general, the term "earnings quality" can be used to encompass earnings, cash flow, and balance sheet quality. This section, however, focuses specifically on earnings quality. High

---

[11] A summary of research on predicting accounting misstatement is provided in Dechow, Ge, Larson, and Sloan (2011).

earnings quality is often considered to be evidenced by earnings that are sustainable and rep-resent returns equal to or in excess of the company's cost of capital.[12] High-quality earnings increase the value of the company more than low-quality earnings, and the term "high-quality earnings" assumes that reporting quality is high. In contrast, low-quality earnings are insuf-ficient to cover the company's cost of capital and/or are derived from non-recurring, one-off activities. In addition, the term "low-quality earnings" can also be used when the reported information does not provide a useful indication of the company's performance.

A variety of alternatives have been used as indicators of earnings quality: recurring earnings, earnings persistence and related measures of accruals, beating benchmarks, and after-the-fact confirmations of poor-quality earnings, such as enforcement actions and restatements.

4.1.1. Recurring Earnings

When using a company's current and prior earnings as an input to forecast future earnings (for example, for use in an earnings-based valuation), an analyst focuses on the earnings that are ex-pected to recur in the future. For example, earnings from subsidiaries that have been selected for disposal, which must be separately identified as "discontinued operations," are typically exclud-ed from forecasting models. A wide range of other types of items may be non-recurring—for example, one-off asset sales, one-off litigation settlements, or one-off tax settlements. Reported earnings that contain a high proportion of non-recurring items are less likely to be sustainable and are thus considered lower quality.

Enron, an energy distribution company and a company famous for misreporting, pre-sented non-recurring items, among other reporting issues, in such a way that they created an illusion of a solidly performing company. Example 6 shows aspects of Enron's reporting.

EXAMPLE 6   Non-Recurring Items

Enron Corp.

EXHIBIT 6   Excerpts from Enron and Subsidiaries Consolidated Income Statement, Year-Ended December 31

(In millions, except per share amounts)	2000	1999	1998
Total revenues	$100,789	$40,112	$31,260
Total costs and expenses	98,836	39,310	29,882
Operating income	$1,953	$802	$1,378
Other income and deductions			
Equity in earnings of unconsolidated equity affiliates	$87	$309	$97
Gains on sales of non-merchant assets	146	541	56
Gain on the issuance of stock by TNPC, Inc.	121	0	0
Interest income	212	162	88
Other income, net	–37	181	–37
Income before interest, minority interests, and income taxes	$2,482	$1,995	$1,582

---

[12] The residual income model of valuation is most closely linked to this concept of high earnings quality.

1. How does the trend in Enron's operating income compare with the trend in its income after other income and deductions (i.e., Income before interest, minority interests, and income taxes)?
2. What items appear to be non-recurring as opposed to being a result of routine operations? How significant are these items?
3. The Enron testimony of short seller James Chanos before US Congress referred to "a number of one-time gains that boosted Enron's earnings" as one of the items that "strengthened our conviction that the market was mispricing Enron's stock" (Chanos 2002). What does Chanos's statement indicate about how Enron's earnings information was being used in valuation?

Solution to 1: Enron's operating income varied dramatically from year to year, declining from 1998 to 1999 and then more than doubling in 2000. In contrast, Enron's income before interest, minority interests, and income taxes shows a smooth, upward trend with significant increases each year. The increases were 24% and 26% for 2000 and 1999 relative to 1999 and 1998, respectively.

Solution to 2: Items that appear to be non-recurring are gains on sales of non-merchant assets and the gain on the issuance of stock by TNPC. Although gains from sales of non-merchant assets do recur in each year, this type of activity is not a part of Enron's energy distribution operations. In addition, two other non-operating items—the amount of equity in earnings from unconsolidated subsidiaries and the amount of other income—are highly variable. Two aspects of these items are significant. First, the smooth, upward trend in Enron's income is the direct result of these items. Second, these items collectively represent a significant percentage of the company's income before interest, minority interests, and income taxes, particularly in 1999 when these items represent 52% of the total: ($309 + $541+ $181)/ $1,995 = $1,031/$1,995.

Solution to 3: Chanos's statement suggests that at least some market participants were mistakenly using Enron's reported income as an input to earnings-based valuation, without adjusting for non-recurring items.

Although evaluating non-recurring items for inclusion in operating metrics is important for making appropriate historical comparisons and for developing appropriate inputs in valuation, another aspect of non-recurring items merits mention. Because classification of items as non-recurring is a subjective decision, classification decisions can provide an opportunity to inflate the amount potentially identified by a user of the income statement as repeatable earnings—those earnings expected from the company's business operations, which investors label as "recurring" or "core" earnings. In the absence of special or one-time items (such as restructuring charges, employee separation costs, goodwill impairment charges, or gains on disposals of assets), operating income is representative of these kinds of earnings. So-called classification shifting, which does not affect total net income, can inflate the amount reported as recurring or core earnings. This could be accomplished by re-classifying normal expenses to special items or by shifting operating expenses to income-decreasing discontinued operations. Anecdotal evidence of classification shifting exists (see Exhibit 7), but the evidence only emerges after the fact.[13] From an analyst's perspective, after-the-fact evidence of earnings management is not particularly useful for anticipating issues with earnings quality. Although it may not be possible to identify whether a company might be engaging in classification shifting, an analyst should nonetheless give special attention to income-decreasing special items, particularly if the company is reporting unusually high operating earnings for the period or if the classification of the item enabled the company to meet or beat forecasts for operating earnings.

EXHIBIT 7   Anecdotal Evidence of Classification Shifting

- Borden, a food and chemicals company: The SEC determined that the company had classified $146 million of operating expenses as part of a special item (restructuring charges) when the expenses should have been included in selling, general, and administrative expenses (Hwang 1994).
- AmeriServe Food Distribution Inc., which declared bankruptcy only four months after completing a $200 million junk bond issuance: A bankruptcy court–appointed examiner found that the company's financial statements "classified substantial operating expenses… as restructuring charges," which "masked the company's serious financial underperformance and delayed recognition by all parties of the severity of the problems faced by the company (Sherer 2000)."
- Waste Management, which, in 1998, issued the then-largest restatement in SEC history: The enforcement documentation indicates that the company had improperly inflated operating income by netting non-operating gains from the sale of investments and discontinued operations against unrelated operating expenses (SEC 2001b).
- IBM: Revised disclosures, prompted by SEC scrutiny and analysts' requests, showed that the company had classified intellectual property income as an offset to selling, general, and administrative expenses. This classification resulted in an understatement of operating expenses and thus an overstatement of core earnings by $1.5 billion and $1.7 billion in 2001 and 2000, respectively (Bulkeley 2002).

Companies understand that investors differentiate between recurring and non-recurring items. Therefore, in addition to presenting components of income on the face of the income statement, many companies voluntarily disclose additional information to facilitate the differentiation between recurring and non-recurring items. Specifically, companies may disclose both total income and so-called *pro forma* income (or adjusted income, also referred to as non-GAAP measures, or non-IFRS measures if IFRS is applicable) that has been adjusted to exclude non-recurring items. Disclosures of *pro forma* income must be accompanied by a reconciliation between *pro forma* income and reported income. It is important to be aware, however, that determination of whether an item is non-recurring involves judgment, and some companies'

---

[13] Archival evidence of classification shifting is presented in McVay (2006). McVay first models "expected core earnings" and then documents a relationship between reported-minus-expected core earnings and the number of special items. But in any given year, a company's management could attribute the unexpectedly high core earnings to economic improvements related to the special items; therefore, only the *ex post* evidence that unexpectedly high core earnings tend to reverse in the following year is suggestive of earnings management through classification shifting.

managers may be motivated to consider an item non-recurring if it improves a performance metric relevant to investors. For example, Groupon, an online discount provider, included in its original initial public offering (IPO) filing a *pro forma* (i.e., non-GAAP) measure of operating income that excluded online marketing costs. The SEC determined that the measure was misleading and subsequently required the company to eliminate that measure as reported. Overall, although voluntarily disclosed adjustments to reported income can be informative, an analyst should review the information to ensure that excluded items are truly non-recurring.[14]

4.1.2. Earnings Persistence and Related Measures of Accruals

One property of high earnings quality is earnings persistence—that is, sustainability of earnings excluding items that are obviously non-recurring and persistence of growth in those earnings. The assumption is that, for equity valuation models involving earnings forecasts, more persistent earnings are more useful inputs. Persistence can be expressed as the coefficient on current earnings in a simple model:[15]

$$\text{Earnings}_{t+1} = \alpha + \beta_1 \text{Earnings}_t + \varepsilon$$

A higher coefficient (β_1) represents more persistent earnings.

Earnings can be viewed as being composed of a cash component and an accruals component. The accrual component arises from accounting rules that reflect revenue in the period earned and expenses in the period incurred—not at the time of cash movement. For example, a sale of goods on account results in accounting income in the period the sale is made. If the cash collection occurs in a subsequent period, the difference between reported net income and cash collected constitutes an accrual. When earnings are decomposed into a cash component and an accruals component, research has shown that the cash component is more persistent (Sloan 1996). In the following model, the coefficient on cash flow (β_1) has been shown to be higher than the coefficient on accruals (β_2), indicating that the cash flow component of earnings is more persistent:

$$\text{Earnings}_{t+1} = \alpha + \beta_1 \text{Cash flow}_t + \beta_2 \text{Accruals}_t + \varepsilon$$

Because of the greater persistence of the cash component, indicators of earnings quality evolved to measure the relative size of the accruals component of earnings. Earnings with a larger component of accruals would be less persistent and thus of lower quality.

An important distinction is between accruals that arise from normal transactions in the period (called "non-discretionary") and accruals that result from transactions or accounting choices outside the normal, which are possibly made with the intent to distort reported earnings (called "discretionary accruals"). Outlier discretionary accruals are an indicator of possibly manipulated—and thus low-quality—earnings. One common approach to identifying abnormal accruals is first to model companies' normal accruals and then to determine outliers. A company's normal accruals are modeled as a function of economic factors, such as growth in credit sales and the amount of depreciable assets. Growth in credit sales would be expected to result in accounts receivable growth, and depreciable assets would be associated with the

---

[14] A survey of non-GAAP earnings in the S&P 500 is presented in Ciesielski and Henry (2017). In the article, the authors provide key prescriptions in evaluating non-GAAP earnings disclosure.

[15] Descriptions of certain indicators in this section follow Dechow, Ge, and Schrand (2010).

amount of depreciation. To apply this approach, total accruals are regressed on the factors expected to give rise to normal accruals, and the residual of the regression would be considered a proxy for abnormal accruals.

This approach was pioneered by academics and subsequently adopted in practice.[16] The SEC describes its approach to modeling abnormal accruals:

> Our Accounting Quality Model extends the traditional approach [often based on the popular Jones Model or the Modified Jones Model] by allowing discretionary accrual factors to be a part of the estimation. Specifically, we take filings information across all registrants and estimate total accruals as a function of a large set of factors that are proxies for discretionary and non-discretionary components…. Discretionary accruals are calculated from the model estimates and then used to screen firms that appear to be managing earnings most aggressively. (Lewis 2012)

One simplified approach to screening for abnormal accruals is to compare the magnitude of total accruals across companies. To make a relevant comparison, the accruals would be scaled—for example, by average assets or by average net operating income. Under this approach, high amounts of accruals are an indicator of possibly manipulated and thus low-quality earnings.

A more dramatic signal of questionable earnings quality is when a company reports positive net income but negative operating cash flows. This situation is illustrated in Example 7.

EXAMPLE 7 Discrepancy between Net Income and Operating Cash Flows

Allou Health & Beauty Care, Inc.
Allou Health & Beauty Care, Inc. was a manufacturer and distributor of hair and skin care products. Exhibit 8 presents excerpts from the company's financial statements from 2000 to 2002. Following the periods reported in these statements, Allou's warehouses were destroyed by fire, for which the management was found to be responsible. Allou was subsequently shown to have fraudulently inflated the amount of its sales and inventories in those years.

EXHIBIT 8   Illustration of Fraudulent Reporting in which Reported Net Income Significantly Exceeded Reported Operating Cash Flow, Annual Data 10-K for Allou Health & Beauty Care, Inc., and Subsidiaries

Years ended March 31	2002	2001	2000
Excerpt from Income Statement			
Revenues, net	$564,151,260	$548,146,953	$421,046,773
Costs of revenue	500,890,588	482,590,356	367,963,675
Gross profit	$63,260,672	$65,556,597	$53,083,098

---

[16] See Jones (1991) and Dechow, Sloan, and Sweeney (1995). These seminal academic papers produced the Jones Model and the Modified Jones Model.

EXHIBIT 8   (Continued)

Years ended March 31	2002	2001	2000
	⋮	⋮	⋮
Income from operations	27,276,779	28,490,063	22,256,558
	⋮	⋮	⋮
Income from continuing operations*	$6,589,658	$2,458,367	$7,043,548

Excerpt from Statement of Cash Flows			
Cash flows from operating activities:			
Net income from continuing operations	$6,589,658	$2,458,367	$7,043,548
Adjustments to reconcile net income to net cash used in operating activities:			
[Portions omitted]	⋮	⋮	⋮
Decrease (increase) in operating assets:			
Accounts receivable	(24,076,150)	(9,725,776)	(25,691,508)
Inventories	(9,074,118)	(12,644,519)	(40,834,355)
Net cash used in operating activities	$(17,397,230)	$(34,195,838)	$(27,137,652)

* The difference between income from operations and income from continuing operations included deductions for interest expense and provisions for income taxes in each year and for a $5,642,678 loss on impairment of investments in 2001.

Referring to Exhibit 8, answer the following questions:

1. Based on the income statement data, evaluate Allou's performance over the period shown.
2. Compare Allou's income from continuing operations and cash flows from operating activities.
3. Interpret the amounts shown as adjustments to reconcile income from continuing operations to net cash used in operating activities.

Solution to 1: Based on the income statement, the following aspects of Allou's performance are notable. Revenues grew in each of the past three years, albeit more slowly in the latest year shown. The company's gross margin declined somewhat over the past three years but has been fairly stable. Similarly, the company's operating margin declined somewhat over the past three years but has been fairly stable at around 5%. The company's income from continuing operations was sharply lower in 2001 as a result of an impairment loss. The company showed positive net income in each year. Overall, the company showed positive net income in each year, and its performance appears to be reasonably stable based on the income statement data.

    Note: Gross margin is gross profit divided by revenues. For example, for 2002, $63,260,672 divided by $564,151,260 is 11.2%. The ratios for 2001 and 2000 are 12.0% and 12.6%, respectively.

    Operating margin is income from operations divided by revenues. For example, for 2002, $27,276,779 divided by $564,151,260 is 4.8%. The ratios for 2001 and 2000 are 5.2% and 5.3%, respectively.

Solution to 2: Allou reported positive income from continuing operations but negative cash from operating activities in each of the three years shown. Persistent negative cash from operating activities is not sustainable for a going concern.

Solution to 3: The excerpt from Allou's Statement of Cash Flows shows that accounts receivable and inventories increased each year. This increase can account for most of the difference between the company's income from continuing operations and net cash used in operating activities. The company seems to be accumulating inventory and not collecting on its receivables.

   Note: The statement of cash flows, prepared using the indirect method, adjusts net income to derive cash from operating activities. An increase in current assets is subtracted from the net income number to derive the cash from operating activities.

Similar to Allou, the quarterly data for Enron shown in Exhibit 9 shows positive net income but negative cash from operating activities in quarters that were subsequently shown to have been misreported.

EXHIBIT 9   Quarterly Data 10-Q: Enron and Subsidiaries

Three months ended March 31 ($ millions)	2001	2000
Net income	425	338
Net cash used in operating activities	(464)	(457)

Annual Data 10-K: Enron and Subsidiaries

Year ended December 31 ($ millions)	2000	1999	1998
Net income	979	893	703
Net cash provided by operating activities	4,779	1,228	1,640

An analyst might also question why net cash provided by operating activities was more than double that of net income in 1998, almost 50% greater than net income in 1999, and almost five times net income in 2000.

Although sizable accruals (roughly, net income minus operating cash flow) can indicate possibly manipulated and thus low-quality earnings, it is not necessarily the case that fraudulently reporting companies will have such a profile. For example, as shown in Exhibit 9, Enron's annual operating cash flows exceeded net income in all three years during which fraudulent financial reporting was subsequently revealed. Some of the fraudulent transactions undertaken by Enron were specifically aimed at generating operating cash flow. It is advisable for investors to explore and understand why the differences exist. The company's ability to generate cash from operations ultimately affects investment and financing within the company.

Similarly, as shown in Exhibit 10, WorldCom showed cash from operating activities in excess of net income in each of the three years shown, although the company was subsequently found to have issued fraudulent reports. WorldCom's most significant fraudulent reporting was improperly capitalizing (instead of expensing) certain costs. Because capital expenditures are shown as investing cash outflows rather than operating cash outflows, the company's fraudulent reporting had the impact of inflating operating cash flows.

EXHIBIT 10   Example of Fraudulent Reporting in which Reported Net Income Did Not
Significantly Exceed Reported Operating Cash Flow, WorldCom Inc. and Subsidiaries ($ millions)

For the years ended December 31	1999	2000	2001
Net income (loss)	$4,013	$4,153	$1,501
Net cash provided by operating activities	11,005	7,666	7,994

In summary, although accrual measures (i.e., differences between net income and operating cash flows) can serve as indicators of earnings quality, they cannot be used in isolation
or applied mechanically. WorldCom shows how comparing cash-basis measures, such as cash
provided by operating activities, with net income may provide a false sense of confidence
about net income. Net income is calculated using subjective estimates, such as expected life of
long-term assets, that can be easily manipulated. In each year shown in Exhibit 10, the cash
provided by operations exceeded net income (earnings), suggesting that the earnings were of
high quality; an analyst looking at this without considering the investing activities would have
felt a false sense of security in the reported net income.

4.1.3. Mean Reversion in Earnings

A key analyst responsibility is to forecast earnings for the purpose of valuation in making
investment decisions. The accuracy and credibility of earnings forecasts should increase when
a company's earnings stream possesses a high degree of persistence. As already discussed, earnings can be viewed as being composed of a cash flow element plus an accruals element. Sustainable, persistent earnings are driven by the cash flow element of earnings, whereas the accruals
element adds information about the company's performance. At the same time, the accruals
component can detract from the stability and persistence of earnings because of the estimation
process involved in calculating them.

Academic research has shown empirically what we already know intuitively: Nothing lasts
forever. Extreme levels of earnings, both high and low, tend to revert to normal levels over
time. This phenomenon is known as "mean reversion in earnings" and is a natural attribute
of competitive markets. A company experiencing poor earnings performance will shut down
or minimize its losing operations and replace inferior managers with ones capable of execut-
ing an improved strategy, resulting in improved earnings. At the other extreme, a company
experiencing abnormally high profits will attract competition unless the barriers to entry are
insurmountable. New competitors may reduce their prices to gain a foothold in an existing
company's markets, thereby reducing the existing company's profits over time. Whether a company is experiencing abnormally high or low earnings, the net effect over time is that a return
to the mean should be anticipated.

Nissim and Penman (2001) demonstrated that the mean reversion principle exists across
a wide variety of accounting-based measures. In a time-series study encompassing companies
listed on the New York Stock Exchange and the American Stock Exchange between 1963 and
1999, they tracked such measures as residual income, residual operating income, return on
common equity, return on net operating assets, growth in common equity, core sales profit
margins, and others. Beginning with data from 1964, they sorted the companies into 10 equal
portfolios based on their ranking for a given measure and tracked the median values in each
portfolio in each of the next five-year periods. At the end of each fifth year, the portfolios were
re-sorted. The process was extended through 1994, yielding means of portfolio medians over
seven rankings. The findings were similar across the metrics, showing a clear reversion to the
mean over time.

For example, looking at the pattern for return on net operating assets (RNOA),[17] they found that the range of observed RNOAs was between 35% and –5% at the start of the observations but had compressed to a range of 22% to 7% by the end of the study. Their work illustrates the point that extremely strong or weak performance cannot be sustained forever. They also found that the RNOAs of the portfolios that were not outliers in either direction in Year 1—outperformance or underperformance—did not stray over time, staying constant or nearly so over the entire observation period.

The lesson for analysts is clear: One cannot simply extrapolate either very high or very low earnings into the future and expect to construct useful forecasts. In order to be useful, analysts' forecasts need to take into account normalized earnings over the relevant valuation time frame. As discussed, earnings are the sum of cash flows and accruals, and they will be more sustainable and persistent when the cash flow component dominates earnings. If earnings have a significant accruals component, it may hasten the earnings' reversion to the mean, even more so when the accrual elements are outliers relative to the normal amount of accruals in a company's earnings. In constructing their forecasts of future earnings, analysts need to develop a realistic cash flow model and realistic estimates of accruals as well.

4.1.4. Beating Benchmarks

Announcements of earnings that meet or exceed benchmarks, such as analysts' consensus forecasts, typically result in share price increases. However, meeting or beating benchmarks is not necessarily an indicator of high-quality earnings. In fact, exactly meeting or only narrowly beating benchmarks has been proposed as an indicator of earnings manipulation and thus low-quality earnings. Academic research has documented a statistically large clustering slightly above zero of actual benchmark differences, and this clustering has been interpreted by some as evidence of earnings management.[18] There is, however, disagreement about whether exactly meeting or only narrowly beating is an indicator of earnings manipulation.[19] Nonetheless, a company that consistently reports earnings that exactly meet or only narrowly beat benchmarks can raise questions about its earnings quality.

4.1.5. External Indicators of Poor-Quality Earnings

Two external indicators of poor-quality earnings are enforcement actions by regulatory authorities and restatements of previously issued financial statements. From an analyst's perspective, recognizing poor earnings quality is generally more valuable if it can be done before deficiencies become widely known and confirmed. Therefore, the external indicators of poor earnings quality are relatively less useful to an analyst. Nonetheless, even though it might be better to recognize poor earnings quality early, an analyst should be alert to external indicators and be prepared to re-evaluate decisions.

---

[17] Nissim and Penman define return on net operating assets as Operating income$_t$/Net operating assets$_{t-1}$. Net operating assets are operating assets (those assets used in operations) net of operating liabilities (those generated by operations).

[18] See Brown and Caylor (2005); Burgstahler and Dichev (1997); and Degeorge, Patel, and Zeckhauser (1999).

[19] See Dechow, Richardson, and Tuna (2003).

4.2. Evaluating the Earnings Quality of a Company (Cases)

The aim of analyzing earnings is to understand the persistence and sustainability of earnings. If earnings do not represent the financial realities faced by a company, then any forecast of earnings based on flawed reporting will also be flawed. Choices and estimates abound in financial reporting; and with those choices and estimates, the temptations for managers to improve their companies' performance by creative accounting are enormous. All too often, companies that appear to be extraordinary performers turn out to be quite ordinary or worse once their choice of accounting methods, including fraudulent choices, is uncovered by a regulator.

To avoid repeating the mistakes of the past, it may be helpful for analysts to learn how managers have used accounting techniques to enhance their companies' reported performance. Some cases provide useful lessons. In a study of 227 enforcement cases brought between 1997 and 2002, the SEC found that the most common accounting misrepresentation occurred in the area of revenue recognition (SEC 2003). Revenue is the largest single figure on the income statement and arguably the most important. Its sheer size and its effect on earnings, along with discretion in revenue recognition policies, have made it the most likely account to be intentionally misstated. For those reasons, investors should always thoroughly and skeptically analyze revenues. Too often, however, the chief concerns of analysts center on the quantitative aspects of revenues. They may ponder the growth of revenues and whether growth came from acquisitions or organically, but they rarely focus on the quality of revenues in the same way. A focus on the quality of revenues, including specifically on how they were generated, will serve analysts well. For example, were they generated by offering discounts or through bill-and-hold sales?

4.2.1. Revenue Recognition Case: Sunbeam Corporation

Premature/Fraudulent Revenue Recognition   Sunbeam Corporation was a consumer goods company focused on the production and sale of household appliances and outdoor products. In the mid- to late 1990s, it appeared that its new CEO, "Chainsaw Al" Dunlap, had engineered a turnaround at Sunbeam. He claimed to have done this through cutting costs and increasing revenues. The reality was different. Had more analysts performed basic but rigorous analysis of the financial statements in the earlier phases of Sunbeam's misreporting, they might have been more skeptical of the results produced by Chainsaw Al. Sunbeam engaged in numerous sales transactions that inflated revenues. Among them were the following:

- Sunbeam included one-time disposals of product lines in sales for the first quarter of 1997 without indicating that such non-recurring sales were included in revenues.
- At the end of the first quarter of 1997 (March), Sunbeam booked revenue and income from a sale of barbecue grills to a wholesaler. The wholesaler held the merchandise over the quarter's end without accepting ownership risks. The wholesaler could return the goods if it desired, and Sunbeam would pick up the cost of shipment both ways. All of the grills were returned to Sunbeam in the third quarter of 1997.
- Sunbeam induced customers to order more goods than they would normally through offers of discounts and other incentives. Often, the customers also had return rights on their purchases. This induced ordering had the effect of inflating current results by pulling future sales

into the present. This practice is sometimes referred to as "channel stuffing." This policy was not disclosed by Sunbeam, which routinely made use of channel-stuffing practices at the end of 1997 and the beginning of 1998.

- Sunbeam engaged in bill-and-hold revenue practices. In a bill-and-hold transaction, revenue is recognized when the invoice is issued while the goods remain on the premises of the seller. These are unusual transactions, and the accounting requirements for them are very strict: The buyer must request such treatment, have a genuine business purpose for the request, and must accept ownership risks. Other criteria for justifying the use of this revenue recognition practice include the seller's past experience with bill-and-hold transactions, in which buyers took possession of the goods and the transactions were not reversed.

There was no real business purpose to the channel stuffing and bill-and-hold transactions at Sunbeam other than for the seller to accelerate revenue and for the buyers to take advantage of such eagerness without any risks on their part. In the words of the SEC, "these transactions were little more than projected orders disguised as sales" (SEC 2001a). Sunbeam did not make such transactions clear to analysts, and many of its disclosures from the fourth quarter of 1996 to the middle of 1998 were inadequate. Still, its methods of inflating revenue left indicators in the financial statements that should have alerted analysts to the low quality of its earnings and revenue reporting.

If customers are induced into buying goods they do not yet need through favorable payment terms or given substantial leeway in returning such goods to the seller, days' sales outstanding (DSO) may increase and returns may also increase. Furthermore, increases in revenue may exceed past increases and the increases of the industry and/or peers. Problems with and changes in collection, expressed through accounts receivable metrics, can give an analyst clues about the aggressiveness of the seller in making sales targets. Exhibit 11 contains relevant annual data on Sunbeam's sales and receivables from 1995 (before the misreporting occurred) through 1997 (when earnings management reached its peak level in the fourth quarter).

EXHIBIT 11 Information on Sunbeam's Sales and Receivables, 1995–1997

($ millions)	1995	1996	1997
Total revenue	$1,016.9	$984.2	$1,168.2
Change from prior year	—	−3.2%	18.7%
Gross accounts receivable	$216.2	$213.4	$295.6
Change from prior year	—	−1.3%	38.5%
Receivables/revenue	21.3%	21.7%	25.3%
Change in receivables/revenue	0.7%	0.4%	3.6%
Days' sales outstanding	77.6	79.1	92.4
Accounts receivable turnover	4.7	4.6	4.0

Source: Based on information in original company 10-K filings.

What can an analyst learn from the information in Exhibit 11?

- Although revenues dipped 3.2% in 1996, the year the misreporting began, they increased significantly in 1997 as Sunbeam's various revenue "enhancement" programs were implemented. The important factor to notice—the one that should have given an analyst insight into the quality of the revenues—is the simultaneous, and much greater, increase in the accounts receivable balance. Receivables increasing faster than revenues suggests that a company may be pulling future sales into current periods by offering favorable discounts or generous return policies. As it turned out, Sunbeam offered all of these inducements.

- The percentage relationship of receivables to revenue is another way of looking at the relationship between sales and the time it takes a company to collect cash from its customers. An increasing percentage of receivables to revenues means that a lesser percentage of sales has been collected. The decrease in collection on sales may indicate that customers' abilities to repay have deteriorated. It may also indicate that the seller created period-end sales by shipping goods that were not wanted by customers; the shipment would produce documentation, which serves as evidence of a sale. Receivables and revenue would increase by the same absolute amount, which would increase the percentage of receivables to revenue. Customers would return the goods to the seller in the following accounting period. The same thing would happen in the event of totally fictitious revenues. Revenues from a non-existent customer would simultaneously increase receivables by the same amount. An increase in the relationship between revenue and receivables provides analysts with a clue that collections on sales have declined or that there is a possible issue with revenue recognition.

- The number of days sales outstanding [Accounts receivable/(Revenues/365)] increased each year, indicating that the receivables were not being paid on a timely basis—or even that the revenues may not have been genuine in the first place. DSO figures increasing over time indicate that there are problems, either with collection or revenue recognition. The accounts receivable turnover (365/DSO) tells the same story in a different way: It is the number of times the receivables converted into cash each year, and the figure decreased each year. A trend of slower cash collections, as exhibited by Sunbeam, shows increasingly inefficient cash collections at best and should alert an analyst to the possibility of questionable sales or revenue recognition practices.

- The accounts receivable showed poor quality. In 1997, it increased 38.5% over the previous year, while revenues gained 18.7%. The simple fact that receivables growth greatly outstripped the revenue growth suggests receivables collection problems. Furthermore, analysts who paid attention to the notes might have found even more tiles to fit into the mosaic of accounting manipulations. According to a note in the 10-K titled "Accounts Receivable Securitization Facility," in December 1997 Sunbeam had entered into an arrangement for the sale of accounts receivable. The note said that "At December 28, 1997, the Company had received approximately $59 million from the sale of trade accounts receivable." Those receivables were not included in the year-end accounts receivable balance. As the *pro forma* column in Exhibit 12 shows, the accounts receivable would have shown an increase of 66.1% instead of 38.5%; the percentage of receivables to sales would have ballooned to 30.4%, and the days' sales outstanding would have been an attention-getting 110.8 days. Had this receivables sale not occurred, and the receivables been that large, perhaps analysts would have noticed a problem sooner. Careful attention to the notes might have alerted them to how this transaction improved the appearance of the financial statements and ratios.

EXHIBIT 12   Information on Sunbeam's Sales and Receivables, 1995–1997, and *Pro Forma* Information, 1997

($ millions)	1995	1996	1997	1997 *Pro Forma*
Total revenue	$1,016.9	$984.2	$1,168.2	*$1,168.2*
Change from prior year	—	−3.2%	18.7%	*18.7%*
Gross accounts receivable	$216.2	$213.4	$295.6	*$354.6*
Change from prior year	—	−1.3%	38.5%	*66.1%*
Receivables/revenue	21.3%	21.7%	25.3%	*30.4%*
Change in receivables/revenue	0.7%	0.4%	3.6%	*8.7%*
Days' sales outstanding	77.7	79.2	92.3	*110.8*
Accounts receivable turnover	4.7	4.6	4.0	*3.2*

Source: Based on information in original company 10-K filings.

Analysts observing the trend in days' sales outstanding would have been rightly suspicious of Sunbeam's revenue recognition practices, even if they were observing the days' sales outstanding simply in terms of Sunbeam's own history. If they took the analysis slightly further, they would have been even more suspicious. Exhibit 13 compares Sunbeam's DSO and accounts receivable turnover with those of an industry median based on the numbers from a group of other consumer products companies—Harman International, Jarden, Leggett & Platt, Mohawk Industries, Newell Rubbermaid, and Tupperware Brands.

EXHIBIT 13   Comparison of Sunbeam and Industry Median, 1995–1997

Sunbeam	1995	1996	1997
Days sales outstanding	77.7	79.2	92.3
Accounts receivable turnover	4.7	4.6	4.0
Industry median			
Days sales outstanding	44.6	46.7	50.4
Accounts receivable turnover	8.2	7.8	7.3
Sunbeam's underperformance relative to median			
Days sales outstanding	33.0	32.5	41.9
Accounts receivable turnover	(3.5)	(3.2)	(3.3)

Source: Based on information in company 10-K filings.

There was yet another clue that should have aroused suspicion in the analyst community. In the December 1997 annual report, the revenue recognition note had been expanded from the previous year's note:

The Company recognizes revenues from product sales principally at the time of shipment to customers. *In limited circumstances, at the customer's request the Company* *may sell seasonal product on a bill and hold basis provided that the goods are completed, packaged and ready for shipment, such goods are segregated and the risks of ownership and legal title have passed to the customer. **The amount of such bill and hold sales at December 29, 1997 was approximately 3% of consolidated revenues.*** [Italics and emphasis added.]

Not only did Sunbeam hint at the fact that its revenue recognition policies included a method that was of questionable quality, a clue was dropped as to the degree to which it affected operations. That 3% figure may seem small, but the disclosure should have aroused suspicion in the mind of a thorough analyst. As shown in Exhibit 14, working through the numbers with some reasonable assumptions about the gross profit on the sales (28.3%) and the applicable tax rate (35%), an analyst would have seen that the bill-and-hold sales were significant to the bottom line.

EXHIBIT 14   Effect of Sunbeam's Bill-and-Hold Sales on Net Income ($ millions)

1997 revenue	$1,168.18
Bill-and-hold sales from note	3.0%
Bill-and-hold sales in 1997	$35.05
Gross profit margin	28.3%
Gross profit contribution	$9.92
After-tax earnings contribution	$6.45
Total earnings from continuing operations	$109.42
Earnings attributable to bill-and-hold sales	5.9%

An analyst questioning the genuineness of bill-and-hold sales and performing a simple test of the degree of exposure to their effects might have been disturbed to estimate that nearly 6% of net income depended on such transactions. This knowledge might have dissuaded an analyst from a favorable view of Sunbeam.

4.2.2. Revenue Recognition Case: MicroStrategy, Inc.

Multiple-Element Contracts   MicroStrategy, Inc. was a fast-growing software and information services company that went public in 1998. After going public, the company engaged in more complex revenue transactions than it had previously. Its revenue stream increasingly involved less outright sales of software and began tilting more to transactions containing multiple deliverables, including obligations to provide services.

Product revenue is usually recognized immediately, depending on the delivery terms and acceptance by customers, whereas service revenue is recognized as the services are provided. The relevant accounting standards for multiple-deliverable arrangements at the time permitted recognition of revenue on a software delivery only if the software sale could be separated from the service portion of the contract and only if the service revenues were in fact accounted for separately.

Analysts studying MicroStrategy's financial statements should have understood the effects of such accounting conventions on the company's revenues. MicroStrategy's revenue recognition policy in the accounting policies note of its 1998 10-K stated that the standards' requirements were, in fact, its practice:

> Revenue from product licensing arrangements is generally recognized after execution of a licensing agreement and shipment of the product, provided that no significant Company obligations remain and the resulting receivable is deemed collectible by management... Services revenue, which includes training and consulting, is recognized at the time the service is performed. The Company defers and recognizes maintenance revenue ratably over the terms of the contract period, ranging from 12 to 36 months. (p. 49)

MicroStrategy took advantage of the ambiguity present in such arrangements, however, to mischaracterize service revenues and recognize them earlier than they should have as part of the software sale. For example, in the fourth quarter of 1998, MicroStrategy entered into a $4.5 million transaction with a customer for software licenses and a broad array of consulting services. Most of the software licenses acquired by the customer were intended to be used in applications that MicroStrategy would develop in the future, yet the company recognized all of the $4.5 million as software revenue (SEC 2000).

Similarly, in the fourth quarter of 1999, MicroStrategy entered into a multiple-deliverable arrangement with another customer that included the provision for extensive services. Again, the company improperly allocated the elements of the contract, skewing them toward an earlier-recognized software element and improperly recognizing $14.1 million of product revenue in the quarter, which was material.

How could analysts have recognized this pattern of behavior? Without in-depth knowledge of the contracts, it is not possible to approve or disapprove of the revenue allocation with certainty. The company still left a trail that could have aroused the suspicion of analysts, had they been familiar with MicroStrategy's stated revenue recognition policy.

Exhibit 15 shows the mix of revenues for 1996, 1997, and 1998 based on the income statement in MicroStrategy's 1998 10-K:

EXHIBIT 15   MicroStrategy's Mix of Licenses and Support Revenues, 1996–1998 ($ millions)

	1996	1997	1998
Licenses	$15,873	$36,601	$72,721
Support	6,730	16,956	33,709
Total	$22,603	$53,557	$106,430
Licenses	70.2%	68.3%	68.3%
Support	29.8	31.7	31.7
Total	100.0%	100.0%	100.0%

Between 1996 and 1997, the proportion of support revenues to total revenues increased slightly. It flattened out in 1998, which was the first year known to have mischaracterization between the support revenues and the software revenues. With perfect hindsight, had the $4.5 million of consulting services not been recognized at all, overall revenues would have been $101.930 million and support revenues would have been 33.1% of the total revenues. What could have alerted analysts that something was amiss, if they could not examine actual contracts?

Looking at the quarterly mix of revenues might have aroused analyst suspicions. Exhibit 16 shows the peculiar ebb and flow of revenues attributable to support services revenues.

EXHIBIT 16   MicroStrategy's Revenue Mix by Quarters, 1Q1998–4Q1999

Quarter	Licenses	Support
1Q98	71.8%	28.2%
2Q98	68.3	31.7
3Q98	62.7	37.3
4Q98	70.7	29.3
1Q99	64.6	35.4
2Q99	68.1	31.9
3Q99	70.1	29.9
4Q99	73.2	26.8

The support services revenue climbed in the first three quarters of 1998 and dropped sharply in the fourth quarter—the one in which the company characterized the $4.5 million of revenues that should have been deferred as software license revenue. Subsequently, the proportion rose again and then continued a downward trend, most sharply in the fourth quarter of 1999 when the company again mischaracterized $14.1 million of revenue as software license revenue.

There is no logical reason that the proportion of revenues from licensing and support services should vary significantly from quarter to quarter. The changes should arouse suspicions and generate questions to ask management. Management's answers, and the soundness of the logic embedded in them, might have made investors more comfortable or more skeptical.

If an analyst knows that a company has a policy of recognizing revenues for contracts with elements of multiple-deliverable arrangements—something apparent from a study of the accounting policy note—then the analyst should consider the risk that misallocation of revenue can occur. Observing trends and investigating deviations from observed trends become important habits for an analyst to practice in order to isolate exceptions. Although a study of revenue trends may not pinpoint a manipulated revenue transaction, it should be sufficient to raise doubts about the propriety of the accounting for transactions.

Enhancing the recognition of revenue is a way for managers to increase earnings, yet it can leave indicators that can be detected by analysts vigilant enough to look for them. Exhibit 17 provides a summary of how to assess the quality of revenues.

EXHIBIT 17   Summary: Looking for Quality in Revenues

Start with the basics

The first step should be to fully understand the revenue recognition policies as stated in the most recent annual report. Without context for the way revenue is recognized, an analyst will not understand the risks involved in the proper reporting of revenue. For instance, analysts should determine the following:
- What are the shipping terms?
- What rights of return does a customer have: limited or extensive?
- Do rebates affect revenues, and if so, how are they accounted for? What estimates are involved?
- Are there multiple deliverables to customers for one arrangement? If so, is revenue deferred until some elements are delivered late in the contract? If there are multiple deliverables, do deferred revenues appear on the balance sheet?

(continued)

EXHIBIT 17   (Continued)

Age matters

A study of DSO can reveal much about their quality. Receivables do not improve with age. Analysts should seek reasons for exceptions appearing when they
- Compare the trend in DSOs or receivables turnover over a relevant time frame.
- Compare the DSO of one company with the DSOs of similar competitors over similar time frames.

Is it cash or accrual?

A high percentage of accounts receivable to revenues might mean nothing, but it might also mean that channel-stuffing has taken place, portending high future returns of inventory or decreased demand for product in the future. Analysts should
- Compare the percentage of accounts receivable to revenues over a relevant time frame.
- Compare the company's percentage of accounts receivable to revenues with that of competitors or industry measures over similar time frames.

Compare with the real world when possible

If a company reports non-financial data on a routine basis, try relating revenues to those data to determine whether trends in the revenue make sense. Examples include
- Airlines reporting extensive information about miles flown and capacity, enabling an analyst to relate increases in revenues to an increase in miles flown or capacity.
- Retailers reporting square footage used and number of stores open.
- Companies across all industries reporting employee head counts.

As always, analysts should compare any relevant revenue-per-unit measure with that of relevant competitors or industry measures.

Revenue trends and composition

Trend analysis, over time and in comparison with competitors, can prompt analysts to ask questions of managers, or it can simply evoke discomfort with the overall revenue quality. Some relationships to examine include
- The relationships between the kinds of revenue recognized. For example, how much is attributable to product sales or licenses, and how much is attributable to services? Have the relationships changed over time, and if so, why?
- The relationship between overall revenue and accounts receivable. Do changes in overall revenues make sense when compared with changes in accounts receivable?

Relationships

Does the company transact business with entities owned by senior officers or shareholders? This is a particularly sensitive area if the manager/shareholder-owned entities are private and there are revenues recognized from the private entity by a publicly owned company; it could be a dumping ground for obsolete or damaged inventory while inflating revenues.

Overstating revenues is not the only way to enhance earnings; according to the SEC study of enforcement cases brought between 1997 and 2002, the next most common financial misreporting was improper expense recognition (SEC 2003). Improper expense recognition typically involves understating expenses and has the same overstating effects on earnings as improper revenue recognition. Understating expenses also leaves indicators in the financial statements for the vigilant analyst to find and assess.

4.2.3. Cost Capitalization Case: WorldCom Corp.

Property/Capital Expenditures Analysis   WorldCom was a major global communications company, providing phone and internet services to both the business and consumer markets. It became a major player in the 1990s, largely through acquisitions. To keep delivering the earnings expected by analysts, the company engaged in the improper capitalization of operating expenses known as "line costs." These costs were fees paid by WorldCom to third-party telecommunications network providers for the right to use their networks, and the proper accounting treatment for them is to classify them as an operating expense. This improper treatment began in 1999 and continued through the first quarter of 2002. The company declared bankruptcy in July 2002; restatements of financial reports ensued.

The company was audited by Arthur Andersen, who had access to the company's records. According to the findings of the special committee that headed the investigation of the failure (Beresford, Katzenbach, and Rogers 2003), Arthur Andersen failed to identify the misclassification of line costs, among other things, because

> Andersen concluded—mistakenly in this case—that, year after year, the risk of fraud was minimal and thus it never devised sufficient auditing procedures to address this risk. Although it conducted a controls-based audit—relying on WorldCom's internal controls—it failed to recognize the nature and extent of senior management's top-side adjustments through reserve reversals with little or no support, highly questionable revenue items, and entries capitalizing line costs. Andersen did not conduct tests to corroborate the information it received in many areas. It assumed incorrectly that the absence of variances in the financial statements and schedules—in a highly volatile business environment—indicated there was no cause for heightened scrutiny. Andersen conducted only very limited auditing procedures in many areas where we found accounting irregularities. Even so, Andersen still had several chances to uncover problems we identify in this Report. (p. 230–231)

If auditors failed to detect fraud, could analysts really be expected to do better? Analysts may not have been able to pinpoint what was going on at WorldCom, all the way down to the under-reported line costs, but if they had focused on the company's balance sheet, they certainly could have been suspicious that all was not right. If they were looking for out-of-line relationships between accounts—something that the auditors would be expected to do—they might have uncovered questionable relationships that, if unsatisfactorily explained, should have led them to shun securities issued by WorldCom.

For an operating expense to be under-reported, an offsetting increase in the balance of another account must exist. A simple scan of an annual time-series common-size balance sheet, such as is shown in Exhibit 18, might identify the possibility that capitalization is being used to avoid expense recognition. An analyst might not have known that line costs were being under-reported, but simply looking at the time series in Exhibit 18 would have shown that something unusual was going on in gross property, plant, and equipment. The fraud began in 1999, and gross property, plant, and equipment had been 30% and 31% of total assets, respectively, in the two prior years. In 1999, property, plant, and equipment became a much more significant 37% of total assets and increased to 45% in 2000 and 47% in 2001. The company had not changed strategy or anything else to justify such an increase.

EXHIBIT 18   Common Size Asset Portion of Balance Sheet for WorldCom, 1997–2001

	1997	1998	1999	2000	2001
Cash and equivalents	0%	2%	1%	1%	1%
Net receivables	5	6	6	7	5
Inventories	0	0	0	0	0
Other current assets	2	4	4	2	2
Total current assets	7%	12%	11%	10%	8%
Gross property, plant, and equipment	*30%*	*31%*	*37%*	*45%*	*47%*
Accumulated depreciation	3%	2%	5%	7%	9%
Net property, plant, and equipment	27%	29%	32%	38%	38%
Equity investments	NA	NA	NA	NA	1
Other investments	0	0	0	2	1
Intangibles	61	54	52	47	49
Other assets	5	5	5	3	3
Total Assets	100%	100%	100%	100%	100%

Note: NA is not available.

Source: Based on information from Standard & Poor's Research Insight database.

A curious analyst in 1999 might not have *specifically* determined that line costs were being understated, but the buildup of costs in property, plant, and equipment should have at least made the analyst suspicious that expenses were under-reported somewhere in the income statement.

Capitalizing costs is not the only possible way of understating expenses. Exhibit 19 provides a summary of how to assess the quality of expense recognition, including some things to consider.

EXHIBIT 19   Summary: Looking for Quality in Expense Recognition

Start with the basics

The first step should be to fully understand the cost capitalization policies as stated in the most recent annual report. Without context for the costs stored on the balance sheet, analysts will not be able to comprehend practice exceptions they may encounter. Examples of policies that should be understood include the following:
- What costs are capitalized in inventory? How is obsolescence accounted for? Are there reserves established for obsolescence that might be artificially raised or lowered?
- What are the depreciation policies, including depreciable lives? How do they compare with competitors' policies? Have they changed from prior years?

EXHIBIT 19   (Continued)

Trend analysis

Trend analysis, over time and in comparison with competitors, can lead to questions the analyst can ask managers, or it can simply evoke discomfort with overall earnings quality because of issues with expenses. Some relationships to examine include the following:

- Each quarter, non-current asset accounts should be examined for quarter-to-quarter and year-to-year changes to see whether there are any unusual increases in costs. If present, they might indicate that improper capitalization of costs has occurred.
- Profit margins—gross and operating—are often observed by analysts in the examination of quarterly earnings. They are not often related to changes in the balance sheet, but they should be. If unusual buildups of non-current assets have occurred and the profit margins are improving or staying constant, it could mean that improper cost capitalization is taking place. Recall WorldCom and its improper capitalization of "line costs": Profitability was maintained by capitalizing costs that should have been expensed. Also, the overall industry environment should be considered: Are margins stable while balance sheet accounts are growing and the industry is slumping?
- Turnover ratio for total assets; property, plant, and equipment; and other assets should be computed (with revenues divided by the asset classification). Does a trend in the ratios indicate a slowing in turnover? Decreasing revenues might mean that the assets are used to make a product with declining demand and portend future asset write-downs. Steady or rising revenues and decreasing turnover might indicate improper cost capitalization.
- Compute the depreciation (or amortization) expense compared to the relevant asset base. Is it decreasing or increasing over time without a good reason? How does it compare with that of competitors?
- Compare the relationship of capital expenditures with gross property, plant, and equipment over time. Is the proportion of capital expenditures relative to total property, plant, and equipment increasing significantly over time? If so, it may indicate that the company is capitalizing costs more aggressively to prevent their recognition as current expenses.

Relationships

Does the company transact business with entities owned by senior officers or shareholders? This is a particularly sensitive area if the manager/shareholder-owned entities are private. Dealings between a public company and the manager-owned entity might take place at prices that are unfavorable for the public company in order to transfer wealth from the public company to the manager-owned entity. Such inappropriate transfers of wealth can also occur through excessive compensation, direct loans, or guarantees. These practices are often referred to as "tunneling" (Johnson, LaPorta, Shleifer, and Lopez-de-Silanes 2000).

In some cases, sham dealings between the manager-owned entity and the public company might be falsely reported to improve reported profits of the public company and thus enrich the managers whose compensation is performance based. In a different type of transaction, the manager-owned entity could transfer resources to the public company to ensure its economic viability and thus preserve the option to misappropriate or to participate in profits in the future. These practices are often referred to as "propping" (Friedman, Johnson, and Mitton 2003).

Assessing earnings quality should be an established practice for all analysts. Earnings quality should not automatically be accepted as "high quality" until accounting problems emerge and it is too late. Analysts should consider the quality of earnings before assigning value to the growth in earnings. In many cases, high reported earnings growth, which turned out to be fraudulent, preceded bankruptcy.

4.3. Bankruptcy Prediction Models

Bankruptcy prediction models address more than just the quality of a company's earnings and include aspects of cash flow and the balance sheet as well.[20] Various approaches have been used to quantify the likelihood that a company will default on its debt and/or declare bankruptcy.

4.3.1. Altman Model

A well-known and early model to assess the probability of bankruptcy is the Altman model (Altman 1968). The model is built on research that used ratio analysis to identify likely failures. An important contribution of the Altman model is that it provided a way to incorporate numerous financial ratios into a single model to predict bankruptcy. The model overcame a limitation of viewing ratios independently (e.g., viewing a company with poor profitability and/or solvency position as potentially bankrupt without considering the company's strong liquidity position).

Using discriminant analysis, Altman developed a model to discriminate between two groups: bankrupt and non-bankrupt companies. Altman's Z-score is calculated as follows:

$$Z\text{-score} = 1.2 \text{ (Net working capital/Total assets)} + 1.4 \text{ (Retained earnings/Total assets)}$$
$$+ 3.3 \text{ (EBIT/Total assets)} + 0.6 \text{ (Market value of equity/Book value of liabilities)}$$
$$+ 1.0 \text{ (Sales/Total assets)}$$

The ratios in the model reflect liquidity, profitability, leverage, and activity. The first ratio—net working capital/total assets—is a measure of short-term liquidity risk. The second ratio—retained earnings/total assets—reflects accumulated profitability and relative age because retained earnings accumulate over time. The third ratio—EBIT (earnings before interest and taxes)/total assets, which is a variant of return on assets (ROA)—measures profitability. The fourth ratio—market value of equity/book value of liabilities—is a form of leverage ratio; it is expressed as equity/debt, so a higher number indicates greater solvency. The fifth ratio—sales/total assets—indicates the company's ability to generate sales and is an activity ratio.

Note that Altman's discriminant function shown in his original article (1968) was

$$Z\text{-score} = 0.012X_1 + 0.014X_2 + 0.033X_3 + 0.006X_4 + 0.999X_5$$

with each of the X variables corresponding to the ratios just described. Altman (2000) explains that "due to the original computer format arrangement, variables X_1 through X_4 must be calculated as absolute percentage values. For instance, the company whose net working capital to total assets (X_1) is 10% should be included as 10.0% and not 0.10. Only variable X_5 (sales to total assets) should be expressed in a different manner: that is, a S/TA [sales/total assets] ratio of 200 percent should be included as 2.0" (p. 14). For this reason, the Z-score model is often expressed as shown in the first equation of this section.

---

[20] Recall that the term "earnings quality" is used broadly to encompass the quality of earnings, cash flow, and/or balance sheet items.

The interpretation of the score is that a higher *Z*-score is better. In Altman's application of the model to a sample of manufacturing companies that had experienced losses, scores of less than 1.81 indicated a high probability of bankruptcy, scores greater than 3.00 indicated a low probability of bankruptcy, and scores between 1.81 and 3.00 were not clear indicators.

4.3.2. Developments in Bankruptcy Prediction Models

Subsequent research addressed various shortcomings in the Altman prediction model. One shortcoming is the single-period, static nature of the Altman model; it uses only one set of financial measures, taken at a single point in time. Shumway (2001) addressed this shortcoming by using a hazard model, which incorporates all available years of data to calculate each company's bankruptcy risk at each point in time.

Another shortcoming of the Altman model (and other accounting-based bankruptcy prediction models) is that financial statements measure past performance and incorporate the going-concern assumption. The reported values on a company's balance sheet assume that the company is a going concern rather than one that might be failing. An alternative is to use market-based bankruptcy prediction models. For example, market-based prediction models building on Merton's concept of equity as a call option on the company's assets infer the default probability from the company's equity value, amount of debt, equity returns, and equity volatility (Kealhofer 2003). Credit default swap data and corporate bond data can also be used to derive default probabilities. Other research indicates that the most effective bankruptcy prediction models include both accounting-based data and market-based data as predictor variables. For example, Bharath and Shumway (2008) model default probability based on market value of equity, face value of debt, equity volatility, stock returns relative to market returns over the previous year, and the ratio of net income to total assets to identify companies likely to default.

5. CASH FLOW QUALITY

Cash flow statements are free of some of the discretion embedded in the financial statements based on accrual accounting. As a result, analysts may place a great deal of importance and reliance on the cash flow statement. However, there are opportunities for management to affect the cash flow statement.

5.1. Indicators of Cash Flow Quality

Operating cash flow (OCF) is the cash flow component that is generally most important for assessing a company's performance and valuing a company or its securities. Therefore, discussions of cash flow quality typically focus on OCF.

Similar to the term "earnings quality," when reported cash flows are described as being of high quality, it means that the company's underlying economic performance was good (i.e., value enhancing) and it also implies that the company had high reporting quality (i.e., that the information calculated and disclosed by the company was a reasonable reflection of economic reality). Cash flow can be described as "low quality" either because the reported information correctly represents bad economic performance (poor results quality) or because the reported information misrepresents economic reality (poor reporting quality).

From an economic perspective, the corporate life cycle and industry profile affect cash flow and must be considered when analyzing the statement of cash flows. For example, a start-up company might be expected to have negative operating and investing cash flows, which would be funded from borrowing or from equity issuance (i.e., financing cash flows). In contrast, an established company would typically have positive operating cash flow from which it would fund necessary investments and returns to providers of capital (i.e., dividends, share repurchases, or debt repayments—all of which are financing cash flows).

In general, for established companies, high-quality cash flow would typically have most or all of the following characteristics:

- Positive OCF
- OCF derived from sustainable sources
- OCF adequate to cover capital expenditures, dividends, and debt repayments
- OCF with relatively low volatility (relative to industry participants)

As always, high quality requires not only high results quality, as in the previous list, but also high reporting quality. The reported cash flows should be relevant and faithfully represent the economic reality of the company's activities. For example, classifying a financing inflow as an operating inflow would misrepresent the economic reality.

From the perspective of cash flow reporting quality, OCF is generally viewed as being less easily manipulated than operating or net income. Large differences between earnings and OCF or increases in such differences can be an indication of earnings manipulation. The statement of cash flows can be used to highlight areas of potential earnings manipulation.

Even though OCF is viewed as being less subject to manipulation than earnings, the importance of OCF may create incentives for managers to manipulate the amounts reported. Therefore, quality issues with cash flow reporting can exist. One issue that arises with regard to cash flow reporting quality is timing. For example, by selling receivables to a third party and/ or by delaying paying its payables, a company can boost OCF. An increase in such activities would be reflected as a decrease in the company's days' sales outstanding and an increase in the company's days of payables. Thus, an analyst can potentially detect management choices to decrease current assets or increase current liabilities, choices that will increase OCF, by looking at asset utilization (activity) ratios, changes in balance sheet accounts, and disclosures in notes to the financial statements. Another issue that arises with regard to cash flow reporting quality is related to classification of cash flows: Management may try to shift positive cash flow items from investing or financing activities to operating activities to inflate operating cash flows.

5.2. Evaluating Cash Flow Quality

Because OCF is viewed as being less subject to manipulation than earnings, the statement of cash flows can be used to identify areas of potential earnings manipulation. The financial fraud at Satyam Computer Services, an Indian information technology company, was described earlier in this chapter. In that case, the use of a computer model based on accruals may have failed to detect the fraud. A *New York Times* article (Kahn 2009) provides anecdotal evidence:

> In September, [an analyst] used a computer model to examine India's 500 largest public companies for signs of accounting manipulation. He found that more than 20 percent of them were potentially engaged in aggressive accounting, but Satyam was not on the list. This is because the automated screens that analysts ... use to pick up

signs of fraud begin by searching for large discrepancies between reported earnings and cash flow. In Satyam's case, the cash seemed to keep pace with profits.

In other words, a computer model that screened for companies with operating cash flow persistently lower than earnings would not have identified Satyam as a potential problem because its reported operating cash flow was relatively close to reported profits.

It may be helpful to examine pertinent indicators using a more qualitative approach. Exhibit 20 presents an excerpt from the statement of cash flows for Satyam for the quarter ended June 30, 2008.

EXHIBIT 20   Excerpt from Satyam's IFRS Consolidated Interim Cash Flow Statement (All amounts $ millions except per share data and as otherwise stated.)

	Quarter ended June 30, 2008 (unaudited)	Quarter ended June 30, 2007 (unaudited)	Year ended March 31, 2008 (audited)
Profit before income tax	**143.1**	**107.1**	**474.3**
Adjustments for			
Share-based payment expense	4.3	5.9	23.0
Financial costs	1.3	0.8	7.0
Finance income	(16.2)	(16.4)	(67.4)
Depreciation and amortization	11.5	9.3	40.3
(Gain)/loss on sale of premises and equipment	0.1	0.1	0.6
Changes in value of preference shares designated at fair value through profit or loss	0.0	0.0	(1.6)
Gain/(loss) on foreign exchange forward and option contracts	53.0	(21.1)	(7.4)
Share of (profits)/losses of joint ventures, net of taxes	(0.1)	0.0	(0.1)
	197.0	**85.7**	**468.7**
Movements in working capital			
— Trade and other receivables	(81.4)	(64.9)	(184.3)
— Unbilled revenue	(23.5)	(6.0)	(39.9)
— Trade and other payables	34.1	2.2	48.8
— Unearned revenue	5.8	2.4	11.4
— Other liabilities	(6.3)	30.3	61.2
— Retirement benefit obligations	3.7	1.3	17.8
Cash generated from operations	**129.4**	**51.0**	**383.7**
Income taxes paid	−3.8	−9.8	−49.4
Net cash provided by operating activities	**125.6**	**41.2**	**334.3**

Source: Based on information from Satyam's Form 6-K, filed July 25, 2008.

One item of note on this statement of cash flows is the $53 million non-cash item labeled "Gain/(loss) on foreign exchange forward and options contracts" (i.e., derivative instruments) in the quarter ended June 30, 2008. The item appears to be shown as a gain based on the labeling; however, it would not be correct to add back a gain in this calculation of operating cash flow because it is already included in profit before tax. When the company was asked about this item in the quarterly conference call with analysts, no answer was readily available. Instead, the company's manager said that he would "get back to" the questioner. The fact that the company's senior executives could not explain the reason for an item that represented almost 40% of the total pre-tax profit for the quarter ($53/$143.1 = 37%) is clearly a signal of potential problems. Refer to Exhibit 21 for an excerpt from the conference call.

EXHIBIT 21   Excerpt from Conference Call regarding Quarterly Results of Satyam, July 18, 2008

George Price, analyst at Stifel Nicolaus:	One question which is on the cash flow statement. You had a—you had $53 million in unrealized gain on derivative financial instruments in the quarter and it's a line item that just, on quick check, I don't think we've seen in past quarters. Can you comment on exactly what that is? … On the comparison periods, there were more modest losses. What drove that large benefit? How should we think about timing of cash flow maybe over the next couple quarters? Any one-time issues like that?
Srinivas Vadlamani:	I—can you repeat that, please?
George Price:	Srinivas, there's was a $53 million unrealized gain in the cash flow statement, and I'm just wondering if you could explain that in a little bit more detail…. The magnitude is a little surprising.
Srinivas Vadlamani:	No, let me—let me check on that. I'll get back to you.

Another item of note on the statement of cash flows is the steady growth in receivables. Analysts examine a company's ratios, such as days' sales outstanding. Exhibit 22 presents selected annual data for Satyam. The large jump in days' sales outstanding from 2006 to 2007 could cause concern. Furthermore, the management commentary in the company's Form 20-F indicated that "Net accounts receivable… increased… primarily as a result of an increase in our revenues and increase in collection period." An increase in the collection period of receivables raises questions about the creditworthiness of the company's customers, about the efficiency of the company's collection efforts, and about the quality of the revenue recognized.

EXHIBIT 22   Selected Annual Data on Accounts Receivable for Satyam, 2005–2008

($ millions)	2008	2007	2006	2005
Total revenue	$2,138.1	$1,461.4	$1,096.3	$793.6
% Change from previous year	*46.3%*	*33.3%*	*38.1%*	
Gross accounts receivable	$539.1	$386.9	$238.1	$178.3
% Change from previous year	*39.3%*	*62.5%*	*33.5%*	
Allowance for doubtful debts	$31.0	$22.8	$19.1	$17.5
% Change from previous year	*36.0%*	*19.4%*	*9.1%*	
Gross receivables/revenue	25.21%	26.47%	21.72%	22.47%
Change in receivables/revenue	*−4.8%*	*21.9%*	*−3.3%*	
Days' sales outstanding	92.0	96.6	79.3	82.0
Accounts receivable turnover	4.0	3.8	4.6	4.5

Source: Based on data from Satyam's 20-F filings.

A signal of problems related to cash, which would not have appeared on the statement of cash flows, was the purported use of the company's cash. Satyam reported increasing amounts invested in current accounts. On a conference call excerpted in Exhibit 23, an analyst asked for a specific reason why such large amounts would be held in non-interest-bearing accounts. Instead of providing a reason, the company officer instead stated that the amounts would be transferred to higher-earning accounts soon.

EXHIBIT 23   Excerpt from Conference Call regarding Quarterly Results for Satyam, October 17, 2008

Kawaljeet Saluja, analyst at Kotak Institutional Equities:	Hi, my questions are for Srinivas. Srinivas, any specific reason why you have $500m parked in current accounts which are not [gaining] any interest?
Srinivas Vadlamani:	No, that is basically—as on the quarter ending, but there is a statement to that [inaudible] to the deposit accounts. We have [inaudible] deposits now.
Kawaljeet Saluja:	But, Srinivas, if I look at the deposit accounts for the last four quarters, that number has remained absolutely flat. And most of the incremental cash that is parked in current accounts and this is not something which is this quarter changed. Would you highlight some of the reasons for it?
Srinivas Vadlamani:	No, basically, what will happen is these amounts will be basically in different countries. And then we will be bringing them to India based on the need. So we will be—basically, some of them are in overnight deposits and all that. So, now we have placing them into normal current deposits. So, next quarter onwards, we will see that as part of the deposits.

In Satyam CEO's January 2009 letter of resignation, he confessed that "the Balance Sheet carries as of September 30, 2008 [i]nflated (non-existent) cash and bank balances of Rs. 5,040 crore[21] (as against Rs. 5,361 crore reflected in the books)...."[22] In other words, of the amount shown as cash on the company's balance sheet, more than 90% was non-existent. It is suggested that some of the cash balances had existed but had been "siphoned off to a web of companies controlled by Mr. Raju and his family." (Kahn 2009)

Overall, the Satyam example illustrates how the statement of cash flows can suggest potential areas of misreporting. In Satyam's case, two items that raised questions were a large non-cash gain on derivatives and an increase in days' sales outstanding. Potential areas of misreporting can then be investigated by reference to the company's other financial reports. The following example illustrates how the statement of cash flows can highlight earnings manipulation and also illustrates how the cash flow information corresponds to information gleaned from analysis of the company's earnings.

Example 8 covers the application of cash flow evaluation to determine quality of earnings.

---

[21] Crore is used in India to denote 10,000,000.

[22] From Mr. B. Ramalinga Raju's resignation letter attached to Form 6-K that was filed with the SEC on January 7, 2009.

EXAMPLE 8   Sunbeam Statement of Cash Flows

As noted in the previous section, Sunbeam engaged in various improper accounting practices. Refer to the excerpt from Sunbeam's statement of cash flows in Exhibit 24 to answer the following questions:

1. One of the ways that Sunbeam misreported its financial statements was improperly inflating and subsequently reversing restructuring charges. How do these items appear on the statement of cash flows?
2. Another aspect of Sunbeam's misreporting was improper revenue recognition. What items on the statement of cash flow would primarily be affected by that practice?

EXHIBIT 24   Excerpt from Sunbeam's Consolidated Statement of Cash Flows, 1995–1997 ($ thousands)

Fiscal Years Ended	Dec. 28, 1997	Dec. 29, 1996	Dec. 31, 1995
Operating Activities:			
Net earnings (loss)	109,415	(228,262)	50,511
Adjustments to reconcile net earnings (loss) to net cash provided by (used in) operating activities:			
Depreciation and amortization	38,577	47,429	44,174
Restructuring, impairment, and other costs	—	154,869	—
Other non-cash special charges	—	128,800	—
Loss on sale of discontinued operations, net of taxes	13,713	32,430	—
Deferred income taxes	57,783	(77,828)	25,146
Increase (decrease) in cash from changes in working capital:			
Receivables, net	(84,576)	(13,829)	(4,499)
Inventories	(100,810)	(11,651)	(4,874)
Account payable	(1,585)	14,735	9,245
Restructuring accrual	(43,378)	—	—
Prepaid expenses and other current assets and liabilities	(9,004)	2,737	(8,821)
Income taxes payable	52,844	(21,942)	(18,452)
Payment of other long-term and non-operating liabilities	(14,682)	(27,089)	(21,719)
Other, net	(26,546)	13,764	10,805
Net cash provided by (used in) operating activities	(8,249)	14,163	81,516

Note: The reason that an increase in sales is shown as a negative number on the statement of cash flows prepared using the indirect method is to reverse any sales reported in income for which cash has not yet been received.

Solution to 1: Sunbeam's statement of cash flows is prepared using the indirect method (i.e., the operating section shows a reconciliation between reported net income and operating cash flow). This reconciliation highlights that the amount of non-cash charges recorded in 1996 for restructuring, impairment, and other costs totaled about $284 million ($154.869 million + $128.8 million). In the following year, the reversal of the restructuring accrual was $43 million. By inflating and subsequently reversing restructuring charges, the company's income would misleadingly portray significant improvements in performance following the arrival of its new CEO in mid-1996.

Solution to 2: The items on the statement of cash flows that would primarily be affected by improper revenue recognition include net income, receivables, and inventories. Net income and receivables would be overstated. The statement of cash flows, in which an increase in receivables is shown as a negative number, highlights the continued growth of receivables. In addition, Sunbeam's practice of recording sales that lacked economic substance—because the purchaser held the goods over the end of an accounting period but subsequently returned all the goods—is highlighted in the substantial increase in inventory in 1997.

An issue that arises with regard to cash flow reporting quality is classification shifting: shifting positive cash flow items from investing or financing to inflate operating cash flows. A shift in classification does not change the total amount of cash flow, but it can affect investors' evaluation of a company's cash flows and investors' expectations for future cash flows.

Flexibility in classification exists within accounting standards. For example, IFRS permits companies to classify interest paid either as operating or as financing. IFRS also permits companies to classify interest and dividends received as operating or as investing. In contrast, US GAAP requires that interest paid, interest received, and dividends received all be classified as operating cash flows. Thus, an analyst comparing an IFRS-reporting company to a US GAAP-reporting company would want to ensure comparable classification of interest and dividends and would adjust the reported amounts, if necessary. In addition, an analyst examining an IFRS-reporting company should be alert to any year-to-year changes in classification of interest and dividends. For example, consider an IFRS-reporting company that changed its classification of interest paid from operating to financing. All else equal, the company's operating cash flow would appear higher than the prior period even if no other activities occurred in the period.

As another example of the flexibility permitted by accounting standards, cash flows from non-trading securities are classified as investing cash flows, whereas cash flows from trading securities are typically classified as operating cash flows. However, each company decides what constitutes trading and non-trading activities, depending on how it manages its securities holdings. This discretion creates an opportunity for managers to shift cash flows from one classification to another.

Example 9 illustrates a shift of cash flows from investing to operating.

EXAMPLE 9   Classification of Cash Flows

Nautica Enterprises[23]
An excerpt from the statement of cash flows from the fiscal 2000 annual report of Nautica Enterprises, an apparel manufacturer, is shown as Exhibit 25. An excerpt from the statement of cash flows from the company's fiscal 2001 annual report is shown in Exhibit 26. Use these two excerpts to answer the questions that follow.

EXHIBIT 25   Excerpt from Nautica Enterprises' Consolidated Statement of Cash Flow from Annual Report, filed May 27, 2000 (amounts in thousands)

	Year ended March 4, 2000
Cash flows from operating activities	
Net earnings	$46,163
Adjustments to reconcile net earnings to net cash provided by operating activities, net of assets and liabilities acquired	
Minority interest in net loss of consolidated subsidiary	—
Deferred income taxes	(1,035)
Depreciation and amortization	17,072
Provision for bad debts	1,424
Changes in operating assets and liabilities	
Accounts receivable	(6,562)
Inventories	(3,667)
Prepaid expenses and other current assets	(20)
Other assets	(2,686)
Accounts payable: trade	(548)
Accrued expenses and other current liabilities	9,086
Income taxes payable	3,458
Net cash provided by operating activities	62,685
Cash flows from investing activities	
Purchase of property, plant, and equipment	(33,289)
Acquisitions, net of cash acquired	—
Sale (purchase) of short-term investments	21,116
Payments to register trademark	(277)
Net cash used in investing activities	(12,450)

---

[23] Example adapted from Mulford and Comiskey (2005).

EXHIBIT 26   Excerpt from Nautica Enterprises' Consolidated Statements of Cash Flows
from Annual Report, filed May 29, 2001 (amounts in thousands)

	Year Ended March 3, 2001	Year Ended March 4, 2000
Cash flows from operating activities		
Net earnings	46,103	46,163
Adjustments to reconcile net earnings to net cash provided by operating activities, net of assets and liabilities acquired		
Minority interest in net loss of consolidated subsidiary	—	—
Deferred income taxes	(2,478)	(1,035)
Depreciation and amortization	22,968	17,072
Provision for bad debts	1,451	1,424
Changes in operating assets and liabilities		
Short-term investments	28,445	21,116
Accounts receivable	(17,935)	(768)
Inventories	(24,142)	(3,667)
Prepaid expenses and other current assets	(2,024)	(20)
Other assets	(36)	(2,686)
Accounts payable: trade	14,833	(548)
Accrued expenses and other current liabilities	7,054	3,292
Income taxes payable	3,779	3,458
Net cash provided by operating activities	78,018	83,801
Cash flows from investing activities		
Purchase of property, plant, and equipment	(41,712)	(33,289)
Acquisitions, net of cash acquired	—	—
Purchase of short-term investments	—	—
Payments to register trademark	(199)	(277)
Net cash used in investing activities	(41,911)	(33,566)

1. What amount does Nautica report as operating cash flow for the year ended March 4, 2000 in Exhibit 25? What amount does Nautica report as operating cash flow for the same year in Exhibit 26?
2. Exhibit 25 shows that the company had investing cash flows of $21,116 thousand from the sale of short-term investments for the year ended March 4, 2000. Where does this amount appear in Exhibit 26?
3. As actually reported (Exhibit 26), how did the company's operating cash flow for fiscal year 2001 compare with that for 2000? If Nautica had not changed the classification of its short-term investing activities, how would the company's operating cash flows for fiscal year 2001 have compared with that for 2000?

Solution to 1: In Exhibit 25, Nautica reports operating cash flow for the year ended March 4, 2000 of $62,685 thousand. In Exhibit 26, Nautica reports operating cash flow for the same year of $83,801 thousand.

Solution to 2: The $21,116 thousand (i.e., the difference between the amounts of operating cash flow reported in Exhibits 25 and 26) that appears in Exhibit 25 as investing cash flows from the sale of short-term investments for the year ended March 4, 2000 has been reclassified. In Exhibit 26, this amount appears under changes in operating assets and liabilities (i.e., as a component of operating cash flow).

Solution to 3: As reported in Exhibit 26, the company's cash flows declined by 7% from fiscal year 2000 to fiscal year 2001 (= 78,018/83,801 − 1 = −7%). If Nautica had not changed the classification of its short-term investing activities, the company's operating cash flows for fiscal year 2001 would have been $49,573 thousand (=78,018 − 28,445), and would have shown a decline of 21% from fiscal year 2000 to fiscal year 2001 (= 49,573/62,685 − 1 = −21%).

An analyst could have identified Nautica's classification shift by comparing the statement of cash flows for 2000 in the fiscal year 2000 annual report with the statement in the fiscal year 2001 annual report. In general, comparisons of period-to-period reports issued by a company can be useful in assessing financial reporting quality. If a company restates prior years' financial statements (because of an error), recasts prior years' financial statements (because of a change in accounting policy), omits some information that was previously voluntarily disclosed, or adds some item, such as a new risk disclosure that was not previously disclosed, an analyst should aim to understand the reasons for the changes.

6. BALANCE SHEET QUALITY

With regard to the balance sheet, high financial *reporting* quality is indicated by completeness, unbiased measurement, and clear presentation. High financial *results* quality (i.e., a strong balance sheet) is indicated by an optimal amount of leverage, adequate liquidity, and economically successful asset allocation. Balance sheet strength is assessed using ratio analysis, including common-size financial statements, which is covered by the financial statement analysis chapters. There are no absolute values for ratio analysis that indicate adequate financial strength; such analysis must be undertaken in the context of a firm's earnings and cash flow outlook, coupled with an understanding of the environment in which the firm operates. In this section, the focus is on high financial reporting quality.

An important aspect of financial reporting quality for the balance sheet is *completeness*. Significant amounts of off-balance-sheet obligations could be a concern for an analyst because exclusion of these obligations could understate the company's leverage. One common source of off-balance-sheet obligation is purchase contracts, which may be structured as take-or-pay contracts. Analysts typically adjust reported financial statement information by constructively capitalizing, where material, purchase obligations. Constructive capitalization means that the analyst estimates the amount of the obligation as the present value of future purchase obligation payments and then adds the amount of the obligation to the company's reported assets and liabilities.

The use of unconsolidated joint ventures or equity-method investees may reflect off-balance-sheet liabilities. In addition, certain profitability ratios (return on sales, also called "net profit margin") may be overstated because the parent company's consolidated financial statements include its share of the investee's profits but not its share of the investee's sales. If disclosures are adequate, an analyst can adjust the reported amounts to better reflect the combined amounts of sales, assets, and liabilities. A company operating with numerous or material unconsolidated subsidiaries for which ownership levels approach 50% could be a warning sign of accounting issues. Understanding why a company structures its operations in such a manner—industry practice or need for strategic alliances in certain businesses or geographies—can allay concerns.

Another important aspect of financial reporting quality for the balance sheet is *unbiased measurement*. Unbiased measurement is particularly important for assets and liabilities for which valuation is subjective. The following list presents several examples:

- As previously discussed, understatement of impairment charges for inventory; plant, property, and equipment; or other assets not only results in overstated profits on the income statement but also results in overstatement of the assets on the balance sheet. A company with substantial amounts of reported goodwill but with a market value of equity less than the book value of shareholders' equity may indicate that appropriate goodwill impairments have not been taken.
- Similarly, understatement of valuation allowance for deferred tax assets would understate tax expenses and overstate the value of the assets on the balance sheet. (Overstatement would have the opposite effect.) Significant, unexplainable variations in the valuation account can signal biased measurement.
- A company's investments in the debt or equity securities of another company would ideally be based on observable market data. For some investments, no observable market data exist and the valuation must be based solely on management estimates. The balance sheet of a company with a substantial portion of its assets valued using non-observable inputs likely warrants closer scrutiny.
- A company's pension liabilities require various estimates, such as the discount rate at which future obligations are present valued. If pension obligations exist, the level and changes for the discount rate should be examined.

Example 10 shows a company with overstated goodwill.

EXAMPLE 10   Goodwill

Sealed Air Corporation
In August 2012, a *Wall Street Journal* article listed six companies that were carrying more goodwill on their balance sheets than the companies' market values (Thurm 2012). At the top of the list was Sealed Air Corporation, a company operating in the packaging and containers industry. Exhibit 27 presents an excerpt from the company's income statement for the following year, and Exhibit 28 presents an excerpt from the company's balance sheet.

EXHIBIT 27   Sealed Air Corporation and Subsidiaries Consolidated Statements of Operations ($ millions, except per share amounts)

Year ended December 31	2012	2011	2010
Net sales	$7,648.1	$5,550.9	$4,490.1
Cost of sales	5,103.8	3,950.6	3,237.3
Gross profit	2,544.3	1,600.3	1,252.8
Marketing, administrative, and development expenses	1,785.2	1,014.4	699.0
Amortization expense of intangible assets acquired	134.0	39.5	11.2
Impairment of goodwill and other intangible assets	1,892.3	—	—
Costs related to the acquisition and integration of Diversey	7.4	64.8	—
Restructuring and other charges	142.5	52.2	7.6
Operating (loss) profit	(1,417.1)	429.4	535.0
Interest expense	(384.7)	(216.6)	(161.6)
Loss on debt redemption	(36.9)	—	(38.5)
Impairment of equity method investment	(23.5)	—	—
Foreign currency exchange (losses) gains related to Venezuelan subsidiaries	(0.4)	(0.3)	5.5
Net gains on sale (other-than-temporary impairment) of available-for-sale securities	—	—	5.9
Other expense, net	(9.4)	(14.5)	(2.9)
(Loss) earnings from continuing operations before income tax provision	(1,872.0)	198.0	343.4
Income tax (benefit) provision	(261.9)	59.5	87.5
Net (loss) earnings from continuing operations	(1,610.1)	138.5	255.9
Net earnings from discontinued operations	20.9	10.6	—
Net gain on sale of discontinued operations	178.9	—	—
Net (loss) earnings available to common stockholders	$(1,410.3)	$149.1	$255.9

EXHIBIT 28   Excerpt from Sealed Air Corporation and Subsidiaries Consolidated Balance Sheets ($ millions, except share data)

Year Ended December 31	2012	2011
ASSETS		
Current assets		
Cash and cash equivalents	$679.6	$703.6
Receivables, net of allowance for doubtful accounts of $25.9 in 2012 and $16.2 in 2011	1,326.0	1,314.2
Inventories	736.4	777.5
Deferred tax assets	393.0	156.2
Assets held for sale	—	279.0
Prepaid expenses and other current assets	87.4	119.7
Total current assets	$3,222.4	$3,350.2

EXHIBIT 28   (Continued)

Year Ended December 31	2012	2011
ASSETS		
Property and equipment, net	$1,212.8	$1,269.2
Goodwill	3,191.4	4,209.6
Intangible assets, net	1,139.7	2,035.7
Non-current deferred tax assets	255.8	112.3
Other assets, net	415.1	455.0
Total assets	$9,437.2	$11,432.0

1. Sealed Air Corporation's financial statements indicate that the number of common shares issued and outstanding in 2011 was 192,062,185. The price per share of Sealed Air Corporation's common stock was around $18 per share in December 2011 and around $14 in August 2012; the *Wall Street Journal* article (Thurm 2012) was written in 2012. What was the company's market value?
2. How did the amount of goodwill as of December 31, 2011 compare with the company's market value?
3. Why did the *Wall Street Journal* article state that goodwill in excess of the company's market value is "a potential clue to future write-offs"?
4. Based on the information in Exhibit 28, does the *Wall Street Journal* article statement appear to be correct?

Solution to 1: Sealed Air Corporation's market cap was about $3,457 million (= 192,062,185 shares × $18 per share) in December 2011 and around $2,689 million (= 192,062,185 shares × $14 per share) when the *Wall Street Journal* article was written in August 2012.

Solution to 2: The amount of goodwill on Sealed Air Corporation's balance sheet as of December 31, 2011 was $4,209.6 million. The amount of goodwill exceeded the company's market value. (Also note that goodwill and other intangible assets represented about 55% of Sealed Air Corporation's total assets as of December 31, 2011.)

Solution to 3: If the market capitalization exactly equaled the reported amount of goodwill, the value implicitly assigned to all the company's other assets would equal zero. In this case, because the market capitalization is less than the reported amount of goodwill, the value implicitly attributed to all the company's other assets is less than zero. This suggests that the amount of goodwill on the balance sheet is overvalued, so a future write-off is likely.

Solution to 4: Yes, based on the information in Exhibit 28, the *Wall Street Journal* article statement appears correct. In the fiscal year ending December 31, 2012 after the article, Sealed Air Corporation recorded impairment of goodwill and other intangible assets of $1,892.3 million.

Finally, *clear presentation* is also important for financial reporting quality for the balance sheet. Although accounting standards specify many aspects of what appears on the balance sheet, companies have discretion, for example, in determining which line items should be shown separately and which should be aggregated into a single total. For items shown as a single total, an analyst can usually consult the notes for information about the components. For example, in consulting the inventory note, an analyst may learn that inventory is carried on a last-in, first-out basis and that, consequently, in an inflationary environment, the inventory is carried on the balance sheet at a cost that is significantly lower than its current cost. This information would provide the analyst with comfort that the inventory is unlikely to be overstated.

7. SOURCES OF INFORMATION ABOUT RISK

A company's financial statements can provide useful indicators of financial, operating, or other risk. For example, high leverage ratios (or, similarly, low coverage ratios) derived from financial statement data can signal financial risk. As described in a previous section, analytical models that incorporate various financial data can signal bankruptcy risk, and others can predict reporting risks (i.e., the risk of a company misreporting). Operating risks can be indicated by financial data, such as highly variable operating cash flows or negative trends in profit margins. Additional information about risk can be obtained from sources other than the financial statements.

An audit opinion(s) covering financial statements (and internal controls over financial reporting, where required) can provide some information about reporting risk. However, the content of an audit opinion is unlikely to be a timely source of information about risk. A related item that is potentially a signal of problems (and thus potentially represents information about risk) is a discretionary change in auditor. For example, Allou Health & Beauty Care, discussed in Example 7, had a different auditor for 2000, 2001, and 2002.

The notes are an integral part of the financial statements. They typically contain information that is useful in understanding a company's risk. Beyond the information about risk that can be derived from a company's financial statements and notes, various other disclosures can provide information about financial, operating, reporting, or other risks. An important source of information is the management commentary, which provides management's assessment of the important risks faced by the company. Although risk-related disclosures in the management commentary sometimes overlap with disclosures contained in the financial statement notes or elsewhere in regulatory filings, the commentary should reveal the management perspective, and its content often differs from the note disclosures.

Other required disclosures that are specific to an event, such as capital raising, non-timely filing of financial reports, management changes, or mergers and acquisitions, can provide important information relevant to assessing risk. Finally, the financial press, including online media, if used judiciously, can be a useful source of information about risk.

7.1. Limited Usefulness of Auditor's Opinion as a Source of Information about Risk

An auditor's opinion is unlikely to be an analyst's first source of information about a company's risk.[24] For financial statements, a clean audit opinion states that the financial statements

---

[24] Regulators globally are considering changes to increase the usefulness of audit reports. For example, the Financial Reporting Council in the UK requires auditors to include more information in their reports on risks identified during the audit and on how the concept of materiality was applied.

present the information fairly and in conformity with the relevant accounting principles. For internal controls, a clean audit opinion states that the company maintained effective internal controls over financial reporting. A negative or going-concern audit opinion on financial statements or a report indicating an internal control weakness would clearly be a warning sign for an analyst. However, an audit opinion relates to historical information and would, therefore, typically not provide information on a timely enough basis to be a useful source of information about risk.

For example, Eastman Kodak Company filed for bankruptcy on January 19, 2012. The audit opinion for fiscal 2011 (dated February 28, 2012) is shown in Exhibit 29. The opinion is identical to the company's audit opinion for the prior fiscal year except for two differences: (1) the years have been updated, and (2) the paragraph highlighted in bold has been added. The added paragraph states that the financial statements were prepared under the "going-concern" assumption; the company has subsequently declared bankruptcy, which raises doubt about the company's ability to continue as a going concern; and the financial statements have not been adjusted to reflect the bankruptcy. An analyst would have learned about Eastman Kodak's bankruptcy on January 19, so the audit opinion is not useful as a source of that information. In addition, the audit opinion addresses financial statements that had not been adjusted to reflect the bankruptcy, which would limit usefulness to an analyst.

EXHIBIT 29   Post-Bankruptcy Audit Opinion for Eastman Kodak

Report of Independent Registered Public Accounting Firm

To the Board of Directors and Shareholders of Eastman Kodak Company:

In our opinion, the consolidated financial statements listed in the index appearing under Item 15(a)(1) present fairly, in all material respects, the financial position of Eastman Kodak Company and its subsidiaries at December 31, 2011 and 2010, and the results of their operations and their cash flows for each of the three years in the period ended December 31, 2011 in conformity with accounting principles generally accepted in the United States of America. In addition, in our opinion, the financial statement schedule listed in the index appearing under Item 15(a)(2) presents fairly, in all material respects, the information set forth therein when read in conjunction with the related consolidated financial statements. Also in our opinion, the Company maintained, in all material respects, effective internal control over financial reporting as of December 31, 2011, based on criteria established in *Internal Control - Integrated Framework* issued by the Committee of Sponsoring Organizations of the Treadway Commission (COSO). The Company's management is responsible for these financial statements and financial statement schedule, for maintaining effective internal control over financial reporting and for its assessment of the effectiveness of internal control over financial reporting, included in Management's Report on Internal Control over Financial Reporting appearing under Item 9A. Our responsibility is to express opinions on these financial statements, on the financial statement schedule, and on the Company's internal control over financial reporting based on our integrated audits. We conducted our audits in accordance with the standards of the Public Company Accounting Oversight Board (United States). Those standards require that we plan and perform the audits to obtain reasonable assurance about whether the financial statements are free of material misstatement and whether effective internal control over financial reporting was maintained in all material respects. Our audits of the financial statements included examining, on a test basis, evidence supporting the amounts and disclosures in the financial statements, assessing the accounting principles used and significant estimates made by management, and evaluating the overall financial statement presentation. Our audit of internal

(continued)

EXHIBIT 29   (Continued)

control over financial reporting included obtaining an understanding of internal control over financial reporting, assessing the risk that a material weakness exists, and testing and evaluating the design and operating effectiveness of internal control based on the assessed risk. Our audits also included performing such other procedures as we considered necessary in the circumstances. We believe that our audits provide a reasonable basis for our opinions.

The accompanying financial statements have been prepared assuming that the Company will continue as a going concern. As more fully discussed in Note 1 to the financial statements, on January 19, 2012, the Company and its US subsidiaries filed voluntary petitions for relief under chapter 11 of the United States Bankruptcy Code. Uncertainties inherent in the bankruptcy process raise substantial doubt about the Company's ability to continue as a going concern. Management's plans in regard to these matters are also described in Note 1. The accompanying financial statements do not include any adjustments that might result from the outcome of this uncertainty.

A company's internal control over financial reporting is a process designed to provide reasonable assurance regarding the reliability of financial reporting and the preparation of financial statements for external purposes in accordance with generally accepted accounting principles. A company's internal control over financial reporting includes those policies and procedures that (i) pertain to the maintenance of records that, in reasonable detail, accurately and fairly reflect the transactions and dispositions of the assets of the company; (ii) provide reasonable assurance that transactions are recorded as necessary to permit preparation of financial statements in accordance with generally accepted accounting principles, and that receipts and expenditures of the company are being made only in accordance with authorizations of management and directors of the company; and (iii) provide reasonable assurance regarding prevention or timely detection of unauthorized acquisition, use, or disposition of the company's assets that could have a material effect on the financial statements.

Because of its inherent limitations, internal control over financial reporting may not prevent or detect misstatements. Also, projections of any evaluation of effectiveness to future periods are subject to the risk that controls may become inadequate because of changes in conditions, or that the degree of compliance with the policies or procedures may deteriorate.

/s/ PricewaterhouseCoopers LLP

PricewaterhouseCoopers LLP
Rochester, New York
February 28, 2012

Note: Bold-face type is added for emphasis.

In the case of Kodak, an analyst would not have obtained very useful information about risk from the auditor's report. Other sources of information—financial and market data—would have provided clear and timely indications of the company's financial difficulty.

Groupon provides another example of the timing of availability of information about risk in external auditors' reports. Exhibit 30 presents a timeline of events related to the company's material weakness in internal controls. Note that no negative external auditor opinion appeared before or during the timeframe in which the weakness existed. No external opinion was required for the first annual filing, and the weakness had been remedied by the second annual filing.

EXHIBIT 30   Material Weaknesses in Internal Controls at Groupon

November 2011:	The company goes public (initial public offering)
March 2012:	The company revises financial results and discloses that management concluded there was a "material weakness" in internal controls over financial reporting, as of December 31. Shares fall 17%. (Because of an exemption for newly public companies, no external auditor opinion on the effectiveness of internal controls was required.)
May 2012:	In its first-quarter filing, the company discloses that it is "taking steps" to correct the weaknesses but cannot provide assurance that internal controls will be considered effective by the end of the year.
August 2012:	Second-quarter filing includes a disclosure similar to that in first-quarter filing.
November 2012:	Third-quarter filing includes a disclosure similar to that in first-quarter filing.
February 2013:	Full-year filing indicates that the company "concluded that we have remediated the previously identified material weakness as of December 31, 2012." (As required for public companies, the filing includes Groupon's first external auditor opinion on the effectiveness of internal controls. The company received a clean opinion.)

In the case of Groupon, an analyst would not have obtained any useful information from the auditor's report. Other data would have given more useful indicators of the company's reporting difficulties. For example, the company was required to change its revenue recognition policy and to restate the amount of revenue reported in its IPO filing—clearly a sign of reporting difficulties. Another item of information providing a signal of likely reporting difficulties was the company's extensive number of acquisitions and explosive growth. Groupon's reported revenues for 2009 were more than 300 times the amount of 2008 reported revenues, and 2010 reported revenues were 23 times larger than 2009 revenues. As described in an August 2011 accounting blog (Catanach and Ketz 2011):

> It is absolutely ludicrous to think that Groupon is anywhere close to having an effective set of internal controls over financial reporting having done 17 acquisitions in a little over a year. When a company expands to 45 countries, grows merchants from 212 to 78,466, and expands its employee base from 37 to 9,625 in only two years, there is little doubt that internal controls are not working somewhere.

The growth data, particularly coupled with disclosures in the IPO filing about management inexperience, are a warning sign of potential reporting risks. These reporting risks were observable many months before the company disclosed its internal control weakness, and the control weaknesses did not appear in an audit opinion.

Although the content of an audit opinion is unlikely to provide timely information about risk, a change in the auditor—and especially multiple changes in the auditor—can signal possible reporting problems. For example, one of the largest feeder funds for Bernie Madoff (the perpetrator of a multi-billion-dollar Ponzi scheme) had three different auditors for the three years from 2004 to 2006, a fact highlighted in testimony as a huge warning sign indicating "auditor shopping."[25] Similarly, the use of an auditor whose capabilities

---

[25] From the testimony of Harry Markopolos, CFA, given before the US House of Representatives Committee on Financial Services, February 4, 2009.

seem inadequate for the complexity of the company can indicate risk. For example, the accounting/auditing firm that audited Madoff's $50 billion operation consisted of three people (two principals and a secretary). The small size of the auditing firm relative to the size of Madoff's operations should have caused serious concern for any potential investor. In general, it is important to understand the relationship between the auditor and the firm. Any questions about the auditor's independence would be a cause for concern—for example, if the auditor and company management are particularly close or if the company represents a substantial portion of the auditing firm's revenue.

7.2. Risk-Related Disclosures in the Notes

The notes, an integral part of the financial statements, typically contain information that is useful in understanding a company's risk. For example, both IFRS and US GAAP require specific disclosures about risks related to contingent obligations, pension and post-employment benefits, and financial instrument risks.

Disclosures about contingent obligations include a description of the obligation, estimated amounts, timing of required payments, and related uncertainties.[26] Exhibit 31 shows excerpts from two of Royal Dutch Shell's financial statement notes disclosing information about provisions and contingencies. The year-to-year changes in management's estimated costs for items such as future decommissioning and restoration could have implications for risk evaluation. The disclosure also emphasizes the uncertain timing and amounts.

EXHIBIT 31   Disclosures about Contingent Obligations, Excerpt from Royal Dutch Shell's Note 19 and Note 25

19. Decommissioning and Other Provisions

	Current		Non-Current		Total	
	Dec 31, 2012	Dec 31, 2011	Dec 31, 2012	Dec 31, 2011	Dec 31, 2012	Dec 31, 2011
Decommissioning and restoration	1,356	894	14,715	13,072	16,071	13,966
Environmental	366	357	1,032	1,078	1,398	1,435
Redundancy	228	406	275	297	503	703
Litigation	390	256	307	330	697	586
Other	881	1,195	1,106	854	1,987	2,049
Total	3,221	3,108	17,435	15,631	20,656	18,739

The timing and amounts settled in respect of these provisions are uncertain and dependent on various factors that are not always within management's control. Additional provisions are stated net of reversals of provisions recognised in previous periods.

---

[26] Contingent losses are recognized (i.e., reported on the financial statements) when it is probable the loss will occur and the amount can be reasonably estimated. Contingencies are disclosed (but not recognized) when the occurrence of a loss is less than probable but greater than remote and/or the amount cannot be reliably estimated. The concepts are similar under IFRS and US GAAP despite differences in terminology. IFRS makes a distinction between "provisions," which are recognized as liabilities because they meet the definition of a liability, and "contingent liabilities," which are disclosed but not recognized.

Of the decommissioning and restoration provision at December 31, 2012, an estimated $4,666 million is expected to be utilized within one to five years, $3,483 million within six to ten years, and the remainder in later periods.

Reviews of estimated decommissioning and restoration costs are carried out annually, which in 2012 resulted in an increase of $1,586 million ...

25. Legal Proceedings and Other Contingencies

Groundwater contamination

Shell Oil Company (including subsidiaries and affiliates, referred to collectively as SOC), along with numerous other defendants, has been sued by public and quasi-public water purveyors, as well as governmental entities. The plaintiffs allege responsibility for groundwater contamination caused by releases of gasoline containing oxygenate additives. Most of these suits assert various theories of liability, including product liability, and seek to recover actual damages, including clean-up costs. Some assert claims for punitive damages. Fewer than 10 of these cases remain. On the basis of court rulings in SOC's favor in certain cases claiming damages from threats of contamination, the claims asserted in remaining matters, and Shell's track record with regard to amounts paid to resolve varying claims, the management of Shell currently does not believe that the outcome of the remaining oxygenate-related litigation pending, as at December 31, 2012, will have a material impact on Shell.

Nigerian claims

Shell subsidiaries and associates operating in Nigeria are parties to various environmental and contractual disputes. These disputes are at different stages in litigation, including at the appellate stage, where judgments have been rendered against Shell. If taken at face value, the aggregate amount of these judgments could be seen as material. The management of Shell, however, believes that these matters will ultimately be resolved in a manner favorable to Shell. While no assurance can be provided as to the ultimate outcome of any litigation, these matters are not expected to have a material effect on Shell.

Other

In the ordinary course of business, Shell subsidiaries are subject to a number of other loss contingencies arising from litigation and claims brought by governmental and private parties. The operations and earnings of Shell subsidiaries continue, from time to time, to be affected to varying degrees by political, legislative, fiscal and regulatory developments, including those relating to the protection of the environment and indigenous groups, in the countries in which they operate. The industries in which Shell subsidiaries are engaged are also subject to physical risks of various types. The nature and frequency of these developments and events, as well as their effect on future operations and earnings, are unpredictable.

Disclosures about pensions and post-employment benefits include information relevant to actuarial risks that could result in actual benefits differing from the reported obligations based on estimated benefits or investment risks that could result in actual assets differing from reported amounts based on estimates.

Disclosures about financial instruments include information about risks, such as credit risk, liquidity risk, and market risks that arise from the company's financial instruments, and how they have been managed.

EXAMPLE 11   Use of Disclosures

Use the excerpts from Royal Dutch Shell's note disclosing information about financial instruments in Exhibit 32 to answer the following questions:

1. Does Shell appear to take a centralized or decentralized approach to managing interest rate risk?
2. For the year ended December 31, 2012, Shell reported pre-tax income of $50,289 million. How significant is Shell's exposure to a 1% increase in interest rates?
3. For the year ended December 31, 2012, what would be the impact on Shell's pre-tax income of a 10% appreciation of the Australian dollar against the US dollar?

EXHIBIT 32   Disclosures about Financial Instruments, Excerpt from Royal Dutch Shell's Note 21

21 Financial Instruments and Other Derivative Contracts
A – Risks

In the normal course of business, financial instruments of various kinds are used for the purposes of managing exposure to interest rate, currency and commodity price movements.

. . . .

Interest rate risk

Most debt is raised from central borrowing programs. Interest rate swaps and currency swaps have been entered into to effectively convert most centrally issued debt to floating rate linked to dollar Libor (London Inter-Bank Offer Rate), reflecting Shell's policy to have debt principally denominated in dollars and to maintain a largely floating interest rate exposure profile. Consequently, Shell is exposed predominantly to dollar Libor interest rate movements. The financing of most subsidiaries is also structured on a floating-rate basis and, except in special cases, further interest rate risk management is discouraged.

On the basis of the floating rate net debt position at December 31, 2012, and assuming other factors (principally foreign exchange rates and commodity prices) remained constant and that no further interest rate management action were taken, an increase in interest rates of 1% would decrease pre-tax income by $27 million (2011: $146 million).

Foreign exchange risk

Many of the markets in which Shell operates are priced, directly or indirectly, in dollars. As a result, the functional currency of most Upstream companies and those with significant cross-border business is the dollar. For Downstream companies, the local currency is typically the functional currency. Consequently, Shell is exposed to varying levels of foreign exchange risk when it enters into transactions that are not denominated in the companies' functional currencies, when foreign currency monetary assets and liabilities are translated at the reporting date and as a result of holding net investments in operations that are not dollar-functional. The main currencies to which Shell is exposed are sterling, the Canadian dollar, euro and Australian dollar. Each company has treasury policies in place that are designed to measure and manage its foreign exchange exposures by reference to its functional currency.

Exchange rate gains and losses arise in the normal course of business from the recognition of receivables and payables and other monetary items in currencies other than individual companies' functional currency. Currency exchange risk may also arise in connection with capital expenditure. For major projects, an assessment is made at the final investment decision stage whether to hedge any resulting exposure.

Hedging of net investments in foreign operations or of income that arises in foreign operations that are non-dollar functional is not undertaken.

Assuming other factors (principally interest rates and commodity prices) remained constant and that no further foreign exchange risk management action were taken, a 10% appreciation against the dollar at December 31 of the main currencies to which Shell is exposed would have the following pre-tax effects:

$ millions	Increase (decrease) in income		Increase in net assets	
	2012	2011	2012	2011
10% appreciation against the dollar of:				
Sterling	(185)	(58)	1,214	1,042
Canadian dollar	131	(360)	1,384	1,364
Euro	30	458	1,883	1,768
Australian dollar	246	153	142	120

The above sensitivity information is calculated by reference to carrying amounts of assets and liabilities at December 31 only. The pre-tax effect on income arises in connection with monetary balances denominated in currencies other than the relevant entity's functional currency; the pre-tax effect on net assets arises principally from the translation of assets and liabilities of entities that are not dollar-functional.

Solution to 1: Shell appears to take a centralized approach to managing interest rate risk based on its statements that most debt is raised centrally and that interest rate swaps and currency swaps have been used to convert most interest rate exposure to dollar Libor. In addition, Shell states that apart from structuring subsidiary financing on a floating-rate basis, it discourages subsidiary's further interest rate risk management.

Solution to 2: For the year ended December 31, 2012, Shell's exposure to a 1% increase in interest rates is relatively insignificant. An increase in interest rates of 1% would decrease pre-tax income by $27 million, which is less than 0.1% of Shell's 2012 reported pre-tax income of $50,289 million.

Solution to 3: The impact on Shell's pre-tax income of a 10% appreciation of the Australian dollar against the US dollar would be an increase of $246 million, which is about 0.5% of Shell's 2012 reported pre-tax income of $50,289 million.

These disclosures, along with expectations about future market conditions, can help an analyst assess whether the company's exposures to interest rate risk and foreign exchange risks pose a significant threat to the company's future performance.

7.3. Management Commentary (Management Discussion and Analysis, or MD&A)

The IFRS Practice Statement, *Management Commentary*, issued in December 2010, is a non-binding framework for commentary related to financial statements prepared in accordance with IFRS. One purpose of the commentary is to help users of the financial reports in understanding the company's risk exposures, approach to managing risks, and effectiveness of risk management. The practice statement includes five elements that should be contained in the commentary: (1) nature of the business; (2) objectives and strategies; (3) resources, risks, and relationships; (4) results and prospects; and (5) performance measures and indicators. The section on risks can be particularly useful (IFRS 2010).

> Management should disclose its principal strategic, commercial, operational, and financial risks, which are those that may significantly affect the entity's strategies and progress of the entity's value. The description of the principal risks facing the entity should cover both exposures to negative consequences and potential opportunities.... The principal risks and uncertainties can constitute either a significant external or internal risk to the entity. (p. 13)

Public US companies are required to include an MD&A as Item 7 of Form 10-K. The MD&A disclosures include information about (1) liquidity, (2) capital resources, (3) results of operations, (4) off-balance-sheet arrangements, and (5) contractual arrangements. Information about off-balance-sheet arrangements and contractual arrangements can enable an analyst to anticipate future impact on cash flow. Companies are required to present quantitative and qualitative information about the company's exposure to market risks as Item 7A of the 10-K. This disclosure should enable analysts to understand the impact of fluctuations in interest rates, foreign exchange, and commodity prices.[27]

The IFRS Practice Statement states specifically that companies should present only the principal risks and not list all possible risks and uncertainties. Similarly, the SEC Division of Corporation Finance's internal reference document, *Financial Reporting Manual*, states, "MD&A should not consist of generic or boilerplate disclosure. Rather, it should reflect the facts and circumstances specific to each individual registrant" (p. 296). In practice, disclosures do not always reflect the intent. One challenge faced by analysts is identifying important risks and distinguishing between risks that are generic and thus relevant to all companies and risks that are more specific to an individual company.

---

[27] Although not part of the MD&A, disclosures about risk factors relevant to the company's securities are also required as Item 1A of Form 10-K.

This challenge is illustrated by an excerpt from the "Key Risks and Uncertainties" section of Autonomy Corporation's 2010 Annual Report, its last annual report before it was acquired by Hewlett-Packard Company (HP) for $11.1 billion in 2011.[28] As shown in Exhibit 33, Autonomy's risk disclosures contain many items that are arguably generic, such as the inability to maintain the competitive value of its technology, loss of key executives, and continued unfavorable economic conditions. These types of risks would be faced by any technology company. This significant amount of generic commentary (two pages) could potentially distract a reader whose aim was to identify the specific and important risks faced by the company.

EXHIBIT 33   Autonomy Corporation, Key Risks and Uncertainties

Risk	Description	Impact/Sensitivity	Mitigation/Comment
Technology	Business depends on our core technology, and our strategy concentrates on developing and marketing software based on our proprietary technology.	Since substantially all of revenues derive from licensing our core technology, if unable to maintain and enhance the competitive value of our core technology, our business will be adversely affected.	Continue to invest heavily in research and development to maintain competitive advantage. Monitor market to maintain competitiveness. Apply core technology to new and additional vertical market applications.
Competition	Technology which significantly competes with our technology.	Could render our products out of date and could result in rapid loss of market share.	Invest heavily in new product development to ensure that we have products at various stages of the product life cycle.
Variability and visibility	There may be fluctuations in results due to quarterly reporting, and variability in results due to late-in-the-quarter purchasing cycles common in the software industry.	Although quarter-to-quarter results may not be meaningful due to the short periods, negative sentiment may arise based on interpretation of results. Due to late purchasing cycles common in the software industry, variability in closure rates could become exaggerated resulting in a negative effect on operations.	Close management of sales pipelines on a quarterly basis to improve visibility in results expectations. Close monitoring of macro and micro economic conditions to understand variability in closure rates. Annual and quarterly target setting to enable results achievement.

(continued)

---

[28] HP subsequently took a multi-billion-dollar write-down on its investment, which it attributed to misreporting by Autonomy Corporation, stating that "the majority of this impairment charge is linked to serious accounting improprieties, disclosure failures and outright misrepresentations at Autonomy Corporation plc that occurred prior to HP's acquisition of Autonomy and the associated impact of those improprieties, failures and misrepresentations on the expected future financial performance of the Autonomy business over the long-term" (HP earnings announcement, November 20, 2012). Of course, HP's due diligence prior to purchasing the company would have gone far beyond the published financial reports; HP would have had access to all of the company's internal reporting as well.

EXHIBIT 33   (Continued)

Risk	Description	Impact/Sensitivity	Mitigation/Comment
Margins	Expenditures increasing without a commensurate increase in revenues, and rapid changes in market conditions.	If increased expenses are not accompanied by increased revenues, we could experience decreased margins or operating losses.	Close monitoring by management of revenue and cost forecasts. Adjustment to expenditures in the event of anticipated revenue shortfalls.
Average selling prices	The average selling prices of our products could decrease rapidly.	May negatively impact revenues and gross margins.	Monitor market prices on an ongoing basis. Pricing responsibility at a senior level of management for deviations from standard.
Market conditions	The continuation of unfavourable economic and market conditions.	Could result in a rapid deterioration of operating results.	Regular monitoring of economic conditions. Adjustments to costs and product offerings to anticipate and match market conditions.
Resellers	Our ability to expand sales through indirect sellers and our general reliance on sales of our products by third parties.	Inability to recruit and retain resellers who can successfully penetrate their markets could adversely affect our business.	Invest in training resources for resellers. Close monitoring of reseller sales cycles. Investment in direct sales channel.
Management	The continued service of our executive directors.	The loss of any key member of management may affect the leadership of the company.	Establish succession plan. Maintain effective management training program. Attract and retain senior personnel.
Hiring	The hiring and retention of qualified personnel.	Without the appropriate quality and quantity of skills throughout the organization, it would be difficult to execute the business plans and grow.	Use of external recruiters and internal bonuses. Rigorous talent management plans and reviews. Provide competitive compensation packages. Ensure that work is challenging and rewarding.
Product errors	Errors or defects in our products.	Could negatively affect our revenues and the market acceptance of our products and increase our costs.	Invest in quality control programs. Monitor integrity and effectiveness of software. Solicit and act on customer feedback.
Acquisitions	Problems encountered in connection with potential acquisitions.	We may not successfully overcome problems in connection with potential acquisitions, which could lead to a deterioration in our results.	Carefully evaluate transactions. Conduct thorough due diligence on all targets. Carefully plan for post-acquisition integration.

EXHIBIT 33   (Continued)

Risk	Description	Impact/Sensitivity	Mitigation/Comment
IP infringement	Claims by others that we infringe on their intellectual property rights.	If our technology infringed on other parties' intellectual property rights, we could be exposed to costs and injunctive relief.	Monitor market developments closely to identify potential violations of our patents, and by the company, and take action where necessary. Maintain a significant number of patents to support our business and protect competitive advantage.
Growth	Our ability to effectively manage our growth.	Expansion places demands on management, engineering, support, operations, legal, accounting, sales and marketing personnel, and other resources. Failure to manage effectively will impact business and financial results.	Recruitment and retention of key personnel. Investment in corporate infrastructure, including support, operations, legal, and accounting personnel. Focus on internal controls.
International risks	Additional operational and financial risks as we continue to expand our international operations.	Exposure to movements in exchange rates and lack of familiarity with local laws could lead to infractions.	Pricing of contracts in US dollars to the extent possible to minimize exchange risk. Retention of local staff and local advisors, reporting to headquarters, to manage risk.
Security breaches	Any breach of our security measures and unauthorized access to a customer's or our data.	Could result in significant legal liability and negative publicity.	Establish and maintain strict security standards. Test security standards on a regular basis.

Source: Section from Autonomy Corporation's 2010 Annual Report.

7.4. Other Required Disclosures

Other required disclosures that are specific to an event, such as capital raising, non-timely filing of financial reports, management changes, or mergers and acquisitions, can provide important information relevant to assessing risk. In the United States, public companies would report such events to the SEC in a Form 8-K (and NT—"notification of inability to timely file"—when appropriate). Delays in filing are often the result of accounting difficulties. Such accounting difficulties could be internal disagreement on an accounting principle or estimate, the lack of adequate financial staff, or the discovery of an accounting fraud that requires further examination. In general, an NT filing is highly likely to signal problems with financial reporting quality.

For public companies in Europe, the Committee of European Securities Regulators (CESR)[29] has published guidance concerning the types of inside information that must be disclosed on an ad hoc basis to the market. Examples of such information include changes in control; changes in management and supervisory boards; mergers, splits, and spinoffs; legal disputes; and new licenses, patents, and registered trademarks. Companies use the disclosure mechanisms specified by their relevant national authorities to make such disclosures. For example, in the United Kingdom, a company would release an announcement to the market via an approved regulatory information service.

In these cases, an examination of the information announced would be necessary to determine whether reporting quality would be affected. For example, an announcement of the sudden resignation of a company's most senior financial officer or external auditor would clearly be a warning sign of potential problems with financial reporting quality. As another example, an announcement of a legal dispute related to one of the company's important assets or products would warrant attention because it could negatively affect the company's future earnings. Announcements of mergers and acquisitions, although they might indicate future positive developments for the company, could also indicate changes in the company's risk profile, particularly during the transaction.

7.5. Financial Press as a Source of Information about Risk

The financial press can be a useful source of information about risk when, for example, a financial reporter uncovers financial reporting issues that had not previously been recognized. For example, a *Wall Street Journal* financial reporter, Jonathan Weil (2000), was one of the first people to identify problems with the accounting at Enron (and other companies that were using "gain-on-sale" accounting, an aggressive policy allowing immediate revenue recognition on long-term contracts). Indeed, the well-known investor James (Jim) Chanos cites an article by Weil as the catalyst of his investigation of Enron (Chanos 2002).

It is important to emphasize that even if an initial idea comes from a news article, further investigation is essential—first, by using definitive sources (i.e., regulatory filings) to confirm any accounting and financial disclosures and, second, by seeking supporting information from other sources, where available. For example, although a financial press article was the initial source of information for Chanos, the first step in his research was to analyze Enron's annual SEC filings (Form 10-K and 10-Q). In addition, Chanos obtained information about insider stock sales, the company's business strategy and tactics, and stock analysts' perspectives.

It is also important—and likely will become increasingly important as electronic media via the internet expands—to consider the source of any particular news article. Information reported by a well-known financial news provider is more likely to be factual than information from less-established sources. Similarly, stories or blogs written by financial journalists are more likely to be unbiased than those written by individuals with a related service or product to sell.

8. SUMMARY

Assessing the quality of financial reports—both reporting quality and results quality—is an important analytical skill.

- The quality of financial reporting can be thought of as spanning a continuum from the highest quality to the lowest.

---

[29] CESR has been replaced by the European Securities and Markets Authority (ESMA).

- Potential problems that affect the quality of financial reporting broadly include revenue and expense recognition on the income statement; classification on the statement of cash flows; and the recognition, classification, and measurement of assets and liabilities on the balance sheet.
- Typical steps involved in evaluating financial reporting quality include an understanding of the company's business and industry in which the company is operating; comparison of the financial statements in the current period and the previous period to identify any significant differences in line items; an evaluation of the company's accounting policies, especially any unusual revenue and expense recognition compared with those of other companies in the same industry; financial ratio analysis; examination of the statement of cash flows with particular focus on differences between net income and operating cash flows; perusal of risk disclosures; and review of management compensation and insider transactions.
- High-quality earnings increase the value of the company more than low-quality earnings, and the term "high-quality earnings" assumes that reporting quality is high.
- Low-quality earnings are insufficient to cover the company's cost of capital and/or are derived from non-recurring, one-off activities. In addition, the term "low-quality earnings" can be used when the reported information does not provide a useful indication of the company's performance.
- Various alternatives have been used as indicators of earnings quality: recurring earnings, earnings persistence and related measures of accruals, beating benchmarks, and after-the-fact confirmations of poor-quality earnings, such as enforcement actions and restatements.
- Earnings that have a significant accrual component are less persistent and thus may revert to the mean more quickly.
- A company that consistently reports earnings that exactly meet or only narrowly beat benchmarks can raise questions about its earnings quality.
- Cases of accounting malfeasance have commonly involved issues with revenue recognition, such as premature recognition of revenues or the recognition of fraudulent revenues.
- Cases of accounting malfeasance have involved misrepresentation of expenditures as assets rather than as expenses or misrepresentation of the timing or amount of expenses.
- Bankruptcy prediction models, used in assessing financial results quality, quantify the likelihood that a company will default on its debt and/or declare bankruptcy.
- Similar to the term "earnings quality," when reported cash flows are described as being high quality, it means that the company's underlying economic performance was satisfactory in terms of increasing the value of the firm, and it also implies that the company had high reporting quality (i.e., that the information calculated and disclosed by the company was a good reflection of economic reality). Cash flow can be described as "low quality" either because the reported information properly represents genuinely bad economic performance or because the reported information misrepresents economic reality.
- For the balance sheet, high financial *reporting* quality is indicated by completeness, unbiased measurement, and clear presentation.
- A balance sheet with significant amounts of off-balance-sheet debt would lack the completeness aspect of financial reporting quality.
- Unbiased measurement is a particularly important aspect of financial reporting quality for assets and liabilities for which valuation is subjective.
- A company's financial statements can provide useful indicators of financial or operating risk.
- The management commentary (also referred to as the management discussion and analysis, or MD&A) can give users of the financial statements information that is helpful in assessing the company's risk exposures and approaches to managing risk.

- Required disclosures regarding, for example, changes in senior management or inability to make a timely filing of required financial reports can be a warning sign of problems with financial reporting quality.
- The financial press can be a useful source of information about risk when, for example, a financial reporter uncovers financial reporting issues that had not previously been recognized. An analyst should undertake additional investigation of any issue identified.

REFERENCES

"Ahold: Europe's Enron." 2003. *The Economist* (February 27).

Altman, Edward I. 1968. "Financial Ratios, Discriminant Analysis and the Prediction of Corporate Bankruptcy." *Journal of Finance*, vol. 23, no. 4 (September):589–609. doi:10.1111/j.1540-6261.1968.tb00843.x

Altman, Edward I. 2000. "Predicting Financial Distress of Companies: Revisiting the Z-Score and Zeta[*] Models." Working paper (July).

Beneish, Messod D. 1999. "The Detection of Earnings Manipulation." *Financial Analysts Journal*, vol. 55, no. 5 (September/October):24–36. doi:10.2469/faj.v55.n5.2296

Beneish, Messod D., Charles M.C. Lee, and D. Craig Nichols. 2013. "Earnings Manipulation and Expected Returns." *Financial Analysts Journal*, vol. 69, no. 2 (March/April):57–82. doi:10.2469/faj.v69.n2.1

Bens, Daniel A., Theodore H. Goodman, and Monica Neamtiu. 2012. "Does Investment-Related Pressure Lead to Misreporting? An Analysis of Reporting Following M&A Transactions." *Accounting Review*, vol. 87, no. 3 (May):839–865. doi:10.2308/accr-10210

Beresford, Dennis R., Nicholas deB. Katzenbach, and C.B. Rogers. Jr. 2003. "Report of Investigation by the Special Investigative Committee of the Board of Directors of WorldCom, Inc." (March 31): www.sec.gov/Archives/edgar/data/723527/000093176303001862/dex991.htm.

Bharath, Sreedhar T., and Tyler Shumway. 2008. "Forecasting Default with the Merton Distance to Default Model." *Review of Financial Studies*, vol. 21, no. 3 (May):1339–1369. doi:10.1093/rfs/hhn044

Bhasin, Madan. 2012. "Corporate Accounting Frauds: A Case Study of Satyam Computers Limited." *International Journal of Contemporary Business Studies*, vol. 3, no. 10 (October):16–42.

Brown, Lawrence D., and Marcus L. Caylor. 2005. "A Temporal Analysis of Quarterly Earnings Thresholds: Propensities and Valuation Consequences." *Accounting Review*, vol. 80, no. 2 (April):423–440. doi:10.2308/accr.2005.80.2.423

Bulkeley, W. 2002. "Questioning the Books: IBM Annual Report Shows Stronger Core Earnings." *Wall Street Journal* (Match 12).

Burgstahler, D., and Ilia Dichev. 1997. "Earnings Management to Avoid Earnings Decreases and Losses." *Journal of Accounting and Economics*, vol. 24, no. 1 (December):99–126. doi:10.1016/S0165-4101(97)00017-7

Catanach, Anthony H., and J. Edward Ketz. 2011. "Trust No One, Particularly Not Groupon's Accountants," Grumpy Old Accountants (August): http://blogs.smeal.psu.edu/grumpyoldaccountants.

Chanos, James. 2002. "Anyone Could Have Seen Enron Coming: Prepared Witness Testimony Given Feb. 6, 2002 to the House Committee on Energy and Commerce," *Wall \$treet Week with FORTUNE* (http://www.pbs.org/wsw/opinion/chanostestimony.html).

Ciesielski, Jack T., and Elaine Henry. 2017. "Accounting's Tower of Babel: Key Considerations in Assessing Non-GAAP Earnings." *Financial Analysts Journal*, vol. 73, no. 2:34–50.

Dechow, Patricia M., Richard G. Sloan, and Amy P. Sweeney. 1995. "Detecting Earnings Management." *Accounting Review*, vol. 70, no. 2 (April):193–225.

Dechow, Patricia M., Scott A. Richardson, and Irem Tuna. 2003. "Why Are Earnings Kinky? An Examination of the Earnings Management Explanation." *Review of Accounting Studies*, vol. 8, no. 2–3 (June):355–384. doi:10.1023/A:1024481916719

Dechow, Patricia M., Weili Ge, and Catherine Schrand. 2010. "Understanding Earnings Quality: A Review of the Proxies, Their Determinants and Their Consequences." *Journal of Accounting and Economics*, vol. 50, no. 2–3 (December):344–401. doi:10.1016/j.jacceco.2010.09.001

Dechow, Patricia, Seili Ge, Chad Larson, and Richard Sloan. 2011. "Predicting Material Accounting Misstatements." *Contemporary Accounting Research*, vol. 28, no. 1 (Spring):17–82. doi:10.1111/j.1911-3846.2010.01041.x

Degeorge, François, Jayendu Patel, and Richard Zeckhauser. 1999. "Earnings Management to Exceed Thresholds." *Journal of Business*, vol. 72, no. 1 (January):1–33. doi:10.1086/209601

Fuji Electric. 2013. "Announcement of Impairment Losses on Noncurrent Assets (Extraordinary Losses)." memo (April 25): www.fujielectric.com/company/news/box/doc/130425_evaluation.pdf.

Erickson, Merle, and Shiing-wu Wang. 1999. "Earnings Management by Acquiring Firms in Stock for Stock Mergers." *Journal of Accounting and Economics*, vol. 27, no. 2 (April):149–176. doi:10.1016/S0165-4101(99)00008-7

Erickson, M., S. Heitzman, and X.F. Zhang. 2012. "The Effect of Financial Misreporting on Corporate Mergers and Acquisitions." Working paper.

Friedman, Eric, Simon Johnson, and Todd Mitton. 2003. "Propping and Tunneling." *Journal of Comparative Economics*, vol. 31, no. 4 (December):732–750. doi:10.1016/j.jce.2003.08.004

Hwang, S.L. 1994. "Borden to Reverse, Reclassify 40% of 1992 Charge." *Wall Street Journal* (March 22).

IASB. 2010. *Conceptual Framework for Financial Reporting 2010*. International Accounting Standards Board (September).

IFRS. 2010. *Management Commentary, A Framework for Presentation*. IFRS Practice Statement (December).

Johnson, S., R. LaPorta, A. Shleifer, and F. Lopez-de-Silanes. 2000. "Tunneling." *American Economic Review*, vol. 90, no. 2 (May):22–27. doi:10.1257/aer.90.2.22

Jones, Jennifer J. 1991. "Earnings Management during Import Relief Investigations." *Journal of Accounting Research*, vol. 29, no. 2 (Autumn):193–228. doi:10.2307/2491047

Kahn, Jeremy. 2009. "In India, Clues Unfold to a Fraud's Framework." *New York Times* (January 26).

Kealhofer, Stephen. 2003. "Quantifying Credit Risk I: Default Prediction." *Financial Analysts Journal*, vol. 59, no. 1 (January/February):30–44. doi:10.2469/faj.v59.n1.2501

Leuty, Ron. 2012. "Elan Will Shutter South S.F. Center as It Shifts R&D to New Company." *San Francisco Business Times* (October 5 2012): www.bizjournals.com/sanfrancisco/blog/biotech/2012/09/elan-neotope-onclave-alzheimers.html?page=all.

Lewis, Craig M. 2012. "Risk Modeling at the SEC: The Accounting Quality Model," Speech given at the Financial Executives International Committee on Finance and Information Technology (13 December):www.sec.gov/news/speech/2012/spch121312cml.htm.

McVay, Sarah E. 2006. "Earnings Management Using Classification Shifting: An Examination of Core Earnings and Special Items." *Accounting Review*, vol. 81, no. 3 (May):501–532. doi:10.2308/accr.2006.81.3.501

Mulford, Charles W., and Eugene E. Comiskey. 2005. *Creative Cash Flow Reporting: Uncovering Sustainable Financial Performance*. Hoboken, NJ:John Wiley & Sons.

Nissim, Doron, and Stephen H. Penman. 2001. "Ratio Analysis and Equity Valuation: From Research to Practice." *Review of Accounting Studies*, vol. 6, no. 1 (March):109–154. doi:10.1023/A:1011338221623

SEC. 2000. "Accounting and Auditing Enforcement, Release No. 1350." US Securities and Exchange Commission (December 14): www.sec.gov/litigation/admin/34-43724.htm.

SEC. 2001a "Accounting and Auditing Enforcement, Release No. 1393." US Securities and Exchange Commission (May 15): www.sec.gov/litigation/admin/33-7976.htm.

SEC. 2001b. "Accounting and Auditing Enforcement, Release No. 1405." US Securities and Exchange Commission (June 19): www.sec.gov/litigation/admin/34-44444.htm.

SEC. 2003. "Report Pursuant to Section 704 of the Sarbanes-Oxley Act of 2002" US Securities and Exchange Commission (January 24): www.sec.gov/news/studies/sox704report.pdf.

Sherer, P. 2000. "AmeriServe Examination Finds Financial Woes." *Wall Street Journal* (July 3).

Shumway, Tyler. 2001. "Forecasting Bankruptcy More Accurately: A Simple Hazard Model." *Journal of Business*, vol. 74, no. 1 (January):101–124. doi:10.1086/209665

Sloan, Richard G. 1996. "Do Stock Prices Fully Reflect Information in Accruals and Cash Flows about Future Earnings?" *Accounting Review*, vol. 71, no. 3 (July):289–315.

Thurm, Scott. 2012. "Buyers Beware: The Goodwill Games." *Wall Street Journal* (August 12).

Weil, Jonathan. 2000. "Energy Traders Cite Gains, But Some Math is Missing," *Wall Street Journal* (September 20).

PRACTICE PROBLEMS

The following information relates to Questions 1–4

Mike Martinez is an equity analyst who has been asked to analyze Stellar, Inc. by his supervisor, Dominic Anderson. Stellar exhibited strong earnings growth last year; however, Anderson is skeptical about the sustainability of the company's earnings. He wants Martinez to focus on Stellar's financial reporting quality and earnings quality.

After conducting a thorough review of the company's financial statements, Martinez concludes the following:

Conclusion 1: Although Stellar's financial statements adhere to generally accepted accounting principles (GAAP), Stellar understates earnings in periods when the company is performing well and overstates earnings in periods when the company is struggling.

Conclusion 2: Stellar most likely understated the value of amortizable intangibles when recording the acquisition of Solar, Inc. last year. No goodwill impairment charges have been taken since the acquisition.

Conclusion 3: Over time, the accruals component of Stellar's earnings is large relative to the cash component.

Conclusion 4: Stellar reported an unusually sharp decline in accounts receivable in the current year, and an increase in long-term trade receivables.

1. Based on Martinez's conclusions, Stellar's financial statements are *best* categorized as:
   A. non-GAAP compliant.
   B. GAAP compliant, but with earnings management.
   C. GAAP compliant and decision useful, with sustainable and adequate returns.

2. Based on Conclusion 2, after the acquisition of Solar, Stellar's earnings are *most likely*:
   A. understated.
   B. fairly stated.
   C. overstated.

3. In his follow-up analysis relating to Conclusion 3, Martinez should focus on Stellar's:
   A. total accruals.
   B. discretionary accruals.
   C. non-discretionary accruals.

4. What will be the impact on Stellar in the current year if Martinez's belief in Conclusion 4 is correct? Compared with the previous year, Stellar's:
   A. current ratio will increase.
   B. days sales outstanding (DSO) will decrease.
   C. accounts receivable turnover will decrease.

The following information relates to Questions 5–12

Ioana Matei is a senior portfolio manager for an international wealth management firm. She directs research analyst Teresa Pereira to investigate the earnings quality of Miland Communications and Globales, Inc.

Pereira first reviews industry data and the financial reports of Miland Communications for the past few years. Pereira then makes the following three statements about Miland:

Statement 1:   Miland shortened the depreciable lives for capital assets.
Statement 2:   Revenue growth has been higher than that of industry peers.
Statement 3:   Discounts to customers and returns from customers have decreased.

Pereira also observes that Miland has experienced increasing inventory turnover, increasing receivables turnover, and net income greater than cash flow from operations. She estimates the following regression model to assess Miland's earnings persistence:

$$\text{Earnings}_{t+1} = \alpha + \beta_1 \text{Cash flow}_t + \beta_2 \text{Accruals}_t + \varepsilon$$

Pereira and Matei discuss quantitative models such as the Beneish model, used to assess the likelihood of misreporting. Pereira makes the following two statements to Matei:

Statement 4:   An advantage of using quantitative models is that they can determine cause and effect between model variables.
Statement 5:   A disadvantage of using quantitative models is that their predictive power declines over time because many managers have learned to test the detectability of manipulation tactics by using the model.

Pereira collects the information in Exhibit 1 to use the Beneish model to assess Miland's likelihood of misreporting.

EXHIBIT 1   Selected Beneish Model Data for Miland Communications

	Last Year	Current Year
Days' sales receivable index (DSR)	0.90	1.20
Leverage index (LEVI)	0.75	0.95
Sales, general, and administrative expenses index (SGAI)	0.60	0.75

Pereira concludes her investigation of Miland by examining the company's reported pretax income of $5.4 billion last year. This amount includes $1.2 billion of acquisition and divestiture-related expenses, $0.5 billion of restructuring expenses, and $1.1 billion of other non-operating expenses. Pereira determines that the acquisition and divestiture-related expenses as well as restructuring expenses are non-recurring expenses, but other expenses are recurring expenses.

Matei then asks Pereira to review last year's financial statements for Globales, Inc. and assess the effect of two possible misstatements. Upon doing so, Pereira judges that Globales improperly recognized EUR50 million of revenue and improperly capitalized EUR100 million of its cost of revenue. She then estimates the effect of these two misstatements on net income, assuming a tax rate of 25%.

Pereira compares Globales, Inc.'s financial statements with those of an industry competitor. Both firms have similar, above-average returns on equity (ROE), although Globales has a higher cash flow component of earnings. Pereira applies the mean reversion principle in her forecasts of the two firms' future ROE.

5. Which of Pereira's statements describes an accounting warning sign of potential overstatement or non-sustainability of operating and/or net income?
   A. Statement 1
   B. Statement 2
   C. Statement 3

6. Which of Pereira's statements about Miland Communications is *most likely* a warning sign of potential earnings manipulation?
   A. The trend in inventory turnover
   B. The trend in receivables turnover
   C. The amount of net income relative to cash flow from operations

7. Based on the regression model used by Pereira, earnings persistence for Miland would be highest if:
   A. β_1 is less than 0.
   B. β_1 is greater than β_2.
   C. β_2 is greater than β_1.

8. Which of Pereira's statements regarding the use of quantitative models to assess the likelihood of misreporting is correct?
   A. Only Statement 4
   B. Only Statement 5
   C. Both Statement 4 and Statement 5

9. Based on Exhibit 1, which variable in the Beneish model has a year-over-year change that would increase Miland's likelihood of manipulation?
   A. DSR
   B. LEVI
   C. SGAI

10. Based on Pereira's determination of recurring and non-recurring expenses for Miland, the company's recurring or core pre-tax earnings last year is *closest* to:
    A. $4.3 billion.
    B. $4.8 billion.
    C. $7.1 billion.

11. After adjusting the Globales, Inc. income statement for the two possible misstatements, the decline in net income is *closest* to:
    A. EUR37.5 million.
    B. EUR112.5 million.
    C. EUR150.0 million.

12. Pereira should forecast that the ROE for Globales is likely to decline:
    A. more slowly than that of the industry competitor.
    B. at the same rate as the industry competitor.
    C. more rapidly than that of the industry competitor.

The following information relates to Questions 13–19

Emmitt Dodd is a portfolio manager for Upsilon Advisers. Dodd meets with Sonya Webster, the firm's analyst responsible for the machinery industry, to discuss three established companies: BIG Industrial, Construction Supply, and Dynamic Production. Webster provides Dodd with research notes for each company that reflect trends during the last three years:

BIG Industrial:

Note 1: Operating income has been much lower than operating cash flow (OCF).
Note 2: Accounts payable has increased, while accounts receivable and inventory have substantially decreased.
Note 3: Although OCF was positive, it was just sufficient to cover capital expenditures, dividends, and debt repayments.

Construction Supply:

Note 4: Operating margins have been relatively constant.
Note 5: The growth rate in revenue has exceeded the growth rate in receivables.
Note 6: OCF was stable and positive, close to its reported net income, and just sufficient to cover capital expenditures, dividends, and debt repayments.

Dynamic Production:

Note 7: OCF has been more volatile than that of other industry participants.
Note 8: OCF has fallen short of covering capital expenditures, dividends, and debt repayments.

Dodd asks Webster about the use of quantitative tools to assess the likelihood of misreporting. Webster tells Dodd she uses the Beneish model, and she presents the estimated *M*-scores for each company in Exhibit 1.

EXHIBIT 1   Beneish Model *M*-scores

Company	2017	2016	Change in *M*-score
BIG Industrial	−1.54	−1.82	0.28
Construction Supply	−2.60	−2.51	−0.09
Dynamic Production	−1.86	−1.12	−0.74

Webster tells Dodd that Dynamic Production was required to restate its 2016 financial statements as a result of its attempt to inflate sales revenue. Customers of Dynamic Production were encouraged to take excess product in 2016, and they were then allowed to return purchases in the subsequent period, without penalty.

Webster's industry analysis leads her to believe that innovations have caused some of the BIG Industrial's inventory to become obsolete. Webster expresses concern to Dodd that although the notes to the financial statements for BIG Industrial are informative about its inventory cost methods, its inventory is overstated.

The BIG Industrial income statement reflects a profitable 49% unconsolidated equity investment. Webster calculates the return on sales of BIG Industrial based on the reported income statement. Dodd notes that industry peers consolidate similar investments. Dodd asks Webster to use a comparable method of calculating the return on sales for BIG Industrial.

13. Which of Webster's notes about BIG Industrial provides an accounting warning sign of a potential reporting problem?
    A. Only Note 1
    B. Only Note 2
    C. Both Note 1 and Note 2

14. Do either of Webster's Notes 4 or 5 about Construction Supply describe an accounting warning sign of potential overstatement or non-sustainability of operating income?
    A. No
    B. Yes, Note 4 provides a warning sign
    C. Yes, Note 5 provides a warning sign

15. Based on Webster's research notes, which company would *most likely* be described as having high-quality cash flow?
    A. BIG Industrial
    B. Construction Supply
    C. Dynamic Production

16. Based on the Beneish model results for 2017 in Exhibit 1, which company has the highest probability of being an earnings manipulator?
    A. BIG Industrial
    B. Construction Supply
    C. Dynamic Production

17. Based on the information related to its restatement, Dynamic Production reported poor operating cash flow quality in 2016 by understating:
    A. inventories.
    B. net income.
    C. trade receivables.

18. Webster's concern about BIG Industrial's inventory suggests poor reporting quality, *most likely* resulting from a lack of:
    A. completeness.
    B. clear presentation.
    C. unbiased measurement.

19. In response to Dodd's request, Webster's recalculated return on sales will *most likely*:
    A. decrease.
    B. remain the same.
    C. increase.

CHAPTER 18

INTEGRATION OF FINANCIAL STATEMENT ANALYSIS TECHNIQUES

Jack T. Ciesielski, CPA, CFA

LEARNING OUTCOMES

After completing this chapter, you will be able to do the following:

- demonstrate the use of a framework for the analysis of financial statements, given a particular problem, question, or purpose (e.g., valuing equity based on comparables, critiquing a credit rating, obtaining a comprehensive picture of financial leverage, evaluating the perspectives given in management's discussion of financial results);
- identify financial reporting choices and biases that affect the quality and comparability of companies' financial statements and explain how such biases may affect financial decisions;
- evaluate the quality of a company's financial data and recommend appropriate adjustments to improve quality and comparability with similar companies, including adjustments for differences in accounting standards, methods, and assumptions;
- evaluate how a given change in accounting standards, methods, or assumptions affects financial statements and ratios;
- analyze and interpret how balance sheet modifications, earnings normalization, and cash flow statement related modifications affect a company's financial statements, financial ratios, and overall financial condition.

1. INTRODUCTION

It is important to keep in mind that financial analysis is a means to an end and not the end itself. Rather than try to apply every possible technique and tool to every situation, it is essential for the investor to consider and identify the proper type of analysis to apply in a given situation.

The primary reason for performing financial analysis is to help in making an economic decision. Before making such decisions as whether to lend to a particular long-term borrower or to invest a large sum in a common stock, venture capital vehicle, or private equity candidate, an investor or financial decision-maker wants to make sure that the probability of a successful outcome is on his or her side. Rather than leave outcomes to chance, a financial decision-maker should use financial analysis to identify and make more visible potential favorable and unfavorable outcomes.

The purpose of this chapter is to provide examples of the effective use of financial analysis in decision making. The framework for the analysis is shown in Exhibit 1. The case study follows the basic framework shown in Exhibit 1.

EXHIBIT 1   A Financial Statement Analysis Framework

Phase	Sources of Information	Examples of Output
1. Define the purpose and context of the analysis.	• The nature of the analyst's function, such as evaluating an equity or debt investment or issuing a credit rating • Communication with client or supervisor on needs and concerns • Institutional guidelines related to developing specific work product	• Statement of the purpose or objective of the analysis • A list (written or unwritten) of specific questions to be answered by the analysis • Nature and content of report to be provided • Timetable and budgeted resources for completion
2. Collect input data.	• Financial statements, other financial data, questionnaires, and industry/economic data • Discussions with management, suppliers, customers, and competitors • Company site visits (e.g., to production facilities or retail stores)	• Organized financial statements • Financial data tables • Completed questionnaires, if applicable
3. Process input data, as required, into analytically useful data.	• Data from the previous phase	• Adjusted financial statements • Common-size statements • Ratios and graphs • Forecasts
4. Analyze/interpret the data.	• Input data and processed data	• Analytical results
5. Develop and communicate conclusions and recommendations (e.g., with an analysis report).	• Analytical results and previous reports • Institutional guidelines for published reports	• Analytical report answering questions posed in Phase 1 • Recommendation regarding the purpose of the analysis, such as whether to make an investment or grant credit
6. Follow-up.	• Information gathered by periodically repeating above steps, as necessary, to determine whether changes to holdings or recommendations are necessary	• Updated reports and recommendations

2. CASE STUDY: LONG-TERM EQUITY INVESTMENT

The portfolio manager for the food sector of a large public employee pension fund wants to take a long-term equity position in a publicly traded food company and has become interested in Nestlé S.A., a global company. In its 2014 annual report, Nestlé's management outlined its long-term objectives for organic growth, margin and earnings per share improvement, and capital efficiency. The management report indicated the following general strategic direction: "Our ambition is not just to be the leader but the industry reference for Nutrition, Health and Wellness. In recent years we have built on the strong foundations of our unrivalled food and beverage portfolio, exploring the benefits of nutrition's therapeutic role with Nestlé Health Science." Nestlé's stated objectives, including expansion of the company's mission into "nutrition's therapeutic role," captured the portfolio manager's attention: She became intrigued with Nestlé as an investment possibility. She asks an analyst to evaluate Nestlé for consideration as a large core holding. Before investing in the company, the portfolio manager has several concerns that she has conveyed to the analyst:

- What are Nestlé's sources of earnings growth? How sustainable is Nestlé's performance? Do the company's reported earnings represent its economic reality? And if Nestlé's performance is fairly reported, will it be sustainable for an extended period, such as 5 to 10 years, while the pension fund has the common stock as a core holding?
- In determining the quality of earnings over a long-term time frame, the portfolio manager wants to understand the relationship of earnings to cash flow.
- Having started out in the investment business as a lending officer, the portfolio manager wants to know how well Nestlé's balance sheet takes into account the company's full rights and obligations. She wants to know whether the capital structure of the company can support future operations and strategic plans. Even if the investor is primarily concerned with the earnings potential of a possible investee, the balance sheet matters. For example, if asset write-downs or new legal liabilities decrease a company's financial position, it is difficult for a company to sustain profitability if it has to repair its balance sheet. Worse still for an investor: If "repairing the balance sheet" means the issuance of dilutive stock, it can be even more costly to existing investors.

The analyst develops a plan of analysis to address the portfolio manager's concerns by following the framework presented in Exhibit 1. Phases 3 and 4 will be the focus of most of the work.

2.1. Phase 1: Define a Purpose for the Analysis

The analyst states the purpose and context of the analysis as identifying the factors that have driven the company's financial success and assessing their sustainability. He also states the need to identify and understand the risks that may affect the sustainability of returns.

2.2. Phase 2: Collect Input Data

The analyst finds that Nestlé has an extensive collection of financial statements on its website. After gathering several years of annual reports, he is ready to begin processing the data.

2.3. Phase 3: Process Data and Phase 4: Analyze/Interpret the Processed Data

The analyst intends to accomplish his purpose stated in Phase 1 through a series of financial analyses, including

- a DuPont analysis;[1]
- an analysis of the composition of Nestlé's asset base;
- an analysis of Nestlé's capital structure;
- a study of the company's segments and the allocation of capital among them;
- an examination of the company's accruals in reporting as they affect earnings quality;
- a study of the company's cash flows and their adequacy for the company's continued operations and strategies; and
- a decomposition and analysis of the company's valuation.

While processing the input data consistent with the needs of these analyses, the analyst plans to simultaneously interpret and analyze the resulting data. In his view, Phases 3 and 4 of the framework are best considered jointly.

2.3.1. DuPont Analysis

The analyst decides to start the assessment of Nestlé with a DuPont analysis. The investment is expected to be in the company's common stock, and ultimately, the DuPont analysis separates the components affecting the return on common equity. Furthermore, the disaggregation of return on equity (ROE) components leads to more trails to follow in assessing the drivers of Nestlé's performance. The analyst also intends to investigate the quality of the earnings and underlying cash flows, as well as to understand the common shareholders' standing in the Nestlé capital structure.

One basic premise underlying all research and analysis is to constantly look beneath the level of information presented—to constantly search for meaningful insights through disaggregation of the presented information, whether it is a single line on a financial statement or within segments of an entire entity. This constant reduction of information into smaller components can reveal a company's earnings drivers; it can also highlight weaker operations being concealed by stronger ones in the aggregate. That premise of "seeking granularity" underlies DuPont analysis: By isolating the different components of ROE, it helps the analyst discover a company's strengths and allows the analyst to assess their sustainability.[2] Seeking granularity also helps the analyst find potential operational flaws and provides an opening for dialogue with management about possible problems.

The analyst begins to process the data gathered in Phase 2 in order to assemble the information required for the DuPont analysis. Exhibit 2 shows the last three years of income statements for Nestlé; Exhibit 3 shows the last four years of Nestlé balance sheets.

From his study of the income statement, the analyst notes that Nestlé has a significant amount of "income from associates and joint ventures" (hereafter referred to in the text as

---

[1] A reminder to the reader: This case study is an example, and starting the financial statement analysis with a DuPont analysis is not a mandate. Alternatively, another analyst might be more interested in the trends of various income and expense categories than in the sources of returns on shareholder equity as a financial statement analysis starting point. This analyst might have preferred starting with a time-series common-size income statement. The starting point depends on the perspective of the individual analyst.

[2] ROE can be decomposed in a variety of ways:

ROE = Return on assets × Leverage

ROE = Net profit margin × Asset turnover × Leverage

ROE = EBIT margin × Tax burden × Interest burden × Asset turnover × Leverage

income from associates) in all three years. In 2014, this income amounted to CHF8,003 million, or 53.7%, of Nestlé's net income (referred to by Nestlé as "profit for the year"). The income from associates[3] is a pure net income figure, presented after taxes and with no related revenue in the income statement. Much of the income from associates relates to Nestlé's 23.4% stock ownership of L'Oréal, a cosmetics company.

In 2014, L'Oréal affected the amount of income from associates in a variety of ways. In 2014, Nestlé reduced its L'Oréal ownership by selling 48.5 million shares of its holding back to L'Oréal. In return, Nestlé gained full ownership of Galderma, a joint venture it had with L'Oréal. The partial disposal of L'Oréal shares resulted in a net gain of CHF4,569 million. Income from associates included a revaluation gain of CHF2,817 million from the increase in ownership of Galderma. Nestlé had owned 50% of Galderma, with L'Oréal holding the other 50%. When Nestlé bought the remaining ownership from L'Oréal, its original 50% ownership position was revalued at current fair value, which was based on the price paid. As of July 2014, Galderma became an affiliated company that was fully consolidated. Because of its L'Oréal stock ownership, Nestlé recognizes a share of L'Oréal's net income.

The share of results at other companies that Nestlé included in income from associates was CHF828 million in 2014.

The analyst wants to decompose the company's financial results as much as possible in order to identify any problem operations or to find hidden opportunities. Including the net investments and returns of associates with the full reported value of Nestlé's own assets and income would introduce noise into the analytical signals produced by the DuPont analysis. Unlike the "pure Nestlé" operations and resources, the returns earned by associates are not under the direct control of Nestlé's management. To avoid making incorrect inferences about the profitability of Nestlé's operations, the analyst wants to remove the effects of the investments in associates from the balance sheet and income statement. Otherwise, such DuPont analysis components as net profit margin and total asset turnover would combine the impact of pure Nestlé operations with that of the operations of associated companies: Conclusions about Nestlé-only business would be flawed because they would be based on commingled information.

EXHIBIT 2   Nestlé S.A. Income Statements, 2014–2012 (CHF millions)

	2014	2013	2012 (restated)[d]
Sales	91,612	92,158	89,721
Other revenue	253	215	210
Cost of goods sold	(47,553)	(48,111)	(47,500)
Distribution expenses	(8,217)	(8,156)	(8,017)
Marketing and administration expenses	(19,651)	(19,711)	(19,041)
Research and development costs	(1,628)	(1,503)	(1,413)
Other trading income	110	120	141
Other trading expenses[a]	(907)	(965)	(637)
Trading operating profit[b]	**14,019**	**14,047**	**13,464**

(continued)

[3] Associates are companies in which Nestlé has the power to exercise significant influence but does not exercise control. Associates and joint ventures are accounted for by the equity method.

EXHIBIT 2   (Continued)

	2014	2013	2012 (restated)[d]
Other operating income	154	616	146
Other operating expenses[c]	(3,268)	(1,595)	(222)
Operating profit (EBIT)	**10,905**	**13,068**	**13,388**
Financial income	135	219	120
Financial expense	(772)	(850)	(825)
Profit before taxes, associates, and joint ventures (EBT)	**10,268**	**12,437**	**12,683**
Taxes	(3,367)	(3,256)	(3,259)
Income from associates and joint ventures	8,003	1,264	1,253
Profit for the year	**14,904**	**10,445**	**10,677**
of which attributable to non-controlling interests	448	430	449
of which attributable to shareholders of the parent (net profit)	14,456	10,015	10,228
Earnings per share			
Basic earnings per share	4.54	3.14	3.21
Diluted earnings per share	4.52	3.13	3.20

Excerpted information from notes to the financial statements:	2014	2013	2012 (restated)
[a] Other trading expenses include:			
Restructuring costs	(257)	(274)	(88)
Impairment of PP&E	(136)	(109)	(74)
Impairment of intangible assets (other than goodwill)	(23)	(34)	—
Litigation and onerous contracts	(411)	(380)	(369)
Unusual charges contained within operating profit	(827)	(797)	(531)
[b] Expenses allocated by function:			
Depreciation of PP&E	(2,782)	(2,867)	(2,655)
Amortization of intangible assets	(276)	(301)	(394)
	(3,058)	(3,168)	(3,049)
[c] Other operating expenses include:			
Impairment of goodwill	(1,908)	(114)	(14)

[d] The 2012 information came from the 2013 Annual Report; 2012 comparatives were restated by Nestlé following the implementation of IFRS 11 and IAS 19 revised, as described in Note 22.

EXHIBIT 3   Nestlé S.A. Balance Sheets, 2014–2011 (CHF millions)

	2014	2013	2012 (restated)[a]	2011 (revised)[b]
Assets				
Current assets				
Cash and cash equivalents	7,448	6,415	5,713	4,769
Short-term investments	1,433	638	3,583	3,013
Inventories	9,172	8,382	8,939	9,095
Trade and other receivables	13,459	12,206	13,048	12,991
Prepayments and accrued income	565	762	821	879
Derivative assets	400	230	576	722
Current income tax assets	908	1,151	972	1,053
Assets held for sale	576	282	368	16
Total current assets	**33,961**	**30,066**	**34,020**	**32,538**
Non-current assets				
Property, plant, and equipment (PP&E)	28,421	26,895	26,576	23,460
Goodwill	34,557	31,039	32,688	28,613
Intangible assets	19,800	12,673	13,018	8,785
Investments in associates and joint ventures	8,649	12,315	11,586	10,317
Financial assets	5,493	4,550	4,979	7,153
Employee benefits assets	383	537	84	127
Current income tax assets	128	124	27	39
Deferred tax assets	2,058	2,243	2,899	2,408
Total non-current assets	**99,489**	**90,376**	**91,857**	**80,902**
Total assets	**133,450**	**120,442**	**125,877**	**113,440**
Liabilities and equity				
Current liabilities				
Financial debt	8,810	11,380	18,408	15,945
Trade and other payables	17,437	16,072	14,627	13,544
Accruals and deferred income	3,759	3,185	3,078	2,780
Provisions	695	523	452	575
Derivative liabilities	757	381	423	632
Current income tax liabilities	1,264	1,276	1,608	1,379
Liabilities directly associated with assets held for sale	173	100	1	—
Total current liabilities	**32,895**	**32,917**	**38,597**	**34,855**

(continued)

EXHIBIT 3   (Continued)

	2014	2013	2012 (restated)[a]	2011 (revised)[b]
Non-current liabilities				
Financial debt	12,396	10,363	9,008	6,165
Employee benefits liabilities	8,081	6,279	8,360	6,912
Provisions	3,161	2,714	2,827	3,079
Deferred tax liabilities	3,191	2,643	2,240	1,974
Other payables	1,842	1,387	2,181	2,113
Total non-current liabilities	**28,671**	**23,386**	**24,616**	**20,243**
Total liabilities	**61,566**	**56,303**	**63,213**	**55,098**
Equity				
Share capital	322	322	322	330
Treasury shares	(3,918)	(2,196)	(2,078)	(6,722)
Translation reserve	(17,255)	(20,811)	(17,924)	(16,927)
Retained earnings and other reserves	90,981	85,260	80,687	80,184
Total equity attributable to shareholders of the parent	**70,130**	**62,575**	**61,007**	**56,865**
Non-controlling interests	1,754	1,564	1,657	1,477
Total equity	**71,884**	**64,139**	**62,664**	**58,342**
Total liabilities and equity	**133,450**	**120,442**	**125,877**	**113,440**

[a] The 2012 information came from the 2013 Annual Report; 2012 comparatives were restated by Nestlé following the implementation of IFRS 11 and IAS 19 revised, as described in Note 22.
[b] The analyst revised the 2011 balance sheet from that reported in the 2012 Consolidated Financial Statements of the Nestlé Group.

To keep the DuPont analysis as logically consistent as possible throughout all the periods of study, the analyst revises the 2011 balance sheet (from that reported in the 2012 Consolidated Financial Statements of the Nestlé Group) for the effects of implementing IFRS 11 and IAS 19 revised. He identifies the January 1, 2012 adjustments from the 2013 financial statements and revises the December 31, 2011 year-end balances accordingly. The analyst's revisions to the as-reported 2011 balance sheet are shown in Exhibit 4.

EXHIBIT 4   Modifications to 2011 Balance Sheet (CHF millions)

	2011 (as reported)	Effects of IAS 19 (1)	Effects of IFRS 11 (2)	2011 (revised)
Assets				
Current assets				
Cash and cash equivalents	4,938	—	(169)	4,769
Short-term investments	3,050	—	(37)	3,013
Inventories	9,255	—	(160)	9,095

EXHIBIT 4   (Continued)

	2011 (as reported)	Effects of IAS 19 (1)	Effects of IFRS 11 (2)	2011 (revised)
Trade and other receivables	13,340	—	(349)	12,991
Prepayments and accrued income	900	—	(21)	879
Derivative assets	731	—	(9)	722
Current income tax assets	1,094	—	(41)	1,053
Assets held for sale	16	—	—	16
Total current assets	**33,324**	**—**	**(786)**	**32,538**
Non-current assets				
Property, plant, and equipment	23,971	—	(511)	23,460
Goodwill	29,008	—	(395)	28,613
Intangible assets	9,356	—	(571)	8,785
Investments in associates and joint ventures	8,629	—	1,688	10,317
Financial assets	7,161	—	(8)	7,153
Employee benefits assets	127	—	—	127
Current income tax assets	39	—	—	39
Deferred tax assets	2,476	(5)	(63)	2,408
Total non-current assets	**80,767**	**(5)**	**140**	**80,902**
Total assets	**114,091**	**(5)**	**(646)**	**113,440**
Liabilities and equity				
Current liabilities				
Financial debt	16,100	—	(155)	15,945
Trade and other payables	13,584	—	(40)	13,544
Accruals and deferred income	2,909	—	(129)	2,780
Provisions	576	—	(1)	575
Derivative liabilities	646	—	(14)	632
Current income tax liabilities	1,417	—	(38)	1,379
Liabilities directly associated with assets held for sale	—	—	—	—
Total current liabilities	**35,232**	**—**	**(377)**	**34,855**
Non-current liabilities				
Financial debt	6,207	—	(42)	6,165
Employee benefits liabilities	7,105	(91)	(102)	6,912
Provisions	3,094	—	(15)	3,079
Deferred tax liabilities	2,060	18	(104)	1,974
Other payables	2,119	—	(6)	2,113
Total non-current liabilities	**20,585**	**(73)**	**(269)**	**20,243**
Total liabilities	**55,817**	**(73)**	**(646)**	**55,098**

(continued)

910 International Financial Statement Analysis

EXHIBIT 4 (Continued)

	2011 (as reported)	Effects of IAS 19 (1)	Effects of IFRS 11 (2)	2011 (revised)
Equity				
Share capital	330	—	—	330
Treasury shares	(6,722)	—	—	(6,722)
Translation reserve	(16,927)	—	—	(16,927)
Retained earnings and other reserves	80,116	68	—	80,184
Total equity attributable to shareholders of the parent	**56,797**	**68**	**—**	**56,865**
Non-controlling interests	1,477	—	—	1,477
Total equity	**58,274**	**68**	**—**	**58,342**
Total liabilities and equity	114,091	(5)	(646)	113,440

(1) IAS 19 Revised 2011—Employee Benefits was implemented in 2013, with comparative restatement made to January 1, 2012. This standard revised the calculation of benefit plan obligations. The January 1, 2012 adjustments were imposed on the December 31, 2011 balance sheet by the analyst, taken from Note 22 (Restatements and adjustments of 2012 comparatives) of the 2013 Annual Report.

(2) IFRS 11—Joint Arrangements was implemented in 2013, with comparative restatement made to January 1, 2012. Nestlé had used proportional consolidation for two of its joint arrangements (Cereal Partners Worldwide and Galderma), and the standard required that they be accounted for using the equity method of investments. The January 1, 2012 adjustments were imposed on the December 31, 2011 balance sheet by the analyst, taken from Note 22 (Restatements and adjustments of 2012 comparatives) of the 2013 Annual Report.

The analyst considers what information he needs for a DuPont analysis. He extracts the data shown in Exhibit 5 from Exhibits 2 and 3:

EXHIBIT 5 Data Needed for DuPont Analysis (CHF millions)

	2014	2013	2012	2011
Income Statement Data:				
Sales	91,612	92,158	89,721	
Operating profit (EBIT)	10,905	13,068	13,388	
Profit before taxes, associates, and joint ventures (EBT)	10,268	12,437	12,683	
Profit for the year	14,904	10,445	10,677	
Income from associates and joint ventures	8,003	1,264	1,253	
Profit, excluding associates and joint ventures	6,901	9,181	9,424	
Balance Sheet Data:				
Total assets	133,450	120,442	125,877	113,440
Investments in associates and joint ventures	8,649	12,315	11,586	10,317
Total assets, excluding associates and joint ventures	124,801	108,127	114,291	103,123
Total equity	71,884	64,139	62,664	58,342

The five-way decomposition of ROE is expanded to isolate the effects of the investment in associates in Nestlé's asset base and earnings. The necessary modifications to the reported financial data to isolate these effects are shown in Exhibit 5. Subtracting income from associates from the net income (profit for the year) gives the profits generated by Nestlé's own asset base. Subtracting the amount of investment in associates from total assets results in a figure that more closely represents Nestlé's own asset base. With this information, the analyst can assess the profitability and returns of the largest and most relevant part of the entire Nestlé entity: the core Nestlé company.

Exhibit 6 shows the results of expanding the DuPont analysis. The net profit margin component and the asset turnover component require adjustments to remove the impact of the associates on the return on assets. To adjust the net profit margin component, the analyst subtracts the associates' income from the net income and divides the result by sales. For 2014, the Nestlé-only net profit margin was 7.53% (= Profit excluding income from associates/Sales = 6,901/91,612). To adjust the asset turnover, the analyst subtracts the investment in associates from total assets to arrive at the assets used by the core Nestlé company. Sales divided by the average of the beginning and ending assets (excluding investment in associates) gives the Nestlé-only asset turnover. For 2014, the Nestlé-only asset turnover was 0.787 {= 91,612/[(108,127 + 124,801)/2] = 91,612/116,464}. Including the investment in associates in total assets, the asset turnover was 0.722 {= 91,612/[(120,442 + 133,450)/2] = 91,612/126,946}. The difference between the asset turnover based on unadjusted financial statement amounts and the Nestlé-only asset turnover gives the effect on total asset turnover of the investment in associates: a decrease of 0.065 in 2014.

The net profit margin can be decomposed into three components: EBIT margin × Tax burden × Interest burden. The tax and interest burdens indicate what is left for the company after the effects of taxes and interest, respectively. To adjust the tax burden component, the analyst divides profit (excluding income from associates) by profit before taxes and income from associates (EBT). For 2014, the tax burden was 67.21% (= 6,901/10,268). The interest burden is calculated by dividing the profit before taxes, associates, and joint ventures (EBT) by operating profit (EBIT). For 2014, the interest burden was 94.16% (= 10,268/10,905). The EBIT margin is earnings before interest and taxes (operating profit) divided by revenue (sales). For 2014, the EBIT margin was 11.90% (= 10,905/91,612).

Multiplying the three components together yields the Nestlé-only net profit margin. In 2014, the Nestlé-only net profit margin was 7.53% (= 67.21% × 94.16% × 11.90%). Calculating the net profit margin without excluding income from associates gives 16.27% (= Net income/Revenue = Profit for the year/Sales = 14,904/91,612), which is not representative of the Nestlé-only operations. Dividing the net profit margin by the net profit margin *without* the associates' income (16.27%/7.53% = 216.07%) quantifies the magnifying effect of the associates' income on Nestlé's own margins. The "Nestlé-only" entity earned 7.53% on every sale, but including the associates' income in net profit increases the net profit margins by 116.07% [(100.00% + 116.07%) × 7.53% = 16.27%]. A 16.27% level of profitability is not representative of what Nestlé's core operations can generate.

EXHIBIT 6   Expanded DuPont Analysis

	2014	2013	2012
Tax burden (excl. associates)	67.21%	73.82%	74.30%
× Interest burden	94.16%	95.17%	94.73%
× EBIT margin	11.90%	14.18%	14.92%

(continued)

EXHIBIT 6   (Continued)

	2014	2013	2012
= Net profit margin (excl. associates)	7.53%	9.96%	10.50%
× Associates' effect on net profit margin	216.07%	113.76%	113.33%
= **Net profit margin**	**16.27%**	**11.33%**	**11.90%**
Total asset turnover (excl. associates)	0.787	0.829	0.825
Effect of associates' investments on turnover	(0.065)	(0.081)	(0.075)
× **Total asset turnover**	**0.722**	**0.748**	**0.750**
= Return on assets	11.75%	8.47%	8.93%
× **Leverage**	**1.87**	**1.94**	**1.98**
= **Return on equity (ROE)**	**21.97%**	**16.44%**	**17.67%**
Traditional ROE calculation (CHF millions):			
Net income	14,904	10,445	10,677
÷ Average total equity	68,012	63,402	60,503
= **ROE**	**21.91%**	**16.47%**	**17.65%**

Note: Differences in ROE calculations because of rounding.

In 2012 and 2013, the net profit margin (including income from associates) was fairly stable at 11.90% and 11.33%, respectively. But it increased significantly in 2014—to 16.27%—as a result of the increase in income from associates attributable to the L'Oréal disposal and Galderma revaluation. The analyst, however, is interested in the ongoing operations of Nestlé, unaffected by such non-repeating types of gains. The net profit margin excluding income from associates shows a disturbing trend: It decreased each year in the 2012–2014 period. This finding prompts the analyst to try to identify a reason for the declining profitability of the Nestlé-only business. Searching the income statements and notes in the annual reports, he notices that Nestlé has recorded goodwill impairments over the period under study, with a particularly large one, CHF1,908 million, occurring in 2014. This impairment was related to Nestlé's acquisitions of ice cream and pizza businesses in the United States. He also notices that Nestlé has recorded provisions each year for restructuring activities, environmental liabilities, litigation reserves, and other activities. To see how much these events affected the Nestlé-only profitability, he constructs the table shown in Exhibit 7. He calls these events "unusual charges" for convenience of presentation.

The analyst notices that the adjusted profits and the adjusted profit margins were more stable over the three-year period than the profits and profit margins excluding associates. However, the adjusted profits and profit margins and the profits and profit margins excluding associates decreased over the same period. Although the provisions and impairment charges potentially explain the significant decrease in the Nestlé-only profit margins, in particular from 2013 to 2014, the analyst decides *not* to adjust the remaining DuPont analysis to exclude these charges. They involve decisions by management, they recur regularly, and they affect the returns to shareholders. In assessing the company's prospects, he believes that these charges are important variables that should not to be ignored.

EXHIBIT 7   Profitability Adjusted for Provisions and Impairment Charges (CHF millions)

	2014	2013	2012
Sales	91,612	92,158	89,721
Profit excluding income from associates (from Exhibit 5)	6,901	9,181	9,424
Impairment of goodwill	1,908	114	14
Total provisions for restructuring, environmental, litigation, and other (not tax-affected: assumed non-taxable in year of recognition)	920	862	618
Profit adjusted for unusual charges	9,729	10,157	10,056
Net profit margin: excl. associates, with all unusual charges incl.	7.53%	9.96%	10.50%
Net profit margin: excluding associates and unusual charges	10.62%	11.02%	11.21%
Profit margin consumed by unusual charges	3.09%	1.06%	0.71%

Returning to the DuPont analysis, he now realizes the significance of the associates' earnings to the entire Nestlé entity. The margin is greater in each year if the associates' earnings are included in net profit as opposed to looking at Nestlé alone. Consistently, the company's profit margins are smaller without the boost from associates' earnings. Asset turnover is consistently lower when assets include the investment in associates.

The adjustments thus far have isolated the operational aspects of Nestlé's performance and the assets that produced them from non-Nestlé operations. The financial leverage ratio has not been adjusted by the analyst in similar fashion to profit margin and asset turnover. The profit margin and asset turnover components of the DuPont analysis are relatively easy to consider when including or excluding associates: Both the Nestlé assets and the non-Nestlé assets produce a certain pre-tax return. Isolating those assets and their respective returns from each other makes it possible to see the contributions of each to the aggregate performance. It might be tempting to likewise adjust the financial leverage ratio by subtracting the investment in associates from total assets and equity, but the financial leverage component need not be adjusted. The analyst assumes that there will be no change in the Nestlé capital structure and that a similar blend of debt and equity in the company's capital structure finances the investment in associates' assets and the Nestlé-only assets.

From Exhibit 6, multiplying the three conventionally calculated components of ROE (net profit margin, total asset turnover, and leverage) yields the ROE when the effect of associates is included (top row of Exhibit 8). The ROE exhibits an overall increasing trend when examined without adjusting for investment in associates. The analyst wants to compare the ROE for Nestlé alone with the ROE including associates. Calculating the ROE on a Nestlé-only basis is done by multiplying the net profit margin excluding associates by the total asset turnover excluding associates by the financial leverage. For 2014, the Nestlé-only ROE was 11.08% (7.53% × 0.787 × 1.87 = 11.08%).

Exhibit 8 shows the ROE including and excluding the effects of associates. The difference between the two sets of ROE figures reveals the amount of ROE contribution from the associates. The trend in the ROE including associates, which shows a significant increase in 2014, is largely the result of the gains in 2014 from the transactions involving the investments in associates (exchange of L'Oréal shares for complete ownership of Galderma). Nestlé only shows a different trend: decreasing in each of the last two years.

EXHIBIT 8   ROE Performance Due to Investment in Associates

	2014 (%)	2013 (%)	2012 (%)
ROE including associates	21.97	16.44	17.67
Less Nestlé-only ROE	11.08	16.02	17.15
Associates' contribution to ROE	10.89	0.42	0.52

The analyst is particularly troubled by the sharp drop-off in the Nestlé-only ROE in 2014. He knows that there was an unusually large goodwill impairment charge in 2014, which may explain the sudden decrease. To see the role played by such unusual charges in the ROE trend, he reworks the Nestlé-only ROE figures on the basis of revised net profit margins (excluding associates and unusual charges) as shown in Exhibit 7. For 2014, the Nestlé-only ROE was 15.63% ($10.62\% \times 0.787 \times 1.87 = 15.63\%$). The results are shown in Exhibit 8A.

EXHIBIT 8A   Nestlé-Only ROE, with Unusual Charges Removed from Pre-tax Margins

	2014	2013	2012
Nestlé-only ROE	15.63%	17.73%	18.31%

Absent the unusual charges, the magnitude of the Nestlé-only ROE improved significantly in all three years, but the trend remained on a downward slope. This trend is a genuine concern to the analyst; the investment in associates might provide incremental returns, but he believes the biggest part of the entire entity should be the most significant driver of returns.

Underscoring the significance of the investment in associates—and the deterioration of the Nestlé-only business—is the increasing spread between the as-reported and the Nestlé-only net profit margins in a with- and without-associates comparison (Exhibit 9). The profit margins include all the previously identified unusual charges because the analyst believes that they should not be excluded. They are real costs of doing business and seem to recur; they were actually incurred by the managers, who should be accountable for their stewardship of the shareholders' resources.

EXHIBIT 9   Net Profit Margin Spread

	2014	2013	2012
Consolidated net profit margin based on as-reported figures	16.27%	11.33%	11.90%
Nestlé-only profit margin	7.53%	9.96%	10.50%
Spread	8.74%	1.37%	1.40%

The analyst decides to focus on learning more about the drivers of Nestlé-only growth and revenues. He makes a note to himself to investigate the valuation aspects of the investment holdings later.

2.3.2. Asset Base Composition
The analyst examines the composition of the balance sheet over time, as shown in Exhibit 10.

EXHIBIT 10   Asset Composition as a Percentage of Total Assets

	2014 (%)	2013 (%)	2012 (%)	2011 (%)
Cash and equivalents	5.6	5.3	4.5	4.2
Short-term investments	1.1	0.5	2.8	2.7
Inventories	6.9	7.0	7.1	8.0
Trade and other receivables	10.1	10.1	10.4	11.5
Other current	1.8	2.0	2.2	2.4
Total current	**25.5**	**24.9**	**27.0**	**28.8**
Property, plant, and equipment, net	21.3	22.3	21.1	20.7
Goodwill	25.9	25.8	26.0	25.2
Intangible assets	14.8	10.5	10.3	7.7
Other non-current	12.5	16.4	15.6	17.7
Total	**100.0**	**99.9***	**100.0**	**100.1***

* Does not add to 100% because of rounding.

Although he expected significant investments in current assets, inventory, and physical plant assets—given that Nestlé is a food manufacturer and marketer—he is surprised to see so much investment in intangible assets, indicating that Nestlé's success may depend, in part, on successful acquisitions. Apparently, the company has been actively acquiring companies in the last four years. Goodwill and intangible assets, hallmarks of a growth-by-acquisition strategy, composed 40.7% of total assets in 2014; at the end of 2011, they amounted to 32.9% of total assets. The investing section of the statement of cash flows (Exhibit 11) shows that there have been acquisitions.

EXHIBIT 11   Nestlé Investing Activities, 2012–2014 (CHF millions)

	Total	2014	2013	2012
Capital expenditure	(14,115)	(3,914)	(4,928)	(5,273)
Expenditure on intangible assets	(1,236)	(509)	(402)	(325)
Acquisition of businesses	(13,223)	(1,986)	(321)	(10,916)
Disposal of businesses	884	321	421	142
Investments (net of divestments) in associates and joint ventures	3,851	3,958	(28)	(79)
Outflows from non-current treasury investments	(573)	(137)	(244)	(192)
Inflows from non-current treasury investments	4,460	255	2,644	1,561
Inflows/(outflows) from short-term treasury investments	115	(962)	400	677
Other investing activities	668	(98)	852	(86)
Cash flow from investing activities	(19,169)	(3,072)	(1,606)	(14,491)
Acquisitions' percentage of total investing activities	69.0%	64.6%	20.0%	75.3%

Except for a slowdown in acquisitions in 2013, Nestlé had been very active in devoting resources to acquisitions. For the full three-year span, 69.0% of the cash expenditures for investing activities were devoted to acquisitions. The largest single acquisition occurred in 2012, when Nestlé acquired the nutritional business of Wyeth for CHF10,846 million; this acquisition was 74.8% (= 10,846/14,491) of the cash used for investing activities in 2012.

2.3.3. Capital Structure Analysis

From the DuPont analysis, the analyst understands that Nestlé's overall financial leverage was rather stable over the last three years, which does not completely satisfy the analyst's curiosity regarding Nestlé's financing strategies. He knows that one shortcoming of financial leverage as a capital structure metric is that it says nothing about the nature, or riskiness, of the different financing instruments used by a company. For example, the financial burden imposed by bond debt is more onerous and bears more consequences in the event of default than do employee benefit plan obligations.

He decides to investigate Nestlé's capital structure more deeply by constructing a chart on a common-size basis, shown in Exhibit 12. The DuPont analysis indicated that the company's financial leverage remained within a narrow range over the last three years, from a low of 1.87 to a high of 1.98. A look at Exhibit 12, however, shows that Nestlé has been making its capital structure financially riskier over the last four years. Not only is the proportion of equity financing decreasing—from 74.2% in 2011 to 71.5% in 2014—but long-term financial liabilities have become a significantly greater part of the capital mix, increasing to 12.3% in 2014 from 7.8% in 2011. The "other long-term liabilities" (primarily employee benefit plan obligations and provisions) decreased from 17.9% in 2011 to 16.2% in 2014.

EXHIBIT 12   Percentages of Long-Term Capital Structure

	2014	2013	2012	2011
Long-term financial liabilities	12.3	11.8	10.3	7.8
Other long-term liabilities	16.2	14.9	17.9	17.9
Total equity	71.5	73.3	71.8	74.2
Total long-term capital	100.0	100.0	100.0	99.9*

* Does not add to 100% because of rounding.

Given the increased leverage in the long-term capital structure, the analyst wonders whether there have also been changes in the company's working capital accounts. He decides to examine Nestlé's liquidity situation. From the financial statements in Exhibits 2 and 3, he constructs the table shown in Exhibit 13.

The analyst notices that the current and quick ratios improved slightly in 2014, after three years of relative stability. He also notices that the defensive interval ratio improved in 2014 after a significant decrease in 2013 from its prior levels. The improvements were modest; given the increase in long-term leverage, he was expecting more of a liquidity cushion in the working capital accounts. He found the cushion in that the speed of cash generation has been increasing: Since 2011, days' sales outstanding has decreased, as has days on hand of inventory, and the number of days payables has increased. In fact, the management of the working capital accounts has changed so much that Nestlé now has a negative eight days for its cash conversion cycle, mostly attributable to its steadily increasing delay in paying its vendors. In effect, Nestlé has been generating cash from its working capital accounts eight days before applying the cash to accounts payable.

EXHIBIT 13   Nestlé Working Capital Accounts and Ratios, 2011–2014

	2014	2013	2012	2011
Current ratio	1.03	0.91	0.88	0.93
Quick ratio	0.68	0.59	0.58	0.60
Defensive interval ratio*	106.6	91.9	110.0	110.5
Days sales outstanding (DSO)	51.1	50.0	53.0	54.7
Days on hand of inventory (DOH)	67.4	65.7	69.3	70.4
Number of days payables	(126.5)	(117.8)	(108.6)	(105.3)
Cash conversion cycle	(8.0)	(2.1)	13.7	19.8

* From Exhibit 2, for 2014: Daily cash expenditure = Expenses – Non-cash items = [Cost of goods sold + Distribution expenses + Marketing and administration expenses + R&D expenses – (Depreciation of PP&E + Amortization of intangible assets) + Net trading expenses – (Impairment of PP&E and intangible assets) + (Net other operating expenses – Impairment of goodwill) + Net financial expenses]/365 = [47,553 + 8,217 + 19,651 + 1,628 – 3,058 + 797 – 159 + (3,114 – 1,908) + 637]/365 = 209.5. The defensive interval ratio is 22,340/209.5 = 106.6.

2.3.4. Segment Analysis and Capital Allocation

The DuPont analysis showed the declining profitability of Nestlé in its core operations, leading the analyst to subsequently learn more about the composition of the assets and to study the company's financing. He knows that asset turnover has been slowing at Nestlé and that the company has been looking to acquisitions for growth. But he still wonders about the health of the different businesses under the Nestlé umbrella and how effectively management has allocated capital to them. DuPont analysis does not provide answers to these kinds of questions, and he knows there is more information in the financial statements that might shed light on how management allocates capital internally as opposed to making acquisitions.

To understand any geopolitical investment risks, as well as the economies in which Nestlé operates, the analyst wants to know which geographic areas are of the greatest importance to the company. One issue the analyst identifies is that Nestlé reports segment information by management responsibility and geographic area (hereafter referred to as "segment"), not by segments based exclusively on geographic areas. From the segment information in Exhibit 14, he notes that the sales and operating profit of the European segment decreased in absolute terms and as a percentage of total business in 2014 compared with 2012. The decrease in profits has been consistent over the period. The sales of the Americas segment have also become a smaller contributor to the whole company's revenue base in the same period and, like the European segment, have decreased slightly since 2012. The Americas operating profit has decreased consistently since 2012, and like the European segment, the Americas contribution to total operating profit in 2014 is a smaller proportion than in 2012. The Asia, Oceania, and Africa segment repeated the pattern: lower sales and operating profit, with a decrease in both measures in each of the two years following 2012. The smallest segment, Nestlé Waters, was not a true geographic segment. It showed minor growth in revenues and operating profit between

2012 and 2014 and contributed essentially the same proportion of sales and operating profit in 2014 as it did in 2012. Nestlé Nutrition grew significantly during the period: It contributed 10.5% of revenues in 2014 (only 8.8% in 2012), and its operating profit contributed 14.2% of revenues in 2014 compared with 11.2% in 2012. The analyst remembers that Nestlé acquired the Wyeth Nutritionals business in 2012, which would explain the solid growth. "Other businesses," which is a collectively large group of disparate businesses, also increased in importance between 2012 and 2014, accounting for 15.2% of sales in 2014 (13.2% in 2012) and 18.9% of operating profit (15.3% in 2012). Both measures (sales and operating profit) grew in 2014, and the analyst attributes that growth to Nestlé's gaining full control of Galderma in 2014.

EXHIBIT 14   Sales and EBIT by Segment (CHF millions)

Sales	2014		2013		2012		Year-to-Year % Change	
	Amount	% Total	Amount	% Total	Amount	% Total	2014	2013
Europe	15,175	*16.6*	15,567	*16.9*	15,388	*17.2*	−2.5	1.2
Americas	27,277	*29.8*	28,358	*30.8*	28,613	*31.9*	−3.8	−0.9
Asia, Oceania, and Africa	18,272	*19.9*	18,851	*20.5*	18,875	*21.0*	−3.1	−0.1
Nestlé Waters	7,390	*8.1*	7,257	*7.9*	7,174	*8.0*	1.8	1.2
Nestlé Nutrition	9,614	*10.5*	9,826	*10.7*	7,858	*8.8*	−2.2	25.0
Other businesses[a]	13,884	*15.2*	12,299	*13.3*	11,813	*13.2*	12.9	4.1
	91,612	*100.0*	92,158	*100.0*	89,721	*100.0*		

Trading operating profit	2014		2013		2012		Year-to-Year % Change	
	Amount	% Total	Amount	% Total	Amount	% Total	2014	2013
Europe	2,327	16.6	2,331	16.6	2,363	17.6	−0.2	−1.4
Americas	5,117	36.5	5,162	36.7	5,346	39.7	−0.9	−3.4
Asia, Oceania, and Africa	3,408	24.3	3,562	25.4	3,579	26.6	−4.3	−0.5
Nestlé Waters	714	5.1	665	4.7	640	4.8	7.4	3.9
Nestlé Nutrition	1,997	14.2	1,961	14.0	1,509	11.2	1.8	30.0
Other businesses[a]	2,654	18.9	2,175	15.5	2,064	15.3	22.0	5.4
Unallocated items	(2,198)	−15.7	(1,809)	−12.9	(2,037)	−15.1	21.5	−11.2
	14,019	100.0	14,047	100.0	13,464	100.0		

[a] Group mainly includes Nespresso, Nestlé Professional, Nestlé Health Science, and Nestlé Skin Health.

For several reasons, the analyst is somewhat frustrated by the segment information presented by Nestlé. He would like to look at trends over more than just three years, but the change in accounting principles in 2013 (for IFRS 19) was not carried back in the segment information prior to 2012. That accounting change eliminated the proportional consolidation method of accounting for joint ventures and made the 2011 segment information non-comparable with the figures presented for 2012 and later. The earlier amounts included proportional amounts of sales and operating profits for the segments, and a comparison with later years would be flawed.

Another problem with the segment information is that it is not defined by category with fully geographic information or product information. The analyst notes that three geographically classified segments accounted for 66.3% of revenues in 2014 and 70.1% in 2012; the operating profit for the same three segments amounted to 77.4% in 2014 and 83.9% in 2012. Thus, these segments are declining in importance to Nestlé as a whole, whereas Nestlé Waters and Other businesses are increasing in size and importance. Yet, it would seem likely that both of these segments have geographically different operations as well, which are not being accounted for in the other three geographic segments. These segments are growing in relevance, and more information about them would be useful. For instance, the Other businesses segment includes a coffee product line, professional products, health care products, and skin care products. Together, they amount to almost 19% of operating profit, yet they seem unlikely to have similar distribution channels, profitability levels, and growth potential.

The segment information is presented on the basis that management uses to make decisions. The analyst moves on with his segment analysis and evaluation of capital allocation, gathering the segment information shown in Exhibit 15 regarding Nestlé's capital expenditures and assets.

EXHIBIT 15   Asset and Capital Expenditure Segment Information (CHF millions)

	Assets*			Capital Expenditures		
	2014	2013	2012	2014	2013	2012
Europe	11,308	11,779	11,804	747	964	1,019
Americas	20,915	21,243	22,485	1,039	1,019	1,073
Asia, Oceania, and Africa	15,095	14,165	14,329	697	1,280	1,564
Nestlé Waters	6,202	6,046	6,369	308	377	407
Nestlé Nutrition	24,448	22,517	24,279	363	430	426
Other businesses[a]	21,345	9,564	9,081	573	642	550
	99,313	85,314	88,347	3,727	4,712	5,039

*Assets do not equal total assets on the balance sheet because of inter-segment assets and non-segment assets.
[a]Group mainly includes Nespresso, Nestlé Professional, Nestlé Health Science, and Nestlé Skin Health.

Using the information from Exhibit 14 to calculate EBIT margins, as well as the information about the asset and capital expenditure distribution from Exhibit 15, the analyst constructs the table in Exhibit 16, ranking by descending order of EBIT profitability in 2014.

EXHIBIT 16   EBIT Margin, Asset, and Capital Expenditure Proportions by Segment

	EBIT Margin %			% of Total Assets			% of Total Capital Expenditures		
	2014	2013	2012	2014	2013	2012	2014	2013	2012
Nestlé Nutrition	20.77	19.96	19.20	24.6	26.4	27.5	9.7	9.1	8.5
Other businesses[a]	19.12	17.68	17.47	21.5	11.2	10.3	15.4	13.6	10.9
Americas	18.76	18.20	18.68	21.1	24.9	25.5	27.9	21.6	21.3
Asia, Oceania, and Africa	18.65	18.90	18.96	15.2	16.6	16.2	18.7	27.2	31.0
Europe	15.33	14.97	15.36	11.4	13.8	13.4	20.0	20.5	20.2
Nestlé Waters	9.66	9.16	8.92	6.2	7.1	7.2	8.3	8.0	8.1
				100.0	100.0	100.1*	100.0	100.0	100.0

*Does not add to 100% because of rounding.
[a]Group mainly includes Nespresso, Nestlé Professional, Nestlé Health Science, and Nestlé Skin Health.

Although the segmentation is not purely geographic, the analyst can still make some judgments about the allocation of capital. On the premise that the largest investments in assets require a similar proportion of capital expenditures, he calculates ratios of the capital expenditure proportion to the total asset proportion for the last three years and compares them with the current EBIT profitability ranking. The resulting table is shown in Exhibit 17.

EXHIBIT 17   Ratio of Capital Expenditure Percentage to Total Asset Percentage Ranked by EBIT Margin

	EBIT Margin %	Ratio of Total Capital Expenditure % to Total Asset %		
	2014	2014	2013	2012
Nestlé Nutrition	20.77	0.39	0.34	0.31
Other businesses[a]	19.12	0.72	**1.21**	**1.06**
Americas	18.76	**1.32**	0.87	0.84
Asia, Oceania, and Africa	18.65	**1.23**	**1.64**	**1.91**
Europe	15.33	**1.75**	**1.49**	**1.51**
Nestlé Waters	9.66	**1.34**	**1.13**	**1.13**

[a] Group mainly includes Nespresso, Nestlé Professional, Nestlé Health Science, and Nestlé Skin Health.

A ratio of 1 indicates that the segment's proportion of capital expenditures is the same as its proportion of total assets. A ratio of *less than* 1 indicates that the segment is being allocated a lesser proportion of capital expenditures than its proportion of total assets; if a trend develops, the segment will become less significant over time. A ratio of *greater than* 1 indicates the company is growing the segment; the segment is receiving a "growth allocation" of capital spending. Comparing the ratio with the EBIT margin percentage gives the analyst an idea of whether the company is investing its capital in the most profitable segments. (In Exhibit 17, the ratios greater than 1 are bolded for ease of viewing.)

Equipped with these premises, the analyst is puzzled by the capital allocation taking place within Nestlé. The most profitable segment is Nestlé Nutrition, but over the last three years, it has received the lowest proportion of capital expenditures. The company has invested in the nutrition segment by acquisition, such as the Wyeth Nutritionals business in 2012. One would expect that a more substantial operation would require more capital expenditures on maintenance. The capital expenditures for the nutrition segment have increased only nominally since 2012.

The Other businesses segment is the next most profitable segment in EBIT margin terms. The analyst has difficulty understanding just why the profit margins are high in this segment because of the variety of businesses it contains. It appears that the company's managers are allocating capital to it in a significant way. Although it did not receive a "growth allocation" of capital expenditures in 2014, it received a growth allocation in the previous two years. The Americas segment and the Asia, Oceania, and Africa segment have similar EBIT margins, which are in the same range as those of the Nestlé Nutrition and Other businesses segments. Given their profitability levels and substantial operations, the analyst is encouraged to see that they are receiving "growth allocations" of capital spending.

Less encouraging, however, is the past and continuing significant allocation of capital spending to the European segment. Even more questionable is the high proportional allocation of capital spending to the Nestlé Waters segment, which has had the lowest profit margins. The analyst is uncomfortable with growth investments in such a low-return business but notes that the absolute levels of capital expenditures are the lowest of all the segments in each year.

In a worst-case scenario, if the company were to continue making growth allocations of capital toward the lowest-margined businesses, such as Europe and Nestlé Waters, the overall Nestlé-only returns might be affected negatively. As a result, Nestlé might become more dependent on its investment in associates to sustain performance.

The analyst knows that accrual performance measures, such as EBIT, can produce results that do not indicate an entity's ability to generate cash flow, and he wonders whether this limitation has any effect on Nestlé management's capital allocation decisions. He also knows that at the segment level, cash flow information is not publicly available. He decides to at least approximate cash flow by adding depreciation expense to operating profit and then relate the approximated cash flow to the average total assets of each segment. This approach provides an approximation of cash return relative to the continued investment in a particular segment.

The analyst combines the segment operating profit from Exhibit 14 and the segment depreciation and amortization in Exhibit 18 to estimate the segment cash generation shown in Exhibit 18. Because he wants to eliminate the effects of any investment peaks or valleys, he also averages the total assets for each segment in Exhibit 18. The average total assets in 2012 include the 2011 total assets that were prepared on a pre–IFRS 19 basis, for which no adjustment is available. The analyst is aware of the irreconcilable difference but believes that the averaging of the two years' amounts will help dilute the difference. He notes that if any resulting measures based on 2011 data points appear to be outliers, he will dismiss them.

EXHIBIT 18   Segment Depreciation and Amortization, Segment Cash Generation, and Average Assets (CHF millions)

	Depreciation and Amortization			Segment Cash Generation			Average Total Assets*		
	2014	2013	2012	2014	2013	2012	2014	2013	2012
Europe	473	517	533	2,800	2,848	2,896	11,544	11,792	11,683
Americas	681	769	899	5,798	5,931	6,245	21,079	21,864	22,783
Asia, Oceania, and Africa	510	520	553	3,918	4,082	4,132	14,630	14,247	14,068
Nestlé Waters	403	442	491	1,117	1,107	1,131	6,124	6,208	6,486
Nestlé Nutrition	330	337	176	2,327	2,298	1,685	23,483	23,398	18,564
Other businesses[a]	525	437	295	3,179	2,612	2,359	15,455	9,323	10,009

*Average of total assets at beginning and end of the year.
[a]Group mainly includes Nespresso, Nestlé Professional, Nestlé Health Science, and Nestlé Skin Health.

In Exhibit 19, the analyst computes each segment's cash operating return on total assets and compares the results with the 2014 ranking of capital expenditures (Exhibit 17) as well as the EBIT margins. They are ranked in descending order of the ratio of capital expenditure percentage to percentage of total assets. The lighter shading indicates the highest EBIT margin and cash return on assets for each year, and the darker shading indicates the lowest EBIT margin and cash return on assets for each year.

EXHIBIT 19   Segment Cash Operating Return on Assets

	2014		Segment Cash Return on Average Total Assets		
	Capex %/ Asset %	EBIT %	2014 (%)	2013 (%)	2012 (%)
Europe	1.75	15.3	24.3	24.2	24.8
Nestlé Waters	1.34	9.7	18.2	17.8	17.4
Americas	1.32	18.8	27.5	27.1	27.4
Asia, Oceania, and Africa	1.23	18.7	26.8	28.7	29.4
Other businesses[a]	0.72	19.1	20.6	28.0	23.6
Nestlé Nutrition	0.39	20.8	9.9	9.8	9.1

[a] Group mainly includes Nespresso, Nestlé Professional, Nestlé Health Science, and Nestlé Skin Health.

The analyst is surprised to see that the Nestlé Nutrition segment, which has the highest EBIT profit margin, consistently has the lowest cash return on total assets. When he looks at the segments with respect to EBIT margins, he is disappointed with the allocation of capital spending to Nestlé Nutrition, thinking that it is too low. When he looks at it using the cash return on total assets measure, the low allocation of spending makes much more sense. He is pleased to see that the segments with the highest cash return on total assets each year—the Americas and the Asia, Oceania, and Africa segments—are receiving growth allocations of capital spending. He is also encouraged that the European segment, though a poor performer with respect to EBIT margin, has cash returns on total assets that are competitive with the other segments and far ahead of Nestlé Waters and Nestlé Nutrition. Even Nestlé Waters, which had not appeared very attractive with respect to EBIT margin, is generating strong cash returns on total assets. The exercise restores the analyst's confidence that management is allocating capital in a rational manner. It makes sense to him that if management makes capital budgeting decisions on a cash flow basis, they should be evaluated on a cash flow basis also.

He decides to look at Nestlé's capital allocation process from a product group standpoint. The sales and EBIT information is shown in Exhibit 20. From the table, he notes that the Nutrition and Health Science product group is the only one with significant growth in either sales or EBIT, and that is the segment in which the company has been making its acquisitions in the last few years. He also notes that the EBIT margin for the Nutrition and Health Science product group has increased in each of the last two years, and although it is among the highest over the last three years, the Powdered and Liquid Beverages product group has consistently shown higher EBIT margins. The Powdered and Liquid Beverages product group EBIT margins far exceed the lowest-ranking EBIT margins of the Water product group.

Unfortunately for purposes of his analysis, Nestlé does not provide capital expenditure information by product group. Compared with the segment analysis he performed, the analyst's scope is more limited in examining product groups. All that can be done is to look at the return on assets with respect to EBIT rather than on a cash-generated basis. Nevertheless, the analyst decides to work with all the available information. To further examine capital allocation decisions, he gathers the asset information by product group from the financial statements, as shown in Exhibit 21. The reported total assets differ by segment and product group presentation because Nestlé reports its assets on an *average* basis for product groups and on a *year-end* basis for segments. A significant amount of assets is unallocated to segments, but there is no unallocated amount by product group. He calculates the EBIT return on assets as EBIT divided by average assets and determines the proportion of total average assets devoted to each product group. The highest EBIT percentage, EBIT return on assets, and percentage of total assets each year are lightly shaded, and the lowest are shaded darker.

EXHIBIT 20   Sales and EBIT Segment Information by Product Group (CHF millions)

Sales	2014	% Total	2013	% Total	2012	% Total	Year-to-Year % Change 2014	2013
Powdered and Liquid Beverages	20,302	22.2	20,495	22.2	20,248	22.6	−0.9	1.2
Water	6,875	7.5	6,773	7.3	6,747	7.5	1.5	0.4
Milk Products and Ice Cream	16,743	18.3	17,357	18.8	17,344	19.3	−3.5	0.1
Nutrition and Health Science	13,046	14.2	11,840	12.8	9,737	10.9	10.2	21.6
Prepared Dishes and Cooking Aids	13,538	14.8	14,171	15.4	14,394	16.0	−4.5	−1.5
Confectionery	9,769	10.7	10,283	11.2	10,441	11.6	−5.0	−1.5
Pet Care	11,339	12.4	11,239	12.2	10,810	12.0	0.9	4.0
	91,612	100.0	92,158	100.0	89,721	100.0		

EBIT								
Powdered and Liquid Beverages	4,685	33.4	4,649	33.1	4,445	33.0	0.8	4.6
Water	710	5.1	678	4.8	636	4.7	4.7	6.6
Milk Products and Ice Cream	2,701	19.3	2,632	18.7	2,704	20.1	2.6	−2.7
Nutrition and Health Science	2,723	19.4	2,228	15.9	1,778	13.2	22.2	25.3
Prepared Dishes and Cooking Aids	1,808	12.9	1,876	13.4	2,029	15.1	−3.6	−7.5
Confectionery	1,344	9.6	1,630	11.6	1,765	13.1	−17.5	−7.6
Pet Care	2,246	16.0	2,163	15.4	2,144	15.9	3.8	0.9
Unallocated items	(2,198)	−15.7	(1,809)	−12.9	(2,037)	−15.1	21.5	−11.2
	14,019	100.0	14,047	100.0	13,464	100.0		

EBIT margin	2014	2013	2012
Powdered and Liquid Beverages	23.1%	22.7%	22.0%
Water	10.3%	10.0%	9.4%
Milk Products and Ice Cream	16.1%	15.2%	15.6%
Nutrition and Health Science	20.9%	18.8%	18.3%
Prepared Dishes and Cooking Aids	13.4%	13.2%	14.1%
Confectionery	13.8%	15.9%	16.9%
Pet Care	19.8%	19.2%	19.8%
Total	15.3%	15.2%	15.0%

EXHIBIT 21 Asset Segment Information by Product Group (CHF millions)

	Average Assets			EBIT %	EBIT Return on Assets			% Total Assets		
	2014	2013	2012	2014	2014	2013	2012	2014	2013	2012
Powdered and Liquid Beverages	11,599	11,044	10,844	23.1%	40.4%	42.1%	41.0%	11.6%	11.5%	12.4%
Water	5,928	6,209	6,442	10.3%	12.0%	10.9%	9.9%	6.0%	6.4%	7.4%
Milk Products and Ice Cream	14,387	14,805	14,995	16.1%	18.8%	17.8%	18.0%	14.4%	15.4%	17.1%
Nutrition and Health Science	32,245	28,699	19,469	20.9%	8.4%	7.8%	9.1%	32.4%	29.8%	22.2%
Prepared Dishes and Cooking Aids	13,220	13,289	13,479	13.4%	13.7%	14.1%	15.1%	13.3%	13.8%	15.4%
Confectionery	7,860	8,190	8,343	13.8%	17.1%	19.9%	21.2%	7.9%	8.5%	9.5%
Pet Care	14,344	14,064	13,996	19.8%	15.7%	15.4%	15.3%	14.4%	14.6%	16.0%
	99,583	96,300	87,568	15.3%	14.1%	14.6%	15.4%	100.0%	100.0%	100.0%

The analyst uses this information to make some important observations:

- The Nutrition and Health Science product group—which the company has been investing in over the last several years—has the lowest EBIT return on assets in each of the last three years and makes up the greatest portion of total assets.
- The EBIT return on assets for the Nutrition and Health Science product group is even lower than that of the Water product group, which has the lowest EBIT margin.
- The Nutrition and Health Science product group's EBIT return on assets is well below the total company's EBIT return on assets (8.4% versus 14.1% in 2014, 7.8% versus 14.6% in 2013, and 9.1% versus 15.4% in 2012).
- The Nutrition and Health Science product group drags down the overall return in each year as it becomes a bigger part of the whole.
- The EBIT return on assets is highest for the Powdered and Liquid Beverages product group, possibly because it might not need much in the way of assets or capital spending: It is one of the lesser components of total assets. Furthermore, it has the highest EBIT margin of all the product groups. Given the high EBIT margin, the high EBIT return on assets, and the low dedication of total assets, the analyst wonders whether the company is allocating capital among its product offerings effectively. It would make sense to devote as many resources as possible to where returns are best.
- He also wonders about management's capital allocation skills regarding acquisitions. The EBIT return on assets in the Nutrition and Health Science product group is weak, and the company has been making acquisitions in that group. He finds it troubling that Nestlé took a goodwill impairment charge of CHF1,908 million in 2014—something directly related to management's skill in making past acquisitions.

2.3.5. Accruals and Earnings Quality

At this point, the information reviewed by the analyst has not increased his enthusiasm for Nestlé's operating and capital allocation prowess. He considers a worst-case possibility: Could the company try to make up for weak operating performance by manipulating accounting inputs? He makes it a point to understand whether accruals play a role in the company's performance.

He decides to examine the balance-sheet-based accruals and the cash-flow-based accruals over the last few years. From the Nestlé financial statements, he assembles the information and intermediate calculations shown in Exhibit 22.

The analyst calculates the balance-sheet-based and cash-flow-based accruals ratios, which are measures of financial reporting quality.[4] The ratios are calculated as follows:

Balance sheet accruals ratio for time $t = (NOA_t - NOA_{t-1})/[(NOA_t + NOA_{t-1})/2]$, and
Cash flow accruals ratio for time $t = [NI_t - (CFO_t + CFI_t)]/[(NOA_t + NOA_{t-1})/2]$,

where NI is net income, CFO is cash flow from operations, and CFI is cash flow from investing.
The accruals ratios for the last three years are shown in Exhibit 23.

---

[4]If you are interested in subcomponents of accrual activity, simply focus on the relevant line item from the balance sheet. For example, looking at the change in net receivables over a fiscal period deflated by average NOA will give you a sense of the magnitude of accrued revenue attributable to net credit sales.

EXHIBIT 22 Selected Information from Balance Sheet and Statement of Cash Flows (CHF millions)

	2014	2013	2012	2011
Balance sheet accrual info:				
Total assets	133,450	120,442	125,877	113,440
Cash and short-term investments	8,881	7,053	9,296	7,782
Operating assets (A)	124,569	113,389	116,581	105,658
Total liabilities	61,566	56,303	63,213	55,098
Long-term debt	12,396	10,363	9,008	6,165
Debt in current liabilities	8,810	11,380	18,408	15,945
Operating liabilities (B)	40,360	34,560	35,797	32,988
Net operating assets (NOA) [(A) − (B)]	84,209	78,829	80,784	72,670
Balance-sheet-based aggregate accruals (year-to-year change in NOA)	5,380	(1,955)	8,114	6,218
Average NOA	81,519	79,807	76,727	69,561
Statement of cash flows accrual info:				
Profit from continuing operations	14,904	10,445	10,677	
Operating cash flow	(14,700)	(14,992)	(15,668)	
Investing cash flow	3,072	1,606	14,491	
Cash-flow-based aggregate accruals	3,276	(2,941)	9,500	

EXHIBIT 23 Accruals Ratios (CHF millions)

	2014	2013	2012
Balance-sheet-based aggregate accruals (year-to-year change in NOA)	5,380	(1,955)	8,114
Divided by: Average NOA	81,519	79,807	76,727
Balance-sheet-based accruals ratio	**6.6%**	**−2.4%**	**10.6%**
Cash-flow-based aggregate accruals	3,276	(2,941)	9,500
Divided by: Average NOA	81,519	79,807	76,727
Cash-flow-based accruals ratio	**4.0%**	**−3.7%**	**12.4%**

The analyst notes that the absolute level of accruals on the balance sheet is minor relative to the size of the operating assets, on either an ending balance basis or an average basis. Similarly, the fluctuation in the balance-sheet-based accruals ratio is low. The analyst would have been more concerned if the absolute levels of the accruals ratio were high; even more worrisome would have been if they were consistently trending higher. That was not the case. The cash-flow-based accruals ratio exhibits a similar pattern. For the most recent two years, both ratios are lower than in 2012 and indicate that accruals are not a large factor in the financial results. The analyst still decides to examine the quality of Nestlé's cash flow and its relationship to net income.

2.3.6. Cash Flow Relationships

He begins his analysis with the compilation of Nestlé's statements of cash flows shown in Exhibit 24.

EXHIBIT 24   Nestlé's Statement of Cash Flows, 2012–2014 (CHF millions)

	2014	2013	2012
Operating activities			
Operating profit	10,905	13,068	13,388
Non-cash items of income and expense	6,323	4,352	3,217
Cash flow before changes in operating assets and liabilities	17,228	17,420	16,605
Decrease/(increase) in working capital	(114)	1,360	2,015
Variation of other operating assets and liabilities	85	(574)	(95)
Cash generated from operations	17,199	18,206	18,525
Net cash flows from treasury activities	(356)	(351)	(324)
Taxes paid	(2,859)	(3,520)	(3,118)
Dividends and interest from associates and joint ventures	716	657	585
Operating cash flow	**14,700**	**14,992**	**15,668**
Investing activities			
Capital expenditure	(3,914)	(4,928)	(5,273)
Expenditure on intangible assets	(509)	(402)	(325)
Acquisition of businesses	(1,986)	(321)	(10,916)
Disposal of businesses	321	421	142
Investments (net of divestments) in associates and joint ventures	3,958	(28)	(79)
Outflows from non-current treasury investments	(137)	(244)	(192)
Inflows from non-current treasury investments	255	2,644	1,561
Inflows/(outflows) from short-term treasury investments	(962)	400	677
Other investing activities	(98)	852	(86)
Cash flow from investing activities	**(3,072)**	**(1,606)**	**(14,491)**
Financing activities			
Dividends paid to shareholders of the parent	(6,863)	(6,552)	(6,213)
Dividends paid to non-controlling interests	(356)	(328)	(204)
Acquisition (net of disposal) of non-controlling interests	(49)	(337)	(165)
Purchase of treasury shares	(1,721)	(481)	(532)
Sale of treasury shares	104	60	1,199
Inflows from bonds and other non-current financial debt	2,202	3,814	5,226
Outflows from bonds and other non-current financial debt	(1,969)	(2,271)	(1,650)
Inflows/(outflows) from current financial debt	(1,985)	(6,063)	2,325

(continued)

EXHIBIT 24   (Continued)

	2014	2013	2012
Cash flow from financing activities	(10,637)	(12,158)	(14)
Currency retranslations	42	(526)	(219)
Increase/(decrease) in cash and cash equivalents	1,033	702	944
Cash and cash equivalents at beginning of year	6,415	5,713	4,769
Cash and cash equivalents at end of year	7,448	6,415	5,713

The analyst's most pressing concerns include the following: Are Nestlé's operating earnings backed by cash flow? Are the accrual measures telling the whole story? Are the operating earnings the result of accounting choices? To convince himself of the representativeness of the Nestlé earnings, he first compares the cash generated by operations with the operating profit as shown in Exhibit 25. The amounts in Exhibit 25 are found in the cash flow statements in Exhibit 24.

EXHIBIT 25   Operating Cash Flow to Operating Profit, 2012–2014 (CHF millions)

	2014	2013	2012
Cash generated from operations	17,199	18,206	18,525
Operating profit	10,905	13,068	13,388
Cash generated from operations/Operating profit	1.58	1.39	1.38

The cash generated from operations is comparable to accrual basis operating income *but on a cash flow basis*. If the cash flow generated by operations was significantly or consistently less than operating profit, one would have reason to be suspicious about the quality of the operating profit. The analyst is encouraged by the fact that the cash generated from operations substantially exceeded the operating profit in each of the last three years.

Knowing that Nestlé has made a number of acquisitions, the analyst decides to examine the relationship between operating cash flow and total assets. *Cash flow* is a measure of the operational success of the company's investment projects: Successful investments generate cash rather than absorbing it. *Total assets* reflect the sum total of management's resource allocations over time. Cash generated by total assets indicates the kind of cash return that is generated by all investments. The relationship is shown in Exhibit 26.

EXHIBIT 26   Ratio of Operating Cash Flow to Total Assets, 2012–2014 (CHF millions)

	2014	2013	2012
Cash generated from operations	17,199	18,206	18,525
Average total assets	126,946	123,160	119,659
Cash return on total assets	13.5%	14.8%	15.5%

Again, the analyst finds himself concerned about the effectiveness of management's asset allocation decisions. Although the 13.5% cash return on total assets is a high return on investment, the trend is declining. The analyst thinks back to the 2014 goodwill impairment and the poor EBIT return on assets in the Nutrition and Health Science product group, in which acquisitions have been occurring lately.

Given the negative trend in asset returns, the analyst looks at Nestlé's liquidity and funding ability relative to cash flow. He decides to compare cash flow with reinvestment, debt, and debt-servicing capacity, as shown in Exhibit 27.

The analyst sees that reinvestment needs have been covered by cash flow by a factor of 3.89 in 2014, 3.42 in 2013, and 3.31 in 2012. Even better, the trend is improving.

He also sees that based on the relationship of cash flow to total debt, the company is not highly leveraged, with cash generated from operations at 78.3% of total debt at the end of 2014. The ratio is high enough to indicate that additional borrowing could be arranged should an investment opportunity arise. Furthermore, the analyst notes that Nestlé has the capacity to pay off its debt in approximately two years even while maintaining its current reinvestment policy [21,963/(17,199 − 4,423)].

Finally, the cash flow interest coverage ratio indicates more than satisfactory financial strength in the current year, with cash flow 33.2 times the interest paid. Like the ratio of cash flow to total debt, it indicates that the company has sufficient financial capacity to add more debt if there is an investment opportunity.

EXHIBIT 27   Ratio of Operating Cash Flow to Reinvestment, Debt, and Debt-Servicing Capacity, 2012–2014 (CHF millions)

	2014	2013	2012
Cash flow to reinvestment: *			
Cash generated from operations	17,199	18,206	18,525
Capital expenditures	3,914	4,928	5,273
Expenditure on intangible assets	509	402	325
Total reinvestment spending	4,423	5,330	5,598
Ratio of cash flow to reinvestment	**3.89**	**3.42**	**3.31**
Cash flow to total debt:			
Cash generated from operations	17,199	18,206	18,525
Current debt (short-term financial liabilities)	8,810	11,380	18,408
Current derivative liabilities	757	381	423
Long-term debt (long-term financial liabilities)	12,396	10,363	9,008
Total debt	21,963	22,124	27,839
Ratio of cash flow to total debt	**78.3%**	**82.3%**	**66.5%**
Cash flow interest coverage:			
Cash generated from operations	17,199	18,206	18,525
Cash interest paid	518	505	559
Cash flow interest coverage	**33.2**	**36.1**	**33.1**

*Information is from Exhibit 24.

2.3.7. Decomposition and Analysis of the Company's Valuation

At this point, the analyst believes he has obtained sufficient information about the company's sources of earnings and returns on shareholders' equity, its capital structure, the results of its capital allocation decisions, and its earnings quality. Before he makes his report to the portfolio manager, he wants to study the company's market valuation. During his reading of the annual reports, he noted that Nestlé has a significant equity position (23.4%) in L'Oréal (Paris exchange: OR), a French cosmetics company. L'Oréal is accounted for in the financial statements as an investment in associates because Nestlé's ownership position does not give it control. Although L'Oréal contributes to the earnings of Nestlé as a whole, it is also valued separately in the public markets, and its discrete valuations may be very different from its embedded Nestlé valuation. To determine the value that the market places solely on Nestlé operations, the analyst first removes the value of the L'Oréal holding from the Nestlé market value, as shown in Exhibit 28.

EXHIBIT 28   Nestlé Market Value without L'Oréal as of December 31, 2014 (Currency in millions, except share prices)

L'Oréal value:	
31 Dec 2014 share price	€139.30
Shares held by Nestlé (millions)	129.881
L'Oréal holding value	€18,092
31 Dec EUR/CHF rate	1.202
L'Oréal holding value	CHF21,747
Nestlé market value, with and without L'Oréal:	
Nestlé 29 Dec 2014 share price	CHF72.95
Shares outstanding (millions)	3,168.400
Nestlé market capitalization	CHF231,135
Value of L'Oréal holding	(21,747)
Implied value of Nestlé operations	CHF209,388
Pro rata market value:	
L'Oréal	9.4%
Nestlé	90.6%
	100.0%

The value of the L'Oréal holding is slightly less than 10% of the value of Nestlé's market capitalization. The analyst now wants to remove the earnings of L'Oréal from the earnings of the combined entity (Exhibit 29) to make a price-to-earnings comparison for Nestlé earnings alone. For L'Oréal, this comparison is simple: Nestlé discloses in its annual report that L'Oréal has contributed CHF934 million to current year earnings. After isolating the different earnings sources, the analyst prepares the table shown in Exhibit 30, which compares the different market values and price-to-earnings ratios.

EXHIBIT 29   Calculation of Nestlé Earnings without
L'Oréal as of December 31, 2014 (CHF millions)

Calculation of Nestlé standalone earnings:	2014
Nestlé consolidated earnings	14,904
Less: L'Oréal earnings	(934)
Nestlé standalone earnings	13,970
Less: Non-controlling interests	(448)
Nestlé standalone earnings to shareholders	13,522

At the time of the analysis (early 2015), Nestlé's common stock traded at a price-to-earnings multiple of 16.0 based on its year-end market value of CHF231,135 million and trailing earnings (attributable to controlling interests) of CHF14,456 million: a discount of 20% to the price-to-earnings multiple of 19.9 for the S&P 500 Index at year-end 2014. Once the earnings and available market value of the L'Oréal holding are taken out of the price-to-earnings valuation, the shares of the "Nestlé-only" company are selling at a slightly higher discount: At 15.5 times earnings, the discount to the overall market's price-to-earnings multiple was a steeper 22%. At first, the analyst is surprised by Nestlé's discount to the market multiple, given that the company has consistently demonstrated meaningful cash flows and earnings and possesses low financial leverage. He considers whether the discount might be attributable to Nestlé's slipping core profitability. The analyst concludes that Nestlé shares may be discounted by the market because investors may be developing a skeptical attitude toward the company.

EXHIBIT 30   Comparison of Decomposed Nestlé Earnings and Price-to-Earnings Ratios

Earnings (CHF millions)	Market Value	Earnings (Group Shareholder Level)	Respective Price-to-Earnings Ratios
L'Oréal	21,747	934	23.3
Implied Nestlé-only	209,388	13,522	15.5
Actual earnings available to Nestlé parent company shareholders	231,135	14,456	16.0

Recap (%):	Market Value	Earnings
L'Oréal	9.4	6.5
Implied Nestlé-only	90.6	93.5
	100.0	100.0

At this point, the analyst believes that he has processed and analyzed the data sufficiently to pull together his findings and make his report to the portfolio manager.

2.4. Phase 5: Develop and Communicate Conclusions and Recommendations (e.g., with an Analysis Report)

As a result of the analyses performed, the analyst has gathered sufficient evidence regarding many of Nestlé's operational and financial characteristics and believes he is able to address the concerns initially expressed by the portfolio manager. Summary points he will cover in his report are divided into two classes: support for an investment in Nestlé shares and causes for concern.

2.4.1. Support for an Investment in Nestlé Shares

- Nestlé has the financial stability to fund growth in its existing operations and carry out its growth-by-acquisition strategy. The company's current liquidity and cash flows are more than adequate for future operating and investment purposes. The company has low leverage, and the capital structure is capable of supporting future operations and strategic plans.
- The operating cash flows have consistently exceeded the operating earnings. The ratio of operating cash to operating profit has been consistently favorable, providing confidence in the quality of the earnings. Measures comparing cash flow with reinvestment, debt, and debt-servicing capacity indicate strength in financial capacity.
- Decomposing earnings into Nestlé-only and L'Oréal and considering the respective price-to-earnings ratios, it appears that the implied Nestlé-only portion is undervalued. The implied Nestlé-only portion has a far lower price-to-earnings ratio than L'Oréal or the market. This finding should be considered an opportunity, given Nestlé's demonstrated cash flows and low financial leverage.

2.4.2. Causes for Concern

- Although Nestlé has significant, world-class brands and global reach, its core business has deteriorated in profitability in the last several years, as shown by the decomposition of the ROE. Even when taking into account the unusual items affecting profit margins, core operations still show decreases in profitability.
- The negative trend also shows in the cash returns on total assets. They have decreased each year since 2012.
- The acquisition activities in the Nutrition and Health Science product group do not appear to build on the company's traditional strengths. They do not seem to provide a remedy for the deterioration in the core profitability.
- The company's priorities in the allocation of capital in making acquisitions are of some concern. Although the Nutrition and Health Science product group and the Nestlé Nutrition segment show excellent EBIT margins, they rank very low in return on assets. This finding raises the question of whether management is overpaying for acquired companies.
- The company's write-down of goodwill from earlier acquisitions may signal ineffective allocation of capital. It is troubling that Nestlé has taken write-downs on previous acquisitions while actively making new ones.

The analyst concludes that Nestlé is not clearly a good investment opportunity *at this time* and recommends waiting to see whether a further discount makes it more attractive or the operations improve.

2.5. Phase 6: Follow-up

The portfolio manager is surprised by the analyst's findings and recommendations. The portfolio manager is convinced that the purchase of shares is justified because of the discount and because, in her opinion, Nestlé is experiencing only temporary issues. She commits the pension fund to a cautious, less-than-core investment holding of Nestlé common stock. The size of the holding is less than originally anticipated because, despite her enthusiasm for the company, the portfolio manager is troubled by the analyst's observations about the resource allocation within the company. She wants him to continually re-evaluate the holding. Unproductive capital spending may be a trigger for eliminating the holding. The analyst is asked to update his findings in the initial research report at each reporting period, emphasizing the quality measures expressed by the accruals tests and the cash flow support of earnings, with particular regard to return on assets.

3. SUMMARY

The case study demonstrates the use of a financial analysis framework in investment decision making. Although each analysis undertaken may have a different focus, purpose, and context that result in the application of different techniques and tools, the case demonstrates the use of a common financial statement analysis framework. The analyst starts with a global, summarized view of a company and its attributes and digs below the surface of the financial statements to find economic truths that are not apparent from a superficial review. In the case of Nestlé, the analyst applied disaggregation techniques to review the company's performance in terms of ROE and then successively examined the drivers of ROE in increasing detail to evaluate management's skills in capital allocation.

An economic decision is reached, which is consistent with the primary reason for performing financial analysis: to facilitate an economic decision.

PRACTICE PROBLEMS

The following information relates to Questions 1–7

Quentin Abay, CFA, is an analyst for a private equity firm interested in purchasing Bickchip Enterprises, a conglomerate. His first task is to determine the trends in ROE and the main drivers of the trends using DuPont analysis. To do so he gathers the data in Exhibit 1.

EXHIBIT 1   Selected Financial Data for Bickchip Enterprises (€ Thousands)

	2020	2019	2018
Revenue	72,448	66,487	55,781
Earnings before interest and tax	6,270	4,710	3,609
Earnings before tax	5,101	4,114	3,168
Net income	4,038	3,345	2,576
Asset turnover	0.79	0.76	0.68
Assets/Equity	3.09	3.38	3.43

After conducting the DuPont analysis, Abay believes that his firm could increase the ROE without operational changes. Further, Abay thinks that ROE could improve if the company divested segments that were generating the lowest returns on capital employed (total assets less non-interest-bearing liabilities). Segment EBIT margins in 2020 were 11 percent for Automation Equipment, 5 percent for Power and Industrial, and 8 percent for Medical Equipment. Other relevant segment information is presented in Exhibit 2.

EXHIBIT 2   Segment Data for Bickchip Enterprises (€ Thousands)

Operating Segments	Capital Employed			Capital Expenditures (Excluding Acquisitions)		
	2020	2019	2018	2020	2019	2018
Automation Equipment	10,705	6,384	5,647	700	743	616
Power and Industrial	15,805	13,195	12,100	900	849	634
Medical Equipment	22,870	22,985	22,587	908	824	749
	49,380	42,564	40,334	2,508	2,416	1,999

Abay is also concerned with earnings quality, so he intends to calculate Bickchip's cash-flow-based accruals ratio and the ratio of operating cash flow before interest and taxes to operating income. To do so, he prepares the information in Exhibit 3.

EXHIBIT 3   Earnings Quality Data for Bickchip Enterprises (€ Thousands)

	2020	2019	2018
Net income	4,038	3,345	2,576
Net cash flow provided by (used in) operating activity[a]	9,822	5,003	3,198
Net cash flow provided by (used in) investing activity	(10,068)	(4,315)	(5,052)
Net cash flow provided by (used in) financing activity[b]	(5,792)	1,540	(2,241)
Average net operating assets	43,192	45,373	40,421
[a] includes cash paid for taxes of:	(1,930)	(1,191)	(1,093)
[b] includes cash paid for interest of:	(1,169)	(596)	(441)

1. Over the three-year period presented in Exhibit 1, Bickchip's return on equity is *best* described as:
   A. stable.
   B. trending lower.
   C. trending higher.

2. Based on the DuPont analysis, Abay's belief regarding ROE is *most likely* based on:
   A. leverage.
   B. profit margins.
   C. asset turnover.

3. Based on Abay's criteria, the business segment *best* suited for divestiture is:
   A. medical equipment.
   B. power and industrial.
   C. automation equipment.

4. Bickchip's cash-flow-based accruals ratio in 2020 is *closest* to:
   A. 9.9%.
   B. 13.4%.
   C. 23.3%.

5. The cash-flow-based accruals ratios from 2018 to 2020 indicate:
   A. improving earnings quality.
   B. deteriorating earnings quality.
   C. no change in earnings quality.

6. The ratio of operating cash flow before interest and taxes to operating income for Bickchip for 2020 is *closest* to:
   A. 1.6.
   B. 1.9.
   C. 2.1.

7. Based on the ratios for operating cash flow before interest and taxes to operating income, Abay should conclude that:
   A. Bickchip's earnings are backed by cash flow.
   B. Bickchip's earnings are not backed by cash flow.
   C. Abay can draw no conclusion due to the changes in the ratios over time.

GLOSSARY

Accelerated methods   Depreciation methods that allocate a relatively large proportion of the cost of an asset to the early years of the asset's useful life.

Accounting profit   Income as reported on the income statement, in accordance with prevailing accounting standards, before the provisions for income tax expense. Also called *income before taxes* or *pretax income*.

Accounts payable   Amounts that a business owes to its vendors for goods and services that were purchased from them but which have not yet been paid.

Accrued expenses   Liabilities related to expenses that have been incurred but not yet paid as of the end of an accounting period—an example of an accrued expense is rent that has been incurred but not yet paid, resulting in a liability "rent payable." Also called *accrued liabilities*.

Accumulated benefit obligation   The actuarial present value of benefits (whether vested or non-vested) attributed, generally by the pension benefit formula, to employee service rendered before a specified date and based on employee service and compensation (if applicable) before that date. The accumulated benefit obligation differs from the projected benefit obligation in that it includes no assumption about future compensation levels.

Acquisition method   A method of accounting for a business combination where the acquirer is required to measure each identifiable asset and liability at fair value. This method was the result of a joint project of the IASB and FASB aiming at convergence in standards for the accounting of business combinations.

Activity ratios   Ratios that measure how efficiently a company performs day-to-day tasks, such as the collection of receivables and management of inventory. Also called *asset utilization ratios* or *operating efficiency ratios*.

Allowance for loan losses   A balance sheet account; it is a contra asset account to loans.

Amortisation   The process of allocating the cost of intangible long-term assets having a finite useful life to accounting periods; the allocation of the amount of a bond premium or discount to the periods remaining until bond maturity.

Amortised cost   The historical cost (initially recognised cost) of an asset, adjusted for amortisation and impairment.

Antidilutive   With reference to a transaction or a security, one that would increase earnings per share (EPS) or result in EPS higher than the company's basic EPS—antidilutive securities are not included in the calculation of diluted EPS.

Asset utilization ratios   Ratios that measure how efficiently a company performs day-to-day tasks, such as the collection of receivables and management of inventory.

Assets   Resources controlled by an enterprise as a result of past events and from which future economic benefits to the enterprise are expected to flow.

Available-for-sale   Under US GAAP, debt securities not classified as either held-to-maturity or held-for-trading securities. The investor is willing to sell but not actively planning to sell. In general, available-for-sale debt securities are reported at fair value on the balance sheet, with unrealized gains included as a component of other comprehensive income.

Back-testing   With reference to portfolio strategies, the application of a strategy's portfolio selection rules to historical data to assess what would have been the strategy's historical performance.

Balance sheet ratios   Financial ratios involving balance sheet items only.

Balance sheet   The financial statement that presents an entity's current financial position by disclosing resources the entity controls (its assets) and the claims on those resources (its liabilities and equity claims), as of a particular point in time (the date of the balance sheet). Also called *statement of financial position* or *statement of financial condition*.

Basic EPS   Net earnings available to common shareholders (i.e., net income minus preferred dividends) divided by the weighted average number of common shares outstanding.

Bottom-up analysis   An investment selection approach that focuses on company-specific circumstances rather than emphasizing economic cycles or industry analysis.

Capital structure   The mix of debt and equity that a company uses to finance its business; a company's specific mixture of long-term financing.

Carrying amount   The amount at which an asset or liability is valued according to accounting principles.

Cash conversion cycle   A financial metric that measures the length of time required for a company to convert cash invested in its operations to cash received as a result of its operations; equal to days of inventory on hand + days of sales outstanding – number of days of payables. Also called *net operating cycle*.

Cash flow from operations   The net amount of cash provided from operating activities. This is sometimes called cash flow from operating activities.

Classified balance sheet   A balance sheet organized so as to group together the various assets and liabilities into subcategories (e.g., current and noncurrent).

Common shares   A type of security that represent an ownership interest in a company.

Common stock   See *common shares*.

Common-size analysis   The restatement of financial statement items using a common denominator or reference item that allows one to identify trends and major differences; an example is an income statement in which all items are expressed as a percent of revenue.

Comprehensive income   The change in equity of a business enterprise during a period from nonowner sources; includes all changes in equity during a period except those resulting from investments by owners and distributions to owners; comprehensive income equals net income plus other comprehensive income.

Contra account   An account that offsets another account.

Coupon rate   The interest rate promised in a contract; this is the rate used to calculate the periodic interest payments.

Credit analysis   The evaluation of credit risk; the evaluation of the creditworthiness of a borrower or counterparty.

Credit risk   The risk of loss caused by a counterparty's or debtor's failure to make a promised payment. Also called *default risk*.

Cross-sectional analysis   Analysis that involves comparisons across individuals in a group over a given time period or at a given point in time.

Current assets   Assets that are expected to be consumed or converted into cash in the near future, typically one year or less. *Also called liquid assets*.

Current cost   With reference to assets, the amount of cash or cash equivalents that would have to be paid to buy the same or an equivalent asset today; with reference to liabilities, the undiscounted amount of cash or cash equivalents that would be required to settle the obligation today.

Current exchange rate   For accounting purposes, the spot exchange rate on the balance sheet date.

Current liabilities   Short-term obligations, such as accounts payable, wages payable, or accrued liabilities, that are expected to be settled in the near future, typically one year or less.

Current rate method   Approach to translating foreign currency financial statements for consolidation in which all assets and liabilities are translated at the current exchange rate. The current rate method is the prevalent method of translation.

Days of inventory on hand   An activity ratio equal to the number of days in the period divided by inventory turnover over the period.

Dealing securities   Securities held by banks or other financial intermediaries for trading purposes.

Debt-to-assets ratio   A solvency ratio calculated as total debt divided by total assets.

Debt-to-capital ratio A solvency ratio calculated as total debt divided by total debt plus total shareholders' equity.

Debt-to-equity ratio A solvency ratio calculated as total debt divided by total shareholders' equity.

Deductible temporary differences Temporary differences that result in a reduction of or deduction from taxable income in a future period when the balance sheet item is recovered or settled.

Defensive interval ratio A liquidity ratio that estimates the number of days that an entity could meet cash needs from liquid assets; calculated as (cash + short-term marketable investments + receivables) divided by daily cash expenditures.

Deferred income A liability account for money that has been collected for goods or services that have not yet been delivered; payment received in advance of providing a good or service.

Deferred revenue A liability account for money that has been collected for goods or services that have not yet been delivered; payment received in advance of providing a good or service.

Deferred tax assets A balance sheet asset that arises when an excess amount is paid for income taxes relative to accounting profit. The taxable income is higher than accounting profit and income tax payable exceeds tax expense. The company expects to recover the difference during the course of future operations when tax expense exceeds income tax payable.

Deferred tax liabilities A balance sheet liability that arises when a deficit amount is paid for income taxes relative to accounting profit. The taxable income is less than the accounting profit and income tax payable is less than tax expense. The company expects to eliminate the liability over the course of future operations when income tax payable exceeds tax expense.

Defined benefit pension plans Plan in which the company promises to pay a certain annual amount (defined benefit) to the employee after retirement. The company bears the investment risk of the plan assets.

Defined contribution pension plans Individual accounts to which an employee and typically the employer makes contributions during their working years and expect to draw on the accumulated funds at retirement. The employee bears the investment and inflation risk of the plan assets.

Defined contribution pension plans Individual accounts to which an employee and typically the employer makes contributions, generally on a tax-advantaged basis. The amounts of contributions are defined at the outset, but the future value of the benefit is unknown. The employee bears the investment risk of the plan assets.

Depreciation The process of systematically allocating the cost of long-lived (tangible) assets to the periods during which the assets are expected to provide economic benefits.

Derivatives A financial instrument whose value depends on the value of some underlying asset or factor (e.g., a stock price, an interest rate, or exchange rate).

Diluted EPS The EPS that would result if all dilutive securities were converted into common shares.

Diluted shares The number of shares that would be outstanding if all potentially dilutive claims on common shares (e.g., convertible debt, convertible preferred stock, and employee stock options) were exercised.

Diminishing balance method An accelerated depreciation method (i.e., one that allocates a relatively large proportion of the cost of an asset to the early years of the asset's useful life).

Direct financing leases Under US GAAP, a type of finance lease, from a lessor perspective, where the present value of the lease payments (lease receivable) equals the carrying value of the leased asset. No selling profit is recognized at lease inception. The revenues earned by the lessor are financing in nature.

Direct format With reference to the cash flow statement, a format for the presentation of the statement in which cash flow from operating activities is shown as operating cash receipts less operating cash disbursements. Also called *direct method*.

Direct method See *direct format*.

Direct write-off method An approach to recognizing credit losses on customer receivables in which the company waits until such time as a customer has defaulted and only then recognizes the loss.

Dividend payout ratio The ratio of cash dividends paid to earnings for a period.

Double declining balance depreciation   An accelerated depreciation method that involves depreciating the asset at double the straight-line rate. This rate is multiplied by the book value of the asset at the beginning of the period (a declining balance) to calculate depreciation expense.

Downstream   A transaction between two related companies, an investor company (or a parent company) and an associate company (or a subsidiary) such that the investor company records a profit on its income statement. An example is a sale of inventory by the investor company to the associate or by a parent to a subsidiary company.

DuPont analysis   An approach to decomposing return on investment (e.g., return on equity, as the product of other financial ratios).

Earnings per share   The amount of income earned during a period per share of common stock.

Effective interest rate   The borrowing rate or market rate that a company incurs at the time of issuance of a bond.

Equity   Assets less liabilities; the residual interest in the assets after subtracting the liabilities.

Exercise date   The date when employees actually exercise stock options and convert them to stock.

Expenses   Outflows of economic resources or increases in liabilities that result in decreases in equity (other than decreases because of distributions to owners); reductions in net assets associated with the creation of revenues.

Exposure to foreign exchange risk   The risk of a change in value of an asset or liability denominated in a foreign currency due to a change in exchange rates.

Face value   The amount of cash payable by a company to the bondholders when the bonds mature; the promised payment at maturity separate from any coupon payment.

Fair value   The amount at which an asset could be exchanged, or a liability settled, between knowledgeable, willing parties in an arm's-length transaction; the price that would be received to sell an asset or paid to transfer a liability in an orderly transaction between market participants.

FIFO method   The first in, first out, method of accounting for inventory, which matches sales against the costs of items of inventory in the order in which they were placed in inventory.

Finance lease   From the lessee perspective, under US GAAP, a type of lease which is more akin to the purchase of an asset by the lessee. From the lessor perspective, under IFRS, a lease which "transfers substantially all the risks and rewards incidental to ownership of an underlying asset."

Financial flexibility   The ability to react and adapt to financial adversity and opportunities.

Financial leverage ratio   A measure of financial leverage calculated as average total assets divided by average total equity.

Financial leverage   The extent to which a company can effect, through the use of debt, a proportional change in the return on common equity that is greater than a given proportional change in operating income; also, short for the financial leverage ratio.

Financing activities   Activities related to obtaining or repaying capital to be used in the business (e.g., equity and long-term debt).

Fixed charge coverage   A solvency ratio measuring the number of times interest and lease payments are covered by operating income, calculated as (EBIT + lease payments) divided by (interest payments + lease payments).

Fixed costs   Costs that remain at the same level regardless of a company's level of production and sales.

Float   Amounts collected as premium and not yet paid out as benefits.

Foreign currency transactions   Transactions that are denominated in a currency other than a company's functional currency.

Free cash flow   The actual cash that would be available to the company's investors after making all investments necessary to maintain the company as an ongoing enterprise (also referred to as free cash flow to the firm); the internally generated funds that can be distributed to the company's investors (e.g., shareholders and bondholders) without impairing the value of the company.

Functional currency   The currency of the primary economic environment in which an entity operates.

Gains   Asset inflows not directly related to the ordinary activities of the business.

Goodwill An intangible asset that represents the excess of the purchase price of an acquired company over the value of the net assets acquired.

Grant date The day that stock options are granted to employees.

Gross margin Sales minus the cost of sales (i.e., the cost of goods sold for a manufacturing company).

Gross profit margin The ratio of gross profit to revenues.

Gross profit Sales minus the cost of sales (i.e., the cost of goods sold for a manufacturing company).

Grouping by function With reference to the presentation of expenses in an income statement, the grouping together of expenses serving the same function (e.g. all items that are costs of goods sold).

Grouping by nature With reference to the presentation of expenses in an income statement, the grouping together of expenses by similar nature (e.g., all depreciation expenses).

Growth investors With reference to equity investors, investors who seek to invest in high-earnings-growth companies.

Held-to-maturity Debt (fixed-income) securities that a company intends to hold to maturity; these are presented at their original cost, updated for any amortisation of discounts or premiums.

Historical cost In reference to assets, the amount paid to purchase an asset, including any costs of acquisition and/or preparation; with reference to liabilities, the amount of proceeds received in exchange in issuing the liability.

Historical exchange rates For accounting purposes, the exchange rates that existed when the assets and liabilities were initially recorded.

Horizontal analysis Common-size analysis that involves comparing a specific financial statement with that statement in prior or future time periods; also, cross-sectional analysis of one company with another.

If-converted method A method for accounting for the effect of convertible securities on earnings per share (EPS) that specifies what EPS would have been if the convertible securities had been converted at the beginning of the period, taking account of the effects of conversion on net income and the weighted average number of shares outstanding.

Income tax paid The actual amount paid for income taxes in the period; not a provision, but the actual cash outflow.

Income tax payable The income tax owed by the company on the basis of taxable income.

Income Increases in economic benefits in the form of inflows or enhancements of assets, or decreases of liabilities that result in an increase in equity (other than increases resulting from contributions by owners).

Indirect format With reference to cash flow statements, a format for the presentation of the statement which, in the operating cash flow section, begins with net income then shows additions and subtractions to arrive at operating cash flow. Also called *indirect method*.

Indirect method See *indirect format*.

Intangible assets Assets lacking physical substance, such as patents and trademarks.

Interest coverage A solvency ratio calculated as EBIT divided by interest payments.

Inventory turnover An activity ratio calculated as cost of goods sold divided by average inventory.

Investing activities Activities associated with the acquisition and disposal of property, plant, and equipment; intangible assets; other long-term assets; and both long-term and short-term investments in the equity and debt (bonds and loans) issued by other companies.

Investment property Property used to earn rental income or capital appreciation (or both).

Lessee The party obtaining the use of an asset through a lease.

Lessor The owner of an asset that grants the right to use the asset to another party.

Liabilities Present obligations of an enterprise arising from past events, the settlement of which is expected to result in an outflow of resources embodying economic benefits; creditors' claims on the resources of a company.

LIFO layer liquidation With respect to the application of the LIFO inventory method, the liquidation of old, relatively low-priced inventory; happens when the volume of sales rises above the volume of recent purchases so that some sales are made from relatively old, low-priced inventory. Also called *LIFO liquidation*.

LIFO method   The last in, first out, method of accounting for inventory, which matches sales against the costs of items of inventory in the reverse order the items were placed in inventory (i.e., inventory produced or acquired last are assumed to be sold first).

LIFO reserve   The difference between the reported LIFO inventory carrying amount and the inventory amount that would have been reported if the FIFO method had been used (in other words, the FIFO inventory value less the LIFO inventory value).

Liquidity ratios   Financial ratios measuring the company's ability to meet its short-term obligations.

Liquidity   The ability to purchase or sell an asset quickly and easily at a price close to fair market value. The ability to meet short-term obligations using assets that are the most readily converted into cash.

Local currency   The currency of the country where a company is located.

Long-lived assets   Assets that are expected to provide economic benefits over a future period of time, typically greater than one year. Also called *long-term assets*.

Losses   Asset outflows not directly related to the ordinary activities of the business.

Market rate of interest   The rate demanded by purchasers of bonds, given the risks associated with future cash payment obligations of the particular bond issue.

Market-oriented investors   With reference to equity investors, investors whose investment disciplines cannot be clearly categorized as value or growth.

Matching principle   The accounting principle that expenses should be recognized in the same period in which the associated revenue is recognized.

Monetary assets and liabilities   Assets and liabilities with value equal to the amount of currency contracted for, a fixed amount of currency. Examples are cash, accounts receivable, accounts payable, bonds payable, and mortgages payable. Inventory is not a monetary asset. Most liabilities are monetary.

Monetary/non-monetary method   Approach to translating foreign currency financial statements for consolidation in which monetary assets and liabilities are translated at the current exchange rate. Non-monetary assets and liabilities are translated at historical exchange rates (the exchange rates that existed when the assets and liabilities were acquired).

Multi-step format   With respect to the format of the income statement, a format that presents a subtotal for gross profit (revenue minus cost of goods sold).

Net asset balance sheet exposure   When assets translated at the current exchange rate are greater in amount than liabilities translated at the current exchange rate. Assets exposed to translation gains or losses exceed the exposed liabilities.

Net book value   The remaining (undepreciated) balance of an asset's purchase cost. For liabilities, the face value of a bond minus any unamortized discount, or plus any unamortized premium.

Net income   The difference between revenue and expenses; what remains after subtracting all expenses (including depreciation, interest, and taxes) from revenue.

Net liability balance sheet exposure   When liabilities translated at the current exchange rate are greater than assets translated at the current exchange rate. Liabilities exposed to translation gains or losses exceed the exposed assets.

Net profit margin   An indicator of profitability, calculated as net income divided by revenue; indicates how much of each dollar of revenues is left after all costs and expenses. Also called *profit margin* or *return on sales*.

Net realisable value   Estimated selling price in the ordinary course of business less the estimated costs necessary to make the sale.

Net revenue   Revenue after adjustments (e.g., for estimated returns or for amounts unlikely to be collected).

Non-current assets   Assets that are expected to benefit the company over an extended period of time (usually more than one year).

Non-current liabilities   Obligations that broadly represent a probable sacrifice of economic benefits in periods generally greater than one year in the future.

Non-monetary assets and liabilities   Assets and liabilities that are not monetary assets and liabilities. Non-monetary assets include inventory, fixed assets, and intangibles, and non-monetary liabilities include deferred revenue.

Operating activities Activities that are part of the day-to-day business functioning of an entity, such as selling inventory and providing services.

Operating cash flow The net amount of cash provided from operating activities.

Operating efficiency ratios Ratios that measure how efficiently a company performs day-to-day tasks, such as the collection of receivables and management of inventory.

Operating lease An agreement allowing a lessee to use some asset for a period of time; essentially a rental.

Operating leverage The use of fixed costs in operations.

Operating profit margin A profitability ratio calculated as operating income (i.e., income before interest and taxes) divided by revenue. Also called *operating margin*.

Operating profit A company's profits on its usual business activities before deducting taxes. Also called *operating income*.

Ordinary shares Equity shares that are subordinate to all other types of equity (e.g., preferred equity). Also called *common stock* or *common shares*.

Other comprehensive income Items of comprehensive income that are not reported on the income statement; comprehensive income minus net income.

Other post-employment benefits Promises by the company to pay benefits in the future, such as life insurance premiums and all or part of health care insurance for its retirees.

Owners' equity The excess of assets over liabilities; the residual interest of shareholders in the assets of an entity after deducting the entity's liabilities. Also called *shareholders' equity* or *shareholders' funds*.

Pension obligation The present value of future benefits earned by employees for service provided to date.

Period costs Costs (e.g., executives' salaries) that cannot be directly matched with the timing of revenues and which are thus expensed immediately.

Permanent differences Differences between tax and financial reporting of revenue (expenses) that will not be reversed at some future date. These result in a difference between the company's effective tax rate and statutory tax rate and do not result in a deferred tax item.

Premiums Amounts paid by the purchaser of insurance products.

Prepaid expense A normal operating expense that has been paid in advance of when it is due.

Present value (PV) The present discounted value of future cash flows: For assets, the present discounted value of the future net cash inflows that the asset is expected to generate; for liabilities, the present discounted value of the future net cash outflows that are expected to be required to settle the liabilities.

Presentation currency The currency in which financial statement amounts are presented.

Pretax margin A profitability ratio calculated as earnings before taxes divided by revenue.

Price to book value A valuation ratio calculated as price per share divided by book value per share.

Price to cash flow A valuation ratio calculated as price per share divided by cash flow per share.

Price to earnings ratio (P/E ratio or P/E) The ratio of share price to earnings per share.

Price to sales A valuation ratio calculated as price per share divided by sales per share.

Profit and loss (P&L) statement A financial statement that provides information about a company's profitability over a stated period of time. Also called the *income statement*.

Profit margin An indicator of profitability, calculated as net income divided by revenue; indicates how much of each dollar of revenues is left after all costs and expenses.

Profitability ratios Ratios that measure a company's ability to generate profitable sales from its resources (assets).

Property, plant, and equipment Tangible assets that are expected to be used for more than one period in either the production or supply of goods or services, or for administrative purposes.

Provision for loan losses An income statement expense account that increases the amount of the allowance for loan losses.

Purchasing power gain A gain in value caused by changes in price levels. Monetary liabilities experience purchasing power gains during periods of inflation.

Purchasing power loss A loss in value caused by changes in price levels. Monetary assets experience purchasing power loss during periods of inflation.

Realizable (settlement) value   With reference to assets, the amount of cash or cash equivalents that could currently be obtained by selling the asset in an orderly disposal; with reference to liabilities, the undiscounted amount of cash or cash equivalents expected to be paid to satisfy the liabilities in the normal course of business.

Return on assets (ROA)   A profitability ratio calculated as net income divided by average total assets; indicates a company's net profit generated per dollar invested in total assets.

Return on equity (ROE)   A profitability ratio calculated as net income divided by average shareholders' equity.

Return on sales   An indicator of profitability, calculated as net income divided by revenue; indicates how much of each dollar of revenues is left after all costs and expenses. Also referred to as *net profit margin*.

Return on total capital   A profitability ratio calculated as EBIT divided by the sum of short- and long-term debt and equity.

Revaluation model   Under IFRS, the process of valuing long-lived assets at fair value, rather than at cost less accumulated depreciation. Any resulting profit or loss is either reported on the income statement and/or through equity under revaluation surplus.

Revenue   The amount charged for the delivery of goods or services in the ordinary activities of a business over a stated period; the inflows of economic resources to a company over a stated period.

Sales   Generally, a synonym for revenue; "sales" is generally understood to refer to the sale of goods, whereas "revenue" is understood to include the sale of goods or services.

Sales-type leases   Under US GAAP, a type of finance lease, from a lessor perspective, where the present value of the lease payments (lease receivable) exceeds the carrying value of the leased asset. The revenues earned by the lessor are both a selling profit at inception and financing (interest) revenues.

Scenario analysis   Analysis that shows the changes in key financial quantities that result from given (economic) events, such as the loss of customers, the loss of a supply source, or a catastrophic event; a risk management technique involving examination of the performance of a portfolio under specified situations. Closely related to stress testing.

Screening   The application of a set of criteria to reduce a set of potential investments to a smaller set having certain desired characteristics.

Sensitivity analysis   Analysis that shows the range of possible outcomes as specific assumptions are changed.

Service period   For employee stock options, usually the period between the grant date and the vesting date.

Shareholders' equity   Assets less liabilities; the residual interest in the assets after subtracting the liabilities.

Simulation   Computer-generated sensitivity or scenario analysis that is based on probability models for the factors that drive outcomes.

Single-step format   With respect to the format of the income statement, a format that does not subtotal for gross profit (revenue minus cost of goods sold).

Solvency ratios   Ratios that measure a company's ability to meet its long-term obligations.

Solvency   With respect to financial statement analysis, the ability of a company to fulfill its long-term obligations.

Specific identification method   An inventory accounting method that identifies which specific inventory items were sold and which remained in inventory to be carried over to later periods.

Statement of changes in equity   (statement of owners' equity) A financial statement that reconciles the beginning-of-period and end-of-period balance sheet values of shareholders' equity; provides information about all factors affecting shareholders' equity. Also called *statement of owners' equity*.

Statement of financial position   The financial statement that presents an entity's current financial position by disclosing resources the entity controls (its assets) and the claims on those resources (its liabilities and equity claims), as of a particular point in time (the date of the balance sheet). This is sometimes called the statement of financial condition.

Statement of operations   A financial statement that provides information about a company's profitability over a stated period of time.

Straight-line method   A depreciation method that allocates evenly the cost of a long-lived asset less its estimated residual value over the estimated useful life of the asset.

Sustainable growth rate   The rate of dividend (and earnings) growth that can be sustained over time for a given level of return on equity, keeping the capital structure constant and without issuing additional common stock.

Tax base   The amount at which an asset or liability is valued for tax purposes.

Tax expense   An aggregate of an entity's income tax payable (or recoverable in the case of a tax benefit) and any changes in deferred tax assets and liabilities. It is essentially the income tax payable or recoverable if these had been determined based on accounting profit rather than taxable income.

Tax loss carry forward   A taxable loss in the current period that may be used to reduce future taxable income.

Taxable income   The portion of an entity's income that is subject to income taxes under the tax laws of its jurisdiction.

Taxable temporary differences   Temporary differences that result in a taxable amount in a future period when determining the taxable profit as the balance sheet item is recovered or settled.

Temporal method   A variation of the monetary/non-monetary translation method that requires not only monetary assets and liabilities, but also non-monetary assets and liabilities that are measured at their current value on the balance sheet date to be translated at the current exchange rate. Assets and liabilities are translated at rates consistent with the timing of their measurement value. This method is typically used when the functional currency is other than the local currency.

Top-down analysis   An investment selection approach that begins with consideration of macroeconomic conditions and then evaluates markets and industries based upon such conditions.

Total comprehensive income   The change in equity during a period resulting from transaction and other events, other than those changes resulting from transactions with owners in their capacity as owners.

Total invested capital   The sum of market value of common equity, book value of preferred equity, and face value of debt.

Trade payables   Amounts that a business owes to its vendors for goods and services that were purchased from them but which have not yet been paid.

Trading securities   Under US GAAP, a category of debt securities held by a company with the intent to trade them. Also called *held-for-trading securities*.

Transaction exposure   The risk of a change in value between the transaction date and the settlement date of an asset of liability denominated in a foreign currency.

Treasury stock method   A method for accounting for the effect of options (and warrants) on earnings per share (EPS) that specifies what EPS would have been if the options and warrants had been exercised and the company had used the proceeds to repurchase common stock.

Unearned revenue   A liability account for money that has been collected for goods or services that have not yet been delivered; payment received in advance of providing a good or service. Also called *deferred revenue* or *deferred income*.

Units-of-production method   A depreciation method that allocates the cost of a long-lived asset based on actual usage during the period.

Upstream   A transaction between two related companies, an investor company (or a parent company) and an associate company (or a subsidiary company) such that the associate company records a profit on its income statement. An example is a sale of inventory by the associate to the investor company or by a subsidiary to a parent company.

Valuation allowance   A reserve created against deferred tax assets, based on the likelihood of realizing the deferred tax assets in future accounting periods.

Valuation ratios   Ratios that measure the quantity of an asset or flow (e.g., earnings) in relation to the price associated with a specified claim (e.g., a share or ownership of the enterprise).

Value investors   With reference to equity investors, investors who are focused on paying a relatively low share price in relation to earnings or assets per share.

Variable costs   Costs that fluctuate with the level of production and sales.

Vertical analysis   Common-size analysis using only one reporting period or one base financial statement; for example, an income statement in which all items are stated as percentages of sales.

Vested benefit obligation   The actuarial present value of vested benefits.

Vesting date   The date that employees can first exercise stock options.

Weighted average cost method   An inventory accounting method that averages the total cost of available inventory items over the total units available for sale.

Working capital   The difference between current assets and current liabilities.

ABOUT THE EDITORS

Thomas R. Robinson, PhD, CFA, is managing director of the Americas at CFA Institute. He leads a cross-functional team that participates in developing global strategy, implements the global strategy regionally, and engages with stakeholders regionally. He also has direct responsibility for Member and Candidate Services and the Future of Finance Initiative globally. Previously, Dr. Robinson served as managing director of education at CFA Institute, providing vision and leadership for a 100-member global team producing and delivering educational content for candidates, members, and other investment professionals.

Prior to joining CFA Institute, Dr. Robinson had a 25-year career in financial services and education, having served as a tenured faculty member at the University of Miami, managing director of a private wealth investment advisory firm, and director of tax and consulting services at a public accounting firm. He has published regularly in professional journals and has authored or co-authored many books on financial analysis, valuation, and wealth management. He is a CFA charterholder, a Certified Public Accountant (CPA) (Ohio), a Certified Financial Planner (CFP®), and a Chartered Alternative Investment Analyst (CAIA). He holds a bachelor's degree in economics from the University of Pennsylvania and a master's and doctorate from Case Western Reserve University.

Elaine Henry, PhD, CFA, is a Clinical Associate Professor of Accounting at Fordham University. Previously, she taught at the University of Miami from 2005 to 2012. Courses have included financial accounting, financial statement analysis, international financial reporting standards, and equity valuation. Dr. Henry's research areas include international accounting, computational linguistics in financial analysis, restatements, and related party transactions. She has published articles in a number of journals, including *Journal of International Accounting Research, Journal of Emerging Technologies in Accounting, Accounting Horizons,* and the *Journal of Business Finance & Accounting.* Dr. Henry served as project team leader for the PCAOB (Public Company Accounting Oversight Board) research synthesis project on Related Party Transactions in 2006 and 2007. She serves on the editorial board of the *Financial Analysts Journal.*

Prior to her academic career, Dr. Henry worked in corporate finance at Lehman Brothers, strategy consulting at McKinsey & Company, and corporate banking at Citibank (Athens, London, and New York). She received her BA and BBA from Millsaps College, her MBA with high distinction from the Harvard Business School, and her PhD from Rutgers University. Dr. Henry has been an active volunteer at CFA Institute, CFA Society Miami, the Harvard Business School Club of London, and the American Accounting Association.

Michael A. Broihahn, CFA, is Associate Professor of Accounting at Barry University in Miami Shores, Florida. Mr. Broihahn received his BS, MBA, and MS degrees from the University of Wisconsin, majoring in accounting and finance. He is licensed as a Certified Public Accountant in Florida and Wisconsin and also holds the professional credentials of Certified Internal

Auditor, Certified Management Accountant, Certified in Financial Management, Certified Financial Planner, and Certified Fund Specialist.

Mr. Broihahn began his business career in 1976 with Price Waterhouse in Milwaukee, Wisconsin, where he worked on the audits of Fortune 500 manufacturing companies. He has worked with Fox & Carskadon Financial Corporation in San Mateo, California, as a portfolio controller and with ComputerLand Corporation as Corporate Controller and Director of Financial Reporting. In 1985, he returned to Milwaukee as the CFO for ComputerBay, also a franchisor of computer retail stores. In 1988 he joined the faculty of the Andreas School of Business at Barry University, where he presently teaches courses in financial accounting, auditing, and financial statement analysis. He has been a CFA charterholder since 1990 and currently serves CFA Institute in a number of capacities.

ABOUT THE
CFA PROGRAM

The Chartered Financial Analyst® designation (CFA®) is a globally recognized standard of excellence for measuring the competence and integrity of investment professionals. To earn the CFA charter, candidates must successfully pass through the CFA Program, a global graduate-level self-study program that combines a broad curriculum with professional conduct requirements as preparation for a wide range of investment specialties.

Anchored by a practice-based curriculum, the CFA Program is focused on the knowledge identified by professionals as essential to the investment decision-making process. This body of knowledge maintains current relevance through a regular, extensive survey of practicing CFA charterholders across the globe. The curriculum covers 10 general topic areas, ranging from equity and fixed-income analysis to portfolio management, all with a heavy emphasis on the application of ethics in professional practice. Known for its rigor and breadth, the CFA Program curriculum highlights principles common to every market so that professionals who earn the CFA designation have a thoroughly global investment perspective and a profound understanding of the global marketplace.

www.cfainstitute.org

INDEX

Page numbers followed by italic *e* refer to exhibits.